THE 1993 PLAYS AND PLAYERS THEATRE YEARBOOK

EDITED BY Gwyn Morgan

PUBLISHED BY:
Multimedia Publishing Ltd.
Pickwick House
995 High Road
London N12 8QX

ISBN I-897742-00-2 Hardback

ISBN I-897742-01-0 Paperback

Editor: Gwyn Morgan
Research and Marketing Manager: Norman Dalzell

Internal design and origination by TechniGraphics
Additional design by Laura Gershfield, Louisa McCabe and Marie Sullivan.

Computer system for index and searchline listings supplied by Heathmill Multimedia; programmed by Harry Railing, Marc Surry, Paul McDonald and Mark Oliver.

Promotion Managers: Rory Bourke, Rosamund Dunford, Samuel Garrick and John Skillings.

Production: Kevin Salisbury and Joanna Pyke.

Printed and bound in Great Britain by William Clowes Limited, Beccles and London

Contributors

Michael Arditti
Pat Ashworth
Kate Bassett
Clare Bayley
Michael Billington
Jim Burke
Betty Caplan
Gerry Colgan
William Cook
Della Couling
Tim Cronin
Terry Diab
Rod Dungate
Max Findlay
Mark Fisher
Graham Hassell
Malcolm Hay
Lynda Henderson
Martin Hoyle
Donald Hutera
Nick James
Caroline Kay
Roy Kift
Reva Klein
Ariane Koek
Jeremy Kingston
Gina Landor
John McVicar
Charles Morgan
Gwyn Morgan
Sheridan Morley
Jim O'Quinn
Nina Pasco
Ingeborg Pietzsch
Kenneth Rea
Timothy Ramsden
Simon Reade
Helen Rose
Allen Saddler
Ann St Clair-Stannard
Prunella Scales
Ian Shuttleworth
Ned Sherrin
Penny Simpson
Tom Soper
Mia Soteriou
Sheila Starns
Anne Vanhaeverbeke
Christopher Webber
Andrew Wickes
Robert Workman

The contributors' biographies begin on page 405.

CONTENTS

The West End

The Fringe

Beyond the Fringe

The Royal Court

The National Theatre

The Royal Shakespeare Company

The Regional Guide – Scotland

Regional – The East

Regional – The South West

Regional – The South East

Commercial Tours

Touring Companies

Festivals

Children's Theatre

International View

The Media

Books

An Actor's Life

Serious Money

Where Acting Helps

Obituraries

Contributors

FOREWORD

Welcome to the Plays & Players Yearbook. Here at last is a book about the whole of British theatre.

The Yearbook records what's been going on in regional theatre from Perth to Plymouth. The Bristol Old Vic, the Glasgow Citizens, the Manchester Royal Exchange, the West Yorkshire Playhouse, (that's in alphabetical order) – the festivals at Chichester and Stratford (that's alphabetical order, too) – all are covered, together with touring theatre of every kind. If you want to know what happened in London in 1992, in the West End, at the National, the Royal Court, the RSC, at Stratford East, on the Fringe – it's all described here.

For actors, there is lots of essential information. In the Searchline Players listing, we can look up where friends and colleagues have been appearing throughout 1992. In the section "An Actor's Life", there's an account of Equity's year, a report on agents, and an article on how computer technology may affect our existence in years to come. For future and aspiring actors, there's information on drama schools, and some fascinating insights into the actor's career – from tough beginnings through the tough middle years to the tough problems of trying to maintain a position in the profession in later life.

For those members of the public who simply love and enjoy the theatre, there is plenty here too – features on the work of the director, on lighting design, on sound. The Yearbook leads you through the labyrinthine complications of theatre funding in these days of sparse government subsidy. There are articles on the "angel" system, and contributions from the National Campaign for the Arts and from the Association for Business Sponsorship of the Arts (ABSA).

There is so much in this book: children's theatre, festivals, films, broadcasting, an international section, and to round it off, articles on how theatre can help people – in education, in management training, and in prisons – (although I don't want to imply that's a natural progression). Theatre is around us in many and various forms: the Plays & Players Yearbook describes and celebrates them all.

Indeed the only people who shouldn't buy it are the ones I'm going to give it to for Christmas.

Prunella Scales.

EDITOR'S INTRODUCTION

In the world of theatre, amazing and fascinating things happen all the time. 1992 has been no exception. In Lancaster, the Dukes theatre mounted a production of "The Wizard of Oz" in a local park – and turned the space into a wonderland, complete with yellow brick road. In Bangor, a girl who had once worked as an usher in the Theatr Gwynedd took the leading role in a professional production of "The Glass Menagerie", while, on the stage of the Derby Playhouse, the company of "On the Piste" zoomed down a thirty five foot ski slope, only just managing to stop short of the audience's front row.

The most wonderful thing of all about British theatre is the spirit of inventiveness and resilience which abounds. Subsidies may be cut and sponsorship hard to come by, but actors and directors continue to come up with new ideas. If you read the arts pages of the national press, it's easy to believe that British theatre is dying on its feet. Look at the Yearbook and you can see what's going on right across the country: times may be tough but new plays, new writers keep on cropping up; directors find ever more ingenious ways of producing the classics; and audiences simply can't be kept away from plays by Alan Ayckbourn and John Godber, both of whom continue to develop their material which, while it amuses, genuinely relates to people's lives.

As Prunella Scales points out in her Foreword, the Yearbook is about the whole of British theatre – not just what's new, not just what's in the capital. As editor, I am particularly proud to have assembled such a splendid collection of writers who describe that huge world of activity. Prunella herself heads a list of multi-talented performers who can wield a word processor as happily as they can grace a stage. Joining these thespians, we have a fine collection of Britain's best writers about the theatre – Michael Arditti, Michael Billington, Jeremy Kingston, Sheridan Morley, Ned Sherrin and many, many, more.

The book is divided into sections. After pointing the spotlight at some wonderful "Players of the Year" and looking at some emerging talent with Ned Sherrin, there are three sections which explain things you may have long wanted to know about the theatre but never quite liked to ask...What does a director actually do?...How do they build those amazing sets?...Who are the directors and designers of the moment? Look at our sections "Who Does What in the Theatre", "How Theatre Happens" and "Designers and Directors".

The real meat of the Yearbook is in the middle: our encyclopaedic coverage of productions, theatres and festivals throughout London and the regions. After that, we look at children's theatre, the international scene and theatre in the media. This book is for actors as well as being about them and we hope that they will particularly enjoy "An Actor's Life", a section which is packed with information about the day to day reality of the professional's existence.

We round off with "Serious Money" which analyses the pounds and pence (even the ecus) of the business, "Where Acting Helps", and, finally, obituaries – not forgetting those Searchline Lists which all readers of "Plays & Players" magazine love to pore over.

British theatre is one of the country's greatest assets. Forceful, vibrant and, above all, courageous, it is something to be proud of and to enjoy. I hope that the "Plays & Players" Yearbook will enhance your knowledge and encourage your even greater appreciation of Britain's remarkable plays and players.

GWYN MORGAN

PLAYERS OF THE YEAR

Overworked, undervalued and sought after all over the world, British actors are our theatre's most precious resource. Unlike many of their counterparts in Europe or USA, British actors tend not to specialize. Some of our greatest performers tend not to pay the mortgage by working on film and television alone. Instead, they also choose to display their considerable talents in the theatre – sometimes in the classics, sometimes in new plays.

At the same time, new actors emerge, often through the impoverished fringe and touring companies. Soon, they too will be pursuing dual carreers, entertaining the nation on screen and (we hope) returning to the stage to delight new generations of theatregoers.

In each issue of "Plays & Players", ROBERT WORKMAN selects and photographs a "Player of the Month". The following twelve pages contain his selection for the Yearbook, reflecting some of the acting triumphs of 1992. Some are familiar faces and some are exciting new prospects: all of them are "Players of the Year".

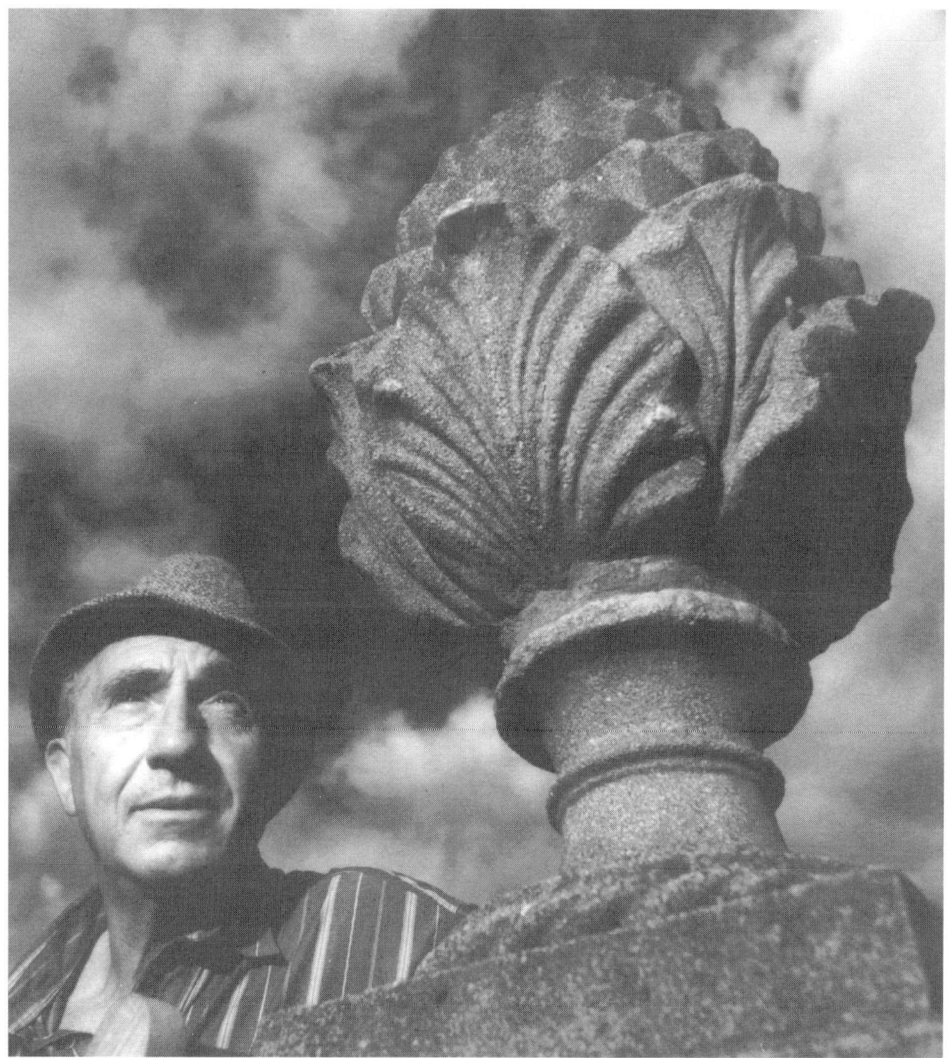

Nigel Hawthorne

Nigel Hawthorne gave the performance of his life in "The Madness of George III" at the Lyttleton theatre. "We know Mr Hawthorne to be a deft comedian" said Michael Billington in the Guardian, " but here he gives us the King's tyrannical humours, surreal babblings, unconscious desires and helpless vulnerability. The genius of the performance lies in the suggestion that under the status-conscious monarch lies a prosaic, domesticated man who likes nothing better than to curl up with 'Mrs King'."

Felicity Kendal

Well known for her success on television and in contemporary plays, Felicity Kendal has played the classics this year. As Dorine in "Tartuffe" at the Playhouse, she drew praise from Alistair Macaulay in the Financial Times: "I love the way she has let the bubbly soubrette charm of her youth deepen and gather force." As Ariadne Utterword in "Heartbreak House" at the Haymarket theatre, she was a no-nonsense siren with a voice that both smarted and caressed.

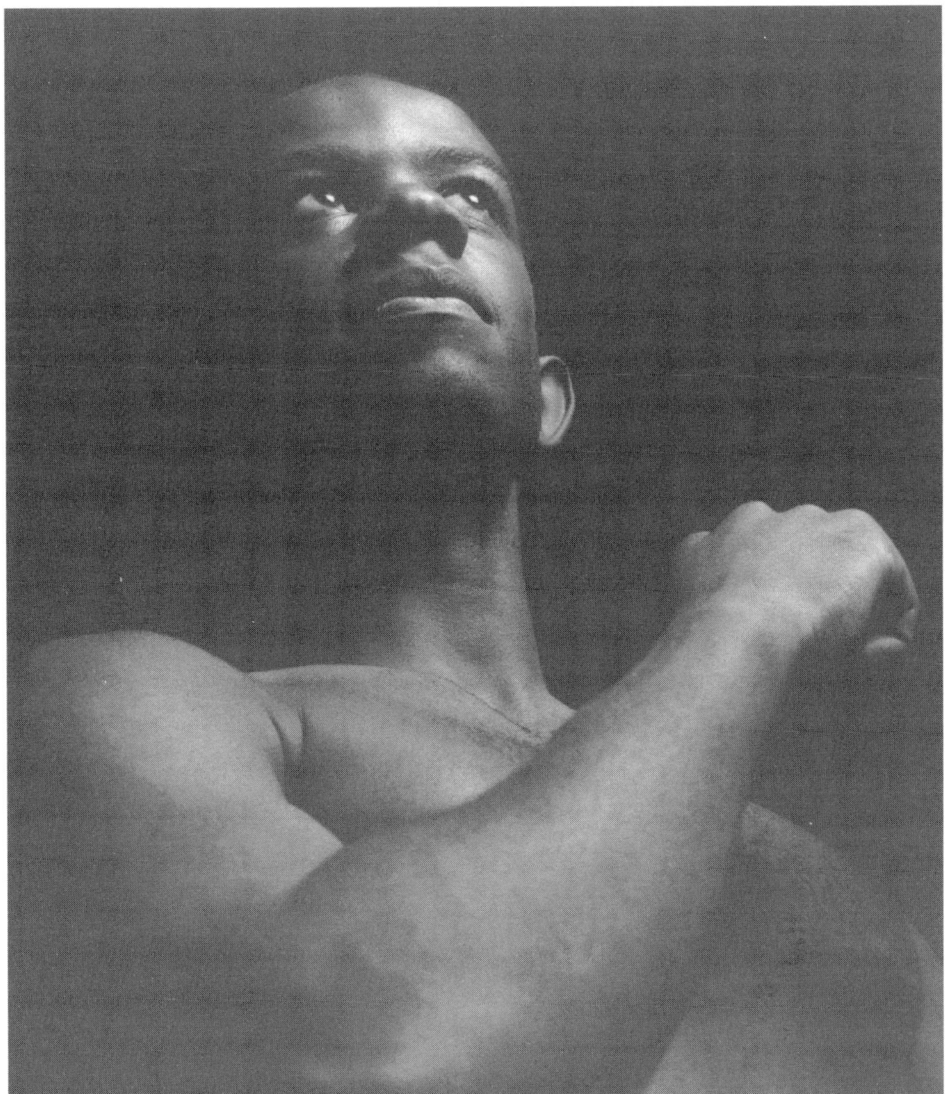

Adrian Lester

Extraordinarily cast in Cheek by Jowl's "As You Like It", Irving Wardle of the Independent on Sunday considered Adrian Lester the most breathtakingly sensuous Rosalind since Vanessa Redgrave. And in John Guare's "Six Degrees of Separation"(Royal Court), the Daily Mail's Jack Tinker described his performance as "an object lesson in dazzling charisma". As the seductive trickster who gate-crashes a Manhatten dinner party, Lester had just the right amount of wonder and charm, seeming – dangerously – to believe in his own lies.

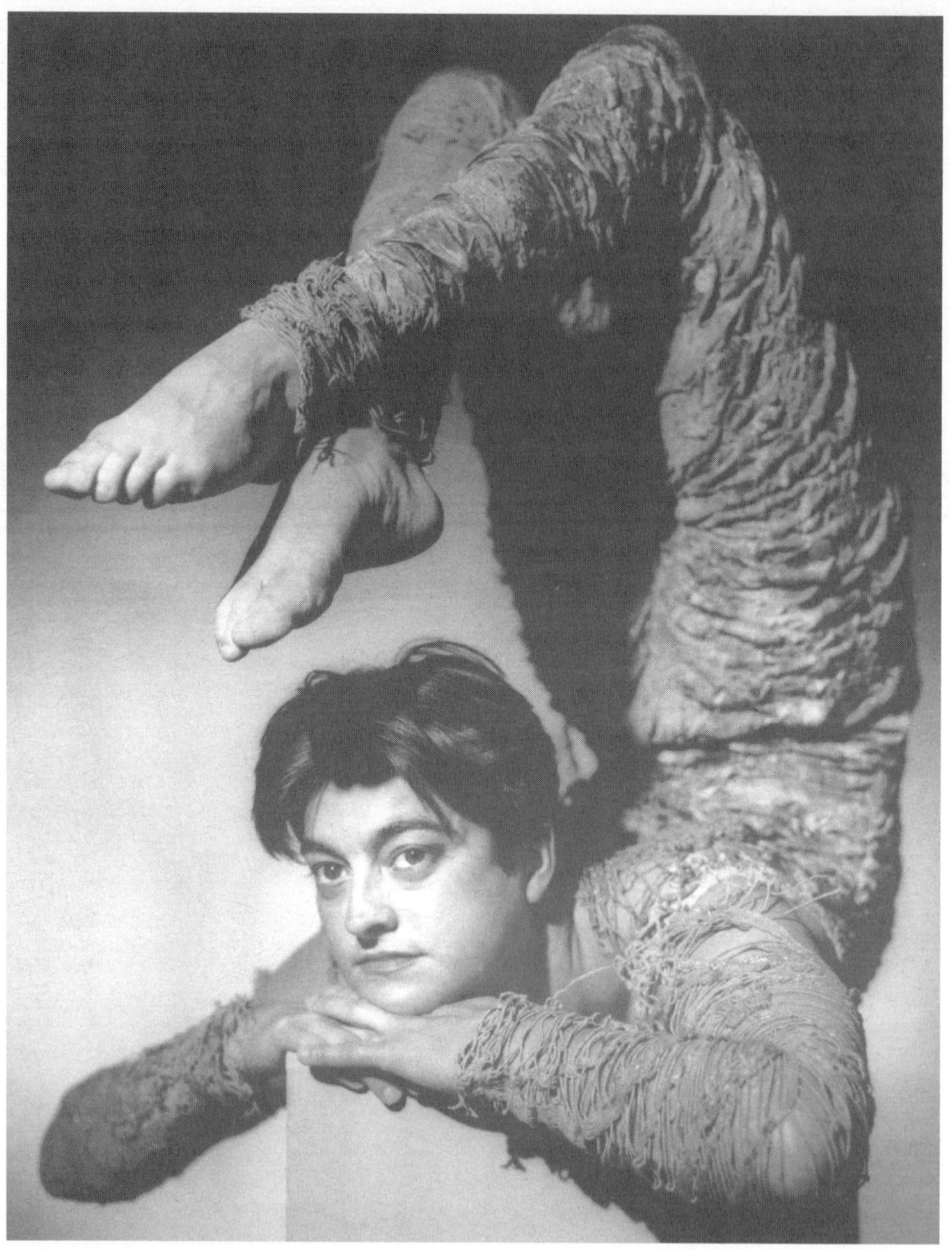

Angela Laurier

Angela Laurier's Puck was surely the most astonishing performance of the year. Robert Lepage's production of "A Midsummer Night's Dream" turned the Olivier stage into a muddy fantasy in the animal kingdom. Laurier could swish through water like a crab, reversing the functions of her hands and feet; she put a girdle round the world by twirling on a high rope in a gravity defying spin; and she even played Bottom's ass's ears – with her double jointed feet!

Barry Foster

As busy in the theatre as on televsion, Barry Foster has enjoyed as varied a year as an actor could hope for. At the Almeida, he gave a heart-catching rendition of JDW King, the quack psychologist in Tom Murphy's "The Gigli Concert". Turning to the world of musicals, Foster delighted with an eye-patched, morphine-addicted Colonel Doctor Otternschlag who oversaw the sophisticated comings and goings at "The Grand Hotel" at the Dominion.

Jane Horrocks

Jack Tinker in the Daily Mail praised Jane Horrocks in "The Rise and Fall of Little Voice" at the Cottesloe. "It's a performance which must surely ensure that some of her borrowed stardust rubs off on her own career." Horrocks played a loveless girl with a miraculous gift for impersonating famous performers such as Piaf and Judy Garland. "She all but breaks one's heart conjuring the elements of the greatest singers from within her fragile, bird-like frame."

Samuel West

Samuel West is an actor to catch in the theatre before films (Hollywood even?) take up too much of his time. He played Willy Carson, the young man who staggered ashore during a thrilling storm on the Lyttleton stage at the opening of Edward Bond's "The Sea". Finding love amidst the restrictions of an Edwardian coastal village, an honest truth shone out as he eloped with his fiancee, leaving the old regime to vanish under the waves of history.

Josette Bushell-Mingo

With her marvellously striking looks, Josette Bushell-Mingo brought an exuberant sexuality to her portrayal of one of a pair of nieces in Phyllida Lloyd's witty production of "The Virtuoso" for the RSC. As a much-chased nymphette with big wide eyes and a pink dress, she demurely swapped her suitor with her sister in a deliriously funny sexual carousel. Also contributing to the RSC's "The Thebans", Bushell-Mingo has made a notable start to her career.

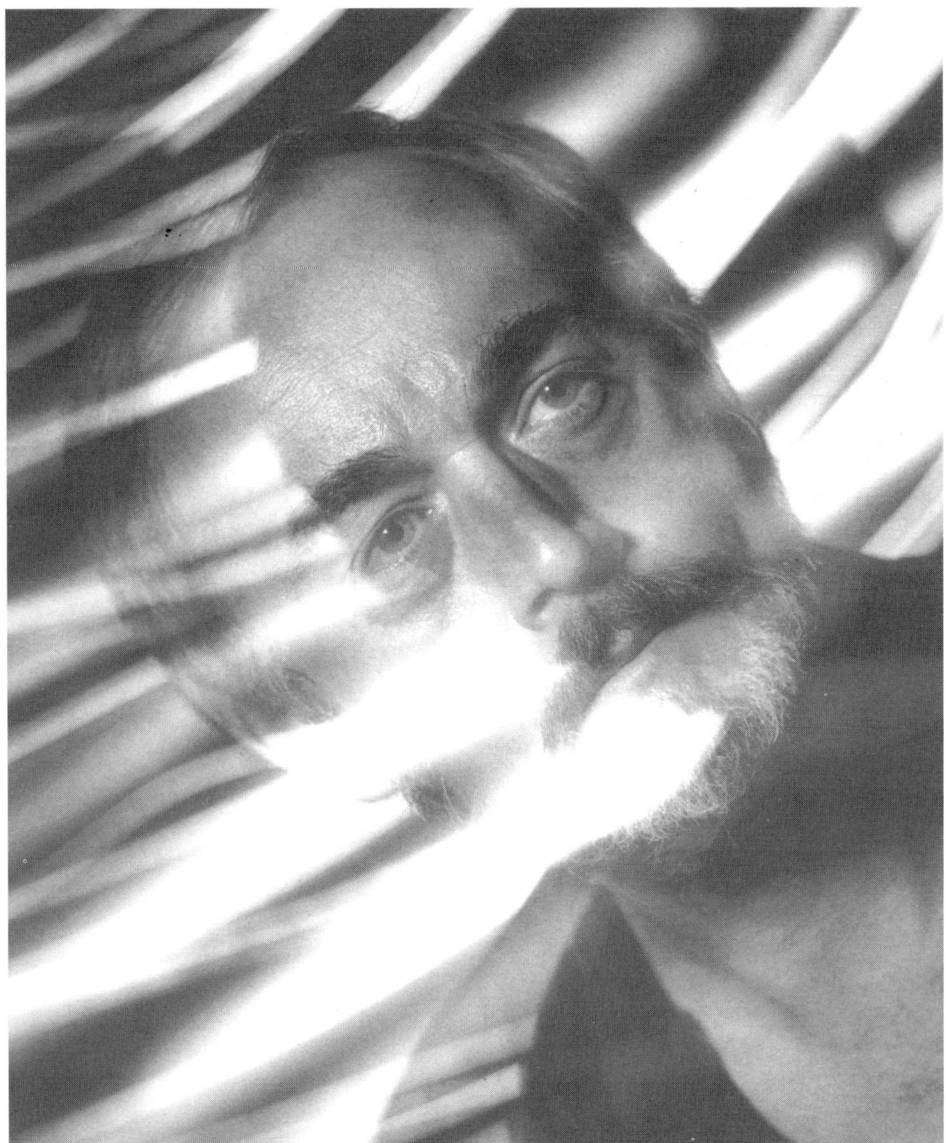

Peter Egan

Peter Egan surpassed himself in "Dejavu" at the Comedy theatre, creating one of the most controversial characters of the year. (Was it Jimmy Porter grown old or John Osborne himself?) Bullying those around him, reciting long bigoted speeches, or playing the trumpet, he was by turns camp, mordant or flirtatious. "His magnificent portrayal lets you see that, however real his hatred for the things he attacks, his disillusion with himself is deeper and more painful" – Paul Taylor, the Independent.

Lesley Sharp

Two superb creations from Lesley Sharp. First, in the Olivier theatre, the straight-thinking WPC in David Hare's "Murmuring Judges". Then a heart-rending Sonya in "Uncle Vanya" at the Cottesloe. "With her drab London accent and gauche manner, she captures all the grief and kindness of this plain woman, aching with a love she knows will never be returned. Her magnificent final speech of sympathy, endurance and desperate hope for a brighter life in the hereafter cuts to the quick" – Charles Spencer, Daily Telegraph.

Andy Serkis

Andy Serkis made a stunning debut at the Royal Court in April de Angelis' "Hush". He played Dogboy, a tramp who is infected by the spirit of a dog he kills. He had an amazing entrance, highlighted at an upstage door, stark naked under his matted hair, howling for his soul. Yelping and quivering, Serkis brought fresh observation and vigour to a part which symbolised everything wild, untameable and primitive. No wonder Michael Billington called it the bravest performance of the season.

Eileen Atkins

The much loved Eileen Atkins won critical superlatives this year for her contribution to "The Night of the Iguana" at the Lyttleton. Paul Taylor, writing in the Independent, said:"In a performance that makes powerful use of those large, sensitive, searching eyes and her tall, thin frame, Atkins lets you see the refined, drily humourous hustler as well as the ethereal saint, the weary woman who has to brazen out constant humiliations as well as the luminously protective grand-daughter."

New Players of the Year

All theatre lovers like to spot talent. Who will be the players of the year in future editions of the Yearbook? NED SHERRIN decribes the performances which have caught his eye.

Emerging Talent

I accepted the brief for this article with some misgivings. Trying to spot emerging talent is a risky business. Just after the war, my late friend and collaborator Caryl Brahms sent one of her novels ("No Bed for Bacon") to Alec Guinness suggesting that he might play the leading character (Shakespeare) brilliantly in a movie. She got a very sharp reply. The letter read "Dear Miss Brahms, I could never forgive you for telling my public that I have a face like a dispirited haddock." This sent her hopping to her files where, to her relief, she found an article she had written about emerging talents and in which she had marvelled at his Fool in "Lear", his Richard II and his Abel Drugger – all the more remarkable as these roles wrought a sublime transformation on his "dispirited haddock face".

Ned Sherrin

Her card sped back. "Dear Mr Guinness, Just which are you disputing: "dispirited" or "haddock"? A few days later a voice on the telephone announced itself as that of "Mr Haddock Guinness" and invited her to lunch – founding a firm friendship.

So perhaps a stern word here or there among the plaudits may do the same for me.

Let us start with a prime candidate. One of the most talented and arresting young presences I have witnessed this year belongs to a beanpole, a maypole, a streak, a wraith, an exclamation mark who is billed by the RSC as Guy Henry. This is a wonderfully diverse actor whom I have seen in "The Alchemist", "The Virtuoso" and "'Tis Pity she's a Whore". I marvelled at his ability to make his extraordinary mark and yet stay wittily within the context of each piece.

The RSC has also belatedly granted leading actor status to a man who will be a powerful leading actor – if he can summon up a soupcon of selfishness in pursuing his career – Michael Siberry. His rough, young Jaques in "As You Like It" at Stratford dominated an enjoyable evening and I look forward to seeing his Parolles in Peter Hall's production of "All's Well" which garnered good reports. In Hall's Dustin Hoffman "Merchant of Venice" a year or so ago, he was the most spendid Gratiano I have seen, but then, Gratiano – like Jaques and Parolles- is a scene stealing role. Derek Jacobi enthused about his Hamlet in Melbourne some years ago. Perhaps it is not too late to mount it here. If Alan Rickman (a natural Claudius) can get away with it Siberry surely could.

Michael Siberry

At the National, a wonderful new presence erupted in Marcus D'Amico in "Angels in America". I saw from the programme that he had been a dancer in "A Chorus Line" in New York. He brought a mature power and yet a vulnerability to his eye-catching role. A much harder task was undertaken by Nick Reding who played the pivotal role of the young mormon, a thankless part which he invented with a seriousness which gave Declan Donellan's breath-taking production of this tremendous (if over-written) play a still sure centre from which the rest of the cast could work. Henry Goodman has been much praised in the same show. He was sinister, yes, but my one breakfast with the late Roy Cohn – the role, taken from real life, which he was playing – was much more chilling, especially when my host turned to a flunkey and said in sardonic vein, "Did you mail that cheque to the judge?"

Rachel Robertson

We should perhaps move on to the girls. I have to declare an interest in Tara Fitzgerald, Peter O'Toole's leading lady in Keith Waterhouse's "Our Song" which we brought to the West End in the autumn. However, I saw her in the movie "Hear my Song" and in her two television appearances, "The Camomile Lawn" and "Anglo Saxon Attitudes". In the latter she played the young Dorothy Tutin and created a wonderful past history for the character played by our most valuable, underrated, great classical actress.

On the whole the new British girls shine out most brightly in musicals. This is no time to celebrate the established and incandescent Fiona Duncans and Juliet Stevensons. You need look no further than the cast of Stephen Sondheim and George Firth's "Merrily We Roll Along" which played the latest version of that musical which I saw in Leicester. Maria Friedman, Louise Gold and Jacqui Dankworth are part of a totally new generation of British musical ladies – serious, dedicated, funny and blessed with glorious voices. And it doesn't stop there. Kelly Hunter served us a "Blue Angel" in a hamfisted text by Pam Gems and a naive and clumsy proscenium staging by Trevor Nunn. The part had nothing to do with the myth of Marlene but it was beautifully acted and refreshingly sung with that sensibility which she always brings to music which challenges or excites her. And then there was Claire Moore revitalising "The Card" – alongside Peter Duncan (back to the chaps) infectious in Jim Dale's old role.

Out of "Spread a Little Happiness" at the Whitehall, there emerged a very promising, still unproved but fresh personality in Rachel Robertson. She will have to work hard to achieve the raw distinction of her acting near-namesake Rachel Roberts; but there is a spark in her which should be fanned. In the same show, Maurice Clarke confirmed the promise he showed as an actor-singer in "Brigadoon" a couple of seasons ago.

This brings us back to musical men. At the Dominion, there was an impeccable company and a charismatic leading man in "Grand Hotel". Brent Barratt sang a small role in a Noel Coward compilation I directed disastrously in Connecticut eleven years ago and it was glorious to hear him again centre stage, in full voice, with bags of panache.

At the Edinburgh Festival, I caught a National Youth Music Theatre revival of the musical "Billy" – an amateur cast led by a professional, Andrew O'Connor, who could be a valuable leading man for "Me and My Girl" in any of the twenty five more years it looks likely to run. And at last I caught up with this ambitious company's "The Ragged Child". Directors Jeremy James Taylor and Frank Whately came up with a breathtaking kaleidescope of stage pictures and Stephen Graham who played the crossing sweeper Tommy should go into the professional theatre with distinction.

Brian Friel's "Philadelphia Here I Come" announced Donald Donnelly's talent to the world back in the 1960s. Dan Crawford's revival at the King's Head and at Wyndham's pitchforked another marvellous pair playing the two sides of the character Gareth O'Donnell into contention. Jonathon Arun's public Gareth and Brendan Coyle's private version were both warm and funny and beautifully differentiated.

One mystery remains. Is the story of the tragic consequences of a jock-strap lobbed into the audience of middle-aged matrons by a Chippendale at the Strand Theatre true? False? Or a Brand New Folk Myth? If you know, please write to me at the Yearbook!

WHO DOES WHAT IN THEATRE

Even the most regular theatre-goer may not always know who does what in the theatre. Who owns the theatre building in which you are sitting? What does a director actually do? CHRISTOPHER WEBBER explains.

Theatre Owners

Britain's theatres are in the hands of a motley crew of companies, corporations, trusts and individuals; and it is curiously difficult to be completely sure who administers them. Quite a large proportion of the capital's best known theatres are built on land which is held freehold by Oxbridge colleges or minor public schools, whilst the leaseholds on the bricks and mortar change hands with alarming rapidity. This makes the shifting empires of the big West End players, like the Maybox Group (who own Wyndham's Theatre) or Stoll Moss, very difficult to compete with.

Wyndham's Theatre

The RSC's London base at the Barbican is owned and administered by the City of London, though the National Theatre stands on ground held freehold by its own governing body. Some famous old foundations, such as Sadler's Wells, are governed by established trusts; others (notably Ed Mervish's Old Vic) are controlled by individual, one-off companies.

Things are not much simpler in the provinces. Most theatres are civic owned, though some (such as Southampton's Nuffield or Exeter's Northcott) are integrally built into modern University Campuses, and many others are in the private control of independent boards of self-appointed enthusiasts.

Subsidised Theatres and their Boards

However the debate may rage over the merits of public spending on the arts, subsidised and commercial theatres manage to coexist fairly happily. Southampton, for example, enjoys profit-making tours at the 2,000-seat Mayflower as well as quality repertory work at the smaller, subsidised Nuffield.

With the exception of a few summer-season theatres (such as Jill Freud's at Southwold) which almost manage on box-office returns alone, all professional reps need subsidy. Money must be found elsewhere if they are to function over and above the Farce and Thriller level of operations.

Theatre's governing boards draw their members from as wide a cross-section of influence as possible – academics as well as civic dignitaries, captains of industry as well as local enthusiasts; and in a time when money from traditional, public sources (the newly devolved regional Arts Councils and Civic Committees) is falling in real terms, cash support from private companies is increasingly necessary to balance the books.

Although the new reliance on business sponsorship has its dangers, the spectre of the RSC putting on a "Hamlet" just to advertise cigars is still some way off. Meanwhile, the hard-pressed reps are only too grateful for the lifeline that corporate funding offers them.

Artistic Directors

There can't be many people with an interest in theatre who haven't cherished some brief day-dream about the marvellous things they would do if they were Artistic Director of the National, the RSC or even their local rep. The actuality might prove less alluring than the dream, especially in the provinces.

Richard Eyre

Artistic Directors of major companies (currently Richard Eyre at the National, Adrian Noble at the RSC) are responsible for artistic staffing, short-term programming of plays and long-term policy. How they operate is down to personal style, but clearly the huge number of shows rolling off, say, the RSC conveyor-belt means that their personal involvement is likely to be confined to a few keynote productions – particularly as they must spend some time away as ambassadors for the company at home and abroad.

At least the flagship companies provide a huge battery of associate directors, literary advisers and casting assistants to help them. Some theatres, notably Manchester's Royal Exchange, have a team of four or five joint-supremos to spread the workload; but in the smaller reps Artistic Directors won't have the budgetary resources to do much other than run the ship pretty well alone. For some of them, the dream is more like a nightmare.

Executive Directors

If an Artistic Director is lucky, she or he will be supported by an administrative or executive director. Some executive directors have hands-on experience as Artistic Directors themselves, more are recruited from other areas of arts administration; perhaps the majority in repertory theatre are trained in money management or accountancy.

Certainly financial survival is the overriding priority for most executive directors. The expertise and tact required to cope with the complexities of managing running costs of the theatre itself, hiring staff and drafting contracts, are equally useful when hammering out production budgets with the Artistic Director. To these chores must be added the main weight of negotiations with funding bodies such as the Arts Council and local corporations.

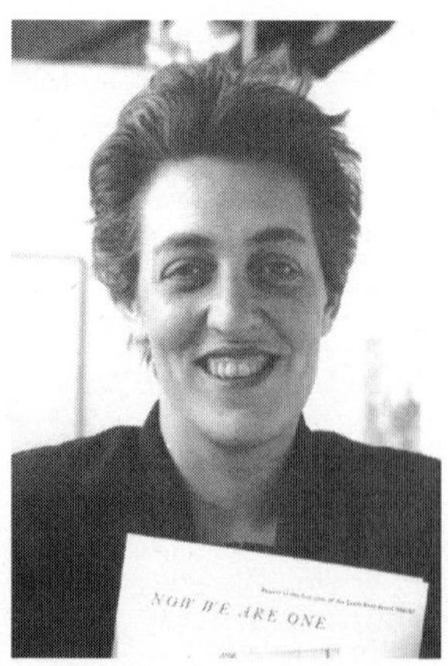

Ruth Mackenzie, executive director of Notingham Playhouse

At Nottingham Playhouse, for instance, executive director Ruth Mackenzie sees her task as essentially supportive, freeing her artistic director, Pip Broughton, from the need to spend time and energy running the building or pursuing sponsorship and enabling her to do what she does best – directing the plays. The organisational and imaginative grasp of an executive director can certainly make or mar an artistic regime.

Fund Raising

Lucy Stout, head of development at the National

The heady days when theatre costs were reliably covered by Arts Council guarantees to top up flagging box-offices are gone. As theatre does its best to respond to economic necessity (and the complications caused by the recent decentralisation of Arts Council financing) new funding strategies and sales ploys have led to the creation of ever more sophisticated marketing departments. Meanwhile, the scramble for corporate sponsorship has become a major preoccupation.

At grass-roots, the last ten years have seen drastic efforts made to maximise ticket receipts. Old-style publicity has been eclipsed by media ploys, subscription schemes and special offers. Many companies now use specialist press and advertising firms to raise public awareness and cultivate the all-important profile, which is indispensable when trying to attract vital money from business sources.

Organisations like ABSA (Association for Business Sponsorship of the Arts) exist to help match potential sponsors to artistic product, and the government's initiative on linked funding for the major companies, by which treasury grants are made to match private sponsorship on a pound for pound basis, offers further temptation to push live theatre away from Arts Council subsidy towards the arms of the new, corporate purseholders.

Producers

Cameron Mackintosh

If funding in the subsidised sector is a complicated balancing act, the prospects of the independent producer being able to turn an honest penny have become even more perilous during the last few years. Many formerly great moguls of commercial theatre have gone into at least temporary hibernation, and even Sir Andrew Lloyd Webber's Really Useful Theatre Company has drawn in its horns.

Few of these independent production companies are large or powerful enough to finance their own shows without recourse to outside backers, or angels. Many individuals (and a few specialist organisations) play the West End and commercial touring game much like the stockmarket. If a show has a successful run, they may see a healthy return on their investment; but many large-scale musicals can take years before they even reach the break-even point.

The new commercial spirit has seen independent producers such as Cameron Mackintosh and Bill Kenwright going into partnership with the major companies (and ailing provincial reps) on projects such as "Les Miserables", which started life as an RSC show at the Barbican. Nowadays actors are even driven to become angels on their own shows – sometimes (as witness "Return to the Forbidden Planet") with spectacular success.

Directors

Deborah Warner

A handful of venerable actors can recall the Good Old Days when the humble stage manager was in charge of mounting the show. Sadly, the growing sophistication of staging has led to the rise of that omnipotent coordinator, The Director. Some writers regret this, though only a few (notably Ayckbourn) have proved clear-minded enough to direct their own plays well. Even democratic acting groups like Shared Experience find the need to have someone in charge of the production process.

What do directors do? Usually the first person contracted by the management, they appoint the rest of the creative team – designers, composers and choreographers; they have the final say in casting the actors; they run rehearsals; they explain the production to the marketing department. What the director says goes, because he or she will finally take much of the blame (or praise) for the finished product.

Directors may be democrats or despots. The best ones, like politicians, develop a knack for conjuring good work from the diverse talents on their team, whether by coercion or persuasion. Current market leaders (such as Deborah Warner or Richard Jones) reject the mandarin approach of some of their predecessors in favour of a more open, non-combative style.

Designers

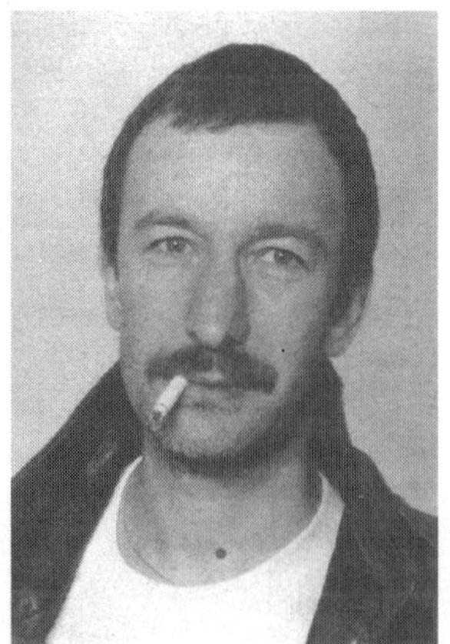

Philip Prowse

Designers help the director to devise and create the production. Most designers specialise in either settings or costume, though many are adept at both. Lighting design is a vital specialist skill, and nowadays the sound designer is just as indispensable, given the complex demands of mixing for big-stage musicals.

Today's designers have to keep abreast of scientific advancements in fields such as engineering, laser and fabric technology, and their work on shows like "Cats" and "Starlight Express" has unquestionably pushed forward the boundaries of theatrical possibility. Indeed, many directors would admit to owing their success to imaginative and sympathetic design; and in great partnerships (such as Sir Peter Hall's with designer John Bury) the input of one can hardly be evaluated independently of the other.

Recently, designers like Philip Prowse at Glasgow Citizens' theatre have gone a step further and chosen to direct their own productions. Where sets and costumes create such unique visual worlds that much of a director's work has to be geared towards helping the actors feel at home, there is sense in this. However, to those actors and writers weary of Directors Theatre, the movement towards Designer's Theatre offers cold comfort.

HOW THEATRE HAPPENS

Actors, writers and directors are all fascinating - but their work could not start without the support of the people who make theatre happen. From lighting designers to choreographers, the Yearbook analyses the talented work going on behind the scenes.

Lighting

Lighting designers are the unsung heroes of the theatre. Critics rarely mention them, and if they do editors tend to find space lacking. Yet the contribution of the lighting team is vital and the need for expertise has become greater than ever. Since 1976, computerised lighting boards have become the norm, giving lighting designers freedom to multiply effects and so play a massive part in creating the theatrical extravaganzas of the 1980s.

Television, video and pop music have all been responsible for enhancing our visual level of expectation. The theatre has, willy-nilly, been forced to compete. Nowadays,the technical "get in" for a musical like "Miss Saigon" can last as long as the rehearsal period. One of the most remarkable of recent innovations is the use of vari lights - motorised, mobile follow-spots which are so sophisticated that a single vari can do the work of a hundred conventional lamps. The effect is to provide precise and subtle lighting for small, defined areas.

Perhaps one reason why lighting designers are ignored is that their skill provides the glue which holds a show together, and which therefore only calls attention to itself when things have gone wrong. Their work must be integral with the design and direction as a whole, just as the actor becomes one part of the vehicle which carries the author's intentions.

Away from the commercial musicals, the scene is very different. In the major houses, equipment is at a standstill and lighting designers have no ongoing budget with which to invest, despite the availability of a vast range of new equipment. Absence of funds is certainly to blame, but some in the profession detect a shortage of assertive newcomers: too many simply follow the director's orders.

Theatrical lighting designers also work in other art forms such as opera and dance - something which greatly enriches their understanding of the theatrical process. And they enjoy variety within the theatre, too: a successful lighting designer like David Hersey, who designed the lights for "Cats" and "Miss Saigon" finds something challenging about the typical fifty lamp rig to be found in fringe venues.

Before moving into a theatre, the designer draws the positions of the chosen lights on a huge piece of paper rather like an architect's drawing. Once inside the building, there are usually between three to five days to fix and focus the lamps, compose the lighting arc, and put the cues into a running order - all of which is fed onto a computer disk. During this concentrated time, the lighting designer is competing with the set builders and the rehearsal process for access to the stage.

Many designers will look to paintings for inspiration and as concrete reference points between them and the directors. Paintings can offer useful clues about the colour, nature and angle of light.

Surprising though it may seem, there are in this country no training courses in lighting design unlike the USA where they are legion. Like so many of their colleagues, lighting workers learn everything on the job. Although the technical side of lighting has become so complex, simple visual images can often provide the most riveting theatre. This year, at the National Theatre, Robert Lepage's "Needles and Opium" (designed by himself) and "A Midsummer Night's Dream" (lighting by Jean Kalman) were noted for their stunning effects. These included huge shadows and starry nights. Lighting can be simple but so powerful that its effects remain to haunt the memory.

BETTY CAPLAN

Music

Mia Soteriou

The presence of the composer in theatre is strong. The West End is humming with musicals, with originals such as "Moby Dick" appearing along with a clutch of shows using existing songs such as "From a Jack to a King" and "Cotton Club". Stalwarts have been revived and new operas such as "Gawain" welcomed.

Composers working in straight theatre may not have as high a profile as composers of musicals or of film and TV themes, but they are an essential part of the team who create the atmosphere and style of a production. The advantage of original music is that it is integral (imagine "Psycho" or "Star Wars" with different music). The composer can create specific themes and moods, written to exact timings. He or she can offer live or recorded sound - which may be instrumental or choral. The music can be used to underscore scenes, punctuate the action, or even add musical content to enhance the play.

Whereas the writers of musicals will often generate and sell their own product, the drama composer is commissioned. He or she then has meetings with the director. Artistic ideas such as appropriate themes, period and instrumentation are propounded alongside practicalities such as budgetary - and human - resources. While fulfilling the brief as creatively as possible, the composer has to consider factors such as whether the venue is open air or whether the company has state-of-the-art equipment.

A plan is made of where music might occur. Some cues are prescribed, as when songs appear within the text. Other cues are artistic decisions. Whether a scene-change requires a song or should be instrumental, which musical theme is relevant at what point, where silence will have the most impact - all these matters must be considered before research and writing begin.

Every composer works differently. Some use keyboards and computers to record arrangements. Others write using instruments and arrange in their heads. Eventually, a score is produced for the musicians to read while vocal parts are often taught to the performers aurally. Recognising and adapting to the standard of skills available is vitally important.

Flexibility is the key to the whole process. For example, during rehearsal, it may emerge that a cast member has a skill which the composer did not know of at the original planning stage. Once discovered, this skill may be highlighted to best effect.

Sometimes, the composer gives a presentation to the company, demonstrating the research done with examples of potential themes to introduce the cast to the world of the production's music. The cast starts learning songs and music early. Where there are separate musicians, these are brought in towards the end of the rehearsal period. Recording is always left as late as possible to allow the maximum opportunity to take exact timings of scenes which are underscored or scene-changes which are to be covered.

Good planning is essential and saves time. It's worth remembering that an actor/musician who is involved in a quick change will not be able to play while changing ! The technical run highlights this sort of problem. At this stage, stage-management will confirm the timing of all the cues and sound-levels are plotted. Where musicians play off-stage, cue-lights will be arranged to signal to them when to start playing. Decisions are made about where the musicians or speakers will be placed - which will sometimes be under the stage or in the auditorium.

Dress runs and previews afford opportunities for the director and composer to make any necessary artistic adjustments. Then on to the first night - when the composer's job is effectively over.

MIA SOTERIOU

Sound

Theo Massos in "Buddy"

Greek theatres were intended to hold the entire population of a town, so their acoustics had to be excellent. Because they were not enclosed, there were no echoes and no reverberation, and all that was necessary was to project the sound effectively: the actors were raised on a platform to allow the sound to carry further; a rear wall reflected voices forward; and there was a hard floor in front to reinforce the direct sound with upward reflections. That this arrangement was remarkably effective can still be heard today at Epidaurus.

When theatre went indoors, acoustical problems grew more complex. Over the years, solutions have been more a matter of luck than judgement, though the excellent acoustic properties of wood were first recognised by the Romans, exploited by the Elizabethans and reached their apotheosis in Wagner's Festspielhaus at Bayreuth. Sadly, wood burns, and other materials must now predominate in our theatre buildings. Even the introduction of computer-aided design techniques has not produced uniformly successful results. The discovery of electronic methods of amplifying and changing sound has opened up many interesting possibilities. Attempts have been made to improve the poor acoustics of an auditorium by hiding loudspeakers in the walls and using them to simulate non-existent resonances. This effect purports to be undetectable, but the results are usually unconvincing.

The technology can be used as an aid to the actor: modern opera performances invariably relay the orchestral sound to the singers through loudspeakers positioned behind the proscenium. A recent development even allows singers to wear individual ear-pieces, to which the sound is transmitted by infra-red beams.

A more interesting use of the technology is in manipulating the sound made by the performers before sending it into the auditorium through loudspeakers. Straight plays and operas rarely use amplification, though it can be useful for special effects, such as adding extra reverberation for a dungeon or a church scene. However, the full range of sound technology is usually on display in a modern performance of a musical. In fact, few major musicals could now take place without the collaboration of the sound designer, his assistants and a wide range of up-to-the-minute devices, including microphones, amplifiers, loudspeakers and many miles of cable. Here, the aim is to facilitate a simpler and more natural style of singing than in opera, yet ironically the means of achieving that end are highly complex.

The multi-track techniques of the recording-studio are now applied to the theatre: the sound produced by each singer and each instrumentalist is picked up by individual microphones, allowing the sound designer great latitude in the way he mixes the final sound - some reverberation behind that solo voice, a little more clarinet, a little less chorus.

In particular, the radio-microphone has proved a very useful tool: small in size, it can be concealed in the hair or on the costume of a performer, and is attached by a thin wire to a small transmitter-pack concealed somewhere on the body. It has the advantage of remaining at a fixed distance from the source of the sound and has a small range, meaning that even if another sound-source is nearby, the microphone will not detect it: thus the sound-desk receives a very clean version of the sound being produced.

The possibilities grow more complex as the technology advances. we have come a long way since the Roman architect Vitruvius (c70-15 BC) tried to enhance the resonances of his amphitheatre by the simple method of placing acoustic vases or "echeia" in cavities under the seats.

ANDREW WICKES

JOHN CAMPBELL
SCENIC ARTIST

PHOTOGRAPHIC BACKINGS

SCENE PAINTING

SPECIAL EFFECTS
LANDSCAPES
ETC

LONDON
TEL: 081-748 7266
FAX: 081-748 1421

SCENERY

FOR ALL PRODUCTIONS

JAS. FREDERICKS STUDIO

Langford Road,
Weston-super-Mare
Tel: 0934 624791

STAGE SETS

Tabs, Legs, Borders & all Stage Drapes-Hire and Sale

Aniline Dyed cloths for Hire - over 300 Subjects, plus Cyc's

Gauzes Plain, Painted, for Hire - over 100 subjects

Excellent selection of period furniture, for Hire

Scenery for all Productions to Hire and built to Order

Exhibition, Video and Photo Sets built & painted to order

Tab Tracks, Wipe Tracks, Rostra Braces & Weights for Hire

Steel Deck Rostra for Hire
Star Cloths (Inc. Fibre Optics)

Unit L Delta Wharf, Blackwall Ind. Estate, Tunnel Avenue, Greenwich, London SE10 OQH.
Tel: 081-853 2370
Fax: 081-853 5683

HI-FLI

FOR FLYING EFFECTS

CONTACT HI-FLI FOR ALL SAFE AND ECONOMICAL FLYING.

HI-FLI Ltd.
16, Compton Close
Kinver, Stourbridge, West Midlands DY7 6DW
Tel: 0384 872710 and 021-550 1088
FAX: 021-550 7249

VELVETFIELD LTD

SCENERY CONSTRUCTION
STAGE ENGINEERING
PROP MAKING
SCENE PAINTING
METAL WORK
PORTABLE STAGING

12 Hillfoot Road Neepsend, Sheffield S3 8AA
Tel: (0742) 756772

SPECIALISTS IN THE ENTERTAINMENT & LEISURE INDUSTRY

We can provide all your scenery, props and model making needs from small scale touring productions to large scale purpose built sets. We will even come to you to build and paint your sets on location. We adapt any set to fit your production. Collection and delivery anywhere in the UK. Anything considered so call us first!

9 Keppel Road, Gorleston, Great Yarmouth
Norfolk, NR31 6SN

Telephone: Studio 0493 657093 24 Hours
Workshop: 0693 652055
Represented by Roger Carey Mangement
Telephone: 081 995 4477

Robert Knight

Stage and Television Scenery Contractors

Production Services:

Production Management. Hires - *serge and velour drapes, black masking, gauzes, cycloramas, revolves, motorised winches, wardrobe equipment, skips and costume containers - for Theatre, Studio and Location.*
Theatre front of house displays.

Tel: 071–277 1704
Fax: 071–277 1722

Set-Building

The designer has completed a 1:25 scale model of the set, and the technical drawings are ready: what next? The execution of the designs is now in the hands of a technical director or production manager; it is his task to superintend the construction process, keep costs down and eventually deliver a completed and fully operational set to the stage.

One of the first decisions to be made is where to have the set built. The national companies and some of the larger repertory theatres have their own workshops which can cope with everything but the most specialised jobs; but the majority of sets will be farmed out to one or more of the many private firms who work exclusively in the field of set-building for theatre, television or film.

Between 1945 and 1960, theatre design in Britain was largely a matter of creating pictures within the frame of the proscenium, by means of an arrangement of backcloths, cut-cloths, canvas flats and rostra: these were sets that could readily be constructed by traditional methods and from traditional materials.

But by the 1960s, a new generation of directors had begun to appear, new kinds of theatres (such as the Chichester Festival Theatre) were making new demands, stage design became established as an academic discipline within colleges of art, and there were huge advances in technology. Sean Kenny's set for "Oliver!" (1960) marked a turning-point: it was architecturally-based, mechanical and three-dimensional; it featured revolves within revolves, and large built pieces moving and turning within one another; there was no backcloth in the traditional sense - a panorama of London was painted directly onto the brick wall at the back of the stage.

Sean Kenny died young, but the baton was taken up by John Bury, who began to experiment with mechanical workings: his flying gods on painted clouds in "La Calisto" (1970) and his moving trees in "A Midsummer Night's Dream" (1981) clearly point the way towards the complex engineering feats of "Cats" (1981) and "The Phantom of the Opera" (1986).

So construction for the modern theatre is no longer a simple matter of joinery and carpentry. Engineering has assumed a much greater importance, and specialist firms who have not up till now been involved in the theatre are able to solve complex constructional and mechanical problems with ease.

New materials have meant that designers can ask for effects which in the past were either impossible or prohibitively expensive. A small scenic piece (say, a ship's figure-head) might be sculpted out of polystyrene, sealed with latex, and covered with fibreglass; architectural details (such as relief mouldings, brickwork or even columns) need no longer be carved individually because they are available in cheap, lightweight vacuum-formed sheets; larger built pieces (say, a full-size horse) are probably a fibreglass shell reinforced with an inner framework of wood or metal.

New materials, new methods of using traditional materials, advances in electronics which have brought the cost of sophisticated control mechanisms within limited theatre budgets: these are some of the factors which have brought about a revolution in methods of set-construction, a revolution which is still in progress today. The watch-words, however, are the same as they always were: effectiveness, ingenuity and economy.

ANDREW WICKES

NEED TO GET THINGS MOVING ?
CONTACT
R ELIABILITY
A DVICE AND BACK-UP
D ISCOUNTED PRICING
C ONTACT 24 HOURS A DAY
L EADING EXPERTS
I DEALLY SUITED VEHICLES AND EQUIPMENT
F RIENDLY AND HELPFUL STAFF
F AST AND EFFICIENT RESPONSE
E XPERIENCE OF THEATRE, FILM AND TELEVISION
S ERVICE – SECOND TO NONE!

LONDON 081 687 2344
BIRMINGHAM 0455 890163
MANCHESTER 061 8650071
24 HOURS 0836 242811

Made to Measure
CASES
For protection, organisation, security, and peace of mind
contact Jeremy, Fred or Nichola.
PRO-tech
Tel: 0562 822906 Fax: 0562 823025

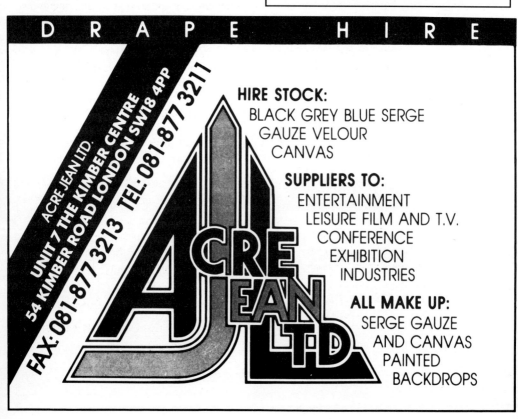

Le Mark

Stage Management

In a large building-based theatre company, like the National Theatre or the Royal Shakespeare Company, several stage managers work together in concert, interacting with a wide range of specialists, from carpenters and wig-makers via set designers and scene painters to sound specialists and lighting engineers.

In a small fringe theatre, the situation is entirely different. There will probably be only one stage manager, as opposed to an integrated team, and far from co-ordinating a range of individual experts, this catch-all title can cover virtually everything in the production apart from actually acting – from set building and selling tickets to sweeping up and making tea.

Joe Orton – one-time ASM

In theory, however, the stage management team consists of a stage manager (SM), deputy stage manager (DSM) and any number of assistant stage managers, commonly known as ASMs. In the heyday of repertory theatre, the post of "Acting ASM" was a common route into the profession, combining assistant stage management tasks with small roles. Inevitably, it remains a less specialised role than SM or DSM.

The stage management team's job is to organise and co-ordinate rehearsals and performances. During rehearsal, this consists of notating blocking and prompting, but it's once the rehearsals finish and the run begins that a stage manager really comes into his or her own. The stage manager is responsible for time cues to the technical staff who provide sound and lighting effects and for "setting" (putting on) or "striking" (taking off) furniture and scenery. Again, on the fringe, stage managers are often expected to perform a lot of these functions themselves. In a big auditorium, he or she co-ordinates the stage crew. In a little theatre the stage manager is the stage crew – and a lot else besides.

Subsidiary responsibilities include preparing and setting out props. Such "properties" (anything handled by an actor or used to dress the set) will often have been hunted down and bought by the stage managers in person, usually on a very limited budget. They tend to be period pieces from cheap junk shops rather than expensive antiques. 60's playright Joe Orton started out as an acting ASM at Ipswich Rep, spending most of his time trudging the street looking for props. Orton later said that the only thing Ipswich Rep taught him was "not to write in too much because it is so awfully hard on the assistant stage managers to fix that sort of thing".

If props cannot be found, then someone has to make them. Again, such tasks are assigned to an entire department in a few of the largest companies, but in smaller troups, it's often the job of the stage manager. And whoever buys, begs, borrows, steals or makes them, it's the stage manager's responsibility to make sure that all the properties are in the right places before the show starts. Common sense and a cool head are essential for a stage manager. He or she must be able to act decisively in the event of a crisis – of which there are inevitably several during the most smoothly run show.

A generation ago, drama schools taught acting only, and stage management was still largely regarded as an unskilled job rather than a career. Now all that has changed. Of the seventeen accredited drama schools in Britain, thirteen offer stage management courses, including Bristol Old Vic Theatre School, Central School of Speach and Drama and the Royal Academy of Dramatic Art. Courses range from two to three years, but this is no back door into acting. The best stage managers are usually artistic – but without even the slightest trace of artistic temperament.

WILLIAM COOK

Make-up

Cats

Make-up in the theatre began as a form of stylisation. It was used to turn the actor's face into a mask and allow him to represent something unusual or impossible. In the religious dramas of medieval Europe, the faces of God and Christ were traditionally painted white and gold, and those of the cherubim in red; Elizabethan actors whitened their features if they were to play ghosts, and Moors were presented with coal-black faces. Not until the seventeenth century, when actors began to perform by artificial light, were cosmetics used to enhance or elaborate the features, and the art of theatrical make-up began to develop.

Natural daylight is reflected onto us, but in the theatre, light is thrown directly onto the performer: this alters natural colour, light and shade, and tends to flatten the features. These conditions present a problem, and offer a possibility: if an actor requires his face to appear normal under stage lighting, corrective make-up is necessary; but the process allows elaborate changes to the natural features. By the early eighteenth century, the use of make-up for disguise was well established. Garricks's skill in this area was well known, and according to the French actor Noverre, even his friends sometimes failed to recognize him.

So make-up has come to serve one of two purposes: "straight" make-up restores natural colour, lines shadows and features, and is ideally undetected by the spectator, while "character" make-up changes the shape, colour and texture of the face, and with the aid of nose putty, false teeth and other devices, can produce an effect far removed from the real appearance of the actor.

Most actors prefer to apply their own make-up, and treat it as an important part of the process of preparing to perform. It is rare that a make-up artist will be available before each performance, though when specialised effects are required, it is more common. Few modern actors know how to use nose-putty effectively, or how to create convincing broken noses, open wounds, burns or deformities.

Make-up comes in two basic forms: grease paint and pancake. Grease-paint, sold in round sticks, was the invention of the Wagnerian singer Ludwig Leichner, who worked on the chemical formula in the 1860s, manufactured the sticks privately, and when professional demand grew, founded a company in 1873. The numbers he gave to each colour are still in use today. It is a hard foundation paint, grease-based and available in stick form or in jars, in a great many colours. The colours are easily mixed, skin blemishes or joins are easily covered and it is inexpensive; but it is messy to use, rubs off on clothing, encourages perspiration and requires powdering, which often obliterates detail. Cake make-up is a greaseless, water-soluble foundation paint, applied with a damp sponge from a flat, round container. It is also available in liquid form. Simple and clean to apply, it has a smooth finish and does not encourage perspiration; however, it is relatively costly, the colours are impossible to mix and during performance, it dissolves quickly.

In recent years we have seen radical changes in methods of stage lighting: not only is light used more indirectly, reproducing more accurately the effect of reflected natural light, but colour is employed with more subtlety. The use of lanterns without coloured gelatine but with corrective filters to remove the warm glow of the tungsten filament is common: three-dimensional lighting does much of the work. Corrective make-up has become less necessary, and convincing character make-up not only impossible but hopelessly old-fashioned. Except in a stylised play, the general rule of make-up nowadays is "as little as possible".

ANDREW WICKES

Hairdressing and Wigs

Wigs have been used on the stage since earliest times: about 1600, John Ogle was paid twenty-six shillings and eight pence for "four yeallowe heares for head attires for women". How convincing these early wigs were we don't know, but with the advent of cinema and changes in modern lighting practice, the art of making a wig undetectable at close quarters has advanced greatly.

Phillip Schofield

The largest theatre companies have wig and make-up departments, which are capable of making everything:- wigs, beards, moustaches, eyebrows, etc. For companies without their own facilities, a freelance wig supervisor may be employed to provide everything either from his own stock or from a hire company; or more frequently the whole business of wigs is left in the hands of the over-worked wardrobe department.

When a wig supervisor receives the designs, he or she looks at the actors who will be wearing them and decides on the technical choices which can be made. Very often an actor's own hair, dressed or coloured differently, can be used for the character he is playing. This is the simplest and most economical solution and certainly preferable to wearing a wig of poor quality or one that fits badly.

If this is not possible, then the desired effect might be achieved with a hairpiece. These are of two kinds: a "toupee", which supplies a front hairline and blends into the natural hair at the back and on the sides; or a "fall", which is attached to the natural hair in order to lengthen it at the back. Alternatively, a full wig must be used. Wigs come in every conceivable shape, colour and size; the only thing that they have in common is that the hair is attached to a base or foundation which is worn on the head. Foundations can be made of cotton or imitation silk net, treated silk lace, nylon net, hairlace, silk gauze or a combination of nylon/lace and terylene net. Each one is different to fit individual measurements.

The hair which is attached to the foundation is mostly human, but yak hair is sometimes employed where greater stiffness is required. It may either be knotted in long strips called weft or more usually nowadays attached by a process called ventilating: hairs are knotted on to the base individually at the front and never more than two or three at a time where the hair would naturally grow thicker. When glued to the performer's face with spirit gum, the transparent net is almost undetectable and gives the illusion of a natural hairline.

Only the minimum amount of hair is used. A typical wig will weigh about two ounces, and it is crucial that it should be light enough for an actor wearing one to look natural next to someone without a wig. At the same time it has to be very durable, and to be able to withstand cleansing with acetone and re-dressing after every performance.

For moustaches and beards, satisfactory effects are possible with crepe hair, but it requires considerable skill and patience to apply, and the result can only be used once or twice. More convenient (though unfortunately much more expensive) are beards and moustaches made of real hair and knotted into net foundations in the same manner as wigs.

Artificial hair is not without its dangers: in 1864, the actor Louis Kramer was playing King Lear at Geneva, and in his excitement swallowed a portion of his artificial beard, which stuck in his windpipe and choked him.

ANDREW WICKES

Costume

Juliet Stevenson as Hedda Gabler, NT 1989

With the minimal era of the black boiler suit behind us, contemporary theatrical costumes are now ranging freely from traditional Restoration to modern naturalism via all points in between. From hats to shoes, the roles of costume designer and costume maker have never been more exciting – or more daunting.

The work of the costume and wardrobe departments can be worlds apart in different theatres. In a big building-based company like the RSC or National, there are separate departments for specialist areas like wigs and make-up, and the costume designer employs a wardrobe supervisor to select fabrics and to oversee the cutting and sewing staff, who do much of the manual work. Star actors in large theatres even enjoy the luxury of personal dressers, to help them with quick costume changes. In a small-scale touring company, all of these contrasting functions may well be performed by a single person.

Yet even in large theatres, the costumes are usually designed by the same person who designs the set, as both these elements must dovetail neatly to create the overall appearance of the production. Costumes must be practical as well as aesthetic. Excessive weight is a common pitfall, especially with period costume. The costume must not constrict the actor, although a heavy cloak or a suffocating corset sometimes fits the tenor of the character.

At the NT or the RSC, wardrobe staff can use or alter clothes from stock or, failing that, buy or hire them. On the Fringe, it's more likely to be a case of improvising, and a good costume designer is someone who can use their ingenuity and imagination. Some minor alterations can transform a commonplace piece of clothing, and unusual juxtapositions of everyday dress can create a more powerful effect than an expensive costume.

Practicalities dictate that cast members are measured for costumes at the first rehearsals, so that costumes are completed by the beginning of technical rehearsals. Actors such as Antony Sher and Alison Steadman have complained that, when discovering a character, this is putting the cart before the horse.

Dressmaking, embroidery, weaving, patterning and millinery (hat making) are all important skills in costume-making, along with silk screen printing, dyeing and "breaking down" costumes, so as to make them look old and worn. More rudimentary tasks include everyday repairs and maintenance. Costume makers are an invaluable part of the creative process, but they mustn't superimpose their own interpretations over those of the designers.

Painstaking research is an essential pre-requisite for designing and theatrical history. A realistic production requires historically accurate costumes, whereas a non-naturalistic interpretation demands a deeper insight into the dramatic intentions of the playwright and the director.

Those who hope to be the costume designers or costume makers of the future can attend specialist courses. Bristol Old Vic Theatre School runs a one year wardrobe course. At Edinburgh College of Art, it is possible to take a degree in fashion and theatre costume. Diplomas are available at Liverpool City College, Staffordshire Technical College and the London College of Fashion.

WILLIAM COOK

Front-of-House

The Lyttelton Foyer

Front-of-House refers to those parts of a theatre in front of the proscenium: the auditorium, foyers, bars, cloakrooms and the box-office. All these public areas are under the control of the house manager and his or her staff, who try to arrange everything for the safety, comfort and convenience of paying audiences: an easy, relaxed and friendly atmosphere will put an audience in the mood to enjoy their theatre experience, and persuade them to return.

The box office is under the control of the box office manager; he and his staff aim to provide a pleasant, courteous service to the public. Life in the box-office often gets very busy, and an equable nature is an asset: the telephone seldom stops ringing, methods of payment become ever more complex and the public more demanding.

In the foyers are the cloakrooms, which must not only be able to take in and store the audience's personal belongings, but must return them at the end of the performance in a very short space of time. Sufficient lavatories on all levels are essential, as anyone who has been caught up in the interval rush will testify.

Adequate provision for the disabled is patchy, but the situation is gradually improving. Access and spaces for wheelchairs, adapted lavatories and induction loops are some of the facilities which are gradually becoming standard. Given sufficient notice, most theatres will make a special effort and provide helping hands.

Income from front of house sales is an essential supplement to ticket revenue. Theatre bars, providing alcoholic drinks, coffee and snacks, are often over-priced and under-staffed but remain profitable. Many theatres now offer a proliferation of show-related merchandise for sale: T-shirts, mugs, CDs, books and souvenirs. "Plays & Players" magazine is on sale in an increasing number of theatres.

Theatre programmes are expensive to produce, but can be self-financing if enough advertising space can be sold: this sometimes forces out information about the production itself, but on the whole modern programmes are informative and good value. A useful practice in some theatres is to provide free cast-lists.

On the way into the auditorium, ushers are on hand to sort out any problems, to check that your tickets are for that particular performance, that you are in the right part of the theatre and that you are not carrying cameras or tape-recorders.

Few older theatres can boast modern standards of comfort and convenience, and the house manager is generally well-used to dealing with complaints about this and other matters. One of the most common concerns is latecomers: nowadays, a television show-relay is often provided in the foyer, and a suitable point in the performance is identified when their admission will cause minimum disruption.

Safety regulations are often cursed by actors, directors and particularly by lighting designers, whose effects are frequently ruined by over-bright exit signs, but no one seriously doubts that the rules are necessary. The licensing authorities usually require that the public can leave at the end of the performance by all available doors, which must be kept open; that all gangways are free from obstructions; that there is no standing in any of the gangways; that smoking is not permitted in the auditorium; and that the safety-curtain is raised and lowered in the presence of each audience.

ANDREW WICKES

Fights

Michael Maloney and Owen Teale

What do the following objects all have in common ? Battleaxes, bayonets, broadswords, chains, claymores, coshes, cutlasses, flicknives, knuckledusters, maces, machetes, pickaxe-handles, pikes, quarterstaffs, rapiers, sandbags, scimitars, spears and truncheons..... All of them are fearsome weapons, designed to maim or murder. But they're also the everyday tools of the theatrical fight director. And those are only some of the more normal ones. Oddities include dustbin lids, handbags, oil drums and scissors – all used by the RSC over the last twenty years.

At first glance, the job of fight director might seem rather marginal to theatre. After all, there are plenty of plays with no fighting in them whatsoever, and even in the few that do boast a brawl, the action is all over very swiftly – as many a disgruntled schoolboy, dragged along to watch "Henry V" or "Richard III" under the false promise of battle will agree.

And yet so much drama lives on the edge of fighting – many fine scenes and speeches are located the moment just before battle is joined. Without the threat of violence, comedy would lack the friction that begets laughter, and stripped of its dark premise, tragedy would be empty. Fights are integral to every dramatic genre, from ancient Greek to the kitchen sink.

A good stage fight must be endemic – a natural development of the drama, not a subsiduary showpiece – and the audience should not be able to see the join. Actors must fight in character – and the fight cheorography must allow them to. Almost all classical fighters are portrayed as proficient warriors, but in a modern play, there's no point in staging a fight between two drunken professors that incorporates amazing stunts or proficiency with unusual weaponry, even though every director always wants to create a contest no audience has seen before.

The fight must fit the space. A meticulous little struggle in a gigantic auditorium will be lost beyond the front stalls. Likewise, a huge operatic battle in a tiny studio theatre will come across as hammy and overplayed. The audience must see enough, but if they see too much they'll spot the tricks of the trade.

These include working with fixed rhythms, so that thrusts and parries are anticipated. Actors are also trained never to cut or thrust across another actor's face. "Thrusting out of point" is another useful tactic, aiming directly at the actor – but only when he's ever so slightly out of reach. If one actor aims to miss, their audience will be able to smell it. Stage fights are built on the flimsiest thin ice of suspended disbelief.

Laurence Olivier (who always did his own stunts) was famous for his uncompromising attitude to staged fights, and in particular for his energetic swordplay, but far from making more dangerous, this full blooded approach was actually much safer – opponents were never left in any doubt about were they stood. Ultimately, the best safety procedure is thorough rehearsal.

Fencing is now an endemic part of basic drama school training, and indeed physically proficient swordsmanship can shed new light on characterisation. The medieval two handed broadsword is a world away from the delicacy of the Restoration rapier.

Fight directors' tastes and techniques vary widely. Retractable daggers aren't popular at the RSC, because if and when they stick, they can become frighteningly real. There are currently twenty fight directors recognised by the actors union, Equity. Until recently, all training was ad hoc, but the Society of Fight Directors now runs its own course.

WILLIAM COOK

Voice and Accent Work

Frances Barber as Eliza in Pygmalion NT 1992

Work on accent has become more scientific and professional in the last ten years. Factors of geography and physiology both come into play with key coaches like Joan Washington having minutely analysed effective techniques for reproducing a huge variety of local sounds. Vowels and consonants vary subtly over the vast range of places where English is spoken and actors are frequently surprised to discover that an accent can be structured like a different language.

Writers generally reproduce the rhythms of the speech they know best. The actor's duty is to ensure that those rhythms are respected. Eugene O'Neill's "Long Day's Journey into Night", which is about Americans of Irish descent, cannot be delivered in Jewish or Italian American tones without making a mockery of the author's intentions. And a play like J.M.Synge's "Playboy of the Western World" with its connection to Irish folklore must stay close to the spirit of its origins. Actors have to resist the temptation to caricature. Working with a competent dialect coach can enable them to steer a path through what might otherwise be a sea of cliches. The most successful work is when the audience fails to notice the accent, the actor having allowed it to become such an integral part of the performance.

Cicely Berry, for many years the RSC's chief voice teacher, has commented that until recently the training of actors was dominated by singing teachers and that until the 1930's the voice required was one that sounded musically acceptable. The voice as an instrument was removed and didn't necessarily reflect what was going on inside the actor.

Nowadays, social attitudes to speaking have changed and the insistence on the necessity for received standard pronunciation and the middle class voice onstage have been questioned. Cicely Berry is quick to point out that Shakespeare did not write in that accent. The theatre profession has widened to include the working classes who were previously unable to afford drama school fees. A worrying trend is the withdrawal of many local authority discretionary grants which could mean that this welcome step is reversed.

Actors are now trained to work in terms of truth and feeling, to examine their own internal landscapes in order to find the right musical cadence. Texts are likely to be spoken as soon as possible in rehearsal. Trying to discover the thought and feeling embodied in the words is an active and ongoing process which does not end on opening night.

BETTY CAPLAN

Movement and Choreography

Fuente Ovejuna, NT 1990/1/2

In Britain, theatre has until very recently been dominated by concern for the text and its vocal delivery. New playwrights have even kept to this formula and the Royal Court has only allowed "performance" work (which is dominated by actions rather than words) under the umbrella of a special season sponsored by Barclays entitled "New Stages." In the last ten years, however, there has been a revolution which has left its mark on everyone.

Partly this has been due to the cross-fertilisation which has been taking place between the arts. There have been some extraordinary collaborations: Siobhan Davies' dance company Second Stride working with playwright Caryl Churchill on "The Lives of the Great Poisoners", and the Womens' Playhouse Trust commissioning Deborah Levy to write the libretto for a new operatic version of Lorca's "Blood Wedding." In recognition of the breaking down of solid boundaries between different art forms, the Arts Council recently set up a multi-disciplinary fund entitled "New Collaborations" to encourage arts practitioners to co-operate rather than compete.

Where did this revolution begin? The impact of dance, still the Cinderella of the arts in this country, has vastly increased since Martha Graham's visit in the late 1960's instigated the establishment of the first contemporary dance school in London. A new sophisticated audience has grown up which is increasingly open to the idea that gesture is an integral part of performance, and that the physical can no longer be separated from the psychological. In recognition of these developments, the National Theatre has opened its arms to companies like Theatre de Complicite, Tara Arts, and to the work of Robert Lepage - all known for their strikingly physical approach.

A whole generation of new directors has sprung up with a passionate commitment to movement. Katie Mitchell who, though only twenty-seven, has worked extensively in Eastern Europe has adopted Polish styles of performance. Her vigorous chorus of athletes with its Bulgarian songs in "The Women of Troy" transformed the Gate's tiny theatre into a miniature Greek amphitheatre, spiriting back the ghost of Euripides' original. And Julia Pascal's highly acclaimed production of the "Dybbuk" at the New End theatre featured a German expressionist dance choreographed and performed by Thomas Kampe, taking a section of the narrative most difficult for modern audiences (the joining of the spirit of the betrayed lover with his betrothed) and making it immediate and real.

Pascal is not the first to recognise that movement can express meanings not available in words. Both Declan Donnellan of Cheek by Jowl and Annable Arden of Theatre de Complicite have been influenced by European work, the later particularly by the school of Jacques Le Coq in Paris and Phillipe Gaulier.

The destruction of barriers in Eastern Europe has meant that directors like Zofia Kalinska from Poland and Robert Sturua from Georgia have for the first time been free to work in this country. Coming from traditions which extol the virtues of body work, they have done an enormous amount to broaden our horizons and release our imaginations.

BETTY CAPLAN

DIRECTORS AND DESIGNERS

Despite moves towards democracy and actor power, to those who work in the theatre, two people still seem to be in charge: the director and the designer. These are the ones who organise, encourage and make crucial decisions. SHEILA STARNS talks to the young director Jake Lushington about the director's role in 1992 and then goes on to acknowledge the directors and designers of the year.

The Director's role

Sometimes it seems as if plays, audience, actors and critics alike exist merely to serve the Cult of The Director. Until mid-Victorian times arbitration between performers was provided by the author, the stage manager or (most often) the chief actor. Given that adjectives like "tyrannical", "dictatorial" and "autocratic" litter the biographies of many leading practitioners of The Art, it is perhaps significant that the first recognisable director was an aristocrat – George II, Duke of Saxe- Meiningen (1826-1914). His methods, largely based on the practices of Edmund Kean and contemporary English stagecraft, spread quickly across Europe, through the good offices of such converts as Antoine in France and Stanislavsky in Russia.

Jake Lushington

If there is a recognisable tradition in England, it dates back to the solidly detailed work of W.S.Gilbert, whose control over staging of the operas he wrote with Sullivan went far beyond authorial niceties of interpretation. Since then, and especially since the last World War, the director has become entrenched as the Person of Power, the arbiter between author and actor who makes all the important decisions on the production he or she has chosen to present.

Jake Lushington's production of the neglected Russian comedy classic "Wit's End" at the New End Theatre, Hampstead in September has already marked him down as a good bet for future honours. He is in no doubt what his job is about: "The director is like a marriage-broker. He brings bride and bridegroom – author and actors – together: he chooses the church and organises the decorations. The trouble starts if he's more interested in the flower arrangements than in the service". Would it be better if directors, especially those who set out to impose an overriding idea or "Concept", didn't have to exist? "I'm not ashamed. A director is there to direct, to bring his own ideas into the rehearsal room and share them with the actors before making decisions on what goes and what doesn't. I'm not going to apologise for that."

Jonathan Miller once said that a director's best work was done by the age of thirty. Lushington agrees, in one sense: "I think every rehearsal has got to be a learning process. As soon as that stops, you're creatively dead. Younger people are more interested in learning". The current problem comes from the ultra-competitive intensity of theatre in a recession, when pressure on the careerist wunderkind to attract notice (or notoriety) at any cost often produces slipshod, showy results that do disservice to play, performers and audience alike. Lushington sympathises with actors, in particular: "They've been very badly treated over the last few years. It's much easier working with young actors – they're so much more open. I suppose the truth is they haven't been around long enough to get hurt".

If the wunderkind market has reached saturation, one thing that hasn't changed much since the late fifties is the perpetual promotion of white, middle-class Oxbridge graduates (preferably male) to the higher echelons of the major companies. Is there an Oxbridge Mafia? "I'll come clean: I'm ex-Cambridge myself – though I didn't go to public school! No, I don't think the old boy network exists; but this is a competitive business, and Cambridge equips student directors to cope with it. You have to lobby for the theatre slots, get your own production team together before you can even think about actually directing your show – if you survive that, you'll survive anything".

Are there misconceptions about the director's role? "It's very difficult to avoid getting known for doing just one kind of thing, whether comedy, classic revivals, new plays or whatever; and that doesn't help develop anybody's talent. What's more, some critics seem out to convince the public that directors are Svengalis who conjure minutely planned, patterned readings. The truth is more prosaic. Great directors are above all great pragmatists, adept at getting the best they can out of what's available to them. Much of their creative energy is spent organising rather than interpreting, and sometimes the critics forget that".

A deeper question must be addressed. Just as the politician is possibly the person least suitable to wield power, so the ambitious director careering from project to project is probably the person least fitted to direct. "I've struggled with that one hard over the last two years. I think if you hold on to your integrity – in other words remember that your job is to make the "marriage" work, and that success only comes from thorough study and preparation – there's less contradiction. Complacency kills. Laissez-faire direction is responsible for a lot of bad work, though the operatic approach – casting actors as mere pawns to fit in with a design concept – is just as big a cop-out".

Lushington is representative of a brisk new tide in directorial affairs, in his passionate belief that verbal values can rescue us from the design-based slough of despond that has oozed over too much modern theatre. "It's that dangerous, suspended moment in time with a fine actor playing a fine text, when you're held in thrall, not quite sure what's going to come next. I want to help prepare that moment. That's why I'm doing this job".

Directors of the Year

Six Degrees of Separation

What makes for a deserving Director of the Year? It's easy for directors to draw attention to their talent by repetition of clever stage tricks (with variations) from production to production. This often passes for personal style, but very few have a vision compelling enough to justify their intrusion. The more praiseworthy approach is the stony road of self-effacement, where play and performances have been brought into such harmonious focus that an audience forgets that there's been any director at all. The bouquets should be handed to those directors who've helped actors make the best case for their authors, alive or dead.

No coincidence, then, that many of the choicest blooms for 1992 go to all-rounders. Alan Ayckbourn is an authentic Renaissance Man – he even makes the sound tapes – and his direction of his own "Time of My Life" (Scarborough, April) demonstrated his knack of getting the best from text and actors alike.

Next up, an actor-writer. Sean Mathias' studio production of "Uncle Vanya" (National Theastre, Cottesloe , February), all restraint and elegance, never fell into the trap of allowing its galactic cast enough rope to hang themselves. Ian McKellen's graceful, unshowy Vanya was an especial beneficiary of this sensitive approach. Never flamboyant, faithfully papering over some prosaic lapses in Pam Gems' version, this was a production which made audiences forget that "Vanya" was always supposed to be Chekhov's most problematic play.

Across London at the Almeida, Ian McDiarmid has proved yet again that actors can, after all, make good Artistic Directors. His stage production of Howard Barker's "A Hard Heart" (February) worked the oracle on a wondrously rich text that might have seemed more suited to radio. McDiarmid sensibly resisted the temptation to foist a "production job" on this austerely beautiful lattice of words, providing the quiet forum that allowed Anna Massey's wry, icy Riddler to ride Barker's well-mettled language as it deserved.

It hasn't been a good year for the visionaries. Robert Lepage's infamous "A Midsummer Night's Dream" (National Olivier Theatre, July) prompted the thought that insurance ought to be available for actors against directorial silliness. Only David Glass really managed to buck the trend, his Ensemble's thrilling "Gormenghast" (BAC, March) achieving the impossible by compressing two, mammoth novels into one stage extravaganza. The baroque fantasy of Mervyn Peake's imagination was brilliantly evoked in Glass' outrageous blend of Kabuki and poor-theatre, grotesque mime and puppetry. There was much chanting and mumbling – yet the performers' skills were harnessed, the story told clearly enough to make for a monstrously satisfying experience.

Every year, one or two new champions catch the critical imagination strongly enough to join the lists of the unshakeably successful. Recent recruits have included Richard Jones, who made a sad National debut with Moliere's "Le Bourgeois Gentilhomme"; and Sam Mendes, much better received at Stratford and the National for "The Alchemist" and "The Rise and Fall of Little Voice" respectively.

This year's entrant is Phyllida Lloyd, who has been waiting in the wings for longer than is customary – though she's probably none the worse for that. A steady progress through the provinces culminated late in 1991 with an eighty-minute "Medea" which hit Manchester's Royal Exchange Theatre like a force-ten gale. Euripides' drama of jealousy and revenge was staged for all of its shock potential, with Claire Benedict's brimstone Medea at its heart. If there's one thing in drama which certainly needs directing, it's a Greek Chorus: Lloyd deployed her nine- strong group tellingly on the cracked stone of the stage, integrating them easily into the fabric of a searing story.

Although Lloyd's RSC debut production of "The Virtuoso" opened in Stratford, this year's substantially recast revival for at the Pit (March) saw it honed to a sharper edge and gaining immense popularity in the process. Shadwell's rather silly piece about dilettante scientific dabblers is living proof that, dusted down by an enthusiastic hand, great theatre doesn't have to be great drama. Lloyd's hallmark is the infectious, buoyant energy which she injects into her work – and this dotty comedy of sex and science was carried joyously through to the wire.

Her biggest splash was probably "Six Degrees of Separation", starring Stockard Channing (Royal Court and West End, August), a production which caught the spirit of John Guare's well-made and deliriously funny play set in up-market New York to perfection. If the satire was presented with little finesse (Lloyd's achilles heel) it was none the less gloriously ripe for that. "Six Degrees" proved – if proof were needed after "The Virtuoso" – that Phyllida Lloyd's range extends well beyond the safe, subsidised classics.

Of the apprentices, Matthew Warkus took pride of place. A production of Calderon's "Life is a Dream" (West Yorkshire Playhouse, May) is rare enough: a production which leaves its audience cheering in the aisles has to be something special. By giving space and time enough to the huge slabs of metaphysical rhetoric with which this Spanish classic is littered, Warkus allowed his actors to develop them with that particular white-hot intensity which makes good stage debate so compelling. Production touches weren't lacking, but the director let nothing muddy the actors' passionate advocacy of Gwynne Edwards' clean-cut translation.

Last, a word for the Old Guard. Sir Peter Hall (whose own company has had rather a rocky ride this year) returned freelance to his old domain at Stratford for the first time in many years, with an outstandingly felicitous "All's Well That Ends Well" (RSC Swan Theatre, June). His spare, even austere approach to Shakespeare's quirky fable lent the plot a classical shape which freed a redoubtable cast – led by Barbara Jefford's Countess – to explore the text with a sophistication, wit and expertise that the Young Guard would do very well to ponder.

Designers of the Year

Heartbreak House

"Thank God for the recession" is not a phrase much bandied about in theatre foyers, but that was exactly what one contented critic came out with at a recent Barbican first night. He went on to explain that he was talking about cuts in the design budget. Cash cuts are indeed a wonderful challenge to the imagination, and it may not be too much to suggest that the art of theatre design never progresses faster than when times are hard.

In fact, the move towards designer-theatre, where the image rules OK, may not have stopped with the funding crisis. In a culture which is hooked on sight rather than sound, the pressure to increase visual sophistication is ever growing. However, designing on a shoestring has forced artists to turn away from the seventies solution of out-gunning the film and TV competition by sheer lavishness. Good design nowadays uses finesse to create images which are special to live theatre and could not be reproduced by the mechanical media. If an evening at the theatre still threatens to be about the set changes, at least the imaginative level is higher.

Curiously enough, the front-runner in the Designer of the Year Stakes is a seventies child. William Dudley (who likes to spend his Saturday nights playing folk music in a South London pub!) has long been up with the pace, but a recent run of London successes makes him a classic contender yet again. Two Shaw productions, "Heartbreak House" (London Haymarket, March) and "Pygmalion" (Olivier Theatre, April) were swiftly followed by the opening of Jim Cartwright's "The Rise and Fall of Little Voice" at the Cottesloe Theatre in June. His work added immeasurably to the power of each production.

There is a sea-change in Dudley's work. He seems to have entered a "skew-whiff" phase, and perhaps that's what gave "Heartbreak House" in particular its extraordinary potency. Two ship-like settings, subtly tilted and twisted a la Stanley Spencer in a Paul Nash landscape, wonderfully evoked both the dotty comedy and topsy-turvy moral logic of Shaw's masterpiece. This magnificent visual image of England afloat demanded inspired playing from Trevor Nunn's cast, which – on the whole – it got.

The strange perspectives of Shotover's mansion could not have come across in any other medium, and the same distortions were at work in Dudley's otherwise realistic setting for "Little Voice". Burnt cookers, brown-stained lino and dirty-tiled kitchens couldn't be further removed from the pristine neo-Georgian greens and blues of "Heartbreak House", but they provided a brilliant visual metaphor reflecting Cartwright's unique voice, vibrant Bolton speech-rhythms straining towards packed poetry.

Philip Prowse, master-fabricator of the silk purse from the sow's ear, had a good year, too: the stark abstractions (inevitably black and white) for his production of Craig Raine's "1953" (Glasgow Citizens', February) forcefully projected the chill at the marble heart of the piece. Richard Hudson's set for "La Bete" (Lyric Hammersmith, January), all sharply-angled cream walls and steeply raked floors in crazed perspectives, elegantly supported the baroque trickery of an intriguing pastiche. Mention should also be made of the ingenious efforts of Saul Radomsky to rescue Ronald Harwood's ill-fated "Reflected Glory" (Vaudeville Theatre, April) from oblivion by placing an entire theatre on stage – acting area, auditorium and all. This was designer's theatre with a vengeance.

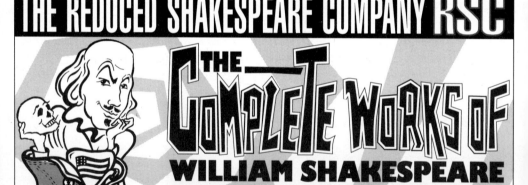

THE WEST END

Even in a recession, theatres in the West End continue to attract visitors from all over the world. This is the heart of British theatre. The Yearbook provides the unique service of describing every production which has been on in the West End during 1992 – from the record breaking "Mousetrap" through to the most recent openings. SHERIDAN MORLEY comments on the surprisingly good fortunes of the theatres this year and CLARE BAYLEY and GRAHAM HASSELL provide details of all the shows.

West End '92

Funny things, statistics: there we were in midsummer '92 lamenting what appeared to be the worst West End summer since the war, what with the recession and the Olympics and the IRA and (perhaps the most devastating of all) radical changes to parking laws around Shaftesbury Avenue which ensured the dreaded clamp for hundreds of unwary theatre goers. One management went bankrupt, others pulled in their reins and at least one show closed prematurely when its star Albert Finney declared a no pay – no play policy.

But then, in the midst of all such doom and gloom, along comes a report from the Society of West End Theatres pointing out that, contrary to popular belief, audiences for the first half of 1992 were running five per cent up on the previous year, with a total of over 820,000 tickets sold in central London up to the end of June. More theatres were in fact open this year than last, and thus far the takings were only two per cent down on the record summer of 1990.

Whether those figures will be sustained to the year's end or not, they show a clear gap between journalistic perceptions of what is going on around the West End and what is actually happening there. One explanation is that a record number of long-runners, from "Miss Saigon" and "Les Miserables" through "Cats" to "Me and My Girl" and "Joseph and the Dreamcoat" and even "Starlight Express", all of which continue at least in the short term to be sold out at least at weekends, are somehow massaging the figures so that the big hits increasingly disguise an ever-growing number of small flops.

But this is something more than a "Phantom" economy: three theatres (the Playhouse, the Criterion and the Warehouse) actually reopened during the autumn, not the usual sign of an industry in deep depression, while of the other forty or so that constitute our commercial West End there were precious few dark for more than a week or two, even in the summer doldrums.

Despite a record number of flops, a quintet of major musicals ("Which Witch ?", "Valentine's Day", "Assassins", "Kiss of the Spider Woman" and "Radio Days") was announced for the autumn, as though managements were willing themselves to believe that all would come right once the weather changed or the right kind of tourists arrived.

Their optimism has yet to be validated, but at the time of this writing there are still twice as many mainstream shows playing in London as in Paris or New York. One trend is strongly detectable however: these shows are seldom if ever originating in their London homes. More and more the West End is, like Broadway, coming to resemble a transfer zone or shop window for the best of theatre from elsewhere. Thus the Theatre Royal Haymarket was occupied for most of the year by the RSC's "A Woman of No Importance" from the Barbican; the Royal Court gave "Death and the Maiden" to the Duke of York's and "Six Degrees of Separation" to the Comedy; the King's Head and the National Theatre were accountable for the two Brian Friels ("Philadelphia, Here I Come" and "Dancing at Lughnasa") which came to rest side by side in the lower Charing Cross Road. Hampstead gave "Someone Who'll Watch Over Me" to the Vaudeville and the National gave "The Rise and Fall of Little Voice" to the Aldwych. If there are still any commercial managements out there with new straight plays they seem to be hiding, who can blame them in the current economy ?

Musicals

Cats

New London

Stephen Tate and Susan Jane Tanner

Though not quite able to match "the Mousetrap"'s longevity, Andrew Lloyd Webber's international award-winning show is nevertheless a recordbreaker in its own field, being London's longest-ever running musical. On 11 May this year it celebrated its eleventh birthday. And unlike the Agatha Christie thriller, there were seven different productions of "Cats" around the world in 1992, including New York, Hamburg, Budapest and Zurich. In London it has been seen by over 5.5 million people. The format puts lyrics gleaned from T.S. Eliot's "Old Possum's Book of Practical Cats" to Lloyd Webber's music. The outstanding song "Memory" has been recorded by many famous singers. Trevor Nunn directed the show, the cat-like choreography was created by Gillian Lynne and the alleyway designs were by John Napier. "Cats" was produced by Cameron Mackintosh and The Really Useful Company and the latest cast had Jackie Scott as Grizabella, Luke Baxter as Mr Mistoffelees and Mark Wynter as Gus.

Starlight Express

Apollo Victoria

This year was "Starlight Express"'s ninth at the Apollo Victoria, making it the second longest running musical in British Theatre history. It opened on 27 March 1984 and proved Andrew Lloyd Webber is nothing if not eclectic. Of all the subjects chosen by the composer for adaptation – from Christ to Parisian actresses, from poetic cats to phantoms – this was surely the riskiest. Trevor Nunn directed this multi-media musical with lyrics by Richard Stilgoe about a race to find the fastest engine on the American railroad. It had most of a forty-strong cast roller skating around tracks which circle the specially adapted auditorium. With designs by John Napier, costumes co-designed by Liz Da Costa, choreography by Arlene Phillips and lighting by David Hersey, plus separate credits for sound and production musical director, it was more spectacle/extravaganza than musical theatre. Produced by The Really Useful Theatre Company, it won Lloyd Webber a gold disc for sales of the album of the show.

Me and My Girl

Adelphi Theatre

Gary Wilmot and Jessica Martin

An old-fashioned, warm-hearted, comic musical with book and lyrics by L. Arthur Rose and Douglas Furber and music by Noel Gay, first produced by Lupino Lane at the Victoria Palace in 1937. Noel Gay's son Richard Armitage produced this version, directed by Mike Ockrent and updated by Stephen Fry which opened at the Adelphi on February 12 1985. A rags to riches tale of a cockney lad (Les Dennis to March 9 1992, then Jonathon Morris) who inherits a fortune and a title much to the dismay of his long-lost huntin', shootin' and fishin' relatives. With his cheeky charm he wins over the family, but love interest is added when they try and persuade him to abandon his cockney "girl" Sally (Louise English until March 9 this year, now Joanna Riding). It all ends happily, however, after a good few rousing numbers including the famous "Lambeth Walk", "Me and My Girl", "The Sun Has Got His Hat On", "Love Makes The World Go Round" and "Leaning On a Lamp Post".

Les Miserables

Palace

After a sell-out season at the Barbican where it opened on October 8 1985, Trevor Nunn and John Caird's RSC production was taken up by Cameron Mackintosh and opened at the Palace on December 4 1985. Based on the novel by Victor Hugo, adapted by Alain Boublil and Claude-Michel Schonberg, it had lyrics by Herbert Kretzmer, music by Schonberg, original text by Boublil and Jean-Marc Natel and additional material by James Fenton. Colm Wildinson was the original Jean Valjean, a former convict who breaks parole after nineteen years on the chain gang and rises up to become a Mayor in Paris. Dave Willetts, the current Valjean, made his West End debut in the role in 1986. Despite unlikely subject matter, it became one the most popular musicals in the world (there are productions in eight different countries and in New York it won eight Tony Awards) and presented the first serious challenge to the Lloyd Webber strangle-hold, both musically and in its relatively low-tech staging. It still earns the RSC £1million a year.

The Phantom of the Opera

Her Majesty's Theatre

Based on the much-adapted gothic tale by Gaston Leroux, Andrew Lloyd Webber's blockbuster musical had lyrics by Charles Hart, with additional lyrics by Richard Stilgoe and book by Stilgoe and Lloyd Webber. Designed by Maria Bjornson and directed by Harold Prince, it opened at Her Majesty's Theatre on October 9 1986, produced by Cameron Mackintosh and The Really Useful Theatre Company. Michael Crawford was the original Phantom, starring opposite Sarah Brightman as Christine, the young soprano who fell under the mesmeric spell of the hideously deformed "Phantom" living in the eerie underground chambers beneath the Paris Opera. The leading roles are currently played by Peter Karrie and Shona Lindsay, with John Barrowman as Raoul. Famous for its special effects (floating gondolas, walk-through mirrors, falling chandaliers) and the unexpected appearances and disappearances of the Phantom, though not necessarily its profoud insights, there are currently productions in ten different cities in Europe and the Americas.

Rosemary Ashe and Sarah Brightman

Blood Brothers

Phoenix

Willy Russell's Liverpudlian musical about twin boys separated at birth got another twelve months under its belt in 1992, giving host theatre the Phoenix its longest running show for years.

This particular revival got under way at the Albery on 28 July 88, transferring to its current home on 21 November 91 where it has been directed by Bob Tomson (musical direction Ron Edwards) with Stephanie Lawrence, Carl Wayne, Russell Boulter and Jan Graveson leading the cast. Yet the show's origins lie further back. It premiered in Liverpool and came to the Lyric Theatre in 1983 with Barbara Dickson as the Catholic, working-class mother forced by poverty to give one twin to her barren, middle-class employer.

It won the 1983 SWET award for best musical but had to close despite its success to let in a previously booked play. The Albery revival starred Kiki Dee with Con O'Neill and Robert Locke as the twins before this year's cast changes.

Stephanie Lawrence and Billy Fellows

Aspects of Love

Prince of Wales

Zoe Hart and Michael Ball

"Aspects of Love" opened at the Prince of Wales on 17 April 1989 with lyrics by Don Black and Charles Hart, and directed by Trevor Nunn. This new musical (more properly an operetta – there was no spoken dialogue), based on an obscure novel by David Garnett, traced the course of an affair between a young English boy and a penniless French actress through the story of a group of five, vaguely bohemian people who, over a period of fourteen years, drift in and out of each others lives and beds. Intended star Roger Moore withdrew prior to previews with a mixture of voice doubts and lack of confidence – partly his and partly The Really Useful Group's. Michael Ball stepped in to play opposite female lead Ann Crumb. Warm critical acclaim, audience confidence in the Lloyd Webber reputation and some casting changes which occasionally put Sarah Brightman in the role of Rose kept the show on the road until 20 June 1992 clocking up 1,325 performances.

Miss Saigon

Theatre Royal Drury Lane

Lea Salonga and Jonathan Pryce

Second only in musical blockbuster terms to Andrew Lloyd Webber is the song writing team of Alain Boublil and Claude-Michel Schonberg. They followed up "Les Miserables" with this sumptious show produced by Cameron Mackintosh, directed by Nicholas Hytner, designed by John Napier with costumes by Andreane Neofitou and lighting by David Hersey. Additional lyrics were by Richard Maltby Jnr.

Opening at Drury Lane on 20 Sept 89 it won instant critical and public acclaim. The story, based loosely on Puccini's "Madam Butterfly", conjures the last days of the Vietnam war and the powerful pull of the American dream on would-be escapees. The production was at its most poignant depicting the fate of half-caste children left fatherless by evacuating GIs. Although original stars seventeen-year-old Lea Salonga and Jonathan Pryce are no longer in the show, box office takings have not been affected – the show is booking until March 1993 and is carrying £2m in box office advance.

Carmen Jones

Old Vic

Wilhelmenia Fernandez and Damon Evans

Simon Callow's celebrated, now multi-award winning (including three 1992 Olivier Awards) production at the Old Vic sailed majestically through another year. This version of Oscar Hammerstein II's 1943 musical with music by Georges Bizet and based on his opera "Carmen" had its London premiere on 8 April 1991. The production was designed by Bruno Santini and choreographed by Stuart Hobbs. Musical arrangements were courtesy of Dave Cullen with lighting by Mark Henderson. The show was produced by Howard Panter and Eddie Kulukundis.
Hammerstein re-locates the action in America during WW2 where the the cigar factory seductress of nineteenth century Seville becomes "Carmen Jones" a worker in a military parachute factory, soldier Don Jose becomes military policeman "Joe" and bullfighter Escamillo becomes champion boxer "Husky Miller". Uniquely in the West End the production had two Carmens playing alternate nights – originally American opera star Wilhelmenia Fernandez and Sharon Benson, most recently Jennifer Chase and Patti Boulaye.

Joseph and the Amazing Technicolor Dreamcoat

London Palladium

Jason Donovan

Andrew Lloyd Webber's revival of his 1968 Biblical rock musical with lyrics by Tim Rice opened at the London Palladium on June 12 1991. Originally written as a forty-minute piece for a school play, it was expanded to a full-length show in 1972.
The trendy team for this production consisted of Steven Pimlott directing, Anthony van Laast choreographing, Mark Thompson designing extravagantly (the stage took the form of an enormous Bible) and Jason Donovan starring.
Nobody thought the Australian soap star would be able to act, let alone sing, but all had to admit a certain charm, and his appeal to the teeny-boppers (enhanced by his skimpy loin-cloth costumes, bare biceps and manly gold breastplate) ensured a sell-out run. Another TV celebrity, Phillip Schofield, succeeded him in the role.

A Swell Party

Vaudeville

A musical biography and celebration of Cole Porter to mark the centenary of his birth, "A Swell Party" was conceived by David Kernan (in the same format as his "Side By Side with Sondheim"), written by John Kane and directed by David Gilmore with the lyrics of the great songwriter himself (including "I Get A Kick Out of You", "Anything Goes", "I've Got You Under My Skin", "Begin The Beguine", "Night And Day"). It opened at the Vaudeville on October 3 1991 with Nickolas Grace as Porter, bearing an "uncanny" resemblance to him. From his early college days to his marriage to an heiress, their separation, the riding accident which confined him to a wheelchair for the last twenty-eight years of his life until his death in 1964, the show alluded to Porter's homosexuality – too much for Sheridan Morley but not enough for Nicholas de Jongh. Angela Richards played his wife and Anne Wood made her West End debut after the abrupt disappearance of Maria Friedman shortly before opening night.

Nickolas Grace

Phantom of the Opera

Shaftesbury

Ken Hill rightly prefaced his show's title "The Original Stage Musical" when it opened at the Shaftesbury on 18 Dec 1991. His "Phantom" had premiered at the Theatre Royal Stratford East in 1984, and was not jumping on the Andrew Lloyd Webber bandwagon, even if subsequently Webber's 1986 blockbuster tended to overshadow Hill's more modest effort. This show was very much a musical spoof of the classic Gaston Leroux tale about a disfigured man in a mask who secretly coaches the chorus girl protege he loves to sing the great operatic roles before abducting her to his lair in the sewers beneath the Paris Opera House. For music, Hill used actual arias from Offenbach, Gounod, Verdi and Weber, with lyrics adapted to fit his plot. Peter Straker played the Phantom to a backdrop of evocative sets by Sarah-Jane McClelland. Although well received the show closed on 11 April 1992.

Peter Straker

Moby Dick

Piccadilly

In a year that fairly groaned under the weight of musical compilations, much hope was pinned on the arrival of impresario Cameron Mackintosh's£1.2m "Moby Dick". When it opened at the Piccadilly on 17 March 1992 it was the only original musical due in the West End for the rest of the year. Certainly the idea of Robert Longden's musical comedy (he wrote the book and lyrics with Hereward Kaye co-composing and contributing additional lyrics) sounded different enough to be fun. This had a group of St Trinian's-like schoolgirls staging Herman Melville's great nineteenth century novel in the school swimming pool to raise funds for their impoverished academy. The critics, however, were not amused and dwindling audiences seemed to concur, leading to the show's closure on 4 July.

Tony Monopoly

Some Like It Hot

Prince Edward

Tommy Steele's unquenchable enthusiasm for musical movies led him to mount this £2m show based on Billy Wilder's 1959 Hollywood film. Originally presented at the Churchill Theatre, Bromley it opened at the Prince Edward on 19 March 1992. This time though Steele's judgement had erred and by 20 June the show had closed. The offical reason for the flop was that illness kept Steele out of the show and advance bookings fell away. The critics, however, had been fairly damning. The production invited comparison on every level with the much respected film and was found wanting. Who could hope to match the celluloid efforts of Jack Lemmon, Tony Curtis and Marilyn Monroe? The show utilised the original Peter Stone book, Jule Styne's music and Bob Merrill's lyrics, but Steele and co-stars Billy Boyle and Mandy Perryment couldn't pull it off.

Tommy Steele, Mandy Perryment and Billy Boyle

Sikulu

Queen's

Bertha Egnos devised and wrote the music for this all-black South African musical with lyrics by Gail Lakier, decor by Anthony Farmer and choreography by Lynton Burns. A cast of thirty included Andy Chabeli, who starred in Egnos's legendary "Ipi Tombi" in 1975. Intended as a follow-up to "Ipi Tombi", it celebrated African culture from its tribal past to now, expressing hope for a democratic future. A simple story told of a young man leaving his village in search of his father Sikulu (which roughly translated as "leader") who was imprisoned for political reasons. His search exposed him to big city life – dancing vicars, yuppies brandishing mobile-phones, keep-fit classes – and the hardship of life in Soweto. After a reunion with his father, he returned home to continue the struggle. The musical's political credibility was tenuous – ANC voiced reservations about it – and it arrived in London shortly after South Africa's watershed referendum voted "yes" to ending apartheid. Reviews were unanimously critical, dismissing it as bland, commercial and naive. It closed on July 4 1992.

Grand Hotel

Dominion

Boldly checking in at the vast and lavishly renovated Dominion, where only the Dave Clark rock musical "Time" has survived a run of more than a year in recent memory, was director/ choreographer Tommy Tune's Tony Award-winning and much heralded Broadway musical "Grand Hotel". It opened on 6 July 1992. The production came replete with eight Broadway principals, among them the star Liliane Montevecchi, while British back-up included Barry Foster. Famously made into a Hollywood film which had Greta Garbo decreeing "I vant to be alone", the story is set in a sumptuous Berlin hotel where the assorted guests and staff – a suave baron, an ageing ballerina, a business tycoon, a book keeper and a pregnant typist – all face personal dilemmas mirroring Berlin's depression five years before Hitler seized power. Warm critical response added to the generally agreed visual splendour – decor Tony Walton, costumes Santo Loquasto – and helped to keep the show affloat in harsh economic times.

Liliane Montevecchi and Debbie de Coudreaux

Lady Be Good

Open Air

Samantha Spiro, Gavin Muir and Bernard Cribbins

The 1992 New Shakespeare Company production of the 1924 Gershwin musical was directed by Ian Talbot. The Gershwin estate had agreed to the addition of some interpolated numbers from other Gershwin shows. The prize specimen was "Just Another Rhumba" which had not been seen on stage before. Other numbers included "Fascinating Rhythm", "A Wonderful Party" and the title song "Oh Lady, Be Good", all strung along to the story about a brother-and-sister dance act who lose all their money and later restore their fortunes when the sister impersonates an heiress. The leading roles were played by Simon Green and Joanna Riding with support from a cast of ten including Bernard Cribbins. The designer was Paul Farnsworth, the musical director Catherine Jayes and the choreographer Kenn Oldfield. The show played in rep between 28 July and 10 September.

Valentine's Day

Globe Theatre

Ruthie Henshall, Edward Petherbridge and Helen Way

Adapted from George Bernard Shaw's play "You Never Can Tell," "Valentine's Day" was adapted by Benny Green and David William. It opened at the Globe on September 17 produced by Brian Brolly for ROSC Theatre. Gillian Lynne directed and choreographed, with design by Paul Farnsworth, lighting by Nick Richings, orchestrations by Chris Walker and musical direction by Ian Smith. A strong cast was led by Edward Petherbridge as William, a singing and dancing waiter, who provided a sardonic commentary on Shaw's bright young things as they stumbled across their father while visiting a dentist's surgery. He was joined by Elizabeth Counsell, John Turner, Edward De Souza, Alexander Hanson, Teresa Banham, Robert Hands, John Berlyne and Nicky Adams.

Which Witch

Piccadilly Theatre

A musical by Scandinavian pop star duo Benedicte Adrian (who also took the lead role) and Ingrid Bjornov (the conductor), with libretto by director Piers Haggard, lyrics by Kit Hesketh-Harvey, musical arrangements by Ingrid Bjornov and orchestrations by Martin Koch. Richard Hudson was the designer with costumes by Mark Bailey, choreography by William Tucket and lighting by Mark Henderson. It opened at the Piccadilly Theatre on October 22 1992. From humble beginnings, the show's popularity had gathered momentum – a concert in Oslo in June attracted an audience of 18,000 and the live double CD of the concert version sold more than 50,000 copies. Described as an operamusical, the score blended pop with opera to tell the story of a seventeenth century love affair between a young Italian woman and Bishop Daniel from Germany, set against the tumultuous background of the Reformation, the Inquisition and culminating in a witch-hunt in Heidelberg.

Assassins

Donmar Warehouse

The re-vamped Donmar Warehouse, which began its theatre life as one of the London homes of the RSC, is now under the artistic directorship of Sam Mendes. It was re-launched on October 23 with the world premiere of a new musical by Stephen Sondheim. In recent years, Sondheim's musicals such as "Sunday in the Park with George" and "Into the Woods" have met with critical acclaim but limited popular success. Based on the stories of eight mis-fits who have assassinated, or attempted to kill American presidents, "Assassins" was a shrewd examination of American history. The cast included Louise Gold, Paul Bentley, Jack Ellis, Cathryn Bradshaw, Michael Cautwell, Henry Goodman and David Firth. The director was Sam Mendes. The long-awaited Donmar Warehouse embarked on a programme of new and classic works, run by one of the country's most popular young directors.

Anthony Barclay and Henry Goodman

Blood Wedding

Jacob Street Studios

One of the most ambitious projects to date of Jules Wright's Women's Playhouse Trust, the musical of Lorca's classic play had a libretto by Deborah Levy and was composed by Nicola LeFanu, conducted by Anne Manson. The Endymion Ensemble, who played on Opera Factory's tour and the Channel 4 production of Harrison Birtwhistle's "Punch and Judy," provided the orchestra. Fotini Dimou, who had worked with the RSC, the National Theatre and London Contemporary Dance, was the designer. The opera was premiered in London on October 26 before a world tour ending in Jules Wright's home town, Sydney, Australia. It was the first time the converted riverside warehouse, Jacob Street film studios, had been used as an opera house.

Kiss of the Spiderwoman

Shaftesbury Theatre

Manuel Puig's celebrated novel adapted into a musical by a starry team: directed by Harold Prince the lyrics were by Fred Ebb, who wrote "Cabaret"," Chicago" and "Zorba", the book was by Terence McNally, who wrote "Frankie and Johnny", and music was by John Kander. It starred Chita Rivera ("West Side Story") as the illusive Spiderwoman of the title, and opened at the Shaftesbury Theatre on October 20. Set in a South American jail, the novel centred on two cell-mates, one an imaginative and sensitive gay dreamer, the other a macho, up-tight political prisoner not at all in touch with his emotions. It was first adapted for the stage at the Bush Theatre in 1985, directed by Simon Stokes and starring Simon Callow and Mark Rylance, but had never before been a musical.

Chita Rivera

All Nations Club

4 Martello Street
(Top of London Lane)
HACKNEY, LONDON,E8
071 249 2168 071 254 2674

We are open on:
1 **Sundays** - 9.00pm - 4.00 am
2 **Saturdays** - 9.00pm - 6.00 am
Sound by Power Jam - Sweet 'G' and Curry B
3 **Sundays** - 9.00pm - 3.00 am

606 CLUB

JAZZ 7 NIGHTS A WEEK
90 LOTS ROAD, LONDON SW10
Tel: 071–352 5953
8.00pm til 2.00am

A (late night) basement club. Here young up-and-coming musicians are encouraged to play alongside more established names. The good food is a must at this relaxed and informal club where musicians come to eat, drink and join in the impromptu sessions. – *Sunday Times*

Music charges:
Members £3.70 Non-Members £3.95 Sun-Thurs • £4.20 Fri & Sat

– Non-members welcome –

• Please note Alcohol can only be served with meals •

Plays And Players Magazine

Features • Reviews • Listings • Angels Corner

AND LOTS MORE
Available every month from your newsagents or call
081–343 9963

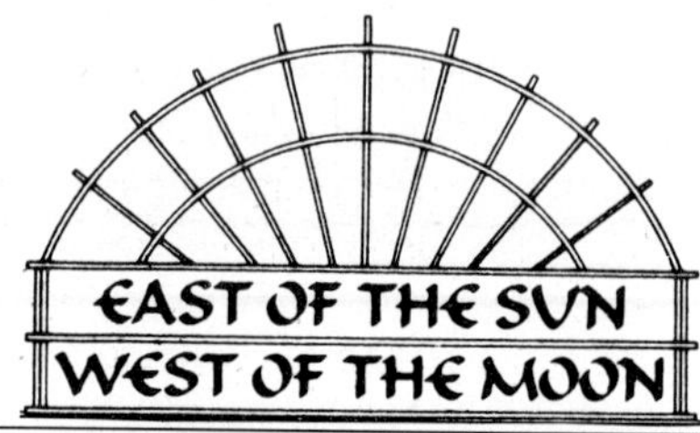

Dining Room & Brasserie

Far Eastern & Western European Cuisine overlooking spectacular Riverfront views close to the National Theatre on Queen's Walk.

Gabriel's Wharf, 56 Upper Ground, London SE1 Open daily 11am to 1am
071 620 0596

TUDOR LODGE

BROMLEY HIGH STREET (BROMLEY BY BOW), E3 (*Near flyover*)

THURSDAY - KARAOKE PLUS DISCO
FRIDAY & SATURDAY OVER 27s DISCO

Smart dress essential (no jeans, TRAINERS)

OPEN 8PM TILL LATE

WE CATER FOR WEDDINGS AND ALL PRIVATE FUNCTIONS

KARAOKE available for any occasion - competitive rates

ENQUIRIES Margaret phone: 081 554 8407

La Scarpetta

"Fully Licensed".
Opening Times:
Mon-Fri 12.00 pm 3.00pm
Pre-Post Theatre Dining Ideal-
Open 6.30 pm - Late.
Sat & Sun: Closed for lunch.
Eves 6.30 pm - Late
Tel:071 503 0393

AUTHENTIC FRENCH CUISINE IDEAL FOR PRE OR AFTER THEATRE DINING

Set price menus plus full a la carte selection and daily specials
Special menus for large party bookings
Vegetarian and other diets are catered for upon request

Lunch Monday - Friday 12.30 - 2.30 pm
Dinner Monday to Saturday 6 - 11pm
Closed all day Sunday

61 THE CUT WATERLOO LONDON SE1 8LL RESERVATIONS: 071-928 8645

La Dordogne

La Dordogne specialises in an all French menu served by French staff using only fresh food. Oysters, langoustines and lobsters are served during their seasons.

5 Devonshire Road, Chiswick, W4
Tel: 081-747 1836
Restaurant Francaise

Radio Times

Queen's Theatre

Kathryn Evans, Tony Slattery, Harriet Benson and Jeff Shankley

A romantic musical comedy built around Noel Gay songs, devised by Alex Armitage with a book by Abi Grant, from an original script by Robin Miller. Produced by Alex Armitage for Waldgrave Productions, it opened at the Queen's Theatre on October 15 1992 after a four week run at Birmingham Rep. Starring Tony Slattery it was directed by David Gilmore, with set and costumes by Terry Parson, lighting by Paul Pyant and Anthony van Laast devising choreography and musical staging. Portraying the life and romantic entanglements of the cast and crew of a radio variety show, it was set in the underground BBC radio stations in London's West End during 1940, and told of the arrival of a censor intending to purge the show of doubles entendres and jokes about the Royal Family. It featured Noel Gay's popular songs, including "Run, Rabbit, Run", "Only A Glass of Champagne", "There's Something About A Soldier", "Hey Little Hen", "You've Done Something To My Heart" and "I Took My Harp To A Party".

Annie Get Your Gun

"Annie Get Your Gun", a major new production of Irving Berlin's famous musical, opened in London in November following a tour.

Please refer to the Yearbook's section on **Commercial Tours** for further details.

Entertainments

Return to the Forbidden Planet

Cambridge Theatre

Kraig Thornber and Allison Harding

Bob Carlton's first musical, born from late night jamming sessions during his time at London Bubble, consisted of a series of sketches set to classic hits of the '50s and '60s ("Great Balls of Fire", "A Teenager In Love", "Don't Let Me Be Misunderstood") and drew inspiration from both "The Tempest" and a '50s sci-fi B-movie loosely based on Shakespeare called "Return to the Forbidden Planet". Brought to the West End by Pola Jones on September 18 1989, it quickly became a cult to rival the "Rocky Horror Show", featuring a roller-skating robot called Ariel, tacky space-ship special effects and a cameo appearance by Patrick Moore on satellite as The Chorus. It controversially won the 1990 Olivier Award for best musical even though none of the songs were original. Productions are planned for Sydney, New York and Tokyo.

Buddy

Victoria Palace

Peter Gallagher, Joe Lutton and Theo Massos

Perhaps no popular icon in the modern era save James Dean has had their reputation and work so lauded after death as Buddy Holly. When it comes to dying young – he was twenty-two when killed in an aircrash – he makes Elvis and John Lennon look like senescence victims. And where Presley is prey to crude impersonation and the ex-Beatle too serious to ape, Holly falls neatly in between. It's not too difficult to find personable young lookalikes (most recently Joe Lutton) who do the man himself no harm by singing his famous songs and mimicking his style of presentation. Old fans are not offended and new ones appreciate it. Hence the massive success of "Buddy", now in it's fourth year at the Victoria Palace having opened on 12 October 89. Alan Janes' story, directed by Rob Bettinson, quite simply charted the rise to fame and untimely death of one of rock's greatest legends and spliced the action with all Holly's big hits -"That'll Be The Day","Peggy Sue," "Rave On","True Love Ways" etc. The Sun newspaper, stuck for superlatives, called it "Buddy brilliant".

Five Guys Named Moe

Lyric

Clarke Peters, Peter Alex Newton, Paul J. Medford, Omar Okai and Kenny Andrews

The Theatre Royal Stratford East doesn't rely on its West End transfers for survival, but they do come as a welcome reward for the effort and enterprise shown by Artistic Director Philip Hedley and his team. Never was this more true than with "Five Guys Named Moe". Commissioned and developed by the East End venue with the aid of a Prudential Award for Theatre, Clarke Peters' musical celebration of the 1940s jazz star Louis ("Is You Is Or Is You Ain't My Baby?") Jordan opened there on 22 October 1990 to rave reviews. Sell-out business soon had Cameron Mackintosh pick the show up for production at the Lyric where it opened on 14 December and has continued to play throughout 1992. The original cast, which included author Peters, transferred with the show but has changed since and most recently featured Johnny Amobi, Colin Charles, Horace Oliver, Kenny Andrews, Peter Alex Newton and Dig Wayne. It was directed and choreographed by Charles Augins with musical arrangements by Neil McArthur and vocal arrangements by Chapman Roberts.

Thunderbirds F.A.B. The Next Generation

Ambassadors

Paul Kent and Wayne Forester

Another cult show, this one a stage spoof version of Gerry Anderson's children's puppet TV show of the same name, which opened at the Mermaid Theatre on June 3 1991. Created and directed by Andrew Dawson and Gavin Robertson, it was produced by John Gore for Titan productions as a follow-up to the sell-out earlier version which began life at the Edinburgh Fringe festival in 1987 then enjoyed a record-breaking run at the Apollo Theatre. Its humour lay in the fact that it was performed by just two actors, Paul Kent and Wayne Forester, with spaceships stuck to their heads, playing many characters (from Lady Penelope to Captain Scarlet via Parker, the villainous Mr X and the President of the USA) and miming an action-packed story involving collapsing bridges, exploding champagne bottles and the invasion of Earth by the Mysterons. It transferred to the Ambassadors on September 19 1992, and has been seen in Japan, Hong Kong and New Zealand.

A Tribute to the Blues Brothers

Whitehall

Not so much a theatre production, more a slickly staged concert – that was the verdict of most critics on emerging from the Whitehall on 12 August 91. The show had got into London via an earlier life as a cult hit in a Brighton pub. The real Blues Brothers were Jake and Elwood, characters invented by Dan Aykroyd and John Belushi, and enshrined in John Landis's 1980 movie. They dressed like hoodlums in mourning (pork-pie hats, Ray-Bans and liquorice ties) and sang old blues and R&B numbers. As directed by film-maker David Leland, the stage show eschewed any storyline and stuck to the music, with English actors Con O'Neill and Warwick Evans as the deshabille duo belting out more than twenty songs from "Rawhide" to "Gimme Some Lovin'",backed up by support band, The Bluettes. The show exceeded expectations and ran until 20 June 1992, by then starring replacements Brian Hibbard and Simon John Foster.

Con O'Neill and Warwick Evans

Good Rockin' Tonite

Prince of Wales

A tribute to Jack Good devised, written and directed by Jack Good, the man who introduced British youth to Rock 'n' Roll in the '50s with two subversive programmes, "The Six-Five Special" and "Oh Boy!". The show was presented by Bill Kenwright in association with the Liverpool Playhouse, as an antidote to the compilation musicals of the '20s and '30s. It opened at the Strand on January 28 with Philip Bird as Good, David Howarth as Tommy Steele and Tim Whitnall as Cliff Richard. The real Cliff Richard, Lonnie Donegan and Jess Conrad were in the audience on the first night, thoroughly enjoying the spirited imitations of themselves and their contemporaries. It loosely told the life-story of Good, an Oxford graduate and aspiring classical actor who got sidetracked by success. Despite some sneering reviews, the show ran and ran, transferring to the Playhouse on March 18 1992 and to the Prince of Wales on July 21 1992.

The Cotton Club

Aldwych

A musical entertainment celebrating the Harlem nightclub of the title, with book by Douglas Barron, presented by Monica Strotmann and Henk van der Meyden for Stardust Productions, directed and choreographed by Billy Wilson. It ran from January 29 to June 27 1992, featuring sumptous costumes by Maya Schroder. Set in the days of prohibition and depression and featuring an all black cast of twenty-six, the show just hinted at the grimmer side of the lavish and glitzy Club through the story of topliner Millie (Joanne Campbell) who succumbed to drugs, and talented novice (Debby Bishop) who fell for the company Casanova. A thin plot provided the excuse for twenty-six songs and/or dance routines, (including "Stormy Weather", "Bye Bye Blackbird", "I'm Just Wild About Harry"), some of which unfortunately coincided with numbers from "Sophisticated Ladies", running concurrently at the Globe.

Sophisticated Ladies

Globe Theatre

A compilation musical based on the music of Duke Ellington with "concept" by Donald McKayle directed by Roger Haines, presented by Frank and Woji Gero, Frederick Zollo and Michael Rose. After runs in New York and Paris, the show finally came to London, opening on January 6 1992 at the Globe. Partly set in Harlem's Cotton Club where Ellington made his name, the show was a non-stop rendition of thirty-two song and dance routines including "I Got It Bad and That Ain't Good" and "In A Sentimental Mood". Stars Jacqueline Dankworth (daughter of Cleo Laine and John Dankworth) and Jacqui Dubois led a vigorous cast of twelve, supported by Charles Miller's twelve piece band. Choreography was by Gillian Gregory and David Morgan Young and Horace Oliver's tap rountines were singled out for praise by otherwise curmudgeonly critics, irritated by the lack of plot and the fact that this was the fourth West End show which anthologised vintage show business personalities. It ran until March 28 1992.

Richie Pitts and Dollie Henry

'Allo 'Allo

Dominion

There was no disguising the collective groan from theatre critics as this TV spin-off nestled into the Dominion on 12 February 1992, as though some grotesque cuckoo's egg was displacing fledgling dramas. True, the Dominion is not noted for its attention to theatrical pedigree, but the only real drama being played out was in getting the reviewers into their press night seats without tears. Their mission was to see the return of the comedy by Jimmy Perry and David Croft, adapted from the famous BBC series and first put on the stage in 1986. Then it had had a successful run at the Prince of Wales, returning three years later for a packed out season at the Palladium in 1989. This latest revival marked a triumpant return to the stage for star Gordon Kaye (playing Rene) following a near fatal accident in January 1990. Despite a poor press, Peter Farago's production successfully completed it's short run to 7 March.

Gordon Kaye

From a Jack to King

Ambassadors

The irony for the small Boulevard theatre is that a West End transfer could see its shows go further out of town. The Boulevard is just 100 yards into Soho from Piccadilly Circus. The move for "From A Jack To A King" has been relatively local and to a theatre almost as intimate. The transfer to the Ambassadors took place on 21 July 1992 and followed the success of the show at the Boulevard where it played to appreciative houses from 13 February to 30 May 1992. Bob Carlton's rock 'n' roll version of "Macbeth" was a ripping yarn put to the thumping beat of classic '60s and '70s pop songs. There was little dramatic development beyond a thin storyline spun out in bastardised bard-speak by the nine-strong band,who, instruments in hand,were ready to illustrate certain motifs with musical raves from the grave. Matthew Devitt played the lead, one Thane Cawdor, and directed the show for West Stage/Rhythm Productions.

Annie Miles and Matthew Devitt

The Complete Works of William Shakespeare (Abridged).

Arts

Reed Martin, Adam Long and Austin Tichenor

Divining the West End's guilt at not always being as culturally as it is commercially concerned, the Reduced Shakespeare Company comedy outfit arrived from America this year and proceeded to exploit the situation, offering to bridge the gap with a show that had everything, almost – i.e. the whole of the Shakespearean canon (including sonnets), made funny, condensed into two hours with, in between times, fire-eating and a tonsil-tapping rendition of the William Tell overture. This other RSC was made up of three Californians – Reed Martin, Jess Borgeson and Adam Long – who, having honed their work at several Edinburgh Fringe Festivals, had finally brought "The Complete Works of William Shakespeare (Abridged)" to the West End. It opened at the Arts on 23 March to only luke warm reviews but had it's run extended twice to a final date of 3 October.

The Chippendales

Strand

The brainchild of American impressario Steve Banerjee, The Chippendales appeared in London at the Strand on March 30 1992. The show was directed by Anthony Van Laast and choreographed by Steve Merritt. Simultaneously, three other troupes of Chippendales toured Britain and Europe, and four troupes were operating in the US. Targeting female "hen partys" audiences the Chippendales were so successful in the US that Banerjee set up a permanent Chippendales nightclub in LA, and another in New York which subsequently closed. The troupe of ten Chippendales and eight dancers performed partial stripteazes accompanied by a live band doing cover versions of chart hits and specially written Chippendale songs, such as Gary Hastings' "Give me your body". London theatre critics were not invited to press night, but media commentators and social pundits dedicated column inches to wondering whether or not the Chipppendales represented "every woman's dream".

Mad, Bad and Dangerous to Know

Ambasssadors

Jane McCulloch's two-hander, a compilation from Byron's letters, journals and poems, arrived at the Ambassadors on 26 May this year, where it ran for a planned six-week season ending on 4 July. Basically a theatrical biography, "Mad, Bad and Dangerous To Know" had started life fifteen years ago as a small cast touring production starring Derek Jacobi entitled "The Lunatic, the Lover and the Poet". Since then it has been changing in style, content and presentation. In this latest manifestation, presented by Michael White, Derek Jacobi remained as the errant poet while support now came from a solitary Isla Blair as assorted women in his life, with music by Donald Fraser, designs by Liz Da Costa and lighting by Jenny Cane. Here Jacobi rendered up the various facets of the poet's character, accompanying each adventure with the limp caused by the famed lame foot. Jane McCulloch directed.

Derek Jacobi and Isla Blair

Spread a Little Happiness

"Spread a Little Happiness" Played in the Whitehall theatre during June and July.

It had transferred from the King's Head theatre in Islington.

Please refer to the Yearbook's section on **The Fringe, King's Head** for further details of this production.

Plays

The Mousetrap

St Martin's

Madeline Smith, Paul Imbusch, Pamela Lane, Paul Wimsett and Nicholas Smith

The world's longest-running play (its run has spanned ten American Presidents and nine British Prime Ministers), "The Mousetrap" opened at the Ambassadors' on November 25 1952 with Richard Attenborough as Detective Sergeant Trotter and Sheila Sim as Mollie Ralston, directed by Peter Cotes and produced by Sir Peter Saunders. There have since been twenty-one directors, a new one every year since 1977, and annual cast changes (Ray Cooney played the Detective in 1965). A conventional whodunnit set in a snowbound bed and breakfast, it was originally written as a radio play called "Three Blind Mice" at the request of Queen Mary for her eightieth birthday in 1947. Now little more than a curiosity or a museum piece, the final revelation of who did it is one of the best kept secrets in London. This year, Trotter was played by Simon Tate, Molly by Maeve Alexander and the director was David Turner.

The Woman in Black

Fortune

Michael Siberry

Stephen Mallatratt's adaptation of a Susan Hill ghost story, directed by Robin Herford, designed by Michael Holt, produced by Peter Wilson. It originally opened at the Stephen Joseph Theatre in Scarborough in 1988, then transferred to the Lyric Hammersmith on January 11 1989, to the Strand, then the Playhouse on April 18 1989 and finally to the Fortune where it has been since June 7 1989.

Now starring Milton Johns and Dominic Letts, "The Woman in Black" is a clever ghost story, set in the very theatre it is performed, with the literary conceit that in middle age a solicitor engages an actor to act out the story of an experience in his youth which has been haunting him ever since: cut to a creepy house in a remote and marshy part of Norfolk, where the solicitor as a young man has been sent to wind up the affairs of a recently deceased old lady...

Dancing at Lughnasa

Garrick

Brian Friel's multi award-winning play was originally an Abbey Theatre, Dublin production, directed by Patrick Mason. It then went to the National Theatre where it received excellent notices (many regarded it as Friel's best play to date), transferred to the Phoenix on March 25 1991, and to the Garrick on December 19 1991. Set in a remote Irish farmhouse in 1936, it focused on a family of five unmarried sisters whose repressed lives were disrupted by the pagan harvest festival of Lughnasa (the hard-to pronounce title was referred to in New York as "Dancing as Lasagna"), associated with dancing and sex. The situation was complicated by the arrival of two men: one a feckless lover and the other the sister's long-lost missionary brother who was considerably affected by the African religions of the people he spent a lifetime trying to convert. After winning several Olivier awards, the original cast took the production to Broadway where they won a clutch of Tonys.

Brid Brennan and Alec McCowen

The Ride Down Mount Morgan

Wyndham's

Michael Blakemore pulled off something of a coup by getting hold of Arthur Miller's first new play for six years and staging the world premiere in London. It was produced by Robert Fox and opened on October 31 1991 with design by Tanya McCallin and lighting by Nick Chelton. Described as a comedy, it starred Tom Conti as the bigamist, Lyman, in plaster up to his neck after a car accident and confronted by two wives (Gemma Jones and Clare Higgins) after the police unwittingly informed both. The play's preoccupations were characteristic of Miller – memory, guilt and deceit – treated with uncharacteristic levity. Miller's unprecedented decision to premiere a new play in London seemed to be a vote of confidence in the West End, but critics pronounced it an inferior play and objected to the production's insistence on treating serious issues lightly. It closed on February 16 1992.

Tom Conti and Gemma Jones

An Evening with Gary Lineker

Duchess Theatre

This play by stand-up comic Arthur Smith and Chris England was directed by Audrey Cooke and originally presented at the Edinburgh Fringe Festival where it was a runaway success. It opened in the West End on December 19 1991, presented by PW Productions and Rupert Gavin for Incidental Theatre Ltd. Set in Majorca at the time of the 1990 World Cup, it used football as an extended metaphor for love, relationships and the differences between the sexes, as a couple of Brits and ill-assorted companions watched the England vs West Germany semi-final. The original production featured co-writer Chris England and frequent Arthur Smith collaborator, Caroline Quentin. The cast of comedians was later replaced by actors Michael Garner, Suzie Aitchison, James Gaddas, Owen Brenman and Georgia Mitchell. Clever, funny, astute and praised by critics, it opened up new audiences among football fans, and tapped into the already large numbers of regulars from the comedy circuit who wouldn't normally venture inside a West End theatre.

Painting Churches

Playhouse

Rosemary Harris and Frank Middlemass in Southampton

Patrick Sandford directed this three-hander by acclaimed US playwright Tina Howe about an elderly, cultured, eccentric couple packing up their Boston apartment and preparing to move to the country. They were visited by their portait artist daughter with some old scores to settle while painting them (hence the title). First seen at the Nuffield Theatre, Southampton in March 1991, it was presented in London by Tim Siracusa, Leila Witkin and Michael Lander in association with the Nuffield Theatre, Southampton, opening at the Playhouse on January 22 1992. With Sian Phillips as the mother and Leslie Phillips as the father, it marked Josie Lawrence's West End straight acting debut as their daughter. Carl Toms designed. Despite having run for months in New York the play was unanimously slated in London for being sentimental, boring and banal. It closed just two weeks after the opening night.

Talking Heads

Comedy

Patricia Routledge

If sometimes the quality of theatre in the West End is taken to task, there are always exceptions to the rule. Alan Bennett's "Talking Heads", which ran at the Comedy this year from 27 January to 28 March, was such a one. Presented by Duncan C Weldon, with decor by Simon Higlett and music by Jeremy Sams, it comprised three separate monologues originally written for BBC television – "A Woman of No Importance", "A Chip in the Butter" and "A Lady of Letters". The first was a portrait of an office busybody who, when hospitalized with stomach cancer, came to understand the depth of her solitude. The last depicted a compulsive, poisonous letter writer who found a new lease of life in the communual warmth of prison. These were played by Patricia Routledge. In between was Bennett himself, playing a mentally-retarded mother's boy driven to Oedipal fury when his seventy-two-year-old mum fell for a fancy man.

La Bete

Lyric, Hammersmith

John Rogan, Alan Cumming and Sarah Crowden

A verse satire on the philistine times we live in by US playwright David Hirson. "La Bete" was produced on Broadway by Andrew Lloyd Webber who lost £2 million on it. The Really Useful Company then pulled out all the stops to resurrect it in the West End, but played safe with a try-out run at the Lyric Hammersmith which opened on February 5 1992. "La Bete" had all the advantages: the award-winning creative team of director Richard Jones and designer Richard Hudson, and a script which acted as a star vehicle for the young but accomplished Alan Cumming, ably supported by a cast which included Timothy Walker as the Prince and Jeremy Northam. Richard Hudson's design and costumes were impressively lavish as usual (the set alone allegedly cost £171,000), but the production did no better in London than it did in New York and when the Hammersmith run ended on March 14 1992 after playing to nearly empty houses, it was abandoned.

Death and the Maiden

Duke of York's

Geraldine James

Ariel Dorfman's multi award-winning play had a peculiarly chequered route to the West End. First seen in a rehearsed reading at the ICA as part of Harold Pinter's Censored Theatre Project, it was directed in July 1991 by Linsday Posner at the Royal Court Upstairs then transferred to the main house and finally opened at the Duke of York's on February 19 1992. Juliet Stevenson recreated her seering performance as Paulina, the South American torture victim whose husband (Bill Paterson) unwittingly brought home the man she believed was her torturer (Michael Byrne). The play was brilliantly structured to allow no alleviation of dramatic tension, while dealing with complex moral issues of forgiveness and retribution in a newly democratic country. There was a flurry of interest from the States, with Jack Nicholson flying in to see the production and the possibility of a film mooted. Stevenson was eventually followed in the role by Geraldine James, and then Penny Downie, with Hugh Ross and Danny Webb.

Straight and Narrow

Wyndham's/Aldwych

Nicholas Lyndhurst and Carmel McSharry

A sharply observed new comedy of family life, Jimmy Chinn's "Straight and Narrow" arrived at Wyndham's Theatre on 18 March this year to mixed critical acclaim, but held on to good houses and eventually extended its run by transferring to the Aldwych on 30 June where it closed on September 12. It was directed by Allan Davis and starred Nicholas Lyndhurst with Neil Daglish and Carmel McSharry.

Chinn dared to be different by writing a mainstream comedy about homosexuality and pulled it off. The trick was not to highlight the difference between homosexuals and heterosexuals, but to portray a gay couple whose lives are just as "dreary and respectable" as the rest of the family who are married. Most of the humour was generated by McSharry as Lyndhurst's's battleaxe mum, determinedly avoiding any knowledge of her son's sexuality.

Reflected Glory

Vaudeville

Albert Finney and Stephen Moore

This show should have been one of the dream tickets of the West End year. "Reflected Glory" had it all. It was written by one of our best playwrights, Ronald Harwood, who knows a little about theatre – he scored a huge hit with "The Dresser" in 1980. It starred Albert Finney with Stephen Moore, Nicky Henson, Mark Tandy, Katherine O'Toole, Stephen Greif and Holly Wilson in support. The director was Elijah Moshinsky, who had already successfully directed Finney in a Harwood play "Another Time" (1989). But it all went wrong.

Harwood's play asked whether an artist's cannibalisation of his own family background is morally legitimate through the story of a feud between two brothers, one a brash restaurateur, the other an arrogant playwright. But critical acclaim for the show when it opened at the Vaudeville on 8 April was only lukewarm, and that was won mostly by Finney's performance. Audiences dwindled quickly and when Finney walked out of the show claiming non-payment it closed abruptly on Thursday 4 June.

The Pope and the Witch

Comedy Theatre

Frances de la Tour and Berwick Kaler

Dario Fo's latest play was translated and adapted by Andy de la Tour and directed by Jude Kelly, Artistic Director of the West Yorkshire Playhouse, where it packed in audiences. For the West End production, which opened on April 13 1992, Frances de la Tour was brought into the cast as the "witch"/wise woman Elisa, playing opposite Berwick Kaler as Pope John Paul II. Rob Jones did the design, Leonard Tucker the lighting and choreography was by Gillian Gregory.

In Italy, the flagrant attack on the Pope's policy on contraception and abortion was joyously received, but in London, as so often happens with translations of Fo's plays, it was not. Despite Andy de la Tour cutting many of the Italian references to make the script more relevant to an English audience (he worked from a literal translation by Ed Emery) the message seemed dated rather than inflammatory and the broad, comic sweep of the production and its farcical plot did not go down well with critics. It closed on May 16 1992.

A Slip of the Tongue

Shaftesbury

John Malkovitch and Kara Zediker

Of that tiny band of American stars who have impressed West End audiences - in recent years Al Pacino in "American Buffalo", Dustin Hoffman in "The Merchant of Venice" and Alan Alda in "Our Town" – John Malkovich is the latest. His performance in the Hampstead Theatre's "Burn This" last year helped it to a West End transfer. And certainly his reappearance on the London stage this year boosted the success of Dusty Hughes' new play "A Slip of the Tongue". Malkovich and the Steppenwolf Theatre Company premiered the play in Chicago in February and brought the show into the Shaftesbury Theatre opening night on 11 May. The casting included the French Clotilde Courau , British Lizzy McInnerny, American Kara Zediker and Lithuanian Ingeborga Dapkunaite. The play was set in an Eastern European country before and after the revolution of 1989 and was about a dissident writer's relationship with four female students. The play was directed by Simon Stokes and closed after its scheduled fifteen-week run.

Body and Soul

Albery

Robert Hardy and Angela Thorne

Given the paucity of new plays about comtemporary issues in the West End it seemed rather a shame that Roy Kendall's "Body and Soul", which puts the topic of the ordination of women on stage, got such a grudging welcome and received no better promotion than a three week booking from 21 May to 6 June at the Albery. It certainly wasn't short of theatrical clout. The cast was headed by Robert Hardy and Angela Thorne and it was directed by Val May. Kendall's drama centred on the core question of the Church of England's refusal to allow women to give absolution and administer communion – the fundamental sacraments. By using the device of a sex-change vicar, Kendall brought other moral certainties crashing down while building up his work into a many layered thing of emotional drama, aphoristic comedy, political machinations and theological debate. Sheridan Morley was moved to call the play one of that endangered species "a well-made moral drama" vital to the West End.

The Blue Angel

Globe

Kelly Hunter and Philip Madoc

Trevor Nunn's Royal Shakespeare Company production of "The Blue Angel" opened at the Globe Theatre on 20 May. Classified "a new musical play" it was written by Pam Gems and based on Heinrich Mann's 1905 novel "Professor Unrat", though clearly equally inspired by the 1930 Josef Von Sternberg film starring Marlene Dietrich. Kelly Hunter played "Lola" and Philip Madoc "Raat" in the classic story in which a fuddy-duddy academic is infatuated with a tawdry night-club singer. The show was designed by Maria Bjornson, lighting was by Chris Parry, musical arrangement by Steven Edis and choreography by David Toguri. The action was updated to Hamburg in the late 1920s and incorporated seventeen songs including the famous "Falling In Love Again". But although highly regarded by critics when it premiered at the Other Place in Stratford-upon-Avon on 7 August 1991 prior to a sell-out tour, and again praised in London, the production fell prey to the dramatic West End slump in business, and closed prematurely on 27 June.

Dejavu

Comedy

Peter Egan

Opinion was not unanimous about John Osborne's most famous play "Look Back In Anger" when it opened in 1956. Ken Tynan loved it, Milton Shulman hated it. Some think it changed the face of English theatre, others beg to differ.

This sequel, "Dejavu", which opened at the Comedy on 10 June this year, directed by Tony Palmer and presented by Bill Kenwright, divided the critics a second time, though not so wholeheartedly. The central character remained, Jimmy Porter (Peter Egan in the role Peter O'Toole quit earlier in the year after differences with the author), the original "angry young man" who loathed the thought of being a member of the public. And plot-wise the play had moved on little, with Jimmy still performing misanthropic double acts with his chum Cliff (Gareth Thomas). Even the ironing board featured prominently again. It was deja vu, indeed, but the older Jimmy had less theatrical puff and expired after eight weeks closing on 1 August.

Murder by Misadventure

Vaudeville/Whitehall

William Gaunt and Gerald Harper

Stage thrillers know all about mounting murders most foul. Sadly, today's theatrical climate has meant the genre's coming to terms with its own untimely demise. Edward Taylor's "Murder By Misadventure", coming into the West End after several months on the road, brought the number of thrillers in town to only three. The new play,a Theatr Clwyd production directed by Val May, opened at the Vaudeville on 13 July. Though a veteran writer for television, this was Mr Taylor's first work for the stage. In the cast were Gerald Harper, William Gaunt, Angela Down and Greg Hicks. The plot had a popular TV thriller-writing duo stuck in a stale partnership. One was blackmailing the other, tempting the victim to do away with his erstwhile chum. A perfect murder was plotted and then ingeniously put into action, but as in all thrillers, the plan misfired. The show transferred to the Whitehall in August and kept audiences on the edge of their seats until the end of the year.

Shades

Albery

Pauline Collins and James Cosmo

A new play by Sharman MacDonald, directed by Simon Callow, starring Pauline Collins and designed by Christopher Morley, "Shades" opened at the Albery on July 23 following a world premiere as the inaugural production at the spanking new New Victoria Theatre in Woking on June 16. Collins, returning to the West End stage for the first time since her award-winning performance in both the play and the film of "Shirley Valentine", played Pearl, a widowed sales assistant with a ten-year-old son, Alan (played on different nights by either by Matthew Steer or Ben Chapman) living in a smart but only two-roomed home in 1950s Glasgow. The two confronted each other in scenes of domestic poignancy. As the mother dressed up for a rare night out the son played on her guilt at leaving him. Touching if slight, this was McDonald's fifth play. The last four have yet to match the acclaim and commercial success of her first, "When I Was A Girl, I Used To Scream And Shout".

It Runs in the Family

Playhouse

Ray Cooney, John Quayle, and Windsor Davies

"It Runs In The Family", a new comedy written and directed by Ray Cooney, opened at The Playhouse on 14 September 1992 following previews from 17 August. The cast featured John Quayle, Sandra Dickinson, Wanda Ventham, Henry McGee, Dennis Ramsden, Jacqueline Clarke, Doris Hare, Michael Fenner, Jennifer Hill, William Harry, Windsor Davies and Ray Cooney himself. Set designs were by Douglas Heap and lighting by Mark Doubleday. Farce master Cooney's convoluted plot had Dr David Mortimore, neurologist, about to give the Ponsonby Lecture, a certain stepping stone to Head Physician and a Knighthood. However, eighteen years and nine months previously he had enjoyed a romantic association. The result of this liaison is now wandering the hospital corridors in search of the father he's never seen. Dr. Mortimore, for obvious reasons, wishes it to remain that way and goes to ridiculous lengths to hide his parental identity. The show was still running at the end of the year.

Our Song

Apollo

Tara FitzGerald and Peter O'Toole

"Our Song", a new play by Keith Waterhouse, adapted from his best selling novel of the same name published in 1988, opened at the Apollo on November 3 after a two week run at the Theatre Royal Bath. It starred Peter O'Toole and was directed by Ned Sherrin and produced by Michael Redington. "Our Song" re-united the team that created the hugely successful "Jeffrey Bernard Is Unwell" which won the Evening Standard Comedy of the Year Award in 1990 and helped the real Jeffrey Bernard, if not to perfect health, at least to a position of being able to afford BUPA membership. "Our Song" told the story of a dazzling but ultimately doomed love affair between a married, middle-aged, middle rung advertising executive and an attractive young self-styled "freelance factotum", Angela Caxton, who, dressed all in black, gatecrashed his son's christening party. The story concerned his astonishing helter-skelter experience of falling unsuitably but violently in love. Tara Fitzgerald played the part of Angela.

Lost in Yonkers

Strand

Maureen Lipman and Benny Grant

Duncan C Weldon presented the latest slice of Neil Simon autobiography opening on November 12 1992 after a national tour which opened in Guildford on September 21 1992. The story of two young boys unwillingly dumped on elderly relations in New York in 1942, the British premiere starred Maureen Lipman as the fragile aunt, with Rosemary Harris repeating her acclaimed Broadway performance as the autocratic Grandma and thirteen year-old Benny Grant (also from the New York production) as the younger brother. David Taylor directed. Set and costumes were by Santo Loquasto and lighting was by Tharon Musser, both of whom worked on the original production.

"Six Degrees of Separation"

John Guare's highly acclaimed "Six Degrees of Separation" opened at the Comedy theatre on 5 August.

It had transferred from the Royal Court.

Please refer to the Yearbook's section on **The Royal Court** for further details of this production.

"Someone Who'll Watch Over Me" and "Making it Better"

Two West End transfers for Hampstead theatre this year, "Someone Who'll Watch Over Me" to the Vaudeville from 8 September and "Making it Better" at the newly refurbished Criterion from 21 October.

For further coverage, please turn to the Yearbook section on **Fringe Theatre, Hampstead**.

"The Rise and Fall of Little Voice"

The Aldwych became the home for this National Theatre production from 14 October.

There are more details in the Yearbook's section on **The National Theatre**.

Revivals and Classics

Becket

Theatre Royal, Haymarket

A revival of Jean Anouilh's 1959 play newly translated by Jeremy Sams and starring Robert Lindsay as Henry II and Derek Jacobi as Becket, it was directed by Elijah Moshinsky and produced by Duncan C Weldon. Bayeux tapestry-inspired sliding panels formed Michael Yeargan's design. "Becket" explored the relationship between the sprightly young Norman king of England with his Saxon friend (lover?) and protege, who later rose to become Chancellor, opposed the king and was murdered in Canterbury cathederal. Not seen in this country since 1961, the producer perhaps hoped to cash in on the success of Anouilh's "The Rehearsal" at the Almeida which successfully transferred. But critics agreed that the play was weak and not even bravura performances from the two stars, Jeremy Sams' lively translation (which changed that much-quoted line "who will rid me of this turbulent priest?" to "this measly priest") and ebullient direction (more than one critic compared it to "Black Adder") were enough. It closed on March 7 1992.

Robert Lindsay and Derek Jacobi

The Cabinet Minister

Albery

The revival of Sir Arthur Wing Pinero's 1891 farce by Braham Murray, which opened on 21 November 1991 at the Albery, seems to have been prompted more by considerations of centennial celebration than actual merit. Pinero's theme is social propriety, the butt of his humour insider trading and politicians with scandalous private lives. Derek Nimmo and Maureen Lipman starred as the dithering Rt Hon Sir Julian Twombley MP, who criminally exploited Cabinet secrets, and his spendthrift wife Lady Kitty, herself in hock to a pushy dressmaker, Mrs Gaylustre (Sara Kestelman), and her money-lending brother, Joseph Lebanon (Teddy Kempner). Yet 100 years on the play's contemporary relevance was more apparent than real and most critics were disturbed by the baldly stated snobbery and prejudice, as when the Jewish Lebanon is shamelessly mocked. Elsewhere the production's sets – an elegant conservatory and a Scottish castle interior – by Simon Higlett were praised. The show closed on 15 February 1992.

Maureen Lipman and Sara Kestelman

The Pocket Dream

Albery

A reworking of "A Midsummer Night's Dream" by Elly Brewer and Sandi Toksvig, it opened at the Albery on March 4 1992. Originally presented at Nottingham Playhouse it was directed by that theatre's Artistic Director, Pip Broughton. "The Pocket Dream" was a play within a play about a travelling company's disaster-ridden production of Shakespeare's Dream, left with only two actors when the rest of the cast decamped en masse to the pub. The performance was predictably disastrous – wigs fell off, scenery fell over, and so on. The production was bolstered with names from the world of stand-up, including writer/ performer Sandi Toksvig , Phelim McDermott, and Mike McShane. Warmly received in the spirit in which it was presented in Nottingham, in the metropolis it met with barely veiled contempt. As John Peter wrote in the Sunday Times, "It takes some nerve to do a send-up of a play which includes the funniest send-up of the theatre ever written". It closed on May 9 1992.

Sandi Toksvig and Mike McShane

Don't Dress for Dinner

Apollo

Director Peter Farago scored an unexpected hit with this modern French boulevard comedy. Written by Marc "Boeing Boeing" Camoletti the show was premiered in Paris in 1985, ran for two years and was still touring successfully in the country of origin when this production opened at the Apollo on 26 March 1991. Theatrical hits don't always weather a Channel crossing, but Richard Hawdon adapted the comedy for an English audience while leaving the characters French and the action still in a restored farmhouse an hour from Paris. The recipe appealed. The plot involved a husband's attempt to spend a weekend with his mistress, using a best friend as an alibi who, unknown to him, was his wife's lover. Being French, there was also the involvement of an attractive young gourmet chef. The original cast was Simon Cadell, Su Pollard, Jane Howe and John Quayle. The show closed on October 24.

Sue Hodge and Tim Perrin

Heartbreak House

Haymarket

A star-studded Duncan C Weldon revival of George Bernard Shaw's flawed masterpiece directed by Trevor Nunn and starring Vanessa Redgrave, Imogen Stubbs, Felicity Kendal, Paul Scofield, Daniel Massey, David Calder and Oliver Ford Davies with design by William Dudley and lighting by Mark Henderson. Coming in the wake of "Moby Dick" and "Some Like it Hot", it was a bid for some serious drama in a sea of showbiz frivolity. Shaw described the play as "A Fantasia in the Russian Manner on English Themes". Set in country house (built by Dudley to look like a ship) it was an allegory of the English chattering classes indolently playeing while the country drifted towards the First World War, which, prophesied Shaw, would bring about their own destruction. Lasting a good three hours played with two intervals, it was universally praised by the critics and ran until June 20 1992.

Paul Scofield & Imogen Stubbs

A Midsummer Night's Dream

Open Air

As hardy perennials go, "A Midsummer Night's Dream" is about as hardy and as perennial as you can get, especially as played in the Open Air Theatre in Regent's Park. It has, after all, been in regular production here, come wind and high weather, since 5 July 1933. A succession of inclement summers, from showery to plain capricious, have been thwarted in their attempts to stop the show going on. This summer's New Shakespeare Company production, playing in rep from 29 May to 12 September, was a revival of last season's show directed by Artistic Director Ian Talbot. Only the cast had changed, with Dinsdale Landen replacing Roy Hudd as Bottom. Sarah-Jane Holm played Hermia, Nigel Hastings Lysander, Oliver Parker Demetrius, Anna Patrick Helena, Ken Bones Oberon and Jane Maud Titania. But the star of the show was once again the amazingly animated Ass's Head created by Steven Gregory – a furry cranium, all twitching ears, chattering teeth, raising eyebrows and great rolling eyes.

Gavin Muir

As You Like It

Open Air

Sarah-Jane Holm

The second to join the New Shakespeare Company's summer repertory season was Maria Aitken's production of Shakespeare's "As You Like It". Her designer was Bruno Santini, her choreographer Kenn Oldfield, musical director Mark Emney, lighting designer Jason Taylor and fight director Peter Woodward. It ran from 15 June to 8 September. The cast included Bette Bourne as Jaques, Oliver Parker as Orlando, Cathryn Harrison as Rosalind and Sarah-Jane Holm as Celia. Miss Aitkin's decision to present the play as if a 1930-ish director were making a film of it failed to amuse most critics, leading one to comment – "Lovely woman, amusing actress. But as a director, well, she thinks the title means as she likes it." Jaques, Shakespeare's melancholy outsider, was played as a movie director who has spotted that all the world's a stage and the Forest of Arden is the place where you go to shoot on location.

A Woman of No Importance

Theatre Royal, Haymarket

Cherry Morris and Leonard Kavanagh

The trend which has the Royal Shakespeare Company transfer its most successful and commercially viable productions to the West End, to date most significantly "Les Miserables" and "Les Liaisons Dangereuses", saw Oscar Wilde's "A Woman of No Importance", directed and designed by Philip Prowse, move into the Haymarket on 24 June. Most of the original cast stayed in the show with John Carlisle playing Lord Illingworth who employs a young secretary, Gerald (Andrew Havill), unaware that he is in fact his son by Mrs Arbuthnot (Carol Royle), a woman he has dismissed as "of no importance". Although this play has tended to be overshadowed by the success of "The Importance of Being Earnest", it contains all the essential elements of Wildean comedy and at its heart lies a dilemma – English society has one law for men and another for women. Prowse's sets created a gold-green fantasy of an English estate garden, a drawing room draped and cushioned in sumptuous reds and golds, and a doom-laden sitting room overwhelmed by huge black curtains.

Cyrano de Bergerac

Theatre Royal, Haymarket

The first West End production for nine years of Edmund Rostand's 1897 classic "Cyrano de Bergerac" arrived on 8 December. The unenviable task of taking on the mantle of Derek Jacobi's barnstorming portrayal of the chivalrous French knight in the glorious 1983 Terry Hands production at the Barbican for the RSC fell to Robert Lindsay. (Mind you, Lindsay had had ample chance to study Jacobi's style – the two were on stage together as Henry II and Thomas Becket respectively in Anouilh's "Becket" at the Theatre Royal Haymarket earlier in the year.) This "Cyrano" was a Duncan Weldon production directed by Elijah Moshinsky.The story, of course, is of a man with a noble heart but an impossibly long nose. Cyrano is not only fearless, but excels in everything – everything, that is, except romance. He loves, instead, vicariously, using his eloquence to help another more handsome but without his panache to win Roxeanne, his beautiful cousin and ideal woman.

Derek Jacobi in the 1983 production

The English Shakespeare Company

This globe-trotting company came to rest in the West End very briefly from November 27 to December 12.

Details of their work will be found in the Yearbook section **Touring Companies, the English Shakespeare Company**.

Philadelphia, Here I Come

Wyndham's became the home for this play by Brian Friel from July 29.

The production transferred from the King's Head in Islington and there are more details in the Yearbook section **Fringe Theatre, King's Head**.

Hayfever

An exciting liaison between the Theatre of Comedy and the Theatr Clwyd.

This production of Noel Coward's classic came to the West End but was first seen at the Theatr Clwyd in Mold.

Please refer to the regions section of the Yearbook, **Wales, Theatr Clwyd**.

THE FRINGE

Many a hardened critic will tell you that his or her most exciting evenings in the theatre have taken place on London's Fringe. IAN SHUTTLEWORTH describes the Fringe in 1992 and goes on to review the work of the principal fringe theatres.

The Fringe '92

London theatre lacks the distinction available to New Yorkers, between off-Broadway and off-off-Broadway; the single label 'Fringe' covers everything beyond the West End and the subsidised flagship houses. In this volume, however, a semi-artificial boundary has been drawn: major Fringe venues (what might be called off-Shaftesbury Avenue) are considered individually, and the plethora of smaller venues relegated to the homogenising process of the "Beyond The Fringe" section. This division has its drawbacks as well as its advantages: while many pub theatres simply book in any company that can afford to hire the space, an increasing number of venues are beginning to operate not only a quality threshold but a coherent artistic policy – resulting, for instance, in work of the calibre of the Mu-Lan company's "Porcelain" transferring from the Etcetera Theatre, Camden, to the Royal Court's Theatre Upstairs.

The premier-division Fringe venues, however, possess a prestige that perpetuates itself: their prominence enables them to draw prominent names to work there, whose presence in turn maintains the venue's profile in a kind of virtuous circle. They certainly can't compete financially, and indeed therein lies a paradox – as Jonathan Kent of the Almeida has noted, "An Alan Bates is more able to afford to work for six weeks at Equity minimum rates than some actor who's still up-and-coming." It is to be hoped that Carling's withdrawal of sponsorship for the 1992-93 Fringe Awards will not have a deleterious effect on the prestige to be earned from putting in high quality performances at Fringe level.

Where the motivation in Fringe theatre was once to constitute an alternative to conventional culture, it is now complementary to the proper channels – indeed, the very notion of impropriety seems faintly ludicrous. A symbiosis exists, as major Fringe venues furnish West End transfers – the likes of Theatre de Complicite perform at the National Theatre – while the NT's studio arm co-produces plays at the Bush and elsewhere. It becomes a pointless semantic question whether Steven Berkoff's "Kvetch" and "Acapulco" transferred to the West End from the King's Head or whether they were simply previewed on the Fringe.

All this healthy crosstalk, however, can obscure an important question: where do opposing voices go to be heard? If nostalgia for vigorous dissenting voices in theatre is regarded as callow romanticism, this says as much about the prevailing cultural climate as about the nostalgist. Of course, talented writers like April De Angelis, Billy Roche and Roy MacGregor are constantly being discovered, but they move now through licensed channels.

The idea that culture must pay its own way has hit Fringe theatre particularly heavily. One aspect of the problem has been the progressive drought of subsidy to smaller, issue- or community-based groups. The reign of market forces produces a kind of self-censorship: theatre which sets out conscious of the need to sugar its pills may, if not losing the message completely in confection, come up with a substance no more powerful than aspirin. Increasingly, vigorous heterodox views are to be found more in non-theatre-based or interdisciplinary work; while vestigial funding quotas remain, the situation can be paradoxically more healthy on the very margins – a kind of licensed wilderness.

And yet for all that, the imminent death of the Fringe is annually bewailed, and it never quite happens. Far from it, as in the past year both Talawa and Soho Theatre Companies have acquired permanent homes (the Cochrane and the Cockpit respectively). As with the Edinburgh Festival, the Fringe long ago grew to strapping adulthood, in many ways outstripping its more staid parent but retaining close family ties. Judge, then, by its deeds what kind of a way this youngster's been making for itself in the world.

Almeida

The converted warehouse of the Almeida remains more or less the most dynamic venue on the Fringe. Under the joint Artistic Directorship of Jonathan Kent and Ian McDiarmid, it was the most vocal opponent of the swingeing cuts proposed in London Boroughs Grant Scheme funding in 1991, and has retained an edge of defiance in its high-profile programming since. Now broadening its focus to place greater emphasis upon opera and contemporary dance seasons, but without slackening its commitment to theatre, its 1991 coup of the Harold Pinter premiere "Party Time" was followed up last autumn by staging that author's return to acting in his own "No Man's Land". A little less broadly based in its patronage than some other venues, which has led to jibes that it's the theatrical equivalent of a wine bar. However, the warm acclaim given to both "The Gigli Concert" and "The Rules Of The Game" gives the lie to such accusations.

The Gigli Concert

Tony Doyle and Barry Foster

Exiled alcoholic Englishman JPW King, living in a Dublin garret and professing the mumbo-jumbo cult of Dynamatology, is visited by a nameless millionaire, who wants King to cure his depression by enabling him to sing like the great tenor Beniamino Gigli. Through an intricate and at times pugnacious series of confessions, the Irishman is released from his impossible longing and King from his narrowness of vision. Karel Reisz's direction made the intricacies of Tom Murphy's play digestible without denying or diluting them; Barry Foster, as King, rumbled and leapt around an attic whose skewed perspectives (designed by Ashley Martin-Davies) reflected his own unsteadiness; Tony Doyle lowered magnificently as a man embarrassed by the wildness of his fancy and Ruth McCabe as Mona, King's mistress, conjured "a mixture of sensuality and disenchantment: a very Irish blend." (John Peter, Sunday Times).

A Hard Heart

Anna Massey

Howard Barker's play, commissioned by Radio 3, was poorly received on its stage premiere. In an unnamed European city under siege, Queen Praxis calls upon awkward genius architect Riddler to save the city, but Riddler's plan involves the destruction of all in the city that might be worth defending. The central duo, Angela Down's subdued Praxis and Anna Massey's granite Riddler, were augmented primarily by James Clyde as Riddler's cowardly, sycophantic son Attila. But neither actors nor Ian McDiarmid's direction could relieve the remorselessly heavy going of Barker's script, discursive and stuffed with abstract nouns demanding capital letters as in German. The production closed a fortnight early, to be replaced (perhaps ironically) by a brief run of Ken Campbell's one-man show "Pigspurt!" (see Riverside Studios).

The Rules of the Game

David Yelland

The sharpness of Jonathan Kent's direction perfectly matched David Hare's new translation of Luigi Pirandello's sardonic 1918 knot of revenge and counter-revenge in a failed marriage. Nicola Pagett's Silia – a creature of sensuality and self-dramatisation – easily manipulates her lover Guido, played with a core of bourgeois stolidity by David Yelland. But the compelling focus was Richard Griffiths' husband Leone, the spider at the centre weaving others' webs into one of his own. A streak of unfussy amusement at the absurdity of a figure as ample as his being party to amorous manoeuvrings, let alone fighting a duel, overlaid a "marvellous malign blandness" (Michael Billington, the Guardian) in Griffiths' performance. The only dissatisfying aspect of the production was its lack of a West End transfer.

Almeida Opera

In a new collaboration with the English National Opera, the Almeida scheduled a season of four operas along with concerts, recitals and cabaret in July. The chamber operas "What Price Confidence" by Ernst Krenek and "False Love/True Love" (based on "Jane Eyre" by Nils Vigeland) were given one or two performances, but the mainspring of the schedule was the British premiere of "Terrible Mouth" by Nigel Osborne with text by Howard Barker. David Pountney directed Osborne and Barker's meditation upon the life, work and creative obsessions of the painter Francisco Goya: Ian McDiarmid spoke text which was expanded musically around him. Oliver's Thomas Mann adaptation (directed by Tim Hopkins) worked with sensitivity and discretion upon the original story, slightly playing up the identification of magician Cipolla with Mussolini and placing the words in an "easy and natural" musical setting (Rodney Milnes, The Times), although those words "might make it sound anodyne, which it emphatically wasn't."

Medea

Michael Billington of the Guardian noted that Jonathan Kent's production was the seventh Medea to be seen in London in a decade. This version, however, was among the strongest. Alistair Elliot's translation and Diana Rigg's performance left no room for qualms or uncertainties as the outraged queen set about murdering her children in revenge for being discarded by her husband. Further, the deus ex machina was discarded, leaving Medea grimly exulting at her deed with no shade of divine redemption. Rigg expertly evoked both Medea's consciousness of the enormity she plans and the implacability of her resolve, creating a knot of motivations more complex and satisfying than modish and facile wronged-woman interpretations.

Diana Rigg

The Bush

With its audience seated on two sides upon large carpeted steps, the Bush physically recalls the last incarnation of the Traverse Theatre in Edinburgh. Nor does the comparison stop there: its concentration on new writing complements the Gate's taste for neglected classics and contemporary work in translation to make it the most consistently vibrant pub theatre in London. The first full year of Dominic Dromgoole's tenure as Artistic Director confirmed both its policy and its standing: after a shaky start with Public Parts' devised biography of Chatterton, "The Marvellous Boy", the following clutch of shows proved consistently worthy of attention, and in some cases (arguably the Rough Magic company's vivid "Digging For Fire", indubitably Bush discovery Roy MacGregor's "Phoenix") brilliant. It also celebrated its twentieth anniversary with a series of rehearsed readings (using, where possible, the original casts) of its greatest hits including "Duet For One", "Kiss of The Spiderwoman" and "The Fosdyke Saga".

The Cutting

Paul Freeman and Sian Thomas

When a play is a two-hander, and one character is mute for the first forty-five minutes, the demands made upon all concerned are heavy. In Dominic Dromgoole's delicate production of Maureen O'Brien's first stage play, those demands were met. Judith (Sian Thomas) has not spoken since her imprisonment for murdering her mother. Psychiatrist Alex has the task of coaxing her into speech again, finding out exactly what happened and why. The title refers both to a stretch of railway line where Judith fed the gulls, and to the act whereby she enabled herself to feed them little pieces of her mother. When Judith rediscovers speech, the play loses track somewhat, ending with Alex's final declaration of love. A first-rate production of a play which, given a couple more drafts, would also have been first-rate.

Digging for Fire

Peter Hanly

Dublin-based Rough Magic scored the hit of the 1991 Dublin Theatre Festival with what author Declan Hughes gets angry if he hears glibly described as an Irish "Big Chill". Still, it does centre upon a reunion after ten years of a group of college friends during a progressively more drunken evening which sours friendships and shreds marriages. Hughes follows this with a finely anticlimactic morning after in which his protagonists have to face up to what they've done. Lynne Parker directed a searingly unpleasant set of characterisations, particularly Gina Moxley's brittle radio executive Breda. A few months later the company visited the Tricycle with a similarly feted production of Farquhar's "Love And A Bottle".

White Woman Street

Roy Hanlon, Kevork Malikyan and Jim Norton

"No more, and no less, than a good Irish tale" was Malcolm Rutherford's verdict (in the Financial Times) on Sebastian Barry's elegiac oddball Western. Set in the hills of Ohio in 1910, a motley collection hailing from Sligo, Grimsby, Tennessee and Brooklyn set out to rob a gold train, but become sidetracked by Trooper O'Hara's compulsion to return to White Woman Street (former location of the only caucasian prostitute within 500 miles) to atone for past misdeeds there. Jim Norton as Trooper led an excellent cast, including Kevork Malikyan as a comically over-punctilious Indian brothel-keeper. Barry's script sketched atmosphere better than it delineated character, and Caroline FitzGerald's direction concentrated rightly on bringing out the brooding tone of the piece, against Kendra Ullyart's mural of a desolate Midwestern landscape.

Pond Life

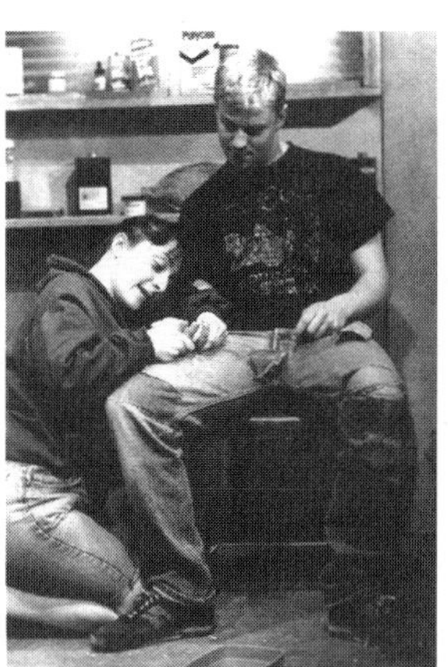

Joanna Robinson and Richard Standing

Richard Cameron's generosity and skill at mapping the vague terrain of adolescence was evidenced in this slight but entrancing comedy, co-produced with the National Theatre Studio and directed with gentle humour by Simon Usher. Trevor (Richard Standing) ties fishing flies and records songs in his shed, which provides a social hub for a group of teenagers at various stages of growing up. Notable among these are the slightly backward Pogo – a fine, sensitive performance from Joanna Robinson – and James Hooton's Malcolm (besotted with Trevor's sister Cassie), who was all gawk and gangle, living in "that desperate twilight state between boy and adult when a chap might enthuse equally and in the same breath about girls and train sets" (Nicholas de Jongh, Evening Standard).

Phoenix

Trevor Ray

Roy MacGregor's first play "Our Own Kind", staged at the Bush in 1991, won the first Meyer-Whitworth Award. "Phoenix" triumphantly confirmed that early promise. As the Berlin Wall comes down, '60s radical-turned-media brat Bruno (Nick Dunning, engagingly sardonic but with a core of deep feeling) travels east where his former lover Renata (Nicola Redmond) is in hiding after a bomb outrage twenty years ago. The phoenix of the title stands for all kinds of political and personal resurrections, evoked by direction (from Dominic Dromgoole) as densely yet quietly patterned as the script. Mark Viner's versatile set design was overlaid with between-scenes slides of Germany past and present. A production that epitomised the role of the Fringe in keeping theatre intelligent and vital.

The Gate

While only seating sixty and not paying its actors (each Monday night's take is divvied up, and that's it), the Gate has seen its reputation as the most consistently successful theatre in the country – fringe or mainstream, critically or pound-for-pound commercially – recognised both by the bestowal of the Kenneth Tynan Award at the Oliviers and Stephen Daldry's appointment at the Royal Court. Their policy of programming brief series of plays has paid remarkable dividends: 1991's Spanish Golden Age season was followed last year, (after a brief run of Talking Tongues' patchy "Guided Tours" double-bill and Venedict Erofeyev's "Walpurgis Night", by a Beyond Europe season including Judith Thompson's "The Crackwalker" from Canada, Nigerian Bode Sowande's "Flamingo" and "Bad Blood" by Argentine Grizelda Gambaro. Jonathan Guy Martin's version of Marivaux' "The False Servant" then preceded Six Plays For Europe – Laurence Boswell's first programme as Daldry's successor – which spanned nations and periods from Euripides' "Hecuba" and Lope de Vega's "Madness In Valencia" (Lope being rather a Gate speciality) to Thomas Bernhard's "Elisabeth II" and Michel Vinaver's "The Television Programme".

Walpurgis Night

Venedict Erofeyev's only play, written in 1984, centres on dissident poet Gurevich who (like the author) is committed to a mental hospital. A bleak exposure of Soviet psychiatric imprisonment changes tack on Walpurgis Night when, in pagan celebration of the end of winter, the inmates rebel, revel and escape. Erofeyev's writing (the play was only finished because his friends rewarded him for each completed page with a glass of vodka) loses coherence in the second half, and Snoo Wilson's clear translation and Lithuanian-born Dalia Ibelhauptaite's direction weren't enough to keep the proceedings focused. Each patient (played by Allan Corduner, Robin Soans and George Irving amongst others) was given time in a spotlight to recount their own history while Nicholas Farrell's Gurevich pulled their strings.

Nicholas Farrell and Beatie Edney

The Crackwalker

Judith Thompson's play, set among the Toronto underclass, includes wife-beating, alcohol, child abuse and the rape of a retarded woman – not a light evening, but in James Macdonald's production a fiery, compelling one that never lapsed into phoney poeticism. Kathy Burke gave a detailed, touching performance as the simple Theresa whose life with nervy Alan (Robert Bowman) deteriorates horrifically with his slide into boozy paranoia and the birth of a defective baby; Kathryn Pogson's long-suffering Sandy showed dogged, but pitifully inadequate, compassion. Amidst all this pity and terror, the crackwalker ingredient (an unexplained figure from native Canadian mythology) was provided by Kennetch Charlette's lurking, incoherent Indian. As often, the tiny Gate brought out the best in a set designer, and Ian MacNeil worked wonders with the space.

Cathryn Pogson

Flamingo

Susan Aderin

The idealistic Moniran sets out, as security chief, to rid Nigeria of the corruption that had been so endemic before a recent coup in Bode Sowande's play, but he fails and resigns in despair. The coup is juxtaposed against the threat of a popular uprising (the Operation Flamingo of the title), and personal against national politics. Director Topher Campbell, however, while giving full rein to the punctuation of drumming and dancing, could not overcome the handicap that Bowande's script plunged into oratory whenever weighty subjects arose. Colin McFarlane played the doomed Moniran with dignity and precision, and Jo Charles was the president who failed to sweep the corridors of power clean; Patrice Naiambana and Elkan Ola Ogunde provided the musical accompaniment. Although Sowande's rhetoric had obviously dated, his ideals remained powerful and infectious.

The False Servant

Marivaux' 1724 satire is based on the old conceit of cross-dressing disguise: "Le Chevalier", really an heiress, dons breeches to investigate her suitor Lelio, who subsequently enrols her/him to woo a countess on his behalf, but the Countess falls for Le Chevalier and Lelio is finally revealed as mercenary and amoral. Jonathan Guy Martin's production was lacking something for everyone. His (and Mary Ann Vargas') translation, sometimes crisp and alert to nuance, occasionally fell prey to alliterative excess ("how many reputations have you wrecked on the rocks of ruthlessness?"). As Le Chevalier, Christabelle Dilks was trapped in panto principal-boy mode and Crispin Redman's Lelio hard put to take the weight of all the play's nastinesses upon his shoulders. Marivaux remains an acquired taste on this side of the Channel.

The Television Programme

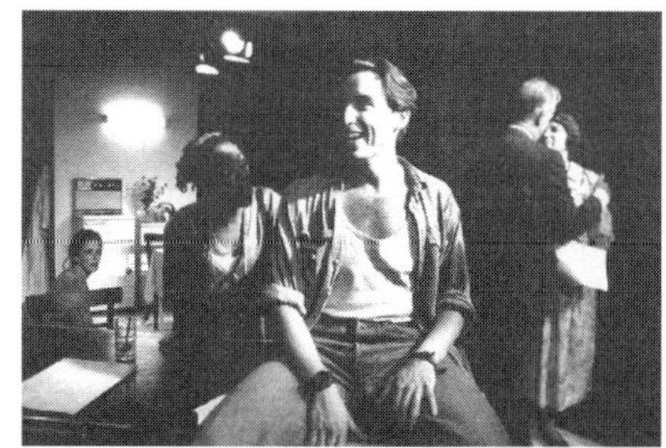

Marva Alexander and Toby Whithouse

The Gate's Six Plays For Europe season began with Michel Vinaver's 1990 play about two long-term unemployed men who become rivals for media attention when a pair of TV researchers (played by Esther Turnage and Devon Scott) approach them to take part in a documentary. When one of the men is murdered, the play's dual time-scheme intercuts the life of the survivor, Pierre Delile (John Muirhead) with a judge's (Guy Burgess) preliminary inquiries into the crime. Kim Dambaek directed with brio, steering characters through each other's lives like sleepwalkers in overlapping scenes and buoying up John and Hannah Bradby's rather pedestrian translation. There was a feeling, though, that Vinaver's whole should somehow have added up to more than the sum of its parts.

Greenwich

Greenwich hasn't quite succeeded in forging the strong image for itself that it both needs and deserves, perhaps due to the very distinctiveness of the district in which it's situated. It carries an air of "out of town" – an impression both reinforced by, and probably a primary cause of, less adventurous programming than comparable venues: less inclined to new work, albeit that its revivals are of ignored or underrated plays or are overdue British premieres. The advantage of such a policy on Matthew Francis' part is that the theatre isn't over-reliant on any particular age or social group. Its Christmas show "The Innocents" having been poorly received, Francis' production of Shaw's "Caesar And Cleopatra" drew warm but not passionate responses. The theatre then played host to the Croydon Warehouse "Playing Sinatra", and a brief re-staging of "The Corn Is Green". Jeremy Sams' directorial debut "Schippel, The Plumber", however, brought unrestrained plaudits.

Caesar and Cleopatra

Shaw's play, written in 1898 and here receiving its first serious revival in forty years, is both a corrective to Shakespeare's romantic view and a comedy of Victorian imperialist manners. Caesar, part brute, part woman and part god, is in the Shavian way an assembly of parts rather than a whole, but Alec McCowen succeeded in making him a paragon rather than a prig. Cleopatra, as played by Amanda Root, could have been the original inspiration for the word kittenish, but remained a devious politician. Matthew Francis' version was brisk and crisp, staged in Victorian dress and on a set (designed by Julian McGowan) that launched a thousand quips about the Egyptian Room of the British Museum.

Alec McCowen and Amanda Root

As You Like It

1992 was the year of "As You Like Its": Cheek By Jowl's triumphant all-male version drew to a close in the New Year, April saw David Thacker's production at Stratford, and the Open Air Theatre in Regent's Park staged Maria Aitken's 1930s-film interpretation in the summer (to say nothing of Christine Edzard's actual film). Robert James Carson, realising that amongst such company he would have to write his messages large, chose to do so literally, with a huge neon sign above the stage reading "nos cedamus amori", ("let us yield to love"). Jemma Redgrave's Rosalind was pleasant if unexceptional, and Philip Franks' Jacques an admirable clinical depressive rather than an affected melancholic.

Sue Flack and Tom Bowles

Schippel, the Plumber

James Saxon

Accomplished translator and composer Jeremy Sams showed himself an agile director to boot, with his production of an adaptation by CP Taylor of Carl Sternheim's mordant 1913 class comedy. The tenor of a bourgeois lieder quartet drops dead, and in order to retain their laurels in a royal competition they are forced to replace him with an angelic-voiced plumber and a bastard. James Saxon's Schippel was vulgar but engaging, ready to exploit his value to the quartet, led by the monstrously uppity Hicketier (a joyous creation from David Bamber). Kate Buffery was the deceased tenor's widow Thekla, now pursued both by Schippel and by Philip Franks' braided Prince. The laurels, though, were primarily Sams': "What does he do for kicks in his spare time," wondered Paul Taylor in the Independent -" a bit of light choreography?"

The Mother Tongue

Prunella Scales & Gwen Taylor

It was with palpable glee that reviewers rushed to decry this play written by a journalist, Alan Franks of the Times. His mechanical generation-conflict saga made concrete the apercu that mother and daughter often speak different languages – in the case of mother Dorothy, a blend of public-school argot and the Spanish of the Argentine where she has been living for decades, whereas daughter Harriet goes in for the jargon of her crudely-drawn women's support group – but it did so in a somewhat heavy-handed way. As Dorothy, Prunella Scales turned in an accomplished performance, as did Gwen Taylor in the role of the daughter Harriet.

Who Shall I Be Tomorrow

Joanna Lumley and Harry Landis

Bernard Kops' "Playing Sinatra" transferred to Greenwich from the Croydon Warehouse earlier last year, and in the autumn Matthew Francis directed Kops' new play which, like the earlier work, hinged upon two people sealed off from the outside world in a milieu of their own. The role of Rosalind Fraser, dowdy nobody who basically dreams of being Joanna Lumley, was daringly taken by Joanna Lumley in her first London appearance since the disappointment of Ayckbourn's "Revengers' Comedies" in late 1991. Her admiring audience, the decrepit Gerald, was played by Harry Landis. Stephen Brimson Lewis designed.

Hampstead

An erratic year for Jenny Topper's NW3 venue. Bruce Myers' two-person version of "The Dybbuk" was undoubtedly warm and affirmative, but too consciously theatrical for many. James Saunders' response to the ongoing Eastern European situation, "Making It Better", was seen as skilled though safe, and "Back Up The Hearse" widely viewed as a second-hand "Glengarry, Glen Ross". With "The Fastest Clock In The Universe", opinion took a turn for the better, as the promise of Philip Ridley's earlier play the "Pitchfork Disney" came closer to fruition; and Frank McGuinness's Beirut hostage play "Someone Who'll Watch Over Me" drew almost universal acclaim. The Hampstead acts more as a small, intelligent theatre, seldom moving far out of the mainstream, than as a ground-breaking experimental venue – as a seed-bed for the serious side of Shaftesbury Avenue rather than as a fringe theatre in the sense of a couple of decades ago.

A Dybbuk for Two People

Erstwhile Peter Brook associate Bruce Myers and his wife Corinne Jaber had been touring their version of Solomon Anski's play for some years before their appearance on the 1991 Edinburgh Fringe led to this London run. The story (young rabbinical scholar is tempted into darkness by the force of his love; he dies, and his spirit possesses the body of his beloved; the spirit is exorcised, but the couple are reunited in death) was framed within a Sabbath evening meal; table, chairs and napkins served as set and costumes as Myers played the various parts of Leye's obsessive suitor Khonen, of her father, her grandmother and the exorcising rabbi. Myers' performance, though skilful, occasionally veered into ostentatious actorliness – but over all there was a warm affirmation of the joy and potency of love.

Corinne Jaber

Making it Better

James Saunders' long association with the Hampstead continued with his meditation on the collapse of the eastern bloc.Jane Asher, as World Service radio producer Diana, finds herself a rival to her estranged platonic husband for the attentions of young Czech exile Tomas (Rufus Sewell) as well as the lover of older writer Josef (a comically fastidious David de Keyser). Even in the London of 1989, even in Diana's flat, factions of Czech ideology come into bitter conflict. Despite a strong and sensual central performance from Asher, the play was only a qualified success; Saunders' characters were perhaps too persistently bemused by both global and intimate events. Nominated for a Carling Fringe award, it lost out to Billy Roche's "Belfry", but finally entered the West End with the reopening of the Criterion.

Rufus Sewell & Jane Asher

Back up the Hearse And Let Them Sniff The Flowers

Lesley Dunlop & Paul Bown

Where the salesmen in David Mamet's "Glengarry, Glen Ross" sold useless plots of real estate, William Gaminara's protagonists peddled that '90s accessory, water filters. (The title refers to a salesman's gambit of frightening someone into buying.) A full set of office politics and commercial pressures are brought into play: the struggle to keep jobs, crises of conscience, a sales race, shady business dealings... the lot. But Gaminara's sharp ear for dialogue is not matched either by a flair for dramatic structure or a coherent overview. Danny Webb played Steve, the star salesman defending his top slot from comedian Brian (James Purefoy) to win a colour TV while office manager Sharon (Lesley Dunlop) struggled in vain to keep everything above board.

The Fastest Clock in the Universe

Con O'Neill & Jonathan Coy

Screenwriter, children's author, film director and (with "The Pitchfork Disney") playwright, Philip Ridley brings a disturbing East End Gothic flavour to his work. The characters' names hinted at the grotesquerie to come: narcissistic Cougar Glass (Con O'Neill, all quiff, shades and languor) enlists the aid of the unwilling but spinelessly devoted Captain Tock (Jonathan Coy) to seduce schoolboy Foxtrot Darling at Cougar's nineteenth birthday party, but Foxtrot (Jude Law) brings along his new fiance Sherbet Gravel, and a not-so-covert duel begins between Cougar and Sherbet (a sweetly acidic Emma Amos) in the decaying loft of a Bethnal Green factory building. Matthew Lloyd's tight direction kept the sex and violence looming in the shadows but Ridley's promise – though tantalisingly in evidence here – has yet to be fully realised in a play.

Someone Who'll Watch Over Me

Stephen Rea and Alec McCowen

As "Making It Better" tackled Eastern Europe, Frank McGuinness's new play grew from the Beirut hostage situation. An American doctor, an Irish journalist and an English teacher are chained in a cell with a bottle of water a day and each other's foibles for constant company. McGuinness dwells not at all on politics, but on the intense pressures and necessities of relationships in such conditions. The shooting of Adam (Hugh Quarshie) leaves Stephen Rea's sardonic but insecure Edward and Michael (Alec McCowen, illuminating the foundations of the stiff-upper-lip stereotype) to help each other through the unnumbered days ahead. From a hilarious re-enactment of the 1977 Wimbledon Ladies' final to the quiet emotion of Michael's beloved Middle English poetry, this was a production that justified the cliche "funny and moving", and deserved its subsequent trip to the Vaudeville.

The King's Head

The King's Head bar still affects pre-decimal prices, although a pint costs £1-14-0 rather than 3/6; a similar air of anachronism hangs over the theatre to its rear, one of the first wave of pub theatres to arise in the early 1970s. Apart from La Bonne Crepe (which is primarily a restaurant), it's the only permanent dinner theatre on the fringe, and its long refectory tables and bank of seating to one side create an atmosphere which can enhance the right kind of show or make the wrong sort look wildly out of place. Founder Artistic Director Dan Crawford, though, has the measure of the place after twenty-one years, and of the productions detailed below only the ill-advised self-indulgence of "Once Upon A Song" sat uncomfortably in the venue. It's a seedbed for the West End: both "Philadelphia, Here I Come!" and "Spread A Little Happiness" moved up west (though the latter, beset by problems, closed after less than a month). Steven Berkoff opened "Kvetch" here in 1991. In addition to evening shows, the King's Head hosts frequent lunchtime productions by Syd Golder's Elephant company.

Spread a Little Happiness

Rachel Robertson

The wave of compilation musicals inundating Shaftesbury Avenue splashed daintily on the fringe with Sheridan Morley's tribute to the music of Vivian Ellis, the now neglected songwriter of the '30s and '40s. Morley's assemblage both unearthed some little gems and revealed why Ellis was never elevated to the pantheon with the likes of the Gershwins and Cole Porter: music largely unimpassioned, songs written to be delivered with airs of forced jauntiness in implausible period accents. Dan Crawford and his cast, however, fashioned a frequently entertaining evening by utilising seasoned performers Thelma Ruby and the gloriously deadpan Frank Thornton, and energetic nineteen-year-old Rachel Robertson. The West End transfer was torpedoed by the eleventh-hour withdrawal of Thornton's replacement Ron Moody and an overall inability to create warmth in a much larger venue.

Once Upon a Song

Created by Antohony Newley,of whom Lyn Gardner wrote in the Independent, "He once wrote a rather good song which posed the question "What Kind Of Fool Am I?" The answer is the kind of fool who writes, directs and stars in this sort of shoestring musical." Playing The Father to Diane Langton's The Mother (with Natalie Wright and Leonard Kirby as... you've guessed it), Newley recycled his old songs into a trite, unedifying meditation upon family life. His vibrato now so great it moved between neighbouring postal districts, his attempts to renew his acquaintance with an adoring audience made an unpleasant and embarrassing sight. For all the strength of her performance here, "Bernadette" is no longer the darkest hour in Natalie Wright's career.

The Chalk Garden

Tessa Wyatt, Kellie Bright and Jean Marsh

"Look Back In Anger" arrived at the Royal Court a month after Enid Bagnold's play opened in the West End in 1956, and this revival highlighted the dangers of rewriting theatrical history to consign the well-made play to oblivion. Director Mark Rayment assembled a number of actors of the finest calibre: Constance Cummings as Mrs. St. Maugham, a grand old lady taking care in a country house of her disturbed granddaughter; Jean Marsh as Mrs. Madrigal, who answers an advertisement to be the granddaughter's companion; and Robert Flemyng as a retired judge who, when visiting Mrs. St. Maugham, recognises Mrs Madrigal as the woman he sentenced to death fifteen years ago. A universal welcome for the dusting-off of this neglected play.

Baby, Baby

Sophie Lovell Smith, Gráinne Byrne, Maggi Morrison

Three fairy godmothers sit outside a labour ward waiting for a celebrity named Angela to give birth; they toss dice to determine the baby's characteristics, engage in musings upon child-rearing and genetic engineering and boogie absurdly. Anne Caulfield's script (as directed by Birte Pedersen, now of Ra Ra Zoo, and performed by the Scarlet Theatre Company) was intermittently engaging, but lacked focus, insufficient either as pure comedy or as food for thought. It was, opined Michael Arditti of the Evening Standard, quintessential pub theatre – complete with missed lighting cues and references to interval drinks. Grainne Byrne, Maggi Morrison and Sophia Lovell Smith worked hard at their distinct characters, but the evening never cohered into a satisfying whole.

Philadelphia, Here I Come !

Brendan Coyle and Jonathan Arun

With "Dancing At Lughnasa" now a West End fixture and "Faith Healer" enthusiastically received at the Royal Court, Brian Friel has become a bankable name. His first major play ran only briefly in London in 1964, so it was gratifying to see London catching on at last to its unostentatious charms. Jonathan Arun and Brendan Coyle dovetailed superbly as the public and private sides of Gar O'Donnell, a young man spending his last evening in Friel's fictional Donegal village of Ballybeg before emigrating to USA. Dan Crawford's direction brought out the sterility both of village life and Gar's own relationships with his father (Eamon Kelly) and the woman he leaves behind (Orla Brady). No less enthralling for the knowledge that Friel went on to much greater achievements, its transfer to Wyndham's was all but preordained.

Riverside Studios

The Riverside primarily books shows in, rather than growing them at home – although the size of its performance spaces (two converted television studios in Hammersmith) does mean that it can accommodate more grandiloquent ventures, and allows for a lean towards interdisciplinary work. (The complex also includes a cinema, two gallery spaces and a bookshop.) Beginning the year with the final few days of Deborah Warner's stunning "Electra", the temperature cooled off with Green Light Music Theatre's atmospheric but hollow production of "The Bells" before the more enjoyable emptiness of "4 Marys" and Ken Campbell's triumphant lump of weirdness, "Pigspurt!". Paines Plough's "Down And Out In Paris And London" was given a muted reception, and the circus antics of Ra Ra Zoo in "The Gravity Swing" met with enjoyment but bewilderment; then followed two brief seasons, France En Direct and the London Opera Festival before Thelma Holt's disappointing production of "Hamlet", directed by Robert Sturua and starring Alan Rickman.

4 Marys

Martin Duncan and Ian Spink devised their piece for Second Stride from the sole piece of information that Mary, Queen of Scots was accompanied to France in 1548 by four ladies-in-waiting, all called Mary. (So why not "5 Marys"?) What they built upon that base was a performance piece blending the skills of theatre and dance to frequently astounding momentary effect but no real end. The Marys got seasick on the boat; scrubbed and vacuumed; tried to contact Elizabeth by phone and gradually retreated into their own private worlds. Second Stride had only just been saved from loss of funding by the establishment of a Combined Arts Department within the Arts Council; this show demonstrated that, accomplished as their work is, it's not just grant-awarding bodies who have yet to learn to accommodate it.

Pigspurt!

After his anarchic Roadshow and Science-Fiction Theatre of Liverpool ventures of the '70s, Ken Campbell's current streak of solo storytelling (begun with "Furtive Nudist" in 1990) proved no less strange or startling for having fewer people onstage. Campbell himself supplied a large and varied cast – from Ken Dodd to a paedophilic Bishop of Colchester – all invoked upon his schizophrenic face. Indeed, his face supplied him with a bizarre slavering half-brother of a plot. Not only does he discover his facial split personality (his right side a spiritualist lady, Sophie Firebright, his left the debauched and demonic Pigspurt), but he also seeks the person whose bottom is reproduced exactly in miniature in the form of Campbell's own nose. Incomprehensible as such a synopsis may be, the show proved hilarious and captivating.

Ken Campbell

Down and Out in Paris and London

Geoffrey Greenhill and Andy McEwan

Nigel Gearing's adaptation for Paines Plough of George Orwell's book was staged with seven professional actors and thirty five local extras from the area around whatever venue the show happened to be playing in. An admirable (and, of course, timely) exercise in principle, it never quite came off in practice. The first-person narration on which the book depends was represented on stage by inter-weaving biographical details of Eric Blair/Orwell's life, but for all Andy McEwan's efforts, Blair seemed rather an upper-class twit. Anna Furse directed individual episodes powerfully but couldn't supply the missing through line. Elaine Caxton as Hampstead socialist Kathleen O'Neill, Michael Benson as a smooth clergyman and Jonathan Burn as a Russian vagrant named Boris were among the most succulent lumps in the stew.

The Gravity Swing

One of two pieces performed in London by Ra Ra Zoo in 1992 ("Angels And Amazons" was seen immediately afterwards at the Drill Hall), "The Gravity Swing" set out to make some connections with chaos theory, but at root was entirely dependent for impact upon the skill of the performers. A clownish Chris Cresswell offered little useful comment upon the exertions performed to Merlin Shepherd's music. The second half of the work, performed upon an enormous rhomboidal framework suspended above the stage, allowed the performers' dexterity to be seen as impressive in itself, rather than wishing to see it employed to some comprehensible end. (The "gravity swing" itself was devised by Sue Broadway's co-director Dave Spathaky.) Sean Gandini's juggling (seven balls!) and Lindsey Butcher's aerial work, along with Jeremy Robins' tumbling, drew particular praise.

France en Direct and London Opera Festival Seasons

France en Direct

Space only allows a list: France En Direct culminated in performances of Sophocles' "Ajax" by Stephane Braunschweig's Lievin-based Theatre Machine, a bizarre "Ubu" by N.A.D.A. featuring a bunch of red grapes as the King of Poland and assorted vegetables as the Russian army, and the Kantor-influenced "Chant Du Bouc" by Francois Tangny's Theatre Du Radeau. The London Opera Festival opened with the premiere of Priti Paintal and Richard Fawkes' "Biko" (for the Royal Opera House Garden Venture and Birmingham Rep), followed by David McVicar's acclaimed 1991 production of Stravinsky's "The Soldier's Tale". The Pocket opera of Nuremberg presented Rossini's "Semiramide", and the Belgian contemporary music theatre company Ensemble Leporello presented the London premiere of "A Song Of Satyrs – Antigone", built upon a fragment of Holderlin's version of the Greek tale.

Theatre Royal, Stratford East

The legacy of Joan Littlewood remains at Stratford East, in a penchant for using popular cultural references in the supposedly high-cultural medium of theatre. The more comfortable financial standing which has come with the continuing West End run of their production of "Five Guys Named Moe" hasn't noticeably changed their artistic policy either by encouraging further moneyspinners or enticing subsidy of obviously slower shows at the box-office – the theatre's first responsibility has always been to the community, but it combines this with an admirable policy of producing only new work. Last year's programme was typical of the breadth that these dual priorities can accommodate: from Patrick Prior's third political comedy "Cut And Trust" and the biographical portrait of James Keir Hardie, "A Better Day", to the live bebop of "A Night In Tunisia" and the Posse's observations on black British life in their "Armed And Dangerous" revue.

A Night in Tunisia

The haunting fear of mediocrity was a major factor in the decline of bebop saxophonist Morgan Peters – a fear perhaps more valid of Paul Sirett's play itself. Alan Cooke was both dramatically and musically impressive as the young Morgan, leading a quartet in 1960s Soho while, on the other side of Jenny Tiramani's crazily-raked stage, Doyle Richmond portrayed present-day Morgan, frail and dependent on medication but still with some vestiges of dignity, looking back on how he lost whatever it was that he had. The production fell between two stools: not musical enough (despite an onstage band) to be a musical, nor dramatic enough to satisfy as a play. Director Jeff Teare failed to charge the atmosphere in performance that was so lacking in the play as a script.

Alan Cooke and Kate McKenzie

Goin' Local

In the days when Canary Wharf still symbolised a dying economic culture rather than a dead one, a representation of it glittered on Jenny Tiramani's set for this comedy (by writer in residence Tunde Ikoli) set in a Docklands minicab office. Act One's night-shift set the scene: everyone (boss included) claiming dole as well, a collection of types ranging from a New Age visionary (Tony Armatrading) to the local villain, not to mention the obligatory long-suffering night controller Nora (Stratford stalwart Kate Williams). Act Two brought a 0-60 acceleration, as two wide-boy newcomers, having whipped the firm away from owner Lol, set out to make it yuppie-friendly and the set design transformed into... well, designer chic. Philip Hedley directed with a sharp satirical eye but a slight lack of energy.

Ron Pember, Kate Williams, Steve Edwin, Alan Ford and Tony Armatrading

Cut and Trust

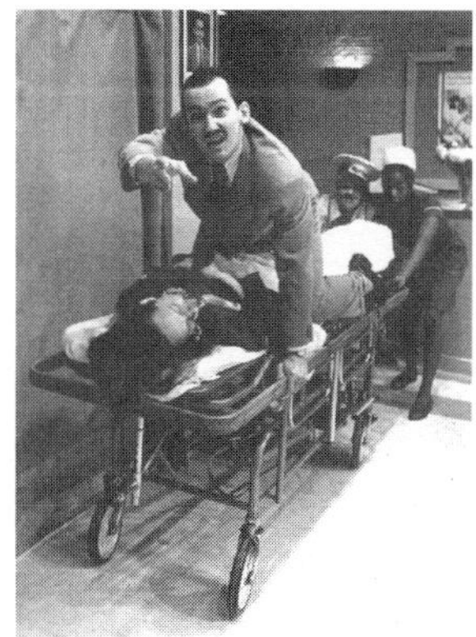

Em Parkinson, Jonathan Coote, Reginda Freedman and Maureen Hibbert

Patrick Prior's trilogy of broadsides against Conservative reforms ("Revolting Peasants" about the poll tax, "The Blackboard Bungle" on school opt-outs) concluded with a symphony of tub-thumping on the topic of hospital privatisation-by-trust. Director Jeff Teare did justice to a script where circumstances called for salvage as well, from a welter of antediluvian sitcom jokes clumsily interspersed with fervent Serious Messages. The plot turned on that wrinkled, desiccated chestnut, mistaken identity: two mental cases discharged into care in the community are mistaken for a Health Minister and her advisor. Yvonne Edgell and (especially) Alan Cowan were amusing as the lunatics taking over the asylum; Regina Freedman turned in a clutch of telling cameos, and Jonathan Coote was an oleaginous but rather vapid hospital administrator.

The Posse: Armed and Dangerous

Victor Romero Evans, Gary McDonald, Michael Buffong and Robbie Gee

Not a play, but a revue: The Posse are eight young black actors who, fed up with not getting the work they deserve (although many are familiar faces from theatre and television), come together for occasional shows of their own. The reviews given to "Armed And Dangerous" are probably not the best index to the show's reception: white middle-class critics dutifully recorded the audience's wild response while remaining palpably bemused themselves. However, when The Posse went beyond comedy of recognition (Jamaican gangster culture) and even satire (Victor Romero Evans as chatshow host Killjoy Acrylic), they sometimes left the audience behind: a Romeo and Julian sketch repeatedly fell prey to the homophobia it was trying to question. However, they hit the targets both of entertainment and intelligence consistently enough to warrant their show an unquestioned success.

A Better Day

Susan Widler, Elizabeth Mansfield and Shona Morris

The team which proved so impressive with "Self Portrait" at the Orange Tree earlier in the year – writer Sheila Yeger and director Annie Castledine – could not repeat that success in this portrait of Keir Hardie. Clive Mendus as Jack Clubley, the master of ceremonies orchestrating the series of vignettes and musical interludes, was vigorously opposed by Rose Britannia (Lynn Anderson), a kind of politically articulate Everyprole, with the result that Keir Hardie's life took on the character of one long dialectic. Ian Angus Wilkie's Keir Hardie did not have the chance to present himself at any length – whether as inspiring politico, hopeless philanderer or despairing husband and father – without being, as it were, overcome by the footnotes of Jack and Rose. An unfortunate victory of style over substance.

The Young Vic

David Thacker departs his job as Artistic Director at the end of the year. During his tenure, this venue has become characterised by a growing speciality in Arthur Miller, and the consistent strength of its youth theatre work. The only London Fringe theatre with a comprehensive youth programme last year staged successful versions both of "The Crucible" and "The Caucasian Chalk Circle" (the first of which won Jud Charlton an acting commendation at the National student Drama Festival) in the Young Vic's studio space, as well as an exuberant "Guys And Dolls" in the main house. Thacker, meanwhile, directed Miller's "All My Sons" and hosted the straightforward but enjoyable musical "In The Midnight Hour" – the two productions being separated by a run of Trevor Nunn's RSC "Measure For Measure". Autumn saw Francesca Annis and Corin Redgrave in Annie Castledine's production of Ibsen's "Rosmersholm".

All My Sons

Ian Bannen and Matthew Marsh

After the disappointment of Arthur Miller's new play "The Ride Down Mt Morgan", his stock rose again with Thacker's gripping production of Miller's post-war study of guilt and responsibility. As former armaments manufacturer Joe Keller, Ian Bannen seemed to grow into the part during previews, settling into a fine portrayal of benevolence progressively racked by deceit over the issue of having sold faulty goods to the government. Equally strong was Marjorie Yates, wilfully refusing to believe in son Larry's death in action. Miller's debt to Ibsen – allowing moral issues generated well before the action to come through and dominate the present – proved too direct and stodgy for a few critics, but Thacker refused to force the pace of the play; what remained was an admiration for the great strengths which Miller was then still developing.

Measure for Measure

David Haig

The word "clarity", grievously overused by critics, should be reserved for the like of Trevor Nunn's detailed, logical, deceptively unproblematic reading of Shakespeare's notorious "problem play". Nunn set the action in the Vienna of Freud and Strauss, underpinning the central sexual and moral dilemma of the play. Claire Skinner as the novice Isabella exuded innocent ardour when pleading alike for her brother Claudio (Jason Durr)'s life to be spared, when repelling the venal advances of David Haig's Angelo (a dedicated manager aroused to – to him – alien and incomprehensible lusts by Isabella) and finally suing for mercy on Angelo himself to the returned Duke (Philip Madoc, in a low-key performance leaving the way clear for the antagonists' respective passions to dominate). Nunn's "return to Shakespeare, after his decade in blockbuster musicals" (Sheridan Morley, Herald Tribune) was universally welcomed.

In the Midnight Hour

Gillian Bevan

When some reviewers carped at the volume of this '60s Northern-Soul compilation musical, Charles Spencer of the Daily Telegraph tartly rejoined, "If it's too loud, you're too old". Philip Ryan's show is set in a Merseyside dance-hall, re-creating his own youthful weekends of dancing, fighting, pills and birds. Among an eleven-strong ensemble of actors/singers/dancers/multi-instrumentalists, Amanda Symonds and Gillian Bevan stood out as innocent Rita and cynical Roxy. Directors Karen Stephens and Chris White concentrated on evoking the atmosphere of an all-nighter; they, and Keith Strachan's arrangements, succeeded well enough to get even Neil and Glenys Kinnock dancing on the first night. Opinion was divided, however, on the dramatic content – although the proceedings had an edge, they weren't necessarily felt to be more than gritty-teenage-by-numbers.

The Crucible and The Caucasian Chalk Circle

The Caucasian Chalk Circle

The Young Vic Youth Theatre complemented David Thacker's main house "All My Sons" with Karen Stephens and Chris White's production in the studio of Miller's modern classic parable of McCarthyism. Performances were honed to fit the smaller space, and the witch-hunting villagers of Salem had a simmering intensity. Jud Charlton conveyed the painfully human imperfection of John Proctor in the face of the inquisitorial storm. In May, the same company acquitted themselves more honourably than most when Nick Stimson and Jon Lee directed them in Brecht's "The Caucasian Chalk Circle." Juliet Aghion's tender-hearted maid Grusha and Mark Fleischmann's quirky rather than maniacal judge Azdak proved effective twin foci in a production which made constructive use of Brecht's passages of narration and comment.

Guys and Dolls

Nicola Kingston and Ben Caplan

The indefatigable Karen Stephens and Chris White took the helm yet again, directing a company of thirty in how "to part and converge on stage like so many ballbearings on a magnetic field" (Sabine Durrant, the Independent) in a warm and winning version of Frank Loesser's musical. Nicola Kingston as Miss Sarah was praised for her impressive portrayal of a journey through temptation to maturity, and was partnered by Ben Caplan's Sky Masterson. Nathan Detroit (Simon Meacock) and his hoods also made a strong team, but understandably, most of the energy was reserved for the big production numbers – ranging off the stage and up steps into the higher levels of the auditorium. Enthusiasm naturally had the upper hand over fully matured abilities, but to call its appreciative critical reception condescension would be gravely unjust.

BAC (formerly Battersea Arts Centre)

BAC has been given a renewed sense of direction under Paul Blackman's adroit helmsmanship – anyone who can stage an adaptation of the Marquis de Sade's "120 Days Of Sodom" (in 1991), inviting dignitaries from Tory Wandsworth to the performance, and still retain his venue's borough grant, is an operator to be reckoned with. In many ways this anecdote typifies BAC's approach, which seems to be one of upholding the now-unfashionable notion of the "right to fail", but moving so swiftly that mistakes don't catch up with them. The closest major venue (along with the Riverside Studios) to the experimental fringe ethos of old, BAC is a principal venue for the annual London International Mime Festival (in January), and hosts its own Festival of Visual Theatre each autumn. Last year they opened a second studio space, expanding the versatility of the complex beyond that of its Hammersmith counterpart.

Mary Stuart

Dacia Marainiss adaptation reshapes Schiller's play for her own ends: she rewrites patriarchal myths and concentrates on the pragmatic but reluctant decision by Elizabeth I to have her cousin executed despite the belief that "ties between women are strongest and most lasting". Anne Firbank's Elizabeth drank beer from the can and wore Doc Martens beneath her velvet skirts; Louise Jameson's Mary showed more tenderness and passion. Some reviewers, while noting the power of Maraini's sentiments, had problems with aspects of Nicolette Kay's production, such as its location in a dressing-room (designed by James Helps), or the frequent snatches of Simply Red. What remained were two riveting performances and an overdue re-evaluation of a moment in history.

Louise Jameson

Manslaughter

The case of Sara Thornton, jailed for killing a man who persistently and brutally mistreated her, was transmuted into a disappointing, self-consciously feminist piece by Robin Brown. Jill Dowse and Jeremy Peters played Laura and George, entangled both in a sterile marriage and in Andrew Phillips' set design of ropes, nets and cages. Between scenes of domestic angst they presented fragments from "Women Beware Women" and "Middlemarch", and (confusingly) a recording of a letter from Thornton herself. The self-conscious artiness of the piece trivialised the case which inspired it. Ann McFerran (in Time Out) summed up: "The author, whose hero suffocates himself in clingfilm, has admitted that the show is a form of guilt-trip. Next time he feels the urge, he should do it elsewhere."

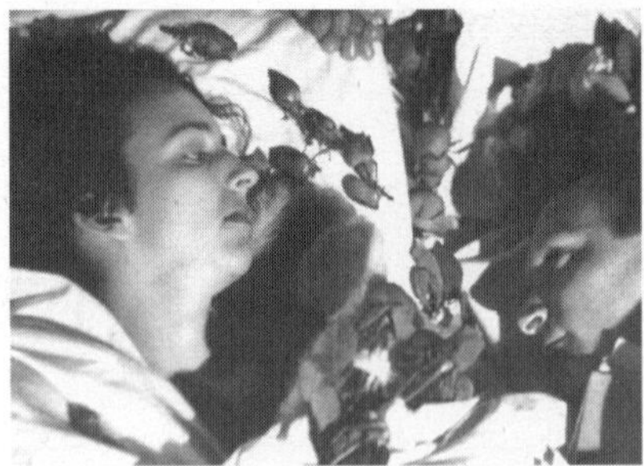

Jill Dowse and Jeremy Peters

Croydon Warehouse

The Warehouse is preparing to move, having last Summer launched its appeal to carry it a few hundred yards east into specially-built new premises. The mere fact that a Croydon venue constitutes one of the first division of London fringe theatres is testimony enough to Ted Craig's skills as Artistic Director, marrying intelligence and commerciality in seasons which are always worth a look, at the very least. That said, 1992's first show, the Sphinx (formerly Women's Theatre Group)'s production of Claire Luckham's "The Roaring Girl's Hamlet", was a beautiful idea almost entirely unrealised in a tedious, dreary three-hour-plus version of Shakespeare's play. Guy Jenkin's "Fighting For The Dunghill" was much better received, though there was less enthusiasm for "Turner's Crossing" by Sheila Dewey. For "On Top Of The World", Craig presented a co-production with the Sydney Theatre Company from his native land; most people were glad they'd made the journey.

Fighting for the Dunghill

Guy Jenkin, co-writer of Channel 4's "Drop The Dead Donkey", won the South London Playwriting Festival in 1991 with this treatment of the life of eighteenth-century cartoonist James Gillray, played with wit and malice by James Bolam. Jenkin framed the play in Gillray's mad, drunken last years, allowing him to indulge in the traditional dramatic pastime of flashback to his prime, when he bitterly opposed attempts by both Whigs and Tories to shackle him to their standard. Michael Fenton Stevens as George Canning and Geoffrey McGivern as Charles James Fox were oily and bluff respectively, but Richard Osborne's production suffered from lack of clarity – caused by the necessity for his five actors to play numerous roles.

James Bolam and Di Langford

On Top of the World

Surfers' Paradise in Queensland is where Australians go to die. In Michael Gow's play, cancer-ridden Clive is awaiting his fate when he and his vitriolic daughter Stephanie are visited by his taciturn son Marcus and the dramatic catalyst, septuagenarian battleaxe Baby. Wayne Harrison's Sydney Theatre Company trod "an uneasy line between humour and emotional realism without winching the two convincingly together" (James Christopher, Time Out), but the performances by Ronald Falk, Carol Burns, Todd Boyce and Lois Ramsey were (once Burns had gauged the size of the small Warehouse space) exquisite, and one rather felt that critics were actively seeking shortcomings to criticise, rather than that the show was marred by major flaws. As a corrective to daytime soaps and a broadening of British knowledge of Australian drama, it was a welcome arrival.

Lois Ramsay and Carol Burns

Orange Tree

Sam Walters' Richmond theatre finally acquired its new premises in 1991, and last year he fulfilled his second main goal by setting up a house repertory company. The Orange Tree's in-the-round space suits Walters' programming, allowing reappraisals of neglected older plays and granting an intimacy to reflective new work. The theatre's Christmas show "The Little Match Girl" ran through January, giving way to Sheila Yeger's acclaimed play about artist Gwen John, "Self Portrait". The "Dark River" constituted half of a Rodney Ackland revival during the Spring ("A Dead Secret" at the Theatre Royal, Plymouth forming the other half), and was followed by Adrian Brine's production of his own translation of Victor Slavkin's "Cerceau". The Orange Tree's contribution to the Edinburgh International Festival's Harley Granville Barker retrospective, "His Majesty", returned to its home patch in September, and was followed by Marston's "The Dutch Courtesan" and Christmas show "A Penny For A Song".

The Dark River

Liz Crowther and Belinda Lang

Rodney Ackland's 1943 success was first revived by the Orange Tree in 1984. Sam Walters staged this second production in tribute to the author's death. This time round, though, the earlier cries of forgotten masterpiece and English Chekhov modulated into more measured appraisal. Catherine Lisle, a former ballet dancer, spends the summer on the upper Thames with Mrs Merriman while wrestling with herself over leaving her unfaithful husband. The play, set in 1937 (the year in which Ackland began writing it) foresees the stormclouds looming over Europe. Although the flaws in the writing were now visible, Walters' light, crisp production made excellent use of the new Orange Tree's in-the-round arrangement, and drew first-rate performances from Belinda Lang, Malcolm Sinclair and Stephanie Cole.

Cerceau

Richard O'Callaghan and Maria Miles

When "Rooster" Petushok inherits a large country house, he invites a number of friends, acquaintances and one total stranger to visit it with him, in the hope of persuading them to live communally there. Victor Slavkin's 1983 prophecy of glasnost divided opinion sharply, between those who admired its precognition and those who found its slow narrative and blatant indebtedness to Chekhov tedious and overwrought. Richard O'Callaghan's Petushok was a wide-eyed mixture of wonder and discontent and Sam Walters returned to the stage to play a devious would-be capitalist door-upholsterer out to embezzle the house away from him. Adrian Brine directed his own translation a little too lovingly to notice the play's longueurs, but created the requisite blend of elegy and anticipation of the unknown.

Tricycle

Nicolas Kent's theatre is usually conscious of its "Co. Kilburn" location; apart from the occasional performance at Aras na nGael, the Tricycle is the sole focus of Irish theatre in London. A solid if unadventurous revival of Mary O'Malley's "Once A Catholic" ran on into February, followed by "Viva Detroit" by Derek Walcott, from Black Theatre Co-Operative and Shared Experience's adaptation of "Anna Karenina". The remainder of the year up to the time of writing was dedicated to the ould sod: Eamon Morrissey's one-man ramble through the delights of the hard stuff, "Just The One", giving way to Rough Magic's masterful production of Farquhar's "Love And A Bottle" and Michael Harding's semi-supernatural comic drama "Una Pooka". The threatened withdrawal of funding from the borough of Brent was mercifully averted, allowing the theatre and its adjoining gallery to continue as much-needed facilities.

Love and A Bottle

Rough Magic went from present-day thirtysomething Dublin ("Digging For Fire" at the Bush above) to the late-seventeenth century London of George Farquhar's first play, where the arrival of Irish rake Roebuck (played with verve by Phelim Drew) creates the usual web of Restoration intrigue and bawdiness. Declan Hughes' adaptation enlarged the character of Lyrick (Peter Ballance), a destitute playwright who has created the character of Roebuck but finds that his creation is out of control. Hughes and director Lynne Parker, realising that energy rather than finesse was the key to bringing such a project off, went at it hell for leather – loud, brash, often missing their humorous or dramatic stride – but in their determination to escape from normal shapely Restoration conclusions and leading the audience into an unaccustomed moral zone, they pulled it off.

Helene Montague and Frankie McCafferty

Gamblers

Dalia Ibelhauptaite directed this visually flamboyant though occasionally sluggishly paced version by Chris Hannan of Nikolai Gogol's story about a card-sharp taken in by three even sharper operators. Oleg Sheintsis' impressive design set the entire play in the coachyard of a hotel, with characters appearing from and scrambling around a number of carriages in what was seldom more than half-light. As protagonist Ikharev, Oleg Menshikov (familiar from his performance in "When She Danced"), in his first English-speaking role, was obviously hampered by the language factor, but his grandiosity of speech and gesture overcame much of the handicap. Mark Rylance was charismatically commanding as a smooth Irish-American, the most devious of the trio practising the "sting". The over-familiarity of the tale was more than outweighed by the confident theatricality of Ibelhauptaite's production.

Oleg Menshikov

BEYOND THE FRINGE

IAN SHUTTLEWORTH continues his survey with a look at what's going on beyond the main fringe theatres.

Beyond the Fringe '92

As stated in the general Fringe section introduction above, this category is largely artificial and by no means homogenous. It ranges from the like of the Lilian Baylis Theatre and the Drill Hall Arts Centre, through small houses with identifiable aims and programmes such as the New End, the Old Red Lion and the Finborough, to a plethora of rooms above pubs in Richmond, Turnham Green or Kennington, which often have little continuity or choice in their bookings. This doesn't mean that they consistently put on rubbish, but it does underline that casual theatregoers turning up at their local Fringe venue will more often than not be taking pot luck.

With one or two exceptions, these venues are not producing houses with their own theatrical companies: they will book in small independent companies, many of which struggle to stage one production a year and few of which can hope to turn a profit after venue hire, box-office splits and other overheads have been deducted. In short, "off-off-Shaftesbury Avenue" Fringe theatre is a proving ground for those (individually and collectively) with the abilities and energies to keep from going under, and on occasion the stage equivalent of "vanity press" publishing – affording those with more money than talent an opportunity to buy themselves ill-deserved exposure. That's not to castigate venues for acquiescing to such demands; the spirit of Michael Caine's remark, "If you want a very high standard of living you have to have a very low standard of film", is even truer for those running a pub venue, for whom the main priority has to be securing the funds to continue and, hopefully, once in a while uncover a gem of a production.

Last year showed, too, how small theatres can be subjected to pressure both from individual and corporate landlords. The Finborough Theatre fought a long and tenacious battle with their pub landlords, who had attempted to ban managers Cathryn Horn and Mary Peate from booking Hawaiian gay company Starving Artists, whose previous appearance had been the most critically and commercially successful the Finborough had seen. Last year, too, the Trustees of the Victoria & Albert Museum shot themselves in the foot by deciding drastically to curtail the use of the Theatre Museum studio for theatrical work, just as the venue was beginning to forge a discernible identity for itself.

In addition, a number of venues cater to a greater or lesser extent for less conventionally theatrical performance-based work: one thinks naturally of the Institute of Comtemporary Arts, but the likes also of the Holborn Centre for the Performing Arts and Arts Threshold in Paddington (whose "Sex And Violence At The Fantasy Cafe" appeared in Edinburgh under the wing of Richard Demarco) are also adventurously catholic in their policies. Very little site-specific performance occurs in London, however, and virtually none in even-numbered years between biennial London International Festivals of Theatre. (Michael Clark's dance work "Mmmm" was less site-specific than simply the opening show in a new converted space.) Apart from "The Criminal Prosecution And Capital Punishment of Animals" in the London Diorama and American Connexion's "Boardroom Shuffle" staged in the corporate opulence of the Cottons Centre by London Bridge, this aspect has been limited to the occasional single performance in a business plaza.

The following pages cannot claim to detail the finest, all the finest and none but the finest works from these areas last year, but they do constitute a selection (hopefully a representative one) of the best and most important work seen in small fringe theatres, and (though not always on such a small scale) the major performance-oriented events.

Plays

You Never Know Who's Out There

Drill Hall

Debbie Isitt's Snarling Beasties company came to general attention with their 1989-91 trilogy of domestic upheaval plays "Punch And Judy", "Femme Fatale" and "The Woman Who Cooked Her Husband". "You Never Know...." focused on Northern night-club comedian Bobby Vincent (a poisonous James Gaddas) and the tensions and power-politicking with his wife, brother and manager. Beverly Klein, as relentlessly sarcastic wife Fay, once more demonstrated her grasp of black comedy. There was disappointment that Isitt the writer still lagged behind Isitt the director in terms of power and originality, and a feeling that this was "an interim work" (Jeremy Kingston, the Times) but it was certainly enough to be going on with.

Mark Killmurray and Ken Sharrock

A Woman is a Weathercock

Pentameters

Jacobean actor Nathan Field "vexed with vile plays" sets out to do better himself. Last performed in 1667, this comedy of mismatched and rearranged nuptials constituted the inaugural production of the Trampoline company. Director Graham Watts' rediscovery of a folio of the play deserves thanks, but it turned out to be hardly a major work. There were, however, some excellent comic performances, notably by Paul Ritter as the sardonic servant Pendant, and Grant Russell as the malcontent soldier Captain Pouts. The play's reception was not helped by being staged amid extensive refurbishment being undertaken both to Pentameters theatre and the pub beneath it, but the company showed distinct promise.

Malcolm Freeman

Jordan

Lilian Baylis

The true story of Shirley Jones – who was tried in 1987 for murdering her thirteen-month old son Jordan, acquitted, and killed herself on the day of her release – was co-written by Anna Reynolds and Moira Buffini, and directed by Fiona Buffini for the Dark Horse company. This was a magnificent production playing to frustratingly poor houses despite universal rave reviews. The sole prop, an outsize chair, symbolised the various authorities and pressures which dwarfed Shirley's every move; both the script and Buffini's performance resolutely avoided unremitting earnestness with a rich vein of humour which made the story more piquant. "Important", "rare and moving" and "almost too painful to watch" were among the accolades heaped upon the show.

Moira Buffini

Steam Factory

Man In The Moon

Rather than a single play, praise for a company's consistently entertaining and intelligent work in the course of the year. The Steam Factory first appeared in late 1991 with "Stealing The Scene", Phil Willmott's comedy about a stage-struck burglar heavying a Fringe actor to teach him the ropes. The play was revived in April last year, and rapidly followed up with Pete Lawson's mosaic of urban automobile stories "Traffic Hearts" and Willmott's seaside shuffle "Mermaid Sandwich" by which time the Steamers had been adopted more or less as the Man In The Moon's house company. Willmott also turned out a brace of Shakespearean re-examinations: "Iago" and "The Wax King" (better known as Henry VI). The deftness and humorous sensitivity with which Willmott handles issues of gayness suggests affinities with John Binnie of Clyde Unity, but the Steam Factory work within the commercial Fringe sector rather than touring among various communitities. A company to watch.

The Dybbuk

New End

Director Julia Pascal used this story as a skeleton upon which to build an unrelenting examination of Jewish cultural identity and a harrowing piece of holocaust drama. A number of secular Jews, in hiding in a ghetto, enact the tale to pass the time: but they revolt against its roles, and the attitudes it embodies prove inflexible against the performers' attempts to digest them. Most disturbingly, the story was never completed: at the climactic moment of exorcism an explosion signalled the storm troopers' arrival, and events mutated into a horrific, endless procession of annihiliation as the actors filed downstage, fell, and moved to rejoin the queue for destruction.

Kate Margram and Thomas Kampe

A Stop in the Desert

Watermans

Grupa Chwilowa from Lublin brought their haunting, heartbreaking play to Edinburgh in 1991 during the Soviet coup: it returned there last year, before making the overdue journey to London. Authors/directors Krzysztof Borowiec and Jerzy Luzynski, and Russian actors Alexei Zeitsev and Irina Nabatova, wove a captivating tapestry of images, from the mourning of dead friends present in photographs (including Venedict Erofeyev, author of "Walpurgis Night", seen at the Gate) to the comical smashing of a birthday cake with a hammer and sickle, before distributing cake and vodka to the entire audience. Nabatova and Zeitsev created the feeling of a truly communal event. Visually enchanting and strongly emotional, it was the most powerful Eastern European theatre of the London year.

Performance Works

Gormenghast

BAC

Richard Attlee

Rae Smith's design wisely left most of the details of Gormenghast Castle to the imagination, providing only a row of doors and mobile (actor-propelled) flats around and through which the human, or near-human grotesques lurched and shambled as Titus, 78th Earl of Groan, (Peter Bailie) simultaneously rebelled against ossified feudal rituals and tried to combat the machiavellian plottings of the sinister Steerpike (a protean performance from Richard Attlee). John Eacott's arresting score added to the air of chaotic decay and grim nastiness.

The Year They Changed The Wires

ICA

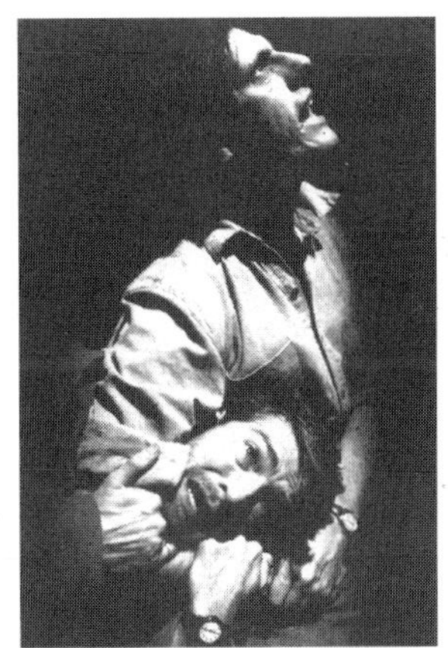

Steve Shill and Graeme Miller

Steve Shill and Graeme Miller played a flash film director and a put-upon novelist collaborating on a rewrite of the latter's 600-page doorstop into a viable screenplay, fuelled by a variety of chemicals from scotch to mushrooms. Oscillating between the story of the rewrite and the mutating plot itself, Shill and Miller become too engrossed in the arsenal of deconstructive effects at their disposal to use them tellingly. Miller's ironic Hollywoodesque score commented wryly upon the goings-on, and John Mckinnon's lighting worked wonderful transformations on the set, but the charm and "cack-handed grace" (Terence Dominic, Time Out) of the performers could have been (and, in the past, has been) more expertly marshalled.

Shaker

ICA

Alison Edgar

Annie Griffin and Alison Edgar's piece (from a play by Nicholas McInerny) began with the biography of Mother Ann Lee, founder of the Shaker sect, then mutated into a watercolour of life in the Shaker community in New England. Visually arresting (Dafydd Llwyd Lewis' spare, elegant set was based around the sect's famous furniture) and with several moments of simple brilliance, the work nevertheless contained a soul-shaped hole at its core: the rigorous asceticism of Shaker life was conveyed, but with none of the passion which, we are told, informs both their beliefs and their industrious lifestyle. Edgar seemed not to be inhabiting the role to the necessary degree, and what could indeed have been a revelation remained a mere series of statements and allusions.

Don Juan

Queen Elizabeth Hall

The audience filed into the theatre to find the seats barred and occupied by the performers in eighteenth-century rouge and frocks (both sexes). They were questioned as to sexual preference, invited to participate in one-to-one question sessions with their fellows, sexually appraised by the company, groped in darkness, and finally, the request was made that one of their number stand naked in the middle for two minutes. This was Sydney Front's first visit to London since 1988's "The Pornography Of Performance" and the themes remained the same. Their determinaton to disorient attitudes toward both nudity and the performer/audience relationship often paid off but in many ways the nature of theatrical performance (and of obscenity laws) prevented them, beribboned penises notwithstanding, from going far enough.

Sweet Temptations

Queen Elizabeth Hall

Belgian Jan Fabre arrived on the South Bank for two performances stooping beneath the weight of his reputation as a writer/director of performance works: in 1987 "The Power Of Theatrical Madness" had, over more than four hours of playing time, both irritated and captivated. "Sweet Temptations" was desperately lacking in captivation. Occasional passages of energetic, mechanistic dance by a number of lycra-clad women mesmerised, but these poor oases were amid a desert of inconsequential dialogue about owls from wheelchair-bound Stephen Hawkingesque twins, high-decibel harangues through microphones, a couple of dispiriting orgies and several gradually overlaid versions of Iggy Pop's "Lust For Life". Many of the audience left; some returned, in a triumph of hope over experience. In basing this work around a definite written text, Fabre seemed paradoxically to have lost the clarity which had given his earlier pieces their sparks of brilliance. Not tempting, and far from sweet.

My Mathematics

Queen Elizabeth Hall

Rose English's latest venture also proved a disappointment.. Recounting a series of disconnected anecdotes punctuated by the mantra, "Yes, yes indeed !", lashing members of the audience with her six-inch eyelashes and vaguely adopting the persona of a faded circus performer, English left the audience wondering impatiently when the much-touted mathematical horse would enter. When she did (accompanied by English in a fringed cowgirl leotard cut high on the buttock), Goldie the palomino's rapport with her partner seemed thin. English played only a single performance on the South Bank, after a single one in New York (with a different horse) and the lack of coherence and dynamism suggested that this time she had put the stylistic cart before.

Rose English with her horse

THE ROYAL COURT

MICHAEL BILLINGTON discusses the fortunes of the Royal Court during 1992 and KATE BASSETT describes the productions which have been on view at Britain's most famous home for new writing.

The Royal Court '92

This was the year in which the Royal Court, traditional bastion of new writing, witnessed a gradual changing of the guard: in the Court's case, a peculiarly prolonged and tortuous process. Stephen Daldry became Artistic Director Designate in April working alongside the present incumbent, Max Stafford-Clark. In October, 1993 Daldry takes over as Artistic Director with Stafford-Clark staying on for eighteen months as his associate. Clearly the two men have different tastes. Daldry, imported from the Gate, is widely seen as a flamboyant cavalier and Stafford-Clark as a puritanical roundhead. But it is too early to say how Daldry will modify the Court's long-standing commitment to socially inquiring, morally purposeful new drama.

In one sense, 1992 was very much business as usual at the Court: the programme was a familiar mix of Irish imports, new women's writing and analyses of the state of Britain. But, in another way, it was a very unusual year. Two productions originating at the Court – Ariel Dorfman's "Death and the Maiden" and John Guare's "Six Degrees of Separation" – enjoyed spectacularly successful West End transfers. No matter that the former was the brainchild of the London International Festival of Theatre and the latter an acclaimed, and extremely superficial, New York hit. It was still good to see the Court, which has often seemed suspicious of stars and commerce, establishing a bridgehead in the West End.

But 1992 was also a year in which the radical Court was forced to confront the collapse of European Communism and the declension of Britain into one-party, right wing governmnent. What exactly is the function of a left wing theatre in a post-Socialist world ? The Court's answer was to present a number of challenging plays exploring a world suddenly shorn of certainties and convictions.

Howard Brenton's "Berlin Bertie" was a big, bold, brassy play about universal loss of faith: in do-gooding liberalism, iron-clad Marxism, devout Christianity. Brenton implied that the end of history was the beginning of despair and that the new world order would produce psychic disorder but at least he retained his bilious humour and corrosive poetry. Klaus Pohl's underrated "Karate Billy Comes Home" in the Theatre Upstairs looked, more specifically, at the bitter legacy of enforced East German collaboration with the Communist secret police. And April de Angelis' "Hush" – a promising Court debut by a young woman writer – was a piece of English surrealism about the personal crises induced by the decline of the Left. We are constantly told that issue plays are dead and people bored stiff with politics: the Court's 1992 programme exposed that as shallow and dangerous nonsense.

The Court's loyalty to political drama was also matched by fidelity to Irish isuues (a legacy perhaps of Stafford-Clark's education at Trinity College, Dublin). Brian Friel's "The Faith Healer", in a marvellously acted Joe Dowling revival, came in from the Abbey Theatre and Ron Hutchinson's "Pygmies in the Ruins" from the Lyric Theatre, Belfast. Women also featured strongly on the agenda. Not only Ms de Angelis but also Heidi Thomas with the nonsensical "Some Singing Blood" – resembling a 1952 British Pinewood Colonialist movie – in the Theatre Upstairs and Timberlake Wertenbaker with a revival of her big 1991 hit, "Three Birds Alighting on a Field".

It was, in short, a year in which the Court stayed loyal to the cause. When a final assessment is made of the Stafford-Clark years – apparently some time in the mid-nineties – I suspect we will say that he gave women dramatists a major platform and retained his faith in left wing drama during a period of right wing domination.

Plays at The Court

Faith Healer

Donal McCann

In spite of its potentially undramatic structure – four successive monologues lasting three hours in total – Brian Friel's "Faith Healer" (Main House, January 21 – February 15) proved a richly complex, mesmerising piece of theatre. Retrospectively, indeed posthumously, Frank tells the story of his life as an itinerant faith healer (all parish halls and cheap hotels), a story subsequently retold – with intriguing discrepancies, particularly regarding the stillbirth and burial of Frank's child – by his ex-wife Grace, now strung out on drink and pills in a Paddington bedsit, and then by Ted, Frank's sad yet comic ex-manager, effortlessly played by Ron Cook.

Sinead Cusack (replacing Judy Geeson from the original cast of the Abbey theatre Dublin production) captured Grace's vulnerable stoicism and half-confessed despair, while Donal McCann's Frank could seem at once a fraudulent mountebank and a frustrated genius – an indirect image of all creative artists, including Friel himself.

Superbly directed by Joe Dowling, the performers' technique was invisible and Friel's lyricism beautifully paced. Frank Hallinan Flood's set – sometimes a tacky inerior, sometimes bleak bare boards, a Beckettian leafless tree and a stormy sky – allowed the dream-like to enter this tragicomic masterpiece of Irish theatre.

Outside of Heaven

James Kerr and Lennie James

The award-winning play, "Outside of Heaven", by the young Bradford playwright Martin Sadofski – subsequent writer in residence at the National Theatre studio – created a bleak world of anger and teenage angst. Ruari Murchison's off-kilter, planked promenade served as pier, squat, bridge and park for a play set in early '80s Southport and late '80s London.

The action follows the character changes of two friends. Paul (Lennie James), an exuberant punk, ends up a viciously aggressive long-term unemployee. His nerdy side-kick – all anorak and thick specs – becomes a got-a-job John. The latter, outstandingly played by James Kerr, turns up at Paul's squat and makes a move on his girlfriend Moony (Katrina Levon). This turns the tables on Paul, who got the girl – Lori (Connie Hyde) – back in Southport.

Praised for ideas and dialogue but needing clearer structure and better explanations for behaviour,(such as Lori's eventual suicide), "Outside of Heaven" received mixed reviews during its run at the Theatre Upstairs (January 30th – February 22). However, Penny Ciniewicz's direction shone out in the comic scenes, most memorably in the farce of trying to dump a real dead Doberman in a river. A vibrant cast gave punch to Sadofski's dark vision.

Some Singing Blood

Anton Rodgers, Prunella Scales and Julia Ford

Alison turns up from England with a biscuit tin. Inside are her father's ashes. She's come crunching up the gravel drive of this thatched, rain-beaten bugalow in Zimbabwe (beautifully designed by Fontini Dimou) to entrust the parental remains to Tudor Philips – the deceased's secret obsession since their days of unconsummated intimacy in the army.

Alison and Tudor cut their losses by bedding each other; his possessive manservant telephones her preposterous mother; and the fight is on.

Heidi Thomas' play was a quirkily plotted piece that rather lost control, lapsing into implausibility and muddling its moods. Though neatly compact linguistically, it came problematically close to "Mills and Boon" and didn't really get to grips with its black and gay issues.

Still, Jules Wright's direction was sure-footed and the cast outshone the play in the Theatre Upstairs during March and April. Julia Ford played Alison with intensity; Anton Rodgers, looking wittily like an outsized schoolboy in his ex-pat shorts, managed to manoeuvre comic eccentricity towards the tragic; and Prunella Scales, playing Iris Corless, the hausfrau from hell,was a little two-dimensional but carried the play through with her theatrical aplomb and perfect comic timing.

Berlin Bertie

Susan Lynch and Penny Dowie

South-of-the-river Sandy, his girlfriend Alice (a suspended social worker) and Joanne (a meditating mime artist) live on drugs and drink in a council flat overlooking a cityscape as bleak as their interior squalor (design by Paul McCauley). Alice's sister, Rosa, turns up from Berlin with high hopes of London and hatred of her husband whom she believes is a spy. Brenton's new play is about East Germany, collapsing European dreams, and the inescapable ties between private and political life, yet it also depicts women outliving these traumas and uniting to solve problems.

The characters sometimes sounded like caricatures (naive idealism, working class myopia, and middle class guilt), contradicting Brenton's claim that he had turned to psychological drama. Still, the set pieces were skillfully written and poetry mingled successfully with tough prose.

As Joanne, Susan Lynch beautifully combined fragility and anger, and Penny Downie's troubled, tearful Alice contrasted with Diana Rigg's ice-cool Rosa. Nicholas Woodeson made an excellent, sinisterly smiling Stasi insinuator while Kevin Allen's Sandy could be impressively foul-mouthed. Though sometimes implausible and unfocused in its anger, "Berlin Bertie" proved a passionate and comic play under Danny Boyle's sensitive direction. It was seen in the Main House during April.

Karate Billy Comes Home

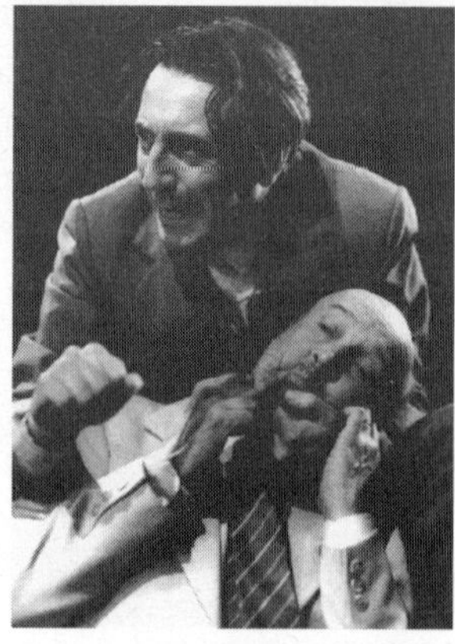
Kevin McMonagle and Glen David

"Karate Billy", by Klaus Pohl, was originally commissioned by Michael Bogdanov and was performed to great acclaim throughout Germany in 1991. Its British premiere, in a translation by David Tushingham, was directed by Stephen Unwin at the Theatre Upstairs, from 30 April, forming a coda to "Berlin Bertie" which had been playing in the Main House. Set in 1990 in a small East German town – with echoes of Durenmatt's "The Visit" – it focused on the Stasi, collective guilt, the bond between state and psyche, and on exorcising history.

Billy was once an Olympic standard athlete but is now brain-damaged and has been imprisoned in an asylum for years as a potential defector. Now released, he embarks on a witch-hunt,tracking down those who were responsible for his internment and unravelling – whodunnit style – a web of complicity and betrayal.

The piece was guilty of some contrived melodrama, heavy allegory, and a rather too easy ending, but was nevertheless enthralling and unsettling, charged with bouts of confession, aggression and suspense. Beth Goddard, Stephen Boxer, and David Bamber shone out, alongside Clare Holman playing Billy's menacingly sweet incestuous sister. As Billy himself, Kevin McMonagle presented a mixture of madness and lucidity, of bestial savagery and pathos.

Six Degrees of Separation

Stockard Channing

He claims he's the son of Sidney Poitier. He's memorised Fifth Avenue addresses, histories of couples' Ivy League offspring and facts about the Arts. That's how Paul – a pioneering, gay, black street kid – cons his way into Manhattan's highlife.

John Guare's play is a witty satire on the superficiality and falsity of the uppercrust art world. Avoiding the emotionally searing and the intellectually delving, it nonetheless intelligently worries simplistic categorisations of class, morality and truthfulness. Incidentally, this is real life turned into theatre, which bizarrely doubled back with the original conman claiming rights to his story and other writers asserting that Guare had copied their works.

Stockard Channing, transferring from the New York production, was truly accomplished as the initially hard-hearted, ultimately self-questioning Ouisa, wife of an art dealer, Flan (Paul Shelley). The cast worked excellently as an ensemble and Adrian Lester oozed enjoyment as Paul, acting with precision, verve and charm. Phyllida Lloyd directed with delightful slick panache, brilliantly supported by Mark Thompson's "modern art" design – receding white frames and bright blocks of colour. Throughout its Main House run in June and July, "Six Degrees" was a huge hit. Like "Death and the Maiden", it transferred to the West End.

Porcelain

Adam Matalon, Daniel York and Julien Ball

In August, Mu-Lan's Theatre Company – true to its founding aim of staging new work with Oriental themes – came to the Theatre Upstairs after a successful run of "Porcelain" at the Etceteras in Camden. Jointly directed by Mu Lan's Artistic Director, Glen Goei, and Stephen Knight, this is a first full length play from Chay Yew, whose earlier short piece, "As If He Hears" was the first Far East drama dealing with AIDS and was banned in Singapore.

In "Porcelain", a British-born Chinese gay confesses how he killed his caucasian lover and faces the heterosexual hostility of an interrogating criminal psychologist. The play investigates the grief and fury that spring from homosexual and racial alienation.

Only slightly repetitive and occasionally contrived, this was a delicately performed, stylishly presented production, ranging from flashes of brutality and eroticism to austere minimalism, as when four whites in a row on kitchen chairs, hedged in a solitary Chinese man who, all in white, compulsively folded blood-red origami birds. The cast – including the outstanding mimic, Adam Matalon – supplied all the sound effects and moved between roles as chorus and characters. Highly acclaimed.

Hush

Andy Serkis and Stephen Dillane

Jo – CND campaigner and symbol of the Far Left – is dead. She drowned at sea a year ago, perhaps intentionally. Her sister Louise and Tony – a hopelss right-on writer – now revisit Jo's home with her daugher Rosa (the broody Dervla Kirwan), who gets pregnant by a young down-and-out. He turns into a mad dog – an underdog whom Rosa's Guardian-reading guardians aren't magnanimous enough to accept.

Max Stafford-Clark's direction was fluid, deftly comic, and steered carefully between stylisation and naturalism, supported by Sally Jacobs' cunning "house becomes beach" set. Marion Bailey resisted caricaturing the clipt Louise, instead turning her into a complicated, almost sympathetic character. Debra Gillett was extremely funny as the ditsey New Age cleaner who dreams of travelling to Tibet while Andy Serkis (Dogboy) laid himself emotionally and literally naked in a performance of great bravery.

Writer April De Angelis came in for some serious criticism for cliched characterisation and over-obvious, rapidly dating political satire. Still, she was strong on symbolism and wit while suggesting intense alienation and pain with a touch of Edward Bond's shockingness. For all its cliches, "Hush" had the range to criticize the hypocrisies of middle class superficial philanthropy alongside the hackneyed cliches of communism. It played in the Main House during August and September.

Colqhoun and MacBryde

David O'Hara and Ken Stott

A decade after the Royal Court production of the "Slab Boys Trilogy", John Byrne's work returned to the Main House from September 17. This time, his piece was about two anti-conformist painters.

Though not household names today, Robert Colquhoun and Robert MacBryde were part of the dynamic arts set that formed in Soho in the 1950s and which had Dylan Thomas and George Baker among its members. Byrne's play follows the story of the two artists – life-long friends and now lovers – as they visit Florence and attain success in Bond Street and renown via the pages of the "Picture Post".

The two drunken protaganists were played by Duncan Bell (Colqhoun) and Ken Stott (MacBryde) who both displayed consummate skill in portraying the various levels of intoxication in which the two artists lived their confused lives. Byrne, whose television series "Tutti Frutti" won six BAFTA awards, proved just how multi-talented he is by designing the set himself. Lindsay Posner, of "Death and the Maiden" fame, directed.

Pygmies in the Ruins

From February 20, the Main House featured "Pygmies in the Ruins" by Ron Hutchinson.

This was a production from the Lyric theatre, Belfast.

Readers will find a review of this production in the regional section of the Yearbook. Please see **Northern Ireland, Lyric**.

Women Laughing

From September 4 to October 3, the Theatre Upstairs presented Richard Wilson's production of "Women Laughing".

This production began its life at the Royal Exchange Theatre, Manchester. Please refer to the Yearbook's regional section, **the North West, Royal Exchange, Manchester**.

THE NATIONAL THEATRE

It's hard to believe that the National Theatre (now Royal National) has only been open on the South Bank for sixteen years. It is now the fixed centre of the London theatre-goer's life. MICHAEL ARDITTI reviews this year at the National and discusses the plays that have been in performance in 1992.

The National '92

The extra-curricular activities at the National continue to thrive. During 1992 you might have heard dozens of major novelists from Peter Ackroyd to Alice Walker reading and discussing their work; you might have taken tea with Frances Barber or Alan Howard, performed alongside Anita Dobson in the 1000th Interaction Workshop, listened to Nicholas de Jongh on homosexuality, Maria St Just on Tennessee Williams or Dirk Bogarde on himself.

With such a rich programme of peripheral activities and a recessionary tightening of belts on stage, it can sometimes seem - to steal a phrase from another cultural institution - as if the National has become an ace platform with productions attached. But, if the theatre's volume of work has decreased, its range and standards have been maintained, with enough cross-fertilisation to satisfy even Polonius, and "An Inspector Calls", "Le Bourgeois Gentilhomme" and "A Midsummer Night's Dream" the only downright duds.

The company's eclecticism can be a problem. "The National Theatre is Yours" may have been a marketing ploy, but "Something For Everyone" has often seemed its only policy. But, while many may consider the inclusion of JB Priestley's relentlessly middle-brow "An Inspector Calls" to be taking its "Something old, something new, something borrowed, something blue" ethos to extremes, few could complain of such dramatic resuscitations as Howard Davies' "Pygmalion", which rescued the play from Julie Andrews and Rex Harrison, despite an extended use of staircases which would not have disgraced "Hello Dolly".

The year's repertoire can be divided many ways, but most productively into four new plays, three European classics, two modern revivals, two Shakespeares, two English classics, two one-man shows, one literary adaptation, one children's play and one musical; with the "Wind in the Willows", "Murmuring Judges", "Arturo Ui", "The Sea", "The Madness of George III", "The Little Clay Cart" and "Blood Wedding" remaining from 1991. It's heartening that the new work was both the largest category and the greatest success, with "Angels in America" my own choice for play and production of the year, and "The Rise and Fall of Little Voice", though flawed, rewarded with a West End transfer.

It proved to be a very egalitarian year with a focus on ensemble work rather than individual virtuosity. With the exception of Eileen Atkins' radiant Hannah Jelkes, the great performances were both held over from last year: Judi Dench's indomitable matriach in "The Sea" and Nigel Hawthorne's ill-used monarch in "The Madness of George III". Indeed, the return of Alan Bates and the rehabilitation of Alan Howard notwithstanding, the spotlight shifted from our senior actors on to the next generation: Frances Barber, Alex Jennings, Sally Dexter and Alison Steadman, and to such shining new talents as Marcus D'Amico and Jane Horrocks.

Directors were more likely to be thirty- than fifty-something, with the familiar faces of Declan Donnellan and Nicholas Hytner joined by debutants Stephen Daldry and Richard Jones. But the year's major disappointment was the recruitment of the Canadian Robert Lepage. The National pursued its international associations more fruitfully by importing productions of Goldoni and Pirandello from veterans Giorgio Strehler and Franco Zeffirelli, and housing a mini European Festival for Young People, involving five companies from four countries and using marionettes, mime, song and dance. It maintained its commitment to the regions with a major tour of the sixties classic, "Billy Liar".

Finally, perhaps the year's most significant event, although sadly the least reported, was the first ever TIE play to be given a National run: Y Touring Theatre's adaptation of Patricia Loughrey's "The Inner Circle" which, through performance, demonstration and discussion, introduced thousands of children to issues of AIDS and HIV.

The Madness of George III

Janet Dale and Nigel Hawthorne

The humiliation of royalty is nothing new. For twentieth century tabloids read eighteenth century doctors. Louis XIV, as a matter of course, had the consistency of his "stools" recorded by court physicians; while the colour and texture of George III's urine were a constant preoccupation for his.

The "1066 and All That" view that "George III was a bad king. He was, however, to a great extent insane" has long been accepted. But modern historians have argued that he was suffering from a blood disease - porphyria. Alan Bennett, whose fascination with royalty recently led to the first appearance of the Queen on the National Theatre stage, sets his play in the gap between received opinion and medical fact.

Its effect is more anecdotal than dramatic, and, apart from chronicling the absurdities of doctors a la Moliere, it's hard to see what the author actually has to say. But it was squeezed for every ounce of theatricality by Nicholas Hytner in one of his most stylish and simple productions which began in the Lyttleton in the Autumn of 1991.

As the King, Nigel Hawthorne gave the performance of a lifetime, depicting with pathos and power the crippling weight of responsibility and the indignity of his misdiagnosed condition, at times reaching the tragic heights of a latterday Lear.

The Sea

Judi Dench

The sea, for Edward Bond, is not only a symbol of nature's mystery and power, but of the swelling tide of social change. When a young man drowns off the Norfolk coast, it prompts a series of reactions and realignments which expose the tensions the author sees in British life.

In one sense, the play serves as a Tempest to Bond's Lear, and indeed Evans (Alan MacNaughton), the old beachcomber, shares Prospero's philosophical garrulity, if none of his magical and poetical power. But Bond himself makes more overt reference to the Orpheus myth, with Samuel West's diffident, soft-spoken Willy leading Sarah Woodward's Rose, like Eurydice, from a small-town hell.

Earlier, Bond shows the ladies of the town rehearsing their version of the Orpheus story for a charitable performance; and it is this scene, together with a farcical funeral, that provided the choicest moments in Sam Mendes' otherwise too evenly paced production.

The glory of the evening was Judi Dench's Mrs Rafi. Whether dominating the rehearsal like a female Wolfit or describing the indignities of old age with unbearable poignance, she constantly revealed the comic brilliance, tragic power and psychological truth that make her incomparably the greatest actress on the British stage.

Angels in America

Lou Hirsch

"Mr President, your family has AIDS" claimed a woman at the recent Republican Convention. Tony Kushner in his "Gay Fantasia on National Themes" reveals the extent of that family - not just fast-lane New Yorkers but mid-western Mormons and, most sinisterly, the closeted McCarthyite Roy Cohn: a man who loves "La Cage Aux Folles", but despises homosexuality - especially his own.

Mr Kushner's greatest strength is that he treats AIDS lightly and the Mormons seriously. He eschews "The Normal Heart's" bleeding heart realism in favour of a roller-coaster scenario which takes in brutal leather sex in Central Park, romantic eskimos in Antartica, visitations from seventeenth century puritans, the ghost of Ethel Rosenberg, and an angelic apotheosis which proves that Heaven is simply Hollywood-on-cloud.

A good angel must have guided the match between Kushner's script with its blood, sweat, tears and lethal one-liners, director Declan Donnellan's sensitive showmanship, designer Nick Ormerod's chinese box minimalism and an expert cast, including Sean Chapman, Henry Goodman, Felicity Montagu and, particularly, Marcus D'Amico who employed a knock-out combination of naked emotion and febrile charm. "Angels in America" played to a packed Cottesloe from 23 January.

The Night of the Iguana

Alfred Molina

St John of the Cross' Dark Night of the Soul has nothing on Tennessee Williams'. His characters, like the titular iguana, are tied down and at the end of their tether. In particular, the Reverend Shannon, like one of Graham Greene's whisky priests, is tortured by self-doubt and torn between his flesh and his calling, and, more immediately, between the two women who represent the author's somewhat schematic view of the Eternal Female: Hannah and Maxine, madonna and whore.

Although the dialogue with its overladen sentences and the drama with its overlaid sensationalism verge on self-parody - at this stage of Williams' career, the elements of erotic perversity appear to have been assembled from a kit - Richard Eyre's atmospheric production (in the Lyttleton from February) gave full weight to the shifting moods of passion, pathos and humour, rooting Williams' idiosyncratic symbolism in the verdant vegetation of Bob Crowley's set.

As Maxine, Frances Barber was impressively steamy if insufficiently raddled and with patently synthetic sweat. Alfred Molina's Shannon was a disappointment: gangling and ungainly with extraordinarily inexpressive shoulders, he seemed more overgrown seminarian than over-wrought priest. But Eileen Atkins' Hannah was a magnificent portrait of delicacy and dignity, worldly compassion and world-weary despair.

Uncle Vanya

Ian McKellen

The English love affair with Chekhov continues apace. Whenever there's an actor-led company, it rapidly reverts to Russia. The McKellen-Petherbridge Actors Company gave us "The Wood Demon"; the McKellen-Petherbridge National Company gave us "The Cherry Orchard". Now Ian McKellen and Antony Sher have jointly instigated "The Wood Demon's" successor, "Uncle Vanya".

Chekhov's attraction to actors is surely not just the range of good parts but that his typical structure - the gathering of a group for a short, intense period, its fraught relationships and subsequent dispersal - mirrors the experience of putting on a play.

Director Sean Matthias assembled some distinguished actors at the Cottesloe in February. They included Eric Porter as a definitively tetchy Professor and the magnificent Janet McTeer investing the underwritten Yelena with unsuspected reserves of disappointment and desire. But I found McKellen's performance unduly solipsistic: feeling but failing to project Vanya's pain, and Sher's quite the opposite: researched rather than experienced; a distracting accumulation of incidental details - the breathless entry, the paint-smattered arms.

This has been the most acclaimed "Vanya" since Olivier's, but I found it strangely uninvolving and was particularly conscious of the problems of focus on the three-sided stage. Democracy, but not drama, was served by the profusion of backs.

The Recruiting Officer

Alex Jennings

Farquhar takes us out of fashionable London and into the market-town of Shrewsbury - anathema to his manifestly metropolitan predecessors. Similarly Nicholas Hytner's production (in the Olivier from March) removed us from the now standard post-Brechtian stagings, where every beauty spot hides a pock mark, and restored the exuberance and artifice to Restoration comedy.

Farquhar worked as a recruiting officer himself and, although the play was originally perceived as a slander on Marlborough's army, clearly retained much affection for military life... the members of the regiment indulge in more mutual kissing than the Boys in the Band. Mr Hytner's reading was post-modern - but not post-Falklands - finding the comedy rather than the cruelty in the soldiers' manipulation of rural youth.

Farquhar's detailed description of Shrewsbury somewhat disappeared in Ashley Martin-Davis' toytown set, complete with cut-out barn-yard animals, more suited to Farmer Giles than Justice Balance. But the cast provided authentic comic portraits, particularly Sally Dexter, aping not only male disguise but male manners when she socked Suzanne Burden's simpering Melissa on the jaw, Alex Jennings' insouciantly lecherous Captain Plume, Desmond Barrit's mountainous Captain Brazen and Ken Stott's sweaty Sergeant Kite.

Pygmalion

Alan Howard

I could have danced all night after Howard Davies' sumptuous revival of "Pygmalion". A play that has been obscured on the one hand by the musical, like an extra swamped in one of Cecil Beaton's Ascot hats, and on the other by innumerable Rep productions, with RADA-trained actresses fighting against type and Received Pronunciation, was given a new lease of life.

For, although the director offered no new insights into Shaw's sexual or social politics, his masterstroke was to integrate material from the Leslie Howard-Wendy Hiller film. This had its longeurs - the bath scene was a delight but the ball scene tedious, and poor Frances Barber had to run down more moving stairs than a Harrods shoplifter - but it fulfilled the vital function of fitting the play to the stage.

The Olivier production may have been conventional, but several minor characters were radically reinterpreted: Alison Fiske's prim Mrs Pearce, clearly carrying a torch for Higgins, and Gillian Barge's blue-stocking Mrs Higgins were superb. Robin Bailey was a clubbable Colonel Pickering. Alan Howard, with his richly percussive voice, seemed a born teacher of phonetics, and Frances Barber's touching, sensual, defiant Eliza was her finest performance to date.

Needles and Opium

Robert Lepage

Suspended for much of the performance in mid-air, Robert Lepage was part Peter Pan, part Icarus. In the close confines of the Cottesloe the cords of his flying harness were plainly - and intentionally - visible. This is a theatrical magician who lets you see each stage of the trick but still creates an incomparable illusion.

The image of flight is central to his work, which is at once dream, drugged hallucination and free-wheeling imagination. He crosses cultures and continents, relishing bizarre coincidences and connections. Here, he performed alone for the first time since "Vinci", in contrast to the epic canvases of "The Dragons' Trilogy" and "Tectonic Plates".

There are three main strands to the piece. A Canadian actor, in Paris to narrate a film about Miles Davies' earlier visit to the city, pines for his former lover in America. This is interweaved with Davis' own experience as he falls in with Sartre and the Existentialists and in love with Juliette Greco. Hovering over them, like a guardian angel, is the figure of Jean Cocteau, writing his "Letter to the Americans" on a plane from New York.

The link between erotic obsession and narcotic addiction may be tenuous, but the visuals were magnificent and the magic real.

Le Bourgeois Gentilhomme

Timothy Spall

Moliere's titles pose problems in English. "The Imaginary Invalid" sounds more like a children's story than a social satire and yet "The Hypochondriac" doesn't quite have the ring of "Le Malade Imaginaire". For his new translation of an earlier comedy, Nick Dear keeps the original "Le Bourgeois Gentilhomme". Unfortunately, that's all he keeps.

Mr Dear relocates Moliere's world somewhere to the east of Stephen Berkoff's. He fatally confuses scatalogy with verbal energy. The "would-be gentleman" himself, with vowels as coarse as his vocabulary, is the chief culprit. His exchanges are peppered with "shut your gob", "shitbag", "don't give a monkey's" and "stick it up your bum".

Moliere's parable of social climbing and parody of artistic pretensions requires a production rooted in a domestic world as real as Alan Ayckbourn's. In this production, which played in the Lyttleon from 5 May, the designers the Brothers Quay gave us pop-up book, puppet-theatre stylisation. The over-elaborate conceits of the early scenes robbed the climactic Turkish sequences of their true effect. The cast led by Timothy Spall, Anita Dobson and Janine Duvitski, was left floundering.

Director Richard Jones' last production "La Bete" showed an insufferable upstart torturing a thinly disguised Moliere: a fault he committed here himself.

Richard III

Ian McKellen

Anyone pining for repeats of TV's "Edward and Mrs Simpson" will find much to enjoy in this "Richard 111". It was Shakespeare for people more fascinated by the House of Windsor than those of Lancaster and York. Richard Eyre's production was a throwback to the days of Jonathan Miller, when one bright idea (repressed sexuality and Vienna equals a Freudian "Measure For Measure") served to define - and confine - the production as a whole.

Eyre's idea hung on the Duke of Windsor's flirtation with fascist ideology, while Ian McKellen's performance in the title role seemed modelled less on the Duke than his most famous interpreter, Edward Fox. All clipped vowels, languid drawl and poker-back, he escaped the shadow of Olivier's hump and Antony Sher's crutches by underplaying the disability, making a virtuoso display of one-handedly lighting a cigarette.

Although the pre-World War Two period offered an ideal setting for one of McKellen's increasingly minimalist performances, it made nonsense of the play's medieval morality and dynastic politics. The early court scenes alone adapted to a world of butlers and Balmoral. The large banner of a naked McKellen seemed a particularly strange choice for a 1930s army.

This revival of the 1990 production played for eight performances in May before a sixteen week tour of the United States.

The Rise and Fall of Little Voice

Alison Steadman

Thirty years ago in "Roots", Arnold Wesker showed a Norfolk girl finding her voice, escaping both the cultural deprivation of her family and the intellectual influence of her London boyfriend. She ends her set-piece speech "D'you hear it? Did you listen to me? I'm talking.... I'm not quoting no more."

Jim Cartwright has written a "Roots" for the nineties, in which another young working-class woman finds her voice. She too has to escape her family - most obviously, her monstrous mother, but also the legacy of her father and his records of great singers. For, in perfecting her impersonations of Shirley Bassey, Judy Garland et al, she is hiding behind their emotions rather than admitting her own.

Jane Horrocks' precise talent for such musical "quotations" was the evening's chief pleasure; her Bassey, Garland and Monroe were spot-on - although her Piaf was simply all-purpose French. There were charming performances from Annette Badland as an obese, insanitary neighbour and Adrian Hood as a love-lorn Telecom engineer. But Alison Steadman as the mother went way over the top, painting her character in even cruder colours than her clothes.

Sam Mendes directed on a set by William Dudley, the oblique angles of which corrected any expectations of gritty Northern realism. The production played in the Cottesloe from June until November, when it transferred to the Aldwych Theatre.

Fuente Ovejuna

Rachel Joyce

Since this production premiered three years ago, the golden age of Spanish drama has been plundered as rapaciously as were its treasure ships by English pirates at the time. The vast output of writers like Calderon and Lope de Vega permits the magic words "British premiere"; while the Gate has virtually declared itself the National Theatre of Spain.

It was Declan Donnellan's brilliantly realised vision that blazed the trail. Nick Ormerod's microcosmic design exploited the Cottesloe's flexibility more fully than any since the 1985 "Mysteries". The play became a tournament with the audience sitting on two sides of a traverse, at one end of which sat the heraldic figures of Ferdinand and Isabella and at the other hung a backcloth of rural Spain.

The play deals with the rape and pillage of a Spanish village by a tyannical military commander (the excellent James Laurenson), together with the villagers' revenge and refusal to betray the culprits even under torture - such rough rural justice being a feature of "Cider With Rosie" over three-hundred years later. The performers were uniformly excellent, but the choric playing and exuberant choreography were the production's most outstanding feature.

A programme postscript informed us that soon afterwards the monarchs had the village destroyed. Fortunately, the National has been more protective of one of its finest works, which returned to the Cottesloe from 23 June.

A Midsummer Night's Dream

Indra Ove and Rupert Graves

The most eagerly awaited opening of the summer turned out to be the most disappointing. Robert Lepage's Shakespearian mudbath provoked a critical bloodbath, as barbs were aimed at the most earth-bound interpretation of recent years which played in the Olivier from July.

That the "Dream" has a dark side is a truism; no one now offers Mendelssohn's music and picturesque elves... unless it's a pack of brownies raising funds for a village hall. But Lepage chose to rub our faces - and more specifically his actors' - in the primordial mire.

He made no distinction between the various worlds of the play; Athens and the forest were represented by the same murky lake. The fairies wallowed in it; the lovers wrestled in it; the mechanicals "died" in it. For, if nothing else, the production proved that it's impossible to play comedy in mud.

Only one performance survived the debacle - Sally Dexter's Titania, who retained her dignity even when sleeping, bat-like, on a rope. Rudi Davies' Helena was inaudible from the sixth row of the stalls. Timothy Spall's cockney wide-boy Bottom was given highly imaginative asses' ears in Puck's feet; but it was an idea, and a position, that could not be sustained. Puck him/herself was the Canadian acrobat Angela Laurier, whose bodily contortions had nothing on her mangling of the verse.

The Street of Crocodiles

Eric Mallett, Lilo Baur and Stefan Metz

Simon McBurney adapted and directed the short stories of Bruno Schulz in "The Street of Crocodiles" at the Cottesloe from 13 August. The piece gave a new lease of life to the work of Schulz, who was described by the novelist David Grossman as "possibly the most important Polish writer between the two world wars".

Schulz' writing is packed with magical and mysterious metamorphoses and this most delightfully unliteral of literary adaptations gives them full weight. The stories, in which mundane events and everyday objects are invested with hidden significance, are ideally suited to the style McBurney has evolved with Theatre de Complicite, giving rise to his most successful show to date.

The production combined many influences, from conventional mime to music hall to the performance art of the Polish Tadeusz Kantor, whose "Dead Class" was recalled by McBurney's sustained sequences with desks. From the gravity-defying opening to the serenity of the close, the images were by turn funny, poignant and horrific and were superbly executed by a multi-national and multi-lingual cast.

Gerard McBurney's music, Rae Smith's design and Paule Constable's lighting all contributed to a production which deftly, unassumingly, conjured up a vanished middle-European world.

An Inspector Calls

Richard Pasco, Robert Bowman and Louis Hilyer

JB Priestley's play, with its creaking construction and middle-brow metaphysics, is a strange choice for the National's repertory, but not even a confirmed Priestley-sceptic like myself believes that it merits the treatment meted out by Stephen Daldry.

Although set in a dining room, it's a conventional drawing room drama spiced up with some once fashionable theories about time. Priestley presents a parable about the complicity of respectability and the responsibility of privilege. Mr Daldry distorted it into a Pirandellian exercise in theatrical ambiguity and a sub-Bunuelian social satire.

A dining room clearly being too limited an arena for a fashionable young director, he and his designer, Ian MacNeil, opted instead for a bomb-damaged street, complete with extraneous, attention-grabbing urchins. Indeed when a design upstages the play so shamelessly, one wonders why the National doesn't cut out the middleman and simply organise tours of the set.

Every movement was exaggerated and every emotion underlined, often by Stephen Warbeck's absurdly portentous score. Kenneth Cranham's Inspector was over-emphatic, Richard Pasco's Birling bombastic and Barbara Leigh-Hunt clearly wished she were still playing Wilde.... Never have I seen a production which evinced so little faith in a play.

Kings

Alan Howard

"Kings", a version of Books One and Two of Homer's "Iliad", is the latest instalment of Christopher Logue's reworking of the greatest of Greek epics. This one and a half hour piece centres on Achilles and Agamemnon's quarrels prior to the storming of Troy.

It captures the spirit of the author by a free and idiosyncratic rendition rather than a literal translation. Occasional anachronistic imagery - Ajax is described as "grim under his tan like Rommel after Alamein" - ensures that the events of the story never seem remote.

Logue originally collaborated with actor Alan Howard and director Liane Aukin on "War Music", an account of three later books of "The Iliad" in 1981. And "Kings" itself was first broadcast on both Radios Two and Three in 1991, before playing to great acclaim on that year's Edinburgh Fringe. It was brought to the Cottesloe in September.

Alan Howard, the only actor in living memory to play the full line of Shakespeare's kings from Richard II to Richard III, was perfectly pitched to capture both the martial rhetoric and domestic detail of Homer's poem. With occasional interpolations from Logue, he delineated a large cast of characters in a dramatic tour-de-force.

Square Rounds

Paola Dionisotti and Jenny Galloway

Not since the heyday of TS Eliot and Christopher Fry has a poet written as successfully for the stage as Tony Harrison. His brilliant versions of Moliere and Aeschylus have inspired a new generation of translators such as Ranjit Bolt; while, more recently, he extended his range with "The Trackers of Oxyrhynchus", which inserted fragments of a Sophoclean satyr-play, "The Ichneutae", in a drama of its discovery by two Oxford dons.

Now he goes further with an entirely original piece, again written in verse. "Square Rounds" examines the ambiguity of science, its power at once to create and destroy, as chemists desperate to bring new fertility to the fields of Europe become the inventors of mass destruction for the twentieth century.

He also tackles the sexual imbalance of contemporary drama by writing a large-scale play predominantly for women. Leading roles were taken by Sara Kestleman, Paola Dionisotti, Maria Friedman and Gillian Barge. Harrison himself directed, with designs by Jocelyn Herbert, music by Dominic Muldowney, choreography by Lawrence Evans and lighting by Mick Hughes. The production played at the Olivier theatre from October 1.

Dragon

The National's annual children's show playing in the Olivier from November, was a new version of Yevgeny Shvarts' "Dragon" by actor Alan Cumming and director/designer Ultz. The play, written in 1943 in Stalinist Russia combines an ancient folk-tale with a number of Hans Anderson stories.

But this is no ordinary folk-tale. There is a typical dragon out for blood and a typical hero, name of Lancelot, out to defeat him, and yet the villagers under seige claim to love their dragon, just as they do their tyrannical President. Small wonder that the first production was considered subversive and the play banned until 1962.

For this new staging Ultz called on a variety of talents, including the creators of Spitting Image to realise Shvarts' bizarre bestiary of animals and characters and the musician M.C.Kinky to provide the reggae rhythms for a band of gypsies. No two performances were ever alike as the cast, including Christopher Campbell, Lolita Chakrabarti, Mark Heap, Paul J Medford and Mark Saban, swapped roles every day.

Stages

Alan Bates

Of all the great writer-director partnerships of the sixties and seventies, Edward Bond's with William Gaskill... Harold Pinter's with Peter Hall, the only one to have survived into a third decade is that of David Storey and Lindsay Anderson. Storey may be better known as a novelist and Anderson as a film-maker, but their theatrical collaborations uniquely match the former's pellucid prose with the latter's meticulous rhythms.

Their particular blend of radical humanism appeared to be out of fashion in the eighties when, after a prolific partnership, they broke their silence only with "Early Days" at the Cottesloe and "The March on Russia" at the Lyttleton; now they return with a study of an artist facing old age.

Alan Bates, a long-term interpreter of Storey's work and one who, with his performances in Osborne, Pinter and Gray, must have created more significant contemporary roles than any other actor, played the central figure of Richard Fenchurch, a painter and writer looking back on the passion that informed his life and work - and eventually drove him to madness.

Other leading roles were taken by Joanna David and Rosemary Martin and the design was by Jocelyn Herbert. "Stages" opened in the Cottesloe on November 18.

Carousel

Nicholas Hytner

Its final song, the rousing "You'll never walk alone", may have become the most popular anthem on the football terraces, but "Carousel" has not had a major revival in London since its original 1950 run at Drury Lane. Based on Ferenc Molnar's play, "Liliom", its mix of Capraesque fantasy and New England realism makes it the most dramatically sophisticated of Rodgers and Hammerstein's shows.

From his vantage point in the clouds, Billy Bigelow looks down at his unhappy teenage daughter and back at the events that led to his death shortly before her birth. He recalls his work as a fairground barker, his doomed love for the young factory girl, Julie Jordan, and the desperate poverty that drove him to crime. He is given the chance to return to earth for a day to try to help his child.

The score contains several of Rodgers and Hammerstein's best-loved songs, including "If I loved you", "June is busting out all over" and "When the children are asleep". The director was Nicholas Hytner with choreography by Sir Kenneth Macmillan and designs by Bob Crowley. The cast was led by Patricia Routledge, Joanna Riding, Janie Dee and Clive Rowe with the young American, Michael Hayden, making his British debut as Billy.

THE ROYAL SHAKESPEARE COMPANY

Our oldest national company, the RSC, has become a famous British institution. It is based in both London and Stratford. Its London home is the Barbican, where there is a main stage and a small theatre, The Pit. At Stratford, the large Royal Shakespeare Theatre and the middle-sized Swan were joined by a small and gleamingly refurbished The Other Place in 1991. JEREMY KINGSTON looks back at the RSC in 1992 and NINA PASCO describes their remarkable contribution to our theatrical fare.

The RSC '92

For his second year as Artistic Director, Adrian Noble continues the long-established RSC pattern that mixes a lot of old with a little new. The 1992 season has given us a proper preponderance of Shakespeare, twelve plays in all, eight of them new productions and all but two staged in the main theatres at Stratford and the Barbican; an excellent variety of other old English plays, "Tamburlaine" the earliest in date, "The Beggar's Opera" the latest; two foreign plays ("The Dybbuk" and Ostrovsky's "Artists and Admirers") and a light peppering of modern pieces. Noble also revived his own production of Sophocles' Theban plays, which by any reckoning must count as "very old".

A system that requires, on average, eight new Shakespeare productions every year is bound to repeat frequently the plays that audiences favour. "Timon" and "All's Well" are given revivals only once in a generation. The RSC can fortunately still afford to revive a play because it is worth doing rather than because parties of tourists will always book for "As You Like It" but there is only so far the company can go down this not-so-commercial road. Occasionally, as with Trevor Nunn's "Timon" a couple of years ago, a problem play is re-thought so vitally that it packs the theatre.

The delight felt in seeing life breathed into rare Shakespeare, or into Elizabethan and Stuart plays unstaged since their authors died, comes not from the jaded critic's craving for novelty but out of longing to rediscover all that lies forgotten from that rich, remote period. I should like to see the company's interest in the works of Shakespeare's contemporaries extended to take in a couple of the plays in which he appears to have had a hand. "Two Noble Kinsmen" was given an airing six years ago. Perhaps "Sir Thomas More", with three of its manuscript pages in Shakespeare's handwriting, has been too savaged by the Elizabethan censor to merit a major revival – though a production was staged at the Shaw theatre two years ago. The anonymous "Edward III" (revived at Theatr Clwyd in 1987) is a better bargain. With its giveaway line "Lilies that fester smell far worse than weeds", the play contains patriotism, much slaughter and some subtlety in the way it treats the king's thwarted wooing of a virtuous countess. It would be good to see what RSC actors could make of it.

Twelve directors shared with Noble the season's workload, and these included two of the three former Artistic Directors: Sir Peter Hall directed "All's Well" and Terry Hands "Tamburlaine the Great". The missing AD, Trevor Nunn, brought "Measure for Measure" and "The Blue Angel", his two productions from The Other Place, to London in the course of the year, while the Artistic Directors of four other theatres also staged work: Max Stafford-Clark, Bill Alexander, David Thacker and Sam Mendes. Four other directors made their debut productions for the company, indicating that Noble's concern to balance old and new is not restricted to his repertoire of plays.

The Shakespeare revivals included some unillustrious items but the only production to come seriously unstuck was Richard Nelson's "Columbus". The wonder is that it was ever thought capable of sticking together. Nelson's past work has adorned the company but this commissioned epic for Columbus Year was mounted in a form several drafts too early. This is not the first time the RSC has come a cropper in catching hold of fashion. Noble's directors, in this case John Caird, should steel themselves on such occasions to say, courteously yet firmly, "No".

The Strange Case of Dr Jekyll and Mr Hyde

This new version of Robert Louis Stevenson's familiar chiller was by David Edgar, whose previous, highly distinguished work with the RSC includes "Destiny", "The Jail Diary of Albie Sachs", "Maydays" and the award-winning "Nicholas Nickleby".

Edgar uses the nightmarish story as the vehicle for a sermon on Victorian values and the human psyche at war with itself. But however valid his points may be, this meant that Peter Wood's stagy but sometimes effective production tended to drag a little.

Jekyll and Hyde were played by Roger Allam and Simon Russell Beale respectively. (In a nice touch, Jekyll had a light Edinburgh accent while Hyde was plainly from the mean streets of Glasgow.)

Simon Russell Beale and Roger Allam

Edgar dutifully related Jekyll's emotionally deprived childhood and bundled in references to every Victorian social issue imaginable. But this worked against the effect of Stevenson's original – a short, dark tale as hard as granite. If Stevenson had made "Jekyll and Hyde" as discursive as "Middlemarch" or "Bleak House" it would have been forgotten a long time ago. In Edgar's version, neither the doctor nor the monster managed to find the jugular.

The Bright and Bold Design

"The Bright and Bold Design", directed by Bill Alexander and designed by Kit Surrey, was the fourth play by Peter Whelan to be premiered by the RSC. In mood and style it was much of a piece with his earlier "The Accrington Pals" and "Clay". Set among the potteries of Staffordshire in the 1930s, it treated us to the sight of actors painting pots and cups on stage (having been specially trained to do so).

Alex Kingston

The play centres on Jim Rhys, an ambitious and political designer who joins a highly conservative firm of potters, intent on adding stylised pylons and radio sets to their traditional floral designs. In Jessie Frost, a young woman employed as a pot painter, Rhys recognises a real artist and, he thinks, a soul mate. But although Frost (loosely based on the real designer Clarice Cliff) is talented, she has a very different outlook and concerns.

Katy Behean and Clive Russell took the parts of Frost and Rhys well. Veterans Bill McGuirk and Paul Webster were excellent as the alcoholic Ulik Mountford and Hector Brabant, Rhys's boss and instinctive enemy. Among the women on the production line, Clare Lawrence stood out as Violet Chappel.

Much Ado About Nothing

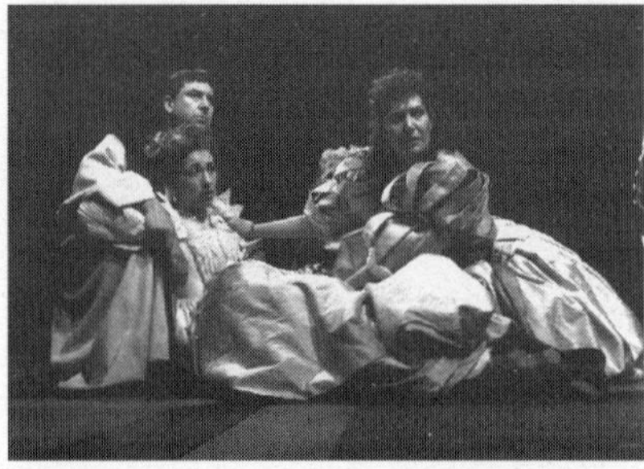
Mike Dowling, Alex Kingston and Susan Fleetwood

The RSC seems to be concentrating much more on Shakespeare's comedies at the moment than on his tragedies. As part of this rash of happy endings, "Much Ado About Nothing" finished off the 1991/1992 season on the main stage in the Barbican, having previously opened in the Royal Shakespeare Theatre in Stratford in April 1990.

Bill Alexander's production of one of Shakespeare's best-loved comedies was a popular and pleasurable RSC success, uniting Susan Fleetwood's spirited and funny Beatrice with Roger Allam's compelling Benedick. Although the play naturally focuses on this duo, Alex Kingston's Hero and John McAndrew's Claudio deserved mention, as did George Raistrick's reliable Dogberry. John Carlisle was a satisfyingly stern Don Pedro. Ken Shorter played Borachio and Paul Webster was Leonato.

If the staging, which was lit by Brian Harris and designed by Kit Surrey with music by Ilona Sekacz, provided no radical new insights into the play, it was at least an enjoyable and fresh visit from an old friend.

Troilus and Cressida

Norman Rodway and Amanda Root

This was the RSC at its small-scale best, in a play that provided a desperate (and blackly funny) showcase for its extremely talented young director Sam Mendes and its able designer Anthony Ward. Paterson Joseph was Troilus, having taken over the part from Ralph Fiennes in September, and Amanda Root was an excellent Cressida. The uniformly strong cast also included Alfred Burke as Nestor, Sally Dexter as Helen, Mike Dowling as Aeneas, Ciaran Hines as Achilles, Paul Jesson as Ulysses, Sylvester Morand as Agamemmnon, Richard Ridings as Ajax, Grant Thatcher as Diomedes, David Troughton as Hector and John Warnaby as Paris.

Troilus and Cressida used to be one of the plays Shakespeare got told off for writing. From time to time people tried to prove it wasn't by him at all. But it seems to have grown in stature over our century, and it is hard to imagine a better production of the play than this. Few actors are likely to provide a Thersites as compelling scabrous as Simon Russell Beale's magnificent monster or another Pandarus as dangerously bland as Norman Rodway's.

The production, which was originally staged in The Swan in Stratford in April 1991, ended the 1991/1992 season in The Pit.

Henry IV Parts One and Two

Robert Stephens

The RSC's tenth season in the Barbican opened in March with Adrian Noble's majestic production of Henry IV Part One, joined five weeks later by Part Two. If anything, Part One was a little too majestic, with more than its fair share of Queen's Award for Export standard-bearing, flag waving and running about the stage in RSC standard-issue doublets and singlets. But it also had three first-rate performances in Robert Stephens' Falstaff (incredibly, this was Stephens' first season with the RSC), Julian Glover's Henry and Michael Maloney's Hal.

This trio made a fascinating comparison with Joss Ackland, Patrick Stewart and Gerard Murphy who took the parts when Trevor Nunn's 1982 production opened the Barbican Theatre. All three came out of such a test well, with the black-robed and icily ill-at-ease Glover proving particularly strong. Maloney was an infectiously energetic and funny but wilfully callow Hal whose tense, flirtatious relationship with Falstaff was doomed to its harsh end from long before curtain-up. Stephens gave us a very singular but winning Falstaff, aggressive, coarse, loving, pathetic and dainty by turns.

Bob Crowley's memorable set boasted an astonishing and hellishly maze-like Boar's Head Tavern for Albie Woodington's Pistol to run riot in. Edward Gregson's driving score seemed to use more musicians in the battle scenes than Noble had soldiers.

Not all the cast were strong. Bernard Kay's Glendower was surprisingly flat and David Bradley's Shallow, although extremely funny, was too thoroughly shallow for his reminiscences to be very moving. Philip Voss was a dependable Worcester in Part One and a very human Lord Chief Justice in Part Two. Linda Bassett was Mistress Quickly and Joanne Pearce was Doll Tearsheet. Kenn Sabberton was Bardolph, Rob Edwards was Poins and Scott Ransome was Peto. Sylvestra le Touzel was an intense wife and widow to Owen Teale's somewhat underwhelming Hotspur. Denys Hawthorne was Northumberland, Gary Powell was Westmorland and Ian Hughes was John of Lancaster. The production was lit by Alan Burrett and the costumes were designed by Deirdre Clancy.

Romeo and Juliet

David Leveaux's uninspired "Romeo and Juliet" transferred to the Barbican, having first been seen in Stratford. The obligatory moan about declining standards in verse speaking might as well be made here as anywhere: what *do* they teach at RADA these days?

Michael Maloney was the best of the stars as a sensitive if not unduly distinctive Romeo. What he saw in Clare Holman's Juliet was never clear. Tim McInnerny's Mercutio was astonishingly undangerous, and the entire cast seemed slightly lost among Alison Chitty's impressive, depressing sets. Kevin Doyle was Benvolio, Ian Hughes was Tybalt and Sheila Reid (perhaps feeling slightly typecast) played the Nurse. Denys Hawthorne was Prince Escalus, Robert Langdon Lloyd was Friar Lawrence, and Jonathan Newth and Jan Shand played Capulet and Lady Capulet.

Michael Maloney and Clare Holman

"Romeo and Juliet" works best if taken at a passionate rush, skating over the cruder mechanics of the tale and some of Shakespeare's less felicitous moments while energetically exploiting the play's many set pieces. John Patten, the Secretary of State for Education, wants all the fourteen year old schoolchildren in the country to be examined on this text (or on "Julius Caesar", God help them, or on "A Midsummer Night's Dream"). If the RSC can't provide something more vital than this it will find it hard to hold its young audience's attention.

The Alchemist

Sam Mendes' production of Jonson's best-known play transferred to the big stage in London after a sell-out season in the smaller confines of the Swan.

The action begins when Lovewit leaves his London house for fear of the plague and Face, his housekeeper, unites with a charlatan called Subtle and Doll Common to use the premises as a base for taking as much money from gullible people as possible, under a variety of pseudonyms and guises. As the house begins to overflow with customers seeking wealth and love through astrology, alchemy, demonology and the like, the trio become the victims of their own success.

Christopher Luscombe and Jonathan Hyde

David Bradley (Subtle), Jonathan Hyde (Face) and Joanne Pearce (Doll Common) kept the farcical action running along at an appropriate speed, supported by a gallery of gulls and grotesques including Richard Bonneville as Surly, Alexis Daniel as Kastril, Bernard Gallagher as Lovewit, Guy Henry as a memorably sanctimonious Ananias with Robert Langdon Lloyd as his sidekick Tribulation, Philip Voss as an equally memorable Sir Epicure Mammon and Albie Woodington as Drugger the tobacconist.

The production was designed by Anthony Ward, with music by Paddy Cunneen.

Columbus and the Discovery of Japan

Jonathan Hyde

Due to a lack of bums on seats this new play, directed by John Caird and written by the American Richard Nelson, ended seven performances short of its advertised run.

Nelson aimed to question the Columbus story which was being celebrated wholesale elsewhere in 1992. Columbus was a landlubber who reached America (which he thought was Japan); a Genoese sailing from Spain; someone who began by raising money in the Jewish quarter but found Spanish Jews looking to him for help as the country expelled them. However, Nelson's irony was swallowed up by the play's scale. And while the earth may have been round it turned out that the writing was decidedly flat.

Some of Timothy O'Brien's design was clever – Jonathan Hyde's Columbus began the play stretched out like an anatomical drawing by Leonardo and ended it cased in robotic armour. But the cleverness often looked forced and over-elaborate.

The cast tried hard in the face of adversity, with particular mention due to Philip Voss as Roderigo Pulgar. But in the end one was left wondering whether a smaller Pit piece on the same subject might not have been far more rewarding.

Two Gentlemen of Verona

Barry Lynch

David Thacker's exhilarating production of this relatively unfamiliar Shakespearean comedy transferred to the Barbican Theatre in the autumn after a sell-out run in The Swan last year.

Perhaps inspired by the astonishing success of various "revival" and "compilation" musicals in the West End, Thacker took the view that there's no tune like an old tune and filled his show with songs from the likes of Cole Porter, Irving Berlin and George Gershwin. Sung by Hilary Cromie, these guaranteed crowd-pleasers transported the play instantly and successfully into the world of light romantic comedies, matching perfectly the tried and tested plot of "boy falls in love with best friend's girlfriend".

The cast included Richard Bonneville as Valentine, Clare Holman as Julia, Barry Lynch as Proteus and Josette Bushell-Mingo as Silvia. Terence Wilton was the Duke of Milan. Richard Moore as Launce deserved an award for not being upstaged by the large and loveable shaggy dog playing Crab.

Design was by Shelagh Keegan, with lighting by Jim Simmons and original music by Guy Woolfenden.

The Theban Trilogy

Gerard Murphy

London theatre has gone Greek in a big way recently. We have seen, among many others, Fiona Shaw as Electra, Diana Rigg as Medea and Janet Suzman in "Hippolytus". Poets such as Tony Harrison, Seamus Heaney and Derek Walcott have produced new works based on their reading of Greek sources.

The RSC's "Theban Trilogy" of Sophocles' plays "Oedipus Tyrannos", "Oedipus at Colonus" and "Antigone" was directed by Adrian Noble and began life in Stratford before moving to the Barbican Theatre. The plays were performed in a new version – good, bare and serviceable – by the award-winning playwright Timberlake Wertenbaker

The plays are a trilogy in that they depict events involving the same characters. However, they were not written as a group and were almost certainly never performed as one by the Greeks.

"Oedipus at Colonus", the "middle" play of the trilogy, was not performed until after Sophocles' death in 405 BC and may well have been his last work. "Antigone", the final play, was probably written in about 440 BC, with "Oedipus Tyrannos" coming some ten years later.

Gerard Murphy as Oedipus went from strutting the stage as Heseltine Tyrannos to being a pathetic mud-covered mendicant who achieved some sort of supernatural atonement and transfiguration in his (off-stage) death. John Shrapnel was wonderful as irritable, dangerous and bullying Creon who never quite understood what was going on around him. Clifford Rose was an insistent, grumbling Tiresias. The adult Antigone, first leading her father through exile and then mesmerically challenging Creon for the body of her dead brother, was Joanne Pearce. Philip Voss was a grave and stately Theseus, and Linda Marlowe played Jocasta. Linda Bassett was Oedipus' other daughter, Ismene.

Among the other roles, Valerie Sarruf stood out as Creon's wife Eurydice and as a messenger (Greek tragedy is probably the only drama in the world which gives the messengers more to say than some of the protagonists). Christopher Saul was a priest of Zeus, Rob Edwards was Polynices and Paul Kiernan was Haemon.

Noble's staging was genuinely thrilling, although some critics objected to the large balloons suspended over the stage and the auditorium, presumably to suggest the presiding gods. The chorus was well received despite sometimes crossing the line that separates intense theatrical movement from morris dancing.

The production was designed by Ultz (balloons) and lit by Alan Burrett. Ilona Sekacz wrote some highly atmospheric music and Sue Lefton was the movement director.

Scandinavian Season

Michael Maloney

"Tender is the North" mounted by the Barbican Centre, encompassed music, art, theatre, cinema and literature and was the largest festival of Scandinavian culture ever to take place in the UK. The RSC mounted several events in The Pit as part of the festival.

There were four performances of "Bellman's Opera" a celebration of the work of Sweden's poet-songwriter Carl Mikael Bellman in an adaption by Martin Best and Clifford Williams.

Julian Glover's gripping one-man version of "Beowulf" (strictly speaking an Anglo-Saxon rather than a Scandinavian piece), fresh from the 1992 Stratford Fringe Festival, had one performance. In addition, there were one-off rehearsed readings of "Rain Snakes" by Per Olov Enquist, "Autumn and Winter" by Lars Norén, and "Burnt Njal" a new play by Peter Whelan based on an ancient Icelandic saga.

It seems a shame that the RSC's contribution to "Tender is the North" should have been confined to a few single performances of loosely Scandinavian pieces. To have properly put on even a single play would have seemed a good deal less half-hearted.

The Virtuoso

Barry Lynch, Richard Bonneville and Sean Murray

Last year's Stratford production, directed by Phyllida Lloyd, was the first time Thomas Shadwell's 1676 comedy had seen the light of day in over two hundred years. Its huge success both in Stratford and on transfer makes this neglect seem unaccountable.

Christopher Benjamin returned to the RSC as Sir Nicholas Gimcrack, the Virtuoso, a role taken by Freddie Jones in Stratford. He was joined by Richard Bonneville (a rather Rik Mayallesque Sir Samuel Hearty), Guy Henry (a glorious Sir Formal Trifle), Linda Marlowe (a hammily voluptuous Lady Gimcrack) and Ken Wynne (an acceptably snarling Snarl). The lust-crossed lovers were well portrayed by Barry Lynch, Sean Murray, Saskia Reeves and in particular Josette Bushell-Mingo. Deborah Winckles was an unexpectedly sympathetic Mrs Figgup.

The RSC gets academic brownie points for reviving a forgotten satire on the young Royal Society and the stranger excesses of seventeenth century gentlemen-scientists. (It also did well to leave off the silly ending added in Stratford where Gimcrack split the atom.) But the play's chief appeal is as a comedy of desire and sexual hypocrisy – something as up-to-date as ever.

What price a revival of Shadwell's last comedy "Bury Fair"?

A Woman Killed With Kindness

Jonathan Cullen and Sylvestra Le Touzel

The year's second production in The Pit was first aired in The Other Place in 1991 and marked the RSC debut of Katie Mitchell, founder of the theatre company Classics on a Shoestring. With the two shoestrings allowed by the RSC's budget she produced a memorable account of this powerful tragedy, a very early English domestic drama, first performed in 1603 and written by Thomas Heywood, one of the most prolific Elizabethan and Jacobean playwrights.

John and Anne Frankford, the tragic protagonists, were movingly portrayed by Michael Maloney and Saskia Reeves. Barry Lynch was Wendoll, the friend whose embrace of Anne Frankford sets the disastrous events in motion. Other leading roles were taken by Jonathan Cullen as Sir Charles Mountford, Sean Murray as Nicholas, Valentine Pelka as Sir Francis Acton, Kenn Sabberton as Jenkin and Sylvestra le Touzel as Susan Mountford.

The set was designed by Vicki Mortimer and lit by Dave Ludlam and Mark Ager. The music was by Ben Livingstone. Movement was by Emma Rice.

'Tis a Pity She's a Whore

Jonathan Cullen

April saw a third transfer from Stratford to The Pit. This time it was David Leveaux's gripping and sometimes very bloody production of John Ford's most famous play – tender, funny and tragic by turns.

Jonathan Cullen and Saskia Reeves (who successfully cornered this year's market in doomed Jacobean heroines in The Pit) gave us an intense Giovanni and Annabella in what the RSC rather coyly called "this masterpiece about forbidden love between brother and sister". After her film role in "Close My Eyes", is there any danger of Reeves cornering the market in arty incest as well? She certainly displayed exactly the right mixture of erotic innocence for Ford's passionate but naive Annabella.

Jonathan Hyde was a notably nasty Vasques and Sheila Reid a refreshingly down to earth Putana. Tim McInnerny was Soranzo and Jonathan Newth was Bonaventura. Kenny Miller designed the production, which was lit by Rick Fisher and had some particularly moody music composed by Corin Buckerridge.

The Dybbuk

Joanne Pearce

This production was directed, designed, lit and composed for by the team responsible for the excellent "A Woman Killed With Kindness". But their "Dybbuk" showed what might happen if Merchant-Ivory filmed "Fiddler on the Roof". It was perfectly well done, but its concern to be faithful to the atmosphere of a nineteenth century community of Hasidic Jews in the Ukraine meant that it lost sight of the most nightmarish aspects of Solomon Anski's play, which was first performed (and filmed) as a more expressionistic and far less nostalgic piece.

The RSC's desire for authenticity extended to the employment of Yiddish coaches and the recruitment of a klezmer band. But in the end the mysterious tale stayed resolutely earthbound, despite a few genuinely powerful moments in Kate Mitchell's staging of Mira Rafolowicz's new version of the play and despite Joanne Pearce's gripping performance as the hysterical Leah, betrothed to one man and married to another, only to be possessed by a dybbuk, the spirit of her dead and vengeful ex-fiancee, on her wedding day.

John Shrapnel was an authoritative Reb Azrielke and Charles Daish played Khonen.

Amphibians

Sean Murray

This new play by award-winning playwright Billy Roche is set firmly in the coastal town of Wexford in Ireland, like his other recent works "A Handful of Stars", "Poor Beast in the Rain" and "Belfry".

The fishing industry of Wexford is in decline and its old skills and customs are gradually disappearing. The play shows how community life changes as the local workforce is gradually netted by industry and drawn up through the factory gates into a newly industrialised life. Movingly, but also with great humour, Roche shows how Eagle the fisherman (strongly portrayed by Ian McElhinney) tries to hand down the trade of his lifetime to his young son, played by Kevin Burke.

The cast included Richard Bonneville as Brian, Hilary Cromie as Bridie, Jane Gurnett as Veronica, Sean Murray as Broaders and Albie Woodington as Dribbler. Barry Lynch was particularly fine as Zak and Lesley Maguire was an excellent Sonia. The production marked Michael Attenborough's directorial debut with the RSC.

Artists and Admirers

Sylvestra le Touzel

"Artists and Admirers" (given in a new version by Kevin Elyot based on a literal translation by Helen Rappaport) is the third play by the nineteenth century Russian writer Alexander Nikolayevich Ostrovsky that the RSC has mounted in the past ten years.

The play (also known in English as "Talents and Suitors", "Fiancee without a Future" and even "Career Woman", and seen in the 1980s at the Riverside Studios) is a funny and affecting tale of provincial thespians in which the talented and admired young actress Negina finds her career in jeopardy when she spurns the advances of a lecherous prince.

Directed by Phyllida Lloyd and designed by Anthony Ward, "Artists and Admirers" opened in the Pit in October. It starred Linda Bassett as the peasant Domna Pantelyevna, Christopher Benjamin as the prince, Kevin Doyle as the student Melusov, Rob Edwards as Bakin, Sylvestra le Touzel as Negina and Philip Voss as an excellent Narokov, the landowner who sacrifices his social position for privilege of being a stage manager.

Julius Caesar

Jonathan Hyde

On the whole this was not a success. Steven Pimlott's first production for the RSC, began with the entrance of a mysterious cloaked figure, who arrived centre stage before most of the audience had found their seats and lurked on the set until scene two before revealing itself as Owen Teale's Mark Antony. From the word go this was obviously "director's theatre".

Things went on in much the same vein. The actors wore renaissance costumes but Tobias Hoheisel's flashy set – a million miles away from the Elizabethan theatre the costumes implied – dwarfed them for most of the time. The exception to this was Robert Stephens' impressively clapped-out Caesar who managed to introduce his own rhetoric rather than being trapped by the production's concern with the show and style of politics.

Cassius was played by David Bradley and Casca by Bernard Gallagher. Jane Gurnett was Portia and Jonathan Hyde was Marcus Brutus. Scott Ransome played Octavius. Lighting was by Paul Pyant and music by Peter Salem.

Twelfth Night

Ken Wynne, Jane Gurnett and Freddie Jones

Griff Rhys Jones is of course a well-known comedian but on the evidence of this production his direction of Shakespearean comedy leaves something to be desired. It wasn't particularly Shakespearean and, to be honest, it wasn't desperately comical. But any staging of "Twelfth Night" is bound to bring its pleasures and this one certainly boasted an able cast well-versed in comedy.

Freddie Jones, although in some ways too agreeable a fellow to be Malvolio, at least has enormous stage presence, and Bill Wallis gave us an excellent Sir Toby Belch. Tim McInnerny's flaxen-haired, bespatted Sir Andrew Aguecheek was an odd interpretation of the role, but one which carried no particular conviction.

Sylvestra le Touzel was a compelling Viola. Other members of the cast included Jane Gurnett as a somewhat pre-Raphaelite Olivia, Terence Hillyer as Duke Orsino, Ian Hughes as Sebastian, Linda Marlowe as Maria, Gary Powell as Antonio and Ken Wynne as Feste.

The production was designed by Ultz and lit by Mick Hughes. The music was provided by Ilona Sekacz.

The Taming of the Shrew

Geoffrey Freshwater and Graham Turner

The 1992 season in the RST opened with "The Taming of the Shrew", directed by Bill Alexander, designed by Tim Goodchild and starring Amanda Harris as an agreeably brash Katherine with Anton Lesser as Petruchio.

The production was based on the 1990 Royal Shakespeare Company/ British Telecom touring version, which also starred Amanda Harris.

Richard McCabe was Tranio and Trevor Martin was Baptista. Geoffrey Freshwater and Paul Webster were the confusingly-named Grumio and Gremio respectively. Rebecca Saire was Bianca.

The production used some of the problematic and unreliable 1594 quarto. This is a very different text from the one we normally see. Christopher Sly, the drunk for whom the Petruchio/ Katherine play is performed, does not vanish quietly from the story but reappears several times to comment on the action. He also provides the "punchline" at the end of the piece, saying that he now knows how to deal with his own wife. The big laugh this always gets may be partly due to the fact that Sly is no Petruchio.

This framing device is funny but puts the emphasis back on the foolish Sly and sidesteps an issue that has increasingly worried critics. Does Shakespeare think women ought to be treated like this?

As You Like It

Kate Buffery

David Thacker's this forest of Arden, designed by Johan Engels and lit by Jim Simmons, was a black and white affair. Phyllida Hancock's Celia and Samantha Bond's Rosalind (later played by Kate Buffery), stood out in the gloomily oppressive court of Andrew Jarvis' Duke Frederick like candles in a sudden draught. Anthony O'Donnell's Touchstone was a Victorian dream of a cap-and-bells jester, not a nervous clown or Sher-like red-nosed fool. In this deliberately naive approach, some of the play's deeper concerns with role-playing, sexuality and worldly power were inevitably lost and Michael Siberry's darkly cynical Jacques looked out of place. It was no great news (or relief) that the good guys won.

Shaw found the main attraction of "As You Like It" to be the wrestling scene, adding that "it is so much easier to find a man who knows how to wrestle than one who knows how to act." But "As You Like It" is always in danger of being lost beneath its own terminally nice surface spectacle. It is easier to find actors who know how to charm their way through the piece than directors prepared to wrestle with its ambiguities.

The Winter's Tale

Richard McCabe

Adrian Noble's "Winter's Tale" was the most impressive Shakespeare to be found at Stratford in 1992 but may have pulled in the passing crowds more because of the presence of John "Bergerac" Nettles as Leontes.

For some reason "The Winter's Tale" seems always to bring the frock coats out of the RSC wardrobe, but the most memorable thing about this Tale was its brilliant Bohemian summer, designed by Anthony Ward and lit by Chris Parry. It also had a lot of little balloons, which were presumably the result of the big balloons being used in "The Thebans Trilogy" having pupped.

It is odd that such a seemingly arbitrary play can be spoiled by slight miscalculations of tone. Perhaps its very eccentricity increases the chances of directors coming unstuck. In the end, however, Noble hit exactly the right note of edgy pastoral. Even his balloons were anchored to Richard McCabe's wonderful Autolycus. And his stunning finale began with the "statue" of Samantha Bond's Hermione facing away from the audience so that, when she moved, the audience saw only the astonished, unbelieving joy of Nettles' Leontes, Alan Cox's Florizel and Phyllida Hancock's Perdita.

The Merry Wives of Windsor

After a trio of popular hits at the RSC with "Pericles", "Two Gentlemen of Verona" and "As You Like It", David Thacker directed a "Merry Wives" that missed quite substantially.

The production always risked suffering from comparisons with a universally acclaimed RSC "Merry Wives" which transported the play into the Tudorbethan home counties of the 1950s. Indeed, after the year's revelations about what goes on in Windsor Castle and thereabouts, the RSC might have commissioned a "Merry Wives Mark II" from someone like Steve Berkoff or Howard Brenton. But it didn't, and what we got instead was a tame, even boring, show redeemed only by Anton Lesser's Ford, a study in jealousy that made a fascinating comparison with John Nettles' Leontes in "The Winter's Tale". Benjamin Whitrow's Falstaff lost in straight sets to Robert Stephens' brazen and vulnerable giant in "Henry IV" – although we might blame Shakespeare for that as much as Whitrow or Thacker.

John Nettles played Page, Cheryl Campbell was Mistress Page, and Ron Cook was an agreeable Dr Caius. Jeffery Dench was Shallow, Nick Holder was Simple, Barbara Jefford was Mistress Quickly, Pearce Quigley was Slender and Paul Webster was Sir Hugh Evans. William Dudley designed the set.

Antony and Cleopatra

This was the first main house production of "Antony and Cleopatra" in Stratford since Peter Brook's 1978 version, and was the final show to open in the Royal Shakespeare Theatre in 1992. Historically the play could be seen as a sequel to "Julius Caesar", but John Caird's production mercifully had little in common with Steven Pimlott's grim "Caesar", mounted in Stratford a year earlier.

Clare Higgins

Richard Johnson played Antony, a part he took opposite Janet Suzman's Cleopatra in Trevor Nunn's RSC production twenty years ago. His other leading Shakespearean roles have included Romeo, Pericles and Sir Andrew Aguecheek. Clare Higgins rejoined the RSC as Cleopatra, having taken several leading roles in the 1989 season.

Charmian was played by Claire Benedict. Paul Jesson was a movingly disillusioned and shattered Enobarbus. John Nettles played the clinical Octavius Caesar and Toby Stephens was Pompey. Sue Blane designed the set and the production was lit by David Hersey. The music was by Ilona Sekacz.

The Beggar's Opera

John Caird's production of "The Beggar's Opera" kicked the Swan season off in style.

John Gay's 1728 "Newgate Pastoral", a send-up of fashionable Italian operas, allegedly made Gay rich and made Rich (the theatre manager at Lincoln's Inn Fields) gay. This production could hardly make such an impression as the original, but was certainly an RSC success.

Ilona Sekacz joined the notables such as Benjamin Britten who have arranged music for the play. The resulting pastiches, ranging from heavy metal music to cabaret songs, were livelier and more entertaining than some of the RSC's past attempts at "real" musicals. They certainly captured the parodic spirit of the original and gave the cast the chance (which they took) to fill Kendra Ullyart's sets with some enjoyably rumbustious acting. David Burt starred as Macheath with Susie Lee Hayward as Jenny and Elizabeth Renihan as Polly Peachum.

What was lost, however, was the political and social satire of the original. It is hard to imagine Brecht being inspired to write "The Threepenny Opera" by Caird's anarchic, pantomimic spectacle. Only Nick Holder's Matt of the Mint held on to some of Gay's outraged cynicism.

A Jovial Crew

Ron Cook

1992 was a good year for beggars in the Swan. Richard Brome's worried Caroline comedy (possibly the last play to be mounted before war and the puritans closed down the English theatres for two decades) concerns the fortunes of the "jovial crew" of England's vagrants. Its topicality in that respect was not lost on the audience.

The RSC described the play as "rarely-performed". This was the understatement of the century – indeed of the last two and a half centuries – since the last time anybody wheeled it out was in 1724.

But what we got in The Swan was not what Brome wrote. Max Stafford-Clark, whose Stratford debut this was, brought in award-winning writer Stephen Jeffreys to revise the play, changing Brome's words and adding to them. And asking Ian Drury of Blockheads fame (who also wrote the songs for Caryl Churchill's "Serious Money") to provide the songs was a guarantee of not getting too much olde England.

Paul Jesson was an appealing Squire Oldrents, with Rebecca Saire and Emily Raymond as his daughters who run away to a band of beggars. Ron Cook was touching as Springlove, Oldrent's steward, an ex-beggar tormented by the call of the wild.

All's Well That Ends Well

Michael Siberry and Rebecca Saire

"All's Well" saw Sir Peter Hall return to Stratford after twenty-five years and Richard Johnson (playing the King of France) rejoin the RSC after an absence of two decades. Guy Woolfenden was celebrating his thirtieth season as a composer for the company. As you would expect, these veterans can do a "problem comedy" and make it look as easy as falling off a log.

This comedy, though, was very short on laughs. Toby Stephens' Bertram and Sophie Thompson's Helena seemed blind and blinkered respectively. Any sort of understanding to which their sufferings might have led them was a fragile one. Michael Siberry's wretched Parolles learnt little from his painful humiliation. Johnson's King and Barbara Jefford's Countess were authority-figures wearied by their own status.

Was Hall giving us a cynical old stager's view of youthful certainties? His bare and powerful production emphasised the emotions and relationships in the play. But the characters seemed, if not exactly two dimensional, at least the victims of their fairy story and even of their happy ending, capable of suffering but not reacting.

Surprisingly, this was the first time Hall has directed "All's Well". His jury is clearly still out on just how well it is really.

Tamburlaine the Great

Anthony Sher and Jasper Britton

Terry Hands' production of Marlowe's epic "Tamburlaine" compressed, as the RSC tactfully put it, both parts of the play into a single evening. To be fair, it is hard to imagine punters turning out in droves for two evenings of "Tamburlaine", even if enticed by the prospect of Anthony Sher as another nasty but irresistible nutter. It is an accepted practice to cut lengthy works – Noble's "Henry IV", for instance, shed some 800 lines between page and stage. But something vital was lost in this huge reduction of the plays' span and Marlowe was not wholly well-served by the result.

Sher, however, was extremely well-served by this chance to shine in a wonderfully overwritten role, no matter how truncated it was. His fiery Tamburlaine completely dominated the stage, obscuring many other fine actors, including Jasper Britton as Calyphas and Trevor Martin as the Soldan of Egypt. Malcolm Storry was a striking and imperious Bazajeth and Claire Benedict was a moving Zenocrate. But Sher's mesmeric performance stole the show and everything in it that wasn't nailed down.

The Changeling

Cheryl Campbell

The final play of the season in the Swan was Thomas Middleton and William Rowley's 1622 tragi-comedy "The Changeling", directed by RSC Executive Producer Michael Attenborough.

The RSC last mounted "The Changeling" in 1978 in a version directed by Terry Hands.

Like most Jacobean plays of this kind, "The Changeling" provides chill laughs, black humour and the guarantee of a bloody ending. And like most of them it is deeply concerned with lust and murder. (For good measure it also throws in corruption and madness.)

Cheryl Campbell (who joined the company as Mistress Page in "The Merry Wives of Windsor") played Beatrice-Joanna and Malcolm Storry was an impressive De Flores.

Other roles were taken by Stephen Casey as Tomazo, Jeffery Dench as Vermandero, Geoffrey Freshwater as Lollio, Emily Raymond as Isabella, Michael Siberry as Alsemero, Paul Webster as Alibius and David Westhead as Antonio.

The set was designed by Julian McGowan and Andreane Neofitou was responsible for the costumes. The production was lit by Alan Burrett and had music by Paddy Cunneen.

The Odyssey

Sophie Okonedo

Although better-known as a poet, Derek Walcott, the winner of the 1992 Nobel Prize for literature, is a veteran playwright. "The Odyssey" arises from his reading of Homer and is a striking and successful piece of work, with a text that is richly sensuous, complex and sometimes allusive, but which always manages to maintain the comfortable momentum of a familiar story well told.

Gregory Doran's production grew out of a workshop held at The Other Place in 1991. The leading role of Odysseus was taken by Ron Cook, fresh from playing a different type of wanderer in "A Jovial Crew", who was a streetwise (or seawise) and funny, non-too-heroic hero. Amanda Harris was his Penelope. Claire Benedict was Eurycleia and Bella Enahoro was Circe.

The designer Michael Pavelka gave us a highly dramatic view of Walcott's Caribbean-style Mediterranean, with a brilliantly theatrical storm, the dead rising ghoulishly from Hades, and several other startling and memorable coups de théâtre.

Richard III

Simon Russell Beale

Sam Mendes' production of "Richard III" was the second production of the year in Stratford's Other Place. It will deservedly be seen in London at the reopened Donmar Warehouse after touring nationally (like several other recent Richards) and before returning to Stratford in 1993.

Simon Russell Beale has played several larger than life villains in recent RSC productions, including Mr Hyde and Thersites. He has also given us Edward II and a shattering and subtle Konstantin in "The Seagull". His astonishing Richard III was a menacing comic grotesque, aptly referred to by one critic as "toad-like". If the jet black humour sometimes blunted the play's harsh edge it at least reminded us of the origins of Shakespeare's Richard in the rough and tumble world of medieval morality plays. This Richard was as distinctive as any by Olivier, McKellen or Sher.

Annabelle Apsion was Lady Anne, Stephen Boxer was Buckingham, Simon Dormandy was Clarence, Kate Duchene was Queen Elizabeth, Chris Hunter was Hastings, Mark Lewis Jones was Richmond and Cherry Morris was Queen Margaret. The production was designed by Tim Hatley and lit by Paul Pyant.

The School of Night

Bill Alexander

"The School of Night" is a new play by Peter Whelan. It was directed by Bill Alexander, who was also responsible for last year's fine production of Whelan's "The Bright and Bold Design" in The Pit. It was the last play to open in The Other Place in 1992.

"The School of Night" is a political thriller set in the late sixteenth century. It is actually a play dealing – imaginatively, since documentary evidence is hard to come by – with the strange life and violent death of Christopher Marlowe, played by Richard McCabe as the unstable twin brother of his Autolycus in "The Winter's Tale". The world of spies (in which Marlowe was undoubtedly mixed up) and the world of theatrical pretence become inextricably entwined as the hunted Marlowe takes refuge in a deserted theatre that once presented his violent, political plays. (The RSC was not slow to point out that Marlowe's "Tamburlaine the Great" just happens to be running at the Swan.)

The cast included Bella Enahoro as Rosalinda Benotti, Jack Klaff as Sir Walter Ralegh, Adrian Lukis as Thomas Kyd, John McAndrew as Thomas Walsingham, Rebecca Saire as Audry Walsingham and Graham Turner as Ingram Frizer.

THE REGIONAL GUIDE

The Yearbook offers a unique coverage of theatre across the United Kingdom. Locally-based journalists provide a survey of the theatrical year in the their region and then review the work of the key theatre in each area.

SCOTLAND

by MARK FISHER

Scotland '92

It was a year of new theatres north of the border. Despite the recession, a quite remarkable number of new or up-graded performance spaces came into being. The single most important of these involved the Traverse's relocation from the less salubrious end of Edinburgh's Grassmarket to the custom-built underground site next door to the Usher Hall and the Royal Lyceum. Vying for the limelight was the Citizen's Theatre in Glasgow which trebled its output at a stroke at the beginning of the year, with the introduction of two studio theatres to complement its traditional main-stage space.

These would be developments enough for the eager Scottish play-goer, but 1992 heralded a surfeit of new theatres including the Lemon Tree in Aberdeen, the Drama Centre at Ramshorn, Glasgow, the Mercat Theatre, Drumchapel and the Corn Exchange, Edinburgh. Meanwhile, Glasgow's ill-fated Third Eye Centre (which had established a reputation in the field of performance art to rival that of London's ICA before the receivers were called in to sort out a massive accumulated debt in 1991), returned to the scene re-christened the Centre for Contemporary Arts, first in Mayfest and then full-time in September. And just in time for Glasgow's spring jamboree, the Tron Theatre unveiled its welcome new seating plan which got rid of the awkward old balcony and increased its seating capacity. All this, less than a year after major renovation work at both Edinburgh's Royal Lyceum and Theatre Workshop, and with the opening of the capital's Empire Theatre still to come (due to open summer 1994).

Such developments were clearly welcome, but the year wasn't all rosy. Both the Royal Lyceum and Wildcat went through perilous financial crises, bringing home how vulnerable even our most successful companies are when funding is restricted and the recession bites. The artistic output throughout Scotland was a lot lower than it was only a couple of years ago and much of what was produced was thanks to the dedication of theatre professionals who were prepared to work for next to nothing. Glasgow's Arches Theatre, a remnant of the city's Year of Culture celebrations, was a case in point; it would not have survived without the tireless input of Artistic Director Andy Arnold who mounted a series of solid, low-budget productions of plays including "V", "The Caretaker" and "A Taste Of Honey". In contrast, fully professional theatres, notably The Tron and Cumbernauld Theatre, were restricted in the amount of in-house work they could stage – a great shame when Michael Boyd's "Good" and "The Guid Sisters", Caroline Hall's "The Bloody Chamber" (all for the Tron) and Liz Carruthers' productions of "To", "Me, Myself, Us" and "Lust" (for Cumbernauld) were popular and critical successes. The pioneering work of Glasgow's Tramway continued to fill in the gaps by inviting foreign companies as diverse as the Maly Theatre of St Petersburg "Gaudeamus", Els Joglars "I have an Uncle in America" and the Wooster Group "Brace Up" to Scotland.

But perhaps most of all, 1992 was a year of transition. As well as the many new theatres, there were new directors at Mull Little Theatre, the Brunton Theatre, Musselburgh, Scottish Youth Theatre, Dundee Rep, TAG and the Edinburgh International Festival, and in most cases, caution was the key policy. In the year of the biggest ever Edinburgh Fringe and some of the most important front and back stage developments in decades, Scottish theatre gave itself a firm foundation on which to build.

Citizens' Theatre, Glasgow

Just when it looked as if the Citizens' might have been running out of energy after twenty-odd years in the business of producing challenging theatre, it came up with an idea that caught everyone by surprise but – typically for the Citz' – that made instant and perfect sense. Holding on to its existing 600-seater auditorium, the theatre covered some of the bar area in its spacious foyer into two performance spaces of 130 seats and 70 seats respectively. The new theatres liberated the directorial truimvirate of Giles Havergal, Robert David MacDonald and Philip Prowse from the commercial pressure of the big stage, and allowed them to introduce experimental, obscure and new pieces, as well as plays that simply were better suited to a more intimate environment. With characteristic lack of fanfare, the company casually began its year by opening three plays at a time, giving audiences a chance to tune in much more clearly to the styles and ideas of the respective directors, and bringing two welcome additions to Glasgow's increasingly healthy stock of theatres.

Niagara

Baptising the smallest of the two new studio spaces with a two-hander about the balancing feats of Charles Blondin across the waters of Niagara Falls, Robert David MacDonald both starred in and translated this play by Chilean writer Alonso Alegria. MacDonald played Blondin, presented as a skilled artisan at the height of his powers – and giddy heights they were. Daniel Illsey played the boyish admirer, Carlo, who while in awe of the tightrope-walker, is also aware of his little deceits. Together they form a pact to cross the falls with one on the other's back. It is a simple enough plot, but one which gives rise to an existential debate full of dazzling speeches which the two actors tackled with poise and low-key control. Kenny Miller designed.

Daniel Illseley and Robert David MacDonald

1953

One of the exciting aspects of the shows in the Citizens' studios was that the various designers were unintimidated by the confined spaces; they just went ahead and filled them with their usual flair and flamboyance. Thus "1953", Philip Prowse's debut production in the 130-seat Second Theatre of a startling play by Craig Raine (first performed on Radio Three in 1990). Projecting a less favourable end to World War II, Raine sets his play in Fascist Rome where a Nazi delegation threatens to undermine an edgy status quo as passion and duty come into conflict. A reworking of Racine's "Andromache", the play came across as powerful, violent and poetic – a certain highlight of the Citizens' year – and was graced with thrillingly intense performances from Greg Hicks, Tristram Jellinek, Julia Blalock and others.

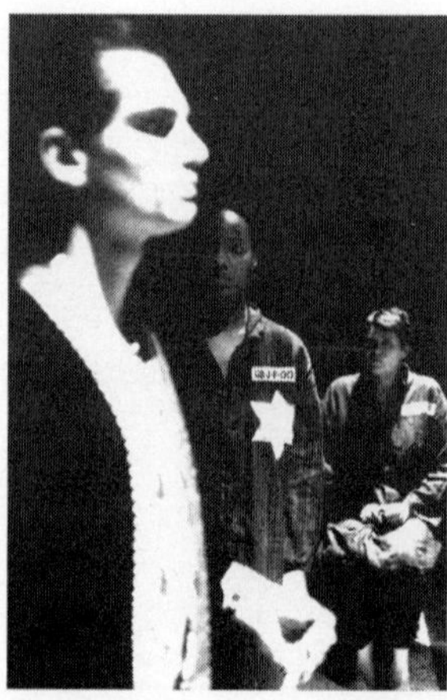

Patrick O'Kane, Julie Saunders and Ellen Sheean

Summer Lightning

Matthew Radford and Colin Wells

Directed and adapted by Giles Havergal, this staging of P.G. Wodehouse's eleven Blandings novels confirmed the theatre's commitment to elegant popular productions, while more esoteric experiments took place in its studios. Gathering its own crazy momentum over two-and-a-half hours, Havergal's production had a lightness of touch that made the trivial tale both very funny and – like his version of Graham Greene's "Travels with my Aunt" which was revived for a national tour during the year – unhampered by the mix of dialogue and narration. The cast of seven, which cut effortlessly from character to character, included Stephen McDonald, Anne Myatt, Siobhan Stanley, Matthew Whittle, Matthew Radford, Helen Baxendale and Colin Wells. Kenny Miller was the designer.

The Pelican

Anne Myatt and Helen Baxendale

One of the most memorable sets of the Citizens' spring season was for Strindberg's little-known one-act drama about a middle-class Swedish mother whose children force her to hear the truth about herself after many years of deceit. Designed by the director, Ian Spink, better known from the world of choreography, the set in the tiny Third Theatre was a murky pool of water which lapped at up-turned period furniture and soaked the logs for the fire. A good deal of climbing and splashing ensued from a strong cast including Anne Myatt a the mother, Matthew Whittle as the disillusioned and wasted son, and Helen Baxendale as the highly-charged daughter. The production drew an interesting parallel with Strindberg's own Intimate Theatre which he dedicated to experimental drama.

Casanova Undone

Siobhan Stanley and Tristram Jellinek

One of the developments brought in with the new spaces at the Citizens', was the increased opportunity to stage new plays by writers not otherwise associated with the directorial triumvirate. One such play was Dic Edwards' pacey comedy about the last days of the infamous lover Casanova. Played here forcefully by Tristram Jellinek, Casanova has become impotent with age and has only his reputation and memories on which to survive. While the French Revolution rages outside, his assistant Costa, played with plucky pragmatism by Roberta Taylor, helps him carry off his deceit with a string of eligible young women. Robert David MacDonald directed an intelligent and sexy production with a typically opulent set by Kenny Miller.

Lulu

Julie Saunders

Jon Pope, Artistic Director of Lancaster's Dukes Theatre, renewed his relationship with the Citizens' with this modern-dress production of Frank Wedekind's long two-part play about a sexually promiscuous young woman and the men who crumble in her wake. With charming Julie Saunders in the title role, the play came across as strikingly contemporary in its detail of child abuse, drug abuse, prostitution and AC/DC sexual activity. Pope also took the design credit – an airy black and white set, spliced in two by a silver-foil curtain and graced with the wreck of a bright red car. Both lighting (Michael Lancaster) and musical score (Adrian Johnston) were given high-profile – the music repeatedly cutting in mid-scene and the lights self-consciously casting unnatural shadows about the stage.

Other Places

Ellen Sheean and Jill Spurrier

The highlight of this compilation of three plays by Harold Pinter was Ellen Sheean's portrayal of Deborah in "A Kind of Alaska", a woman who "wakes" after having spent all her adult life in a state of inertia. Based on the research of Oliver Sacks, the play gave Sheean the chance to turn in a harrowing performance as a woman coming suddenly to terms with her losses and her gains. This play followed "One for the Road", an uncompromising vision of state torture, and "Family Voices", an amusing look at the nature of filial love. Giles Havergal directed the trio in the Third Theatre with a cast comprising Derwent Watson, Matthew Radford and Jill Spurrier. Kenny Miller designed.

Edward II

Patrick O'Kane, Henry Ian Cusiack and Tristram Jellinek

The mainstage offering during Mayfest was Philip Prowse's production of Brecht's "Edward II", a relatively little-known reworking of Marlowe's tragedy about the misplaced allegiances of a king. As ever, Prowse was the designer, staging the action on and around a set of wooden palettes with an ecclesiastical backdrop which by the second act had been stripped down to leave only metallic greys and brutal blacks. In the lead role was Laurence Rudic who turned in perhaps his best performance of the year in a part that took him from Buddhist tranquillity to defiant sexuality to soulful lament. His lover, Gaveston, was played by Patrick O'Kane, and his wife, Queen Anne, by Julie Blalock. Also appearing in this uncut version were Tristram Jellinek, Stephen MacDonald and Colin Wells.

Royal Lyceum

It was a year of consolidation for Edinburgh's Royal Lyceum, which sought to attract back the large audiences that had been built up before the company's itinerant 1990-91 season while renovation work took place at its Grindlay Street site. There was a crisis in the spring when money got tight for the extensive rebuilding programme, but happily the District Council confirmed its support at the eleventh hour. After nine years in the job, Artistic Director Ian Wooldridge announced that he was to resign after his spring 1993 season, but only after he had unveiled another varied line-up of classic and contemporary drama and comedy. Highlights of the autumn season included Moliere's "School for Wives", Pinter's "Old Times" and Tom McGrath's "Laurel and Hardy".

Arsenic and Old Lace

Cavada Humphrey and Elizabeth Tyrell

The Royal Lyceum likes to ease us gently from the panto season and appropriately, Joseph Kesselring's comedy-thriller, staged by guest-director Ben Twist, kicked off the theatre's year with a shot of black humour. Starring Cavada Humphrey and Elizabeth Tyrell as the aged, weird sisters with a penchant for collecting dead bodies, the play emerged as much more than a 1940s period piece thanks to the durability of its well-crafted plot and the company's pacey staging. Stuart McQuarrie played the part of the eager young journalist, and Michael Atwell (of Eastenders fame) and Clive Mendus (a regular with Theatre de Complicite) effectively took the parts of the psychotic criminals once played by Raymond Massey and Peter Lorre. Neil Warmington's bright and airy realistic set played against the drama's morbid associations.

The Marriage of Figaro

Robert Carr and Ann Louise Ross

A huge and unqualified hit with critics and audience alike, this production threw off its operatic associations and returned to the original satirical comedy by Pierre Beaumarchais. Directed by Ian Wooldridge with carefree abandon, "The Marriage of Figaro" became an over-the-top romp which showed some of Scotland's finest comic actors at their best. Jimmy Chisholm was particularly memorable for his camp interpretation of Cherubin, but he was just one of a sparkling cast that included Michael Nardone (in the lead role), Tam Dean Burn (who, ironically, while playing the count was standing as a Communist candidate in the General Election), Muriel Romanes, Kern Falconer, Robert Carr and others. Full marks to designer Gregory Smith for joining in the fun too. The production also played in Stirling and Glasgow.

Uncle Vanya

This interpretation of Chekhov's ironic character comedy was directed by Hugh Hodgart with a mature and sensitive attention to detail. Performed with Scots accents, the play was newly translated by Stuart Paterson (Scotland's most successful writer of Christmas shows) who did much justice to the original, bringing out its earthiness as well as its eloquence. The spacious set, with just an evocative smattering of period furniture, was designed by Gregory Smith who had a big influence on lifting the gloominess so often associated with Chekhov. Communicado's Gerry Mulgrew played the lead role with a nice line in ironic humour, while Ruth Gemmell as Yelena Andreyvna gave a quiet, but controlled performance full of nervous mannerisms and distracted twitches. Also appearing were Michael MacKenzie, Mabel Aitken, Nancy Mitchell, Alexander Morton, Steve Owen and Primrose Milligan.

Ruth Gemmell, Gerard Mulgrew and Mabel Aitken

Merlin

An incredibly ambitious production, pulled off with flair and imagination, "Merlin" was a three-hour adaptation of Tankred Dorst's German epic that in some versions runs to twelve hours. Tom McGrath, Scottish Arts Council Literary Director, worked from a literal translation by Ella Wildridge and created an earthy, Scottish version of this eclectic Knights of the Round Table drama. Ian Wooldridge directed, stretching the Royal Lyceum's technical forces to the full, with a visual and musical feast that emulated the avant-garde European flavour of the original. So successful was the production that the theatre later committed itself to mounting a follow-up in 1993. Kern Falconer played Merlin from stark-naked baby to wise but eccentric wizard, supported by a large and exuberant cast. The script was published in "Theatre Scotland" magazine.

Michael Nardone and Carol Ann Crawford

Cuttin' A Rug

Directed by Ben Twist after his success earlier in the year with "Arsenic and Old Lace", "Cuttin' A Rug" began the theatre's summer season of comedy that also included Tom Stoppard's "Travesties", Noel Coward's "Hay Fever" and P G Wodehouse's "Good Morning Bill". The second part of John Byrne's "Slab Boys Trilogy" first performed at the Traverse in the late 70s and early 80s, "Cuttin' A Rug" is a kind of Glaswegian "Stags and Hens" in which the loveable rogues from the first play go courting at the company Christmas dance. Primarily a vehicle for Bryne's punchline Paisley patter, the play was given a tight, pacey production. Nick Sargent came up with a reversible, skeletal set which inventively marked the outline of the dance hall.

Lewis Howden, John Straiton and Simon McCallum

Traverse Theatre

A major chapter in the history of one of Britain's foremost houses for new writing was begun when the Traverse Theatre finally said goodbye to its dilapidated though atmospheric Grassmarket home and moved into a custom-built basement theatre next door to the Usher Hall and the Royal Lyceum. The old building had served it well and many were deeply sorry to see it go, but the opportunities opened up by the arrival of a theatre nearly three times the size were embraced with enthusiasm by Artistic Director Ian Brown and his company. Arguing that this was the first purpose-built theatre for new writing since Shakespeare's Globe, Brown renewed his commitment to producing challenging provocative and, most of all, entertaining new work by Scottish and international writers. As ever, a major centre in the Edinburgh Fringe, the Traverse made a bold and confident move that set it in a favourably strong position for the future.

Your Turn To Clean The Stair

Louise Ironside

In a city dominated by tenement accommodation where a great many households of all classes share a common stair, Rona Munro's play was bound to be a hit with local audiences. A murder-mystery which the playwright described as less of a whodunnit than a whydunnit, "Your Turn to Clean the Stair" had a backdrop of nosy neighbours, illicit relationships and domestic disputes. And Munro, the writer of the award winning "Bold Girls" and a member of comedy duo The Misfits, mixed in a healthy helping of humour and feminism. John Mitchell, a founder-member of Edinburgh's lunchtime theatre company Oxygen House, directed a production that starred Janet Dye, Louise Ironside, John Ramage, Graham Di Banzie and Kay Gallie, and put his trademark stamp of atmospheric lighting and moody music on top.

Columbus: Blooding the Ocean

Akim Mogaji and Stuart Hepburn

Appropriately for a theatre that was setting sail into unknown waters, the first production at the Traverse's new Cambridge Street home was about a great explorer. 500 years after Columbus set eyes on the Americas, "Columbus: Blooding the Ocean" was one of several plays, films and documentaries which sought to re-assess this major historical event. Written by the Italian-born Michele Celeste, whose "Hanging the President" was a big Fringe hit in 1989, the play was set on board ship on the return leg of one of the explorer's transatlantic journeys. Jacqeline Gunn's realistic wooden set filled the stage for the theatre's debut production which starred Stuart Hepburn as Columbus. Artistic Director Ian Brown was at the helm of a play which returned to the theatre in the Edinburgh Fringe.

The Life of Stuff

Stuart McQuarrie

One of the most distinctive – and distinguished – new plays of the year in Scotland was Simon Donald's urban comedy set in a drug-crazed underworld warehouse where a party is about to be thrown to celebrate the establishment of a new gangland order. Donald came up with a hilarious black comedy written with economy and precision and involving everything from an amputated toe to an Ecstasy-overdose. Stuart McQuarrie played Leonard, the thug with an excema problem, Kern Falconer played Arboghast, Brian McCardie played Fraser, spending much of the play in his underwear, Duncan Duff played Dobie, the in-coming underworld boss, and Mable Aitken and Shirley Henderson turned in inspiring performances as Holly and Evelyn, the pill-popping party-goers. John Mitchell directed and design was by Nick Sargent.

The House Among The Stars

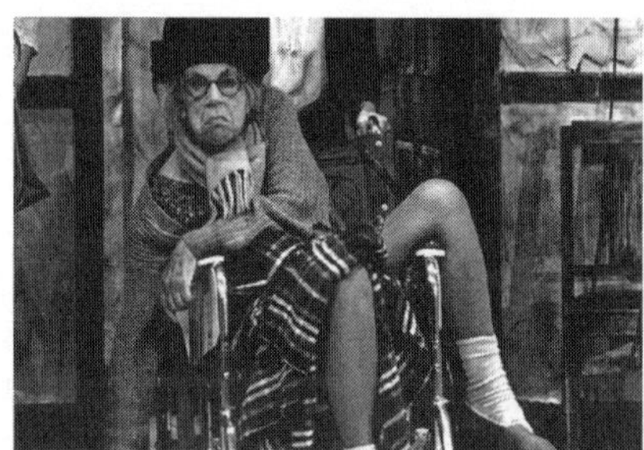

Bill Findlay and Martin Bowman's most successful translation of a Michel Tremblay play was the Tron Theatre's "The Guid Sisters".

The first of two autumn shows, "The House Among The Stars" is a recent play by the prolific French-Canadian writer, Michel Tremblay, which was first performed in Montreal in 1990. Translated by Bill Findlay and Martin Bowman, the play takes place in a country log cabin which has been the refuge of three generations of a family from the early 1900s, the 50s and the present day. All three eras eerily appear on stage together and echo each other's speeches, completely unaware of anyone outside their own generation. The family's history emerges in poignant fragments and draws on characters that Tremblay has used in previous plays and novels. Ian Brown was the director and Geraldine Pilgrim the designer, with a cast that included Eileen Nicholas, Jennifer Black and Stuart McQuarrie.

Unidentified Human Remains and the True Nature of Love

While most theatres were in full swing with their annual pantomime, the Traverse offered a substantial alternative with the British premiere of a recent play by Canadian writer, Brad Fraser. Described as a cross between "Tales of the City" and "Twin Peaks", "Unidentified Human Remains and the True Nature of Love" is a racy, sexy, witty and chilling play. David, a waiter who used to be a soap-opera star, cruises gay bars for fast sex. Candy his flatmate and ex-lover, has problems with food and is re-examining her own sexual preferences. They live in a big city in Central Canada where a serial killer is stalking the streets. The killings are bizarre, mysterious and unmotivated and have a profound effect on the relationships of a group of friends who are strangely caught up with the lives of the murder victims. This sharp and wickedly funny play – the second Canadian play in a row at the Traverse – was directed by Artistic Director Ian Brown and designed by Nick Sargent.

Dundee Rep

After a financially insecure start to the year, Dundee Rep welcomed on board Hamish Glen who took over as Artistic Director from Robert Robertson who left to further his acting career. Glen, who came from touring company Winged Horse after stints with Edinburgh's Royal Lyceum and Glasgow's Tron, began his first season in August with a commitment to providing classic plays (Scottish, British and foreign) presented in an accessible way. Thus he kicked off with plays by C P Taylor, Moliere and Edward Albee, all delivered in an authentic Scottish register. A further element to Glen's strategy for attracting audiences was the integration of the writers' group, the dance company and the community programme in order to build a coherent image for the theatre.

Michael Duke was appointed associate director with special responsibility for the Rep's much-praised community drama and brought with him an impressive track-record of work in the field.

Walter

The first play of Hamish Glen's debut season was actually a commission by the Edinburgh International Festival as part of director Brian McMaster's C P Taylor season. It fitted nicely into Glen's programme of Scots-accented work and it made obvious sense for him to make his first mark with a production from the prestigious EIF. Freely based on the life of Glasgow music hall star, Walter Jackson, Taylor's play is about the aspirations and achievements of an entertainer more deeply rooted in his Jewish culture than he cares to admit. Originally written in two parts, this production was adapted and integrated by playwright Michael Wilcox. Kenny Miller's imposing set was graced by Tom Watson as Walter with support from Vincent Friell, Phil McCall, Tom McGovern, Sandra Voe and Tracey Wilkinson.

Tom Watson and Tracey Wilkinson

Tartuffe

Much of Hamish Glen's work has been with Scottish versions of classic plays, so it was no surprise to see him turning to Liz Lochhead's celebrated treatment of Moliere, a writer whose work adapts remarkably well to a Scottish idiom. This translation was first performed by Edinburgh's Royal Lyceum Theatre Company in 1986 and was published by Polygon. In Lochhead's own words, the translation is "proverbial, slangy, couthy cliched, catch-phrasey and vulgar"; it's also very funny and true to the satirical spirit of Moliere. For Dundee's production Glen assembled a strong cast including the excellent Jimmy Chisholm as Tartuffe, with Ida Schuster, Isabella Jarrett, Vicki Masson, Tony Cownie, Billy Riddoch, David Tennant and Bill Murdoch.

Perth Theatre

After reaching an average of ninety per cent capacity audiences in its spring season, Perth Theatre extended the length of each run from two weeks to three for the autumn, meaning that the building will be open for almost the whole year round. A major achievement by any standards – Perth can boast that it is Scotland's most successful repertory theatre - and even more so given that Artistic Director Joan Knight has been a remarkable thirty years in the job. After delaying her departure, she will finally say goodbye to the theatre at the start of next year and will be remembered with great fondness. As well as its traditional varied programme of plays by Tennessee Williams – "The Glass Menagerie" – Michael Frayn – "Noises Off" – Gilbert and Sullivan – "The Mikado" – Liz Lochhead – "Mary Queen of Scots Got Her Head Chopped Off" - and others, the theatre also had an entertaining package of bar entertainment, including comedy, poetry, music and even wine tastings.

Wuthering Heights

Sharon Small and Colin Gourley

Artistic Director Joan Knight came up with a faithful adaptation of Emily Bronte's classic tale of unbreakable love, passion and revenge on the Yorkshire Moors, for this production which was directed by Ken Alexander. Keeping the original nineteenth century setting, the played starred Sharon Small, on her first appearance at Perth, as Catherine Earnshaw, the respectable farmer's daughter, and Colin Gourley, who has been seen on "Taggart" and "Eastenders", as the wild and untamed gypsy boy, Heathcliffe. With music specially written by John Scrimger and played by Ian Strachan, the production boasted a period set design by Janet Scarfe. Also in the cast were Martin James, Alec Heggie, Paul Nivison, Amanda Beveride, Jean Rimmer, Anthony Houghton, Steven Wren, Astrid Wilson, Gordon MacArthur and Sandra Grieve.

Little Shop of Horrors

Andrew Wrightman and Michael Roberts

The climax of Perth's spring season was a production of this popular musical with lyrics by Howard Ashman and music by Alan Menken, who won the Oscar for Best Original Score for Disney's "Beauty and the Beast" this year. Set in downtown Skid Row, a fantasy 50s American suburb, the show is set in Mushnik's flower shop where a bizarre plant, named Audrey II, begins to grow and grow.........and grow. This production made use of the original West End plant puppets. Averill Cameron, Anthea Ferrell and Ruby-Marie Huthison recreated the girl-group backing band, and Sharon Small, fresh from her leading role in "Wuthering Heights", played the plant's namesake, Audrey. Ken Alexander directed the show which also starred Andrew Wrightman, Michael Roberts, Steven Wren, Amanda Beveridge and Ian Grieve.

Pitlochry Festival Theatre

Opening at the beginning of May with an extended seven-play season and, as usual several plays running concurrently, Pitlochry Festival Theatre's big pull was to have popular Scottish variety and comedy star Jimmy Logan starring in three plays in the season. Ambitiously, the company opened with the complete "Norman Conquests" trilogy by Alan Ayckbourn, with all three instalments opening in the first two days. Logan made his debut appearance at the theatre in Bob Larbey's gentle comedy "The Dominion of Fancy", and in Arthur Miller's "Death of a Salesman" as Willy Loman. Agatha Christie's "Spider's Web" and Fay Weldon's adaptation of "Jane Eyre" were also in the season. Festival Director Clive Perry announced his intention to support new writing where possible and unveiled plans to embark on a programme of building repairs and improvements that will last until 1994.

The Norman Conquests

Alan Ayckbourn's famous comedy trilogy comprising "Table Manners", "Living Together" and "Round and Round the Garden", three self-contained plays in which the action overlaps in time and place, opened the 1992 season at Pitlochry. The company ran a series of special trilogy Saturdays on which the audience could enjoy all three plays and indulge in a bit of nostalgia – a tent was erected in the theatre grounds to provide a picnic supper for the all-day audiences and to remind them of the first thirty years of the company's history which was all under canvas. Directed by Clive Perry, the plays, which Ayckbourn claimed to have written in a single week, starred Graham McTavish, Angela Chadfield, Anne Kidd, Colin Mace, Rosaleen Pelan and Eric Barlow. Design was by Trevor Coe.

Colin Mace

The Dominion of Fancy

This was the year that Stewart Conn, a highly-respected drama producer with Radio Scotland, resigned his position with the BBC in protest at increasing bureaucracy and in order to concentrate on his own writing career. "The Dominion of Fancy", which was premiered at Pitlochry at the end of July, was a comedy by Conn set in 1820s Glasgow and based on the real-life rivalry between actor-managers John Henry Alexander and Francis Seymour. In increasingly outlandish attempts to steal each other's thunder, they set up neighbouring theatres and mount competing productions. With spectacular set and costumes appropriate to the period, the production was designed by Ken Harrison and directed by Clive Perry. Starring in the twenty-strong cast were Eric Barlow as Alexander and Colin Mace as Seymour.

Graham McTavish, Colin Mace, Jimmy Logan, Eric Barlow, James Murray and Rosaleen Pelan

Tron Theatre, Glasgow

A good year for the Tron which began in 1992 by unveiling a refitted auditorium with the kind of professional-looking seating that its productions had long suggested. The new single-tier rake got rid of the distancing effect of the old balcony and increased seating capacity by 52 to 272. It also allowed for a proper lighting box. Yet the converted church space lost none of its cosy atmosphere.

As well as contributing to Mayfest and the Edinburgh International Festival, the company remounted its excellent production of Michel Tremblay's "The Guid Sisters" ("Les Belles Soeurs") for an international tour with Dorothy Paul taking the lead role, and mounted an impressive season of imported Irish theatre in the autumn. It rounded off the year in typically robust style with a new pantomime by the increasingly successful Forbes Masson (star of TV's "My Dead Dad").

Good

The highlight of the C P Taylor retrospective in the Edinburgh International Festival and also a hit at Glasgow's Mayfest, Michael Boyd's revival of "Good" matched the brilliance of the writing with a rich, psychologically-considered production. Graham Johnstone designed a splendidly-balanced neo-classical set consisting of five doors out of which the action – sometimes frightening, sometimes bizarre – would emerge. Telling the story of Halder (Conrad Asquith), a German intellectual who compromises and compromises until the point where he finds himself working for the Nazis, the play is a powerful reminder that it was ordinary people not evil monsters who facilitated the fascist regime. One of the many delights of Boyd's production was the five-strong band which would appear at the most unexpected moments to entertain or haunt Halder (musical director Gordon Dougall). Also in the cast were Derek Anders, Fiona Bell, Jennifer Black, Eliza Langlands, Ronnie Letham, Edith MacArthur, Billy McColl and Tom Smith.

The Bloody Chamber

Peter Mullan, Vanya Eadie and Anne Lacey

Performed in the Centre for Contemporary Arts, this Tron theatre production directed by Caroline Hall owed much to the kind of experimental work seen in the CCA under its old guise as the Third Eye Centre. Hall, however, made this adaptation of Angela Carter's short story very much her own in an entrancing production that gave equal weight to visuals, music and text. Based on the Bluebeard story and developing the music from Bartok's "Bluebeard's Castle", the production was short but totally satisfying, using the great depth of the upstairs performance space to stunning effect. The cast who because of the nature of their work, made a particularly important contribution, were Vanya Eadie, Anne Lacey and Peter Mullan. Jane Gardner was the composer and Angela Davies the designer.

NORTHERN IRELAND

by LYNDA HENDERSON

Northern Ireland '92

The most potentially influential events of 1992 were the publication of the Deane Report on Training for the Arts in Northern Ireland, strongly recommending the establishment here for the first time, in Belfast or Derry, of a Theatre School, with an attached theatre and resource centre for the arts; and of the Priestley Report on Structures and Arrangements for Funding the Arts in Northern Ireland, recommending sweeping changes in the operation of the Arts Council.

Professional theatre in Northern Ireland is largely limited to the major cities and a few towns where there are theatres and arts centres: Belfast and Derry; Coleraine, Downpatrick, Enniskillen and Newry. Derry and Belfast also house the province's two major touring companies, respectively Field Day and Charabanc. Both tour extensively outside Ireland, earning respectful international reputations. A third company, Theatre Ulster, is currently moribund, but an exciting addition is The O'Casey Company, set up by Shivaun O'Casey, based in Newry with its second international tour this year. Coleraine has the Riverside Theatre and Enniskillen the Ardhowen Theatre, each offering programmes largely drawn from touring productions. Newry and Downpatrick have attractive Arts Centres, Newry's with a small purpose-built and flexible theatre space.

Belfast's Grand Opera House has reopened after sustaining bomb damage during an attack nearby - the contingent difficulties of arts managements in the province. The city also houses The Lyric, Northern Ireland's only repertory theatre; The Arts Theatre, a mixed-programme venue; and the little Group Theatre, used by amateur and small professional companies. The Crescent and The Old Museum are lively arts centres; and there are a growing number of fringe companies, many of which have survived beyond the usual butterfly's lifespan: Belfast Community Circus, NOW, Replay, Tinderbox, Out and Out, Sightlines and the Ulster Youth Theatre, sponsored by the Arts Council. Citywide and Scarecrow are new on the scene, the latter notably organising Armada, an adventurous three city, nationwide autumn tour by six new alternative theatre companies. One of the major events of the arts year is the Belfast Festival at Queen's, the largest all-arts festival in Great Britain and Ireland, outside Edinburgh.

It is fair to say that the most creative and inventive energies in the arts here are to be found in Derry, funded whole-heartedly by the forward looking Derry City Council. There is a genuine and popular sense that the language of art can best express the identity of the city. There is, as yet, no purpose built theatre there but there are a range of usable venues such as The Rialto and St Columb's Hall, the Foyle Arts Centre and the recent edition of The Playhouse, with the young 4D company based there. This year, Derry has mounted a running arts festival, IMPACT 92, featuring international companies from a range of art forms. It has also run another International Theatre Workshop Festival, an annual collaboration with cities such as Glasgow and Bristol who are in a similar phase of self-regeneration.

The Lyric Theatre

Built upon the reputation of the Lyric Players in 1966 and by the energies of Mary and Pearse O'Malley, who had begun this then semi-professional company and mounted its productions in their own home, the Lyric Theatre continues to pay annual tribute to W B Yeats. The O'Malleys and the early Lyric were dedicated to his work in attempting to formulate a post-colonial Irish identity.

A large thrust stage with a raked 300 seater auditorium, the theatre's current Artistic Director is Charles Nowosielski with administrator, Mike Blair and literary adviser, the playwright John Boyd. The theatre is grant-aided by the Arts Council of NI and seeks business sponsorship for specific enterprises. The artistic policy centres on the classical repertory with an emphasis on the Irish and, latterly, on as much support for new Irish writing as is consistent with the pressure of the times to generate serious income at the box office.

Pygmies in the Ruins

Harry Towb and Stella McCusker

1992 began with the Lyric's completion of its London run, at the Royal Court, of Ron Hutchinson's new play, "Pygmies in the Ruins", premiered in November 1991, to great interest, at the Belfast Festival at Queens. "Pygmies" is set concurrently in the Belfast's of 1871 and 1991, concentrating on the efforts of police photographer, Harry Washburn, to discover the truth about a murder which had been committed 120 years previously on Cave Hill, the landmark mountain behind the city. "Pygmies" refers to the stunting effect upon the present of the Irish obsession with the past. The production was presented with BBC Radio Drama and Belfast 1991. Director was Eoin O'Callaghan with designer, Kathy Strachan.

Rebecca

Patrick Duncan, Mal White and Noel McGee

A very astute and profitable piece of programming, the Lyric's January production of Rebecca adapted by Clifford Williams from the novel by Daphne du Maurier proved hugely popular. The widely-known suspense thriller, with its strong psychological emphasis on character and motivation readily lent itself to a theatrical realisation which gripped the imagination of its audiences. The production played to packed houses, sold-out and was retained for an extended run. The theatre trailed the show with the query as to whether Rebecca would appear on stage where she is not seen in the novel and was not portrayed in the film. It would be a pity to give the game away here but a ghostly entertainment it certainly was.

Dockers

In March the Lyric produced a revival of Martin Lynch's first professional play, "Dockers" premiered at the Lyric in 1981 and greeted then with universal acclaim. The playwright had himself been a docker and came from a family with a long history of working at Belfast Docks. The action centres around a Trade Unionist who attempts to change unfair practices in the employment of dockers in "the pen" and is opposed by some of his fellows who are afraid of any change in traditional patterns and have a vested interest in the status quo. The philosophy of the play is broadly socialist and its energies centre on stereotypical local characters and on the sharp and irreverent wit of the verbal idiom of the Belfast working-class. For all of these similarities, Martin Lynch has sometimes been referred to as Belfast's O'Casey.

Eileen McCluskey and Stuart Graham

Swansong

In May the Lyric presented a version of Chekhov's "Swansong". Described by the writer as "A Vaudeville for one actor", a tired-and-emotional old thespian indulges in nostalgia about his actual and fantasy career (as they all do) - parts he played, parts he might have played and parts he imagines he did play. To locate the piece in time, Chekhov had inserted short extracts from some notable literary pieces of the day; and the Lyric's production relocated the action by exchanging these insertions for three short Irish plays, Synge's "Riders to the Sea", Yeats's "Purgatory" and Beckett's "Catastrophe". Directed by Charles Nowosielski with musical director, Richard Cherns, designer, Paul Ambrose Wright and lighting designer, Martin Palmer, this made a compendium entertainment which, with its combination of its specific verbal texture with music and dance, provided a lively conclusion to that season's programme.

John Hewitt and Peter O'Meara

Round The Big Clock

One of John Boyd's first plays "The Flats", confronted secrarian violence in Belfast. Something of a cause celebre at the time, the play toured to Dublin and the UK. John Boyd was invited to join the Board of the Lyric Theatre and remains today its literary adviser. November saw perhaps his most ambitious, play "Round the Big Clock", directed by Charles Nowosielski. A docudrama on the rise of Belfast, his native city, the writer's aim has been to show how an early settlement, Beal Feirste, described as "a swampy crossing-place in the Lagan valley" managed to attract settlers ranging from indigenous people to outsiders, and become a major industrial city. John Milton evidently described the place as "a barbarous nook noted for its liars and impostors" without ever having been there. Plus ca change...

John Boyd

Civic Arts Theatre, Belfast

The building in which the Arts Theatre is currently housed was designed as a ballroom and had its purpose diverted, midway through building in the late 1950s, to become a theatre. It seats around 550, with a raised proscenium stage. Its fortunes have fluctuated. It had a period of several years in the 80s where it housed the Ulster Actors Company and had an emphasis on in-house productions with a regular focus on new Ulster writing.

With financial pressures, this emphasis shifted progressively to a mixed programme of variety and popular music with periods of hire and a couple of annual plays produced either under its own or the aegis of Theatre Ulster. Managed alternately by the Arts Theatre and the Riverside Theatre, Coleraine, funded by the Arts Council and producing two or three shows a year, the position of Theatre Ulster is under review. Executive administrator is Paul Maurel.

Sleeping Beauty

This pantomime production - part nightmare, part fantasy, directed by Michael Poynor with Rod McVey composing an original score and acting as musical director, ushered in the year for the Arts Theatre. Usually able to produce only a couple of shows in-house each year, the Christmas show is always one of them. With a guaranteed family following for the bright, energetic productions of this kind there is a healthy impact on the box office. Poynor has an eye for the spectacular, a refreshing irreverence in updating the traditional and predictable, and a keen understanding of the abilities of local actors who are generally effectively cast. This show featured a very memorable dragon whose inevitable death simultaneously underlined received moral values and caused many a moist eye in the house.

A Slice of Saturday Night

Geared to attract the ageing members of the post-war baby boom, offering an evening of restored youth and nostalgia, directed by Peter Quigley with Eddie Friel as musical director and drawing on local performing attractions including downtown radio presenters, this show, which had run for almost a month in 1991, was brought back in March of this year for a further two weeks. Like the pantomime above, it is included in this selection because it typifies a particular approach to in-house entertainments produced by the Arts Theatre. Centred on the Belfast of the 60s, with the rock music of the time, a variety of relevant dance routines, mini-skirts and jokes on the bluer side of pale, this provided an uninhibited romp for the audiences who had made it something of a local cult musical.

THE NORTH WEST

by JIM BURKE

The North West '92

The North West, and more particularly Manchester, is the cradle of the repertory movement. It was here that Annie Horniman, taking advantage of its comparatively low rates, set up her Gaiety Theatre, and since then the area has developed into one of intense theatrical activity, second only to London. Recognition of this fact was recently conferred in the shape of a £250,000 Arts Council cheque, naming Manchester as City of Drama, 1994, for the end-of-the-millenium Arts 2000 initiative. No doubt a feast of sponsorship deals and local authority aid for the area's theatres and companies will follow in its train – £10 million is the conservative estimate. Welcome news indeed, but already a cautionary note is being struck from some quarters, namely those who fear that the jamboree will serve mainly to veil the withholding of necessary core funding. City of Drama will provide a much needed (and much deserved) shot in the arm for ailing companies in the North West, but it is really no substitute for a sustained treatment of subsidy and encouragement. That such treatment has been less than vigorously applied of late is evidenced by certain disturbing trends in the region throughout 1992. There has been an inexorable drift towards playing it safe after 1991's year-of-living-dangerously (relatively speaking), particularly in the less secure reps outside the city centres. Risk taking is fast becoming a thing of the past as light musicals, even lighter comedies and "classic" popular drama elbows aside provocative, challenging and fresh works. With heroic efforts of the likes of Bolton Octagon's Andrew Hay being rewarded with crippling deficits, it is unrealistic, under present circumstances, to expect other artistic directors to follow his lead.

Still, sterling work is being done. The list of reps operating in the area remains impressive, while reps such as Crewe's Century Theatre continue to tour homegrown products around the country.

More new writing is being produced the North West than anywhere in the country. Two major outlets encourage this state of affairs; one is the Mobil Prize (of which more later), the other is the annual North West Playwrights Workshop, based at Contact Theatre, and which offers advice to aspiring writers and professional script-in-hand performances for their work. The event was extended this year to include talks and workshops by, amongst others, Trevor Griffiths, Charlotte Keatley, David Edgar and Peter Flannery.

In addition to all this, there are the massed ranks of the fringe companies based in the North West, of which the attempt at a comprehensive list would be futile. But among those making waves in 1992 have been Roar Material, Mayhew and Edmunds, Kaboodle, 061, Northern Edge, One Step, GW, New Breed and Altered States as well as TIE/community groups such as M6 and Pit Prop.

An extensive network of fringe venues accommodates the work of these groups – venues such as the Abraham Moss in Hulme, the Leigh Drama Centre, The Citadel in St Helen's and Hulme's Nia Centre, the only venue in the country completely given over to Afro-Caribbean arts. Foremost of these venues is Manchester's Green Room, a railway arch in its previous life, now a 165-seat theatre that attracts a wide variety of acts, both national and international. Its artistic policy leans heavily towards the performance based and experimental rather than script-based works, but it has served as a valuable space for the promotion of new plays. Among its initiatives for 1992 has been a major festival of lesbian and gay theatre, "It's Queer Up North".

The Royal Exchange, Manchester

Sometimes referred to as the National Theatre of the North, the Royal Exchange attracts the biggest names, the biggest audiences, and, not surprisingly, the biggest subsidies and sponsorship deals in the North West. Situated in Manchester's salubrious St Anne's Square, its glass and steel, 740 seat theatre-in-the-round is considered one of the most unique auditoria in the country. Another less welcome reputation has continued to dog it throughout 1992; that it plays too safe and that it cares more about soothing its sponsors than presenting exciting, challenging theatre.

As a riposte to these views, one could point to the peaks of excellence this theatre has achieved: Phyllida Lloyd's stunning production of Soyinka's "Death and the King's Horsemen" or Braham Murray's production of Ron Wooden's vitriolic "Your Home in the West", recipient of the Royal Exchange-based Mobil prize, which, with £40,00 in prize money, is the leading international contest for playwrights.

As far as the question of money goes, in national terms it is arguable that the Exchange gets something of a bum deal. It recently increased its proportion of self-generated income from 48% to 56% and the proportion of its grants fell accordingly. Artistic Director Braham Murray sees this as a case of the North being penalised for success, something unheard of in the South.

Nevertheless, its detractors do have a point. The programming for 1992, like many years before it, has been less than visionary. The autumn season had two nineteenth century novel adaptations back to back, while contemporary playwrights remain largely unrepresented. And then there's that legendary local story that the Exchange spent more on a piece of cloth used only for five minutes in their 1990 "Tempest" than was spent on the entire budget for Oldham Coliseum's concurrent and far more exciting production of John Godber's "Teechers".

Good work has been achieved by the longstanding directorial triumvirate of Braham Murray, Gregory Hersov and James Maxwell, whilst guest directors come and go like blasts of fresh air, most notably Phyllida Lloyd and Richard Wilson. Perhaps some kind of shake-up is required. The recent appointment of Harriet Walter to the directorial team may result in some such cataclysm: among other things, Walter has already declared a commitment to developing new writing.

The Miser

The Royal Exchange invariably eschews the traditional Christmas panto, a fact for which many of us were truly grateful in that they gave us Tom Courtenay in "The Miser" for Christmas. Courtenay's Harpagon was a truly appalling creation. Whether clutching at his threadbare tails, hurling demonically about the stage, arranging ludicrous marriages, or languishing pathetically for his lost love (a cashbox containing six million francs), his was an hilarious, inspired, fully committed performance. In the rest of the cast, William Armstrong was particularly memorable as Cleante, Harpagon's wretched son. Armstrong played him as a hopelessly flapping booby going rapidly to seed under Harpagon's well-worn heel. Under Braham Murray's punchy direction, the production fair pelted along, with enough comic business to ensure that each belly laugh merged into the next.

Tom Courtenay

Sidewalk Sidney

Eddie Osei and Charlie Caine

"Sidewalk Sidney" was a Mobil Prize runner-up, and, as one critic rather unkindly put it at the time, I would have hated to have seen what came third. It was a tale of racism and its aftershocks in urban Britain, a subject which, you would have thought, could hardly fail to pack some kind of emotional wallop. Something, though, went horribly wrong here. Despite a strong performance from Eddie Osei, and some good writing along the way, its two-handed structure imposed limits upon the dramatic possibilities that writer Randhi McWilliams was evidently not equipped to overcome. And its sluggardly pace made it look as though James Maxwell had directed it with a lead weight dangling from each wrist. The Mobil Prize has yielded some gems in the past. This, unfortunately, wasn't one of them.

Romeo and Juliet

Kate Byers and Michael Sheen

The Royal Exchange usually includes at least one Shakespeare in a year, and sometimes it has seemed a rather tedious duty for actors and audience alike. Not so with Gregory Hersov's crackling production of "Romeo and Juliet". Hersov updated the setting and the body language to the rave scene. Michael Sheen and Kate Byers played the doomed lovers with a minimum of dewy-eyed sentimentality, and were all the more affecting for it. A superb supporting cast included Judd Meyers' swaggering, near psychotic Mercutio, Jonathan Hackett's movingly humanist Friar Lawrence, and Amelia Bullmore and John Branwell as Juliet's selfish, washed-up parents. The civic brawls were convincingly nasty, and the general tone dark, almost nihilistic. But it was played with an exuberance that made it the ideal production for the company's nationwide tour.

A View From The Bridge

Jonathan Hackett

Accompanying "Romeo and Juliet" on tour was this production of Arthur Miller's "A View From The Bridge", again directed by Gregory Hersov and using the same cast. Hersov has an impressive track record with Miller but, disappointingly, this was his weakest to date. Jonathan Hackett's Eddie Carbone was a desperately raging bull, but, ultimately, he failed to convince, partly because his histrionic excesses seemed too calculated, partly because they left him nowhere to go. Morever, the majority of the cast seemed to follow suit and simply bellowed their way through the more emotional scenes. Still, David Short's set was impressive enough, especially in the opening sequence, a representation of the blood, sweat, and toil of the docks over which hung the hook of a giant crane like a malignant engine of fate.

Women Laughing

Patricia Kerrigan, Christopher Fulford and Hetty Baynes

Another new play enjoyed a short run in May, this time the late Michael Wall's "Women Laughing", a black comedy about upward mobility and insanity. Christopher Fulford and Stephen Tomkinson gave fine performances as yuppies Colin and Tony, engaging in matey chitchat in the garden while becoming increasingly paranoid over their wives' offstage hilarities. In the second half, Patricia Kerrigan and Hetty Baynes came into their own as the bemused Steph and Maddy, trying to come to terms with their by now institutionalised husbands. Director Richard Wilson gave us a sharply focused production which never relinquished the play's deep sense of tragedy, even at its most hilarious. Morever, it was a painful reminder that Michael Wall's death in 1991 robbed the theatre of a considerable new talent.

The Recruiting Officer

Derek Griffiths

It was back to the past in June, to the Restoration in fact, with Braham Murray's hit-and-miss production of George Farquhar's "The Recruiting Officer". On the plus side was Haydn Gwynne's earthy, sensible Silvia, swaggering convincingly when she pulled on the breeches for her disguise as Jack Wilful. Emil Wolk's manic, cartoon-like Captain Brazen was a big hit with members of the audience, but critics were appalled at his self-indulgent hugging of the stage to the exclusion of whoever happened to be there at the time. Far more effective was Derek Griffiths' superbly controlled performance as Sergeant Kite, especially in the scene during which he drums up recruits while disguised as a mystic. Small wonder he got star billing for what was, after all, a supporting role.

An Ideal Husband

Rebecca Lacey, Emily Morgan and Una Stubbs

Sad to report, the season ended with something of a whimper. James Maxwell's production of Oscar Wilde's "An Ideal Husband" contained all those elements that have, on occasion, left the Royal Exchange open to some derision from the critics. This was middle-of-the-road, middle-class nineteenth century costume drama delivered with too much reverence and an obsessive and prodigal antiquarianism in its design. Wilde's story of a respectable politician's threatened fall from grace over a murky past failed to ignite, and the endless stream of "Oscarisms" was delivered with ponderous relish. Against such a drab background, Robert Glenister's Lord Goring gleamed all the more brightly. It was a performance that engagingly captured the languorous cynicism and impassioned humanity of this Wildean alter-ego.

The Library Theatre Company

The Library Theatre Company is unique in two ways: one, that it is the only regional company to be funded entirely by local authority grant aid; two, that it is the only company that has responsibility for two auditoria eight miles apart. The main auditorium is in the basement of Manchester's Central Library, where the emphasis is mainly on new and contemporary work, though this year they have given us Ibsen's "Ghosts" and their first Shakespeare for seven years, "The Merchant of Venice". Over the last couple of years, the Library Theatre has hit upon a winning formula of presenting contemporary American drama in the accessible shapes of Neil Simon and Arthur Miller. 1992 saw the production of Miller's "Two-Way Mirror" (following 1991's "The Price") and Neil Simon's "Broadway Bound" (following 1991's "Brighton Beach Memoirs" and "Biloxi Blues"). New work is usually the province of the company's writer-in-residence – Marvin Close took over from John Chambers this year, and he himself was succeeded by Jayne Hollinson in September. The LTC's other venue, The Forum, is part of the civic complex in Wythenshawe, where its non-central location has dictated a more circumspect approach to programming. Here, the popular drama, musical and farce reigns.

Robin Hood And The Raven's Revenge

John Chambers' last show as writer-in-residence was this yuletide attempt to capitalise on the vogue then being enjoyed by that legendary, green-tighted, merry olde Englishman, Kevin Costner. This wasn't a panto in the traditional sense; few incitements to audience participation, very few songs, and even fewer dreadful puns – just jokes about the poll tax and Manchester's Olympic bid and the like. Political correctness was further made manifest by the appearance of Marcia Rose's Big Joan – Little John, of course, was at home minding the kids. Sir Guy of Gisborne was played with hissable superciliousness by James Quinn, while Claude Close (brother of incoming writer-in-residence Marvin) played a dyspepsic Friar Tuck.

Barbara Dryhurst and Tom Higgins

Two-Way Mirror

Arthur Miller's more recent works rarely surface at the reps, but the LTC brought us his 1982 double-bill, "Two-Way Mirror" in January, directed by Sue Sutton Mayo. The two-strong cast (husband and wife Ray Jewers and Colette Stevenson) faltered a little in the first play, "Elegy For A Lady", a short, gentle, but rather tricky piece about a grieving man quizzing a shop proprietress over what he should buy his dying lover. They fared better with the second play, "Some Kind Of Love Story", on the surface, a hard-boiled detective story that pitches a world-weary Irish-American gumshoe against a schizophrenic hooker. The parts were played with considerable panache, indeed some thought Colette Stevenson invested her role with more complexity than her somewhat cypher-like character deserved.

Ray Jewers and Colette Stevenson

The Writing Game

Joanna Hole and Lawrence Werber

David Lodge's first stage play, "The Writing Game" received its premiere in Birmingham in 1991, and the LTC revived it in the spring of this year. "The Writing Game" takes a hard, cynical, but ultimately fond look at a trio on a writing course. Lodge's main concern is with the writing process itself, and he carries the debate in sinewy, accessible and, for the most part, entertaining and witty mode. Pity about the rather shaky sexual politics though, which have Maude, a writer of frothy romances, expressing disapproval of her fellow writer's aggressive sexual fantasies while really saying "Yes, give it to ME!". Nevertheless, Chris Honer directed a strong cast, including Roy Barraclough whose quivery tones on the ansaphone as Maude's abandoned, domestically-mystified hubby received the biggest laugh of the evening.

Closer Than Ever

Andrew C. Wadsworth and Meredith Rich

In 1991, LTC scored a big hit with the Maltby and Shire musical, "Baby". So this year they tried with another musical from the same team. I must confess, I found David Shire's tunes instantly forgettable, and Richard Maltby's rhyme schemes quite mind-boggling in their fatuousness. Set in a recording studio in New York, it provides four performers with the opportunity to run the whole gamut of emotion – unhappy parents, remorseful sons, unfulfilled lovers, despairing loners. All life was here, and the performers, accompanied by two very talented musicians, delivered it all with a skill and relaxed charm that clearly warmed the audience to them. Apart, of course, from those who found the huggy-huggy sentiment and cutesy knowingness too glutinous to swallow.

Working

Faith Tingle and Robert Calvert

Inspired by living history projects, "Working" was, if nothing else, a monument to the colossal effort undertaken by LTC writer-in-residence, Marvin Close. It was transcribed from a veritable mountain of tapes recorded and edited by Close, and brought the working experience of Manchester's working population to the stage. Receptionists, kissograms, roadsweepers, cinema projectionists, prostitutes, firemen, drug-dealers, librarians – all imagineable facets of working life were represented by the eight-strong cast. And not one word uttered was invented by Close. It was certainly energetic, and it yielded some startling insights into the deceptive ordinariness of everyday lives. If it wasn't a complete success, it was at least a heroic attempt, and a demonstration that here was a theatre prepared to explore possibilities, whatever the risk.

The Forum, Wythenshawe

Cinderella

Tania Rodrigues and Polly Highton

The Forum pantos have always been relatively humble affairs. While other theatres were pursuading such luminaries as Lionel Blair, Dana, and even Derek Hatton onto their boards, the best the Forum could boast of was somebody called Tania Rodrigues who had apparently turned up on Coronation Street a couple of times. Still, this lack of star attraction didn't work to the detriment of "Cinderella", especially as it featured such capable players as Jane Hollywood, and Mel Taylor as the Ugly Sister's scheming mother, Mrs Joy Da Palma (a cross between Little Richard and Peter Cushing, as one critic put it at the time).

On Golden Pond

Martino Lazzeri and Willoughby Gray

When the LTC at the Wythenshawe Forum aren't producing musicals and light comedies, they can often be caught putting on "serious" drama that everybody will have heard of because its been on the telly. Hence their February production of Ernest Thompson's autumnal tear-jerker, "On Golden Pond", which, you may recall, was on the telly with no less than two Fondas and a Hepburn. There was nobody at the Forum of such crowd-pulling stature, but Willoughby Gray, as the caustic, death-fixated octagenarian, Norman, brushed the heart strings with the best of them. Daphne Oxenford, Regina Reagan and Ian Flintoff were among those offering solid support, while Judith Croft designed a suitably faded New England lodge.

A Marginal Affair

Jane Hollywood and Bruce Montague

Four weeks before the general election, Dave Simpson's new play, "A Marginal Affair" appeared at the Forum. Bruce Montague played the bluff northern Labour man who wakes up after one of those nights to find a girl in his soup. Just to complicate matters, she also happens to be the wife of the Liberal Democrat candidate. And so all was set for those farcical strategems that get the characters in the most compromising position at the least convenient moment. Thus booze-befuddled Jill topples Jack onto the sofa just as the Tory candidate walks through the door. The performances, from a quality cast including Jane Hollywood and Diane Whitely, kept things rolling along.

Bolton Octagon

The national press once dubbed Bolton Octagon as the best regional theatre in the country. That was in Andrew Hay's day, with his outstanding seasons of Berkoff, O'Neill, Potter, Beckett, and a wealth of new work, not least from wunderkind writer-in-residence Jim Cartwright. Hay left for Bristol Old Vic at the beginning of the year, and the Octagon at present has no writer-in-residence. But with the installation of new Artistic Director Lawrence Till, the Octagon's reputation has continued to flourish, though for different reasons. Till's programming has little of the cosmopolitan intrepidity of Hay, being dominated by vintage pieces by the likes of Wilde, Naughton, Ayckbourn, and Delaney, but the execution of these works has been of a consistently high standard. Till's most valuable contribution to date, though, has been in his determined drive to make theatre accessible to the handicapped, particularly the deaf. His British sign language version of Medoff's "Children Of A Lesser God" was rapturously received, and the theatre was recently awarded £25,000 as part of the Arts Council's Be Bold initiative. The money will be used to stage a sign-language production of "Titus Andronicus", using an integrated hearing and deaf company.

Spring And Port Wine

Bill Naughton was himself from Bolton, and he died shortly before this production, Lawrence Till's first at the Octagon, began its run. Set around a Boltonian working-class living room, it deals with intransigent patriarch Rafe Compton's turbulent voyage of discovery, launched by his rebellious daughter and a slice of uneaten haddock. Alan Rothwell's Rafe managed to be formidable without being an ogre, and his sardonic interplay with the rest of the cast skilfully endeared him to the audience. The comic elements of the play tended to work best in this production, and, as such, much of the evening was stolen by Mary Cunningham as the slovenly, scrounging neighbour, and especially by John Lloyd Fillingham's spineless, would-be-rebellious Harold. But under Till's sensitive direction the whole cast barely put a foot wrong.

John Lloyd Fillingham, Stefan Escreet, Andy Wear and Alan Rothwell

The Norman Conquests

In May, the Octagon tackled Ayckbourn's vintage trilogy, "The Norman Conquests". Ayckbourn is on record as saying that he has since moved away, both aesthetically and philosophically from that stage of his career, so perhaps something a little fresher might have been in order. The action of the trilogy takes us through one weekend at a country house where the shabby, implausibly charming Norman has set his beady sights on the womenfolk gathered there. Director Romy Baskerville handled the structurally complicated material competently enough, and the cast made fine use of the peccadilloes Ayckbourn had allocated to their characters. Particularly memorable was Bob Mason's gormless, vetinary suitor, Tom. And Robert Pickavance, as Norman, soon settled down to give a funny portrait of a seemingly innocent, almost maligned philanderer.

Robert Pickavance

Chester Gateway

Chester Gateway serves Cheshire, the Wirral and North Wales. It has a 440 seat capacity, and an impressive foyer and bar area that once earned it the reputation for being the most attractive rep in the region. At the time of writing, the theatre has no Artistic Director, but one is soon to be appointed. Plans are also afoot for the creation of a new 100-plus seat studio theatre, small scale community touring, and outreach and education work. 1992 has seen a programme dominated by lower-middle to middle-brow comedies, including Stoppard's "Hapgood", Richard Harris' "The Maintenance Man", and Godber's "Bouncers". Next year, the theatre commemorates its twenty-fifth anniversary, and a series of special events is currently being planned.

It's A Girl

John Burrow's "ante-natal comedy for the nuclear age" was delivered with much aplomb in May. Critics responded warmly to this acappella musical following the fortunes of five members of the Bradstow Regain Your Shape After Pregnancy Coffee Circle. The all-female cast (backed by a virtually all-female production team) tackled a multitude of characters and lustily performed the play's thirteen acappella song and dance numbers. Rachel Clarke played Linda who retrospectively tells of her two-fisted battle to give birth at home and keep the nuclear waste off her doorstep. This was as much a series of cabaret songs and sketches as a play, and the cast rose to it with bags of energy – including, I might add, Janys Chambers, who was eight months pregnant at the time.

Bouncers

John Godber's "Bouncers" is an exceedingly popular play in this region (as indeed are most of his plays). Hardly a year goes by without a quartet of actors donning the monkey suits to drag this less than sacred guild of "ejection technicians" and their customers/victims through two hours of merciless lampoonery. Director Robert Sian left hardly a grimy stone unturned in his quest for easy laughs. Vomit, sputum, and jokes about colossal genitalia were the order of the evening. Whatever subleties and truths might be lurking in the script were buried under the deluge. But the four actors launched themselves into their thirty-two roles with the kind of protean adaptability Godber's script demands. Juliet Wilkinson's set, approximating a 70s nightclub, was suitably ghastly.

Contact Theatre, Manchester

Contact theatre is very much the young person's venue in Manchester, not least because it is situated right in the heart of University life. Sixty per cent of its audience are under thirty, and, accordingly, Artistic Director Brigid Larmour endeavours to effect a degree of dynamism in her programming. Challenging, sometimes provocative works are the norm here, with the likes of Dario Fo, Caryl Churchill, Harvey Feirstein and Liz Lochead crowding its flexible stage in recent times. Even when Contact do the classics, they are presented in innovative and revisionist ways, sometimes, though by no means always, with satisfactory results.

Up until recently, Contact offered an annual Brecht production, a practice that added to the company's reputation for coming down from the political fence – though perhaps the withdrawal of this practice suggests that repetition resulted in staleness.

Contact also has its own Community Theatre Team (for the twelve to twenty-five age range), of which Contact Youth Theatre is a major part. No writer-in-residence is employed there at present, the most recent being the award-winning James Stock.

Oedipus Tyrannos

Contact's first production of 1992 was Timberlake Wertenbaker's translation of Sophocles' "Oedipus Tyrannos". Richard Foxton's stunning set had the audience gasping even before the first words had been spoken. Surrounded by wire mesh and with the debris of a post-catclysmic society hanging over their heads, the audience became the plague-stricken citizens of Thebes. It was a wonderful idea, with sudden, startling shifts of focus contributing to the excitement, although Kenny Ireland's production didn't quite match the boldness of the design – apart from those brief moments in which the characters mingled with the audience or unexpectedly popped up from one corner or another. Philip Glenister's Oedipus was a little too rigidly autocratic to make this the tragedy of a flawed but otherwise admirable human being.

Philip Glenister

Measure For Measure

As if to outdo the darkness at the heart of the Royal Exchange's "Romeo and Juliet", Contact gave us a brooding, doom-laden "Measure For Measure", in which Simon Banham's mirrored set was only just perceptible under the strangled glimmer of lights. This may be one of Shakespeare's less merry comedies, but even so, director Brigid Larmour was taking a chance with such a morose interpretation. As it happened, it was a risk worth taking. The oppressive atmosphere gave extra depth to its story of puritanism and sexual hypocrisy, almost as though we were being offered an expressionistic rendering of Angelo's dour psyche (sympathetically portrayed by a frock-coated Simon Andrews). Katherine Rogers gave a strong willed Isabella, and Paul Brightwell lent the Duke's paternalistic benevolence the ambiguity which some feel the part deserves.

Diane Adderley and Cristopher Penney

Duke's Playhouse, Lancaster

Lancaster's Dukes is a relatively new rep whose mainhouse is a proscenium-stage theatre with a 307 capacity, and which also contains an in-the-round studio theatre. Perhaps the most notable feature of the theatre, however, is the company's annual promenade season in Lancaster's Williamson Park. For the last five years, this Victorian setting has seen a summertime children's show and a Shakespeare, although executive director Jon Pope is planning to break away from this tradition to offset predictability. Next year the company have ambitions to stage an outdoor "War Of The Roses", possibly in two parts. This year, the promenade productions were "The Taming Of The Shrew", set in Second World War Padua, and "The Wizard Of Oz". The company reached its twenty-first anniversary in 1992, and their achievement of average 81% capacity for their indoor productions and huge critical and public acclaim for their promenade productions ensured they had something to celebrate.

Look Back In Anger

Just as Osborne was blowing the dust off Jimmy Porter for "Deja Vu", Lancaster Dukes were reviving his '50s incarnation under Robert Pickavance's direction, which was perhaps informed by Osborne's recent claim that his play has been misconceived over the years; Porter is really a comic character. Julian Protheroe's portrayal emphasised the humour more than the anger, which left some critics bemoaning the consequent lack of passion. He was backed by Meriel Scholfield's Alison and Ian Puleston-Davies as Cliff. Caroline Fenton gave a spiky, cynical Helana, and Tony Broughton, recently seen as businessman Kevin Taylor in the satire "Get Stalker!" brought a world-weary pathos to imperialist buffer, Colonel Redfern. Special mention should also go to whoever designed the terrific publicity poster which featured a recumbent Brando being threatened by a giant iron.

Julian Protheroe and Meriel Scholfield

The Wizard Of Oz

Though the Dukes company have been more than adequately drilled in outdoor playing by five years of Williamson Park promenade productions, this adaptation of "The Wizard Of Oz" was their first attempt at extending their talent to full-blown outdoor musicals. The results were exemplary, earning them some unbridled enthusiasm from press and public. Jon Pope was joined by Adrian Johnston and Joe Sumsion in directing this piece which involved five locations around the park, a specially-built Yellow Brick Road, forty-five Munchkins (played by local children), a firework finale, and four dogs drilled in the nuances of playing Dorothy's pet, Toto, on separate evenings. The whole cast delivered exuberant performances, but most praise went to James Duke's pantomime-dame-like Wicked Witch of the West.

James Dukes and Anna Palmer

Liverpool Everyman

Founded in the '60s by Terry Hands, Liverpool's Everyman soon established itself as one of the most adventurous reps in the country, influencing other theatres near and far. Its premises were originally built as a Non Conformists' meeting house, became a music hall, a cinema, and then a rock venue.

In more recent times, like Liverpool's Playhouse, the Everyman was threatened with closure, the besieged City Council having little money for theatre and the Arts Council allegedly considering two reps to be one too many in Liverpool. Thankfully, the Everyman survived, and, under thirty-six year old John Doyle's energetic direction, continues to offer an exciting programme of classic and contemporary works.

Othello

John Doyle's production of "Othello" featured a passionate performance from Ray Fearon as the Moor, and a steely, cold-hearted Iago from Tony Turner. Joanne Stoner provided a convincing Emilia. Some critics were less sure about other roles, pointing to the lack of polish in vocal delivery in some of the younger cast members. But the look of the production didn't fail to impress, with India Smith's sparse wooden rakes and field tables conjuring the atmosphere of matters military. (Robin Thornber of *The Guardian* placed it more precisely as Italy's pre-World War One exploits in Africa).

Tony Turner and Ray Fearon

Candide

John Doyle also directed Bernstein's musical version of Voltaire's "Candide" in June, and, according to some critics, it was very nearly the best of all possible productions. India Smith's designs gave it the nursery feel, with alphabet blocks and a mini-adventure playground, while the cast of ten gave life to the whole teeming population of Voltaire's satire. Mike Afford played both Voltaire himself, the narrator of the piece, and the beamingly optimistic tutor, Pangloss, while Philip Rham played Candide, doomed to a thousand ignominious ends but blessed with an obliviousness as to both himself and the world's wretched state. The actors, immensely versatile bunch that they were, in addition to enacting this cruel and carnivalesque world, joined musicians Rob Mitchell and Helen Ireland to provide orchestral backing for their own exuberant singing.

Jenny Galloway

Liverpool Playhouse

Opened in 1911, the Liverpool Playhouse is distinguished by the fact that it is the oldest surviving rep in the country. In its early days, it found it difficult to shrug off a rather conventional image, and the same might be said of it in the year in question. In the interim, though, it gave rise to that highly influential and prolific "Gang Of Four", Alan Bleasdale, Chris Bond, Bill Morrison and Willy Russell, and, in 1989, managed to ruffle a few tabloid feathers with its staging of "Fears And Miseries Of The Third Term", a Brechtian satire on Thatcherism. Recently, the theatre's financial difficulties threatened it with permanent closure, until producer Bill Kenwright rode in on his white charger and rescued it with a lucrative programme of his big star, populist shows. Autumn's "The Nineteenth Hole", written by Johnny Speight and starring Eric Sykes, was symptomatic of this strategy. The theatre now functions largely as a space for touring productions and West End transfers such as Peter Hall's production of Poliakoff's "Sienna Red".

99 Heyworth Street

Perhaps yearning back to its Gang Of Four heyday, the Playhouse's new musical, "99 Heyworth Street" was an affectionate portrait of Liverpool Irish working class life with strong echoes of Willy Russell's "Blood Brothers". Very much a family affair, it was written by Tony Bryan, featured music by John Bryan, and told the story of their mum and their aunt, twin sisters struggling against the odds in working class Liverpool. Critics' responses ranged from those praising its truthfulness, to those poo-pooing it for its triteness, while others cried "Foul!" at its use of taped, synthesized music. Easy to carp, but finding money for such luxuries as live music is less so.

Imagine

Mark McGann

While the Everyman, under John Doyle, has managed to shun its occasional habit of wallowing in Scousery, the Playhouse let rip with this unflinchingly sentimental and reverent tribute to The Beatles, and more specifically, John Lennon. Russell's "John, Paul, Ringo ... and Bert" had strongly hinted at the limitations of fickle fame, but Keith Stracham's script hinted at very little beyond how simply fab these boys were. There was little dramatic meat, even less continuity, but it did have a live band who delivered the tunes with considerable faithfulness. Mark McGann continued in his bid to corner the market in playing Lennon, and Andy Walmsley earned some praise for his city-scape design. But he last word will probably go to The Times' Martin Hoyle who quipped, "In comparison, "Buddy" is a Brechtian epic".

Oldham Coliseum

Another Artistic Director to depart from the region this year was the Coliseum's Paul Kerryson, who moved on to Leicester Haymarket. Kerryson miraculously helped pull the theatre from the mire of deficit with a series of glittery, populist, often critically-derided shows which subsequently toured the country with huge success. It's difficult to forget (and God knows some of us have tried) such ultra-camp extravaganzas as "Ladies Night", "Hold Tight, It's Sixties Night", and "Hot Stuff". Alongside these Kerryson presided over a number of musical productions of the highest standard, while slipping in the Berkoffs, the Shermans, and the lesser-known Shakespeares by the back door. New Artistic Director Warren Hooper seems to be pursuing a similar populist policy (though we've yet to see anything remotely controversial, weighty, or innovative). His seasons have thus far consisted of rather insubstantial musicals and comedies, all of which have earned him a reputation for playing it too safe. But it's easy to carp, particularly if one forgets the disastrous Strindberg ("Miss Julie") that kept people away in droves at the end of 1991. Under such circumstances, Hooper can hardly be blamed for choosing the safest weapons available to defeat the demon deficit.

Yakety Yak

Sally Sagoe and Sarah Ingram

Warren Hooper inaugurated his stay as Artistic Director at the Coliseum with "Yakety Yak", billed as a '50s musical. It's about two brothers who live on a derelict site in New York, who fall in love with the same girl, squabble, and make up. The famous, and the not so famous, rock 'n' roll numbers were exuberantly performed, to be sure, but the characterisations were like soggy cardboard, and the yakety-yak between the songs was embarrassing in its puerility. Did it matter ? Not if you were just there to appreciate the well-packaged nostalgia, helped along by India Smith's suitably garish set, Kevin Quarmby's bass-throated drug dealer (he also doubled as a cop) and Sally Sagoe's Mama, whose mournful rendition of "Is That All There Is ?" almost made the evening worth it.

Dames At Sea

Kim Ismay, Catherine Terry and Karen Clegg

Much more in keeping with the high reputation Paul Kerryson achieved for this theatre was Lindsay Dolan's production of "Dames At Sea", a wonderfully preposterous skit on the Hollywood musical. Its familiar tale of a 42nd Street theatre down on its luck and ready for the scrap heap was carried by its six-strong cast with just the right balance of wide-eyed ingenuousness and lampoonery. India Smith's sets gave us both a down-at-heel theatre which collapsed under the bulldozers just before the interval, and a big, camp glitzy battleship, complete with exploding gun turrets, for the second half. It was all quite irresistible, with spot-on song and dance routines, one-hundred-and-one showbiz cliches, and a finale that offered six hundred (imaginary) dancing sailors.

THE NORTH EAST

By TIMOTHY RAMSDEN

The North East '92

Huge industrial areas dominate South and West Yorkshire, and they are served by major theatres, the Crucible in Sheffield, which by the end of the year looked set to recover its artistic nerve, and in Leeds the West Yorkshire Playhouse, where classics startled in unconventional productions and new plays mostly disappointed.

North Yorkshire, with its smaller urban areas, has a string of three repertories, the ever-inventive Harrogate Theatre, whose adventures in classic texts belies its staid if elegant setting, York Theatre Royal, shrugging off its old pretensions to be a major tourist trap, with West End style prices, and the Stephen Joseph Theatre in the Round at Scarborough. York hosted a five-hour indoor version of England's greatest drama, the Mystery Plays, in June and July, then settled into a so-so season of "What the Butler Saw", "Lend Me A Tenor", and "The Importance of Being Earnest". Scarborough is the unlikely home of an experimental theatre-in-the-round. The experiment was made by Stephen Joseph, who died in 1967. On the cafe wall in the Stephen Joseph Theatre, there is a poster which explains how that Theatre has survived. It is advertising a play in an early season called "The Square Cat" and it is written by ingenue author Roland Allen, who stayed in Scarborough and went on to write much more under his own name, Alan Ayckbourn. This year the house dramatist had two new offerings, "Time of My Life" and the musical (more accurately, with-music play) "Dreams From A Summer House".

Much of North Yorkshire is rural, with scattered small communities; each year Harrogate's Theatre in Education company undertakes two-day residencies in village schools. These include a play – in 1992 the "Beowulf" – based "Grendel Speaks" – used as the source of work in schools, and repeated as an evening performance to bring theatre to the villages.

Further north, the rural/urban mix also determines the form of theatre provision. For the major company, Newcastle-upon-Tyne's Northern Stage, it has been a year of reorganisation rather than production, following several years of horrendous problems over finding a suitable home base. However, autumn saw a new Artistic Director down from Scotland in Alan Lyddiard and a season starting at the Edinburgh Festival with C.P.Taylor's "And A Nightingale Sang".

Among the small-scale touring companies set up to visit the local network of village halls, schools and art venues, Newcastle's Live Theatre and Northumberland Theatre Company have been most active, the latter even taking its autumn show, Stewart Howson's "Staying Here" to Hampshire for a weekend. Howson is a master of the local play based on oral record, and in his new piece about holiday homes and rural and urban expectations he has found a subject perfectly fitted to the region.

West Yorkshire Playhouse

Artistic Director Jude Kelly is keen her Leeds theatre serves the entire West Yorkshire community, which as she has pointed out, consists of many communities. Between them the large, fan-shaped Quarry Theatre and the smaller, 400 seater Courtyard, hold some seventeen productions in a year, plus visiting companies chosen to represent production styles and areas such as ethnic drama which the in-house productions do not cover. The repertoire has retained a pleasingly eclectic flavour since the Playhouse opened in March 1990; one exciting thing about the theatre in Leeds is you can never predict what the next season will contain. When it is announced, there are always surprises. Another positive aspect is that programming of the two theatre spaces in the building is determined by artistic rather than commercial priorities. So, in March John Godber's "Happy Families", a domestic play, was put in the Courtyard though such a popular playwright could well have filled the Quarry. Then in June a rare classic, Calderon's "Life is A Dream" was given in the Quarry where the production's epic nature could breathe, though it was clearly not destined to be a box office puller.

Cinderella

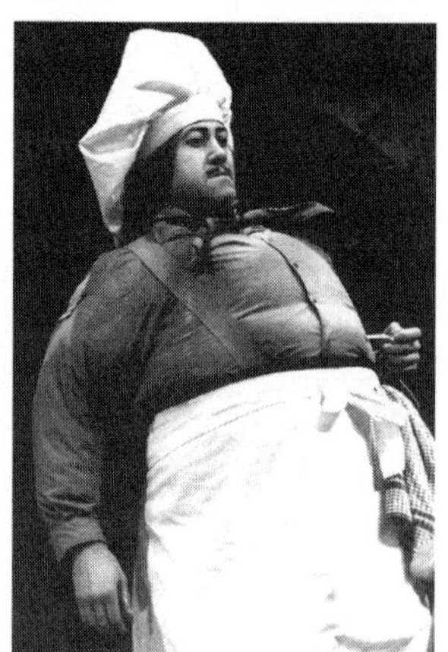

James Hornsby

1992 in the Courtyard opened with Michael Birch's production of "Cinderella" by Stuart Paterson. Birch, a Drama lecturer at Leeds University, has also been involved with the Playhouse Community and Education programmes, an interest evident in this high energy production. The usual Courtyard end-stage format was transformed to give a large corner acting area which lacked any single point of focus. To ensure visibility from all parts of the usually packed house, and to add a touch of youth credibility, a black-clothed figure on stage wielded a video camera, with large screens showing the action magnified. The black video operator soon became "invisible" – ignored as he was clearly not part of the action. This was a version of the black-clad figures, supposedly invisible, in Noh drama. This sort of cultural question did not occupy audiences overmuch at "Cinderella"; nor was it a pantomime but became, in Birch's hands, as much a party as a play.

The Gulf Between Us

Paul Slack

Written and directed by Trevor Griffiths, this play was timed to open on the first anniversary of the outbreak of the Gulf War. The production was presented in association with The Building Company, set up by Griffiths and others in 1991 to produce new plays on contemporary themes.

Set in the middle east, "The Gulf Between Us" shows a group of British brickies working on the reconstruction of a bombed Mosque wall. The wall was rebuilt nightly during the play; the cast included former bricklayer Paul Slack.

The play's problem lay in the unclear narrative, which only cloudily established that the mosque was in use both by the military and for the care of children. Hayden Griffin designed the building site Quarry set and Mic Pool concocted a culminating barrage of war sounds.

The Revenger's Tragedy

Andy Serkis

Jude Kelly directed in the Quarry, from February 15 – March 14, with designs by Pamela Howard. Two huge walls speckled with skulls spiralled apart to create the large main acting area. The effect was to dwarf the human actor, lost in this Renaissance world of corruption and intrigue. Visually, settings and costumes suggested the period while also making modern references – the Duke ("royal lecher") was in a business suit.

Vindice, seeking revenge for his beloved's death from the ducal family of nasties and weirdos he holds responsible, emerged from behind these huge walls. Reece Dinsdale adopted a northern accent for the part, only putting on a posh southern voice when disguised as the Duke's hired hitman Piato.

One of the highlights of the production was Kelly's use of a women's chorus, whose role as silent cleaners, Mme Defarge-like knitters and streetwalkers eerily intensified the play's atmosphere.

Happy Families

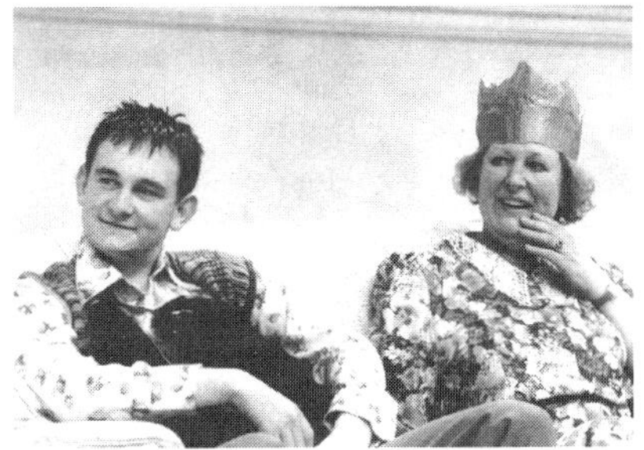

Nicholas Lane and Judith Barker

John Godber's play was written for simultaneous premieres by almost fifty amateur groups in 1991. This was the professional premiere, given in the Courtyard during the spring. Its popular success was such that an extra matinee had to be provided – which sold out speedily. "Happy Families" turned out to be as easily assimilable and as diverting a way of passing the time as the card game from which it is named, delineating a northern family that has begun to grope its way upwards on the lower rungs of social advance.

Godber directed his play expertly, Nicholas Lane gave a strong performance as John, experienced Godber actor Jane Clifford was Auntie Doris, while another habitue of the Godber stable, Andrew Livingstone provided another full-belted portrayal as Vic.

Three Girls in Blue

Helen Ryan

Russian author Ludmila Petrushevskaya was already known in Britain through her drinking-session play "Cinzano". This production, in the Courtyard during April and May, was directed by Michael Birch and designed by Pamela Howard. The translation was by Stephen Mulrine.

There was plenty of liquid on display here, from the vodka that was drunk to the rain which swept down in summer storms around the decrepit dacha where the action is set. Though this is not a play of great external action, rather of talk and, frequently, argument. The old Soviet ways are criticised through Ann Penfold's quarrelsome Marya, often seen with her feet in a bucket of water. Generally, the play was held to be more interesting as a report of Russian mores and morale than in its own dramatic right.

Tess of the D'Urbevilles

Shelley Willetts

Helena Kaut-Howson directed Fay Weldon's new adaptation of Thomas Hardy's novel, which played in the Quarry Theatre in April. Weldon's version related Tess's story to the changing seasons and Wessex landscape and developed the theme of relations between men and women. The production exploited the epic possibilities of the Quarry stage, above which there was suspended a crown of thorns, symbolically drawn at once from religion and the natural world.

The director's European style, strongly visual and physical, employed strong ensemble work. The result divided critical opinion into those who saw the production as a radical, theatrically alive interpretation and others who found it an unsatisfying amalgam of literal script ornamented by a series of staging tricks. There was, though, general agreement that Shelly Willetts gave an impressive performance as Tess.

Life is a Dream

James Larkin

Summertime saw Calderon's philosophical, religious drama, translated by Gwynne Edwards, in the first Playhouse production by the newly appointed resident director Matthew Warchus. It had designs by Neil Warmington. Calderon's story of a malignant prince Segismundo who is given a day's release from his perpetual captivity, then rearrested and made to believe he had been dreaming his freedom, had its central ideas expanded. Rosaura, the traveller in male disguise who opens the play, descended to earth from a large suspended bed. During the action, parts of the stage emerged, descended or disappeared in a dreamlike way until, in a final staging coup, the whole set vanished to leave a bare stage, upon which the whole cast appeared. Theatre, the play and its life were all shown as a dream, an act of the imagination.

The Wicked Old Man

Edward Jewesbury, Rebecca Charles and John Arthur

A political writer like John McGrath did not find the 1980s easy. Of the two 7:84 theatre companies he founded in the seventies, the English group went out of existence while the Scottish one was effectively wrested from his control. Jude Kelly has stated the importance of sustaining existing writers as well as finding new ones; presenting McGrath's play represented an important aspect of the Playhouse's wide-ranging repertory.

Harry Trowbridge (Edward Jewesbury) decides, in his seventies and following his wife's funeral, to go gay – or, as he puts it, queer. He grows sweet on Sugar, his black houseboy who is on the fringes of drugs and crime. The play shows how Harry's acquisitive relatives become increasingly frenzied as they see their inheritance vanishing. Jude Kelly's production played in the Courtyard June 4 – July 11.

Absent Friends

Susie Blake

By his recent standards, Ayckbourn's 1974 play is slender and slight, though in its day it was seen as evidence of his deepening gloom. Peter James' production (in the Quarry, June and July) cast Gary Bond as the bereaved Colin, a model of superficiality, for whom Pope might have written "Eternal smiles his emptiness betray". A strong cast tore themselves and their marriages apart around him. Susie Blake, as Diana, caught precisely the mix of anguish and laughter the character's progressive breakdown can elicit from an audience. Jane Slavin managed the feat of making the taciturn, gum toting Evelyn a real and funny character. Overall the revival entertained well without persuading us that a near-masterpiece had been resurrected.

When We Are Married

Mark Jax, Stephen McKenna, Sebastian Abineri and Robert Mcintosh

In the autumn, director John Adams and designer Patrick Connelan repeated their collaboration; they had worked together at the Playhouse in spring on "The Rivals". Their unconventional version of J.B. Priestley's backwards look at conventional respectability was the first of four regional revivals of English plays supported by English Estates.

Set on a raked diamond shaped stage, the two back walls were covered with pictures of sheep (the men work in the wool exchange); among them was the marriage portrait of the three couples who find that they like sheep have gone astray. Organist Gerald Forbes, who spitefully tells the three couples their marriages are invalid, entered and left through the floor while playing a towering church organ upon which characters climbed when trying to top others' points in argument.

A Working Woman

Kate Gartside

The Courtyard's final production before the Christmas period was an adaptation of Zola's "L'Assinniur". It is the story of a woman, Gervaise, struggling unsuccessfully to establish a business among the drink-ravaged slums. It also introduces us to a future Zola protagonist, the prostitute Nana, seen here as a child.

The adaptation was made by Stephen Wyatt, with directors Sue Lefton and Jane Gibson, from the movement departments of the RSC and National. They had earlier presented "Nana" in an acclaimed production for Shared Experience and their free-flowing strongly visual style suited the novel's structure. Belinda Davison, who had been the Shared Experience Nana, played that part again, with Kate Gartside as Gervaise, Ewan Stewart as Copeau, Stephen Marcus as Goujet and Jack Chiswick as Monsieur Lorilleux.

Stephen Joseph Theatre, Scarborough

"The warmest of Yorkshire welcomes and the best of world theatre" is the Stephen Joseph Theatre in the Round's proclamation. It can be interesting to judge whether warmth topples over into cosiness and to ask whether the best of world theatre can be summed up in the 1992 repertory of two new Ayckbourns, a couple of new English plays, a revival of "Abigail's Party" plus two twentieth century American pieces.

This year saw an earlier than usual start to the season, catching the Easter trade, while the summer season saw the usual mix of lunchtime and late-night events.

As Artistic Director Alan Ayckbourn continued to cast with his customary eye for strong young performers and to obtain from established northern actors such as Claude Close and James Tomlinson some of their strongest work. And – something which always lifts a Scarborough season a notch or two – actor Russell Dixon was back to create two more of his hollow monsters, Gerry Stratton in Ayckbourn's season – opening "Time of My Life" and Gordon in Tim Firth's "Neville's Island".

Time Of My Life

Ayckbourn directed his new play which opened the season mid-April and remained in the Scarborough repertory until August, before opening designer Roger Glossop's new Lake District theatre. Set in Calvinu's restaurant, "Time of My Life" begins with bustling merriment as Gerry and Laura Stratton enjoy a celebratory meal out with their two sons and the sons' partners. As the night progresses, the family splits apart and Laura's past adultery comes to light. This is interspersed with scenes of tete-a-tetes at Calvinu's between the sons and their womenfolk.

As the relationships reflect upon each other, often though not exclusively comically, the family becomes increasingly to be seen as an oppressive, and repressive, institution.

Russell Dixon and Terence Booth

Rocket to the Moon

Clifford Odets' 1938 play, set in a New York dentists reception area, was directed by Malcolm Hedben, who, it is tempting to say, never put a tooth wrong. The central relationship is between middle-aged dentist Ben Stark, played with suitable bemused weariness by Kenneth Price, and his new, young, attractive, inefficient receptionist Cleo Singer. Sarah-Jane Fenton avoided stereotyping Cleo and Christine Cox made the suspicious wife Belle a dignified and sensible person. Other characters were also established strongly and Juliet Nicholls' set gave the actors space while creating two distinct acting areas and suggesting the existence of several surgeries offstage.

"Rocket" held up the quality of period detail and freshness of acting brought to these Scarborough events.

James Tomlinson and Kenneth Price

Neville's Island

Russell Dixon, Adrian McLoughlin and Kenneth Price

Tim Firth's new play was directed by Connal Orton in repertory from June to September. It showed four businessmen coming adrift on an initiative taking exercise in the Lake District. Having elected the eponymous Neville (Adrian McLoughlin) as leader, they are led astray and end up marooned.

Like Ayckbourn, Tim Firth lets darker moods grow out of comedy. Act One was hilarious, as the stranded foursome decided what last call to make on the dying battery of a portable 'phone and attempted to dry out a floating sandwich. Act Two was much bleaker, as matters went far beyond a joke. Russell Dixon's explosive Gordon, always attacking what is precious to others because of his own inadequacy, cracked the religious faith of Kenneth Price's Roy, upon which Roy had rebuilt his life after a breakdown.

Dreams From a Summer House

Janie Dee and Jan Hartley

The year's second Ayckbourn premiere, directed by the author, was a play with music by the regular Stephen Joseph composer John Pattison. Set in the garden of an affluent household, its central character is the hard-drinking artist Robert (Dale Rapley) whose idealised female, drawn for a children's book, comes to life.

The play's central device lies in the fairy characters, Beauty and the Beast, who only understand and express themselves in song. Beauty was beautifully sung by Jan Hartley and Juliet Nicholls' sets suited both real and fantasy sequences. However, the new piece carried an uncertainty of tone, as if Ayckbourn wanted to believe in fantasy and show us he was aware it was unreal at the same time.

Prince on a White Bike

James Tomlinson

December saw a revival of Ayckbourn's "My Very Own Story"' a children's piece, which played mostly daytimes, leaving the evening slot for "Prince on a White Bike", by octogenarian Charles Thomas. It was directed by Ayckbourn. As with "Dreams", the play mixes real life with fantasy. In this case the prince, supposedly on a white charger, arrives on more prosaic transport. The setting is the east end of London in the 1930s.

As end-of-the-year entertainment, the play provided a variation on standard Christmas fare, and showed once again that a theatre run by a writer can be open in access to unsolicited scripts and willing to stage a new work by an unknown dramatist.

The Crucible, Sheffield

It's not been an easy year for the 1,000 seater thrust stage Crucible. When the theatre opened in 1971 many Sheffielders lamented the passing of the proscenium touring house, the Lyceum. But, though dead the Lyceum did not lie down. As a listed building it stayed up, if shut. Then last year it reopened as a touring house and brought the likes of Robert Lindsay and Julie Walters to within 100 yards of the Crucible's front door. But it was the Lyceum's stage door they went through, and the Lyceum which attracted the crowds.

Crucible and Lyceum operate under the Sheffield Theatres umbrella with Stephen Barry as Chief Executive, but Crucible Artistic Director Mark Brickman resigned in late 1991 when the decision was made to axe his classical ensemble season. So 1992 opened without "The Front Page" and "Hedda Gabler" but with a revival of an old local documentary, tours and "Cabaret" plus "Adrian Mole".

By autumn new Artistic Director Michael Rudman had arrived, kicking off his regime with the "Dream" followed by Annie Castledine's production of "Jane Eyre".

The Stirrings in Sheffield on Saturday Night

Andrew Readman, Joanna Swain and David Birrell

This was a revival of Alan Cullen's 1966 play about the century old union outrages, when pub landlord William Broadhead organised the dynamiting of recalcitrant bosses' homes. Writer Tony Robinson was drafted in to prepare a new version of the script. Withered laurels were chucked out and the music hall idea, from the last scene of the 1966 show, was incorporated as a framing device for the entire piece.

New music was provided and the cast of Richard Stone's production (designer Michael Vale) was made up largely of local actors.

Best of all, after its January 30 – February 22 run, it went on to play a week at the Lyceum.

Cabaret

Sally Ann Triplett

Roger Haines directed the revival of the John Kander (music) and Fred Ebb (lyrics) musical, designed by Lez Brotherston and with Robert Scott as musical director, running June 4 – 27.

"Cabaret" always runs the risk of glamourising an increasingly unpleasant, intolerant society and as neo-Nazis strike in modern Germany the danger of this becomes greater. Lez Brotherston made Berlin a cold, harsh place. Equipped with a red stick, Andy Serkis made Emcee (the Master of Ceremonies) a sinister, mechanistic figure. As the Isherwood figure, Simon Burke was strong, as was Sally Ann Triplett as the cabaret singer Sally Bowles. Any idea of a cosy night out was squashed at the swastika-swathed conclusion. Again, the Crucible had given artistic validity to what might have seemed an easy commercial option.

Harrogate Theatre

Anyone expecting a plain roast beef and Yorkshire pub menu in Yorkshire theatres will be surprised. In February, you could have compared Leeds and Harrogate (under twenty miles apart) in Jacobaean tragedy, in September seen unconventional versions of Priestley (Leeds) and Coward (Harrogate), with a bomb-site "Blithe Spirit".

The difference is, Leeds is deservedly much sung about; Harrogate goes largely unnoticed. Yet over seven years Andrew Manley has brought this theatre from near closure to a vibrant state attracting a new, alert and younger audience. Once a black Eliza Doolittle brought reproaches and controversy; now among the Godber and Ayckbourn, the theatre fills for Middleton, Tennessee Williams "The Glass Menagerie" and play-opera mixes such as 1991's "The Marriage of Figaro" and this November's "The Barber of Seville". In what he calls the lowest funded repertory theatre in Britain (a particular anxiety is the inability to incorporate previews into what are often mere two and a half week runs) Manley has built a distinctive, bold production style aimed at making classic texts speak clearly to modern audiences.

The Changeling

Jane Robbins

Running in February and March, Manley's production of Middleton's tragedy (William Rowley's secondary plot was cut) was mounted on Julie Henry's ornate, candle-strewn set, backed by a huge mirror from which a white sheet was torn at the start. Updated costumes mixed formality with sexuality in the women's short-skirted, button-up suits. Jane Robbins played Beatrice-Joanna, seen first in dark glasses, as a manipulative sophisticate. De Flores (Vincent Franklin), crawling, smelling Beatrice-Joanna's cast-off glove, putting it on and watching himself in the mirror as he felt his face with the gloved hand on the line "I know she hates me" epitomised the intensity and passion of the production. Even murder became sexual, De Flores eventually lying by his victim after a paroxysm of stabbing, like an exhausted lover.

Blithe Spirit

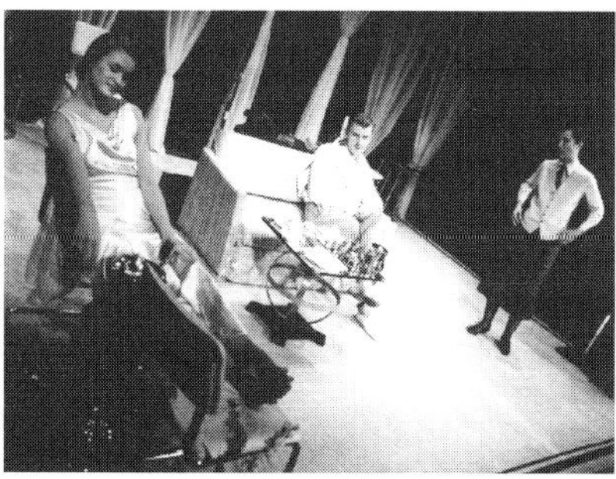

Catherine Prendergast, Charles Edwards and Rebecca Charles

Opening the autumn season, Andrew Manley's production of Noel Coward's play was the first of four shows set on the same basic design – a huge, ruined building which could have been church, factory or even a large house. In front of this a fashionable late thirties set was laid (and at the very end removed). The contrast of private lives and historical events was also established through characters repeatedly turning off radio programmes broadcasting Churchill's messages or an account of blitzed London. Avoiding the death outside, these characters performed in their brightly lit room. The cast, playing on Julie Henry's set, mostly caught the Coward style for this 1941 play, with strong work from Rebecca Charles as Ruth and Katy Secombe, in her first professional role as the maid Edith.

THE MIDLANDS

By PAT ASHWORTH and ROD DUNGATE

The Midlands '92

Mixed fortunes over such a very diverse region of the country, but a deservedly good year on the whole for Midlands theatre. Theatres under new direction included Birmingham Rep, where Bill Alexander took over from John Adams in November, and Derby Playhouse, where Mark Clements took up his appointment in January to initiate the theatre's most successful season ever at the box office.

Space was gained and space was lost: the Richardson Studio at the Everyman Theatre, Cheltenham, reopened after a year in darkness in September, with a regional premiere of Jean Binnie's "Lady Macbeth", but Northampton Royal Theatre lost its Derngate Studio. Like Northampton, some theatres played safe with traditional programming policies: others, such as Cheltenham, committed themselves to regional premieres and risked the wrath of the public.

Oxford Playhouse, under the joint direction of Tish Francis and Hedda Beeby, had a successful first year after their four-year closure, not only surviving but exceeding financial targets and eliciting ongoing support from an increasingly committed audience. In a programme that varied from contemporary dance through opera to the classics, the season also saw their first co-production with the Oxford Stage Company.

New work could be found in pockets throughout the region, principally at Birmingham Rep which developed its links with local writers and put on a season of new writing in the Studio. Coventry Belgrade, which under Robert Hamlin has always been willing to take the odd risk and mount adventurous things in the Studio, put on Stephen Clark's new play, "A Twitch on the Thread" and also - as a theatre wholly committed to involving its public - put on a massive, devised community play in the main house. The Swan at Worcester - which receives no Arts Council funding - put on "Anzacs over England", also by a local writer.

The Arts Centre at the University of Warwick, Coventry, continued to be the place where you could pick up all sorts of innovative work. The season here, under the direction of Jodi Myers, saw the return of the English Shakespeare Company to premiere Macbeth, and the development of a unique series of events, "Seeing is Believing". This included the first performances in England by Welsh performance group Brith Gof; from France NADA Theatre's acclaimed "Ubu", and the commissioning of the world's largest laser-scanned hologram - "Cyclops". The Midlands Arts Centre at Cannon Hill Park, Birmingham, a favourite venue for touring companies, committed itself to a policy of putting theatre and dance into residencies and outreach rather than into one and two-night stands.

Major venues like Nottingham and Leicester continued to thrive, Leicester's outrageous '70's compilation musical, "Hot Stuff" going out on national tour. Sponsorship was generally worked hard for and achieved, enabling many theatres to embark on improvements to seating and to hospitality areas to make sponsorship even more attractive. And the new M42 link from the M1 to Birmingham should encourage theatregoers in the major Midlands cities to be more adventurous in travelling to other venues.

Birmingham Repertory Theatre

Bill Alexander took over as Artistic Director , in November, from John Adams who left in the summer. The Birmingham Rep produced nine home-grown productions in their main house (of which one was jointly produced with Yorkshire Playhouse.) In addition there were two collaborations, "Biko", a new opera by Priti Paintal and Richard Fawkes in conjunction with Royal Opera House Garden Venture, and "Radio Times", featuring Tony Slattery, a new reminiscence musical in conjunction with Waldgrave productions, destined for the West End. Their studio continued as a venue for small-scale touring companies, but in September they launched a policy of presenting home-grown work - three new plays and a special project devised by associate director Gwenda Hughs for people with severe learning difficulties. The company mounted two community tours ("Island" adapted by Guy Hutchins from Scot O'Dell's novel "Island of the Blue Dolphins", and "The Devil's only Sleeping" by Nick Stafford); they also toured the main house "Kafka's Dick" by Alan Bennett. The Birmingham Rep's policy of integrated casting resulted in an acrimonious debate in the Birmingham local press.

The Rivals

This was a co-production with the West Yorkshire Playhouse where it was first seen in March: it was sponsored by Ansells brewery. Under John Adams' intelligent direction this was a highly stylish production. Patrick Connellan's imaginative set was also a delight. David Harewood played Captain Absolute and Jean Fergusson, Mrs Malaprop. The Birmingham Rep has long suffered at the hands of its local press who seem not to have realised the world has moved on since 1930, and this production was no exception. The national press said "The joy of John Adams' production is that it confidently achieves a mannered style without appearing to be affected" [Robin Thornber, The Guardian] but the best the Birmingham press could muster was "I found neither humour nor intimacy in John Adams' production" [Richard Edmonds, Birmingham Post].

David Harewood and Kate Duchene

My Mother Said I Never Should

Anthony Clark directed: in some senses a return visit, the play was originally commissioned by Contact Theatre in Manchester during his time as Artistic Director there. It is an intimate play which Charlotte Keatley says, "I wrote because I didn't know of any plays about mothers and daughters." It is easy to get trapped into believing that the huge Rep space needs huge plays, but this production showed it not to be the case - it's quality that counts. It was also a rare opportunity to see the work of a woman playwright in the Rep main house. Beautiful ensemble acting came from Margery Mason (Doris), Christine Absalom (Margaret), Janice McKenzie (Jackie) and Louise Yates (Rosie). Fran Thompson's designs, in which giant suitcases featured, ensured the play sat easefully into the space.

Christine Absalom, Louise Yates, Margery Mason and Janice McKenzie

The Last Carnival

Jill Brassington, Peter Woodward and Haydn Forde

While "My Mother Said . . ." was a rare chance to hear a woman's voice in the Rep main house, Derek Walcott's "The Last Carnival" was a rare chance to hear a black person's voice there. Set in Trinidad between 1947 and 1970 it was a sensitive account of a French Creole family faced with the emergence of the Black Power movement. John Adams directed, with set designs by Roger Butlin and costumes by Sue Plummer: the result was a highly atmospheric evocation of the island. Jill Brassington played Agatha, the white English socialist governess and Peter Woodward, Victor Delafontaine her employer. "Carnival" called for a cast of fifteen and it was pleasing to see a regional rep take a chance with a play like this. Unfortunately, while it was critically well received, audiences were disappointing.

New Plays in the Studio

Jason Yates, Ian Pepperell, Robin Pirongs and James Dreyfus in Playing By The Rules

The Rep launched a policy of presenting new work in September. Three world premieres appeared between then and December - "Playing By The Rules" by Rod Dungate, "Nervous Women" by Sarah Woods and a specially commissioned adaptation by Lisa Evans of Mrs Henry Woods' "East Lynne" for Christmas. The Rep is developing close links with local writers and both "Playing By the Rules" and "Nervous Women" are a result of those links.

All three plays had strong contemporary themes. Rod Dungate's looked at the issue of male prostitution from the boys' point of view. It was a tough, no-holds-barred, play, which was about "survival, about caring and about whether there is any place for love in the entrepreneurial '90s." Ruari Murchison's wild designs perfectly captured the play's theatrical tone. Sarah Woods' extraordinary play concerned the lives of two women, living a hundred years apart in the same house. It parallelled the sexual suppression of a Victorian wife with the growing agoraphobia of a present day woman. Both plays were directed by Anthony Clark. Gwenda Hughes directed Lisa Evans' adaptation which was more than simply telling the story of the novel to save us reading it. It was a healthily critical examination of Mrs Henry Woods' stern and unforgiving sense of sin and retribution and her wholehearted embracing of what we now call "Victorian values."

Belgrade, Coventry

Robert Hamlin continues as Artistic Director, with Rumu Sen-Gupta this year appointed as associate director. This talented young woman director completed her traineeship at the Belgrade this year. The theatre mounted ten productions during the year, and played host to a number of tours. The programming accent tends to be on modern popular theatre with some notable, more adventurous exceptions. The theatre seriously endeavours to address the diverse cultural backgrounds of the people living in and around Coventry. The theatre houses the prestigious Theatre in Education team - the Belgrade TIE company was the first in the country.

Firestone

The Belgrade got 1992 off to a pounding start with a production of this "sex, drugs and rock 'n' roll" musical by Peter Fieldson and Stephen Warbeck, first seen at the Contact Theatre in Manchester. It's a rollicking tale of four young adventurers who set out on a perilous quest to free the benighted land of Zamethess from Suckerax the Sorceress and liberate the mortal men imprisoned in the Sucksisters' bordello. Songs lurk under titles such as "The Masculine Feminist", "Advertisiac", "Black Widow" and "Sexual Pursuits". It was all good clean fun! "Firestone" was directed by Peter Fieldson, directing his second show for the Belgrade, his other having been "Accidental Death of An Anarchist".

Mandy Travis

Safe in Our Hands

The Belgrade presented Andy de la Tour's political farce in conjunction with Bill Kenwright during April. It was greeted with mixed reactions of hilarity and accusations of bad taste - much what Mr de la Tour would wish, I suppose. But it was generally agreed that his political observation is sharp and to the point and that the company as a whole showed a sense of timing and flair for comedy which made for a racy and stylish evening's entertainment. It was directed by Glen Walford. Adrian Rees' set was a cause of delight in itself, on two levels, it came complete with lifts, sliding doors and flashing lights. Among the cast were Kenneth Cope (Barnes), Tony Osoba (Roland Dixon), Frances Dodge (Deirdre Holbrook) and Susan Jameson (Jill Robinson).

Kenneth Cope

A Twitch on the Thread

Peter Hamilton Dyer and Prim Cotton

Stephen Clark's professional writing debut was made in the Belgrade Studio during May, in this production directed by Robert Hamlin. "A Twitch on the Thread" is an absorbing trilogy of plays for two performers - in this production Prim Cotton and Peter Hamilton Dyer. The first is a monologue for the woman - "Mary's Story", the second a monologue written in fluent verse for the man - "Steven's Fish". The third play "Tree" brings the two actors together; all three plays are loosely linked by the theme of death. Full marks to Robert Hamlin for taking time to invest in the development of this new playwright - while opinions had a healthy degree of divergence, it was unanimously agreed that the sensitivity of the performance team showed the promise of this new writer to great advantage.

Leave Taking

Eddie Osie and Lorren Bent

Ms Pinnock's 1991 George Devine Award winner, received its first post-award production at the Belgrade during May. It is a play, says Ms Pinnock that "highlights the upheaval and confusion faced by many generations of families struggling to find their roots in a new cultural environment." It was the first time it had been played on a large main house stage, and was a bold venture for Rumu Sen-Gupta's main house directing debut. The entire Belgrade got into the spirit of the play with pre-show performances, Caribbean food-tasting, art and craft exhibitions and samba music: the TIE team developed a special programme. The cast included two Coventry born actors, Lorren Bent and Doreene Blackstock with Anni Domingo, Vivienne Rochester and Eddie Osie completing the team. Design was by Trudy Marklew.

Diamonds in the Dust

Devising in action

A very special first for the Belgrade in November when they presented the country's first devised community play: it incorporated about one hundred people and was devised under the leadership of Janice Dunn. They aimed to create a piece of theatre which would truly allow participants to address the issues which concerned them, yet celebrated the varied natures of the community in which we live. Community participants were involved in all aspects including design (headed up by Ali McLaurin) and even finance - the production was sponsored by Peugot. "Diamonds" dealt with an urban community which is inhabited by many varied and exciting characters. The whole place is blown wide open by the arrival of a group of outsiders who alter the fabric of people's everyday existence, and change some peoples' lives forever.

Derby Playhouse

Always a lot of politics in Derby, but things may settle down following the resignation earlier in the year of the highly controversial County Council leader, David Bookbinder. The Playhouse is currently enjoying both stability and success after turbulent times which saw the departure of Annie Castledine in the mid-1990's followed by a 1991 season programmed by the theatre's executive director, David Edwards, and members of his Board.

Mark Clements was appointed Artistic Director in January 1992, following a long period as assistant and associate director at the Royal Theatre, Northampton, and has done some notable work to make this season the most successful ever at the box office. Now virtually clear of deficit despite the shortfall induced by the loss of its city council grant, the theatre has been able to invest in new seating in the auditorium and extensive improvements to its bar and coffee bar areas, spaces which are used more than ever to complement and enhance productions.

And a Nightingale Sang

Mark Clements' first production here and one with very broad appeal. This lovely piece of wartime nostalgia by C.P.Taylor, set in Newcastle-upon Tyne, was wry, at times almost crazy stuff, a love story in which momentous world events happen outside to throw into focus the everyday preoccupations of a working-class family. Beautifully staged on the revolve, it was very poignant, with the "nightingale" a crooner set high aloft the stage, and all the songs very artlessly delivered under the musical direction of David Roper.Designed by Charles Cusick-Smith, and beautifully paced so as to produce a series of action-stoping punchlines, there were exceptional performances from Margo Stanley, Sheila Tait and Geoffrey Banks as the irrepressible Granda. This was a production which laid the foundations of the new era at the theatre.

Geoffry Banks, Sheila Tait and Margo Stanley

On the Piste

John Godber's outrageous ski and sex comedy broke box office records at Derby, being so successful during its initial three-week run in March/April that it returned for a further season in the autumn. It's rumoured that people would have killed for tickets. Designer Chris Crosswell produced a set that was the talk of the town: an artificial ski-slope thirty-five feet high and angled at thirty degrees , down which the actors glided, toppled and stumbled with varying expertise, to stop short within breathtaking inches of the front row. Mark Clements directed, Sheila Tait and Sharon Mayer returned to play Alison and Melissa, and Shaaron Jackson (a seasoned Godber player, principally with Hull Truck Theatre Company) made her Derby debut as Bev. The play attracted sponsorship by the local Swadlincote Ski Centre and earned an award under the Government's business sponsorship incentive scheme.

Shaaron Jackson

The Innocents

William Peterson and Anna Bowtell

Robin Midgely came to Derby as guest director for this haunting and atmospheric ghost story by William Archibald, based on Henry James' "The Turn of the Screw". This was a psychological thriller that played on the nerves in a subtle and measured way, producing cutting shocks out of prolonged periods of silence and evincing those collective intakes of breath that demonstrate an audience totally at one with what is happening on stage.The subject matter had extraordinary power to shock: full of sexual undercurrents and sexual ambivalence, it opened up a can of worms to reveal the corruption to which two seemingly innocent children had been exposed. A dark play indeed, with outstanding performances from Jane Montgomery (the governess) and Margo Stanley (the housekeeper). Two local children performed remarkably as Flora and Miles.

Far from the Madding Crowd

Anna Skye and Timothy Watson

Another success for Mark Clements in Sally Hedges' dramatisation of one of Hardy's best-loved novels: the production, with a running time of three and a half hours and a cast of just eight, won high praise for its powerful staging and presentation. Charles Cusick-Smith's design, in conjunction with Chris Ellis's lighting, produced a very ingenious, three-tiered set depicting the waste of Egdon Heath at the upper level, a whole host of authentically depicted Wessex households at middle level and, in what is normally the orchestra pit, the malthouse. This device was a refreshing departure from the ubiquitous use of the revolve when dramatising huge novels. Anna Skye played Bathsheba; Tom Knight, Gabriel Oak; Robert Ashby, Farmer Boldwood and Timothy Watson, Sergeant Troy.

My Sister Next Door

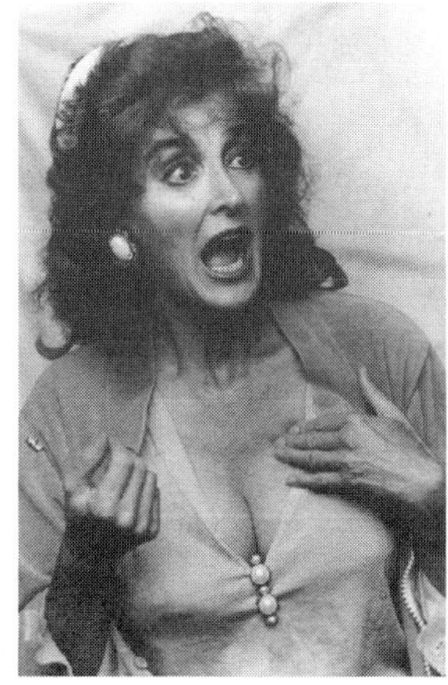

Anna Barry

This was a gem of a solo presentation written and directed by Michael Burrell, enjoyed a run of almost four weeks and demonstrated the power and flexibility of Derby's studio space.Anna Barry played the twin roles of two ageing sisters living in adjacent rooms in their family home in Derby: Anthea, the dancer, romanticising and embellishing the details of her career; Gwen, a clerk at the Belper and Nelson Building Society, and the sister who stayed home to look after Father. Different in appearance, style, bearing and voice, the sisters were beautifully portrayed by Anna Barry, in a witty and clever script that has seen performance in Canada and at London's Latchmere Theatre. Designed by Anne Curry and much appreciated by the Derby audience for its wealth of local references.

Leicester Haymarket

The joint Artistic Directorship of performance artist Julia Bardsley and Paul Kerryson produced a season of memorable work at the Haymarket, a theatre which has always profitably indulged its audience's passionate love of lavish musicals whilst maintaining a varied programme of classic and modern drama and producing some splendid and innovative work in the studio.

So whilst audiences flocked to the moneyspinning "The King and I", "Hot Stuff" and "West Side Story", they also had the rare opportunity to see T.S Eliot in the main house and the UK premiere of Kroetz's "Dead Soil" in the studio. The theatre received a major award of £100,000 from the Sports and Arts Foundation, which has provided new seating in the studio - heartfelt thanks for that. It will also fund two multi-lingual community touring projects as part of its outreach programme under a new head of Outreach, Julia Smith. Julia Bardsley received special enhancement funding from both the Arts Council and the European Arts festival for her powerful production of Lorca's "Blood Wedding".

Hot Stuff

Undoubtedly the sensation of the year, even by Leicester standards. An outrageous compilation musical co-devised by Paul Kerryson and Maggie Norris and directed by Kerryson, it was the Faust legend never before so demonic, with David Dale as Lucy Fur, Guy Oliver-Watts as Gary Glitter, and Chris Talman as the fall guy, Joe Soap, who sells his soul to Lucy Fur and crashes his way through glam-rock, punk and disco, in the wildest imaginable rendering of '70's music. This was an extraordinary, ear-splitting gallop through the decade, which packed in every song you thought you'd forgotten from Abba, Kate Bush, David Bowie, Slade and the rest whilst maintaining a credible, even poignant story-line. Co-designers were Charles Cusick-Smith and Phil R.Daniels; musical director Julian Kelly, and lighting designer Chris Ellis.

David Dale

Dead Soil

Directed in the studio by Julia Bardsley, in a translation by Anthony Vivis, Kroetz's grim, disturbing and frequently repellent play couldn't have presented a greater contrast to the licentiousness of "Hot Stuff". Heavily laden with religious symbolism, it is the odyssey of a farming family who take Jesus with them on their tractor into the city, hoping for something better than rural life can offer. Disillusion, degeneration and despair follow, but there's a wholly unexpected hint of resurrection at the end.

Aldona Cunningham's set

Played promenade style, it confronted the audience at every turn with grotesque and horrifying images, such as a foetus placed into the maggot-ridden belly of a dead woman. Extraordinarily detailed and complex and certainly not for the faint-hearted, it left open-mouthed an audience who hadn't seen anything quite like this before.

Merrily we Roll Along

Maria Friedman

"The musical may be dead as an art form in the West End...but musicals with something to say and a sense of irony, style and versatility are still to be found in subsidised regional theatres." (Robin Thornber, The Guardian). And how. Sondheim and Furth were both in rehearsal at Leicester for this bittersweet story of lost dreams, lost innocence and lost idealism, which flopped on Broadway but which - re-written up to the very last minute - received wide critical rather than popular acclaim here.

Directed by Paul Kerryson, a consistently good company included Michael Cantwell as the composer of Hollywood and Broadway musicals and Evan Pappas as his lyricist: praise too for Maria Friedman, Jacqueline Dankworth and Louise Gold as well as for the musical direction of Julian Kelly. "..The sheer sensual excitement of the narrative set pieces make up the most stirring episodes currently available in the British theatre." (Michael Coveney, The Observer)

The Family Reunion

John Joyce, Phyllida Hewat, Vivienne Burgess, Jonathan Cecil, and John Quentin

T.S.Eliot isn't everyone's cup of tea and this particular play is seldom performed these days - but this production demonstrated the boldness and confidence of the Haymarket's policy. Directed by Julia Bardsley, this wasn't tucked away in the studio but flaunted in the main house where it toweringly filled the stage and the mind.

A strong cast did more than justice to the cadences and complexities of Eliot's verse, but there was more to it than words in this extraordinarily visual production. The Eumenides were grotesque, masked miniatures of the Aunts and Uncles; at portentous moments, the chandelier would swing massively like a pendulum in a hurricane; blood-red lighting suffused the stage at moments of spiritual enlightenment.

Anna Karenina

This extraordinary and awesome piece of theatre was from Shared Experience, directed by Nancy Meckler who was associate director at the Haymarket from 1984 to 1987 and returns frequently to work there.

This production is described in full in the Yearbook's section on **Touring Companies**.

Nottingham Playhouse

A second successful season under Ruth Mackenzie, executive director; Pip Broughton, Artistic Director; and Stuart Rogers, administrative director, has earned the Playhouse a growing reputation for its commitment to bringing the best of world theatre to Nottingham: the Maly Theatre of St.Petersburg was a sell-out here and Sturua's "Hamlet", with Alan Rickman and Geraldine McEwan, sold out within ten hours - believed to be the fastest-selling production since the theatre opened in 1948. Bookings for the autumn season were 50% up on 1991, and the theatre's own productions included a Godber premiere and a major new "Doctor Faustus." Audiences now include increased numbers of students and young people.

Generous sponsorship by Home Brewery, increased for the 1992/3 season, is detailed in the **Serious Money** section of the Year Book. Nottingham can also boast one of the most successful pantomimes in the region, written, directed and starring the theatre's former director, Kenneth Alan Taylor, which has itself attracted major sponsorship from McDonalds.

What the Butler Saw

Ultz both designed and directed this new production of Joe Orton's high farce, which allowed the elegance and complexity of Orton's language and the dazzle of his words to come to the fore. One of those unforgettably manic nights in the theatre, and one to which the Nottingham audience responded after some initial bafflement - the notion of the madhouse in which unusual behaviour is the order of the day does take some getting used to, as does the delight taken in nymphomania, incest and transvestism. Helen Atkinson Wood played the redoubtable Mrs Prentice and Mark Arden Doctor Prentice, with Nigel Pivaro as Sergeant Match. Quite a romp, with the descent by rope to the stage of the half-naked, bloodstained sergeant in a leopard-skin dress the dramatic high point of the evening.

Helen Atkinson Wood and Bill Thomas

Les Miserables - the Play

This specially commissioned stage adaptation by Belfast-born playwright, Christina Reid, opened at just around the time that the Trevor Nunn-devised musical adaptation was making its northern debut in Manchester, providing some interesting contrasts. Reid's device of using the ghosts of Gavroche and Eponine, killed at the barricades, to tell their own story, gave the play a good narrative framework. Technical brilliance - particularly in the staging of the siege - on a steeply raked set designed by Ruari Murchison and Geraldine Pilgrim and lit by Mark Ridley, was matched by some exceptional performances, notably from Kevin Quarmby as the stocky, bear-like Valjean; Roger McKern as his ruthless adversary, Javert; and Angela Clerkin as a spirited Eponine. Directed by Peter Rowe.

Francis Johnson, Roger Leach, Kevin Quarmby and Angela Clerkin

The Rivals

Ann Mitchell

A very authentic, stylish and well researched production of the Sheridan classic, directed by James Macdonald and designed by Geraldine Pilgrim, who was also much acclaimed here for her sets and costumes for "Les Miserables". Mild embarrassment to the theatre on this one: for some inexplicable reason, their pre-publicity described the production as "raunchy" (since known as "the R word") - thankfully, it was about as raunchy as "Little Women", and notable for the dazzle and the sharpness of the wit.

Ann Mitchell played a droll, endearing and slightly batty Mrs Malaprop, and Robin Soans gave a delicious performance as Sir Anthony Absolute, as tetchy and testy as could be imagined. A strong cast included David Fielden, Simon Roberts, John Keegan, Jason Watkins, Nirjay Mahindru, Sandy McDade, Lucy Briers, Victoria Scarborough and Sean Hannaway, and particularly memorable was Ace McCarron's lighting, producing startling prismatic effects on an ingenious revolving set.

The Office Party

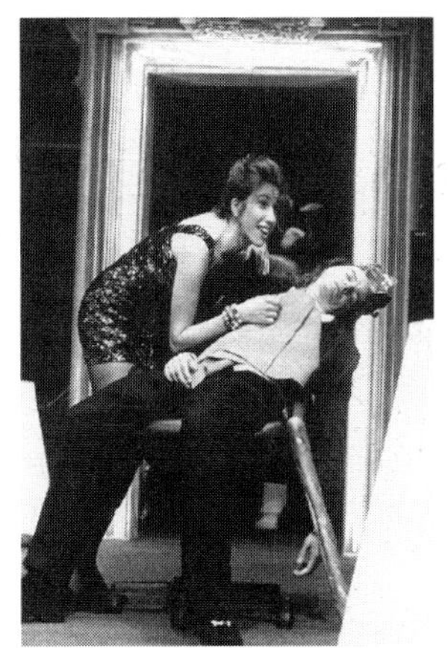
Gaynor Faye and Gareth Tudor Price

John Godber's eagerly awaited new play received its premiere at Nottingham Playhouse before embarking on a nationwide tour. A co-production with Hull Truck Theatre Company, it followed the success of "April in Paris" and "Happy Families" which played to capacity audiences and received widespread critical acclaim. An outrageous and highly visual comedy of manners, "The Office Party" was directed by John Godber and designed by Robert Jones.

Funny, dangerous, entertaining and menacing, the play features the office romp at Chapman and Howard, a successful, high-profile marketing firm who have just won a prestigious health drink contract, and explores - in an innovative style combining verse and flashback - the direction in which we are moving as a consumer-led society.

The Pocket Dream

Having had its premiere in Nottingham in 1992, when it was hugely enjoyed by the local audience, "The Pocket Dream" by Elly Brewer and Sandi Toksvig returned to the Playhouse prior to its London run. As before, it was received with much mirth and its poor reception in London seemed surprising. Please see the Yearbook's section on **The West End**.

Everyman, Cheltenham

Martin Houghton is Artistic Director, with Sheila Mander as associate director. They mounted nine or eleven shows in their main house - depending on whether you count Ayckbourn's "Intimate Exchanges" as one or three! New work appeared in the form of a new translation of Ibsen's "A Doll's House" by Karina Micallef as part of the 1992 Cheltenham Literature Festival. In September they re-opened their Richardson Studio and presented three plays, one of which, Tom McGrath's "Laurel and Hardy", directed by Sheila Mander, toured locally – the Everyman's ability to tour is under threat due to financial constraints. The theatre plays host to several touring companies, including a fair spread of shows specially for children. The Everyman also launched its own paper in August; they hope to increase understanding of their policies, achievements and difficulties - the "Everyman News" will appear in all programmes.

A Family Affair

Dan Milne, Mark Chatterton and Sharon Muircroft

Martin Houghton thought he'd blow a few cobwebs off the Everyman's proscenium when he decided to programme Nick Dear's vigorous and very funny version of this Ostrovsky play about greed, hypocrisy and lust. Robin Polley played Bolshov, the merchant, Pat Rossiter, Agrafena, his wife, Sharon Muircroft, their daughter, Lipochka and Mark Chatterton Lazar, Bolshov's assistant with murky intentions, in a production in which people are as turned on by money as they are by sex. In Nettie Edwards' design, Bosch's Garden of Delight towered over all. If the stage is a mirror, then Cheltenham audiences were shocked by what they saw of themselves, and reactions were extreme - positive and negative.

Over a Barrel

Jackie Smith-Wood

Bravely following his policy of not "playing safe", but continuing his policy of "regional premieres", Martin Houghton programmed Stephen Bill's uncompromising comedy/farce. Sure enough, letters of complaint followed - one patron suggesting that the theatre's "Everyman" name was no longer appropriate. Sheila Mander's design was impressive, a non-realistic house setting which beautifully fitted the Everyman's high narrow proscenium. The kitchen itself (in which all the action takes place) earned its own production credit - "Born in Germany . . . Currently on tour but looking to retire permanently . . . please contact the star's agent, Carol Bowen, In-toto Kitchens . . ." The owners of the kitchen, the Bartletts were played by Jackie Smith-Wood and Mac Andrews, with Mark Chatterton as Ray, the local builder, adding some good comic touches.

The New Victoria Theatre, North Staffordshire

The first professional company in Britain to perform permanently in the round - in the stunning surroundings of the 1986 building - the New Vic in the largely working-class area of the Potteries maintains its international reputation as a prime example of a community theatre, despite frequently falling victim to loss of local funding in avoidance of rate-capping. Its dynamic director, Peter Cheeseman, has been with the company for thirty years and finds here every creative challenge he wants in "creating the circumstances in which wonderful things can happen."

Ten major productions this year have included two Shakespeare's, "Julius Caesar" and "The Comedy of Errors"; Brecht's "Threepenny Opera"; Ayckbourn's "Henceforward"; "Hobson's Choice" by Harold Brighouse, and "To" by Jim Cartwright, in addition to the highlights detailed below - both in the fine tradition of Staffordshire documentaries which dates back to the days of the Old Vic.

The Bright and Bold Design

Julia Righton, Louise Tomkins and Katie London

Commissioned by the RSC from Peter Whelan and premiered at the Barbican Pit in 1991, where it continued into 1992, "The Bright and Bold Design" was soon seen in a fresh production in what can fairly be regarded as its home town. The play was described by Robin Thornber of The Guardian as "probably the most substantial play to come out of the Potteries this century - maybe ever." Whelan was born in the Potteries in 1931 and set this play amongst the paintresses whose freehand decoration adorned teasets before the second world war. Authentically researched and directed by Peter Cheeseman in a production described by The Guardian as "meticulously real", it featured twenty-two-year-old Kay Pope as Jessie and Sean O'Callaghan as Jim Rhys. The production was designed by the New Vic's resident designer, Lis Evans.

The Jolly Potters

"And we were brought to poverty..."

Originally staged in 1964, this outstanding musical documentary was devised by the company from historical accounts of the Chartist riots in the Potteries in 1842. It was to mark the 150th anniversary that Cheeseman revived "The Jolly Potters", with a new script reworked by Romy Robinson and new music by John Kirkpatrick. It was described by The Guardian as a version which "retained the gutsy integrity of the Vic tradition, enhanced with the more sophisticated resources of the New Vic theatre." Performed by a consistently strong company of twelve, many of whom were fresh from drama school, the first half of the show depicted the harsh living and working conditions in the Potteries in the 1830s and the second half the riots and subsequent trials, with detail drawn from contemporary accounts. Designed by Lis Evans.

Royal Theatre, Northampton

Michael Napier Brown continues as Artistic Director of the charming Victorian Royal Theatre in Northampton. 1992 saw nine productions in the theatre's only auditorium of which two, "Martin Chuzzlewit" and "To Serve them All my Days" were new adaptations (Lynn Robertson Hay and Shaun McKenna respectively.) This year saw the last Royal production in the nearby Derngate studio - Nicholas Wright's "Mrs Klein". Michael Napier Brown has a traditional programming policy (the theatre has to pay its way!) and the most "daring" he dare be in the main house is Orton's "Entertaining Mr Sloane". The loss of the use of the Derngate space is to be regretted. From February onwards it became the Royal's policy to sign one performance of each play, and one performance is orally introduced for visually impaired clients. Lynn Wyfe joined the Royal as Director of TIE and also directed the theatre's community tour of John Christopher-Wood's "Elsie and Norman's Macbeth".

Blithe Spirit

Corinna Powlesland

Coward's classic comedy was presented during June in a production sponsored by Express Lifts. It was directed by a young visiting director, Philip Howard and included Michael Cadman as Charles, Jane Hollowood as Ruth and Mellee Hutton as a laid back Elvira. Bridget Turner played Madam Arcati in an unusual portrayal that attempted to shake off the "Rutherford" image. This Arcati was more like a highly professional headmistress. Corinna Powlesland was a valuable comic addition to the team as Edith, the maid. Design was by associate designer Alison Heffernan, who placed the Condomine's famous living room in a realistic setting - a long corridor along the front of the set and a hill side for Arcati to ride down along the set's rear. Even the theatre's bars got into the spirit - "Spirit of Elvira" cocktails were readily available.

To Serve Them All My Days

Marie Critchley and Gwynn Beech

John Napier Brown directed this large cast adaptation, specially commissioned by the Royal. The production itself fits into a theatre policy of annually programming something that uses significant numbers of local youngsters. In this production the theatre was well served by all twelve of them. The many locations required by the adaptation were lovingly recreated in great detail by resident designer Ray Lett, ingeniously using every inch of the small stage. A strong acting company was headed up by Gwynn Beech as a moving protagonist, David Powlett Jones, Robert Vahey as the humane "old guard headmaster" Rev Algy Herries, Marie Critchley as P-J's lively first wife, Beth, and Lynette Edwards as the elegant widow, Julia Darbyshire.

Swan Theatre, Worcester

The Swan, built in 1965, is the only professional repertory company in the county of Hereford and Worcester. It is under the directorship of Pat Trueman: Jonquil Panting is her assistant. The theatre has no Arts Council funding and is reliant on West Midlands Arts, and the city and county councils. The Worcester Theatre Company (the professional company) plays host to the Swan Theatre Company (the amateur company) who mount shows regularly throughout the year. The professional company mounted seven plays during the year and the amateur company three. Of the Worcester Theatre Company's plays, one, an adaptation of "Stig of the Dump", was for children. The theatre hosts a wide variety of touring shows, varying from Phil Cool, to Hull Truck to Phoenix Dance.

The Curse of the Mummy's Tomb

Sayan Kent

The Worcester Theatre Company produced this lively musical in March -it was directed by Pat Trueman. Originally written for and performed by the London Bubble Theatre in 1985 during author Bob Eaton's period there as Artistic Director, it was substantially rewritten and updated. It is set in 1928, and Professor Hugh Cartwright is to guide the audience on their first Egyptian tour. Naturally, nothing is straightforward, and the audience is quickly caught up in a tale of danger, mystery and suspense. Kate Edgar was musical director (as she was on the original Bubble production) and Claire Southern designer. Lennox Greaves played Professor Hugh Cartwright and Jenny Coulston his daughter Bunty. Inspector Ernest Ransome was played by Peter Alexander with Donovan Cary keeping a wary eye open as Selim, the Sphinx night-club owner.

Anzacs Over England

Miranda Pleasence and Richard S. Huggett

In September the company presented a new play "Anzacs Over England" by a local writer, David Goodland. The play tells the story of a training school for Australian fighter pilots which was set up in the Cotswold Hills in World War I. It explores the clash of cultures when two worlds meet - the rural communities of the Cotswolds and the "bronzed gods from down under". The play started life as a television documentary shown throughout Australia, and was also recorded by BBC Bristol with the Worcester cast. Directed by Pat Trueman, and designed by Jill Amos, the play had Richard S Huggett (of "Neighbours" fame) making his British stage debut as Lieutenant Jeff Rylands. Annie, the girl with whom he falls in love, was played by Miranda Pleasence, making her professional debut.

WALES

by PENNY SIMPSON

Wales '92

Previous years have shown that is is the small-scale experimental companies, often existing with minimal funding and no settled base, that best reveal the state of Welsh theatre.

This year was no exception. The most challenging productions were often first seen away from the four repertory theatres, new performance works in both Welsh and English from companies like Y Cwmni, Dalier Sylw, Volcano Theatre, Man Act and Brith Gof.

Typically, the majority of these companies have first had to achieve recognition outside of their native Wales. In this, Y Cwmni are following an established pattern - their triology of new plays by Ed Thomas ("House of America", "Flowers of the Dead Red Sea" and "East From The Gantry") was initially presented by Glasgow's Tramway, who backed the project with an enthusiasm that was at the start lacking in Wales itself.

The newly refurbished Chapter Arts Centre probably boasted the most innovative theatre programming, now a base for Y Cwmni, as well as regular venue for internationaly acclaimed companies such as Brith Gof and Volcano. In addition, they presented Dalier Sylw's latest production "Y Forwyn Goch"/"The Red Virgin", an exploration in film, slide and poetic text of the life of French philosopher Simone Weil. A relative newcomer to Welsh theatre, Dalier Sylw have marked out a place for themselves as the only company in Cardiff presenting innovative new writing in the Welsh language.

A new start too for the Sherman Theatre and the St Stephen's Theatre Space, who are now interlinked in a way not anticipated at the beginning of the year. Once the home of Moving Being, St Stephen's is now a production resource for the thriving community of independent theatre and film companies found in Wales. The Sherman is its new caretaker following a dispute over the future of the converted dockland church base after Moving Being ran up a deficit and had to pull out of presenting an annual body of work that incorporated lunchtime dance and drama and classical texts. It will still occasionally act as a performance centre and has already welcomed Moving Being back ("The Changing Light") and Poland's Akademia Ruchu.

The refurbishment of seven former miners institutes and workmen's halls in the Valleys offered up improved facilities for touring community groups like Hijinx Theatre. Although small in scale, in impact these companies reach the parts that many larger and more nationally recognised groups fail to reach with their devised shows that target audience needs, but still provide an exciting theatricality often absent in mainstream works.

Wales's repertory theatres bucked a trend and in many cases saw box office takings rise. The Torch Theatre and the Sherman Theatre both backed new writing by Welsh playwrights, Theatr Gwynedd adaptations of the classics in Welsh. The English Shakespeare Company, the Peter Hall Company, the Royal Shakespeare Company and Simon Callow's production of "My Fair Lady" were all seen at Cardiff's New Theatre.

Sherman Theatre, Cardiff

The Sherman continued its policy of providing plays predominantly in the English language for younger audiences. The adoption of this policy two years ago by Artistic Director Phil Clark paid early dividends. Clark's view remains that the theatre's role should be that of a major community resource, one that ensures theatrical traditions flourish and stay put on the leisure agenda of young people. The programme reflected this concern with further commissions from playwright Mike Kenny, who wrote the two Christmas shows, one aimed at a family audience and one for the under-five's, as well as the Sherman Theatre Company's production of "Fern Hill", a rites of passage drama. "The Merchant of Venice" was a hit with schools - particularly the Playdays in which Portia played Blind Date to underline the Bard's themes. The theatre also hosted the first Welsh International Children's Theatre Festival, introducing companies from Alaska, Quebec, and Australia. The Sherman made a commitment to local writers, commissioning two new plays from Rhondda's Frank Vickery and an adaptation of Saunders Lewis' "Blodeuwedd" from Sion Eirian.

The Merchant of Venice

Simon Harris, Patrick Brennan and Kenneth Gardnier

Guest director Jamie Garven took an upbeat approach, fleshing out some of the minor characters to develop an unexpectedly humorous show. The scenes of reconcilation benefited, transforming the bartering courtiers as well as the revengeful Shylock in a manner that stressed the more fabulous elements of the play.

Jane Linz Roberts' design was a highlight of the production, swags of netting and a floor that tilted up like a ship's prow. The sensation of peeling back that curling floor and watching the darker shadows emerge was a strong one, an uneasy atmosphere aided by Matthew Bailey's evocative music - unaccompanied voices singing in Italian and Latin.

Fern Hill

Ian Saynor and Geraint Morgan

May saw a new play by Mike Kenny that used a familiar poem by Dylan Thomas to explore life's rites of passage. He took the poem's language and themes and translated them very broadly into a new drama that had at its centre psychological transitions experienced by schoolteacher John Stone.

A chronological narrative was overturned in favour of a constantly shifting world inhabited by Stone's reluctant pupils, members of his family - both dead and alive - and imagined arguments with the poet himself. Director Phil Clark, designer Jane Linz Roberts and all the production team have had strong ties with community theatre in the past and "Fern Hill" reflected these influences with its roots in improvisation, conducted partly in Dylan Thomas' home town Laugharne.

Leading the cast in the final version was Ian Saynor as schoolteacher Stone.

Sleeping with Mickey Mouse

Menna Trussler

Last year, the Sherman Theatre Company gave the first professional production of a work by Rhondda writer Frank Vickery. "A Kiss On The Bottom" was a bitter sweet drama set in a hospital ward and its star was actress Menna Trussler.

From out of this collaboration came "Sleeping With Mickey Mouse", a one-woman show exploring experiences of loneliness and the restorative powers of the imagination.

Set on New Year's Eve, Trussler's character Eileen sketches out why she is now alone. The heart of the play was found in the second Act where the wrtier captured the strength of a woman on the edge, but fighting back with strange rituals that conjured up a past lover and a dead daughter.

The play later toured to Swansea's Grand Theatre.

Erogenous Zones

Stuart Hulse

Playwright Frank Vickery established a strong working relationship with the Sherman's Artistic Director Phil Clark over the year. They teamed up for a second time to work on this drama, shortlisted for the LWT's Plays On Stage awards. Set in three city flats, "Erogenous Zones" explored the complex web of relationships that develop between five people. Experimental in form, the play marked a radical departure from Vickery's previous work.

Designer John Elvery returned to the Sherman to create a non-naturalistic set inspired by the sculptures of Rodin.

Once again, Clark employed a cast of Welsh actors, relying on strong ensemble acting rather than "star" names to draw in audiences, including Katherine Dimery, Erica Eirian and Geraint Morgan.

Blodeuwedd, Woman of Flowers

"A woman created out of flowers."

Actors Touring Company and the Sherman Theatre Company worked together for the first time in this new adaptation of a Welsh classic by Saunders Lewis based on a tale taken from The Mabinogion. One of the highlights of the autumn season, the production later toured throughout England and Wales before closing at London's Baylis Theatre, Sadlers Wells in November.

Director Ceri Sherlock was concerned to draw out the contemporary references in this re-telling of a medieval myth, based around the figure of Blodeuwedd, a woman created out of flowers.

Jane Linz Roberts and lighting designer Nick MacLiammoir worked closely together on producing the final set, influenced by eighteenth century paintings exploring the relationship between art and science.

The original poetic drama written in 1947 was translated by Sion Eirian, a contemporary playwright and crowned Eisteddfod Bard.

Theatr Clwyd, Mold

Theatr Clwyd celebrated one of their most successful years in 1992 - and welcomed a new Artistic Director Polish born Helena Kaut-Howson. Her arrival marked a change in approach for the Theatr Clwyd Company with the introduction of a policy that would help develop an identity for the North Walian arts centre in Europe as well as within Wales. A start was made with the invitation to Polish designer Pawel Dobrzycki to work on a new production of John Whiting's "The Devils".

But for a time, theatre staff enjoyed the rare opportunity of working alongside two Artistic Directors. Toby Robertson continued to direct in the early part of the year, with productions of "The Seagull" and "Marching Song". There were guest directors too, most notably actress Maria Aitken, who has had a long association with the Theatr Clwyd Company. She directed a production of "The School For Scandal" with a large cast headed by Sarah Crowe.

In addition to the Theatr Clwyd Company's progamme, there were performances from visiting companies and artists, among them Cardiff's dance company Diversions, dancers with The Russian Connection, and Theatr Gwynedd.

The Guardsman

A rarely staged play by Hungarian playwright Molnar, this production boasted an all female production team, led by director Lucy Parker. Set in the early nineteenth century, designer Claudia Mayer indicated the divided location (the play is set partly in a flat and partly at the opera) by a stunning painted curtain decorated with the faces of the audience seated at the opera.

The choice of Molnar's work marks out the theatre's policy of performing a range of European classic texts. Whilst the play might be unfamiliar, the names in the cast often help draw the good box that Theatr Clywd has enjoyed this year. The Guardsman starred Jenny Seagrove, making her first appearance with the Theatr Clywd Company, Oliver Parker and Mark Wing-Davey.

Mark Wing-Davey and Oliver Parker

Marching Song

The policy of reviving little known classics in action once again - this time dramatist John Whiting's "Marching Song". The symbolism of the text was drawn out in Simon Higlett's impressive and stunning design, which saw the actors placed on a perspex stage, above the remains of a destroyed city.

Toby Robertson directed a cast that included Clive Swift, Rupert Frazer and Graham Crowden.

This stylistic approach has marked out several productions in the 1992 season, and offered a continuity of approach with the arrival of Helena Kaut-Howson, who is also interested in creating atmospheric, stylized settings in her productions.

Higlett is just one of many top-line designers working at Mold in recent months, attracted by an artistic vision which enables technical staff and actors to collaborate on challenging, innovatively designed productions.

Clive Swift

The Seagull

Toby Robertson's swansong and another visual tour de force with sets by Australia's Paul Edwards and lighting design by Theatr Clwyd regular Jenny Cane, also responsible for spotlighting the perspex marvels found in "Marching Song".

Edwards created a versatile pine structure that was forest and home in one, cleverly lit to evoke the changing landscapes. The detailed period costumes provided more colour in what was a highlight of the summer programme. The cast included Dorothy Tutin in the role of the actress Irina Arkadina, Ian Hogg (Boris Trigorin) and Ronald Fraser (Pyotr Sorin).

This was the premiere of a new adaptation of Chekhov's play by Gwynedd-based writer Jeremy Brooks.

Dorothy Tutin and Ian Hogg

The Devils

This was a second chance for audiences in Clwyd to enjoy a rarely performed drama by John Whiting. It was also an opportunity to compare the very different directing styles of Toby Robertson, who directed Whiting's "Marching Song" earlier in the season, and his replacement Helena Kaut-Howson. She also opted to present a play by Whiting for her debut production with Theatr Clwyd. She put the play on in the Emlyn Williams Theatre, a small studio space, which turned out to be ideally suited for acting out a drama about political intrigue and conspiracy.

Olivier award winner Kathryn Hunter led the cast in a stylized production that was noted for its strong atmospheric feel, a sensation aided by the designs of Poland's Pawl Dobrzycki. He is chief scenographer of Krakow's Teatr Stary.

The Director: Helena Kaut-Howson

Hay Fever

Maria Aitken once again to the fore in the autumn season at Clwyd. After directing "The School For Scandal", she joined director Alan Strachan to play the lead of Judith Bliss in "Hay Fever", the only leading Coward role Aitken had left to play.

This was the first co-production to be set up between the Theatr Clwyd Company and the Theatre of Comedy Co Ltd and it boasted a high profile with an invitation to screen designer Anthony Powell to design the exquisite period costumes and Tudor timber interior.

Premiered in the main theatre, the play went on to tour England and then transferred into the West End.

Maria Aitken

Theatr Gwynedd, Bangor

Theatr Gwynedd is the only producing house in Wales to offer plays in both Welsh and English. The Artistic Director Graham Laker has continued this year to provide a range of work, including plays by Welsh writers Saunders Lewis and Emlyn Williams, and adaptations of classic texts by Tennessee Williams "Y Werin Wydr"/"The Glass Menagerie" and Lope De Vega "Y Gosb Ddiddial". These latter commissions were both awarded to two contemporary writers Gareth Miles and Annes Gruffydd, who both have strong connections with theatre companies providing experimental and challenging drama productions in Wales. There has been one major policy change this year, the invitation to Ceri Sherlock, formerly Artistic Director of Actors Touring Company, to direct "Y Gosb Ddiddial" by Gareth Miles for Cwmni Theatr Gwynedd. The emphasis was on a strikingly visual interpretation of a classic text, developing a style of performance that was first unveiled last year when the two collaborated on Dalier Sylw's reworking of Euripides' "The Bacchae". There were also touring shows from Compass Theatre Company "King Lear"/"Hamlet", Snap Theatre Company "Cyrano de Bergerac" and the Sherman Theatre Company "Fern Hill".

The Druid's Rest

Theatr Gwynedd was able to stage a summer production this year after savings made in last year's budget when the Sherman Theatre Company brought "Under Milk Wood" into the theatre for a season.

There was also sponsorship from a local company Mico Link Electronics for the run.

Set in a pub in North Wales at the turn-of-the-century, Emlyn Williams's comedy originally starred a young Richard Burton in one of his first stage roles. This new production featured an all Welsh cast, led by popular Welsh actress Myfanwy Talog.

The storyline revolves around Job Edwards, a landlord determined that his choir wins a National Eisteddfod competition.

The Glass Menagerie/Y Werin Wydr

Graham Laker directed a cast of four on John Jenkins' striking set, which consisted of a raised glass platform backed by plain brick walls.

Amongst the cast were two performers making their stage debuts - Nia Dryhurst, a former usher at Theatr Gwynedd, who played Laura, and Huw Charles (Jim), a graduate from the Welsh College of Music and Drama.

Christine Pritchard, who was in S4C's popular soap "Dinas", played the role of the domineering mother of a disturbed family. Arwel Gruffydd returned to Cwmni Theatr Gwynedd to play the narrator Tom.

This was a new adaptation in Welsh by Annes Gruffydd, part of a policy aimed at introducing modern classic texts to the theatre's regular audiences.

Torch Theatre

The Torch Theatre in Milford Haven made the commitment to continue touring as widely as possible this year.

They have just completed a three-week run at the Brewhouse in Taunton in a new production of Alan Ayckbourn's "Season's Greetings". While for audiences in Milford Haven, the festive offering was "The Lion, The Witch and The Wardrobe" as the Torch became the only repertory company this year to be granted performing rights for the work.

Artistic Director Kit Thacker is fighting substantial cutbacks in funding - they have lost £85,000 from their annual grant this year - but an encouraging sign was the unexpected upturn in box office sales.

Other works in the 1922 programme were chosen for their popular appeal, but the emphasis was also on presenting quality writing - John Godber's "Up 'n' Under", Frederick Knott's "Dial M For Murder" for the summer season and Shakespeare's "Antony and Cleopatra".

Antony and Cleopatra

Shakespeare's classic played from Febraury 13 February 29. Director Kit Thacker transported the play to pre-war fascist Italy offering soldiers dressed in Mussolini blackshirt uniforms and stormtrooper boots and a cocktail party atmosphere for Cleopatra's court.

Vikie Le Sache created a striking matt black high- tech sculptural set to highlight this approach further. The opposing camps were indicated by two large flags, whilst the final scenes were acted out against a large granite mausoleum.

The cast included Elizabeth Downes, who returned to the Torch Theatre Company to play Cleopatra, Alister Cameron (Antony) and Colin Mayes (Octavius Caesar/Philo). This production also went on tour to Aberdare and to the Sherman Theatre, Cardiff.

Alister Cameron and Elizabeth Downes

The Final Appearance of Miss Mamie Stuart

The Torch commissioned this new play from Cardiff-based actor/playwright Phil Michell following its successful tour to the Edinburgh Fringe Festival last year. The writer's company Equinox also undertook a small-scale tour of the three-hander play in England and Wales. The show played at Milford during October.

Mike James, former Artistic Director of the Sherman in rehearsal with Iain Stuart Ferguson

Mamie Stuart worked in the music halls before marrying and moving to Swansea. Her disappearance and the discovery of her body some forty years later make up the subject matter of the play, with playwright Michell offering up the theory that her husband murdered her. Local newspaper accounts of the disappearance and the gruesome discovery lent weight to the dramatic arguments, staged using the conventions of music hall to produce a stylish and unusual "whodunnit". Mike James directed.

THE EAST

By TIMOTHY RAMSDEN

The East '92

East Anglia is a large chunk of agricultural England, its main cultural association being the music of Benjamin Britten. That link had at least one effect in 1992, the programming of Paul Godfrey's play about Britten and tenor Peter Pears, "Once in a While the Odd Thing Happens" as the second main show in the Wolsey Theatre's new Studio. But infiltrating this traditional rural England is the advance of the east side of the London conurbation and commuting, associated especially with Essex but nowadays spread more thoroughly through the region. The result has been a conservative theatre scene. No urban area has the size or will to support two or more theatres that might develop distinct artistic identities. In Southend, during October, the Palace Theatre produced a new play, "Time's Window" by Michael Wilcox, but it took the town's centenary to make it happen. Once in a century a new play happens ?

Up north, in Ipswich the boast is a new play every two years, and the first studio season will offer a new piece by Judith Cook on Christopher Marlowe, plus a Gogol adaptation by local writer Kelvin Seggar. Seggar is a member of the Wolsey Writers Workshop, a group that meets at the theatre to develop writing skills monthly. This is Artistic Director Antony Tuckey's move to help new writers and exiguous as it seems by the side of some parts of the country, it is a shining beacon in East Anglia.

Otherwise the region relies heavily on touring companies. The Eastern Touring Agency organises new work and exciting prospects from the classics (such as the Gate's "Madness in Valencia") to come to the several small-scale venues, while larger scale work finds a home in receiving houses such as the Cambridge Arts Theatre and the Theatre Royal Bury St Edmunds. This is worth a visit in its own right, as the only theatre building in the care of the National Trust.

1992 has seen some good news and bad. The good news has been the reopening at the end of the year of the Theatre Royal in Norwich. Under the late Dick Condon, the Theatre Royal had a fine reputation for audience-pulling and book balancing. Rebuilding has been beset with problems, but following the reopening in time for the Christmas season, it is to be hoped 1993 will see the new management able to repeat Condon's success.

They must be hoping to avoid the fate of a major receiving theatre further down the line. On election night in April it was the Conservative's retention of Basildon that signalled the national result. A month later, the conservative takeover of Basildon council in the local election certainly signalled the end for the Towngate Theatre. The new council came to power on a cost-cutting pledge and the Towngate was in their sights as a cost to be cut. The precipitate closure of the theatre in response to subsidy cuts left booked companies unable to perform and angry ticket holders with no show to see. The anger organised itself into protests but the Towngate remained shut.

The Mercury, Colchester

Opened in 1972, the Mercury has an adaptable stage allowing proscenium staging or a shallow thrust, seating capacity varying between some 400 to 500 depending on stage shape; there is also a studio theatre in the same building.

In 1992 the Mercury offered a programme which could be taken as a survey of popular twentieth century British theatre. Spring opened with "What the Butler Saw" and also included "Beyond A Reasonable Doubt", "The Winslow Boy", Ayckbourn's reworking of the first Aldwych farce "Tons of Money" and Emlyn Williams' thriller "Night Must Fall". Autumn brought "The Three Musketeers", Godber's "On the Piste" and Rob Bettinson's stage version of Catherine Cookson's "The Fifteen Streets".

Apart from this cautious policy, the theatre mounted "Wicks's Folly", a community play by Jill Burrows about how a clean water supply was brought to Colchester, and David Storey's "Jubilee". The studio has seen a co-production of "Peculiar People" with touring company Eastern Angles and a short programme of plays by young writers.

What the Butler Saw

Orton's farce, which provoked outrage at its London premiere, faced the post-pantomime Colchester audience, where it seemed its sixties shock value had diminished with time, or with more realistic expectations as to what an Orton play would involve. It was notable for a suitably clinical set from the Mercury's head of design Karen Bartlett, her first set for this stage. Julie Bramall presented a confused, ever-perplexed Geraldine Barclay, while Michael Tudor Barnes played Dr Rance as a formidable figure in whom the anarchic possibilities of excessive order were brought to the surface. Some felt the production, by Richard Digby Day with Mercury Artistic Director Michael Winter, needed more fury and savagery; others felt the production hotted up after taking time to lets its farcical trousers down.

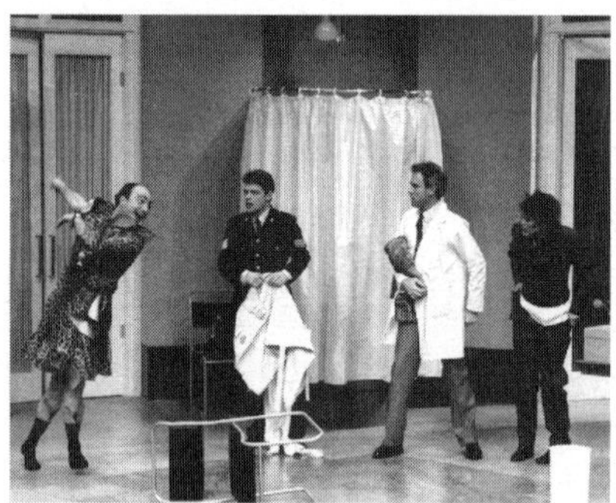

Cameron Stewart, Russell Porter, Michael Walker and Julie Bramall

Until Death Do Us Part

One of the most adventurous events at the Mercury this year was the Young People's Writing Competition, held during the spring with workshops at the theatre led by the project's director Elizabeth Gorla and writer in residence Stuart Browne. Four of the plays were chosen for performance and the final half-hour provided a knockout blow. Written by fifteen year old Sarah Duggan, "Till Death Do Us Part" started with a group of youngish women at the funeral of their friend Robyn. After the funeral, one of them, Fay, discovered Robyn's diaries. These set her off on a trail through the group's relationships. Focussing upon Fay's betrayals, the play handled sufficiently familiar ideas – the lure of new friends, sexual betrayal – but handled them with an assurance that required no allowance for the author's youth.

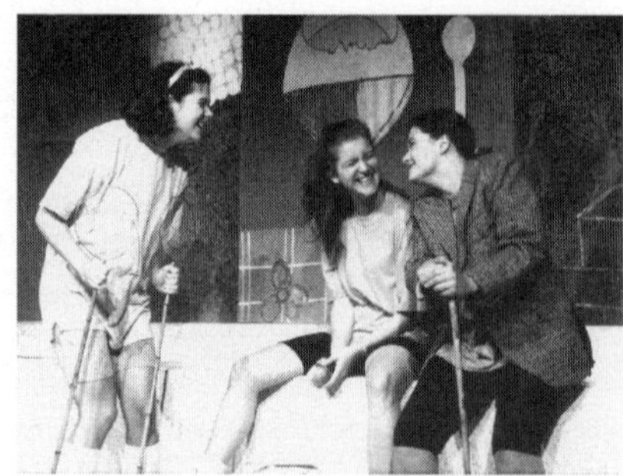

Kate Lawton, Connie Hyde and Susan Gott

Queens, Hornchurch

The year has seen a continuation of the theatre's broad policy, to present a wide programme of plays and musicals for the whole community. So far, new Artistic Director Marina Calderone has continued predecessor Bob Tomson's policy of a hefty musical section to the repertoire. Spring saw a revival of Denise Deegan's schoolgirl mock-romp "Daisy Pulls It Off", then Daphne Du Maurier's "Rebecca"; a new thriller in the Heather Brothers' "Cold Sweat", and the musical "Blues in the Night", while autumn opened with Tony Roper's "Talk of the Steamie" followed by "Gaslight" and another Heather Brothers show, "Lust". This was a musical based on Wycherley's Restoration rudery "The Country Wife".

Queen's publicity has always emphasised their casting of well-known TV actors; it's a place particularly for soap stars to clean up their act and wash down their theatrical credentials. "Daisy" cast "Eastenders" Sophie Lawrence, "Gaslight" Sally Ann Matthews from "Coronation Street". And so on.

Rebecca

Julie-Kate Olivier and Michael Cashman

Young director Tal Rubins mounted this production, which was notably designed by John Jenkins and ran March 6 – 28 with Michael Cashman and Julie-Kate Olivier as Max and the second Mrs De Winter.

Rubins' production created the play's sinister atmosphere through striking visual images, on a near all-black set dominated by a huge fireplace. The darkness was accentuated by a scattering of contrasting white objects, and by Rebecca Janaways' costumes in grey and black. There was a particular interest in the conflict between the innocence and vulnerability of Olivier's young bride and the formidable presence of Pamela Ruddock as the dominating housekeeper Mrs Danvers. Rubins used the household servants forcefully, watching, noticing and increasing the pervading sense of fear.

Talk of the Steamie

Kate Williams, C.P. Grogan, Morar Kennedy and Eileen Gourlay

It was brave of Artistic Director Marina Calderone to open her autumn season by directing Tony Roper's tribute to the working women of mid-century Glasgow, though it became clear that the underlying sense of old communal values coming into conflict with new, improved materialism with its tendency to break up old values (there's no one to talk to over a washing machine in the kitchen) applies to any once-strong community. And it has songs, plus a number of strong roles that could be seized on by the Hornchurch cast. East-ender specialist Kate Williams took the tough-talking part of Magrit McGuire.
Designer Rebecca Janaway created the Carnegie Street, Glasgow, steamie of 1953.

The Wolsey, Ipswich

Opened in 1979, the Wolsey consists of a single raked auditorium seating some 500 facing an open-end stage. The company boasts high attendance figures – in 1990-91 its productions of "The Double Dealer" and "A Christmas Carol" were among the three best attended shows in the country. The kind of programming that brought this about continued in 1992. Spring saw a collection of crowd-pleasers: "Absent Friends", "Shadowlands", and "Noises Off" stiffened by a mix of classical drama, "A Midsummer Night's Dream" and "A Doll's House". Autumn saw a similar mixture, "Deathtrap" being followed by "Candida" and a new play "Goodnight Mr Tom", adapted from her novel by Michelle Magorian. The year opened with the Wolsey occupied by the highly successful musical "Into the Woods": it ended with another musical, "High Society".

The year will be memorable also for the opening of the Wolsey studio in late October. Most of the studio season (running to spring 1993) has been in the hands of Wolsey associate director Hettie MacDonald, whose presence in Ipswich already during the year had given the theatre a notable lift.

Into the Woods

Sondheim's musical had only a moderate London run, but it was widely agreed that this Ipswich production was a runaway success. It was directed by Antony Tuckey, with James Simpson as musical director and musical staging by Lorelai Lynn. The design of a fairy-tale forest was by David Knapman and played a major part in the triumph of the show.

Among a fine cast, Marily Cutts as the Wife and David Timpson's Baker gave a strong centre, with Debbie Paul's Cinderella and Don Gallacher's Prince Charming (a character boasting little else than charm, as Gallacher made clear) catching the right tone for this wry (and awry) retelling of familiar stories.

A Midsummer Night's Dream

Following the favourable impression created with their Sondheim production, the Wolsey could have been forgiven for advertising this as "Into The Wood II" (they didn't). Antony Tuckey's production ran March 19 – April 11. Tuckey wanted to set the play in a straight-laced society, so chose the Victorian period. In such a milieu, fantasies and desires force their ways into dreams. Theseus and Hippolyta re-emerged as the darker Oberon and Titania; Barry McCarthy and Suzette Llewellyn doubled the appropriate roles. Similarly, Michael Winsor doubled Theseus' Master of the Revels Philostrate and Oberon's right-hand creature Puck. The mechanicals, led by Kenneth Gilbert's Peter Quince and David Timpson's larger-than-life Bottom, were an especial success.

THE SOUTH WEST

by ALLEN SADDLER

The South West '92

The main story of 1992 was the resurgence of the Bristol Old Vic, threatened with complete closure at the end of 1991. Director Andrew Hay mounted four major productions in the first half by economising on scenery and the same in the second. The studio theatre, the New Vic re-opened after a two year closure and there was a new venue, called The Basement. No less than seven new plays were premiered. Public and critics spoke about a new spirit, a combination of good will on all sides, willing the theatre to succeed.

The recession altered the style and content of theatres in the region. The legitimate theatre saw less home grown productions, causing an influx of touring in. There were less new plays, more tried and tested revivals. But there was a spread of shoe string companies, willing to experiment, more and larger amateur productions, community theatre and touring productions from training companies finding it easier to occupy the stage at main venues. The Cygnet training company had six productions on the road, including a new play, "Double Concerto", which was seen at the Northcott in Exeter, and Cygnet productions were often seen in the studio adjacent to the Theatre Royal, Plymouth, the Drum.

Ex-drama students from Exeter, Bristol and Dartington continued to strike out, forming acting groups, usually with improvised scripts, launching themselves into a low scale professional career. Professional directors got involved in amateur productions. New plays attracted the help of professional actors "resting". The staging of new plays from new writers became a cause at the BOV, but also were greatly helped by the Exeter & Devon Arts Centre with its tiny cafe theatre, and by the Barbican Theatre in Plymouth, where a large scale community play with a topical punch, "Ill At Ease", played to packed houses for a week.

Main house productions at Plymouth's Theatre Royal continued the tradition for musicals with "A Little Night Music" and "Annie Get Your Gun". The programme was a good deal slimmer because of the cancellation of a musical version of "Rain", as a vehicle for Stephanie Powers, much in the manner of the shock cancellation of "Gold Diggers" last year. The tour in of "Noel and Gertie" also failed to materialise.

It has been a thin time at the Northcott Theatre in Exeter, with rumours about going dark after the Christmas splurge. The theatre kept open with amateur productions, training company shows, only broken, in the first half of the year by a production of Willy Russell's four hander, "One For The Road".

A vital element in the survival of South West theatre has been the South West Consortium, a mutual self help umbrella between the Theatre Royal, Plymouth, the Northcott, Exeter, the Orchard, a touring company based in Barnstaple, North Devon, Kneehigh a knockabout commedia company from Cornwall, Theatre Alibi, a company of physical actors based in Exeter and Rent-A-Role, based at the Barbican Theatre, Plymouth, who tour schools with topical productions. The Consortium co-ordinates activities and venues and is essential to the existence of the smaller companies.

As the established groups (Orchard, Kneehigh) make for the larger towns smaller companies (Common Players) take over the rural touring to villages, which has always been a feature in the far South West, where mainstream theatre maybe over an hour's drive away. The form of theatre activity has become less viable to Equity companies, but continues through the noble spirit of actors' self sacrifice.

Bristol Old Vic

Andy Hay

At the end of last year it looked as though one of Britain's oldest provincial theatres was to close. The studio theatre, the New Vic had been dark for two years. Grants were being cut and the theatre was not full. Andrew Hay's appointment as Artistic Director seemed like offering the last breakfast; but skill, ingenuity and enthusiasm has not only kept the theatre open, but re-opened the New Vic and a further studio venue, The Basement.

Hay used the same basic set for his first three productions and re-instituted the repertory system. A group of actors were put on long term contracts and were used for any of the three venues. The system meant that male parts, (in "Romeo and Juliet") were filled by female actors, but the theatre had a genuine buzz of excitement.

Another new innovation was "The Raw Tour of Two" and "Blood Brothers", in stripped down versions, to outlying areas. The second half of the year saw seven new plays premiered, (eight, if you count the panto).

A lot will depend on the figures, but it looks as though the BOV is not only saved, but is expanding in all sensible directions.

Romeo and Juliet

"Romeo and Juliet" was generally judged as a good start to Andrew Hay's tenure at Bristol Old Vic. There was a liveliness and spirit of innovation, with the stage thrust forward to allow seating at the side and the rear. This was a production uncluttered by props, but supported by an effective sound track.

The production marked the start of the repertory ensemble and critics were undecided about a female playing Mercutio, but found little fault with the black actor Clarence Smith as Romeo. Geraldine Somerville's Juliet was a witty and tender performance, described as "bold" and "shy", and possessing a sensible scepticism.

Caroline Bliss as the Nurse opted for broad comedy of a gap toothed variety. This production was noted for its pace and bustle, for Mick Bearwash's design, and the general clarity of the spoken text.

Fuente Ovejuna

The second stage of Andrew Hay's regeneration of the Bristol Old Vic was a fine ensemble display of Lope de Vega's "Fuente Ovejuna", written in 1614. It is a story of a popular uprising against tyranny, of a unity of peasants in the face of repression.

Adrian Mitchell adapted this melodramatic bloodthirsty play, taming its fury slightly from the original. The play, which was much performed in communist Eastern Europe, has a revolutionary core, but is not anti Catholic.

Lope de Vega was a prolific playwright, writing for the popular theatre of his day. "Fuente Ovejuna" is written in verse and the company did not let this fact inhibit their treatment of the words. The production was clear and colourful, with the sweep of inevitability as events unfolded. At times it seemed more Latin American than Spanish but it contained a powerful punch that was well worth its revival.

The cast

Epsom Downs

Howard Brenton's "Epsom Downs" made an engaging romp. The small social dramas formed a background to the 1977 Derby when The Minstrel, with Lester Piggott, fulfilled all hopes.

Opinions varied, some thought it was acute social commentary while others found it to be condensed soap opera. Within the framework is a dissection of the English class system, with its levels marked out between the popular and the enclosure. There are aristocrats and gypsies, peers and tinkers, middle class families and drunks, and the ghost of the suffragette Emily Davidson. The martyred suffragette is a presence that broods over the caricatures that enliven the scene.

Ian Hastings directed a cast of nine with deftness and wit. The actors doubled up cheerfully, enjoying the chance of quick change acting. The actual race was well staged and exciting. A warm hearted play with lots of colour, but full of sharp truths and insights.

Northcott Theatre, Exeter

The Northcott celebrates twenty-five years this year. The celebration production "The Three Musketeers", was designed to raise spirits in a difficult year and the splendid full scale production of David Pownall's adaption did show a new air of confidence. The best play, "Inventing a New Colour", seemed to baffle the Northcott audience, despite the fact that it was based in the city. The Christmas show, "Merlin's Dream", based on the Arthurian legend had several sword fights too many and did not settle between panto and epic theatre. "One For The Road" was a stop gap suitable for the economic climate and seemed strangely dated, despite the fact that it was only written in 1976. John Durnin continues as Artistic Director, showing his talent when he gets the chance, as in "The Three Musketeers".

The Three Musketeers

Rupert Wickman and Jon Glentoran

David Pownall's adaptation of "The Three Musketeers" contained all the vainglorious boasting and sword fights, but was more than an historical romp. In this version the central figure is Lady de Winter, who emerges as a double agent in the war between France and England. She is a seductress and a plotter, but is taken advantage of by D'Artagnan, betrayed and condemned. She is the most rounded character and we follow her exploits with more interest than the jolly trio. The change gave the familiar tale another dimension and Jacqueline Dutoit's performance was powerful enough to hold the interest. The musketeers were all characters in their own right, but sketched in. John Glentoran (Athos), Simon Armstrong (Porthos) and Francis Middleditch (Aramis), with Rupert Wickham (D'Artagnan) captured the stage and audience with bounding leaps.

Inventing A New Colour

Michael Tudor Barnes and Ann Firbank

Paul Godfrey's play "Inventing A New Colour", is set in Exeter in 1942. It displayed a simple strength that should have captured the city. 1942 was the time when the bombs fell on Exeter; but this was not another "blitz" play, for the death and destruction plays a background part to a story about personal relationships. Mother, father and teenage son dream aloud about the present, the past and the future as though the chance of a quick end was hardly a possibility. Directed by the playwright, the sombre sturdy characters try to confront their lives but are baffled, not by the turn of events, but by each other. There were moments when ordinary speech turned into poetic understatement. It was in these moments that the play was at its most moving.

Salisbury Playhouse

There has been live professional theatre in Salisbury for nearly fifty years with the present purpose built Playhouse being built and opened in 1976. It has developed into a major producing theatre putting on plays in its two auditoria (a main house seating 516 and a studio seating 100) as well as running theatre services for young people (including work with schools and colleges and a thriving 200 strong youth theatre).

In October 1990 the current Artistic Director, Deborah Paige, was appointed. Her policy has been to appeal to a broader range of audiences by mounting a wider range of plays and to raise production standards overall.

The Choice

Robert Bathurst and Jane Maud

During March, in the studio, there was a world premiere production of a play written by Claire Luckham. Originally commissioned by Derby Playhouse, Salisbury Playhouse took over the commission and Luckham became writer-in-residence in Salisbury for a year. The play, which concerns a couple who discover their child will be born with Down's Syndrome, starred Toyah Willcox. It was directed by Annie Castledine and designed by Bill Pinner, and received considerable national acclaim. The Daily Telegraph called it "gripping, emotionally overwhelming drama..... it combines heart-wrenching emotion with intellectual vigour". And The Observer commented "Hooray for Claire Luckham's "The Choice" at Salisbury Playhouse - a rich, challenging and extraordinary drama".

Relative Values

Nigel Lindsay

Summertime in the main theatre saw a revival of a rarely performed play by "The Master", Noel Coward. "Relative Values" was directed by Artistic Director, Deborah Paige and designed by Kit Surrey, with Richard Addison, Holly De Jong and Barbara Thorn in the leading roles.

Always popular with audiences, this Coward revival was particularly well received, with a good reception from press and public alike. The Daily Telegraph showered praise "Deborah Paige's production exudes a winning confidence. First rate performances..... great comic scenes." And The Guardian spoke of an "enterprising revival" in a "crisp production".

Theatre Royal, Plymouth

The Theatre Royal celebrated its tenth year, started some small scale touring, continued with its policy of mounting large scale musicals for national touring and transfer to London, and had its first year in the black. The theatre is still in debt from previous years of deficit, but the financial improvement cheered everyone. A catastrophe was the cancellation of "Rain", a musical version of Somerset Maugham's Sadie Thompson story, which was booked for a national tour and a London opening. The big musical event was Tommy Steele in "Some Like It Hot" which ran three weeks before the London transfer. The best touring in production was the English Shakespeare Company in "Macbeth".

Director Roger Redfarn expanded the theatre's links with the community with "The Music Of The Night", an outdoor show pageant to celebrate the Royal Citadel, a fortress on Plymouth Hoe. Literally hundreds of dancers, singers, local bands and operatic societies combined with military and Marine bands for this spectacular event. The studio theatre, The Drum, saw visits from the Orchard and Compass, Birmingham Rep, and training groups Cygnet, The Hub (from Cornwall), and the local youth theatre, under the direction of assistant director, Amanda Knott.

A Little Night Music

Stephen Sondheim's stage musical oozes old world sophistication and cynicism, a mixture of Schnitzler's "La Ronde" and Noel Coward in his "Bitter Sweet" mood. A staid lawyer realises his mistake in taking a young wife, who remains a virgin after ten months of marriage. An actress with whom he has had a previous liaison arrives in town on a tour and this event sparks off a whole series of new couplings. The sheer cleverness of Sondheim's way with words and his attractively sour harmonies elevate the trite romantic story into a minor masterpiece of musical drama. Roger Redfarn's production was a large scale ambitious and attractive attempt to realise Sondheim's wry fairytale, with Rula Lenska playing the world weary actress Desiree with good humoured charm and all the cast in good voice.

A Dead Secret

Rodney Ackland, who died last year, had a worthy tribute with Roger Redfarn's production of his play "A Dead Secret". It is the story of Frederick S Dyson, a man with a severe disorder of the ego, brought about by Lloyd George's plans to tax property and income. This large rambling untidy play contains an acute psychological study, and an evocation of London life in 1910 that made the audience gasp with its assumptions. Edward Woodward as Dyson gave a performance of prosaic menace. Michelle Dotrice played his wife at the end of her tether. It was a part that required much sitting and listening without the reward of a juicy outburst. But you could feel the seething discontent, the bewilderment of a woman who knows her husband is insane but dares not challenge his authority.

THE SOUTH AND SOUTH EAST

By ANN StCLAIR-STANNARD

The South and South East '92

While some West End theatres have gone dark during the recession ridden months of 1992, regional theatres in the South-East have continued to draw reasonable, and at certain periods of the year, increased audiences. In trying to analyse the reasons for this, I have come to the conclusion that people develop an allegiance to their neighbourhood playhouse, especially if, like the Redgrave Theatre in Farnham, Surrey, it has an "in house" atmosphere. Volunteers sell programmes and ice-cream, you trustingly hang your coat on a hook and go into the auditorium where you know the standard of production is consistently good. So encouraging would the scene appear to be in the South East that a bold new venture – the Peacocks Arts & Entertainment Centre – has been set up in Woking, Surrey. The management company for this centre is Woking Turnstyle Ltd – a joint venture between the developers of the Peacocks, London & Edinburgh Trust plc and entertainment specialists Turnstyle Group Ltd. The new centre includes the 1,300 seat New Victoria Theatre, 230 seat Rhoda McGaw Theatre and a three-screen 1000 seat cinema complex, night club, bars, and entertainment and conference suites as well as a shopping mall. The investor is obviously confident that he can draw audiences.

Further south, Chichester Festival Theatre, couched in its grassy knoll, pennants flying gaily in the wind, and sprouting its comparatively new annex, continues to attract audiences from further inland as well as from all along the coast. The standard of work compares well with that of the West End. Directors such as Sir Peter Hall are just as likely to launch a new production from, say, the Yvonne Arnaud Theatre, Guildford or the Chichester Festival Theatre as they are in London. Gone are the days when local repertory theatres employed half-trained actors and, managing with one permanent group, presented a new play each week. There are many good drama schools training young actors to a high standard. Community theatre, street theatre and school tour productions, as well as fringe productions such as are performed at Brighton's Pavilion and Sallis Benney theatres, often give ex-students a chance to gain experience. Seat prices have been kept within reasonable bounds, although administrators tell me they depend on ancillary services such as theatre bars, restaurants and club membership to make their ventures viable. When you consider that the cheapest reserved seat for the Benson & Hedges County Cricket final at Lord's costs £26.00, theatre seats are modestly priced by comparison.

There is a continued strong commitment by managements to provide a balance between the classics, new work and popular revivals. Bearing in mind that box office receipts must show a profit, this is no easy task. My impression, however, is that theatre in the South and South-East of England is cradled in skilled, experienced and dedicated hands.

Chichester Festival Theatre

Chichester opthalmist Leslie Evershed-Martin CBE once saw a television programme about Canada's Stratford Ontario Shakespeare Memorial Theatre and, quite simply, set about making possible the erection of such a building in his own home town. The late Tyrone Guthrie pledged himself right behind the project and, on 3 July 1962, it opened under the directorship of the then Laurence Olivier. The money was raised from private and commercial sources as well as from the Arts Council which made possible the building of a hexagonal theatre, seating 1,374 people in the round. No member of the audience is more than sixty feet from the stage. In 1989, the second venue, which had been housed in the "Tent" was rehoused in the new Minerva complex.

The highlight of Chichester's year is the summer festival which this year featured the Renaissance Company in "Coriolanus". (See the Yearbook section on **Touring Companies**.) Under Artistic Director Patrick Garland, the theatre remains primarily dependent upon the private sector. Nissan UK Ltd have provided sponsorship which stands at £1,000,000.

Venus Observed

A revival of Christopher Fry's verse play first presented in 1950, "Venus Observed" tells a fairy tale story about the Duke of Altair, in the autumn of his life, trying to make up his mind which of his three former mistresses to marry, when his agent's nubile young daughter arrives on the scene to captivate him. Rich in philosophy and wit, this play starred Donald Sinden as the Duke, Denis Quilley as his agent, Kate O'Mara, Jean Boht and Alexandra Bastedo as his three mistresses. Susannah Harker played Perpetua with whom the Duke falls in love. James Roose-Evans directed, the set was designed by Poppy Mitchell, lighting by Nigel Hollowell-Howard and music by Kevin Malpass.

Donald Sinden and Robert Portal

King Lear in New York

Melvin Bragg's first attempt at writing a stage play embraced an ambitious analogy between the tale of Shakespeare's King Lear and a saga of present times. Using his long experience of media interviewing Bragg weaves in scenes representing this genre with great verisimilitude. Every character in Shakespeare's "Lear" has its counterpart in Bragg's play, although his plot stands alone for those not aware of the comparison. The staging at Chichester lent itself particularly to the constant scene changes in the second half where an exciting backdrop of downtown New York, complete with elevated railway and neon lights, served to link progression of events. Tim Supple directed and Bunny Christie designed. Lighting was by Ben Ormerod and Andrew Poppy wrote the music.

John Stride

She Stoops to Conquer

Denis Quilley and Susannah Harker

Strangely enough "She Stoops to Conquer" has never before been presented at Chichester. The score has now been put straight with Oliver Goldsmith's ebullient comedy being given the full treatment by director Peter Wood, who directed Sheridan's "School for Scandal" at the National Theatre. Recognised as a master of Georgian theatre, Wood cast Jean Boht as Mrs Hardcastle, Denis Quilley as her spouse, Jonathon Morris as Tony Lumpkin, Susannah Harker as their daughter Kate, while Iain Glen appeared as the handsome young Marlow with Leonie Melinger as Constance. Sets were by David Walker, lighting by Bill Bray and music by Carl Davis.

Me and My Friend

Tom Hollander and Jonathon Morris

First performed in 1988 when it won the Verity Bargate Award, "Me and My Friend" by Gillian Plowman focusses on two pairs of ex-psychiatric patients trying to reconstruct their lives. Humourous and compassionate, the play has moments of high comedy and great poignancy.

Mike Ockrent directed in the Minerva Studio and the cast included Jonathon Morris, Tom Hollander and Theresa Fresson. The psychological realism of Plowman's piece proved especially suited to the intimate atmosphere at the Minerva.

Double Take

Lisa Harrow, David Cardy and Jeremy Brudenell

Deborah Moggach, one of our foremost novelists and television writers, gave us her first stage play dealing with the idea that, if we were to be given the chance to live our lives again with another partner, we would be different people – or would we ?

The piece was perceptively performed by peppy Lisa Harrow, well-known for her wide ranging television work and for triumphant seasons with the RSC, Helga Brindle, Jeremy Brudenell and David Cardy. The direction was by Hugh Wooldrige and Simon Higlett designed set and costumes.

Churchill Theatre, Bromley

Sir Arthur Sullivan, in partnership with W.S. Gilbert, opened a drill hall in East Street, Bromley in 1872 and offered a thousand seated patrons pantomime, variety shows and plays from provincial houses. In 1889 Bromley proved itself capable of supporting two entertainment houses, and the Grand Hall in the High Street was opened by a local butcher who offered similar fare. Eventually re-named The New, this theatre kept going until one fateful night in 1971 during a run of "The Heiress" when it was gutted by fire. Seven years later the Churchill Theatre opened on the same site. The Churchill follows the policy of generating some of their own work which they hope will tour and earn revenue to help buy in quality plays from other touring companies. Artistic Director John Wallbank joined the Churchill in July 1991. He began his career at Joan Littlewood's famous Theatre Workshop at Stratford East as stage manager, carpenter and musician.

Rule of the Game

It gives an added dimension to a play when you know the story to be a true one and that the characters represented, however bizarre, actually behaved this way in real life. "Rule of the Game" shows us the dramatic situation where Philip Gale Drew, a larger-than-life actor from the American West, is accused of murder while in his cups. Although he goes free, the audience is left in grave doubt whether this should be so. Patrick Mower gave a bravura performance as Drew while Sally Knyvette and Denis Clinton played Marion and Frank Lindo (real life parents of the well-known actress Olga Lindo) who employed Drew in their theatrical company. Michael Latimer directed, Douglas Heap designed and Chris Nicholls lit the show, which played during May 1992.

Patrick Mower

Elvis

Veterans Jack Good and Ray Cooney devised this fun musical which did well at Bromley and went on to play a summer season in Bournemouth. Clayton Mark bears an amazing likeness to Elvis Presley and has talent to match. Bo Wills and Ian Salisbury played other leading characters.

Carole Todd directed this nostalgia trip. Alan Miller Bunford and Annette Sharville developed the costumes from original designs by Patrick Robertson and Rosemary Vercoe. Graham McClusky was lighting designer.

Clayton Mark

Haymarket, Basingstoke

Adapted from the original building which used to be the town's Corn Exchange, this theatre owes much to the inspiration of Guy Slater, whose dream of a resident repertory company was fulfilled with the setting up of the new Basingstoke Theatre Trust in April 1986. He left after six years to join the BBC, but it has continued to thrive under subsequent directors Tony Craven and then Ian Mullins. The present Artistic Director, Adrian Reynolds, took over in 1990 bringing with him a fine reputation gained at the Byre Theatre, St Andrews in Fife. This last season, prior to the Haymarket's £2,500,000 refurbishment, has set the resident Horseshoe Theatre Company a series of epic challenges. All the plays were dramatically testing and technically demanding. The world premiere of the David Pomeranz musical about Charlie Chaplin, "The Little Tramp", offered the Company immense potential to place it sharply in the national focus. The Horseshoe Theatre Company have a studio theatre at Queen Mary's College where alternative shows have a chance to be seen. The Haymarket is due to re-open in September 1993.

A Streetcar Named Desire

The year began with Mel Martin as Blanche DuBois in Tennessee Williams' steamy tragedy. The management imaginatively invited the public to a demonstration by the director, cast and technicians of the process of preparing and rehearsing a professional stage production.

Adrian Reynolds directed, Elroy Ashmore designed the set and Graham Walne was in charge of the lighting. Other parts were played by Hildegarde Neil, Ralph Arliss and Shelagh McLeod.

Mel Martin

The Little Tramp

David Pomeranz wrote the book and the lyrics for this show based on the life of Charlie Chaplin. A world premiere, "The Little Tramp" spans a wide spectrum of time from Lambeth in 1894, where Charlie suffered an impoverished childhood, through his triumphs on the silent screen, his battle with the political lobby and his subsequent exile from America. Following its premiere at Basingstoke the musical was geared for a major tour.

Paul Tomany, Peter Duncan, John Altman and Patrick Jamieson

The same team of Adrian Reynolds as director, Elroy Ashmore as designer and Graham Walne as lighting expert were responsible for those disciplines. Peter Duncan played Charles Chaplin and Jacinta Mulcahy Oonah his wife. They were supported by a large cast, many of whom played several parts.

Nuffield Theatre, Southampton

Some of the most powerful theatre of the past few years has come from venues not originally built to present drama. One such is the Nuffield, built as a large lecture hall in the University of Southampton. Seating 500, since 1976 it has enjoyed increasingly strong seasons as a producing theatre. One of the reasons for the Nuffield to be noticed and appreciated is its policy of forging innovative work – a brave policy which has paid off well.

Patrick Sandford, Artistic Director since 1988, came from the Redgrave Theatre, Farnham, where he had gained an admirable reputation, particularly for selecting plays by comparative newcomers such as Christina Reid and Louise Page. After winning the TMA/Martini Regional Theatre Award for Best Director in 1991 Patrick Sandford has not let his standards drop during 1992.

Leo In Love

This drama by Jean Sarment, translated by Ann Queensberry, serves to show the playwright's affinity to Jean Anouilh, especially in his ambiguous attitude towards the role of illusion in human affairs. Directed by Patrick Sandford and starring Angela Pleasance, Sarah Badel and Martin Jarvis, "Leo in Love" was well enough received to encourage the management to arrange a first time tour of one of their productions. The success that ensued has stimulated them to plan other tours. Sets and costumes were created by Robin Don, and lighting designed by Stephen Watson.

Martin Jarvis

A New World and the Tears of the Indians

An ambitious production with music, based on the work of Spaniard Lope de Vega, the most prolific dramatist of all time, "A New World and the Tears of the Indians" treats with scenarios in Spain, Portugal and the West Indies. It involves Christopher Columbus (Hugh Quarshie), the King of Portugal (David O'Keefe), King Ferdinand and Queen Isabella of Spain (Keith Woodham and La Verne Williams) plus many, many other characters played by a large cast most of whom have more than one role.

Again, Patrick Sandford directed and Robin Don designed the sets. Costumes were by Frances Tempest.

Hugh Quarshie

Palace, Watford

One of the finest examples of an Edwardian playhouse the Palace Theatre, Watford, was built in 1908 and was, for many years, known as the Watford Palace of Varieties. Now a flourishing repertory company it earns approximately 70% of its revenue. The remaining 30% is provided by the Civic Theatre Trust and by the Arts Council of Great Britain.

The past year has seen important developments with several projects coming to fruition. Following the successful visit in August 1991 of their twin city theatre, the Novgorod Regional Theatre, who gave Watford audiences their production of Dostoevsky's "The Devils", the creation of an education department has resulted in 2000 young people being gathered in to enjoy experience of theatre. A new marketing department has also been set up.

Lou Stein has been Artistic Director at Watford for five years. He founded The Gate at Nottinghill and the Latchmere theatre in Battersea. His artistic policy of producing new and international work has led to twenty of Watford's last fifty plays being UK or world premieres.

Stitched Up

Lynda Rooke and Michael Mears

Stephen Bill, who wrote this comedy, first shown at the Octagon Theatre, Bolton in 1990, is a prolific promoter of plays for stage and television. He has won several awards from "Plays and Players London Critics", the "Evening Standard", "Drama Magazine" and The Writers Guild. Bill's play "Curtains" dealt with the taboo subject of euthanasia with both horror and comedy. "Stitched Up" turns to the topical subject of debt. Bill manages to leave his audience feeling better rather than worse, having first given them some hope. Bob Carlton directed the play which starred Philip Whitchurch, Lynda Rooke, Marjie Campi, Michael Mowby and Michael Mears. Norman Coates designed and Paul Armstrong lit the show.

Baby

Sarah Berger and Simon Slater

In the present tradition of the Palace Theatre "Baby" is a world premiere production of a play by Jon Canter. Canter has had much experience of writing radio, television and video scripts, but this is his first stage play. The advertising world is the setting and the programme gave the audience a useful glossary of terms bandied about by the players.

The cast of four included Simon Slater, Andrew Searr, Sarah Berger and Jim Dunk. Lou Stein directed, Martin Sutherland provided designs and Mark Henderson the lighting. The production followed "All Stitched Up" and played during June.

The Redgrave, Farnham

The Redgrave has consistently featured among the top seven best attended theatres in the country, and has an enviable record for the quantity and quality of its work. During the year 1991/1992 it has played to 68% capacity with average seat prices of £7.37.

The Regrave uses its auditorium, foyer and restaurant for much ancillary entertainment in the forms of children's theatre, youth productions, one-off concerts and summer supper cabaret. On Sundays there are free lunch-time jazz sessions. Seating 362, the theatre provides an extremely well-designed seating arrangement with plenty of leg room, and splendid acoustics.

Graham Watkins, who took up his appointment in 1988, is resident Artistic Director. He has master-minded over twenty productions, many of which have subsequently toured. Watkins has a great gift for appropriate casting; and concentrates on choosing his shows with a view to pleasing a very wide age group. The Redgrave receives £243,480 per year from combined grants given by six district councils and South-East Arts. Sponsorship of £25,000 came from Johnson's Wax, £5,000 from Racal, £2,000 from Courage and £1,500 from the Redgrave Theatre Club.

Mansfield Park

Mark Aiken, Terence Langton and Clare Owen

Simon Ward adapted for the stage Jane Austen's classic tale of Fanny Price, the poor relation brought up amongst her more prosperous cousins at Mansfield Park. Julie-Kate Olivier played Fanny in this charmingly stylised production, while Terence Langton was her uncle, Sir Thomas Bertram. The vapid Lady Bertram was played by Clare Owen. Graham Watkins directed. Colin Winslow designed the elaborate yet flexible sets, and Peter Edwards lit the show. Back projection was effectively used to depict coach journeys; and the music used was by English composers between years 1750-1800.

Don't Rock the Boat

Michael Sharvell-Martin and Garfield Morgan

Robin Hawdon, author of this comedy, had another play, "Revenge" premiered at the Redgrave in January 1991. The two could not be more of a contrast and serve to show what a versatile playwright he is. "Revenge" was a cunningly constructed thriller, whereas "Don't Rock the Boat" verges on farce. The latter used a most realistic set consisting of a complete cross-section of a converted river barge – all of it on the same scale except where set designer Janey Gardiner had allowed the stage apron to provide more floor space. Graham Watkins directed and the cast included Pauline Yates, Michael Sharvell-Martin, Sarah Reed, Garfield Morgan, Jane Rossington and Sally Geoghegan. Mark Doubleday did the lighting.

Yvonne Arnaud, Guildford

Yvonne Arnaud Theatre

The past year has seen the Yvonne Arnaud go from strength to strength, presenting a wide variety of shows. Val May, Artistic Director for the last sixteen years, handed over the reins during the summer to James Barbour. The new Artistic Director has devoted his entire theatrical career to this theatre, starting as an assistant stage manager and working his way to the top. He understands the underpinnings, audience reactions, financial structure and community significance of the venue intimately. Moreover, he is often to be seen in the audience at other regional theatres, which indicates that he keeps his eye on the whole theatrical scenario.

The Yvonne Arnaud has generated some of its own productions and intends to increase this practice in the future. The more it can generate good shows, which may then be toured, the more money it will have in order to buy in quality entertainment. A new restaurant has now been added, making three places in the building where you can eat. There's a really comfortable snack bar in the foyer; the Harlequin, which provides full meals; and Figaro's, serving pasta and salad which you can enjoy to the accompaniment of live piano music.

The Yvonne Arnaud receives no funding from the Arts Council of Great Britain but has a small grant from the Surrey County Council and the Guildford Borough Council. There has been no sponsorship in the past year.

On Approval

Frederick Lonsdale's comedy of contemporary manners, first shown in London in 1927, starred Penelope Keith, Judy Clifton, Edward de Souza and Michael Cochrane. David Giles directed. The truly stunning designs were by Robin Frazer Paye and the lighting by Richard M Parker.

Penelope Keith is especially loved by Guildford audiences since she lives nearby and gives generously of her time to local charities. She has made two successful appearances at the Arnaud in the past – Terence Rattigan's "The Deep Blue Sea" and in 1991 as Lady Bracknell in Oscar Wilde's "The Importance of Being Earnest" which went on to become a successful tour.

Edward de Souza, Penelope Keith, Judy Clifton and Michael Cochrane

COMMERCIAL TOURS

Being "on the road" is a traditional part of theatrical life. TOM SOPER looks at shows that have toured in 1992.

Commercial Tours '92

Commercial tours, as the name suggests, are simply those that receive no regional or governmental funding. They are the traditional form you might say, made more practical by the advent of the railways. Before steam it might have been possible for players to tour from town to town by coach but obviously this was far more difficult for entire companies. Once the network of tracks grew, in the Victorian days, when most medium size towns were proud to boast at least one theatre, and many could offer a variety, tours proliferated in many shapes and sizes. There were acts going to the music halls, which also catered for racier "burlesque" shows. Alongside the repertory theatres there were medium size houses that took in touring dramas and musicals. And also, there where the largest theatres, the Hippodromes and the Opera Houses, capable of staging the grand touring shows that originated mainly in the capital. Not that this thriving community offered the majority of its players anything like opulence. Those at the lower end might be "shilling-a-night" men – named after the cost of a boarding house room. Those higher up might find a good wage while employed but faced continual uncertainty. Commercial or not, even in those boom days few people have ever made theatre solely for money.

During the spread of radio and film, theatre audiences naturally shrank. The second world war saw the virtual demise of repertory theatre while the cinemas flourished. This, in part, promoted the development of the Arts Council, in 1946, to fund theatre for the provinces. A decade later the public had returned to live performance with renewed interest; new theatres were established and old ones revamped, but the easier days had gone. Higher standards were expected. Commercially, touring came into ascendancy, because all the diverse artistic skills needed for a show, and the financial backers, could be gathered together from the whole of the country, put to work on a project and then laid off as soon as the run was finished.

Commercial tours tend to visit "receiving theatres" (rather than "producing theatres") . These are theatres (the Manchester Opera House is an example) which produce none of their own work.Today's tours are often criticised as mere pot-boilers relying on television names to pull in a crowd, but, as the list below reflects, the true picture is far more varied. Many West-End bound plays try out on the road before facing the capital's critics, often adapting the show along the country run. Many plays come out of the West-End to play to a larger audience. And there is, as well, a wide spectrum of projects that someone has believed in, felt was necessary or downright entertaining, and took to the road to find punters. Commercial tours nowadays are really a cross-section of the shows that would have been split amongst all the old theatres, catering to a broad theatre-going public, appraising themselves at the box-office.

Annie Get Your Gun

One of the great hits of the golden era of Broadway, "Annie Get Your Gun" is probably Irving Berlin's best known musical, not least because it contains some of the standards of musical theatre, including the rollicking anthem, "There's no Business Like Show Business". On August 15 this year Kim Criswell took the title role, originally written for Ethel Merman, at a newly refurbished Theatre Royal, Plymouth. Birmingham Hippodrome, King's Theatre, Edinburgh, and King's Theatre, Glasgow were the only other venues on a tour produced by Ronald S. Lee which went to the West End by Christmas. But then you don't move a cast of over forty and a full orchestra around too much. Instead, you make sure that word of mouth imitates another number from the show,"They say its wonderful."

Kim Criswell

Barnum

Paul Nicholas was on stage all evening, and singing in every number, as Phileas T Barnum, the nineteenth century impresario who founded "The Greatest Show on Earth" with James Bailey. The book for this extravaganza, written by Mark Bramble, covers the master showman's life up to their collaboration. On stage all manner of circus stunts illustrated the action- a tight rope walk when Barnum's marriage to "Charity" seems in trouble, juggling as he makes a decision. A cast of over fifty performers plus high spirited musical numbers (music by Cy Coleman, lyrics by Michael Stewart) added to the spectacle. Apollo Leisure's tour started in 1991, began 1992 in Edinburgh and took in seven more venues, winding down at the Theatre Royal in Nottingham the first week of December.

Paul Nicholas

Bazaar And Rummage

Sue Townsend centres her comedy around the goings-on at an Acton church hall where a self-help group of female agoraphobics is holding a rummage sale. Through some bawdy humour (that shocked a few provincial audiences expecting nothing more unseemly than acne from Adrian Mole's creator) and some subtle crisis points as the roots of each of the women's despairing lives are brought out into the open. This funny-to-sad play was produced by Live Wire Theatre Productions and toured from Croydon in March to Oxford in May, and after a change of cast (all still well known television actresses) played a further ten venues from Bristol in September to Eastbourne by November.

Lesley Joseph, Liza Tarbuck, Linda Davidson, Dilys Watling and Eve Ferret

Breaking The Code

Derek Jacobi and Rachel Gurney

Derek Jacobi returned to a role he created six years ago as mathematics genius Alan Turing. Duncan Weldon produced a tour which began in Sheffield, July 6, reaching the Chichester Festival Theatre in mid October. Hugh Whitemore's play celebrated the idiosyncratic and tragic man, who broke the German Enigma Code- so vital to the early success of the U-Boats- then dreamt up the concept of a "thinking machine", and finally, and disastrously in post-war Britain, admitted his homosexuality to a policeman. Mr Jacobi was much praised for a portrayal full of neurotic stammering and vocal jerkiness. Referring to an obvious problem for all scripts laden with mathematical theorem one reviewer explained, "in this form Jacobi could read the telephone directory to rapt attention."

Buddy

Joe Lutton and Besienka Blake

Simultaneously in the West End, Buddy Holly has been re-cloned again this year to tour on several continents, including an itinerary covering the full twelve months at fourteen large theatres in the U.K. Joe Lutton gets the work as our latest bespectacled one in Alan James' biog-musical. It has been said that the plot is barely a thin, sanitised version of Holly's brief life, but reviewers consistently remark on a massing of middle-agers twisting something nasty in the aisles when the high energy rock and roll numbers kick in. Also endorsed by John Major, this show looks set to run and run. This tour is produced by International Artists.

The Corn Is Green

Brendan O'Hea and Patricia Routledge

Stout, philanthropic Miss Moffat (Patricia Routledge) sets up a school in a remote Welsh village to educate a few bright boys out of the pits. All too speedily, however, the bossy old blue-stocking sacrifices her communal aims to concentrate on the progress of Morgan Evans (Brendan O'Hea), the lad who might get to Oxford if only he can keep away from naughty Bessie Watly (Candida Rundle). Emlyn Williams' partly autobiographical play wryly examines the prejudices of a small, late nineteenth century mining community and the burden of collective ambitions resting on a young man destined to escape from it. Originally a Greenwich Theatre production, Duncan Weldon's tour began at Greenwich on April 15, tested itself most strenuously at Cardiff in the second to last week, and then ended at Bradford, on June 22.

Dancing At Lughnasa

Five women and a seven year-old boy are cutting wood, striking matches and getting on with life and each other in rural Ireland around the harvest of 1936. Like the ripe golden corn on stage everything is coming to a head. An old relation returns from missionary work with distinct pagan leanings, the boy's father makes a poignant visit and the women ponder whether they will allow themselves a chance of some wild life, dancing at the Lughnasa festival. Patrick Mason directed Bill Kenwright's touring production of Brian Friel's masterpiece that started at Bristol Theatre Royal, August 3, and, after visiting sixteen other large theatres, ended in Sheffield on December 20. The West End production continues to run.

The Haunted Hotel

Sian Webber and Glyn Houston

A spooky supernatural presence waits for revenge in Room 13a. So television actors Glyn Houston, Hilary Croson and Sian Webber were forced to go in there and deal with it. Wilkie Collins' ghost story set in Victorian London and Venice was adapted for stage by Philip Dart who also directed. It was produced with lavish sets for the luxurious hotel by Channel Theatre Company and their autumn tour set off from Epsom Playhouse on September 10. It was later spotted at some smaller and medium size receiving venues and finally possessed the Connaught Theatre, Worthing, on November 23.

The Heiress

Nichola McAuliffe and Anthony Head

Dr. Sloper threatens to disinherit his shy daughter if she won't desist from her proposed match to a charming wastrel, Morris Townsend. Thus, Ruth and Augustus Goetz's adaptation of the Henry James novel, Washington Square brings ancient passions and Victorian prejudices into battle. In a tour produced by Lee Denn, Frank Finlay led the cast as the martinet father, with Nichola McAuliffe as Catherine, the put-upon offspring. This production carefully plotted the claustrophobic relationships and jarring finale of what is a pot-boiler by James'(and the programme's) own admission, but from Bromley in February to Richmond late July, one done to a turn.

The House of Stairs

Anita Harris

Ruth Rendell, also known as Barbara Vine, is fast becoming a new queen of the crime and thriller genres, which makes her books prime material for the commercial stage. This adaptation by Don Taylor weaves together past present and future at the house of Cossette (Virginia Stride), a rich widow who takes younger "courtiers" under her roof in a vain attempt to keep herself from growing old. Seen through the eyes of Elizabeth (Anita Harris), suppressed desperation and covert passions climb to the fore. Produced by Bill Kenwright's well established company, "The House of Stairs" played the larger venues later on in the year.

The Kingfisher

Dinah Sheridan and Charles Stapley

House lights down for gentle escapism into a land of lost but not forgotten love where Sir Charles Warburton (Charles Stapley) tries to rekindle a flame with the gal (Dinah Sheridan) he should have married fifty years previously. But do watch out for the butler. Nostalgia was mixed with jokes on old age into a somnambulant rhythm, lulling the audience through two hours beside a beech tree, during this revival,produced by Channel and directed by Philip Dart, that celebrated the eightieth birthday of playwright William Douglas Home before his sad death later in the year. It proved at the same time that the quintessentially English play which Osborne hoped to eradicate in the fifties has never been entirely overcome.

Ladies Night

For the third year running Stephen Sinclair and Anthony McCarten's male strip show, produced by Newpalm Productions, has covered the country from Blackpool to Aberdeen, stopping to liberate Tunbridge Wells and fifteen other towns besides. The basic plotline goes: the boys try to earn a few pennies taking off their underpants but are useless. Then they meet empowered and understanding Glenda who shows them the tricks. They become freshly oiled stars. Proving that such simple ideas are always the greatest the lads- Gaz, Baz, Nor, Wes, Gra, Craig and Bern- have had audiences shrieking with laughter and, well, with lust, wherever they showed.

Macbeth

Paul Darrow

1992 saw D.P. Productions press ahead with their intention of presenting accessible and fine Shakespearean shows on the commercial circuit- a laudable aim indeed considering the cast-size and budgets involved. This season's "Macbeth", staring Paul Darrow as the ambitious nobleman, was set in Scotland around the time of the Jacobite Rebellion, thus keeping to a clear, traditional interpretation. Pamela Salem played the evil Lady behind the evil Lord with noteworthy passion as the tour moved through thirty regional theatres, stopping to workshop occasionally with younger play-goers. The critical response was generally favourable, though the sound, the lighting and the witches' lycra suits often got much of the attention.

M. Butterfly

D.C. Chan and George Chakiris

David Henry Hwang takes on Western preconceptions about oriental culture in his tale of love, submission and espionage. Set in a Paris prison, 1989, the action flashes back to the years 1960-86 in Beijing and Paris, fictionalising real events of one of the biggest spy trials of this century, and confronting myths intrinsic to Puccini's opera. D.C. Chan played Song Lilling, who turned out not to be a madame, and George Chakiris tackled the meatier role of Rene Gallimard. Bill Kenwright's tour trucked from the Thorndike Theatre, Leatherhead, after three weeks beginning March 23, played fifteen venues and ended in Woking on July 25.

My Cousin Rachel

Jill Greenacre, Anita Harris, Steven Pinner and Robert Grange

The last of Daphne du Maurier's romantic Cornish novels, adapted for stage by Diana Morgan and directed by the irrepressible Charles Vance, questions whether enigmatic and beautiful Rachel (Anita Harris) has murdered to have her way at Barton Hall or whether she is really an ill fated innocent. As the contradictory evidence mounts, dashing Philip Ashley (Steven Pinner) can only decide that he loves her. This Prestige Plays production boiled first at the Churchill Theatre, Bromley, January 27, then simmered its way through twenty venues to Salisbury Playhouse at the end of July.

My Fair Lady

Michael Medwin, Sheila Burrell, Helen Hobson and Michael Dewdney

Edward Fox provided a big star name as Professor Henry Higgins, Helen Hobson did the Eliza Doolittle, Simon Callow directed, while fashion guru Jasper Conran designed costumes and the cast numbered over forty performers, the orchestra twenty. Such is the scale that can be reached on the commercial circuit when the basic vehicle is such a sure fire winner as Lerner and Loewe's musical.Pola Jones assembled this impressive line-up which toured twelve of the largest theatres throughout the country starting at Manchester's Opera House for three weeks (February to March) and finally rested after the Mayflower Theatre in Southampton on September 26. Cor Blimey!

On Golden Pond

Googie Withers and John McCallum

Two crinklies are seeing out their forty-eighth summer beside a Maine pond when Chelsea (Julia Foster), their daughter in her forties, turns up with her new fiance- Bill- and his son- Bill Jr- in tow. Her attempt at a new life provokes recriminations across the generation gap bringing old family tensions to the surface, but a surprising affection between the young boy and the old grandpa starts a change towards reconciliation. Husband and wife, John McCallum and Googie Withers, played the old couple made so famous on film by Henry Fonda and Catherine Hepburn in a Bill Kenwright production that toured from the Royal Theatre Windsor, May 11, to the Theatre Royal Bath, August 22, stopping at nine others.

70, Girls,70

Out on tour after a lukewarm reception at the West-End's Vaudeville theatre Dora Bryan starred as Ida in Kander and Ebb's unlikely musical comedy. Now the '80s are gone, there is some implausibility in the question of whether any evil developers would want to take over the dilapidated hotel where the action is set. Still vitality, not credibility, is the hook in this show and the cast displayed it admirably, touring from Bath in May to Edinburgh just before the festival, then back to London. Newpalm Productions were the backers.

Dora Bryan

Shirley Valentine

Kate Fitzgerald

When a Liverpudlian housewife downs the chip pan, drops the hubby and heads off to a climate where they actually grow the grape that goes in the glass in your hand she peels back years of stifling domesticity and finds her original self. Willy Russell's warm-hearted play took to the road in September of 1991 and kept going until July 4 this year, when it finished at Bournemouth. Kate Fitzgerald was the third and final middle-aged traveller to unravel under a Mediterranean sun on this huge tour produced by Bill Kenwright and directed by Richard (son of Laurence) Olivier.

A Slice of Saturday Night

Alvin Stardust filled a dinner jacket recently vacated by Gary Glitter in this year's extensive tour (York on February 10 to Aberdeen, Aug 24, via twenty-three other venues) of the Heather Brother's musical. As Eric "Rubber Legs" De Vern, Mr Stardust presided over The Club-A-Go-Go where he consoled and cajoled three boys and four girls through a medley of '60's pastiche numbers and some amusing home-truths about teenage sexuality- mainly revealed through in-the-toilet conversations. Regional critics felt that the show was feather -weight plotwise, but full of infectious good humour and buoyant tap-along songs. Ivan Hale Ltd produced.

The Sound of Music

Christopher Cazenove and Liz Robertson

"Doe a deer, a female deer, ray a drop of.." But doesn't it just carry you along? I know it's schmaltz, it's tear-jerk sentimentalism, but can anyone resist Rodgers and Hammerstein's 1959 musical? Revived and toured in 1992 with a cast that looked so similar to the Julie Andrew's film no one who has sat through a small screen Christmas special would feel betrayed, The S of M toured, with Christopher Cazenove and Liz Robertson as the Baron and the postulate, from Birmingham's Alexandra Theatre at the beginning of the year to a final date in June at Sadler's Wells, where the remarkable Wendy Toye, director, must have felt quite at home having danced there at the beginning of her career in the '20s.

Ronald S. Lee produced.

Stageland

Amanda Kirby, Trevor Bannister and Terence Singleton

Jerome K. Jerome was an actor from 1877 to 1880 before he turned to writing so the rough life of touring, the villainous managers and shady agents described in his book are not merely funny but accurate for their times as well. Michael Friend's loving adaptation kept much of the humour of the original but also too much of the prose making for a unwieldy piece in performance- narration threatening to stifle action. The actors entertained nonetheless, each displaying his or her talents in a number of roles, while overall a good balance was struck between the melodramatic style of the time and a modern naturalism. "Stageland" played in ten regional theatres from May 19 to July 27.

Stepping Out

A tap dancing class in North London offers release to nine women and one man from their everyday trudges. Postures and poses are comically struck, steps and stances ridiculously tried, as Mavis attempts to drive them towards their first public performance. But she isn't the only one who thinks she knows how the show should run. The professionals who performed the tricky business of deliberately dancing badly in Richard Harris' perennial laugh-along created an excellently silly amateur night, under the direction of Martin Connor, that started at the Towngate Theatre in Poole on May 25 and reached the Theatre Royal, Windsor, on August 24. Bill Kenwright produced.

Witness For the Prosecution

John Barron

Typical of Agatha Christie's best loved crime stories the plot hinges around a legal technicality (that a man cannot be tried twice for the same crime) and ends with a twist that shakes off most audience sleuths. Billed as The Queen of Crime's second most successful piece of stagecraft after "The Mousetrap", this courtroom drama has also been made into a multi-Oscar nominated film in 1957 and an all star television production in 1982. Prestige Plays Ltd gave audiences a chance to guess the outcome from Wimbledon Theatre in March to Glasgow in November. Derek Waring took over from John Barron as Sir Wilfrid Robarts, QC, around the halfway point at Oxford.

You Must Be The Husband

Tim Brooke-Taylor and Carola Stewart

Another farce that skims the surface of cosy, suburban concerns, Colin Bostock-Smith's hardly new play was most often noted for its surplus of puns. Tom (Tim Brooke-Taylor) discovers his wife has written a sexy best seller, so the poor old chap must now come to terms with her success, his neighbour's innuendo, and his fictional (or is he?) rival in the bedroom, Steve. Brigit Forsyth partnered the ex-Goody on Bryan Hands Productions' spring tour that started at Wakefield Theatre Royal, February 10 (after a standard, but brief, two weeks of rehearsal) and ended at Taunton Brewhouse early in April. After a change of cast (Jeffrey Holland and Sue Holderness in the leads) a summer tour carried on from Wimbledon, June 16, to Westcliff, August 23.

Hot Stuff, A Woman of no Importance, Shades

All three shows toured. "Hot Stuff" emanated from Leicester and is fully covered in the **Midlands** in the Yearbook's **Regional Guide**. "Shades" toured prior to its West End run, as did "A Woman of no Importance". Both shows are described in the Yearbook's section on **The West End**.

TOURING COMPANIES

"Commercial tours" tend to involve a single show. When it's over, the company disbands and the producer moves on to another play. The touring companies have an identity and a life which stretches beyond any one production. There are very many such companies – all with their own style. The Yearbook describes a selection and looks at their current work.

Touring Companies '92

The touring company is a phenomenon which began to grow up between ten and twenty years ago. Unable or unwilling to enlist with a building based company, young actors and directors decided to go on the road on their own. Perhaps they wished to produce plays with a clear message – such as the group of women ex-prisoners who started Clean Break Theatre Company. Perhaps they felt that some aspect of Britain's cultural mix needed reflecting in the theatre – as has been achieved by Talawa and Tara Arts. Such companies eschewed the need for purpose-built theatres and took their productions around the country and the world, bringing in new audiences and widening people's perceptions.

With the decline in central and local authority funding in the 1980s, a plethora of these little companies sprung up – all with their own ethos and policies, united in their determination to put on plays despite an inauspicious environment. At the helm of many such enterprises were figures of immense drive and talent. Outstanding examples are Deborah Warner, who attracted attention with Kick Theatre, and the collaborators Declan Donnellan and Nick Ormerod, whose Cheek by Jowl was regarded by many as the highspot of British theatre in the 1980s: innovative, challenging and unapologetically intellectual.

Cheek by Jowl's simple, even minimalistic, style was formed in part by the limitations of touring sets and small budgets. Other companies were similarly challenged by necessity and this led to their great contribution: while the musical extravaganzas became ever more spectacular and opulent, the touring companies were putting thoughtful work into productions which relied on ingenuity and simplicity for their effects.

With their openness to new ideas and their experience of travel, the new companies increasingly adopted approaches to theatre which they had learned from abroad – Europe, in particular. Theatre de Complicité was influenced by the work of the Parisian master, Jacques le Coq. They have brought his emphasis on physical technique to the fore. This has had a strong influence on the present generation of actors. Whereas fifteen years ago, a young actor would work on his voice, the young performer today spends as much time on his back-flips and cartwheels.

The 1990s have seen the pioneers reap their rewards. Warner and Donnellan are now associate directors at the National Theatre and Complicité have been embraced by the establishment – so warmly embraced that their major project of 1992 was "The Street of Crocodiles" at the National's Cottesloe. (This means that they do not appear in the following pages but in the **National Theatre** section of the Yearbook.)

Some of the so-called touring companies have always had a fixed base. This is particularly true in the regions: Eastern Angles, for example, operate out of the Sir John Mills theatre in Ipswich. Some of the companies, such as Shared Experience and Talawa, have acquired bricks and mortar and feel this to be a great achievement. Others, notably the English Shakespeare Company, regard touring as their raison d'etre. Some tour in just one region, as Orchard do in the South West. Others travel mainly abroad. The range in approach and ambition is enormous. In their unpredictability, their refusal to chase after material success and their happy resignation to the discomforts of travel, the touring companies represent British theatre's enduring strength.

GWYN MORGAN

Actors Touring Company

Tasso

The Actors Touring Company was set up in 1978 by John Retallack (who remained their Artistic Director until 1986). Its aim was to ensure that British audiences outside London had the opportunity to see high quality productions of neglected European classics. Over fourteen years of small scale touring, ATC has produced twenty four shows, including six British premieres, earning a strong following and many awards. BBC Radio 4's Kaleidoscope called them "the company with a history of brilliant, inventive productions."

ATC has been Arts Council funded since 1984 and currently has "three year franchise" funding. In April this year, they were awarded an increase of 35.4% on their revenue grant following an appraisal of work during the last five years. Nick Philippou will become the fourth Artistic Director in March 1993, following predecessors Ceri Sherlock (1989-92) and Mark Brickman (1986-1988).

Recent successes include the British premiere of "Tasso" by Goethe in a new version by Robert David MacDonald, in which actor Ian Hughes won the 1991 Ian Charleson Award for an outstanding performance in a classic role; and the British premiere of Marina Tsvetayeva's "Phaedra" in a version by Michael Glenny and Richard Crane, which The Guardian described as an "intravenous injection of raw passion". Both productions were directed by Ceri Sherlock.

La Ronde and Blodeuwedd, Woman of Flowers.

Victoria Scarborough and Colin Watson

From January to April, the company produced Schnitzler's "La Ronde", in a new version by Ceri Sherlock, directed by Nicholas Bone and Ceri Sherlock, and designed by Birte Meyer and Idit Nathan.

Actors Victoria Scarborough and Colin Watson played a national tour which trucked through twenty five venues.

The Observer praised the production most highly, describing it as "careful and stylish".

"Blodeuwedd, Woman of Flowers" by Saunders Lewis, in an English version by Sion Eirian, was a co-production with the Sherman theatre, Cardiff. Details may be found in the Yearbook's Regional Guide – **Wales**.

MIA SOTERIOU

Baroque

Nick Mattingley

Nicolas Brook

One of the more significant initiatives of 1992 may turn out to have been the founding of Baroque, under Nicolas Brooke and Nick Mattingley. Fresh out of drama school, determined to avoid the long dole queues in an overcrowded profession, they have formed their own company and employed themselves. Two things set them apart from scores of similarly hopeful venturers: their practicality, and a highly imaginative casting policy.

Company strategy is to balance commercial tours with new-look classic revivals, but the keynote is to cast beginners alongside well-established professionals. With the decline in scope of regional repertory theatre, a traditional proving-ground for young performers has been lost, and Baroque's determination to promote opportunities for accredited drama school leavers up to about eighteen months "out" is a welcome breath of fresh air.

Funding has come from sources as diverse as the Cameron Mackintosh Trust, ABSA and a major business sponsor, General Portfolio. There is also a flourishing "Friends" structure, with Geraldine McEwan as patron. Next year comes another national tour, a musical dramatisation of the Maria Marten ("Murder in the Red Barn") story; and the young directors already have plans to take Baroque to Europe in the none too distant future.

See How They Run

David Kelsey, Nicolas Brooke, Claudia McNulty, Alastair Evans-Gordon, John Iles, Andy Whip and Philip Ives

The first fruit of the two Nicks' efforts has been a successful national tour of Philip King's 1945 classic "See How They Run", the first major West End comedy of the post-war era. Its subject is the Church of England, its method a choice mixture of clerical bungling and manic farce, its climax famously involves no less than five vicars evading the fury of an outraged bishop. Judging from reviews and public reception of the Baroque tour it has lost none of its point and power to please.

Under the direction of the highly experienced Wendy Toye, Baroque, in accordance with their casting policy, used an ensemble mixing familiar faces from TV soaps with a batch of young hopefuls. The result was an encouraging first outing, no less in box-office than in critical terms.

With the examples before them of Jon Iles, David Kelsey and Josephine Tewson (an established farceur of impeccable Whitehall pedigree) the younger members of the company acquitted themselves well – Maxine Evans, in the role of a dotty maid, came in for especial praise. The high quality of the acting, and meticulous preparation of the staging, augured well for the future of the company.

CHRISTOPHER WEBBER

Brith Gof

Patagonia

Brith Gof are probably Wales's best known experimental theatre company. Since forming eleven years ago, they have achieved recognition both overseas and at home for a distinctive style of performance that is rooted in the Welsh language, culture and history.

A large number of their projects have taken place outside the confines of the proscenium arch theatre, transferring the company in to disused factories, a quarry, an ice-hockey stadium and a railway terminus.

In 1992, however, they returned to traditional theatre spaces to present a new work, "Patagonia", a project assisted by a sponsorship award from the Barclays New Stages scheme. This enabled them to work in England for the first time, taking in the Royal Court Theatre and the University of Warwick Arts Centre on a short tour.

They also launched a major new site specific work called "Haearn" ("Iron") in October in a disused Valleys factory and collaborated with acclaimed German saxophonist Peter Brotzmann for a performance at the 1992 Cardiff Festival.

And there were showings of an earlier work, "Los Angeles", in festivals in Switzerland, Grenoble and Argentina.

Patagonia

Six years ago, Brith Gof travelled to visit Welsh communities in Patagonia, the direct descendants of a group of settlers who sailed to Argentina in the nineteenth century. Patagonia was based around research material collected on that trip, a show that used a complex web of ideas, allusions, anecdotes - even lists of words and the flickering movements of early silent movies - to relate an episode in history and to question its wider meaning in a contemporary context.

The blending of these two different cultures provided some striking images, which were worked into the show - parrots flying over chapels and farmers dancing the paso doble.

The contradictory impressions were deliberate, a device to debate the different readings of this experience. Scenographer Cliff McLucas, a trained architect, created a simple framework structure for the four performers to work against, using just a few props - apples, sand and a rifle - to suggest changing scenes. The performers, dressed in period costume, moved across a series of thresholds, as if tracing their way into an architectural drawing.

A specially developed miking and amplification system gave an audience the impression of being surrounded by the individual voices, a means employed to draw closer together the performers and spectators.

PENNY SIMPSON

Cambridge Theatre Company

Mike Alfreds

Under its Artistic Director Mike Alfreds, Cambridge Theatre Company continues to provide high-quality touring theatre throughout the country, presenting a mix of classic drama, new writing and adaptations. It performs an average of thirty-two weeks each year, of which between six and eight are spent in Cambridge; for the remaining weeks, the company visits venues all over Britain, from Berwick to Brighton. This year has seen the further development of an extensive programme of educational and community work: each production being supported by a network of workshops, talks, seminars and residencies, and informative background packs are available. At the beginning of the year, Shaw's anti-romantic comedy "Arms and the Man" was directed by Nick Philippou and designed by Stewart Laing, and in September the same team tackled Frank Wedekind's "Lulu" in a clear-eyed and uncompromising version by Edward Bond and Elisabeth Bond Pable. In April, Mike Alfreds and designer Paul Dart mounted a 1940s New York version of "The Revengers Tragedy" "by Cyril Tourneur or Thomas Middleton", as the billing had it; and the year finished with a notable revival of "The Game of Love and Chance".

The Game of Love and Chance

This new production of Pierre Marivaux's glittering comedy "The Game of Love and Chance" was first seen in October at Poole, before moving on to Worthing, Oxford, Warwick, Eastbourne, Cambridge and Malvern. A co-production with Gloria, this was the first in what it is hoped will become a series of artistic collaborations with other companies. Mike Alfreds co-directed with Neil Bartlett (who provided a new translation), the music was by Nicolas Bloomfield and Leah Hausman was in charge of movement; Bartlett, Bloomfield and Hausman are all members of Gloria. The action was transplanted to our own century, Stefan Bednarczyk (as Maurice) was an on-stage pianist and there were stunning frocks by Paul Dart; the cast was Maggie Steed (Silvia), Caroline Quentin (Lisette), Trevor Baxter (Mr Prowde), Marcello Magni (Arlecchino) and Peter Wingfield (Mr Dorant). The production was presented in association with the National Theatre, and after the tour it joined the repertoire at the Cottesloe.

ANDREW WICKES

Charabanc

The company was formed in 1983 by five Belfast-based women actors - largely because the city's theatres offered few serious roles for women. Initially dedicated to devising and performing plays "from and for the community", their first production was "Lay Up Your Ends"' about the Belfast linen mill workers at the time of the strike in Belfast in 1911, led by James Connolly. This was scripted by Martin Lynch with Marie Jones and directed by Pam Brighton, fresh from Hull Truck. The company's development saw Lynch become less central, Marie Jones began to write more; Pam Brighton had a pronounced impact on their performance style through directing a series of shows; and Marie Jones became a playwright in her own right and move on, leaving Carol Scanlan and Eleanor Methven as directors. They developed what had become a more flexible approach to programming, with the performing of existing scripts by other writers, usually female and where the concerns of the play related to women's experience. The company have toured annually throughout Ireland; often to the UK and internationally - to America, Canada, Germany, Moscow, Leningrad and Vilnius. Funded by the Arts Council, company administrator is Patricia McBride.

Eleanor Methven

Carol Scanlan

October Song

In April and May of this year Charabanc toured with "October Song" by Andy Hinds, the Derry-born director facing the challenge to write his own plays. Developed in workshops with company members, Carol Scanlan and Eleanor Methven from an idea of his about two sisters meeting after a twenty-year-long breach, the scenario acquired a third sister, a teenage son, a husband and a father. Hinds was born in Derry, where Charabanc had recently worked, taking workshops, so the decision was taken to locate the action of the play there and to premiere it in the city. This was supported by the Derry City Council and by Impact 92, the year-long Derry festival. An intensive research period in the city developed the storylines and Hinds then wrote the performance script, squirrelling himself away at Annaghmakerrig, the Tyrone Guthrie Centre. The production was undertaken in association with the Open House project, founded by Andy Hinds to offer training to selected young directors (three of whom worked with Hinds on this show); to help writers to develop their work - even Hinds himself; and to explore methods of collaborative playmaking. This last allowed a fruitful exploration of the psychological and social complexities surrounding the twenty year estrangement between the sisters.

Eleanor Methven

LYNDA HENDERSON

Cheek by Jowl

Wick Ormerod and Declan Donnellan

Cheek by Jowl - the brainchild of the director-designer partnership Declan Donnellan and Nick Ormerod - was founded in 1981 as a small-scale company touring classic plays. Ambitious and expansionist, it flourished during its first decade and is now popular the world over.

Shakespeare productions and British premieres of European classics - stripping away preconceived performance notions, allowing the actors to present the raw text on a bare stage, using nothing but their physical dexterity and nimble ideas (less means more) inspired by Donnellan's freely associative approach - was recognised by numerous awards (from a Scotsman Edinburgh Fringe First to three Oliviers). Behind cultural innovation a mischievous social frisson loomed, both in the narrative of the plays chosen and in the style of the productions: a collective celebration dwarfing the authority of the self-important individual.

Donnellan and Ormerod now have a second home in Richard Eyre's catholic National Theatre, where their productions of "Fuente Ovejuna" and "Angels in America" have been seen this year. Cheek by Jowl and its progenitors will continue to be a major theatrical force throughout the next decade.

Cheek by Jowl present Alfred de Musset's "Don't Fool With Love" in 1993, with plans for "Measure for Measure" in 1994.

As You Like It

Adrian Lester

Beginning with one of its hallmarks - actors and audience natter with unforced familiarity - Cheek by Jowl's all-male "As You Like It" inserted a prologue: Jaques' "All The World's A Stage" (Joe Dixon won the Ian Charleson Award for his performance). "And All The Men And Women Merely Players" drove Adrian Lester (Rosalind: a boy plays a girl pretending to be a boy pretending to be that girl) and Tom Hollander (Celia) into a coy corner, separated from the remainder of the company.

Despite homoerotic expectations, love transcended sexuality. The women were not camp drag-queens; they conveyed an abstract beyond gender. Simplicity allowed the company to unpick a play peopled by a range of individuals with contrasting desires and expectations. Ormerod's designs moved from the black-and-white, ugly machismo of a de-bagging Court retinue, to an overcoated, bleak Arden in winter - which then burst into summer hues. It was a mature production.

Cheek by Jowl has been recognised nationally and internationally as a potent force; it is "sans doute l'une des compagnies les plus originales et passionantes travaillant actuellement dans le théâtre européen" (Tageblatt, Luxembourg).

SIMON READE

Clean Break

Clean Break is a company working with and for women ex-prisoners. It all started with two inmates of Askham Grange, York, in 1979, who decided to devise and perform their own shows. Thirteen years on, the company has expanded hugely, with permanent premises in Camden and funding from, among others, the Arts Council and the Home Office.

There are two distinct parts to their work. At the Camden premises, there is a training programme in performance arts for ex-offenders. Those who have benefitted from this programme can go on to the other branch of the company, who mount professional productions, employing both ex-prisoners and theatre professionals as writers, directors and production staff.

The professional show tours throughout the UK and internationally. The show is seen both inside and outside prisons – though much of the work done within institutions consists of workshops allowing for maximum involvement of the inmates who may be encouraged to attend the Camden centre on release.

Director Alex Ford is assisted by an artistic course director, an administrator and a financial administrator. The increasing professionalism of the company's administration is mirrored in the standard of their performance work which attains ever greater polish and style.

Headrot Holiday

Written by Sarah Daniels, formerly writer in residence at the Royal Court, this new play was concerned with the experience of women put into special hospitals, such as Broadmoor. Clean Break set up research periods with a number of women who had undergone treatment in "specials" as well as sessions with psychiatrists and nurses working in this field.

The play explores the secret world of special hospitals through presenting three women: Dee, who feels that, at twenty two, she has reached the end of the road, Ruth, who can't remember if her life is real or part of a song, and Claudia, who has been judged too arrogant to be well. Women can be transferred to a hospital from a conventional prison for disruptive behaviour. In the "special", the prisoner has no definite end to her prison sentence. She remains an inmate until she can prove herself sane.

Daniels' challenging piece raises many issues about how madness and mad women are perceived, posing the question of whether seeing life from a feminist perspective is regarded by some as a form of insanity. It was directed by the highly effective Paulette Randall, author of last year's disturbing piece about racism and the prison system, "24%".

GWYN MORGAN

Communicado

Tom McGovan and Cara Kelly in "Thérèse Raquin"

With five Fringe Firsts picked up from various Edinburgh Festivals, Communicado is Scotland's most critically and popularly acclaimed touring company. Dedicated to the craft of clear-sighted story-telling, tackling grand themes in a highly theatrical style, the company has earned a reputation for producing ambitious epics on the one hand, and fresh interpretations of the classics on the other.

Its remarkable "Jock Tamson's Bairns" was a lasting highlight of Glasgow's Year of Culture in 1990, analysing the Scottish psyche in a hypnotic visual and musical feast, and in 1991 the company performed a similarly large-scale adaptation of "The Cone Gatherers" in which the audience sat among the trees and wood-chips of a recreated forest.

More conventionally, Gerry Mulgrew's company has tackled plays including "Antigone", "Danton's Death" and, this year, an adaptation directed by Jennifer Black of "Thérèse Raquin", but always with a touch of theatrical flair that sets it apart.

Cyrano de Bergerac

Tom Mannion

Edmond Rostand's epic tragi-comedy about a supremely gifted but large-nosed soldier who courts the woman he loves under the guise of another man, was given a sparkling Scots translation by the poet Edwin Morgan. Keeping the rhyming-verse form of the original, Morgan had an eclectic frame of reference that gave the piece its special contemporary edge.

In a brilliant piece of ensemble acting, directed by Gerry Mulgrew, with assistant Andrew Farrell, "Cyrano" was a high-energy production that brought laughter and tears to packed houses in Communicado's early-autumn tour. Starring Tom Mannion with a suitably elongated nose, Kenneth Glenaan as Christian, and Sandy McDade as Roxanne, the play was rich in live music in true Communicado style, performed here by Iain Johnstone and the company.

Cygnet

Linda Mills and Louis Dempsey in "Arms and the Man"

Cygent is a training theatre; but it differs from other training establishments in two ways. Students are treated as working actors, and a lot of training is in actual performances before a paying public.

Director Monica Shallis firmly believes in a good deal of practical experience. Therefore Cygnet will have as many as six productions on tour at once. Cygnet travel around the south west in small venues, experiencing the difficulties of setting up in village and school halls. They send their productions to the Edinburgh Festival and run a summer season at Lyme Regis. The working actors appear in everything from Shakespeare to farce, getting ensemble experience in large scale productions of "The Beggars Opera" and the intense glow of "Miss Julie".

This is a remarkably successful operation which has grown over the years and this year has been made a member of the Conference of Drama Schools, which should help with local authority fees.

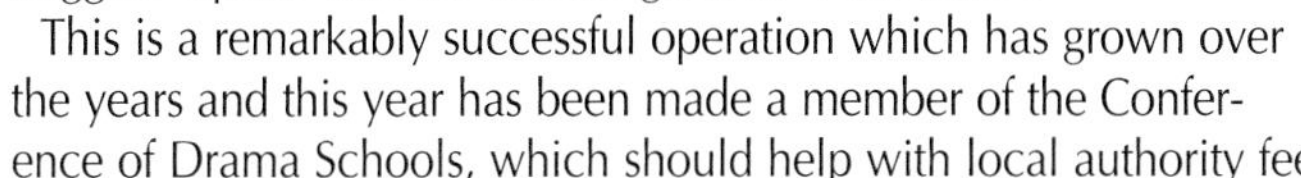

Monica Shallis still directs most of the productions, with Alistair Ganley as assistant director taking on the director's mantle for some productions.

Cygnet was founded by Monica Shallis and the hardworking administrator, Mary Evans.

Double Concerto

Lynda Mills and Janet Howd

"Double Concerto", a new play by Sarah Palinkov, deals with the psychological shifts that occur during a prolonged interrogation. The victim is an internationally acclaimed violinist, the daughter of a dissident mother, who is a composer, and a thorn in the side of an unspecified totalitarian regime.

A tough female investigator is assigned to break down the violinist's resolve, to extract from her the address of her mother. The subtle interplay between the two women is the substance of the play.

The investigator tries to weaken her prisoner by the classic ploy of alternate moods, by deprivation and humiliation, cold blooded threats and offers of help and good will. The violinist is aware of the tactics, but, even so, is manipulated against her will. There is a satisfying conclusion that retains a certain amount of ambiguity. The close relationship leaves a mark on the investigator as much as the prisoner.

Lynda Mills gave a controlled performance as the violinist, never descending into hysterics, trying to find some logic in a mechanical madness. Janet Howd cleverly showed touches of humanity behind a steely surface, sensed in voice and gesture, while her expression remained set in unswerving obedience to an intractable party line. Louis Dempsey played the prison guard as an automaton; no sense, no feeling.

ALLEN SADDLER

Eastern Angles

"Peculiar People"

Eastern Angles was formed in 1982 by five actors returning to their home in East Anglia after theatre training. The Artistic Director, Ivan Cutting, was one of those founder members. It was felt that East Anglia lacked a touring company which was specifically committed to the region. Reflecting the rural nature of East Anglia, the company set out to visit professional and non-professional venues, in both rural and urban settings.

Experience has shown that it is the annual tour of non-professional venues – mainly village halls- which allows most room for experiment. Eastern Angles has built up a list of places who ask them to return. As they also search out new places to perform, tour schedules get longer and longer: the autumn tour is now twelve weeks long and the spring tour lasts up to sixteen weeks.

Based at the Sir John Mills theatre just outside Ipswich, the company travels many miles. The home county of Suffolk is sizeable enough. Norfolk and Essex are also large – and there are occasional forays elsewhere on the Eastern side of Britain. This is an area not noted for its fast roads.

The company raises almost half its income from fees and box office. Subsidy has come from Eastern Arts and various councils amounting to £130,000 for 1992-1993.

Peculiar People

"Peculiar People"

Spring brought a new play, Robert Rigby's "Peculiar People", which Eastern Angles mounted in association with Colchester's Mercury theatre. After opening in the Mercury studio in February, it toured until the 9th of May.

Ivan Cutting directed with designs by Karen Bartlett, head of design at the Mercury. The peculiar people in question were a nineteenth century religious sect founded in Essex. The play concerns a late Victorian Peculiar casting a long shadow over a 1990s couple, newly arrived from London.

Other productions this year included "When the Boats Came In", a company devised piece about the Lowestoft herring industry, and "Song of Provence", inspired by the novels of Jean Giono.

TIMOTHY RAMSDEN

English Shakespeare Company

Jenny Quayle and Michael Pennington in "Macbeth"

The English Shakespeare Company was formed in 1986 by director Michael Bodganov and actor Michael Pennington, both of whom had previously worked for the Royal Shakespeare Company. The reputation of the company was quickly made; between 1987 and 1989 the "Wars of the Roses", Shakespeare's complete history cycle toured nationally and internationally to enormous critical acclaim. The plays, seven in all, were performed at eighteen venues in Britain including the Old Vic in London and then toured to Japan, the United States, Australia, the Netherlands, and Germany. Michael Bogdanov was awarded the 1990 Lawrence Olivier award for Best Director.

By 1990 the programme of work was expanded so that three companies were touring nationally and internationally at the same time, and the company's educational group was developed. This now provides a full time educational service consisting of practical workshops, teacher's development courses, summer school courses and prison visits.

The company has always been supported by the Arts Council and the British Council, but has also received extensive sponsorship from individuals and businesses. Between 1990 and 1991 Michael Bogdanov was also Artistic Director of the Deutsches Schauspielhaus in Hamburg, Germany, and has recently directed productions in Dublin and Cologne.

Macbeth

Michael Pennington

Michael Bogdanov has a reputation for exciting visual and physical theatre, accessible particularly to the young, combining contemporary and historical sources in the same production. Macbeth was no exception. The stage was dominated by a form of travelling crane, dubbed a Macbethescope, which served as a battle-cannon, a battering ram, the ramp to a throne and a support for Banquo's Ghost. Battle scenes were indicated by strobe lighting and helicopter sound effects and modern weapons appeared alongside swords and daggers. The production was designed by Claire Lyth, lighting design was by Chris Ellis and the fights were directed by Malcolm Ranson.

Paradoxically the anachronistic nature of the production placed, if anything, even greater responsibility on the performers. Michael Pennington and Jenny Quayle gave performances of great depth and sublety, belying the programme note that "Macbeth is not about a metaphysical concept or an individual subject". The witches, played by Vivienne Munn, Allie Burne and Tracey Mitchell were extremely effective, especially in the cauldron scene which was set in a rubbish skip.

The production received many excellent reviews particularly for Michael Pennington's Macbeth. As well as playing eleven venues in Britain it toured to Korea, Japan and the United States.

TERRY DIAB

Field Day

Stephen Rea

Funded by the Arts Council and founded by playwright Brian Friel and actor Stephen Rea, Field Day has become one of the foremost influences in contemporary Irish theatre. It produces, almost exclusively, new commissioned plays either by Irish writers or dealing with issues central to the creation of a post-colonial Irish identity. Its first production was Friel's "Translations", a play which entered the international repertoire very quickly. Featuring writers from both traditions in Ulster, the company produced "Pentecost", which turned out to be the last play by the much missed Stewart Parker before his premature death from cancer. The board was expanded to include the poet Seamus Heaney, scholar/poets Seamus Deane and Tom Paulin, musician David Hammond and, later, Galway-based playwright, Tom Kilroy. With this new expertise, the company diversified into publishing. It produced several series of the "Field Day Pamphlets", exploring more abstractly the issues confronted by the dramas. It has published and distributed internationally the ambitious "Field Day Anthology of Irish Writing", edited by Seamus Deane. The company has held an autumn reading of an early play by David Rudkin and plans a touring production for the spring of 1993. Based in the Foyle Arts Centre in Derry, Company Manager is Gary McKeone.

The Madame MacAdam Travelling Theatre

Julian Curry, Amanda Hurwitz, Helen Ryan and Tina Kellegher

This production by author Tom Kilroy who had earlier written "Double Cross" for Field Day, finished its Irish tour with a London run. The apparent matter of the play is the fate of a run-down English theatre company touring wartime rural Ireland. They run out of steam in a remote town and become involved in its life. A little girl goes missing, an actor seduces a local girl and one of the company is lynched by a local posse. The assimilation of the company into the town is resisted and remains incomplete. The powerhouse at the centre of the company is the Madame herself; and the range of disguises adopted by the locals extends the theatrical metaphor. The earlier play, "Double Cross", may well be the progenitor of the deeper concerns of the play. It can be read - and played - as an exploration of the relationship of a colony to an imperial force in decline. The chosen role of roving entertainment, the preferred theatrical diet of abridged Shakespeare and patriotic heroics about Robert Emmett seems to underline an ambivalence and insecurity in the English group's sense of itself and its role. Disappointingly, the play seemed to be understood only shallowly by its audiences throughout its tour.

LYNDA HENDERSON

Fifth Estate

Gordon Dougal, George Drennan, Gary Grochla and Julia Dow in "The Ballachulish Beat"

The biggest success story of the last two years in Scottish theatre is that of Fifth Estate, a company of experienced actors and directors operating out of the tiny Netherbow Theatre in Edinburgh. Fifth Estate are not, strictly speaking, a touring company - but they have been invited to perform in places as far apart as Hampstead and the Tron Theatre, Glasgow. Committed to literate Scottish drama, both forgotten classics and previously-unseen plays, the company quickly won favour with critics and audiences, though funding was less forthcoming. It is remarkable that such established stage-hands should be so foolhardy as to set up a new theatre company instead of lucrative TV or mainstage work, but perhaps more remarkable still that such a young company should be invited to perform in the Edinburgh International Festival as part of Brian McMaster's CP Taylor's retrospective with the previously unseen "The Ballachullish Beat". That was just one instalment of a year-round programme that challenged the bigger repertories to look again at the range of work to which they were restricting themselves. Like the younger West Coast company Raindog, Fifth Estate was seen as part of a broader movement to assert and redefine the nature of Scottish identity.

The Jesuit

Sandy Neilson

One of Fifth Estate's characteristic abilities is to make the tiny Netherbow Theatre stage appear to be as big as any classical rep theatre. It's part of the company's tendency to think big - big plays, big casts, big ideas - and Paul Ambrose Wright's cell-block set for "The Jesuit" was no exception. Donald Campbell's play had gone unproduced since 1976 despite an enthusiastic response to it at the time, so it was with some missionary fervour that Fifth Estate returned to it. Set in seventeenth century Scotland, the play is a moral battle of wills between Ogilvie - the Jesuit of the title - and Spottiswoode, the Archbishop of Glasgow. Ogilvie is arrested, tortured and finally hanged for his beliefs, while an intense debate rages about faith, morality, piety and self-doubt. Directed with much energy by Alan Sharpe, the play starred Sandy Neilson as Ogilvie and Robin Thomson as Spottiswoode. Also in the cast were Douglas Sannachan, Andrew Barr, Steven McNicholl, Iain Stuart Robertson and Muriel Romanes.

MARK FISHER

Gloria

Gloria is an association of theatre-making artists set up in 1988 to produce the work of Neil Bartlett (writer, director, performer), Nicholas Bloomfield (composer), Leah Hausman (director, choreographer) and Simon Mellor (producer). Their shows combine live music and song with striking visuals and unusual subject matter. Past projects include "A Vision Of Love Revealed in Sleep" (1989), inspired by the work and life of gay Victorian painter Simeon Solomon, and "Sarrasine" (1990), a monumental, gender-bending adaptation of Balzac's novella about an eighteenth century nobleman's obsessive love for a castrato. These and the company's other pieces do not fit easily into any particular category (performance art, musical, gay theatre, contemporary opera, etc.), yet they share a passionate, heightened performing style and recurring themes of social acceptability and separation, sex and sexuality, and the use and abuse of power. Gloria has toured nationally and internationally both in non-traditional venues (art galleries, a derelict warehouse) and more mainstream spaces. Following their successful application for franchise funding from the Arts Council, the company embarked on the creation of five works to be staged in theatres between 1992 and 1995. The first of these was "A Judgement In Stone".

Sheila Hancock in "A Judgement in Stone

A Judgement In Stone

Gloria's adaptation of popular thriller writer Ruth Rendell's short novel was something of a departure for the company. Their intention was to present a more accessible piece in larger, more commercial venues than they had previously been seen in. Thematically, the choice of this particular Rendell novel made sense. The story of an illiterate, middle-aged housekeeper who murders a family of four in their genteel country home, it calls into question the degree of society's responsibility for its outsiders. This clearly links it to Gloria's earlier work. Co-directors Neil Bartlett (who also wrote the script) and Leah Hausman and composer Nicholas Bloomfield converted Rendell's grimly detached modern tragedy into a fluid piece of musical theatre. Traipsing about Mark Bailey's lurid-coloured domestic set, the characters expressed themselves in a pastiche of song styles ranging from light opera to music hall. The show opened at Glasgow's Tramway as part of the 1992 Mayfest, then played at the Playhouse, Nottingham and Blackpool's Grand Theatre before its London presentation at the Lyric, Hammersmith. It was generally very well-received by the press, with special mention going to Sheila Hancock's alienated, homicidal housekeeper; Time Out aptly described her as "horribly brilliant". Beverly Klein's demonically hammy performance as prostitute-turned-busybody-postmistress was, in some quarters, regarded as a sensationally entertaining if somewhat misguided vaudeville turn. The gay press was less favourable, one reviewer advising Bartlett in particular to "go back to your roots in radical gay theatre". DONALD HUTERA

Sheila Hancock and Beverly Klein

Graeae

Graeae was founded in 1980 by Nabil Shaban and Richard Tomlinson to encourage the active participation of disabled people in all types of creative performance. The name was chosen from the three Greek mythological sisters who shared an eye and a tooth between them. The plays have toured to theatres and arts centres here and abroad. Specially commissioned work spans a variety of themes all related to disability. Previous productions include "Sideshow", "Casting Out", "Working Hearts" and the critically acclaimed "Hound" by Maria Oshodi. The company's Theatre-in-Education programme is available to schools and residential centres which may not normally have access to theatre and live performance. Funded principally by the London Arts Board, London Borough of Camden, London Borough Grants Committee and Sir John Cass' Foundation, Graeae has been instrumental in offering individually designed workshops and projects to schools, voluntary sector organisations, youth clubs and community centres and in ensuring that disabled people have access to high quality training in all aspects of theatre. The company believes that the Theatre-in-Education work is particularly important in challenging the casual, destructive stereotyping of disabled people.

Maria Oshidi

Hound

"Hound" by Maria Oshodi is a sharp and witty account of the experiences of three blind people who find themselves thrown together at a guide-dog training centre where they soon discover that their only common link is their mutual desire for independent lives. With the arrival of a television producer keen to film their experiences for a "caring" documentary, they are forced to confront the way they are treated by the media. "Hound" is the first ever professional play to be performed by blind people and written by a writer who is herself blind.

Maria Oshodi has been widely praised for her work with the Royal Court, Riverside Studios and Cockpit Theatres. Her previous work includes: "The 'S' Bend" (Young Writers' Festival, Royal Court Theatre) "Blood Sweat and Fears" (Riverside Studios and national tour) and Mug for Channel 4. Key roles were played by David Bowen, Veronique Christie, Dave Kent, Marvel Opara, Kate Portal and Giles, a working guide dog. Directed by Ewan Marshall and designed by Sue Mayes, "Hound" featured music by James Mackie and lighting by Ace McCarron. True to its name, the company combined forces to choreograph the dog's training sequences.

Graeae Theatre Company in "Hound"

BETTY CAPLAN

Hull Truck

Nigel Betts, Jonathon Deverell, Stan and Adrian Hood

Hull Truck was formed in 1971 by its founder Artistic Director Mike Bradwell. Barry Nettleton, the current administrator joined in 1975, and John Godber, the present Artistic Director joined in 1984. From very modest beginnings, it has developed into a multi-faceted theatre operation, balancing community/ educational work with regional touring and commercial exploitation of its own shows.

There are many members of the general public for whom Hull Truck will have been their first introduction to theatre. The company remains committed to building new audiences and presenting popular, entertaining and accessible theatre. Now in its twenty-first year, Hull Truck has survived grant cuts, revision of arts policies, swingeing VAT rates, pop star actors and two major artistic changes. In spite of these setbacks, it has performed numerous times in London's West End, toured to the USA and Europe regularly and to the Edinburgh Festival annually. This year John Godber's "Up 'n Under" has undertaken a large scale tour and Godber's new comedy "April in Paris" and Jim Cartwright's "To" have been shown in tandem at the Wakefield Season in Yorkshire. Garry Lyons' new play "Frankie and Tommy" played at the Edinburgh Festival in August before touring nationally and, bowing to popular demand, "Bouncers" returned to the company's Spring Street home before its Edinburgh Festival appearance. Another new play by John Godber, "Office Party" (a co-production with Nottingham Playhouse) embarked on a large-scale tour in August.

Up 'n Under

Robert Hudson, Susan Cookson, Martin Barrass, Malcolm Scates and Ian Rogerson

Since joining Hull Truck in 1984, John Godber has given the company a unique profile with his idiosyncratic brand of ebulliently popular theatre. "Up 'n Under" which he both wrote and directed featured William Ilkley, Mark Addy, Gareth Tudor Price, Andrew Livingston, Martin Barrass and Nicola Vickery. "Up 'n Under" is a realisation of Godber's desire to create a truly physical style of theatre in which form and content fuse. When the author left teaching in 1984 and went to live in Hull, he felt the need to take a potent local theme and develop it in a theatrical way. "Rugby League is in the air in Hull," he says. "You can cut through it." "Up 'n Under" was Godber's first original play for Hull Truck. As well as receiving many honours including the prestigious Laurence Olivier Comedy of the Year award, it played for almost two years in the West End and has been seen in many parts of the world. The company has brought "Up 'n Under" back into its twenty-first anniversary season as a worthy showpiece.

BETTY CAPLAN

Kaboodle

The company

Liverpool based Kaboodle have been going since the late 1970s, but far from running out of steam, they combine the verve and enthusiasm of a new company with the solid skills of experienced professionals. Over the years, under Lee Beagley's energetic leadership, they have given physical, sometimes stunning productions of plays ranging from Buchner, to Shakespeare, to company-devised pieces such as "The Delivery Man" and "The Ugly Duckling". Their recent version of Miller's "A View From The Bridge" was received with every superlative under the sun, and rightly so. With Beagley taking the lead, it was a tough, blistering experience from start to finish. In the autumn, they embarked upon a major tour of "King Lear", again with Beagley in the lead and co-directed by the RSC's Josette Bushell-Mingo. Unfairly dogged by the "small scale" label, Kaboodle are now the largest, most successful independent touring company in the north west. Despite this, and despite winning Granada TV's Flying Start Award in 1991 (and being nominated for several others), Kaboodle thus far are without a permanent base. If outstanding merit is any recommendation, that is a situation that should change very soon.

Threepenny Story

"Threepenny Story"

Kaboodle's "Threepenny Story" is the first part of a planned state-of-the-nation epic trilogy beginning just after the Boer War and bringing us up to present times. As the title suggests, it is strongly influenced by Brecht and Gay, as well as Dickens' "Hard Times", but the raw energy, breakneck pace, and prodigious theatrical invention are all Kaboodle's own. Its length led some critics to accuse it of self-indulgence, and at three hours it could arguably profit from some cuts. Nevertheless, this is the kind of committed, bravura theatre that makes the majority of companies look timid in comparison. Written and directed by Lee Beagley, it featured excellent performances from Russ Edwards as wounded, much-put upon veteran Private Filch, Angela Bullock as a posturing Polly Peachum, Sean Kearney as the amoral Mac - but the list could go on and on. There wasn't a weak link in the nine-strong cast. The frantic goings-on were eccentrically backed by the excellent Wizards of Twiddly, whose songs ranged from jazz to music hall to raucous Kurt Weill-like creations.

JIM BURKE

The London Bubble

Linda Dobell in "The Good Person of Sezuan"

The Bubble is a theatre in a tent. It tours the parks of London during the summer months, June to September. It usually resides in each park for a week at a time, where it presents nine performances of three different shows. It seats 242 people and is totally self contained, including dressing rooms, a bar tent, food trailer, box office and toilets. When it is too cold to tour the tent, the Bubble company leave it behind and take their annual Christmas production to arts centres, community centres, civic centres, and anywhere else that can accommodate a show. They then mount another tour in the spring.

The company was started in 1972 by Glen Walford and the current Artistic Director is Jonathan Petherbridge. Its aim has always been to make theatre accessible, and it achieves this not only by literally, physically bringing shows to people who may never have set foot inside a theatre, but also by its upfront house style and the easy welcome it manages to convey to both old and young.

Other London Bubble projects include Forum Theatre, which actively involves its audiences; Cardboard Citizens, a group of homeless people who devise and tour shows dealing with the issues of homelessness; two youth theatre groups, an adult drama group, and several one-off community projects.

Measure For Measure

Sandra Yaw and Barry Killerby

1992 was the London Bubble's twenty-first anniversary season, and the summer programme in the Theatre Tent included Brecht's "The Good Person Of Sezuan", Nona Shepherd's "Brainpower" - for seven to eleven year olds, a Friday late-night cabaret spot, and Shakespeare's "Measure For Measure". With two classics in its anniversary repertoire, in true Bubble spirit the company set out to transform the Brecht into a "high-spirited musical morality tale for the nineties", and to turn Shakespeare's "problem play" into popular entertainment.

"Measure For Measure" was designed by Hannah Mayall. The setting was simple and modernised; watches were consulted, gum chewed, and the costumes included several oversized, flowing overcoats. A few liberties were taken with the text, but not to the detriment of the play. It was performed unabridged, with typical Bubble pace and gusto, by a strong and truly integrated cast.

Appropriately for a Bubble show, the comedy was brilliantly exploited by Mark Saban (Lucio) and Linda Dobell (Pompey), who played Shen Teh in "Good Person". And the tension between Claudio and Isabella, played by Barry Killerby and Sandra Yaw, was electric. It is no mean feat to tell this story successfully in a tent, often competing with noisy traffic and cold weather, and most of the critics were enthusiastic about this typically engaging Bubble production. It was directed by Jonathan Petherbridge, with Adrian Jackson assisting.

GINA LANDOR

Meeting Ground

Tanya Myers and Stephen Lowe

Meeting Ground Theatre Company is committed to celebrating meetings of artists from different disciplines and cultures, particularly between Eastern and Western Europe. Artistic Directors Tanya Myers, Stephen Lowe and Jonathan Chadwick together with associate director Zofia Kalinska aim to work collectively with members of the company in order to reach a wider audience. New work, both text based and devised, is central to their concern, requiring interactive workshops with artists and the wider community. Education and training, combined with project research and the documentation of work are all considered vital to the company's development.

Past productions include "Strive", a one act play by Stephen Lowe which opened in May 1985 as part of the Nottingham Festival, "Fat Cats and Hot Dogs", a community play staged in Newark Town Hall, "Paradise" a musical written by Stephen Lowe with music by David Wilson, and "The Sale of the Demonic Women". "City of Women", a documentary for Central Television transmitted in 1987 examined the lives of women working in Nottingham's famous textile industry. "Plaisirs d'Amour" based on the story of Eloise and Abelard is currently being developed following its Scotsman's Fringe First award at the 1991 Edinburgh Festival.

The Sale of the Demonic Women

Isabel Whitaker

"The Sale of the Demonic Women" was directed by Zofia Kalinska and devised by an international cast. The text is based on the writings of Polish playwright author, philosopher and painter Stanislaw Witkiewicz whose work pre-dates the absurdists Beckett, Ionesco and Genet by some twenty years. Designed by Zofia de Innes Lewcuk, this was the second production on the theme of demonic women following "Nominate Filiae" in 1988 produced under the auspices of the Magdalena International Womens' Theatre Project in Cardiff. It toured nationally in the autumn of 1990 and Spring 1991 and in Germany in the summer and autumn of 1991. The British Council funded a tour to the Krakow festival in June of this year, which was an outstanding success.

Using figures from Witkiewicz's work interlaced with quotations from Heiner Muller's "Medea Material" and Ronald Duncan's "Eloise and Abelard", Kalinska enabled the company to find their own relationships to the archetypes which shape our lives. Kalinska who was for over twenty years a leading actress in Tadeusz Kantor's Cricot 2 company has for the past five years with her all female troupe Akne been trying to realise a form of art which celebrates women's creativity without resorting to stereotypes or reproducing male perceptions of womanhood. A spare text is interwoven with sound, music, and movement to create lasting and vivid images.

BETTY CAPLAN

Millstream

A Madhouse in Goa

Millstream, founded by Christopher Masters in 1981 at the Yvonne Arnaud Theatre, Guildford, soon established a reputation for consistently high quality productions of recent work. Touring has been the primary focus of company policy, with three Arts Council funded productions per year (including musicals) going out to a wide range of provincial centres.

It's comparatively easy for contemporary writers to get a first run mounted at a leading London venue, such as The Royal Court or Hampstead Theatre; but without the kudos of a "world premiere" tag to offer, second showings are rare. Millstream has proved invaluable in nurturing such new-born pieces as "Tom and Viv", "The Road to Mecca" and Martin Sherman's "A Madhouse in Goa". They've also presented world or British premieres of plays by, amongst others, Tom McGrath ("Laurel and Hardy") and Arthur Miller ("Two Way Mirror").

The late 1992 tour of David Hare's "The Secret Rapture" marked a new phase in the company's development under the artistic and administrative direction of Masters and Peta Honey. Now resident at Trinity Theatre, Tunbridge Wells, Millstream are aiming for longer runs at larger theatres with a higher national profile – though artistic policy will remain as vigorous as ever.

Mrs Klein

Eliza Hunt as Mrs Klein

The choice of Nicholas Wright's play for its 1992 spring tour was a good example of Millstream's imaginative policy in reviving successful London work for new audiences. Previewed at the National Theatre before a West End run, "Mrs Klein" had been produced in at least eight countries abroad before the company took it up for its first national tour, playing venues as diverse as Basildon, Spalding and Jersey.

One of the most controversial psychoanalysts, Melanie Klein pronounced awesome judgements upon an entire generation of babies based on experiments on her own children. In 1934 her son, Hans, was reported killed in a climbing accident. The play shows the aftermath of his death on three women – all German, Jewish and analysts – as they battle to unravel the events leading up to the incident. The question provides an intriguing, psychoanalytical "whodunit".

Christopher Masters' production, designed by company regular Tim Shortall, featured a needle-sharp performance from Eliza Hunt as Mrs Klein, sensitively supported by Francine Morgan and Polly Irvin as Melitta and Paula. The play proved as captivating in it's smaller-scale touring incarnation as it had in the West End, and further consolidated Millstream Touring's reputation as vigorous champion of high-quality modern work.

CHRISTOPHER WEBBER

Orchard

Bill Buffery

Orchard Theatre is in its twenty fifth year. Originally formed for rural touring the company has switched its policy to appear in the larger towns and suburbs. 17,500 people saw the Christmas show, "The Little Mermaid" and over 10,000 saw "The Tempest". This year the sponsorship from British Telecom amounted to £30,000. The Orchard has always supported new writing and currently has Charles Way as resident dramatist. Way adapted Mary Shelley's "Frankenstein", which toured in tandem with "The Tempest'. He also contributed a new play about the "Wild West", "Dead Man's Hat". A notable success was Alex Shearer's "The Dream Maker", a comedy based in Newton Abbot.

Director Bill Buffery has formed a core company of actors, which are expanded according to the needs of the production. The Orchard cover the whole of the South West, from Bristol to Lands End. They also appear at the theatres in Exeter and The Drum in Plymouth. The Orchard took its name from the last line of their first production, John Arden's "Sergeant Musgrave's Dance", "Let's start an orchard".

The Dream Maker

Andrea Gascoigne and Andrew Howard

Hope against hope was the mainspring of Alex Shearer's new play for Orchard, "The Dream Maker". Set in more innocent days it features a conman who arrives in Newton Abbot and fraudulently establishes a reputation for foretelling the future. He calls himself The Professor and soon becomes the focus of all local hopes and dreams, his achievements magnified by local gossip. The story is told from the view of a youth, the son of the landlady where The Professor rents a room. At first the constant stream of narration seemed irritating, but, when accepted, is an ironic running commentary against the action. This warm, self-contained and gently humorous tale of human falibility has elements of The Wizard Of Oz.

The characterisation in this piece was well realised, with Andrew Howard carrying the burden of exposition on a note of fear and mounting excitement. Ian Bailey played the conman racked with self doubt, with an air of shabby pride. "The Dream Maker" demonstrated that new plays, which are locally set, need not be historical or a rehash of a local scandal. "The Dream Maker" was popular accessible theatre, which gathered an audience during its tour.

ALLEN SADDLER

Oxford Stage Company

John Retallack

The Oxford Stage Company began life as the Oxford Playhouse Company in 1974, producing ten plays a year and performing mainly in the Playhouse in Beaumont Street. Funding problems caused the closure of the theatre in 1987 and the company's name was changed. Having already established its reputation as a middle-scale touring company in the early 1980s, this policy was continued and strengthened as productions of both classical and modern plays were seen all over Britain. In 1991 the Playhouse re-opened, enabling the company to perform in the city again, while many productions also toured abroad.

Under Artistic Director John Retallack, founding director of the Actors Touring Company and previously Artistic Director of the Coliseum, Oldham, the company now aims to produce one classical work, a new translation, a new play for children and a devised show each year.

Oxford Stage Company has an integrated casting policy and its reputation for innovative and energetic theatre means it can attract established performers and directors, both from Britain and abroad. It is funded by the Arts Council, Oxford County Council, and Oxford City Council; in 1992 British Telecom sponsored sign language performances of their productions.

Much Ado About Nothing

Tony Forsyth, Diane Parish, Trevor H. Laird and Richard Evans

The company's 1992 production of "Much Ado About Nothing" was directed by a Romanian, Alexandru Darie, resident director of the Comedy Theatre, Bucharest, and designed by Maria Miu, designer at Teatrul Mic, Bucharest. This was the director's first production for a British company.

Drawing inspiration from the text, costumes and music reflected a diversity of sources ranging from the Far East to the Balkans. The deliberately simple set, of timber and drapes, gave the impression it could be packed up and moved if necessary. Alexandru Darie saw the play as relevant to the upheavals taking place in Europe, feeling that while no escape from conflict seems possible, people still strive for happiness. Consequently the set was people with animated characters who appeared to live life fully.

Despite the vibrant costumes and spectacular dance, the central relationship of Beatrice and Benedick was still one of the main attractions, as played by Marie Francis and James Simmons. The music was composed by Karl James, who also appeared as Borachio, and the lighting designer was Raymond Cross. The company's nation wide tour ended with appearances at the Tokyo Globe Theatre in Japan and the Petaling Jaya Civic Centre in Kuala Lumpur, Malasia.

TERRY DIAB

Paines Plough

Former A.D., Pip Broughton

Paines Plough is Britain's leading touring company specialising in new theatre by new writers. Founded in 1974, it now mounts two or three productions a year frequently in co-operation with repertory theatres and international organisations. The current Artistic Director is Anna Furse who both wrote and directed the key production of the year "Augustine (Big Hysteria)" which toured extensively in the UK and to countries of the former Soviet Union. Nigel Gearing's adaptation of George Orwell's "Down and Out in Paris and London" featured in the British Theatre season at the Gennevilliers Theatre in Paris. It was exceptional in that between twenty and fifty local onstage extras were recruited from each venue visited. "Scenic Flights an Act of Tourism" was written and performed by Cindy Oswin in collaboration with Anna Furse, composer Nigel Piper and lighting designer Chahine Yavroyan.

An active policy of writers development offers workshops, residencies and courses, and the literary manager Robin Hooper responds to over two hundred unsolicited scripts per annum. Some of these are offered Playbacks (informal rehearsed readings) or Showcases (readings in public venues to which the public and press are invited.) Two new developments for 1992 onwards are site specific productions and international exchanges.

Augustine (Big Hysteria)

Wolfe Morris, Anne Wood, James Dreyfus and Shona Morris

"Augustine (Big Hysteria)" was based on the actual events surrounding the treatment of Augustine, a young "grande hysterique" by the famous neurologist Charcot in the Salpetriere Hospital, Paris, at the end of the nineteenth century. Augustine became the star of Charcot's outlandish public lectures on hypnosis. His work was documented with disturbing photographs and sketches of the young woman in her various moods. Anna Furse imagined a meeting between Charcot, Augustine and the youthful Freud who was at that time studying with Charcot. Blending image, movement, music and text, she teases out the contradictions between the three characters. James Dreyfus played Freud, Shona Morris Augustine and Wolfe Morris Charcot. Violinist Anne Wood provided onstage musical accompaniment which added greatly to the play's subtlety and complexity.

The production was written and directed by Anna Furse and designed by Sally Jacobs. Most recently this team was responsible for Stephen Jeffrey's play "The Clink." Anna Furse has previously worked with the Womens Theatre Group, Graeae and Blood Group which she founded. Sally Jacobs is well known for her extensive work in theatre and opera and designed the legendary Peter Brook "Midsummer Night's Dream". The music for "Augustine (Big Hysteria)" was composed by Graeme Miller. The production toured regionally before leaving for Kiev and Moscow.

BETTY CAPLAN

Red Shift

Fiona McAlpine and Ruth Mitchell

Red Shift was founded by Jonathan Holloway, Charlotte Humpston and a group of (initially unpaid) actors in 1982, with the aim of producing work which married accessible storytelling with high theatricality. The intense, sometimes pyrotechnic style revealed in productions like "X Equals Murder" soon made its mark, but it was not until 1986 ("The Double") that Arts Council money allowed the company to tour productions without inevitable compromises.

Since then, Red Shift has continued to develop its commitment to radical adaptation of classic texts, filtered through a uniquely acrobatic and elegantly stylised visual approach. Perhaps the productions of "Mill on the Floss" (1987) and "Timon of Athens" (1989) came close to performance art but Holloway and Humpston have succeeded in winning broad audiences to their challenging work.

Since the company gained Arts Council "revenue" (more permanent) status the range of subjects chosen has covered the spectrum from detective thrillers through Wedekind's "Lulu" to "Fanny Hill". 1992 has been typically adventurous, with a touring revival of Samuel Butler's novel "The Way of All Flesh" preceding the new production of "Orlando". Future plans include expansion into repertory main houses and open-air performance.

Orlando

Vanessa Keywood

Red Shift's major new offering (and tenth anniversary production) during the year was "Orlando", a new play based on the work of Virginia Woolf. Premiered at the Edinburgh Festival prior to a season at the Lyric Studio, Hammersmith and a National Tour, "Orlando" charts Woolf's fantastic, fictional biography of her lover and friend Vita Sackville West.

During the four-century course of the novel Orlando changes sex and ages thirty-five years. Starting the play as a page at the court of Elizabeth I and a beau at the court of James I, he/she survives a bloody Turkish uprising, outdoor life with a band of picaresque gypsies, the salons of Dryden and Pope, and – not least – sombre Victorian dinner-parties. She ends up shopping in Oxford Street, motoring away from the urban sprawl on the novel's publication day in October 1928.

Woolf's sensuous vision, lush wordscapes and colourful intensity proved a natural vehicle for the company's highly distinctive "European" style of presentation. The usual hallmarks – arresting live music, performed with quality by dedicated actor-musicians, atmospheric design, powerfully pointed theatricality and physical invention – combined to convey Orlando's story with what was seen as arresting skill, and haunting imagination.

CHRISTOPHER WEBBER

Renaissance

Susannah Harker and Kenneth Branagh in "Corolanus"

Since its launch in 1987 by actors David Parfitt and Kenneth Branagh, Renaissance, with its sister film company, has tackled a catholic cross-section of theatre, television, radio and film (the award-winning "Henry V"). Shakespeare has been at the heart of the company's work; but from John Sessions' one-man shows through Chekhov's "Uncle Vanya", Osborne's "Look Back in Anger" (with Branagh and Emma Thompson) to plays by Ingmar Bergman and Branagh himself, the repertoire has never been predictable.

The mainspring of Renaissance's success has been its refusal to give the obvious jobs to the obvious people: directing, for example, has been in the hands of actors, with Judi Dench, Geraldine McEwan and Derek Jacobi all making directorial debuts. This element of calculated risk-taking has guaranteed a freshness of approach which has communicated strongly to audiences at home and abroad.

1992 has seen activity on a broad front. The film company has released "Peter's Friends", and there has been a complete "Hamlet" (Radio 3 and CD/cassette) with a cast including Branagh, Dench, Sir John Gielgud and Renaissance stalwart Richard Briers. Late in the year came another all-star "Hamlet" in collaboration with the RSC, which is likely to be filmed during 1993.

Coriolanus

Iain Glen

The theatrical centrepiece of the year was undoubtedly "Coriolanus" presented at the Chichester Festival, directed by Tim Supple and featuring Dame Judi Dench and Richard Briers along with Kenneth Branagh in the title role. The patterning of Shakespeare's granite-like artifice was forcefully mirrored in Supple's staging and Andrew Poppy's metallic music. This was a vigorous approach which illuminated the colossal scale of the public scenes, rather than the more intimate moments of human tragedy at the play's heart.

Dench's Volumnia was a study in contained agony, whilst Briers' touching old Menenius and Iain Glen's tricky Aufidius gave strong support. The ranks of professional actors were memorably swelled by fifty or so amateur volunteers from the Chichester area, which made for plebeian bread riots and battles more energetic and powerfully convincing than we've grown used to in these minimalist casting days.

Kenneth Branagh's assumption of the title role was less notable for physical prowess or verbal intensity than for the sheer ferocity with which he laid into battle at home as well as abroad. His was an articulate, calculated Coriolanus which undeniably held the attention - a summary judgement which was repeated in critical response to the production as a whole.

CHRISTOPHER WEBBER

(Scotland)

7:84

At the beginning of the year, David Hayman, Gerard Kelly (Artistic Directors) and Jo Beddoe (general manager) completed their three-year tenure at the head of 7:84 which had begun after the enforced departure of its founding member John McGrath. Taking over as Artistic Director was the young and very promising Iain Reekie, who had worked with 7:84 and his own company Theatre Positive to much acclaim. The new regime relaunched the company in the autumn with a season of plays that included a contribution to the Tron's Irish season - Dermot Bolger's "The Lament For Arthur Cleary". Reekie regards the company's name - taken from the statistic that seven per cent of the population owned eighty-four per cent of the wealth - as a challenging discipline and not a restriction and believes that prejudice and social inequality are central to most drama. Thus he began his directorship in the spirit of the company's founder-members, but with an outlook appropriate to the 1990s.

Iain Reekie

Scotland Matters

Reviving the format of a show called "Long Story Short, Scotland Matters" was an interesting experiment to see what happened when some of the country's leading writers were asked to contribute short playlets relating to the subject of life in contemporary Scotland. Directed by Iain Reekie (although he was commissioned to do it before he became Artistic Director), the production ran through ten mini-dramas written by Peter Nardini, Ann Marie di Mambro, John Binnie, Jan Natanson, Iain Heggie and Gurmeet Mattu. The diverting compilation format was framed by a series of scenes in a TV studio which held the disparate pieces together. The evening covered sectarianism, education cut-backs, homosexuality, pacifism and hairdressing even before the interval; a fact that demanded much adaptability from a cast that included Stuart Bowman, David Tennant, Matthew Costello, Emma Currie and Marion Sangster. Rae Smith was the designer.

Marion Sangster and Matthew Costello

MARK FISHER

Shared Experience

Nancy Meckler

Shared Experience Theatre was founded in 1975 under the directorship of Mike Alfreds, who remained as Artistic Director until Nancy Meckler took over in 1987. Central to the distinctive style, established in the earliest shows, "Arabian Nights" and "Bleak House", was a belief in the importance of the performer, the openness of each performance and the uniqueness of the relationship between the performers and the audience. Each performance was felt to be a collaborative venture. Rehearsal periods and performances were both lengthy - "Bleak House" was ten hours long after a rehearsal period of nine months.

Later the company continued to explore the dramatic potential of narrative forms but also applied their expansive vision of theatre to diverse existing texts such as "Cymbeline" (1979) and "Happy Days" (1984). Similarly varied, productions directed by Nancy Meckler have included "The Bacchae" (1988), "Heartbreak House" (1989) and "The Birthday Party" (1990).

In 1985 Shared Experience Theatre acquired its own building in the centre of London and thus the Soho Laundry became their base. Westminster City Council now funds the Shared Experience Youth Theatre offering young people the chance to involve themselves in a variety of projects, including a community play every two years.

Anna Karenina

Helena Edmundsen's much acclaimed adaptation of Tolstoy's "Anna Karenina" took the parallel but contrasting journeys of Anna and Levin and placed them equally on stage, providing a narrative framework for the complexities of the action. Within this, director Nancy Meckler interwove characters and situations and depicted stations, ballrooms and peasants' fields using the physical skills of the actors to maximum effect. Central to the production was the stylised movement used to convey both the passions of the individual and the reactions of the society in which their great drama was enacted. The choreography was by Liz Ranken and design by Lucy Weller.

The most enduring image of the play was the climactic racing scene in which Anna became Vronsky's horse, the horse whose spine Vronsky fractured. Anna Karenina was played by Annabelle Apsion and Vronsky by Max Gold, while the other couple, Levin and Kitty, were played by Richard Hope and Pooky Quesnel. Other characters were skilfully portrayed by Katherine Barker, Tilly Blackwood, Gregory Floy and Nigel Lyndsay.

"Anna Karenina" was a box-office success in a number of venues in Britain and received unanimously enthusiastic reviews. The production was sponsored by Aqua Libra. The company is funded by the Arts Council.

TERRY DIAB

The Sphinx

Sue Parrish with Harriet Walter

Until last January The Sphinx had been The Women's Theatre Group, standard-bearing tour company for women. Over twenty years it has nurtured a generation of actresses, and writers including Claire McIntyre and Timberlake Wertenbaker. Sustained Arts Council support has enabled it to maintain its subsidiary role as a forum for debate beyond the stage.

Is the name change a mere marketing ploy? Artistic Director Sue Parrish points to the common association of "Group" with a worthy, lost ideal – for as the company has grown, the original collective principle has withered away: "It implied a heavy feminist evening in the theatre . . . . women right, men wrong". The newly adopted Sphinx image, with its woman's head and lion's body, is certainly potent.

1992 has seen a play about Bessie Smith, "Every Bit of It" by Jackie Kay; as well as "The Glass Ceiling", a lively debate on women in culture with panellists as diverse as Fiona Shaw and Marina Warner. The new name and company structure won't imply any reduced commitment to the issues – rather a new maturity, a broader vision of the changing perceptions, identities and values (of men as well as women) from within the theatrical mainstream.

The Roaring Girl's Hamlet

Angela Walsh and Ruth Mitchell

The Sphinx's most ambitious project of 1992 was "The Roaring Girl's Hamlet", directed by Sue Parrish, which enjoyed a sell-out national tour to decidedly mixed reviews. In Claire Luckham's framework, the play is acted out by a group of seventeenth century "roaring girls", women illicitly disguised as men, led by the notorious Moll Cutpurse – who herself takes the role of Claudius.

The rebellious Moll begins by warning the audience that the performance they are about to witness, with eight women sharing out eighteen roles, is strictly secret and illegal. This ingenious presentation of Shakespeare's great tragedy as an "outlawed act" served to highlight the subversive danger implicit in the casting; and the result was a vigorous, thought-provoking production which polarised critical and audience opinion.

There was plenty of praise for the effectiveness of Alexandra Mathie's robust Claudius, doubling Moll Cutpurse; and for Ruth Mitchell's finely drawn, sensitive portrait of the scholar-prince himself. Not everything about the production was equally admired – although there was no dissent about the impact of Philip Croskin's spectacular duel, which helped provide a memorable and moving end to an evening which certainly kept The Sphinx in the vanguard of risk-taking, controversial theatre.

CHRISTPHER WEBBER

Talawa

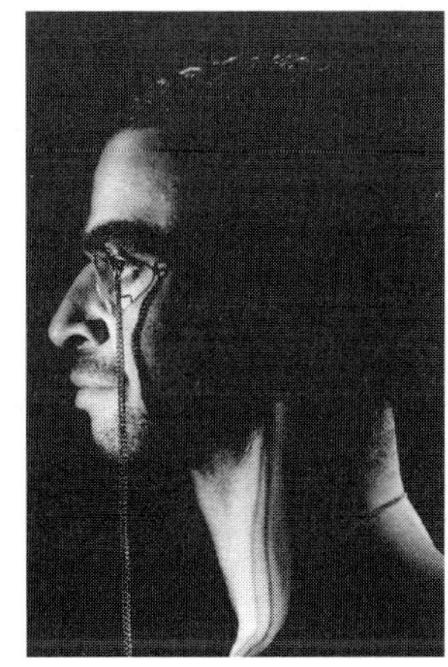
"The Road"

February 1992 marked a historic moment in Talawa's development when the Cochrane Theatre reopened after a stunning redesign by Nigerian architect Abiodun Odedina to provide a new home for black theatre in the heart of London.

The residency provides an annual programme of three or four plays a year and hosts a mixed programme of dance, music and mime by black artists. As a building-based company Talawa is able now to offer much needed training opportunities to young black performers, stage managers and designers as well as having a comprehensive brief to serve the wider community.

Since being resident at the Cochrane, Talawa has developed an Education programme which is providing an impressive outreach to schools and colleges. The department has forged links with The British Museum, The Horniman Museum and the School for Oriental and African Studies and there are plans for future work with the Museum of Mankind.

The company - founded in 1985 by Yvonne Brewster, Mona Hammond, Carmen Munroe and Inigo Espejel to provide middle scale, high quality productions that would demonstrate the serious creative role that black theatre had to play within the UK - feels justly proud of its progress. Plans for 1993 include a co-production with the Contact Theatre when Annie Castledine directs "From the Mississippi Delta" by Endestra Ida Mae Holland.

The Road

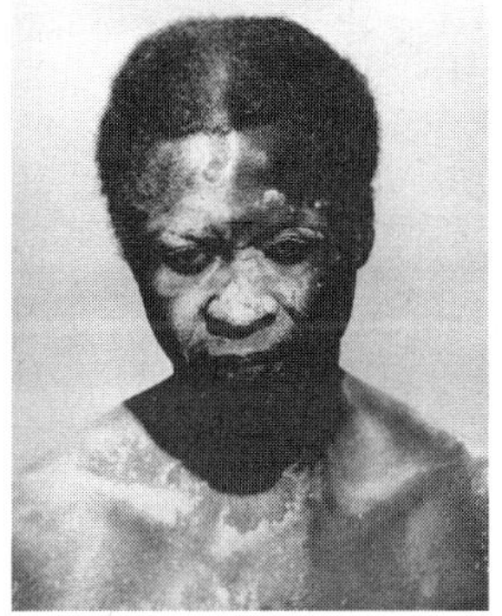
"The Road"

Talawa chose "The Road" by Nobel prize winning writer Wole Soynika - seldom performed in Britain, despite his international standing - for its opening production at the Cochrane.

Designer Sue Mayes was presented with the remarkable challenge of transposing to London WC1 the Nigerian motorpark in which the drama is played out, and her impressive set of fourteen vehicles stacked one on top of the other provided the performers with an urban playground for a highly physical production.

Offering a challenging insight into the power and consequence of roleplaying, the world of "The Road" moved between the harsh reality of lives spent in unemployment and bribery, the choir music of the Christian church and the surreal spirit world of the Yoruba Gods. The production was very much evidence of the serious creative role of black theatre within the UK, Europe and the wider world, and established "The Road" as part of an international canon of classic texts available to British audiences.

Tara Arts

PAT ASHWORTH

Founded by South Asian immigrants in 1976, Tara Arts has today become Britain's leading exponent of cross-cultural theatre. Its repertoire includes European classics re-interpreted through Indian theatre techniques as well as Indian classics made accessible to European audiences.

Jatinder Verma

Tara Arts is led by Artistic Director Jatinder Verma whose highly original productions of Moliere's "Tartuffe" (set in Mughal India) and the Indian classic "The Little Clay Cart" were shown at the National Theatre, the first Asian company to be given the opportunity. Jatinder Verma's adaptation of Sophocles' "Oedipus the King" was the British offering at the second European Theatre Convention in Bologna.

A documentary on Jatinder Verma and Tara Arts' work was produced by the BBC for the Late Show in December 1991.

In its fifteenth anniversary year, the company is establishing a project entitled "Beyond the Stage" to fully develop the educational and cultural industries' potential of its major touring productions. Project co-ordinators Sophie Robson and Matthew Jones will be producing work-packs for video and television, presenting workshops in schools and colleges and networking with European arts organisations in particular those concerning minority communities.

Heer Ranjha

"Heer Ranjha, the Legend of an Epic Love" is based on a seventeenth century Punjabi poem by Varis Shah and Shakespeare's "Romeo and Juliet". Tara Arts have devoted an entire year to the exploration of this story of a love which crosses borders. Set against the backdrop of the Chenab, one of the five great rivers of the Punjab in Pakistan, it tells of a young woman, Heer who, though forcibly married by her family to another man cannot ignore her love for Ranjha, youngest son of a neighbouring landlord. Driven apart by family and circumstance, the lovers marry secretly with the help of the gods. Returning to their home town they are reconciled with Heer's family and promised an official wedding, but Heer's wicked uncle Kaidu, believing the family honour to have been stained, sees a fatal dose of poison as the only possible solution.

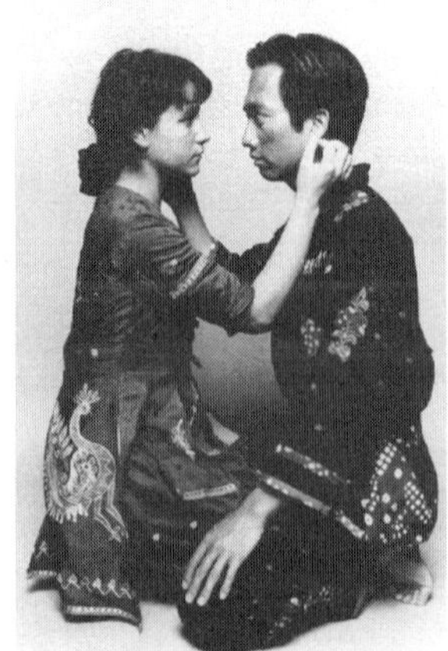

David Tse and Tassia Messimeris

A legend in its own time and a living text for contemporary Asians, the story of Heer and Ranjha has been interpreted many times on stage and in film in India and Pakistan.

The cast for this production was drawn from two continents with four visiting artists including a musical consultant who joined the company from India for the duration of the project. After opening at the Theatre Royal in Stratford (co-producers) in October a national tour continues until February 1993 to be followed by an international tour.

BETTY CAPLAN

Trestle

A group of students on the Performing Arts course at Middlesex Polytechnic got together with their tutor to experiment in a unique style of mask theatre and formed Trestle Theatre Company in 1981. Since then, the company has developed its own original style of popular mask theatre, touring an average of 300 performances a year to over 37,000 people. Trestle's productions combine comedy with a sense of the unexpected, frequently relying on the power of masks and visual images rather than words to convey meaning.

Together with its touring productions, the company conducts workshops and residencies for both the experienced and the uninitiated. Regular tours in the UK have alternated with visits to Europe, Hong Kong, Australia, New Zealand and the Phillipines.

State of Bewilderment

The company has been rewarded for its initiative by the Arts Council with "three year franchise" funding. Recent work includes "Ties that Bind", "The Edge", "Crime of Love" and a new version of "The Soldier's Tale" commissioned by the Birmingham Contemporary Music Group, with Simon Rattle not only conducting, but dressed as a devil, taking part in the action.

Trestle Theatre Company is based in Bedford.

State of Bewilderment

Based on the work of the celebrated Australian cartoonist Michael Leunig, the company's flagship production of the year "State of Bewilderment" is a show filled with humour, irony and absurdity. It deals with life in the city where misunderstandings abound, panic spreads, and loneliness and misery proliferate in tower blocks. The hero, a forlorn observer, looks on in horror but finds no understanding. He sets out to discover what is missing from his life armed only with a broken teapot and a duck. He travels to distant lands where he meets strange people, trying to arrive at a sense of harmony before it is too late.

Trestle's new piece blends comic and poetic imagery, live music, puppetry, illusion, and of course, masks, appealing to young and old.

After previewing in Bedford, the company's home town, the show opened in the brand new Platform theatre in Lindfield, West Sussex before a fifteen week tour of the UK and a three week run in London's Cochrane Theatre as part of the fifteenth London International Mime Festival. Finally the production went "down under" for a further three month tour of Australia and New Zealand.

BETTY CAPLAN

Festivals

The long-standing and famous Edinburgh Festival has been joined in recent years by Glasgow's Mayfest and other annual beanfeasts of the arts. The Yearbook covers the theatrical events at a selection of these celebrations, beginning with MARTIN HOYLE'S view of Edinburgh together with his choice of key shows.

Edinburgh '92

"What a place for a festival" said Audrey Mildmay to Rudolf Bing as they gazed at the most picturesque urban view in Britain. Bing had worked at Glyndebourne, Mildmay was the wife of its founder-owner, John Christie. Inevitably the early years of the post-war Edinburgh Festival favoured music. The greatest arts festival in the world remained one of the most prestigious under directors like Peter Diamand, Lord Harewood and John Drummond. As picturesque as Salzburg, it cast its net much wider. The growth of the Fringe made Edinburgh, for a brief period, a microcosm of the performing arts, the Festival throwing up Maggie Smith and Maria Callas, "The Cocktail Party" and "Beyond the Fringe", or Albert Finney and Rex Harrison in new plays.

The rich mixture has turned into a thin gruel in recent years. A combination of Frank Dunlop's small-scale populism, the city's endemically parochial meanness and the absence of quality-control over the Frankenstein-monster Fringe results in provincial dowdiness illuminated by the odd star musician that the blasé London concert-goer takes for granted anyway. Under its new regime Edinburgh has reverted to the old idea of consistent themes. For theatre this proved a mixed blessing: Granville Barker turned out as boring as he was brilliant; C P Taylor's average was rather worse. But a shape emerges: the ragbag days are over – and not before time. With Salzburg now turning to theatre, Edinburgh should look to its faded laurels. Quality rather than anything-goes quantity should be the priority. The Fringe should be genuinely innovative rather than a try-out for the London cabaret circuit. And let's stop pretending that the Traverse is Fringe when it often provides the Festival's most stimulating events ("The Life of Stuff") as well as the most pretentiously misguided ("Cyrano de Bergerac").

The Voysey Inheritance

Harley Granville Barker is constantly praised for his "beautifully written" plays, a phrase as suspect as "ravishingly photographed" in a film review. You know it means boring.

William Gaskill's production at the Royal Lyceum held the attention thanks to the quivering intensity of Peter Lindford as heir to a family business run on lies, embezzlement and fraud. The problems posed by this discovery – should he continue the cover-up, trying to replace lost funds, or reveal everything, ruining family and clients ? – emerged as personal rather than moral drama. As the shamelessly buccaneering old father, Tenniel Evans provided suave charm rather than sharklike ruthlessness. Peter Blythe's booming major tended to steal the scene. Katherine Rogers should note that neither "droring-room" nor "neether" was or is acceptable genteel usage.

The Ballachulish Beat

Gordon Dougal, George Drennan, Gary Grochla and Julia Dow

In theory it's a good wheeze: a season devoted to a vaguely well thought-of but almost forgotten writer, including the first performance of an unproduced play. This is one of the functions of a festival with its (ideally) favourable conditions for preparation and its enthusiastic and knowledgeable public.

The choice of C P Taylor went very much agley at Edinburgh this year. At the Corn Exchange "The Ballachulish Beat" summed up his strengths and weaknesses: sprawling narrative shapelessness, the blurred line between irony and seriousness, thumping over-emphasis – and political anger and idealism.

Allan Sharpe's direction aimed at a Viz-style romp but ended in confusion – despite Paul Ambrose Wright's comic-strip designs – in this already tired-looking satire on pop and politics.

Mad

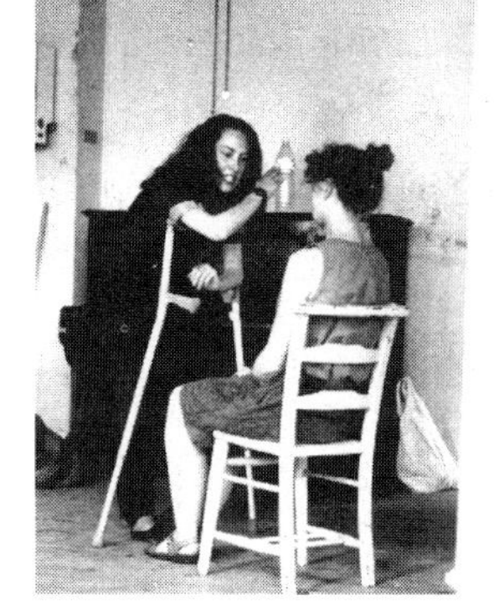

At what level should we take this ? As with director Jeremy Weller's other products ("Glad", "Bad"), the number of non-professional actors suggested real-life stories, raw-edged documentary. The dramatic framework (the action was set in an audition – for "Mad") and a fortnight's run imply selection, polishing up, artifice. Paradoxically, I felt a cast with real actors would have seemed less – well, insincere.

The piece tries to pre-empt this criticism with conscious re-enactments by the eight women and one man with varying experiences of mental illness. When Carolyn Raeburn relives the break-up of her marriage, she switches off the intensity and asks "How's that ?" Fine; but does this mean you're playing games with us ? Some critics complained the performers were exploited. Me, I think it was the spectators who were emotionally toyed with.

Desdemona – If Only You Had Spoken !

Eleanor Bron

Of course, she *did* speak. Only the most old-fashioned Shakespeare productions still give us the obedient milksop instead of a spirited young woman making free choices.

The title of Christine Bruckner's book from which Eleanor Bron drew her one-woman show reflects the woolly-mindedness of the whole enterprise. The original collection of monologues was touted as giving vent to "years of frustration and anger".

Not here they didn't. The three cameos selected for performance were Mrs Martin Luther (Eleanor Bron with a Scottish accent kneading dough), Petrarch's Laura (Eleanor Bron lying on a sickbed) and Goethe's fat, common wife (Eleanor Bron with northern accent swigging port).

Familiar Bron elegance, ruefulness, wry amusement; not much anger, just commonplace objections at cooking being taken for granted or at local snobbery. The result was bland, pleasant and superficial.

Persona

Sandra Duncan

Sandra Duncan's solo portraits, inspired by the Canadian novelist Margaret Laurence, brilliantly showed up Eleanor Bron's sell-out turn as an anodyne party-piece.

To judge by the adaptation by director Terence Shank, Laurence is in the great tradition of gently – painfully – probing women writers. Ms Duncan ranges from the recollected death of a small girl's father in the Depression to the rigidly unbending ninety-year-old whose cantankerous bitterness at marrying beneath her stopped her admitting the physical pleasure her husband gave her.

In between there was the blonde of thirty-nine, tending to slobbishness and secret vodka, tearful, funny, self-aware; and the middle-aged writer coldly slapping down unhappy childhood memories. Vocal and physical variety – and impeccable Canadian, not just North American, accents – made this a hauntingly powerful show which should travel further.

Revelations – The Testament of Salome

Wendy Buonaventura

Susannah York and Penny Cherns shared directing credits at the Traverse for this interpretation of history's first stripper as a betrayed feminist.

Narrator Deirdra Morris is co-author with dancer Wendy Buonaventura. Their story sees Salome as dedicated to the goddess Ishtar, the only field where women have influence. The advent of John the Baptist merely emphasises Christo-Judaic contempt for women.

Against an evocative set of broken pillars, actress and dancer presented the story of hope, moral blackmail and disappointment. Buonaventura, an expert in Middle Eastern movement, avoided belly-dancing cliches except in deliberate mockery. Only the language ("You screwed up!") suggested that the seventh veil concealed a right-on militant nearer a UCLA campus than Ramoth-Gilead.

Frankie and Tommy

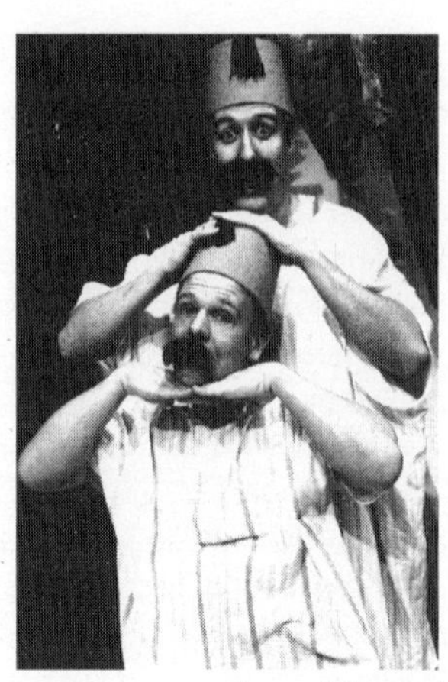
Steven Spiers and Charlie Dickinson

Garry Lyons has capitalised on his father's memories of working a comedy duo when in the army to write a sombre, uncomfortable reflection on the theme of public clown as private neurotic. For though Lyons senior never made showbiz in Civvy Street, his partner was Tommy Cooper who achieved stardom but, like Hancock, Sid Field, Little Tich – most great comics you can name – was driven by demons.

The play shows Cooper's obsessive lust for perfection erupting into aggression, even as in a chilling comedy boxing sketch – violence. Steven Spiers was a good lookalike but indistinct diction muffled some punchlines. Damian Cruden's direction, for Hull Truck hinted at deep, dark compulsion. Cooper's death on stage in mid-act wasn't just a good way to go: for him it was the only way.

Play, Boy !

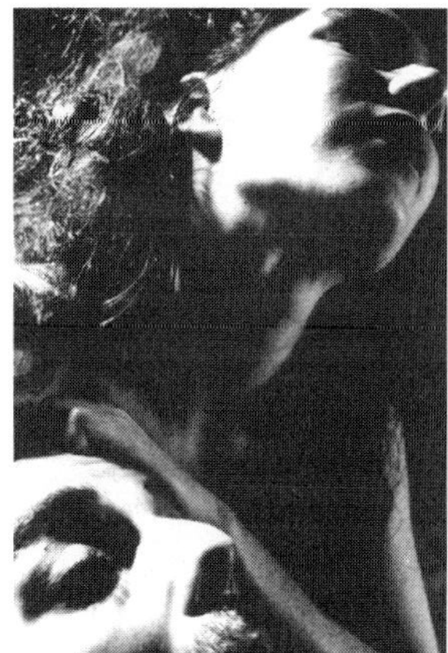

This was a good fringe for women. Among the most cogent and stylish Feminist advocates was the Boilerhouse company whose late-night allegory pulled no punches, showed no self-pity.

Three sexily-clad lovelies (the Soho terminology is unavoidable), all black frills and heavy breathing, state their cases to Ariel (Jenny Fraser, a wonderfully vulnerable embodiment of dewy freshness). Each one attempts to lure the newcomer to her side.

Electra lives by phone sex ("great money and no mess"); Chamelea is the career climber, via sex and abortions; Medusa refuses to disturb her comfortable marriage even when her husband abuses their daughter.

Paul Pinson's stylised, thrusting direction got charismatic performances, and never overstated the uncomfortable message that women behave like this because of men's expectations. No wonder Ariel storms off.

Studs

The Dublin-based Passion Machine homed in on the urban community and youth culture. This cheerfully engaging football saga at first glance resembles "Up'n Under" shipped across the Irish sea and transplanted to a soccer pitch. But the direction (by author Paul Mercier) was more stylised, the characterisations more abrasive with the psychological interest concentrated on the figure of a fallen idol whose illusions are more creative than mundane truth – a familiar theme in Irish drama from Synge onwards.

Wonderfully drilled; fine ensemble work; some difficulty with the accents. Above all, the feeling of a communal background and shared values. Despite their laudable emphasis on new work, Passion Machine would be worth seeing in "Playboy of the Western World".

Serpent Kills

M. Green, G. Ferrabee, A. Curtis and D. Clarke

Canada's One Yellow Rabbit company presented the fascinating story of Charles Sobhraj, a plausible charmer who smuggled, thieved and murdered his way through Asia in the 1970s. His victims were often laid-back youngsters on the drug-trail to Katmandu.

The play evokes an era not just by platform shoes and comic drop-out Gerry, but by the exotic substances apparently puffed by the cast and such terrifyingly insincere remarks as Charles' "I'm a people person; I like people".

But the piece fails to explore the killer's amorality, apart from revealing that Sobhraj was inspired by James Bond. And Gerry, blandly narrating from a respectable distance years later, is morally queasy. But the direction, choreography (dancing unfolding the story as much as speech) and flexible set had a serpentine power.

Mayfest

Reaching its tenth birthday, Glasgow's annual arts jamboree brought together another large selection of local, national and international drama, dance, music, comedy and art for three weeks in May. Mayfest director Robert Robson, in his second year in charge, made a move towards making the festival more of an outward looking celebration of Scottish culture than the echo of other festivals – notably Edinburgh – that it was threatening to become. To this end, Robson set aside a small amount of money to commission shows as well as simply to book them. Keen to promote new and ambitious Scottish work, Robson put money into four productions which had an emphasis on mixed media presentation. This, he felt, was a policy that could flourish in future years should financial resources allow. As Britain's second largest festival, Mayfest continued to provide a large choice for a wide range of people, especially as its community programme was as strong as ever.

Gaudeamus

A brilliantly comic look at the lives of new military recruits in the Russian army, "Gaudeamus" was the big Mayfest hit of 1992. Ironically pointing to the moral decay of Russian society, it was performed by a forty-strong company made up from the Maly Drama Theatre in St Petersburg. Energetically performed with a level of skill, timing and imagination rarely seen in Britain, it drew on music, song and dance to look a the generation trapped between childhood and adulthood. Directed by the internationally acclaimed Lev Dodin, the production was based on a short story by Sergei Kaledin which was banned until 1989 when it was published by a literary journal. For all the games, pranks and jokes in the show, it was underscored by a constant note of condemnation for the brutality of the military.

The World's Edge

Young Glasgow performance group, Clanjamfrie, was one of four companies to receive special funding from Mayfest and it used it for this idiosyncratic contemplation of our relationship with the Americas. Performed in a rickety old boiler shed round the back of Tramway, the show was performed on a sand floor against the same bare brick walls that give the main building such charm. Created by company stalwarts Emma Davie and Jules Dorey-Richmond in collaboration with a group of performers from South America, "The World's Edge" used live video, Super 8 footage, dance, percussion and a specially commissioned score. Produced in response to the Columbus quincentenary, the show drew on many different American images – Hollywood musicals, for example – so as not to simplify the reaction down to a condemnation of Columbus' colonialist exploits.

Me, Myself, Us

John McKay and Forbes Masson

It was a good year for John McKay whose sitcom "My Dead Dad" – based on the Traverse hit "Dead Dad Dog" – was screened on Channel 4. The playwright and performer maintained his relationship with the theatre, however, and in Mayfest he teamed up with Forbes-Masson (who starred in "My Dead Dad") for a two-hander comedy. Directed by Liz Carruthers "Me, Myself, Us" told the story of a successful young novelist who has only one week left to write his new book or pay back the advance he's already spent. The typical John McKay twist is that the novelist wakes up with his own creative self lying next to him in bed – separate and uncooperative. What followed was a witty, enjoyable comedy that also touched on the down-side of creativity.

MacWizard fae Oz

Stephen Docherty and Mari Binnie

Clyde Unity Theatre, probably Scotland's busiest touring company, launched another long community tour at Mayfest with John Binnie's Glaswegian reworking of Hollywood's "Wizard of Oz". Shifting the action to the town of Kilsyth, the musical play – with original songs by Binnie and Lorna Brooks – told the story of a girl who is sucked into her TV on Christmas Day and ends up on set with Judy Garland. Garland, needless to say, is not amused about being upstaged by a wee lassie from Kilsyth. Binnie made points about the influence of Hollywood on our lives and our need for fantasy in times of recession, but above all, the show was a rollicking, spring pantomime with goodies, baddies and positive gender models.

A Judgement in Stone

This adaptation of a Ruth Rendell murder-mystery was a major feature of Mayfest. It was brought to the festival by Gloria and a full description of the company and production will be found in the Yearbook's section **Touring Companies**.

MARK FISHER

Brighton '92

Brighton - otherwise known as London-by-the-Sea - has always striven to be all things to all people, in its architecture as well as its entertainment. The town itself is a heady cocktail of British seaside kitcsh with amusement arcades, chips and ice-cream on the beach, mixed together with a dash of Georgian white-washed splendour, cosy old world tea rooms and lanes studded with antique shops. The Brighton Festival, now in its twenty-fifth year, matches the town's aspiring everyman image. With an extensive programme, this year totalling nearly 500 events over three weeks in May, England's largest festival covers everything from the mainstream to the avantgarde, and from local to international productions.

Mainstream theatrical events, this year including the National Youth Theatre's production of Sheridan's "The Rivals", and Frank Finlay starring in "The Heiress" at Brighton's Theatre Royal, rub shoulders with experimental work from the likes of Brighton- based dance group Divas or the Didier Theron Dance Company from France. Classical music, rock and pop, cabaret, film, and outdoor events also figure prominently in the festival's programme.

Every year this extraordinary mixture of events is yoked loosely to a theme - in 1992, that of "Saints and Sinners" reflecting the naughty but nice image of both the festival and town. And under the directorship of Gavin Henderson, the festival has made significant steps forward. Not only has it established close links with France – reflected in this year's dance programme – but it has also added in the last three years a special comedy programme, and Showcase – a weekend devoted to British performance art. At a time of economic uncertainty, the Brighton Festival still manages to be forward-looking.

Laughing Gas

For the last two years comedy has been one of the main highlights of the Brighton Festival. The brainchild of the celebrated stand-up comedian Simon Fanshawe, and local promoter Lucy Barry, "Laughing Gas" as it is called, this year consisted of thirty-three different shows. Many of the best loved names of British comedy featured in the line-up - among them Barry Cryer and Willie Rushton, self-confessed Two Old Farts, and stand ups Jeremy Hardy, John Hegley and Eddie Izzard.

Louise Rennison

But there were newer names too. Louise Rennison, who won both Comedy festival awards last year with her first solo show, the award-winning "Stevie Wonder Felt My Face", continued to explore her comic style of racy monologues couched in the form of real-life memories with her show "Bob Marley's Gardener Sold My Friend." And two short comic plays by Ollie Parker, "Killers" and "Get Up and Be Somebody" earned the accolade of being compared by critic Michael Billington with the writing of the early Harold Pinter because of their sense of menace.

In the first play performed by Ben Miller and Martin Jones, the term serial killers was given a new meaning: a reclusive pair plot the murder of their housepartner over the breakfast table. In the second play, two men wake up in bed together - much to their mutual surprise. "I'm not homosexual" one of the men says. "Prove it" the other replies, coldly.

Showcase Weekend

Snuffhouse-Dustlouse

Now in its second year, the performance art Showcase weekend presented in association with the British Council and The Arts Council of Great Britain, included homegrown talent Liz Aggiss in a dance piece inspired by the writings of the South American writer Lorca, and the physical comedy and lunacy of the Canadian The Right Size Theatre Company.

With fifteen events in all, the most outstanding ones were the most visual in which text played little part in the action. Faulty Optic Theatre of Animation presented "Snuffhouse-Dustlouse", a surreal, wordless drama of eccentricity, in which a hermit-like figure catalogues and guards his quirky objects in a world of Heath-Robinson like contraptions, pulleys and sound machines.

Music Theatre

Cinderella

This year music theatre took a more prominent position in the Brighton Festival. The Festival opened with a theatrical coup - Fiona Shaw starring in the title role in "Joan of Arc at the Stake" - a rare concert drama by Arthur Honegger set to the words of the poet Paul Claudel, and directed by Clare Venables.

Music Theatre London/Vienna, straight from their success in the Vienna Festival, presented an updated version of Rossini's opera "Cinderella" - directed by Nick Broadhurst and conducted by Tony Britten. This partnership also adapted and translated this work -drawing on the English obsession with class and some of the more bizarre conventions of the English pantomime to produce a witty update in which social-climbing oiks and sneering green-welly brigade vie for attention in Rossini's social comedy of manners.

Community Theatre

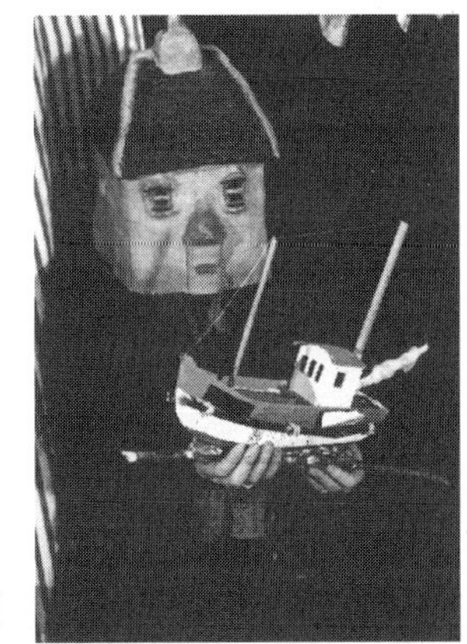

Horse and Bamboo

Every year Horse and Bamboo travel through the British Isles with a horse and a new show. This year they came to Sussex, with their latest show - "A Strange and Unexpected Event! The Life and Death of JG Posada." The show was based in the story of the legendary and influential Mexican artist, combining puppetry techniques, masks and live music - appealing to young and old alike.

Another Brighton first was Walk the Plank - a performing company who use the Fitzcarraldo, Europe's first touring theatre ship, as their stage. Anchored in Brighton Marina and Newhaven Harbour this extraordinary venture presented a daytime family show "The Blue," written by the poet and playwright Adrian Mitchell. This ecological fairy tale was told through pantomime and puppetry, live music, song and spectacular images winched from the sea and unfurled from the bows.

ARIANE KOEK

The Festival of Europe

The European Arts Festival, celebrating the UK's presidency of the European Community, had government funding to the tune of £6,000,000. It set out to reach all parts of the country (250 locations), with its 600 events covering foreign companies and local groups and helping both small scale performances and "mega-events" in music, theatre, dance and the visual arts. Theatrical shows ranged from street and children's theatre up to big names like Mnouchkine's Théâtre du Soleil, Giorgio Strehler's Piccolo Teatro coming from Milan to the National Theatre along with Franco Zefferelli's production of Pirandello's "Six Characters in Search of an Author". The scale of the whole project did cause administrative inefficiencies, unevenness, and a certain randomness of selection, but some events were outstanding and only such large-scale funding can enable the otherwise impossible importation of vitalising top-quality work from across the Channel into Britain. Anyway, it's about time two-way travel between the UK and the continent – both for productions and theatre research – got more serious support.

Les Atrides

After twenty-one years, Ariane Mnouchkine's Théâtre du Soleil were back in Britain – at a wool mill outside Bradford. Within a wooden bull ring – a setting transcending any specific society – this collective company acted out an epic of political and familial treachery and revenge, "Les Atrides" (the "Oresteia" and "Imphigénie à Aulis"). Mnouchkine's production proved visually stunning with boldly-painted faces and beautiful choreography, much indebted to Japanese and Indian drama. Jean-Jaques Lemetre, the composer, conducted three musicians who managed a hundred or more exotic instruments. Meanwhile the chorus turned from light-footed girls to hobbled old-age to four-footed Furies (like lion-maned baboons), and the five multi-roled principals combined athleticism and emotional daring with crystal-clear gesture and delivery.

The Travelling Tent

Yllana

The travelling tent's Saturday at Chatham Docks (11th July) was, unfortunately, a bit of a wash-out what with rain and no publicity. Still none of that reflected on the performers. Yllana from Spain presented a satire using mime plus pop music to mock toreadors' machismo with great comedy, physical agility and absurd exuberance. Kim Mandini – filling the yawning gap between events – provided a private magic show. Goldfish tumbled out of newspapers, fans swished and snapped like curious aerial creatures, and a red ball kept popping up everywhere. Mandini is an inspired, dedicated, eternal performer with mesmerising intensity alongside a knowing twinkle of amusement. The Tent also housed Umbrella Theatre's Parisian cabaret, Polka's children's show, and folk, opera and jazz music from Spain, France and the UK.

KATE BASSETT

Barclays New Stages '92

New Stages is Barclays Bank's six-year programme – now in its second year – which supports fringe theatre all over Britain. Firstly, it sponsors companies to create and tour new productions and, secondly, it finances an annual festival held at the Royal Court. This year's festival of four shows combined theatre, music and dance. Brith Gof are a widely-travelled Cardiff-based company used to site-specific projects (quarries, factories etc.) exploiting amplified soundtracks and physical action. Their show, "Patagonia", was an intriguing collage of music and mime, story-telling and snatches of dialogue, investigating the little-known world of Welsh pioneers in Argentinian Patagonia. "Time Spent In The Company Of Bad People" demonstrated the ferocious physicality of V-TOL Dance Company, creating a surreally vertiginous interior of domestic urban angst with dancers (and three-piece suites) driven, literally, up the wall. It was sexy, tightly-choreographed apparent anarchy. All credit to Barclays for branching out.

Stomp

"Stomp" was irresistibly exuberant, an hour of banging on dustbins and miraculously making music out of anything to hand – rubbish bags, buckets, matchboxes, whatever. All crew-cuts, T-shirts, cut-offs, and steel toecaps, the eight-strong Yes/No People (now including two women) had been a huge hit at the Assembly Rooms in Edinburgh before bringing their electrifying, ritualistic show of "street percussion" to The Royal Court – pure stamping and shaking with not a word spoken. Full of energy and inventiveness (abseiling included), "Stomp" was also perfectly choreographed with geometric rigour and synchronised professional team-work. The show had raw primitive boldness and yet, simultaneously, sensitized the audience to the slightest sound: the click of a zippo lighter; the sweep of a broom; the jangle of car keys. The mood occasionally darkened into aggressive menace.

Birthday

The Cholmondeleys and The Featherstonehaughs: get your mouth round that. These reunited, co-founded companies – one all-female, one all-male – indulged in some synchronised snogging having been going single between now and 1989. "Birthday" scrutinized the physical quirks of party-goers in a series of short episodes (dressing up; giving presents; playing games etc.), the piece proved richly eclectic ranging from drills to folk dances, from bathrobes and flippered feet to a funereal sword dance where black-kilted men stepped over women in the place of the traditional weapons. The Cholmondeleys and The Featherstonehaughs (incidentally pronounced Chumleys and Fanshaws) work with "found" movement emerging from rehearsals and street observation, subsequently honed by choreographer Lea Anderson who, here, characteristically isolated then patternistically multiplied minute telling gestures. Astute, stylish work.

KATE BASSETT

We offer a range of workshops for all situations – from the classroom to the theatre. What better way to discover and explore the world we live in than through Active Involvement

For further information and to book phone 0895 422 040

6.15 THEATRE CO

James Tillitt
Artistic Director

Specialists in writing and producing TIE plays for children on curriculum based subjects which entertain and educate

22 Brookfield Mansions, Highgate West Hill, London N6 6AS
Tel: 081-340 5430 Fax: 081-340 5696

Quicksilver

Theatre for Children

perform in theatres and schools for children aged 3-12

Forthcoming productions include a co-production with Trestle and plays commissioned from Mike Kenny and Roger McGough.

Contact Leila Jancovich on 071 241 2942
Quicksilver, The Glass House, 4 Enfield Road, London N1 5AZ

THE MAGICAL WORLD OF PUPPET THEATRE

(formerly Cannon Hill Puppet Theatre).

All enquiries about design, direction, performance and workshops for theatre and television to :

John Blundall
021 784 8757

Britain's National Theatre for Children

Productions 1992/3

DREAMS OF ANNE FRANK
A new play for Young People by Bernard Kops
Directed by Leona Heimfeld Designed by Fran Cooper

THE WIZARD OF OZ
Directed by Vicky Ireland Designed by Fran Cooper
Musical Direction by Neil Brand

THE BRAVE MAGICIANS OF MANGALORE
A play for Infants by Kenneth Rae
Directed by Vicky Ireland Designed by Bridge tKimak
Choreography by Shobana Jeyasing

THE BOY WHO TALKED TO WHALES
A play for Juniors by Webster Smalley
Directed by Ian Good Designed by Fran Cooper
Choreography by Shobana Jeyasing

240 The Broadway, London, SW19 1SB
tel: 081-543 4888

Soapbox

Each year SOAPBOX gives over 200 performances in schools (nursery, Primary & Secondary) to a total audience of over 26,000. Our productions encompass a wide range of issues, such as equal opportunities, racial prejudice, disability awareness, homelessness, and environmental concern, as well as performances of works by established playwrights. Where appropriate, comprehensive teachers' packs are supplied, related to the National Curriculum attainment targets.

Durning Hall, Earlham Grove, Forest Gate, London E7 9AB
071-511 6711

BOOKS TODAY

A FREE Service from Plays And Players

Brecht...Brenton... Checkov...Fo... Guare... Miller...Minghella...Poliakoff...Strindberg...

You name it we will find it!

081–343 9963

CHILDREN'S THEATRE

Too long the Cinderella of the theatre world, drama provision for children and young people is traditionally neglected and under-funded. But, like Cinderella, children's theatre remains remarkably resilient. HELEN ROSE reports.

Children's Theatre '92

Now the dust is beginning to settle after the legislative and structural upheavals of the past five years (introduction of the poll tax, charge capping, arts funding, re-structure, the Education Reform Act, the Child Act, the national curriculum and the introduction of local management of schools) children's theatre is, on the whole, even worse off and remains grossly underfunded (particularly in comparison with Europe), generally unrecognised as an art form and, like the rest of us, struggling with economic recession.

Children's theatre has always been the poor relation of grown-up theatre and sadly many of the changes over recent years have served to reinforce both the situation and the attitudes towards it. There has never been sufficient recognition of the value and scope of children's theatre (notably in the under fives bracket) – national paper critics rarely, if ever, review children's theatre and at grass roots level there is no specific training for practitioners in the art. Now the effects of the various changes are compounding to marginalise and squeeze out one of the most valuable and important art forms for children, but in spite of this, children's theatre continues to produce some of the most important work around.

The shift to local management of schools has generally meant less drama in schools, partly due to an inability or unwillingness of schools to pay companies' fees, partly because it is now illegal for schools to ask for money from parents for trips and visits, and discretionary donations from parents can, in poorer areas, fall short of target funds resulting in the cancellation of a theatre visit. The impact of the national curriculum among the various other reforms led to a drop in drama in schools as much through confusion as anything else and although a slow rise is now perceptible it is not to a level prior to these changes.

Finally, although larger companies have been able to benefit from the vogue of corporate sponsorship, smaller companies are feeling the squeeze as the recession has meant that funders give less and for shorter periods. Sponsorship and awards schemes, although very welcome, tend to be aimed more at youth theatre (over twelves) than at children's theatre.

All this said there is still a huge amount of excellent work being done and many companies I would like to have included are not represented simply due to lack of space. The following is a selection from the enormous body of fine, often pioneering new work being produced for our next generation.

Pantomime

Derived ultimately from commedia dell'arte, via the French harlequinade, British pantomime is now a unique genre of its own. It is a hybrid form borrowing from burlesque for the principal boy being played by a woman and the dame a man; from the music hall for the solo turns and group acts and on folk tales for the plot line. In recent years however, most notably on the Fringe, the annual Christmas panto has become a more political animal using the traditional fairy-tale as a hook on which to hang pertinent political comment and acerbic wit. Recent years have seen poll-tax pantos, green pantos, nuclear free pantos and lesbian and gay pantos which at best, have challenged and revitalised what had become a tired and worn tradition.

Jack and the Beanstalk

The big West End panto of '91/'92 was at the Piccadilly Theatre and was a blatant mix of commercial enterprise and traditional staging. Directed by Tudor Davies, who turned in the best spot of the show with his wittily rude Dame Trot, the production featured Cilla Black, as herself rather than her assigned role as Jack, but warm, giggly and girl-next-doorish as ever. Elsewhere Bob Carolgees (his T-shirt with sponsor Cadbury's logo emblazoned across it) was an endearingly oafish Simple Simon who did great things with his disgusting puppet Spit the Dog and Patrick Mower made an eminently hissable Demon Blackspider. But much of the show was tacky. If Davies had put as much into his production as he did his performance it would have been altogether better.

Bob Carolgees and Spit the Dog

The Snow Queen

Last Christmas the Young Vic staged an excellent production of Hans Christian Anderson's "The Snow Queen", adapted by Nick Stafford and co-directed by Chris White and Karen Stephens. Due in part to the success of the show and also for sound financial reasons the theatre is reviving it this year with a new cast. The appeal of the production was a skill in achieving maximum effect with minimal props – Bethia Jane Green's design was simple but imaginative: the warm security of the home, the swirling snowstorms of Gerda's journey or the Snow Queen's glittering, frozen palace were evoked with equal eloquence and ease. It was an assertive show with obvious Freudian psychological resonances in the Gerda/Kai/Snow Queen tug-of-love, but also a simple tale of the triumph of virtue and love over cold hearted possession.

Fraser James and Sarah-Jane Holm

Aladdin

David Dale

The Oldham Coliseum has a deserved reputation for offering the best traditional, family panto in the area. Paul Kerryson's version of Aladdin, directed by Adrian Howell, filled the auditorium with an action packed audience (made to do keep fit) and a vibrantly funny show. David Dale's splendid Widow Twankey descended onto the stage à la Miss Saigon on a helicopter and then proceeded to romp gloriously through old jokes and new frocks – appearing at one stage in Oldham Athletic strip. Elsewhere the non-star cast turned in star performances with great gusto and fun. Warren Hooper, the new Artistic Director, has written a traditionally based "Robin Hood" for this year which none the less delights in a variety of crazy anachronisms – Robin Hood begins the show by being away on his hols in Benidorm.....

Mother Goose

Bill Thomas

The Theatre Royal, Stratford East, doesn't need a celebrity to prop up a thin panto or entice the punters in. The theatre has built up a well earned reputation for high class, well acted family entertainment – no smut here, just a sly political jibe or two, some contemporary jokes and plenty of fun and slapstick. Where most theatres have to persuade punters to participate, at the Theatre Royal they almost have to be restrained from taking over – friendly hecklers do their best to steal the show and the actors have to work hard sometimes to keep to script and storyline. Last year's "Mother Goose" featured some wonderfully camp detail and an impressive transformation from woodland to the feathery splendour of Duckingham Palace – home of young Irma La Goose's royal parents. This year Philip Hedley will direct "Aladdin".

Dick Whittington

The Hackney Empire, a crumbling Victorian theatre with a worn and faded interior and roomy auditorium has become a popular venue for the annual traditional panto. "Dick Whittington", the third panto here by Kevin Hood in collaboration with the resident management company Roland Muldoon's Hackney New Variety, was the familiar mix of television stars and slapstick. Pauline Quirke and Linda Robson (of TV Birds of a Feather fame) starred with ex-Blue Peter presenter Peter Duncan. The show was given a certain dramatic edge by the fact that Linda Robson began the panto eight months pregnant and there was always the lurking possibility that the panto could one night become a nativity play.

The Polka Theatre

The Polka Theatre in Wimbledon, Britain's only purpose built children's theatre, is invariably a delight to visit for not only is it friendly and devoted to children's needs with playground, railway carriage cafe and spacious foyer, but Artistic Director Vicky Ireland has programmed an excellent season of in-house productions which have been entertaining, educational and relevant.

For the very young the intimate Adventure Playroom has welcomed a variety of touring companies from home and abroad, and also presented Ireland's own "Star Dog" tales – all ideal shows for little children first experiencing the magic of theatre.

Ireland's strength has been in specially commissioning work from both new and established dramatists and maintaining the kind of production standards usually considered the preserve of grown-up theatre.

Yoshi and the Tea Kettle

Nancy McClean and David Tse

This Christmas show was an astute piece of commissioning to fit in with Japanese Festival Year and Lynne Reid Banks came up with a fabulous adventure story which featured a young Samurai girl Yoshi, a bone-less (but not spineless) god who takes on the earthly form of a Badger Tea Kettle and a monk poet. In a Japan ravaged by plague, the unlikely trio set off to find the only cure – a magic flower which only blossoms inside a volcano. Traditional Japanese theatrical effects of billowing lengths of silk completed designer Fran Cooper's transformation of the auditorium into a Hokusai-style hall. The story showed how the protagonists were able then to conquer not just the plague but their own fears. Vicky Ireland's production was a triumph of design, magical staging and strong storyline.

Androcles and the Lion

Dramatist in residence Bernard Kops adapted the famous Aesop fable for eight year olds upwards and created in Androcles an amiable wimp with a line in feeble jokes and a fear of creepy crawlies. Vicky Ireland's production gently guided David Jarvis' comic, naive Androcles through the adventures which make him confront his own cowardice and learn to face reality. Kops' version featured two strong women – Androcles' wife and a fellow slave, who acted as beacons on Androcles' journey of physical hardship and spiritual self discovery. In the key scene where Androcles removes the thorn from the lion's paw Jarvis clearly showed his character recognising the animal's pain rather than seeing the lion as beast. The play addressed issues of courage and self-esteem in an accessible, amusing narrative which was played out against Verity Hawkes' sun bleached set.

Indigo Mill

Socialist textile designer William Morris would not at first appear an ideal subject for a play for eight to twelve year olds but Nick Fisher's specially commissioned work wove intrigue and mystery into the life and times of this famous Victorian figure. A sweat-shop seamstress, thrown onto the streets by her employer, ends up pickpocketing and is caught by William Morris who takes her on as part of a wager and social experiment. With strong elements of Victoria melodrama and yet intelligently well written, Fisher's play explored the social and economic structure of Victorian London and the pioneering work of William Morris. Beautifully designed (with help from William Morris prints of course) by Helen Skillicorn the play moved dramatically from back street squalor to country house elegance with ease in Caroline Smith's brisk paced production.

Sally Ann Matthews, Christopher Robbie and Jo-Anne Knowles

The Giraffe, the Pelly and Me

Less consciously educational, more obviously a summer crowd puller the world premiere of Roald Dahl's tale of the thief-catching, window-cleaning trio of the title proved to be the least artistically exciting of the year's shows. Roald Dahl's imaginative flights of fantasy, notably the Pelican's patented beak, proved too much for the technical production team who made a disappointing stab at compromise using small rod puppets. However, under Roman Stefanski's capable direction the show rose to the occasion with a general exuberance and a delight in Dahl's idiosyncratic storyline. Fran Cooper's design pleased purists and Dahl afficianados by evoking Quentin Blake's original drawings.

Dystin Johnson, Richard Ashro, and Edward Brittain

Anne Frank

Fifty years ago this year a young Jewish girl called Anne Frank was holed up in an Amsterdam attic with her family in order to escape the sweeping Nazi round-up. The diary she kept during this claustrophobic period of silent, secret fear has become a powerful and poignant testament of Hitler's brutal programme of racial purification. Bernard Kops wrote a play exploring the world into which Anne escaped during those months of inner exile. Blending reality with Anne's dreams the play, under Leona Heimfeld's subdued direction, showed a teenage girl living out her trapped life through her diary and her imagination. The play very gently and subtley addressed issues of war and suffering but concentrated mainly on the hopes, dreams, loves and philosophy of Anne's life. Richly rewarding, very moving piece of theatre.

Elizabeth Chadwick, Edward Halsted and Kitty Alvarez

The Unicorn Theatre

Richard Williams, already an accredited and award winning director of adult theatre who has worked as a freelance director for Vanessa Ford Productions, began his Artistic Directorship of the Unicorn in 1990 and opened a season of distinguished productions in September 1991 which combined ambitious programming with top quality production standards. The Unicorn, the only professional children's theatre in the West End, has always had a commitment to producing the best of theatre for children and Williams has continued the tradition with shows which have been educational and entertaining. Biology was made fun with Andy Rashleigh's comic look at the inside workings of a schoolboy's body; specially commissioned adaptations of Hans Christian Anderson tales provided unusual dramatisations of familiar stories; the Columbus bandwagon was given comic alternative treatment in Rashleigh's domestic history lesson and Williams himself adapted some of the Ahlberg "Happy Families" stories for the stage. The year was rounded off with the talented writer-in-residence Rashleigh's version of "Pinocchio" for the Christmas season.

Body Talk

Biology lessons will never be the same for those who saw Andy Rashleigh's hilarious view of the inside of eleven year old Mudge's body. Run by Bods from a space capsule style Mission Control and overseen by the authoritarian Brain, Mudge's insides are a fractious lot; Tum is always hungry; Mouth is ever open and Memory isn't very good at remembering things especially Geography tests. Things are thrown into even greater chaos when Germ enters the system, upsets Tum and causes Mudge to throw up spectacularly over the headmaster – witnessed from Mudge's point of view through four video screens (design David Collis). Bodily functions are always a source of amusement to kids but Rashleigh injected his own brand of humour to make an uproarious comedy of an informative educational lesson.

Hans Christian Anderstories

Hans Christian Anderson has always provided rich source material for the stage and Richard Williams commissioned five established writers to each adapt a story in a joint venture with Warwick Arts Centre. The five pieces were linked by a plot-line by Andy Rashleigh. The coup of the venture was the diversity of writing talent grouped under one umbrella – each writer bringing his or her own style to the tale being told so Fay Weldon's "Ugly Duckling" had a wise pathos and beauty of its own; Adrian Mitchell gave a straight narrative telling of the "Tin Soldier" and Claire Luckham had her "Little Mermaid" falling in love with a pop star. Ken Campbell's "Magic Goloshes" was predictably anarchic and wild while Charles Causley gave a sharpness and edge to the familiar "Emperor's New Clothes".

Happy Families

Few children can resist the Ahlberg books; the quirky illustrations, accessible humour and slightly ridiculous sense of fun quickly established them as children's classics. This year Richard Williams followed his earlier Unicorn success, his dramatisation of the Ahlberg "Ten in a Bed", with another stage version – this time a selection from the "Happy Families" series. Directed by Orit Azaz, the musical retained the delightful Edwardian flavour of the original illustrations through music hall pastiche (music by Alisdair Nicolson) and the occasional nod towards Gilbert and Sullivan. Faithful to the original text, Williams' adaptation enhanced the quirky detail and comic oddness of Ahlberg's characters, enriching the already larger-than-life personalities like Mrs Lather the Laundry or the outrageous Mrs Plug the Plumber to suit the style and scope of the stage.

Columbus

This is the year of Columbus – plays about Christopher Columbus have been popping up all over the place – and the Unicorn obviously decided not to be the exception. With typical insight and with one eye on education and the other on fun Andy Rashleigh brought his Columbus into the front room making text book history into a tale of family histrionics. An Anglo American family, whose children have been set a school project on Columbus, rally round to help the kids out with riotous results. The uncle from New York and the aunt from Milan have wildly different views of what Columbus was like and in the end the family re-create their own version of Columbus' voyages of discovery and discover a few truths of their own. Funny, poignant and excellently performed.

Pinocchio

The prolific writer-in-residence Andy Rashleigh turned his pen to an adaptation of Carlo Collodi's famous Victorian tale of Pinocchio, which was first published in Britain 100 years ago this year. Sweeping aside the more heavy Victorian threads of morality and vengeance which run through the original, Rashleigh chose the most dramatic scenes from this episodic tale of the puppet with a mind of his own, to weave into a new, highly original stage version directed by Richard Williams. With a score by Alisdair Nicolson, the show followed Pinnocchio's adventures with friend Lampwick, the Blue Fairy and his narrow escape from death at the hands of the evil puppet master to realisation of the value of life and truth.

Puppet Theatres

There are only six full time puppet theatres in the UK and Ireland, four in Britain and one each in Scotland and Ireland, and although there has been a greater use of puppets in children's theatre generally there still does not exist any formal training or school for puppeteers in this country. The Gulbenkian Foundation funded a national enquiry into puppetry, published this year, which significantly showed a serious lack of funding for puppetry and a general attitude to the craft which classified it, in a derogatory sense, as being just for kids. Compared to Europe, puppetry in Britain and Ireland, is unsupported and so even well established resident companies like Purves Puppets in Scotland or the Movingstage Marionette Company in London receive no funding. The result is an emphasis on revivals because new shows, especially those where puppets are hand made for each production (this takes weeks), are expensive and time-consuming to mount. Puppetry on the whole is regarded as entertainment and some companies suffered as a result of the new stringencies of the National Curriculum.

Puppet Theatre Barge

The Movingstage Marionette Company, with its unique, hand-carved wooden marionettes, this year celebrated its tenth anniversary year aboard the company's barge home, with a programme made up largely of revivals of past successes. These included their excellent "Tales of Brair Rabbit" and, for older children and adults, Lorca's beautifully poignant love story "The Butterfly's Spell" in a presentation which brought to life the poet's world of the imagination where mystery, beauty and the spirit of freedom are the treasures of the mind which prove far greater than the material constraints of reality. The company's new production was, like so much of their work, inspired by poetry, in this case Robert Louis Stevenson's "A Child's Garden of Verses" which provided a springboard for a careful blending of poetry, puppetry and music.

The Little Angel Marionette Theatre

The small auditorium with its beautifully carved proscenium arch, pretty frescoes and surprisingly spacious stage is a favoured venue in the East of London. Here the puppets, (all made in the company's workshop), are operated using the black theatre technique, and have no strings but are animated by velvety shadowed figures who manage the most extraordinarily eloquent feats of puppetry with their tiny characters. This year, due largely to the death last year of founder and Artistic Director John Wright, the Little Angel ran a series of revivals, with the Christmas show for the very young "Cindermouse" their only new production. With the arrival in early 1993 of the new Artistic Director Christopher Leith the company hopes to be back on its feet again with three new shows.

Brog Puppets

Dennis and Juliet Harkness, alias Mr and Mrs Brog, are a travelling puppet theatre who tour schools, theatres and parks across the country with a mixed programme of plays designed to engage the audience in active participation. From Mrs Brog's gentle, endearing show "Humpty Dumpty, Quite Contrary" for the very young, where audience members are invited to help stick the broken pieces of Humpty back together again, or assist Mary in finding the silver bells and cockle shells to grace her garden trellis; to Mr Brog's version of the medieval classic "Sir Gawain and the Green Knight" or his Tibetan tale of "King of the Mice" – the shows have a seductive warmth and openness, a kind of homeliness which gives even the shiest child the confidence to take part in the action.

Punch and Judy

Due in part to adverse criticism of the innate sexism and scenes of domestic violence displayed in traditional Punch and Judy this uniquely British puppet show has become an endangered species, but there are a few "Professors" of the art still practising and Martin Bridle, also known as Martin the Puppet Man, is one of the country's best and most devoted traditional profs. Martin has performed regularly at the National Theatre's foyer, around Britain and at international puppet fairs and was the first solo performer in Britain to be invited to the Moscow State Theatre. Martin's Punch and Judy show, although making concessions to contemporary attitudes, is very much in the spirit of the classical tradition. By including modern variations to classic scenarios he has kept alive an old tradition by breathing fresh new life into it.

Martin Bridle

Norwich Puppets

The Norwich Puppet Theatre, housed in a beautifully converted medieval church close to Norwich cathedral, is one of the few building based puppet companies in the UK. Founded by Ray and Joan DaSilva as a base for DaSilva Puppets, the Norwich Puppet Theatre has become one of the leading puppet centres in the country. Last year Luis Boy was appointed as new Artistic Director and brought his own special interest and experience to the theatre. The year's productions included John Roberts' enchanting "Hansel and Gretel", and the touring shows of "The Travelling Storyteller" which was a colourful piece taking the audience on an exotic journey into India, Vietnam and the Caribbean – the play used rod, glove and banraku puppets. Beautiful, large, animal puppets featured in Rudyard Kipling's "Just So" stories in the summer season.

Commercial Tours

Where subsidised children's theatre aims on the whole to educate and entertain (and make money if possible), the commercial sector is there to entertain and make money and although book adaptations proliferate in both areas they dominate, almost to exclusion, in commercial companies. In an age of TV-literate children companies have expediently turned to the "box" for inspiration. Like using TV soap stars in Christmas pantos, children's companies have cashed in on the advantages of using ready-made characters in familiar situations to draw the punters in and have not always backed this up with a strong or interesting script.

One of the most recent success stories (in commercial terms) has been that of Leyston Productions, headed by Dudley Russell who took his cue from his own kids and staged the hugely popular "Postman Pat". Russell followed that with "Fireman Sam" and later "Rupert the Bear". Vanessa Ford Productions cornered the market for slightly older children with faithful, popular adaptations of the C S Lewis Narnia books. Elsewhere Roald Dahl crops up regularly in more or less successful stage versions.

Postman Pat

When Dudley Russell decided to stage "Postman Pat", he hit a goldmine. Kids up and down the country, already devotees of the TV series, thrilled to the sight of Postman Pat driving a real little red Post Office van round the stage. The actors, dressed like puppets (and acting like them too) peopled the stage with familiar scenarios from Pat's daily routine of postal deliveries in the hills and valleys of Greendale. It was a formula to be repeated in the similar "Fireman Sam" show, also based on the popular TV animation, which targeted the same young audience with an almost identical product. Russell has now bought the rights to "Rupert the Bear", so watch out for a stage version next year.

The BFG

Mary-Ann Coburn

Roald Dahl has a way of capturing the imaginations of the young; his unique use of language, his way of tapping into children's secret fears and balancing that with warmth and security makes him still Britain's favourite children's author. "The BFG", Dahl's tale of a potentially threatening but immensely likeable giant whose abduction of the orphan Sophie develops into a firm friendship, is an adventure story full of magic, fantasy, monsters and love. It was a tall order of a tale to adapt for the stage, but David Wood, commissioned by Clarion Productions, came up with an artistic and commercial success, now touring into its second year. Designed by Susie Caulcutt who used puppets ingeniously, the play was dominated by Anthony Pedley's endearingly gentle giant. Wood is adapting Dahl's "The Witches" for the upcoming season.

Singing Kettle

The Singing Kettle is the most popular and well known children's theatre company in Scotland. The founding trio of folk musicians began doing set pieces around the street songs of their youth (in Kingskettle, Fife) and their children's shows evolved from there and moved on with great success to include four TV series, a BBC and a BAFTA award.

The stage shows are characterised by plenty of participation from the children. This year's "The Wild West Show" was an action-packed adventure involving thieving bandits who stole the company's hallmark kettles. The kids were invited on stage to help retrieve them and fight the desperados Six Gun Spike, Gold Diggin Gabby and Dirty Dollar Bill. The company is original, commercial and hugely successful – ask any kid in Scotland.

Pied Piper

The Pied Piper company founded by writer, director and sometime performer Tina Williams is another of the few commercial touring companies to use original scripts and stories rather than adaptations. The company generally produces one Christmas show plus one or two educational touring shows. "Bertie Badger's Christmas Adventure" is a charming tale for the very young which encourages awareness of and care for woodland animals and the environment without any tub-thumping evangelism. Here was a Christmassy show about a bored badger who wakes his friend tortoise from hibernation to go on an adventure. The tale included the case of the lost necklace, a thieving magpie and a vivacious girl called Clare. Tina Williams creates a warm, friendly atmosphere with magic and fun.

The Lion, The Witch and The Wardrobe

James Mathews and Mary Conlon

Vanessa Ford Productions has become the company associated with C S Lewis's Narnia books, with Glyn Robbins' adaptation of "The Lion, the Witch and the Wardrobe" probably the most popular of their shows. Robbins is a faithful adaptor who captures the magic and fantasy of Narnia in all its picaresque Edwardian style while shedding some of the more dated values and attitudes of the original. The shows are unassuming, competent and well presented and although this year the family-run company has been troubled with personal health problems, it will still be presenting two shows in the West End, the above mentioned Lewis show plus their seasonal special – Ron Pember's musical adaptation of Dickens' "A Christmas Carol" with Pember himself as a humorous, redeemable old Scrooge in a lively singing, dancing version.

Touring Companies

A survey of children's theatre last year by the Children's Theatre Association found that the majority of companies questioned did not consider themselves "building based". Nearly 80% of children's theatre is small-scale, low budget touring with almost all companies involved in tours of some sort or another. Compared to adult theatre, children's theatre (notably the under fives) boldly goes into uncharted areas of entertainment – parks, clubs, nurseries and community centres as well as more established arts centres, small theatres and schools. In addition to this nearly all the work produced is devised or created by the company and children's theatre companies in general commission more new work and produce more new performances than adult theatre. There is a whole body of new work being generated and with the Education Reform Act ruling on charges for theatre visits there has been a move to more public performances and slightly less Theatre In Education. Many of these companies are addressing important issues and display an acute awareness of the social, emotional and physical needs of their audience.

Neti-Neti

Neti-Neti, always a company to address delicate or taboo subjects in an accessible form, followed their previous, highly acclaimed work on bullying and grief with "Shabbash !" a vibrant new show on self-esteem. Writer and director Penny Casdagli approached the subject both directly through colour-coded characters and indirectly through puppet play. The characters played out classroom, domestic and social scenes while using the stick puppets in their pockets to express hidden emotions of anger, fear, sadness etc. Performed, like all their work in English, Bengali and Sign, the play occasionally confused some of its messages but still showed clearly that self-esteem is not just possible for anyone, whatever their personal experience, but also the right of everyone.

Molecule

This year the Molecule Theatre of Science celebrated its twenty-fifth anniversary with a commitment to continue the dream of founders Lord and Lady Miles "to enthuse young children with the wonders of science and the natural world through the impact and drama of live theatre". The theatre company continues to exist almost entirely from sponsorship and this year's project, "Satellite", by Gerry Nowicki was sponsored by BP. The nature of the work entailed week-long residencies in schools where investigative research by the students was combined with and incorporated into the drama of Nowicki's script – written to involve children actively in strategic decision-making in the plot. Not only did the work introduce children to the concept of satellite technology but offered the opportunity of exploring a sense of personal and global responsibility through group activities.

Oily Cart

Over ten years this small touring company has established itself as a pioneering group taking shows to young audiences. The company, the founding production team of writer Tim Webb and musical director Max Reinhardt, presents plays specifically for children with severe learning difficulties, for the under fives and for school children. There were three productions this year : "Dinner Ladies from Outer Space" for students with severe learning difficulties concentrated on the sense of taste using highly visual, tactile experiences for the audience. "Greenfingers" humorously sorted the bugs from the boys and showed three to five year-olds how to exploit nature's own eco-system to make their garden bloom and grow. "Gobble and Gook" for five to nine year-olds explored questions of language with emphasis on Europe and our continental neighbours.

Greenfingers

Theatre Centre

Based at Hanover School in Islington, Theatre Centre presents highly visual theatre which challenges young audiences into questioning given values and concepts. The works presented often address contemporary issues in an oblique, subtle way, drawing the audience into a network of visual images which are thought provoking and instructive. Storytelling seemed to be the theme this year starting with a piece devised with Hijinx Theatre, "A World Turned Upside Down" which explored solitude and security, friendship and the outside world. This was followed by Noel Greig's "Lie of the Land" which told of giants and storytellers and explored the nature of truth and lies, the power of stories in a land shadowed by fear. A retelling of the Rapunzel classic "The Tower Without Stairs" used sign language, music, drama and visual imagery to recreate an old text.

Pop Up

Pop Up theatre has established itself as one of the country's leading companies for theatre for the under-fives. The company takes the very young seriously and gives them seriously good theatre. "Feeling Fine" was about Didi (a quiet dreamer in blue) and Krumpcracker (vibrant and loud in red). Didi discovers a beautiful butterfly locked inside her cocooned nature which the bullying Krump cannot destroy. Graeme Miller, an award winning performance artist in adult theatre worked with Penny Bernard on a new work "Inside Out" which told of the rich, beautiful and magical world a child is able to show to a weary, luggage laden traveller lost in the dark of despair. Again a play of stylish simplicity and gentle instruction for the under fives.

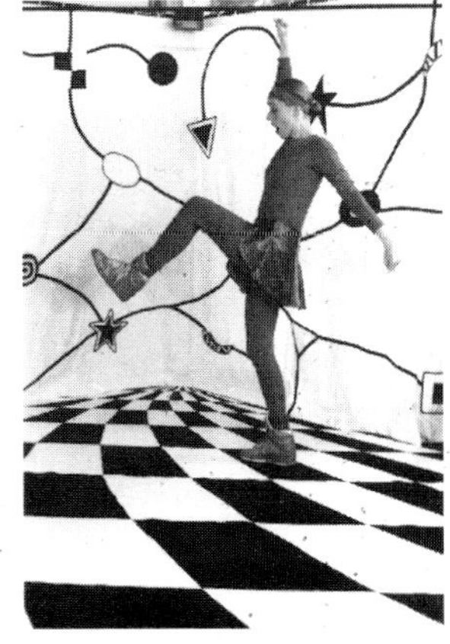

Tag Theatre

The Dance and the Railroad

Tag Theatre in Glasgow is Scotland's leading theatre for young people. Established in 1967, the company has created its own style of dance/theatre. Their 1992 programme, under new Artistic Director Tony Graham, reflects both the diversity and ambitious scale of projects. "The Dance and the Railroad" by David Hwang brought together the Singapore Leling Beijing Opera Troupe and Tag under Alan Lyddiard's direction in a hybrid production of Eastern art and Western thought where each discipline informed and enhanced the other. This was followed by Noel Greig's version, for primary schools, of the epic poem "Beowulf".

Anthony Burgess' "A Clockwork Orange" was updated and given a Scottish setting (Alex and his Droogs in kilts) in a production in which dance brought a fluid, stylised sense of horror to the violence in the story.

Manchester Actors Company

Jack Spratt

Although not exclusively a children's company, the Manchester Actors Company has a commitment to community theatre, part of which includes a maximum of three shows a year for children. This year saw a double-bill aimed at primary kids "Jack Spratt" and "The Beastly Creatures" which addressed environmental issues on food, while the summer playscheme tour was a science fiction musical which invited children to participate in the plot by climbing aboard the Starship Timeslicer in a quest for septic alien cheeses and herbal slime on a voyage of discovery under the domestic kitchen sink; "It Came from Under the Sink" took its cue from popular Nintendo computer games to include children in an epic theatrical adventure.

Quicksilver

Bagdancing

Quicksilver is one of the many excellent companies touring schools and theatres with plays which challenge and inform. Their summer production "Bag Dancing", by Mike Kenny, took a humorous but poignant look at the lives of two of society's misfits – Imelda Baglady and Neville Child. She's a grubby, drunken itinerant who lives out of a collection of bags, while Neville is an obsessive cleaner in a hostel for the homeless. A series of stories are taken from Imelda's bags telling of the personal tragedies and disappointments which brought both Neville and Imelda to their current situations. Storytelling of a different sort was the key to a retelling of the Pied Piper tale – "No. 3 Pied Piper Street" found two children entering a world of dreams and fantasy where wishes come true.

INTERNATIONAL VIEW

The Yearbook is primarily a survey of theatre in Britain. But British theatre is increasingly influenced by what happens abroad. In previous years, many countries in the Eastern Bloc would have provided separate sections in a chapter of this kind. Because of recent events, all those countries are covered in a single, extended section. Seven other countries have been chosen to provide a taste of what's going on around the world.

France

Like many other European countries, in France productions in the more important theatres, thanks to government subsidies, tour the country after their premiere in their "home" theatre, and often today initial production costs are shared between more than one theatre. This was the case for actor turned playwright Jean-Gabriel Nordmann's "La mangeuse de crottes" (The female glutton), directed by the author and produced by Le Grand Nord and the Théâtre de l'Invisible. A man/woman two-hander, of an ill-assorted petit bourgeois couple, this is the rather acid Gallic equivalent of Alan Bennett country.

French playwrights tend to direct first productions of their work (which possibly tells us something of their opinion of French directors), such as Gérard Dessalles, whose eighth play, "Carnaval", produced by Les Projecteurs de Rêves and the Théâtre Jean-Marie Serreau, is a very stylish view of upper-class fun and games with dark overtones at a Venice carnival, reminiscent of Hofmannsthal.

A mega-event was Claude Confortès' "Les Olympiennes", about three woman athletes, which required months of athletic training for the actresses and had the surprise twist of three different endings, depending on which "athlete" won in any particular performance.

Another spectacular was Philippe Genty's "Ne m'oublie pas" at the Théâtre de la Ville, containing dance, mime and puppets as well as acting roles, on a stage covered with huge air-filled structures. A nightmarish vision of human conflicts with more than a nod in the direction of the darker moments of "A Midsummer Night's Dream".

Roger Planchon also directed his diptych "Le vieil hiver/Fragile forêt", an intense indictment of man's eternal urge to self-destruction, to great acclaim in early spring at the Théâtre National de la Colline.

"Roberto Zucco", the last play of Bernard-Marie Koltès, who died last year at the age of forty, and is arguably France's finest recent playwright, was directed at the Théâtre de la Ville in Paris not by Patrice Chéreau, who directed most of Koltès work while he was still alive, but by Bruno Boëglin, and the part of Zucco was played by the Polish actor Jerzy Radziwilowicz, known to international audiences mainly from Wajda films.

Chéreau is now championing in France the plays of Germany's leading playwright, Botho Strauss, and his production of "Time and the Room" at the Odéon in Paris won the Prix Molière as the best production of the 91/92 season.

The Comédie-Française, besides offering the usual classics, revived Victor Hugo's "Le roi s'amuse" at the beginning of the year in a sumptuous period costume production directed by Jean-Luc Boutté. Written in 1832, the play has suffered the peculiar fate of being totally overshadowed by Verdi's operatic version, "Rigoletto", which effectively stifled the original work. Another Hugo, "Ruy Blas", was revived at the Théâtre des Bouffes du Nord by Georges Wilson, using star actor Lambert Wilson in the main role, in a successful attempt to attract a young audience.

Otherwise, plenty of Molière everywhere, and plenty of new writing of wildly varying standard.

DELLA COULING

Germany

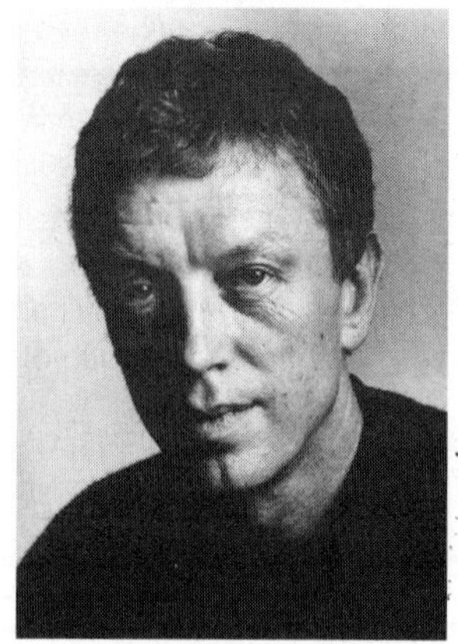

Terry Hands: his "Buffalo Bill Show" was not a success

Three years after the collapse of the communist regime in East Germany the German theatre is still dominated by the social, artistic and financial consequences of unification. When the two cultural capitals of Berlin became one it was clear that even the most generously subsidised theatre system in the world could not afford to maintain for long three opera houses, two ballet ensembles, three musical theatres and eleven fully-subsidised straight theatres. Things came to a head this year in July when the Freien Volksbühne in West Berlin – original home of the legendary director Erwin Piscator whose productions of Heinar Kipphardt ("Oppenheimer"), Peter Weiss ("The Investigation") and Rolf Hochuth ("The Representative") sent ripples of furore round the world in the 1960's – closed its doors as all subsidy was withdrawn by the grant-giving bodies. At the same time the old directorial regime at Bert Brecht's legendary Berliner Ensemble finally capitulated to the forces of capitalism, bowing out with an ironic final performance of Brecht's greatest hit "The Threepenny Opera". The shark indeed has very sharp teeth !

Meanwhile audiences in the East of the country have dropped away alarmingly. The population's struggle to survive economically has resulted in theatre-going being regarded as at best a luxury and at worst an irrelevance. Indeed many of the major city theatres in this part of the country – a typical example is the northern sea port of Rostock – are in real danger of permanent closure not for lack of subsidy, but of bums on seats. Throughout Germany as a whole the unexpectedly high burden of unification has meant that the pfennigs of public money are being counted as never before with the result that artistic directors have tended to play even more safe than usual with their choice of repertoire. New plays, always a rare commodity here, have become even rarer. Klaus Pohl's fall-of-the-wall comedy "Karate Billy comes back" (staged at the Royal Court in May) was the most performed new play with over twenty productions nationwide. But, for my money, the most interesting new works were Joshua Sobol's comedy "A and B", and the premiere of a hitherto unknown one-actor by Jean Genet entitled "She" about an encounter between a photographer and the Pope. The fringe continued to show little or no life apart from the remarkable Teatr Kreatur company in Berlin, led by a Pole Andrej Woron, whose production of an adaptation of Isaac Babel's "The End of the Poorhouse" created history by being selected as one of the best productions of the year for the prestigious Berlin Theatre Festival. Prize for the biggest flop of the year has to be shared between Peter Zadek's production of "The Blue Angel" starring the singer Ute Lemper, a show which proved to be about as substantial as the smoke of its own publicity; and former RSC director Terry Hands' dismal re-staging of Arthur Kopit's "Indians" in a circus tent with the unwanted remains of the former East German National Circus. Retitled "The Buffalo Bill Show" ostensibly to pull in the crowds, the resulting farrago managed to dissatisfy circus and theatre fans alike and collapsed in a financial disaster unparalleled since the same Mr Hands' attempt to revive the fortunes of the RSC some years back with a musical adaptation of a Steven King novel. A sad case of "Carrie on, Terry".

ROY KIFT

Holland

Usually an ideal place to catch up on what has been happening in Dutch and Flemish theatre is the annual Theatre Festival, which runs for about two weeks each year in August/September, organized by the indefatigable Arthur Sonnen, former long-term director of the Holland Festival.

This year the now familiar companies were again represented: Discordia, Blauwe Maandag, Onafhankelijk Toneel, Theatergroep Hollandia, in the now familiar deconstructions of Chekhov, O'Neill et al., which, outrageous though many of them are at first sight, start to look rather boringly similar after a few years – the Festival's poster this year, of a piece of not very exciting wallpaper, proved rather apt.

A rather surprising choice was the Toneelschuur Produkties' "Frankenstein or the landscapes of the soul", played with some panache by a largely young cast, who sent up the whole melodramatic genre of Gothic horror with a great sense of comedy and not much else.

The distinguished Belgian playwright Hugo Claus was represented by an early work, "Thyestes". First performed in the 1960s, this study of brotherly envy, hatred and revenge is sadly still relevant and given a spare but striking production by the Zuidelijk Toneel company, directed by Dora van der Groen. (There were two other Claus plays this season: "Richard Everzwijn" in Ghent, and "Winteravond" (Winter evening) in a large-scale production in Amsterdam, the latter about an ageing actress, played by Kitty Courbois, an ex-girlfriend of Claus).

The Theatre Festival jury's choice has always been idiosyncratic, but this year it verged on the wilful: omitting the great hit of the season, Karst Woudstra's "Een zwarte Pool" (A "black"-i.e. illegal immigrant-Pole). This is Woudstra's usual territory, of family conflicts and power struggles, but by inserting a young Polish student, Woudstra, in this extremely funny comedy, extends the battle to a world stage, and conversely skilfully reduces glasnost and perestroika to the personal level. Premiered at The Hague's Royal Theatre in April, it then toured the Netherlands and Belgium – as do most main productions in both countries.

Another giant omission is Frans Strijards' latest play, "Sporen" (Traces), possibly owing to its late premiere in July. Strijards and Judith Herzberg (no new play by her this year) are the joint flagship of Dutch drama abroad, enjoying considerable success in Germany in particular.

International as ever, Dutch and Flemish theatres also put on a lot of modern European plays, among others by Thomas Bernhard, Botho Strauss, and Lars Noren (the latter translated as always by Karst Woudstra, who has been responsible for promoting Lars Noren's work in the Netherlands).

An intriguing also-ran of 1992 was "Prins Karel, Graaf van Vlaanderen", by Rudy Geldhof (who tragically died in July at the age of 48). About a womanizing uncle of the present King of the Belgians, the play unfortunately was not seen outside Flanders, mainly, one suspects, owing to a not very brilliant script. A pity, as the subject has a certain topicality.

DELLA COULING

Irish Republic

The Gate Production of "A Month in the Country"

It was a year marked by the tried and true, rather than the new. The National Theatre, universally known as the Abbey, led the way with a brilliant refurbishing of Tom Murphy's "Conversations on a Homecoming". The director was Garry Hynes, who was having something of a renaissance after a controversial 1991 debut as the Abbey's Artistic Director, and reminded her critics of the reason she got the job in the first place – her nurturing of Galway's Druid Theatre to international fame.

She brought with her some actors from that memorable pioneering in the west, and two in particular, Sean McGinley and Marie Mullen, gave astonishing performances in the Murphy play. They epitomized the loss of hope, dreams and finally self-respect of those who miss the tide of life. Throughout the year, indeed, as in a later revival of a much older play – Lennox Robinson's barbed comedy, "Drama at Inish" – they reaffirmed their exceptional talents.

There was one new play at the Abbey of considerable interest, partly for the return of Tony Award-winning Hugh Leonard after an absence of some years. "Moving" was not in the author's familiar comic vein, being instead a sober view of social evolution via a Dublin family going through the hoops twice, with a thirty year interval. Elsewhere, Kerry's veteran John B Keane had audiences massing to his revived "The Man from Clare", a local wine of some character.

The Abbey moved this year to disband the remnants of its permanent company in favour of short contracts. It has been a traumatic process for those directly involved, and a source of sadness for many observers. But change is inevitable, and there is the consolatory gift of new lamps for the old.

Brian Friel's "Dancing at Lughnasa" , still gathering international awards, was revived at the Abbey, but his latest work was launched by the Gate Theatre. The author finds the classic Russian simpatico, and has used his wizardry before to provide versions with a modern Irish flavour. Turgenev's "A Month in the Country" was his latest choice, and he harmonized the old with the new so as to satisfy critics and public alike.

As always in the Gate, the standards dictated by supremo Michael Colgan were observed; a beautiful set, perfectly lit, and a cast of top-liners led by Donal McCann and Catherine Byrne.

Regional theatre, though living on its usual financial knife-edge, still thrived. Waterford's Red Kettle company launched a new light comedy, "Forty-Four, Sycamore", by the popular Bernard Farrell, and toured profitably with it throughout the year. Galway's Druid, still a force in the land, had a mixed bag of polished revivals. Limerick's Island Theatre group took a giant leap forward with an anarchic production of "A Midsummer Night's Dream", and is now on the aficionados' short list of venues worth travelling to.

That last, indeed, encapsulates a year in which Irish theatre travelled hopefully, with many a rewarding halting site, and pleasing prospects ahead – and is not that the name of the game ?

GERRY COLGAN

Italy

A lot of Italian classics this year, headed by Giorgio Strehler's production at the Teatro Lirico in Milan of Goldoni's "Le Baruffe Chiozzotte" (The Chioggian Quarrels), which, after travelling to Expo 92 in Seville, was also seen at the National Theatre in London in the autumn. Pirandello too, has been well represented, including "Trovarsi" (Meeting) at the Quirino in Rome with Valeria Moriconi heading a distinguished cast, and a Milan production at the Teatro Carcano of "L'Uomo, la bestia e la virtù" directed by Gabriele Lavia, who made his name with very full-blooded versions of Ibsen, Strindberg and Schiller and can always be relied on to nail you to your seat. Catania saw a new production of "Nuova Colonia".

That more recent Italian classic writer, De Filippo was also well represented, including a stylish production of his "Uomo e galantuomo" at Rome's beautiful Teatro Valle, and Alberto Moravia's widow, Dacia Maraini, has reworked Moravia's "Il Diavolo non puo salvare il mondo" (The devil cannot save the world) at the Piccolo Teatro in Milan, and also another of his stories, "Delitto" (Crime), bringing the total of her performed plays to over thirty.

As Italy has no recognized national centre where theatre is concerned – Milan, Florence, Turin, Rome and indeed other cities can all claim to have equally good theatre – many productions are shared between two or more cities, and most important productions automatically tour. Arguably the most talked about production of the year, "Ulisse e la balena bianco" (Ulysses and the White Whale) provided the most mind-boggling tour of the year. Written and directed by Vittorio Gassman (who also plays Melville/Ishmael), with sets by the architect Renzo Piano, this monster hybrid out of Melville and Homer was premiered in Genoa in July in a piazza in the old port, to a background of sea and ships. It is a co-production of the Teatro di Genova with the Genova 92 exhibition in honour of their most famous son, and Seville's Expo 92 on the same theme. It was enthusiastically received everywhere (at least by the audiences), and after Seville there were performances on the Tiberina island in Rome in September, and in November again indoors at the Teatro Argentina.

The other mega-event of the year was the return of Dario Fo to the one-man show format, after some rather disastrous ventures in recent years. This show, "Johan Padan a la Descoverta de le Americhe", is also on the Columbus theme, but typically from the point of view of the under-dog, crew member Johan Padan, who, in a peculiar dialect, invented by Fo but somehow always understandable, presents a predictably iconoclastic view of the whole Colombian enterprise. At a stroke, with this show Fo has regained his position as Italy's best loved man of the theatre – even the critics liked it.

Austria's Thomas Bernhard is posthumously conquering Italy, with top-notch productions in some of Italy's most prestigious theatres, ditto Bernard-Marie Koltès – Italian theatre is nothing if not international in outlook. Not that Italians are slouches at new writing: Luigi Squarzina's "Siamo Momentaneamente Assenti" (We're not here for the moment), which won the coveted Italian Drama Institute prize for 1991, had another successful production at the Piccolo Teatro in Milan this year. Just one of a wealth of new Italian plays.

DELLA COULING

Japan

East met West during the 1991 Japan festival

The genius of the Japanese theatre rests in the fact that it had centuries to develop its acting traditions in undisturbed isolation, but when it did finally open to the outside world, it was able to learn from western techniques, make them its own and often go one better. As the Japan Festival 1991 showed, the Japanese can also lay on impressive versions of Shakespeare and Lloyd Webber as well as fine home-grown plays in the Brechtian vein.

Much of the excitement in contemporary productions springs from the tension between tradition and change. Every Japanese director lives and works in the shadow of an awesome theatrical heritage that includes Kabuki, Bunraku and Noh. Some directors draw their inspiration from it, but most rebel against it.

At the same time, Kabuki is often accused of being a museum piece though it is the brilliance of flamboyant star actors like Ennosuke Ichikawa III and Bando Tamasaburo (who dazzled London audiences at the National Theatre in the Japan Festival 1991) which keeps it very much alive. Similarly the consummate art of actors like Hideo Kanze and Makio Umewaka make Noh theatre a journey into the past that is well worth taking.

Much harder to keep alive is the contemporary theatre. It struggles on without the kind of subsidy British companies are used to, heavily reliant on market forces and the dedication of its artists, most of whom have day jobs to support themselves.

There is a sharp conflict between the older generation of directors such as Koichi Kimura and Yukio Ninagawa, who are concerned with developing high quality serious theatre, and the younger generation, such as Hideki Noda and Shoji Kokami, who seem to derive their inspiration from television, disco dancing and the junk culture that envelops the affluent young. But the past year has seen the evaporation of much of this energy from the younger groups. As Ninagawa's producer Tadao Nakane commented, "The younger generation never had enough power to attack the older generation so they played at being children and refused to grow up. But now many of them are well into their thirties and it's ridiculous to pretend they're still children. Besides, since the fall of the Berlin Wall the world has become much more serious".

Significantly, Hideki Noda, aged thirty-seven, one of the young generation's most influential directors, announced his intention to fold up his company, Yume no Yumin-sha in October and travel to London to study theatre.

Meanwhile the older directors seem increasingly torn between developing their ideals for a committed audience in Japan and being tempted abroad where their work is warmly acclaimed. No sooner had Ninagawa opened his production of Chekhov's "Three Sisters" in Toyko in October, than he was preparing to bring a revival of "The Tempest" to the Barbican Theatre in December.

Ironically this leaves the door open for even more foreign work to be seen in Japan. Indeed British musicals continue to dominate the commercial theatre, among them, "Miss Saigon" which has been running in Japan for over a year now.

But the most surprising trend is the revival of interest in Kabuki among very young people. A new breed of young Kabuki stars is breathing fresh life into the old museum piece and enjoying rock star status. There lies the secret of Kabuki's survival: it has always adapted to a changing world without ever losing its identity.

KENNETH REA

U.S.A.

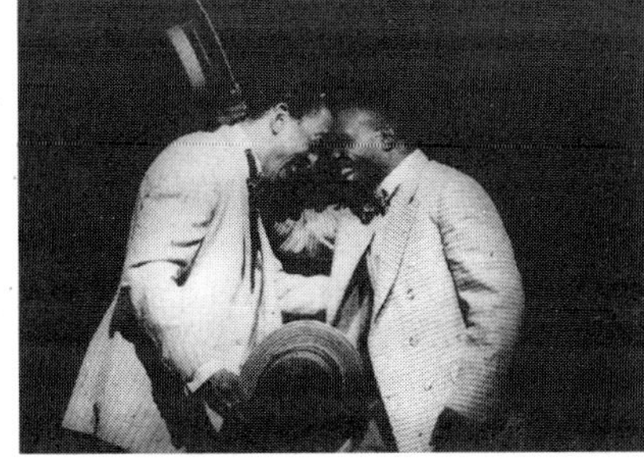

Jelly's Last Jam

It was the year that "Angels in America" came home. Tony Kushner's ambitious, politically-charged, seven-hour "Gay Fantasia on National Themes", sporting the shiny badge of its runaway-hit status in London, opened in November in Los Angeles's Mark Taper Forum in an atmosphere of feverish anticipation. Why did so much seem to hinge on the home-turf success of Kushner's epic? Perhaps because, as serious writing for the American stage grows ever more constricted in its scope and aspirations, the thirty-six-year-old playwright's committed posture and unabashedly grandiose vision suddenly seemed the elixir that might revitalize the nation's theatrical corpus.

No such tonic was forthcoming from Broadway, where Hollywood star power (Close, Hackman and Dreyfus in Ariel Dorfman's "Death and the Maiden", Alda in Neil Simon's "Jake's Women") and a $3.16 average increase in the price of a ticket sent box-office grosses to all-time highs. Despite the pre-Tony surge that lit twenty-one marquees with new productions in the spring, by September only a lonely pair of non-musicals "Dancing at Lughnasa" and Herb Gardner's conventional but insightgful "Conversations with My Father" were holding on. That meant that "Two Trains Running", the latest entry in August Wilson's cycle of plays about the lives of black Americans, had a preternaturally short run despite Frank Rich's critical embrace, and that John Guare's "Four Baboons Adoring the Sun" at Lincoln Center met an even quicker end. Playgoers in search of ideas on Broadway were more likely to discover them set to music, in George C Wolfe's brave and complex bio-musical about jazz pianist Jelly Roll Morton, "Jelly's Last Jam"; and William Finn's AIDS-decade amalgam "Falsettos". The arrival of two nonprofit producers new to Broadway – the Roundabout Theatre Company, which moved to a Times Square address, and Tony Randall's critically skewered National Actors Theatre – pointed up the growing independence of US commerical and nonprofit undertakings.

A bumptious presidential campaign raised some theatrical eyebrows - four regional companies unearthed the 1931 Gershwin slapstick musical satire "Of Thee I Sing" around election time - and the AIDS crisis continued to merit compassionate attention in Paula Vogel's elegant and funny memory play "The Baltimore Waltz", one of the season's most-produced works. Tensions between women and men seem to be occupying major playwrights David Mamet (whose "Oleanna" takes an iconoclastic view of sexual harassment) and Wendy Wasserstein (who casts a seriocomic eye on the lives of three siblings in "The Sisters Rosenweig"). Of the nation's leading experimental ensembles, the commedia-trained Theatre de la Jeune Lune set about filling its new 6,000 square-foot performance space in Minneapolis with "Children of Paradise", a spectacle based on the famous French film; and the Manhattan-based Wooster Group undertook the potentially controversial deconstruction of O'Neill's "The Emperor Jones". But it may have been visitors to America that made the year's strongest impact. A sellout international festival of puppet theatre at New York's Joseph Papp Public Theatre, extravagantly funded by the Jim Henson Foundation, opened the eyes of startled audiences and performers to the form's untapped possibilities. South African playwright Athol Fugard took up residence in Atlanta for a sixtieth-birthday festival of his work, including the joint La Jolia Playhouse-Alliance Theatre debut of his new two-hander "Playland". And Theatre du Soleil of France spun out its acclaimed environmental saga of the House of Atreus, "Les Atrides", in a cavernous armory in Brooklyn. Angels come in many forms.

JIM O'QUINN

The Former Eastern Bloc

Vaclav Havel, the playwright turned politician whose work is now rarely performed

In the beginning, euphoria reigned. In all the eastern European socialist countries those involved in theatre had played a considerable part in the "change", "velvet revolution" or overthrow. Afterwards, everything seemed possible: putting on plays that had been prohibited for decades, catching up on what had until then been proscribed (the theatre of the absurd in the GDR, for example), public discussion of social grievances. But - lo and behold - things turned out differently.

It is of course extremely difficult to sum up the theatre situation of the individual countries in one short article and I am forced to resort to some generalized assessments, nevertheless the problems arising in the former eastern block states are proving similar in many respects. Before 1989 it was mainly the intellectuals from the arts world who voiced criticism of the system (often in a way only comprehensible to the initiated). This criticism was conveyed indirectly - via association, simile, metaphor and symbol, in parables and historical plays, but above all via the master works of world literature. And audiences picked up these messages and information, otherwise denied them in the media, readily and with great sensitivity. But once newspapers, radio and television were able to report on political changes in an unvarnished and realistic way, the theatre lost its former compensatory function. Interest in political theatre just died from one moment to the next. And plays that had been lying for years at the back of the drawer because they criticised too openly the social reality of "real socialism", proved in most cases artistically inadequate and overtaken anyway by the new social situation. But often - surprisingly - the playwrights had nothing at all in the drawer.

There are many different reasons for the identity crisis in the theatre in Eastern Europe, and the economic crisis is aggravating this situation. Censorship and ideological dictatorship have disappeared, but now the market is making its own demands - without quarter. As the Hungarian writer György Spiró observed bitterly: "Of course the laws of the market place apply to culture too - but surely not at the level of the potato stall".

The wretched economic situation in all the former socialist countries frequently leads theatres to kow-tow to the public. A lot of West-End type plays of tawdry standard are being presented, (For example, in the Russian Ekaterinenburg the former artistically renowned Academic Drama Theatre is fading fast, degenerating into a French Drama and Comedy Theatre: in one season alone eight French comedies were put on). The gulf between those holding the purse-strings and making decisions on the theatres - often "without the faintest idea" of culture and art, as Gábor Zsámbeki, director of the Katona Jószef Theatre in Budapest, laments - and the theatres themselves, is enormous. For it is no longer artistic quality that counts here, merely financial profit. State-subsidizing of the theatres has decreased in nearly every country. The result: ticket prices have shot up; and it is precisely the young intellectual audiences who are missing out. In Poland hardly any theatres are subsidized at all by the state any more; even the world-famous Stary Theatre with director Andrej Wajda is threatened with closure; some theatres have already had to close. In the former Soviet Union, once hugely popular houses, playing constantly to packed houses, such as Yuri Lyubimov's Taganka, or Oleg Yefremov's Moscow Arts Theatre, are struggling.

Contemporary authors largely remain silent. A gifted writer like György Spiró has given up writing for the time being and is now Artistic Director of the theatre in the Hungarian provincial city of Szolnok. No sign of life from once productive and widely performed playwrights such as Alexander Gelman, Victor Rosov or Mikhail Schatrov, often too, because the problems are too close to home, it is too difficult to write about them with enough detachment or objectivity. The plays of István Eörsi or Vaclav Havel, which were on the programme of many theatres immediately following 1989, now rarely turn up on the repertoire. But the public is not even showing much interest in plays attacking present realities, for example the Austrian Peter Turrini's "Der Minderleister" (The under-achiever). People don't want to see their social predicaments reflected on the stage, preferring the distractions of light entertainment or world classics.

Contradictions emerge: while in Prague the director Otomar Krejca, who had been driven into exile in 1968, is struggling hard to make artistic sense out of a brutal epoch which has now ended, in Romania - in spite of the extremely stressful financial situation - the returned exiled directors Liviu Ciulei and Lucian Pintilei are celebrating real triumphs.

But in every country - mainly because of the complex economic state of affairs - the situation is precarious, although there are differences. For example, in Czechoslovakia the alternative theatres (such as the "Shoestring Theatre" in Brno under Peter Scherhaufer or the Prague "Studio Ypsilon" under Jan Schmid) are being taken up by the public, while the big state theatres are not receiving much attention at all. In general in Czechoslovakia there is a lot of interest for innovative, improvisatory theatre. In contrast, in Hungary the public seem to greatly prefer the artistically highly qualified, state subsidized theatres such as the Budapest Katona Jószef Theatre and the provincial theatre in Kaposvár. Other theatres are on their last legs.

In Bulgaria only a few artistic productions of exceptional quality attract an audience - for example, the productions of the highly gifted director Leon Daniel - although it is in Bulgaria that theatre tickets are still relatively cheap. What is striking is that in this country too, important authors, such as Jordan Raditschkov remain silent; it is mainly small-scale productions that have a chance of being put on, such as the two-handers of Konstantin Iliev ("Nirvana" or "Red Wine for Farewells", in both of which pairs of lovers come to grief through the present political conditions in Bulgaria).

In the former GDR too, economic and consequently existential uncertainty prevails. In all probability, in the coming years several houses will close. Imported artistic directors from West Germany, ignorant of past times and experiences, have created a climate of insecurity. Dismissals of artistic personnel are often the result, but are sometimes too a necessary consequence, due to the new and complicated situation.

The most significant artistic achievements are still to be seen in the renowned Deutsches Theater under Thomas Langhoff and in the small but artistically very flexible Maxim Gorki theatre in Berlin. That is no coincidence: in these two houses the new age has been welcomed as a challenge and correspondingly reflected in artistic practice.

INGEBORG PIETZSCH

THE MEDIA

While delighting in and encouraging the unique experience of live performance, the Yearbook recognizes the importance of film, TV and radio in the theatre world. NICK JAMES begins the Yearbook's coverage of the media with his view of the year's films and MALCOLM HAY makes his choice of television and radio plays.

Films '92

The ever-advertised decline of the British film industry reached a new low this year with two productions – "Leon the Pig Farmer", a comedy starring Janet Suzman, Connie Booth and Brian Glover about a nice Jewish boy who discovers he may not after all be semitic, and "The Mystery of Edwin Drood", an adaptation of the Dickens ghost story starring Robert Powell – both having to rely on cast and crew working almost for thin air in order to be made. Happily, "Leon the Pig Farmer" went on to win the critics' prize at the Venice Film Festival, making up for the failure of Sally Potter's adaptation of Virginia Woolf's "Orlando" (starring Tilda Swinton) to win anything potlike.

Other British triumphs this year included Anthony Hopkins' Best Actor Oscar for "The Silence of the Lambs", and a special prize at Cannes for his follow up film, the Merchant Ivory adaptation of EM Forster's "Howards End". The latter was outstanding enough to overcome the kind of built-in critical prejudice against costume drama which ironically scuppered the chances of Britain's other Cannes entry, Terence Davies' evocation of his Liverpool childhood, "The Long Day Closes".

Christine Edzard, whose previous films "Little Dorrit" and "The Fool" had been tailored to the Merchant Ivory Eng Lit formula, moved away from costume drama to direct a modern dress adaptation of Shakespeare's "As You Like It" – one of few directly adapted plays released this year. By unflattering coincidence, it was released at the same time as the newly restored reissue of Orson Welles' "Othello", the 1959 expressionist masterpiece whose troubled production was so vividly etched in Iago Michael MacLiammoir's acid memoir "Put Money In Thy Purse".

The most popular play adaptation however was undoubtedly Australian Baz Luhrmann's enthralling exploration of the besequined world of suburban dance, "Strictly Ballroom", and it was nostalgia for pre-rock 'n' roll leisure pursuits that also helped the unlooked for success of Peter Chelsom's spry fable about the search for ageing tenor Joseph Locke, "Hear My Song"; which starred Adrian Dunbar and ubiquitous newcomer Tara Fitzgerald. Meanwhile, Kenneth Branagh continued to wow the Americans, following up his bizarre Hitchcockian thriller "Dead Again", with a very British comedy-drama, "Peter's Friends" starring Branagh's friends and thematically very similar to the '80s US drama "The Big Chill".

The year's disappointments must include Peter Kosminsky's outdoor pursuits remake of "Wuthering Heights", along with all the movies that have "Columbus" connections, and it took American director Michael Mann (with the help of Daniel Day Lewis and Stephen Waddington) to show us how to make musket and breeches films of epic proportions with "The Last of the Mohicans". However, if asked to name my British movie of the year, Neil Jordan's tender film "The Crying Game" starring Stephen Rea, Miranda Richardson and newcomer Jaye Davidson – just edges Terry Davies' elegy out of the frame.

The Crying Game

Forest Whittacker and Stephen Rea

IRA volunteer Jude (Miranda Richardson) lures Black British trooper Jody (Forest Whittacker) into a trap at a fairground in the North. Behooded and held hostage for an exchange that he's wise enough to know will never happen, Jody befriends a sympathetic voice who he learns is called Feargus (Stephen Rea), asking if the gunman will look up Jody's girl Dil (Jaye Davidson) for him after he's been executed. After Jody is killed in the confusion of an army raid, the guilt ridden Feargus disappears to London and indeed begins an affair with Dil. But she is not what she seems, and the IRA are hot on Feargus' tail. Director Neil Jordan here returns to "Mona Lisa" form with a complex, and moving film about political and sexual identity, and the meaning of betrayal in a world of crumbling values and certainties. With finely tuned performances from Rea and newcomer Davidson.

Noises Off

Carol Burnettt, Michael Caine, Mark Linn-Baker and John Ritter

In bringing Michael Frayn's classic play-within-a-play to the cinema screen, controversial American director Peter Bogdanovitch ("The Last Picture Show", "Nickelodeon") wisely elects to stick as closely as possible to the play's dramatic context, avoiding tricksy camera stunts. A strong international cast in hand, he manages both the on-stage farce and offstage shenanigans with appropriate fizz. Michael Caine is suitably insouciant as Lloyd Fellowes, the cravat-wearing director of "Nothing On" who is simultaneously entangled with Julie Hagerty's ASM, Poppy Taylor, and Nicollette Sheridan's wide-eyed innocent, Brooke Ashton. Carol Burnett makes the fraught star Dotty Otley a sympathetic luvvie monster, forever spatting with her young lover Garry Lejeune (John Ritter). With the late Denholm Elliot resisting temptation to do his usual seedy, sardonic turn with the alcoholic has-been Selsdon Mowbray, Bogdanovitch's film comes close enough to replication to make the tacked-on smash hit happy ending almost forgivable.

Glengarry Glen Ross

Al Pacino and Alan Arkin

With David Mamet himself scripting, and such a heavyweight and bankable cast at his disposal, one might have forgiven director James Foley (best known for his work in rock video) if he had shown signs of being overawed. His confidence abounds however, and he brings an imagist's enhancement to Mamet's arena of terse masculine conflict. A crooked real estate company puts its four salesmen on the line – first prize, a Cadillac; second, a set of steak knives; third, the elbow. When the office is burgled and records of potential customers disappear, what looks like a comfortable situation for hot-shot Ricky Roma (Al Pacino), is a desperate one for old timer Shelley Levine (Jack Lemmon). Lemmon's portrait of despair won him the best actor prize at the Venice film festival.

Howards End

Emma Thompson and Vanessa Redgrave

There's a real sense that an entire variety of film making – period costume drama cruelly characterised by critics as the film equivalent of Marx and Spencer foodstuffs – redeems itself in this, the finest film version of an EM Forster novel yet made. It's not that any concessions have been made to Hollywood, it's more that this time James Ivory's craft coalesces perfectly with the understated performances, so that the texture remains filmic rather than taking on the set-bound statis of so many Merchant Ivory films. But then, this is Forster's finest novel, with an acute sense of Edwardian social disintegration that requires no touristic Italian contrast to bring it off. The cast includes Anthony Hopkins, Sam West and Vanessa Redgrave.

Peter's Friends

Given the matey cast and Branagh's reputation for smuggery, the prospect of a film about an Oxbridge University singing troupe's ten-year-on reunion could not have been more unappetising. All power to Ken and pals then that they not only manage to banish such prejudices, but produce a sharp and witty film (scripted by Rita Rudner). Aristocrat Peter (Stephen Fry) gathers all the gang together for a weekend – Hollywood emigre Andrew (Branagh) and his apalling soap star wife Carol (Rudner), boring couple Roger (Hugh Laurie) and Mary (Imelda Staunton) whose marriage is rocky, batty brick Maggie (Emma Thompson), and sexy but diffident Sarah (Alphonsia Emmanuel) with her current beau Brian (Tony Slattery). Together they disentangle past relations through tears, laughter and sex before Peter reveals the real reason for the get-together.

Television Drama '92

The major television drama event of the year was an extensive retrospective on BBC 2 of the work of Alan Bennett. No other playwright can rival his ability to show how bitterly people regret their missed opportunities in life, or to reveal a whole world of possibilities barely glimpsed, rarely grasped, lost through fear of change or sheer force of circumstance. Bennett's plays are about quiet, ordinary lives but they are rich in meaning.

Even the best new plays and screenplays of 1992 failed to measure up to this exacting standard. Bennett himself, in the course of introducing a selection of some of his favourite programmes from the archives, looked back with open nostalgia to the days when our TV drama was the envy of the world: "Now the death wind of accountancy, which has done so much to revivify British industry, has done the same for television drama which is leaner, more competitive – and on its last legs." Many cash-starved drama producers would doubtless say "amen" to Bennett's caustic analysis of the situation. Yet new plays – or, more often, new serials or series – continue to be made. As the following entries indicate, there is a lot of talent within the industry. But writing talent needs careful nurturing and more needs to be done to support and encourage the TV dramatists of the future.

Red Nose Of Courage

Presented by the Comic Strip and performed by a hugely talented cast which included Alexei Sayle, Dawn French and Adrian Edmondson, "Red Nose Of Courage" (BBC2) told the story of John Major's rise to power. Sayle played Major's dad, head of the travelling circus into which John was born; Edmondson turned in a delightful performance as the budding politician struggling to combine his night-time duties as Coco the Clown with a career at Westminster; French was suitably dynamic in her role as Glynis Kinnock, leader of the Labour opposition in the House, implacable in her dislike of Major but hopelessly in love with a certain circus clown. An excellent script by Peter Richardson effortlessly mixed biting satire with a curiously gentle treatment of their passionate but ill-fated affair. The overall message, though lightly expressed, was inescapable. As the truth about Major's double life was about to be revealed, the Speaker of the House of Commons asked with indignation: "Are you suggesting that a top British politician is a clown ?"

Alexei Sayle

Natural Lies

Denis Lawson and Bob Peck

David Pirie's three-part thriller on BBC1 deftly wove together a doom-laden ecological theme and a plot worthy of Hitchcock at his best. The storyline was concerned with a conspiracy to suppress information that a BSE-like virus had entered the food chain from infected cattle. Bob Peck was ideally cast as an advertising executive possessed with a conscience. His relentless pursuit of the truth led him to being framed for the murder of a young woman and a climactic showdown with his best friend, the flash editor of a national newspaper, at the Grand Hotel in Brighton. Other dramatic set-pieces included a scene where Peck's wife was chased around a country cottage by a psychopath with a shotgun and a long sequence where Peck laboured to move the young woman's corpse from his living-room rug to the boot of his car without arousing the curiosity of his mother-in-law who had dropped in to enquire about his state of mind. Idle to pretend that every step in the narrative was wholly convincing. No matter: this was a fast-paced and totally absorbing serial, full of atmosphere and intelligent in its treatment of human relationships.

An Ungentlemanly Act

Bob Peck and Ian Richardson

Bob Peck once again – this time as Major Mike Norman, the Royal Marine Officer in command of the garrison on the Falkland Islands at the time of the Argentinian invasion. Writer/director Stuart Urban ruffled many feathers with his film for BBC2 which treated the first thirty-six hours of the Falklands conflict as a latter-day Ealing Comedy. That's to say he refused to indulge in any mock heroics. Ian Richardson was admirably cool and unflappable as Sir Rex Hunt, the Governor, faced with impossible odds and certain defeat but frustrated most of the time by the inefficiency of the Foreign Office. This was an ambitious project on a subject still loaded with political and national significance. It is to Urban's credit that he succeeded in balancing a sense of the momentous nature of the events with a keen sense of humour. The only real failing was its length. At two hours and a half the film seemed unnecessarily protracted.

The Reconstructed Heart

Robert Llewellyn

Robert Llewellyn's comic disquisition on changes in male behaviour over the last two decades (on Channel 4) made frequent use of graphs and diagrams to explore the concept of the Reconstructed Man, a wholly sensitive and deeply considerate male forever seeking to build more honest and less exploitive relationships with members of the opposite sex. Llewellyn himself delivered this spoof lecture in the guise of a psycho-sexual consultant committed to the idea that reconstruction could only be achieved when modern man accepted his share of the blame for 5000 years of patriachal oppression – though without allowing himself to wallow in guilt. We were told that the main obstacle to reconstruction was the male's tendency to deal with uncomfortable emotions by taking refuge in fishing trips, model railways and bouts of violence. Llewellyn's tongue-in-cheek acting style and the sly humour in the writing made this short solo piece one of the most intelligent comic programmes on television in the course of the year. The most revealing graph showed the amount of wine that a woman has to drink before she decides that all men are out-and-out bastards.

Root Into Europe

Pat Heywood and George Cole

William Donaldson, creator of the best-selling book "The Henry Root Letters", co-wrote this splendidly funny five-part series (Central TV) together with its director Mark Chapman. George Cole, of "Minder" fame, was the awful Henry Root, true-blue British patriot, late middle-aged chauvinist, and conceiver of an audacious plan to undertake a "fact-finding mission" on the Continent before our country became engulfed by the European Community and foreign culture. His aggressive modern-day equivalent of the Grand Tour threw up any number of hilarious situations. Root's patronising attitudes and inability to tolerate any form of unfamiliar behaviour were the mainspring of the humour but Patricia Heywood, as his long-suffering wife, contributed enormously to the comic effects by providing a steady thread of cool-headedness and common sense. Despite Root's dogmatic blustering, his often silent spouse was all too clearly the senior partner in a fascinating double act.

Bye Bye Columbus

Playwright Peter Barnes made a characteristically quirky and irreverent contribution to the large batch of programmes commemorating Columbus' journey to the New World with this studio-based drama for BBC2. It was filmed in just four days and directed by Barnes himself. The famous explorer was depicted as a bitter neurotic looking back over his life in conversation with his parrot. A star-studded cast featured Daniel Massey as Columbus (an incompetent "who couldn't sail a boat in a bathtub"), Harriet Walter as "the Castilian windbag" Queen Isabella, Simon Callow in a cameo part as the chief map-maker in Spain, and Jack Shepherd as the voice of the parrot. Barnes boldly declared the style of this production with an opening scene where the ceremony claiming the newly discovered land for Spain broke up in confusion as Columbus' crew scrambled off to sit bare-arsed in a row and discharge their diarrhoea-ridden bowels. That was only the beginning. The play got wilder still as it went along.

Daniel Massey

The Lost Language of Cranes

The difficulty faced by some homosexuals in "coming out" was the main theme of this film (for "Screenplay" on BBC2), written by Sean Mathias and based loosely on a novel by David Leavett. Angus McFadyen played a young man in his early twenties who was faced with the problem of telling his parents that he was gay. His father (Brian Cox), a university lecturer, struggled with the much greater problem of acknowledging to himself, and then to his wife (Eileen Atkins), that he had a sexual preference for men. This was a highly charged and ruthlessly honest account of the emotional consequences. Three finely judged performances enabled the viewer to make connections with equivalent situations: the characters showed a remarkable determination, despite their anguish, to talk through their responses. Director Nigel Finch made intelligent use of a number of London locations. The scenes of homosexual love, filmed without any sense of coyness, registered feelings of great tenderness to the point of becoming positively erotic.

Angus MacFadyen (front), Eileen Atkins and Brian Cox

Man To Man

Tilda Swinton

In this BBC2 "Screenplay" Tilda Swinton re-created her stunning stage performance as a young, working-class German widow who assumes her dead husband's identity during the 1920s, purely in order to survive, and then lives and works as a man for a period of forty years. She endures Hitler's Germany and the Second World War. She survives on her wits and her ability to convince other people that she's a man. But she ends up an embittered old woman, swilling beer and railing against the work-shy dossers outside her front door. Manfred Karge's one-woman play was transferred to television with great inventiveness by director John Maybury. He successfully combined actual newsreel footage and expressionist effects while maintaining a steady focus on Swinton's character and her amazing physical transformations. This was a compelling portrayal of an admirable though not wholly sympathetic individual whose resourcefulness provoked admiration, since one realised that traditional morality had little to offer her as she faced the man-made horrors of a society which had abandoned any form of caring.

Bad Girl

Jane Horrocks

Guy Hibbert's tough but humane study of a young single mother, locked in a never-ending struggle with the Social Services to regain custody of her child, rightly drew from many critics favourable comparisons with "Cathy Come Home", that classic drama-documentary from the distant past. The overall message was clear: here was an individual intent on living her own life without continually being told by others how she should behave. But Hibbert was careful to ensure this was no one-sided account of freedom against authority – the woman's rebellious attitudes meant that she often appeared to be her own worst enemy. Jane Horrocks made herself a front runner for every TV acting award on offer with her finely judged portrayal of a woman whose resourcefulness and determination made you want, at one and the same moment, to weep and cheer.

The Treaty

Ian Bannen

Brian Phelan's play (produced by Thames for ITV) showed that some television blockbusters can treat the viewer as intelligent human beings. It marked the seventieth anniversary of the treaty inaugurating the Irish Free State and dealt with the discussions, wranglings, in-fighting, plotting and counter-plotting on each and every side of the many political divides. No doubt historians could quibble over some of the finer points of Phelan's interpretation of the events. But this prime-time drama exerted a strong hold on the attention and at the same time offered illuminating insights into the historical context of the current situation in Northern Ireland. Ian Bannen gave a wily performance as "Welsh wizard" and British PM Lloyd George. Brendan Gleason as Michael Collins (pugnacious leader of the Irish Republican Brotherhood, more gunman than politician) and Barry McGovern as Eamon de Valera headed an excellent supporting cast.

Anglo-Saxon Attitudes

Richard Johnson

Adapter par excellence Andrew Davies took the well known novel by Sir Angus Wilson and, with the help of any number of superb directorial touches from Diarmuid Lawrence, fashioned it into an absorbing three-part serial (Thames for ITV). The complex narrative involved much use of flashbacks as the action switched backwards and forwards across a large span of time from 1912 to the 1950s. But the firmly drawn central characters and the powerful ebb and flow of their relationships came across with great clarity. Part family saga and part detective story, part comedy of manners but most of all the story of an old man's quest for the truth and passion he'd been hiding from, this magnificently executed Euston Films production contained a string of riveting performances – most notably from Richard Johnson as the troubled historian making sense of his own past and from Elizabeth Spriggs as his extravagantly sentimental Danish wife.

Radio Drama '92

It was not a good year for radio drama. There were a number of interesting new plays. There was also a new production of "Hamlet" featuring Kenneth Branagh. Otherwise the best that can be said is that producers in the BBC Radio Drama Departments in London and the regions maintained the standard of excellence that we've long come to expect from them. The bad news came halfway through the year when plans for a revamped Radio 3 were unveiled. Nicholas Kenyon, controller of the network, claimed that the redefining of Radio 3 as "Music Plus" was a response to the growing audience for classical music and opera. More cynical souls felt that it might be in part a reaction to the threat from Classic FM. The effect of "Music Plus" was to reduce Radio 3's drama output.

"Drama Now" disappeared from the Tuesday night schedules and instead alternated on Sundays with seasons of "The Sunday Play". The sense of loss was palpable. It was not remedied by any increase in the programming of drama on Radio 4. All this at a time when Geoffrey Strachan, publisher at Methuen London, felt moved to declare: "Radio drama is a quite extraordinary medium: it can be very private and very public. But its special contribution to the cultural life of our society and of our world has never been more needed than now."

Hamlet

Kenneth Branagh and Glyn Dearman co-directed this fascinating new production of the world's most famous play. It was presented by the Renaissance Theatre Company in association with BBC Radio Drama and released on audio cassette and CD. The basic approach was to treat the story as a taut psychological thriller: Branagh, as the Prince of Denmark, showed us an impressionable young man, clearly suffering a degree of inner turmoil but mainly bent on taking some form of action to relieve the situation. This straightforward and uncomplicated reading went hand in hand with a considerable emphasis on pace. Although this was an uncut version of the play, the co-directors maintained a strong feeling of tension throughout. They also conveyed a vivid sense of the settings: the intrigue-ridden court, the graveyard, and every nook and cranny – or so it seemed – of the castle. John Gielgud's Ghost and Richard Briers' Polonius stood out head and shoulders amongst a host of fine performances from a cast including Judi Dench (Gertrude), Derek Jacobi (Claudius), Michael Hordern (the Player King) and Michael Elphick (First Gravedigger).

Napoli Milionaria

The Royal National Theatre production of Eduardo De Filippo's play, written in 1945, was transferred to Radio 3 by Chris Barton and sounded a lot more interesting and enjoyable than some critics of the original production on the South Bank would have led us to believe. Peter Tinniswood's new version of the play converted the Neapolitan dialect into Scouse. The effect was to create a kind of Naples on the Mersey. Ian McKellen and Frances Barber turned in immaculate performances as the shambolic but virtuous nominal head of the household and his hard-as-nails profiteering wife. There is no escaping the fact that De Filippo serves up an impossibly sentimental ending. But his thoughtful and humane account of the death of a family corrupted by the war for the most part switches deftly between seriousness and comedy. Even on radio the scene where the father has to impersonate a corpse was riotously funny.

The Way We Are Now

Radio drama exists in an infinite variety of forms. Susan Sontag's strikingly effective piece, adapted for radio by Valerie Seigel and broadcast on Radio 3, was in no way a conventional play but instead a collage of voices lasting less than half an hour. A group of New Yorkers expressed their emotions as they were faced with the impending death of a close friend from AIDS. Their thoughts and comments combined to pose a series of questions: when did their friend first know that he had contracted the illness ? Should one arrive at the hospital with chocolates or flowers ? What do you say to someone in that situation ? How should one respond to his curious detachment from what's happening ? Do the doctors really know what they're doing ? Are any of us likely to end up in the same position ? Can one learn how to die ? All this and a lot more besides. The production by Michael Fox was undemonstrative, quiet and contained, wholly admirable. This will surely become a classic of its kind.

Caves of Steel

Isaac Asimov's classic science fiction story, dramatised for radio by Bert Coules, afforded a kind of childlike knee-hugging pleasure that could only be compared with listening to old radio serials like "Dick Barton" or "Journey Into Space". This fast-moving detective thriller, set in New York in the distant future and involving a murder which threatened to cause the destruction of the planet, had all the virtues of a novel by Raymond Chandler. The futuristic setting was admirably created by director Matthew Walters who also showed great skill in handling action scenes (always a problem on radio). It would be idle to pretend that this play held any great significance in terms of the ideas. But it was a timely reminder of the delight that comes from listening to a rattling yarn. That's a rare commodity in any form of drama nowadays.

Unmade Movies II

Imagine a meeting between T.S. Eliot and Groucho Marx. The Brothers have decided they need to make one more movie and Groucho recognises they're too old to chase women and throw themselves around. This time they need some really classy lines. So who better for them to approach than the world's best known poet? Eliot leaps at the opportunity: "Groucho, Chico, Harpo – and Tommo", he muses. David Stafford's inventive comic play (Radio 3), subtitled "A Night at the Wasteland", offered Michael Roberts and Frank Lazurus (Groucho and Chico) a heaven-sent chance to mimic the patterns of the old Marx Brothers routines. Kerry Shale was impressive as the pompous and self-regarding man of letters. Harpo's persistent honkings disrupted Eliot's erudite explanation of his intentions with the screenplay. We heard enough to know that Groucho would play a mangy lover called J. Alfred Prufrock and Harpo's eventual fate was to be crucified on an anthill.

BOOKS

There have been many fascinating books about the theatre this year. "Plays & Players" magazine reviews theatre books as they arrive on the shelves month by month. MAX FINDLAY provides a resumé of some of the reviews which have appeared in 1992.

The Theatre of Steven Berkoff

Methuen Drama (£20)

This is a stunning array of photographs of Berkoff productions in an oddly organised volume matched with an uninspiring text. The pictures - by photographers such as John Haynes, Martha Swope and Nobby Clark - encapsulate the raw physicality of the man's work but too often the accompanying descriptions tumble into the mundane. The group photograph of "East", for example, is thrillingly entitled "Barry Philips, Matthew Scurfield, David Delve, Anna Nygh and Me". The theatrical hell-raiser of "East" and "Greek" depressingly metamorphoses into the family snapshot caption writer. This book is more radical cheek than chic and does little justice to Berkoff's own plays.

The Methuen Book of Shakespeare Anecdotes

Compiled/Edited by Ralph Berry, Methuen Drama (£15.99)

Given a large enough slice of theatrical history and a famous enough cast of characters, it isn't what you tell about them but how you tell it. Despite certain minor eccentricities (Why didn't Mr Berry talk to some actors ?), this book has some very funny stories. In particular, the anonymous actor playing Othello who, realising that Iago always got the best notices (however appalling his performance), hired the best Othello he could and played Iago himself. For people who like stories such as Alec Guinness reading his bad notices to a second night audience and Kenneth Branagh asking Prince Charles how to play Henry V, this is the sort of book they will like.

Shakespeare Comes to Broadmoor

Edited by Dr Murray Cox, Jessica Kingsley Publishers (£12.95 paperback/£25 hardback)

This important book looks at the impact on actors and audience of a series of Shakespearean tragedies performed at Broadmoor in front of patients and medical staff between 1989 and 1991. The plays included Deborah Warner's "King Lear" for the National Theatre and the RSC's "Hamlet". Performed in the round, with the audience much closer to the actors than usual, and followed up with workshop sessions, the actors were compelled to re-evaluate the plays, what they as performers were trying to achieve and their own prejudices about the mentally ill. The details of this interaction are sensitively edited by Murray Cox into a compelling publication.

The Presence of the Actor

Joseph Chaikin, Theatre Communications Group (£7.99)

First published twenty years ago, this collection of notes is an absorbing account of Chaikin's exploration (as actor, director and producer) of all aspects of theatrical experience. He himself describes the book as "notes from several layers of myself" and his central concern is the individual discovering the splinter of truth within him or herself. This is encapsulated in his advice on acting: "Don't sing your voice. Find and sing the song." He is plainly a man who welcomes change, who is prepared to admit that he is wrong and who creates afresh from an understanding of his own (and his colleagues') deficiencies and failings.

Not in Front of the Audience: Homosexuality on Stage

Nicholas de Jongh, Routledge (£10.99)

Critic de Jongh's central thesis is that we have virtually come full circle from the starting point of homosexuality as sin to the present day belief of gay man as the carrier of the AIDS plague. Although there is a US survey of the subject entitled "We Can Always Call Them Bulgarians", this is the first UK appraisal and de Jongh has had the benefit of being the first outsider to see the Lord Chamberlain's confidential files. Even after the relaxation of censorship on homosexuality in 1958, the topic remained under theatrical wraps until John Osborne's "A Patriot For Me" in 1965. It is a well researched book.

Noel Coward

Clive Fisher, Weidenfeld and Nicholson (£17.99)

This book adds little that is new and deals with Coward's plays without reference to actual performances. It does, however, boast a strong line in accompanying publishing hype to the effect that it is the first biography to deal openly with the vexed question of its subject matter's homosexuality. Quite how a book would deal secretly with a subject everyone has known about for years is anyone's guess. The Coward estate apparently refused Fisher permission to quote from the great man's works. This is a pity. Coward's plays were often thin on plot or even witty dialogue but a literary minute steak would have been better than literary gruel.

Theatre Criticism

Irving Wardle, Routledge (£25 hardback/£7.99 paperback)

Wardle believes that the theatre critic is a messenger in possession of an exceptional treasure which must be conveyed to the readers. He is sharply critical of the indolent reviewer who unthinkingly follows fashionable opinion or simply shows off. He reappraises some of his own work, particularly his response to the baby-stoning scene in Bond's "Saved" which distorted his judgment of the play itself. It is an analytical and informative investigation of the art of criticism which is certain of the reviewer's importance, whether he or she is merely a tipster or (as in the case of Hazlitt's account of Kean's Richard III or Tynan's descriptions of Olivier's performances) a historian.

AN ACTOR'S LIFE

The Yearbook looks at the realities of life in the acting profession. CHRISTOPHER WEBBER interviews three actors at varying stages in their career; he then analyses the role of agents and computers, compares rates of pay and reports on Equity. GINA LANDOR choses eleven drama schools which are worth a second look.

Jane Asher

Jane Asher has been an actress since she was five. Forty years on, a glance at her credits reveals a happy balance between film, TV and theatre work - and impressive success in all three. There's no grand strategy behind this: "I don't believe you can plan a career. I've simply done what seemed right for me at the time. The only real rule I've followed has been to aim for quality".

Early on, it must have been tempting to ditch quality - and straight theatre - for the host of lucrative film offers promising to cash in on the fashionable appeal of the Asher "Ice Maiden". Her refusal to be pigeon-holed has led to some unwelcome press attention, but in retrospect she feels that living dangerously has made for a more satisfying career.

Perhaps this fear of falling into an easy casting line accounts for Jane's periodic changes of agent - though her tally of five is not unusual. "In some ways I envy Judi (Dench) for having had just the one. But once you've made your mark, an agent is really there to keep things ticking over, and for me a change is a good way of recharging the batteries". She has benefited in turn from the support that smaller personal managers can provide, and from the special ability of large, cosmopolitan agencies to offer financially tempting "packages" of star clients to producers. With wages on the slide in all areas ("I always seem to be on a "special low" at the BBC these days!") that's very important to an actress with substantial family and business commitments.

Those commitments have left little space for morbid thoughts during the inevitable breaks between jobs - "I've known business people understandably devastated when they're made redundant, yet it can happen to us five or six times a year". This positive attitude extends to people some actors may feel less than enthusiastic about - such as directors: "I need them. I'm intensely grateful for the help I've had over the years. For instance Michael Rudman, director of "Making it Better", opened my eyes to aspects of the piece which I'd never have seen by myself". Even the press are welcome: "I've learnt a lot from reviews, at least some of the critical ones, though nowadays I avoid reading them till late in the run!".

At root, acting is a craft: "Writers are the genuine creative people. Sometimes I feel that acting is really rather silly - which is why I admire actors like Michael Gambon who seem to take it all rather lightly. We can get so terribly serious - it is "play", after all". Her own delight in the work, and the recognition it has brought her, is evident: "I quite enjoy walking into a room and knowing they're not all thinking "Who on earth is she?". And it does take the pressure off you at that first read-through.".

Her advice to a young hopeful thinking of joining the business would be simple: "Don't". She's seen too many talents starved and disappointed to give false encouragement. Yet ironically enough, the actress so memorably touching as the robot in Ayckbourn's futuristic "Henceforward" points to one, faint gleam of light: "At least the microchip can't completely replace the performer - so perhaps there's hope for us yet!".

Mairead Carty

Shortly after Mairead Carty joined the RSC at Stratford she enjoyed a momentary thrill of achievement. But it wasn't when she trod those famous boards for the first time. "It was in the dressing-room loo. I found myself thinking, Helen Mirren's sat on this same seat!". The qualities of openness and humour that saw a relatively untried actress sail through the series of rigorous interviews before she joined the company in 1991 are plain to see.

Mairead was spotted by the RSC in an adaptation of "Adam Bede" at the Orange Tree in Richmond - not the first pub to feature in her life, as she was brought up by Irish parents in the lively atmosphere of the "Duke" on London's Portobello Road. She's been a sociable soul ever since ("I'm no wilting violet") and set her mind on an acting career as early as fourteen.

After school, she took a working sabbatical to get her own flat, before joining The Academy of Live and Recorded Arts at nineteen. She firmly believes that year off helped her get more out of her training. Whatever the cause, unlike most young hopefuls she's hardly stopped work since leaving college "One job has really led to another. I've been very lucky". Not that luck seems to enter into it so much as determination: she once plucked up the courage to gatecrash "A Winter's Tale" auditions for the Wolsey, Ipswich. She got the audition, and the part of Perdita.

So for one young actress at least, life as a small fish at the RSC didn't prove too daunting. Her first role was the important cameo of Philotis in "'Tis Pity She's a Whore". More significant for the future, though, was her assignment to understudy Juliet. She developed great rapport in the "cover" rehearsals with assistant director Julie Anne Robinson ("I learned to stop flailing around") and Romeo understudy, Sean Murray, winning golden praise from Artistic Director Adrian Noble for her playing of the balcony scene in a stage run-through. She looks forward with relish to playing Juliet "for real" sometime, somewhere in the not-too-distant future.

Why did she leave the company last June? Despite the loss of financial security, for practical and logical reasons. "I think the truth is that the RSC "ladder" only really operates for male actors. After all, there simply aren't that many middle-sized roles for women, particularly in Shakespeare". She'd love to go back, but next time it would have to be at the top of that ladder. Meanwhile, she can look back with pleasure on her RSC apprenticeship - especially the Irish Festival she organised with Denys Hawthorne, and studio performances as the Dark Lady in Shaw's "Man of Destiny".

Now happily under the wing of top agents Scott Marshall, she's enjoyed her first TV experiences ("It's the round-the-clock buffet they provide that's so fabulous"), notably as a young Irish terrorist in "Good Guys". When filming Simon Gray's "Running Late" (Screen 2) she worked with actor Peter Bowles, which led to his recommending her for her most recent job, as a go-getting young novelist in a prestigious national tour of another Gray play, "Otherwise Engaged".

Future dreams? "Juliet, of course. Pegeen Mike in "Playboy of the Western World". Some Chekhov. But what I really like about this part in "Otherwise Engaged" is that it challenges me a bit". One thing is sure: if talent and application are anything to go by, Mairead Carty won't need the luck of the Irish to meet many such challenges, in what already bids fair to be more than just another "promising" career.

John Arthur

The name may not be familiar. The face almost certainly will be. That lanky frame, quizzical eye and effortless comedy technique make John Arthur one of those instantly recognisable actors who are the backbone of the business. Never a household name, he has nonetheless enjoyed a consistent work record since leaving Birmingham Drama School in 1970 which would be the envy of many less durable "stars" - "I've never been rich; but it has paid the bills, so far!".

A long list of jobs over two decades includes regular roles in a host of soaps and serials, such as "Fresh Fields" and "Close to Home" (Paul Nicholas' fellow vet, Tom); countless police detectives and doctors in one-off TV dramas; poetry readings and plays for Radio 4; and more parts in theatre than he's able to remember, in seasons for long-gone rep. companies like Hull, Rotherham and Crewe.

After a formative three-year stint committed to street theatre, conjuring, stand-up comedy and just about everything else in the East Midlands ("I even played the ASDA supermarket car park in Nottingham, twice") John joined Alan Ayckbourn's regular company at Scarborough from 1977 to 1980. Those years were the making of him: the many parts written for him by Ayckbourn and others (his hilarious Roland Crabbe in "Taking Steps" stands out) gave him the momentum to gravitate down south, pick up a top London agent - before that he'd gone it alone - and set up a solid TV and West End career.

Like many working actors, he has had to ration the time he could afford to spend in live work: "There was a brief period in the late seventies when you could almost earn decent money in theatre. Today it's not possible". However, as the recession hits even TV producers' pockets, John finds himself going back to repertory: "I think it's good for the quality of the reps. that so many highly experienced actors are having to go in there again".

Unlike many actors, he's nothing but praise for his agent. David Daly has worked hard with him to ensure that work has led to more work, by tirelessly bullying casting directors and TV producers into catching his performances. Still, many people in conventional jobs would be amazed at the amount of time even well-known actors spend "out". This keen bird-watcher and music lover claims not to find that too traumatic, "though my wife (actress Jeni Giffen) might tell you a different story about me. Actually, unemployment isn't necessarily related to financial success. Some of my best years have involved a lot of sitting around after a good "telly" or advert. This year hasn't been so hot - and yet ironically I've spent a lot of time away".

As far as the future is concerned, he'd love to do more radio work than he's been able to fit in lately, and have a go at some of the classics that have eluded him ("Until recently, they just weren't in my arsenal"). John Arthur isn't interested in stardom, with its attendant ills "During "Fresh Fields" particularly I was recognised a lot, buttonholed by people on the tube and so forth. I'm not sure I could have put up with it for long". He's happy to be able to continue earning a reasonable living in a job which he knows he does well - many would say superbly. Yet is his generation at the end of a great line of British character actors? - "I wish I could feel more confident for the future of the business. Probably I've been lucky to catch the Golden Age....".

Agents and others

Having a credit card certainly doesn't make you money, but without one you've limited means of getting hold of any. An agent is an actor's credit card, and acquiring influential representation (such as provided by Jeremy Conway or ICM) can make all the difference between the breadline and comparative comfort.

Actors' agents (some prefer to call themselves "personal managers"), exist to ferret out work, introduce their clients to the company or director concerned, and then negotiate the contract of employment. Most charge between 10% and 15% (plus VAT) for their services, though many may reduce rates for poorly paid repertory or Theatre-In-Education work, and some charge more on lucrative advertising contracts.

Agent-less actors can buy the Stage newpaper, which still contains a sprinkling of job adverts. They can also subscribe to PCR ("Professional Casting Report", £85 per quarter), a chatty journal with more-or-less up- to-date news which sees itself as the parish pump of the agency world. They cannot subscribe to the more high-powered SBS ("Script Breakdown Service", £90 per quarter for bona fide agents only), which contains reliable casting information and guards its exclusivity fiercely - agents taking it must agree to keep its contents confidential.

Most of an agent's real effort on their clients' behalf, however, comes in the less tangible form of cultivating contacts, personally and by telephone. The actor can only sit back and hope that the director on the other end of the line trusts in the reputation and judgement of the agent.

Increasing numbers of actors are preferring to take their destiny into their own hands. The number of actors' cooperatives is growing and many of them, such as Actorum and The Actors' Exchange (which have between sixteen and twenty members looking after their own and each others' careers) are thriving whilst lesser personal managers are going to the wall. The cooperatives work in exactly the same way as conventional agents, except that the office is manned by its own currently out-of-work members, and commission rates tend to be lower. The Actors' Exchange, for example, currently takes between 5% and 10% - and as the company is non-profitmaking, there's no VAT to pay on top.

The current economic climate is forcing most actors and their agents to cast the nets ever wider in the search for a living income. The days when top actors might flinch away from commercials, for example, are long gone; and corporate work - training films, in-house videos, voice-overs and role-play - accounts for an increasingly large slice of the annual wage. This is one area where an agent's work for his client is invaluable: keeping tabs on the shifting multitude of companies likely to provide corporate work would be an expensive nightmare for the individual actor.

Indeed, the main challenge facing the agent is the sheer complexity of the system. It is no longer a question of ringing up individual directors or TV producers to ask them what they are casting. Most repertory theatre directors, for example, are guarded by proficient secretaries, who sift through casting submissions themselves before passing the best down the line. Some of the larger provincial theatres, and London-based organisations like the RSC and National, employ one or more casting directors whose whole job is to garner suggestions and initiate the casting process themselves.

Most ITV, BBC and Independent film, video and commercial producers use specialist firms such as The Casting House or S & K to conduct availability checks on likely actors, arrange interviews and talk money when the offer of a job is made. Unravelling who is doing what and for whom is the agent's bread and butter task.

Any agent, personal manager or coop member, has to be much more to their actor than simple job-getter or negotiator. Theatre people spend much time not working, and the good agent must be adept at keeping up confidence, so that when the audition or interview does come along the actor stands the best chance of doing themself - and the agent justice. Surrogate social work is as much a part of the job as career promotion. Despite this, the agent will be first in the firing line when a career has gone stagnant or an actor feels they weren't put up for this or that ideal role. Perhaps 10% isn't so unreasonable - with or without VAT.

Rates of Pay

Acting is vocational. In other words, job satisfaction is meant to compensate for low pay. The recently challenged directive of the Inland Revenue to remove young actors' schedule D status - taking tax out of pay packets and allowing fewer expenses against income - has made a career in theatre still more unstable; and only a very few star names have been made anything like rich by "the business".

As might be expected, subsidised theatre rarely pays well. Many reps operate a company wage and pay all actors equally, rarely more than £190-£210 for a sixty-or-so hour week. Some pay according to experience, and one (New Victoria, Newcastle) on a sliding scale of wage-for-age. On top of this, subsistence is payable (£48 p.w.) to help actors on short contracts keep up with the cost of trying to live in two places at once. Even actors working in the lower ranks at the National Theatre can only expect gross pay in the region of £210 p.w.

Commercial and West End rates are better (£280 average). Touring allowance is reasonable (£70 average), and travelling costs (plus overtime for Sunday travel) are met by managements. Names known from TV will expect a percentage of box-office take; but market forces operate savagely, and many "inner-circle" actors (i.e. those who are generally in demand) find that they have to ration the time they actually spend doing live theatre, topping up their income with better paid work in television or commercials.

TV companies no longer provide a licence to print money, and reduced budgets have meant reduced employment. The BBC categorises actors by size of role, type of programme, and experience - the more work you've done for the BBC, the higher up the particular scale you start. A reasonably experienced actor doing a small part in one episode of, say, "House of Elliot" could expect to earn in the region of £600 for a week's contract: this covers rehearsal fees, wardrobe calls and a first repeat. The minimum total fee for an actor in a speaking role is £258.

Fees for in-house ITV and independent productions are roughly comparable. A regular on "The Bill", for example, could be earning £35,000 p.a. or more, and a single episode might mean about £700. Extra payments for "special skills" (e.g. truck-driving), use of own clothing, special haircuts, extracts and trailers all boost the occasional TV actor's wage.

Getting the Big Commercial is the ordinary working actor's dream - almost like winning the pools. Even here, though, a recent change in the system by which fees are calculated may hit actors' pockets. Payments had been based on the number of repeat broadcasts, multiplied by a fixed percentage of the BSF ("Basic Studio Fee"). This was a lottery, but at best long-running adverts could net the actor fees stretching into tens of thousands of pounds.

The new system introduced by the advertisers depends instead on a TV Rating system (TVR) - the more who watch, the higher the fee - allowing block payments for fixed periods, no matter how often the advert is shown. Many actors now prefer to choose the safer, less lucrative option of the "buy out", whereby fees are paid in advance for unlimited use.

Lastly, many fringe theatre companies, and even some film producers, now pay on a profit-sharing basis - film work is currently only a paying proposition for stars and extras. Actors work for nothing and then divide box-office profits at the end of the run, or are paid shares if a film is sold to major distributors. This usually means payment by job satisfaction - only.

PAY – SOME MINIMUM RATES

THEATRE – *weekly rates*

WEST END

Once Nightly	£209.82
Twice Nightly	£244.71

PROVINCIAL (COMMERCIAL & TOURING)

Once Nightly – lower	£157.50
Twice Nightly – lower	£166.95
Once Nightly – higher	£182.70
Twice Nightly – higher	£199.50
Touring Allowance	£48.00

Note: higher minimum conditions apply in most cases, e.g. where 1,000,000+ people live within a twenty five mile radius of any theatre on the tour.

SUBSIDISED THEATRE

Lowest minimum	£165.00
Highest minimum	£219.50
Subsistence	£48.00

Note: most repertory theatres are at the lower end of these bands.

SMALL-SCALE THEATRE

Most TIE and small tours	£194.00
Subsistence	£45.00

RADIO — *daily minimum*

National radio	£128.00
Local radio	£87.00
World Service	£82.00
Rehearsal days	£77 £60 (W.Service)

TELEVISION

ITV — daily minimum

Walk-on 1 (extra)	£55.50
Walk-on 2 (non-speaking)	£105.15
Speaking roles	£125.20

Note: the last two include recording fees. Higher fees/weekly rates are generally negotiable.

BBC — minimum aggregate weekly fee

Speaking roles	£278.00

COMMERCIALS

"BSF" for major commercials averages £250. Fees now based on "TVR" (see article).

DIRECTORS — *some weekly minimums*

Resident Art. Dirs. (Reps)	£273.00
Guest Dirs. (Reps)	£323.50

Computers

Jane Asher's claim that the microchip can never replace people may well be justified, if only on her side of the footlights. Even so, in time only the livest of "live" theatrical events may be truly safe. The video explosion has already ensured that mechanical duplication of performances by the dead departed happens on a huge scale; and the living actor also feels the competitive squeeze from modern computerised inlay and film separation techniques, which have enabled commercially astute production teams (aided by grey areas in the laws of copyright) to rifle the classic treasure trove of great film performances from the past.

On the stage, a handful of computer-generated holograms have replaced live actors - most effectively in the case of Laurence Olivier's eerie spectre in "Time". Still, for the moment, the computer revolution promises to offer artistic gains to designers rather than job losses to actors - though the future is not so rosy for backstage workers, given the new labour-saving power and reliability of, say, computerised lighting technology.

From the actor's point of view the most noticeable computer-aided change is occurring in the field of casting - and it has come from an unexpected quarter. Virtually all professional actors pay an annual subscription to place their photos in the famous Spotlight directory, a hefty tome appearing biannually. At the end of 1992 male actors were surprised to receive along with their annual renewal notice a new form from the Spotlight requesting details about recent work, physical characteristics, language/accent abilities and other skills.

What has happened is that Spotlight has acquired Lasercast, which together with Showbase has been the pioneer in the computer casting field. "Lasercast (originally a BBC Enterprises brainchild) never really caught on", says Paul Sinclair of Spotlight. "The system was good, though the previous owners had difficulty demonstrating its effectiveness to casting directors. What's more, actors didn't see the need to pay for another shop window beyond our tried and trusted directory. There was a feeling that non-equity actors might jump on the bandwagon, and reduce its credibility".

The credibility gap closed when Spotlight, seeing the potential of Lasercast's CD-Rom format when wedded to their own huge directory, bought out and developed the system, which will be launched as Spotlight CD in early summer. At "virtually no extra cost" to actors, users of the old directory - casting directors, TV companies and major theatres - will be encouraged to get hold of the Apple-Mac hardware needed to run the system, and purchase Spotlight's regularly updated laser disks, packed with digitized images and information on 20,000 performers.

What does Paul Sinclair believe the new system will do? "Sadly, it won't make more work for actors! It will simplify the whole casting process, especially given some of the gadgets you can use". For example, it's possible to call up details of actors with similar physical statistics, and compare up to nine different faces on screen at any one time - useful if, for example, you need to quickly cast a look-alike family for a commercial. There is even a capability to add sound, though Spotlight CD has no current plan to expose casting directors to potentially countless renditions of "To be or not to be", or "Memory".

Late in 1992 there are only about twenty working machines around - albeit with important employers such as the BBC, Granada TV, commercial supremos Saatchi and Saatchi, and Edinburgh's Royal Lyceum Theatre. But Spotlight is spreading the gospel to casting directors at home and abroad, as well as encouraging companies like the RSC and the National Theatre to come on board in time for the launch. Nigel Seale, Spotlight's Managing Director, expects the CD database to be very firmly established with most major users by 1997.

His persuasive enthusiasm is not likely to be shared by agents, fearful of losing some influence on TV and commercial casting to this impressive, centralised casting tool. Some actors harbour the understandable concern that, in a time when opportunities to develop their craft are few and far between, computerised casting may result in even more parts being awarded on the basis of "being" a character rather than on the ability to "act" it. The microchip may not defeat the actor, but it may dictate its own terms for survival.

Equity

"The British Actors' Equity Association", to give Equity its full title, draws its membership from the ranks of professional actors, stage management, theatre designers and directors, choreographers, dancers, singers, stand-up comics, circus performers - in fact, anyone who is active in the entertainment industry. Under the newly elected General Secretary, Ian McGarry, there is an active recruitment drive, particularly in the under-represented club and circus fields.

It was formed in 1929 by the amalgamation of two previous groups, the Actors' Association and the Stage Guild; and registered as a trade union the following year, taking its name and many of its ideas from the already existing American Equity. Membership has grown from 4,000 in the 1930s to today's figure of about 45,000. The subscription system is calculated on a sliding scale according to gross annual earnings, starting at £20 for £3,000 or less, rising to £1,000 maximum for earnings over £100,000.

There are two main variants on normal full membership. Provisional cardholders (who've done less than twenty weeks total on Equity contracts) work with certain restrictions - for instance, they're not usually considered for West End Theatre - but otherwise enjoy the same benefits as full members. There is also a temporary cardholders' scheme, for recent graduates of registered drama colleges and short-term workers from abroad.

Equity's primary function is to secure the best possible terms and conditions of work for its members through negotiation of standard contracts and minimum rates of pay with employers in virtually every section of entertainment: theatre, television (BBC and Independent), films, commercials, radio and recording, variety and clubs. In most areas, casting agreements have been made with the employers which stipulate that only artists with previous professional experience (i.e. Equity members) are eligible to be considered for work, though there will usually be an agreed quota of new memberships available. Recent government legislation on closed shops, however, has weakened the force of these agreements. The quota system, which effectively limited the number of new cardholders, particularly in theatre, can no longer be applied rigorously. Now, anyone who wishes may apply for any job in professional theatre, and adverts stipulating "Equity Members Only" are no longer valid.

Beyond this, Equity offers important services to all members in full benefit - i.e. those less than thirteen weeks in arrears with subscriptions. The regular Equity Journal gives news and information on the union and its members - including full black lists of employers in dispute with the union. There is advice about contractual disputes and injury cases; accident insurance and backstage cover; low premiums (through Equity Insurance) on all insurance including personal pensions; help with mortgages, and death benefits.

Perhaps most usefully for an association the majority of whose members spend so much time out of work, Equity offers confidential advice from full-time staff on all welfare matters. This includes help with problems concerning National Insurance, Social Security, Restart job scheme interviews, and representation at benefit appeals. Currently, one area presents special problems - the new Inland Revenue directive on the favourable schedule D tax status, which has put many younger actors working in theatre straight into the PAYE scheme. Equity advisors advise those members hardest hit by these restrictions.

There exist a number of voluntary registers, available to potential employers, which list members skilled in particular fields, such as foreign languages, stunt work and puppetry; as well as groups like the disabled, Afro-Asian artists, and twins/triplets. Sadly, the Equity Grapevine, a phone hotline with some up-to-date casting information, no longer exists.

Michael Caine, in the official Equity leaflet "Working for you", speaks for most members: "All artists, whether at the beginning of their careers or established need each other. It is that fact that has kept the Union strong and united". In what is undoubtedly a difficult time for unions, where Equity's hands as negotiator are tied by the double bind of Government legislation and economic stringency, the additional benefits and support the union provides to its lower-paid workers provide the best argument for its continued existence.

Patrons: Richard Briers, Edward De Souza, Sir Michael Hordern CBE

London's first

Full-Time Evening Drama Course

Training *by* working actors, for those who wish to *become* working actors.

Five nights per week and all day Saturday plus some Sundays. The course is of two years, three 12 week terms per year. £850 per term.

The theatre is our business.
We'd like to help you make it yours.

ALSO -

SATURDAY COURSE (Audition Preparation)
DAYTIME POSTGRADUATE REPERTORY COURSE
DAYTIME MEDALLION COURSE (16-18 year olds)
PART-TIME EVENING COURSE
EVENING SUMMER COURSE

For prospectus or information Tel: 071-377 8735

DRAMA CENTRE LONDON

MEMBER OF THE CONFERENCE OF DRAMA SCHOOLS

President: The Earl of Harewood
Vice-Presidents: Sean Connery, Sir Peter Hall, Neville Shulman OBE
Principal: Christopher Fettes
Associate Director: Yat Malmgren

COURSES

ACTING DIPLOMA
3 year course accredited by the National Council for Drama Training

PROFESSIONAL INSTRUCTORS
2 year course

WEEKEND FOUNDATION COURSE
One year part-time

DRAMA CENTRE LONDON
176 PRINCE OF WALES ROAD
LONDON NW5 3PT TEL: 071 267 1177

PRS AND MUSIC IN THEATRES

1. General

The normal practice of the Performing Right Society (PRS) is to issue a blanket annual licence to a music user, in return for payment of royalty charges. This authorises the licence holder to perform in public any of the millions of copyright musical works under PRS's control. The royalties collected are distributed to the members of PRS and its affiliated societies world-wide: composers, lyricists and music publishers whose works have been performed.

However, with particular regard to theatrical presentations, there are some types of musical work and performances *not controlled by PRS*. Here we try to provide a guide for amateurs who may have found the matter rather confusing. What follows are outline checklists only.

2. What you need a PRS licence for

Pre-existing music accompanying plays: Overture, entr'acte, exit; curtain and incidental music are readily licensed by PRS. However, music interpolated into the stage action of a play, or making up a compilation show must be notified to PRS in advance so that the rights/licensing situation can be examined in each instance.*
Musical compilation shows: These shows are made up of pre-existing music on the life or career of a particular composer or performer, or concerning a period or style of music.*
Variety shows: These have a mixture of musical and non-musical items on the programme.
Music Hall entertainments: Many songs written at the turn of the century are still in copyright, which normally lasts for 50 years after the death of the creator.
Concerts: Both *classical* music concerts and recitals, and concerts of *popular* music of all descriptions (pop, rock, jazz, folk, etc.).
Films which include music: Including those of ballets, operas, musical plays and the like.
Miscellaneous presentations with music: Such as fashion shows, exhibitions, trade fairs, etc.
Mechanically-performed music: By record/CD/tape players, juke boxes, television, radio, etc., whether *featured* (e.g. discos) or as *background* music in theatre bars, restaurants and foyers.

3. What you don't need a PRS licence for

Grand Right Works: i.e. musicals/operas for which all the music has been specially written - go direct to rights owners for your licence; ballet/contemporary dance/mime - whether or not the music is specially written - go direct to rights owners/music publishers (do not confuse with dance displays/tap dancing etc., which is PRS-controlled).
Dramatic Excerpts: You should also apply direct to rights owners for permission to perform dramatic (staged) excerpts from operas and musical plays (of specially written music); songs from a show amounting to over 25 minutes in duration; music covering a complete act or which forms a "potted" version of the show.
Music specially written for a dramatic work in a theatre: Permission to perform e.g. music specially written for a straight play, accompanying a performance of that play, should be obtained direct from the rights owner (e.g. the composer).

Before you commit your group to the production of works outside PRS control, you must obtain prior permission from the rights owners as they are entitled to withhold permission (without necessarily stating a reason). Unauthorised productions have been halted at the eleventh hour. It is your legal obligation to obtain permission before a copyright work is performed.

* Note that in some instances, by special arrangement with PRS, a music publisher can license music interpolated in a play or music making up a compilation show.

These notes are not exhaustive, so if you have any queries please contact the Theatres Section at PRS. 29/33 Berners Street, London W1P 4AA. Tel:071-580 5544.

BARBARA SPEAKE STAGE SCHOOL & AGENCY

AND C.S.M. (ARTISTES) LTD

Licensed by the London Borough of Ealing

WELL DISCIPLINED AND EXPERIENCED CHILDREN, TEENAGERS (All ages & many nationalities) AND ADULTS
for STAGE, TV, FILMS, MODELLING, ETC

Children's Agency under the direction of Mrs JUNE COLLINS

BARBARA SPEAKE STAGE SCHOOL
EAST ACTON LANE, W3 7EG
081-743 1306; 081-743 6096 (day)
081-998 6596 (night)
Fax 081-740 6542

C.S.M. (ARTISTES) LTD (Adults)
under direction of Mrs Carole Deamer
Communications: 49 Churchfield Road, Acton W3 6AY
081-992 8668

Drama Schools

The last few years have seen a marked decrease in the number of Local Education Authority Grants being given to drama students. This is because the authorities have been forced to cut back on discretionary awards, the main source of funding for drama students. According to research conducted by the Conference of Drama Schools, the figures over the last three years show that there has been a 20% decrease in the number of LEA's giving full discretionary awards, 35% of LEA's have stopped awarding full fees and maintenance , and some of them are no longer giving any discretionary grants at all. The Conference of Drama Schools, with the support of other organisations such as Equity and the TMA, is campaigning to protest about this situation, which they feel could ultimately lead to the falling of standards in the profession.

This is a serious cause for concern for every drama school in the country, none of whom wants to turn talented students away because of lack of funding. In most cases the schools will do their utmost to help students to whom they have offered a place if the student in question cannot get a Local Authority grant. They will advise students about other sources of funding, for example from charitable trusts, and some of the larger schools have several internal scholarships to offer. It is adviseable for applicants who need grants to make inquiries about funding from their Local Education Authorities as soon as they apply to any drama school.

The Arts Educational Schools

Five schools under one roof comprise the Arts Educational Schools: the dance school, drama school, musical theatre school - which are all three year courses, and the acting company and theatre arts school. The schools are continuing to expand, and have recently introduced a one year postgraduate course in musical theatre and a one year playwrights course. The Arts Educational Schools are situated in what used to be Chiswick Polytechnic, and their programme is probably the largest and most varied in the country.

The theatre arts school is a five year foundation course for eleven to sixteen year olds which includes academic studies as well as vocational training. The pupils specialise in dance or drama and can choose the musical theatre option from the fourth year. The drama school provides the standard three year acting training, and the acting company is an unusual one year course designed for mature students. Applicants can include postgraduates from other acting schools or training programmes, people whose vocation has developed late in life, as well as professional actors, dancers, and singers who want to re-focus their careers. The course functions like a professional acting company, presenting plays regularly in and outside London as well as incorporating an intense training programme.

The playwrights' course is run in association with the acting company, who present workshop performances of the writers' work in progress. The premises for both of these courses is in Errol Street in the City of London, apart from the rest of the school.

Birmingham School of Speech and Drama

The school's main building is in pleasant grounds in Edgbaston near the centre of Birmingham. It has responded to the recession in recent years by expanding its premises to cater for a larger student population and new courses - a one year post graduate acting course and a two year stage management course. In addition to these there is a three year professional theatre course and a two year teaching course.

The school was founded in 1936 by Pamela Chapman, and her daughter, Patricia A. Yardley is now the principal. The cultivation of the voice has always been, and still is, of primary importance at this school. In recent years several changes and additions have been made to the curriculum of the theatre course in response to the ever increasing competition in the profession and therefore the demand for actors to be more and more versatile. These include classes in television and radio technique and specialist skills such as puppetry, as well as more singing classes. The acting students are also all required to help with stage management at various times throughout their training.

The competition for places in the school has not only increased in numbers, but also as regards the ability of the applicants. The lower age limit for applicants is eighteen years old, and there is no upper age limit.

Central School of Speech and Drama

Central has an exceptionally wide variety of courses divided into three areas: art, design and performing arts; education; and therapy. The art, design and performing arts area is further divided into disciplines which are either performance related or production related. Most of the courses offered are either diploma courses, B.A. or B.Sc. honours degree courses, or MA courses. There is also a continuing education programme, offering evening classes and summer courses.

The diploma in acting, a three year full time course, accepts about forty five students each year, fifteen of whom will be admitted to the musical theatre pathway and the rest of whom will follow the theatre pathway. For most of their training these two groups work together, and the theatre students also perform in musicals. There is no method as such to the training, which is divided into four integrated strands - acting and stagecraft, movement, musicality, and voice.

The school is constantly changing, adapting and expanding in a variety of ways, throughout all of the disciplines and provisions. Because so many of the courses are directly related to one another, interaction between the students and teachers from other departments is a valuable advantage. Central also has links with several other educational institutions and is currently undertaking a major new building project on the premises.

BASINGSTOKE ACADEMY OF ACTING

Colin Flaherty A.L.A.M. L.L.A.M.

Professional approach to acting or drama, whether for leisure or career purposes.

Tuitions and examinations to the standard of London Academy of Music and Dramatic Arts

& ACORN THEATRICAL AND MODEL AGENCY

14 Winchester Street, Basingstoke
Telephone or write for our prospectus
Tel. (0256) 818987

Principal:
Ian Horsbrugh FGSM FRCM FRSA

Director of Drama:
Virginia Snyders

Director of Technical Theatre Department : Sue Thornton

COURSES IN DRAMA AND TECHNICAL THEATRE

These courses are accredited by the National Council for Drama Training

Details of all courses are given in the prospectus but a comprehensive syllabus of the Stage Management course is also available. The prospectus and syllabus may be obtained from the Registrar

Silk Street, Barbican, London EC2Y 8DT
Tel: 071 6282571
Fax: 071 256 9438

THE BIRMINGHAM SCHOOL OF SPEECH AND DRAMA

Three-Year Full-Time Course for the Professional Theatre
(this course is accredited by the National Council for Drama Training)

Two-Year Full-Time Course for the Teaching of Speech & Drama

Two-Year Full-Time Stage Management Course

One-Year Post Graduate Course

Prospectus from:
THE REGISTRAR
45 CHURCH ROAD
EDGBASTON
BIRMINGHAM 15 3SW
Tel: 021-454 3424

BLAIR THEATRE SCHOOL

AUDITIONING NOW!

PRINCIPAL:
LESLEY BLAIR L.G.S.M.

For futher details contact:
Office:
Highgate, London N6 5XA
Tel: 081 348 2975

One Year Foundation Acting Course 16 + (Full-time Sep 93)

One Year 'A' Level Theatre Studies and Acting Course (Mon-Fri Sep 93)

Ten Week Evening Acting Course (Jan 1993)

Saturday classes in Dance, Drama or Voice. 4-16 yrs (No audition required)

DRAMA STUDIO LONDON

1966-1992

Now Commencing Our 26th Year

LONDON

Drama Studio London
Grange Court
1 Grange Road
London W5 5QN
Tel: 081 579 3897
Fax: 081 566 2035

One year acting course
(Accredited by the National Council for Drama Training)

One year directing course

Summer Programme

Drama Studio London is the only major drama school in Great Britain, offering exclusively a one-year training programme for graduate and other advanced students

Executive Director Peter Layton

AUDITIONS HELD THROUGHOUT THE YEAR 1993

The Drama Studio

All three full time courses at the Drama Studio are one year intensive post-graduate courses; in acting, directing, and theatre administration. The Drama Studio was established in 1966 to answer a demand for post-graduate training and requires that recruits be over twenty one years of age, preferably with previous experience or related experience in the area in which they will train. They are interested in students who are mature and pragmatic, and committed to a career in the theatre.

No single philosophy or method is espoused. The school prides itself on the practical and flexible nature of its courses, and aims to expose students to the circumstances they will encounter in the real world by employing tutors who are all professional practitioners with different ways of working. Always open to change, and with a constant eye on the demands of the profession, the Drama Studio approach is above all realistic.

The premises are in a Victorian Building in Ealing containing a studio theatre and four rehearsal rooms as well as seminar rooms, common room, etc. Because the courses are so compact, some students who are accepted on the acting course are advised to do a nine week preparatory course, run by the Drama Studio, in the summer. And recently, because of the economic climate, the school has found it expedient to introduce two additional short, self contained summer courses.

East 15

The current principal,Margaret Walker, founded East 15 in 1961 in order to continue the teachings and methods of Joan Littlewood, with whom she had worked as an actress for fourteen years.

The philosophy of the school is based on the belief that before an actor can act, before he can investigate the character and actions of other people, he must first know and understand himself. This does not mean that the basic disciplines are ignored of course, but students must be prepared to study their own behaviour and open themselves to scrutiny and change before attempting to create the life of another human being on stage. This approach extends to all aspects of the actor's training, including voice, movement and text study. Risk, hard work and fun are all important ingredients in the process.

The courses offered are a three year acting course, one year post-graduate acting course, a three year director's course, one year stage management course, and one year tutor's course. Summer drama workshops provide an introduction to the East 15 method.

The school has two premises; Hatfields, near Epping Forest outside London, and Sheriff Hutton Hall, ten miles from York. The summer drama workshops are based at Sheriff Hutton Park, and the three year courses use both locations. The school's main performing space, the Corbett Theatre, is at Hatfields.

Guildhall School of Music and Drama

The dynamism of the Guildhall is largely due to the fact that music and drama are taught side by side, and when appropriate, there is interaction between the two. The location of the Guildhall in the Barbican Centre is another factor, for there are strong links between the school and the resident companies the Royal Shakespeare Company and the London Symphony Orchestra - and with the Centre itself. Both music and drama students take part in all the major festivals at the Barbican, as well as performing regularly in lunchtime concerts and platform performances.

The school of music is an international conservatoire which trains both singers and instrumentalists. The school of drama offers a three year professional acting course and a two year course in stage management and technical theatre studies. There is also a junior department in both music and drama open to pupils aged between thirteen and eighteen years.

The international character of the music school is extending more and more to the drama department. Links are being forged with drama schools abroad, especially Hungary, the United States and Russia, and Guildhall student productions have also toured abroad.

The acting course aims to train versatile actors to recognise and meet the demands that will be made on them in the profession. The school employs tutors who are working professionals and regularly invites speakers to talk about practical aspects of the business. No particular method is pushed, but there is a constant emphasis on the students' imaginative response to language.

The London Academy of Music and Dramatic Art

LAMDA, founded in 1861, is one of the oldest drama schools in the country. No particular method or philosophy is preached and it no longer puts more emphasis on music than other schools. Like the others however, it recognises musical skills as an important part of an actor's training.

The three year acting course concentrates in the first year on freeing, developing and strengthening an actor's use of his voice and body. With a good grounding in these technical skills the process of acting and the inner life of characters are then explored. Specialist classes in mask and clown work, and television and radio technique are offered in the second year. LAMDA believes that a thorough traditional training for the stage will prepare its drama students for work in any media, and indeed graduates of the school have proved it.

The other courses offered are a two year stage management technical theatre course, and a one year acting course for overseas students which concentrates on the classics. This course began in 1956 following a request from the Fulbright Commision. Overseas students are also eligible for the first two years of the three year course, as well as the Shakespeare summer workshops, and LAMDA hold auditions in London, New York, Los Angeles, Toronto and Vancouver.

Mountview

Mountview's approach to acting is eclectic; it does not adhere to any dogma. The school employs a broad range of teachers and directors and each year looks for as wide a range of students as possible. Auditions are sometimes held abroad for overseas students. The ethos of the school is to train students to be versatile and employable.

The courses offered are a three year acting and musical theatre course, a one year postgraduate acting course, a two year stage management, technical theatre and design course, and a one year postgraduate director's course, as well as summer courses in British theatre and musical theatre. Mountview has three performance spaces: one proscenium arch theatre, and two studio theatres.

The school evolves according to the demands of the profession, so the curriculum is always under review. In both of the acting courses it is possible for students to specialise in musical theatre. There is more time spent on television technique than before, and the school now has a professionally equipped studio for video and film work, and radio technique is also studied. A lot of attention is also given to practical ways of increasing the students' chances of employment, including basics such as letter writing and interview technique. The students are encouraged to make regular visits to the theatre.

Oxford School of Drama

Situated on the edge of the Blenheim Palace Estate in Woodstock, the Oxford School of Drama is an eighteenth century farmhouse which has been converted into three main studios. Although most of the students choose to live in Oxford, the work is conducted in this rural setting and daily transport is available to and from the school.

Three full time courses are offered: a one year acting course, a two year acting course, and a theatre administration/stage management course. Public performances are presented regularly at The Old Fire Station in Oxford as well as at various central venues in London. Short summer courses are also offered in Oxford, as well as an Edinburgh Festival performance course.

The acting courses are Stanislavsky based and designed to thoroughly investigate the process of acting and to concentrate on exploring and developing the inner life of the character, as well as to give the students a solid foundation in the craft and basic skills of the actor. The two year course offers additional practical options such as theatre for young people, contemporary and traditional dance, circus skills, mime and stage management.

The school seeks students who are focussed, determined, and fully aware of the harsh realities of a career in the theatre, so commitment and resilience are high on the list of qualities sought. And at the end of each course, the school aims to place students on secondment, in any aspect of production.

The Poor School

Founded seven years ago largely as a reaction to the increasing difficulty drama students were having getting grants, The Poor School continues to thrive as the recession hits harder elsewhere and local education authorities cut back even further. Classes are held in the evenings and on weekends which allows students to work in the daytime, and the fees are less than half what most other drama schools charge.

Consequently the competition for places is very high and growing all the time. The working week demands more than twenty hours of intense training, and the course runs for two years. In the final two terms some daytime work is required. The classes offered are the standard mix of acting, voice and movement classes but they are constantly modifed in response to the demands of the profession and the students. The course itself is down-to-earth and fundamental but by no means superficial.

The last two terms are devoted to rehearsals and public performances which are normally presented at the Duke of Cambridge (DOC) Theatre. Currently they are building their own 900 square foot theatre on their premises near Kings Cross, set to open in March 1993. An appeal has been launched, with a target of £22,000.

The Royal Academy of Dramatic Art

RADA offers a nine term diploma acting course and a two year diploma course in stage management and theatre production. There are also four-term specialist diploma courses in scenic design, scene painting, stage carpentry, stage electrics and property making as well as shorter summer courses in Shakespearean acting and set design. Auditions for the full time acting course are now held in Manchester and New York as well as in London, reflecting the school's determination to recruit talent from all areas and backgrounds. Competition for places in RADA is extremely fierce.

Because of the ever increasing competition in the profession and in order to give students exposure to working professionals, RADA employs professional directors and choreographers from outside the school for all public performances. The acting course is Stanislavsky based. All students are given individual tuition in Alexander technique and singing and encouraged to develop their particular individual skills. However, equal emphasis is placed on contributing these skills wholeheartedly to the work of the group. The acting students are also required to do a term of technical training which includes company management and front of house management.

The school boasts three fully equipped theatres and a central London location in Gower Street, where it was established soon after its foundation at the beginning of the century.

SERIOUS MONEY

Who pays for Theatre? Not just the punter at the box office. The Yearbook examines finances in this year of recession by inviting a spokesman from the National Campaign for the Arts to analyse the present position. A representative of the Association for Business Sponsorship of the Arts (ABSA) explains the role of sponsorship with some intriguing examples. And in a year when Europe has been on everyone's mind, the Secretary General of Cerec, the European arts sponsorship association, throws light on how sponsorship works in the context of Britain's European partnership. This is followed by updates on the angel system and on the marketing of tickets.

Finances '92

With the appointment of a new Heritage Minister, it seems appropriate to look back over the period of Conservative Government and examine the trends which have led to the present situation.

It seems unlikely that many will look back at the Thatcher years as a golden age for the theatre. The decade began with a promise that there would be "no candle-end economies in the arts", closely followed by £1.1m clawback from the Arts Council grant and an increase in the rate of VAT from 8% to 15%; it ended with thirty out of thirty two of the Arts Council building-based theatres sharing an accumulated deficit of more than £4 million.

It would be too easy to concentrate on the financial stringencies of that time. The character of the decade was determined not only by money but by the wide range of local authority legislation – the abolition of the GLC and MCCs, the introduction of the poll tax and Uniform Business Rate, rate and poll tax capping – education reforms and changes in company law, which posed a series of threats to theatrical activity at all levels, even if that had never been part of the Government's intention. Quite simply, the arts were never considered important enough to have a voice in Cabinet discussion.

Nobody could argue that there was insufficient discussion about the needs of the theatre – the House of Commons Select Committee Report of 1982, the Priestley Report into the finances of the Royal Shakespeare Company, the Arts Council's own "Glory of the Garden" strategy and the Cork Report "Theatre Is For All". It might have been fair to expect that all of those reports would have produced some positive action but there was too little sign of policy being put into practice.

It is remarkable how well theatrical activity survived the onslaught. Many theatre companies were successful in adapting to the market philosophies of the 1980s; despite rising ticket prices, the audience for live theatre continued to increase; and theatre-in-education, youth and community theatre and amateur activity continued to flourish against a background of inadequate support.

Thanks to better information gathering there was hard evidence to show that theatre-going could not be dismissed as a marginal, minority activity. Independent research, subsequently verified by the Treasury, also brought a long overdue acknowledgement of the important contribution made to the economy by the arts and cultural industries – and at subsidy levels which are still less than half those of our major European neighbours.

But those successes were achieved at painful cost – fewer productions, fewer new plays, smaller cast sizes, inadequate remuneration for artists made even worse by new interpretation of tax regulations. Performance, it seemed, had more to do with what was happening in the accounts office than on stage.

So far, the new decade has been dominated by the much amended conclusions of the Wilding Report – the reorganisation of the Arts Council and Regional Arts Boards, the development of the National Arts and Media Strategy – and a continuing flood of new legislation. Further reorganisation of local authority finance and structures, the continuing reform of education and training and broadcasting, and a new Charities Act all promise further uncertainty and insecurity for the arts. Europe is making its presence felt, too, with its data protection, health and safety and working-time directives.

At least the squeeze on direct central government funding which persisted throughout the 1980s was lifted, even if only temporarily. Three years of increases in Arts Council grant exceeded not only inflation – by 13.7% in real terms – but also expectations, though in truth they did little more than to allow the larger companies a small breathing space.

Pressure on local authority funding, declining since the early 1980s, has been exerted with tighter and tighter control. The problems for locally-funded venues and companies, theatre-in-education and community theatre, the provision of drama in schools and of discretionary grants for students seeking to train for a career in theatre continue with renewed force. The threat of CCT hangs over venues round the country, notwithstanding the comment of the Audit Commission as recently as January 1991 that the theatres, concert halls and arts centres provided and operated by local authorities "are the essential infrastructure without which many people would have no access to live entertainment."

Business sponsorship had grown to approximately £50m by 1990/91, though theatre's share of that amounted to only just over £5m. Arts Council reports confirm that sponsorship amounted to only 4.2% of their main drama clients' income in 90/91; Independent Theatre Council surveys indicate that sponsorship contributes an even lower percentage at 3%. And that is gross income; it would be interesting to know how much had to be spent to raise this "additional" money.

In creating a Department of National Heritage with a Minister at the cabinet table and promising a National Lottery, John Major and his colleagues seemed to recognise at the last Election that there might be votes in the arts. Both were developments which have been welcomed by many. But the Conservative manifesto's declaration that the new department "will aim to encourage private sector enterprise" and "continue to develop schemes for greater sponsorship in cooperation with business and private individuals" does not suggest that the Government have accepted their responsibility to support the arts here at the level of our new European partners.

The National Lottery is still at least a year away and while it could be an extremely welcome source of additional funds for long overdue capital expenditure and endowment, it must not become an excuse for Government to cut or freeze continuing revenue grant. Nor must the publicity value of a National Lottery be allowed to distract from more urgent demands – a secure place for drama in every child's education, an equitable grant system to provide for the professional training of actors, technicians and designers, and theatres which can afford to produce new work and maintain affordable seat prices without exploiting their artists, writers and backstage workers.

None of those are new demands; it is a sad truth that they have been talked about – but not acted upon – for so long. But that's what you are there for, Mr Brooke – isn't it?

CHARLES MORGAN

Charles Morgan is the spokesman for the National Campaign for the Arts. The Yearbook is most grateful to him for contributing his views.

Sponsorship

Since the birth of theatre in Ancient Greece there have been sponsors. The Athenian Festival of Dionysus was supported by a mixture of civic funding, box office revenue and private patrons, and in that private patronage the roots of modern sponsorship can be seen. Those private patrons supported the arts for two reasons. Primarily, they wished to boost their public image and show their influence: there was a secondary bonus that if they had supported the winning play, they would receive tax breaks for a year.

This philosophy still holds today, though we have moved on to an era where, although private patronage still plays an important part, the visible sponsors come from the corporate sector. Today, business sponsorship of theatre amounts to some £5.1m, with a further £1.6m coming from corporate memberships of theatre companies. This represents around 12% of the overall total of business support for the arts in the UK (£57.1m in 1990–91).

The reasons why businesses sponsor the arts are varied, but fall into three main categories: promotion of their corporate or product image; entertainment of clients, customers or opinion formers; and commitment to the community in which they trade and from which they draw their employees.

In turn, theatre companies have developed a number of ways of attracting business support to meet these criteria. As well as offering benefits relating to sponsorship of a particular production, theatres have produced a variety of other "packages", including single-evening sponsorships with corporate entertainment possibilities, gala nights, sponsorship of education and outreach work, and corporate membership schemes. All of these schemes can be enhanced through the Government's Business Sponsorship Incentive Scheme which acts as an incentive to businesses to put new money into the arts and provides matching funding to arts organisations. This range of possibilities is a key to success in raising sponsorship as it allows businesses to become involved with the theatre at the level, and in the manner, that most fits their company objectives.

Another important factor is research. Any sponsorship proposal should be tailored to the needs of the business to whom it is sent and must describe the benefits specific to that business's aims; the quality of the art alone is not a sufficient incentive.

Sponsorship-seeking requires commitment by the theatre company concerned in terms of staff resources and time. Particularly in the present economic climate, it may seem difficult to dedicate already scarce resources to the precarious business of raising private sector funds. However, the title frequently used for sponsorship staff – development officer – indicates that their brief is wider than merely helping out the bottom line through the corporate sector. Most development officers have responsibilities for all aspects of fundraising, including from trusts and foundations as well as private individuals. Plural funding is undoubtedly here to stay, even if the corporate sector may find it hard to take on new projects in the next year or so – and as the market gets more competitive, it is the theatre companies who are well prepared who will ultimately succeed in raising the private sector funds of which so many organisations are seeking a share.

Nottingham Playhouse/Home Brewery

Home Brewery had never sponsored the arts before, but had in the past given small donations to community groups in the Nottingham area. They were looking for a sponsorship opportunity which would promote their name both within and beyond the Nottingham area , offering suitable occasions for corporate hospitality and promotion and involvement with the local community.

The Nottingham Playhouse, meanwhile was under a new management team and the opportunity of a major sponsorship – the largest, at that point, of an English Rep theatre – was a chance to stabilise their financial position as well as developing a highly beneficial relationship with a new partner. The initial sponsorship was so successful that it has been renewed, partly as a result of audience research which showed a very positive attitude towards the sponsor.

Polka Childrens Theatre/Kia-Ora

"The Four Friends"

Kia Ora, another first-time sponsor, wished to promote a caring image through work which focused on educational and learning through play. They wished their orange drink brand to appeal to "Mums and Kids" and they felt that by sponsoring Polka Childrens Theatre they could achieve this aim while allowing the production of "The Four Friends" to be enhanced: by the commission of original music and the employment of musicians, by producing branded material to complement the production and to produce an improved teachers pack. This sponsorship is a good example of brand sponsorship, which is still an under-exploited area in the arts if an appropriate link can be found between the brand and the artistic event in question.

Zenana Theatre Company/Sequin Park Womens' Health Clubs and Gyms

The Zenana Theatre Company's production of "16 Words for Water", by Billy Marshall Stoneking, a play about the life and work of Ezra Pound, was put on at the Old Red Lion fringe venue in Islington North London. The company found a sponsor in Sequin Park, who manage three women's gyms in the North London area, one of which was in the same street as the Old Red Lion. Sequin Park wished to raise awareness of their services and were conscious that the kind of young, professional, local audience which were attracted to the fringe theatre venues of Islington were likely to be the kind of people who were also likely to use their facilities.

Horse and Bamboo Theatre Company/ Arrow Oil

Arrow Oil, winner of the ABSA Northern Ireland Award for best first-time sponsorship in 1991, is a confederation of six independently owned small oil distributors. In 1990 they launched the new brand of Arrow Oil and they wished to introduce the brand amongst the communities it served on Northern Ireland's North coast. Horse and Bamboo is a travelling theatre company which toured the Antrim coast for six weeks, walking from Larne to Derry with its three horses, showman's wagon and two flat-bed drays. It gave thirty-three performances en route, covering the precise territory in which the distributors operated. This innovative sponsorship brought brand awareness for the sponsor and brought, by day and night, street theatre, masque, mime, music and drama to twelve villages and towns. This sponsorship shows how an imaginative link between the aims of the sponsor and the schedule of the arts organisation can provide a real business benefit while achieving excellent and unusual artistic aims at the same time. The sponsorship came about because an approach was made to an established, large oil company who themselves felt the sponsorship was not appropriate for them but passed the information on to their contacts at Arrow. Horse and Bamboo also appeared at Brighton this year and a further description of their work appears in the Yearbook's Festival section under **Brighton**.

The National Theatre Corporate Contributors' Scheme

Corporate members' schemes are a way of involving businesses in supporting a theatre for defined benefits but with less financial commitment than a full-blown sponsorship might cost.

The National Theatre Corporate Contributors' Scheme has four levels of annual membership, as follows: Platinum (£10,750 + VAT), Gold (£7,650 + VAT), Silver (£4,350 + VAT) and Bronze (£2,150 + VAT). Benefits of membership of the scheme, which vary according to the level of contribution, include complimentary and reduced price tickets, guest entertainment, special events available only to contributors, priority booking, free car parking, complimentary programmes and many other privileges at the National Theatre and when the company is on tour.

Other theatres running such schemes include the Royal Exchange, Manchester and the Basingstoke theatre. Or course, each theatre sets levels of membership appropriate to the kind of businesses they are likely to attract. In Manchester, the core joining level is £1,850 + VAT. Basingstoke has a Business Friends Scheme where the majority pay £250 + VAT.

CAROLINE KAY

Caroline Kay is Head of External Affairs at ABSA. The Yearbook is indebted to her and to ABSA for this contribution.

Sponsorship in Europe

Despite the difficult economic climate, interest in business support for the arts has continued to grow in all European countries. Although budgets may be cut as a result of the recession, statistics show that an increasing number of companies are turning to arts sponsorship, that once they have tried it they stay with it, and that long-term support programmes are finding favour over expensive one-night events.

Business sponsorship of the arts is regarded as an important supplement to state subsidy, local authority funding and revenue from the box office. In 1986, the Council of Ministers for Cultural Affairs declared that "the European cultural heritage and cultural activities in general benefit from a combination of public and private support . . . business sponsorship can enhance the cultural heritage and increase the production and dissemination of artistic activity . . . it should provide supplementary funding for cultural activities, not a substitute . . . ".

In response to this and parallel calls from the European Parliament for the promotion of business support for the arts Europe-wide, the national sponsorship associations in existence at the time approached the European Commission in 1988 with a view to setting up a European secretariat. Cerec (Comité européen pour le rapprochement de l'économie et de la culture), the European arts sponsorship association, was created in March 1991 and is funded by the European Commission and the private sector. It comprises the ten national associations for business support for the arts currently operating in Europe and has access, through its members, to over 1300 businesses, many more arts organisations, national press lists, government ministries and local authorities.

Cerec activities focus on three major areas: co-ordinating the activities of its national member associations, informing the business community on EC matters which have a bearing on sponsorship (such as, for example, the proposed directive on tobacco advertising restrictions), and thirdly, encouraging the business community to consider the pan-European sponsorship of the arts as an important new business activity.

Country	Sponsorship Estimate
Austria	1991: £12m
Belgium	1991: £15m
France	1991: £80m
Germany	1991: £80m
Greece	no figures available
Denmark	£200m from company foundations
Italy	1991: £200m
Netherlands	1991: £52.2m
Republic of Ireland	1990: £2.5m
Sweden	£10m
United Kingdom	1990/1991: £57m

While there are differences in attitudes towards the balance set up between the private sector, the public sector and the arts, Cerec's job is to highlight the similarities. Across Europe, "good corporate citizenship" is taking the place of expensive, gala-based sponsorship which is good for the arts as it favours long-term and committed business support. This new mood means, however, that increasingly, the arts are having to compete for business money with other fields (the environment, health, education & research). Countries are in agreement that incentives (legal, fiscal, government "matching" schemes), while affecting the amount companies give to the arts, do not affect giving per se. A new French law passed in 1991 making it easy for French companies to set up foundations has had a positive influence on the sponsorship climate, while in Italy, where sponsorship is regarded as indicative of good managment, businesses spent £200m on the national heritage last year despite no obvious fiscal incentive. However, there is no doubt that the British Business Sponsorship Incentive Scheme run by ABSA, which matches new or increased sponsorship with government money, has had a catalytic effect on arts sponsorship in Britain. Since the scheme was introduced in 1984, sponsorship figures have risen from £600,000 to close on £60m. Cerec is currently developing plans for a "seal of approval" scheme for sponsorship at a European level and a European awards scheme which would enhance those already awarded at a national level.

Across Europe, arts sponsorship is becoming more beneficial to both sides and development managers more professional about seeking and maintaining sponsorship. There is growing involvement from local authorities, as opposed to central government, and from Small and Medium-sized Enterprises (SMEs) as opposed to large corporations. The French association on the Cerec network, Admical, took this trend towards decentralised activity into account when choosing Arles, rather than Paris, as the setting for their 1992 conference on business sponsorship, and seminars run by the various associations are increasingly focussing on the potential for involvement by the smaller players.

Simultaneously, arts sponsorship has become more international, with American and Japanese countries sponsoring pan-European. Cerec was created in order to cater for this multi-national development. The recently-launched Northern Telecom Arts Europe programme (NTAE) is a first European partnership initiative for the arts between Cerec and Northern Telecom. With NTAE, the Canadian telecommunications company demonstrates a commitment to encouraging cross-frontier communication in an exciting new open environment. The programme is designed to promote collaboration and exchange between young European artists from all art forms and will ultimately embrace six European countries. Cerec advised Northern Telecom Europe on developing the programme and Cerec will be represented on the jury selecting the projects to benefit from it. While the NTAE programme is the first truly pan-European arts sponsorship programme (as opposed to a series of several national sponsored events), it is certainly not the first to look beyond national frontiers. Reasons for developing European rather than, or in addition to, national programmes vary. When Guinness Brewing Worldwide sponsored the UK's National Theatre's European tour of "King Lear" and "Richard III", which travelled to Cork, Madrid, Hamburg, Paris, Milan and Belgium, the company was keen to present a strong pro-European profile while at the same time linking its name to the best of British culture.

In the Maastricht treaty, the new article on culture puts the arts on the European agenda for the first time by providing the legal basis for proposing cultural policy, administering a larger budget and taking culture into account in the formulation of other Commission policies. The European Commission views its priorities as encouraging cultural diversity, bringing the common heritage to the fore, promoting young artists and improving knowledge and dissemination of the arts. In addition, it wishes to increase co-operation with non-member countries, especially those in central and eastern Europe. Proposed agreements with Poland, Hungary and Czechoslovakia include a cultural clause. This interest in central and eastern Europe is reflected by the national associations for sponsorship, and, as part of its future training programme, Cerec hopes to develop exchange opportunities for arts managers working outside the EC.

While the new work undertaken by the EC is much welcomed, the geographical boundaries of the European Community do not ultimately determine cultural activities and national differences in levels of state and private intervention will continue to prevail. Maastricht or not, from a cultural viewpoint, Europe is already a reality, with its identity defined by its diversity.

ANNE VANHAEVERBEKE

Anne Vanhaeverbeke is Secretary General of Cerec. The Yearbook thanks her for contributing this piece.

Angels

In theatre's commercial sector, there is an area of investment which has been in operation for years but of which few people are aware. The angel system involves individuals putting up money to finance the production of a show. If the show is not a success, the investor loses his or her money. If it's a hit, the investor will recoup and see some return. Often this return is minimal but if the show is a long running success, then the reward can be substantial.

Those who invested in the unlikely sounding all singing, all dancing stage adaptation of T.S. Eliot's cat poems back in 1980 are still laughing all the way to the bank. According to Phillippe Carden and Bee Huntley in their recently published book on how to be a West End angel, an investment in "Cats" of £750 will have, to date, seen profits in excess of £16,000.

The trick, therefore, is to back a winner. Angels – so called, it is thought, because they are more likely to get their reward in that great theatre in the sky than in the bank – are invariably people who invest more through a love of the theatre than from a desire for financial gain. This is not to say that angels invest unwisely or without hope of profit but they are essentially gamblers who like a flutter in the arts.

Of course, there are some names which are associated with success: Andrew Lloyd-Webber, Cameron Mackintosh and Michael Codron. These people tend to have private lists of regular investors who are unlikely to let their coveted places go. It is said that there are angels waiting in the wings to occupy dead men's shoes.

Other producers and companies have to advertise for investors. Strictly speaking, it is illegal to tout for angels, so notices tend to be carefully worded invitations to invest. Some angels will put money in a particular show and never be seen again. Others invest regularly, sometimes as individuals and sometimes in syndicates. These people may not be rich (the minimum sum is usually around £1,000) but they will have sufficient funds to be able to partake in a particularly fickle gamble.

The origin of the angel system is shrouded in mystery. It probably emerged out of the old style patronage that was prevalent in Shakespeare's day. Certainly, by the 1920s, angel syndicates were in operation. Certain famous theatre families, such as the Littlers, have long been associated with theatrical investment. Other angels are just keen theatre goers with a bit of cash to spare.

With productions (particularly big musicals) becoming more and more costly, producers are relying on angels more than ever. Units of investment are offered to potential investors in carefully drafted legal documents. In 1980, the Society of West End Theatres (SWET) opened a service which acts as a go-between for producers and potential angels. This takes the form of a list of investors who receive information about current investment possibilities.

In the subsidised sector, the angel system cannot exist: many theatres have charity status which bars any form of commercial investment. However, increasing numbers of shows are launched in a subsidised theatre and then make a transfer into the West End. At the transfer stage, all the rules change and the producers will need to raise money from as many willing sources as they can.

The King's Head – that quirky time-warp pub theatre in Islington where the drinks are still charged in pounds, shillings and pence is run by Artistic Director Dan Crawford who regularly comes up with shows which transfer to the West End. Over the last twelve years, the King's Head has built up a faithful collection of between four and five hundred angels to back these commercial ventures. Units can cost as little as £250 and have allowed a whole new bracket of investor into the angel arena. As Rick Locker, the general manager, says:"Lots of angels have been coming to the theatre for years and I find it quite sweet that they invest just because they want to put back into the theatre some of the enjoyment they've had over those years."

The National Theatre has recently launched a sponsorship scheme which in appearance is similar to the angel system in that it is open to individuals rather than their usual corporate bodies (whose contribution is discussed by Caroline Kay, above). However, this scheme is strictly sponsorship, not investment, as the contributors provide money as a gift and have no hope of seeing any return on it.

The National's scheme was born out of an awareness that it was able to hang on to its corporate investors despite the recession and it was felt that there was perhaps the potential for individual sponsorship, too. The scheme was launched in September 1991 with the aim of raising around £50,000 in the first year. Amazingly, over £100,000 was raised in the first six months, enabling the National to fund an entire production – "The Recruiting Officer".

The "angelic" contributors to the National's resources are entitled to use the Ashcroft room. (Dame Peggy was the scheme's patron but sadly died before it came to fruition. Penelope Wilton has taken over the mantle.) The Ashcroft room is not an elitist corner: there are no free drinks and sponsors have to pay for their tickets, too. It is simply a function room specifically for sponsors' use. Contributors enjoy priority booking and a hotline to the finance office where information is available on "their" show.

The National's development manager, Lucy Stout, finds that most sponsors are regular theatre goers who want to keep theatre alive. She recalls a letter from an elderly woman in Yorkshire who said she was no longer able to go to the theatre but that her fondest memories were of productions at the National. These perhaps are the true angels. Without such generous and affectionate spirits, British theatre would be in a sorry state.

HELEN ROSE

Tickets

Booking a West End theatre ticket via one of the main ticket agencies such as Ticket Master or First Call is very much like booking a holiday with a travel agent: the service provided is essentially one of convenience. Anyone who has attempted to purchase a ticket for a popular show such as "Joseph and his Amazing Technicolor Dreamcoat" by ringing the venue's box office directly will know how frustrating it can be to be left waiting in a very long and costly telephone queue only to find that the show is sold out.

Obviously, nobody can guarentee that a ticket will be available for the show you want to see on the night you want to see it, but by ringing a major ticket agency you will at least have your call answered almost straight away as there will be many more telephone lines. Should your chosen theatre be full, you will be offered alternatives which you will be able to take immediately. When you receive your tickets, you will also be sent information as to how to get to and from the theatre which can be a useful service for those not used to London. It all adds up to increased convenience – but of course it is the customer who pays for it.

The booking fee and handling charge vary according to where you obtain your tickets and also to a certain extent on how successful the show is. I tried to book two top price tickets for "Grand Hotel" at the Dominion Theatre. My first call was the venue's box office where I was told the tickets were £30 each and could be booked over the phone with a credit card and collected on the night of the performance. This way I wouldn't pay any extra charges. Next I phoned First Call where once again each ticket was £30 but I would also have to pay a booking fee of £6 on each ticket. There wasn't time for them to send it to me so again I would have to collect the tickets on the evening of the show. Finally I rang the Credit Card Hotline and was offered the tickets at face value with no charges whatsoever. All the numbers I rang were able to offer me tickets at relatively short notice – four days.

It is a legal requirement for an agency to inform customers about any extra charge at least twice before a booking can be accepted. It is also worth noting that if you have an Amex Gold card you will receive preferential treatment on the phone. What's more, some tickets are held back exclusively for Amex card holders and are not released to the general public until 8.30 am on the day of the performance.

The lesson to be learned from all this is that it is best to ring as many different numbers as possible and find the best deal before you let go of any money. One last thing worth bearing in mind is that the large agencies will offer some sort of refund should the show close. Even if this is theatre tokens or a only a percentage of what you paid, it is still better than nothing.

TIM CRONIN

WHERE ACTING HELPS

Those who were lucky enough to see the award-winning "Our Country's Good" at the Royal Court a few years ago must have been impressed with the play's vision of how acting can do you good. The Yearbook looks at Theatre in Education, drama in prisons and at role-playing in management training.

Theatre In Education

TIE in action

It is one of those grim ironies that Theatre In Education (TIE) is taking off in Europe and North America at a time when it has sunk to the level of endangered species here, in the country of its birth. Directors of TIE companies are lecturing and giving demontstrations in their methodologies to eager, curious, newly enlightended followers from all over the place, who see the interactive, participatory, forum theatre techniques embodied in the genre for what they are: intellectually challenging ways of tackling just about any subject on - or outside - the curriculum.

The reasons for TIE's decline in Britain are various. Pioneered in the 1960s and popularised in the 1970s through the work of drama in education theorists Dorothy Heathcote and Gavin Bolton, it is a methodology that has been used largely with issue-based work. Some of the issues depicted have been overtly "political", such as colonialism, homophobia, the troubles in Northern Ireland, Nazism in the 1930s, racism, sexism, etc. Others more recently have moved to areas to do with relationships and self-image. Whether political with a small or a large "P", TIE has taken a knocking from the national curriculum. The child-centredness implicit in a methodology which allows its audience to explore, confront and analyse does not rest easily in the goal and fact orientated curriculum.

Hand in hand with the national curriculum, other aspects of the Education Reform Act have contributed to the travails of TIE. Local management of schools has meant that budgets previously controlled by education authorities (many of whom directly funded TIE companies) are now in the hands of headteachers and governors - some of whom will have no interest in or understanding of the value of TIE as a learning resource. That by now proverbial choice between mending the roof and buying in an all day TIE programme for a couple of hundred pounds has meant a sorry ending for those companies who have had to compensate for their loss of local authority or arts board funding by charging commercial rates to schools who previously enjoyed their services for free.

As a result, only a handful of companies remain. One estimate has it that of the seventy odd companies operating full-time three years ago, less than half have survived today. Apart from the handful of original companies who have managed to hold on, there has surfaced a newer breed. Where, in the days of LEA funding, companies would have revenue funding to enable them to plan their programmes a year in advance and in close consultation with schools and curriculum development advisors, the new economic climate has engendered the phenomenon of project-based TIE. This is a system in which companies find funding for a particular project and then tour it to whoever is prepared to pay for it. Curricular orientated projects are all the rage, as you can imagine in the current education climate. Science plays on everything from internal combustion to nuclear power are regaling audiences up and down the country: plays made possible thanks to the benevolence of companies like Shell, BP, British Gas and British

Nuclear Fuels, among others.

You don't need to be a conspiracy theorist to realise that sponsorship such as this carries the risk of compromising the integrity of the piece. What would BNF make of a Theatre In Education programme that was critical of its waste disposal practices, for instance ?

Along with the risk to free speech is that to artistic integrity. Many of the newer, project-based companies are being formed by students recently out of drama school who do not always have the acting and teaching experience required to devise and perform TIE satisfactorily. Theatre In Education is anything but a cushy way to earn an Equity card.

Traditionally, it has been devised and performed by actor-teachers who are experienced in both. Pedagogic theory and an understanding of young people are as important as good acting; so is the credibility that comes with that understanding. Plugging into the curriculum in itself is no bad thing. Indeed, demand from teachers for help from theatre companies has never been greater, particularly since advisors are no longer there to turn to. But TIE must be done properly if it is to be of use to its audience. For that to happen, some kind of quality control mechanism would be of enormous use to its consumers.

REVA KLEIN

Theatre in Prisons: Geese Theatre Company

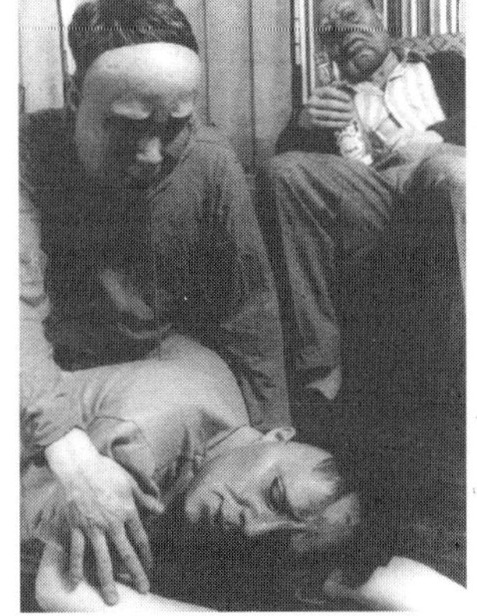
"Violent Illusion Part I"

Since it began in 1987, Geese Theatre has toured prisons, young offender institutions and probation centres throughout Great Britain and Ireland. The company is an offshoot of the award-winning Geese Theatre Company USA formed in 1980 by expatriate British director John Bergman. The group's credo is that "theatre in prison and probation can be a valuable teaching, learning and rehabilitative tool". Their work includes live performances; workshops on a wide variety of themes designed to examine offenders' problems, thinking and behaviour; long-term programmes as an alternative to custody and extensive probation periods; training institutional staff in drama techniques; and week-long residencies to form and train inmate and ex-offender drama groups.

Central to the company's work is the actors' use of masks which allows rapid changes in characterisation. When the characters in a play wear their masks, they are role playing. When they lift them, they must say truthfuly what is on their mind.

Two of the company's current productions – "The Plague Game" and "Lifting the Weight" – are structured improvisations which rely heavily on suggestions from the audience. At vital moments, onlookers are asked to direct the action on stage. The idea is that the plays become inter-active dramas, where new ideas of how to behave and react are examined.

"The Plague Game" is about two families who have to deal with the combined pressures of prison visiting and everyday problems such as housing, debt and raising children as a single parent. The play seeks to explore new ways of protecting families and friendships from cracking under the strain of imprisonment. To win the game, Geese say that "the characters have to learn to accept changes, to listen, to talk honestly about feelings and problems and plan effectively for release". Painting a picture of the difficulties facing offenders leaving prison, "Lifting the Weight" is also played out as a game. Here, the characters confront five key areas: survival, family, work, authority and free-time. Each area contains tokens focusing on issues such as relationships, peer pressure, alcohol and drug abuse, and the potential to re-offend which players have to win in order to stop themselves returning to prison.

"Are You Positive?" is a traditional scripted play designed to educate the audience about HIV and AIDS. It looks at high risk sexual activities and, says Geese, "advocates responsible sexual behaviour". The play looks at the myths surrounding AIDS and how sufferers cope both with the disease and the attitude of those around them. After the performance, the company holds a question and answer session in small groups.

The company's newest production is "The Violent Illusion", which is a series of performances and workshops examining cycles of violent and sexual abuse within the family. Part One is mimed by actors wearing full masks. It tells the story of a young child growing up in a violent environment. The family in Part Two comes from a similar background to the family in Part One but are not violent. The final part of the trilogy (which will be performed in 1993) will explore the consequences of a meeting between the now adult child of Part One and the family of Part Two.

MAX FINDLAY

A Response to Geese

Not a lot of people know this but it's a fact: I wrote the script for the film "McVicar". The script wasn't very good, which probably had something to do with the movie's success. Unfortunately I turned out to be an even worse deal-maker than I was a scriptwriter, which is why I rarely talk about it. I only mention it here to establish my credentials as a scriptwriter rather than a hack at the end of the media food chain.

After the financial pains of seeing "McVicar" run and run on video, then go the rounds on TV without a pee in royalties accruing to me, I wasn't tempted to go near another script until twelve years later when, in 1991, a government agency asked me to write and present a video that advised ex-offenders about getting a job. Part of the programme was a sketch, written and played by the Geese Theatre Company, which dramatised the problems ex-cons face.

I thought the sketch was fatuous in how it portrayed the choice of crime and, since I was presenting the programme and therefore tied to its general approach, I decided to rewrite it. I kept to the playlet's original context but jazzed up the dialogue and tightened the interplay between the characters. Geese adopted most of my suggestions, so presumably they saw some merit in my version. However, although I did not raise the matter, I thought that the view of the self on which much of the company's work is predicated was dogshit.

Geese perform their works wearing masks. When characters talk the truth or voice their conscience, they raise their masks. Of course, the origins of this epistemic framework go back a long way, not least to Christianity. That is, in every person there is a sacred, god-given part, which can be consulted in times of trouble either by one's own methods or divination or with the help of the registered mediators. Then there is all that perilous stuff that we have inherited by our epoch's love affair with Marxism and Freudianism. The latter two perspectives also provide methods for liberating the alienated or repressed self but, as befits their this- worldly orientation, recommend action now rather than leaving such issues for the afterlife.

Meanwhile a ragbag of secular shamans, who present themselves as having a scientific insight into the human condition, plagues our culture, offering various forms of treatment or counselling to an ever-expanding range of unhappy or politically incorrect people. Their lingua franca is a vulgar mishmash of sociological and psychological jargon, concepts and theories. These soul doctors are to be found in the "case-work" social services, the counselling industry, the human potential movement and wherever experts with a social engineering disposition set up shop. Now they are contaminating drama.

Drama has become therapy for the disturbed, an outlet for the angry and reform for the deviant. Geese epitomise this trend.

Karl Popper said recently: "I feel we intellectuals are obliged to those who are not as lucky as we are to help them understand what happens in the world." Whatever else scriptwriters or playwrights do – and it should be plenty – they are directly involved in just what Popper identifies. Indeed, their responsibilities extend not merely to holding up a mirror to nature but also offering us new and original possibilities.

Drama – in our time no longer theatre but film and television – has always had this purpose. Ever since the invention of the form, and Aristotle's analysis, the basics of drama have proved impressively enduring: character being tested by conflict and being changed in the process. And there is a profound, eternal truth about selfhood in drama's creed that action makes, forms, constructs character.

We can only be made human by being exposed to language in a time and place. There is no alternative. If you do not learn language you remain an ape: unless you are programmed by a culture you default to the instincts. Neither the gods nor your genes give you a self – the mind is a social artefact. That's a fact, whether you know it or not.

Oscar Wilde certainly understood this. "Most people are other people," he wrote. Their thoughts are someone else's opinions, their lives a mimicry, their passions a quotation." In the same essay, "De Profundis", he also pointed out that "every little action of the common day makes or unmakes character, and that therefore what one has done in the secret chamber one has some day to cry aloud on the hilltop." As we all know, the box-office claims of drama have to make a crisis of the everyday happenings of the common day. Nonetheless, the more enduring and bounteous drama has always used this principle to convey its understanding of the way the world works. The school of drama that uses the divinised self to further the action is, in fact, a deformed throwback to the deus ex machina school. One of the fruits of modernity, which surely we should eat with relish, is that sky-godders no longer have a voice either from above or within.

Masks have always been at the metaphorical heart of the theatre. Actors put on a mask to play a part – just as we do in society. Consequently, I don't object to the Geese masks per se. They express a truism of both stage and life. What is not allowed is the assumption that behind all the masks is the real or true or authentic – however you want to tag it – self. Like romantic, for-ever-after love, this – in computer-speak – is not available. Under one mask is merely another; and if you take away all the masks there is nothing. The best you can do is create a more useful mask, a more ironical one, a more self-willed one.

JOHN MCVICAR

Management Training

John Cleese

Using actors to advertise the product is an old idea. Using them in training videos is a newer one. There is a world beyond. Today's captains of industry understand the need for good verbal and psychological skills, whether the job involves relating to customers, patients or colleagues; and many firms, in the public as well as the private sector, are discovering that actors can do much more than present the glamorous front to help sell their wares. The buzz-word in modern training is "role-play".

Actors are no strangers to the business world. Over the years, many specialist video companies have produced training films providing employers with more or less useful material, featuring stars such as John Cleese or Penelope Keith in formats not dissimilar from TV sitcoms. At the humbler end of the market, companies have commissioned cut-price productions geared to their own specific training needs.

The latest development has been role-play – using actors in simulated real-life situations to help staff develop communication techniques, examine emotional reactions and improve both effectiveness and job satisfaction. Not everyone has a natural talent for personal presentation, but these skills can be learned. Working opposite a professional actor versed in the particular demands of role-play work can often be an illuminating experience.

The leading specialist company providing this service is Role Call, a consultancy formed by actresses Deborah Manship and Sharon Rose. "Until fairly recently, trainees in role-play sessions were encouraged to act out scenes with their associates – but how good is a bank manager at playing a hairdresser on the verge of bankruptcy?", asks Deborah. "Our actors are all working professionals, with great experience in theatre, film and TV. Their job demands the ability to portray different personalities convincingly".

Drawing on that special expertise, Role Call can devise tailor-made exercises involving characters, events and problems likely to confront the staff of any organisation. The team spans a wide range of age, type and race; but all are expert at working to a brief and are skilled at improvising with flexibility, imagination, and a vital eye on the point of the exercise. "We work closely with the managers, to make absolutely sure that the simulations are as close to real life as humanly possible".

For actors and actresses like Deborah, role-play has much to offer aside from a useful contribution to income. "It really forces you to get right back to basics. It's very easy for actors to hide behind tricks and techniques, especially in today's "instant acting" media world. But when you're playing opposite a real person doing a real job, you've got to be real, too – anything less than that just won't wash!".

Commerce and industry have realised that a happy workforce, confident in its ability to deal with any situation that arises, will improve the competitive edge – whether the aim is profit or service. Training is increasingly important, and the new emphasis on communication skills should prove a financially fertile – and professionally satisfying – ground for the modern actor.

CHRISTOPHER WEBBER

OBITUARIES

MAX FINDLAY remembers personalities from the world of theatre who have died this year.

Dame Judith Anderson

Australian-born Dame Judith Anderson began her stage career in Sydney in 1915 and made her first appearance in New York three years later. Following a series of leading roles spanning twenty years, she appeared as Gertrude in "Hamlet" with Sir John Gielgud and soon appeared at London's Old Vic as Lady Macbeth and as Olga in "The Three Sisters". Continuing a career on both sides of the Atlantic, she performed as Irina Arkadina in "The Seagull" at the Edinburgh Festival and at the Old Vic. Her many film roles included Mrs Danvers in Hitchcock's "Rebecca". She became a Dame Commander of the British Empire in the Birthday Honours in 1960. At the age of eighty four, she starred as the grand dame in the TV soap opera, "Santa Barbara".

Maxine Audley

The granddaughter of Herbert Beerbohm Tree's general manager, Maxine Audley died aged sixty-nine. She made her first stage appearance in a walk-on role at the Open Air, Regent's Park, in 1940. Following extensive repertory and war work, her West End debut was in the musical "Clarissa" at the Palace in 1948. After a stint at Stratford-on-Avon (playing, for example, Goneril in "King Lear"), she joined Laurence Olivier at the St James', appearing in "Anthony and Cleopatra" and "Caesar and Cleopatra". Thereafter she combined West End appearances with seasons at the Old Vic, Bristol Old Vic and Stratford. She enjoyed a succesful film career in the 1950s, starring in movies such as "The King in New York" (playing opposite Charlie Chaplin) and "The Prince and the Showgirl".

Geoffrey Axworthy

Geoffrey Axworthy – the director and lecturer – established the UCI Travelling Theatre which toured Nigeria in the 1960s on a collapsible stage mounted on the back of a trailer. He became the Principal of London's Central School of Speech and Drama in 1967. Six years later, he became the Artistic Director of the new Sherman Theatre in Cardiff. He had originally been invited by University College, Cardiff, to act as consultant on the project; and Axworthy was responsible for pushing through the plans for the theatre's two auditoria. He died in April aged sixty nine.

Robert Beatty

Canadian-born Robert Beatty started his career as a cashier in a gas and fuel company but first appeared in London in the 1938 production of "Idiot's Delight" at the Apollo Theatre. He first appeared in films the same year and his film credits included "Captain Horatio Hornblower RN" (1951); "Albert RN" (1953); "The Amorous Prawn" (1962); "2001: A Space Odyssey" (1968); "Where Eagles Dare" (1969); "The Spaceman and King Arthur" (1979); and "Superman III" (1983). He also performed frequently on television. He appeared regularly on the London stage throughout the 1940s; toured South Africa in "The Aspern Papers" in 1960; and acted in several UK national tours in the 1960s and 1970s. Beatty was eighty two when he died.

Linda Brandon

Linda Brandon, the ICA's Director of Talks, died of cancer aged thirty two in June. Even during her last illness, she was organising the ICA's first major international writers' forum. When Vaclav Havel was on an official visit to London, Brandon managed to involve him in her East European Arts Forum. Under the aegis of her Censored Theatre Project, she was also responsible for arranging the first public reading of Ariel Dorfman's "Death and the Maiden" which was read by Penelope Wilton, Michael Maloney and Jonathan Hyde, directed by Peter James. In the debate which followed, Dorfman said that if the play had been put on in Chile, a bomb would have been dropped on the theatre.

Georgia Brown

Born in the East End in 1934 as Lily Klot, Georgia Brown began in West End cabaret but in 1956 she appeared as Lucy in the first London production of "The Threepenny Opera". In 1957, she duplicated the role on Broadway. Mainly based in the USA throughout her career, she enjoyed her greatest success playing Nancy in "Oliver", repeating her triumph on Broadway in 1962. In 1965, she took over from Rachel Roberts the role of Maggie May in the musical which Bart had written especially for her. She returned frequently to Britain to appear in films such as "Lock Up Your Daughters" and "The Seven Per Cent Solution"; and in the 1980s played in "42nd Street" at Drury Lane and Steven Berkoff's play "Greek".

Yvonne Bryceland

Yvonne Bryceland, who died at the age of sixty seven, was born in South Africa and enjoyed a successful classical career there before coming to London in Athol Fugard's "Statements after an Arrest under the Immorality Act" at the Royal Court in 1974. She later joined the National Theatre where she appeared in Fo and Rame's "Female Parts" in 1981. She won the Olivier award for best actress and international acclaim for her performance in Fugard's "Road to Mecca" in 1985. Writing in The Independent, Fugard paid tribute to Bryceland as one of theatre's "unique and most courageous talents".

William Douglas-Home

William Douglas-Home died aged eighty. He studied at RADA and made his stage debut at the Brighton Repertory Theatre in 1937, appearing later the same year at the New Theatre in London in "Bonnett Over the Windmill". His plays were the last of the type seen frequently between the wars and (despite their lack of modernity) attracted big name stars such as Ralph Richardson and Celia Johnson. He wrote two autobiographies and was deeply interested in politics. In a playwriting career lasting half a century, he wrote (among others) "Great Possessions", "The Thistle and the Rose", "The Reluctant Debutante", "The Drawing Room Tragedy", "The Secretary Bird", "The Grouse Moor Image", "Lloyd George Knew My Father", "The Dame of Sark", "The Kingfisher", "You're All Right, How Am I?", "After the Ball is Over" and "Portraits".

Adele Dixon

Adele Dixon, who died aged eighty three, first appeared on the London stage aged thirteen in "Where the Rainbow Ends" at the Apollo Theatre. Her last West End appearance was at the Palladium in 1953, as Prince Charming to Julie Andrews' Cinderella. After RADA, she joined Robert Atkins' Shakespeare company on a 1927 tour of Egypt, playing a series of major female roles. In 1928, she joined the Old Vic company, where her leads included Juliet to Gielgud's first Romeo and Ophelia to his first Hamlet. Her performance as Susie Dean in the 1931 stage adaptation of JB Priestley's "The Good Companions" (again opposite Gielgud) was widely acclaimed. During the 1930s, she enjoyed many starring roles in West End musical comedies, including Cole Porter's "Anything Goes" in 1935. Her films included "Banana Ridge" (1941).

Denholm Elliott

Probably better known for his work on screen than on stage, Denholm Elliott died in October aged seventy. In the 1940s and 1950s, he played in Christopher Fry's "Venus Observed" at the St James's; Anouilh's adaptation of "Ring Round the Moon"; TS Eliot's "The Confidential Clerk"; and Tennessee Williams' "Camino Real". His film career began in earnest with "The Sound Barrier" (1952) and "The Cruel Sea" (1953). The late 1950s were a comparatively barren period and he was rescued by the cinema, in particular by his performances in "King Rat" (1965) and famously as the backstreet abortionist in "Alfie" (1966). Specialising in playing charming but seedy characters, he went on to star in a wide range of extremely popular TV and cinema films. His last West End appearance was in David Mamet's "A Life in the Theatre" in 1989.

Ronald Eyre

Director Ronald Eyre died in April aged sixty two. He made his debut as a theatre director in 1963, producing "Titus Andronicus" at Birmingham Rep. He was equally happy working in the West End and in television and with both the major companies and the smaller subsidised theatres. He directed "Mrs Warren's Profession" at the National Theatre in 1971; and " The Marquis of Keith" (1974) and Donald Sinden's 1979 Stratford "Othello" for the RSC. In the year after his stint with the National, he directed Charles Wood's "Veterans" (Royal Court) and Boucicault's "London Assurance" (New Theatre), as well as Alec Guinness in John Mortimer's "A Voyage Round My Father" (Haymarket). Sixteen years later, he again worked with Alec Guinness, this time in Lee Blessing's "A Walk in the Woods" at the Comedy Theatre.

Jose Ferrer

The American actor and director Jose Ferrer began his career as an opera singer and made his Broadway debut in 1935 in a "A Slight Case of Murder". He was much praised for his performance as Iago to Paul Robeson's Othello in 1943, moving on to achieve fame as a screen actor in the title role in "Cyrano de Bergerac"(1950) and as Toulouse Lautrec in "Moulin Rouge" (1952). Ferrer directed Keith Michell as Cyrano at the Chichester Festival Theatre and later appeared on the Chichester stage in "Ring Round the Moon" and in Peter Hall's production "Born Again". Continuing to appear in films and TV dramas throughout his later years, Ferrer died at the age of eighty.

Dame Gwen Ffrangcon-Davies

Known mainly for classical roles, Dame Gwen made her stage debut in a walk-on part in "A Midsummer Night's Dream" at Her Majesty's in 1911, having been encouraged onto the boards by Ellen Terry after accosting her backstage and giving a rendition of Juliet's potion speech. She went on to play Juliet and a string of leading ladies, particularly in the plays of GB Shaw. Famous as Gielgud's partner in many Shakespearean and Chekhovian roles, she is remembered by many as the impossibly correct Gwendolen Fairfax in the Gielgud/Edith Evans "The Importance of Being Earnest". She continued to work after the age of a hundred, most recently in the TV "Poirot".

Margaret Hotine

Margaret Hotine was a Shakespearean scholar providing intellectual weight to theatrical productions. There were many companies who profited from her considerable expertise (frequently displayed in their programme notes). She trained at RADA and her acting roles (spread either side of her taking an economics degree in the mid-1960s and subsequent teaching career) included Ellie May in the London production of "Tobacco Road", first witch in Kenneth McClellan's "Macbeth" in the 1980s, and a wide range of fringe productions. Ironically (given her cause of death), these included a play at the Latchmere Theatre set in a women's cancer clinic. For many years she worked for the Equity Members Job Grapevine until it was finally abolished.

Frankie Howerd

Born in 1921, Frankie Howerd made his first professional appearance on the stage at the London Palladium in 1950. In 1953, he appeared in the revue "Pardon My French" at the Prince of Wales's Theatre which ran for 759 performances. Famous for his stage, film and television career as a comic, his film roles included "The Ladykillers" (1955), "The Great St Trinian's Train Robbery" (1966) and two "Carry On" films; and he starred in a wide range of TV programmes including "That Was the Week That Was" and "Up Pompeii". Besides his pantomime roles, he played Lord Fancourt Babberley in "Charley's Aunt" at the Globe in 1955; Bottom in "A Midsummer Night's Dream" at the Old Vic in 1957; and Prologue and Pseudolos in "A Funny Thing Happened on the Way to the Forum" in 1963.

Robert Locke

Aged only thirty five, Robert Locke died in July. Locke began his career in the 1970s in touring productions which included the Oxford Stage Company's "Macbeth" and "Psycho". He soon exploited his considerable talent as a singer, appearing in a tour of "Annie" and in "Jesus Christ Superstar" in Norwich and York.

His West End debut was as Charlie Brown in "Snoopy" at the Duchess Theatre. Later, his most famous role was as Eddie in "Blood Brothers" in 1988. Returning to the role at the Phoenix Theatre in October 1991, he played Eddie until illness forced his retirement in March. Following his death, the Phoenix was the venue for a midnight matinee of the show in aid of research into multifocal progressive leukoencephalopathy.

Robert Morley

Robert Morley made his first stage appearance in 1928 in "Dr Syn" at the Hippodrome, Margate, and his London debut in 1929 as a pirate in "Treasure Island" at the Strand. His first major London role was the title part in "Oscar Wilde" (1937), having toured the provinces for several years and (together with Peter Bull) established repertory at Perranporth in Cornwall. He subsequently starred as Henry Higgins in "Pygmalion" at the Old Vic and in the New York production of "Oscar Wilde". He named his son, the writer and critic Sheridan Morley, after the character Sheridan Whiteside in "The Man Who Came to Dinner", which he played in 1941. His film appearances included "The African Queen" and "Theatre of Blood". He died aged eighty four.

Nan Munro

South African-born Nan Munro died shortly before her eighty seventh birthday. She originally trained as a gymnastics teacher and masseuse before moving onto RADA. Her first appearance was in 1931 in Noel Coward's "The Young Idea" at the Pavilion, Weymouth. She made her West End debut in "The Moon in the Yellow River" in 1934, later followed by a noted performance in "Dear Octopus" at the Queen's. She returned to South Africa in 1941, formed her own company and toured widely. On her return to London seven years later, she starred in "Waters of the Moon" at the Haymarket and subsequently Geoffrey Lumsden's farce "Caught Napping". She also made numerable film and television appearances.

Laurence Naismith

Laurence Naismith had a distinguished stage career before moving to the USA to work in films. He joined the Bristol Repertory Company in 1930 (having been in the chorus line of "Oh Kay !" in 1926). After the war, he returned to the stage in the 1948 production of Odet's "Rocket to the Moon" at St Martin's Theatre. Subsequent stage roles included Proteus opposite Noel Coward in Shaw's "The Apple Cart"; Dr Pangloss in Bernstein's "Candide"; and as the father in the 1970 production of "The Winslow Boy". His films included "A Night To Remember", "Solomon and Sheba", "The Angry Silence", "The Trials of Oscar Wilde", "Greyfriars Bobby", "Cleopatra", "Camelot", "Scrooge" and "Diamonds are Forever". He died in June aged eighty three.

Stephen Oliver

Composer and librettist Stephen Oliver died in April. Oliver will be remembered for taking music and musical enthusiasm to unusual places and to new people. His opera scores include "The Duchess of Malfi", "Tom Jones" and "Timon of Athens", which was a recent success at English National Opera. He staged musical work at the King's Head, hoping to introduce opera to a new kind of audience. His scores for radio were celebrated: the music for the series "The Lord of the Rings" was particularly popular.

His full-length musical "Blondel" (lyrics by Tim Rice) was, sadly for him, not a major commercial or critical success. His scores for theatre productions included several for the RSC, especially his celebrated accompaniment to "Nicholas Nickleby".

Peter Radmore

Peter Radmore joined the lighting department at the Old Vic in 1964, moving from the Oxford Playhouse. He managed the lighting for the Chichester Festival seasons contemporaneously with his work at the Old Vic, as well as acting as chief electrician on all Laurence Olivier's major provincial and overseas tours and West End seasons at the Albery, Queen's and Cambridge Theatres. Subsequently, he became the chief electrician of the Olivier Theatre. He lit several plays for the National, including "The Beggar's Opera" and "Futurists" for Richard Eyre; "Bedroom Farce" for Peter Hall and Alan Ayckbourn; and "The Hunchback of Notre Dame" for Michael Bogdanov. He also worked regularly with students, creating a student attachment scheme within his department. In 1988, he became the National's technical manager.

Harriet Reynolds

Harriet Reynolds died of cancer in June, aged forty seven. She was probably most widely known for her role as Sue (Abigail's mother) in Mike Leigh's "Abigail's Party" at Hampstead Theatre in 1977 and again in the TV version five years later. Her last appearance was in an episode of the television series "Jeeves and Wooster", recorded in October 1991. She played a wide variety of comic roles in major repertory theatres. In 1985, she took over the part of The Headmistress in "Daisy Pulls It Off" at the Globe Theatre (a theatre she revisited three years later playing Sergeant Fire in "Dry Rot"). Her many TV appearances included roles in "Lovejoy", "A Very Peculiar Practice" "London's Burning" and "The New Statesman".

John Stratton

John Stratton, who died at the age of sixty six and whose recreations included shop window gazing, made his first appearance at the Empire Theatre, Dewsbury, in 1943 as Freddie Eynsford-Hill in "Pygmalion". He first appeared in London five years later in "No Trees in the Street" at St James's Theatre. In a career lasting a quarter of a century, his credits included a 1949 tour of England and Germany as Morgan Evans in "The Corn is Green"; Paul in "Colombe" in 1951 and Rapcev in "An Act of Madness" at the Edinburgh Festival in 1955 (his two favourite parts); McCann in "The Birthday Party" at the Lyric, Hammersmith, in 1958; as well as many films and television productions including "Fall of Eagles".

Joan Sanderson

Joan Sanderson made her first professional stage appearance at Stratford-on-Avon immediately before World War II. During the war, she acted extensively in repertory and toured Italy and North Africa in productions for the troops. In the 1953 Stratford season, she played Goneril to Michael Redgrave's King Lear. Best known for her comedy roles, her first West End appearance was in "See How They Run" just after the war; and she starred in "Simple Spymen", "Banana Ridge", "Anyone for Denis?" and Alan Bennett's "Habeas Corpus" at the Lyric. Her first major TV success was in "Please, Sir". Since then, she starred in TV series such as "All Gas and Gaiters", "Fawlty Towers", "Upstairs, Downstairs" and, more recently, with Prunella Scales in "After Henry". She died aged seventy nine.

CONTRIBUTORS

The Yearbook has collected together a large number of writers in order to produce this book. CAROLINE KAY, CHARLES MORGAN AND ANNE VANHAEVERBEKE have generously contributed pieces as spokesmen for their various organisations and details of their postions in those organisations appear with their contributions. The remaining contributors are listed here.

Michael Arditti is a drama critic for The Evening Standard and regularly contributes arts features to various papers. He has had several plays produced on the stage and radio and his first novel, "The Celibate" will be published in January 1993 by Sinclair-Stevenson.

Pat Ashworth began her working life as an English teacher in secondary schools. The mother of two children, her second career is in journalism. She has edited the monthly magazine, Nottingham Topic, for ten years and has written widely in the national press, in particular The Guardian, for which she has reviewed the arts since 1986. She regularly writes and directs her local pantomime.

Kate Bassett is a theatre director and freelance arts journalist. She currently writes on theatre for Plays & Players, The New Statesman and City Limits. She has also reviewed theatre for The Guardian, Time Out and The List, and is a book reviewer for The Literary Review and The Daily Telegraph.

Clare Bayley is a co-editor of Hybrid, the new cross-art form bi-monthly. She is a former theatre editor of What's On in London and a freelance contributor to publications including The Independent, The Guardian and Plays & Players.

Michael Billington has been drama critic of The Guardian since 1971 and of Country Life since 1987. He also broadcasts regularly on the arts on radio and television and has written and presented profiles of Peggy Ashcroft, Peter Hall and Alan Ayckbourn. He has also written a number of books on the theatre. He began his reviewing career on Plays & Players in 1964.

Jim Burke is the theatre editor of City Life, Manchester's arts and entertainment listings magazine. He is one of the founders of the theatre collective, Northern Edge, and co-author of the skinhead musical "Suedehead" which was nominated for a Manchester Evening News Fringe Award, 1992.

Betty Caplan is a freelance critic and writer who has written regularly for The Guardian and New Statesman since 1987. Short stories and plays include "No Place for a Lady", broadcast on Radio 3, "Another Life"(Blackie 1981) and, most recently, "Demeter's Daughter."

Gerry Colgan has worked as a freelance writer on theatre and books for many Irish newspapers and periodicals for over twenty five years. For the last ten years, he has been a regular theatre critic and columnist for The Irish Times and Irish correspondent for Plays International.

William Cook is a freelance journalist specialising in the performing arts and popular culture. He has contributed to The Times and The Independent and is the comedy critic of The Guardian. He also writes for The Scotsman and City Limits and works as a reader for Channel 4.

Della Couling is a theatre and opera critic for The Independent and other British publications. Her special interest is European theatre. She also writes widely in various European newspapers and specialist journals. She has translated several plays.

Tim Cronin is a musician, song-writer and freelance journalist.

Terry Diab has worked extensively as an actress, including a two year spell at the National Theatre, appearing in "The Romans in Britain", "The Mayor of Zalemea" and as Minnehaha in "Hiawatha". She is also the mother of two children and is a broadcaster – working mainly for the BBC's World Service – and a writer.

Rod Dungate is a playwright whose works include "Up the Pole!", "A Little Light Orienteering", "King James' Ear" and "Picking Over the Icefloes". He is chair of Stagecoach, an organisation developing the arts in the West Midlands. He is also drama advisor to West Midlands Arts. He is a regular contributor to Plays & Players and Tribune.

Max Findlay is a writer on a wide variety of subjects whose work has appeared in many national publications. He has also published a book of poetry, "If They Gave Medals".

Mark Fisher is theatre editor of The List, Glasgow and Edinburgh's event guide. He is also one of the editorial group of Theatre Scotland, a quality theatre quarterly that was launched in 1992.

Graham Hassell has been a regular contributor to Plays & Players since 1989. He started writing theatre reviews in 1981, working as the drama critic for London Alternative Magazine. Since then his theatre pieces have appeared in many publications. He is currently assistant editor of What's On in London magazine.

Malcolm Hay has contributed to many national newspapers and magazines on theatre, comedy and the media. He is the author of a book about Edward Bond. He has worked as a lecturer on drama in many academic institutions, including the University of Massachusetts. He currently lectures at the University of East London and is comedy editor of Time Out.

Lynda Henderson is a theatre critic, editor and publisher who teaches theatre studies at the University of Ulster at Coleraine and was a founding editor of the magazine *Theatre Ireland* which she now designs.

Martin Hoyle has been a theatre critic for The Financial Times, The Times and others for a decade. He is classical music and opera editor of Time Out.

Donald Hutera is a freelance writer on the arts currently living in Minneapolis, USA. He has written for a wide variety of publications, most particularly for the New York publication, London Theatre News. His specialities are dance and performance art and he is co-author of "The Dance Handbook" and a major contributor on dance to Chambers Biographical Dictionary.

Nick James was a member of various punk outfits throughout the 1980s and then started writing about cinema for City Limits, The Producer and The Venue. He joined City Limits as TV editor in 1989 and is now cinema editor on that magazine.

Roy Kift is a German playwright whose works have been translated into over twenty languages. As well as winning several literary prizes and awards for his work in Germany, he is also a translator of plays (including the work of Moliere, Goldoni, Kipphardt and Patrick Suskind) and a contributor to various journals on contemporary German theatre.

Reva Klein is a freelance writer who has written widely in the national press. She now writes mainly for The Times Educational Supplement, for which she is comissioning editor on Theatre In Education and to which she contributes a column on theatre.

Ariane Koek is a freelance writer and a producer with BBC Radio 4's Woman's Hour.

Jeremy Kingston is a theatre critic on The Times. At one time he was a playwright: two of his plays were presented in the West End and "Oedipus at the Crossroads" at the King's Head, Islington. For ten years he was the theatre critic for Punch.

Gina Landor is an actress and has played many leading roles with major repertory and touring companies as well as with companies in London and abroard. She also teaches drama.

John McVicar is an ex-criminal who served a long prison sentence. He is now a commentator and writer on law and order and has written widely in the national press.

Gwyn Morgan practised as a barrister until shortly before she became a mother in 1982. She is a long-standing contributor to Plays & Players. She has written for Time Out, City Limits, The Independent on Sunday and many other publications.

Sheridan Morley is the film critic of The Sunday Express and drama critic of The International Herald Tribune and several other publications both in UK and abroard. He has made major contributions to The Times and Punch. He has appeared on numerous occasions on radio and television and hosts the Radio 2 "Arts Programme". On stage, he has narrated several shows including his own "Spread a Little Happiness". His books include biographies of Noel Coward, David Niven and Oscar Wilde.

Jim O'Quinn is the founding editor of the US monthly, American Theatre. His articles and reviews have appeared in New York Native, Theater heute and The Tatler. He has worked on The Drama Review and The New Orleans States-Item. He is also a composer and music arranger, with work including a children's opera, "The Littlest Emperor".

Nina Pasco writes on a variety of topics – ranging from fantasies on computer technology to biographical studies: her latest subject is Viennese composer Alban Berg.

Ingeborg Pietzsch was a staff journalist on the East German magazine Theater der Zeit for over twenty years. Her specialisation was not only theatre in GDR but also in the Eastern bloc as a whole. Theater der Zeit closed in the early months of 1992, the victim of the financial pressures of reunification.

Kenneth Rea is a theatre critic for The Guardian. He also writes for The Times and teaches drama at Guildhall School of Music and Drama.

Timothy Ramsden has taught, reviewed and written programme notes for other people's plays. Recently he has started writing his own, with Theatre In Education pieces, "Finding Jake" and "Lifestyles" on HIV and "No Half Measures" on alcohol. "Hard Cases", which is about bullying, is in preparation.

Simon Reade is a critic and dramaturg. Since 1990, he has been literary manager of the Gate theatre, Notting Hill. He is author of "Cheek by Jowl: Ten Years of Celebration" published by Absolute Classics.

Helen Rose worked on Time Out's picture desk for three years before joining that magazine's theatre section where she worked for seven years before the birth of her first child in 1988. She now works as a freelance theatre journalist, contributing particularly to Time Out and Plays & Players.

Allen Saddler is the regular West country reviewer for The Guardian. He has written over twenty radio plays and the comedy series "I Should Say So" for Michael Williams. He is a novelist and writes books for children, the most recent of which, "Sam's Swap Shop", will be published by OUP in spring 1993 and will be heard on Radio 5.

Ann St Clair-Stannard was trained at RADA and worked in theatre and television (she played Jane in the first TV adaptation of "Pride and Prejudice") before marrying and having children. She has been the theatre correspondent for Monocle magazine for eight years. She is also an artist and has exhibited at the Royal Society of Miniaturists and at Day and Bird of Old Bond Street.

Prunella Scales is an actress whose numerous theatre performances include "Single Spies", "An Evening with Queen Victoria", "School for Scandal" and "A Long Day's Journey into Night". Her directing credits include "The Woodcarver" (Bristol Old Vic) and "Uncle Vanya" (Perth, Australia). Her TV appearances, in programmes as varied as "After Henry" and "My Friend Walter" have been extensive and her films include "A Chorus of Disapproval" and "Howard's End."

Ian Shuttleworth has been theatre and books editor of City Limits since 1991 and has contributed to The Sunday Times, The Independent, The Stage and Plays & Players. He founded the Belfast-based electronic music label Cemental Health Records. He has appeared on Radio 4's "Kaleidescope", BBC 1's "Joker in the Pack" and in the film "White Knuckle Ride" in which he played a sinister behavioural psychologist.

Ned Sherrin worked for the BBC during the 1960s and directed the original "That Was the Week that Was". He has written novels,newspaper columns, stories, songs, plays, musicals and radio and television plays – sometimes in collaboration with Caryl Brahms – including the play "Beecham". He has directed numerous stage shows, notably "Side by Side by Sondheim" and "Jeffrey Bernard is Unwell". He often broadcasts on radio and television and currently presents the award-winning "Loose Ends" on Radio 4.

Penny Simpson is a Cardiff-based journalist who has written about the visual arts, theatre and style for regional and national newspapers. In 1991, she was awarded the TMA regional critic of the year award. She also edits the Welsh arts supplement Prime Time.

Tom Soper is a playwright and freelance journalist.

Mia Soteriou is an actress, a singer, a composer and a musician. She has composed music for plays for the BBC, RSC, Greenwich theatre, and Chichester Festival theatre. She has acted in the West End – notably as Yoko Ono in "Lennon" – the Royal Court, the National and in television and radio plays. She has played in various bands and has worked as a recording artist.

Sheila Starns is an academic, freelance journalist and photographer. Formerly a department head for the British Library, she now divides her time between London and Glasgow where she lectures at Strathclyde University.

Christopher Webber is an actor who has appeared in the West End, in tours, in repertory and on the London Fringe. He is also a director, a writer and broadcaster. His recent publications include "Bluff Your Way at the Races" and "Tatyana" for Nottingham Playhouse, starring Josie Lawrence.

Andrew Wickes has directed five Gilbert and Sullivan operas for the D'Oyly Carte, has acted in repertory and in the West End and has written a number of stage adaptations including "The History of Tom Jones."

Robert Workman photographs operas, musicals, plays, actors, actresses and singers. He, too, has appeared on stage. At school, he acted in "Henry V" as the Chorus and in "Oliver's Island" as a Dusky Maiden.

Searchline Listings

EVERY :

-PLAY - 1,252 Productions
-PLAYER - 5,018 actors
-PLAYHOUSE - 772 Theatres

PLUS:

-660 PLAYWRIGHTS
-669 PRODUCERS
-171 DIRECTORS

Produced Exclusively for
PLAYS and PLAYERS

The information contained in the following pages, is compiled by us - with the untiring assistance of the VAST majority of production companys and theatres - for which we thank you. However, as the data has to be entered by people - mostly actors! - there will be errors, for which we apologise. Therefore, we cannot accept responsibility for any errors and omissions. If we are notified, we will gladly amend our record and correct our mistake.

The Searchline Database is designed by the Eazy Software Company and operated on computers supplied by HeathMill MultiMedia

PLAYS LISTING

We have attempted to give a full listing of productions shown in 1992, together with productions scheduled to be shown in 1993.
We regret any errors or ommissions and apologise unreservedly if you find any.

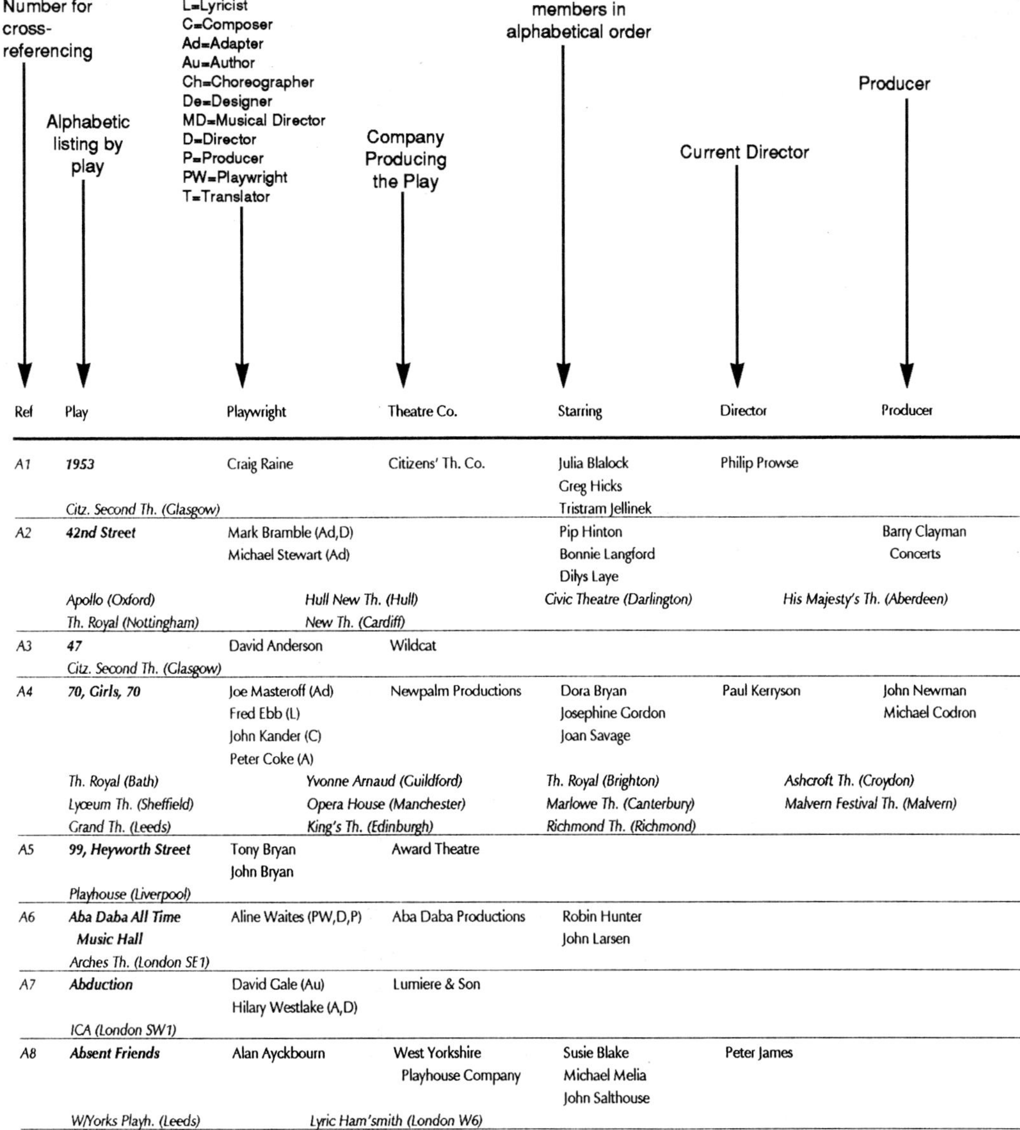

Ref	Play	Playwright	Theatre Co.	Starring	Director	Producer
A1	***1953***	Craig Raine	Citizens' Th. Co.	Julia Blalock Greg Hicks Tristram Jellinek	Philip Prowse	
	Citz. Second Th. (Glasgow)					
A2	***42nd Street***	Mark Bramble (Ad,D) Michael Stewart (Ad)		Pip Hinton Bonnie Langford Dilys Laye		Barry Clayman Concerts
	Apollo (Oxford) *Th. Royal (Nottingham)*	*Hull New Th. (Hull)* *New Th. (Cardiff)*		*Civic Theatre (Darlington)*	*His Majesty's Th. (Aberdeen)*	
A3	***47***	David Anderson	Wildcat			
	Citz. Second Th. (Glasgow)					
A4	***70, Girls, 70***	Joe Masteroff (Ad) Fred Ebb (L) John Kander (C) Peter Coke (A)	Newpalm Productions	Dora Bryan Josephine Gordon Joan Savage	Paul Kerryson	John Newman Michael Codron
	Th. Royal (Bath) *Lyceum Th. (Sheffield)* *Grand Th. (Leeds)*	*Yvonne Arnaud (Guildford)* *Opera House (Manchester)* *King's Th. (Edinburgh)*		*Th. Royal (Brighton)* *Marlowe Th. (Canterbury)* *Richmond Th. (Richmond)*	*Ashcroft Th. (Croydon)* *Malvern Festival Th. (Malvern)*	
A5	***99, Heyworth Street***	Tony Bryan John Bryan	Award Theatre			
	Playhouse (Liverpool)					
A6	***Aba Daba All Time Music Hall***	Aline Waites (PW,D,P)	Aba Daba Productions	Robin Hunter John Larsen		
	Arches Th. (London SE1)					
A7	***Abduction***	David Gale (Au) Hilary Westlake (A,D)	Lumiere & Son			
	ICA (London SW1)					
A8	***Absent Friends***	Alan Ayckbourn	West Yorkshire Playhouse Company	Susie Blake Michael Melia John Salthouse	Peter James	
	W/Yorks Playh. (Leeds)	*Lyric Ham'smith (London W6)*				

Ref	Play	Playwright	Theatre Co.	Starring	Director	Producer
A9	***Absent Friends*** *Palace Th. (Westcliff-On-Sea)*	Alan Ayckbourn	Palace Theatre, Westcliff		Christopher Dunham	
A10	***Absent Friends*** *Wolsey Theatre (Ipswich)*	Alan Ayckbourn		Marilyn Cutts Michael Garner Stephen Tompkinson	Hettie MacDonald	Wolsey Theatre Company Ltd
A11	***Absurd Person Singular*** *Belgrade Th. (Coventry)*	Alan Ayckbourn	Belgrade Theatre Company	Eliza Hunt Elizabeth Mickery Paul Rattfield	Robert Hamlin	
A12	***Acapulco*** *King's Head Th. (London N1)*	Steven Berkoff (PW,D)		Paul Bentall Steven Berkoff Rory Edwards		
A13	***The Actor's Nightmare & Identity Crisis*** *Th. Museum (London WC2)*	Christopher Durang	No Wall Theatre Company			
A14	***Adult Child/Dead Child*** *King's Head Th. (London N1)* *Pavillion (Brighton)* *The Green Room (Manchester)*	Claire Dowie	One in the Eye Theatre Company	Mem Morrison	Jens Thordal	Simon Drysdale
A15	***Adult Child/Dead Child*** *BAC (London SW11)*	Claire Dowie	Starving Artists Theatre Co	Claire Dowie	Colin Watkeys	
A16	***After You With The Milk*** *Playhouse Th. (Salisbury)*	Ben Travers	Salisbury Theatre Company	Sarah Carpenter James Mansfield Alan Moore	Deborah Paige	
A17	***Aladdin*** *Palace Th. (Watford)*	Roy Hudd	Palace Theatre, Watford		Martin Connor	Palace Theatre
A18	***Aladdin*** *Apollo (Oxford)*	Rhys Nelson (D & Ch)		Amelia Frid Ashley Paske Bradley Walsh		Barrie C Stead
A19	***Aladdin*** *Thorndike Th. (Leatherhead)*		Thorndike Theatre	Sophie Lawrence		Bill Kenwright
A20	***Aladdin*** *Opera House (Manchester)*			Michael Barrymore Dooby Duck Val Lehman		Manchester Theatres Ltd
A21	***Aladdin*** *Lyceum Th. (Sheffield)*		Crucible Theatre			
A22	***Aladdin*** *Theatr Colwyn (Colwyn Bay)*			Phil Batty Maxwell Slater		
A23	***Aladdin*** *Swan Theatre (Worcester)*	Christopher Lillicrap Jeanette Ranger	Worcester Theatre Company		Pat Trueman	
A24	***Aladdin*** *Palace Theatre (Newark)*					
A25	***Aladdin*** *Bristol Old Vic (Bristol)*	Chris Denys Chris Harris	Bristol Old Vic Ensemble	Chris Harris		
A26	***Aladdin*** *Arts Centre (Horsham)*			Josephine Blake Lorraine Chase Jess Conrad	Lynda Baron	New Pantomime Productions
A27	***Aladdin Bolton*** *Octagon Th. (Bolton)*	Bob Carlton	Octagon Theatre Company	Paul Kissaun Carol Noakes Bernard Wrigley	Noreen Kershaw	
A28	***The Alchemist*** *Playhouse (Newcastle/u/Tyne)* *Barbican Th. (London EC2)*	Ben Jonson	Royal Shakespeare Company	David Bradley Jonathan Hyde Joanne Pearce	Sam Mendes	RSC
A29	***Alfie*** *Hull New Th. (Hull)* *Grand Th. (Leeds)* *King's Th. (Edinburgh)* *Lyceum Th. (Sheffield)* *Th. Royal (Newcastle/u/Tyne)* *Opera House (Manchester)* *Grand Th. (Swansea)*	Bill Naughton		Adam Faith	Frank Dunlop	

Produced exclusively for Plays & Players by SEARCHLINE

Ref	Play	Playwright	Theatre Co.	Starring	Director	Producer
A30	*Alfie* *Octagon Th. (Bolton)*	Bill Naughton	Octagon Theatre Company	Eithne Browne Liz Fraser Gary Webster	Lawrence Till	
A31	*Aliens 4* *ICA (London SW1)*		Dogs In Honey			
A32	*All My Sons* *Palace Th. (Watford)*	Arthur Miller	Palace Theatre, Watford	Diane Fletcher Julian Glover Mark McGann	Lou Stein	
A33	*All My Sons* *Young Vic Th. (London SE1)*	Arthur Miller	Young Vic Company	Ian Bannen Amanda Boxer Marjorie Yates	David Thacker	
A34	*All On Top* *Etcetera (London NW1)*	Marcus Brent	Stretch Theatre	Mark Monero	Richard Bridgland	
A35	*All's Well That Ends Well* *Swan Th. (Stratford-upon-Avon)*	William Shakespeare	Royal Shakespeare Company	Alfred Burke Barbara Jefford Richard Johnson	Peter Hall	RSC
A36	*'Allo,'Allo* *Opera House (Manchester)* *Dominion (London W1)*	David Croft		Gordon Kaye Richard Marner Carmen Silvera	Peter Farago	Mark Furness Ltd
A37	*Amahal And The Night Visitors* *Little Angel (London N1)*	Menotti (C)	Little Angel Marionette Theatre			
A38	*American Heart* *Tabard Th. (London W4)*	Sean Eve	Tabard Theatre Company		Patrick Marmion	
A39	*American Buffalo* *Hen & Chickens (London N1)*	David Mamet	The Film & Theatre Foundation	Richard Brake Steve James Jack Panter	Jonathan Robinson	
A40	*Amphibians* *Barbican/The Pit (London EC1)*	Billy Roche	Royal Shakespeare Company	Richard Bonneville Hilary Cromie Jane Gurnett	Michael Attenborough	RSC
A41	*An After Taste Of Sherry* *BAC (London SW11)*	Alison West	Black Theatre Co operative		Joan-Ann Maynard	
A42	*An Evening With John Mills* *Yvonne Arnaud (Guildford)*			John Mills		Duncan C Weldon
A43	*And A Nightingale Sang* *Playhouse (Derby)*	C.P. Taylor	Derby Playhouse	Sharon Mayer Sheila Tait	Mark Clements	
A44	*And Hunger For All* *Man in the Moon (London SW3)*	Mary Bonner	Pathos	Mary Bonner	Esty Zakhem	
A45	*Androcles And The Lion* *Polka Th. (London SW19)*	Bernard Kops	Polka Theatre	Donald Allen Amanda Edwards David Jarvis	Vicky Ireland	
A46	*Angelo* *Little Angel (London N1)*		Little Angel Marionette Theatre			
A47	*Angels In America* *NT/Cottesloe (London SE1)*	Tony Kushner	Royal National Theatre	Sean Chapman Marcus D'Amico Lou Hirsch	Declan Donnellan	RNT
A48	*Angels & Amazons*		Ra Ra Zoo	Sue Broadway Angela de Castro Valerie Griffiths	Sue Davis	

Ryan Centre (Stranraer)
Prema Arts Ctr. (Dursley, Glos.)
The Theatre (Chipping Norton)
The Junction (Cambridge)
Dartington Arts (Totnes)
Leigh Drama Ctre (Leigh)
Ocean Room (Weymouth)
Spring St. Th. (Hull)
Arts Workshop (Newbury)
Strode Theatre (Street, Somerset)
The Green Room (Manchester)
Trinity Arts (Gainsborough)
Drill Hall (London WC1)
Civic Theatre (Oswaldtwistle)
Arts Centre (Birmingham)
Beaford Art Ctr. (Beaford, Devon)
Parr Hall (Warrington, Cheshire)
Civic Th. (Ayr)
West End Centre (Aldershot)
Bluecoat Arts (Liverpool)
Harlequin Th (Northwich)
Leisure Centre (Ullapool)
King's Lynn Arts (King's Lynn)
21 South Street (Reading)
MacRobert Arts (Stirling)
Island Arts (Broadstairs)
The Gantry (Southampton)
Colchester Arts (Colchester)
Tron Th. (Glasgow)

Ref	Play	Playwright	Theatre Co.	Starring	Director	Producer
A49	***Animal Farm***	George Orwell (A) Roger Parsley (Ad)	Snap Theatre Company	Jeremy Hutton Joanne McInnes James Traherne	Andy Graham	
	Beck Th. (Hayes, Middx) *Palace Th. (Westcliff-On-Sea)* *Library Theatre (Solihull)* *Regal Arts Ctre (Worksop)* *Spring St. Th. (Hull)*					
A50	***Anna Karenina***	Leo Tolstoy	Shared Experience	Annabelle Apsion Gregory Floy Max Gold	Nancy Meckler	
	W/Yorks Playh. (Leeds) *Haymarket Studio (Leicester)* *Tricycle Th. (London NW6)* *Brewhouse Th. (Taunton)* *Playhouse Th. (Salisbury)*					
A51	***Annie Get Your Gun***	Irving Berlin (C & L)	Theatre Royal Plymouth	Kim Criswell John Deidrich Brian Glover	Roger Redfarn	Ronald Lee
	Th. Royal (Plymouth) *Hippodrome (Birmingham)* *King's Th. (Edinburgh)* *King's Th. (Glasgow)* *Prince of Wales Th. (London W1V)*					
A52	***Antigone***	Jean Anouilh	The Acting Company		David Harris	
	Th. Museum (London WC2)					
A53	***Antony and Cleopatra***	William Shakespeare	Royal Shakespeare Company	Clare Higgins Paul Jesson Richard Johnson	John Caird	RSC
	RST (Stratford-upon-Avon)					
A54	***Antony And Cleopatra***	William Shakespeare	Torch Theatre Company		Kit Thacker	
	Torch Theatre (Milford Haven)					
A55	***Anybody for Murder?***	Clemens & Spooner	Back To Back Theatre Company	Val Lehman Ian Lindsay David Roper	Brian Clemens	Daryl Back
	Granville Th. (Ramsgate) *Ashcroft Th. (Croydon)* *Lichfield Civic Hall (Lichfield)* *Gaiety Theatre (Ayr)* *King's Theatre (Southsea)* *Forum Th. (Manchester)* *Arts Centre (Horsham)* *Civic Theatre (Scunthorpe)* *Tameside Th (Ashton-under-Lyne)* *Lyceum Th. (Crewe)* *Arts Centre (Aberystwyth)* *Towngate Th. (Poole)* *Th. Royal (Lincoln)* *Opera House (Buxton)* *Playhouse (Epsom)* *Towngate Th. (Poole)*					
A56	***Anzacs Over England***	David Goodland	Worcester Theatre Company	Richard Huggett	Pat Trueman	
	Swan Theatre (Worcester)					
A57	***Apple Blossom Afternoon***	David Sheasby	Stephen Joseph Theatre Company		Malcolm Hebden	
	S. Joseph Studio (Scarborough)					
A58	***April In Paris***	John Godber (PW,D)	Hull Truck Theatre Company	Jane Clifford John Godber		
	Spring St. Th. (Hull) *Theatre Royal (Wakefield)*					
A59	***Armed And Dangerous***		The Posse	Brian Bovell Michael Buffong Robbie Gee		
	Crucible Th. (Sheffield)					
A60	***Arms and the Man***	George Bernard Shaw	Cambridge Theatre Company	Jack Fortune Anastasia Hill Paul Mooney	Nick Philippou	
	Arts Th. (Cambridge) *Ashcroft Th. (Croydon)* *Arts Centre (Warwick)* *Towngate Th. (Poole)* *Oxford Playhouse (Oxford)* *Grand Th. (Blackpool)*					
A61	***Arms And The Man***	George Bernard Shaw	Lyric Players Theatre		Charles Nowosielski	
	Lyric Players (Belfast)					
A62	***Arsenic and Old Lace***	Joseph Kesselring	Salisbury Theatre Company		Sonia Fraser	
	Playhouse Th. (Salisbury)					
A63	***The Artifice***	Susannah Centlivre	Orange Tree Theatre		Sam Walters	
	Orange Tree Th. (Richmond)					
A64	***Artists and Admirers***	Alexander Ostrovsky Helen Rappaport (T) Kevin Elyot (Ad)	Royal Shakespeare Company	Linda Bassett Christopher Benjamin	Phyllida Lloyd	RSC
	Barbican/The Pit (London EC1)					
A65	***As Time Goes By***	Mark Brailsford	Cackophonics Theatre Company	Mark Brailsford David Callahan Angus M. Glen	Claire Storey Mark Helyar (MD)	
	Canal Cafe Th. (London W2)					
A66	***As You Desire Me***	Luigi Pirandello	Powerhouse Pictures	Sandra Fox	Derek Wax	Powerhouse Pictures
	New End Th. (London NW3)					

Produced exclusively for Plays & Players by SEARCHLINE

Ref	Play	Playwright	Theatre Co.	Starring	Director	Producer
A67	***As You Like It*** *RST (Stratford-upon-Avon)*	William Shakespeare	Royal Shakespeare Company	Samantha Bond Peter de Jersey Michael Siberry	David Thacker	RSC
A68	***As You Like It*** *Greenwich Th. (London SE10)*	William Shakespeare	Greenwich Theatre	Philip Franks Jemma Redgrave	James Robert Carson	
A69	***As You Like It*** *Ludlow Festival (Shrops)*	William Shakespeare		John Gordon-Sinclair Sylvester McCoy Victoria Wicks	Alan Cohen	Sarah Parkin
A70	***As You Like It*** *Seven Dials Ctre (London WC2)*	William Shakespeare	Centre Stage	Francesca Agati Barbara Mathieson Rebecca Mays	Julie Somers	
A71	***As You Like It*** *Open Air Th. (London NW1)*	William Shakespeare	New Shakespeare Company	Bette Bourne Cathryn Harrison	Maria Aitken	
A72	***Aspects Of Love*** *Prince of Wales Th. (London W1V)*	Andrew Lloyd Webber	Really Useful Theatre Company Ltd.	Susannah Fellows Barrie Ingham Michael Praed	Trevor Nunn	Really Useful Group
A73	***Assassins*** *Donmar Warehouse (London WC2H)*	Stephen Sondheim (C) John Weidman (A)	Donmar Warehouse	Louise Gold Henry Goodman Ciaran Hinds	Sam Mendes Jeremy Sams (MD)	
A74	***At Fifty She Discovered The Sea*** *Playhouse (Liverpool)*	Denise Chalem Sian Evans (T)	Liverpool Repertory Theatre	Kerry Peers Jennie Stoller	Rumin Gray	
A75	***The Author's Voice*** *La Bonne Crepe (London SW11)*	Richard Greenburgh	La Bonne Crepe		Ned Seago	
A76	***Away Alone*** *Peacock Th. (Dublin)*	Janet Noble	Abbey Theatre Dublin		Fionnula Flannagan	
A77	***An Awfully Big Adventure*** *Playhouse (Liverpool)*	Beryl Bainbridge	Liverpool Repertory Theatre	Rodney Bewes Eithne Browne Rudi Davies	Ian Kellgren	
A78	***Ay Carmela!*** *BAC (London SW11)*	Jose Sanchis Sinisterra John London (Ad)	Loose Change	Philip Bliss Janet Steel	Tessa Schneideman	
A79	***Babes in the Wood*** *New Th. (Cardiff)*	Roy Hudd (PW,D)		Roy Hudd Geoffrey Hughes June Whitfield		
A80	***Babes in the Wood*** *Theatre Royal (York)*	Berwick Kaler	York Theatre Royal Company	Martin Barrass Berwick Kaler David Leonard	Derek Nicholls	
A81	***Babes In The Wood*** *Civic Theatre (Darlington)*		Nick Thomas Enterprises	Cannon & Ball	Jonathan Kiley	Nick Thomas
A82	***The Baby*** *Palace Th. (Watford)*	Jon Canter	Palace Theatre, Watford	Sarah Berger Jim Dunk Simon Slater	Lou Stein	
A83	***Baby Baby*** *King's Head Th. (London N1)*		Scarlet Theatre Co.	Grainne Byrne Sophie Lovell-Smith Maggi Morrison		
A84	***Back Up The Hearse*** *Hampstead Th. (London NW3)*		Hampstead Theatre Company	Paul Bown Lesley Dunlop Debra Gillett		
A85	***Bad Blood*** *Gate Th. Club (London W11)*	Grizelda Gambaro			Kate Rowland	
A86	***Bad Girl*** *Old Red Lion Th. (London EC1)*	Kay Trainor	First Productions	Tricia Kelly Sandy McDade	Anna Birch	
A87	***Bag Dancing*** *Lyric Ham'smith (London W6)* *BAC (London SW11)* *St George's Th. (Luton)* *Old Town Hall (Hemel/Hemp)* *Trinity Arts (Tunbridge Wells)* *Colchester Arts (Colchester)* *Tricycle Th. (London NW6)* *Brewhouse Th. (Burton-on-Trent)* *Old Bull Arts (Barnet)* *Lyric Ham'smith (London W6)*	Mike Kenny	Quicksilver Theatre For Children	Carey English Nigel Greenhalgh	Steve Byrne	

Ref	Play	Playwright	Theatre Co.	Starring	Director	Producer
A88	***Ballard of the Limehouse Rat***	Tim Newton	Louder Than Words	Tim Newton	Ruth Ben-Tovim	
	Haymarket Studio (Leicester); Lemon Tree (Aberdeen); Andrews Lane (Dublin); Central Studio (Basingstoke); Harrow Arts (Harrow); Nuffield Studio (Southampton); Unity Theatre (Liverpool); Rotherham Arts (Rotherham); Angles Centre (Wisbech, Cambs); Arts Centre (Birmingham); Bowen West Th. (Bedford)					
A89	***The Barber Of Seville***	Ranjit Bolt (a) Pierre Beaumarchais	Palace Theatre, Watford	Helena Bonham-Carter Lee Cornes Oliver Parker	Lou Stein	
	Palace Th. (Watford)					
A90	***The Barber of Seville***	Pierre Beaumarchais Rossini (M)	Harrogate Theatre Company		Roger Delves-Broughton Andrew Manley	
	Harrogate Th. (Harrogate)					
A91	***Barefoot in the Park***	Neil Simon	Blue Box Theatre Company		Ellis Jones	
	Century Th. (Keswick)					
A92	***Barnstormers***	Mitch Binns	Century Theatre Touring	Kerry Angus Peter McNally Debbie Paul	Han Duijvendak	
	Lyceum Th. (Crewe); The Playhouse (Harlow); Playhouse (Newcastle/u/Tyne); Towngate Th. (Poole)					
A93	***Barnum***	Mark Bramble (B) Cy Coleman (C) Michael Stewart (L)	Apollo Leisure UK Ltd	Paul Nicholas	Buddy Schwab Simon Lowe (MD)	
	Mayflower (Southampton); Opera House (Manchester); Apollo (Oxford); Th. Royal (Nottingham); Dominion (London W1)					
A94	***Bazaar and Rummage***	Sue Townsend	Live Wire Theatre Productions	Jill Gascoine Anna Karen Sophie Lawrence	Richard Haddon	Arthur Bostrom James Tapp Charles H. Simpson
	King's Theatre (Southsea); The Hawth (Crawley); Grand Theatre (Wolverhampton); Th. Royal (Brighton); Wimbledon Th. (London SW19); Marlowe Th. (Canterbury); Empire Theatre (Sunderland); Malvern Festival Th. (Malvern); Apollo (Oxford); Hippodrome (Bristol); Th. Royal (Plymouth); Hull New Th. (Hull); Theatre Royal (York); Forum Theatre (Billingham); Civic Th. (Chelmsford); Grand Th. (Lancaster); New Victoria Th. (Woking); Th. Royal (Hanley); Winter Gardens (Eastbourne)					
A95	***Beardsley***	Donald S Olson	Stage One Theatre Company	Catherine Barrett Giles Foreman Martin Head	Michael Walling	Richard Jackson Stage One
	Offstage D/Stair (London NW1)					
A96	***Beardsley***	Tony Peters	Level Five Theatre Company			
	Th. Museum (London WC2)					
A97	***Beauty And The Beast***	Stuart Paterson (A)	Royal Lyceum Theatre Company	Carol Ann Crawford Stephen Hogan Maria Miller	Hugh Hodgart	
	Royal Lyceum Th. Co (Edinburgh)					
A98	***Beauty And The Beast***	J. Planche	Players Theatre	Gerardine Arthur Josephine Baird Nigel Williams	Dudley Stevens	
	Players Th. (London WC2H)					
A99	***Beauty and the Beast***	David Holman	Birmingham Rep.	David Crean Roger Watkins Rita Wolf	Gwenda Hughes	
	Birmingham Rep. (Birmingham)					
A100	***Beauty And The Beast***	Devised By The Company	Snap Theatre Company	Peter MacNally Colin Stevens Claire Waller	Jeremy James	
	Oakengates Th (Telford); Guildhall Th. (Brecon); Village Hall (Parsons Drove); Village Hall (Benwick); Village Hall (Friday Bridge); Arts Centre (Birmingham); The Playhouse (Harlow); Theatr Gwynedd (Bangor); Beck Th. (Hayes, Middx); Guildhall Centre (Grantham); Maltings Arts (St Albans); Magdalene Sch (Newark); Sutton Centre (Sutton In Ashfield); Roundhill School (Beeston); Minster School (Nottingham); (W. Bridgeford); Mansfield Leis. (Mansfield); Old Laundry Th (Bowness); Thameside Th. (Grays); Regal Arts Ctre (Worksop); The Metropolitan (B. St Edmunds); Brewhouse Th. (Burton-on-Trent); Platform Theatre (Haywards Heath); Arts Centre (Southport)					
A101	***Beauty and the Bat***	Aline Waites (PW,D) Robin Hunter	Aba Daba Productions			
	Arches Th. (London SE1)					
A102	***Beauty And The Beast***	Mike Carter (Ad)	Palace Theatre, Watford		Christopher Dunham	
	Palace Th. (Westcliff-On-Sea)					
A103	***Becket***	Jean Anouilh		Derek Jacobi Andrew Jarvis Robert Lindsay	Elijah Moshinsky	Duncan C Weldon
	Haymarket (London SW1)					

Ref	Play	Playwright	Theatre Co.	Starring	Director	Producer
A104	**Bedroom Farce**	Alan Ayckbourn		Michael Denison Dulcie Gray	Caroline Smith	Bill Kenwright Ltd
	Belgrade Th. (Coventry) *Forum Theatre (Billingham)* *Th. Royal (Brighton)* *Festival Th. (Chichester)* *Richmond Th. (Richmond)* *Theatre Royal (York)* *Crucible Th. (Sheffield)* *Th. Royal (Glasgow)* *Grand Th. (Leeds)* *Churchill Th. (Bromley)*					
A105	**Bedside Manners**	Derek Benfield Charles Vance (D,P)	Prestige Plays			
	Opera House (Buxton) *The Playhouse (Harlow)*					
A106	**The Beggar's Opera**	John Gay	Royal Shakespeare Company	David Burt Elizabeth Renihan	John Caird	Michael Attenborough
	Swan Th. (Stratford-upon-Avon)					
A107	**Belle Reprieve**		Split Britches & Bloolips			
	Grand Th. (Blackpool)					
A108	**The Bells**	Daryl Runswick	Green Light Music Theatre	Mary King Philip Langridge James Meek	Stephen Langridge	
	Riverside Std. (London W6)					
A109	**Berlin Bertie**	Howard Brenton	Royal Court Theatre	Kevin Allen Penny Downie Diana Rigg	Danny Boyle	
	Royal Court Th. (London SW1)					
A110	**The Best Man**	David Richard-Fox	Art Depot	Veronica Geary James Griffiths Carol Harvey	Bardy Thomas	
	Warehouse Th. (Croydon)					
A111	**A Better Day**	Sheila Yeger	Theatre Royal Stratford East	Madeline Blakeney Clive Mendus Ian Angus Wilkie	Annie Castledine	
	Th. Royal (Stratford East)					
A112	**Between the Lines**	Alan Ayckbourn Paul Todd	Etcetera Theatre Company	Stefan Bednarczyk Janie Dee Simon Green	Vivienne Cozens	David Bidmead Etcetera Theatre Company
	Etcetera (London NW1)					
A113	**Beyond Reasonable Doubt**	Jeffrey Archer	Mercury Theatre	Michael Tudor-Barnes Michael Walker Helen Weir	Michael Winter	
	Mercury Th. (Colchester)					
A114	**Beyond Reasonable Doubt**	Jeffrey Archer	Wolsey Theatre Company	Geoffrey Hodson Brian Ralph William Whymper	Antony Tuckey	
	Wolsey Theatre (Ipswich)					
A115	**Beyond Reasonable Doubt**	Jeffrey Archer	Thorndike Theatre	Nyree Dawn Porter Richard Todd	Roger Clissold	
	Thorndike Th. (Leatherhead)					
A116	**The BFG**	Roald Dahl (A) David Wood (Ad,D) Peter Pontzen (C)	Clarion Productions	Lucy Fenwick Fiona Grogan Anthony Pedley		
	Marlowe Th. (Canterbury) *Hippodrome (Bristol)* *Grand Th. (Swansea)* *Th. Royal (Nottingham)* *Alhambra Th. (Bradford)* *Th. Royal (Plymouth)* *Towngate Th. (Poole)* *Derngate (Northampton)* *Orchard Th. (Dartford)* *Eden Court Th. (Inverness)* *Apollo (Oxford)* *Opera House (Manchester)* *Hippodrome (Birmingham)* *New Th. (Cardiff)* *Empire Th. (Liverpool)* *Regent Th. (Ipswich)* *Th. Royal (Newcastle/u/Tyne)*					
A117	**Biboff**	Yossi Hadar	Theatre Beneath The Sand	Kay D'Arcy David Futcher Richard Gofton	Shai Bar Yaacov	
	Theatro Technis (London NW1)					
A118	**Big Maggie**	John B. Keane	Birmingham Rep.		Gwenda Hughes	
	Birmingham Rep. (Birmingham)					
A119	**Big Night Out At The Little Sands Picture Pa**	Sandi Toksvig	Nottingham Playhouse		Pip Broughton	
	The Playhouse (Nottingham)					
A120	**A Bigger Slice of the Pie**	Tim Firth	Stephen Joseph Theatre Company		Connal Orton	
	S. Joseph Studio (Scarborough)					
A121	**Biko**	Richard Fawkes Priti Paintal (C)	Birmingham Rep.	Damon Evans Hyacinth Nicholls Daniel Washington	Wilfred Judd	
	Birmingham Rep. (Birmingham) *Riverside Std. (London W6)*					

Ref	Play	Playwright	Theatre Co.	Starring	Director	Producer
A122	***Billy Liar*** *Oxford Playhouse (Oxford)* *Gulbenkian Th. (Canterbury)* *Brewhouse Th. (Burton-on-Trent)* *Riverside Th. (Coleraine)* *Theatr Hafren (Newtown)* *Minerva Studio (Chichester)* *Gardner Arts Ctr (Brighton)* *Sherman Th. (Cardiff)* *Brewhouse Th. (Taunton)* *Alhambra St (Bradford)* *Trinity Arts (Tunbridge Wells)* *Contact Th. (Manchester)* *Tron Th. (Glasgow)* *Whitley Bay P/h. (Whitley)* *Riverbank Theatre (Dublin)* *Warwick Arts (Coventry)* *Arts Theatre (Belfast)* *NT/Cottesloe (London SE1)*	Keith Waterhouse Willis Hall	Royal National Theatre	James Grant June Watson Paul Wyett	Tim Supple	RNT
A123	***Billy the Kid*** *Etcetera (London NW1)*	Paul Bishop	Classic Theatre Productions		Stanley Morris	
A124	***The Birthday Party*** *Citz. Second Th. (Glasgow)*	Harold Pinter	Citizens' Th. Co.	Henry Cusick Andrew Joseph John Muirhead	Antony McDonald	
A125	***Blithe Spirit*** *Playhouse (Derby)*	Noel Coward	Derby Playhouse	Robert Ashby Anna Skye	Mark Clements	
A126	***Blithe Spirit*** *Haymarket Th. (Basingstoke)*	Noel Coward	Horseshoe Theatre Company	Maria Charles	Philip Grout	
A127	***Blithe Spirit*** *Royal Th. (Northampton)*	Noel Coward	Royal Theatre, Northampton	Michael Cadman Jane Hollowood Corinna Powlesland	Philip Howard	
A128	***Blithe Spirit*** *Harrogate Th. (Harrogate)*	Noel Coward	Harrogate Theatre Company		Andrew Manley	
A129	***Blodeuwedd - Woman Of Flowers*** *Sherman Th. (Cardiff)* *Little Theatre (Middlesborough)* *Merlin (Frome)* *Gardner Arts Ctr (Brighton)* *Island Arts (Broadstairs)* *Lilian Baylis (London EC1)* *Theatr Mwldan (Cardigan)*	Saunders Lewis Sion Eirian (T)	Actors Touring Company	Katherine Aughton Terence Dauncey Simon Harris	Ceri Sherlock	ATC & Sherman Theatre
A130	***Blood Brothers*** *New Vic (Bristol)*	Willy Russell	Bristol Old Vic Ensemble	Caroline Bliss Simon Day Suzanne Packer	Foz Allan	
A131	***Blood Brothers*** *Phoenix Th. (London WC2)*	Willy Russell		David Bardsley Stephanie Lawrence Carl Wayne	Bob Tomson	Bill Kenwright Ltd
A132	***Blood Wedding*** *Lyric Ham'smith (London W6)*	Federico Garcia Lorca	Odyssey			
A133	***Blood Wedding*** *Bridge Lane Th (Battersea)*	Federico Garcia Lorca	About Time Theatre Company	David Callahan Lucy Capito Raphael McAuliffe	Yuval Zamir	Nigel Barden
A134	***Blood Wedding*** *Haymarket Th. (Leicester)*	Federico Garcia Lorca Gwynne Edwards (Tr)	Haymarket Theatre Company		Julia Bardsley	
A135	***Blood Whispers*** *La Bonne Crepe (London SW11)*	Paul Prescott (PW,D)	La Bonne Crepe	Mark Caven Paul Prescott Penny Smith		Carlo Lange
A136	***The Bloody Chamber*** *Tron Th. (Glasgow)*	Angela Carter (a) Caroline Hall (Ad,d)	Tron Theatre Company			
A137	***Bloody Poetry*** *Turtle Key Arts (London SW6)*	Howard Brenton	About Time Theatre Company	Sarah Bishop Ben Robertson Jonathan Wilmot	Caroline Hetherington	Raphael McAuliffe
A138	***The Blue Angel*** *Globe Th. (London W1)*	Heinrich Mann (A) Friedrich Hollander (C D) Pam Gems (Ad)	Royal Shakespeare Company	Judith Bruce Kelly Hunter Philip Madoc	Trevor Nunn	John Newman Mark Furness Ltd
A139	***Blue Remembered Hills*** *Bristol Old Vic (Bristol)*	Dennis Potter	Bristol Old Vic Ensemble	Nigel Betts Caroline Bliss Lesley Nicol	Andrew Hay	
A140	***The Deep Blue Sea*** *Watermill Th. (Newbury)*	Terence Rattigan	Watermill Theatre	Jean Harvey Barbara Kellerman Steven Mann	Euan Smith	Watermill Theatre

Ref	Play	Playwright	Theatre Co.	Starring	Director	Producer
A141	***Blues Angels***	Marsha Raven & Beverly Andrews		Marsha Raven	Beverly Andrews	
	Bloomsbury Th. (London WC1H)					
A142	***A Tribute to the Blues Brothers***			Simon John Foster Brian Hibbard	David Leland	David Pugh Ltd
	Whitehall Th. (London SW1A)					
A143	***Blues for Mister Charlie***	James Baldwin	Royal Exchange Theatre Company	Nicholas Le Prevost Wyllie Longmore David Schofield	Gregory Hersov	
	Royal Exchange (Manchester)					
A144	***Blues In The Night***	Sheldon Epps	Queen's Theatre, Hornchurch	Patti Boulaye Jacqui Dubois Paul Kissaun	Sean O'Connor	
	Queen's Th. (Hornchurch)					
A145	***Boardroom Shuffle***	Gregg Ward	The American Connexion			
	Court Th. (London N1)					
A146	***Body And Soul***	Roy Kendall	Yvonne Arnaud Theatre	Robert Hardy Nicola Redmond Angela Thorne	Val May	Mark Furness Ltd
	Yvonne Arnaud (Guildford) *Albery Th. (London WC2)*		*Alexandra Th. (Birmingham)*	*Th. Royal (Brighton)*	*Malvern Festival Th. (Malvern)*	
A147	***Body Talk***	Andy Rashleigh	Unicorn Theatre	Richard Bryan Ray Emmet-Brown Emma Gibbons	Richard Williams	
	Arts Theatre (London WC2H)					
A148	***Bodycount***	Les Smith	Bristol Old Vic Ensemble	Toshie Ogura	Kristine London-Smith	
	New Vic (Bristol)					
A149	***Bold Girls***	Rona Munro	Abbey Theatre Dublin		John Dove	
	Peacock Th. (Dublin)					
A150	***Bouncers***	John Godber	Belgrade Theatre Company			
	Belgrade Th. (Coventry)					
A151	***Bouncers***	John Godber	Hull Truck Theatre Company	Anthony Dunn John Kirk Jake Nightingale	Damian Cruden	
	Spring St. Th. (Hull)		*George Square Th. (Edinburgh)*			
A152	***Bouncers***	John Godber	Chester Gateway Theatre		Robert Sian	
	Gateway Th. (Chester)					
A153	***Le Bourgeois Gentilhomme***	Nick Dear (Ad) Moliere	Royal National Theatre	Anita Dobson Janine Duvitski Timothy Spall	Richard Jones	RNT
	NT/Lyttelton (London SE1)					
A154	***Boy With Beer***	Paul Boakye	This is Now Theatre Company			
	Man in the Moon (London SW3)					
A155	***The Boy's Own Story***		Boy's Own Productions	Peter Flannery	Richard Digby Day Tony Yates	
	Chelsea Centre (London SW10)					
A156	***Brace Up!***		Wooster Group	Willem Dafoe Roy Faudree Scott Renderer	Elizabeth LeCompte	
	Tramway (Glasgow)					
A157	***Brand***	Henrik Ibsen	The Troupe	Robin Cameron Harriet Keevil Keith Matthews	Astrid Hilne	Annette Moskowitz Alexander Racolin
	Emerald Centre (London W6) *Stamford Arts C. (Stamford)*		*Maltings Arts (St Albans)* *Cumbernauld Th. (Cumbernauld)*	*Merlin Theatre (Sheffield)* *Civic Th. (Ayr)*	*Library Arts Th. (Skelmersdale)*	
A158	***The Brave Magicians of Mangalore***	Kenneth Rea	Polka Theatre			
	Polka Th. (London SW19)					
A159	***Breaking the Code***	Hugh Whitemore		Rachel Gurney Derek Jacobi Nicholas Selby	Clifford Williams	Duncan C Weldon
	Alexandra Th. (Birmingham) *Alhambra Th. (Bradford)* *Ashcroft Th. (Croydon)* *Festival Th. (Chichester)*		*Th. Royal (Newcastle/u/Tyne)* *Richmond Th. (Richmond)* *Lyceum Th. (Sheffield)*	*Yvonne Arnaud (Guildford)* *Th. Royal (Brighton)* *King's Th. (Edinburgh)*	*Th. Royal (Bath)* *Th. Royal (Nottingham)* *Opera House (Belfast)*	
A160	***Breathless***	April De Angelis	Cold Fish	Deborah Goodman Carolyn Wildi	Deborah Shaw	
	Canal Cafe Th. (London W2)					

Ref	Play	Playwright	Theatre Co.	Starring	Director	Producer
A161	***The Bright And Bold Design*** *New Victoria Th. (New/u/Lyme)*	Peter Whelan	New Victoria Theatre	Katie London Kay Pope Rosie Timpson	Peter Cheeseman	
A162	***Brighton Beach Memoirs*** *Byre Theatre (St Andrews)*	Neil Simon	Byre Theatre Company		Ken Alexander	
A163	***Broadway Bound*** *Library Th. (Manchester)*	Neil Simon	Library Theatre Company		Roger Haines	
A164	***Broken Folk*** *Finborough Th. (London SW10)*	Godfrey Hamilton	Starving Artists Theatre Co	Don Boydell Mark Pinkosh	Colin Watkeys	
A165	***Broken Heads*** *BAC Studio 2 (London SW11)*	Simon Blake (PW,D)	Changeinspeak			
A166	***The Brothers Karamazov*** *Royal Exchange (Manchester)*	Dostoyevsky (AU) Gerard McLarnon (A)	Royal Exchange Theatre Company		Braham Murray	
A167	***Buchanan*** *Traverse Th. (Edinburgh)*	Tom McGrath	Traverse Theatre Company		John Mitchell	
A168	***Buddy*** *Opera House (Manchester)* *Lyceum Th. (Sheffield)* *Hull New Th. (Hull)* *Hippodrome (Bristol)* *Alhambra Th. (Bradford)* *Th. Royal (Nottingham)* *Mayflower (Southampton)* *Opera House (Belfast)* *King's Th. (Edinburgh)* *King's Th. (Glasgow)* *Opera House (Blackpool)* *Empire Th. (Liverpool)* *Th. Royal (Plymouth)*	Alan Janes	E & B Productions		Rob Bettinson	Paul Elliott
A169	***Buddy*** *Victoria Palace Th. (London SW1)*	Alan Janes	E & B Productions		Rob Bettinson	Paul Elliott
A170	***Building Blocks*** *Nuffield Th. (Southampton)*	Bob Larbey	Nuffield Theatre Company	Phil Bretherton Kate Spiro Christopher Timothy	Patrick Sandford	
A171	***Bulldog Drummond*** *Nuffield Th. (Southampton)*	Sapper Peter Woodward (A)	Nuffield Theatre Company	Granville Saxton Peter Woodward	Jeremy Sinden	
A172	***Burbage and the Bard*** *Robin Hood Th. (Averham)* *The Crown (Matlock, Derbys)* *Brewhouse Th. (Burton-on-Trent)* *Comm. Arts Centr (Mansfield)* *Battle Festival (Battle)* *Hay-on-Wye Fest. (Hay-on-Wye)* *Georgian Theatre (Richmond)* *Hunstanton Fest. (Hunstanton)* *Haybridge School (Stourbridge)*	Stan Pretty (PW,D) Jonathan Milton (PW,D)	Travelling Light Shakespeare Company	Jonathan Milton Stan Pretty		
A173	***The Business of Murder*** *Century Th. (Keswick)*	Richard Harris	Blue Box Theatre Company		Ellis Jones	
A174	***The Business Of Murder*** *Theatr Colwyn (Colwyn Bay)*	Richard Harris	Theatr Colwyn Summer Rep	Reg Large David Middleton Helen Parkinson	Gareth ap Gwylim	
A175	***The Business Of Murder*** *Royal Th. (Northampton)*	Richard Harris	Royal Theatre, Northampton	Felicity Goodson Michael Kirk Glynn Sweet	Gareth Armstrong	
A176	***Cabal and Love*** *Lyric Ham'smith (London W6)*	Friedrich Schiller David Paisey (Tr)			Patrick Wilde	
A177	***Cabaret*** *Crucible Th. (Sheffield)*	John van Druten Fred Ebb (L) John Kander (C) Joe Masteroff (A)	Crucible Theatre			
A178	***Cabaret*** *Arts Theatre (Belfast)*	Joe Masteroff Fred Ebb (L) John Kander (M) John van Druten	Arts Theatre, Belfast		Peter Quigley	Arts Theatre Prod.
A179	***The Cabinet Minister*** *Albery Th. (London WC2)*	Arthur Wing-Pinero	Triumph Productions	Sara Kestleman Maureen Lipman Derek Nimmo	Braham Murray	Duncan C Weldon

Produced exclusively for Plays & Players by SEARCHLINE

Ref	Play	Playwright	Theatre Co.	Starring	Director	Producer
A180	***Caesar And Cleopatra*** *Greenwich Th. (London SE10)*	George Bernard Shaw	Greenwich Theatre	Sheila Ballantine Alec McCowen Amanda Root	Matthew Francis	
A181	***Cain*** *Minerva Studio (Chichester)*	George Byron	Chichester Festival Theatre	Maria Miller Kate O'Mara Richard Warwick	Edward Hall	
A182	***Call Blue Jane*** *ICA (London SW1)*	Devised By The Company	Man Act	Phillip Mackenzie Simon Thorne		
A183	***Candida*** *Wolsey Theatre (Ipswich)*	George Bernard Shaw	Wolsey Theatre Company		Antony Tuckey	
A184	***The Candidate*** *Man in the Moon (London SW3)*	Stash Kirkbride		Stash Kirkbride	Stephen Wyllie	Rebecca Snell
A185	***Candide*** *Everyman Th. (Liverpool)*	Leonard Bernstein (C) Hugh Wheeler (Ad) Stephen Sondheim (L)	Everyman Theatre Company	Oliver Beamish Elena Ferrari Philip Rham	John Doyle Helen Ireland (Md)	
A186	***Caprice*** *Century Th. (Keswick)*	Alfred de Musset	De Musset & Co			
A187	***The Card*** *Watermill Th. (Newbury)*	Keith Waterhouse Willis Hall	Watermill Theatre	Lesley Duff Peter Duncan Claire Moore	Jeremy Sams	Cameron Mackintosh Watermill Theatre
A188	***The Caretaker*** *The Playhouse (Nottingham)*	Harold Pinter	Nottingham Playhouse		Steve Shill	
A189	***Carmen Jones*** *Old Vic (London SE1)*	Oscar Hammerstein		Patti Boulaye Jennifer Chase Gary Wilmot	Simon Callow	Turnstyle
A190	***Carousel*** *NT/Lyttelton (London SE1)*	Richard Rodgers (M) Oscar Hammerstein III (L)	Royal National Theatre	Michael Hayden Joanna Riding Patricia Routledge	Nicholas Hytner Kenneth MacMillan (Ch)	RNT
A191	***Casanova Undone*** *Citz. Second Th. (Glasgow)*	Dic Edwards	Citizens' Th. Co.	Tristram Jellinek Siobhan Stanley Roberta Taylor	Robert David MacDonald	
A192	***The Case of the Frightened Lady*** *Palace Th. (Watford)*	Edgar Wallace	Palace Theatre, Watford	Sheila Ballantine Rowland Davies William Osborne	Frith Banbury	
A193	***The Case Of The Dead Flamingo Dancer*** *Churchill Th. (Bromley)*	Donald Oliver Dan Butler		Josephine Blake Tim Flavin Jessica Martin	Martin Connor	
A194	***Cats*** *New London Th. (London WC2)*	Andrew Lloyd Webber	Really Useful Theatre Company Ltd.	Luke Baxter Donald Francke Jackie Scott	Trevor Nunn	Cameron Mackintosh
A195	***Cerceau*** *Orange Tree Th. (Richmond)*	Victor Slavkin Adrian Brine (T,D)	Orange Tree Theatre	Maria Miles Richard O'Callaghan Sam Walters		
A196	***The Chalk Garden*** *King's Head Th. (London N1)*	Enid Bagnold	King's Head Theatre	Constance Cummings Robert Flemyng Jean Marsh		Lance Spiro
A197	***The Changeling*** *Swan Th. (Stratford-upon-Avon)*	William Rowley Thomas Middleton	Royal Shakespeare Company	Cheryl Campbell Stephen Casey Malcolm Storry	Michael Attenborough	RSC
A198	***The Changing Reason*** *Royal Court Th. (London SW1)*	Noel MacAoidh	Royal Court Theatre			Carl Miller
A199	***Charlemagne*** *Old Fire Station (Oxford)*	Sarah Miles		Lindy Alexander Greg Hicks Sarah Miles	Lisa Forrell	

Ref	Play	Playwright	Theatre Co.	Starring	Director	Producer
A200	***Charley's Aunt*** *Th. Royal (Bury St Edmunds)* *Devonshire Park Th. (Eastbourne)* *Lyceum Th. (Sheffield)* *Marlowe Th. (Canterbury)* *Oxford Playhouse (Oxford)* *Towngate Th. (Basildon)* *Th. Royal (Bath)* *Eden Court Th. (Inverness)* *Civic Theatre (Darlington)* *Arts Th. (Cambridge)* *New Tyne Th. (Newcastle/Tyne)* *Grand Th. (Blackpool)* *Opera House (Manchester)* *Wimbledon Th. (London SW19)*	Brandon Thomas	Mobil Touring Theatre	Patrick Cargill Felicity Duncan Frank Windsor	Peter Wilson	
A201	***Chasing The Hypnotist*** *The Vox Theatre (London SW12)*	Phil Viner (PW,D)	Building With Bone	Lesley Albiston Gregory Gray Georgina Griffiths		
A202	***The Cherry Orchard*** *Everyman Th. (Cheltenham)*	Anton Chekhov	Everyman Theatre Company	Naomi Buch Sandor Eles Alison Fielding	Martin Houghton	
A203	***The Cherry Orchard*** *Gate Theatre (Dublin)*	Anton Chekhov	Gate Theatre Dublin	Cyril Cusack Sara Kestleman T McKenna	Michael Bogdanov	
A204	***Chester Cycle of Mystery Plays*** *Mermaid Th. (London EC4)*		London Theatre Ensemble		Mark Dornford-May	Westhead
A205	***Children of a Lesser God*** *Playhouse (Derby)*	Mark Medoff	Derby Playhouse			
A206	***Children Of A Lesser God*** *Octagon Th. (Bolton)*	Mark Medoff	Octagon Theatre Company	Paula Garfield Tom Higgins Jane Lancaster	Lawrence Till	
A207	***The Chimes*** *New Vic (Bristol)*	Les Smith (Ad) Charles Dickens (A)	Bristol Old Vic Ensemble		Ian Hastings	
A208	***Chitty Chitty Bang Bang*** *Gordon Craig Th. (Stevenage)*	Ian Fleming (A)	Nextage	Paul Laidlaw Claire Massie Richard Whitmore	Matthew Townshend Michael Jeffrey (MD)	
A209	***The Choice*** *Playhouse Th. (Salisbury)*	Claire Luckham	Salisbury Theatre Company	Toyah Willcox	Annie Castledine	
A210	***A Chorus of Disapproval*** *Redgrave Th. (Farnham)*	Alan Ayckbourn	Redgrave Theatre Company	Richard Bartlett Prim Cotton Edward Hardwickle	Jane McCulloch	
A211	***A Chorus of Disapproval*** *Playhouse (Derby)*	Alan Ayckbourn	Derby Playhouse			
A212	***A Christmas Carol*** *Mermaid Th. (London EC4)*	Ron Pember (Ad,D) Charles Dickens (A)	Vanessa Ford Productions	Ron Pember		
A213	***A Christmas Carol*** *Ashcroft Centre (Fareham)*	Jeff Young (Ad) Charles Dickens (A)	Rejects Revenge			
A214	***A Christmas Carol*** *Theatr Clwyd (Mold)*	Christopher G Sandford (Ad,D) Mike Read (Ad) Charles Dickens (A)	Theatr Clwyd Company			
A215	***Christmas Rubbish*** *Arches Th. (London SE1)*	Aline Waites (PW,D)	Aba Daba Productions			
A216	***Christmas Cat And The Pudding Pirates*** *Warwick Arts (Coventry)*	Christopher Lillicrap (PW,D) Jeanette Ranger	Muffin Productions			
A217	***A Christmas Carol*** *Library Th. (Manchester)*	Charles Dickens (Au) David Holman (A)	Library Theatre Company	Peter Macqueen	Sue Sutton Mayo	

Produced exclusively for Plays & Players by SEARCHLINE

Ref	Play	Playwright	Theatre Co.	Starring	Director	Producer
A218	***Christopher Street Columbus*** *Drill Hall (London WC1)*	Jimmy Camicia (PW,D)	Hot Peaches	Jimmy Camicia Mark Hannay Ron Jones		
A219	***Cinderella*** *Pavilion Theatre (Bournemouth)*	Carole Todd (D,Ch)	Cadbury's Pantomime Season	June Brown Windsor Davies Stefan Dennis		Brian Hewitt-Jones Chris Moreno
A220	***Cinderella*** *Th. Royal (Brighton)*	Christopher Wren (PW D)	Theatre Royal Brighton	Barbara Windsor Christopher Wren		Kevin Wood Prod.
A221	***Cinderella*** *Th. Royal (Norwich)*		Theatre Royal Norwich	Lionel Blair Annabel Croft Gary Webster	Peter Wilson Lionel Blair	
A222	***Cinderella*** *Mercury Th. (Colchester)*	Michael Winter (PW,D) Brian Parr	Mercury Theatre	Catherine Duncan Felicity Goodson Jacquie Toye		
A223	***Cinderella*** *Towngate Th. (Poole)*	Michael Rose (D,P)		Matthew Kelly		
A224	***Cinderella*** *Th. Royal (Bath)*		E & B Productions	Rolf Harris Lesley Joseph Sylvester McCoy		Paul Elliott
A225	***Cinderella*** *Arts Th. (Cambridge)*	Christopher Lillicrap Jeanette Ranger		Michelle Hatch Wayne Morris Carmen Silvera	Michelle Hardy	Muffin Productions
A226	***Cinderella*** *Dukes Theatre (Lancaster)*	Kenneth Alan Taylor	Dukes Theatre Company	Vicky Blake Ian Blower	Jon Pope Ian Blower	
A227	***Cindermouse*** *Little Angel (London N1)*		Little Angel Marionette Theatre			
A228	***Cindermouse*** *Little Angel (London N1)*		Little Angel Marionette Theatre			
A229	***Chinese State Circus*** *Granada Car Park (Manchester)* *Clapham Common (London SW12)*		Chinese State Circus			
A230	***Clockwork Orange*** *Traverse Th. (Edinburgh)*	Anthony Burgess (A)	Tag Theatre Company		Tony Graham	
A231	***Closer Than Ever*** *Library Th. (Manchester)* *Opera House (Buxton)*	David Shire (C) Richard Maltby Jr (L)	Library Theatre Company	Barry James Meredith Rich Andrew C. Wadsworth	Roger Haines	Michael Rose
A232	***Cloud 9*** *Contact Th. (Manchester)*	Caryl Churchill (a)	Contact Theatre	Ian Aspinall David Case Ray Fearon	Burt Caesar	
A233	***Clown For A Day*** *Th. Museum (London WC2)*		Cavalcade Theatre Company			
A234	***Cold Sweat*** *Queen's Th. (Hornchurch)*	The Heather Brothers	Queen's Theatre, Hornchurch	Leslie Grantham Angharad Rees	Marina Caldarone	
A235	***Colquhoun And MacBryde*** *Royal Court Th. (London SW1)*	John Byrne	Royal Court Theatre	David O'Hara Ken Stott	Lindsay Posner	
A236	***Columbus Blooding the Ocean*** *Traverse Th. (Edinburgh)*	Michele Celeste	Traverse Theatre Company		Ian Brown	
A237	***Columbus And The Discovery Of Japan*** *Barbican Th. (London EC2)*	Richard Nelson	Royal Shakespeare Company	Robert Demeger Jonathan Hyde Philip Voss	John Caird	RSC
A238	***Come On Sinderby*** *The Playhouse (Harlow)*	Christopher Lillicrap (Ad) J.L. Carr (A) Mike Fields (Ad)	Jill Freud and Company			
A239	***The Comedy of Errors*** *Redgrave Th. (Farnham)*	William Shakespeare	Redgrave Theatre Company	Mark Arden Mary-Louise Clarke Roger Martin	Graham Watkins	

Ref	Play	Playwright	Theatre Co.	Starring	Director	Producer
A240	***The Comedy of Errors***	William Shakespeare	New Victoria Theatre	Kay Pope John Wild Karl Woolley	Chris Martin	
	New Victoria Th. (New/u/Lyme)					
A241	***The Comedy Of Errors***	William Shakespeare	Royal Shakespeare Company	Desmond Barrit Neil Caple Estelle Kohler	Ian Judge	RSC
	Th. Royal (Nottingham) *Alhambra Th. (Bradford)* *Mayflower (Southampton)* *Barbican Th. (London EC2)*					
A242	***The Comedy Store Players***		The Kaliber No Limits Tour	Josie Lawrence Paul Merton Sandi Toksvig		Nica Burns
	Grand Theatre (Wolverhampton) *Grand Th. (Leeds)* *Regent Th. (Ipswich)* *The Hexagon (Reading)* *Opera House (Manchester)*					
A243	***Coming of Age***	Mark Keegan	Onion Theatre Company		Bob Grove	
	DOC Th. Club (London NW5)					
A244	***Commodities***	Elizabeth Walley	Raison d'etre	Alec Gilbert Elizabeth Walley	John Harris	
	New End Th. (London NW3)					
A245	***The Complete Works Of William Shakespeare***	William Shakespeare	The Reduced Shakespeare Company	Jess Borgeson Adam Long Reed Martin		Edward Snape Charles Stephens Warwick Productions Ltd
	Arts Theatre (London WC2)					
A246	***Confusions***	Alan Ayckbourn	Theatre Unlimited	Lucia Fausset Leigh Rogers Christopher Whittingham	John Link	
	Mermaid Studio (London EC4V)					
A247	***Conundrum***	Robert David MacDonald (PW,D)	Citizens' Th. Co.	Angela Chadfield Daniel Illsley Robert D MacDonald		
	Citz. Third Th. (Glasgow)					
A248	***Coriolanus***	William Shakespeare	Renaissance Theatre Company	Kenneth Branagh Richard Briers Judi Dench	Tim Supple	
	Festival Th. (Chichester)					
A249	***The Corn Is Green***	Emlyn Williams	Greenwich Theatre	Brendan O'Hea Patricia Routledge	Matthew Francis	Duncan C Weldon
	Greenwich Th. (London SE10) *Yvonne Arnaud (Guildford)* *Richmond Th. (Richmond)* *Lyceum Th. (Sheffield)* *Alexandra Th. (Birmingham)* *Th. Royal (Bath)* *New Th. (Cardiff)* *Alhambra Th. (Bradford)*					
A250	***The Cotton Club***	Douglas Barron		Debby Bishop Joanne Campbell Marcel Peneux	Billy Wilson	Stardust Productions
	Aldwych Th. (London WC2)					
A251	***Country Dance***	James Kennaway	Fifth Estate	Becky Baxter Sarah Collier Sandy Neilson	John Bett	
	Dundee Repertory (Dundee)					
A252	***The Country Wife***	William Wycherley	The Harlow Players		Brenda Jones	
	Studio Theatre (Harlow)					
A253	***The Country Wife***	William Wycherley	Oracle Productions		Peter Benedict	
	Holland Park Th. (London)					
A254	***Couples***	W. Gordon Smith	Dundee Repertory Theatre Ltd			
	Dundee Repertory (Dundee)					
A255	***Courting Winnona***	Jonathan Field	Big Dipper		Deidre Harrison	
	Old Red Lion Th. (London EC1)					
A256	***Crackwalker***	Judith Thompson	Gate Theatre Company		James McDonald	
	Gate Th. Club (London W11)					
A257	***Crazy For You***	George Gershwin (C) Ira Gershwin (L) Ken Ludwig (B)			Mike Ockrent Susan Stroman (Ch)	
	Prince Edward (London WC2N)					
A258	***Crime of Love***		Trestle Theatre	Abigail Dulay Debi Mastel Sarah Moore		
	Old Bull Arts (Barnet) *Drama Centre (Glasgow)* *Civic Th. (Ayr)* *Arts Centre (Aberdeen)* *Contact Th. (Manchester)* *Sevenoaks Fest. (Sevenoaks)* *Holland Park Th. (London)* *Arts Centre (Windsor)* *Barnfield Th. (Exeter)*					

Ref	Play	Playwright	Theatre Co.	Starring	Director	Producer
A259	***Criminal Prosecution & Punishment of Animals*** *The Diorama (London W1)*	Geoffrey Cush	Oracle Productions		Peter Benedict	
A260	***The Crucifer of Blood*** *Watermill Th. (Newbury)*	Paul Giovanni	Watermill Theatre		Graham Callan	
A261	***Crying For The Moon*** *Citz. Second Th. (Glasgow)*	Terry Neason	Citizens' Th. Co.	Terry Neason		
A262	***The Curse Of The Mummy's Tomb*** *Swan Theatre (Worcester)*	Bob Eaton Paddy Cunneen (C)	Worcester Theatre Company		Pat Trueman	
A263	***The Curse Of The Egyptian Mummy*** *Open Air Th. (London NW1)*	David Conville David Gooderson	New Shakespeare Company	Simon Harrison Nigel Hastings Rhys Ifans	Delena Kidd	
A264	***Custer's Last Stand*** *Cockpit Th. (London NW8)* *Watermans (Brentford, Middx)*	Andrew Williams	Yorkshire Theatre Company	Mark Alex-Jones Paul Marrow Andrew Williams	Toby Swift	
A265	***Cut and Trust*** *Th. Royal (Stratford East)*	Patrick Prior		Alan Cowan Yvonne Edgell	Jeff Teare	
A266	***Cuttin' A Rug*** *Royal Lyceum Th. Co (Edinburgh)*	John Byrne	Royal Lyceum Theatre Company		Benjamin Twist	
A267	***The Cutting*** *Bush Th. (London W12)*	Maureen O'Brien	Bush Theatre Company	Paul Freeman Sian Thomas	Dominic Dromgoole	Bush Theatre Company
A268	***Cyrano De Bergerac*** *Old Town Hall (Driffield)* *Stamford Arts C. (Stamford)* *Gulbenkian Th. (Canterbury)* *Ward Freeman Sch (Buntingford)* *Drama Centre (Cambridge)* *Arts Centre (Cranleigh)* *Arts Centre (Horsham)* *Arts Centre (Chesterfield)* *King's Lynn Arts (King's Lynn)* *Theatr Gwynedd (Bangor)* *Ellesmere Arts C (Ellesmere)* *Theatr Colwyn (Colwyn Bay)* *Regal Arts Ctre (Worksop)* *Blackpool Coll (St Anne's)* *Village Hall (Northwich)* *Poly Arts Centre (Preston)* *Arts Centre (Southport)* *The Metropolitan (B. St Edmunds)* *Centre Stage (Stockport)* *The Playhouse (Harlow)* *Brewhouse Th. (Burton-on-Trent)* *Campus West (Welwyn Gdn City)* *West Cliff Th. (Clacton)* *Music Hall (Shrewsbury)* *Guildhall Th. (Brecon)* *Dixon Studio (Westcliff-On-Sea)* *M.Rawlings Ctre (Hull)* *Hornsea School (Hornsea)* *Caxton Theatre (Grimsby)*	Nigel Greenhalgh (T) Edmond Rostand	Snap Theatre Company	Doug Brazier Beaux Bryant Kevin Tuer		
A269	***Cyrano De Bergerac*** *Haymarket (London SW1)*	John Wells (Ad) Edmond Rostand		Julian Glover Stella Conet Robert Lindsay	Elijah Moshinsky	Duncan C Weldon
A270	***Cyrano De Bergerac*** *Traverse Th. (Edinburgh)* *Dundee Repertory (Dundee)* *Arts Th. (Cambridge)* *Tron Th. (Glasgow)* *Alhambra St (Bradford)*	Edwin Morgan (Ad) Edmond Rostand	Communicado		Gerry Mulgrew	
A271	***Daisy Pulls it Off*** *Dukes Theatre (Lancaster)*	Denise Deegan	Dukes Theatre Company		Maggie Norris	
A272	***The Dance And The Railroad*** *Contact Th. (Manchester)*	David Henry Hwang	Tag Theatre Company		Alan Lyddiard Goh Siew Geok	
A273	***Dance Of Guns - Women In Resistance*** *Jackson's Lane (London N6)* *All Saints Arts (London N20)* *Waltham Forest (London E17)* *Poly of E London (London E15)*	Nina Rapi	Broadsword Theatre Company	Georgia Clarke Maria Moustaka Anna Savva	Ruth Ben-Tovim	
A274	***Dancing At Lughnasa*** *Garrick Th. (London WC2)*	Brian Friel	Abbey Theatre Dublin	Kate Fitzgerald Helena Little Anny Tobin	Patrick Mason	Bill Kenwright Ltd

Ref	Play	Playwright	Theatre Co.	Starring	Director	Producer
A275	***Dancing at Lughnasa***	Brian Friel	Abbey Theatre Dublin	Alan Dobie Dilly Keane Mary McCusker	Patrick Mason	Bill Kenwright Ltd
	Venues: *Cork Opera House (Cork); Ashcroft Th. (Croydon); Derngate (Northampton); Crucible Th. (Sheffield); Th. Royal (Nottingham); Arts Th. (Cambridge); Th. Royal (Brighton); Alexandra Th. (Birmingham); Forum Theatre (Billingham); Oxford Playhouse (Oxford); Hull New Th. (Hull); Belgrade Th. (Coventry); Marlowe Th. (Canterbury); Th. Royal (Newcastle/u/Tyne); The Hexagon (Reading); Bristol Old Vic (Bristol); Opera House (Manchester); Alhambra Th. (Bradford); His Majesty's Th. (Aberdeen); Eden Court Th. (Inverness); King's Th. (Edinburgh); Th. Royal (Plymouth); Theatre Royal (York); Beck Th. (Hayes, Middx); Grand Theatre (Wolverhampton); The Hawth (Crawley); Malvern Festival Th. (Malvern); Richmond Th. (Richmond); New Th. (Cardiff)*					
A276	***Dangerous Corner*** *Wolsey Theatre (Ipswich)*	J.B. Priestley	Wolsey Theatre Company		Antony Tuckey	
A277	***Dangerous Corner*** *Birmingham Rep. (Birmingham)*	J.B. Priestley	Birmingham Rep.	Marilyn Cutts Hazel Maycock Graham Padden	Gwenda Hughes	
A278	***Dangerous Obsession*** *Royal Th. (Northampton)*	N.J. Crisp	Royal Theatre, Northampton	Eric Carte Chris Matthews Holly Wilson	Michael Brown	
A279	***Dangerous Dolls Mummys Little Girl*** *Lyric Ham'smith (London W6)*	Jenny Eclair		Jenny Eclair	Tom Hunsinger	Icy Productions
A280	***Dangerous Dolls-Soap Crazy*** *Lyric Ham'smith (London W6)*	Julie Balloo		Julie Balloo Ben Holmes Laurel Lefkow	Phil Setren	Icy Productions
A281	***Dangerous Obsession*** *Forum Th. (Manchester)*	N.J. Crisp	Library Theatre Company	Peter Hampson Sally Knyvette Alan Rothwell	David Fleeshman	
A282	***The Dark River*** *Orange Tree Th. (Richmond)*	Rodney Ackland	Orange Tree Theatre	Stephanie Cole Belinda Lang Malcolm Sinclair	Sam Walters	
A283	***The Darling Family: A Duet For Three*** *Old Red Lion Th. (London EC1)*	Linda Griffiths	Furore Theatre Company	Kieron Jecchinis Gina Landor	Janine Wunsche	
A284	***Daughters Of England*** *New End Th. (London NW3)*	Jon Harris (Ad,D) Virginia Woolf (A)	Very Fine Productions	Emma Bown Tracy Cavalier Sarah-Jane Harris	Karen Cass	
A285	***The Day After Tomorrow*** *NT/Cottesloe (London SE1)*	Roel Adam Noel Clark (T)	Royal National Theatre		Anthony Clark	
A286	***The Day After The Fair*** *Royal Th. (Northampton)*	Frank Harvey (Ad) Thomas Hardy (A)	Royal Theatre, Northampton	Eric Carte Liz Edmiston	Michael Brown	
A287	***Dead Heroic*** *Tron Th. (Glasgow)*	Noel Greig	Tag Theatre Company	Keith McPherson Caroline Parker Jane Simpson	Tony Graham	
A288	***Dead Man's Hat***	Charles Way	Orchard Theatre Company	Andrea Gascoigne Andrew Howard James Lailey	Bill Buffery	
	Venues: *Plough Theatre (Exeter); North Devon Col. (Barnstaple); Redgrave Theatre (Bristol); The Regal Th. (Minehead); Victoria Pavilio (Ilfracombe); The Town Hall (Bovey Tracey); College Theatre (Bideford); Mowlem Theatre (Swanage); Northcott (Exeter); Memorial Hall (Exford); Ansford College (Castle Cary); Brewhouse Th. (Taunton); Launceston Coll. (Launceston); The Guildhall (Axminster); Town Hall (Dorchester); Arts Centre (Shaftesbury); Drum Theatre (Plymouth); Blundells School (Tiverton); Arts Centre (Falmouth); Acorn Arts Ctre (Penzance); Treviglas School (Newquay); The Octagon (Okehampton)*					
A289	***A Dead Secret*** *Th. Royal (Plymouth); Richmond Th. (Richmond)*	Rodney Ackland	Theatre Royal Plymouth	Michelle Dotrice Vivienne Martin Edward Woodward	Roger Redfarn	Theatre Royal Plymouth
A290	***Dead Soil*** *Haymarket Studio (Leicester)*	Franz Xavier Kroetz	Leicester Haymarket Theatre	Natasha Pope Peter Sproule	Julia Bardsley	

Ref	Play	Playwright	Theatre Co.	Starring	Director	Producer
A291	***Deadly Nightcap***	Francis Durbridge	Newpalm Productions			
	Thorndike Th. (Leatherhead)					
A292	***Death And Dancing***	Claire Dowie	Starving Artists Theatre Co	Claire Dowie Mark Pinkosh	Colin Watkeys	
	BAC (London SW11)		*Theatre Events (Brighton)*	*Bowen West Th. (Bedford)*	*Traverse Th. (Edinburgh)*	
A293	***Death and the Maiden***	Ariel Dorfman		Penny Downie Hugh Ross Danny Webb	Lindsay Posner	Royal Court Theatre
	Duke of York's (London WC2)					
A294	***Death and the Maiden***	Ariel Dorfman	Theatre Royal Windsor	Tony Anholt Colin Baker Dearbhla Molloy	Lindsay Posner	Bill Kenwright Ltd
	Th. Royal (Windsor, Berks) *Th. Royal (Nottingham)*		*Th. Royal (Brighton)* *Opera House (Buxton)*	*Alhambra St (Bradford)* *Oxford Playhouse (Oxford)*	*Arts Th. (Cambridge)*	
A295	***Death of a Salesman***	Arthur Miller	Derby Playhouse	Vilma Hollingbery Tom Knight Michael Napier Brown		
	Playhouse (Derby)					
A296	***Death of a Salesman***	Arthur Miller	Octagon Theatre Company		Lawrence Till	
	Octagon Th. (Bolton)					
A297	***Death Of A Salesman***	Arthur Miller	Palace Theatre, Watford	Wendy Gifford John Phythian John Ringham	Christopher Dunham	
	Palace Th. (Westcliff-On-Sea)					
A298	***Deathtrap***	Ira Levin	Wolsey Theatre Company	David Mallinson Steven Mann Lise Ann McLaughlin	Hettie MacDonald	
	Wolsey Theatre (Ipswich)					
A299	***Decadence***	Steven Berkoff	London City Actors			
	Salberg Studio (Salisbury)					
A300	***Deceptions***	Paul Wheeler	Mainstream Theatre		Patrick Wilde	
	Etcetera (London NW1)					
A301	***The Decorator***	Donald Churchill	Yvonne Arnaud Theatre	Peter Davison Gabrielle Drake Erika Hoffman	Val May	
	Yvonne Arnaud (Guildford) *The Hawth (Crawley)*		*Derngate (Northampton)* *Civic Theatre (Darlington)*	*Th. Royal (Plymouth)* *Th. Royal (Nottingham)*	*Th. Royal (Brighton)* *Hull New Th. (Hull)*	
A302	***Dejavu***	John Osborne	Bill Kenwright Ltd	Peter Egan Alison Johnston Eve Matheson	Tony Palmer	Bill Kenwright
	Thorndike Th. (Leatherhead)		*Comedy Th. (London SW1)*			
A303	***The Devil's Only Sleeping***	Nick Stafford	Birmingham Rep.	Lorna Laidlaw Janice McKenzie Jonathan Oliver	Theresa Heskins	
	Highbury Th (Sutton Coldfield) *Birm.Rep. Studio (Birmingham)* *Theatregoers (Ashby/Zouch)* *Holly Lodge Sch (Sandwell)*		*Sixth Form College (Stoke)* *Westwood High School (Leek)* *Crestwood School (Dudley)* *Village Inst. (Church Eaton)*	*New College (Telford)* *Ounsdale Sch (Wombourne)* *King Edward VI School (B/ham)* *English Bridge Workshops (Shrewsbury)*	*Perry Common School (Birmingham)* *Holyhead School (Birmingham)* *Arena Th. (Wolverhampton)*	
A304	***The Devils***	John Owen (AD) John Whiting	Theatr Clwyd Company	Kathryn Hunter Philip Madoc Murray Melvin	Helena Kaut-Howson	
	Th.Clywd Studio (Mold)					
A305	***Dial M for Murder***	Frederick Knott	Torch Theatre Company		Kit Thacker	
	Torch Theatre (Milford Haven)					
A306	***Diamonds in the Dust***	Devised By The Company	Belgrade Theatre Company	Tony Caverner Julie Golsworthy Rachel Osmon	Janice Dunn Mike Roberts (MD)	
	Belgrade Th. (Coventry)					
A307	***Dick Whittington***	Peter Denyer			Kenn Michaels	Kevin Wood
	Watermans (Brentford, Middx)					
A308	***Dick Whittington***	Bryan Blackburn Kenn Oldfield (D,Ch)	Churchill Theatre	Susan Maughan George Sewell Jimmy Tarbuck		
	Churchill Th. (Bromley)					
A309	***Dick Whittington And His Cat***		Connaught Theatre, Worthing	Wayne Jackman Hugh Lloyd Sophia Winter		
	Connaught Th. (Worthing)					

Ref	Play	Playwright	Theatre Co.	Starring	Director	Producer
A310	***Dick Whittington*** *Harrogate Th. (Harrogate)*	Jennifer Manley Andrew Manley (PW,D)	Harrogate Theatre Company			
A311	***Dick Whittington*** *The Playhouse (Nottingham)*	Kenneth Alan Taylor (PW,D)	Nottingham Playhouse	Sally Ann Matthews Kenneth Alan Taylor		
A312	***Dick Whittington and his Cat*** *Royal Th. (Northampton)*	Vilma Hollingbery Maurice Merry (M)	Royal Theatre, Northampton	Nelly Morrison Paul Tootnill Kim Wall	Michael Brown	
A313	***Digging for Fire*** *Bush Th. (London W12)*	Declan Hughes	Bush Theatre Company	Pam Boyd Jane Brennan Peter Hanly	Lynne Parker	Rough Magic
A314	***Disobediently Yours, Edmund Kean*** *Hen & Chickens (London N1)*	Michael Futcher		Michael Futcher	Gabrielle Daws	BK Productions
A315	***A Distant Applause*** *La Bonne Crepe (London SW11)*	Paul Prescott (PW,D)		Paul Prescott David Taylor		Carlo Lange
A316	***Doctor Faustus*** *Tabard Th. (London W4)*	Christopher Marlowe	Freelance Theatre Company			
A317	***Doctor Faustus*** *The Playhouse (Nottingham)*	Christopher Marlowe	Nottingham Playhouse	Michael Cashman	Phelim McDermott Lee Simpson	
A318	***Doctor Faustus*** *Dukes Theatre (Lancaster)*	Christopher Marlowe	Dukes Theatre Company		Jon Pope	
A319	***Dog Days*** *Th. Royal (Windsor, Berks)*	Simon Gray	Theatre Royal Windsor	Paul Chapman Tom Conti Caroline Langrishe	Tom Conti	
A320	***A Doll's House*** *Playhouse Th. (Salisbury)*	Henrik Ibsen Christopher Hampton (Tr)	Salisbury Theatre Company	Alastair Galbraith Susannah Hitching	David Massarella	
A321	***A Doll's House*** *Wolsey Theatre (Ipswich)*	Henrik Ibsen	Wolsey Theatre Company	Roger Booth Julia Ford Colin McCormack	Hettie MacDonald	
A322	***A Doll's House*** *Everyman Th. (Cheltenham)*	Henrik Ibsen Karina Micallef (T)	Everyman Theatre Company	Teresa Gallagher Robin Polley Steve Swinscoe	Martin Houghton	
A323	***A Doll's House*** *Village Theatre (London NW2)*	Henrik Ibsen	The Village Theatre Company	John Hug Debbie Radcliffe John Tallents	Dee Hart	
A324	***A Doll's House*** *Bridge Lane Th (Battersea)*	Henrik Ibsen	Wild Iris Theatre Company	Timothy Bentinck Christopher McHallem Sophie Thursfield	Polly Irvin	
A325	***Don Juan In Hell*** *Hazlitt Theatre (Maidstone)* *Malvern Festival Th. (Malvern)* *The Theatre (Chipping Norton)* *Quay Theatre (Sudbury)*	George Bernard Shaw	Lyceum Productions	Knight Mantell Liz Payne		
A326	***Don Juan*** *ICA (London SW1)*		The Sydney Front			
A327	***Don Juan*** *Wolsey Studio (Ipswich)*	Christopher Hampton (Tr) Moliere	Wolsey Theatre Company	Steven Mann Lise Ann McLaughlin Don Williams	Antony Tuckey	
A328	***Don Quixote*** *Warehouse Th. (Croydon)*	Vince Foxall	Warehouse Theatre Company	Graham Christopher Anthony Donne Carmen Gomez	Ted Craig	
A329	***Don't Play With Love*** *French Institute (London SW7)* *Rudolf Steiner (London NW1)*	Alfred de Musset		Dylan Brown Emma Higginson Fay Rusling	Jean-Marc Lanteri	
A330	***Don't Rock The Boat*** *Redgrave Th. (Farnham)* *Orchard Th. (Dartford)* *Th. Royal (Brighton)* *Beck Th. (Hayes, Middx)*	Robin Hawdon		Garfield Morgan Jane Rossington Michael Sharvell-Martin	Graham Watkins	Excalibur Productions

Ref	Play	Playwright	Theatre Co.	Starring	Director	Producer
A331	***Don't Dress For Dinner***	Marc Camoletti Robin Hawdon (Ad)		Sue Hodge Royce Mills Simon Ward	Peter Farago	Mark Furness Ltd
	Apollo Th. (London W1)	*Duchess Th. (London WC2)*				
A332	***The Dorm***		Mandela Theatre Company	John Clyde Jan Knightley Steve Scarron	Paul Pinson	
	Traverse Th. (Edinburgh)	*Theatre in the Mill (Bradford)*		*Watermans (Brentford, Middx)*		
A333	***The Double D***		Small Fish Big Ponds Theatre Company	Charlotte Bellamy Liz Brimilcombe Jan Graveson	Matthew Westwood June Brown	
	Etcetera (London NW1)					
A334	***The Double Bass***	Adam Norton		Adam Norton	Peter Cheeseman	
	New End Th. (London NW3)					
A335	***The Double Dealer***	William Congreve	Gate Theatre, Dublin	Bill Golding Tom Hickey Rosaleen Linehan	Jonathan Miller	
	Gate Theatre (Dublin)					
A336	***Double Double***	Elice & Rees	Salisbury Theatre Company		Sarah Ream	
	Playhouse Th. (Salisbury)					
A337	***Double Double***	Eric Elice Roger Rees	Palace Theatre, Westcliff	Liz Bagley David Bannerman	Eric Standidge	
	Palace Th. (Westcliff-On-Sea)					
A338	***Double Take***	Deborah Moggach	Chichester Festival Theatre	Jeremy Brudenell David Cardy Lisa Harrow	Hugh Wooldridge	
	Minerva Studio (Chichester)					
A339	***Down And Out In Paris And London***	George Orwell (A) Nigel Gearing (Ad)	Paines Plough	Lucinda Curtis Geoffrey Greenhill Harley Loudon	Anna Furse	
	Playhouse Th. (Salisbury) *Tramway (Glasgow)*	*Birm.Rep. Studio (Birmingham)* *Glennevilliers (Paris)*		*Alhambra Th. (Bradford)*	*Riverside Std. (London W6)*	
A340	***The Dracula Spectacular***	John Gardiner (L) Andrew Parr (C)	Tumbling Dice Theatre Company	Roger Ayres David Callahan Sean Connolly	Debbie Wastling	
	Th. Royal (Lincoln)	*Civic Theatre (Doncaster)*		*Civic Theatre (Mansfield)*		
A341	***Dragon***	Ultz (Ad,D) Yevgeny Shvarts (A) Alan Cumming (Ad)	Royal National Theatre	Tony Armatrading Lolita Chakrabarti Paul J Medford		RNT
	NT/Olivier (London SE1)					
A342	***Drama At Inish***					
	Abbey Th. (Dublin)					
A343	***The Dramatic Attitude of Miss Fanny Kemble***	Claire Luckham	Worcester Theatre Company		Pat Trueman	
	Swan Theatre (Worcester)					
A344	***Dreams of Anne Frank***	Bernard Kops David Burman (C)	Polka Theatre		Leona Heimfeld	
	Polka Th. (London SW19)					
A345	***Driving Miss Daisy***	Alfred Uhry	Key Theatre, Peterborough	Colin Blumenau Guy Gregory Val Lehman	Derek Killeen	
	Key Theatre (Peterborough)					
A346	***Driving Miss Daisy***	Alfred Uhry	Salisbury Theatre Company	Maria Charles Okon Jones Alan Moore	Sonia Fraser	
	Playhouse Th. (Salisbury)					
A347	***The Duchess of Malfi***	John Webster	Court Theatre Company		Anthony Cornish	
	New End Th. (London NW3)					
A348	***The Dutch Courtesan***	John Marston	Orange Tree Theatre		Sam Walters	
	Orange Tree Th. (Richmond)					
A349	***The Dybbuk***	Solomon Anski	Royal Shakespeare Company	Charles Daish Joanne Pearce John Shrapnel	Katie Mitchell	
	Barbican/The Pit (London EC1)					

Ref	Play	Playwright	Theatre Co.	Starring	Director	Producer
A350	***The Dybbuk*** *New End Th. (London NW3)*	Solomon Anski	Pascal Theatre Company	Thomas Kampe Kate Margam Ruth Posner	Julia Pascal	
A351	***Dylan Thomas-Return Journey*** *Th.Clywd Studio (Mold)*			Bob Kingdom	Anthony Hopkins	Bob Kingdom
A352	***East Lynne*** *Birm.Rep. Studio (Birmingham)*	Henry Woods (A) Lisa Evans (Ad)	Birmingham Rep.		Gwenda Hughes	
A353	***The Ecstacy*** *Pentameters (London NW3)*	Simon Black		Guy Hemphill Joanne Sergent Rob Slinger	Kate Gielgud	
A354	***Eductaing Rita*** *Opera House (Buxton)* *The Playhouse (Harlow)*	Willy Russell Charles Vance (D,P)	Prestige Plays	Georgia Greeph Hugo Myatt		
A355	***Edward II*** *Citz.First Th. (Glasgow)*	Bertolt Brecht	Citizens' Th. Co.		Philip Prowse	
A356	***Eight to the Bar*** *Citz.First Th. (Glasgow)*	David Anderson David Maclennan (PW,D)	Wildcat	Joanne Brooks George Drennan Phil McCall		
A357	***Ein Traum, Was Sonst?*** *King's Th. (Edinburgh)*	Hans Jurgen Syberberg		Edith Clever		
A358	***Elegies for Angels, Punks and Raging Queens*** *King's Head Th. (London N1)*	Bill Russell (PW,D)		Amanda Mealing Ray Shell		
A359	***The Elephant*** *New End Th. (London NW3)*	Betsuyaka Minoru	Wave Theatre Company	Sarah Ball Jonathan Coyne Alex Harland	Tim Keenan	
A360	***Elidor*** *Contact Th. (Manchester)*	Alan Garner (A) Brian Elsley (Ad,D)	Contact Theatre			
A361	***Elisabeth II*** *Gate Th. Club (London W11)*	Thomas Bernhard Meredith Oakes (T)	Gate Theatre Company	Rob Dixon Joan Geary Ian Gelder	David Fielding	
A362	***Elvis - the Musical*** *Churchill Th. (Bromley)* *New Tyne Th. (Newcastle/Tyne)* *Orchard Th. (Dartford)* *New Victoria Th. (Woking)* *Pavilion Theatre (Bournemouth)* *Th. Royal (Plymouth)* *Alhambra Th. (Bradford)* *Opera House (Belfast)* *Lyceum Th. (Sheffield)* *New Th. (Cardiff)* *His Majesty's Th. (Aberdeen)* *Hippodrome (Birmingham)* *Hull New Th. (Hull)*		E & B Productions	Clayton Mark Ian Salisbury Bo Wills	Jack Good (De) Carole Todd	Paul Elliott
A363	***Emanuelle Enchanted*** *Nuffield Theatre (Lancaster)* *Powerhouse (Nottingham)* *Phoenix Arts (Leicester)* *Prema Arts Ctr. (Dursley, Glos.)* *Warwick Arts (Coventry)* *The Leadmill (Sheffield)* *ICA (London SW1)* *The Green Room (Manchester)* *Alsager Arts C. (Crewe)* *Nth.Riding Coll. (Scarborough)*	Devised By The Company	Forced Entertainment Theatre	Robin Arthur Richard Lowdon Claire Marshall	Tim Etchells	
A364	***The Emperor's New Clothes*** *Wilde Th. (Bracknell)*	John Denny Julie Denny (PW,D)	The Wilde Community Theatre Company			
A365	***The End Of The Tunnel*** *Lilian Baylis (London EC1)* *Bowen West Th. (Bedford)* *North Devon Col. (Barnstaple)* *St George's Th. (Luton)* *Unity Theatre (Liverpool)* *The Theatre (Chipping Norton)* *Stanwix Arts Th (Carlisle)* *The Leadmill (Sheffield)* *Civic Centre (Whitchurch)* *Old Bull Arts (Barnet)* *Arts Centre (Birmingham)* *Warwick Arts (Coventry)* *Arena Th. (Wolverhampton)* *Central Studio (Basingstoke)* *Drama Studio (Exeter)* *Ashcroft Centre (Fareham)* *Collyer Hall Th. (London SW19)*		Compagnie Phillipe Gaulier	Mick Barnfather Abigail Dulay Cal McCrystal	Phillipe Gaulier	

Ref	Play	Playwright	Theatre Co.	Starring	Director	Producer
A366	***The End Of The Beginning***	Sean O'Casey	Winged Horse Touring Productns	Paul Morrow Ian Sexon Kirsty Yuill	Eve Jamieson	
	High School (Castle Douglas) *Mercat Theatre (Glasgow)* *Ardishaig Hall (Ardrishaig)* *Community Venue (Glasgow)* *Old Athenaeum Th (Glasgow)*	*D. Stewart Sch (Newton Stewart)* *St Andrews Sch (Clydebank)* *Borderline Th (Ayr)* *Whitehill Ctr (Hamilton)*		*Wallace Hall (Thornhill)* *Dolphin Arts (Glasgow)* *Arts Centre (Aberdeen)* *Arts Centre (Dundee)*	*Arts Centre (Paisley)* *Th. Workshop (Edinburgh)* *Haddo House (Aberdeen)* *Bishoploch Hall (Glasgow)*	
A367	***Endangered Species*** *Wimbledon Th. (London SW19)*	Peter Brewis (M) Howard J Davidson (M)	The Kosh	Mark Hopkins Sian Williams	Michael Merwitzer Johnny Hutch	
A368	***Endgame*** *Hull New Th. (Hull)*		Hull Freetown Theatre Company	Adrian Berry Maryann Devally Graham Wicinskj	Adrian Berry	
A369	***Enemy To The People***		English Shakespeare Company	Tim Goodwin Terry McGinity Sonia Ritter	Tim Carroll	
	Old Athenaeum Th (Glasgow) *Gardner Arts Ctr (Brighton)* *Ashcroft Centre (Fareham)* *Trinity Arts (Tunbridge Wells)* *Selby High Sch. (Selby)* *Barn Theatre (Dartington)* *Hay-on-Wye Fest. (Hay-on-Wye)*	*Borough Theatre (Abergavenny)* *The Harlequin Theatre (Redhill)* *Cricklade Th. (Andover)* *Hewitt School (Norwich)* *Cirencester Sch (Cirencester)* *Plough Theatre (Exeter)*		*Theatre Cwmtawe (Swansea)* *New Th. Royal (Portsmouth)* *Regent Centre (Christchurch)* *King's Lynn Arts (King's Lynn)* *Forest...College (Stroud)* *Guildhall Centre (Grantham)*	*The Theatre (Chipping Norton)* *The Maltings (Farnham)* *Riverhouse Barn (Walton-on-Th)* *Norwich Art Ctr. (Norwich)* *Lipson Comm Coll (Plymouth)* *Haymarket Studio (Leicester)*	
A370	***The English Kiss*** *Boulevard (London W1)*	Michael Church Betty Tadman	Chadwell Productions	Simon Beresford Toby Sawyer	Alan Ferris	
A371	***Ennio Marchetto*** *Criterion Th. (London W1V)*	*Duke of York's (London WC2)*		Ennio Marchetto		
A372	***Enter The Tragic Muse*** *Th. Museum (London WC2)*	Carol Crowther *(Newcastle Under Lyme)*		Pamela Buchner	Graham Ashe	
A373	***Entertaining Mr Sloane*** *Royal Th. (Northampton)*	Joe Orton	Royal Theatre, Northampton	Lois Baxter Peter Dineen Jonny Lee Miller	Philip Howard	
A374	***Entertaining Mr Sloane*** *Greenwich Th. (London SE10)*	Joe Orton	Greenwich Theatre		Jeremy Sams	
A375	***Epsom Downs*** *Bristol Old Vic (Bristol)*	Howard Brenton	Bristol Old Vic Ensemble		Ian Hastings	
A376	***Eric The Epic*** *New Victoria Th. (New/u/Lyme)*	Rony Robinson	New Victoria Theatre		Rob Swain	
A377	***Erogenous Zones*** *Sherman Th. (Cardiff)*	Frank Vickery	Sherman Theatre Company		Phil Clark	
A378	***The Europeans (Struggles To Love)*** *Greenwich Th. (London SE10)*	Howard Barker	Greenwich Theatre		Kenny Ireland	
A379	***Europe my Country*** *London Ark (London W6)*		Eurobizz			
A380	***Europeans*** *Watermans (Brentford, Middx)*		Talking Pictures		Stephen Daldry	
A381	***EuroVision*** *Drill Hall (London WC1)*	Tim Luscombe (PW,D)	London Gay Theatre Company	James Dreyfus Adam Magnani Michael Matus		
A382	***An Evening With Gary Lineker***	Chris England Arthur Smith	PW Productions Ltd	Andrew Hall Steven Hartley Paul Venables	Audrey Cooke	PW Productions
	Th. Royal (Brighton) *Mayflower (Southampton)* *The Hexagon (Reading)*	*Alexandra Th. (Birmingham)* *Grand Th. (Swansea)* *Civic Theatre (Darlington)*		*Lyceum Th. (Sheffield)* *The Hawth (Crawley)* *Key Theatre (Peterborough)*	*Hippodrome (Bristol)* *Theatr Clwyd (Mold)* *Th. Royal (Norwich)*	

Ref	Play	Playwright	Theatre Co.	Starring	Director	Producer
A383	*An Evening with Gary Lineker* *Duchess Th. (London WC2)*	Chris England Arthur Smith	PW Productions Ltd	Suzy Aitchison Michael Garner Georgia Mitchell	Audrey Cooke	PW Productions
A384	*Everlasting Rose* *Village Theatre (London NW2)*	Judy Upton	Harley Productions		Dee Hart	
A385	*Every Bit Of It* *Warwick Arts (Coventry)*; *Woughton Centre (Milton Keynes)*; *Arena Th. (Wolverhampton)*; *Pegasus Theatre (E. Oxford)*; *Venn Street (Huddersfield)*; *Rotherham Arts (Rotherham)*; *Old Town Hall (Hemel/Hemp)*; *Forum 28 (Barrow-in-Furness)*; *The Polytechnic (Leeds)*; *Live Theatre (Newcastle/U/Tyne)*; *Ashcroft Centre (Fareham)*; *The Junction (Cambridge)*; *Drama Centre (Redbridge)*; *Limelight Th (Aylesbury)*; *21 South Street (Reading)*; *Holloway Prison (London)*; *Old Bull Arts (Barnet)*; *Tron Th. (Glasgow)*; *Traverse Th. (Edinburgh)*; *Sherman Th. (Cardiff)*	Jackie Kay	The Sphinx	Suzanne Bonnar Elizabeth Quinn	Sue Parrish	
A386	*Excess XS* *Contact Th. (Manchester)*	Kevin Fegan	Contact Theatre		Richard Gregory Brigid Larmour	
A387	*Exile* *Bush Th. (London W12)*	David Ian Neville (PW D)	Studio Earth	Corinne Harris Finlay McLean Jane Reilly		
A388	*Experiment In Contraprojection* *Central Studio (Basingstoke)*; *Hornpipe Arts (Portsmouth)*; *Theatr Clwyd (Mold)*; *Tameside Th (Ashton-under-Lyne)*; *The Green Room (Manchester)*; *Melling Tithebarn (Liverpool)*; *The Maltings (Berwick-u-Tweed)*; *Nuffield Theatre (Lancaster)*; *Alsager Arts C. (Crewe)*; *Nth.Cheshire Col (Warrington)*; *Arts Centre (Birmingham)*; *Theatr Hafren (Newtown)*; *Arts Theatre (Belfast)*; *Bowen West Th. (Bedford)*; *Arts Centre (Falmouth)*; *Arts Centre (Cornwall,)*; *St Luke's Th. (Exeter)*; *The CCA (Glasgow)*; *Cowane Centre (Stirling)*		Forkbeard Fantasy	The Brittonioni Brothers		
A389	*Faith Healer* *Royal Court Th. (London SW1)*	Brian Friel	Royal Court Theatre	Ron Cook Sinead Cusack Donal McCann	Joe Dowling	
A390	*Faith Over Reason* *Royal Court Th. (London SW1)*	Sarah Hunter	Royal Court Theatre		Burt Ceaser	
A391	*Fallen Angels* *Thorndike Th. (Leatherhead)*; *Lyceum Th. (Sheffield)*; *Opera House (Manchester)*; *Th. Royal (Bath)*; *His Majesty's Th. (Aberdeen)*; *Malvern Festival Th. (Malvern)*; *Richmond Th. (Richmond)*; *Alexandra Th. (Birmingham)*; *New Victoria Th. (Woking)*; *Th. Royal (Brighton)*; *Forum Theatre (Billingham)*; *Marlowe Th. (Canterbury)*	Noel Coward		Sandor Eles Juliet Mills Hayley Mills	Christopher Renshaw	Bill Kenwright Ltd
A392	*The False Servant* *Gate Th. Club (London W11)*	Pierre Marivaux	Gate Theatre Company		Jonathan Martin	
A393	*A Family Affair* *Everyman Th. (Cheltenham)*	Alexander Ostrovsky	Everyman Theatre Company	Sharon Muircroft Robin Polley Pat Rossiter	Martin Houghton	
A394	*The Family Reunion* *Haymarket Th. (Leicester)*	T.S. Eliot	Haymarket Theatre Company		Julia Bardsley	
A395	*The Fancy Man* *Towngate Th. (Poole)*; *Devonshire Park Th. (Eastbourne)*; *Grand Th. (Swansea)*; *Connaught Th. (Worthing)*; *Gaiety Th. (Isle of Man)*; *Grand Theatre (Wolverhampton)*	Mike Stott	David Kirk Productions	Tracy Brabin Brian Murphy Ian Sharrock	Michael Napier Brown	David Kirk
A396	*Fantasy Island* *Old Red Lion Th. (London EC1)*	Alexander Sisters (PW D)	Barmont Productions	Carolyn Bonnyman Lynn Ferguson		
A397	*Far From The Madding Crowd* *Playhouse (Derby)*	Thomas Hardy Sally Hedges (Ad)	Derby Playhouse	Robert Ashby Tom Knight Anna Skye	Mark Clements	
A398	*The Fastest Clock in the Universe* *Hampstead Th. (London NW3)*	Philip Ridley	Hampstead Theatre Company	Jonathan Coy Jude Law Con O'Neill	Matthew Lloyd	
A399	*Feed* *Octagon Th. (Bolton)*	Tom Elliott	Octagon Theatre Company	Roy Barraclough Lesley Nicol Henrietta Whitsun Jones	Lawrence Till	

Ref	Play	Playwright	Theatre Co.	Starring	Director	Producer
A400	***Fern Hill***	Mike Kenny	Sherman Theatre Company	Marged Esli Geraint Morgan Ian Saynor	Phil Clark	
	Sherman Th. (Cardiff); Taliesin Arts C. (Swansea); Theatr Gwynedd (Bangor); Torch Theatre (Milford Haven); Ystradgynglais W (Swansea); Guildhall Th. (Brecon); Theatr Ardudwy (Gwynedd); Theatr Felinfach (Lampeter); Theatr Mwldan (Cardigan); Arts Centre (Aberystwyth); Theatr Hafren (Newtown); Theatr Colwyn (Colwyn Bay); Borough Theatre (Abergavenny); Montgomery Th. (Sheffield); Wyeside Arts C. (Builth Wells)					
A401	***Fiddler On The Roof*** *W/Yorks Playh. (Leeds)*	Sholom Alaichem (Au) Joseph Stein Jerry Bock (C) Sheldon Harnick (L)	West Yorkshire Playhouse Company	Beverley Klein Bernard Lloyd Alexandra Sumner	Matthew Warchus	
A402	***Fierce Love*** *Drill Hall (London WC1)*	Devised By The Company	Pomo Afro Homos	Djola Bernard Branner Brian Freeman Eric Gupton	The Company	
A403	***The Fifteen Streets*** *Mercury Th. (Colchester)*	Rob Bettinson (Ad) Catherine Cookson (A)	Mercury Theatre	James Allen Sarah Prince Jacquie Toye	Michael Winter	
A404	***Fighting For The Dunghill*** *Warehouse Th. (Croydon)*	Guy Jenkin	Warehouse Theatre Company	James Bolam	Richard Osborne	
A405	***The Final Appearance of Mamie Stuart*** *Torch Theatre (Milford Haven)*	Philip Michell	Torch Theatre Company		Mike James	
A406	***Firestone*** *Belgrade Th. (Coventry)*	Peter Fieldson	Belgrade Theatre Company			
A407	***Five Guys Named Moe*** *Lyric Theatre (London W1)*	Clarke Peters		Johnny Amobi Colin Charles Horace Oliver	Charles Augins	Cameron Mackintosh
A408	***Flamingo*** *Gate Th. Club (London W11)*	Bode Sowande			Topher Campbell	
A409	***Flight To Finland*** *BAC (London SW11)*		The Right Size	Sean Foley Tomas Kubinek Hamish McColl		
A410	***Flowers For Algernon*** *The Courtyard (London N1)*	Daniel Keyes	Tin Drum Theatre Company	Mark Curry	Jasper Holmes	Tindrum Company
A411	***Fool for Love*** *Grace Theatre (London SW11)*	Sam Shepard	Scarlet Edge	Don Fellows Abigail Harrison Tim Smallwood	Don Fellows	Abigail Harrison
A412	***Fooling About*** *Oxford Playhouse (Oxford)*	Renata Allen	Oxford Stage Company	Lucy Briers Simon Cox Peter Jordan	John Retallack	
A413	***Forever Yours Marie Lou*** *BAC (London SW11)*	Michel Tremblay	Thin Language	Susan Ellen Flynn Gary Richards Beth Robert	Natasha Betteridge Simon Harris	
A414	***Four Marys*** *Riverside Std. (London W6)*	Martin Duncan Ian Spink	Second Stride	Marty Cruickshank Linda Dobell Darlene Johnson	Martin Duncan & Ian Spink	
A415	***Frankenstein***	Mary Shelley	Orchard Theatre Company	Andrea Gascoigne Andrew Howard James Lailey	Bill Buffery	Orchard Theatre Company
	Drum Theatre (Plymouth); Northcott (Exeter); Park School (Barnstaple); The Octagon (Okehampton); Bryanston Arts (Blandford); Digby Hall (Sherborne, Dorset); Mowlem Theatre (Swanage); Arts Centre (St Helier); Russell-Cotes (Bournemouth); Corn Exchange (Dorchester); College Theatre (Bideford); The Civic Hall (Totnes); Acorn Arts Ctre (Penzance); Arts Centre (Falmouth); Treviglas School (Newquay); Brewhouse Th. (Taunton); The Regal Th. (Minehead); Merlin (Frome); Victoria Pavilio (Ilfracombe); Eden Arts Trust (Cumbria); Manor Pavilion (Sidmouth); The Parkhouse Centre (Bude); Hope Theatre (Bristol); Town Hall (Lynton)					
A416	***Frankenstein*** *Haymarket Studio (Leicester)*	Mary Shelley (A) Julia Bardsley (Ad,D)	Haymarket Theatre Company			

Ref	Play	Playwright	Theatre Co.	Starring	Director	Producer
A417	***Frankie & Johnny in the Clair De Lune***	Terrence McNally	Theatre Royal Plymouth	Colin Baker Susan Edmonstone	Amanda Knott	
	Brewhouse Th. (Taunton); Drum Theatre (Plymouth); Th. Royal (Winchester); Opera House (Buxton); The Harlequin Theatre (Redhill); Towngate Th. (Poole); Charter Th. (Preston); Octagon (Yeovil); Towngate Th. (Poole)					
A418	***Frankie & Tommy***	Garry Lyons	Hull Truck Theatre Company	Charlie Dickinson Steven Speirs	Damian Cruden	
	Spring St. Th. (Hull); Mad's Little The (Macclesfield); Madeley Court Theatre (Telford); Alhambra St (Bradford); Parr Hall (Warrington, Cheshire); Ellesmere Arts C (Ellesmere); VI Form Coll (Barrow-in-Furness); Ashton Theatre (Shrewsbury); Limelight Th (Aylesbury); Bewdley Festival (Worcs.); Berwyn Centre (Nantymoel); Municipal Hall (Pontypridd); Congress Th. (Gwent); Community Centre (Aberfan); Blackwood Miners'Inst (Gwent); Woughton Centre (Milton Keynes); Quay Theatre (Sudbury); Regal Arts Ctre (Worksop); St George's Th. (Luton); Stanwix Arts Th (Carlisle); Tynedale High School (Blyth); Angles Centre (Wisbech,Cambs); Norwich Art Ctr. (Norwich); Wyvern Th. (Swindon); Sherman Th. (Cardiff); Sutton Centre (Sutton In Ashfield); Dovecot (Stockton on Tees); Forest...College (Stroud); Lion Theatre (Horncastle); Community College (Fareham); Theatr Felinfach (Lampeter); Theatr Ardudwy (Gwynedd); Theatr Mwldan (Cardigan); Guildhall Th. (Brecon); Gardner Arts Ctr (Brighton); Seacombe Centre (Sutton, Surrey); Arena Th. (Wolverhampton); Penyrheol Theatr (Swansea); York Arts Centre (York); Garage Arts Centre (Walsall); Merlin (Frome); Harrow Arts (Harrow)					
A419	***Frankie and Johnny in the Clair De Lune***	Terrence McNally	Derby Playhouse			
	Derby Studio (Derby)					
A420	***From A Jack To A King***	Bob Carlton		John Ashby Matthew Devitt Allison Harding	Matthew Devitt	West Stage Productions
	Boulevard (London W1); Ambassadors Th. (London WC2)					
A421	***Frozen Chicken Parts***		Gone Fishing Theatre Company	Helena Christy Guy Hemphill		
	Pentameters (London NW3)					
A422	***Fuente Ovejuna***	Lope de Vega	Royal National Theatre	Rachel Joyce James Laurenson	Declan Donnellan	
	NT/Cottesloe (London SE1); T. Lope de Vega (Seville, Spain); Sports Complex (Derry); Assembly Hall (Edinburgh)					
A423	***Fuente Ovejuna***	Lope de Vega		Ewen Cummins Clarence Smith Geraldine Sommerville	Andrew Hay	Old Vic Theatre Company
	Bristol Old Vic (Bristol)					
A424	***Gamblers***	Nicolai Gogol Chris Hannan (Ad)	Tricycle Theatre	Phil Daniels John Labanowski Mark Rylance	Dalia Ibelhauptaite	
	Tricycle Th. (London NW6)					
A425	***The Game Of Love And Chance***	Pierre Marivaux Neil Bartlett (Ad,D)	Cambridge Theatre Company	Marcello Magni Caroline Quentin Maggie Steed	Mike Alfreds	RNT Gloria
	Towngate Th. (Poole); Connaught Th. (Worthing); Oxford Playhouse (Oxford); Warwick Arts (Coventry); Arts Th. (Cambridge); Malvern Festival Th. (Malvern); NT/Cottesloe (London SE1)					
A426	***Games***	James Saunders Peter D Norman (D,P)	The Whole in the Wall Gang	Kimberly Bevers Julian Eardley Pete Freeman		
	Etcetera (London NW1)					
A427	***Gargling With Jelly***	Brian Patten	Hull Truck Theatre Company		Damian Cruden	
	Spring St. Th. (Hull)					
A428	***Gaslight***	Patrick Hamilton	Queen's Theatre, Hornchurch	Brian Cant Susanna Dawson Jay Villiers	Sean O'Connor	Queen's Theatre
	Queen's Th. (Hornchurch)					
A429	***Gaslight***	Patrick Hamilton	Chester Gateway Theatre	Felicity Dean Stephen Tindall Robert Vahey	Roland Jaquarello	
	Gateway Th. (Chester)					
A430	***Gaudeamus***	Sergei Kaladin Maly Theatre (Ad)	Maly Theatre Of St Petersburg		Lev Dodin	
	Alhambra Th. (Bradford); The Playhouse (Nottingham); Tramway (Glasgow); Sports Complex (Derry)					
A431	***The Ghost Sonata***	August Strindberg	Sturdy Beggars Theatre Company	Nicholas Gilbrook Stephen Jameson Elizabeth McGrath	Jonas Finley	
	New End Th. (London NW3)					
A432	***Ghosts***	Henrik Ibsen	Theatre Event	Jan Lower Wendy Macadam Geoff Westoby	Pat Lower	
	DOC Th. Club (London NW5)					

Ref	Play	Playwright	Theatre Co.	Starring	Director	Producer
A433	***Ghosts*** *Library Th. (Manchester)*	Henrik Ibsen	Library Theatre Company		Sue Sutton Mayo	
A434	***The Gifts Of The Gorgon*** *Barbican/The Pit (London EC1)*	Peter Shaffer	Royal Shakespeare Company	Judi Dench Jeremy Northam Michael Pennington	Peter Hall	RSC
A435	***The Gigli Concert*** *Almeida Th. (London N1)*	Tom Murphy	Almeida Theatre Co	Tony Doyle Barry Foster Ruth McCabe	Karel Reisz	
A436	***The Giraffe and The Pelly and Me*** *Polka Th. (London SW19)*	Roald Dahl (A) Vicky Ireland (Ad)	Polka Theatre		Roman Stefanski	
A437	***I Can Give You A Good Time*** *New Vic (Bristol)*	Gilly Fraser	Bristol Old Vic Ensemble	Nigel Cooke Heather Williams	Ian Hastings	
A438	***The Glass Menagerie*** *Perth Th. (Perth)*	Tennessee Williams	Perth Theatre Company		Joan Knight	
A439	***The Glass Menagerie*** *Swan Theatre (Worcester)*	Tennessee Williams	Worcester Theatre Company		Pat Trueman	
A440	***The Glass Menagerie*** *Bristol Old Vic (Bristol)*	Tennessee Williams	Bristol Old Vic Ensemble	Paul Brennen Sally Mais Marjorie Yates	Ian Hastings	
A441	***Glassparts*** *Phoenix Arts (Leicester); Brewhouse Th. (Taunton); Bryanston Arts (Blandford); (Swindon)*			David Glass	Peta Lily Leah Hausman	
A442	***Goin' Local*** *Th. Royal (Stratford East); The Playhouse (Nottingham)*	Tunde Ikoli	Theatre Royal Stratford East	Paul Barber Kate Williams	Philip Hedley	
A443	***The Golden Ass*** *Old Red Lion Th. (London EC1)*	Gerald Killingworth (PW,P)		Simon Beresford Richard Tate Chris Tranchell	Mike Ashman	
A444	***Goldilocks And The Three Bears*** *Wimbledon Th. (London SW19)*		E & B Productions	Bobby Davro Victor Spinetti Michaela Strachan	Tudor Davies	Paul Elliott
A445	***Gone With The Wind II*** *Arches Th. (London SE1)*	Aline Waites (D,P) David Kelsey	Aba Daba Productions	Jacqui Cryer Shaun Curry Robin Hunter		
A446	***Good*** *Tron Th. (Glasgow)*	C.P. Taylor	Tron Theatre Company		Michael Boyd	
A447	***Good Morning Bill*** *Royal Lyceum Th. Co (Edinburgh)*	P.G. Wodehouse	Royal Lyceum Theatre Company		Hugh Hodgart	
A448	***The Good Person Of Sezuan*** *Everyman Th. (Liverpool)*	Bertolt Brecht	London Bubble Theatre Company		Jonathon Petherbridge	
A449	***Good Rockin' Tonite*** *Strand Th. (London WC2B); Playhouse (London WC2); Prince of Wales Th. (London W1V)*	Jack Good (PW,D)		Michael Dimitri David Howarth Tim Whitnall	Ian Kellgren	Bill Kenwright Ltd
A450	***Goodnight Mr Tom*** *Wolsey Theatre (Ipswich)*	Michelle Magorian Gary Carpenter (C)	Wolsey Theatre Company	David Cooper Robbie Gill Richard Owens	Antony Tuckey Gerry Tebutt (Ch)	
A451	***Gormenghast*** *Queens Hall Arts (Hexham); BAC (London SW11); Palace Theatre (Newark); Arts Th. (Cambridge)*	Mervyn Peake (A) John Constable David Glass (Ad,d)	The David Glass Ensemble	Peter Bailie Di Sherlock David Tysall		
A452	***Grace*** *Hampstead Th. (London NW3)*	Doug Lucie	Hampstead Theatre Company	Kate Fahy James Laurenson Anna Massey	Mike Bradwell	
A453	***Grand Hotel*** *Dominion (London W1)*	Luther Davis Robert Wright (C) George Forrest (L)		Brent Barrett Debbie de Coudreaux Liliane Montevecchi	Tommy Tune	James Nederlander

Produced exclusively for Plays & Players by SEARCHLINE

Ref	Play	Playwright	Theatre Co.	Starring	Director	Producer
A454	***The Grapes of Wrath***	John Steinbeck (A) Frank Galati (Ad)	Birmingham Rep.	Paul Herzberg Mary Macleod Graham Padden	Anthony Clark	
	Birmingham Rep. (Birmingham)					
A455	***Grave Dancer***	Lizzie Mickery	Finborough Productions		Mary Peate	
	Finborough Th. (London SW10)					
A456	***Grave Plots***	David Kane	Nottingham Playhouse	Patrick Cargill Adrian Edmondson John Gordon Sinclair		Notingham Playhouse Carnival Productions
	The Playhouse (Nottingham)					
A457	***Gravity Swing***	Broadway	Ra Ra Zoo	Lindsay Butcher Chris Cresswell Jeremy Robins	Birte Pedersen	
	Arts Th. (Cambridge)		*Playhouse Th. (Weston-S-Mare)*	*Riverside Std. (London W6)*	*Warwick Arts (Coventry)*	
	Th. Royal (Bury St Edmunds)		*Orchard Th. (Dartford)*	*Crucible Th. (Sheffield)*	*Wyvern Th. (Swindon)*	
	Swan Theatre (Worcester)		*Linkoping (Sweden)*	*Palace Theatre (Newark)*	*Octagon (Yeovil)*	
	Grand Th. (Swansea)		*Little Theatre (Middlesborough)*	*Oxford Playhouse (Oxford)*	*Queens Hall Arts (Hexham)*	
A458	***Grease***	Jim Jacobs Warren Casey	Derby Playhouse	Jane Ashby Vas Constanti	Mark Clements	
	Playhouse (Derby)					
A459	***The Great God Brown***	Eugene O'Neill	Stage One Theatre Company	Oona Beeson Alastair Cumming Miles Harvey	Michael Walling	Stage One
	Georgian Theatre (Richmond)		*Civic Th. (Ayr)*	*Rudolf Steiner (London NW1)*	*Mansfield Leis. (Mansfield)*	
	Stamford Arts C. (Stamford)		*Merlin Theatre (Sheffield)*	*The Theatre (Chipping Norton)*	*Maltings Arts (St Albans)*	
	Riverhouse Barn (Walton-on-Th)		*Arena Th. (Wolverhampton)*			
A460	***Grope***	Jane Eller Michele Howarth	Mad Cow	Antonia Best Julie Hobbs Anthony Wise	Paul Besterman	
	Treadwell's (Bradford)					
A461	***The Guardsman***	Ferenc Molnar	Theatr Clwyd Company	Jo Kendall Jenny Seagrove Mark Wing-Davey	Lucy Parker	
	Theatr Clwyd (Mold)					
A462	***The Gulf Between Us***	Trevor Griffiths (PW D)	The Building Company	Kulvinder Ghir Dave Hill Paul Slack		
	W/Yorks Playh. (Leeds)					
A463	***Hamlet***	William Shakespeare	Compass Theatre Company	Nick Chadwin Carlene Reed Paul Rider	Neil Sissons	
	Little Theatre (Middlesborough)		*Drum Theatre (Plymouth)*	*Crucible Th. (Sheffield)*	*New Tyne Th. (Newcastle/Tyne)*	
	Georgian Theatre (Richmond)		*Brewhouse Th. (Burton-on-Trent)*	*Globe (Tokyo, Japan)*	*Theatr Mwldan (Cardigan)*	
	Guildhall Th. (Brecon)		*Opera House (Buxton)*	*Wilde Th. (Bracknell)*	*Kimberley Comp. School (Notts)*	
	Spring St. Th. (Hull)		*Queens Hall Arts (Hexham)*	*The Maltings (Berwick-u-Tweed)*	*Regal Arts Ctre (Worksop)*	
	Little Theatre (Knutsford)		*The Playhouse (Harlow)*	*Arts Centre (Aberystwyth)*	*Miners Hall (Swansea)*	
	Wyeside Arts C. (Builth Wells)		*Nth.Riding Coll. (Scarborough)*	*Theatr Gwynedd (Bangor)*	*Lilian Baylis (London EC1)*	
A464	***Hamlet***	William Shakespeare	Theatr Clwyd Company		Michael McCaffey	
	Th. Royal (Brighton)		*Th. Royal (Brighton)*			
A465	***Hamlet***	William Shakespeare		David Burke Geraldine McEwan Alan Rickman	Robert Sturua	Thelma Holt City of Nottingham
	Riverside Std. (London W6)		*Alhambra Th. (Bradford)*	*VI Form Coll (Barrow-in-Furness)*	*The Playhouse (Nottingham)*	
	Bradie's (Barrow in Furness)		*(Liverpool)*			
A466	***Hamlet***	William Shakespeare	Royal Shakespeare Company	Richard Bonneville Kenneth Branagh Jane Lapotaire	Adrian Noble	Sponsored by Unilever
	Barbican Th. (London EC2)					

Ref	Play	Playwright	Theatre Co.	Starring	Director	Producer
A467	***Hamlet***	William Shakespeare	Medieval Players	Mark Knight Mark Knox Roy Weskin	Ben Benison	
	Civic Theatre (Scunthorpe)		*The Nave (Uxbridge)*	*Arts Centre (Horsham)*	*Arts Centre (Salisbury, Wilts.)*	
	Univ. of Essex (Colchester)		*Millfield Th. (London N18)*	*Grand Theatre (Wolverhampton)*	*Globe Theatre (Neuss (Germany))*	
	St Magnus Festival (Kirkwall)		*Shetland Island (Shetland Isles)*	*Lyth Arts Centre (Wick)*	*Mill (Thurso)*	
	Village Hall (Durness)		*Village Hall (Rosehall, H'Lands)*	*Leisure Centre (Ullapool)*	*Village Hall (Ullapool, H'land)*	
	Village Hall (Acharacle,H'Lands)		*Broadford Hall (Skye, H'Land)*	*Village Hall (Lochcarron)*	*Village Hall (Findhorn, H'Lands)*	
	Holland Park Th. (London)		*Octagon (Yeovil)*	*King's Lynn Arts (King's Lynn)*	*Cambridge Fest. (Cambridge)*	
	The Faroe Isles (Faroe Isles)		*Eden Court Th. (Inverness)*	*The Hexagon (Reading)*	*Brewhouse Th. (Taunton)*	
	M'brough College (Marlborough)		*Bryanston Arts (Blandford)*	*The Lawn (Lincoln)*	*College of F.E. (Lancs)*	
	The Tithe Barn (Ely)		*Sth Holland Ctr. (Spalding)*	*Norwich Art Ctr. (Norwich)*	*Willyotts Arts C (Potters Bar, Herts)*	
	Grimsby Leis. (Grimsby)		*Live Arts (Grantham)*	*Stanwix Arts Th (Carlisle)*	*Little Theatre (Middlesborough)*	
	Sports & Arts C. (Thame, Oxon)		*Platform Theatre (Haywards Heath)*	*Th. Royal (Bury St Edmunds)*	*Theatr Hafren (Newtown)*	
	Taliesin Arts C. (Swansea)		*Grange Arts Ctr. (Manchester)*	*The Metropolitan (B. St Edmunds)*	*The Marina Th. (Lowestoft)*	
	Trinity Arts (Gainsborough)		*Gatehouse Th. (Stafford)*	*Bowen West Th. (Bedford)*		
A468	***Handsome, Handicapped And Hebrew***	Sara Sugarman (PW,D)	The Film & Theatre Foundation			
	The Grove (London W10)					
A469	***Hanging Around***		Trestle Theatre			
	(Bolton)		*(Newcastle Under Lyme)*			
A470	***Hans Christian Anderstories***	Hans Christian Andersen (A)	Unicorn Theatre	Richard Bryan Ray Emmet-Brown Emma Gibbons	Richard Williams	
	Arts Theatre (London WC2H)					
A471	***Hansel And Gretel***		Norwich Puppet Theatre Trust Ltd			
	Norwich Puppet (Norwich)					
A472	***Hapgood***	Tom Stoppard	Century Theatre Touring	Chris Bramwell Hilary Drake Robert Tunstall	Graham Callan	
	Gateway Th. (Chester)		*Towngate Th. (Poole)*			
A473	***Happy As A Sandbag***	Ken Lee	ARC Theatre Company	Vanessa Collick Celia Jones Helen Pagett	John Ghent	
	Civic Th. (Chelmsford)		*Playhouse Th. (Weston-S-Mare)*	*Th. Royal (Lincoln)*	*Arts Centre (Horsham)*	
	Opera House (Buxton)		*Charter Th. (Preston)*	*Theatre Royal (Wakefield)*	*Wimbledon Th. (London SW19)*	
	Pomegranate Th. (Chesterfield)					
A474	***Happy Days***	Samuel Beckett	Salisbury Theatre Company	Peter Halliday Dilys Laye	David Massarella	
	Salberg Studio (Salisbury)					
A475	***Happy Days***	Samuel Beckett	Citizens' Th. Co.	Anne Myatt Derwent Watson	Kim Dambaek	
	Citz.First Th. (Glasgow)					
A476	***Happy Families***	John Godber (PW,D)	West Yorkshire Playhouse Company	Judith Barker Nicholas Lane Andrew Livingston		West Yorkshire Playhouse
	W/Yorks Playh. (Leeds)					
A477	***A Hard Heart***	Howard Barker	Almeida Theatre Co	James Clyde Angela Down Anna Massey	Ian McDiarmid	
	Almeida Th. (London N1)					
A478	***The Hatchet Man***	Thomas Coyle	Wild Pig	Sally Burnett Karl Draper Robert Horwell	Josephine LeGrice	
	DOC Th. Club (London NW5)					
A479	***The Haunted Hotel***	Wilkie Collins (Au) Mr Philip Dart (Ad)	Channel Theatre Company	Hilary Crowson Glyn Houston Sian Webber	Philip Dart	
	Epsom Playhouse (Epsom)		*Th. Royal (Winchester)*	*Brewhouse Th. (Taunton)*	*Civic Theatre (Scunthorpe)*	
	Theatre Royal (Wakefield)		*Orchard Th. (Dartford)*	*Gordon Craig Th. (Stevenage)*	*Arts Centre (Aberystwyth)*	
	Malvern Festival Th. (Malvern)		*Ashcroft Th. (Croydon)*	*Connaught Th. (Worthing)*		
A480	***Hawks & Doves***	Louise Page	Nuffield Theatre Company		Patrick Sandford	
	Nuffield Th. (Southampton)					
A481	***Hay Fever***	Noel Coward		Maria Aitken Maria Charles Sara Crowe	Alan Strachan	Theatre of Comedy
	Theatr Clwyd (Mold)		*Richmond Th. (Richmond)*	*Th. Royal (Bath)*	*Yvonne Arnaud (Guildford)*	

Ref	Play	Playwright	Theatre Co.	Starring	Director	Producer
A482	***Hay Fever*** *Royal Lyceum Th. Co (Edinburgh)*	Noel Coward	Royal Lyceum Theatre Company		Hugh Hodgart	
A483	***He's So at Peace with Himself*** *Duke's Head (Richmond)*	Jan Booth	Meet The Folks Theatre Co.			
A484	***Head-Rot Holiday*** *BAC (London SW11)* *The Link (London)*	Sarah Daniels	Clean Break Theatre Company		Paulette Randall	
A485	***Heart*** *Young Vic Studio (London SE1)* *New Victoria Th. (New/u/Lyme)* *Bowen West Th. (Bedford)*	Denise Wong (De,D)	Black Mime Theatre Ensemble			
A486	***Heartbreak House*** *Yvonne Arnaud (Guildford)* *Haymarket (London SW1)*	George Bernard Shaw		Felicity Kendal Vanessa Redgrave Paul Scofield	Trevor Nunn	Duncan C Weldon
A487	***Heartless*** *ICA (London SW1)*	Claire MacDonald	ICA Live Arts		Simon Vincenzi	Arts Admin
A488	***Hecuba*** *Gate Th. Club (London W11)*	Kenneth McLeish (T) Euripides	Gate Theatre Company		Laurence Boswell	
A489	***Heer Ranjha*** *Th. Royal (Stratford East)*	Varis Shah (A) Jatinder Verma (Ad,d)	Tara Arts	Bhageerathi Bagi Nirmal Chandra Pandey		
A490	***The Heiress*** *Churchill Th. (Bromley)* *Lyceum Th. (Sheffield)* *Th. Royal (Windsor, Berks)* *King's Th. (Edinburgh)* *Th. Royal (Plymouth)* *Th. Royal (Brighton)* *Lyceum Th. (Crewe)* *Malvern Festival Th. (Malvern)* *Civic Theatre (Darlington)* *Opera House (Manchester)* *New Victoria Th. (Woking)* *Alexandra Th. (Birmingham)* *Oxford Playhouse (Oxford)* *Th. Royal (Glasgow)* *Richmond Th. (Richmond)*	Henry James		Frank Finlay Anthony Head Nichola McAuliffe	John David	Lee Dean Associates
A491	***Henceforward...*** *New Victoria Th. (New/u/Lyme)*	Alan Ayckbourn	New Victoria Theatre	Sophie Heydel Adam Norton Joanna Phillips-Lane	Rob Swain	
A492	***Henry IV Part 1*** *Barbican Th. (London EC2)*	William Shakespeare	Royal Shakespeare Company	Julian Glover Michael Maloney Robert Stephens	Adrian Noble	RSC
A493	***Henry IV Part 2*** *Barbican Th. (London EC2)*	William Shakespeare	Royal Shakespeare Company	Julian Glover Michael Maloney Robert Stephens	Adrian Noble	RSC
A494	***High Society*** *Wolsey Theatre (Ipswich)*	Cole Porter	Wolsey Theatre Company		Gerry Tebutt Antony Tuckey	
A495	***Hindsight*** *Watermill Th. (Newbury)*	Richard Everett	Watermill Theatre	Kay Adshead John Conroy Fiona Hendley	Euan Smith	
A496	***His Brother's Keeper*** *Springfield Th. (London N11)*	J. Madison Johnston Kimberley Ann Herd	London Via Stoke Productions			
A497	***His Majesty*** *St Bride's Centre (Edinburgh)* *Orange Tree Th. (Richmond)*	Harley Granville Barker	Orange Tree Theatre		Sam Walters	
A498	***The Hobbit*** *Redgrave Th. (Farnham)*	J.R.R. Tolkien Graham Watkins (Ad,D) Rony Robinson (Ad)	Redgrave Theatre Company			
A499	***Hobson's Choice*** *New Victoria Th. (New/u/Lyme)*	Harold Brighouse	New Victoria Theatre	Anthony Dutton Richard Hague Rosie Timpson	Rob Swain	
A500	***Hobson's Choice*** *Birmingham Rep. (Birmingham)*	Harold Brighouse	Birmingham Rep.	Janice McKenzie Brian Rawlinson Tom Watt	Gwenda Hughes	
A501	***The Hollow*** *Devonshire Park Th. (Eastbourne)*	Agatha Christie	Newpalm Productions			

Ref	Play	Playwright	Theatre Co.	Starring	Director	Producer
A502	***Home At Seven***	R.C. Sherriff Charles Vance (D,P)	Prestige Plays	Elaine Banham Georgia Greeph Hugo Myatt		
	Opera House (Buxton); The Playhouse (Harlow)					
A503	***The Home Show Pieces***	David Greenspan	Citizens' Th. Co.		Matthew Lloyd	
	Citz. Third Th. (Glasgow)					
A504	***Horse-Radish***	Toby Rodin	Etcetera Theatre Company	Toby Rodin	Sonia Fraser	
	Etcetera (London NW1)					
A505	***The Hostage***	Brendan Behan	Harrogate Theatre Company	Vincent Franklin Leda Hodgson Ted Richards	Andrew Manley	
	Harrogate Th. (Harrogate)					
A506	***Hostages and Hamsters***	Stuart McEnzie	La Bonne Crepe	Mac Andrews Graham Christopher Philip Peacock	Paul Prescott	Carlo Lange
	La Bonne Crepe (London SW11)					
A507	***Hot Italian Nights***	Devised By The Company	Oxford Stage Company	Jan Alphonse Nicola Burnett-Smith Andrew Dennis	John Retallack	
	Warwick Arts (Coventry); Towngate Th. (Basildon); Brewhouse Th. (Taunton); The Playhouse (Harlow); Connaught Th. (Worthing); Richmond Th. (Richmond); Th. Royal (Bury St Edmunds); Towngate Th. (Poole); Th. Royal (Lincoln); Oxford Playhouse (Oxford)					
A508	***Hot Stuff***	Kerryson & Norris	Leicester Haymarket Theatre	David Dale	Paul Kerryson	
	Hippodrome (Birmingham); Wimbledon Th. (London SW19); Grand Th. (Swansea); Derngate (Northampton); Th. Royal (Nottingham); Grand Th. (Leeds); Haymarket Th. (Leicester)					
A509	***Houdini's Death Defying Mystery***	Raymund FitzSimon	Pocket Theatre Cumbria	Sophy Ackroyd David Cole Peter Gerald Amanda MacDonald	Keiran Gillespie	
	Stanwix Arts Th (Carlisle); St Bride's Centre (Edinburgh); Cumbernauld Th. (Cumbernauld); Riverside Th. (Coleraine); Arts Centre (Newry); Square Chapel (Halifax); The Old Laundry (Bowness); Brewhouse Th. (Burton-on-Trent); Kendal Town Hall (Kendal); Victory Hall (Broughton); Coronation Hall (Ulverston); Live Theatre (Newcastle/U/Tyne); Library Theatre (South Shields)					
A510	***Hound***	Maria Oshodi	Graeae Theatre Company	David Bowen Veronique Christie Dave Kent	Ewan Marshall	
	Old Bull Arts (Barnet); The Junction (Cambridge); Cricklade Th. (Andover); South Hill Park (Bracknell); Arts Centre (Birmingham); Sherman Th. (Cardiff); Albany Centre (Bristol); Live Theatre (Newcastle/U/Tyne); Buddle Arts Ctre (Tyneside); Town Hall (Hartlepool); Halton Guildhall (Widnes); Grange Arts Ctre (Ellesmere Port); Everyman Th. (Liverpool); The Green Room (Manchester)					
A511	***The Hour Of The Lynx***	Per Enquist	Exciting Inner City Theatre Company	Deidrie Doone Shona Morris William Oxborrow	Les Miller	Inner City Th. Co.
	Grace Theatre (London SW11); Chelsea Centre (London SW10)					
A512	***House Among the Stars***	Michel Tremblay	Traverse Theatre Company	Jennifer Black Graham di Banzi Kern Falconer	Ian Brown	
	Traverse Th. (Edinburgh)					
A513	***The House Of Stairs***	Ruth Rendell (A) Don Taylor (Ad)	Churchill Theatre	Anita Harris Virginia Stride	Kenneth Alan Taylor	Bill Kenwright Ltd
	Thorndike Th. (Leatherhead); Orchard Th. (Dartford); Lyceum Th. (Sheffield); Forum Theatre (Billingham); Grand Theatre (Wolverhampton); Derngate (Northampton); Richmond Th. (Richmond); Playhouse (Liverpool); Th. Royal (Plymouth); Beck Th. (Hayes, Middx); Marlowe Th. (Canterbury); New Th. (Cardiff); Th. Royal (Brighton); Th. Royal (Glasgow); Th. Royal (Bath); Oxford Playhouse (Oxford); Alexandra Th. (Birmingham); Th. Royal (Nottingham); Churchill Th. (Bromley); Arts Th. (Cambridge); Ashcroft Th. (Croydon); Belgrade Th. (Coventry)					
A514	***The House Of The Spirits***	Isabel Allende Michael Batz (Ad)	The Yorick Theatre Company	Paula Bardowell Nick Bartlett Fisun Burgess		
	Tramway (Glasgow)					
A515	***The House of Bernarda Alba***	Federico Garcia Lorca Matthew Banks (Tr) Katie Mitchell (D,P)	Classics on a Shoestring & Gate Theatre	Alexandra Gilbreath Liz Kettle Dinah Stabb		
	Gate Th. Club (London W11)					

Ref	Play	Playwright	Theatre Co.	Starring	Director	Producer
A516	*House Of America*	Ed Thomas	Y Cwmni	Rhodri Hugh Lisa Palfrey		
	Chapter Arts (Cardiff)	*Tramway (Glasgow)*				
A517	*House of Bernarda Alba*	Federico Garcia Lorca	Court Theatre Company		Peter Gale	
	Court Th. (London N1)					
A518	*The House That Jack Bought*	David Anderson (PW,D) David Maclennan	Wildcat		David MacLellen	
	Traverse Th. (Edinburgh)					
A519	*The House That Henry Built*		Inside Out Theatre Company			
	Th. Museum (London WC2)					
A520	*How The Other Half Loves*	Alan Ayckbourn	Royal Theatre, Northampton			
	Royal Th. (Northampton)					
A521	*Howard Johnson Commits Suicide*		Canadian Phoenix			
	Tabard Th. (London W4)					
A522	*Hush*	April De Angelis	Royal Court Theatre	Marion Bailey Debra Gillett Dervla Kirwan	Max Stafford-Clark	
	Royal Court Th. (London SW1)					
A523	*The Hypochondriacs*	Botho Strauss	Citizens' Th. Co.		David Fielding	
	Citz. Second Th. (Glasgow)					
A524	*I Believe In Love*	Jez Butterworth James Harding	The Wilcot Group		David Bidmead	
	Etcetera (London NW1)					
A525	*I Stand Before You Naked*	Joyce Carol Oates Sydnee Blake (PW,D)	Cakes and Ale Theatre Company	Frances Cuka		
	Offstage D/Stair (London NW1)					
A526	*Iago*	Phil Wilmott (A,D) William Shakespeare	Steam Factory	Howard Sadler Charles Simpson Nicola Wright		
	Man in the Moon (London SW3)					
A527	*An Ideal Husband*	Oscar Wilde	Peter Hall Company	Anna Carteret Hannah Gordon Martin Shaw	Peter Hall	Bill Kenwright Ltd
	Thorndike Th. (Leatherhead)	*Lyceum Th. (Sheffield)*		*Th. Royal (Bath)*	*New Th. (Cardiff)*	
	Richmond Th. (Richmond)					
A528	*An Ideal Husband*	Oscar Wilde	Royal Exchange Theatre Company	Tom Chadbon Emily Morgan Una Stubbs	James Maxwell	
	Royal Exchange (Manchester)					
A529	*The Imaginary Invalid*	Miles Malleson (Tr) Moliere	Masque Theatre Company	John Carter Jeannette Dobney Paulette Lythall	Kay Dudeny	
	Thorndike Th. (Leatherhead)					
A530	*Imagine*	Bob Eaton		Paul Case Karl Lornie Mark McGann	Ian Kellgren	
	Playhouse (Liverpool)					
A531	*The Importance Of Being Earnest*	Oscar Wilde	Royal Theatre, Northampton			
	Royal Th. (Northampton)					
A532	*The Importance of Being Earnest*	Oscar Wilde	Bristol Old Vic Ensemble	Paul Brennen John Lloyd Fillingham Zena Walker	Ian Hastings	
	Bristol Old Vic (Bristol)					
A533	*The Importance Of Being Earnest*	Oscar Wilde	York Theatre Royal Company		Derek Nicholls	
	Theatre Royal (York)					
A534	*In Camera*	Jean-Paul Sartre				
	Duke's Head (Richmond)					
A535	*In Celebration*	David Storey	Tavistock Repertory Company		Harry Landis	
	Tower Theatre (London N1)					

Ref	Play	Playwright	Theatre Co.	Starring	Director	Producer
A536	***In Praise Of Love*** *Dundee Repertory (Dundee)*	Terence Rattigan	Dundee Repertory Theatre Ltd	Neville Barber Kay Gallie David Weston	Terry Wale	
A537	***In The Midnight Hour*** *Theatre Royal (York)*	Philip Ryan	York Theatre Royal Company	Matthew Lloyd Davies Michael Mawby Lynn Whitehead	Greg Palmer (MD) Derek Nicholls	
A538	***In The Midnight Hour*** *Young Vic Th. (London SE1)*	Philip Ryan	Young Vic Company	Anthony Barclay Gillian Bevan Jeremy Brook	Karen Stephens Chris White	
A539	***Indigo Mill*** *Polka Th. (London SW19)*	Nick Fisher	Polka Theatre	Nigel Bowden Joanne Knowles Sally Ann Matthews	Caroline Smith	
A540	***The Innocents*** *Playhouse (Derby)*	William Archibald	Derby Playhouse	Jane Montgomery Margot Stanley	Robin Midgley	
A541	***An Inspector Calls*** *NT/Lyttelton (London SE1)* *Th. Royal (Bath)* *NT/Olivier (London SE1)* *Th. Royal (Newcastle/u/Tyne)* *Alhambra Th. (Bradford)* *New Th. (Cardiff)* *Th. Royal (Glasgow)* *Lyceum Th. (Sheffield)* *Grand Th. (Blackpool)*	J.B. Priestley	Royal National Theatre	Kenneth Cranham Barbara Leigh-Hunt Richard Pasco	Stephen Daldry	RNT
A542	***An Inspector Calls*** *Octagon Th. (Bolton)*	J.B. Priestley	Octagon Theatre Company		Lawrence Till	
A543	***Intimacy*** *Ecology Centre (London W1)*	Jean-Paul Sartre Michael Almaz (Ad,D)	The Artaud Company	Felicity Branagan Eva Coleman-Wood		Cafe Theatre Company
A544	***Intimate Exchanges*** *Everyman Th. (Cheltenham)*	Alan Ayckbourn	Everyman Theatre Company	Elizabeth Elvin Martyn Stanbridge	Ellis Jones	
A545	***Into The Woods*** *Forum Th. (Manchester)*	Stephen Sondheim	Library Theatre Company		Roger Haines	
A546	***Invasion Werewolf*** *Old Red Lion Th. (London EC1)*		Esselen International	Johnny Myers		
A547	***The Invisible Man*** *Th. Royal (Stratford East)*	Ken Hill (PW,D)	Theatre Royal Stratford East	Sarah Berger Brian Murphy Toni Palmer		
A548	***It Runs In The Family*** *Th. Royal (Windsor, Berks)* *Playhouse (London WC2)*	Ray Cooney (PW,D)	Theatre Royal Windsor	Windsor Davies Sandra Dickinson Wanda Ventham		
A549	***It's A Girl*** *Gateway Th. (Chester)*	John Burrows	Chester Gateway Theatre	Janys Chambers Rachel Clarke Kay Purcell	Claire Grove	
A550	***It's Not All Grimm*** *Arts Theatre (London WC2H)*	The Brothers Grimm (Au) Peter Fieldson (A)	Unicorn Theatre		Richard Williams	
A551	***Jack and the Beanstalk*** *The Hexagon (Reading)*			Charlie Drake Timmy Mallett Linda Nolan	Brian Marshall	Nick Thomas Productions
A552	***Jack And The Beanstalk*** *Millfield Th. (London N18)*			Helen Shapiro	Bonnie Lithgoe	
A553	***Jack And The Beanstalk*** *Davenport Th. (Stockport)*			Ian Botham Max Boyce Jane Freeman		International Artistes Ltd
A554	***Jack's Out*** *Bush Th. (London W12)*	Danny Miller	Barmont Productions	John Challis James Clyde Georgiana Dacombe	Ken McClymont	
A555	***Jane Eyre*** *Crucible Th. (Sheffield)*	Charlotte Bronte (A) Willis Hall (Ad)	Crucible Theatre	Emma Fielding Jack Shepherd	Annie Castledine	
A556	***The Jesuit*** *Tron Th. (Glasgow)*		Fifth Estate			

Ref	Play	Playwright	Theatre Co.	Starring	Director	Producer
A557	***The Jolly Potters*** *New Victoria Th. (New/u/Lyme)*	Rony Robinson (Ad) Peter Cheeseman (Ad,D)	New Victoria Theatre	Jon Benoit Matthew Cottle Sally George		
A558	***Jordan*** *Lilian Baylis (London EC1)*	Anna Reynolds Moira Buffini	Dark Horse Theatre Company	Moira Buffini	Fiona Buffini	
A559	***Joseph And The Amazing ... Dreamcoat*** *London Palladium (London W1)*	Andrew Lloyd Webber	Really Useful Theatre Company Ltd.	David Easter Linzi Hateley Phillip Schofield	Steven Pimlott	Really Useful Group
A560	***Josephine*** *BAC (London SW11)*	Maureen Chadwick	BAC Theatre Company	Miquel Brown Dawn Hope	Maggie Norris	
A561	***A Jovial Crew*** *Swan Th. (Stratford-upon-Avon)*	Richard Brome (A) Stephen Jeffreys (Ad)	Royal Shakespeare Company	Ron Cook Paul Jesson Rebecca Saire	Max Stafford-Clark	Nicky Pallot
A562	***Jubilee*** *Mercury Th. (Colchester)*	David Storey	Mercury Theatre	David Goudge Pamela Lane Colm O'Neill	Geoff Bullen	
A563	***A Judgement In Stone*** *Tramway (Glasgow); The Playhouse (Nottingham); Grand Th. (Blackpool); Lyric Ham'smith (London W6)*	Neil Barlett (Ad) Nicholas Bloomfield (C) Neil Bartlett (PW,D)	Gloria	Sheila Hancock	Leah Hausman	Gloria
A564	***Julius Caesar*** *New Victoria Th. (New/u/Lyme)*	William Shakespeare	New Victoria Theatre	Oliver Beamish Roger Llewellyn Ted Richards	Martin Harvey	
A565	***Julius Caesar*** *Rutland Open Air (Stamford)*	William Shakespeare	Stamford Shakespeare Company		Diane Watson	
A566	***Julius Caesar*** *Th. Royal (Newcastle/u/Tyne)*	William Shakespeare	Royal Shakespeare Company	Jonathan Hyde Robert Stephens Owen Teale	Steven Pimlott	RSC
A567	***June Moon*** *Hampstead Th. (London NW3); Vaudeville Th. (London WC2)*	Ring Lardner George Kaufman	Hampstead Theatre Company	Julia Blalock Susannah Fellows Frank Lazarus	Alan Strachan	Theatre of Comedy Hampstead Theatre
A568	***The Jungle Book*** *Citz.First Th. (Glasgow)*	Rudyard Kipling (Au) Myles Rudge (A)	Citizens' Th. Co.	Carol Brannan Edward Brittain Cheryl Innes	Giles Havergal	
A569	***Just Between Ourselves*** *Greenwich Th. (London SE10)*	Alan Ayckbourn	Greenwich Theatre	Martin Jarvis Robin Nedwell Liz Smith	Robin Midgley	
A570	***Just So*** *Norwich Puppet (Norwich)*	Rudyard Kipling (Au)	Norwich Puppet Theatre Trust Ltd			
A571	***Kafka's Dick*** *Birmingham Rep. (Birmingham); Charter Th. (Preston); Marlowe Th. (Canterbury)*	Alan Bennett	Birmingham Rep.	Amelda Brown Andrew Normington Michael Roberts	John Adams	
A572	***Karate Billy Comes Home*** *Th. Upstairs (London SW1)*	Klaus Pohl David Tushingham (T)	English Stage Company	Tom Marshall	Stephen Unwin	
A573	***Killers*** *Th. Upstairs (London SW1)*	Adam Pernak		Sam Kelly Stephen McGann Mark McGann	Ian Rickson	
A574	***A Killing Passion*** *Warwick Arts (Coventry); Drama Hall (Weymouth); Arts Centre (Bridgwater); Strode Theatre (Street, Somerset); Sherbourne School (Dorset); Arts Centre (Birmingham); Harlequin Th (Northwich); The Nave (Uxbridge); College Theatre (Bideford); Hope Theatre (Bristol)*	James Alby & Miss Sheena Wrigley	Temba	Catherine Coffey Charlie Folorunsho Anthony Warren	James Alby	
A575	***King Baby*** *Barbican/The Pit (London EC1)*	James Robson	Royal Shakespeare Company		Simon Usher	RSC

Ref	Play	Playwright	Theatre Co.	Starring	Director	Producer
A576	***King Lear*** *Tabard Th. (London W4)*	William Shakespeare	Tabard Theatre Company		Kate Bone	
A577	***King Lear***		Compass Theatre Company	Nick Chadwin Paul Rider	Neil Sissons	
	Little Theatre (Middlesborough); Drum Theatre (Plymouth); Crucible Th. (Sheffield); New Tyne Th. (Newcastle/Tyne); Holland Park Th. (London); Globe (Tokyo, Japan); Guildhall Th. (Brecon); Opera House (Buxton); Wilde Th. (Bracknell); Minster School (Nottingham); All Saints Schoo (Mansfield); Toot Hill Th. (Nottingham); Palace Theatre (Newark); Spring St. Th. (Hull); Queens Hall Arts (Hexham); The Maltings (Berwick-u-Tweed); Lewis Girls Sch. (Ystrad Mynach); Municipal Hall (Pontypridd); Parc & Dare Th. (Treorchy); Berwyn Centre (Nantymoel); Technical Coll. (Merthyr Tydfil); Club Theatre (Altrincham); Nuffield Theatre (Lancaster); Harlequin Th (Northwich); Theatr Gwynedd (Bangor); The Playhouse (Harlow); Arts Centre (Aberystwyth); Guildhall Th. (Derby); St George's Th. (Luton); Theatr Felinfach (Lampeter); Theatr Ardudwy (Gwynedd); Wyeside Arts C. (Builth Wells); Nth.Riding Coll. (Scarborough); Lilian Baylis (London EC1)					
A578	***King Lear***	William Shakespeare	Kaboodle	Lee Beagley Andrea Earl Paula Simms	Lee Beagley Josette Bushell-Mingo	
	Warwick Arts (Coventry); The Harlequin Theatre (Redhill); Arts Centre (Horsham); Brewery Arts Cen (Cumbria); Stanwix Arts Th (Carlisle); Arts Theatre (Belfast); Riverside Th. (Coleraine); Ardhowen Th. (Co Fermanagh); Taliesin Arts C. (Swansea); Theatr Hafren (Newtown); Univ. of Essex (Colchester); Merlin (Frome); The Hawth (Crawley); Gulbenkian Th. (Canterbury); Forest Arts Ctre (New Milton); Ashcroft Centre (Fareham); Arena Th. (Wolverhampton); Stahl Theatre (Peterborough); The Gantry (Southampton); The Green Room (Manchester); Unity Theatre (Liverpool)					
A579	***King Lear*** *Royal Court Th. (London SW1)*	William Shakespeare	Royal Court Theatre	Tom Wilkinson	Max Stafford-Clark	
A580	***King Lear In New York*** *Festival Th. (Chichester)*	Melvyn Bragg	Chichester Festival Theatre	Kate O'Mara Jenny Seagrove John Stride	Patrick Garland	
A581	***The Kingfisher*** *Theatr Colwyn (Colwyn Bay)*	William Douglas Home	Theatr Colwyn Summer Rep	Gordon Alcock Reg Large Pam Rayner	Gareth ap Gwylim	
A582	***The Kingfisher***	William Douglas Home	Channel Theatre Company	Dinah Sheridan Richard Vernon Paddy Ward	Philip Dart	
	Gordon Craig Th. (Stevenage); Towngate Th. (Poole); Civic Theatre (Scunthorpe); Connaught Th. (Worthing); Brewhouse Th. (Taunton); Malvern Festival Th. (Malvern); Th. Royal (Bath); Alexandra Th. (Birmingham); Palace Th. (Westcliff-On-Sea)					
A583	***Kings*** *NT/Cottesloe (London SE1)*	Christopher Logue	Royal National Theatre	Alan Howard Christopher Logue	Liane Aukin	RNT
A584	***Kiss of the Spiderwoman*** *Shaftesbury Th. (London WC2)*	Fred Ebb John Kander Terence McNally		Brent Carver Anthony Crivello Chita Rivera	Harold Prince Jeffrey Huard (Md)	LIVENT
A585	***Kurt Weill Cabaret*** *Attic Theatre (London SW19)*	Kurt Weill Laurence Evans (c)	Vandyk & Company	Walter Vandyk	Liam Halligan	
A586	***Kvetch*** *W/Yorks Playh. (Leeds)*	Steven Berkoff	West Yorkshire Playhouse Company	Michael Cashman Richard Hahlo Anna Savva	Vicky Featherstone	
A587	***La Bete*** *Lyric Ham'smith (London W6)*			Stephen Beard Sarah Crowden Alan Cumming		
A588	***La Muse De Montparnasse*** *Canal Cafe Th. (London W2)*	Saskia Bosch Geoffrey Osborn				
A589	***La Ronde***	Arthur Schnitzler	Actors Touring Company	Victoria Scarborough Colin Watson	Ceri Sherlock	
	Sherman Th. (Cardiff); Watermans (Brentford, Middx); Arena Th. (Wolverhampton); Spring St. Th. (Hull); Arts Centre (Warminster); Arts Centre (St Helier); Truro City Hall (Truro, Cornwall)					
A590	***La Ronde*** *Questors (London W5)*	Arthur Schnitzler			Wendy Smith	

Ref	Play	Playwright	Theatre Co.	Starring	Director	Producer
A591	***La Voix Humaine*** *King's Head Th. (London N1)*	Poulenc Cocteau (C & L)	MusicTheatre	Gerardine Arthur	Mary Benning	
A592	***Ladies' Night*** *Opera House (Manchester)* *Lyceum Th. (Sheffield)* *Hull New Th. (Hull)* *Grand Th. (Leeds)* *His Majesty's Th. (Aberdeen)* *Gaiety Theatre (Ayr)* *Key Theatre (Peterborough)* *Queen's Th. (Hornchurch)* *Ashcroft Th. (Croydon)* *Orchard Th. (Dartford)* *Th. Royal (Brighton)* *Towngate Th. (Poole)*	Steven Sinclair Antony McCarten	Newpalm Productions	Darrell Bowlby Dominic Cotton Paul Neaum	Paul Kerryson	Newpalm Productions
A593	***Lady Aoi*** *New End Th. (London NW3)*	Yukio Mishima Amy Kassai (Ad,Dir)	Chardonnay Productions	Caroline Bullen Michael Haighton Kate Richmond		
A594	***Lady Be Good*** *Open Air Th. (London NW1)* *Th. Royal (Lincoln)* *Civic Theatre (Darlington)* *Th. Royal (Brighton)* *Oxford Playhouse (Oxford)* *Grand Th. (Blackpool)* *Arts Th. (Cambridge)*	George Gershwin (L) Ira Gershwin	New Shakespeare Company	Bernard Cribbins Simon Green	Ian Talbot	
A595	***Lady Macbeth*** *Everyman Th. (Cheltenham)*	Jean Binnie	Everyman Theatre Company	Mac Andrews Tina Jones	Martin Houghton	
A596	***Lady of the Lilacs*** *Barons Court Th. (London W14)*	Meade Roberts		Kate Hamilton Liz Payne	Silvio Narizzano	
A597	***Lancelot The Lion*** *Little Angel (London N1)*		Little Angel Marionette Theatre			
A598	***The Last Carnival*** *Birmingham Rep. (Birmingham)*	Derek Walcott	Birmingham Rep.	Michael Bertenshaw Jill Brassington Peter Woodward	John Adams	
A599	***The Late Edwina Black*** *Connaught Th. (Worthing)* *Th. Royal (Lincoln)* *Alexandra Th. (Bognor Regis)*	William Diner William Morum		David Banks Lorraine Chase Anna Karen	Alexander Bridge	Barry Stacey
A600	***Late Joys Music Hall*** *Players Th. (London WC2H)*		Players Theatre	Stella Moray Dudley Stevens Julia Sutton		
A601	***Laurel and Hardy*** *Derby Studio (Derby)*	Tom McGrath	Derby Playhouse			
A602	***Laurel and Hardy*** *Royal Lyceum Th. Co (Edinburgh)*	Tom McGrath	Royal Lyceum Theatre Company	Alasdair McCrone Stuart McQuarrie	Richard Baron	
A603	***Laurel and Hardy*** *Everyman Th. (Cheltenham)*	Tom McGrath	Everyman Theatre Company	Greg Banks Shaun Prendergast	Sheila Mander	
A604	***Le Baruffe Chiozzotte*** *NT/Lyttelton (London SE1)*	Carlo Goldoni	Piccolo Teatro Milan		Georgio Strehler	
A605	***Leave Taking*** *Belgrade Th. (Coventry)*	Winsome Pinnock	Belgrade Theatre Company	Lorren Bent Eddie Osei Vivienne Rochester	Rumu Sen-Gupta	
A606	***Lend Me A Tenor*** *Theatre Royal (York)*	Ken Ludwig	York Theatre Royal Company		Derek Nicholls	
A607	***Leo In Love*** *Nuffield Th. (Southampton)* *Oxford Playhouse (Oxford)* *Th. Royal (Bath)* *Richmond Th. (Richmond)* *Wyvern Th. (Swindon)* *Towngate Th. (Poole)* *Th. Royal (Brighton)*	Jean Sarment Ann Queensbury (Tr)	Nuffield Theatre Company	Debra Beaumont Martin Jarvis Angela Pleasance	Patrick Sandford	
A608	***Leonardo - A Portrait Of Love*** *Old Fire Station (Oxford)*	Greg & Tommy Moeller Russell Dunlop Robert Mackintosh (Pr)	Leonardo Productions Ltd	Simon Burke Lucy Dixon Hal Fowler	Hugh Halliday Mike Dixon (MD)	
A609	***Les Atrides*** *Robin Mills (Bradford)*		Le Theatre Du Soleil	Simon Abkarian Catherine Schaub	Ariane Mnouchkine	

Ref	Play	Playwright	Theatre Co.	Starring	Director	Producer
A610	***Les Liaisons Dangereuses***	Christopher Hampton	Royal Shakespeare Company	Anna Carteret Paul Shelley Paula Stockbridge	Stephen Dobbin	RSC
	Grand Th. (Swansea) *Towngate Th. (Poole)* *Opera House (Belfast)*	*Grand Theatre (Wolverhampton)* *Orchard Th. (Dartford)*		*Opera House (Manchester)* *Eden Court Th. (Inverness)*	*The Hexagon (Reading)* *Adam Smith Th. (Kirkcaldy)*	
A611	***Les Miserables***	Victor Hugo (A) Alain Boublil (Ad) Claude-Michel Schoenberg (C)	Royal Shakespeare Company	Meredith Braun Jeff Leyton Philip Quast	John Caird Trevor Nunn	Cameron Mackintosh
	Palace Th. (Manchester)					
A612	***Les Miserables***	Victor Hugo Christina Reid (A)	Nottingham Playhouse	Anthony Cairns Angela Clerkin Kevin Quarmby	Peter Rowe	
	The Playhouse (Nottingham)					
A613	***Les Miserables***	Alain Boublil Claude-Michel Schoenberg		Megan Kelly Andrew C. Wadsworth Dave Willetts	Trevor Nunn	Cameron Mackintosh
	Palace Th. (London W1)					
A614	***Lettice & Lovage***	Peter Shaffer	Everyman Theatre Company	Jacquie Crago Susan Dowdall George Waring	Sheila Mander	
	Everyman Th. (Cheltenham)					
A615	***Lettice And Lovage***	Peter Shaffer	Chester Gateway Theatre	Joanna Van Gyseghem		
	Gateway Th. (Chester)					
A616	***Liar Liar***	Marianne MacDonald	Three's Company	Marianne Mcdonald Kate Worth	Helen Fotheringham	
	Etcetera (London NW1)					
A617	***The Lie Of The Land***	Noel Greig		Adam Annand Yolande Bastide Antonia Coker	Libby Mason	
	Theatre Centre (London N1)					
A618	***A Life In The Theatre***	David Mamet	Theatre Vein	Andy Cadogan Sam Fisher	Anatol Orient	
	Man in the Moon (London SW3)					
A619	***Life is a Dream***	Calderon	West Yorkshire Playhouse Company	Mark Bannister David Killick James Larkin	Matthew Warchus	
	W/Yorks Playh. (Leeds)					
A620	***The Life of Stuff***	Simon Donald	Traverse Theatre Company		John Mitchell	
	Traverse Th. (Edinburgh)					
A621	***Life Support***		Parti Pris	Leah Fletcher Toby Jones Suzy Mitchell		
	Etcetera (London NW1)					
A622	***Light in the Village***	John Clifford	Attic Theatre Company	Sandra Clark Sebastian Craig Sean Jackson	Jenny Lee	
	Attic Theatre (London SW19)					
A623	***The Lion, The Witch And The Wardrobe***	C.S. Lewis	Torch Theatre Company		Kit Thacker	
	Torch Theatre (Milford Haven)					
A624	***The Lion, The Witch And The Wardrobe***	C.S. Lewis Glyn Robbins (Ad)	Vanessa Ford Productions		Vanessa Ford	
	(St Albans)		*Royalty Theatre (London WC1)*			
A625	***The Lion, The Witch And The Wardrobe***	C.S. Lewis	Lyric Players Theatre		Charles Nowosielski	
	Lyric Players (Belfast)					
A626	***Lions of Lisbon***	Willy Maley Ian Auld	The Penny Mob Theatre Company	Vicky Clark Gary Lewis Mac McEleney	Libby McArthur	
	Tron Th. (Glasgow)					
A627	***The Little Clay Cart***	Shudraka	Royal National Theatre	Yogesh Bhatt Nizwar Karanj Shelley King	Jatinder Verma	RNT
	NT/Cottesloe (London SE1)					
A628	***The Little Foxes***	Lillian Hellman	Nuffield Theatre Company		Patrick Sandford	
	Nuffield Th. (Southampton)					
A629	***The Little Mermaid***	Hans Christian Andersen (Au)	Little Angel Marionette Theatre			
	Little Angel (London N1)					

Ref	Play	Playwright	Theatre Co.	Starring	Director	Producer
A630	***A Little Night Music*** *Th. Royal (Plymouth)*	Stephen Sondheim (C)	Theatre Royal Plymouth	Glynis Johns Rula Lenska	Roger Redfarn	
A631	***A Little Older*** *Hampstead Th. (London NW3)*	John Binnie (PW,D)	Clyde Unity Theatre	Mari Binnie Stephen Docherty		
A632	***Little Shop Of Horrors*** *Perth Th. (Perth)*	Alan Menken Howard Ashman	Perth Theatre Company		Ken Alexander	
A633	***Little Shop of Horrors*** *Playhouse (Derby)*	Howard Ashma Alan Menken	Derby Playhouse			
A634	***Little Tramp*** *Haymarket Th. (Basingstoke)*	David Pomeranz	Horseshoe Theatre Company	Peter Duncan Jacinta Mulcahy Jacquie Toye	Adrian Reynolds	Mark Furness Ltd
A635	***Lloyd George Knew My Mother*** *Theatr Colwyn (Colwyn Bay)*	Marjorie Dickinson Michael Vernier	Dan Mold Enterprises	Harry MacDonald Debbie Thomas	Colin Prockter	
A636	***The London Vertigo*** *Andrews Lane (Dublin)*	Brian Friel	Gate Theatre, Dublin	Gemma Craven John Hurt John Kavanagh	Judy Friel	
A637	***Loot*** *Swan Theatre (Worcester)*	Joe Orton	Worcester Theatre Company	Karen Ascoe Campbell Graham Richard Hague	Lennox Greaves	
A638	***Loot*** *Lyric Ham'smith (London W6)*	Joe Orton	Lyric Theatre, Hammersmith	Colin Hurley Dearbhla Molloy David Troughton	Peter James	
A639	***The Lord Of The Rings*** *Watermans (Brentford, Middx)*	J.R.R. Tolkien (A)		Richard Bridges Kenny Forest	Richard Bridges	
A640	***The Lost Child*** *Wolsey Studio (Ipswich)*	Mike Kenny	Wolsey Theatre Company		Andrew Breakwell	
A641	***Lost in Yonkers*** *Yvonne Arnaud (Guildford)*; *Alhambra Th. (Bradford)*; *Th. Royal (Newcastle/u/Tyne)*; *Richmond Th. (Richmond)*; *Alexandra Th. (Birmingham)*; *Th. Royal (Bath)*; *Strand Th. (London WC2B)*	Neil Simon		Benny Grant Rosemary Harris Maureen Lipman	David Taylor	Duncan C Weldon
A642	***Love From Shakespeare To Coward*** *Th. Museum (London WC2)*	Elizabeth Sharland-Jones (Ad)		Corin Redgrave Daniel Thorndike Tamara Ustinov		
A643	***Love and a Bottle*** *Tricycle Th. (London NW6)*	Declan Hughes (Ad) George Farquhar	Rough Magic		Lynne Parker	
A644	***The Love Space Demands*** *Cochrane Th (London WC1B)*	Ntozake Shange	Talawa Theatre Company	Jean "Binta" Breeze	Yvonne Brewster	
A645	***Love's Labour's Lost*** *Royal Exchange (Manchester)*	William Shakespeare	Royal Exchange Theatre Company	John Bennett Bernard Bresslaw Patricia Kerrigan	James MacDonald	
A646	***Love's Labour's Lost*** *Rutland Open Air (Stamford)*	William Shakespeare	Stamford Shakespeare Company		David Roberts Kay Winterbourne	
A647	***Lovers*** *New Vic (Bristol)*	Brian Friel	Bristol Old Vic Ensemble	Jessica Lloyd Brian McGovern	Ian Hastings	
A648	***Lulu*** *Brewhouse Th. (Taunton)*; *Oxford Playhouse (Oxford)*; *The Playhouse (Harlow)*; *Connaught Th. (Worthing)*; *Arts Th. (Cambridge)*; *Towngate Th. (Poole)*; *Th. Royal (Bury St Edmunds)*; *Lilian Baylis (London EC1)*	Elisabeth Bond-Pable (Ad) Frank Wedekind Edward Bond (Ad)	Cambridge Theatre Company	John Baxter Ewen Cummins Susan Lynch	Nick Philippou	
A649	***Lulu*** *Citz.First Th. (Glasgow)*	Frank Wedekind	Citizens' Th. Co.		Jon Pope	

Ref	Play	Playwright	Theatre Co.	Starring	Director	Producer
A650	***Lust*** *Queen's Th. (Hornchurch)*	The Heather Brothers	Queen's Theatre, Hornchurch	Dennis Lawson Judith Paris Myra Sands	David Toguri	Dan Crawford
A651	***M. Butterfly*** *Thorndike Th. (Leatherhead); Churchill Th. (Bromley); Forum Theatre (Billingham); Marlowe Th. (Canterbury); Playhouse (Liverpool); New Th. (Cardiff); Richmond Th. (Richmond); Alexandra Th. (Birmingham); Arts Th. (Cambridge); Th. Royal (Brighton); New Victoria Th. (Woking)*	David Henry Hwang		George Chakiris	Richard Olivier	Bill Kenwright Ltd
A652	***Macbeth*** *Citz.First Th. (Glasgow)*	William Shakespeare	Rain Dog			
A653	***Macbeth*** *New End Th. (London NW3)*	William Shakespeare	Buttonhole Theatre Company	Sally Mortimer Ian Reddington George Sweeney	Chris Geelan	
A654	***Macbeth*** *DOC Th. Club (London NW5)*	William Shakespeare	Astra Theatre Company		Caroline Gardiner	
A655	***Macbeth*** *Festival Th. (Chichester); Th. Royal (Nottingham); Apollo (Oxford); His Majesty's Th. (Aberdeen); Civic Theatre (Darlington); Mayflower (Southampton); Eden Court Th. (Inverness); Warwick Arts (Coventry); Hull New Th. (Hull); Th. Royal (Newcastle/u/Tyne); Th. Royal (Bath); The Hexagon (Reading); Th. Royal (Glasgow); Richmond Th. (Richmond); Grand Th. (Swansea); Th. Royal (Plymouth); Hippodrome (Bristol); New Th. (Cardiff); New Victoria Th. (Woking); Grand Th. (Leeds); Royalty Theatre (London WC1)*	William Shakespeare	English Shakespeare Company	Sean Baker Lynn Farleigh Tony Haygarth	Michael Bogdanov	
A656	***Macbeth*** *Watermill Th. (Newbury)*	William Shakespeare	Watermill Theatre	Douglas Henshall Bill Leadbitter Caroline Loncq	Euan Smith	
A657	***Macbeth*** *Princess Theatre (Torquay); The Playhouse (Harlow); Ashcroft Th. (Croydon); New Pavilion (Rhyl); Opera House (Buxton); Forum 28 (Barrow-in-Furness); Thorndike Th. (Leatherhead); Key Theatre (Peterborough); Charter Th. (Preston); Apollo (Oxford); Civic Hall (Guildford); Octagon (Yeovil); Empire Th. (Liverpool); Opera House (Manchester); Hippodrome (Bristol); Th. Royal (Nottingham); Playhouse Th. (Weston-S-Mare); Gordon Craig Th. (Stevenage); New Tyne Th. (Newcastle/Tyne); Medina Theatre (Newport, I O W); The Marina Th. (Lowestoft); Grand Theatre (Wolverhampton); Grand Th. (Swansea); Towngate Th. (Poole); Th. Royal (Winchester); Gaiety Th. (Isle of Man)*	William Shakespeare	DP Productions	Paul Darrow Pamela Salem Jack Smethurst	Ian Dickens	
A658	***Macbeth*** *Everyman Th. (Cheltenham)*	William Shakespeare	Everyman Theatre Company	Julian Bleach Julian Protheroe Dilys Watling	Martin Houghton	
A659	***Macbeth*** *Grace Theatre (London SW11)*		Point Blank Theatre			
A660	***Macbeth*** *Tabard Th. (London W4)*	William Shakespeare	Tabard Theatre Company	Kirsty Cubberley Edward Harvey	Kate Bone	
A661	***Macbeth*** *Harrogate Th. (Harrogate)*	William Shakespeare	Harrogate Theatre Company		Andrew Manley	
A662	***Macbett*** *Etcetera (London NW1)*	Eugene Ionesco Donald Watson (Tr)	Shattered Fish Theatre Company			
A663	***MacWizard Fae Oz*** *Citz.First Th. (Glasgow)*	John Binnie (PW,D)	Clyde Unity Theatre	Mari Binnie Marjory Hogarth Aileen Ritchie		
A664	***Mad Mash One*** *Polka Th. (London SW19)*		Bodger And Badger			
A665	***Mad,Bad,And Dangerous To Know*** *Richmond Th. (Richmond); Ambassadors Th. (London WC2)*	Jane McCulloch (PW,D)		Isla Blair Derek Jacobi		Michael White
A666	***Madame Mao's Memories*** *Arts Centre (Birmingham); Gulbenkian Th. (Newcastle/Tyne)*	Henry Ong	Mu-Lan Theatre Company	Tsai Chin	Glen Goei	Sacha Brooks
A667	***Madame Mao's Memories*** *Traverse Th. (Edinburgh)*	Henry Ong	Theatreworks	Claire Wong	Ong Keng Sen	

Ref	Play	Playwright	Theatre Co.	Starring	Director	Producer
A668	***Madness in Valencia***	Lope de Vega David Johnston (T)	Gate Theatre Company		Laurence Boswell	
	Gate Th. Club (London W11)					
A669	***The Madness Of George III***	Alan Bennett	Royal National Theatre	Janet Dale Nigel Hawthorne Harold Innocent	Nicholas Hytner	RNT
	NT/Lyttelton (London SE1); *Th. Royal (Newcastle/u/Tyne)*; *Lyceum Th. (Sheffield)*; *Th. Royal (Bath)*; *Alhambra Th. (Bradford)*; *King's Th. (Edinburgh)*					
A670	***The Madras House***	Harley Granville Barker	Lyric Theatre Company		Peter James	
	Royal Lyceum Th. Co (Edinburgh); *Lyric Ham'smith (London W6)*					
A671	***The Magic Island***	Liz Lochhead	Unicorn Theatre		Richard Williams	
	Arts Theatre (London WC2H)					
A672	***The Magic Storybook***	Renata Allen	Oxford Stage Company	Jan Alphonse Nicola Burnett-Smith Ian Davies	John Retallack	
	Warwick Arts (Coventry); *Towngate Th. (Basildon)*; *Brewhouse Th. (Taunton)*; *The Playhouse (Harlow)*; *Connaught Th. (Worthing)*; *Richmond Th. (Richmond)*; *Th. Royal (Bury St Edmunds)*; *Towngate Th. (Poole)*; *Th. Royal (Lincoln)*					
A673	***The Maintenance Man***	Richard Harris	Theatr Colwyn Summer Rep	David Middleton Helen Parkinson Sharon Scogings	Gareth ap Gwylim	
	Theatr Colwyn (Colwyn Bay)					
A674	***The Maintenance Man***	Richard Harris	Chester Gateway Theatre	Tim Block Sunny Ormonde Sian Webber	Karl Hibbert	
	Gateway Th. (Chester)					
A675	***Major Barbara***	George Bernard Shaw	Citizens' Th. Co.		Giles Havergal	
	Citz.First Th. (Glasgow)					
A676	***Mak The Sheepstealer***		Little Angel Marionette Theatre			
	Little Angel (London N1)					
A677	***Making It Better***	James Saunders	Hampstead Theatre Company	Jane Asher David de Keyser Larry Lamb	Michael Rudman	
	Hampstead Th. (London NW3); *Richmond Th. (Richmond)*; *Criterion Th. (London W1V)*					
A678	***Mamahuhu?***	Donald Swan Leon Berger (A,D)	Elektra Ensemble	Gerardine Arthur Kate Dyson Lore Lixenberg		
	Turtle Key Arts (London SW6)					
A679	***Man Cub***	Rudyard Kipling (A) Keiran Gillespie (Ad D)	Pocket Theatre Cumbria	Brian Brittain Eve Keepax Katy Stephens		Pocket Theatre Cumbria
	Century Th. (Keswick); *Blue Box Theatre (Keswick)*; *Mansfield Leis. (Mansfield)*; *Brewhouse Th. (Burton-on-Trent)*; *Arts Centre (Aberdeen)*; *Georgian Theatre (Richmond)*; *Whitley Bay P/h. (Whitley)*; *Little Theatre (Middlesborough)*					
A680	***Man in the Moon***	Jeff Young (PW,d)	Everyman Theatre Company			
	Everyman Th. (Liverpool)					
A681	***The Man Outside***	Wolfgang Borchert	Academy Productions	Will Barton David Battcock Andrew Potts	Andy Lavender	
	Chelsea Centre (London SW10)					
A682	***Man, Beast and Virtue***	Luigi Pirandello Charles Wood (Ad)	Great Eastern Stage	David Annen Bill Britten Sarah Finch	Derek Wax	
	Palace Theatre (Newark); *Plough Theatre (Exeter)*					
A683	***Mansfield Park***	Jane Austen Simon Ward (Ad)	Redgrave Theatre Company	Henry Crawford Terence Longdon Julie-Kate Olivier	Graham Watkins	
	Redgrave Th. (Farnham)					
A684	***Manslaughter***	Robin Brown		Jill Dowse Jeremy Peters	Kate Normington	
	BAC (London SW11)					
A685	***Marching Song***	John Whiting	Theatr Clwyd Company	Bernice Stegers Clive Swift John Turnbull	Tony Robertson	
	Theatr Clwyd (Mold)					
A686	***Marching For Fausa***	Biyi Bandele- Thomas	Royal Court Theatre			
	Th. Upstairs (London SW1)					

Produced exclusively for Plays & Players by SEARCHLINE

Ref	Play	Playwright	Theatre Co.	Starring	Director	Producer
A687	***A Marginal Affair*** *Forum Th. (Manchester)*	Dave Simpson	Library Theatre Company	Robert Calvert Jane Hollowood Martin Reeve	Sue Sutton Mayo	
A688	***Martin Chuzzlewit*** *Belgrade Th. (Coventry)*	Sally Hedges (Ad) Charles Dickens (A)	Belgrade Theatre Company			
A689	***Martin Chuzzlewit*** *Royal Th. (Northampton)*	Lynn Robertson Hay (Ad) Charles Dickens (A)	Royal Theatre, Northampton	Aled Jones	Michael Napier Brown	
A690	***The Marvellous Boy*** *Gulbenkian Th. (Newcastle/Tyne); Warwick Arts (Coventry); Playhouse Th. (Salisbury); Alexandra Th. (Bognor Regis); Old Bull Arts (Barnet); Playhouse (Liverpool); New Vic (Bristol); Spring St. Th. (Hull); The Elgiva (Bucks); Playhouse (Epsom)*	Devised By The Company	Public Parts Theatre Company	Timothy Craven Carrie Wale	Julia Limer	
A691	***Mary Queen of Scots Got Her Head Chopped Off*** *Perth Th. (Perth)*	Liz Lochhead	Perth Theatre Company		Ken Alexander	Perth Theatre
A692	***Massa*** *Etcetera (London NW1)*	Steve Gooch	Academy Company	Hannah Davis Pamela Flint Robert Reina	Tim Reynolds	
A693	***The Master and Margarita*** *Lyric Studio (London W6)*	Mikhail Bulgakov (A) David Graham (Ad)	Four Corners Theatre Company	Anna Gilbert Peter Tate	David Graham-Young	
A694	***Master Harold & The boys*** *North Peckham Ct (London SE15)*	Athol Fugard	Umoja Theatre Company	Patrick Cameron Jason Cheater Jason Rose	Gloria Hamilton	
A695	***Mayor of Casterbridge*** *Turtle Key Arts (London)*	Thomas Hardy (A) Jo Carter (Ad,D)	Du Bois Productions			
A696	***Me And Mamie O'Rourke*** *Palace Th. (Watford)*	Mary Agnes Donoghue	Palace Theatre, Watford	Ron Berglas Diana Hardcastle Patti Love	Robert Chetwyn	Palace Theatre
A697	***Me and My Friend*** *Minerva Studio (Chichester)*	Gillian Plowman	Festival Th.	Theresa Fresson Tom Hollander Jonathon Morris	Ian Rickson	
A698	***Me And My Girl*** *Apollo (Oxford); Empire Th. (Liverpool); Playhouse Th. (Edinburgh); Hippodrome (Bristol); Hippodrome (Birmingham)*	Stephen Fry (A) Noel Gay (C)	Richard Armitage & Noel Gay Prod.	Jessica Martin Nicholas Smith Gary Wilmot	Mike Ockrent	Pola Jones
A699	***Me And My Girl*** *Adelphi Th. (London WC2)*	Stephen Fry (A) Noel Gay (C)		Les Dennis Louise English Alfred Marks	Mike Ockrent	Alex Armitage
A700	***Measure For Measure*** *Young Vic Th. (London SE1)*	William Shakespeare	Royal Shakespeare Company	David Haig Philip Madoc Claire Skinner	Trevor Nunn	RSC
A701	***Measure For Measure*** *Gateway Th. (Chester)*	William Shakespeare	Chester Gateway Theatre			
A702	***Measure For Measure*** *Contact Th. (Manchester)*	William Shakespeare	Contact Theatre	Simeon Andrews Paul Brightwell Katharine Rogers	Brigid Larmour	
A703	***Measure for Measure*** *Blackheath (London SE3)*	William Shakespeare	London Bubble Theatre Company		Jonathon Petherbridge	
A704	***Medea*** *Almeida Th. (London N1)*	Euripides (A) Alistair Elliot (Ad)	Almeida Theatre Co	Diana Rigg Madge Ryan Tim Woodward	Jonathan Kent	
A705	***The Memoirs of a Survivor*** *Salberg Studio (Salisbury)*	Richard Osborne (Ad,D) Doris Lessing (A)	Salisbury Theatre Company	Toyah Willcox		

Ref	Play	Playwright	Theatre Co.	Starring	Director	Producer
A706	***The Merchant of Venice*** *Northcott (Exeter)*	William Shakespeare	Northcott Theatre Company		John Durnin	
A707	***The Merchant Of Venice*** *Sherman Th. (Cardiff)* *Torch Theatre (Milford Haven)* *Theatr Gwynedd (Bangor)*	William Shakespeare	Sherman Theatre Company	Rakie Ayola Patrick Brennan Kenneth Gardiner	Jamie Garven	
A708	***The Merchant of Venice*** *Library Th. (Manchester)*	William Shakespeare	Library Theatre Company	Kate Paul Peter Whitman Chris Wright	Chris Honer	
A709	***Merlin, The Search For The Grail*** *Royal Lyceum Th. Co (Edinburgh)*	Tankred Dorst Ron Shaw (C)	Royal Lyceum Theatre Company		Ian Wooldridge	
A710	***Merlin the Magnificent*** *Dundee Repertory (Dundee)*	Stuart Paterson	Dundee Repertory Theatre Ltd	Russell Hunter	Dave McVicar	
A711	***Merrily We Roll Along*** *Haymarket Th. (Leicester)*	Stephen Sondheim (C)	Haymarket Theatre Company	Michael Cantwell Maria Friedman Evan Pappas	Paul Kerryson	
A712	***The Merry Wives Of Windsor*** *Tower Theatre (London N1)*	William Shakespeare	Tavistock Repertory Company		Noreen Spall	
A713	***The Merry Wives Of Windsor*** *RST (Stratford-upon-Avon)*	William Shakespeare	Royal Shakespeare Company	Samantha Bond Cheryl Campbell Anton Lesser	David Thacker	RSC
A714	***Metamorphosis*** *New Athenaeum (Glasgow)* *Theatr Hafren (Newtown)* *South Hill Park (Bracknell)* *Gardner Arts Ctr (Brighton)* *Arts Centre (Aberystwyth)* *Th. Royal (Lincoln)* *Arts Theatre (Belfast)* *The Hawth (Crawley)* *Th. Royal (Bury St Edmunds)* *Holland Park Th. (London)* *Octagon (Yeovil)* *Arts Theatre (Belfast)*	Franz Kafka (A) Steven Berkoff (Ad)	Birmingham Rep.	Rebecca Harries Iain Ormsby-Knox Gary Sefton	Julia Smith	
A715	***Metamorphosis*** *DOC Th. Club (London NW5)*	Steven Berkoff	Three Legged Company		Larry Jones	
A716	***A Midsummer Night's Dream*** *Playhouse Th. (Salisbury)*	William Shakespeare	Salisbury Theatre Company		Deborah Paige	
A717	***A Midsummer Night's Dream*** *Wolsey Theatre (Ipswich)*	William Shakespeare	Wolsey Theatre Company	Suzette Llewellyn Larry McCarthy David Timson		
A718	***A Midsummer Night's Dream*** *NT/Olivier (London SE1)*	William Shakespeare	Royal National Theatre	Sally Dexter Jeffery Kissoon Timothy Spall	Robert Lepage	
A719	***A Midsummer Night's Dream*** *Rutland Open Air (Stamford)*	William Shakespeare	Stamford Shakespeare Company		Jean Harley	
A720	***A Midsummer Night's Dream*** *Crucible Th. (Sheffield)*	William Shakespeare	Crucible Theatre	Anthony Brown Alex Kingston Michael Mueller	Michael Rudman	
A721	***A Midsummer Night's Dream*** *Open Air Th. (London NW1)*	William Shakespeare	New Shakespeare Company	Ken Bones Dinsdale Landen Jane Maud	Ian Talbot	
A722	***The Mikado*** *Perth Th. (Perth)*		Perth Theatre Company	Donald Maxwell Linda Ormiston	Clive Perry	
A723	***Mirandolina*** *Royal Lyceum Th. Co (Edinburgh)*	Carlo Goldoni (A) Ranjit Bolt (T)	Royal Lyceum Theatre Company		Hugh Hodgart	
A724	***The Miser*** *Ashcroft Th. (Croydon)* *Richmond Th. (Richmond)* *Alexandra Th. (Birmingham)* *Yvonne Arnaud (Guildford)* *Arts Th. (Cambridge)* *Lyceum Th. (Crewe)*	Moliere	The Royal Exchange Company	William Armstrong Tom Courtenay Margo Gunn	Braham Murray	Duncan C Weldon

Produced exclusively for Plays & Players by SEARCHLINE

Ref	Play	Playwright	Theatre Co.	Starring	Director	Producer
A725	***Misery*** *Criterion Th. (London W1V)*	Stephen King (Au) Simon Moore	Carnival Theatre Ltd.	Sharon Gless Bill Paterson	Simon Moore	Brian Eastman Andrew Welch
A726	***Misogynist*** *Bush Th. (London W12)*	Michael Harding (PW,D)		Tom Hickey		
A727	***Miss Saigon*** *Drury Lane Th. (London WC2)*	Alain Boublil (L) Claude-Michel Schoenberg (C)		Simon Bowman Jenine Desiderio Junix Inocian	Nicholas Hytner	Cameron Mackintosh
A728	***Moby Dick*** *Piccadilly Th. (London W1)*	Robert Longden (c,D) Hereward Kaye (c)	Cameron Mackintosh Ltd	Tony Monopoly		Cameron Mackintosh
A729	***The Molecatcher's Daughter*** *Village Theatre (London NW2)*	Tom Leatherbarrow (PW D)	Harley Productions	James Reynard Kate Steavenson-Payne Michael Watson		
A730	***Moll Flanders*** *Mercury Studio (Colchester)*	Daniel Defoe (A) Claire Luckham (AD)	Mercury Theatre	James Allen Kate Arnell Joan Davies	Graham Watts	
A731	***A Moment of Madness*** *Barons Court Th. (London W14)*	Ronald Selwyn Phillips	Deconstruction Theatre Company		Roger Cook	
A732	***Moment Of Weakness*** *Malvern Festival Th. (Malvern)* *Th. Royal (Plymouth)* *Th. Royal (Nottingham)* *Th. Royal (Newcastle/u/Tyne)*	Donald Churchill	Yvonne Arnaud Theatre	Liza Goddard Ruth Hudson Christopher Timothy	Val May	
A733	***Monday After The Miracle*** *Haymarket Th. (Basingstoke)*	William Gibson	Horseshoe Theatre Company	Daryl Back Peter Jason Hildegard Neil	Adrian Reynolds	
A734	***The Monster He Made Me*** *Finborough Th. (London SW10)*	Michael Butt	Finborough Productions	Victoria Davies Deborah McHardy Alister Schofield	Cathryn Horn	
A735	***Monstre, Va!*** *French Institute (London SW7)*	Ludovic Janvier	La Compagnie Des Ours	Luc-Antoine Diquero	Robert Cantarella	
A736	***A Month In The Country*** *Palace Th. (Watford)*	Ivan Turgenev Ariadne Nicolaeff (Tr)	Palace Theatre, Watford	Kate Byers Jonathan Coy Emily Morgan	John Dove	
A737	***Moonstone*** *Royal Exchange (Manchester)*	James Maxwell (Ad,D) Wilkie Collins (A)	Royal Exchange Theatre Company			
A738	***Moose*** *Old Bull Arts (Barnet)* *Rotherham Arts (Rotherham)* *Theatr Hafren (Newtown)* *Arena Th. (Wolverhampton)* *Grand Th. (Blackpool)* *Stanwix Arts Th (Carlisle)* *Colchester Arts (Colchester)* *Bowen West Th. (Bedford)* *Nuffield Theatre (Lancaster)* *Queens Hall Arts (Hexham)* *The Hawth (Crawley)*	Sean Foley	The Right Size	Sean Foley Tomas Kubinek Hamish McColl	Jos Houben Micheline van de Poel	
A739	***Mother Goose*** *Key Theatre (Peterborough)*	Tony Clayton	Key Theatre, Peterborough	Chris MacDonnell	Derek Killeen	
A740	***Mother Goose*** *Playhouse Th. (Salisbury)*	Colin Wakefield Kate Edgar (C)	Salisbury Theatre Company		Deborah Paige	
A741	***Mother Goose*** *Belgrade Th. (Coventry)*	Iain Lauchlan (PW,D) Will Brenton	Belgrade Theatre Company			
A742	***Mother Goose*** *The Theatre (Chipping Norton)*	Jeff Clarke	Chipping Norton Theatre			
A743	***The Mother Tongue*** *Greenwich Th. (London SE10)* *Yvonne Arnaud (Guildford)*	Alan Franks	Greenwich Theatre	Jamie Glover Prunella Scales Gwen Taylor	Richard Cotterell	
A744	***The Mousetrap*** *St Martin's Th. (London WC2)*	Agatha Christie		Maev Alexander Andrew Alston Paul Bacon	David Turner	Peter Saunders Ltd

Ref	Play	Playwright	Theatre Co.	Starring	Director	Producer
A745	**Mowgli - Enfant Loup**	Eric de Dadelsen (A,D)	Theatre Jeune Public (Strasbourg)	Xavier Boulanger Simon Pomara Zakaria Riachi		Dual Control International Theatre
	Marlowe Th. (Canterbury) *Octagon Th. (Bolton)* *Haymarket Th. (Leicester)* *Civic Theatre (Darlington)* *Connaught Th. (Worthing)*					
A746	**Mr A's Amazing Maze Plays**	Alan Ayckbourn	Royal National Theatre	John Branwell Graeme Eton Glyn Grain	Alan Ayckbourn	
	NT/Cottesloe (London SE1) *Towngate Th. (Poole)* *Orchard Th. (Dartford)* *Oxford Playhouse (Oxford)* *Charter Th. (Preston)* *Warwick Arts (Coventry)*					
A747	**Mrs Columbus Speaks Out**	Maria Tolly	Compact Theatre	Maria Tolly		
	Watermans (Brentford, Middx)					
A748	**Mrs Klein**	Nicholas Wright	Millstream Touring	Eliza Hunt Polly Irvin Francine Morgan	Christopher Masters	
	Trinity Arts (Tunbridge Wells) *Quay Theatre (Sudbury)* *Gulbenkian Th. (Canterbury)* *The Theatre (Chipping Norton)* *Arts Centre (St Helier)* *The Hawth (Crawley)* *William Ferrers (Woodham)* *Arts Centre (Swindon)* *Library Theatre (Leighton Buzz.)* *Arts Centre (Warwick)* *Guildhall Centre (Grantham)* *Forest Arts Ctre (New Milton)* *Riverhouse Barn (Walton-on-Th)* *Univ. of Essex (Colchester)* *Maltings Arts (St Albans)* *Old Town Hall (Hemel/Hemp)* *Sth Holland Ctr. (Spalding)* *Arts Centre (Peterborough)* *Th. Royal (Bury St Edmunds)* *Towngate Th. (Basildon)* *Georgian Theatre (Richmond)*					
A749	**Mrs Klein**	Nicholas Wright (KP)	Mrs Klein	Susanna Hamnett Margaret Robertson Liza Sadory	Wyn Jones	
	Royal Th. (Northampton)					
A750	**Much Ado About Nothing**	William Shakespeare	The Village Theatre Company	John Hug Debbie Radcliffe John Tallents	John Strehlow	
	Village Theatre (London NW2)					
A751	**Much Ado About Nothing**	William Shakespeare	Everyman Theatre Company		John Doyle	
	Everyman Th. (Liverpool)					
A752	**Much Ado About Nothing**		Oxford Stage Company	Marie Francis Richard Santhiri James Simmons		
	Lyceum Th. (Sheffield) *Redgrave Th. (Farnham)* *Arts Th. (Cambridge)* *Oxford Playhouse (Oxford)* *Open Air Theatre (Arundel)* *Th. Royal (Bury St Edmunds)* *MacRobert Arts (Stirling)* *The Hawth (Crawley)* *Wyvern Th. (Swindon)* *Warwick Arts (Coventry)* *The Playhouse (Harlow)* *Brewhouse Th. (Taunton)* *Globe (Tokyo, Japan)*					
A753	**Much Ado About Nothing**	William Shakespeare			Robert Clare	
	Little Theatre (Southport)					
A754	**Muder At The Vicerage**		Palace Theatre, Watford		Christopher Dunham	
	Palace Th. (Westcliff-On-Sea)					
A755	**Murder By Misadventure**	Edward Taylor	Theatr Clwyd Company	William Gaunt Gerald Harper Deborah Watling	Val May	Excalibur Productions Ltd
	Theatr Clwyd (Mold) *Th. Royal (Brighton)* *Malvern Festival Th. (Malvern)* *Th. Royal (Bath)* *Marlowe Th. (Canterbury)* *Yvonne Arnaud (Guildford)* *The Hawth (Crawley)* *Th. Royal (Plymouth)* *Belgrade Th. (Coventry)* *Vaudeville Th. (London WC2)* *Whitehall Th. (London SW1A)*					
A756	**A Murder Has Been Arranged**	Emlyn Williams	Newpalm Productions			
	Devonshire Park Th. (Eastbourne) *Thorndike Th. (Leatherhead)*					
A757	**Murder In Green Meadows**	Douglas Post	Nuffield Theatre Company	Ian Redford David Schofield Kate Spiro	Patrick Sandford	
	Nuffield Th. (Southampton)					
A758	**Murmuring Judges**	David Hare	Royal National Theatre	Michael Bryant Richard Pasco Lesley Sharp	Richard Eyre	RNT
	NT/Olivier (London SE1)					

Ref	Play	Playwright	Theatre Co.	Starring	Director	Producer
A759	***The Good Old Days Of Music Hall & Variety***		Hiss And Boo	Edmund Hockridge Ian Liston Barbara Windsor		
	Crucible Th. (Sheffield) *Northcott (Exeter)* *Churchill Th. (Bromley)*					
A760	***Miss Helen Watson's Music Hall***		Watermill Theatre		Helen Watson	
	Watermill Th. (Newbury)					
A761	***My Blood on Glass***	Paul Prescott (PW,D)	La Bonne Crepe	Yvonne Riley David Taylor Valerie Weyland		Carlo Lange
	La Bonne Crepe (London SW11)					
A762	***My Cousin Rachel***	Charles Vance (D,P) Daphne du Maurier	Prestige Plays	Anita Harris Robin Lloyd Vernon Thompson		
	Churchill Th. (Bromley) *His Majesty's Th. (Aberdeen)* *Connaught Th. (Worthing)* *King's Theatre (Southsea)* *Th. Royal (Bath)* *Th. Royal (Winchester)* *Arts Centre (Horsham)* *Devonshire Park Th. (Eastbourne)* *Beck Th. (Hayes, Middx)* *Grand Th. (Blackpool)* *Key Theatre (Peterborough)* *Towngate Th. (Basildon)* *Gordon Craig Th. (Stevenage)* *The Playhouse (Harlow)* *Towngate Th. (Poole)* *Charter Th. (Preston)* *Princess Theatre (Torquay)* *Hull New Th. (Hull)* *Alexandra Th. (Birmingham)* *Civic Theatre (Darlington)* *Wyvern Th. (Swindon)* *Playhouse Th. (Salisbury)*					
A763	***My Fair Lady***	Alan Jay Lerner (L) Frederick Loewe (C)		Edward Fox Helen Hobson Alfred Pringle	Simon Callow	Pola Jones
	Opera House (Manchester) *Hippodrome (Birmingham)* *New Th. (Cardiff)* *Empire Th. (Liverpool)* *Apollo (Oxford)* *Hippodrome (Bristol)* *Playhouse Th. (Edinburgh)* *His Majesty's Th. (Aberdeen)* *Alhambra Th. (Bradford)* *King's Th. (Glasgow)* *Th. Royal (Newcastle/u/Tyne)* *Mayflower (Southampton)*					
A764	***My Heart's A Suitcase***	Clare McIntyre	Theatre Per Se	Glenn Doherty Liz Greenaway Abi Rayment	Mark Heron	
	DOC Th. Club (London NW5)					
A765	***My Mother Said I Never Should***	Charlotte Keatley	Royal Theatre, Northampton			
	Royal Th. (Northampton)					
A766	***My Mother Said I Never Should***	Charlotte Keatley	Birmingham Rep.	Christine Absalom Margery Mason Janice McKenzie	Anthony Clark	
	Birmingham Rep. (Birmingham) *The Harlequin Theatre (Redhill)*					
A767	***My Mother Said I Never Should***	Charlotte Keatley	Not the National Theatre	Joanna Field Victoria Little Judy Wilson	Elizabeth Goria	Roger Gartland
	Playhouse (Epsom) *Arts Centre (Windsor)* *Old Town Hall (Hemel/Hemp)* *Havant Arts Centre (Havant)* *Connaught Th. (Worthing)* *Arts Centre (St Helier)* *Hornpipe Arts (Portsmouth)* *Trinity Arts (Gainsborough)* *Quay Theatre (Sudbury)* *Octagon (Yeovil)* *Arts Centre (Horsham)*					
A768	***My Mother Said I Never Should***	Charlotte Keatley	New Victoria Theatre			
	New Victoria Th. (New/u/Lyme)					
A769	***My Sister Next Door***	Michael Burrell (PW,D)	Derby Playhouse	Anna Barry		
	Playhouse (Derby)					
A770	***Mystery Plays***		Chester Mystery Plays Ltd		Bob Cheeseman	
	The Cathedral (Chester)					
A771	***The Mystery Plays***		Miracle Productions Ltd	Peter Barkworth	Kenneth Pickering	
	C'bury Cathedral (Canterbury)					
A772	***Name (Winner of a Barclay New Stages Award)***	Gary Stevens (PW,D,P)		Andrew Davenport Gary Stevens Caroline Wilkinson		
	Shaftesbury Hall (Cheltenham) *The Leadmill (Sheffield)* *The Green Room (Manchester)* *Haymarket Studio (Leicester)* *Haymarket Studio (Leicester)* *Chisenhale Gall. (London E3)*					
A773	***Natural Causes***	Eric Chappell	Theatre Royal Windsor	George Cole Penny Morrel Simon Williams	Mark Piper	
	Th. Royal (Windsor, Berks) *Richmond Th. (Richmond)* *Yvonne Arnaud (Guildford)* *Th. Royal (Bath)*					

Ref	Play	Playwright	Theatre Co.	Starring	Director	Producer
A774	**Necklaces** *Cochrane Th (London WC1B)*	Tariq Ali	Talawa Theatre Company	Jude Akuwudike Pamela Nomvete Peggy Phango	Topher Campbell	
A775	**Needles And Opium** *NT/Cottesloe (London SE1)* *NT/Lyttelton (London SE1)*	Robert Lepage (PW,D)	Royal National Theatre	Robert Lepage		
A776	**Nervous Women** *Birm.Rep. Studio (Birmingham)*	Sarah Woods	Birmingham Rep.	Robin Pirongs Peter Shorey Victoria Worsley	Anthony Clark	
A777	**Neville's Island** *Stephen Joseph (Scarborough)*	Tim Firth		Claude Close Russell Dixon Adrian McLoughlin	Connal Orton	
A778	**New Man** *Etcetera (London NW1)*	Scott Talbot	Short Sharp Shock Theatre Company		Stuart Wood	
A779	**New Voices** *Royal Court Th. (London SW1)*		Royal Court Theatre			
A780	**A New World And The Tears Of The Indians** *Nuffield Th. (Southampton)*	Bartholome De Las Casas Adrian Mitchell (A) Pete Moser (C) Lope de Vega	Nuffield Theatre Company	Hugh Quarshie Ewart James Walters La Verne Williams	Patrick Sandford	
A781	**Niagara** *Citz. Third Th. (Glasgow)*	Alonso Alegria	Citizens' Th. Co.	Daniel Illsley Robert D MacDonald	Robert David MacDonald	
A782	**The Night Before The Morning After** *New Victoria Th. (New/u/Lyme)*	Bob Eaton (PW,D)	New Victoria Theatre	Oliver Beamish Jeremy Clay Howard Gay		
A783	**A Night in Tunisia** *Th. Royal (Stratford East)*	Paul Sirett		Robert Carter Alan Cooke Alan Cowan	Jeff Teare	
A784	**Night Must Fall** *Mercury Th. (Colchester)*	Emlyn Williams	Mercury Theatre	Darren Bennett Patricia Kneale Tessa Pritchard	Richard Digby Day	
A785	**The Night of the Iguana** *NT/Lyttelton (London SE1)*	Tennessee Williams	Royal National Theatre	Robin Bailey Frances Barber Alfred Molina	Richard Eyre	RNT
A786	**The Nightclub Puppets** *Offstage D/Stair (London NW1)*		La Compania du Soleil			
A787	**Nightmare - The Fright Of Your Life** *Opera House (Buxton)* *Ashcroft Th. (Croydon)* *Civic Theatre (Darlington)*	Roger S. Moss		Peter Byrne David Kershaw Jean Rogers		Michael Rose
A788	**No 3 Pied Piper Street** *Lilian Baylis (London EC1)* *Gulbenkian Th. (Newcastle/Tyne)* *The Theatre (Chipping Norton)* *Redbridge Centre (London E18)* *Queen's Th. (Hornchurch)* *Theatr Hafren (Newtown)* *Whitley Bay P/h. (Whitley)* *Arts Centre (Birmingham)*	Cheryl Moskowitz	Quicksilver Theatre For Children	Mark Hathaway Dystin Johnson Richard Stemp	Guy Holland	
A789	**No Man's Land** *Almeida Th. (London N1)*	Harold Pinter	Almeida Theatre Co	Paul Eddington Harold Pinter	David Leveaux	
A790	**No Remission** *Lyric Studio (London W6)*	Rod Williams	Midnight Theatre Company	Daniel Craig Pip Donaghy Rob Spendlove	Derek Wax	
A791	**No Trams to Lime Street** *Playhouse (Liverpool)*	Alun Owen (A) Marty Wilde (Ad) Ronnie Scott (Ad)			John Cameron	
A792	**Noah** *Little Angel (London N1)*		Little Angel Marionette Theatre			
A793	**Noises Off** *Perth Th. (Perth)*	Michael Frayn	Perth Theatre Company			

Ref	Play	Playwright	Theatre Co.	Starring	Director	Producer
A794	***Noises Off*** *Forum Th. (Manchester)*	Michael Frayn	Library Theatre Company	Ian Lavender Jenny Logan David Stoll	Martin Connor	
A795	***Noises Off*** *Wolsey Theatre (Ipswich)*	Michael Frayn	Wolsey Theatre Company	Jo Kendall Barry McCarthy David Pullan	Antony Tuckey	
A796	***The Norman Conquests*** *Octagon Th. (Bolton)*	Alan Ayckbourn	Octagon Theatre Company	Roberta Kerr Nick Maloney Robert Pickavance	Romy Baskerville	
A797	***Northern Trawl*** *Spring St. Th. (Hull)* *UK Tour ()*	Rupert Creed (PW,D) Jim Hawkins	Remould Theatre Company	Chuck Foley Neville Hutton Gerard McDermott		
A798	***The Nose*** *Wolsey Studio (Ipswich)*	Kelvin Segger	Wolsey Theatre Company		Hettie MacDonald	
A799	***Not About Heroes*** *Citz. Second Th. (Glasgow)*	Stephen MacDonald (PW D)	Citizens' Th. Co.			
A800	***Obsession*** *BAC (London SW11)*	Douglas McFarren	BAC Theatre Company	Douglas Hodge Tessa Peake Jones	Bill Pryde	
A801	***The Odd Women*** *Royal Exchange (Manchester)*	George Gissing (A) Michael Meyer (A)	Royal Exchange Theatre Company		Braham Murray	
A802	***The Odyssey*** *The Other Place (Stratford/Avon)*	Derek Walcott	Royal Shakespeare Company	Claire Benedict Ron Cook Amanda Harris	Gregory Doran	RSC
A803	***The Office Party*** *Civic Theatre (Scunthorpe), The Playhouse (Nottingham), Wimbledon Th. (London SW19), Wimbledon Th. (London SW19), Th. Royal (Bury St Edmunds), Key Theatre (Peterborough), Theatre Royal (York), Civic Th. (Chelmsford), Warwick Arts (Coventry), Congress Th. The (Eastbourne), Arts Th. (Cambridge), Swan Theatre (Worcester), Arts Centre (Aberystwyth), Grand Theatre (Wolverhampton), Spring St. Th. (Hull), Playhouse (Newcastle/u/Tyne), Orchard Th. (Dartford), Th. Royal (Winchester), Th. Royal (Norwich), The Hawth (Crawley), W/Yorks Playh. (Leeds), Grand Th. (Blackpool), New Victoria Th. (Woking), Lyceum Th. (Crewe), Playhouse Th. (Salisbury), Th. Royal (Lincoln)*	John Godber (PW,D)	Hull Truck Theatre Company	Mark Addy Steven Alvey Gareth Tudor Price		
A804	***The Old Country*** *Palace Th. (Watford)*	Alan Bennett	Palace Theatre, Watford		Roger Smith	
A805	***Old Mother Hubbard*** *Queen's Th. (Hornchurch)*	John Halstead	Queen's Theatre, Hornchurch	John Halstead	Marina Caldarone	
A806	***Old Times*** *Royal Lyceum Th. Co (Edinburgh)*	Harold Pinter	Royal Lyceum Theatre Company		Hugh Hodgart	
A807	***On Approval*** *Yvonne Arnaud (Guildford), Richmond Th. (Richmond), Alexandra Th. (Birmingham), Th. Royal (Nottingham), Alhambra Th. (Bradford), Lyceum Th. (Sheffield)*	Frederick Lonsdale		Michael Cochrane Edward De Souza Penelope Keith	David Giles	Pencon
A808	***On Golden Pond*** *Th. Royal (Windsor, Berks), Yvonne Arnaud (Guildford), Grand Th. (Leeds), Alexandra Th. (Birmingham), New Victoria Th. (Woking), Richmond Th. (Richmond), Th. Royal (Brighton), Opera House (Manchester), Th. Royal (Bath)*	Ernest Thompson	Theatre Royal Windsor	John McCallum Googie Withers	Christopher Renshaw	Bill Kenwright Ltd
A809	***On Golden Pond*** *Byre Theatre (St Andrews)*	Ernest Thompson	Byre Theatre Company	Thane Bettany Julie Ellen Kay Gallie	Maggie Kinloch	
A810	***On The Piste*** *Playhouse (Derby)*	John Godber	Derby Playhouse	James Hornsby Shaaron Jackson Michael Nicholson	Mark Clements	
A811	***On The Piste*** *Mercury Th. (Colchester)*	John Godber	Mercury Theatre	James Allen Susan Gott Sarah Prince	Graham Watts	

Ref	Play	Playwright	Theatre Co.	Starring	Director	Producer
A812	**On The Piste**	John Godber	Theatre Royal Windsor	Peter Birch Paul Bown Julia Deakin	Bob Tomson	Bill Kenwright Ltd
	Th. Royal (Windsor, Berks)	*Playhouse (Liverpool)*				
A813	**On The Piste**	John Godber	Library Theatre Company			
	Forum Th. (Manchester)					
A814	**On Top of the World**	Michael Gow	Australian Actors Abroad	Todd Boyce Carol Burns Ronald Falk	Wayne Harrison	
	Warehouse Th. (Croydon)					
A815	**Once a Catholic**	Mary O'Malley	Liverpool Repertory Theatre			
	Playhouse (Liverpool)					
A816	**Once In A While The Odd Thing Happens**	Paul Godfrey	Wolsey Theatre Company		Hettie MacDonald	
	Wolsey Studio (Ipswich)					
A817	**Once Upon A Song**	Anthony Newley (PW,D)	King's Head Theatre	Diane Langton Anthony Newley Natalie Wright		Dan Crawford
	King's Head Th. (London N1)					
A818	**One For The Road**	Willy Russell	Northcott Theatre Company	Peter Lorenzelli Caroline Swift	John Durnin	
	Northcott (Exeter)					
A819	**One For The Road**	Willy Russell	Worcester Theatre Company		Pat Trueman	
	Swan Theatre (Worcester)					
A820	**One Over The Eight**	Peter Robert	Stephen Joseph Theatre Company		Alan Ayckbourn	
	Th. Royal (Brighton)	*Th. Royal (Brighton)*				
A821	**One The Ledge**	Alan Bleasdale	Nottingham Playhouse	Mark McGann Gary Olsen David Ross	Robin Lefevre	RNT
	The Playhouse (Nottingham) *Th. Royal (Newcastle/u/Tyne)*	*0*		*Th. Royal (Glasgow)*	*Alhambra Th. (Bradford)*	
A822	**One-Man Shows**			Rob Inglis		
	Casson Room (Leatherhead)					
A823	**The Open Couple**	Dario Fo Franca Rame	Abacus Arts			
	DOC Th. Club (London NW5)					
A824	**Orlando**	Virginia Woolf (A) Robin Brooks (Ad)	Red Shift Theatre Company	Eric MacLennan Fiona McAlpine Bella Merlin	Jonathan Holloway	
	BAC (London SW11) *Th. Royal (Winchester)* *Evans Theatre (Winslow)* *Jellicoe Theatre (Bournemouth)* *Ashcroft Centre (Fareham)* *Old Town Hall (Hemel/Hemp)*	*Lyric Ham'smith (London W6)* *Rose Theatre (Kidderminster)* *Wyeside Arts C. (Builth Wells)* *Nicool Centre (Cirencester)* *Central Studio (Basingstoke)* *Arena Th. (Wolverhampton)*		*Strode Theatre (Street, Somerset)* *Theatr Mwldan (Cardigan)* *Arts Centre (Aberystwyth)* *Guildhall Arts (Gloucester)* *The Gantry (Southampton)* *Maltings Arts (St Albans)*	*Powell Theatre (Dorset)* *Glynne Wickham (Bristol)* *College of F.E. (Oxford)* *Arts Workshop (Newbury)* *Nuffield Studio (Bailrigg)* *Centrespace (Hounslow)*	
A825	**Oscar**	James Clutton Damian Landi			Jamie Hayes	Edwardian Hotels
	Tricycle Th. (London NW6)					
A826	**Othello**	William Shakespeare	Byre Theatre Company		Maggie Kinloch	
	Byre Theatre (St Andrews)					
A827	**Othello**	William Shakespeare	Everyman Theatre Company	Ray Fearon Gillian Kearney Tony Turner	John Doyle	
	Everyman Th. (Liverpool)					
A828	**Othello**	William Shakespeare	Court Theatre Company			
	Court Th. (London N1)					
A829	**Other Places**	Harold Pinter	Citizens' Th. Co.		Giles Havergal	
	Citz. Third Th. (Glasgow)					
A830	**Otherwise Engaged**	Simon Gray	Yvonne Arnaud Theatre	Peter Bowles	Peter Bowles	
	Yvonne Arnaud (Guildford)	*Richmond Th. (Richmond)*		*Alexandra Th. (Birmingham)*		
A831	**Our Day Out**	Willy Russell	Key Theatre, Peterborough		Derek Killeen Michael Cross	
	Key Theatre (Peterborough)					
A832	**Our Ellen**	Richard Osbourne		Tina Gray	Richard Osbourne	Belgrade Theatre
	Belgrade Studio (Coventry)					

Ref	Play	Playwright	Theatre Co.	Starring	Director	Producer
A833	***Our Song***	Keith Waterhouse		Peter O'Toole Donald Pickering Jack Watling	Ned Sherrin	Michael Redington
	Th. Royal (Bath)					
A834	***Out Of Order***	Ray Cooney			Leslie Lawton	Theatre of Comedy
	Churchill Th. (Bromley)					
A835	***Out Of Order***	Ray Cooney	Palace Theatre, Westcliff	Kenneth Keating Kenneth Price Brian Tully	Christopher Dunham	
	Palace Th. (Westcliff-On-Sea)					
A836	***Out Of The Ordinary***	Debbie Isitt	Snarling Beasties			
	(Newcastle Under Lyme) *West End Centre (Aldershot)* *The Hawth (Crawley)* *Arena Th. (Wolverhampton)*	*Warwick Arts (Coventry)* *Platform Theatre (Haywards Heath)* *Bowen West Th. (Bedford)* *Th. Upstairs (London SW1)*		*Old Town Hall (Hemel/Hemp)* *Haymarket Th. (Leicester)* *The Gantry (Southampton)*	*Ashcroft Centre (Fareham)* *The Junction (Cambridge)* *Arts Centre (Birmingham)*	
A837	***Outside Edge***	Richard Harris	Northcott Theatre Company	Peter Harding Patrick Romer Caroline Swift	Martin Harvey	
	Northcott (Exeter)					
A838	***Outside Edge***	Richard Harris	Derby Playhouse			
	Playhouse (Derby)					
A839	***Outside Of Heaven***	Martin Sadofski	English Stage Company		Penny Ciniewicz	
	Th. Upstairs (London SW1)					
A840	***Over a Barrel***	Stephen Bill	Everyman Theatre Company	Mac Andrews Edmund Kente Jackie Smith-Wood	Sheila Mander	
	Everyman Th. (Cheltenham)					
A841	***Pains of Youth***	Ferdinand Bruckner	The Acting Company		Dana Fainaro	
	Th. Museum (London WC2)					
A842	***Painting Churches***	Tina Howe		Josie Lawrence Sian Phillips Leslie Phillips	Patrick Sandford	M.I. Group
	Playhouse (London WC2)					
A843	***Paradise Garden***		BAC Theatre Company	George Little	Stuart Wood	
	BAC Studio 2 (London SW11)					
A844	***Passion of Marianne***		Theatre Street Ltd	Myriam Cyr		Sacha Brooks
	Etcetera (London NW1)					
A845	***Patagonia***		Brith Gof	Lis Hughes Jones Eddie Ladd Richard Lynch	Mark Pearson	
	Warwick Arts (Coventry)		*Tramway (Glasgow)*	*Th. Upstairs (London SW1)*		
A846	***Peculiar People***	Robert Rigby	Eastern Angles Theatre Company	Oona Besson Ali Walton Leonard Webster	Ivan Cutting	
	Sir J. Mills Th. (Ipswich)					
A847	***The Pelican***	August Strindberg	Citizens' Th. Co.	Helen Baxendale Lucy Bevan Julia Blalock	Ian Spink	
	Citz. Third Th. (Glasgow)					
A848	***A Penny for a Song***	John Whiting	Orange Tree Theatre	Caroline Gruber Caroline John Auriol Smith	Sam Walters	
	Orange Tree Th. (Richmond)					
A849	***Pepys - The Diarist***	James Meredith (Ad)	Staircase Productions	James Meredith	David Alexander	
	Duke's Head (Richmond)					
A850	***Peril At End House***	Agatha Christie	Newpalm Productions			
	Devonshire Park Th. (Eastbourne)	*Thorndike Th. (Leatherhead)*				
A851	***Peter Pan***	J.M. Barrie (A) Marvin Close (Ad)	Crucible Theatre		Alan Cohen	
	Crucible Th. (Sheffield)					
A852	***Peter Pan***	J.M. Barrie (A) Marvin Close (Ad)	Library Theatre Company	Andrew Ballington	Roger Haines	
	Forum Th. (Manchester)					
A853	***Phantom of the Opera***	Ken Hill (PW,D)		Reginald Marsh Toni Palmer Peter Straker		Hot Show Ltd
	Shaftesbury Th. (London WC2)					

Ref	Play	Playwright	Theatre Co.	Starring	Director	Producer
A854	***Phantom Of The Opera*** *Her Majesty's (London)*	Andrew Lloyd Webber (C) Charles Hart (L)	Really Useful Group	Simon Burke Peter Karrie Shona Lindsay	Harold Prince	Cameron Mackintosh
A855	***Pharmaceutical Migraines*** *Etcetera (London NW1)*	Matthew Westwood	Small Fish Big Ponds Theatre Company	Liz Brimilcombe	June Brown	
A856	***Philadelphia Here I Come*** *King's Head Th. (London N1)* *Wyndhams Th. (London WC2)*	Brian Friel	King's Head Theatre	Jonathan Arun Brendan Coyle Pauline Delany	Dan Crawford	
A857	***Phoenix*** *Bush Th. (London W12)*	Roy MacGregor	Bush Theatre Company	Nick Dunning Trevor Ray Nicola Redmond	Dominic Dromgoole	Bush Theatre Company
A858	***The Pied Piper*** *Norwich Puppet (Norwich)*		Norwich Puppet Theatre Trust Ltd			
A859	***Pig In A Poke*** *Towngate Th. (Poole)* *Th. Royal (Winchester)* *Oxford Playhouse (Oxford)* *Connaught Th. (Worthing)* *Arts Th. (Cambridge)* *Th. Royal (Bury St Edmunds)*	Georges Feydeau Kenneth McLeish (Ad)	Oxford Stage Company	Paul Greenwood Linda Spurrier Tessa Wyatt	Mark Dornford-May	
A860	***Pigspurt*** *Riverside Std. (London W6)* *Bowen West Th. (Bedford)* *Millfield Th. (London N18)*	Ken Campbell (PW,D)		Ken Campbell		Colin Watkeys
A861	***Play Strindberg*** *Mermaid Th. (London EC4)*	Friedrich Durrenmatt	Quest Theatre Company	Rod Culbertson Nina Thomas Paul Vaughan-Teague	David Craik	
A862	***The Player*** *Canal Cafe Th. (London W2)*	Rehan Sheikh (PW,D)	Awaaz Theatre Company			
A863	***Playing by the Rules*** *Birm.Rep. Studio (Birmingham)*	Rod Dungate	Birmingham Rep.	James Dreyfus Ian Pepperell David Phelan	Anthony Clark	
A864	***Playing Sinatra*** *Greenwich Th. (London SE10)*	Bernard Kops	Greenwich Theatre	Stefan Bednarczyk Susan Brown Ian Gelder	Ted Craig	
A865	***Playing The Wife*** *Ustinov Studio (Bath)* *Watermans (Brentford, Middx)* *Stranmillis Th (Belfast)*	Ronald Hayman	Compass Theatre Company	Barry Foster Jacqueline Morgan Julia Ormond Paul Spence	Tim Pigott-Smith	
A866	***Please Sir!*** *Connaught Th. (Worthing)*			Roger Hume		
A867	***The Plough & The Stars*** *New Victoria Th. (New/u/Lyme)*	Sean O'Casey	New Victoria Theatre		Peter Cheeseman	
A868	***The Pocket Dream*** *The Playhouse (Nottingham)* *Albery Th. (London WC2)*	Elly Brewer Sandi Toksvig	Nottingham Playhouse	Clive Mantle Mike McShane Sandi Toksvig	Pip Broughton	Theatre of Comedy
A869	***Pond Life*** *Bush Th. (London W12)*	Richard Cameron	Bush Theatre Company	Lyndon Davies Joe Duttine James Hooton	Simon Usher	
A870	***The Pope And The Witch*** *Comedy Th. (London SW1)*	Dario Fo Andy de la Tour (Ad)	West Yorkshire Playhouse Company	Frances de la Tour Berwick Kaler	Jude Kelly	Freeshooter
A871	***Porcelain*** *Etcetera (London NW1)* *Royal Court Th. (London SW1)*	Chay Yew	Royal Court Theatre	Adam Matalon David Tysall Daniel York	Glen Goei	Sacha Brooks
A872	***Powershifts*** *Traverse Th. (Edinburgh)*		Women Are More Waterproof Than Men			

Ref	Play	Playwright	Theatre Co.	Starring	Director	Producer
A873	**The Price** *Theatre Royal (York)*	Arthur Miller	York Theatre Royal Company			
A874	**The Price** *Royal Lyceum Th. Co (Edinburgh)*	Arthur Miller	Royal Lyceum Theatre Company		Richard Baron	
A875	**The Prime of Miss Jean Brodie** *Royal Lyceum Th. Co (Edinburgh)*	Muriel Spark (A) Jay Presson Allen (Ad)	Royal Lyceum Theatre Company		Caroline Hall	
A876	**Prin** *W/Yorks Playh. (Leeds)*	Andrew Davies	West Yorkshire Playhouse Company	John Branwell Stephanie Fayerman Sarah Swingler	Penny Ciniewicz	
A877	**The Prince And The Mouse** *Little Angel (London N1)*	Oliver Goldsmith (Au)	Little Angel Marionette Theatre			
A878	**The Prisoner Of Zenda** *Greenwich Th. (London SE10)*	Anthony Hope	Greenwich Theatre		Matthew Francis	
A879	**The Prisoner's Pumpkin** *New Vic (Bristol)*	Alan McMurtrie	Bristol Old Vic Ensemble	Christian Rodska Jane Wood		Foz Allan
A880	**Private Lives** *Th. Royal (Plymouth)* *The Hexagon (Reading)* *Devonshire Park Th. (Eastbourne)* *Grand Th. (Leeds)*	Noel Coward		Tony Anholt Tracy Childs Gemma Craven	John David	Lee Dean Associates
A881	**Private Lives** *Redgrave Th. (Farnham)*	Noel Coward	Redgrave Theatre Company	Jane Arden Michael David Tim Meats	John David	
A882	**Private Lives** *Gate Theatre (Dublin)*	Noel Coward	Gate Theatre Dublin	Stephen Brennan Amanda Redman Alan Stanford	Robin Lefevre	
A883	**The Professional** *Offstage D/Stair (London NW1)*	Dusan Kovacevic Bob Djurdjevic (Tr & Ad)		Justin Butcher George Irving Illona Linthwaite	Peter Craze	Buddy Dalton Emmy Enterprises Inc
A884	**The Provoked Wife** *New End Th. (London NW3)*	John Vanbrugh	The 1697 Group	John Ashton Jon Harris Corinna Richards	Jon Best	
A885	**Put That Light Out** *Arches Th. (London SE1)*	Aline Waites (PW,D) Robin Hunter	Aba Daba Productions	Maggie Beckit John Larsen		
A886	**Pygmalion** *NT/Olivier (London SE1)*	George Bernard Shaw	Royal National Theatre	Robin Bailey Frances Barber Alan Howard	Howard Davies	RNT
A887	**Pygmies In The Ruins** *Royal Court Th. (London SW1)*	Ron Hutchinson	Royal Court Theatre	Lorcan Cranitch Ian McElhinney	Eoin O'Callaghan	
A888	**Queen Christina** *Man in the Moon (London SW3)*	Pam Gems	Absolute Theatre		Andrew Pratt	
A889	**Radio Times** *Counterpoint (Swansea)* *West End Centre (Aldershot)* *Cricklade Th. (Andover)*	Nigel Thornbury Tean Mitchell	Bone Idol Theatre Company	Tean Mitchell Nigel Thornbory		
A890	**Radio Times** *Birmingham Rep. (Birmingham)* *Queen's Th. (London W1V)*	Abi Grant (A)	Birmingham Rep.	Kathryn Evans Jeff Shankley Tony Slattery	David Gilmore Alex Armitage	Waldgrave Productions
A891	**The Ransom & The Golden Chicken** *Polka Th. (London SW19)*		Sumy Children's Theatre			
A892	**Rat Play** *Old Red Lion Th. (London EC1)*	Michael Skelly	Barmont Productions	Kieran Cunningham Elaine Lordan	Ken McClymont	Barmont Productions
A893	**Raving Beauties** *Playhouse (Liverpool)*	Dave Simpson	Liverpool Repertory Theatre	Michelle Collins Jan Graham Julie Riley	Bob Tomson	

Ref	Play	Playwright	Theatre Co.	Starring	Director	Producer
A894	***Rebecca*** *Queen's Th. (Hornchurch)*	Daphne du Maurier	Queen's Theatre, Hornchurch	Michael Cashman Julie-Kate Olivier Pamela Ruddock	Tal Rubins	
A895	***Rebels And Friends*** *Andrews Lane Studio Th. (Dublin 2)*	Jacqueline Mulhallen William Alderson (D,P)	Lynx Theatre and Poetry	Marianne March Jacqueline Mulhallen		
A896	***The Recruiting Officer*** *NT/Olivier (London SE1)*	George Farquhar	Royal National Theatre	Desmond Barrit Sally Dexter Alex Jennings	Nicholas Hytner	RNT
A897	***The Recruiting Officer*** *Royal Exchange (Manchester)*	George Farquhar	Royal Exchange Theatre Company	Derek Griffiths Greg Wise Emil Wolk	Braham Murray	
A898	***Reflected Glory*** *Civic Theatre (Darlington)* *Alexandra Th. (Birmingham)* *Hippodrome (Bristol)* *Th. Royal (Brighton)* *Palace Th. (Manchester)* *Grand Th. (Leeds)* *Vaudeville Th. (London WC2)*	Ronald Harwood		Albert Finney Nicky Henson Stephen Moore	Elijah Moshinsky	Mark Furness Ltd
A899	***Relative Values*** *Playhouse Th. (Salisbury)*	Noel Coward	Salisbury Theatre Company	Richard Addison Barbara Thorn	Deborah Paige	
A900	***Relatively Speaking*** *Yvonne Arnaud (Guildford)* *Th. Royal (Brighton)* *Th. Royal (Windsor, Berks)* *Lyceum Th. (Sheffield)*	Alan Ayckbourn	Yvonne Arnaud Theatre	Judy Clifton Francis Matthews Graham Seed Angela Thorne	Penelope Keith	
A901	***The Return of the Prodigal*** *Orange Tree Th. (Richmond)*	John Hankin	Orange Tree Theatre			
A902	***The Return of the Native*** *Swan Theatre (Worcester)*	Thomas Hardy (A) Andrew Rattenbury (Ad)	Worcester Theatre Company		Pat Trueman	
A903	***Return To The Forbidden Planet*** *Opera House (Manchester)*	Bob Carlton (PW,D)	Pola Jones			Andrew Fell
A904	***Return to the Forbidden Planet*** *Cambridge Th. (London WC2)*	Bob Carlton (PW,D)		Tim Barron Nina Lucking Stephen Tate		Pola Jones
A905	***Revelations-The Testament of Salome*** *Traverse Th. (Edinburgh)* *Watermans (Brentford, Middx)*	Wendy Buonaventura Deirdra Morris Penny Cherns (AD)	Cinnabar	Wendy Buonaventura Deirdra Morris	Susannah York	
A906	***The Revenger's Tragedy*** *Palace Theatre (Newark)* *Opera House (Buxton)*	Cyril Torneur	Compass Theatre Company		Neil Sissons	
A907	***Revenge*** *Yvonne Arnaud (Guildford)* *Churchill Th. (Bromley)* *Marlowe Th. (Canterbury)* *Forum Theatre (Billingham)* *Lyceum Th. (Crewe)* *Richmond Th. (Richmond)* *Richmond Th. (Richmond)* *Alexandra Th. (Birmingham)* *New Th. (Cardiff)*	Robin Hawdon	Theatre Royal Windsor	Fiona Fullerton Patrick Mower	Graham Watkins	Lee Dean Paul du Fer
A908	***The Revenger's Tragedy*** *W/Yorks Playh. (Leeds)*	Cyril Tourneur	West Yorkshire Playhouse Company	Reece Dinsdale Tom Mannion Dermot Walsh	Jude Kelly	
A909	***The Revenger's Tragedy*** *Th. Royal (Bath)* *Yvonne Arnaud (Guildford)* *Th. Royal (Winchester)* *Towngate Th. (Poole)* *Warwick Arts (Coventry)* *Connaught Th. (Worthing)* *Oxford Playhouse (Oxford)* *Arts Th. (Cambridge)* *Brewhouse Th. (Taunton)*	Cyril Tourneur Thomas Middleton	Cambridge Theatre Company	John Abbott Martin Marquez Eileen Nicholas	Mike Alfreds	
A910	***Richard III*** *The Other Place (Stratford/Avon)* *Meadowside Leis. (Burton/Trent)*	William Shakespeare	Royal Shakespeare Company	Annabelle Apsion Simon Dormandy	Sam Mendes	RSC

Ref	Play	Playwright	Theatre Co.	Starring	Director	Producer
A911	***Richard III*** *NT/Lyttelton (London SE1)*	William Shakespeare	Royal National Theatre	Ian McKellen	Richard Eyre	RNT
A912	***Richard III*** *Marina Boat Head (Hull)*	Barrie Rutter (D,P) William Shakespeare	Northern Broadsides	Mark Addy Brian Glover Barrie Rutter		
A913	***Richard's Cork Leg*** *Canal Cafe Th. (London W2)*	Brendan Behan			Julia Hallawell	Not The Abbey Theatre
A914	***Richard's Cork Leg*** *Arches Th. (Glasgow)*	Brendan Behan	Arches Theatre Company			
A915	***The Ride Down Mt Morgan*** *Wyndhams Th. (London WC2)*	Arthur Miller		Tom Conti Clare Higgins Gemma Jones	Michael Blakemore	Robert Fox Ltd
A916	***Rimbaud And Verlaine*** *Ashcroft Centre (Fareham)*	Adam Darius (PW,D)	Adam Darius Company	Kazimir Kolesnik Thierry Lawson		
A917	***The Rise And Fall Of Little Voice*** *NT/Cottesloe (London SE1)* *Aldwych Th. (London WC2)*	Jim Cartwright	Royal National Theatre	Jane Horrocks Pete Postlethwaite Alison Steadman	Sam Mendes	Michael Codron
A918	***The Rivals*** *W/Yorks Playh. (Leeds)* *Birmingham Rep. (Birmingham)*	Richard Brinsley Sheridan	West Yorkshire Playhouse Company	Kate Duchene Jean Fergusson David Harewood		
A919	***The Rivals*** *The Playhouse (Nottingham)*	Richard Brinsley Sheridan	Nottingham Playhouse	David Fielder Ann Mitchell Jason Watkins	James MacDonald	
A920	***The Rivals*** *Lyceum Th. (Crewe)* *South Hill Park (Bracknell)* *Towngate Th. (Poole)* *Th. Royal (Winchester)* *Arts Th. (Cambridge)* *Forum 28 (Barrow-in-Furness)* *The Playhouse (Harlow)* *Charter Th. (Preston)*	Richard Brinsley Sheridan	Century Theatre Touring	David Gant Di Langford	Robin Midgley	
A921	***The Road*** *Cochrane Th (London WC1B)*	Wole Soyinka	Talawa Theatre Company	Steve Ashton Lenny Aljernon Edwards	Yvonne Brewster	
A922	***Road*** *Wolsey Studio (Ipswich)*	Jim Cartwright	Wolsey Theatre Company		Hettie MacDonald	
A923	***Road To Casablanca*** *Arches Th. (London SE1)*	Aline Waites (PW,P) David Kelsey (PW,D) Robin Hunter	Aba Daba Productions	Jenny Coulston Karen Gisbourne Robin Hunter		
A924	***Roadshow*** *Etcetera (London NW1)*	Peter Simmonds	Stumbling Block Theatre Company	Hilary Creatorex Lynne Hames David Reakes		Alex Rose
A925	***The Roaring Girl's Hamlet*** *Traverse Th. (Edinburgh)* *Sherman Th. (Cardiff)* *Birm.Rep. Studio (Birmingham)* *Venn Street (Huddersfield)* *Arena Th. (Wolverhampton)* *New Victoria Th. (New/u/Lyme)* *Arts Centre (Warwick)* *Lilian Baylis (London EC1)*	William Shakespeare	The Sphinx	Greer Gaffney Alexandra Mathie Ruth Mitchell	Sue Parrish	
A926	***Roberto Calvi Is Alive And Well*** *Finborough Th. (London SW10)*	Roy Smiles		Robin Blades Simon Clayton Maria Fierheller	Gregor Truter	
A927	***Robin Prince Of Sherwood*** *Playhouse (Liverpool)* *Grand Theatre (Wolverhampton)* *Forum Theatre (Billingham)* *Devonshire Park Th. (Eastbourne)* *New Victoria Th. (Woking)* *Hull New Th. (Hull)*	Peter Howarth	Bill Kenwright Ltd	Warwick Evans Mike Holoway Peter Lawrence	Bill Kenwright	
A928	***Robin Hood & The Babes In The Wood*** *Alhambra Th. (Bradford)*			Russ Abbot Bella Emberg	Robin Midgley	Stuart Littlewood
A929	***Robin Hood*** *Ecology Centre (London W1)*	Robert Murray (PW,D)	Cry Havoc Theatre Company	Jamie James Phillip Lewis Robert Murray		Peter Matthews
A930	***Robin of the Wood*** *Northcott (Exeter)*	Karoline Leach	Northcott Theatre Company		John Durnin	

Ref	Play	Playwright	Theatre Co.	Starring	Director	Producer
A931	***The Rock Station*** *Cockpit Th. (London NW8)*	Ger FitzGibbon	Soho Theatre Company	Peter Caffrey Sean Crannitch Emily Fox	Abigail Morris	
A932	***Rocket To The Moon*** *Stephen Joseph (Scarborough)*	Clifford Odets		Claude Close Christine Cox Sarah-Jane Fenton	Malcolm Hebden	
A933	***Rocky Horror Show*** *Wimbledon Th. (London SW19); Orchard Th. (Dartford); Alhambra Th. (Bradford); Playhouse Th. (Edinburgh); Forum Theatre (Billingham); Th. Royal (Newcastle/u/Tyne); Hull New Th. (Hull); The Hexagon (Reading); Th. Royal (Hanley); Th. Royal (Nottingham); Grand Th. (Swansea); Hippodrome (Birmingham); The Hawth (Crawley); Opera House (Manchester)*	Richard O'Brien	Phil McIntyre Promotions Ltd	Daniel Abineri Zalie Burrow Tim Flavin	Christopher Malcolm	Rocky Horror London Ltd
A934	***Roman & Marys*** *Offstage D/Stair (London NW1)*	Wally Daly		Barbara Ewing Helene Kvale Seamus Newham	Cordelia Monsey	Buddy Dalton
A935	***Romeo and Juliet*** *Bristol Old Vic (Bristol)*	William Shakespeare	Bristol Old Vic Ensemble	Suzanne Packer Clarence Smith Geraldine Sommerville	Andrew Hay	
A936	***Romeo and Juliet*** *Royal Exchange (Manchester); Meadowside Leis. (Burton/Trent); Ashington Leis. (Ashington); Mansfield Leis. (Mansfield); Grimsby Leis. (Grimsby); The Sands Centre (Carlisle); Kingsbridge Leis (Nr Totnes); Riverside Leis. (Chelmsford); Shavington Sport (Crewe); Alexander Sports (Bedford)*	William Shakespeare	Royal Exchange Theatre Company	Amelia Bullmore Kate Byers Michael Sheen	Gregory Hersov	
A937	***Romeo and Juliet*** *Barons Court Th. (London W14)*	William Shakespeare	The Deconstruction Theatre Company	Heather Imani Christopher Toba	David Evans Rees	
A938	***Romeo And Juliet*** *Th. Royal (Newcastle/u/Tyne); Barbican Th. (London EC2)*	William Shakespeare	Royal Shakespeare Company	Clare Holman Michael Maloney Tim McInnerny	David Leveaux	RSC
A939	***Rosmersholm*** *Young Vic Th. (London SE1)*	Henrik Ibsen	Young Vic Company	Francesca Annis Miriam Karlin Corin Redgrave	Annie Castledine	
A940	***Round The Big Clock*** *Lyric Players (Belfast)*	John Boyd	Lyric Players Theatre		Michael Poyner	
A941	***Ruby In The Dust*** *London Ark (London W6)*	Patrice Chaplin	Chaplin Lyonhart Productions	Tim Chaplin Frances Lyonhart	Roland Rees	
A942	***Rule Of The Game*** *Churchill Th. (Bromley); Yvonne Arnaud (Guildford)*	Peter Stallwood	Churchill Theatre	Nick Ellsworth Sally Knyvette Patrick Mower	Michael Latimer	E & B Productions
A943	***The Rules Of The Game*** *Almeida Th. (London N1)*	Luigi Pirandello David Hare (T)	Almeida Theatre Co	Richard Griffiths Nicola Pagett David Yelland	Jonathan Kent	
A944	***Run for Your Wife*** *Lyceum Th. (Sheffield); Key Theatre (Peterborough); Belgrade Th. (Coventry)*	Ray Cooney		Trevor Bannister Aimi McDonald		
A945	***Sab*** *Royal Court Th. (London SW1)*	Michael Cook			Ian Rickson	
A946	***The Sacred Penman*** *DOC Th. Club (London NW5)*	Sharon Kennet (PW,D)	Praxis Theatre Company	Denise Bryson Sharon Kennet Martin McDougall	Jonathan Meth	Praxis Theatre Co.
A947	***Safe In Our Hands*** *Belgrade Th. (Coventry)*	Andy de la Tour	Belgrade Theatre Company	Kenneth Cope Francis Dodge Susan Jameson		
A948	***Sailor Beware!*** *Theatr Clwyd (Mold)*	King & Carey	Theatr Clwyd Company	Jane Freeman Hugh Lloyd Kathy Staff	Peter James	Theatr Clywd

Ref	Play	Playwright	Theatre Co.	Starring	Director	Producer
A949	***Saint Oscar*** *Haymarket Studio (Leicester)*	Terry Eagleton	Haymarket Theatre Company	Russell Dixon Tracy Sweetinburgh Steve Weston	Paul Kerryson	
A950	***Salonika*** *Th. Museum (London WC2)*	Louise Page	The Acting Company		Luke Dixon	
A951	***Same Time Next Year*** *Tower Theatre (London N1)*	Bernard Slade	Tavistock Repertory Company	Jill Batty Simon Bullock	Peter Westbury	
A952	***Savage Storm*** *Man in the Moon (London SW3)*	Marion Andre		Paul Ansdell John Bown Norman Dalzell	Hana-Maria Pravda	
A953	***Scenic Flights, An Act Of Tourism*** *Chelsea Centre (London SW10)* *Arts Workshop (Worcester)* *Old Town Hall (Hemel/Hemp)* *Colchester Arts (Colchester)* *Old Bull Arts (Barnet)* *Westminster Th. (London SW1E)* *Arts Centre (Beds.)*	Cindy Oswin	Paines Plough	Cindy Oswin	Anna Furse	
A954	***Schippel, The Plumber*** *Greenwich Th. (London SE10)*	Jeremy Sams (T,D) Carl Sternheim	Greenwich Theatre	David Bamber Kate Buffery James Saxon		
A955	***Schmucks*** *BAC (London SW11)*	Roy Smiles	BAC Theatre Company	William Marsh Dave Mayberry Malcolm Ridley	Paul Blackman	
A956	***The School For Scandal*** *Everyman Th. (Liverpool)*	Richard Brinsley Sheridan	Everyman Theatre Company	Ray Fearon David Monico Keith Woodason	John Doyle	
A957	***The School For Scandal*** *Theatr Clwyd (Mold)*	Richard Brinsley Sheridan	Theatr Clwyd Company	Sara Crowe Audrey Tom John Turnbull	Maria Aitken	
A958	***School For Wives*** *Royal Lyceum Th. Co (Edinburgh)* *Eden Court Th. (Inverness)*	Moliere Neil Bartlett (Trans)	Royal Lyceum Theatre Company		Ian Wooldridge	
A959	***The School of Night*** *The Other Place (Stratford/Avon)*	Peter Whelan	Royal Shakespeare Company	Adrian Lukis John McAndrew Richard McCabe	Bill Alexander	RSC
A960	***The School Of Night*** *Pavilion Theatre (Bournemouth)* *Pavilion Th. (Worthing)* *Warehouse Th. (Croydon)* *(Edinburgh)* *Theatre Events (Brighton)*	Stephen Plaice	Alarmist Theatre	Ralph Higgins Judith Hurley Peter Leabourne	Helena Uren	
A961	***The Sea*** *NT/Lyttelton (London SE1)*	Edward Bond	Royal National Theatre	Judi Dench Celia Imrie Ken Stott	Sam Mendes	RNT
A962	***The Seagull*** *Theatr Clwyd (Mold)*	Anton Chekhov Jeremy Brooks (Ad)	Theatr Clwyd Company	Ian Hogg Dorothy Tutin Nick Waring	Toby Robertson	
A963	***The Seagull*** *Contact Th. (Manchester)*	Thomas Kilroy (Ad) Anton Chekhov	Contact Theatre	Paul Brightwell Christopher Penney Maggie Shevlin	Brigid Larmour	
A964	***The Seagull*** *Th. Museum (London WC2)*	Anton Chekhov	The Acting Company		David Harris	
A965	***Season's Greetings*** *Torch Theatre (Milford Haven)*	Alan Ayckbourn	Torch Theatre Company		Kit Thacker	
A966	***Second From Last In The Sack Race*** *Royal Th. (Northampton)*	David Nobbs (A) Michael Birch (Ad)	Royal Theatre, Northampton	Mark Carey	Michael Brown	
A967	***The Secret Diary Of Adrian Mole...*** *Crucible Th. (Sheffield)*	Sue Townsend Ken Howard & Alan Blaikley (C)	Crucible Theatre		Peter Shepherd	

Ref	Play	Playwright	Theatre Co.	Starring	Director	Producer
A968	***The Secret Rapture***	David Hare	Millstream Touring	Caroline Harding Serena Harragin Susan Kyd	Christopher Masters	
	Th. Royal (Bury St Edmunds) *The Hawth (Crawley)* *Christ's Hosp. (Horsham)* *Bowen West Th. (Bedford)* *Old Town Hall (Hemel/Hemp)*	*King's Lynn Arts (King's Lynn)* *Trinity Arts (Tunbridge Wells)* *Theatr Hafren (Newtown)* *Gulbenkian Th. (Canterbury)* *Connaught Th. (Worthing)*		*Stahl Theatre (Peterborough)* *Th. Royal (Winchester)* *Arts Centre (Falmouth)* *Warwick Arts (Coventry)* *The Theatre (Chipping Norton)*	*Octagon (Yeovil)* *Harlequin Th. (Horsham)* *Brewhouse Th. (Taunton)* *Little Theatre (Middlesborough)*	
A969	***Section 2 Housing Problems*** *Etcetera (London NW1)*	Peter Pilbeam Tracy Redraws			David Whybrow	Peter D Norman
A970	***See How They Run*** *Devonshire Park Th. (Eastbourne)*	Philip King	Newpalm Productions			
A971	***See How They Run***	Philip King	Watermill Theatre	John Iles David Kelsey Josephine Tewson	Wendy Toye	Watermill Theatre
	Watermill Th. (Newbury) *The Harlequin Theatre (Redhill)* *White Rock Th. (Hastings)*	*The Playhouse (Harlow)* *The Marina Th. (Lowestoft)* *Hull New Th. (Hull)*		*Octagon (Yeovil)* *Connaught Th. (Worthing)*	*Gordon Craig Th. (Stevenage)* *Wyvern Th. (Swindon)*	
A972	***See That's Her!*** *Dundee Repertory (Dundee)*	Dorothy Paul *Tron Th. (Glasgow)*		Dorothy Paul	John Brett	
A973	***Self Catering*** *Playhouse Studio (Liverpool)*	Andrew Cullen	Altered States Theatre Company	Ayse Owens Rosie Rowell Andrew Schofield	Kate Rowland	
A974	***Self Portrait*** *Orange Tree Th. (Richmond)*	Sheila Yeger	Orange Tree Theatre	Richard Howard Barbara Marten	Annie Castledine	
A975	***Selling Out*** *St Catherine's (Oxford)*	Daniel Chambers *Old Fire Station (Oxford)*			Alan Ayckbourn	
A976	***September In The Rain*** *Theatr Colwyn (Colwyn Bay)*	John Godber	Theatr Colwyn Summer Rep	Gordon Alcock Ina Clough	Gareth ap Gwylim	
A977	***Serpent Kills*** *Traverse Th. (Edinburgh)*	Blake Brooker (PW,D)	One Yellow Rabbit	Denise Clarke Andy Curtis Gillian Ferrabee		
A978	***Seven Doors*** *Gate Th. Club (London W11)*	Botho Strauss Anthony Meech (T)	Gate Theatre Company		David Farr	
A979	***Sex and Sadness*** *Barons Court Th. (London W14)*	Ronald Selwyn Phillips	Deconstruction Theatre Company		Roger Cook	
A980	***Sex III*** *BAC (London SW11)*	Emily Woolf (PW,P) *Platform Theatre (Haywards Heath)*		Emily Woolf		
A981	***Shades***	Sharman MacDonald	Turnstyle Group	James Cosmo Patricia Hodge	Simon Callow	Howard Panter
	Richmond Th. (Richmond) *Albery Th. (London WC2)*	*New Victoria Th. (Woking)*		*Th. Royal (Brighton)*	*Th. Royal (Bath)*	
A982	***Shadowlands*** *Royal Th. (Northampton)*	William Nicholson	Royal Theatre, Northampton	Michael Napier Brown		
A983	***Shadowlands*** *Belgrade Th. (Coventry)*	William Nicholson	Belgrade Theatre Company	David Allistair Jacqueline Pearce	Rumu Sen-Gupta	
A984	***Shadowlands*** *Palace Th. (Westcliff-On-Sea)*	William Nicholson	Palace Theatre, Westcliff	Philip Anthony Ursula Mohan Brian Tully	Christopher Dunham	
A985	***Shadowlands*** *Wolsey Theatre (Ipswich)*	William Nicholson	Wolsey Theatre Company	Barry McCarthy Shelley Thompson	Antony Tuckey	
A986	***Shaker*** *ICA (London SW1)*	Richard McInerny *Glynne Wickham (Bristol)*	Touchstone Theatre Company	Alison Edgar	Annie Griffin	

Ref	Play	Playwright	Theatre Co.	Starring	Director	Producer
A987	***Shakers***	Jane Thornton John Godber (PW,D)	Hull Truck Theatre Company	Rebecca Clay Tracy Sweetinburgh Nicola Vickery Joanne Wooton		
	Arts Centre (Birmingham) *Arts Theatre (Belfast)* *Playhouse (Newcastle/u/Tyne)* *Sth Holland Ctr. (Spalding)* *Oakham Festival (Oakham)* *Wyvern Th. (Swindon)* *Everyman Palace (Cork)* *Sherman Th. (Cardiff)* *Uppingham Th. (Uppingham)* *Glynne Wickham (Bristol)* *Library Theatre (Leighton Buzz.)* *Hawk's Well Th. (Sligo)* *Forum 28 (Barrow-in-Furness)* *Civic Theatre (Darlington)* *Rawmarsh School (Rotherham)* *Riverside Th. (Coleraine)* *Ryde Theatre (Isle of Wight)* *Theatr Hafren (Newtown)* *Th. Royal (Bury St Edmunds)*					
A988	***Shame, Ignorance and Binoculars*** *Bridge Lane Th (Battersea)*	Sharon Riley (AD)	Heather Productions	Stuart Allen	Stuart Allen	
A989	***The Shawl*** *S. Joseph Studio (Scarborough)*	David Mamet			Malcolm Hebden	
A990	***She Stoops To Conquer*** *New End Th. (London NW3)*	Oliver Goldsmith	Court Theatre Company		Anthony Cornish	
A991	***She Stoops To Conquer*** *Haymarket Th. (Leicester)*	Oliver Goldsmith		Ronald Fraser Richard Gibson Marcia Warren	Paul Kerryson	
A992	***She Stoops To Conquer*** *Festival Th. (Chichester)*	Oliver Goldsmith	Chichester Festival Theatre	Jean Boht Susannah Harker Denis Quilley	Peter Wood	
A993	***She Ventures He Wins*** *Man in the Moon (London SW3)*	Ariadne	The Man in the Moon Theatre Company		Vivienne Cottrell	
A994	***Sherlock Holmes & the Tiger of San Pedro*** *Queens Hall Arts (Hexham)* *Queens Hall Arts (Hexham)* *Richmond Th. (Richmond)* *Little Theatre (Middlesborough)*	Conan Doyle (A) Stewart Howson	Northumberland Theatre Company		Gillian Hambleton	
A995	***Shirley Valentine*** *Crucible Th. (Sheffield)* *Theatre Royal (York)* *Redgrave Th. (Farnham)* *Richmond Th. (Richmond)* *Playhouse (Liverpool)*	Willy Russell		Pamela Power	Richard Olivier	Bill Kenwright Ltd
A996	***Shoot The Women First*** *BAC (London SW11)*		Foursight Theatre Company Ltd	Jill Dowse Kate Joseph	Kate Hale Deborah Barnard	
A997	***Shout Across The River*** *Barons Court Th. (London W14)*	Stephen Poliakoff	The Cloth Horse Theatre Company	Brett Allen Hayley Chiswell Terri Potoczna		
A998	***Sidewalk Sidney*** *Royal Exchange (Manchester)*	Randhi McWilliams	Royal Exchange Theatre Company	Charles Caine Eddie Osei	James Maxwell	
A999	***Sienna Red*** *Alexandra Th. (Birmingham)* *Richmond Th. (Richmond)* *Th. Royal (Bath)*	Stephen Poliakoff	Peter Hall Company	Francesca Annis Martin Shaw	Peter Hall	Bill Kenwright Ltd
A1000	***Signora Joyce*** *New End Th. (London NW3)*	G. O'Connor	The Irish Company	Franchine Mulrooney	Deb Jones	
A1001	***Sikulu*** *Queen's Th. (London W1V)*	Bertha Egnos (C) Gail Lakier (L)			Lynton Burns Andy Chabeli (Ch) Shadrack Twala (Ch)	
A1002	***The Sin Eaters*** *City Centre (Dublin)* *Aman Centre (Ammanford, Dyfed)* *Drill Hall (Chepstow, Gwent)* *Triskel Arts Ctr (Cork, Eire)* *Llanover Hall (Cardiff)* *Lesneven (Lesneven, Brittany)* *Newport Centre (Newport, Gwent)* *Brest, Brittany (Brest)* *Drama Centre (Gwent)*	Ian Rowlands	Wales Actors' Company		Ruth Garnault	
A1003	***Sindbad's Arabian Nights*** *Nuffield Th. (Southampton)*		Nuffield Theatre Company		Patrick Sandford	
A1004	***Single Spies*** *Playhouse Th. (Salisbury)*	Alan Bennett	Salisbury Theatre Company		David Massarella	
A1005	***Single Spies*** *Redgrave Th. (Farnham)*	Alan Bennett	Redgrave Theatre Company		Leona Heimfeld	Redgrave Theatre Company

Ref	Play	Playwright	Theatre Co.	Starring	Director	Producer
A1006	***Sisters*** *Th. Museum (London WC2)*; *Duke's Head (Richmond)*	Stephen Sewell	Missing Twin Productions	Caroline Davenport Allison Hancock	Ian Herbert	
A1007	***Six Characters in Search of an Author*** *NT/Lyttelton (London SE1)*	Franco Zeffirelli (Ad D) Luigi Vanzi (Ad) Luigi Pirandello	Royal National Theatre			
A1008	***Six Degrees of Separation*** *Royal Court Th. (London SW1)*; *Comedy Th. (London SW1)*	John Guare	Royal Court Theatre	Stockard Channing Adrian Lester Paul Shelley	Phyllida Lloyd	Theatre of Comedy Royal Court Theatre
A1009	***Six Fools*** *Old Red Lion Th. (London EC1)*	Lyall Watson	Trampoline Productions	Leigh Funnelle Julia Watson Benny Young	Sian Edwards	
A1010	***Sleeping With Mickey Mouse*** *Sherman Th. (Cardiff)*	Frank Vickery		Menna Trussler	Phil Clark	
A1011	***Sleeping Beauty and the Beast*** *Haymarket Th. (Leicester)*	Paul Kerryson (PW,D)	Haymarket Theatre Company	David Dale		
A1012	***The Sleeping Beauty*** *Th. Royal (Windsor, Berks)*	Mary Kerridge	Theatre Royal Windsor	Bryan Burdon Ernie Wise	Mark Piper	
A1013	***Sleuth*** *Lyceum Th. (Sheffield)*; *New Victoria Th. (Woking)*; *Th. Royal (Nottingham)*; *Towngate Th. (Poole)*	Anthony Shaffer	Excalibur Productions Ltd	Lewis Collins Richard Todd	Ian Kellgren	
A1014	***A Slice of Saturday Night*** *Royal Th. (Northampton)*	The Heather Brothers	Royal Theatre, Northampton	John Ashton	Johnny Worthy	
A1015	***A Slice Of Saturday Night*** *Belgrade Th. (Coventry)*; *Opera House (Manchester)*; *Forum Theatre (Billingham)*; *Marlowe Th. (Canterbury)*; *St George's Hall (Bradford)*; *Lyceum Th. (Sheffield)*; *Towngate Th. (Poole)*; *Opera House (Buxton)*; *New Victoria Th. (Woking)*; *Key Theatre (Peterborough)*; *Th. Royal (Brighton)*; *Everyman Th. (Cheltenham)*; *Queen's Th. (Hornchurch)*	The Heather Brothers	Queen's Theatre, Hornchurch	Alvin Stardust	Lea Heather Keith Hayman (MD)	Ivan Hale
A1016	***A Slip Of The Tongue*** *Shaftesbury Th. (London WC2)*	Dusty Hughes	Steppenwolf Theatre Company	John Malkovich Lizzy McInnerny	Simon Stokes	Turnstyle Howard Panter
A1017	***Smile Orange*** *Cochrane Th (London WC1B)*; *Belgrade Th. (Coventry)*	Trevor Rhone (PW,D)	Talawa Theatre Company	Gordon Case Dona Croll Richard McKeuley		
A1018	***The Sneeze*** *Duke's Head (Richmond)*; *Arts Centre (Horsham)*; *Charles Cryer St.Th. (Sutton)*	Anton Chekhov Michael Frayn (T)	PTC Productions	Julia Farino Bill Newman Vince Penfold	Colin Swift	
A1019	***Snow Queen*** *Norwich Puppet (Norwich)*	Hans Christian Andersen (Au)	Norwich Puppet Theatre Trust Ltd			
A1020	***The Snow Queen*** *Young Vic Th. (London SE1)*	Hans Christian Andersen (Au) Nick Stafford (A)	Young Vic Company	Katherine Barker Neil Clark Marie Critchley	Karen Stephens Chris White	
A1021	***The Snow Queen*** *New Victoria Th. (New/u/Lyme)*	Hans Christian Andersen (A) Bob Eaton (Ad,D)	New Victoria Theatre	Simon Egerton Joanna Phillips-Lane Karl Woolley		
A1022	***Snow White and the Seven Dwarfs*** *Ashcroft Th. (Croydon)*		E & B Productions	Stu Francis Linda Lusardi		Paul Elliott

Ref	Play	Playwright	Theatre Co.	Starring	Director	Producer
A1023	***Snow White and the Seven Dwarfs*** *Richmond Th. (Richmond)*		E & B Productions	Marti Caine Daniella Carson Derek Griffiths		Paul Elliott
A1024	***The Solo Experience*** *Warwick Arts (Coventry)* *Arts Centre (Birmingham)* *Arena Th. (Wolverhampton)* *Old Bull Arts (Barnet)* *Nuffield Studio (Southampton)* *Clarendon College (Nottingham)* *Stamford Arts C. (Stamford)* *Chelsea Centre (London SW10)*	Mark Long	The People Show	Mark Long		
A1025	***Some Like It Hot*** *Prince Edward (London WC2N)*	Peter Stone		Billy Boyle Royce Mills Tommy Steele	Tommy Steele	Mark Furness Ltd
A1026	***Some Singing Blood*** *Th. Upstairs (London SW1)*	Heidi Thomas	English Stage Company	Julia Ford Gary McDonald Prunella Scales	Jules Wright	
A1027	***Some...Atomic Zombie Things From Hell*** *La Bonne Crepe (London SW11)*	Paul Prescott (PW,D)		Jonathan Avery Susi Mowson Jan Revere		Bonne Crepe
A1028	***Someone Who'll Watch Over Me*** *Hampstead Th. (London NW3)* *Vaudeville Th. (London WC2)*	Frank McGuinness	Hampstead Theatre Company	Alec McCowen Hugh Quarshie Stephen Rea	Robin Lefevre	David Pugh Ltd
A1029	***Something's Burning*** *Th. Royal (Windsor, Berks)* *Yvonne Arnaud (Guildford)*	Eric Chappell	Theatre Royal Windsor	Christopher Blake Geoffrey Davies Joanna Van Gyseghem	Mark Piper	
A1030	***Something Missing*** *Etcetera (London NW1)*	Hugh Cruttwell (PW,D)	Hot Tea	Deborah Davies Rudolph Kolias		
A1031	***Song Of Provence*** *Old Town Hall (Hemel/Hemp)* *West Cliff Th. (Clacton)* *King's Lynn Arts (King's Lynn)* *Wolsey Theatre (Ipswich)* *Quay Theatre (Sudbury)* *Stamford Arts C. (Stamford)* *Library Theatre (Leighton Buzz.)* *Princess Th. (Hunstanton)* *Th. Royal (Bury St Edmunds)*	Jean Giono	Eastern Angles Theatre Company		Ivan Cutting	
A1032	***Sophisticated Ladies*** *Globe Th. (London W1)*	Duke Ellington	Gero Productions	Jacqui Boatswain Jacqueline Dankworth Jacqui Dubois	Roger Haines	Michael Rose Frank & Woji Gero
A1033	***The Sound Of Music*** *His Majesty's Th. (Aberdeen)* *King's Th. (Glasgow)* *Alhambra Th. (Bradford)* *Th. Royal (Newcastle/u/Tyne)* *Sadler's Wells (London EC1)*	Rodgers & Hammerstein II		Christopher Cazenove Robin Nedwell Liz Robertson	Wendy Toye	Ronald Lee
A1034	***Speed-The-Plow*** *Pentameters (London NW3)*	David Mamet			Jonathan Best	Tina Marshall
A1035	***Spread A Little Happiness*** *Whitehall Th. (London SW1A)*	Sheridan Morley	Spread A Little Happiness Ltd.	Clare Burt Maurice Clarke Ron Moody	Dan Crawford	Dan Crawford
A1036	***Spring and Port Wine*** *Octagon Th. (Bolton)*	Bill Naughton	Octagon Theatre Company	Mary Cunningham Madge Hindle Lucy Robinson	Lawrence Till	
A1037	***Spring Awakening*** *Mermaid Studio (London EC4V)*	Frank Wedekind Edward Bond (Tr)	About Time Theatre Company	David Glennie Raphael McAuliffe Michael Warburton	Yuval Zamir	Nigel Barden
A1038	***Square Rounds*** *NT/Olivier (London SE1)*	Tony Harrison (PW,D)	Royal National Theatre	Paola Dionisotti Sara Kestleman Sian Thomas		RNT
A1039	***Scrooge The Musical*** *Alexandra Th. (Birmingham)*	Leslie Bricusse (Ad) Charles Dickens (A)		Stratford Johns Anthony Newley Jon Pertwee	Bob Tomson	Graham Mulvin Ltd.
A1040	***Stage Struck*** *Theatr Colwyn (Colwyn Bay)*	Simon Gray	Theatr Colwyn Summer Rep	David Middleton Stewart Morritt Helen Parkinson	Gareth ap Gwylim	

Ref	Play	Playwright	Theatre Co.	Starring	Director	Producer
A1041	***Stageland***	Jerome K. Jerome (A) Michael Friend (Ad,D)		Trevor Bannister		Michael Friend Productions
	Dundee Repertory (Dundee); New Tyne Th. (Newcastle/Tyne); Devonshire Park Th. (Eastbourne); Gaiety Th. (Isle of Man); King's Theatre (Southsea); Yvonne Arnaud (Guildford); Connaught Th. (Worthing); Ashcroft Th. (Croydon); Palace Th. (Westcliff-On-Sea); Marlowe Th. (Canterbury)					
A1042	***Stages***	David Storey	Royal National Theatre	Alan Bates Joanna David Rosemary Martin	Lindsay Anderson	RNT
	NT/Cottesloe (London SE1)					
A1043	***Starlight Express***	Andrew Lloyd Webber (C) Richard Stilgoe (L)		Greg Ellis John Partridge Reva Rice	Trevor Nunn	Really Useful Theatre Co.Ltd.
	Apollo Victoria (London SW1)					
A1044	***State of Bewilderment***		Trestle Theatre			
	Bowen West Th. (Bedford); Platform Theatre (Haywards Heath); The Playhouse (Harlow); Theatre Royal (Wakefield); Th. Royal (Bury St Edmunds); Connaught Th. (Worthing); Brewhouse Th. (Taunton); Warwick Arts (Coventry); Oxford Playhouse (Oxford); Palace Theatre (Newark); Palace Theatre (Newark); Arts Th. (Cambridge); Trinity Arts (Tunbridge Wells); Th. Royal (Winchester); The Hawth (Crawley); Grand Th. (Blackpool); Opera House (Buxton); Arts Centre (St Helier); Phoenix Arts (Leicester); Cochrane Th (London WC1B)					
A1045	***Steel Magnolias***	Robert Harling		Patricia Garwood Val Lehman Ruth Madoc	Derek Killeen	
	Thorndike Th. (Leatherhead)					
A1046	***Stepping Out***	Richard Harris	Bill Kenwright Ltd	Miranda Fellows Teddy Green Valerie Walsh	Martin Connor	Bill Kenwright
	Connaught Th. (Worthing); Wyvern Th. (Swindon); Beck Th. (Hayes, Middx); RST (Stratford-upon-Avon); Crucible Th. (Sheffield); Grand Theatre (Wolverhampton); Grand Th. (Swansea); Wimbledon Th. (London SW19); Forum Theatre (Billingham); Hull New Th. (Hull); Charter Th. (Preston); Orchard Th. (Dartford); Arts Th. (Cambridge); Playhouse (Liverpool); Towngate Th. (Poole); The Hawth (Crawley); Alexandra Th. (Birmingham); Th. Royal (Brighton); The Hexagon (Reading); Grand Th. (Leeds); New Victoria Th. (Woking); Th. Royal (Windsor, Berks); Churchill Th. (Bromley); Harlequin Th (Northwich); Festival Th. (Chichester)					
A1047	***Stig Of The Dump***	Clive King (Au) Richard Williams (A)	Unicorn Theatre		Richard Williams	
	Arts Theatre (London WC2H)					
A1048	***Stig Of The Dump***	Clive King (A) Richard Williams (Ad)	Worcester Theatre Company		Pat Trueman	
	Swan Theatre (Worcester)					
A1049	***Stirrings in Sheffield on Sat Night***	Alan Cullen	Crucible Theatre			
	Crucible Th. (Sheffield)					
A1050	***Stitched Up***	Stephen Bill	Palace Theatre, Watford	Marji Campi Lynda Rooke Philip Whitchurch	Bob Carlton	
	Palace Th. (Watford)					
A1051	***A Stop in the Desert***		Grupo Chwilowa	Irina Nabatova Alexei Zeitsev	Krzystof Borowiec Jerzy Luzynski	
	Watermans (Brentford, Middx)					
A1052	***Stories From The National Enquirer***	Jeanne Murray Walker	The Man in the Moon Theatre Company		Kirstie Gulick	
	Man in the Moon (London SW3)					
A1053	***The Story of the Last of the Just***	Andre Schwarzbart (A) Robbie Gringrass (Ad D)	The Besht Tellers	Olivier Louis Beer Robbie Cringras Nadine Shenton		Rebecca Wolman
	New End Th. (London NW3)					
A1054	***Straight & Narrow***	Jimmie Chinn		Nicholas Lyndhurst Carmel McSharry	Allan Davis	Linnit Productions Allan Davis Ltd
	Th. Royal (Brighton); Wyndhams Th. (London WC2); Palace Th. (Manchester); Aldwych Th. (London WC2)					
A1055	***Strange Domain***	Andrew Lowe-Watson (L) Richard Parsons (C)	Elephant Theatre	Carl Antony Paul Blackwell Lesley Coleman	Marc Urquhart	Syd Golder Barbara Barringer
	Canal Cafe Th. (London W2)					

Ref	Play	Playwright	Theatre Co.	Starring	Director	Producer
A1056	***The Street of Crocodiles*** *NT/Cottesloe (London SE1)*	Bruno Schulz (A) Simon McBurney (Ad,D)	Theatre de Complicite	Annabel Arden Lilo Baur Eric Mallett		
A1057	***Strippers*** *Palace Th. (Westcliff-On-Sea)*	Peter Terson	Palace Theatre, Westcliff	Dorothy Lawrence James Telfer	Christopher Dunham	
A1058	***Summer Lightning*** *Citz.First Th. (Glasgow)*	P.G. Woodhouse	Citizens' Th. Co.	Helen Baxendale Siobhan Stanley	Giles Havergal	
A1059	***Sweet Bird of Youth*** *Citz.First Th. (Glasgow)*	Tennessee Williams	Citizens' Th. Co.		Philip Prowse	
A1060	***A Swell Party*** *Vaudeville Th. (London WC2)*	John Kane Cole Porter (C)		Nickolas Grace David Kernan Angela Richards	David Gilmore	Showpeople 90
A1061	***Sylvia*** *Andrews Lane Studio Th. (Dublin 2)*	Jacqueline Mulhallen	Lynx Theatre and Poetry	Jacqueline Mulhallen	Simone Vause	
A1062	***The Tailor-Made Man*** *Hen & Chickens (London N1)*	Claudio Macor (PW,D)	Torchlight Theatre Company			
A1063	***The Taking of Liberty*** *Man in the Moon (London SW3)*	Cheryl Robson	The Man in the Moon Theatre Company		Jennie Darnell	
A1064	***Taking Steps*** *Century Th. (Keswick)*	Alan Ayckbourn	Blue Box Theatre Company		Ellis Jones	
A1065	***Talk Of The Steamie*** *Queen's Th. (Hornchurch)*	Tony Roper David Anderson (L)	Queen's Theatre, Hornchurch	Eileen Gourlay C.P. Grogan Kate Williams	Marina Caldarone	Harvey Kass
A1066	***Talking Heads*** *Yvonne Arnaud (Guildford)* *Comedy Th. (London SW1)*	Alan Bennett (PW,D)	Duncan C Weldon	Alan Bennett Patricia Routledge		Duncan C Weldon
A1067	***Tamburlaine The Great*** *Swan Th. (Stratford-upon-Avon)*	Christopher Marlowe	Royal Shakespeare Company	Jasper Britton Stephen Casey Antony Sher	Terry Hands	RSC
A1068	***The Taming Of The Shrew*** *RST (Stratford-upon-Avon)*	William Shakespeare	Royal Shakespeare Company	Amanda Harris Anton Lesser	Bill Alexander	RSC
A1069	***The Taming of the Shrew*** *Williamson Park (Lancaster)*		The Duke's Theatre Company	Anna Palmer Lucy Tregear Chris Wright	Jon Pope	
A1070	***The Taming Of The Shrew*** *Royal Lyceum Th. Co (Edinburgh)*	William Shakespeare	Royal Lyceum Theatre Company		Ian Wooldridge	
A1071	***Tamayos*** *New Vic (Bristol)*		Boi De Mamao			
A1072	***Tango 'Til You're Sore*** *Finborough Th. (London SW10)*	Robert Young	Finborough Productions	Tracy Hardwick Andy Lucas Celia Nelson	Richard Georgeson	
A1073	***Tartuffe*** *Dundee Repertory (Dundee)*	Moliere Liz Lochhead (Tr)	Dundee Repertory Theatre Ltd	Jimmy Chisolm Tony Cownie Molly Innes	Hamish Glen	
A1074	***A Taste of Honey*** *Th.Clywd Studio (Mold)*	Shelagh Delaney	Theatr Clwyd Company	Harriette Ashcroft Michael Brogan Eileen Pollock	Caroline Eves	
A1075	***A Taste of Honey*** *Octagon Th. (Bolton)*	Shelagh Delaney	Octagon Theatre Company	Nick Conway Sally Whittaker	Lawrence Till	
A1076	***Teechers*** *Theatr Colwyn (Colwyn Bay)*	John Godber	Theatr Colwyn Summer Rep	Kevin Dyer Tanya Franks Sharon Scogings	Gareth ap Gwylim	
A1077	***Teechers*** *Studio Theatre (Harlow)*	John Godber	The Harlow Players		Simon Mawdsley	
A1078	***Teechers*** *Everyman Th. (Cheltenham)*	John Godber	Everyman Theatre Company	Angela Bain Mark Chatterton Sharon Muircroft	Richard Stone	
A1079	***Telephonebelles*** *Man in the Moon (London SW3)*	Pete Lawson (PW,D)	Steam Factory		Jennie Darnell	

Ref	Play	Playwright	Theatre Co.	Starring	Director	Producer
A1080	***The Television Programme***	Michel Vinaver	Gate Theatre Company		Kim Dambaek	
	Gate Th. Club (London W11)					
A1081	***Telling Tales***	Clayton Buffoni (PW,D)	Aspect Theatre Productions			
	BAC (London SW11)					
A1082	***The Tempest***	William Shakespeare	English Shakespeare Company	Olwen Fouere Ravil Isyanov John Woodvine	Michael Bogdanov	
	Festival Th. (Chichester); Derngate (Northampton); Th. Royal (Nottingham); Grand Theatre (Wolverhampton); Apollo (Oxford); His Majesty's Th. (Aberdeen); Eden Court Th. (Inverness); Grand Th. (Swansea); Th. Royal (Plymouth); Hippodrome (Bristol); New Victoria Th. (Woking); Hull New Th. (Hull); Grand Th. (Leeds); Royalty Theatre (London WC1); New Th. (Cardiff)					
A1083	***The Tempest***	William Shakespeare	Orchard Theatre Company	Andrea Gascoigne James Lailey John Surman	Stephen Powell	
	Drum Theatre (Plymouth); Sth Molton Cllge (South Molton); Victoria Pavilio (Ilfracombe); The Octagon (Okehampton); Merlin (Frome); Queens Hall Th (Barnstaple); Arts Centre (Falmouth); Treviglas School (Newquay); Corn Exchange (Dorchester); Acorn Arts Ctre (Penzance); Town Hall (Tavistock); Northcott (Exeter); Digby Hall (Sherborne, Dorset); Arts Centre (Shaftesbury); Arts Centre (St Helier); Mowlem Theatre (Swanage); College Theatre (Bideford); Barn Theatre (Dartington); Eden Arts Trust (Cumbria); Manor Pavilion (Sidmouth); Hope Theatre (Bristol)					
A1084	***The Tempest***	William Shakespeare			Yukio Ninagawa	RSC
	Barbican Th. (London EC2)					
A1085	***The Tempest***	William Shakespeare	Bristol Old Vic Ensemble			
	Bristol Old Vic (Bristol)					
A1086	***Ten In A Bed***	Alan Ahlberg	Unicorn Theatre	Richard Bryan Ray Emmet-Brown Emma Gibbons	Richard Williams	
	Arts Theatre (London WC2H)					
A1087	***Ten Times Table***	Alan Ayckbourn	Salisbury Theatre Company	Gabrielle Hamilton Janet Rawson Michael Shaw	Graham Callan	
	Playhouse Th. (Salisbury)					
A1088	***The Tender Husband***		Magnificent Theatre Company	John Conroy John Crocker Ben Crocker	Lucie Fitchett	Ben Crocker
	The Playhouse (Harlow); Oxford Playhouse (Oxford); Guildhall Centre (Grantham); Trinity Arts (Gainsborough); Stahl Theatre (Peterborough); Alhambra St (Bradford); Dovecot (Stockton on Tees); Georgian Theatre (Richmond); The Theatre (Chipping Norton); Arts Centre (Birmingham); Christ's Hosp. (Horsham); Trinity Arts (Tunbridge Wells); Drama Centre (Cambridge); The Harlequin Theatre (Redhill); The Gantry (Southampton); Watermans (Brentford, Middx); Stamford Arts C. (Stamford); The Maltings (Berwick-u-Tweed); Queens Hall Arts (Hexham); King's Lynn Arts (King's Lynn); Lyceum Th. (Crewe); Grand Th. (Blackpool); Old Town Hall (Hemel/Hemp); Th. Royal (Bury St Edmunds)					
A1089	***Tess of the D'Urbervilles***	Thomas Hardy Fay Weldon (Ad)	West Yorkshire Playhouse Company	Graeme Henderson Shelly Willetts Richard Willis	Helena Kaut-Howson	
	W/Yorks Playh. (Leeds)					
A1090	***The 19th Hole***	Johnny Speight	Thorndike Theatre	David Lumsden Bruce Montague Eric Sykes	Tony Craven	
	Playhouse (Liverpool); Thorndike Th. (Leatherhead); Ashcroft Th. (Croydon)					
A1091	***The Ballroom***	Peter King	Attic Theatre Company	Doreen Andrew Philip Childs Trevor Jones	David Gilmore	
	Attic Theatre (London SW19)					
A1092	***The Great Exhibition***	David Hare	The Company			
	The Courtyard (London N1)					
A1093	***The Refuge***	Barbara Perkins		Tara Joseph	Janine Clements	
	Ecology Centre (London W1)					
A1094	***The Slicing Edge***	Judith Cook	Wolsey Theatre Company			
	Wolsey Studio (Ipswich)					
A1095	***The Thebans***	Sophocles	Royal Shakespeare Company	Linda Bassett Rob Edwards Linda Marlowe	Adrian Noble	RSC
	Playhouse (Newcastle/u/Tyne); Barbican Th. (London EC2)					

Ref	Play	Playwright	Theatre Co.	Starring	Director	Producer
A1096	***And Then There Were None*** *Perth Th. (Perth)*	Agatha Christie Joan Knight (AD)	Perth Theatre Company		Ken Alexander	
A1097	***Therese Raquin*** *Fife College (Fife); Dundee Repertory (Dundee); Volunteer Hall (Galashiels); Byre Theatre (St Andrews); Palace Th. (Kilmarnock); Arts Centre (Paisley); Tramway (Glasgow); Mill (Thurso); Town Hall (Dingwall); Village Hall (Ballachulish, H'land); High School (Mallaig, H'land); Broadford Hall (Skye, H'Land); Village Hall (Rothshire, H'land); Village Hall (Ullapool, H'land); Town Hall (Pitlochry, Tayside); MacRobert Arts (Stirling); Town Hall (Penicuik, Lothian)*	Emile Zola (A) Stuart Paterson (Ad)	Communicado	Tony Cownie Alyxis Daly Cara Kelly	Jennifer Black	
A1098	***The Thin Soldier*** *Thorndike Th. (Leatherhead)*	Hans Christian Andersen	Thorndike Theatre	Samantha Best Emma Danby David Rowan	Beth Wood	
A1099	***Thirteenth Night*** *Lyric Studio (London W6)*	Howard Brenton	London Actors Theatre Company	David Bauckham Isabel Brook Chris Brown	Chris Fisher	
A1100	***Three Birds Alighting on a Field*** *Royal Court Th. (London SW1)*	Timberlake Wertenbaker	Royal Court Theatre	Harriet Walter	Max Stafford-Clark	
A1101	***Three Girls In Blue*** *W/Yorks Playh. (Leeds)*	Ludmilla Petrushevskaya Stephen Mulrine (Tr)	West Yorkshire Playhouse Company	Jackie Lye Ann Penfold Helen Ryan	Michael Birch	
A1102	***Three Men in a Boat*** *Canal Cafe Th. (London W2)*	Jerome K Jerome (A)			David Woods	Ridiculous Woods
A1103	***Three More Sleepless Nights*** *Orange Tree Th. (Richmond)*	Caryl Churchill	Orange Tree Theatre		Dominic Hill	
A1104	***The Three Musketeers*** *Warehouse Th. (Croydon); Watermans (Brentford, Middx)*	Robert Ballard (PW,D)	Performance Theatre Company	Robert Ballard Patrick Bramwells Steve Gallagher		The Warehouse Theatre Company
A1105	***The Three Musketeers*** *Grand Th. (Blackpool); Playhouse (Newcastle/u/Tyne); Live Arts (Grantham); Warwick Arts (Coventry); Wyeside Arts C. (Builth Wells); Old Town Hall (Hemel/Hemp); Tunisia (Tunisia); Stahl Theatre (Peterborough); Antwerp, Belgium (Belgium); Octagon (Yeovil); Connaught Th. (Worthing); Broxbourne Arts Centre (Hoddesdon); Gardner Arts Ctr (Brighton); Alhambra St (Bradford); Prince Of Wales (Staffordshire); Purcell Room (London SE1)*		Mime Theatre Project	Andrew Dawson Gavin Robertson Robert Thirtle	Toby Sedgwick	
A1106	***The Three Musketeers*** *Northcott (Exeter)*	David Pownall (Ad) Alexandre Dumas (A)	Northcott Theatre Company	Simon Armstrong Peter Harding Rupert Wickham	John Durnin	
A1107	***The Three Musketeers*** *Mercury Th. (Colchester)*	Alexandre Dumas (A) Phil Woods (Ad)	Mercury Theatre	Marcello Marasculchi Daniel O'Brien John Pennington	Michael Winter	
A1108	***Threepenny Story*** *Arena Th. (Wolverhampton); Brewhouse Th. (Burton-on-Trent); Netherfield Comm (Notts); Stanwix Arts Th (Carlisle)*	Lee Beagley (PW,D)	Kaboodle	Angela Bullock Andrea Earl Russ Edwards		
A1109	***The Threepenny Opera*** *New Victoria Th. (New/u/Lyme)*	Bertolt Brecht	New Victoria Theatre	Jeremy Clay Ted Richards Carole Ruggier	Rob Swain	
A1110	***Thumbelina*** *Norwich Puppet (Norwich)*		Norwich Puppet Theatre Trust Ltd			

Ref	Play	Playwright	Theatre Co.	Starring	Director	Producer
A1111	*Thunderbirds FAB*	Gavin Robertson (PW,d) Andrew Dawson (PW,D)	Mime Theatre Project	Wayne Forester Paul Kent		Titan Productions
	Ambassadors Th. (London WC2); Grand Th. (Blackpool); Wyvern Th. (Swindon); Derngate (Northampton); Th. Royal (Lincoln); Th. Royal (Glasgow); Arts Th. (Cambridge); New Pavilion (Rhyl); Th. Royal (Brighton); Royal Northern (Manchester); Everyman Th. (Cheltenham); Opera House (Belfast); Grand Theatre (Wolverhampton); Pavilion Theatre (Bournemouth); George Square Th. (Edinburgh); Assembly Hall (Tunbridge Wells); Crucible Th. (Sheffield); Opera House (Buxton); Th. Royal (Nottingham); Alhambra Th. (Bradford); The Marina Th. (Lowestoft); Pavilion Th. (Worthing)					
A1112	*Time Of My Life*	Alan Ayckbourn (PW,D)	Stephen Joseph Theatre Company	Terence Booth Russell Dixon Karen Drury		
	Stephen Joseph (Scarborough)					
A1113	*Time Windows*	Michael Wilcox	Palace Theatre, Watford	Terence Halliday Roger Heathcott Alan Renwick	Christopher Dunham	
	Palace Th. (Westcliff-On-Sea)					
A1114	*'Tis Pity She's A Whore*	John Ford	Royal Shakespeare Company	Jonathan Cullen Jonathan Hyde Saskia Reeves	David Leveaux	RSC
	Barbican/The Pit (London EC1)					
A1115	*TO*	Jim Cartwright	New Victoria Theatre	Jacqueline Morgan Eddie York	Rob Swain	
	New Victoria Th. (New/u/Lyme)					
A1116	*TO*	Jim Cartwright	Hull Truck Theatre Company	Susan Cookson Ian Rogerson	Damian Cruden	
	Theatre Royal (Wakefield); Spring St. Th. (Hull)					
A1117	*TO*	Jim Cartwright	Not the National Theatre			
	Wilde Th. (Bracknell)					
A1118	*TO*	Jim Cartwright	Theatre Royal Plymouth	Dave Barrass Helen Cotterill	Amanda Knott	
	Drum Theatre (Plymouth)					
A1119	*TO*	Jim Cartwright	Cumbernauld Theatre Company	Blythe Duff Vincent Friel	Les Carruthers	
	Tron Th. (Glasgow); Cumbernauld Th. (Cumbernauld)					
A1120	*TO*	Jim Cartwright	Everyman Theatre Company	Mark Chatterton Sharon Muircroft	Richard Stone	
	Everyman Th. (Cheltenham)					
A1121	*To Kill A Mockingbird*	Harper Lee (A) Christopher Sergel (Ad)	Northcott Theatre Company	Steve Bennett Monica Dolan Peter Harding	John Durnin	
	Northcott (Exeter)					
A1122	*To My Country A Child*	Joe White (PW,D)	Stone Lady Theatre Company			
	Birm.Rep. Studio (Birmingham)					
A1123	*To Serve Them All My Days*	R.F. Delderfield (A) Shaun McKenna (Ad)	Royal Theatre, Northampton	Gwynn Beech Chris Matthews Robert Vahey	Michael Brown	
	Royal Th. (Northampton)					
A1124	*Tomorrow We Do The Sky*	Michael Mears	Citizens' Th. Co.	Michael Mears	Sonia Fraser	
	Citz. Second Th. (Glasgow)					
A1125	*Tons Of Money*	Evans Valentine	Mercury Theatre	Lynette Edwards Sheila Irwin Gavin Muir	David Conville	
	Mercury Th. (Colchester)					
A1126	*Too Clever By Half*	Alexander Ostrovsky Rodney Ackland (Tr)			Simon Meadon	
	Questors (London W5)					
A1127	*Too Much Too Young*	Catherine Johnson	Bristol Old Vic Ensemble	Robert Beach Joanne Campbell Cliff Howells	Andy Hay	
	New Vic (Bristol)					
A1128	*Top of the Town*		King's Head Theatre		Jim McManus	
	King's Head Th. (London N1)					
A1129	*Toronto, Mississippi*	Joan MacLeod	Finborough Productions	Scott Gilmore Laurissa Kalinowsky William Marsh	Charles Siegel	
	Finborough Th. (London SW10)					
A1130	*Tottering Towers*	Devised by cast	Shoestring		Dennis Douglas	
	Pegasus Theatre (E. Oxford); Mill Theatre (Banbury)					
A1131	*A Touch of Danger*	Francis Durbridge	Newpalm Productions			
	Devonshire Park Th. (Eastbourne)					

Ref	Play	Playwright	Theatre Co.	Starring	Director	Producer
A1132	***Towards Zero***	Agatha Christie	Newpalm Productions			
	Devonshire Park Th. (Eastbourne)	*Thorndike Th. (Leatherhead)*				
A1133	***Traffic Hearts***	Pete Lawson Jennie Darnell	Steam Factory			
	Man in the Moon (London SW3)					
A1134	***Travels With My Aunt***	Graham Greene (A) Giles Havergal (Ad,D)	Thorndike Theatre	Simon Cadell Richard Kane John Wells		Bill Kenwright Ltd
	Thorndike Th. (Leatherhead) *Alexandra Th. (Birmingham)* *Wyndhams Th. (London WC2)*		*Th. Royal (Brighton)* *Richmond Th. (Richmond)*	*Th. Royal (Bath)* *Towngate Th. (Poole)*	*Churchill Th. (Bromley)* *Yvonne Arnaud (Guildford)*	
A1135	***Travelling Light***	Ted Moore	Express Theatre Company	Richard Bushell Tanya Crook Alan Palmer	Graham Chinn	
	BAC (London SW11)					
A1136	***Travelling Light***	Ted Moore	Birmingham Rep.		Gwenda Hughes	
	Birm.Rep. Studio (Birmingham)					
A1137	***Travesties***	Tom Stoppard	Royal Lyceum Theatre Company		Richard Baron	
	Royal Lyceum Th. Co (Edinburgh)					
A1138	***Trelawny Of The Wells***	Arthur Wing Pinero	Royal National Theatre	Robin Bailey Michael Bryant Helen McCrory	John Caird	
	NT/Olivier (London SE1)					
A1139	***Trelawny Of The Wells***	Arthur Wing Pinero		Sarah Brightman Jason Connery Michael Hordern	Toby Robertson	Duncan C Weldon
	Yvonne Arnaud (Guildford)		*Th. Royal (Brighton)*	*Comedy Th. (London SW1)*		
A1140	***The Trial***	Kafka	The Mouse People	B. Poraj-Pstrokouski	Julia Smith	
	Birm.Rep. Studio (Birmingham)					
A1141	***Trilby & Svengali***	George Du Maurier	Nuffield Theatre/Shared Experience	Tilly Blackwood Teddy Kempner Mary Roscoe	Nancy Meckler	
	Stahl Theatre (Peterborough) *Theatr Hafren (Newtown)*		*Oxford Playhouse (Oxford)* *Cockpit Th. (London NW8)*	*Nuffield Th. (Southampton)*	*Arts Theatre (Belfast)*	
A1142	***Trouble in Mind***	Alice Childress	Tricycle Theatre	David Blake-Kelly David Carr Carmen Munroe	Nicolas Kent	
	Tricycle Th. (London NW6)					
A1143	***Truth Games In The 21st Century***	Ben Caudell	Virtual Reality Theatre Company		Jo Stuart	
	Etcetera (London NW1)					
A1144	***Turkey Time***	Ben Travers	New Victoria Theatre	Simon Egerton Kay Pope	Peter Cheeseman	
	New Victoria Th. (New/u/Lyme)					
A1145	***Turned Out Nice Again***	Vince Powell Alan Randall		Alan Randall Dorothy Wayne	Duggie Chapman	Alan Randall
	The Playhouse (Harlow) *Pomegranate Th. (Chesterfield)* *Mechanics Theatr (Burnley)* *Civic Hall (Stratford-upon-Avon)* *Pavilion Theatre (Bournemouth)*		*Opera House (Manchester)* *Town Hall Theatr (Cleveland)* *Futurist Theatre (Scarborough)* *Civic Theatre (Cheshire)*	*Empire Theatre (Wisbech)* *Royal Theatre (Leamington Spa)* *Ashcroft Th. (Croydon)* *Civic Theatre (Doncaster)*	*Prince Of Wales (Staffordshire)* *The Theatre (Chipping Norton)* *Charter Th. (Preston)* *Civic Theatre (Rotherham)*	
A1146	***Turner's Crossing***	Shelia Dewey	Warehouse Theatre Company	Caroline Blakiston Marcus Eyre Sabina Franklyn	Ted Craig	
	Warehouse Th. (Croydon)					
A1147	***Twelfth Night***	William Shakespeare			Gillian Diamond	Bill Kenwright
	Thorndike Th. (Leatherhead)		*Playhouse (Liverpool)*			
A1148	***Twelfth Night***		English Shakespeare Company	Timothy Davies Vivian Munn Jenny Quayle	Michael Pennington	
	Warwick Arts (Coventry) *Th. Royal (Bath)*		*Civic Theatre (Darlington)* *The Hexagon (Reading)*	*Mayflower (Southampton)* *Th. Royal (Glasgow)*	*New Th. (Cardiff)* *Richmond Th. (Richmond)*	

Ref	Play	Playwright	Theatre Co.	Starring	Director	Producer
A1149	***Twelfth Night***	William Shakespeare	Factotum	Ben Dudley Lisa Fornara Dione Inman	Alastair Palmer	
	The Lost Theatre (London SW6) Conquest Theatre (Bromyard) Arts Centre (Horsham) Playhouse (Epsom) Brewhouse Th. (Burton-on-Trent) Penyrheol Theatr (Swansea) Prince Of Wales (Staffordshire) Arts Centre (Bridgwater) Tertiary College (Daventry) Redgrave Theatre (Bristol) Belgrave School (Staffordshire) Merlin (Frome) Corn Market Hall (Kettering) Brewery Arts (Gloucester) Hazlitt Theatre (Maidstone) Barn Arts Centre (Littlehampton) The Tithe Barn (Wellingborough)					
A1150	***Twelfth Night*** *Watermans (Brentford, Middx)*	William Shakespeare	Wizzard Productions		David Gillies	
A1151	***Twelfth Night*** *Globe Museum (London SE1)*	William Shakespeare	Ingood Company	Finola Carroll Barnaby Edwards Tanya Roach	Tamsin Habety	
A1152	***Twelfth Night*** *Th. Royal (Newcastle/u/Tyne)*	William Shakespeare	Royal Shakespeare Company	Jane Gurnett Freddie Jones Sylvestra le Touzel	Griff Rhys Jones	RSC
A1153	***A Twitch On The Thread*** *Belgrade Studio (Coventry)*	Stephen Clarke	Belgrade Theatre Company	Prim Cotton Peter Dyer	Robert Hamlin	
A1154	***The Two Gentlemen of Verona*** *Playhouse (Newcastle/u/Tyne) Barbican Th. (London EC2)*	William Shakespeare	Royal Shakespeare Company	Richard Bonneville Josette Bushell-Mingo Clare Holman	David Thacker	RSC
A1155	***The Ugly Duckling*** *Gateway Th. (Chester)*	Neil Duffield (Ad) Hans Christian Andersen (A)	Chester Gateway Theatre			
A1156	***Una Pooka*** *Tricycle Th. (London NW6)*	Michael Harding	Tricycle Theatre		Nicolas Kent Mark Lambert	
A1157	***Uncle Vanya*** *NT/Cottesloe (London SE1)*		Royal National Theatre	Ian McKellen Eric Porter Antony Sher	Sean Mathias	RNT
A1158	***Uncle Vanya*** *Royal Lyceum Th. Co (Edinburgh)*	Anton Chekhov	Royal Lyceum Theatre Company		Hugh Hodgart	
A1159	***Uncle Vanya*** *Th. Museum (London WC2)*	Anton Chekhov	The Acting Company		Dana Fainaro	
A1160	***Under Milk Wood*** *Haymarket Studio (Leicester)*	Dylan Thomas	Haymarket Theatre Company	Una Brandon-Jones Rory Edwards Paul Hamilton	Julia Bardsley	
A1161	***Understanding the Dangers*** *White Bear (London SE11)*	Sheila Goff	Prism Theatre	Michael Bernardin Tselane Tambo Anstey Thomas	Gabriele Meini	
A1162	***Unidentified Human Remains*** *Traverse Th. (Edinburgh)*	Brad Fraser	Traverse Theatre Company	Irene McDougal Dougray Scott	Ian Brown	
A1163	***Up 'N' Under*** *Wimbledon Th. (London SW19) Oxford Playhouse (Oxford) Theatr Clwyd (Mold) Th. Royal (Bury St Edmunds) Arts Th. (Cambridge) Redgrave Th. (Farnham)*	John Godber (PW,D)	Hull Truck Theatre Company	Martin Barrass Dave Barrass Ian Rogerson		
A1164	***Valdorama*** *Grace Theatre (London SW11)*	Peter Oswald	Osney Mead Theatre Company	Elizabeth Banks Dennis Clinton John Food	Michael Latimer	Osney Mead
A1165	***Valentine's Day*** *Globe Th. (London W1)*	Benny Green (Ad) David Williams (Ad) George Bernard Shaw		Elizabeth Counsell Edward Petherbridge John Turner	Gillian Lynne	Brian Brolly
A1166	***Be My Aba Daba Valentine*** *Arches Th. (London SE1)*	Various Aline Waites (D,P)	Aba Daba Productions	Maggie Beckit Robin Hunter Nigel Leach		

Ref	Play	Playwright	Theatre Co.	Starring	Director	Producer
A1167	***Venus and Adonis*** *Citz. Third Th. (Glasgow)*	William Shakespeare	Citizens' Th. Co.		Malcolm Sutherland Matthew Radford	
A1168	***Venus Observed*** *Festival Th. (Chichester)*	Christopher Fry	Chichester Festival Theatre	Kate O'Mara Denis Quilley Donald Sinden	James Roose-Evans	
A1169	***A View From The Bridge***	Arthur Miller	Kaboodle	Lee Beagley Sean Kearney Paula Simms		
	Arena Th. (Wolverhampton) *Stahl Theatre (Peterborough)*		*Brewhouse Th. (Burton-on-Trent)* *Stanwix Arts Th (Carlisle)*	*Music Hall (Shrewsbury)* *Kendal Town Hall (Kendal)*	*Hugh Baird Coll. (Liverpool)*	
A1170	***A View From The Bridge*** *Wolsey Theatre (Ipswich)*	Arthur Miller	Wolsey Theatre Company	Del Henney Rosemary McHale Lisa Orgolini	Hettie MacDonald	
A1171	***A View From The Bridge*** *Royal Th. (Northampton)*	Arthur Miller	Royal Theatre, Northampton	David Hargreaves Katharine Schlesinger Nicola Scott	Michael Napier Brown	
A1172	***A View From The Bridge***	Arthur Miller	Royal Exchange Theatre Company	Amelia Bullmore Jonathan Hackett Paul Higgins	Gregory Hersov	
	Ashington Leis. (Ashington) *Grimsby Leis. (Grimsby)* *Shavington Sport (Crewe)*		*Royal Exchange (Manchester)* *The Sands Centre (Carlisle)* *Alexander Sports (Bedford)*	*Meadowside Leis. (Burton/Trent)* *Kingsbridge Leis (Nr Totnes)*	*Mansfield Leis. (Mansfield)* *Riverside Leis. (Chelmsford)*	
A1173	***Village Wooing*** *S. Joseph Studio (Scarborough)*	George Bernard Shaw			Malcolm Hebden	
A1174	***Villain*** *Hen & Chickens (London N1)*	Tony Longhurst	Aquila Productions		Peter Meineck	
A1175	***Vincent*** *Man in the Moon (London SW3)*	Leonard Nimoy		Roger Ringrose	Roger Ringrose	
A1176	***The Virtuoso***		Royal Shakespeare Company	Christopher Benjamin Richard Bonneville Guy Henry	Phyllida Lloyd	
	Playhouse (Newcastle/u/Tyne)		*Barbican/The Pit (London EC1)*			
A1177	***Vita and Virginia*** *Minerva Studio (Chichester)*	Eileen Atkins (Ad)	Chichester Festival Theatre	Eileen Atkins	Patrick Garland	
A1178	***Viva Detroit***	Derek Walcott	Black Theatre Co Operative	Norman Beaton Marlena Mackey Steve Toussaint	Malcolm Frederick	
	Tricycle Th. (London NW6) *Library Theatre (Sheffield)* *Victoria Centre (Northants)* *Arts Centre (Peterborough)* *Sherman Th. (Cardiff)*		*Wilde Th. (Bracknell)* *Wolsey Theatre (Ipswich)* *John Stripe Th. (Winchester)* *Island Arts (Broadstairs)* *Arts Centre (Birmingham)*	*The Theatre (Chipping Norton)* *Ashcroft Centre (Fareham)* *Warwick Arts (Coventry)* *Charles Cryer St.Th. (Sutton)* *Contact Th. (Manchester)*	*St George's Th. (Luton)* *The Gantry (Southampton)* *Haymarket Studio (Leicester)* *21 South Street (Reading)*	
A1179	***Voice of the Sea*** *Lilian Baylis (London EC1)*	Amy Finegan	Patois Theatre Company		Steffyni Rigold	
A1180	***Voices at Her Elbow*** *Bhasvic Studio (Brighton)*	Steven Deproost	Britannia Theatrical Services	Tony Bannister Nina Downey Lisa Moreno	Robin Yarnton	
A1181	***A Voyage Round Para Handy*** *Byre Theatre (St Andrews)*	Brian Osborne Ronald Armstrong	Byre Theatre Company		Maggie Kinloch	
A1182	***The Voysey Inheritance***	Harley Granville Barker	Edinburgh Int. Festival	Christopher Good Paul Mooney Frederick Treves	William Gaskill	
	Royal Lyceum Th. Co (Edinburgh)		*Th. Royal (Bath)*			
A1183	***Walter*** *Dundee Repertory (Dundee)*	C.P. Taylor	Dundee Repertory Theatre Ltd		Hamish Glen	
A1184	***The War In Heaven***	Joseph Chaikin Sam Shepard Sally Jacobs (Dir)	The Peloton	Michael Sherin		
	Saatchi Coll. (London NW8)		*Spitalfields Mkt (London E1)*			
A1185	***The Wasp Factory*** *Citz. Second Th. (Glasgow)*	Iain Banks	Citizens' Th. Co.		Malcolm Sutherland	

Ref	Play	Playwright	Theatre Co.	Starring	Director	Producer
A1186	***Wasting Reality*** *Perth Th. (Perth)*	Ian Brown	Perth Theatre Company		Joan Knight	
A1187	***Watching And Weighting*** *Man in the Moon (London SW3)*	Susan Gott	The Troupe	Susan Gott		Annette Moscowitz Alexander E Racolin
A1188	***Water Music*** *Cockpit Th. (London NW8)*	Lyndon Morgans	Soho Theatre Company	Lynda Baron Raymond Coulthard Dervla Kirwan	Keith Boak	
A1189	***The Wax King*** *Man in the Moon (London SW3)*	Phil Willmott (Ad,D) William Shakespeare	The Steam Factory			
A1190	***The Way of All Flesh*** *Arts Centre (Eastbourne)* *Stamford Arts C. (Stamford)* *West End Centre (Aldershot)* *The Hawth (Crawley)* *VI Form Coll (Barrow-in-Furness)* *Gulbenkian Th. (Newcastle/Tyne)* *Towngate Th. (Basildon)* *Arena Th. (Wolverhampton)* *Guildhall Centre (Grantham)* *Arts Centre (Warminster)* *Riverhouse Barn (Walton-on-Th)* *New Vic (Bristol)* *BAC (London SW11)* *Quay Theatre (Sudbury)* *Niccol Centre (Cirencester)* *Arts Centre (Birmingham)* *Sth Holland Ctr. (Spalding)* *Th. Royal (Winchester)* *Hornpipe Arts (Portsmouth)* *Arts Centre (Salisbury, Wilts.)* *Stanwix Arts Th (Carlisle)* *Regal Arts Ctre (Worksop)*	Samuel Butler Robin Brown (A)	Red Shift Theatre Company	Iona Kennedy David Prescott Michael Sheldon	Jonathan Holloway	
A1191	***We*** *Traverse Th. (Edinburgh)*	Yevegeny Zamyatin		Peter Ireland	Liz Swift	
A1192	***Weldon Rising*** *Playhouse Studio (Liverpool)* *Th. Upstairs (London SW1)*	Phyllis Nagy Liverpool Playhouse (AP)	Royal Court Theatre	Simon Gregor Melee Hutton Rosie Rowell	Penny Ciniewicz	Royal Court Theatre
A1193	***West Side Story*** *Haymarket Th. (Leicester)*	Bernstein, Sondheim & Robbins	Haymarket Theatre Company	Paulette Ivory Paul Manuel Caroline O'Connor	Paul Kerryson	
A1194	***Wexford Trilogy*** *Bush Th. (London W12)*	Billy Roche	Bush Theatre Company	Ingrid Craigie Gary Lydon Des McAleer	Robin Lefevre	Bush Theatre Company
A1195	***What About Luv?*** *Arts Centre (Horsham)* *Holland Park Th. (London)*	Murray Schisgal Howard Marren (C) Susan Birkenhead (L) Kenn Oldfield (D & C)	Fenton Gray Ltd	Rosemary Ashe Tim Flavin David Janson		Fenton Gray
A1196	***What The Butler Saw*** *The Playhouse (Nottingham)*	Joe Orton	Nottingham Playhouse	Mark Arden Helen Atkinson Wood Nigel Pivaro	Ultz	
A1197	***What the Butler Saw*** *Mercury Th. (Colchester)*	Joe Orton	Mercury Theatre	Delena Kidd Michael Tudor-Barnes Michael Walker	Richard Digby-Day Michael Winter	
A1198	***What The Butler Saw*** *Theatre Royal (York)*	Joe Orton	York Theatre Royal Company		Derek Nicholls	
A1199	***When The Past Is Still To Come*** *Finborough Th. (London SW10)*	Tom Kempinski	Zenana Theatre Company	John Castle Ron Wood	Madeleine Wynn	
A1200	***Which Witch*** *Piccadilly Th. (London W1)*	Adrian & Bjornov (C) Kit Hesketh-Harvey (L)		Benedicte Adrian	Piers Haggard	Theatre Productions Ltd
A1201	***While The Sun Shines*** *Old Rep Th. (Birmingham)*	Terence Rattigan	Birmingham Stage Company	Neal Foster Lucy Scott Virginia Walshaw	Granville Saxton	
A1202	***White Woman Street*** *Bush Th. (London W12)*	Sebastian Barry	Bush Theatre Company	Roy Hanlon Patrick Miller David Yip	Caroline Fitzgerald	
A1203	***Who Shall I Be Tomorrow?*** *Greenwich Th. (London SE10)*	Bernard Kops	Greenwich Theatre	Harry Landis Joanna Lumley	Matthew Francis	

Ref	Play	Playwright	Theatre Co.	Starring	Director	Producer
A1204	***Who Was Hilary Maconochie?*** *Orange Tree Th. (Richmond)*	James Saunders	Orange Tree Theatre	Caroline John Jenny McCracken Auriol Smith	Rachel Kavanaugh	
A1205	***Who's Afraid of Virginia Woolf?*** *Dundee Repertory (Dundee)*	Edward Albee	Dundee Repertory Theatre Ltd	Vicki Masson Sandy Neilson David Tennant	Hamish Glen	
A1206	***Why Things Happen*** *Bowen West Th. (Bedford)* *Thameside Th. (Grays)* *ICA (London SW1)* *The Junction (Cambridge)* *Univ. of Essex (Colchester)* *Old Town Hall (Hemel/Hemp)* *Maltings Arts (St Albans)*	Marty Cruikshank	Second Stride	Joanne Leighton Charles Mutter Timothy Walker	Antony McDonald	
A1207	***The Wicked Old Man*** *W/Yorks Playh. (Leeds)*	John McGrath	West Yorkshire Playhouse Company	Felicity Dean Edward Jewesbury Ann Penfold	Jude Kelly	
A1208	***Wicks's Folly*** *Mercury Th. (Colchester)*	Jill Burrows	Mercury Theatre	Kate Lawton Russell Porter Peter Schofield	Michael Winter	
A1209	***Wild Night Of The Witches*** *Little Angel (London N1)*		Little Angel Marionette Theatre			
A1210	***Wild Night Of The Witches*** *Little Angel (London N1)*		Little Angel Marionette Theatre			
A1211	***The Wind In The Willows*** *NT/Olivier (London SE1)*	Kenneth Grahame	Royal National Theatre	Desmond Barrit Michael Bryant Adrian Scarborough	Nicholas Hytner	RNT
A1212	***The Wind in the Willows*** *Byre Theatre (St Andrews)*	Kenneth Grahame (A) Neil Simmons (Ad)	Byre Theatre Company		Cliff Burnett	
A1213	***The Winslow Boy*** *Mercury Th. (Colchester)*	Terence Rattigan	Mercury Theatre	Peter Harlowe Tam Hoskyns Roger Hume	Geoff Bullen	
A1214	***The Winter's Tale*** *RST (Stratford-upon-Avon)*	William Shakespeare	Royal Shakespeare Company	Samantha Bond Gemma Jones John Nettles	Adrian Noble	RSC
A1215	***The Winter's Tale*** *Swan Th. (Stratford-upon-Avon)* *Oxford Playhouse (Oxford)* *Theatr Hafren (Newtown)* *Arts Th. (Cambridge)* *Connaught Th. (Worthing)* *Th. Royal (Winchester)* *Th. Royal (Bury St Edmunds)* *Lyric Ham'smith (London W6)*	William Shakespeare	Theatre de Complicite	Lilo Baur Kathryn Hunter Simon McBurney	Annabel Arden	
A1216	***Wit's End*** *New End Th. (London NW3)*	Griboedev Stephen Walshe (Tr)	Angel Theatre Company	Adrian Schiller	Jake Lushington	
A1217	***Withering Looks*** *Harrogate Th. (Harrogate)* *Library Th. (Manchester)* *Gulbenkian Th. (Canterbury)* *Warwick Arts (Coventry)* *ADC Theatre (Cambridge)* *Wilde Th. (Bracknell)* *Quay Theatre (Sudbury)* *Maltings Arts (St Albans)* *Brewhouse Th. (Burton-on-Trent)* *Ashcroft Centre (Fareham)* *Coliseum Th. (Oldham)* *Assembly Rooms (Edinburgh)* *Limelight Th (Aylesbury)* *Gulbenkian Th. (Newcastle/Tyne)*	Maggie Fox Sue Ryding	Lip Service	Maggie Fox Sue Ryding	Noreen Kershaw	
A1218	***Witness For The Prosecution*** *Th. Royal (Windsor, Berks)* *Grand Theatre (Wolverhampton)* *Orchard Th. (Dartford)* *Th. Royal (Plymouth)* *The Hawth (Crawley)* *Apollo (Oxford)* *Key Theatre (Peterborough)* *Gordon Craig Th. (Stevenage)* *Eden Court Th. (Inverness)* *Wimbledon Th. (London SW19)* *Devonshire Park Th. (Eastbourne)* *Ashcroft Th. (Croydon)* *Th. Royal (Nottingham)* *Wyvern Th. (Swindon)* *Lyceum Th. (Sheffield)* *Connaught Th. (Worthing)* *Arts Centre (Horsham)* *The Playhouse (Harlow)* *Churchill Th. (Bromley)* *Beck Th. (Hayes, Middx)* *Alexandra Th. (Birmingham)* *The Hawth (Crawley)* *Marlowe Th. (Canterbury)* *Opera House (Manchester)* *Civic Theatre (Darlington)* *Malvern Festival Th. (Malvern)* *Pavilion Theatre (Bournemouth)* *Th. Royal (Lincoln)* *Towngate Th. (Poole)* *Forum Theatre (Billingham)* *Th. Royal (Brighton)* *Hippodrome (Birmingham)* *New Victoria Th. (Woking)* *Opera House (Belfast)*	Charles Vance (D,P) Agatha Christie	Prestige Plays	Prunella Gee Derek Waring Giles Watling		

Ref	Play	Playwright	Theatre Co.	Starring	Director	Producer
A1219	***The Wizard of Oz***	L. Frank Baum (A) Frank Gabrielson (Ad)	Everyman Theatre Company		Peter Fieldson	
	Everyman Th. (Liverpool)					
A1220	***The Wizard of Oz***	Frank Baum	Snap Theatre Company			
	St George's Th. (Luton)					
A1221	***The Wizard of Oz***	L. Frank Baum (A) Frank Gabrielson (Ad)	Polka Theatre		Vicky Ireland	
	Polka Th. (London SW19)					
A1222	***The Wizard of Oz***	L. Frank Baum (A)		Jon Atkins Anna Palmer Lucy Tregear	Adrian Johnston Jon Pope	
	Williamson Park (Lancaster)					
A1223	***The Wizard of Oz***	L. Frank Baum (A) Frank Gabrielson (Ad)	Everyman Theatre Company	Ashley Artus Karen Clegg Brian Kennedy	Sheila Mander	
	Everyman Th. (Cheltenham)					
A1224	***The Wizard of Oz***	L. Frank Baum (A) Frank Gabrielson (Ad)	Birmingham Rep.	Nicky Adams Graeme Henderson Brian Hewlitt	Ian Forrest Lorelei Lynn (Ch)	
	Birmingham Rep. (Birmingham)					
A1225	***The Woman Destroyed***	Simone De Beauvoir		Diana Quick	Vanessa Fielding	Theatre Royal Presentations
	Cockpit Th. (London NW8) *Wolsey Theatre (Ipswich)*					
A1226	***The Woman In Black***	Susan Hill	Thorndike Theatre	Dominic Letts Richard Todd	Ian Kellgren	
	Thorndike Th. (Leatherhead)					
A1227	***The Woman In Black***	Steven Mallatratt	PW Productions Ltd	John Nettleton Patrick Toomey	Robin Herford	PW Productions Ltd
	Fortune Th. (London WC2)					
A1228	***Woman In Mind***	Alan Ayckbourn	Theatre Royal Windsor	Morag Hood Paul Jerricho Michael Stroud	Robin Herford	
	Th. Royal (Windsor, Berks)					
A1229	***A Woman Killed With Kindness***	Thomas Heywood	Royal Shakespeare Company	Sylvestra le Touzel Barry Lynch Saskia Reeves	Katie Mitchell	RSC
	Barbican/The Pit (London EC1)					
A1230	***A Woman Of No Importance***	Oscar Wilde	Royal Shakespeare Company	John Carlisle Cherry Morris Carol Royle	Philip Prowse	Duncan C Weldon
	Yvonne Arnaud (Guildford) *Lyceum Th. (Sheffield)* *Richmond Th. (Richmond)* *Th. Royal (Bath)* *Grand Th. (Leeds)* *Alexandra Th. (Birmingham)* *New Th. (Cardiff)* *Bristol Old Vic (Bristol)* *Th. Royal (Brighton)* *King's Th. (Glasgow)* *Haymarket (London SW1)*					
A1231	***A Woman Plays ...***	France Rame Dario Fo	Tell Us Theatre Company	Nadine Raeburn		
	Man in the Moon (London SW3)					
A1232	***The Woman Who Cooked Her Husband***	Debbie Isitt (PW,D)	Snarling Beasties	Debbie Isitt Mark Kilmurry Lucy Richardson		
	Haymarket Studio (Leicester) *Arts Centre (Birmingham)* *The Green Room (Manchester)* *Bluecoat Arts (Liverpool)* *Limelight Th (Aylesbury)* *Woughton Centre (Milton Keynes)* *Harlequin Th (Northwich)* *Old Museum Arts Centre (Belfast)* *Arches Th. (Glasgow)*					
A1233	***Women in Love***	D.H. Lawrence (A) Steve Chambers (Ad)	Derby Playhouse	Sarah Ball Mark Heal Thomasina Unsworth	Paul Clarkson	
	(Barton-Under-Needwood) *Derby Studio (Derby)* *College of H.E. (Derby)* *Tertiary College (Derby)* *Chellaston Coll (Derby)* *Venture Th (Ashby-de-la-Zouch)* *Melton Th. (Melton Mowbray)* *John Port Sch (Etwall)* *Highfields Sch (Matlock)* *Picture Palace (S.Normanton)* *Brewhouse Th. (Burton-on-Trent)* *Derby College (Ilkeston)* *Village Hall (Castle Donington)* *Q E Grammar Sch (Ashbourne)* *Barleston Ctre (Nuneaton)*					
A1234	***Women Laughing***	Michael Wall	Royal Exchange Theatre Company	Hetty Baynes Christopher Fulford Stephen Tompkinson	Richard Wilson	
	Royal Exchange (Manchester)					
A1235	***Women Laughing***	Michael Wall Bill Kenwright (AP)	Royal Court Theatre	Christopher Fulford John Michie Maggie O'Neill	Richard Wilson	Royal Court Theatre
	Th. Upstairs (London SW1)					
A1236	***Women Of The Dust***	Ruth Carter	Tamasha		Kristine Langdon-Smith	
	New Vic (Bristol) *Riverside Std. (London W6)*					

Ref	Play	Playwright	Theatre Co.	Starring	Director	Producer
A1237	***Women on Top*** *Gardner Arts Ctr (Brighton)*	David Bryer (PW,D)	The French Play Group			
A1238	***A Working Woman*** *W/Yorks Playh. (Leeds)*	Emile Zola (A) Stephen Wyatt (Ad)	West Yorkshire Playhouse Company	Lorcan Cranitch Kate Gartside Ewan Stewart	Jane Gibson Sue Lefton	
A1239	***Working*** *Library Th. (Manchester)*	Marvin Close	Library Theatre Company	Robert Calvert Kathryn Hunt	Chris Honer	
A1240	***A World Turned Upside Down*** *Theatre Centre (London N1)*	Devised By The Company	Hijinx Theatre Company	Molara Adesigbin Penny Green Sonia Hill	Sita Ramamurthy	
A1241	***A World Upon The Moon*** *The Theatre (Chipping Norton)* *Limelight Th (Aylesbury)* *The Menagerie (Northampton)* *State Music Room (Stowe, Bucks)*	Jeff Clarke (T,D) Josef Haydn	The English Players	Naomi Harvey Steven Newman David O'Brien		
A1242	***The Writing Game*** *Library Th. (Manchester)*	David Lodge	Library Theatre Company	David Ericsson Joanna Hole Lawrence Werber	Chris Honer	
A1243	***Wuthering Heights*** *Perth Th. (Perth)*	Emily Bronte Joan Knight (AD)	Perth Theatre Company		Ken Alexander	
A1244	***Wuthering Heights*** *Tabard Th. (London W4)*	Emily Bronte (A) Niall Whitehead (Ad)	Freelance Theatre Company		Damian Bermingham	
A1245	***The Year They Changed The Wires*** *ICA (London SW1)*	Steve Shill Graeme Miller		Graeme Miller Steve Shill		
A1246	***Yerma*** *New Vic (Bristol)*	Frederico Garcia Lorca	Bristol Old Vic Ensemble			
A1247	***York Cycle Of Mystery Plays*** *Theatre Royal (York)*	Liz Lochhead		Robson Green	Ian Forrest	
A1248	***You Must Be The Husband*** *Octagon (Yeovil)* *Devonshire Park Th. (Eastbourne)* *Th. Royal (Winchester)* *Th. Royal (Lincoln)* *Ashcroft Th. (Croydon)* *Wimbledon Th. (London SW19)* *Belgrade Th. (Coventry)* *Redgrave Th. (Farnham)* *Key Theatre (Peterborough)* *Palace Th. (Westcliff-On-Sea)*	Colin Bostock-Smith		Sue Holderness Jeffery Holland Carola Stewart	Ian Talbot Bryan Hands	Bryan Hands Productions Ltd
A1249	***The Young Man Of Cury*** *Polka Th. (London SW19)*		Kneehigh Theatre			
A1250	***Your Home In The West*** *Live Theatre (Newcastle/U/Tyne)*		Live Theatre Company	Robson Green Charlie Hardwick Pauline Moriarty		
A1251	***Yours Sincerely*** *Redgrave Th. (Farnham)*	Maggie Ollerenshaw (Ad)		Maggie Ollerenshaw	Kevin Robertson	
A1252	***Your Turn To Clean The Stairs*** *Traverse Th. (Edinburgh)* *Dundee Repertory (Dundee)*	Rona Munro	Traverse Theatre Company	Graham di Banzi Louise Ironside John Rammage		

Produced exclusively for Plays & Players by SEARCHLINE

PLAYERS

Here we have listed all the performers we are aware of, performing in the productions listed in the PLAYS LISTINGS. Use the cross-referencing to link plays and performers.

Name	Play	Part	Ref
Jackie **Abbey-Taylor**	Wizard of Oz	Aunt Em	A1223
Russ **Abbot**	Robin Hood	As Cast	A928
Gavin **Abbott**	Cyrano De Bergerac	A Cadet/Etc	A269
Geoffrey **Abbott**	The Beggar's Opera	Nimming Ned	A106
John **Abbott**	Revenger's Tragedy	The Duke	A909
Daniel **Abineri**	Rocky Horror Show	Brad	A933
Simon **Abkarian**	Les Atrides	As Cast	A609
Jacob **Abraham**	One The Ledge	As Cast	A821
Christine **Absalom**	Comedy of Errors	Abbess	A240
	Hobson's Choice	Mrs Hepworth	A500
	My Mother Said...	Margaret Bradley	A766
	Snow Queen	Old Woman	A1021
	Turkey Time	Mrs Gather	A1144
Sophy **Ackroyd**	Houdini	As Cast	A509
David **Acton**	All My Sons	George Deever	A32
	Caesar And Cleopatra	Lucius Septinius	A180
David **Adams**	Starlight Express	Wrench	A1043
Nicky **Adams**	Valentine's Day	Dolly	A1165
	Wizard of Oz	Dorothy Gale	A1224
Polly **Adams**	Pygmalion	Mrs Eynsford-Hill	A886
Sonia **Adams**	School for Scandal	Maria	A957
William **Adams**	Starlight Express	C.B.	A1043
Diane **Adderley**	Measure For Measure	Pompey	A702
Richard **Addison**	Relative Values	Crestwell	A899
Mark **Addy**	Office Party	Copywriter	A803
	Richard III	Richmond	A912
Antonia **Adellita**	Carmen Jones	Good Time Girl at Bar	A189
Susan **Aderin**	Flamingo	As Cast	A408
Molara **Adesigbin**	World...Upside Down	As Cast	A1240
John **Adewole**	Murmuring Judges	Second prisoner	A758
Benedicte **Adrian**	Which Witch	Maria Vittoria	A1200
Kay **Adshead**	Hindsight	Rachel	A495
Mike **Afford**	Candide	Dr Voltaire	A185
Francesca **Agati**	As You Like It	Phoebe	A70
Mark **Aiken**	Mansfield Park	Edmund	A683
	Porcelain	Voice IV	A871
Stephen **Aintree**	Buddy	Ensemble	A168
Sean **Aita**	Buddy	Dion	A169
Suzy **Aitchison**	Evening with Gary L.	Birgitta	A383
Mabel **Aitken**	Uncle Vanya	Sonya	A1158
Maria **Aitken**	Hay Fever	Judith Bliss	A481
Bola **Aiyeola**	Flamingo	As Cast	A408
Jude **Akuwudike**	Flamingo	As Cast	A408
	Necklaces	As Cast	A774
Lesley **Albiston**	Chasing The Hypnotist	As Cast	A201
Roger **Alborough**	Buddy	Highpockets Duncan	A169
Richard **Albrecht**	Three Girls In Blue	Nikolai Ivanovich	A1101
Gordon **Alcock**	The Kingfisher	Hawkins	A581
	Safe In Our Hands	Dougall	A947
	September In The Rain	Jack	A976
David **Alder**	The Card (A musical)	Shillitoe	A187
Zoe **Aldrich**	House of Bernarda Alba	As Cast	A515
Joseph **Alessi**	Comedy Of Errors	As Cast	A241
	Romeo and Juliet	Balthasar	A936
	A View From The Bridge	Tony	A1172
Mark **Alex-Jones**	Custer's Last Stand	Custer	A264
Lindy **Alexander**	Charlemagne	As Cast	A199
Maev **Alexander**	The Mousetrap	Molly Ralston	A744
	Television Programme	Jacky	A1080
Marva **Alexander**	A Midsummer Night's Dream	As Cast	A717
	Shadowlands	As Cast	A985
Peter **Alexander**	Imagine	George Martin	A530
Robert **Alexander**	Beyond Reasonable Doubt	Det. Chief Inspector Travers	A114
	Noises Off	Tim Allgood	A795
Sarah **Alexander**	Gaslight	Nancy	A429
Trevor **Alexander**	Beauty And The Beast	Coachman	A98
	Happy As A Sandbag	As Cast	A473
Roger **Allam**	Una Pooka	As Cast	A1156
Arhlene **Allan**	The Blue Angel	As Cast	A138
Peter **Allcorn**	Chorus of Disapproval	As Cast	A210
	Comedy of Errors	As Cast	A239
Brett **Allen**	Shout Across The River	As Cast	A997
Donald **Allen**	Androcles And The Lion		A45
James **Allen**	Fifteen Streets	John O'Brien	A403
	Moll Flanders	As Cast	A730
	On The Piste	Tony	A811
Keith **Allen**	Murmuring Judges	DC Barry Hopper	A758
Kevin **Allen**	Berlin Bertie	Sandy	A109
Sheila **Allen**	Medea	The Chorus	A704
Stuart **Allen**	Shame, Ignorance	One Man Show	A988
Tish **Allen**	Wit's End	Natalia Dmitrievna	A1216

Name	Play	Part	Ref
David **Allistair**	Awfully Big Adventure	Potter	A77
	Shadowlands	C.S.Lewis	A983
Jan **Alphonse**	Hot Italian Nights	Ensemble	A507
	The Magic Storybook	Ensemble	A672
	Much Ado About Nothing	Priest	A752
Andrew **Alston**	The Mousetrap	Giles Rawlston	A744
John **Altman**	Little Tramp	Tippy Gray/Others	A634
Jodie **Alvarado**	Miss Saigon	Tam	A727
Steven **Alvey**	Office Party	Copywriter	A803
Johnny **Amobi**	Five Guys Named Moe	Eat Moe	A407
Emma **Amos**	The Fastest Clock...	Sherbet Gravel	A398
Janet **Amsden**	Dead Soil	Mother/Electric Coil Fitter	A290
Bruce **Anderson**	Macbeth	As Cast	A655
	The Tempest	As Cast	A1082
Douglas **Anderson**	Some Like It Hot	Lt.O'Malley	A1025
Helen **Anderson**	Hecuba	Chorus	A488
Mark **Anderson**	Death Of A Salesman	Howard Wagner	A297
	Ghost Sonata	Colonel	A431
	Time Windows	Patrick	A1113
Tracey **Anderson**	Heart	As Cast	A485
Adjoa **Andoh**	Cloud 9	Ellen	A232
Doreen **Andrew**	The Ballroom	As Cast	A1091
Iain **Andrew**	Cuttin' A Rug	Terry	A266
Kenny **Andrews**	Five Guys Named Moe	Big Moe	A407
Mac **Andrews**	Hostages and Hamsters	Raoul	A506
	Lady Macbeth	As Cast	A595
	Over a Barrel	Ian	A840
Simeon **Andrews**	Measure For Measure	Angelo	A702
Kerry **Angus**	Barnstormers	Jane/Lady Tyreonnel/Mrs	A92
Tony **Anholt**	Death and the Maiden	Roberto	A294
	Private Lives	Elyot	A880
Nikki **Ankara**	Miss Saigon	Ellen	A727
Helen **Anker**	Radio Times	As Cast	A890
Adam **Annand**	The Lie Of The Land	As Cast	A617
David **Annen**	Man, Beast and Virtue	Toto	A682
Francesca **Annis**	Rosmersholm	Rebbeka West	A939
	Sienna Red	Cecelia	A999
Paul **Ansdell**	Savage Storm	As Cast	A952
Mark **Anstee**	Liaisons Dangereuses	Le Chevalier Danceny	A610
Ignatius **Anthony**	Fuente Ovejuna	Man	A422
Philip **Anthony**	Shadowlands	C.S. Lewis	A984
Wayne **Anthony-Cole**	Buddy	Ensemble	A169
Carl **Antony**	Strange Domain	Francois	A1055
Annabelle **Apsion**	Anna Karenina	Anna Karenina	A50
	Richard III	Lady Anne	A910
Yacoub **Arafeh**	Gulf Between Us	Ancient	A462
Annabel **Arden**	Street of Crocodiles	The Mother	A1056
Jane **Arden**	Private Lives	Sybil Chase	A881
Kate **Arden**	Bedroom Farce	Kate	A104
Mark **Arden**	Comedy of Errors	Antipholous	A239
	What The Butler Saw	Dr Prentice	A1196
James **Arlon**	King Lear In New York	TV Crew:Camera	A580
Tony **Armatrading**	Dragon	As Cast	A341
	Goin' Local	Pete	A442
Richard **Armitage**	Annie Get Your Gun	Ensemble	A51
Charles **Armstrong**	Provoked Wife	Heartfree	A884
Gareth **Armstrong**	Cerceau	Vladimir Ivanovitch	A195
Julie **Armstrong**	Merrily We Roll Along	As Cast	A711
Robert **Armstrong**	Annie Get Your Gun	Ensemble	A51
Simon **Armstrong**	Three Musketeers	Porthos	A1106
	To Kill A Mockingbird	Mr. Cunningham	A1121
William **Armstrong**	The Miser	Cleante	A724
Brierley **Arnell**	From A Jack To A King	Evilynne Gore	A420
Kate **Arnell**	Moll Flanders	As Cast	A730
Isobel **Arnett**	Dick Whittington	Tommy The Cat	A309
Debbie **Arnold**	Bazaar and Rummage	Katrina	A94
Jenny **Arnold**	Chitty Bang Bang	The Baroness	A208
Robert **Arnold**	As You Like It	Duke Senior	A69
Ruth **Arnold**	Gone With The Wind II	Melanie	A445
	Valentine	As Cast	A1166
Gerardine **Arthur**	Beauty And The Beast	Fairy Queen of the Roses	A98
	La Voix Humaine	The Woman	A591
	Mamahuhu?	As Cast	A678
John **Arthur**	Absurd Person Singular	As Cast	A11
	Wicked Old Man	Leo	A1207
Robin **Arthur**	Emanuelle Enchanted	As Cast	A363
Rod **Arthur**	Aladdin Bolton	Dame	A27
Ashley **Artus**	Wizard of Oz	Scarecrow	A1223
Jonathan **Arun**	Elegies...	As Cast	A358
	Philadelphia Here I Come	Public Gar	A856
Karen **Ascoe**	Loot	Fay	A637
Allison **Ash**	The Pope And The Witch	Claudia	A870
Elizabeth **Ash**	Tess Of The D'Urbervil	Rettie	A1089
Lorraine **Ashbourne**	Three Girls In Blue	Tatyana	A1101
Jane **Ashby**	Death of A Salesman	As Cast	A295
	Grease	As Char	A458
John **Ashby**	From A Jack To A King	Len Knox	A420
Kate **Ashby**	Grand Hotel	Operator/The Courtesan	A453
Robert **Ashby**	Blithe Spirit	As Cast	A125
	Far From The Madding Crowd	Farmer Boldwood	A397
Harriette **Ashcroft**	Taste of Honey	Jo	A1074
	Tess Of The D'Urbervil	Izzy	A1089
Will **Ashcroft**	Rivals	Fag	A920
Niall **Ashdown**	Evening with Gary L.	Gary Lineker	A383
Robert **Ashe**	Buddy	Highpockets Duncan	A168
Rosemary **Ashe**	Les Miserables	Madame Thenardier	A613
	What About Luv?	As Cast	A1195
Jane **Asher**	Making It Better	Diana Harrington	A677
Sally **Ashfield**	Phantom Of The Opera	Ballet Swing	A854
David **Ashley**	Starlight Express	Bobo	A1043
Jonathan **Ashley**	Arms and the Man	The Russian Officer	A60
Lorraine **Ashley**	Massa	Sarah	A692
John **Ashton**	Provoked Wife	Sir John Brute	A884
	Slice of Saturday	As Cast	A1014
Pat **Ashton**	Beauty And The Beast	Dressalinda	A98
Richard **Ashton**	Giraffe, Pelly, & Me	The Giraffe	A436
Steve **Ashton**	The Road	Murano	A921
Ian **Aspinall**	Cloud 9	Joshua	A232
George **Asprey**	The Sound Of Music	Rolf Gruber	A1033
Colin **Atkins**	Martin Chuzzlewit	Multiple Roles	A689
	A View From The Bridge	Mike	A1171
Eileen **Atkins**	Night of the Iguana	Hannah Jelkes	A785
	Vita and Virginia	Virginia Woolf	A1177
Jon **Atkins**	Merchant Of Venice	Salerio	A707
	Taming of the Shrew	Gremio	A1069

Name	Play	Part	Ref
	Wizard of Oz	Uncle Henry	A1222
Helen **Atkinson Wood**	What The Butler Saw	Mrs Prentice	A1196
Michael **Atkinson**	Blood Brothers	Policeman/Teacher	A131
Edward **Atterton**	Les Miserables	As Cast	A612
Richard **Attlee**	Gormenghast	Steerpike	A451
Geof **Atwell**	King Lear	Gloucester	A578
James **Auden**	Twelfth Night	Antonio	A1151
Katherine **Aughton**	Blodeuwedd	As Cast	A129
Hope **Augusta**	Moby Dick	As Cast	A728
Robert **Austin**	The Chalk Garden	Maitland	A196
Stephen **Austin**	Biko	Policeman	A121
Jack **Auten**	Revenger's Tragedy	Piero	A909
Jonathan **Avery**	Some...Atomic Zombie		A1027
Paul **Aves**	As You Like It	Le Beau	A71
	Lady Be Good	Removal Man	A594
	A Midsummer Night's ..	Philostrate	A721
Diane **Axford**	Bazaar and Rummage	W.P.C.	A94
John **Axon**	The Recruiting Officer	Thomas Appletree	A897
Sophy **Ayckroyd**	Barnstormers	Molly Maklin	A92
Miguel **Ayesa**	Buddy	Ritchie Valens	A169
Rakie **Ayola**	Merchant Of Venice	Portia	A707
Roger **Ayres**	Dracula Spectacular	Father O'Stake Lamdau	A340
Rosalind **Ayres**	Just Between Ourselves	Pam	A569
Daryl **Back**	Monday After Miracle	Helen Keller	A733
Joanna **Bacon**	Gaslight	Elizabeth	A429
	Television Programme	Caroline	A1080
Paul **Bacon**	The Mousetrap	Mr Paravicini	A744
John **Baddeley**	Leo In Love	Monsieur Pince	A607
Sarah **Badel**	Leo In Love	Marie-Therese	A607
Annette **Badland**	Little Voice	Sadie	A917
Bhageerathi **Bagi**	Heer Ranjha	As Cast	A489
Liz **Bagley**	Double Double	Phillipa James	A337
	Out Of Order	Jane Worthington	A835
Harriet **Bagnall**	Voysey Inheritance	Mrs Hugh Voysey	A1182
Anthony **Bailey**	Monday After Miracle	Ed	A733
Marion **Bailey**	Bad Blood	Mother	A85
	Hush	As Cast	A522
Robin **Bailey**	Night of the Iguana	Jonathan Coffin (Nonno)	A785
	Pygmalion	Col. Pickering	A886
	Trelawny Of The Wells	Sir William Gower	A1138
Rosalind **Bailey**	Cain	Angel	A181
	King Lear In New York	Celia	A580
Peter **Bailie**	Gormenghast	Titus	A451
Allister **Bain**	Turner's Crossing	Priest	A1146
Angela **Bain**	Cherry Orchard	Dunyasha	A202
	Dangerous Corner	As Cast	A277
	Lettice & Lovage	Miss Framer	A614
	Teechers	As Cast	A1078
	Wizard of Oz	As Cast	A1224
Imogen **Bain**	Night of the Iguana	Hilda	A785
	The Sea	Rachel	A961
Sherry **Baines**	New World and Tears	Dalifa/Mareama Imagination	A780
Josephine **Baird**	Beauty And The Beast	Beauty	A98
Colin **Baker**	Death and the Maiden	Gerardo	A294
	Frankie & Johnny	Johnny	A417
Gregg **Baker**	Carmen Jones	Husky Miller	A189
Paul **Baker**	Les Miserables	Joly	A611
Sean **Baker**	Macbeth	Banquo	A655
	The Tempest	Stephano	A1082
Kenny **Baker-Brown**	King Lear In New York	TV Crew:Sound/Drug Dealer	A580
	Measure For Measure	Provost	A702
Belinda-Jayne **Baldwin**	Wind In The Willows	Tommy	A1211
James **Baldwin**	Giraffe, Pelly, & Me	Billy	A436
Carol **Ball**	42nd Street	As cast	A2
Julien **Ball**	Porcelain	Voice III	A871
Sarah **Ball**	Elephant	As Cast	A359
	Women in Love	Ursula	A1233
Sheila **Ballantine**	Caesar And Cleopatra	Ftatateeta	A180
	Frightened Lady	As Cast	A192
Robert **Ballard**	The Three Musketeers	Porthos	A1104
Michelle **Ballentyne**	Starlight Express	Buffy	A1043
Andrew **Ballington**	Peter Pan	Peter Pan	A852
	The Recruiting Officer	Costar Pearmain	A896
Julie **Balloo**	Dangerous Dolls-Soap Crazy	Lisa	A280
David **Bamber**	Karate Billy...Home	As Cast	A572
	Schippel, The Plumber	Hikerte	A954
Joshua **Bancel**	Carmen Jones	Corporal Morrel	A189
Elaine **Banham**	Home At Seven	As Cast	A502
Teresa **Banham**	Measure For Measure	Mariana	A700
	Valentine's Day	Gloria	A1165
Christopher **Banks**	Kafka's Dick	Father	A571
David **Banks**	The Late Edwina Black	Gregory Black	A599
Elizabeth **Banks**	Valdorama		A1164
Geoffrey **Banks**	And A Nightingale Sang	Andie	A43
Greg **Banks**	Laurel and Hardy	As Cast	A603
Ian **Bannen**	All My Sons	Joe Keller	A33
David **Bannerman**	Double Double	Duncan McFee	A337
Mark **Bannister**	Life is a Dream	Astolfo	A619
Tony **Bannister**	Voices at Her Elbow	As Cast	A1180
Trevor **Bannister**	Run for Your Wife	As Cast	A944
	Stageland	Jerome K. Jerome	A1041
Gajit **Bansall**	Elegies...	As Cast	A358
Jane **Baptista**	Miss Saigon	Bar Girl	A727
Jeff **Baptista**	Starlight Express	As Cast	A1043
Attlee **Baptiste**	Starlight Express	As Cast	A1043
Marianne **Jean Baptiste**	A Working Woman	Mme Lorilleaux	A1238
Jimmy **Barba**	A Midsummer Night's ..	Lord/Fairy Lord	A720
Frances **Barber**	Night of the Iguana	Maxine Faulk	A785
	Pygmalion	Eliza Doolittle	A886
Neville **Barber**	In Praise Of Love		A536
Paul **Barber**	Goin' Local	Rafty	A442
Anthony **Barclay**	Assassins	As Cast	A73
	In The Midnight Hour	Cliff	A538
Linda **Bardell**	Stepping Out	Dorothy	A1046
Nigel **Barden**	Blood Wedding	The Bride's Father	A133
	Bloody Poetry	Polidori	A137
Paula **Bardowell**	House Of The Spirits		A514
David **Bardsley**	Blood Brothers	Mickey	A131
Gillian **Barge**	Pygmalion	Mrs Higgins	A886
	Square Rounds	As Cast	A1038
David **Bark-Jones**	Macbeth	As Cast	A657
Eve **Barker**	Rocky Horror Show	Phantom	A933
Judith **Barker**	The Card (A musical)	Mrs Machin	A187
	Happy Families	Dot Taylor	A476
Katherine **Barker**	The Snow Queen	As Cast	A1020
Tim **Barker**	Cabal and Love	Mr Miller	A176
	Grapes of Wrath	Grampa	A454

Name	Play	Part	Ref
Peter **Barkworth**	Mystery Plays	God	A771
Eric **Barlow**	Beauty And The Beast	Dunt/Lord Beastiebasher	A97
	Taming Of The Shrew	Vincentio	A1070
Tim **Barlow**	Gamblers	Glob (father)	A424
Marc **Barnaud**	Les Atrides	As Cast	A609
Barbara **Barnes**	Blues for Mr Charlie	Jo Britten	A143
Chris **Barnes**	Coriolanus	As Cast	A248
Michael **Barnes**	Beyond Reasonable Doubt	Sir David Metcalfe Q.C.	A113
Angus **Barnett**	Doll's House	Dr Rank	A320
Mick **Barnfather**	The End Of The Tunnel	As Cast	A365
Lynda **Baron**	Water Music	Milly	A1188
Ian **Barr**	Phantom of the Opera	Ensemble	A853
John **Barr**	In The Midnight Hour	Cliff	A537
Roy **Barraclough**	Feed	Harry Troop	A399
	The Writing Game	Voice On Telephone	A1242
Dave **Barrass**	TO	Various	A1118
	Up 'N' Under	As Cast	A1163
Martin **Barrass**	Babes in the Wood	As Cast	A80
	Up 'N' Under	As Cast	A1163
Brent **Barrett**	Grand Hotel	The Baron	A453
Catherine **Barrett**	Beardsley	Ada Leverson	A95
Ian **Barrett**	Relative Values	Sir Peter	A899
Lydia **Barrett**	Aspects Of Love	Alex's Date	A72
Venetia **Barrett**	Relative Values	Felicity	A899
Constance **Barrie**	Noises Off	Poppy Norton-Taylor	A794
Chris **Barrit**	The Heiress	Arthur Townsend	A490
Desmond **Barrit**	Comedy Of Errors	Antipholus	A241
	The Recruiting Officer	Captain Brazen	A896
	Wind In The Willows	Toad	A1211
Bob **Barritt**	Cyrano De Bergerac	A Cadet/Etc	A269
Jacqueline **Barron**	Phantom of the Opera	Ensemble	A853
James **Barron**	Leonardo	Francesco	A608
John **Barron**	Witness For The Prosecution	Sir Wilfrid	A1218
Tim **Barron**	Forbidden Planet	Captain Tempest	A904
John **Barrowman**	Phantom Of The Opera	Raoul Vicomte de Chagny	A854
Anna **Barry**	My Sister Next Door	Anthea/Gwen	A769
David **Barry**	Home At Seven	As Cast	A502
Michael **Barrymore**	Aladdin	Wishee Washee	A20
Louis **Barson**	Wind In The Willows	Billy	A1211
Ian **Bartholomew**	Radio Times	Wilf	A890
Keith **Bartlett**	Murmuring Judges	PC Dave Lawrence	A758
Nick **Bartlett**	House Of The Spirits		A514
Richard **Bartlett**	Chorus of Disapproval	Guy Jones	A210
Wren **Bartok**	Cats	Jellylorum	A194
Suzy **Barton**	Barnum	As Cast	A93
Will **Barton**	Man Outside	Corporal Beckmann	A681
Linda **Bassett**	Artists and Admirers	Domna	A64
	Henry IV Part 1	Mistress Quickly	A492
	Henry IV Part 2	Mistress Quickly	A493
	The Thebans	Ismene	A1095
Alexandra **Bastedo**	Venus Observed	As Cast	A1168
Yolande **Bastide**	The Lie Of The Land	As Cast	A617
Ben **Batchelor**	Chitty Bang Bang	The Toymaker	A208
Simon **Bate**	A Hard Heart	The Century	A477
Anthony **Bateman**	Beauty And The Beast	John Quill	A98
Alan **Bates**	Stages	Richard Fenchurch	A1042
Timothy **Bateson**	Hamlet	Gravedigger	A465

Name	Play	Part	Ref
Robert **Bathurst**	The Choice	As Cast	A209
David **Battcock**	Man Outside	Alter Ego	A681
Fiona **Battersby**	Elisabeth II	As Cast	A361
Jill **Batty**	Same Time Next Year	Doris	A951
Phil **Batty**	Aladdin	As Cast	A22
Eileen **Battye**	Valentine's Day	Martha	A1165
David **Bauckham**	Caesar And Cleopatra	Centurion	A180
	Thirteenth Night	As Cast	A1099
Michael **Bauer**	Phantom Of The Opera	Monsieur Firmin	A854
Lilo **Baur**	Street of Crocodiles	Adela	A1056
	The Winter's Tale	Perdita	A1215
Helen **Baxendale**	Dangerous Corner	Betty Whitehouse	A277
	Pelican	As Cast	A847
	Summer Lightning	Sue Brown	A1058
Becky **Baxter**	Country Dance		A251
John **Baxter**	Lulu	Schwarz	A648
Lois **Baxter**	Awfully Big Adventure	Dotty	A77
	Entertaining Mr Sloane	Kath	A373
Luke **Baxter**	Cats	Mr Mistoffolees	A194
	Miss Saigon	Marine	A727
Susie **Baxter**	Absurd Person Singular	As Cast	A11
	The Pope And The Witch	Sister Gabriella	A870
Trevor **Baxter**	Game of Love & Chance	As Cast	A425
Nick **Bayley**	Charley's Aunt	Brasset	A200
Sarah **Bayliss**	Barnum	As Cast	A93
Hetty **Baynes**	Women Laughing	Maddy	A1234
Carolyn **Bazely**	Merchant of Venice	Jessica	A708
Robert **Beach**	Too Much Too Young	As Cast	A1127
Lee **Beagley**	King Lear	King Lear	A578
	Threepenny Story	Inspector Lock	A1108
	A View From The Bridge	Eddie	A1169
Richard **Beale**	A Dead Secret	Pa Dyson	A289
Simon **Russell Beale**	Richard III	Richard III	A910
Oliver **Beamish**	Candide	Governor	A185
	Imagine	Neil	A530
	Julius Caesar	Mark Antony	A564
	The Night Before The Morning After		A782
	The Threepenny Opera	Matt Of The Mint	A1109
Stephen **Beard**	Bourgeois Gentilhomme	Music Master	A153
	La Bete	Rene Du Parc	A587
	A Midsummer Night's Dream	Quince	A718
Tom **Beard**	Becket	4th Baron	A103
Norman **Beaton**	Viva Detroit	Doc	A1178
Adrian **Beaumont**	Robin	Will Scarlet	A927
Christopher **Beaumont**	Forbidden Planet	Petty Officer Ray Gunn	A904
Debra **Beaumont**	Leo In Love	Lucienne	A607
Christopher **Beck**	As You Like It	Amiens	A69
Sonia **Beck**	Macbeth	Witch	A653
Stephen **Beckett**	Beyond Reasonable Doubt	Mr Cole	A113
	The Winslow Boy	Dickie Winslow	A1213
Maggie **Beckit**	Aba Daba Music Hall	Various	A6
	Gone With The Wind II	Mammie/Prissie	A445
	Put That Light Out	Various	A885
	Valentine	As Cast	A1166
Philip **Beckwith**	Chitty Bang Bang	Grandfather	A208
Stefan **Bednarczyk**	Between the Lines	Ensemble	A112
	Game of Love & Chance	As Cast	A425
	Playing Sinatra	Phillip	A864

Name	Play	Part	Ref
Gwynn **Beech**	Serve Them All My Days	David	A1123
Christopher **Beeny**	Bedroom Farce	Nick	A104
Olivier **Louis Beer**	Story of the Last	Various	A1053
Oona **Beeson**	Great God Brown	Margaret	A459
Geoffrey **Beevers**	Karate Billy...Home	As Cast	A572
Bronwen **Belcher**	Doll's House	Helen	A323
Emile **Belcourt**	A Judgement In Stone	George	A563
Duncan **Bell**	Bourgeois Gentilhomme	Dorante	A153
Elizabeth **Bell**	Don't Dress For Dinner	Jacqueline	A331
	Medea	The Chorus	A704
Michael **Bell**	Elegies...	As Cast	A358
	Giraffe, Pelly, & Me	Walter/Duke	A436
Tony **Bell**	Barnstormers	Cambell	A92
Charlotte **Bellamy**	The Double D	As Cast	A333
Duccio **Bellugi**	Les Atrides	As Cast	A609
Kate **Belshaw**	Seagull	Mary	A963
Nikki **Belsher**	Carousel	As Cast	A190
Simone **Bendix**	Importance of Being	Gwendolen	A532
Claire **Benedict**	Antony and Cleopatra	Charmian	A53
	The Odyssey	Eurycleia	A802
	Tamburlaine The Great	Zenocrate	A1067
Jill **Benedict**	Ten Times Table	Helen	A1087
Christopher **Benjamin**	Artists and Admirers	The Prince	A64
	Columbus	Martin	A237
	The Virtuoso	Sir Nicholas Gimcrack	A1176
Stewart **Bennet**	Rocky Horror Show	Riff Raff	A933
Alan **Bennett**	Talking Heads	Graham	A1066
Darren **Bennett**	Hot Stuff	As Cast	A508
	Night Must Fall	Dan	A784
Fleur **Bennett**	My Cousin Rachel	Louise Kendall	A762
Helen **Bennett**	Stepping Out	Sylvia	A1046
Jeremy **Bennett**	Home At Seven	As Cast	A502
John **Bennett**	Love's Labour's Lost	Boyet	A645
Pamela **Bennett**	Hecuba	Chorus	A488
Steve **Bennett**	Three Musketeers	Benajoux	A1106
	To Kill A Mockingbird	Jem	A1121
Tracie **Bennett**	She Stoops To Conquer	As Cast	A991
Allan **Bennion**	Becket	Bishop of Oxford	A103
	Life is a Dream	Clotaldo	A619
Holly **Bennion**	Doll's House	Eva	A322
Ishia **Bennison**	Les Miserables	As Cast	A612
	Richard III	Elizabeth	A912
Christopher **Benny**	Run for Your Wife	As Cast	A944
Jon **Benoit**	Jolly Potters	As Cast	A557
Jon **Benolt**	Comedy of Errors	Angelo	A240
Harriet **Benson**	Radio Times	Amy	A890
Michael **Benson**	Down And Out...	Henri	A339
Sharon **Benson**	Carmen Jones	Carmen Jones	A189
Lorren **Bent**	Leave Taking	Viv	A605
Stephen **Bent**	Building Blocks	Piper	A170
	Richard III	Hastings	A912
Paul **Bentall**	Acapulco	As Cast	A12
Timothy **Bentinck**	A Doll's House	Torvald	A324
Marcus **Bentley**	Death Of A Salesman	Stanley	A297
Paul **Bentley**	Aspects Of Love	Marcel Richard	A72
	Assassins	As Cast	A73
Simon **Beresford**	The English Kiss	Young Man	A370
	The Golden Ass	Lucius	A443
Sarah **Berger**	The Baby	Helen	A82
	The Invisible Man	Miss Statchell	A547
Ron **Berglas**	Lost in Yonkers	As Cast	A641

Name	Play	Part	Ref
	Me And Mamie O'Rourke	David	A696
Steven **Berkoff**	Acapulco	As Cast	A12
John **Berlyne**	Twelfth Night	Valentine	A1148
	Valentine's Day	Bohun	A1165
Djola **Bernard Branner**	Fierce Love	As Cast	A402
Michael **Bernardin**	Understanding The Dang	As Cast	A1161
Martina **Berne**	Blood Wedding	The Bridegroom's Mother	A133
Diana **Berriman**	Liaisons Dangereuses	Madame de Volanges	A610
Elizabeth **Berrington**	An Ideal Husband	Lady Basildon	A528
Adrian **Berry**	Endgame	As Cast	A368
Caroline **Berry**	The Devils	Philippe	A304
Michael **Bertenshaw**	The Last Carnival	Oswald	A598
	The Rivals	Sir Lucius O'Trigger	A918
Oona **Besson**	Peculiar People	Elizabeth Carter	A846
Anthony **Best**	The Seagull	Medvedenko	A962
Antonia **Best**	Grope	Fanny Trump	A460
Samantha **Best**	The Thin Soldier	As Cast	A1098
Paul **Besterman**	Revenger's Tragedy	Ambitioso	A909
John **Bett**	School For Wives	Arnold	A958
Thane **Bettany**	A Doll's House	Dr Rank	A324
	On Golden Pond	Norman	A809
Nigel **Betts**	Blue Remembered Hills	Peter	A139
	Epsom Downs	Charles	A375
	Fuente Ovejuna	Mengo	A423
	Romeo and Juliet	Montague	A935
Gillian **Bevan**	In The Midnight Hour	Roxy	A538
Lucy **Bevan**	Pelican	As Cast	A847
Sophie **Bevan**	Blithe Spirit	Mrs Bradman	A128
	The Hostage	Miss Gilchrist	A505
	Macbeth	Weird Sister Porter	A661
Amanda **Beveridge**	Little Shop Of Horrors	Derelict	A632
	Wasting Reality	Sister	A1186
Kimberly **Bevers**	Games	As Cast	A426
Rodney **Bewes**	Awfully Big Adventure	Uncle Vernon	A77
Yogesh **Bhatt**	Heer Ranjha	As Cast	A489
	The Little Clay Cart	The Goddess Parvati	A627
Paul **Bhattacharjee**	Murmuring Judges	DC Abdul "Jimmy"Khan	A758
Ahsen **Bhatti**	Necklaces	As Cast	A774
Graham **Bickley**	Les Miserables	Enjolras	A613
Samantha **Biddulph**	Cats	The Cats' Chorus	A194
	Starlight Express	Wrench	A1043
Georges **Bigot**	Les Atrides	As Cast	A609
Jo **Bingham**	Cats	Etcetera	A194
Roger **Bingham**	Pygmalion	Butler	A886
Mari **Binnie**	A Little Older	Isla	A631
	MacWizard Fae Oz	As Cast	A663
Peter **Birch**	On The Piste	Tony Muller	A812
Jeffrey **Bird**	The English Kiss	Jake	A370
	Spring Awakening	Ernst/Dieter/Prof. Gutgrinder	A1037
Philip **Bird**	Good Rockin' Tonite	Jack Good	A449
Timothy **Birkett**	Macbeth	As Cast	A660
Nick **Birkinshaw**	King Lear	Kent	A578
Peter **Birrel**	Beyond Reasonable Doubt	Lionel Hamilton	A113
	Monster He Made Me	Pirandello	A734

Name	Play	Part	Ref
David **Birrell**	Hamlet	As Cast	A466
	Romeo And Juliet	Balthasar	A938
Debby **Bishop**	The Cotton Club	Dinah Andrews	A250
Diana **Bishop**	Aba Daba Music Hall	Various	A6
Peter **Bishop**	Joseph...	Asher	A559
Sarah **Bishop**	Bloody Poetry	Claire Clairemont	A137
Simon **Bishop**	Joseph...	Judah	A559
Jennifer **Black**	House Among the Stars	Victoire	A512
Joe **Black**	Dick Whittington	Sarah The Cook	A308
Nicola **Blackman**	Barnum	Joice Heth	A93
Doreene **Blackstock**	Leave Taking	Del	A605
Paul **Blackwell**	Strange Domain	Delouche	A1055
Tilly **Blackwood**	Anna Karenina	Dolly	A50
	Trilby & Svengali	Trilby	A1141
Robin **Blades**	Roberto Calvi	As Cast	A926
Kristen **Blaikie**	Buddy	Vi Petty	A168
	The Mikado	Maid	A722
Andrew **Blair**	Barnstormers	Howard Lowes	A92
	Haunted Hotel	Gerald Ivor	A479
Isla **Blair**	Mad,Bad,And Dangerous	Women	A665
Lionel **Blair**	Cinderella	Buttons	A221
Basienka **Blake**	Buddy	Maria Elena	A168
	Old Times	Anna	A806
Christopher **Blake**	Something's Burning	George	A1029
Clinton **Blake**	Flamingo	As Cast	A408
Josephine **Blake**	Aladdin	The Empress	A26
	Dead Flamingo Dancer	As Cast	A193
Peter **Blake**	Alfie	As Cast	A29
	Rocky Horror Show	Frank N Furter	A933
Susie **Blake**	Absent Friends	Diana	A8
Vicky **Blake**	Cinderella	Cinderella	A226
David **Blake-Kelly**	Trouble in Mind	Henry	A1142
Cameron **Blakely**	School for Scandal	William Joseph Surface's Servant	A957
Madeline **Blakeney**	A Better Day	Lillie	A111
	Self Portrait	Nun	A974
Caroline **Blakiston**	Turner's Crossing	Maggie	A1146
Julia **Blalock**	1953	Princess Ira	A1
	June Moon	As Cast	A567
	Pelican	As Cast	A847
Nicholas **Blane**	Single Spies	Guy Burgess/Chubb	A1005
Adam **Blang**	Barnum	As Cast	A93
Helen **Blatch**	Romeo And Juliet	Lady Montague	A938
Mary **Blatchford**	Stepping Out	Mrs Fraser	A1046
Julian **Bleach**	Cherry Orchard	Trofimov	A202
	Macbeth	Macbeth	A658
Nikki **Blesher**	Slice Of Saturday...	Sue	A1015
Brenda **Blethyn**	An Ideal Husband	Mrs Cheveley	A528
Caroline **Bliss**	Blood Brothers	Mrs Lyons	A130
	Blue Remembered Hills	Angela	A139
	Fuente Ovejuna	Juan Rojo	A423
	Romeo and Juliet	Nurse	A935
Philip **Bliss**	Ay Carmela!		A78
Tim **Block**	The Maintenance Man	Bob	A674
Ian **Blower**	Cinderella	Ugly Sister Donna	A226
Colin **Blumenau**	Driving Miss Daisy	Boolie	A345
Tony **Bluto**	Gamblers	Gabriel	A424
Benedick **Blythe**	EuroVision	Hadrian	A381
Mark **Blythe**	Witness For The Prosecution	Warder	A1218
Peter **Blythe**	Voysey Inheritance	Major Booth	A1182
Jacqui **Boatswain**	Sophisticated Ladies	Ensemble	A1032

Name	Play	Part	Ref
Jean **Boht**	She Stoops To Conquer	Mrs Hardcastle	A992
	Venus Observed	As Cast	A1168
James **Bolam**	Fighting For The Dunghill	Gillray	A404
Andrew **Bolton**	Annie Get Your Gun	Waiter	A51
	A Better Day	As Cast	A111
David **Bond**	Blue Remembered Hills	John	A139
	Epsom Downs	Spt. Blue	A375
	Fuente Ovejuna	Sergeant Ortuno	A423
	Kvetch	George	A586
	Romeo and Juliet	Friar Lawrence	A935
Gary **Bond**	Absent Friends	Colin	A8
Samantha **Bond**	As You Like It	Rosalind	A67
	The Merry Wives Of Windsor	Mistress Ford	A713
	The Winter's Tale	Hermione	A1214
Ken **Bones**	As You Like It	Oliver	A71
	Becket	1st Baron	A103
	A Midsummer Night's ..	Oberon	A721
Helena **Bonham-Carter**	The Barber Of Seville	Rosine	A89
	Trelawny Of The Wells	Imogen Parrott	A1139
Yvonne **Bonnamy**	Mansfield Park	Mrs Norris	A683
Suzanne **Bonnar**	Every Bit Of It	Cathy	A385
Mary **Bonner**	And Hunger For All		A44
Richard **Bonneville**	The Alchemist	Surly	A28
	Amphibians	Brian	A40
	Hamlet	Laertes	A466
	'Tis Pity She's A Whore	Bergetto	A1114
	Two Gents Of Verona	Valentine	A1154
	The Virtuoso	Sir Samuel Hearty	A1176
Clare **Bonnin**	Massa	As Cast	A692
Carolyn **Bonnyman**	Fantasy Island		A396
Clare **Bonsu**	Blues Brothers	A Bluette	A142
Steven **Book**	King Lear	Edmund	A578
	Threepenny Story	Black Jack	A1108
	A View From The Bridge	Marco	A1169
Roger **Booth**	A Dolls House	Dr Rank	A321
	Importance of Being	Lane	A532
Terence **Booth**	Time Of My Life	As Cast	A1112
Jess **Borgeson**	The Complete Works	Various	A245
Arthur **Bostrom**	'Allo,'Allo	Crabtree	A36
John **Boswall**	Bourgeois Gentilhomme	Valet	A153
Stephen **Boswell**	Wizard of Oz	Uncle Henry	A1224
Ian **Botham**	Jack And The Beanstalk	The King	A553
John **Bott**	As You Like It	Corin	A67
	The Winter's Tale	Archidamus	A1214
Paula **Bott**	Phantom Of The Opera	Innkeeper's Wife	A854
Michael **Bottle**	Outside Edge	Dennis	A837
	Three Musketeers	Bonancieux	A1106
	To Kill A Mockingbird	Bob Ewell	A1121
Xavier **Boulanger**	Mowgli - Enfant Loup	Baloo	A745
Patti **Boulaye**	Blues In The Night	The Woman	A144
	Carmen Jones	Carmen Jones	A189
Mynam **Boullay**	Les Atrides	As Cast	A609
Peter **Bourke**	Bedroom Farce	Malcolm	A104
Alex **Bourne**	Buddy	Ensemble	A169
Bette **Bourne**	As You Like It	Jaques	A71
Sally **Bourne**	My Fair Lady	Bystander	A763
Brian **Bovell**	Armed And Dangerous	As Cast	A59
Mark **Bowden**	Six Degrees...	Hustler	A1008
Nigel **Bowden**	Indigo Mill	As Cast	A539

Name	Play	Part	Ref
David **Bowen**	Hound	Vince	A510
	Snow Queen	Baa	A1021
	Turkey Time	Warwick Westbourne	A1144
Mark **Bower**	The Sound Of Music	Ensemble	A1033
Robin **Bowerman**	Fallen Angels	Willy Banbury	A391
	Self Portrait	Jacques Maritain	A974
	Tess Of The D'Urbervil	John Durbeyfield	A1089
Raymond **Bowers**	Comedy Of Errors	As Cast	A241
Darrell **Bowlby**	Ladies' Night	As Cast	A592
Peter **Bowles**	Otherwise Engaged	Simon Hench	A830
Tom **Bowles**	As You Like It	Touchstone	A68
Robert **Bowman**	Crackwalker	Alan	A256
	An Inspector Calls	Eric Birling	A541
Simon **Bowman**	Miss Saigon	Chris	A727
Robby **Bowmen**	Courting Winnona	Billy	A255
Emma **Bown**	Daughters Of England	Poll	A284
John **Bown**	Savage Storm	As Cast	A952
Paul **Bown**	Back Up The Hearse	Gary	A84
	On The Piste	Chris Baxter	A812
Amanda **Boxer**	All My Sons	Sue Bayliss	A33
Stephen **Boxer**	Karate Billy...Home	As Cast	A572
	Richard III	Buckingham	A910
Max **Boyce**	Jack And The Beanstalk	Jack	A553
Todd **Boyce**	On Top of the World		A814
Pam **Boyd**	Digging for Fire	As Cast	A313
Don **Boydell**	Broken Folk		A164
Billy **Boyle**	Some Like It Hot	Jerry	A1025
Paul **Boyle**	Wind In The Willows	Stoat/Gipsy	A1211
Tracy **Brabin**	The Fancy Man	Amy Granville	A395
Louise **Bracey**	Carousel	As Cast	A190
Arturo **Brachetti**	Square Rounds	As Cast	A1038
Andrew **Bradley**	Annie Get Your Gun	Train Conductor Waiter	A51
David **Bradley**	The Alchemist	Subtle	A28
	Hamlet	Polonius	A466
	Henry IV Part 2	Shallow	A493
	Julius Caesar	Cassius	A566
Elizabeth **Bradley**	Billy Liar	Florence	A122
	The Fastest Clock...	Cheetah Bee	A398
Matt **Bradley**	On The Piste	Tony Muller	A810
Paul **Bradley**	Bulldog Drummond	Bentons	A171
Cathryn **Bradshaw**	Assassins	As Cast	A73
	Bourgeois Gentilhomme	Lucile	A153
Ken **Bradshaw**	King Lear	Albany	A578
Oliver **Bradshaw**	Witness For The Prosecution	Mr Justice Wainwright	A1218
Orla **Brady**	Philadelphia Here I Come	Kate	A856
Chris **Brailsford**	Romeo and Juliet	Gregory	A936
	A View From The Bridge	Mr Lipari	A1172
Mark **Brailsford**	As Time Goes By	As Cast	A65
Patricia **Brake**	Don't Dress For Dinner	Suzette	A331
Richard **Brake**	American Buffalo	Bob	A39
Geraldine **Bramall**	What the Butler Saw	Geraldine Barclay	A1197
Chris **Bramwell**	Hapgood	Kerner	A472
Patrick **Bramwells**	The Three Musketeers	Athos	A1104
Felicity **Branagan**	Intimacy	Rirette	A543
Kenneth **Branagh**	Coriolanus	Coriolanus	A248
	Hamlet	Hamlet	A466
Graham **Brand**	Buddy	Ensemble	A169
Neil **Brand**	New World and Tears	Pinzon	A780
Nina **Brandon Jones**	Dead Soil	Grandmother/Woman	A290

Name	Play	Part	Ref
Una **Brandon-Jones**	Blood Wedding	The Neighbour	A134
	Under Milk Wood	As Cast	A1160
Susie **Brann**	Dick Whittington	Fairy Dulcimer	A308
Carol **Brannan**	The Jungle Book	As Cast	A568
	Wasting Reality	Sister	A1186
John **Branwell**	Mr A's Amazing Maze	As Cast	A746
	Prin	Boyle	A876
	Romeo and Juliet	Capulet	A936
	A View From The Bridge	Alfieri	A1172
Jill **Brassington**	House of Bernarda Alba	As Cast	A515
	The Last Carnival	Agatha	A598
Meredith **Braun**	Les Miserables	Eponine	A611
Cliff **Brayshaw**	Little Tramp	J Edgar Hoover Others	A634
Doug **Brazier**	Cyrano De Bergerac	De Guiche	A268
Anne **Breckell**	Carousel	As Cast	A190
James **Bree**	Beauty And The Beast	Sir Aldgate Pump	A98
	The Mother Tongue	Mr Bibby	A743
Jean **"Binta" Breeze**	Love Space Demands	As Cast	A644
Alec **Bregonzi**	Comedy Of Errors	As Cast	A241
Owen **Brenman**	Evening with Gary L.	Ian	A383
Jane **Brennan**	Digging for Fire	As Cast	A313
Liam **Brennan**	Taming Of The Shrew	Hortensio	A1070
Patrick **Brennan**	Merchant Of Venice	Bassanio	A707
Stephen **Brennan**	Private Lives	Elyot	A882
Paul **Brennen**	Glass Menagerie	Tom	A440
	Importance of Being	John Worthing	A532
Jonathan **Brent**	Elegies...	As Cast	A358
Bernard **Bresslaw**	Love's Labour's Lost	Don Adriano de Armado	A645
Phil **Bretherton**	Building Blocks	Jim	A170
Linda **Mae Brewer**	Radio Times	As Cast	A890
David **Brice**	Ladies' Night	As Cast	A592
Elizabeth **Brice**	A Judgement In Stone	Jacqueline	A563
Richard **Bridges**	Lord of the Rings	As Cast	A639
Lucy **Briers**	Fooling About	As Cast	A412
Richard **Briers**	Coriolanus	Menenius	A248
Kelly **Bright**	The Chalk Garden	Laurel	A196
Sarah **Brightman**	Aspects Of Love	Rose	A72
	Trelawny Of The Wells	Rose Trelawny	A1139
Paul **Brightwell**	Measure For Measure	The Duke	A702
	Seagull	Mr Aston	A963
Mark **Brignall**	Ten Times Table	Tim	A1087
Liz **Brimilcombe**	The Double D	As Cast	A333
	Pharmaceutical	As Cast	A855
Carl **Brincat**	Monster He Made Me	Lolo	A734
Helga **Brindle**	Coriolanus	As Cast	A248
	Double Take	Vee	A338
Jon **Briones**	Miss Saigon	Vietnamese Customer	A727
Kirstie **Bristow**	Annie Get Your Gun	Nellie	A51
Brian **Brittain**	Man Cub	As Cast	A679
Eddie **Brittain**	Merlin, The Search	As Cast	A709
Edward **Brittain**	Giraffe, Pelly, & Me	The Monkey	A436
	The Jungle Book	As Cast	A568
Katy **Brittain**	Liaisons Dangereuses	Cecile De Volanges	A610
	A Midsummer Night's ..	Hermia	A720
Bill **Britten**	Man, Beast and Virtue	Paolino	A682
Jasper **Britton**	The Beggar's Opera	Ben Budge	A106
	A Jovial Crew	Beggar	A561
	Tamburlaine The Great	Calyphas	A1067

Name	Play	Part	Ref
The Brittonioni Brothers	Experiment In Contra.		A388
Sue Broadway	Angels & Amazons	As Cast	A48
	Gravity Swing	As cast	A457
Stephane Brodi	Les Atrides	As Cast	A609
Michael Brogan	Taste of Honey	Peter	A1074
Isabel Brook	Rimbaud And Verlaine	Various	A916
	Thirteenth Night	As Cast	A1099
Jeremy Brook	In The Midnight Hour	Dunny	A538
Laura Brook	Pygmalion	Lady	A886
Robert Brook	Enemy To The People	As Cast	A369
Judy Brooke	Alfie	Annie	A30
Nick Brooke	See How They Run	The Intruder	A971
Tim Brooke-Taylor	You Must Be The Husband	Tom	A1248
Chris Brooker	Forbidden Planet	Bosun Arras	A904
Diana Brooks	Stand Before You Naked	As Cast	A525
Joanne Brooks	Eight to the Bar	As Cast	A356
Lorna Brooks	MacWizard Fae Oz	As Cast	A663
Nikki Brooks	Slice Of Saturday...	Sharon	A1015
Lee Broom	Little Tramp	Young Sidney	A634
Paul Broughton	One The Ledge	As Cast	A821
	The School For Scandal	Sir Oliver Surface	A956
	Self Catering	Henry Fonda	A973
David Broughton-Davies	Wizard of Oz	Uncle Henry	A1223
Alan Brown	Madness of George III	Sir Selby Markham	A669
Amelda Brown	Kafka's Dick	Linda	A571
Anthony Brown	A Midsummer Night's ..	Bottom	A720
Chris Brown	Thirteenth Night	As Cast	A1099
Darren Brown	As You Desire Me		A66
	The Recruiting Officer	Collier	A897
Dylan Brown	Don't Play With Love	Perdican	A329
Gaye Brown	Trelawny Of The Wells	Mrs Mossop	A1139
Greg Brown	Blues Brothers	A Bluette	A142
Jo Cameron Brown	Cuttin' A Rug	Miss Walkinshaw	A266
June Brown	Cinderella	Fairy Godmother	A219
Kaye Brown	Cats	Tantomile	A194
Miquel Brown	Josephine	Mama Carrie	A560
Ray Brown	Wicked Old Man	Sugar	A1207
Susan Brown	House of Bernarda Alba	As Cast	A515
	Playing Sinatra	Sandra	A864
Wendy Brown	Carmen Jones	Myrt	A189
Eithne Browne	Alfie	Lily	A30
	Awfully Big Adventure	Lilly	A77
Colin Bruce	The Devils	Father Urbain	A304
Judith Bruce	The Blue Angel	Mai Bombler	A138
	Measure For Measure	Mistress Overdone	A700
Mona Bruce	Deathtrap	Helga ten Dorp	A298
Jeremy Brudenell	Double Take	Paul	A338
	Venus Observed	Edgar	A1168
Dora Bryan	70, Girls, 70	As Cast	A4
Richard Bryan	Body Talk		A147
	Hans C. Anderstories		A470
	Ten In A Bed		A1086
Kenneth Bryans	Merlin, The Search	As Cast	A709
	Taming Of The Shrew	Petruchio	A1070
	Travesties	Lenin	A1137
Beaux Bryant	Cyrano De Bergerac	Roxanne	A268
Edward Bryant	Punishment Of Animals	As Cast	A259
Michael Bryant	Murmuring Judges	Justice Cuddeford	A758
	Pygmalion	Alfred Doolittle	A886

Name	Play	Part	Ref
	Trelawny Of The Wells	James Telfer	A1138
	Wind In The Willows	Badger	A1211
James Bryce	Beauty And The Beast	Father	A97
	Cuttin' A Rug	Curry	A266
	School For Wives	Chrysalde/Henry	A958
Judith Brydon	The Golden Ass	Fotis	A443
Ann Bryson	Evening With Gary L.	Monica	A382
Denise Bryson	The Sacred Penman	As Cast	A946
Naomi Buch	Cherry Orchard	Ranyevskaya	A202
	The English Kiss	Margery	A370
Beth Buchanan	Anybody for Murder?	As Cast	A55
Pamela Buchner	Enter The Tragic Muse	Sarah Siddons	A372
	Snow Queen	Grandma	A1021
	Turkey Time	Ernestine Stoatt	A1144
Dawn Buckland	Starlight Express	As Cast	A1043
Bill Buffery	The Tempest	Caliban/Master	A1083
Kate Buffery	Schippel, The Plumber	Phekla	A954
Moira Buffini	Jordan	One-woman show	A558
Michael Buffong	Armed And Dangerous	As Cast	A59
Neil Bull	Macbeth	Weird Sister	A656
Caroline Bullen	Lady Aoi	As Cast	A593
James Buller	Radio Times	Jeeps	A890
Amelia Bullmore	Romeo and Juliet	Lady Capulet	A936
	A View From The Bridge	Catherine	A1172
Angela Bullock	Threepenny Story	Polly Peachum	A1108
Simon Bullock	Same Time Next Year	George	A951
Antony Bunsee	A Jovial Crew	Beggar/Butler	A561
	The Odyssey	Proteus	A802
Wendy Buonaventura	Revelations	As Cast	A905
Suzanne Burden	The Recruiting Officer	Melinda	A896
Bryan Burdon	Sleeping Beauty	As Cast	A1012
Ian Burford	Pig In A Poke	Oakleigh	A859
Christian Burgess	Artists and Admirers	Velikatov	A64
Fisun Burgess	House Of The Spirits		A514
Guy Burgess	Television Programme	Phelypeaux	A1080
Vivienne Burgess	The Family Reunion	Ivy	A394
Sarah Burghard	Cabal and Love	Luise	A176
Alfred Burke	All's Well That Ends Well	Lafeu	A35
	As You Like It	Adam	A67
Andy Burke	Shadowlands	As Cast	A983
	Working	As Cast	A1239
Billy Burke	Annie Get Your Gun	Tommy Keeler	A51
David Burke	Hamlet	Claudius	A465
Kathy Burke	Crackwalker	Theresa	A256
Simon Burke	Leonardo	Leonardo	A608
	Phantom Of The Opera	Raoul Vicomte de Chagny	A854
Richard Burman	Les Miserables	Innkeeper	A611
Jonathan Burn	Down And Out...	Boris	A339
Andrew Burnett	The Dorm	Tim	A332
Cliff Burnett	Hapgood	Ridley	A472
Sally Burnett	The Hatchet Man	As Cast	A478
Scott Burnett	The Trial	Various	A1140
Nicola Burnett-Smith	Hot Italian Nights	Ensemble	A507
	The Magic Storybook	Ensemble	A672
Carol Burns	On Top of the World		A814
Keith Burns	Les Miserables	Enjolras	A613
Mike Burnside	Madness of George III	Sir Boothby Skrymshir	A669
Sheila Burrell	My Fair Lady	Mrs Higgins	A763
Phoebe Burridge	Voysey Inheritance	Mary	A1182

Name	Play	Part	Ref
Zalie Burrow	Rocky Horror Show	Janet	A933
David Burrows	The BFG	Daniel Bloodbottler etc	A116
Clare Burt	Lust	Alithia	A650
	Spread A Little Happ	As Cast	A1035
David Burt	As You Like It	Amiens	A67
	The Beggar's Opera	Macheath	A106
Eddie Burton	Miss Saigon	Marine	A727
Richard Bushell	Travelling Light	As Cast	A1135
Josette Bushell-Mingo	Two Gents Of Verona	Silvia	A1154
	The Virtuoso	Clarinda	A1176
Justin Butcher	The Professional	As Cast	A883
Lindsay Butcher	Gravity Swing	As Cast	A457
Michael Butcher	Dangerous Dolls-Soap Crazy	Various	A280
Paul Butler	The Trial	Various	A1140
Richard Butler	As You Like It	Adam	A71
	Lady Be Good	Rufus Parke	A594
	A Midsummer Night's ..	Quince	A721
Trevor Butler	The Last Carnival	Rafael	A598
Michelle Butt	Hamlet	Gertrude	A467
Sandra Butterworth	Voysey Inheritance	Ethel	A1182
Tyler Butterworth	Natural Causes	Withers	A773
Matthew Byam-Shaw	Voysey Inheritance	Denis	A1182
Sharon Byatt	Grand Hotel	Operator/Tootsie	A453
Kate Byers	A Month In The Country	As Cast	A736
	Romeo and Juliet	Juliet	A936
	A View From The Bridge	Mrs Lipari	A1172
Peter Bygott	Hamlet	As Cast	A466
	Henry IV Part 1	Second Carrier	A492
	Henry IV Part 2	William Cook	A493
	Romeo And Juliet	Friar John	A938
	Two Gents Of Verona	As Cast	A1154
Doyne Byrd	Murmuring Judges	Toastmaster	A758
	Pygmalion	Covent Garden Crowd	A886
	Wind In The Willows	Otter	A1211
Allie Byrne	Twelfth Night	Olivia	A1148
Antoine Byrne	London Vertigo	Katty Farrel	A636
Connor Byrne	Carousel	As Cast	A190
	Joseph...	Dan	A559
Constance Byrne	Romeo And Juliet	As Cast	A938
	Two Gents Of Verona	As Cast	A1154
Grainne Byrne	Baby Baby	As cast	A83
Michael Byrne	Death and the Maiden	Roberto Miranda	A293
	Hamlet	Polonius	A465
Peter Byrne	Nightmare	As Cast	A787
Russell Byrne	Shadowlands	Registrar's Clerk	A984
Bruce Byron	Custer's Last Stand	Terry	A264
Ian Caddick	Bourgeois Gentilhomme	Student/Tailor Cook	A153
Simon Cadell	Travel With My Aunt	As Cast	A1134
Michael Cadman	Blithe Spirit	Charles	A127
Andy Cadogan	A Life In The Theatre		A618
Gary Cady	Cyrano De Bergerac	Christian	A269
Angela Caesar	Biko	Marian	A121
Peter Caffrey	The Rock Station	Peter	A931
Michael Cahill	Starlight Express	Rusty	A1043
Adam Caine	Grand Hotel	Scullery Worker	A453
	Rocky Horror Show	Rocky	A933
Charles Caine	Sidewalk Sidney	Dominic	A998
Charlie Caine	Goin' Local	Tye	A442
Marti Caine	Snow White	Red Queen	A1023
James Cairncross	Taming Of The Shrew	Baptista	A1070
Anthony Cairns	Les Miserables	Gavroche	A612
Jonathan Cake	As You Like It	First Banished Lord	A67
	The Beggar's Opera	Jemmy Twitcher	A106
	The Odyssey	Antinous	A802
David Calder	Heartbreak House	Boss Mangan	A486
Jason Calder	Macbeth	Lennox	A656
Anthony Calf	Madness of George III	Fitzroy	A669
Martin Callaghan	My Fair Lady	Costermonger Footman	A763
Ray Callaghan	Merchant of Venice	Gobbo	A708
David Callahan	As Time Goes By	As Cast	A65
	Blood Wedding	Leonardo	A133
	Dracula Spectacular	Dracula	A340
Andrew Callaway	The Miser	La Merluche	A724
	Taming of the Shrew	Christopher Sly	A1069
	Wizard of Oz	Hunk	A1222
Robert Calvert	A Marginal Affair	Peter Knowles	A687
	Merchant of Venice	Lorenzo	A708
	Noises Off	Tim Allgood	A794
	Working	As Cast	A1239
Wyn Calvin	Aladdin	Widow Twankey	A18
Alister Cameron	As You Like It	Sir Oliver Martext	A71
	Lady Be Good	A Flunkey	A594
	A Midsummer Night's ..	Egeus	A721
Averill Cameron	Carmen Jones	Victoria	A189
	Little Shop Of Horrors	Cyrstal	A632
Craig Cameron	Starlight Express	Espresso	A1043
Gina Cameron	As You Like It	Country Girl	A71
	A Midsummer Night's ..	Hippolyta	A721
Leesa Cameron	Barnum	As Cast	A93
Patrick Cameron	Flamingo	As Cast	A408
	Master Harold & The bo	Willie	A694
Robin Cameron	Brand	As Cast	A157
Sarah Cameron	Story of the Last	Various	A1053
Jimmy Camicia	Christopher Street	As Cast	A218
Cheryl Campbell	The Changeling	Beatrice	A197
	The Merry Wives Of Windsor	Mistress Page	A713
Christopher Campbell	Dragon	As Cast	A341
	Night of the Iguana	Wolfgang	A785
	Pygmalion	Bystander	A886
Colin Campbell	Richard III	Ratcliffe	A912
Joanne Campbell	The Cotton Club	Millie Gibson	A250
	Too Much Too Young	As Cast	A1127
Ken Campbell	Pigspurt		A860
Rory Campbell	Cats	Asparagus	A194
Marji Campi	Stitched Up	May	A1050
George Canning	Starlight Express	Dustin	A1043
Cannon & Ball	Babes In The Wood		A81
Julian Cannonier	Annie Get Your Gun	Ensemble	A51
Brian Cant	Gaslight	Ex-Detective Rough	A428
	Sailor Beware!	The Rev. Oliver Purefoy	A948
Richard Cant	View From The Bridge	Rodolpho	A1170
Sergio Canto	Les Atrides	As Cast	A609
Michael Cantwell	Assassins	As Cast	A73
	Merrily We Roll Along	Frank	A711
Lucy Capito	Blood Wedding	The Bride	A133

Name	Play	Part	Ref
Neil Caple	Comedy Of Errors	Dromio	A241
	Life is a Dream	Clarion	A619
	Wind In The Willows	Norman	A1211
Marco Capozzoli	A Dead Secret	Stacey Crispin	A289
Caron Cardelle	Starlight Express	As Cast	A1043
David Cardy	Coriolanus	As Cast	A248
	Double Take	Harry	A338
Anita Carey	Richard III	Duchess of York	A912
Mark Carey	Martin Chuzzlewit	Multiple Roles	A689
	Second From Last In The Sack Race	Henry Pratt	A966
Richenda Carey	Madness of George III	Lady Pembroke Margaret Nicholson	A669
Patrick Cargill	Charley's Aunt	Stephen Spettigue	A200
	Grave Plots	As Cast	A456
Jeffrey Carl	World Upon The Moon	Ernesto	A1241
Victoria Carling	Thirteenth Night	As Cast	A1099
John Carlisle	Woman Of No Importance	Lord Illingworth	A1230
Hayley Carmichael	Gormenghast	Fuchsia	A451
	Street of Crocodiles	Maria	A1056
Sandra Caron	Alfie	As Cast	A29
Claire Carpenter	The BFG	Katherine Meatdripper etc	A116
Judith Carpenter	Stepping Out	Vera	A1046
Nick Carpenter	Comedy Of Errors	As Cast	A241
Sarah Carpenter	After You With The Mlk	Dotty	A16
	Fifteen Streets	Christine Bracken	A403
	On The Piste	Alison	A811
Bob Carr	Good Morning Bill	Sir Hugo Drake	A447
David Carr	Trouble in Mind	John Nevins	A1142
Jack Carr	The Seagull	Shamrayev	A962
Peter Carr	King Lear In New York	TV Crew:Lights	A580
Robert Carr	School For Wives	Oronte	A958
	Travesties	Bennett	A1137
Andrina Carroll	Bright & Bold Design	Grace Rhys	A161
	Hobson's Choice	Vickey Hobson	A499
Finola Carroll	Twelfth Night	Olivia	A1151
Joan Carroll	Phantom Of The Opera	Madame Firmin	A854
Olivia Carruthers	Indigo Mill	As Cast	A539
Daniella Carson	Snow White	Snow White	A1023
Silas Carson	Taming Of The Shrew	Lucentio	A1070
Ted Carson	Don't Play With Love	Chorus	A329
Eric Carte	Dangerous Obsession	As Cast	A278
	Day After The Fair	As Cast	A286
	M. Butterfly	Marc/Man 2/Consul Sharples	A651
Clive Carter	Les Miserables	Javert	A613
Glenn Carter	Joseph...	Asher	A559
John Carter	The Imaginary Invalid	Monsieur Argan	A529
Patrick Carter	Artists and Admirers	As Cast	A64
	The Virtuoso	Weaver	A1176
Robert Carter	Night in Tunisia	Bishop Jones	A783
Simon Carter	An Ideal Husband	Phipps	A528
Anna Carteret	An Ideal Husband	Mrs Chevely	A527
	Liaisons Dangereuses	Marquise de Merteuil	A610
Mairead Carty	'Tis Pity She's A Whore	Philotis	A1114
Brent Carver	Kiss of Spiderwoman	Molina	A584
David Cary	Romeo and Juliet	Abraham	A936
	A View From The Bridge	Submarine	A1172
Ronnie Caryl	Good Rockin' Tonite	MC	A449

Name	Play	Part	Ref
David Case	Cloud 9	Clive	A232
Gordon Case	The Odyssey	Eurymachus	A802
	Smile Orange	As Cast	A1017
	Tamburlaine The Great	Usumcasane	A1067
Paul Case	Imagine	Ringo	A530
Anna-Jane Casey	Joseph...	Reuben's Wife	A559
Nigel Casey	Starlight Express	Greaseball	A1043
Stephen Casey	The Changeling	Tomazo	A197
	A Jovial Crew	Hilliard	A561
	The Odyssey	Telemachus	A802
	Tamburlaine The Great	Callapine	A1067
Michael Cashman	Doctor Faustus	Mephistophilis	A317
	Kvetch	Frank	A586
	Rebecca	Maxim De Winter	A894
John Castle	When The Past Is Still	Tom	A1199
Jo Castleton	Witness For The Prosecution	Greta/Miss Clegg	A1218
Clare Cathcart	Cloud 9	Maud	A232
	Fooling About	As Cast	A412
Caroline Catz	Six Degrees...	Tess	A1008
Nicholas Caunter	Cyrano De Bergerac	A Cadet/Etc	A269
	Fuente Ovejuna	The Farmer	A422
Tracy Cavalier	Daughters Of England	Rose	A284
Mark Caven	Blood Whispers	As Cast	A135
Tony Caverner	Diamonds in the Dust	As Cast	A306
Belinda Cawdron	Macbeth	Lady Macduff	A653
Christopher Cazenove	The Sound Of Music	Captain Georg von Trapp	A1033
Jonathan Cecil	The Family Reunion	Gerald Piper	A394
Peter Cellier	Body And Soul	As Cast	A146
Danny Cerqueira	Handsome,Handicapped..	As Cast	A468
Andy Chabeli	Sikulu	Ensemble	A1001
Tom Chadbon	An Ideal Husband	Sir Robert Chiltern	A528
Angela Chadfield	Conundrum	As Cast	A247
Helen Chadwick	Square Rounds	As Cast	A1038
Simon Chadwick	Comedy Of Errors	As Cast	A241
Nick Chadwin	Hamlet	Claudius/Marcellus	A463
	King Lear	King Lear	A577
George Chakiris	M. Butterfly	Rene Gallimard	A651
Lolita Chakrabarti	Dragon	As Cast	A341
	A Midsummer Night's Dream	Hippolyta	A718
John Challis	Jack's Out	As Cast	A554
Martin Chamberlain	Dragon	As Cast	A341
	Pygmalion	Taximan	A886
Emma Chambers	Trelawny Of The Wells	Avonia Bunn	A1138
Janys Chambers	It's A Girl	Mary	A549
Lobo Chan	Miss Saigon	Officer of the South Vietnamese	A727
V Chandran	The Little Clay Cart	Musician	A627
Stockard Channing	Six Degrees...	Ouisa	A1008
Mark Channon	Annie Get Your Gun	Mac. Property Man Major Domo	A51
Doreen Chanter	Blues Brothers	A Bluette	A142
Bairbre Ni Chaoimh	Private Lives	Sibyl	A882
Tim Chaplin	Ruby In The Dust		A941
Ben Chapman	Shades	Alan	A981
Duggie Chapman	Jack And The Beanstalk	Dame Trot	A553
Paul Chapman	Dog Days	As Cast	A319
Sean Chapman	Angels In America	Prior Walter	A47
Colin Charles	Five Guys Named Moe	Four-Eyed Moe	A407

Name	Play	Part	Ref
	Miss Saigon	Marine	A727
Joseph **Charles**	Flamingo	As Cast	A408
	The Last Carnival	George	A598
Maria **Charles**	Blithe Spirit	Madame Arcati	A126
	Driving Miss Daisy	Daisy Werthan	A346
	Hay Fever	Clara	A481
	School for Scandal	Mrs Candour	A957
Rebecca **Charles**	Blithe Spirit	Ruth	A128
	Cyrano De Bergerac	As Cast	A269
	Wicked Old Man	Gertie	A1207
Kenneth **Charlette**	Crackwalker	Man	A256
Orla **Charlton**	Dancing At Lughnasa	Chris	A274
Mark **Charnock**	An Ideal Husband	Marquess of Montford	A528
Jennifer **Chase**	Carmen Jones	Carmen Jones	A189
Lorraine **Chase**	Aladdin	Aladdin	A26
	The Late Edwina Black	Elizabeth Graham	A599
Mary **Chater**	Square Rounds	As Cast	A1038
	Woman Of No Importance	Lady Stutfield	A1230
Mark **Chatterton**	Cherry Orchard	Yasha/Passer-by	A202
	Macbeth	Banquo/Doctor	A658
	Over a Barrel	Ray	A840
	Teechers	As Cast	A1078
	TO	Man	A1120
Jason **Cheater**	Master Harold & The bo	Hallie	A694
Peter **Chequer**	Wind In The Willows	Rabbit/Policeman	A1211
Clive **Cherrington**	Hecuba	Guard	A488
Richard **Cherry**	Brand	As Cast	A157
Mary **Chester**	Elegies...	As Cast	A358
Gareth **Chilcott**	Cinderella	Broker's Man	A224
Jeremy **Child**	Madness of George III	Dr Richard Warren	A669
Philip **Childs**	Shadowlands	As Cast	A983
	The Ballroom	As Cast	A1091
Tracy **Childs**	Nightmare	As Cast	A787
	Private Lives	Sybil	A880
Tsai **Chin**	Madame Mao's Memories	As Cast	A666
Jimmy **Chisholm**	Travesties	Tristan Tzara	A1137
Jimmy **Chisolm**	Tartuffe	Tartuffe	A1073
Jack **Chissick**	A Working Woman	Bec Sale	A1238
Hayley **Chiswell**	Shout Across The River	As Cast	A997
Jeffrey **Chiswick**	Angels In America	Rabbi Isidor Chemelwitz/Martin	A47
Wolf **Christian**	Caesar And Cleopatra	Achillas	A180
Nicole **Christie**	Phantom Of The Opera	Page	A854
Veronique **Christie**	Hound	Nazma	A510
Graham **Christopher**	Don Quixote	As Cast	A328
	Hostages and Hamsters	Queue	A506
Helena **Christy**	Frozen Chicken	As Cast	A421
Geoffrey **Church**	Penny for a Song	As Cast	A848
Boyd **Clack**	Seven Doors	As Cast	A978
Adam **Clair**	Miss Saigon	Dragon Acrobats	A727
Jon **Clairmont**	Merrily We Roll Along	As Cast	A711
Patrick **Clancy**	Joseph...	Baker	A559
Anna-Juliana **Clare**	Good Rockin' Tonite	Liebling	A449
Avril **Clark**	EuroVision	Katia	A381
Ernest **Clark**	While The Sun Shines	As Cast	A1201
Lynette **Clark**	Wizard of Oz	Visiting Witch	A1223
Neil **Clark**	The Snow Queen	As Cast	A1020
Sandra **Clark**	Light in the Village	Meena	A622
Simon **Clark**	The Sound Of Music	Herr Zellor	A1033
Vicky **Clark**	Lions of Lisbon	Theresa	A626
Angela **Clarke**	Billy Liar	Rita	A122
Darren **Clarke**	Hamlet	As Cast	A465
Denise **Clarke**	Serpent Kills	As Cast	A977
Frances **Clarke**	The English Kiss	Brenda	A370
Georgia **Clarke**	Dance Of Guns	As Cast	A273
Jacueline **Clarke**	It Runs In The Family	Matron	A548
Lynette **Clarke**	Caesar And Cleopatra	Charmian	A180
Mary-Louise **Clarke**	Chorus of Disapproval	As Cast	A210
	Comedy of Errors	Adriana	A239
Maurice **Clarke**	Spread A Little Happ	As Cast	A1035
Rachel **Clarke**	It's A Girl	Linda	A549
Sharon **Clarke**	Blues In The Night	The Lady	A144
Victoria **Clarke**	Annie Get Your Gun	Jessie	A51
Paul **Clarkson**	Grease	Teen Angel	A458
Elaine **Claxton**	Down And Out...	Worker	A339
Jeremy **Clay**	Julius Caesar	Decius Brutus	A564
	The Night Before The Morning After		A782
	The Threepenny Opera	Macheath	A1109
Nicholas **Clay**	Cerceau	Lars	A195
Rebecca **Clay**	Office Party	Accounts Handler	A803
	Shakers	Nicky	A987
Edward **Clayton**	A Midsummer Night's ..	Egeus	A720
	Taming of the Shrew	Baptista	A1069
	Wizard of Oz	Zeko	A1222
Simon **Clayton**	Roberto Calvi	As Cast	A926
Robin **Cleaver**	Joseph...	Benjamin's Wife	A559
Nicholas **Cleaves**	As You Like It	Silvius	A69
Karen **Clegg**	Wizard of Oz	Dorothy	A1223
Angela **Clerkin**	Les Miserables	Eponine	A612
Edith **Clever**	Ein Traum, Was Sonst?	As Cast	A357
Scott **Cleverdon**	Cuttin' A Rug	Alan	A266
Darren **Clewlow**	Robin	William Of Cloudsley	A927
Jane **Clifford**	April In Paris	Bet	A58
	Happy Families	Auntie Doris	A476
Veronica **Clifford**	Some Like It Hot	Sweet Sue	A1025
Judy **Clifton**	On Approval	Helen Hayle	A807
	Relatively Speaking	Ginny	A900
Dennis **Clinton**	Medea	The Tutor	A704
	Rule Of The Game	Frank	A942
	Valdorama		A1164
Claude **Close**	Neville's Island	Angus	A777
	Rocket To The Moon	Phil Cooper	A932
Richard **Clothier**	Two Gents Of Verona	As Cast	A1154
	The Virtuoso	Weaver	A1176
Ina **Clough**	September In The Rain	Liz	A976
Rebecca **Clow**	Hot Stuff	Ensemble	A508
Gordon **Clyde**	Valentine	As Cast	A1166
James **Clyde**	A Hard Heart	Attila	A477
	Jack's Out	As Cast	A554
John **Clyde**	The Dorm	Alfie	A332
Gary **Coakley**	Lions of Lisbon	Terry Docherty	A626
Callum **Coates**	Romeo and Juliet	Benvolio	A937
Simon **Coates**	A Midsummer Night's Dream	Demetrius	A718
	Murmuring Judges	PC Toby Metcalfe	A758
	Pygmalion	Freddy	A886
John **Cobb**	Bourgeois Gentilhomme	Student/Tailor Cook	A153
	Dragon	As Cast	A341
	A Midsummer Night's Dream	Snug	A718

Name	Play	Part	Ref
Mel Cobb	Annie Get Your Gun	Foster Wilson Pawnee Bill	A51
Anthony Cochrane	Taming Of The Shrew	Tranio	A1070
Michael Cochrane	On Approval	The Duke of Bristol	A807
Gareth Cockin	Hapgood	Joe	A472
Alan Cody	Twelfth Night	Antonio	A1148
Siobhan Coebly	Starlight Express	As Cast	A1043
Catherine Coffey	Killing Passion	Sita	A574
Judith Coke	Murmuring Judges	Woman Under Arrest	A758
	Pygmalion	Whore	A886
	Wind In The Willows	Hedgehog/Monica	A1211
Antonia Coker	The Lie Of The Land	As Cast	A617
David Cole	Houdini	As Cast	A509
George Cole	Natural Causes	Vincent	A773
Sidney Cole	Merchant of Venice	Salerio	A708
Stephanie Cole	The Dark River	Ella Merriman	A282
Chris Coleman	Leonardo	As Cast	A608
Lesley Coleman	Strange Domain	Millie	A1055
Eva Coleman-Wood	Intimacy	Lulu	A543
Esther Coles	The Recruiting Officer	Poacher's Wife	A897
Nicolas Colicos	Joseph...	Reuben	A559
Wilkie Colins	Elisabeth II	As Cast	A361
Danny Coll	Les Miserables	Enjolras	A611
Joseph Collatin	My Fair Lady	Bystander	A763
Nicholas Collett	Hamlet	Laertes	A467
Stephen Colley	Aspects Of Love	Gondolier/Actor Barker	A72
Vanessa Collick	Happy As A Sandbag	As Cast	A473
Christina Collier	Phantom of the Opera	Christine	A853
Sarah Collier	Country Dance		A251
Eliza Collings	Curse Of The Mummy	Pat	A263
Sam Collings	Curse Of The Mummy	Mike	A263
Jayne Collins	Moby Dick	Starbuck	A728
Karl Collins	Fuente Ovejuna	Grand Master Rodrigo	A422
Lewis Collins	Sleuth	Milo	A1013
Michelle Collins	Anybody for Murder?	Suzy	A55
	Raving Beauties	Denise	A893
Paul Collins	Robin	Alan A-Dale	A927
Pauline Collins	Shades	Pearl	A981
Beatrice Comins	The Way of All Flesh	Alethea/Ellen	A1190
James Compton	Good Rockin' Tonite	HLE	A449
Ruairi Conaghan	Elegies...	As Cast	A358
	Othello	Montano/Lodovico	A827
	Philadelphia Here I Come	Ned	A856
	The School For Scandal	Trip/Snake	A956
Brian Conley	Me And My Girl	Bill Snibson	A699
Dennis Conlon	Merlin, The Search	As Cast	A709
	Night in Tunisia	Fitz Fitzimmons	A783
	Taming Of The Shrew	Biondello/Widow	A1070
Mary Conlon	The House Of Stairs	As cast	A513
Christopher Connah	Some Like It Hot	Cop 3	A1025
Jason Connery	Trelawny Of The Wells	Arthur Gower	A1139
James Connolly	The Beggar's Opera	Jack	A106
	A Jovial Crew	Actor/Beggar	A561
John Connolly	Death Of A Salesman	Happy	A297
Sean Connolly	Dracula Spectacular	Genghis/Herr Hans	A340
Joe Connors	Robin	Guy Of Gisbourne Adam Bell	A927
Jess Conrad	Aladdin	Wishee	A26

Name	Play	Part	Ref
Neil Conrich	Revenger's Tragedy	Junior	A909
John Conroy	Hindsight	Colin	A495
	The Tender Husband	Samuel Pounce	A1088
Vas Constanti	Grease	Danny Zuko	A458
Tom Conti	Dog Days	As Cast	A319
	Ride Down Mt Morgan	Lyman Felt	A915
Leo Conville	Curse Of The Mummy	Sam	A263
Nick Conway	Sailor Beware!	Albert Tufnell	A948
	Taste of Honey	Geof	A1075
Jane Cook	Wit's End	Zizi	A1216
Jocelyn Cook	Joseph...	Levi's Wife	A559
Jonquil Cook	Wit's End	Granddaughter Countess	A1216
Ron Cook	Faith Healer	Teddy	A389
	A Jovial Crew	Springlove	A561
	The Merry Wives Of Windsor	Dr Caius	A713
	The Odyssey	Odysseus	A802
Alan Cooke	Night in Tunisia	Young Morgan	A783
Nigel Cooke	Epsom Downs	Sandy	A375
	Give You A Good Time	The Man	A437
	Lovers	The Man	A647
Martin Cookson	Hobson's Choice	Dr. MacFarlane	A500
	Macbeth	As Cast	A657
Sally Cookson	Epsom Downs	Bobby	A375
	Fuente Ovejuna	Pascuala	A423
	Romeo and Juliet	Lady Montague	A935
Susan Cookson	TO	As Cast	A1116
	Up 'N' Under	As Cast	A1163
Ray Cooney	It Runs In The Family	Dr Bonney	A548
David Cooper	Goodnight Mr Tom	Zach	A450
	The Sound Of Music	Kurt	A1033
Emma Cooper	The Sound Of Music	Ensemble	A1033
Lindsay Cooper	Charley's Aunt	Kitty Verdun	A200
	Comedy Of Errors	As cast	A241
Rowena Cooper	Killers	As Cast	A573
Jonathan Coote	Cut and Trust	Wentworth	A265
Kenneth Cope	Safe In Our Hands	Barnes	A947
Kate Copstick	Merrily We Roll Along	As Cast	A711
Gary Cordice	Starlight Express	Rusty	A1043
Alister Cording	Television Programme	Blache	A1080
Allan Corduner	Rosmersholm	Headmaster Kroll	A939
	Three Birds Alighting	Various	A1100
James Cormack	Beyond Reasonable Doubt	Detective Chief Inspector Travers	A113
	Tons Of Money	Henery	A1125
	The Winslow Boy	Desmond Curry	A1213
Lee Cornes	The Barber Of Seville	Figaro	A89
Bryan Cornish	Handsome,Handicapped..	As Cast	A468
Cavin Cornwall	Miss Saigon	Marine	A727
Paul Corrigan	Madness of George III	Braun	A669
Simon Corris	Death Of A Salesman	Bernard	A297
Jim Corry	Your Home In The West	Sean	A1250
James Cosmo	Shades	Callum	A981
Daniel Costelloe	All My Sons	Bert	A33
Don Cotter	Little Tramp	H G Wells	A634
Chrissie Cotterill	Goin' Local	Sue	A442
Helen Cotterill	TO	Various	A1118
Matthew Cottle	Comedy of Errors	Balthasar	A240
	Jolly Potters	As Cast	A557
	Snow Queen	Prince/Ice Troll	A1021
	The Ballroom	As Cast	A1091

Name	Play	Part	Ref
	Turkey Time	David Winterton	A1144
Dominic **Cotton**	Ladies' Night	As Cast	A592
Prim **Cotton**	Chorus of Disapproval	Enid Washbrook	A210
	A Twitch On The Thread		A1153
Andy **Couchman**	Happy As A Sandbag	As Cast	A473
Frank **Coughlan**	Cherry Orchard		A203
Jenny **Coulston**	Aba Daba Music Hall	Various	A6
	Road To Casablanca	Ingrid Bergman	A923
Raymond **Coulthard**	In Praise Of Love		A536
	Water Music	Howard	A1188
Elizabeth **Counsell**	Valentine's Day	Mrs Clandon	A1165
Clotilde **Courau**	A Slip Of The Tongue	Ivana Milosz	A1016
Tom **Courtenay**	The Miser	Harpagon	A724
Paul **Courtenay-Hugh**	Merchant Of Venice	Lorenzo/Morocco	A707
Margaret **Courtney**	Trelawny Of The Wells	Mrs Telfer	A1139
Nicholas **Courtney**	M. Butterfly	M. Toulon/Man 1 Judge	A651
	19th Hole	As Cast	A1090
Amanda **Courtney-Davies**	Joseph...	Apache Dancer	A559
Simon **Coury**	Wit's End	Molchalin	A1216
Sergio **Covino**	Annie Get Your Gun	Wild Horse Dancer	A51
Alan **Cowan**	Cut and Trust	Bill	A265
	Night in Tunisia	Raymond Spinks	A783
Vinnette **Cowan**	Dragon	As Cast	A341
Tony **Cownie**	School For Wives	Alan	A958
	Tartuffe	As Cast	A1073
	Therese Raquin	Camille/Priest Young Man	A1097
Alan **Cox**	As You Like It	Jaques de Boys	A67
	The Beggar's Opera	Filch	A106
	The Winter's Tale	Florizel	A1214
Alison **Cox**	Dracula Spectacular	Nadia Naive	A340
Arthur **Cox**	A Month In The Country	As Cast	A736
Christine **Cox**	Rocket To The Moon	Belle Stark	A932
Gregory **Cox**	Punishment Of Animals	As Cast	A259
Lesley **Cox**	The Sound Of Music	Ensemble	A1033
Philip **Cox**	Joseph...	Simeon	A559
Simon **Cox**	Fooling About	As Cast	A412
	Hobson's Choice	Fred Beenstock	A499
William **Cox**	Pygmalion	Rough	A886
Selby **Coxon**	The Imaginary Invalid	Monsieur Bonnefoy	A529
Simon **Coxon**	Alfie	As Cast	A29
Jonathan **Coy**	The Fastest Clock...	Captain Tock	A398
	A Month In The Country	As Cast	A736
Brendan **Coyle**	Elegies...	As Cast	A358
	Philadelphia Here I Come	Private Gar	A856
	Pygmies In The Ruins		A887
Jonathan **Coyne**	Elephant	As Cast	A359
Jacquie **Crago**	Lettice & Lovage	Lottie	A614
Daniel **Craig**	No Remission	Kevin	A790
Sebastian **Craig**	Light in the Village	Rhodes	A622
Jonathon **Craige**	Cats	Carbucketty	A194
Ingrid **Craigie**	Cherry Orchard		A203
	Wexford Trilogy	Angela	A1194
Nancy **Crane**	Angels In America	The Voice	A47
Kenneth **Cranham**	An Inspector Calls	Inspector Goole	A541
Lorcan **Cranitch**	Pygmies In The Ruins		A887
	A Working Woman	Lantier	A1238
Sean **Crannitch**	The Rock Station	Eddie	A931
Gemma **Craven**	London Vertigo	Mrs Diggerty	A636

Name	Play	Part	Ref
	Private Lives	Amanda	A880
Timothy **Craven**	The Marvellous Boy	Thomas Chatterton	A690
Carol **Ann Crawford**	Beauty And The Beast	Crackjaw	A97
	Merlin, The Search	As Cast	A709
	Travesties	Nadya	A1137
Henry **Crawford**	Mansfield Park	Marc Sinden	A683
Jackie **Crawford**	Moby Dick	As Cast	A728
David **Crean**	Beauty and the Beast	The Beast	A99
David **Crellin**	Three Girls In Blue	Young Man	A1101
Chris **Cresswell**	Gravity Swing	As Cast	A457
Bernard **Cribbins**	Lady Be Good	Watty Watkins	A594
Kim **Criswell**	Annie Get Your Gun	Annie Oakley	A51
Marie **Critchley**	The Snow Queen	As Cast	A1020
	Serve Them All My Days	As Cast	A1123
Stephen **Critchlow**	Macbeth	As Cast	A657
Anthony **Crivello**	Kiss of Spiderwoman	Valentin	A584
Ben **Crocker**	The Tender Husband	Humphrey Gubbin	A1088
John **Crocker**	The Tender Husband	Sir Harry Gubbin	A1088
Annabel **Croft**	Cinderella	Cinderella	A221
Martin **Croft**	Phantom of the Opera	Ensemble	A853
Dona **Croll**	Smile Orange	Miss Brandon	A1017
Hilary **Cromie**	Amphibians	Bridie	A40
	The Virtuoso	Betty	A1176
Michael **Cronin**	Caesar And Cleopatra	Britannus	A180
	The Corn Is Green	The Squire	A249
Tanya **Crook**	Travelling Light	As Cast	A1135
Annette **Crosbie**	Karate Billy...Home	As Cast	A572
Philip **Croskin**	Hamlet	As Cast	A465
Gerard **Crossan**	Pygmies In The Ruins		A887
Howard **Crossley**	Hamlet	As Cast	A466
	Two Gents Of Verona	As Cast	A1154
	The Virtuoso	Steward	A1176
Steven **Crossley**	Hamlet	As Cast	A465
Graham **Crowden**	Marching Song	John Cadmus	A685
Sarah **Crowden**	La Bete	Dorine	A587
Sara **Crowe**	Hay Fever	Jackie	A481
	School for Scandal	Lady Sneerwell	A957
	Woman Of No Importance	Lady Stutfield	A1230
Jeananne **Crowley**	Double Dealer	As Cast	A335
Phyllida **Crowley-Smith**	Phantom Of The Opera	Ballet/Chorus	A854
Hilary **Crowson**	Haunted Hotel	Evelyn Collier	A479
Georgina **Crowther**	Phantom Of The Opera	Ballet/Chorus	A854
Liz **Crowther**	The Dark River	Gwendolen Mulville	A282
Marty **Cruickshank**	Four Marys		A414
Abigail **Cruttenden**	Hay Fever	Sorel	A481
	School for Scandal	Lady Teazle	A957
Marcos **Cruze**	Good Rockin' Tonite	La Bamba Artist	A449
Andrew **Cryer**	As You Like It	Silvius	A67
	The Taming Of The Shrew	Biondello	A1068
Jacqui **Cryer**	Gone With The Wind II	Scarlett O'Hara	A445
Simon **Cryer**	The Hostage	Sean	A505
Kirsty **Cubberley**	Macbeth	Lady Macbeth	A660
Richard **Cubison**	Ten Times Table	Lawrence	A1087
Richard **Cuerdon**	42nd Street	As cast	A2
Sheilah **Cuffy**	Carmen Jones	Frankie	A189
Frances **Cuka**	Stand Before You Naked	As cast	A525
Rod **Culbertson**	Play Strindberg	Kurt	A861
Jonathan **Cullen**	'Tis Pity She's A Whore	Giovanni	A1114

Name	Play	Part	Ref
	A Woman Killed With Kindness	Sir Charles Mountford	A1229
Helena Cullinan	Three Musketeers	Constance	A1106
	To Kill A Mockingbird	Calpurnia	A1121
Alan Cumming	La Bete	Valere	A587
Alastair Cumming	Great God Brown	Dion Anthony	A459
Constance Cummings	The Chalk Garden	Mrs Maugham	A196
Helen Cummings	Blood Wedding	Wife of Leonardo	A134
Ewen Cummins	Blue Remembered Hills	Willie	A139
	Epsom Downs	Hugh	A375
	Fuente Ovejuna	Esteban	A423
	Lulu	Rodrigo	A648
	Romeo and Juliet	Prince	A935
Kieran Cunningham	In The Midnight Hour	Creech	A538
	Rat Play	Parkie	A892
Mary Cunningham	Children Of Lesser God	Mrs Norman	A206
	Spring and Port Wine	Betsy Jane	A1036
Liz Curnick	Cats	Demeter	A194
	Robin	Maid Marion	A927
Susan Curnow	Dancing At Lughnasa	Agnes	A274
Phillip Curr	Robin Hood	Little John	A929
Julian Curry	Elisabeth II	As Cast	A361
Mark Curry	Charley's Aunt	Lord Fancourt Babberley	A200
	Flowers For Algernon	As Cast	A410
Shaun Curry	Gone With The Wind II	O'Kelsnick	A445
	Rule Of The Game	James Berrett	A942
Adam Curtis	EuroVision	As Cast	A381
Andy Curtis	Serpent Kills	As Cast	A977
Dominic Curtis	Cyrano De Bergerac	Page/Child/Etc	A269
Lucinda Curtis	Down And Out...	Mme Farge	A339
	The Seagull	Polena	A962
David Curtiz	Macbeth	Malcolm	A656
Catherine Cusack	The Seagull	Nina	A962
Cyril Cusack	Cherry Orchard		A203
Niamh Cusack	Phoenix	Gabi	A857
Sinead Cusack	Faith Healer	Grace	A389
Joe Cushley	Giraffe, Pelly, & Me	Clive	A436
Henry Cusick	Birthday Party	As Cast	A124
Simon Cutter	School for Scandal	Trip	A957
Marilyn Cutts	Absent Friends	Diana	A10
	Dangerous Corner	Freda Caplan	A277
	Wizard of Oz	Aunt Em/Glinda	A1224
Matthew Cutts	Starlight Express	As Cast	A1043
Susan Cygan	Stand Before You Naked	As Cast	A525
Myriam Cyr	Passion of Marianne	Marianne	A844
Cyrung	Dragon	As Cast	A341
Marcus D'Amico	Angels In America	Louis Ironstone	A47
Kay D'Arcy	Biboff	Nehama	A117
	Massa	Megs	A692
Emma D'Inverno	Rivals	Julia	A920
Simon da Costa	Shadowlands	As Cast	A985
Julian Cameiro da Cunha	Les Atrides	As Cast	A609
Georgiana Dacombe	Jack's Out	As Cast	A554
	Measure For Measure	Juliet	A700
Willem Dafoe	Brace Up!	As Cast	A156
Neil Daglish	Straight & Narrow	Jeff	A1054
Paul Daintry	The Corn Is Green	Glynn Thomas	A249
Amanda Dainty	Valentine's Day	Minnie	A1165
Charles Daish	The Dybbuk	Khonon	A349

Name	Play	Part	Ref
Charles Dale	Cyrano De Bergerac	Carbon de Castel Jaloux/Montfleury	A269
	A Dolls House	Nils Krogstad	A321
David Dale	Hot Stuff	Lucy Fer	A508
	Sleeping Beauty/Beast	Carabossy	A1011
Janet Dale	Madness of George III	Queen Charlotte	A669
Sam Dale	Dancing At Lughnasa	Michael	A274
Robert Dallas	From A Jack To A King	Terry King	A420
Calvin Dallaway	The Trial	Various	A1140
John Dallimore	A Midsummer Night's ..	Robin Starveling	A720
Charles Dalsh	'Tis Pity She's A Whore	Grimaldi	A1114
Alyxis Daly	Therese Raquin	Mme Raquin	A1097
Peter-Hugo Daly	The Blue Angel	Dieter	A138
	Love's Labour's Lost	Costard	A645
	Measure For Measure	Pompey	A700
Norman Dalzell	Savage Storm	Franaschuk	A952
Judy Damas	Murmuring Judges	Accomplice	A758
	Pygmalion	Parlourmaid	A886
	Wind In The Willows	Rabbit	A1211
Emma Danby	The Thin Soldier	As Cast	A1098
Alexis Daniel	'Tis Pity She's A Whore	Citizen/Bandit	A1114
Phil Daniels	Gamblers	Slipper	A424
Jacqueline Dankworth	Merrily We Roll Along	Beth	A711
	Sophisticated Ladies	Ensemble	A1032
Larry Dann	The Invisible Man	Jaffers	A547
Sophie-Louise Dann	A Midsummer Night's ..	Peaseblossom	A721
Ivor Danvers	Me And My Girl	Sir John Tremayne	A699
Ingeborga Dapkunaite	A Slip Of The Tongue	Katya Lipp	A1016
Adam Darius	Rimbaud And Verlaine	Christ	A916
Oliver Darley	Romeo And Juliet	Capulet's Servant	A938
Paul Darnell	Slice Of Saturday...	Gary & Terry	A1015
John Darrell	As You Like It	Corin	A69
	Becket	Bishop of York	A103
	Macbeth	Ross	A655
	The Tempest	Alonso	A1082
Paul Darrow	Macbeth	Macbeth	A657
Terence Dauncey	Blodeuwedd	As Cast	A129
Victoria Davar	Disobediently Yours	As Cast	A314
	Life is a Dream	As Cast	A619
Andrew Davenport	Name	As Cast	A772
Caroline Davenport	Sisters	As Cast	A1006
Kevin Davey	An Ideal Husband	Mason	A528
Alan David	Karate Billy...Home	As Cast	A572
Clare David	Gaslight	Pianist/Muse	A428
Joanna David	Stages	As Cast	A1042
Michael David	Private Lives	Elyot Chase	A881
Peter David	Starlight Express	Espresso	A1043
Linda Davidson	Bazaar and Rummage	Fliss	A94
Lucy Davidson	Death Of A Salesman	Jenny	A297
Bronwen Davies	Cinderella	Prince Charming	A225
Deborah Davies	Something Missing	As Cast	A1030
Geoffrey Davies	Something's Burning	Jim	A1029
Glen Davies	Hostages and Hamsters	George	A506
Huw Davies	The Corn Is Green	Robert Robbach	A249
Ian Davies	Hot Italian Nights	Ensemble	A507
	The Magic Storybook	Ensemble	A672
James Davies	Cats	The Cats' Chorus	A194
Joan Davies	Fifteen Streets	Hannah Kelly	A403
	Moll Flanders	As Cast	A730
	Night Must Fall	Nurse Libby	A784

Name	Play	Part	Ref
John Francis Davies	Starlight Express	Greaseball	A1043
Karen Davies	It's A Girl	Celia	A549
Lyndon Davies	Pond Life	Dave	A869
Meredith Davies	Liaisons Dangereuses	Major Domo	A610
	Love's Labour's Lost	Dumaine	A645
Race Davies	Elegies...	As Cast	A358
Rita Davies	The Golden Ass	High Priest	A443
Rowland Davies	Frightened Lady	As Cast	A192
	Murder By Misadventure	Inspector Egan	A755
Rudi Davies	Awfully Big Adventure	Stella	A77
	A Midsummer Night's Dream	Helena	A718
Timothy Davies	Ten Times Table	Ray	A1087
	Twelfth Night	Malvolio	A1148
Victoria Davies	Monster He Made Me	Annie	A734
Windsor Davies	Cinderella	Baron Hardup	A219
	It Runs In The Family	Police Sgt	A548
Edgar Davis	Philadelphia Here I Come	Ben	A856
Hannah Davis	Massa	Hannah Cullwick	A692
Mark A Davis	Starlight Express	Dustin	A1043
Ray C. Davis	Dead Flamingo Dancer	As Cast	A193
Belinda Davison	A Working Woman	Nana	A1238
Peter Davison	The Decorator	Walter	A301
Bobby Davro	Goldilocks	Silly Billy	A444
Anthony Dawes	Lust	Sir Jasper Fidget	A650
Nicola Dawn	The Sound Of Music	Ensemble	A1033
Andrew Dawson	The Three Musketeers	Various	A1105
Louise Dawson	Much Ado About Nothing	Margaret/Ursula	A750
Susanna Dawson	Gaslight	Mrs Manningham	A428
Ted Dawson	Revenger's Tragedy	Spurio	A909
Philip Day	Merrily We Roll Along	As Cast	A711
Simon Day	Blood Brothers	Mickey	A130
	Fuente Ovejuna	Frondoso	A423
	The Hostage	IRA Officer	A505
	Macbeth	Lennox	A661
	Romeo and Juliet	Tybalt	A935
	Woman Of No Importance	Lord Alfred Rufford	A1230
Michele de Casanove	The Mikado	Maid	A722
Angela de Castro	Angels & Amazons	As Cast	A48
Debbie de Coudreaux	Grand Hotel	Raffaela	A453
Jeni de Haart	Twelfth Night	Servant to Olivia	A1148
Peter de Jersey	As You Like It	Orlando	A67
	The Odyssey	Amphinomous	A802
Holly de Jong	After You With The Mlk	Leila	A16
	Relative Values	Moxie	A899
David de Keyser	Making It Better	Josef Pavlicek	A677
Frances de la Tour	The Pope And The Witch	Elisa Donadoni	A870
Alex De Marcus	Ladies' Night	As Cast	A592
Ava De Souza	Imagine	Yoko	A530
Edward De Souza	On Approval	Richard Halton	A807
	Valentine's Day	Finch McComus	A1165
Richard De Vere	Aladdin	Emperor	A18
Carla de Wansey	Noises Off	Brooke Ashton	A795
Julia Deakin	On The Piste	Alicen Allan	A812
Felicity Dean	Gaslight	Mrs.Manningham	A429
	Wicked Old Man	Imogen	A1207
Matt Dean	Les Miserables	Fauchelevent/Babet	A611
Stephen J Dean	Elvis - the Musical	Jordanaire	A362
Andy Deane	Ladies' Night	As Cast	A592
Julia Dearden	Una Pooka	As Cast	A1156

Name	Play	Part	Ref
Juliet Deardon	Dancing At Lughnasa	Maggie	A274
Morgan Deare	Blues for Mr Charlie	Ellis	A143
	Little Tramp	Mack Sennett Others	A634
Janie Dee	Between the Lines	Ensemble	A112
	Carousel	Carrie Pipperidge	A190
Czarina Deen	Thirteenth Night	As Cast	A1099
Evroy Deer	The Hostage	Princess Grace	A505
	Macbeth	Banquo	A661
Sharon Degan	Stepping Out	Lynne	A1046
Edmund Dehn	As You Desire Me		A66
John Deidrich	Annie Get Your Gun	Frank Butler	A51
Louise Delamere	Cyrano De Bergerac	As Cast	A269
	Good Morning Bill	Lottie	A447
	Hay Fever	Sorel Bliss	A482
Fiona Delaney	Beauty And The Beast	Damask Rose	A98
Gavin Delaney	Twelfth Night	Sebastian	A1151
Pauline Delany	Philadelphia Here I Come	Madge	A856
Roger Delves-Broughton	The Hostage	Ropeen	A505
	Love's Labour's Lost	Sir Nathaniel	A645
Robert Demeger	Columbus	Diego de Harana	A237
Jeffery Dench	As You Like It	Duke Senior	A67
	The Changeling	Vermandero	A197
	The Merry Wives Of Windsor	Shallow	A713
	The Winter's Tale	Old Shepherd	A1214
Judi Dench	Coriolanus	Volumnia	A248
	Gifts Of The Gorgon	Lead Role	A434
	Mowgli - Enfant Loup	Recorded Narration	A745
	The Sea	Louise Rafi	A961
Virginia Denham	Artists and Admirers	Matryona	A64
	Hamlet	As Cast	A466
	Henry IV Part 1	Traveller/Lady	A492
	Henry IV Part 2	Lady	A493
Alexis Denisof	Cain	Lucifer	A181
	Cyrano De Bergerac	Valvert/Cadet/Etc	A269
Michael Denison	Bedroom Farce	Ernest	A104
	An Ideal Husband	Earl of Caversham	A527
Andrew Dennis	Hot Italian Nights	Ensemble	A507
	The Magic Storybook	Ensemble	A672
Caroline Dennis	Imagine	Cynthia	A530
Les Dennis	Me And My Girl	Bill Snibson	A699
Stefan Dennis	Cinderella	Buttons	A219
Tricia Denton	Fiddler On The Roof	Yente	A401
Hilary Derrett	Doll's House	Christine Linde	A323
Clinton Derricks-Carroll	Five Guys Named Moe	Four-Eyed Moe	A407
Jenine Desiderio	Miss Saigon	Kim	A727
Maryann Devally	Endgame	As Cast	A368
Sue Devaney	Love's Labour's Lost	Moth	A645
Janet Devenish	Lust	Ensemble	A650
Colin Devereux	Jack and the Beanstalk	Dame	A551
Matthew Devitt	From A Jack To A King	Eric Glamis	A420
Toni Devonish	Blues Brothers	A Bluette	A142
Michael Dewdney	Aspects Of Love	Doctor/Actor	A72
	My Fair Lady	Freddy	A763
Emma Dewhurst	Tess Of The D'Urbervil	Joan Durbeyfield	A1089
Sally Dexter	A Midsummer Night's Dream	Titania	A718
	The Recruiting Officer	Silvia	A896

Name	Play	Part	Ref
Dhirendra	Dragon	As Cast	A341
Venu **Dhupa**	Shadowlands	As Cast	A983
Graham **di Banzi**	House Among the Stars	Matthieu	A512
	Your Turn To Clean The Stairs	Bobby	A1252
Miguel **Diaz**	Miss Saigon	Vietnamese Customer	A727
Ian **Dickens**	Macbeth	As Cast	A657
Charlie **Dickinson**	Frankie & Tommy	Frankie	A418
Sandra **Dickinson**	It Runs In The Family	Jane Tate	A548
Harry **Dickman**	42nd Street	As cast	A2
Arosemayer **Diedrick**	Heart	As cast	A485
Kevin **Dignam**	Grace	Lance	A452
	Revenger's Tragedy	Officer	A909
Christabel **Dilkes**	The Sea	Jilly	A961
Christabelle **Dilks**	A Working Woman	Virginie	A1238
Michael **Dimitri**	Good Rockin' Tonite	Bill Haley	A449
Penelope **Dimond**	Hot Italian Nights	Ensemble	A507
	The Magic Storybook	Ensemble	A672
	Much Ado About Nothing	Margaret	A752
Peter **Dineen**	Entertaining Mr Sloane	Ed	A373
	The Recruiting Officer	Mr Scruple	A896
	Serve Them All My Days	As Cast	A1123
Emma **Dingwall**	Hay Fever	Jackie Coryton	A482
	Travesties	Cecily	A1137
Reece **Dinsdale**	The Revenger's Tragedy	Vindice	A908
Paola **Dionisotti**	The Family Reunion	Agatha	A394
	Self Portrait	Barbara Robson	A974
	Square Rounds	As Cast	A1038
Luc-Antoine **Diquero**	Monstre, Va!	Ludo	A735
Callum **Dixon**	The Recruiting Officer	Thomas Appletree	A896
Lucy **Dixon**	Leonardo	Lisa	A608
	Merrily We Roll Along	As Cast	A711
Rob **Dixon**	Elisabeth II	As Cast	A361
Russell **Dixon**	Neville's Island	Gordon	A777
	Saint Oscar	Oscar Wilde	A949
	Time Of My Life	As Cast	A1112
Bethan **Dixon-Bate**	The Corn Is Green	Sarah Pugh	A249
Nadja **Djerrah**	Les Atrides	As Cast	A609
Linda **Dobell**	Four Marys		A414
Alan **Dobie**	Dancing At Lughnasa	Father Jack	A274
	Dancing at Lughnasa	As Cast	A275
Jeannette **Dobney**	The Imaginary Invalid	Angelica	A529
Anita **Dobson**	Bourgeois Gentilhomme	Madame Jourdain	A153
Vernon **Dobtcheff**	Cerceau	Nikolai Lvovitch (Koka)	A195
Stephen **Docherty**	A Little Older	Sandy	A631
Francis **Dodge**	Safe In Our Hands	Deirde Holbrook	A947
Glenn **Doherty**	My Heart's A Suitcase	Pest	A764
	Rocky Horror Show	Phantom	A933
	Television Programme	Paul	A1080
Miche **Doherty**	Double Dealer	As Cast	A335
Monica **Dolan**	Outside Edge	Sharon	A837
	Three Musketeers	Anne of Austria	A1106
	To Kill A Mockingbird	Scout	A1121
Anni **Domingo**	Goin' Local	Bertina	A442
	Leave Taking	Enid	A605
Pip **Donaghy**	No Remission	Victor	A790
Alex **Donald**	Sailor Beware!	Carnoustie Bligh	A948
Anthony **Donne**	Don Quixote	As Cast	A328
Charles **Donnelly**	Home At Seven	As Cast	A502
Jason **Donovan**	Joseph...	Joseph	A559

Name	Play	Part	Ref
Aidan **Dooley**	Elegies...	As Cast	A358
	Philadelphia Here I Come	Tom	A856
Deidrie **Doone**	The Hour Of The Lynx	The Pastor	A511
	House of Bernarda Alba	As Cast	A515
Blaise **Doran**	Much Ado About Nothing	Claudio	A750
Simon **Dormandy**	Richard III	Clarence	A910
	The Rivals	Faulkland	A918
Richard **Dormer**	Una Pooka	As Cast	A1156
Michelle **Dotrice**	A Dead Secret	Margaret Dyson	A289
Richard **Doubleday**	From A Jack To A King	Roskoe Scrim	A420
Andrea **Douglas**	Annie Get Your Gun	Ensemble	A51
Andrew **Douglas**	Carmen Jones	Worker	A189
Vernon **Douglas**	Blues for Mr Charlie	Arthur	A143
	Romeo and Juliet	Mercutio	A937
Perry **Douglin**	My Fair Lady	Costermonger	A763
Anthony **Douse**	Hamlet	As Cast	A466
	Henry IV Part 1	Sir Walter Blunt	A492
	Henry IV Part 2	Silence	A493
	Romeo And Juliet	Apothecary	A938
Susan **Dowdall**	Cherry Orchard	Charlotta Ivanovna	A202
	Doll's House	Anne Marie	A322
	Lettice & Lovage	Lettice	A614
Claire **Dowie**	Adult Child/Dead Child	One-woman Show	A15
	Death And Dancing	As Cast	A292
Angela **Down**	A Hard Heart	Praxis	A477
Jackie **Downey**	Candide	Paquette	A185
Nina **Downey**	Voices at Her Elbow	As Cast	A1180
Penny **Downie**	Berlin Bertie	Alice Brine	A109
	Death and the Maiden	Paulina	A293
Paul **Downing**	The Mikado	Nanki-Poo	A722
Jill **Dowse**	Manslaughter	(Two-Hander)	A684
	Shoot The Women First	Gudrun Ensslin	A996
Gerard **Doyle**	Fiddler On The Roof	Mordcha	A401
	Twelfth Night	Sea Captain	A1148
Kevin **Doyle**	Artists and Admirers	Melusov	A64
	Henry IV Part 1	Chamberlain	A492
	Henry IV Part 2	Tom	A493
	Romeo And Juliet	Benvolio	A938
Tina **Doyle**	Steel Magnolias	Annelle	A1045
Tony **Doyle**	The Gigli Concert		A435
Charlie **Drake**	Jack and the Beanstalk	King	A551
Gabrielle **Drake**	Charley's Aunt	Donna Lucia d'Alvadorez	A200
	The Decorator	Marcia	A301
Hilary **Drake**	Hapgood	Hapgood	A472
Karl **Draper**	The Hatchet Man	As Cast	A478
George **Drennan**	Eight to the Bar	As Cast	A356
Phelim **Drew**	Double Dealer	As Cast	A335
James **Dreyfus**	EuroVision	Gary	A381
	Grapes of Wrath	Al	A454
	Playing by the Rules	Sean	A863
Mark **Drummond**	Hapgood	Russian	A472
Karen **Drury**	Natural Causes	Angie	A773
	Time Of My Life	As Cast	A1112
Carmen **Du Sautoy**	Hay Fever	Myra	A481
Jacqui **Dubois**	Blues In The Night	The Girl	A144
	Sophisticated Ladies	Ensemble	A1032
Kate **Duchene**	Richard III	Queen Elizabeth	A910
	The Rivals	Lydia Languish	A918
Dooby **Duck**	Aladdin	As Cast	A20
Neil **Dudgeon**	Crackwalker	Joe	A256

Name	Play	Part	Ref
Ben **Dudley**	Twelfth Night	Orsino/Andrew Aguecheek	A1149
Blythe **Duff**	TO	As Cast	A1119
Lesley **Duff**	The Card (A musical)	As Cast	A187
David **Duffey**	Philadelphia Here I Come	Con	A856
Carol **Duffy**	Barnum	Charity Barnum	A93
Sean **Duffy**	All My Sons	Bert	A32
Veronica **Duffy**	Dancing At Lughnasa	Kate	A274
Graeme **Dufresne**	Candide	1st Army Recruiter	A185
Sandra **Dugdale**	Phantom Of The Opera	Carlotta Guidicelli	A854
Patrick **Duggan**	Philadelphia Here I Come	Boyle	A856
Edward **Duke**	Trelawny Of The Wells	Ferdinand Gadd	A1139
James **Duke**	Taming of the Shrew	Hortensio	A1069
	Wizard of Oz	Witch	A1222
Pierre **Dulaine**	Grand Hotel	The Gigolo	A453
Abigail **Dulay**	Crime of Love	As Cast	A258
	The End Of The Tunnel	As Cast	A365
Andrew **Dumbleton**	The Virtuoso	Hazard	A1176
Catherine **Duncan**	Cinderella	As Cast	A222
Clive **Duncan**	Hot Italian Nights	Ensemble	A507
	The Magic Storybook	Ensemble	A672
Felicity **Duncan**	Charley's Aunt	Ema Delahay	A200
Helen **Duncan**	Phantom Of The Opera	Princess	A854
Peter **Duncan**	The Card (A musical)	Denry Machin	A187
	Little Tramp	Charles Chaplin	A634
Jim **Dunk**	The Baby	Jake	A82
	Caesar And Cleopatra	Rufio	A180
Lesley **Dunlop**	Back Up The Hearse	Sharon	A84
Anthony **Dunn**	Bouncers	Judd	A151
	New World and Tears	Arana	A780
Ian **Dunn**	Six Degrees...	Policeman/Rick	A1008
Frank **Dunne**	Philadelphia Here I Come	Canon O'Byrne	A856
Nick **Dunning**	Phoenix	Bruno	A857
Phillip **Dupuy**	Macbeth	Donalbain	A655
Andrew **Durant**	Thirteenth Night	As Cast	A1099
Kim **Durham**	Beauty and the Beast	Davy	A99
Tom **Durham**	Breaking the Code	As Cast	A159
Barbara **Durkin**	Alfie	As Cast	A29
Peter **Durkin**	My Fair Lady	Jamie	A763
Sara **Durkin**	Starlight Express	As Cast	A1043
Blaise **Durr**	Starlight Express	As Cast	A1043
Jason **Durr**	Measure For Measure	Claudio	A700
Jacqueline **Dutoit**	Outside Edge	Ginny	A837
Monica **Dutoit**	Three Musketeers	Milady	A1106
Joe **Duttine**	A Month In The Country	As Cast	A736
	Pond Life	Maurice	A869
Anthony **Dutton**	Hobson's Choice	Henry Hobson	A499
Janine **Duvitski**	Bourgeois Gentilhomme	Nicole	A153
Clint **Dyer**	Safe In Our Hands	Peterson	A947
Kevin **Dyer**	Teechers	Salty	A1076
Peter **Dyer**	A Twitch On The Thread		A1153
Kate **Dyson**	Mamahuhu?	As Cast	A678
Leon **Eagles**	Body And Soul	As Cast	A146
Julian **Eardley**	Games	As Cast	A426
Andrea **Earl**	King Lear	Regan	A578
	Threepenny Story	Mrs Peachum	A1108
Sandra **Easby**	Starlight Express	Joule/Sleeper	A1043
Mark **East**	The Hostage	Russian Sailor	A505

Name	Play	Part	Ref
Robert **East**	Bedroom Farce	Trevor	A104
David **Easter**	Joseph...	Pharaoh	A559
Joanne **Easter**	Wizard of Oz	Gloria	A1223
Peter **Eastland**	Over a Barrel	Jason	A840
Gillian **Eaton**	Don't Dress For Dinner	Jacqueline	A331
Vincent **Ebrahim**	The Little Clay Cart	Charudatta/Mathura	A627
Jenny **Eclair**	Dangerous Dolls-Mummys Little Girl	Sally Darling	A279
Peter **Edbrook**	70, Girls, 70	As Cast	A4
	Saint Oscar	Richard Wallace	A949
Paul **Eddington**	No Man's Land	Spooner	A789
Alison **Edgar**	Shaker	Ann Lee	A986
Yvonne **Edgell**	Cut and Trust	Mary	A265
Liz **Edmiston**	Dangerous Obsession	As Cast	A278
	Day After The Fair	As Cast	A286
	M. Butterfly	Helga	A651
Adrian **Edmondson**	Grave Plots	As Cast	A456
Susan **Edmonstone**	Frankie & Johnny	Frankie	A417
John **Edmunds**	Shadowlands	Rev. Harry Harrington	A984
Amanda **Edwards**	Androcles And The Lion		A45
Barnaby **Edwards**	Twelfth Night	Malvolio	A1151
Charles **Edwards**	Blithe Spirit	Charles	A128
	The Hostage	IRA Volunteer	A505
	Macbeth	Macduff	A661
Deirdre **Edwards**	Woman Of No Importance	As Cast	A1230
Donna **Edwards**	The Devils	Ninon/Sister Gabrielle of	A304
Lenny **Aljernon Edwards**	The Road	Particulars Joe	A921
Lynette **Edwards**	Serve Them All My Days	As Cast	A1123
	Tons Of Money	Louise Maitland Allington	A1125
Rob **Edwards**	Artists and Admirers	Bakin	A64
	The Dybbuk	Messenger	A349
	Hamlet	Horatio	A466
	Henry IV Part 1	Poins	A492
	Henry IV Part 2	Poins	A493
	The Thebans	Polynices	A1095
Rory **Edwards**	Acapulco	As Cast	A12
	Blood Wedding	Leonardo	A134
	Dead Soil	Younger Actor\Son	A290
	The Family Reunion	Harry	A394
	Under Milk Wood	As Cast	A1160
Russ **Edwards**	King Lear	Edgar	A578
	Threepenny Story	Private Filch	A1108
	A View From The Bridge	Rodolpho	A1169
Yvonne **Edwards**	Phantom Of The Opera	Wardrobe Mistress	A854
Steve **Edwin**	Building Blocks	Mark	A170
	Goin' Local	Ricky	A442
Peter **Egan**	Dejavu	Jimmy Porter	A302
Simon **Egerton**	Candide	Maximilian	A185
	Snow Queen	Fiddle Player Story Teller	A1021
	Turkey Time	Max Wheeler	A1144
Jennifer **Ehle**	Breaking the Code	As Cast	A159
Erica **Eirian**	Fern Hill	Nicola	A400
	Merchant Of Venice	Nerissa	A707
Jackie **Ekers**	The Blue Angel	Hermine	A138
Steven **Elder**	Macbeth	Malcolm	A653
Sandor **Eles**	Cherry Orchard	Gayev	A202
	Fallen Angels	Maurice Duclos	A391

Name	Play	Part	Ref
Chris **Eley**	Macbeth	As Cast	A660
Nigel **Ellacott**	Cinderella	Ugly Sister	A219
Julie **Ellen**	On Golden Pond	Chelsea	A809
Rachel **Ellen**	Phantom Of The Opera	Ballet/Chorus	A854
Hazel **Ellerby**	Square Rounds	As Cast	A1038
Marc **Elliott**	The Winter's Tale	Mamillius	A1214
Tom **Elliott**	Twelfth Night	Toby Belch/Sea Cpt 2nd Officer	A1149
Brendan **Ellis**	Cherry Orchard		A203
Greg **Ellis**	Starlight Express	Electra	A1043
Jack **Ellis**	Assassins	As Cast	A73
Judith **Ellis**	Slice Of Saturday...	Bridget	A1015
Martin **Ellis**	Les Miserables	Thenardier	A613
Steve **Ellis**	Aladdin	Genie Of The Lamp	A18
Ben **Ellison**	Buddy	Ensemble	A168
Nick **Ellsworth**	Rule Of The Game	Jack Harris	A942
John **Elmes**	Absurd Person Singular	As Cast	A11
Mark **Elstob**	Master and Margarita	Yeshua/Behemoth	A693
Femi **Elufowoju**	Much Ado About Nothing	Dogberry	A752
Elizabeth **Elvin**	Intimate Exchanges	Celia	A544
	Macbeth	Lady Macduff Porter	A658
	Over a Barrel	Venetia	A840
Michael **Elwyn**	Penny for a Song	As Cast	A848
	Safe In Our Hands	Stephen Lehy	A947
Ultan **Ely-O'Carroll**	Pygmalion	Footman	A886
Bella **Emberg**	Robin Hood	As Cast	A928
Cecilia **Emerson**	Merlin, The Search	As Cast	A709
Ann **Emery**	70, Girls, 70	As Cast	A4
Alphonsia **Emmanuel**	Murmuring Judges	Irina Platt	A758
Jon **Emmanuel**	Buddy	Jerry Allison	A168
Ray **Emmet-Brown**	Body Talk		A147
	Hans C. Anderstories		A470
	Ten In A Bed		A1086
Ron **Emslie**	Buddy	Norman Petty	A169
Bella **Enahoro**	As You Like It	Court Lady Shepherdess	A67
	The Odyssey	Circe	A802
	School of Night	Rosalinda	A959
	Tamburlaine The Great	Olympia	A1067
Irma **Endrojono**	Elegies...	As Cast	A358
Susan **Engel**	The Dybbuk	Frade	A349
Joanne **Engelsman**	Slice Of Saturday...	Penny & Shirl	A1015
Chris **England**	Evening with Gary L.	Ian	A383
Carey **English**	Bag Dancing	Imelda Baglady	A87
Louise **English**	Me And My Girl	Sally Smith	A699
Vicky **Entwistle**	Night Must Fall	Dora Parkoe	A784
Caroline **Ephgrave**	Cats	Cassandra	A194
David **Ericsson**	The Writing Game	Jeremy Deane	A1242
Stefan **Escreet**	Beauty and the Beast	Master Blake	A99
	Children Of Lesser God	Mr Franklyn	A206
	Spring and Port Wine	Arthur	A1036
Marged **Esli**	Fern Hill	Katey	A400
Liz **Estensen**	Water Music	Ada	A1188
Graeme **Eton**	Mr A's Amazing Maze	As Cast	A746
Christopher **Ettridge**	Colquhoun And MacBryde	As Cast	A235
	Three Birds Alighting	Various	A1100
Barry **Evans**	Anybody for Murder?	Edgar Chambers	A55
Damon **Evans**	Biko	Thomas	A121
Denise **Evans**	A View From The Bridge	Beatrice	A1169
Fiona **Evans**	Punishment Of Animals	As Cast	A259
Howell **Evans**	70, Girls, 70	As Cast	A4

Name	Play	Part	Ref
Joanne **Evans**	Cats	The Cats' Chorus	A194
Kathryn **Evans**	Dead Flamingo Dancer	As Cast	A193
	Radio Times	Olive	A890
Lawrence **Evans**	Square Rounds	As Cast	A1038
Maxine **Evans**	See How They Run	Ida	A971
Richard **Evans**	Much Ado About Nothing	Leonato	A752
Serena **Evans**	Comedy Of Errors	Luciana	A241
	The Recruiting Officer	Lucy	A896
Victor **Romero Evans**	Armed And Dangerous	As Cast	A59
Warwick **Evans**	Blues Brothers	Elwood	A142
	Robin	Sheriff Of Nottingham	A927
Jackie **Everett**	Doll's House	Annie	A323
	Wit's End	Grandmother Countess	A1216
Maxine **Everett**	Annie Get Your Gun	Ensemble	A51
Raymond **Eves**	Home At Seven	As Cast	A502
Barbara **Ewing**	Roman & Marys	As Cast	A934
Judith **Eyre**	Hot Stuff	Ensemble	A508
Marcus **Eyre**	Turner's Crossing	Dan	A1146
Martin **Eyre**	Radio Times	As Cast	A890
Evelyne **Fagnen**	Les Atrides	As Cast	A609
Kate **Fahy**	Grace	Amy Hoffman	A452
Christopher **Fairbank**	Back Up The Hearse	Des	A84
	Hamlet	As Cast	A465
Patanne **Fairfoot**	Beyond Reasonable Doubt	Court Usher	A113
	Fifteen Streets	Maid/Neighbour	A403
DeNica **Fairman**	The House Of Stairs	Belle	A513
Adam **Faith**	Alfie	Alfie	A29
Kern **Falconer**	House Among the Stars	Jean-Marc	A512
	Merlin, The Search	As Cast	A709
	Travesties	James Joyce	A1137
Ronald **Falk**	On Top of the World		A814
Julia **Farino**	Sneeze	As Cast	A1018
Lynn **Farleigh**	Macbeth	Lady Macbeth	A655
	The Tempest	Juno	A1082
Anna **Farnworth**	The Tender Husband	Bridget Tipkin	A1088
Nicholas **Farr**	Buddy	Dion	A168
Colin **Farrell**	Twelfth Night	Feste	A1148
Roy **Faudree**	Brace Up!	As Cast	A156
Lucia **Fausset**	Confusions	Rosemary/Mrs Pearce/Doreen etc	A246
David **Fawcett**	Les Miserables	Brujon	A611
Colin **Fay**	Man, Beast and Virtue	Captain Perella	A682
Susan **Fay**	Annie Get Your Gun	Mrs Yellow Tooth	A51
Gaynor **Faye**	Office Party	Pippa Rowe	A803
Dalia **Fayed**	Spring Awakening	Ilse/Masked Man	A1037
Stephanie **Fayerman**	Prin	Prin	A876
	Self Portrait	Vera Oumancoff	A974
Ray **Fearon**	Blues for Mr Charlie	Pete	A143
	Cloud 9	Betty	A232
	Love's Labour's Lost	Longaville	A645
	Othello	Othello	A827
	The School For Scandal	Charles Surface	A956
Paul **Featherstone**	Hay Fever	Sandy Tyrell	A482
Richard **Felix**	Buddy	Ensemble	A168
Luke **Fell**	Annie Get Your Gun	Little Jake	A51
Don **Fellows**	The Dark River	Edmund Lester Reade	A282
	Fool for Love	Old man	A411
Miranda **Fellows**	Stepping Out	Andy	A1046

Name	Play	Part	Ref
Susannah Fellows	Aspects Of Love	Rose	A72
	June Moon	As Cast	A567
Holly Felton	La Bete	Catherine De Brie	A587
Michael Fenner	It Runs In The Family	Dr Connolly	A548
Sarah-Jane Fenton	Rocket To The Moon	Cleo Singer	A932
Michael Fenton-Stevens	Fighting For The Dunghill	Canning	A404
Lucy Fenwick	The BFG	Mother/Queen Childchewer etc	A116
Cheryl Fergison	The Blue Angel	Tumtum	A138
	Cyrano De Bergerac	As Cast	A269
	Measure For Measure	Nun	A700
Carl Ferguson	Little Tramp	Young Chaplin	A634
Leon Ferguson	Mamahuhu?	As Cast	A678
Lynn Ferguson	A Better Day	As Cast	A111
	Fantasy Island		A396
Jean Fergusson	The Rivals	Mrs Malaprop	A918
Wilhelmenia Fernandez	Carmen Jones	Carmen Jones	A189
Gillian Ferrabee	Serpent Kills	As Cast	A977
Nick Ferranti	Some Like It Hot	Hood 2	A1025
	West Side Story	Bernardo	A1193
Elena Ferrari	Candide	Cunegonde	A185
Marco Ferraro	Starlight Express	Purse	A1043
Anthea Ferrell	Little Shop Of Horrors	Chiffon	A632
Shelaagh Ferrell	Carmen Jones	Sally	A189
Eve Ferret	Bazaar and Rummage	Margaret	A94
Andrew Ferrier	Much Ado About Nothing	Don John/Dogberry	A750
Peter Ferris	Imagine	George	A530
Caren Ferster	Witness For The Prosecution	Clerk of the Court	A1218
Andrew Fettes	The English Kiss	Stan	A370
Georgina Field	In The Midnight Hour	McCaegy	A537
Joanna Field	My Mother Said	Doris	A767
David Fielder	The Choice	As Cast	A209
	The Rivals	Acres	A919
Simon Fielder	Buddy	Ensemble	A168
	Buddy	Tommy	A169
Alison Fielding	Cherry Orchard	Anya	A202
Douglas Fielding	Run for Your Wife	As Cast	A944
Emma Fielding	Jane Eyre	Jane Eyre	A555
Maria Fierheller	Roberto Calvi	As Cast	A926
Sarah Finch	Man, Beast and Virtue	Rosaria	A682
Michelle Fine	The Card (A musical)	Mrs Codleyn	A187
	Merrily We Roll Along	As Cast	A711
Frank Finlay	The Heiress	Doctor Austin Sloper	A490
Jonas Finlay	The Devils	Guillaume De Cerisay/Cardinal	A304
John Finn	Dancing At Lughnasa	Gerry	A274
Albert Finney	Reflected Glory	Alfred	A898
Victoria Finney	Alfie	Gilda	A30
Ann Firbank	Tess Of The D'Urbervil	Mrs D'Urberville	A1089
	A Working Woman	Mme Coujet	A1238
David Firth	Assassins	As Cast	A73
Doug Fisher	Alfie	As Cast	A29
Lucinda Fisher	Trouble in Mind	Judy Sears	A1142
Martin Fisher	Buddy	Joe Mauldin	A169
Sam Fisher	A Life In The Theatre		A618
Dave Fishley	Macbeth	Angus	A655
	The Tempest	Spirit	A1082
Alison Fiske	Night of the Iguana	Judith Fellows	A785

Name	Play	Part	Ref
	Pygmalion	Mrs Pearce	A886
Michael Fitchew	Phantom Of The Opera	Passarino	A854
Caroline Fitzgerald	Chorus of Disapproval	As Cast	A210
	Comedy of Errors	As Cast	A239
	Private Lives	Louise	A881
Kate Fitzgerald	Dancing At Lughnasa	Maggie	A274
Michael Fitzgerald	Madness of George III	The Prince of Wales	A669
Tara Fitzgerald	Our Song	Angela	A833
Sue Flack	As You Like It	Audrey	A68
Peter Flannery	Boy's Own	McKenna	A155
Tim Flannigan	My Fair Lady	Harry	A763
Tim Flavin	Dead Flamingo Dancer	Nick Lambent	A193
	Rocky Horror Show	Frank N Furter	A933
	What About Luv?	As Cast	A1195
Ian Fleet	Provoked Wife	Cornet/Bully Justice	A884
Peter Fleetwood	Don Juan	As Cast	A327
	Goodnight Mr Tom	As Cast	A450
Lucy Fleming	Cold Sweat	As Cast	A234
	Our Song	Judith	A833
John Flemming	Cherry Orchard	Yepikhodov	A202
Robert Flemyng	The Chalk Garden	Judge	A196
Daniel Flerin	Gulf Between Us	Militia	A462
Diane Fletcher	All My Sons	Kate	A32
Leah Fletcher	Life Support		A621
Sarah Flind	The Blue Angel	Bertha	A138
	Measure For Measure	Francisca	A700
Pamela Flint	Massa	Jane	A692
Gregory Floy	Anna Karenina	Karenin	A50
	Macbeth	Macduff	A655
	The Tempest	Antonio	A1082
Daniel Flynn	Madness of George III	Greville	A669
Eric Flynn	Grand Hotel	Rhona	A453
Susan Ellen Flynn	Forever Yours	Manon	A413
Siobhan Fogarty	House of Bernarda Alba	As Cast	A515
Simon Fogg	Buddy	Joe Mauldin	A168
William Folan-Conray	Some Like It Hot	Poker Player	A1025
Chuck Foley	Northern Trawl	Stan	A797
John Foley	The Sound Of Music	Ensemble	A1033
Sean Foley	Flight To Finland	Ensemble	A409
	Moose	Ensemble	A738
Charlie Folorunsho	Killing Passion	Nanda	A574
John Food	Valdorama		A1164
Sonia Forbes Adam	Trelawny Of The Wells	Claire Foenix	A1139
Peter Forbes	The Hostage	Mr Mulleady	A505
	Macbeth	Macbeth	A661
Darryl Forbes-Dawson	Rivals	Sir Lucius O'Trigger	A920
Oliver Ford Davies	Heartbreak House	Mazzini Dunn	A486
Alan Ford	Goin' Local	Albert	A442
Julia Ford	A Dolls House	Nora	A321
	Hamlet	Ophelia	A465
	Some Singing Blood		A1026
Karen Ford	Macbeth	Weird Sister	A656
Michael Ford	Double Dealer	As Cast	A335
Haydn Forde	Hobson's Choice	Fred Beenstock	A500
	The Last Carnival	Daga	A598
	The Snow Queen	As Cast	A1020
	Taste of Honey	Jimmy	A1074
Giles Foreman	As You Desire Me		A66
	Beardsley	Beardsley	A95

Name	Play	Part	Ref
Kenny Forest	Lord of the Rings	As Cast	A639
Wayne Forester	Thunderbirds FAB	Various	A1111
John Forgeham	Building Blocks	Brian	A170
J Formento	Miss Saigon	Vietnamese Customer	A727
Lisa Fornara	Twelfth Night	Viola	A1149
Deirdre Forrest	Merrily We Roll Along	As Cast	A711
Angela Forry	The Sound Of Music	Brigitta	A1033
Glenna Forster-Jones	Trouble in Mind	Millie Davis	A1142
Brigit Forsyth	You Must Be The Husband	Alice	A1248
Julian Forsyth	The Blue Angel	Klaus	A138
	Measure For Measure	Barnardine	A700
Kieron Forsyth	Jack's Out	As Cast	A554
Tony Forsyth	Much Ado About Nothing	Claudio	A752
Jack Fortune	Arms and the Man	Sergius	A60
Barry Foster	The Gigli Concert	J.P.W King	A435
	Grand Hotel	Dr Otternschlag	A453
	Playing The Wife	As Cast	A865
Julia Foster	On Golden Pond	Chelsea	A808
Neal Foster	While The Sun Shines	Lord Harpenden	A1201
Simon John Foster	Blues Brothers	Elwood	A142
Olwen Fouere	Cherry Orchard		A203
	Dancing At Lughnasa	Agnes	A274
	Macbeth	Lady Macduff	A655
	The Tempest	Ariel	A1082
Hal Fowler	Aspects Of Love	Alex's Friend Actor	A72
	Leonardo	Melzi	A608
Jane Fowler	A Midsummer Night's ..	Lady/Mustardseed	A720
Philip Fowler	Strange Domain	Ganache	A1055
Ben Fox	Aladdin Bolton	As Cast	A27
	Loot	Hal	A637
Edward Fox	My Fair Lady	Henry Higgins	A763
Emily Fox	The Rock Station	Viola	A931
Jessica Fox	The Sound Of Music	Gretl	A1033
Maggie Fox	Withering Looks	As Cast	A1217
Sandra Fox	As You Desire Me	The Unknown Woman	A66
Simon Fox	Aladdin	Abanazar	A20
Trevor Fox	Your Home In The West	Mickey	A1250
David Foxxe	The Sea	Carter	A961
Tim Frances	Barnstormers	Sam Hodgson Richard Cawdell	A92
Andrea Francis	Buddy	Ensemble	A168
Marie Francis	Much Ado About Nothing	Beatrice	A752
Martin Francis	Shout Across The River	As Cast	A997
Nigel Francis	Grand Hotel	Bellboy	A453
	Strange Domain	Frantz	A1055
Stu Francis	Snow White...	As Cast	A1022
Donald Francke	Cats	Old Deuteronomy	A194
Laura Frangolides	Phantom Of The Opera	Ballet/Chorus	A854
Douglas Franklin	Cats	Coricopat	A194
Helen Franklin	Wit's End	Sofia	A1216
Vincent Franklin	As You Like It	As Cast	A68
	Blithe Spirit	Dr Bradman	A128
	The Hostage	Pat	A505
	Macbeth	Ross	A661
Sabina Franklyn	Turner's Crossing	Susan	A1146
Philip Franks	As You Like It	Orlando	A68
	Schippel, The Plumber	The Prince	A954
Tanya Franks	Teechers	Hobby	A1076

Name	Play	Part	Ref
Helen Fraser	Fifteen Streets	Beatrice Llewellyn Bella Bradley	A403
	Night Must Fall	Mrs Terence	A784
Joe Fraser	An Ideal Husband	Vicomte De Nanjac	A528
Liz Fraser	Alfie	Ruby	A30
Ronald Fraser	The Seagull	Sorin	A962
	She Stoops To Conquer	As Cast	A991
Helen Frazer	A Dead Secret	Emily Vokes	A289
Rupert Frazer	Marching Song	Rupert Forster	A685
Allan Fredericks	Annie Get Your Gun	Pawnees' Messenger	A51
Susan Freebury	Some Like It Hot	Emily	A1025
Regina Freedman	Cut and Trust	Nurse/Old Woman etc	A265
Brian Freeman	Fierce Love	As Cast	A402
Ethan Freeman	Phantom Of The Opera	Monsieur Andre	A854
Gately Freeman	The Three Musketeers	King Louis XIII	A1104
Jane Freeman	Jack And The Beanstalk	The Fairy	A553
	Sailor Beware!	Emma Hornett	A948
Myles Freeman	Joseph...	Butler	A559
Paul Freeman	The Cutting	Alex	A267
	Death and the Maiden	Gerardo Escobar	A293
Penelope Freeman	The Mousetrap	Miss Casewell	A744
Pete Freeman	Games	As Cast	A426
Polly Freeman	Noises Off	Brooke Ashton	A794
Richard Freeman	Schippel, The Plumber	Krey	A954
Tim Freeman	Ten Times Table	Max	A1087
Shaun French	The Recruiting Officer	Collier	A896
Mark Frendo	Joseph...	Napthali	A559
Thomas Frere	Candide	1st Bulgarian	A185
Geoffrey Freshwater	The Changeling	Lollio	A197
	The Odyssey	Cyclops	A802
	Tamburlaine The Great	Techelles	A1067
	The Taming Of The Shrew	Grumio	A1068
Theresa Fresson	Coriolanus	As Cast	A248
	Me and My Friend	Robin	A697
Amelia Frid	Aladdin	Princess Balroubador	A18
Maria Friedman	Merrily We Roll Along	Mary	A711
	Square Rounds	As Cast	A1038
Vincent Friel	TO	As Cast	A1119
Robin Fritz	Macbeth	As Cast	A657
Richard Frost	Safe In Our Hands	Russell	A947
Roger Frost	A Jovial Crew	Justice Clack	A561
	The Winter's Tale	Gaoler	A1214
Janette Froud	Annie Get Your Gun	Ensemble	A51
Frances Fry	The Sound Of Music	Ensemble	A1033
Charlotte Fryer	Blues for Mr Charlie	Susan	A143
Christopher Fulford	Women Laughing	Colin	A1234
	Women Laughing	As Cast	A1235
Erik Fuller	Ghost Sonata	Johannson	A431
Fiona Fullerton	Revenge	Mary Stanwick	A907
Leigh Funnelle	Savage Storm	As Cast	A952
	Six Fools	As Cast	A1009
David Futcher	Biboff	Mendel	A117
Michael Futcher	Disobediently Yours	Edmund Kean	A314
Josefina Gabrielle	Carousel	As Cast	A190
James Gaddas	Evening with Gary L.	Dan	A383
Rachel Gaffin	The BFG	Rebecca Gizzardgulper etc	A116
Greer Gaffney	Roaring Girl's Hamlet	Ophelia	A925
Alastair Galbraith	Doll's House	Torvald	A320

Name	Play	Part	Ref
Bernard Gallagher	The Alchemist	Lovewit	A28
	Columbus	Miguel Garcia	A237
	Julius Caesar	Casca	A566
	'Tis Pity She's A Whore	Florio	A1114
Don Gallagher	Goodnight Mr Tom	As Cast	A450
Frank Gallagher	Lions of Lisbon	Phil Divers	A626
Peter Gallagher	Buddy	The Big Bopper	A168
Steve Gallagher	The Three Musketeers	Aramis	A1104
Teresa Gallagher	Doll's House	Nora	A322
Kay Gallie	In Praise Of Love		A536
	On Golden Pond	Ethel	A809
Jenny Galloway	Candide	Baroness	A185
	Square Rounds	As Cast	A1038
Lucinda Galloway	The Miser	Mariane	A724
Kay Gally	Your Turn To Clean The Stairs	Mrs Mackie	A1252
David Gant	Coriolanus	As Cast	A248
	Rivals	Sir Anthony Absolute	A920
Kenneth Gardiner	Merchant Of Venice	Shylock	A707
Michael Gardiner	Fuente Ovejuna	Juan Rojo	A422
Jimmy Gardner	Lulu	Schigolch	A648
Susan Gardner	Working	As Cast	A1239
Paula Garfield	Children Of Lesser God	Sarah	A206
Owen Garmon	Merchant Of Venice	Antonio/Old Gobbo	A707
Michael Garner	Absent Friends	Paul	A10
	Evening with Gary L.	Bill	A383
Richard Garnett	Hay Fever	Sandy	A481
	Time Of My Life	As Cast	A1112
Geoffrey Garratt	Cats	Skimbleshanks	A194
	Joseph...	Dan	A559
Kate Gartside	As You Like It	Celia	A68
	A Working Woman	Gervaise	A1238
Henry Garvey	Macbeth	As Cast	A660
Sean Garvey	Safe In Our Hands	Andrews	A947
Amanda Garwood	Kurt Weill Cabaret	As Cast	A585
Patricia Garwood	Steel Magnolias	Clairee	A1045
Andrea Gascoigne	Dead Man's Hat	As Cast	A288
	Frankenstein	Elizabeth Lavenza	A415
	The Tempest	Miranda/Ariel	A1083
Jill Gascoine	Bazaar and Rummage	Gwenda	A94
William Gaunt	Murder By Misadventure	Riggs	A755
Richard Gauntlett	Barnum	The Ringmaster	A93
Howard Gay	In The Midnight Hour	Judd	A537
	Julius Caesar	Metellus Cimber	A564
	The Night Before The Morning After		A782
Richard Gay	Serve Them All My Days	As Cast	A1123
Isabelle Gazonnois	Les Atrides	As Cast	A609
Alan Gear	A Midsummer Night's Dream	As Cast	A717
	Robin	Friar Tuck	A927
Joan Geary	Elisabeth II	As Cast	A361
	The Family Reunion	Amy	A394
Veronica Geary	The Best Man	Dawn	A110
Liz Gebhardt	Curse Of The Mummy	Miss Hylyard	A263
Christopher Gee	Travel With My Aunt	As Cast	A1134
Donald Gee	As You Like It	Duke Senior	A68
Prunella Gee	Witness For The Prosecution	Romaine	A1218
Robbie Gee	Armed And Dangerous	As Cast	A59

Name	Play	Part	Ref
Ian Gelder	Elisabeth II	As Cast	A361
	Playing Sinatra	Norman	A864
Jonathan Geller	Savage Storm	As cast	A952
Ruth Gemmell	Uncle Vanya	Yelena	A1158
Eamon Geoghegan	Starlight Express	As Cast	A1043
Sally Geoghegan	Don't Rock The Boat	Wendy	A330
Ben George	Grand Hotel	The Chauffeur	A453
Martin George	Forbidden Planet	Cookie	A904
Morgan George	Wit's End	Platon Mikailovich	A1216
Sally George	Comedy of Errors	Luciana	A240
	Henceforward...	Rita (video)	A491
	Jolly Potters	As Cast	A557
Trevor Michael George	Carmen Jones	Rum	A189
Nicola Georgia	Chasing The Hypnotist	As Cast	A201
Billy Geraghty	Buddy	Buddy Holly	A169
Sean Geraghty	Buddy	Ensemble	A169
Peter Gerald	Houdini	As Cast	A509
Shahrokh Meshkin Ghalam	Les Atrides	As Cast	A609
Kulvinder Ghir	Gulf Between Us	Chatterjee	A462
Andrea Gibb	Doll's House	Christina	A322
Piers Gibbon	Caesar And Cleopatra	Soldier	A180
Emma Gibbons	Body Talk		A147
	Hans C. Anderstories		A470
	Ten In A Bed		A1086
Francesca Gibbs	Wit's End	Mimi	A1216
Sheila Shand Gibbs	Hamlet	As Cast	A465
Melissa Gibson	Starlight Express	As Cast	A1043
Richard Gibson	Bulldog Drummond	Algernon	A171
	She Stoops To Conquer	As Cast	A991
Wendy Gifford	Death Of A Salesman	Linda	A297
Alec Gilbert	Commodities	John Sinclair	A244
Anna Gilbert	Master and Margarita	Margarita	A693
Chris Gilbert	Flamingo	As Cast	A408
Kenneth Gilbert	Beyond Reasonable Doubt	Lionel Hamilton	A114
	A Midsummer Night's Dream	As Cast	A717
	Noises Off	Selsdon Mowbray	A795
	Shadowlands	Warnie	A985
Alexandra Gilbreath	As You Like It	Phebe	A69
	House of Bernarda Alba	As Cast	A515
Nicholas Gilbrook	Ghost Sonata	The Student	A431
Sean Gilder	Twelfth Night	Fabian	A1148
Ramsay Gilderdale	Me And My Girl	The Hon Gerald Bolingbroke	A699
Don Gilet	Elegies...	As Cast	A358
John Gill	Woman Of No Importance	The Ven Archdeacon Daubeney	A1230
Ravinder Gill	Heer Ranjha	As Cast	A489
Robbie Gill	Goodnight Mr Tom	Young Willie Beech	A450
Aiden Gillen	Wexford Trilogy	As Cast	A1194
Debra Gillett	Back Up The Hearse	Angie	A84
	Hush	As Cast	A522
Jeremy Gilley	Gamblers	Glob (son)	A424
Manda Gilliland	Phantom Of The Opera	Ballet/Chorus	A854
Christopher Gilling	Macbeth	Ross	A653
Mary Gillingham	A Dolls House	Nurse/Anne-Marie	A321
Daniel Gillingwater	As You Like It	Amiens	A71
	Lady Be Good	Removal Man	A594
	Merrily We Roll Along	As Cast	A711

Name	Play	Part	Ref
	A Midsummer Night's ..	Mustardseed	A721
Tracy Gillman	Phantom of the Opera	Carlotta/Dominque Chorus Girl	A853
Scott Gilmore	Toronto, Mississippi	As Cast	A1129
John Gilmour	Hapgood	Maggs	A472
	The House Of Stairs	Gary	A513
Catherine Gisbourne	School Of Night	Dark Lady	A960
Karen Gisbourne	Aba Daba Music Hall	Various	A6
	Put That Light Out	Various	A885
	Road To Casablanca	Yvette	A923
Steven Givnan	King Lear	Burgundy/Oswald	A578
	Threepenny Story	Scally	A1108
	A View From The Bridge	Louis	A1169
David Glass	Glassparts	Various	A441
Amanda Gleave	Phantom Of The Opera	Standby	A854
Brendan Gleeson	Cherry Orchard		A203
Jonathan Gleeson	The House Of Stairs	Harvey/Mervyn Waiter	A513
Lucy Gleeson	The House Of Stairs	Diana/Perdita Doctor	A513
Angus M. Glen	As Time Goes By	As Cast	A65
Christine Glen	Good Rockin' Tonite	Iris	A449
Edward Glen	Miss Saigon	Marine	A727
Iain Glen	Coriolanus	Tullus Aufidius	A248
	She Stoops To Conquer	Marlow	A992
Kenny Glenaan	Merlin, The Search	As Cast	A709
Robert Glenister	Colquhoun And MacBryde	As Cast	A235
	An Ideal Husband	Lord Goring	A528
David Glennie	Spring Awakening	Melchoir	A1037
Jon Glentoran	Three Musketeers	Athos	A1106
	To Kill A Mockingbird	Boo Radley	A1121
Sharon Gless	Misery	Annie Wilkes	A725
Nicola Glick	The Heiress	Marian	A490
Brian Glover	Annie Get Your Gun	Chief Sitting Bull	A51
	Richard III	Buckingham	A912
David Glover	Single Spies	The Tailor/Anthony Blunt	A1005
Jamie Glover	The Mother Tongue	Jeremy	A743
Julian Glover	All My Sons	Joe	A32
	Cyrano De Bergerac	De Guiche	A269
	Henry IV Part 1	Henry IV	A492
	Henry IV Part 2	Henry IV	A493
	Romeo And Juliet	Prince Escalus	A938
Jonathan Glynn	Measure For Measure	Froth	A700
John Godber	April In Paris	Al	A58
Beth Goddard	Karate Billy...Home	As Cast	A572
Liza Goddard	Moment Of Weakness	Audrey	A732
Kate Godfrey	The House Of Stairs	As cast	A513
Patrick Godfrey	Phoenix	Otto	A857
Adam Godley	June Moon	As Cast	A567
Christopher Godwin	Hay Fever	Richard	A481
	Leo In Love	Francois	A607
Richard Gofton	Biboff	Noah	A117
Valerie Gogan	Love's Labour's Lost	Katherine	A645
Louise Gold	Assassins	As Cast	A73
	Merrily We Roll Along	Gussie	A711
Max Gold	Anna Karenina	Vronsky	A50
Bill Golding	Double Dealer	As Cast	A335
Helen Goldwyn	My Fair Lady	Servant	A763
Julie Golsworthy	Diamonds in the Dust	As Cast	A306
Russell Gomer	Merchant Of Venice	Launcelot Gobbo Aragon/Tubal	A707

Name	Play	Part	Ref
Carmen Gomez	Don Quixote	As Cast	A328
	EuroVision	As Cast	A381
Sharon Gomez	Miss Saigon	Bar Girl	A727
Stella Gonet	Cyrano De Bergerac	Roxanne	A269
Christopher Good	Voysey Inheritance	Trenchard	A1182
Robert Goodale	Hamlet	As Cast	A465
Louise Goodall	Lions of Lisbon	Cathy	A626
Rachel Gooderson	Curse Of The Mummy	As Cast	A263
Deborah Goodman	Breathless	Magda	A160
Henry Goodman	Angels In America	Roy Cohn/Prior 2	A47
	Assassins	As Cast	A73
John Goodrum	Martin Chuzzlewit	Multiple Roles	A689
	Second From Last In The Sack Race	The Parrot/The Radio etc.	A966
Neale Goodrum	The Dark River	Stanley Maltby	A282
Felicity Goodson	The Business Of Murder	As Cast	A175
	Cinderella	As Cast	A222
Damien Goodwin	Caesar And Cleopatra	Centinel	A180
Tim Goodwin	Enemy To The People	As Cast	A369
Deborah Goody	Phantom Of The Opera	Page	A854
Howard Goorney	House Of The Spirits		A514
Jennie Goossens	My Fair Lady	Mrs Pearce	A763
John Gordon Sinclair	Grave Plots	As Cast	A456
Hannah Gordon	An Ideal Husband	Lady Chiltern	A527
Josephine Gordon	70, Girls, 70	As Cast	A4
	Beauty And The Beast	A Zephyr	A98
Peter Gordon	As You Like It	Adam	A69
John Gordon-Sinclair	As You Like It	Orlando	A69
Shay Gorman	Wexford Trilogy	Paddy	A1194
Michael Goron	Man Outside	As Cast	A681
	While The Sun Shines	As Cast	A1201
Julia Goss	Phantom Of The Opera	Carlotta Guidicelli	A854
Susan Gott	Fifteen Streets	Nancy Kelly	A403
	Moll Flanders	As Cast	A730
	On The Piste	Bev	A811
	Watching And Weighting	One-Woman Show	A1187
David Goudge	Fifteen Streets	Father O'Malley	A403
	Jubilee	Collin	A562
Maria Gough	June Moon	As Cast	A567
Matthew Gould	Les Miserables	Ensemble	A613
Michael Gould	The Dybbuk	Third Batlon	A349
	Hamlet	As Cast	A466
	Henry IV Part 1	Duke of Clarence	A492
	Henry IV Part 2	Duke of Clarence	A493
Eileen Gourlay	Talk Of The Steamie	Dolly	A1065
Shenagh Govan	Haunted Hotel	Lady Constance Westwick	A479
	Out Of Order	Gladys	A835
Nickolas Grace	A Swell Party	Cole Porter	A1060
Charmian Gradwell	Chorus of Disapproval	As Cast	A210
Josephine Gradwell	Rivals	Lucy	A920
Luciana Gradwell	Comedy of Errors	Luciana	A239
Bruce Graham	Phantom Of The Opera	Fireman	A854
Campbell Graham	Loot	Sergeant Meadows	A637
Denys Graham	Grand Hotel	Victor Witt	A453
Hepburn Graham	The Revenger's Tragedy	Supervacuo	A908
Jan Graham	Raving Beauties	Sue	A893
Jill Graham	Measure For Measure	Escalus	A702
Judy Graham	Don't Dress For Dinner	Suzanne	A331
Julie Graham	Revenger's Tragedy	Castiza	A909
Valerie Grail	Les Atrides	As Cast	A609

Name	Play	Part	Ref
Glyn Grain	Mr A's Amazing Maze	As Cast	A746
Gawn Grainger	No Man's Land	Briggs	A789
Virginia Grainger	Comedy Of Errors	As Cast	A241
Michael Grandage	Caesar And Cleopatra	Appollodorus	A180
	Voysey Inheritance	Hugh	A1182
Robert Grange	My Cousin Rachel	Nicholas Kendall	A762
Benny Grant	Lost in Yonkers	Arty	A641
Deborah Grant	A Little Night Music		A630
Elaine Grant	Hecuba	Chorus	A488
James Grant	Billy Liar	Geoffrey Fisher	A122
Joyce Grant	Comedy Of Errors	As Cast	A241
Leslie Grantham	Cold Sweat	Mike Mason	A234
Steven Granville	Bright & Bold Design	Ulik Mountford	A161
	Comedy of Errors	Egeon	A240
	Jolly Potters	As Cast	A557
	Snow Queen	Crow	A1021
	Turkey Time	Edwin Stoatt	A1144
Rupert Graves	A Midsummer Night's Dream	Lysander	A718
Jan Graveson	The Double D	As Cast	A333
Dulcie Gray	Bedroom Farce	Delia	A104
	An Ideal Husband	Lady Markby	A527
Gregory Gray	Chasing The Hypnotist	As Cast	A201
James Gray	My Fair Lady	Angry Man	A763
Stephen Gray	Buddy	Buddy Holly	A168
Tina Gray	Our Ellen	Ellen Terry	A832
Hilary Greatorex	Roadshow		A924
Christina Greatrex	Bulldog Drummond	Irma	A171
James Greaves	Crime of Love	As Cast	A258
Matthew Green	The Tender Husband	Hezekiah Tipkin	A1088
Penny Green	World...Upside Down	As Cast	A1240
Robson Green	York Mystery Plays	Jesus Christ	A1247
	Your Home In The West	Maurice	A1250
Simon Green	Between the Lines	Ensemble	A112
	Lady Be Good	Dick Trevor	A594
Teddy Green	Stepping Out	Geoffrey	A1046
Jill Greenacre	My Cousin Rachel	As Cast	A762
Liz Greenaway	My Heart's A Suitcase	Hannah	A764
Brian Greene	70, Girls, 70	As Cast	A4
	Trouble in Mind	Bill O'Wray	A1142
Leon Greene	Annie Get Your Gun	Col Wm. F. Cody	A51
Victor Greene	Therese Raquin	Michaud	A1097
Andy Greenhalgh	Love's Labour's Lost	Dull	A645
Nigel Greenhalgh	Bag Dancing	Neville Child	A87
Geoffrey Greenhill	Down And Out...	The Italian Lover	A339
Paul Greenwood	Pig In A Poke	Wembley	A859
Sally Greenwood	Outside Edge	Maggie	A837
	Roaring Girl's Hamlet	Polonius	A925
	Three Musketeers	Kitty	A1106
	To Kill A Mockingbird	Maudy Atkinson	A1121
Georgia Greeph	Eductaing Rita	Rita	A354
	Home At Seven	As Cast	A502
Simon Gregor	Weldon Rising	As Cast	A1192
Celia Gregory	'Tis Pity She's A Whore	Hippolita	A1114
Dave Gregory	Gulf Between Us	Militia	A462
Emma Gregory	As You Like It	Phoebe	A67
	The Beggar's Opera	Dolly Trull	A106
Guy Gregory	Blues for Mr Charlie	Papa D.	A143
	Courting Winnona	Redman	A255
	Driving Miss Daisy	Hoke Colburn	A345
Stephen Greif	Reflected Glory	Robert Jaffey	A898

Name	Play	Part	Ref
Rachel Grendon	Spring Awakening	Frau Gabor	A1037
Nicola Grier	Beauty And The Beast	Hannah/Crabhook	A97
Ian Grieve	Little Shop Of Horrors	Derelict	A632
Gordon Griffin	And A Nightingale Sang	George Stott	A43
Derek Griffiths	The Recruiting Officer	Sgt Kite	A897
	Snow White	Gypsy King	A1023
Georgina Griffiths	Chasing The Hypnotist	As Cast	A201
James Griffiths	The Best Man	Roger	A110
Jaye Griffiths	Woman Of No Importance	Miss Hester Worsley	A1230
John Griffiths	Phantom Of The Opera	Monsieur Lefevre	A854
Joss Griffiths	Gulf Between Us	Militia	A462
Philip Griffiths	Phantom Of The Opera	Monsieur Reyer	A854
Richard Griffiths	The Rules Of The Game	Leone	A943
Roger Griffiths	Armed And Dangerous	As Cast	A59
Sara Griffiths	Cold Sweat	As Cast	A234
Valerie Griffiths	Angels & Amazons	As Cast	A48
Oliver Grig	The Sound Of Music	Friedrich	A1033
John Grillo	Six Degrees...	Doorman/Dr Fine	A1008
Sophie Grimmer	The Bells	Annette	A108
Glyn Grimstead	Goin' Local	Lol	A442
Dale Grimston	Private Lives	Maid	A880
Robbie Gringras	Story of the Last	Various	A1053
C.P. Grogan	Talk Of The Steamie	Doreen	A1065
Fiona Grogan	The BFG	Sophie	A116
Wifred Grove	Happy Families	Jack Hickman	A476
Sam Grover	The BFG	Sam/Bonecruncher etc	A116
David Groves	Six Degrees...	Woody	A1008
Caroline Gruber	Penny for a Song	As Cast	A848
Paul Gruber	The Dorm	Webster	A332
Liam Grundy	Down And Out...	Debt Collector	A339
Candida Gubbins	Life is a Dream	Estrella	A619
Seamus Gubbins	End Of The Beginning	Various	A366
Maggie Guess	Steel Magnolias	Truvy	A1045
Kaleb Gumbs	Dragon	As Cast	A341
Margo Gunn	The Miser	Elsie	A724
Michael Gunn	Kafka's Dick	Sydney	A571
Eric Gupton	Fierce Love	As Cast	A402
Jane Gurnett	The Alchemist	Dame Pliant	A28
	Amphibians	Veronica	A40
	Artists and Admirers	Smelskaya	A64
	Columbus	Beatrice	A237
	Henry IV Part 1	Lady Mortimer	A492
	Julius Caesar	Portia	A566
	Twelfth Night	Olivia	A1152
Caro Gurney	Road To Casablanca	Marlene	A923
Rachel Gurney	Uncle Vanya	Marya Vassilyevna	A1157
Rachel Gurney	Breaking the Code	As Cast	A159
Ben Guy	Romeo And Juliet	Child	A938
Jane Gwilliams	Courting Winnona	Elizabeth	A255
Haydn Gwynne	The Recruiting Officer	Silvia	A897
Michael Gyngell	Starlight Express	As Cast	A1043
Jonathan Hackett	Romeo and Juliet	Friar Laurance	A936
	A View From The Bridge	Eddie Carbone	A1172
Mark Haddigan	Grease	Johnny Casino	A458
Ellie Haddington	The Sea	Mafanwy Price	A961
William Haden	Night Must Fall	Inspector Belsize	A784
Mark Hadfield	Becket	Little Monk	A103
	Bourgeois Gentilhomme	Dancing Master	A153
	A Midsummer Night's Dream	Starveling	A718

Name	Play	Part	Ref
Kenneth **Hadley**	Doll's House	Dr Rank	A322
Roger **Hager**	The Imaginary Invalid	Cleante	A529
Garrick **Hagon**	All My Sons	Jim Bayliss	A32
Richard **Hague**	Hobson's Choice	William Mossop	A499
	Julius Caesar	Cassius	A564
	Loot	Inspector Truscott	A637
	The Night Before The Morning After		A782
	The Threepenny Opera	Filch	A1109
Richard **Hahlo**	Kvetch	Hal	A586
David **Haig**	Measure For Measure	Angelo	A700
Michael **Haighton**	Lady Aoi	As Cast	A593
Ken **Haines**	Little Shop Of Horrors	Audrey II	A632
Georgina **Hale**	Cinderella	Fairy Godmother	A221
Paul **Haley**	Blues for Mr Charlie	Revd. Phelps	A143
Andrew **Hall**	Evening With Gary L.	Bill	A382
Chris **John Hall**	Romeo and Juliet	The Sultan	A937
Jody **Hall**	70, Girls, 70	As Cast	A4
Michael **Hall**	The Dark River	Mr Veness	A282
Walter **Hall**	Murmuring Judges	Nelson	A758
	Wind In The Willows	Hedgehog	A1211
Andrew **Halliday**	Phantom Of The Opera	Porter	A854
Peter **Halliday**	Happy Days	Willie	A474
	Voysey Inheritance	Rev Evan Colpus	A1182
Terence **Halliday**	Time Windows	Constable Williams	A1113
David **Hallinson**	Cloud 9	Harry	A232
John **Halstead**	Goin' Local	Lenny	A442
	Old Mother Hubbard	Old Mother Hubbard	A805
Masayoshi **Hamana**	Starlight Express	Hashamoto	A1043
Lynne **Hames**	Roadshow		A924
Gabrielle **Hamilton**	Ten Times Table	Audrey	A1087
Graham **Hamilton**	Jack And The Beanstalk	Fleshcreep	A553
Kate **Hamilton**	Lady of the Lilacs	As Cast	A596
	Starlight Express	As Cast	A1043
Nick **Hamilton**	Leonardo	As Cast	A608
Paul **Hamilton**	Blood Wedding	Death	A134
	Gormenghast	Flay	A451
	Under Milk Wood	As Cast	A1160
Dilys **Hamlett**	Becket	Queen Mother	A103
	Cyrano De Bergerac	The Duenna/Mother Marguerite	A269
Mona **Hammond**	Fuente Ovejuna	Queen Isabel	A422
Susanna **Hamnett**	Mrs Klein	As Cast	A749
Julia **Hampson**	Rocky Horror Show	Phantom	A933
Peter **Hampson**	Dangerous Obsession	Mark Driscoll	A281
	Mansfield Park	Mr Yates	A683
Richard **Hampton**	Bulldog Drummond	Derbyshire	A171
Allison **Hancock**	Sisters	As Cast	A1006
Gemma **Hancock**	Caesar And Cleopatra	Iris	A180
Nick **Hancock**	Evening with Gary L.	Dan	A383
Phyllida **Hancock**	As You Like It	Celia	A67
	Becket	Gwendoline	A103
	The Beggar's Opera	Suky Tawdry	A106
	The Winter's Tale	Perdita	A1214
Sheila **Hancock**	A Judgement In Stone	Eunice	A563
Robert **Hands**	As You Like It	Orlando	A68
	Valentine's Day	Philip	A1165
Roy **Hanlon**	White Woman Street	Mo Mason	A1202
Peter **Hanly**	Digging for Fire	As Cast	A313
Gillian **Hanna**	Romeo and Juliet	Lady Montague	A936
	A View From The Bridge	Beatrice	A1172
Sean **Hannaway**	The Rivals	David	A919

Name	Play	Part	Ref
Mark **Hannay**	Christopher Street	As Cast	A218
Alexander **Hanson**	Valentine's Day	Valentine	A1165
Nadine **Hanwell**	Fallen Angels	Saunders	A391
Chloe **Harbour**	My Mother Said	Rosie	A767
Edward **Harbour**	The Miser	Brindavoine	A724
Kate **Harbour**	Phantom of the Opera	Jammes	A853
Michael **N Harbour**	The Invisible Man	Griffin	A547
Diana **Hardcastle**	Me And Mamie O'Rourke	Louise	A696
Allison **Harding**	From A Jack To A King	Queenie	A420
Caroline **Harding**	A Dolls House	Mrs Linde	A321
	The Secret Rapture	Katherine	A968
Jeff **Harding**	Me And Mamie O'Rourke	Clark	A696
Peter **Harding**	Outside Edge	Roger	A837
	Three Musketeers	Richelieu	A1106
	To Kill A Mockingbird	Atticus Finch	A1121
Allan **Hardman**	Les Miserables	Bambatabois	A611
Charlie **Hardwick**	Your Home In The West	Jean	A1250
Tracy **Hardwick**	Tango 'Til You're Sore	Vicky	A1072
Edward **Hardwickle**	Chorus of Disapproval	Dafydd ap Llewellyn	A210
Alex **Hardy**	As You Like It	Duke Frederick	A69
	The Miser	Valere	A724
Andrew **Hardy**	An Ideal Husband	Footman	A528
Robert **Hardy**	Body And Soul	Alex	A146
Doris **Hare**	It Runs In The Family	Mother	A548
Andy **Harewood**	Buddy	Ensemble	A169
David **Harewood**	The Rivals	Captain Absolute	A918
David **Hargreaves**	A View From The Bridge	Eddie	A1171
Susannah **Harker**	Coriolanus	Virgilia	A248
	She Stoops To Conquer	Kate Hardcastle	A992
	Venus Observed	Perpetua	A1168
Alex **Harland**	Elephant	As Cast	A359
Kirsten **Harle**	Robin	Ladies Of The Court	A927
Peter **Harlowe**	The Winslow Boy	Sir Robert Morton	A1213
Jacqui **Harman**	Joseph...	Zebulun's Wife	A559
Ricci **Harnett**	Punishment Of Animals	As Cast	A259
Gerald **Harper**	Murder By Misadventure	Harold	A755
Richard **Harradine**	A View From The Bridge	Marco	A1171
Serena **Harragin**	The Secret Rapture	Isobel	A968
Julian **Harries**	Peculiar People	James Baynard	A846
Rebecca **Harries**	Hobson's Choice	Ada Figgins	A500
	Metamorphosis	Greta	A714
Amanda **Harris**	The Odyssey	Penelope	A802
	The Taming Of The Shrew	Katharina	A1068
Anita **Harris**	The House Of Stairs	Elizabeth	A513
	My Cousin Rachel	Rachel Ashley	A762
Chris **Harris**	Aladdin	Widow Twankee	A25
Corinne **Harris**	Exile	As Cast	A387
Emlyn **Harris**	Little Tramp	Sidney	A634
Garner **Harris**	Starlight Express	As Cast	A1043
Jon **Harris**	Provoked Wife	Constant	A884
Nigel **Harris**	Savage Storm	As Cast	A952
Rolf **Harris**	Cinderella	Buttons	A224
Rosemary **Harris**	Lost in Yonkers	Grandma Kurnitz	A641
Sarah-Jane **Harris**	Daughters Of England	Elizabeth	A284
Simon **Harris**	Blodeuwedd	As Cast	A129
	Merchant Of Venice	Gratiano	A707
Trilby **Harris**	Blood Brothers	Linda	A131
Abigail **Harrison**	Fool for Love	May	A411
Cathryn **Harrison**	As You Like It	Rosalind	A71

Name	Play	Part	Ref
Debbie **Lee Harrison**	Barnum	As Cast	A93
Deirdre **Harrison**	June Moon	As Cast	A567
Jeremy **Harrison**	From A Jack To A King	Still Whithers	A420
Phill **Harrison**	Some Like It Hot	Poker Player	A1025
Simon **Harrison**	Curse Of The Mummy	Akela	A263
Stuart **Harrison**	Trelawny Of The Wells	Cpt. de Foenix	A1139
Simon **Harrison-Scott**	Starlight Express	As Cast	A1043
Lisa **Harrow**	Double Take	Alice	A338
William **Harry**	It Runs In The Family	Leslie	A548
Andrea **Hart**	Beauty And The Beast	Hazel/Banshee	A97
	Merlin, The Search	As Cast	A709
Lorraine **Hart**	Late Joys		A600
Veronica **Hart**	Annie Get Your Gun	Winnie Tate	A51
Ian **Hartley**	Artists and Admirers	As Cast	A64
	Romeo And Juliet	Sampson	A938
John **Hartley**	Straight & Narrow	Arthur	A1054
Steven **Hartley**	Evening With Gary L.	Dan	A382
Kim **Hartman**	'Allo,'Allo	Helga Geerhart	A36
Jamie **Harvell**	Coriolanus	As Cast	A248
Alasdair **Harvey**	My Fair Lady	Costermonger	A763
Carol **Harvey**	The Best Man	Sam	A110
Edward **Harvey**	Macbeth	Macbeth	A660
Jean **Harvey**	The Deep Blue Sea	Mrs Elton	A140
	Macbeth	Weird Sister	A656
Miles **Harvey**	Great God Brown	Billy Brown	A459
	Safe In Our Hands	Derek Fisher	A947
Naomi **Harvey**	World Upon The Moon	Clarice	A1241
Kim **Harwood**	In The Midnight Hour	Duffy	A537
	Some Like It Hot	Olga	A1025
Sarah **Hassell**	Les Miserables	Cosette	A613
Ian **Hastings**	Blue Remembered Hills	Donald Duck	A139
Nigel **Hastings**	As You Like It	Silvius	A71
	Curse Of The Mummy	Police Sergeant	A263
	The Devils	Father Rangier/A Sewerman	A304
	A Midsummer Night's ..	Lysander	A721
Michelle **Hatch**	Cinderella	Cinderella	A225
Linzi **Hateley**	Joseph...	Narrator	A559
Mark **Hathaway**	Biboff	Itzik	A117
	No 3 Pied Piper Street	Peter	A788
Stephen **Hattersley**	Fuente Ovejuna	Don Manrique	A422
Andrew **Havill**	Woman Of No Importance	Gerald Arbuthnot	A1230
Nicky **Hawke**	Annie Get Your Gun	Little Jake	A51
Joe **Hawkins**	Macbeth	Fleance	A658
Leader **Hawkins**	Cherry Orchard	Firs	A202
Dominic **Hawksley**	Cabal and Love	Marshall von Kalb	A176
Paul **Hawkyard**	As You Like It	Dennis	A71
	Lady Be Good	Removal Man	A594
	A Midsummer Night's ..	Cobweb	A721
Chris **Hawley**	Massa	As Cast	A692
	Provoked Wife	Treble/Rake/Rasor	A884
Richard **Hawley**	Hamlet	As Cast	A465
Denys **Hawthorne**	Artists and Admirers	The Tragedian	A64
	Henry IV Part 1	Northumberland	A492
	Henry IV Part 2	Northumberland	A493
	Romeo And Juliet	Prince Escalus	A938
	The Thebans	Messenger	A1095
Nigel **Hawthorne**	Madness of George III	King George III	A669
Liza **Hayden**	Man, Beast and Virtue	Nono	A682
Michael **Hayden**	Carousel	Bill Bigelow	A190
Simon **Hayden**	Miss Saigon	Marine	A727

Name	Play	Part	Ref
Abigail **Hayes**	Macbeth	Waiting Gentlewoman	A655
	The Tempest	Spirit	A1082
Georgie **Hayes**	Miss Saigon	Barman	A727
James **Hayes**	Twelfth Night	Sir Andrew Aguecheek	A1148
Tony **Haygarth**	Macbeth	Macbeth	A655
	The Tempest	Trinculo	A1082
Matthew **Haynes**	School Of Night	Southampton	A960
Alan **Haywood**	Hamlet	As Cast	A465
Barry **Haywood**	Robin	King Richard Clym-The-Clough	A927
Pippa **Haywood**	Private Lives	Amanda	A881
Jane **Hazelgrove**	Spring and Port Wine	Hilda	A1036
Anthony **Head**	The Heiress	Morris Townsend	A490
James **Head**	Little Shop Of Horrors	Audrey II	A632
Martin **Head**	Beardsley	Smithers	A95
Mark **Heal**	Handsome,Handicapped..	As Cast	A468
	The Pope And The Witch	Policeman (Colin) Swiss Guard	A870
	Women in Love	Rupert	A1233
Anna **Healy**	Cherry Orchard		A203
Anne **Healy**	Hecuba	Chorus	A488
Emma **Healy**	Macbeth	Witch	A653
Mark **Healy**	Comedy Of Errors	As Cast	A241
	King Lear In New York	As Cast	A580
Michael **Healy**	Much Ado About Nothing	Leonato	A750
David **Heap**	Cherry Orchard		A203
	Macbeth	Lennox	A655
	The Tempest	Francisco	A1082
Mark **Heap**	Dragon	As Cast	A341
Richard **Heap**	Hamlet	Horatio Guildenstern	A463
	King Lear	Gloucester/Albany	A577
Marcus **Heath**	Merchant Of Venice	Solanio/Duke	A707
	Trouble in Mind	Sheldon Forrester	A1142
Tim **Heath**	Punishment Of Animals	As Cast	A259
	Mansfield Park	Mr Rushworth	A683
Maralyn **Heathcock**	Cabal and Love	Mrs Miller	A176
Barrie **Heathcote**	The Imaginary Invalid	Monsieur Beralde	A529
Roger **Heathcott**	Time Windows	Edward Turnbull	A1113
Mark **Heenehan**	Grand Hotel	Scullery Worker	A453
	Rocky Horror Show	Eddie/Dr Scott	A933
Vivien **Heilbron**	Cerceau	Valyusha	A195
Mark **Helyar**	As Time Goes By	As Cast	A65
Polly **Hemingway**	Richard III	Margaret	A912
Caroline **Hemming**	Phantom Of The Opera	Ballet/Chorus	A854
Nolan **Hemmings**	Single Spies	Tolya/Philips	A1005
Guy **Hemphill**	The Ecstacy	Charles	A353
	Frozen Chicken	As Cast	A421
	You Must Be The Husband	Mr Mason	A1248
Graeme **Henderson**	A Midsummer Night's ..	Francis Flute	A720
	Tess Of The D'Urbervil	Angel Clare	A1089
	Wizard of Oz	Scarecrow	A1224
Joyce **Henderson**	Street of Crocodiles	Agatha	A1056
Shirley **Henderson**	Cuttin' A Rug	Lucille	A266
Fiona **Hendley**	Hindsight	Frances	A495
Janet **Henfrey**	Trelawny Of The Wells	Miss Trafalgar	A1139
Dawn **Hennessey**	The English Kiss	Viv	A370
Del **Henney**	View From The Bridge	Eddie Carbone	A1170
Antoni **Henry**	Miss Saigon	John	A727

Name	Play	Part	Ref
David Henry	Carousel	As Cast	A190
	Madness of George III	Charles James Fox	A669
Dollie Henry	Sophisticated Ladies	Ensemble	A1032
Guy Henry	The Alchemist	Ananias	A28
	Hamlet	As Cast	A466
	'Tis Pity She's A Whore	Poggio	A1114
	Two Gents Of Verona	As Cast	A1154
	The Virtuoso	Sir Formal Trifle	A1176
Douglas Henshall	Macbeth	Macbeth	A656
Ruthie Henshall	Les Miserables	Fantine	A613
Nicky Henson	Reflected Glory	Derek Tewby	A898
Shaun Henson	Cats	Mungojerrie	A194
Karen Henthorn	Second From Last In The Sack Race	Nora/Aunty Doris etc	A966
	The Snow Queen	As Cast	A1020
Peter Heppelthwaite	Slice Of Saturday...	Eddie	A1015
Randal Herley	Romeo And Juliet	Montague	A938
	'Tis Pity She's A Whore	Donado	A1114
	Two Gents Of Verona	s Cast	A1154
Valerie Hermanni	Philadelphia Here I Come	Lizzy	A856
John Herriman	Annie Get Your Gun	Ensemble	A51
Galit Hershkovitz	Spring Awakening	Wendla Bergmann	A1037
Paul Herzberg	Grapes of Wrath	Tom Joad	A454
George Heslin	Philadelphia Here I Come	Joe	A856
Caroline Hetherington	Bloody Poetry	Harriet	A137
Jason Hetherington	Grease	Kenickie	A458
	You Must Be The Husband	Steve	A1248
Phyllida Hewat	The Family Reunion	Violet	A394
Simon Hewitt	Monday After Miracle	Pete	A733
Brian Hewlitt	Wizard of Oz	Cowardly Lion	A1224
Kristin Hewson	House of Bernarda Alba	As Cast	A515
Sophie Heydel	Henceforward...	Zoe	A491
	Snow Queen	Princess	A1021
	Turkey Time	Louise Wheeler	A1144
Sophie Heyman	Time Of My Life	As Cast	A1112
Gerald Heys	Macbeth	The Porter/A Murderer	A653
Vanessa Heywood	Elvis - the Musical	Sweet Inspiration	A362
Brian Hibbard	Blues Brothers	Jake	A142
Linda Hibberd	The Sound Of Music	The Mother Abbess	A1033
Maureen Hibbert	Cut and Trust	Staff Nurse	A265
Brian Hickey	Penny for a Song	As Cast	A848
Tom Hickey	Double Dealer	As Cast	A335
	Misogynist	One-man Show	A726
Greg Hicks	1953	Klaus Maria Von Orestes	A1
	Charlemagne	As Cast	A199
Kim Hicks	Self Portrait	Dorelia McNeill	A974
Clare Higgins	Antony and Cleopatra	Cleopatra	A53
	Ride Down Mt Morgan	Leah	A915
Paul Higgins	Romeo and Juliet	Benvolio	A936
	A View From The Bridge	Rodolpho	A1172
Ralph Higgins	School Of Night	Christopher Marlowe	A960
Tom Higgins	Children Of Lesser God	James	A206
Emma Higginson	Don't Play With Love	Rosette	A329

Name	Play	Part	Ref
Michael Higgs	Romeo And Juliet	Gregory	A938
Robert High	Strange Domain	Meaulnes	A1055
Edward Highmore	My Cousin Rachel	Philip Ashley	A762
Polly Highton	Aladdin Bolton	Genie	A27
Jennifer Hilary	Woman Of No Importance	Mrs Allonby	A1230
Anastasia Hill	Arms and the Man	Raina	A60
Dave Hill	Breaking the Code	As Cast	A159
	Gulf Between Us	O'Toole	A462
Jennifer Hill	It Runs In The Family	Sister	A548
Juliet Hill	Hot Italian Nights	Ensemble	A507
	The Magic Storybook	Ensemble	A672
Sonia Hill	World...Upside Down	As Cast	A1240
Beverley Hills	Roaring Girl's Hamlet	Horatio	A925
Terrance Hillyer	Twelfth Night	Duke Orsino	A1152
Peter Hilton	Les Miserables	Foreman/Combeferre	A611
Louis Hilyer	Bad Blood	Jon Pedro	A85
	An Inspector Calls	Gerald Croft	A541
Gary Hind	A Swell Party		A1060
Madge Hindle	Spring and Port Wine	Daisy Crompton	A1036
Becky Hindley	Man Outside	As Cast	A681
Ciaran Hinds	Assassins	As Cast	A73
Pip Hinton	42nd Street	Maggie	A2
Lou Hirsch	Angels In America	Roy Cohn	A47
David Hitchen	Blood Brothers	Mr Lyons	A131
Susannah Hitching	Doll's House	Nora	A320
Graham Hoadly	Some Like It Hot	Greenbaum	A1025
Cecily Hobbs	Bourgeois Gentilhomme	Dorimene	A153
David Hobbs	Dangerous Corner	Charles Stanton	A277
Julie Hobbs	Grope	Mim	A460
Caroline Hobin	Blood Brothers	Ensemble	A131
Helen Hobson	My Fair Lady	Eliza Doolittle	A763
Kiran Hocking	Your Home In The West	Miss Maybank	A1250
Andy Hockley	Coriolanus	As Cast	A248
Edmund Hockridge	Music Hall		A759
Jack Hodd	Henry IV Part 1	Water-bearer	A492
	Romeo And Juliet	Child	A938
Douglas Hodge	No Man's Land	Foster	A789
	Obsession	As Cast	A800
Patricia Hodge	Shades	Pearl	A981
Sue Hodge	'Allo,'Allo	Mimi	A36
	Don't Dress For Dinner	Suzette	A331
Tom Hodgkins	As You Like It	Charles	A69
	While The Sun Shines	American GI	A1201
John Hodgkinson	The Beggar's Opera	Harry Paddington	A106
	A Jovial Crew	Tallboy	A561
	The Winter's Tale	Lord	A1214
Leda Hodgson	Blithe Spirit	Madame Arcati	A128
	The Hostage	Meg	A505
	Macbeth	Weird Sister Gentleman	A661
Michael Hodgson	Tess Of The D'Urbervil	Christian	A1089
Geoffrey Hodson	Beyond Reasonable Doubt	Mr Justice Tredwell	A114
	Shadowlands	As Cast	A985
Steve Hodson	Cabal and Love	Wurm	A176
Alfred Hoffman	Blithe Spirit	Dr Bradman	A127
	Martin Chuzzlewit	Multiple Roles	A689
	A View From The Bridge	Alfieri	A1171
Erika Hoffman	The Decorator	Jane	A301
	Don't Dress For Dinner	Suzanne	A331
Sharon Hogan	Dancing at Lughnasa	Agnes	A275
Stephen Hogan	Beauty And The Beast	Martin/Beast	A97

Name	Play	Part	Ref
Jane Hogarth	Self Catering	Meryl Streep	A973
Marjory Hogarth	MacWizard Fae Oz	As Cast	A663
Ian Hogg	The Seagull	Trigorin	A962
Caroline Holdaway	The Mother Tongue	Jo Jo	A743
David Holdaway	Life is a Dream	As Cast	A619
Ralph Holden	Starlight Express	As Cast	A1043
Roisin Holden	Wit's End	Liza	A1216
Nick Holder	As You Like It	Charles the Wrestler	A67
	The Beggar's Opera	Matt of the Mint	A106
	The Merry Wives Of Windsor	Simple	A713
Roy Holder	Venus Observed	Bates	A1168
Sue Holderness	You Must Be The Husband	Alice	A1248
Joanna Hole	The Writing Game	Maude Lockett	A1242
Florrie Holland	Out Of Order	The Maid	A835
Jeffery Holland	You Must Be The Husband	Tom	A1248
Lisa Hollander	All My Sons	Lydia Lubey	A32
Tom Hollander	Me and My Friend	Oz	A697
Cassandra Holliday	Little Tramp	Lady Anne/Others	A634
Mandy Holliday	Les Miserables	Crone	A611
Vilma Hollingbery	Death of A Salesman	Linda Loman	A295
Christopher Hollis	Cabal and Love	Ferdinand von Walter	A176
Nina Holloway	Sailor Beware!	Mrs Lack	A948
Jane Hollowood	Blithe Spirit	Ruth	A127
	A Marginal Affair	Mary Wilshaw	A687
Sarah-Jane Holm	As You Like It	Celia	A71
	Curse Of The Mummy	Alberts Mum	A263
	A Midsummer Night's ..	Hermia	A721
Clare Holman	Karate Billy...Home	As Cast	A572
	Romeo And Juliet	Juliet	A938
	Two Gents Of Verona	Julia	A1154
Ben Holmes	Dangerous Dolls-Soap Crazy	Various	A280
Simon Holmes	The Tender Husband	Clerimont Snr	A1088
Mike Holoway	Robin	Robin Hood	A927
Amanda Holt	Beauty And The Beast	Rambling Rose	A98
Carole Holt	Provoked Wife	Lady Fanciful	A884
Lewis Holt	Happy As A Sandbag	As Cast	A473
Bill Homewood	Grand Hotel	Zinnowitz	A453
Jessica Honeyball	Wind In The Willows	Tommy	A1211
Adrian Hood	Little Voice	Billy	A917
Morag Hood	Woman In Mind	As Cast	A1228
Joan Hooley	Blues for Mr Charlie	Mother Henry	A143
Brendan Hooper	1953	Fenice	A1
Ewan Hooper	A Hard Heart	Seemore	A477
	The Recruiting Officer	Mr Balance	A897
James Hooton	Phoenix	Rudi	A857
	Pond Life	Malcolm	A869
Dawn Hope	Josephine	Josephine	A560
Luke Hope	Carousel	As Cast	A190
Richard Hope	Anna Karenina	Levin	A50
Hannah Hopkin	Curse Of The Mummy	As Cast	A263
Rachel Hopkin	Curse Of The Mummy	As Cast	A263
Daniel Hopkins	Dracula Spectacular	Nick Necrophiliac	A340
Mark Hopkins	Endangered Species	As Cast	A367
Gerald Horan	Coriolanus	As Cast	A248
Michael Hordern	Trelawny Of The Wells	Sir William Gower	A1139
James Hornsby	Death of A Salesman	Howard	A295
	On The Piste	Chris Baxter	A810
David Horovitch	The Pope And The Witch	Professor Schillaci	A870
Jane Horrocks	Little Voice	Little Voice	A917
Robert Horwell	The Hatchet Man	As Cast	A478
Craig Horwood	Miss Saigon	Marine	A727
Basil Hoskins	Comedy Of Errors	Aegeon	A241
Tam Hoskyns	The Winslow Boy	Catherine Winslow	A1213
Andy Hough	Macbeth	First Murderer	A655
	The Tempest	Mariner	A1082
Royce Hounsell	Murmuring Judges	Illegal immigrant	A758
	The Recruiting Officer	Melinda's Servant	A896
	Wind In The Willows	Parkinson	A1211
David Hounslow	Fuente Ovejuna	Sergeant Ortuno	A422
Glyn Houston	Haunted Hotel	Sir Francis Westwick	A479
Jane How	Don't Dress For Dinner	Jacqueline	A331
Alan Howard	Kings	As Cast	A583
	Pygmalion	Henry Higgins	A886
Andrew Howard	Dead Man's Hat	As Cast	A288
	Frankenstein	Henry Clerval Felix	A415
	The Tempest	Trinculo/Boatswain Ceres/Francesco	A1083
Barry Howard	Rocky Horror Show	The Narrator	A933
Christopher Howard	Cats	Rum Tum Tugger	A194
Helen Howard	Disobediently Yours	As Cast	A314
Richard Howard	A Midsummer Night's ..	Peter Quince	A720
	Self Portrait	Augustus John	A974
David Howarth	Good Rockin' Tonite	Tommy Steele	A449
Joanne Howarth	'Tis Pity She's A Whore	Virgin	A1114
	The Virtuoso	Weaver	A1176
Kathryn Howden	Taming Of The Shrew	Katherina	A1070
Lewis Howden	Cuttin' A Rug	Spanky	A266
	House Among the Stars	Josaphat-Le-Violin	A512
Jenny Howe	Jack And The Beanstalk	The Princess	A553
Len Howe	42nd Street	As cast	A2
Cliff Howells	The Miser	La Fleche	A724
	Too Much Too Young	As Cast	A1127
Antony Howes	Lady Be Good	Jeff White	A594
Juliet Howland	Man, Beast and Virtue	Mrs Perella	A682
John Hoye	Alfie	As Cast	A29
William Hoyland	Macbeth	Duncan	A656
Graham Hubbard	Fiddler On The Roof	Motel	A401
	Outside Edge	Kevin	A837
	Three Musketeers	King Louis	A1106
	To Kill A Mockingbird	Dill	A1121
Roy Hudd	Babes in the Wood	'Orrible' Uddy	A79
John Hudson	The Dark River	Christopher Lisle	A282
Robert Hudson	Up 'N' Under	As Cast	A1163
Ruth Hudson	Moment Of Weakness	Lucy	A732
Tim Hudson	Columbus	Francisco Pinzon	A237
	Hamlet	As Cast	A466
	'Tis Pity She's A Whore	Citizen/Bandit	A1114
	Two Gents Of Verona	As Cast	A1154
	The Virtuoso	Footman/Weaver	A117
Tom Hudson	Tango 'Til You're Sore	Vince	A107
John Hug	Doll's House	Torvald Helmer	A323
	Much Ado About Nothing	Benedick	A750
Richard Huggett	Anzacs Over England	Lt. Jeff Rylands	A56

Name	Play	Part	Ref
Tyrone Huggins	Murmuring Judges	Jason	A758
Rhodri Hugh	House Of America	Boyo	A516
Lis Hughes Jones	Patagonia	As Cast	A845
Geoffrey Hughes	Babes in the Wood	"Orful" Onslow	A79
Ian Hughes	Hamlet	As Cast	A466
	Henry IV Part 1	John of Lancaster	A492
	Henry IV Part 2	John of Lancaster	A493
	Romeo And Juliet	Tybalt	A938
	The Thebans	Messenger	A1095
	Twelfth Night	Sebastian	A1152
Samantha Hughes	Ladies' Night	As Cast	A592
Glenn Hugill	Six Degrees...	Doug	A1008
Stephen Huison	The Lie Of The Land	As Cast	A617
	Richard III	Dorset	A912
Lisa Hull	Phantom Of The Opera	Christine Daae	A854
Roger Hume	Beyond Reasonable Doubt	Mr Justice Treadwell	A113
	Please Sir!	One-Man Show	A866
	The Winslow Boy	Arthur Winslow	A1213
Paul Humpoletz	Kafka's Dick	Hermann K	A571
Anthony Hunt	In The Midnight Hour	Dunny	A537
Eliza Hunt	Absurd Person Singular	As Cast	A11
	Mrs Klein	Mrs Klein	A748
James Hunt	Giraffe, Pelly, & Me	Billy	A436
Jan Hunt	70, Girls, 70	As Cast	A4
Kathryn Hunt	Merchant of Venice	Nerissa	A708
	Working	As Cast	A1239
	The Writing Game	Penny Sewell	A1242
Marsha Hunt	Ride Down Mt Morgan	Nurse Hogan	A915
Chris Hunter	Richard III	Hastings	A910
Kathryn Hunter	The Devils	Sister Jeanne	A304
	The Winter's Tale	Mamillius	A1215
Kelly Hunter	The Blue Angel	Lola	A138
	Trelawny Of The Wells	Avonia Bunn	A1139
Michele Hunter	Spring Awakening	Frau Bergmann	A1037
Robin Hunter	Aba Daba Music Hall	Various	A6
	Gone With The Wind II	Rhett Butler	A445
	Put That Light Out	Various	A885
	Road To Casablanca	Bing Crosby	A923
	Valentine	As Cast	A1166
Russell Hunter	Merlin the Magnificent	Merlin	A710
Peter Hurle	Dick Whittington	Sultan Of Morocco	A308
	The Ballroom	As Cast	A1091
Colin Hurley	Loot	Dennis	A638
	Macbeth	Porter	A656
	A Midsummer Night's Dream	Lysander	A717
Judith Hurley	School Of Night	Queen Elizabeth	A960
Isobel Hurll	The House Of Stairs	Sheila	A513
John Hurt	London Vertigo	Count Mushroom	A636
Maxwell Hutcheon	A Jovial Crew	Hearty	A561
	The Taming Of The Shrew	Sly	A1068
Lloyd Hutchinson	A Jovial Crew	Patrico	A561
	Tamburlaine The Great	Mycetes	A1067
Ruby-Marie Hutchinson	Carousel	As Cast	A190
	Little Shop Of Horrors	Ronnette	A632
Stuart Hutchison	Dancing at Lughnasa	Jack	A275
	Woman Of No Importance	Footman	A1230
Jeremy Hutton	Animal Farm	Ensemble	A49
Joe Hutton	Elegies...	As Cast	A358

Name	Play	Part	Ref
Melee Hutton	Arms and the Man	Louka	A60
	Blithe Spirit	Elvira	A127
	Weldon Rising	As Cast	A1192
Neville Hutton	Northern Trawl	Ron	A797
Shirley Hutton	My Fair Lady	Angry Woman	A763
Connie Hyde	Acapulco	As Cast	A12
Jonathan Hyde	The Alchemist	Face	A28
	Columbus	Columbus	A237
	Julius Caesar	Marcus Brutus	A566
	'Tis Pity She's A Whore	Vasques	A1114
Jacqueline Hynes	Candide	2nd Army Recruiter	A185
Jay Ibot	Miss Saigon	Vietnamese Customer	A727
Rhys Ifans	As You Like It	First Lord	A71
	Curse Of The Mummy	Skip	A263
	Marching Song	Bruno Hurst	A685
	A Midsummer Night's ..	Flute	A721
Alan Igbon	One The Ledge	As Cast	A821
John Iles	See How They Run	Lt Clive Winton	A971
Daniel Illsley	Conundrum	As Cast	A247
	Niagara	Carlo	A781
Heather Imani	Romeo and Juliet	Juliet	A937
Celia Imrie	The Sea	Jessica Tilehouse	A961
Barrie Ingham	Aspects Of Love	George Dillingham	A72
Rob Inglis	One-Man Shows	Various	A822
Dione Inman	Twelfth Night	Olivia	A1149
Mark Inman	Macbeth	As Cast	A657
Cheryl Innes	The Jungle Book	As Cast	A568
	MacWizard Fae Oz	As Cast	A663
Molly Innes	Tartuffe	As Cast	A1073
Harold Innocent	Madness of George III	Sir George Baker	A669
Junix Inocian	Miss Saigon	The Engineer	A727
John Ireland	Taming of the Shrew	Lucentio	A1069
Peter Ireland	We		A1191
Louise Ironside	Your Turn To Clean The Stairs	Kay	A1252
Polly Irvin	Mrs Klein	Paula	A748
Adrian Irvine	The Hostage	Rio Rita	A505
	Macbeth	Seyton	A661
George Irving	The Professional	As Cast	A883
	White Woman Street	Blakely	A1202
Sheila Irwin	Tons Of Money	Miss Mullett	A1125
	The Winslow Boy	Violet	A1213
Clare Isaac	The Devils	Sister Louise of St. John	A304
Debbie Isitt	Woman Who Cooked	Laura	A1232
Kate Isitt	Charley's Aunt	Amy Spettigue	A200
Kim Ismay	Comedy Of Errors	As Cast	A241
Joel Issac	A Dead Secret	Alfie	A289
Ravil Isyanov	Macbeth	Fleance	A655
	Marching Song	Matthew Sangosse	A685
	The Tempest	Caliban	A1082
Philip Ives	See How They Run	Rev Arthur Humphrey	A971
Sian Ivogen	Beardsley	Mabel	A95
Paulette Ivory	Buddy	Ensemble	A169
	West Side Story	Maria	A1193
Catherine Jack	A Better Day	As Cast	A111
Godfrey Jackman	Deathtrap	Porter Milgrim	A298
	Don Juan	As Cast	A327
Wayne Jackman	Dick Whittington	Dick Whittington	A309

Name	Play	Part	Ref
David **Jackson**	Grand Hotel	Jimmy	A453
Jodie **Jackson**	Grand Hotel	Operator/Trude	A453
	Starlight Express	As Cast	A1043
Sean **Jackson**	Light in the Village	Montie	A622
Shaaron **Jackson**	On The Piste	Beverley	A810
Tony **Jackson**	Out Of Order	George Pidgeon	A835
Stephanie **Jacob**	The Winter's Tale	Mopsa	A1214
Derek **Jacobi**	Becket	Becket	A103
	Breaking the Code	Alan Turing	A159
	Mad,Bad,And Dangerous	Lord Byron	A665
Paula **Jacobs**	The Corn Is Green	Mrs Watty	A249
Martial **Jacques**	Les Atrides	As Cast	A609
Paul Jacuson James	Othello	Roderigo	A827
	The School For Scandal	Rowley	A956
Barry **James**	Closer Than Ever	As cast	A231
	Grand Hotel	Otto Kringelein	A453
Bruce **James**	The Late Edwina Black	Det. Henry Martin	A599
Geraldine **James**	Death and the Maiden	Paulina Salas	A293
Jamie **James**	Robin Hood	Robin Hood	A929
Karl **James**	Hot Italian Nights	Ensemble	A507
	The Magic Storybook	Ensemble	A672
	Much Ado About Nothing	Boraccio	A752
Martyn **James**	Hay Fever	David Bliss	A482
	Wasting Reality	Jock	A1186
Polly **James**	The Miser	Frosine	A724
Raji **James**	The Jungle Book	As Cast	A568
Steve **James**	American Buffalo	Don	A39
Stori **James**	Cats	Bill Bailey	A194
Trilby **James**	Absent Friends	Evelyn	A10
	A Midsummer Night's Dream	Hermia	A717
Sandra **James-Young**	Murmuring Judges	Illegal Immigrant	A758
	The Recruiting Officer	Wife	A896
	Wind In The Willows	Goaler's Daughter	A1211
Jacqui **Jameson**	Joseph...	Simeon's Wife	A559
Stephen **Jameson**	Ghost Sonata	The Old Man	A431
Susan **Jameson**	Just Between Ourselves	Vera	A569
	Safe In Our Hands	Jill Robinson	A947
Malcolm **Jamieson**	House Of The Spirits		A514
Patrick **Jamieson**	Little Tramp	Prince Of Wales Others	A634
	Valentine's Day	Jim	A1165
David **Janson**	'Allo,'Allo	Herr Flick	A36
	What About Luv?	As Cast	A1195
Tarcissius **Januel**	Carmen Jones	Bartender	A189
Nina **Jaques**	Elisabeth II	As Cast	A361
John **Jardine**	Cinderella	Baron Hardup	A225
	Far From The Madding Crowd	Henry Fray	A397
	Saint Oscar	The Judge	A949
Isabella **Jarrett**	Tartuffe	As Cast	A1073
Andrew **Jarvis**	As You Like It	Duke Frederick	A67
	Becket	Archbishop of Canterbury	A103
	The Winter's Tale	Antigonus	A1214
David **Jarvis**	Androcles And The Lion		A45
Martin **Jarvis**	Just Between Ourselves	Dennis	A569
	Leo In Love	Leopold	A607
Rob **Jarvis**	Cyrano De Bergerac	Actor/Pastrycook Etc	A269
	In The Midnight Hour	Jazza	A538
Peter **Jason**	Monday After Miracle	John Macy	A733

Name	Play	Part	Ref
Mark **Jax**	The Devils	Mannoury	A304
Kenneth **Jay**	Witness For The Prosecution	Inspector	A1218
Jonathan **Jaynes**	View From The Bridge	As Cast	A1170
Kieron **Jecchinis**	The Darling Family	As Cast	A283
Andrew **Jeffers**	The BFG	Guy/Fleshlumpeater etc	A116
Barbara **Jefford**	All's Well That Ends Well	Countess	A35
	The Merry Wives Of Windsor	Mistress Quickly	A713
Victoria **Jeffrey**	Wit's End	The Princess	A1216
Kimberley **Jehane-Cliffe**	Hot Stuff	Ensemble	A508
Tristram **Jellinek**	1953	Oldenburg	A1
	Casanova	As Cast	A191
Sarah **Jenkin**	Buddy	Mary Lou Sokoloff	A169
Paul **Jenner**	Carousel	As Cast	A190
Alex **Jennings**	The Recruiting Officer	Captain Plume	A896
Paul **Jerricho**	Woman In Mind	As Cast	A1228
Paul **Jesson**	Antony and Cleopatra	Enobarbus	A53
	The Beggar's Opera	Peachum	A106
	A Jovial Crew	Oldrents	A561
	The Winter's Tale	Polixenes	A1214
Melanie **Jessop**	Lulu	Countess Geschwitz	A648
Edward **Jewesbury**	Wicked Old Man	Harry	A1207
Robert **Jezek**	Relative Values	Don Lucas	A899
Brontis **Jodorowsky**	Les Atrides	As Cast	A609
Caroline **John**	Penny for a Song	As Cast	A848
	Who Was Hilary	As Cast	A1204
Patrick **John-Anthony**	The Hatchet Man	As Cast	A478
Glynis **Johns**	A Little Night Music	Madame Armfeldt	A630
Milton **Johns**	The Woman In Black	Arthur Kipps	A1227
Stephanie **Johns**	Aspects Of Love	Pharmacist/Actress Labourer	A72
Stratford **Johns**	Scrooge the Musical	Christmas Present	A1039
Darlene **Johnson**	Four Marys		A414
	The Odyssey	Anticleia	A802
	Tamburlaine The Great	Zabina	A1067
Dystin **Johnson**	Giraffe, Pelly, & Me	The Pelican	A436
	No 3 Pied Piper Street	Natalya	A788
Francis **Johnson**	Les Miserables	As Cast	A612
Gael **Johnson**	Joseph...	Issachar's Wife	A559
Karl **Johnson**	The Sea	Vicar	A961
	Uncle Vanya	Ilya Ilyvitch Telyegin	A1157
Marilyn **Johnson**	The Cotton Club	Emma Washington	A250
Meg **Johnson**	Annie Get Your Gun	Dolly Tate	A51
Neil **Johnson**	Cats	Alonzo	A194
Richard **Johnson**	All's Well That Ends Well	King of France	A35
	Antony and Cleopatra	Mark Antony	A53
Wilbert **Johnson**	Back Up The Hearse	Andy	A84
	Fuente Ovejuna	Frondoso	A422
	The Snow Queen	As Cast	A102
Alison **Johnston**	Dejavu	Alison	A302
Halcro **Johnston**	My Fair Lady	Costermonger	A763
Willie **Jonah**	Flamingo	As Cast	A408
	The Road	Koyunu	A921
David **Jonathan**	Happy As A Sandbag	As Cast	A473
Adam **Jones**	Cats	The Cats' Chorus	A194
Aled **Jones**	Martin Chuzzlewit	Young Martin	A689

Name	Play	Part	Ref
Andrew Michael **Jones**	The Seagull	Yakov	A962
Carolyn **Jones**	Anybody for Murder?	Janet Harrington	A55
	Gaslight	Elizabeth	A428
Celia **Jones**	Happy As A Sandbag	As Cast	A473
Charlotte **Jones**	Love's Labour's Lost	Maria	A645
Chris **Jones**	Elvis - the Musical	Farren	A362
Eluned **Jones**	House Of America	Mam	A516
Freddie **Jones**	Twelfth Night	Malvolio	A1152
Gemma **Jones**	Ride Down Mt Morgan	Theo	A915
	The Winter's Tale	Paulina	A1214
Griffith **Jones**	The Beggar's Opera	Wat Dreary	A106
Huw **Jones**	Blood Brothers	Perkins	A131
Joseph **Jones**	The Recruiting Officer	Poacher	A896
Judy **Jones**	The Seagull	Maid	A962
Lesley **Jones**	The Three Musketeers	Constance	A1104
Maggie **Jones**	A Dead Secret	Mrs Cluff	A289
Mark Lewis **Jones**	Richard III	Richmond	A910
	The Winter's Tale	Florizel	A1215
Michael **Jones**	Coriolanus	As Cast	A248
	Venus Observed	Captain Fox	A1168
Okon **Jones**	Driving Miss Daisy	Hoke Colburn	A346
Oliver **Jones**	Much Ado About Nothing	Friar Frances Borachio	A750
Ria **Jones**	Les Miserables	Fantine	A611
Robin **Jones**	Carmen Jones	Remo the Drummer	A189
Ron **Jones**	Christopher Street	As Cast	A218
Tina **Jones**	Lady Macbeth	As Cast	A595
Toby **Jones**	Life Support		A621
Trevor **Jones**	Noises Off	Frederick Fellowes	A794
	The Ballroom	As Cast	A1091
Wendy **Jones**	Late Joys		A600
Peter **Jonfield**	Straight & Narrow	Bill	A1054
Desmond **Jordan**	While The Sun Shines	As Cast	A1201
Pearl **Jordan**	My Fair Lady	Mrs Hopkins	A763
Peter **Jordan**	Fooling About	As Cast	A412
Andrew **Joseph**	Birthday Party	As Cast	A124
Kate **Joseph**	Shoot The Women First	Ulrike Meinhof	A996
Lesley **Joseph**	Bazaar and Rummage	Gwenda	A94
	Cinderella	Fairy Godmother	A224
Michelle **Joseph**	Grapes of Wrath	Floyd's Wife	A454
	Playing by the Rules	Julie	A863
	Wizard of Oz	As Cast	A1224
Paterson **Joseph**	Blues for Mr Charlie	Richard Henry	A143
	The Recruiting Officer	Mr Worthy	A896
Philip **Joseph**	Dancing At Lughnasa	Gerry	A274
Tara **Joseph**	The Refuge	Tara	A1093
David **Joyce**	Wind In The Willows	Rabbit/Gerald	A1211
Emily **Joyce**	Romeo And Juliet	As Cast	A938
	'Tis Pity She's A Whore	Virgin	A1114
John **Joyce**	Blood Wedding	The Father of The Bride/Woodcutter	A134
	The Family Reunion	Downing	A394
	Under Milk Wood	As Cast	A1160
Rachel **Joyce**	Fuente Ovejuna	Laurencia	A422
Robert **Joyce**	Grope	Lionel Figg	A460
John **Judd**	Jack And The Beanstalk	As Cast	A552
Peter **Judge**	Dancing at Lughnasa	Michael	A275
Danny **Jules**	Carmen Jones	Dink	A189
Susannah **Jupp**	Little Tramp	Lita Gray/Others	A634
K.F.T.D.	Starlight Express	Rocky 1	A1043
Berwick **Kaler**	Babes in the Wood	Nanny Kaler	A80

Name	Play	Part	Ref
	The Pope And The Witch	Pope John Paul II	A870
Laurissa **Kalinowsky**	Toronto, Mississippi	As Cast	A1129
Stefan **Kalipha**	Fuente Ovejuna	Alonso	A422
Mario **Kalli**	Breaking the Code	As Cast	A159
Ismail **Kamara**	Carmen Jones	T-Bone	A189
Thomas **Kampe**	Dybbuk	As Cast	A350
Toni **Kanal**	Jubilee	Wendy	A562
Amanda **Kane**	The Trial	Various	A1140
Georgina **Kane**	Dracula Spectacular	Countess Wrath Gretel	A340
John **Kane**	As You Like It	Touchstone	A71
Richard **Kane**	Hindsight	Howard	A495
	Travel With My Aunt	As Cast	A1134
Ravi **Kapoor**	Heer Ranjha	As Cast	A489
Nizwar **Karanj**	The Little Clay Cart	Maitreya	A627
Anna **Karen**	Bazaar and Rummage	Bell-Bell	A94
	The Late Edwina Black	Ellen	A599
Jane **Karen**	Buddy	Ensemble	A169
Miriam **Karlin**	Rosmersholm	Mrs Helseth	A939
Richard **Karlsson**	Merlin, The Search	As Cast	A709
	Outside Edge	Alex	A837
	Three Musketeers	De Treville	A1106
	To Kill A Mockingbird	Tom Robinson	A1121
Peter **Karrie**	Phantom Of The Opera	The Phantom	A854
Stefan **Karsberg**	King Lear	France/Oswald	A578
	Self Portrait	John Quinn	A974
	Telling Tales	As Cast	A1081
Theresa **Kartell**	Moby Dick	As Cast	A728
Dwan **Kastelle**	Merrily We Roll Along	As Cast	A711
Maurice **Kaufmann**	Trelawny Of The Wells	Charles	A1139
Anne **Kavanagh**	Dancing At Lughnasa	Rose	A274
John **Kavanagh**	London Vertigo	Murrough O'Doherty	A636
Leonard **Kavanagh**	Woman Of No Importance	Sir John Pontefract	A1230
Barnaby **Kay**	A Jovial Crew	Beggar/Constable	A561
	The Taming Of The Shrew	Rt Hon Peter Sinclair	A1068
	The Winter's Tale	Shepherd's Servant	A1214
Bernard **Kay**	Henry IV Part 1	Glendower	A492
	Henry IV Part 2	Glendower	A493
	Romeo And Juliet	Friar Lawrence	A938
Charles **Kaye**	Madness of George III	Dr Francis Willis	A669
Gordon **Kaye**	'Allo,'Allo	Rene Artois	A36
Ivan **Kaye**	On The Piste	Dave Truman	A812
Dilly **Keane**	Dancing at Lughnasa	Maggie	A275
Gillian **Kearney**	Othello	Desdemona	A827
	The School For Scandal	Maria	A956
Sean **Kearney**	Threepenny Story	Mac	A1108
	A View From The Bridge	Alfieri	A1169
Sean **Kearns**	Digging for Fire	As Cast	A313
Kenneth **Keating**	Out Of Order	The Hotel Manager	A835
Michael **Keating**	A Midsummer Night's ..	Snug	A720
Anna **Keaveney**	Straight & Narrow	Nona	A1054
Jonathan **Keeble**	Shadowlands	As Cast	A983
Ashley **Keech**	Robin	Much The Miller	A927
John **Keegan**	Pygmies In The Ruins		A887
	The Rivals	Sir Lucius O' Trigger	A919
Michael **Keegan-Dolan**	Carousel	As Cast	A190
Dawn **Keeler**	Arms and the Man	Catherine	A60
Nicola **Keen**	Joseph...	Gad's Wife	A559

Name	Play	Part	Ref
Bernadette Keenan	The Sound Of Music	Sister Sophia	A1033
John Keenan	Chorus of Disapproval	As Cast	A210
	Comedy of Errors	As Cast	A239
Eve Keepax	Man Cub	As Cast	A679
Harriet Keevil	Brand	As Cast	A157
	The Tender Husband	Lucy Fainlove	A1088
Penelope Keith	On Approval	Mrs Maria Wislack	A807
JD Kelleher	The Little Clay Cart	Sharvilaka/Driver	A627
Barbara Kellerman	The Deep Blue Sea	Hester Collyer	A140
Cara Kelly	Therese Raquin	Therese Raquin	A1097
Colette Kelly	Strippers	Buffy	A1057
Darragh Kelly	Digging for Fire	As Cast	A313
Eamon Kelly	Philadelphia Here I Come	S B O'Donnell	A856
Liz Kelly	Macbeth	First Witch	A655
	The Tempest	Spirit	A1082
Matthew Kelly	Cinderella	Buttons	A223
Megan Kelly	Joseph...	Reuben's Wife	A559
	Les Miserables	Cosette	A613
Pamela Kelly	House Among the Stars	The Fat Woman	A512
Sam Kelly	Killers	As Cast	A573
Tricia Kelly	Bad Girl	Frances	A86
	Voysey Inheritance	Honor Voysey	A1182
David Kelsey	Merchant of Venice	Antonio	A708
	See How They Run	Bishop Of Lax	A971
Sue Kelvin	Assassins	As Cast	A73
	Les Miserables	Madame Thernardier	A613
Dominic Kemp	Barnstormers	Jeremiah Hodgson	A92
Nick Kemp	As You Like It	Le Beau	A67
	The Beggar's Opera	Robin of Bagshot	A106
	Tamburlaine The Great	Basso	A1067
Polly Kemp	Fooling About	As Cast	A412
Teddy Kempner	Bourgeois Gentilhomme	Coveille	A153
	Trilby & Svengali	Svengali	A1141
Felicity Kendal	Heartbreak House	Ariadne Utterword	A486
Clive Kendall	Macbeth	Angus/A Murderer	A653
Jo Kendall	The Guardsman	The Mother	A461
	Noises Off	Dotty Otley	A795
Merelina Kendel	Elisabeth II	As Cast	A361
Ella Kenion	Cabal and Love	Sophie	A176
	The Recruiting Officer	Rose	A897
Andrew Kennedy	Slice Of Saturday...	Rick	A1015
Brian Kennedy	Wizard of Oz	Tin Man	A1223
Fiona Kennedy	Alfie	As Cast	A29
Iona Kennedy	The Way of All Flesh	Christina/Mrs Jupp	A1190
Laurence Kennedy	The Writing Game	Simon Sinclair	A1242
Morar Kennedy	Talk Of The Steamie	Mrs Culfeathers	A1065
Sharon Kennet	The Sacred Penman	As Cast	A946
Christopher Kent	Cyrano De Bergerac	Cadet/Etc	A269
Dave Kent	Hound	Joe	A510
Diana Kent	An Inspector Calls	Sheila Birling	A541
Graham Kent	Barnstormers	Henry Lowes/Lord Delaval	A92
	Rivals	Bob Acres	A920
Paul Kent	Thunderbirds FAB	Various	A1111
Tricia Kent	Shadowlands	Registrar	A984
	Strippers	Barmaid	A1057
Edmund Kente	Macbeth	Duncan/Old Siward	A658
	Over a Barrel	Duncan	A840
Doreen Keogh	Una Pooka	As Cast	A1156
Robin Keogh	Wit's End	Petrushka/Mr N.	A1216
David Kernan	A Swell Party		A1060

Name	Play	Part	Ref
James Kerr	Fuente Ovejuna	Soldier	A422
	A Midsummer Night's ..	Lysander	A720
Louise Kerr	Bourgeois Gentilhomme	Student/Tailor Cook	A153
Nan Kerr	Beyond Reasonable Doubt	Mrs Rogers	A114
Roberta Kerr	The Norman Conquests	Sarah	A796
Dermot Kerrigan	Trilby & Svengali	Little Billy	A1141
Patricia Kerrigan	Love's Labour's Lost	Princess of France	A645
	Women Laughing	Stephanie	A1234
David Kershaw	Nightmare	As Cast	A787
Emma Kershaw	Buddy	Ensemble	A168
Glyn Kerslake	Miss Saigon	Chris	A727
Maria Kesselman	A Judgement In Stone	Melinda	A563
Sara Kestleman	The Cabinet Minister	Mrs Gaylustre	A179
	Cherry Orchard		A203
	Square Rounds	As Cast	A1038
Liz Kettle	House of Bernarda Alba	As Cast	A515
	Roaring Girl's Hamlet	Laertes	A925
Ruth Kettlewell	As You Desire Me		A66
William Key	Spring Awakening	Georg/Rupert/Prof. Tonguetwister	A1037
David Keys	Macbeth	Donalbain	A656
Marjorie Keys	Annie Get Your Gun	Mrs Blacktooth	A51
Shehnaz Khan	The Little Clay Cart	Radanika/Madanika Aryaka	A627
Delena Kidd	Beyond Reasonable Doubt	Mrs Rogers	A113
	What the Butler Saw	Mrs Prentice	A1197
Josie Kidd	Noises Off	Dotty Otley	A794
Jeffrey Kidner	My Cousin Rachel	Antonio Rainaldi	A762
Paul Kiernan	Henry IV Part 1	Sir Richard Vernon	A492
	Henry IV Part 2	Earl of Warwick	A493
	The Thebans	Haemon	A1095
Timothy Kightley	Caesar And Cleopatra	Theodotus	A180
Melanie Kilburn	Straight & Narrow	Lois	A1054
Michael Kilgarriff	Dick Whittington	King Rat	A308
	Late Joys	Chairman	A600
Barry Killerby	One For The Road	Roger	A818
David Killick	Comedy Of Errors	The Duke	A241
	Life is a Dream	Basilio	A619
Tim Killick	Coriolanus	As Cast	A248
Mark Kilmurry	Woman Who Cooked	Kenneth	A1232
Barbara King	Cats	Rumpleteazer	A194
Beryl King	Importance of Being	Miss Prism	A532
Bobby King	Turned Out Nice Again	Harry Scott	A1145
Donna King	Cats	Bombalurina	A194
Lorelei King	Blues for Mr Charlie	Hazel	A143
Mary King	The Bells	Catherine	A108
Neville King	Dick Whittington	Captain and Mate	A308
Richard King	The Cotton Club	Jim Carlton	A250
Shelley King	Cloud 9	Edward	A232
	Heer Ranjha	As Cast	A489
	The Little Clay Cart	The God Shiva	A627
Bob Kingdom	Return Journey	Dylan Thomas	A351
John Kingsley	School for Scandal	Moses	A957
Miranda Kingsley	The House Of Stairs	Felicity	A513
Alex Kingston	Bad Blood	Delores	A85
	A Midsummer Night's ..	Hippolyta/Titania	A720
Philip Kingston	Macbeth	As Cast	A660
Jacqueline Kington	Othello	Bianca	A827
	The School For Scandal	Mrs Candour	A956

Name	Play	Part	Ref
Amanda **Kirby**	Stageland	Amanda/Jane/Tiddy	A1041
Leonard **Kirby**	Once Upon A Song		A817
John **Kirk**	Bouncers	Les	A151
Michael **Kirk**	The Business Of Murder	As Cast	A175
	Macbeth	Rosse	A658
	Martin Chuzzlewit	Multiple Roles	A689
	Second From Last In The Sack Race	Ezra Pratt/Uncle Teddy etc	A966
	Serve Them All My Days	As Cast	A1123
Stash **Kirkbride**	The Candidate	One-Man Show	A184
Keith **Kirkwood**	Barnum	As Cast	A93
Dervla **Kirwan**	Hush	As Cast	A522
	Water Music	Monique	A1188
	Wexford Trilogy	As Cast	A1194
Paul **Kissaun**	Aladdin Bolton	Aladdin	A27
	Alfie	Perc	A30
	Blues In The Night	The Man	A144
Jeffery **Kissoon**	A Midsummer Night's Dream	Oberon	A718
Lynn **Kitch**	Strippers	Cilla	A1057
Wendy **Kitching**	Cats	Electra	A194
Helen **Kitson**	Serve Them All My Days	As Cast	A1123
Rodger **Kitter**	'Allo,'Allo	Captain Bertorelli	A36
Jack **Klaff**	Tamburlaine The Great	Theridamus	A1067
Gertan **Klauber**	Night of the Iguana	Herr Fahrenkopf	A785
	Pygmalion	Gentleman	A886
Beverley **Klein**	Fiddler On The Roof	Golda	A401
	A Judgement In Stone	Joan	A563
Patricia **Kneale**	Night Must Fall	Mrs Bramson	A784
Clive **Kneller**	Fooling About	As Cast	A412
	A Midsummer Night's ..	Philostrate/Puck	A720
Ashley **Knight**	Grand Hotel	Bellboy	A453
Charlotte **Knight**	Brand	As Cast	A157
Mark **Knight**	Hamlet	Corambis	A467
Rebecca **Knight**	Valentine's Day	Millicent	A1165
Rosalind **Knight**	La Bete	Madeline Bejart	A587
Tom **Knight**	And A Nightingale Sang	Norman	A43
	Death of A Salesman	Biff	A295
	Far From The Madding Crowd	Gabriel Oak	A397
	Master and Margarita	Ivan Bezdonny	A693
Jan **Knightley**	The Dorm	Thommo	A332
Darryl **Knock**	Les Miserables	Marius	A613
Duncan **Knowles**	Twelfth Night	Feste/Sebastian 1st Officer	A1149
Joanne **Knowles**	Indigo Mill	As Cast	A539
Pauline **Knowles**	Cuttin' A Rug	Bernadette	A266
	School For Wives	Georgette	A958
Mark **Knox**	Hamlet	Hamlet	A467
Sally **Knyvette**	Dangerous Obsession	Sally Driscoll	A281
	Rule Of The Game	Marion Lindo	A942
Anna **Kohler**	Brace Up!	As Cast	A156
Estelle **Kohler**	Comedy Of Errors	Adriana	A241
Kazimir **Kolesnik**	Rimbaud And Verlaine	Arthur Rimbaud	A916
Rudolph **Kolias**	Something Missing	As Cast	A1030
Cara **Konig**	Our Song	Belle	A833
Jenifer **Konko**	Ghost Sonata	Milkmaid	A431
Richard **Kort**	Robin	George-A-Green	A927
Adam **Kotz**	Bourgeois Gentilhomme	Cleonte	A153
Sarah **Kovar**	Wind In The Willows	Billy	A1211
Dan **Kramer**	Comedy of Errors	Antipholous	A239
Rennie **Krupinski**	The Rivals	Fag	A918

Name	Play	Part	Ref
Tomas **Kubinek**	Flight To Finland	Ensemble	A409
	Moose	Ensemble	A738
Syreeta **Kumar**	House Of The Spirits		A514
	Necklaces	As Cast	A774
Simon **Kunz**	Thirteenth Night	As Cast	A1099
Janos **Kurucz**	Phantom Of The Opera	Joseph Buquet	A854
Helene **Kvale**	Roman & Marys	As Cast	A934
Susan **Kyd**	The Secret Rapture	Marion	A968
Paul **Kynman**	Madness of George III	Ramsden	A669
Ben **Kypreos**	Buddy	Ensemble	A168
Natasha **L-Rotheroe**	Telling Tales	As Cast	A1081
John **Labanowski**	Gamblers	Alexei	A424
Rebecca **Lacey**	An Ideal Husband	Mabel Chiltern	A528
	Sailor Beware!	Shirley Hornett	A948
Eddie **Ladd**	Patagonia	As Cast	A845
Keith **Ladd**	Alfie	Humphrey	A30
Colm **Lagam**	Monster He Made Me	Fino	A734
Simone **Lahbib**	Dead Heroic	Teenage Girl	A287
Lorna **Laidlaw**	Buddy	Ensemble	A168
	Devil's Only Sleeping	Alex	A303
	The Last Carnival	Jean Beauxchamps	A598
Paul **Laidlaw**	Chitty Bang Bang	Caractacus Potts	A208
James **Lailey**	Dead Man's Hat	As Cast	A288
	Frankenstein	Victor Frankenstein	A415
	The Tempest	Ferdinand Sebastian	A1083
Peter **Laird**	Madness of George III	Edmund Burke	A669
Trevor **Laird**	The Revenger's Tragedy	Amitioso	A908
Sarah **Lam**	New World and Tears	Imagination Tacuana	A780
Christopher **Lamb**	Charley's Aunt	Jack Chesney	A200
Larry **Lamb**	Making It Better	Adrian Harrington	A677
Ian **Lambert**	Beyond Reasonable Doubt	Prison Officer	A114
	A Midsummer Night's Dream	As Cast	A717
	Shadowlands	As Cast	A985
Mark **Lambert**	Dancing At Lughnasa	Michael	A274
Glenn **Lamont**	Gulf Between Us	Militia	A462
Andy **Lanai**	Miss Saigon	Mama San	A727
Jane **Lancaster**	Children Of Lesser God	Edna Klein	A206
	Kvetch	Mother-in-law	A586
James **Lance**	Elegies...	As Cast	A358
Peter **Land**	Phantom Of The Opera	Monsieur Andre	A854
Dinsdale **Landen**	A Midsummer Night's ..	Bottom	A721
Harry **Landis**	Ride Down Mt Morgan	The Father	A915
	Who Shall I Be?	As Cast	A1203
Kristine **Landon-Smith**	Fuente Ovejuna	Grand Master Rodrogo	A423
	Romeo and Juliet	Benvolio	A935
Gina **Landor**	The Darling Family	As Cast	A283
Maggie **Lane**	Happy Families	Auntie Edna	A476
Nicholas **Lane**	Happy Families	John Taylor	A476
	Office Party	Lee Cook	A803
Pamela **Lane**	Fifteen Streets	Peggy Flaherty	A403
	Jubilee	Hilda	A562
Samantha **Lane**	Starlight Express	Belle	A1043
Belinda **Lang**	The Dark River	Catherine Lisle	A282
Alex **Langdon**	Dragon	As Cast	A341
	What The Butler Saw	Nicholas	A1196
Bonnie **Langford**	42nd Street	Peggy Sawyer	A2

Name	Play	Part	Ref
Di Langford	Fighting For The Dunghill	Hannah Humphrey	A404
	Rivals	Mrs Malaprop	A920
	Television Programme	Rose	A1080
Philip Langridge	The Bells	Matthias	A108
Caroline Langrishe	Dog Days	As Cast	A319
Diane Langton	Comedy Of Errors	A Courtesan	A241
	Once Upon A Song		A817
Jane Lapotaire	Hamlet	Gertrude	A466
Reg Large	The Business Of Murder	Stone	A174
	The Kingfisher	Cecil	A581
	Stage Struck	Widdecombe	A1040
Chris Larkin	Taste of Honey	Geoffrey	A1074
James Larkin	Life is a Dream	Segismundo	A619
Chris Larner	The Recruiting Officer	Bridewell	A896
	Wind In The Willows	Rabbit/Fred	A1211
John Larsen	Aba Daba Music Hall	Various	A6
	Put That Light Out	Various	A885
John Larson	All My Sons	Bert	A32
Karen Lashinsky	Brace Up!	As Cast	A156
Ruth Lass	Handsome,Handicapped..	As Cast	A468
	Hecuba	Chorus	A488
Max Latimer	Don't Play With Love	Maitre Blazius	A329
Carol Laula	Merlin, The Search	As Cast	A709
James Laurenson	Fuente Ovejuna	Commander Gomez	A422
	Grace	Neal Hoffman	A452
Anthony Laurie	The Three Musketeers	Cardinal Richelieu	A1104
Angela Laurier	A Midsummer Night's Dream	Puck	A718
	Square Rounds	As Cast	A1038
Mark Lavelle	A Dead Secret	Archie Gooch	A289
Sally Lavelle	Hot Stuff	As Cast	A508
	A Midsummer Night's ..	Lady/Cobweb	A720
Ian Lavender	Noises Off	Lloyd Dallas	A794
Samantha Lavender	The Sound Of Music	Ensemble	A1033
Duncan Law	A View From The Bridge	Rodolpho	A1171
Jude Law	The Fastest Clock...	Foxtrot Darling	A398
Andrew Lawden	Grand Hotel	Scullery Worker	A453
William Lawford	A Month In The Country	As Cast	A736
Paul Lawley	Forbidden Planet	Petty Officer Roger Andout	A904
William Lawrance	Hamlet	Horatio	A467
Bernard Lawrence	Macbeth	Duncan	A653
Dorothy Lawrence	Strippers	Wendy	A1057
Josie Lawrence	The Comedy Store	Various	A242
	Painting Churches	Margaret Church	A842
Peter Lawrence	Robin	Earl Of Loxley	A927
Sophie Lawrence	Aladdin	Aladdin	A19
	Bazaar and Rummage	Fliss	A94
Stephanie Lawrence	Blood Brothers	Mrs Johnstone	A131
Caroline Lawrie	The House Of Stairs	Fay	A513
Richard Lawry	Master and Margarita	Pontius Pilate	A693
Dennis Lawson	Lust	Horner	A650
Kate Lawson	Beauty And The Beast	Cabbage Rose	A98
Nicky Lawson	Starlight Express	As Cast	A1043
Thierry Lawson	Rimbaud And Verlaine	Paul Verlaine	A916
Kate Lawton	Wicks's Folly	As Cast	A1208
Lesley Lawton	It Runs In The Family	Dr Mortimore	A548
Simon Lay	Raving Beauties	Chris	A893
Penny Layden	Henceforward...	Geain	A491
	Jolly Potters	As Cast	A557
	Snow Queen	Gerda	A1021
	Turkey Time	Florence	A1144
Dilys Laye	42nd Street	Dorothy	A2
	Happy Days	Winnie	A474
Russell Layton	Comedy Of Errors	As Cast	A241
Paul Lazar	Brace Up!	As Cast	A156
Frank Lazarus	June Moon	As Cast	A567
Dominic le Foe	Late Joys		A600
Nicholas Le Prevost	Blues for Mr Charlie	Parnell James	A143
Sylvestra le Touzel	Artists and Admirers	Negina	A64
	Henry IV Part 1	Lady Percy	A492
	Henry IV Part 2	Lady Percy	A493
	Twelfth Night	Viola	A1152
	A Woman Killed With Kindness	Susan Mountford	A1229
An Le	Miss Saigon	Tam	A727
Peter Leabourne	School Of Night	Raleigh	A960
Nigel Leach	Fuente Ovejuna	Cimbranos	A422
	Gone With The Wind II	Ashley Wilkes	A445
	Me And My Girl	Gerald Bolingbroke	A698
	Valentine	As Cast	A1166
Roger Leach	Les Miserables	As Cast	A612
Bill Leadbitter	Macbeth	Macduff	A656
Jacqueline Lean	Annie Get Your Gun	Nellie	A51
Stephen Leatherland	Blood Brothers	Ensemble	A131
Jane Lebina	Sikulu	Ensemble	A1001
Susie Lee Hayward	As You Like It	Court Lady Hisperia	A67
	The Beggar's Opera	Jenny Diver	A106
Abigail Lee	Goodnight Mr Tom	As Cast	A450
Adrian Lee	The Little Clay Cart	Musician	A627
Dougal Lee	Don't Dress For Dinner	George	A331
Roger Lee	Shout Across The River	As Cast	A997
Kim Leeson	Starlight Express	Pearl	A1043
Laurel Lefkow	Dangerous Dolls-Soap Crazy	Kandy Dean	A280
Janette Legge	Lost in Yonkers	As Cast	A641
Val Lehman	Aladdin	Empress of China	A20
	Anybody for Murder?	As Cast	A55
	Driving Miss Daisy	Daisy Werthon	A345
	Steel Magnolias	Oiser	A1045
Vincent Leigh	Cats	Munkustrap	A194
Barbara Leigh-Hunt	An Inspector Calls	Sybil Birling	A541
	Woman Of No Importance	Lady Hunstanton	A1230
Joanne Leighton	Why Things Happen	Paula	A1206
Sonya Leite	Bourgeois Gentilhomme	Student/Tailor Cook	A153
	The Sea	Davis	A961
	Square Rounds	As Cast	A1038
Alan Leith	A Midsummer Night's ..	Tom Snout	A720
David Lemkin	The Deep Blue Sea	Philip Welch	A140
	Comedy Of Errors	As Cast	A241
	EuroVision	Antinous	A381
Peter Lennon	Macbeth	Bloody Captain	A655
	The Tempest	Boatswain	A1082
Rula Lenska	A Little Night Music	Desiree	A630
David Leonard	Babes in the Wood	As Cast	A80
Paul Leonard	Les Miserables	Javert	A613
	Lust	Quack	A650
Robert Lepage	Needles And Opium	Solo Performance	A775
Sasha Leslie	Spring Awakening	Martha/Prof. Bonebreaker	A1037

Name	Play	Part	Ref
Anton **Lesser**	The Merry Wives Of Windsor	Frank Ford	A713
	The Taming Of The Shrew	Petruchio	A1068
Adrian **Lester**	Six Degrees...	Paul	A1008
Mark **Letheren**	Building Blocks	Dave	A170
Dominic **Letts**	The Woman In Black	The Actor	A1226
	The Woman In Black	The Actor	A1227
Tania **Levey**	Comedy of Errors	Courtesan	A240
	Jolly Potters	As Cast	A557
Helen **Levien**	Hamlet	Rosencrantz Fortinbras	A463
John **Levitt**	Fighting For The Dunghill	Sneyd	A404
Martin **Levy-Anderson**	All My Sons	Bert	A33
Adam **Lewis**	Curse Of The Mummy	Albert	A263
Emma **Lewis**	Grace	Joanna	A452
Gary **Lewis**	Lions of Lisbon	Father O'Hara	A626
Karen **Lewis**	A Month In The Country	As Cast	A736
Phillip **Lewis**	Robin Hood	King John	A929
Rhoda **Lewis**	A Month In The Country	As Cast	A736
Charles **Lewsen**	The Dybbuk	Meyer	A349
Audrey **Leybourne**	Don't Play With Love	Dame Pluche	A329
Jeff **Leyton**	Les Miserables	Jean Valjean	A611
Bo **Light**	Grand Hotel	Bellboy	A453
Gary **Lilburn**	Henceforward...	Mervyn Bickerdike	A491
	Jolly Potters	As Cast	A557
Song **Liling**	M. Butterfly	D.C. Chan	A651
Mary **Lincoln**	Goodnight Mr Tom	Mrs Beech	A450
Stephen **Lind**	Beardsley	Raffalovich	A95
Andy **Linden**	Roberto Calvi	As Cast	A926
Kenny **Linden**	Annie Get Your Gun	Ensemble	A51
Ellis **Linders**	House Of The Spirits		A514
Ian **Lindsay**	Anybody for Murder?	George Ticklewell	A55
Nigel **Lindsay**	Anna Karenina	Stiva	A50
Robert **Lindsay**	Becket	Henry II	A103
	Cyrano De Bergerac	Cyrano De Bergerac	A269
Shona **Lindsay**	Phantom Of The Opera	Christene Daae	A854
Matthew **Line**	The Pope And The Witch	Roberto	A870
Barry **Linehan**	You Must Be The Husband	The Boss	A1248
Rosaleen **Linehan**	Double Dealer	As Cast	A335
Simon **Linnell**	A View From The Bridge	Louis	A1171
Nigel **Linsay**	Relative Values	Nigel	A899
Illona **Linthwaite**	The Professional	As Cast	A883
Lynette **Linthwaite**	The Heiress	Mrs Montgomery	A490
Caroline **Lintot**	Provoked Wife	Belinda	A884
Maureen **Lipman**	The Cabinet Minister	Lady Kitty	A179
	Lost in Yonkers	Aunt Bella	A641
Brian **Lipson**	Bourgeois Gentilhomme	Tailor	A153
	Seven Doors	As Cast	A978
Leon **Lissek**	Cyrano De Bergerac	Ligniere/Capuchin	A269
Ian **Liston**	Music Hall	Chairman	A759
Edward **Little**	Macbeth	Second Murderer	A655
	The Tempest	Adrian	A1082
	Twelfth Night	Curio	A1148
George **Little**	Paradise Garden	Jack Woodcock	A843
Helena **Little**	Dancing At Lughnasa	Chris	A274
Victoria **Little**	My Mother Said	Jackie	A767
Andrew **Livingston**	Happy Families	Vic Taylor	A476
	Richard III	Stanley	A912
Sidney **Livingstone**	The Blue Angel	Friedrich Bombler	A138

Name	Play	Part	Ref
	Measure For Measure	Provost	A700
Lore **Lixenberg**	Mamahuhu?	As Cast	A678
Marc **Lixenburg**	Wind In The Willows	Billy	A1211
Christopher **Llewellyn**	Goin' Local	Young Gentleman	A442
Ray **Llewellyn**	The Corn Is Green	Mr Goronwy-Jones	A249
Roger **Llewellyn**	Julius Caesar	Brutus	A564
Suzette **Llewellyn**	A Midsummer Night's Dream	Titania	A717
Julia **Lloyd Barrie**	A Doll's House	Christine	A324
Matthew **Lloyd Davies**	In The Midnight Hour	Jazza	A537
	Madness of George III	Papandiek	A669
John **Lloyd Fillingham**	Glass Menagerie	Gentleman Caller	A440
	Importance of Being	Algernon Moncrieff	A532
	Spring and Port Wine	Harold	A1036
David **Lloyd Meredith**	The Devils	Louis Trincant Father Ambrose	A304
Bernard **Lloyd**	Fiddler On The Roof	Tevye	A401
	Rosmersholm	Ulrik Brendel	A939
	The Seagull	Dorn	A962
Gabrielle **Lloyd**	Stages	As Cast	A1042
Hugh **Lloyd**	Dick Whittington	Alderman Fitzwarren	A309
	Sailor Beware!	Henry Hornett	A948
Jean **Lloyd**	My Fair Lady	Mrs Eynsford-Hill	A763
Jessica **Lloyd**	Lovers	Magg	A647
Robert **Langdon Lloyd**	Romeo And Juliet	Friar Lawrence	A938
Robin **Lloyd**	My Cousin Rachel	Seecombe	A762
Sharon **Lloyd**	M. Butterfly	Renee/Woman At Party/Girl	A651
Clifton **Lloyd-Bryan**	Carmen Jones	Eddie Perkins	A189
Robert **Locke**	Blood Brothers	Eddie	A131
Thomas **Lockyer**	Blodeuwedd	As Cast	A129
Mark **Lockyer**	Madness of George III	The Duke of York	A669
Kenneth **Lodge**	Death Of A Salesman	Charley	A297
Jenny **Logan**	Goodnight Mr Tom	As Cast	A450
	Noises Off	Belinda Blain	A794
	Stepping Out	Mavis	A1046
Christopher **Logue**	Kings	As Cast	A583
Michelle **Lokey**	Carmen Jones	Myrt	A189
Caroline **Loncq**	Macbeth	Lady Macbeth	A656
Katie **London**	Bright & Bold Design	Violet Chappel	A161
	Hobson's Choice	Ada Figgins	A499
Kate **Lonergan**	All My Sons	Lydia Lubey	A33
	Seagull	Lily	A963
Adam **Long**	The Complete Works	Various	A245
Mark **Long**	The Solo Experience	Various	A1024
Richard **Long**	The Recruiting Officer	Bullock	A897
Terence **Longdon**	Mansfield Park	Sir Thomas Bertram	A683
Brenda **Longman**	The Sound Of Music	Sister Margaretta	A1033
Wyllie **Longmore**	Blues for Mr Charlie	Meridian Henry	A143
Elaine **Lordan**	Rat Play	Mary	A892
Peter **Lorenzelli**	One For The Road	Dennis	A818
Karl **Lornie**	Imagine	Paul	A530
Andrew **Loudon**	Lust	Harcourt	A650
Harley **Loudon**	Down And Out...	Mimi	A339
Dorian **Lough**	Romeo and Juliet	Paris	A936
	A View From The Bridge	Immigration Officer	A1172
Patti **Love**	Me And Mamie O'Rourke	Bibi	A696
	Three Birds Alighting	Various	A1100

Name	Play	Part	Ref
Sophie Lovell-Smith	Baby Baby	As cast	A83
Richard Lowdon	Emanuelle Enchanted	As Cast	A363
Maggie Lowe	Out Of Order	Pamela	A835
Philip Lowe	The Trial	Various	A1140
Jan Lower	Ghosts	Oswald Alving	A432
	Medea	The Chorus	A704
Antonia Loyd	Macbeth	Witch	A653
Andy Lucas	Tango 'Til You're Sore	Ricky	A1072
Nina Lucking	Forbidden Planet	Miranda	A904
Adrian Lukis	As You Like It	Oliver	A67
	School of Night	Thomas Kyd	A959
	Tamburlaine The Great	Alcidamus	A1067
Joanna Lumley	Who Shall I Be?	As Cast	A1203
David Lumsden	19th Hole	As Cast	A1090
Michael Lumsden	The Secret Rapture	Tom	A968
Dennis Lupien	Annie Get Your Gun	Ensemble	A51
Linda Lusardi	Snow White...	As Cast	A1022
Christopher Luscombe	The Alchemist	Dapper	A28
	Artists and Admirers	Vasya	A64
	Henry IV Part 1	Francis	A492
	Henry IV Part 2	Travers	A493
Joe Lutton	Buddy	Buddy Holly	A168
Gary Lydon	Wexford Trilogy	Georgie	A1194
Jackie Lye	Three Girls In Blue	Ira	A1101
Barry Lynch	Amphibians	Zak	A40
	Two Gents Of Verona	Proteus	A1154
	The Virtuoso	Bruce	A1176
	A Woman Killed With Kindness	Wendoll	A1229
Michael Lynch	Christopher Street	As Cast	A218
Richard Lynch	Patagonia	As Cast	A845
Susan Lynch	Berlin Bertie	Joanne	A109
	Lulu	Lulu	A648
Nicholas Lyndhurst	Straight & Narrow	Bob	A1054
David Lyndon	Aspects Of Love	1st Barker	A72
Emma Lyndon	The House Of Stairs	Stanford	A513
Richard Lyndon	A Little Night Music		A630
Victoria Lynson	Some Like It Hot	Nellie Wiesmyer	A1025
David Lyon	Becket	Gilbert Folliot	A103
Frances Lyonhart	Ruby In The Dust		A941
Gary Lyons	Phantom of the Opera	Remy	A853
Jake Lyons	Twelfth Night	Fabian	A1151
Carolyn Lyster	Run for Your Wife	As Cast	A944
Paulette Lythall	The Imaginary Invalid	Toinette	A529
Wendy Macadam	Ghosts	Mrs Alving	A432
Simon Macallum	Cuttin' A Rug	Hector	A266
Amanda MacDonald	Houdini	As Cast	A509
Harry MacDonald	The Guardsman	The Creditor	A461
	Lloyd George	Lloyd George	A635
Robert D MacDonald	Conundrum	As Cast	A247
	Niagara	Blondin	A781
Samantha MacDonald	Les Atrides	As Cast	A609
Stephen MacDonald	Summer Lightning	Beach/Lord Emsworth	A1058
Chris MacDonnell	Mother Goose	Mother Goose	A739
Irene MacDougall	Hay Fever	Myra Arundel	A482
	Merlin, The Search	As Cast	A709
	Old Times	Kate	A806
Claire Machin	My Fair Lady	Mrs Higgins' Maid	A763
Darren Machin	Out Of Order	Ronnie	A835
Ross Mackay	MacWizard Fae Oz	As Cast	A663
Stephen Mackenna	Fiddler On The Roof	Constable	A401

Name	Play	Part	Ref
Ellie Mackenzie	Savage Storm	As Cast	A952
Michael MacKenzie	Hay Fever	Richard Greatham	A482
	Old Times	Deeley	A806
	Uncle Vanya	Serebryakov	A1158
Phillip Mackenzie	Call Blue Jane	As Cast	A182
Marlena Mackey	Viva Detroit	Pat	A1178
Doon MacKichen	Killers	As Cast	A573
Claira Mackie	Macbeth	As Cast	A657
Steven Mackintosh	The Woman In Black	The Actor	A1227
Anna Mackmin	The Norman Conquests	Annie	A796
Quention Maclaine	Phantom of the Opera	Ensemble	A853
Eric MacLennan	Orlando	As Cast	A824
	The Way of All Flesh	Ernest/George Pontifex	A1190
Lewis MacLeod	Jack And The Beanstalk	Simple Simon	A553
Mary Macleod	Grapes of Wrath	Ma	A454
Robbie Macnab	The Sound Of Music	Ensemble	A1033
Peter MacNally	Beauty And The Beast	Beast/Son	A100
Alan MacNaughtan	The Sea	Evens	A961
Peter Macqueen	Christmas Carol	Scrooge	A217
Roy Macready	Me And My Girl	Herbert Parchester	A699
Duncan MacVicar	Carousel	As Cast	A190
Rosemary Macvie	Witness For The Prosecution	Janet McKenzie	A1218
Ritchie Madden	Trilby & Svengali	Taffy	A1141
Karl Maddix	Dragon	As Cast	A341
Alan Maddrell	Macbeth	Donalbain	A658
Philip Madoc	The Blue Angel	Professor Raat	A138
	The Devils	Father Barre	A304
	Measure For Measure	The Duke	A700
Ruth Madoc	Steel Magnolias	M'Lynn	A1045
Dominic Mafham	A Jovial Crew	Oliver	A561
	The Taming Of The Shrew	Lord Simon Llewellyn	A1068
Francis Magee	The Best Man	Phil	A110
Adam Magnani	EuroVision	Kevin	A381
Marcello Magni	Game of Love & Chance	Harlequin	A425
	The Winter's Tale	Autolycus	A1215
Lesley Maguire	Amphibians	Sonia	A40
	Romeo And Juliet	As Cast	A938
Nirjay Mahindru	Comedy of Errors	Duke Of Ephesus	A240
	Jolly Potters	As Cast	A557
	The Rivals	Fag	A919
Peter Mair	The Sound Of Music	Admiral Von Schreiber	A1033
Sara Mair-Thomas	Hecuba	Polyxena	A488
Sally Mais	Glass Menagerie	Laura	A440
	Too Much Too Young	As Cast	A1127
Sandra Maitland	Working	As Cast	A1239
Nigel Makin	Aba Daba Music Hall	Various	A6
Kevorak Malikyan	Hecuba	Odysseus	A488
	White Woman Street	Clerk	A1202
Jessica Malin	Merchant Of Venice	Jessica	A707
Sarah Malin	Hecuba	Chorus	A488
Anastasia Malinoff	Television Programme	Belot	A1080
Clare Malka	House of Bernarda Alba	As Cast	A515
John Malkovich	A Slip Of The Tongue	Dominic Tantra	A1016
Eric Mallett	Street of Crocodiles	Theodore	A1056
Timmy Mallett	Jack and the Beanstalk	Jack	A551
David Mallinson	Deathtrap	Sidney Bruhl	A298
	View From The Bridge	Alfieri	A1170
Michael Maloney	Henry IV Part 1	Prince Hal	A492

Name	Play	Part	Ref
	Henry IV Part 2	Prince Hal	A493
	Romeo And Juliet	Romeo	A938
	A Woman Killed With Kindness	John Frankford	A1229
Nick Maloney	The Norman Conquests	Reg	A796
George Malpas	Single Spies	Shop Assistant Restorer	A1005
Robin Malyon	Kurt Weill Cabaret	As Cast	A585
Caroline Mander	Good Rockin' Tonite	Miss Bushman	A449
Ben Mangham	Hapgood	Merryweather	A472
Karen Mann	Forbidden Planet	Science Officer	A904
Norman Mann	Don't Play With Love	Maitre Bridaine	A329
Steven Mann	The Deep Blue Sea	Freddie Page	A140
	Deathtrap	Clifford Anderson	A298
	Don Juan	Don Juan	A327
Guy Manning	The Deep Blue Sea	Jackie Jackson	A140
Tom Mannion	The Revenger's Tragedy	Lussurioso	A908
Elizabeth Mansfield	A Better Day	Sylvia Pankhurst	A111
James Mansfield	After You With The Mlk	Ricky	A16
	Wit's End	Repetilov	A1216
Marcia Mantack	Romeo and Juliet	Nurse	A937
Knight Mantell	Don Juan In Hell	The Devil	A325
Clive Mantle	The Pocket Dream	Bottom	A868
Collin Mantle	Chorus of Disapproval	As Cast	A210
Paul Manuel	My Fair Lady	Zoltan Karpathy	A763
	West Side Story	Tony	A1193
Stephen Mapes	Time Of My Life	As Cast	A1112
Marcello Marasculchi	Three Musketeers	As Cast	A1107
Yvonne Marceau	Grand Hotel	The Countess	A453
Marianne March	Rebels And Friends	As Cast	A895
Ennio Marchetto	Ennio Marchetto	One-Man Show	A371
Fizz Marcus	Grope	Catherine	A460
Stephen Marcus	A Working Woman	Goujet	A1238
Kate Margam	Dybbuk	As Cast	A350
Paula Margertson	Chorus of Disapproval	As Cast	A210
	Comedy of Errors	As Cast	A239
Peter Marinker	Bad Blood	Father	A85
Clayton Mark	Elvis - the Musical	Mature Elvis	A362
Sara Markland	Hecuba	Chorus	A488
	Importance of Being	Cecily	A532
Alfred Marks	Me And My Girl	Sir John Tremayne	A699
Gareth Marks	Buddy	The Big Bopper	A169
Kristin Marks	Grace	Felicia	A452
Lisa Marks	Macbeth	As Cast	A657
Jonathon Markwood	Charley's Aunt	Charles Wykeham	A200
Lara Marland	Macbeth	As Cast	A657
Clive Marlowe	Chorus of Disapproval	As Cast	A210
	Comedy of Errors	As Cast	A239
	The Sound Of Music	Ensemble	A1033
Linda Marlowe	The Thebans	Jocasta	A1095
	Twelfth Night	Maria	A1152
	The Virtuoso	Lady Gimcrack	A1176
Richard Marner	'Allo,'Allo	Colonel Von Stroam	A36
Alan Marni	Blodeuwedd	As Cast	A129
Martin Marquez	Revenger's Tragedy	Vindice	A909
	View From The Bridge	Marco	A1170
Ian Marr	Ladies' Night	As Cast	A592
Josh Marriott	Twelfth Night	Sir Toby Belch	A1151
Paul Marrow	Custer's Last Stand	Red Cloud	A264
Judi Mars	Buddy	Maria's Aunt	A169
Betty Marsden	Trelawny Of The Wells	Mrs Telfer	A1138
Kate Marsden	Les Miserables	Ensemble	A613
Colin Marsh	Lust	Ensemble	A650
Jean Marsh	The Chalk Garden	Mrs Madrigal	A196
Matthew Marsh	All My Sons	Chris Keller	A33
Reginald Marsh	Phantom of the Opera	M. Richard	A853
William Marsh	Schmucks	As Cast	A955
	Toronto, Mississippi	As Cast	A1129
Claire Marshall	Emanuelle Enchanted	As Cast	A363
Melanie Marshall	Carmen Jones	Cindy Lou	A189
Tom Marshall	Karate Billy...Home	As Cast	A572
Gillian Martell	Voysey Inheritance	Mrs Voysey	A1182
Barbara Marten	Self Portrait	Gwen John	A974
Bernard Martin	Les Atrides	As Cast	A609
	Safe In Our Hands	Ted Wallace	A947
Chris Martin	Henceforward...	Lupus (video)	A491
Corinne Martin	Handsome,Handicapped..	As Cast	A468
Graham Martin	Starlight Express	Dustin	A1043
Jessica Martin	Dead Flamingo Dancer	Gussie	A193
	Me And My Girl	Sally Smith	A698
Reed Martin	The Complete Works	Various	A245
Roger Martin	Chorus of Disapproval	As Cast	A210
	Comedy of Errors	Solinus	A239
Rosemary Martin	Angels In America	Hannah Porter Pitt	A47
	Stages	As Cast	A1042
Stephanie Martin	Les Miserables	Eponine	A613
Tina Martin	Giraffe, Pelly, & Me	Mum/Duchess	A436
Trevor Martin	The Odyssey	Eumaeus	A802
	Tamburlaine The Great	Soldan of Egypt	A1067
	The Taming Of The Shrew	Baptista	A1068
Vivienne Martin	A Dead Secret	Maria Lummus	A289
Antonio Gil Martinez	Street of Crocodiles	Cousin Emil	A1056
Thandi Mashiloane	Sikulu	Ensemble	A1001
Karen Maskill	Ghost Sonata	The Fiancee	A431
Andrea Mason	The Recruiting Officer	Colliers Wife	A897
Bob Mason	The Norman Conquests	Tom	A796
Margery Mason	My Mother Said...	Doris	A766
Matt Mason	King Lear	Cornwall	A578
Anna Massey	Grace	Ruth Hartstone	A452
	A Hard Heart	Riddler	A477
Daniel Massey	Heartbreak House	Hector Hushabye	A486
Claire Massie	Chitty Bang Bang	Truly Scrumptious	A208
Carl Masson	A Better Day	As Cast	A111
Vicki Masson	Tartuffe	As Cast	A1073
	Virginia Woolf	Honey	A1205
Theo Massos	Buddy	Richie Valens	A168
Debi Mastel	Crime of Love	As Cast	A258
Guy Masterson	Cyrano De Bergerac	Bellarose/Spanish Officer	A269
Adam Matalon	Porcelain	Voice II	A871
Eve Matheson	Dejavu	Helena	A302
Alexandra Mathie	Roaring Girl's Hamlet	Claudius	A925
Barbara Mathieson	As You Like It	Rosalind	A70
Chris Matthews	Dangerous Obsession	As Cast	A278
	Serve Them All My Days	As Cast	A1123
Daniel Matthews	Macbeth	Fleance/Young Siward	A653
Francis Matthews	Relatively Speaking	Philip	A900
Keith Matthews	Brand	As Cast	A157
Nicholas Matthews	Romeo And Juliet	Child	A938
Peter Matthews	Night in Tunisia	Tony Lemmon	A783
Sally Ann Matthews	Dick Whittington	Dick Whittington	A311
	Gaslight	Nancy	A428

Name	Play	Part	Ref
	Indigo Mill	As Cast	A539
Seymour Matthews	Pygmalion	Bystander	A886
Stephen Matthews	Death of A Salesman	As Cast	A295
Michael Matus	EuroVision	Andreas	A381
Jane Maud	The Choice	As Cast	A209
	Lady Be Good	Josephine Vanderwater	A594
	A Midsummer Night's ..	Titania	A721
Susan Maughan	Dick Whittington	Dick Whittington	A308
Gary Mavers	Coriolanus	As Cast	A248
Ben Maw	Henry IV Part 1	Water-bearer	A492
Michael Mawby	In The Midnight Hour	Benny	A537
	Stitched Up	Nigel	A1050
Edward Max	As You Like It	Charles	A71
	Lady Be Good	Manuel Estrada	A594
	A Midsummer Night's ..	Snout	A721
Tim Maxwell Clarke	Buddy	Norman Petty	A168
Donald Maxwell	The Mikado	Ko-Ko	A722
Victoria Maxwell	Starlight Express	Ashley	A1043
Rita May	A Working Woman	Ma Coupeau	A1238
William May	Phantom Of The Opera	Slave Master	A854
Dave Mayberry	Schmucks	As Cast	A955
Hazel Maycock	Dangerous Corner	Miss Mockridge	A277
	Grapes of Wrath	Grandma	A454
	Wizard of Oz	Mis Gultch/Wicked Witch	A1224
Sharon Mayer	And A Nightingale Sang	Joyce Stott	A43
	On The Piste	Melissa	A810
Colin Mayes	Death of A Salesman	As Cast	A295
	Far From The Madding Crowd	Joseph Poorgrass	A397
	Grease	Eugene	A458
Mark Mayes	Beyond Reasonable Doubt	Mr Cole	A114
Richard Mayes	A Hard Heart	Plevna	A477
	Importance of Being	Canon Chasuble	A532
Mandy Mayhew	The Golden Ass	Isis	A443
Lottie Mayor	The Sound Of Music	Liesl	A1033
Rebecca Mays	As You Like It	Celia	A70
Peter Maz	Buddy	Murray Deutch	A168
Des McAleer	Wexford Trilogy	Artie	A1194
Fiona McAlpine	Orlando	Vita Sackville-West	A824
John McAndrew	A Jovial Crew	Sentwell	A561
	School of Night	Thomas Walsingham	A959
	The Taming Of The Shrew	Lucentio	A1068
John McArdle	Raving Beauties	Jack	A893
Gerrard McArthur	Birthday Party	As Cast	A124
Neil McArthur	Dragon	As Cast	A341
Shobu McAuley	Night in Tunisia	Naseem Khan	A783
Nichola McAuliffe	The Heiress	Catherine Sloper	A490
Raphael McAuliffe	Blood Wedding	The Bridegroom	A133
	Spring Awakening	Otto/Headmaster Sunstroke	A1037
Robert McBain	The Mother Tongue	Gerald	A743
Simon McBurney	The Winter's Tale	Leontes	A1215
Mike McCabe	Aladdin	Chinese Policeman	A18
Richard McCabe	School of Night	Christopher Marlowe	A959
	The Taming Of The Shrew	Tranio	A1068

Name	Play	Part	Ref
	The Winter's Tale	Autolycus	A1214
Ruth McCabe	The Gigli Concert		A435
Robin McCaffery	All My Sons	Ann Deever	A32
Phil McCall	Eight to the Bar	As Cast	A356
Ross McCall	Lost in Yonkers	Jay	A641
John McCallum	On Golden Pond	Norman Thayer	A808
Donal McCann	Faith Healer	Frank	A389
Ronnie McCann	The Jungle Book	As Cast	A568
Martin McCardie	Lions of Lisbon	Danny	A626
Edith McCarthur	Hay Fever	Judith Bliss	A482
Barry McCarthy	Noises Off	Lloyd Dallas	A795
	Shadowlands	C.S.Lewis	A985
Larry McCarthy	A Midsummer Night's Dream	Oberon	A717
Maggie McCarthy	Night of the Iguana	Frau Fahrenkopf	A785
	Square Rounds	As Cast	A1038
Neil McCaul	June Moon	As Cast	A567
Paul McCleary	Arms and the Man	Nicola	A60
Roger McClenahan	Rule Of The Game	PC Martin	A942
	Valdorama		A1164
Hamish McColl	Flight To Finland	Ensemble	A409
	Moose	Ensemble	A738
Colin McCormack	A Dolls House	Torvald Helmer	A321
	Three Birds Alighting	Various	A1100
Emer McCourt	Cherry Orchard		A203
Alec McCowen	Caesar And Cleopatra	Caesar	A180
	Someone Who'll Watch	Michael	A1028
Sylvester McCoy	As You Like It	Touchstone	A69
	Cinderella	Baron Hardup	A224
Jenny McCracken	Who Was Hilary	As Cast	A1204
Paul McCready	Pond Life	Shane	A869
Alasdair McCrone	Laurel and Hardy	Stan Laurel	A602
Helen McCrory	Fuente Ovejuna	Jacinta	A422
	Trelawny Of The Wells	Rose Trelawny	A1138
Cal McCrystal	The End Of The Tunnel	As Cast	A365
Debra McCulloch	Lust	Mistress Squeamish	A650
Mary McCusker	Dancing at Lughnasa	Kate	A275
Stella McCusker	Pygmies In The Ruins		A887
Sandy McDade	Bad Girl	Moira	A86
	The Rivals	Julia	A919
James McDaniel	Someone Who'll Watch	Adam	A1028
Gerard McDermott	Northern Trawl	Ted	A797
Phelim McDermott	The Pocket Dream	Quince	A868
Aimi McDonald	Run for Your Wife	As Cast	A944
Dorian McDonald	A Jovial Crew	Beggar/Martin	A561
	The Taming Of The Shrew	Rt Hon Hugo Daley Young	A1068
Gary McDonald	Armed And Dangerous	As Cast	A59
	Some Singing Blood		A1026
Leigh McDonald	Moby Dick	As Cast	A728
Marianne Mcdonald	Liar Liar	As Cast	A616
Chris McDonnell	Macbeth	As Cast	A657
Irene McDougal	Unidentified Human	As Cast	A1162
Martin McDougall	The Sacred Penman	As Cast	A946
Mac McEleney	Lions of Lisbon	Inspector Farquar	A626
Michael McElhatton	Handsome,Handicapped..	As Cast	A468
	Water Music	Barry	A1188
Ian McElhinney	Amphibians	Eagle	A40
	Pygmies In The Ruins		A887
Teresa McElroy	Fuente Ovejuna	Woman	A422
	Self Portrait	Ida John	A974
Maria McErlane	Evening with Gary L.	Birgitta	A383

Name	Play	Part	Ref
Alec McEwan	Down And Out...	Eric Blair (Orwell)	A339
David McEwan	Some Like It Hot	M.D (Speakeasy)	A1025
Geraldine McEwan	Hamlet	Gertrude	A465
Myra McFadyen	Bourgeois Gentilhomme	Professor Of Philosophy	A153
	Square Rounds	As Cast	A1038
Colin McFarlane	Flamingo	As Cast	A408
Mark McGann	All My Sons	Chris	A32
	Imagine	John Lennon	A530
	Killers	Brother	A573
	One The Ledge	As Cast	A821
Stephen McGann	Killers	Brother	A573
Henry McGee	It Runs In The Family	Bill	A548
Penelope McGhie	Rocky Horror Show	Magenta/Usherette	A933
Terry McGinity	Enemy To The People	As Cast	A369
Geoffrey McGivern	Fighting For The Dunghill	Joshua	A404
Susan McGoun	House of Bernarda Alba	As Cast	A515
	Night in Tunisia	Margaret Dawes	A783
Brian McGovern	Lovers	Joe	A647
Tom McGovern	Therese Raquin	Laurent	A1097
Paul McGrane	Uncle Vanya	A Workman	A1157
Elizabeth McGrath	Ghost Sonata	The Mummy	A431
Graham McGregor	Taming Of The Shrew	Curtis/Pedant	A1070
Matt McGuire	Lost in Yonkers	As Cast	A641
Bill McGuirk	Woman Of No Importance	Farquhar	A1230
Rosemary McHale	View From The Bridge	Beatrice	A1170
Christopher McHallem	A Doll's House	Nils	A324
Deborah McHardy	Monster He Made Me	Elli	A734
Kieran McIlroy	Grand Hotel	Eric	A453
Lizzy McInnerny	A Slip Of The Tongue	Isabel Brezhinski	A1016
Tim McInnerny	Romeo And Juliet	Mercutio	A938
	'Tis Pity She's A Whore	Soranzo	A1114
	Twelfth Night	Sir Andrew Aguecheek	A1152
Alyson McInnes	Aladdin	Aladdin	A20
Joanne McInnes	Animal Farm	Ensemble	A49
Robert McIntosh	The Rivals	David/Coachman	A918
Ciaran McIntyre	A Jovial Crew	Cook/Soldier Beggar	A561
David McKail	Shadowlands	As Cast	A983
David McKay	The Jungle Book	As Cast	A568
Elizabeth McKechnie	The Rivals	Julia	A918
Sarah-Jane McKechnie	Noises Off	Poppy	A795
Martin McKellan	School for Scandal	Joseph Surface	A957
Ian McKellen	Richard III	Richard III	A911
	Uncle Vanya	Vanya	A1157
Alison McKenna	Night of the Iguana	Charlotte Goodall	A785
Susie McKenna	In The Midnight Hour	Roxy	A537
T McKenna	Cherry Orchard		A203
Janice McKenzie	Devil's Only Sleeping	Myra	A303
	Hobson's Choice	Maggie Hobson	A500
	My Mother Said...	Jackie Metcalfe	A766
Kate McKenzie	Night in Tunisia	Gillian Peters	A783
Abigail McKern	Three Birds Alighting	Various	A1100
Roger McKern	Les Miserables	As Cast	A612
Richard McKeuley	Smile Orange	As Cast	A1017
Dermot McLaughlin	Fiddler On The Roof	Mendel	A401
Gerry McLaughlin	Taming of the Shrew	Biondello	A1069
	Wizard of Oz	Nikko	A1222

Name	Play	Part	Ref
Lise Ann McLaughlin	Deathtrap	Myra Bruhl	A298
	Don Juan	Elvira	A327
	Una Pooka	As Cast	A1156
Finlay McLean	Exile	As Cast	A387
Michael McLean	Phantom of the Opera	Faust	A853
Gary McLeod	Taming of the Shrew	Grumio	A1069
	Wizard of Oz	Chester Marvel	A1222
Adrian McLoughlin	Neville's Island	Neville	A777
	Rocket To The Moon	Willy Wax	A932
Kate McLoughlin	Dancing at Lughnasa	Chris	A275
Pauline McLynne	Double Dealer	As Cast	A335
Jim McManus	Road To Casablanca	Bob Hope	A923
Kevin McMonagle	Karate Billy...Home	As Cast	A572
Lynette McMorrough	The Heiress	Maria	A490
Tim McMullan	Murmuring Judges	Woody Pearson	A758
	Wind In The Willows	Chief Weasel	A1211
Peter McNally	Barnstormers	Billy Johnston	A92
Desmond Mcnamara	The Blue Angel	As Cast	A138
	Measure For Measure	Elbow	A700
Anna McNell	Massa	Anne	A692
Claudia McNulty	See How They Run	Penelope Toop	A971
Lizzie McPhee	Hamlet	Ophelia	A463
	King Lear	Cordelia	A577
Keith McPherson	Dead Heroic	Treasure Collect	A287
Stuart McQuarrie	Good Morning Bill	Bill Paradene	A447
	House Among the Stars	Edouard	A512
	Laurel and Hardy	Oliver Hardy	A602
Hilton McRae	Acapulco	John	A12
Andrew McRobb	A Month In The Country	As Cast	A736
Mike McShane	The Pocket Dream	Theatre Manager	A868
Carmel McSharry	Straight & Narrow	Vera	A1054
Tracy McSmythurs	The Tender Husband	Jenny	A1088
Karen McSween	Barnum	As Cast	A93
Janet McTeer	Uncle Vanya	Yelena Andreyevna	A1157
Tom McVeigh	Phantom Of The Opera	Lionman	A854
J.Mark McVey	Les Miserables	Jean Valjean	A613
Ron Meadows	Othello	Brabantio/Gratiano	A827
	The School For Scandal	Crabtree/Careless	A956
Ray Meagher	Goldilocks	Good Ringmaster	A444
Amanda Mealing	Elegies...	As Cast	A358
Stephen Mear	Grease	Sonny	A458
	Some Like It Hot	Taxi Driver	A1025
Catherine Mears	The Taming Of The Shrew	Lady Sarah Ormsby	A1068
	The Winter's Tale	Lady	A1214
Michael Mears	Stitched Up	Souter/James/etc etc	A1050
	Tomorrow We Do The Sky	As Cast	A1124
Tim Meats	Private Lives	Victor Prynne	A881
Paul J Medford	Dragon	As Cast	A341
	Five Guys Named Moe	Little Moe	A407
Michael Medwin	My Fair Lady	Colonel Pickering	A763
James Meek	The Bells	Christian	A108
Joe Melia	Heartbreak House	Billy Dunn	A486
	Trelawny Of The Wells	O'Dwyer	A1139
Michael Melia	Absent Friends	Paul	A8
Leonie Mellinger	She Stoops To Conquer	Constance Neville	A992
Louis Mellis	Goin' Local	Boy-Boy	A442
Cherith Mellor	Absent Friends	Marge	A8
Kay Mellor	Three Girls In Blue	Svetlana	A1101
John Melvin	Robin	James-The-Dean	A927

Name	Play	Part	Ref
Jules Melvin	Massa	Nell	A692
Murray Melvin	The Devils	Father Mignon	A304
Clive Mendus	A Better Day	Jack	A111
	Street of Crocodiles	Uncle Charles	A1056
Oleg Menshikov	Gamblers	Ikharev	A424
Ian Mercer	The Revenger's Tragedy	Spurio	A908
	The Rivals	Acres	A918
Nick Mercer	Bourgeois Gentilhomme	Student/Tailor Cook	A153
James Meredith	Pepys - The Diarist	Pepys	A849
Robin Meredith	As You Desire Me		A66
Susannah Meredith	Aspects Of Love	Jenny Dillingham	A72
Bella Merlin	Orlando	As Cast	A824
Pamela Merrick	Elephant	As Cast	A359
Jason Merrills	School Of Night	Essex	A960
Clive Merrison	The Pope And The Witch	Cardinal Vialli	A870
Paul Merton	The Comedy Store	Various	A242
Ted Merwood	The Sound Of Music	Baron Elberfeld	A1033
Paul Meston	Bourgeois Gentilhomme	Fencing Instructor	A153
	Dragon	As Cast	A341
	A Midsummer Night's Dream	Philostrate	A718
Stefan Metz	Street of Crocodiles	Leon	A1056
Jud Meyers	Romeo and Juliet	Mercutio	A936
	A View From The Bridge	Mike	A1172
Janet Michael	Wasting Reality	Meg	A1186
Debra Michaels	Carmen Jones	Cleo	A189
Joanna Michaels	Elvis - the Musical	Sweet Inspiration	A362
Yomi A Michaels	Romeo and Juliet	Lord Capulet	A937
Vicki Michelle	'Allo,'Allo	Yvette	A36
John Michie	Women Laughing	As Cast	A1235
Elizabeth Mickery	Absurd Person Singular	As Cast	A11
Francis Middleditch	Three Musketeers	Aramis	A1106
	To Kill A Mockingbird	Mr. Gilmer	A1121
Frank Middlemass	Voysey Inheritance	George Booth	A1182
David Middleton	The Business Of Murder	Hallet	A174
	The Maintenance Man	Bob	A673
	Stage Struck	Robert	A1040
Louise Middleton	Relative Values	Alice	A899
Peter Mielniczek	The Three Musketeers	Rochforte	A1104
Annie Miles	From A Jack To A King	Laura Ross	A420
Ben Miles	Fuente Ovejuna	Leonelo	A422
	Trelawny Of The Wells	Arthur Gower	A1138
Gaynor Miles	Phantom of the Opera	Ensemble	A853
Maria Miles	Cerceau	Nadya	A195
	King Lear In New York	Juliet	A580
Sarah Miles	Charlemagne	As Cast	A199
Clara Miller	Barnum	Jenny Lind	A93
Graeme Miller	...Changed The Wires	Martin Keeble	A1245
Jonny Lee Miller	Entertaining Mr Sloane	Sloane	A373
Maria Miller	Beauty And The Beast	Beauty	A97
	Cain	Adah	A181
	Eight to the Bar	As Cast	A356
Patrick Miller	Too Much Too Young	As Cast	A1127
	White Woman Street	James Miranda	A1202
Primrose Milligan	Uncle Vanya	Marina	A1158
Hayley Mills	Fallen Angels	Jane Banbury	A391
Ian Mills	Starlight Express	As Cast	A1043
John Mills	John Mills	One-Man Show	A42
Juliet Mills	Fallen Angels	Julia Sterroll	A391
Royce Mills	Don't Dress For Dinner	Bernard	A331
	Some Like It Hot	Osgood	A1025
Tim Mills	Mansfield Park	Thomas	A683
Louisa Millwood Haigh	What The Butler Saw	Geraldine	A1196
Gordon Milne	Master and Margarita	Azazello/Bellesez	A693
Anthony Milner	Gamblers	Heathen	A424
Kristopher Milnes	Once Upon A Song		A817
Debora Milton	Elvis - the Musical	Sweet Inspiration	A362
Jonathan Milton	Burbage and the Bard	Various	A172
Hilary Minster	'Allo,'Allo	Von Klinkerhoffen	A36
Simon Mirren	Hostages and Hamsters	Miguel	A506
Linson Miswe	Sikulu	Ensemble	A1001
Allan Mitchell	The Blue Angel	As Cast	A138
	Measure For Measure	Escalus	A700
	A Midsummer Night's Dream	Theseus	A718
Ann Mitchell	Hecuba	Hecuba	A488
	The Rivals	Mrs Malaprop	A919
Brian Mitchell	Prin	Walker	A876
Georgia Mitchell	Evening with Gary L.	Monica	A383
Iain Mitchell	Madness of George III	Sheridan	A669
Mary Mitchell	Pygmalion	Lady	A886
Nancy Mitchell	Hay Fever	Clara	A482
	Uncle Vanya	Maria Vasilyevna	A1158
Norman Mitchell	Hobson's Choice	Jim Heeler	A500
Ruth Mitchell	Orlando	Virginia Woolf	A824
	Roaring Girl's Hamlet	Hamlet	A925
Sheila Mitchell	Wit's End	Miss Khlyostova	A1216
Suzy Mitchell	Life Support		A621
Tean Mitchell	Radio Times	Various	A889
Tracey Mitchell	Twelfth Night	Maria	A1148
Audra Mitcheson	Annie Get Your Gun	Mrs Little Horse Sylvia	A51
Karl Moffatt	The Mousetrap	Christopher Wren	A744
Akim Mogaji	The Road	Salub	A921
Ursula Mohan	Shadowlands	Joy Davidman	A984
Alfred Molina	Night of the Iguana	The Rev Shannon	A785
Alex Mollo	Night of the Iguana	Pedro	A785
Nick Mollo	Night of the Iguana	Pancho	A785
Christopher Molloy	Aspects Of Love	Jerome/Hotelier	A72
Dearbhla Molloy	Death and the Maiden	Paulina	A294
	Loot	Fay	A638
	One The Ledge	As Cast	A821
Mark Monero	All On Top	As Cast	A34
David Monico	The School For Scandal	Sir Peter Teazle	A956
Bill Monks	Awfully Big Adventure	George	A77
Tony Monopoly	Aladdin	Abanazar	A18
	Moby Dick	Headmistress Captain Ahab	A728
Joanna Monro	Blood Brothers	Mrs Lyons	A131
Bruce Montague	19th Hole	As Cast	A1090
Felicity Montague	Angels In America	Harper Amaty Pitt	A47
Joe Montana	Acapulco	As Cast	A12
David Monteath	Breaking the Code	As Cast	A159
Liliane Montevecchi	Grand Hotel	Grushinskaya	A453
Mark Montgomerie	Goin' Local	Cliff	A442
Jane Montgomery	Doll's House	Mrs Linde	A320
	The Innocents	Miss Giddens	A540
Nicholas Monu	Blues for Mr Charlie	Lorenzo	A143
Ron Moody	Spread A Little Happ	As Cast	A1035
Joan Moon	Beyond Reasonable Doubt	Lady Metcalfe	A114
	Noises Off	Belinda Blair	A795

Name	Play	Part	Ref
Paul Mooney	Arms and the Man	Bluntschli	A60
	Voysey Inheritance	Edward	A1182
Lucy Moorby	Joseph...	Asher's Wife	A559
Alan Moore	After You With The Mlk	Don	A16
	Driving Miss Daisy	Boolie (Daisy's Son)	A346
Bonnie Moore	Carousel	Carnival Boy	A190
Claire Moore	The Card (A musical)	Ruth	A187
	Miss Saigon	Ellen	A727
Jason Moore	Joseph...	Benjamin	A559
John Moore	Curse Of The Mummy	Nathan	A263
Mandy Moore	Leonardo	As Cast	A608
Polly Moore	Elegies...	As Cast	A358
Richard Moore	Hamlet	First Gravedigger	A466
	The Thebans	Herdsman/Soldier	A1095
	Two Gents Of Verona	Launce	A1154
Sarah Moore	Crime of Love	As Cast	A258
Stephen Moore	Reflected Glory	Michael	A898
Viv Moore	Fern Hill	Eirwen	A400
Frank Moorey	Caesar And Cleopatra	Pothinus	A180
	Penny for a Song	As Cast	A848
Angela Moran	Me And My Girl	Duchess of Dene	A699
Josh Moran	Merchant of Venice	Leonardo	A708
Justine Moran	Annie Get Your Gun	Ensemble	A51
Tara Moran	Time Windows	Mitch	A1113
Sylvestor Morand	Hecuba	Agamemnon	A488
Stella Moray	Late Joys		A600
Gary Moreline	Shadowlands	Douglas	A984
Lisa Moreno	Voices at Her Elbow	As Cast	A1180
Buddig Morgan	As You Like It	Phoebe	A68
Dorcas Morgan	Trelawny Of The Wells	Sarah	A1139
Emily Morgan	An Ideal Husband	Lady Chiltern	A528
	A Month In The Country	As Cast	A736
Francine Morgan	Dancing at Lughnasa	Rose	A275
	Mrs Klein	Melitta	A748
Garfield Morgan	Don't Rock The Boat	John Coombes	A330
Geraint Morgan	Fern Hill	Gareth/Gwlfa	A400
Jacqueline Morgan	Hobson's Choice	Mrs Hepworth	A499
	Playing The Wife	As Cast	A865
	TO	As Cast	A1115
Ric Morgan	Arms and the Man	Major Petkoff	A60
	The Pope And The Witch	Professor Ridolfi	A870
Sadie Ann Morgan	Carousel	As Cast	A190
Wendy Morgan	As You Like It	Celia	A69
Naoko Mori	Miss Saigon	Bar Girl	A727
Paul Moriarty	Murmuring Judges	Sergeant Lester Speed	A758
Pauline Moriarty	Your Home In The West	Jeanie	A1250
Joshua Morrel	Carmen Jones	Corporal Morrel	A189
Penny Morrel	Natural Causes	Celia	A773
Cherry Morris	Richard III	Queen Margaret	A910
	Woman Of No Importance	Lady Caroline Pontefract	A1230
Deirdra Morris	Beardsley	Ellen	A95
	Revelations	As Cast	A905
Jonathon Morris	Me and My Friend	Bunny	A697
	She Stoops To Conquer	Tony Lumpkin	A992
Keith Morris	Witness For The Prosecution	Carter/Dr Wyatt	A1218
Shona Morris	A Better Day	As Cast	A111
	The Hour Of The Lynx	The Researcher	A511
Wayne Morris	Cinderella	Butons	A225

Name	Play	Part	Ref
Trisha Morrish	Curse Of The Mummy	Mrs Webb	A263
Diana Morrison	Aspects Of Love	Jenny Dillingham	A72
Maggi Morrison	Baby Baby	As cast	A83
Mem Morrison	Adult Child/Dead Child	As Cast	A14
	The English Kiss	Waiter	A370
Nelly Morrison	Dick Whittington	As Cast	A312
Stuart Morrison	70, Girls, 70	As Cast	A4
	Saint Oscar	Jamie	A949
Eamon Morrissey	London Vertigo	Tom Hamilton	A636
Elinor Morriston	The House Of Stairs	Bell	A513
Stewart Morritt	Stage Struck	Herman	A1040
	Strippers	Paulie	A1057
Paul Morrow	End Of The Beginning	Various	A366
Sally Mortimer	Macbeth	Lady Macbeth	A653
Alexander Morton	Uncle Vanya	Astrov	A1158
Liz Moscrop	A Hard Heart	The Women	A477
	Voysey Inheritance	Phoebe	A1182
Alan Mosley	Merrily We Roll Along	As Cast	A711
Abigail Moss	Much Ado About Nothing	Hero	A750
Joe Motsamai	Sikulu	Ensemble	A1001
Anna-Louise Mountford	Starlight Express	Ashley	A1043
Jenny Mountford	Henceforward...	Young Gaien (video)	A491
Maria Moustaka	Dance Of Guns	As Cast	A273
Patrick Mower	Revenge	Bill Crayshaw M.P.	A907
	Rule Of The Game	Philip Yale Drew	A942
Susi Mowson	Some...Atomic Zombie		A1027
Gina Moxley	Digging for Fire	As Cast	A313
Stephen Moyer	Romeo And Juliet	Abraham	A938
David Mucci	Buddy	The Big Bopper	A169
Michael Mueller	A Midsummer Night's ..	Theseus/Oberon	A720
	Twelfth Night	Orsino	A1148
Andrew Muir	Six Degrees...	Ben	A1008
Gavin Muir	Lady Be Good	Bertie Bassett	A594
	A Midsummer Night's ..	Puck	A721
	Tons Of Money	Aubrey Henry Maitland Allington	A1125
Sharon Muircroft	Cherry Orchard	Varya	A202
	Family Affair	Lipochka	A393
	Macbeth	Seyton	A658
	Teechers	As Cast	A1078
	TO	Woman	A1120
John Muirhead	Birthday Party	As Cast	A124
	Television Programme	Delile	A1080
Jacinta Mulcahy	Little Tramp	Oona Chaplin	A634
Gerry Mulgrew	Uncle Vanya	Vanya	A1158
Jacqueline Mulhallen	Rebels And Friends	As Cast	A895
	Sylvia	As Cast	A1061
Dan Mullane	Medea	The Messenger	A704
Stephen Mullane	Medea	Medea's Son	A704
Neil Mullarkey	The Comedy Store	Various	A242
Steve Muller	Forbidden Planet	Navigation Officer	A904
Andy Mulligan	Shadowlands	Christopher Riley	A984
	Strippers	Harry	A1057
Marcia Mullings	Carmen Jones	Dancer	A189
	A Midsummer Night's ..	Lady/Peaseblossom	A720
Ian Mullins	Death of A Salesman	As Cast	A295
Anastasia Mulrooney	The Recruiting Officer	Lucy	A897
Franchine Mulrooney	Signora Joyce	Nora Barnacle Joyce	A1000
Jimmy Mulville	One The Ledge	As Cast	A821

Name	Play	Part	Ref
Vivian Munn	Twelfth Night	Sebastian	A1148
Carmen Munroe	Trouble in Mind	Wiletta Mayer	A1142
Glenn Munroe	Some Like It Hot	Hood 1	A1025
Gregory Munroe	The Road	Chief In Town	A921
Mitch Munroe	Strange Domain	Valentine	A1055
Bill Murdoch	Tartuffe	As Cast	A1073
Vicky Murdock	Night in Tunisia	Julie Dreyer	A783
Brian Murphy	The Fancy Man	Dr P.T. Peach	A395
	The Invisible Man	Thomas Marvel	A547
Gerard Murphy	The Thebans	Oedipus	A1095
John Murphy	Lions of Lisbon	Donaldo	A626
Katrina Murphy	Carousel	As Cast	A190
Barbara Murray	The Heiress	Mrs Lavinia Penniman	A490
Robert Murray	Robin Hood	Guy Gisbourne	A929
Rory Murray	Coriolanus	As Cast	A248
Sean Murray	Amphibians	Broaders	A40
	Romeo And Juliet	Tybalt	A938
	Two Gents Of Verona	Speed	A1154
	The Virtuoso	Longvil	A1176
	A Woman Killed With Kindness	Nicholas	A1229
Paul Murthwaite	The Winslow Boy	Ronnie Winslow	A1213
Michelle-Anne Musty	Starlight Express	As Cast	A1043
Charles Mutter	Why Things Happen	Violinist	A1206
Anne Myatt	Happy Days	Winnie	A475
	Summer Lightning	Lady Constance Keeble	A1058
Hugo Myatt	Eductaing Rita	Frank	A354
	Home At Seven	As Cast	A502
Joseph Mydell	Angels In America	Mr Lies/As Cast	A47
Johnny Myers	Invasion Werewolf	One-Man Show	A546
Richard Mylan	Starlight Express	Flat Top	A1043
Irina Nabatova	Stop in the Desert	As Cast	A1051
Cathy Naden	Emanuelle Enchanted	As Cast	A363
Patrice Naiambana	Flamingo	As Cast	A408
Salwa Nakkarah	Gulf Between Us	Dr Aziz	A462
Fidel Nanton	Alfie	Lofty	A30
	Beauty and the Beast	Lt. Bennett	A99
	A Midsummer Night's Dream	As Cast	A717
Michael Napier Brown	Death of A Salesman	Willy Loman	A295
	Shadowlands	C.S.Lewis	A982
Garth Napier Jones	Rivals	David	A920
David Napier	Roberto Calvi	As Cast	A926
Michael Nardone	Merlin, The Search	As Cast	A709
Alexander Nash	The Hostage	Leslie Williams	A505
	Macbeth	Malcolm	A661
Jane Nash	Square Rounds	As Cast	A1038
Avi Nassa	House Of The Spirits		A514
Gill Nathanson	Dead Man's Hat	As Cast	A288
Terry Neason	Crying For The Moon	One-Man Show	A261
Paul Neaum	Ladies' Night	As Cast	A592
Robin Nedwell	Just Between Ourselves	Neil	A569
	The Sound Of Music	Max Detweiler	A1033
David Needham	Hot Stuff	Ensemble	A508
Peter Needham	The Dybbuk	Sender	A349
Adrian Neil	Revenger's Tragedy	Judge	A909
Hildegard Neil	Monday After Miracle	Annie Sullivan	A733
Kevin Neil	Romeo and Juliet	Tybalt	A937
Michael Neilsen	Blood Brothers	Husband /Teacher	A131
Sandy Neilson	Country Dance		A251

Name	Play	Part	Ref
	Virginia Woolf	George	A1205
Alexander Nelson	Eight to the Bar	As Cast	A356
Celia Nelson	Bloody Poetry	Mary Shelley	A137
	Tango 'Til You're Sore	Anna	A1072
Conrad Nelson	Coriolanus	As Cast	A248
Kenneth Nelson	Dead Flamingo Dancer	As Cast	A193
James Nesbitt	Una Pooka	As Cast	A1156
Sally Nesbitt	The Winslow Boy	Grace Winslow	A1213
Eddie Nestor	Armed And Dangerous	As Cast	A59
John Nettles	Antony and Cleopatra	Octavius	A53
	The Merry Wives Of Windsor	George Page	A713
	The Winter's Tale	Leontes	A1214
John Nettleton	The Woman In Black	Arthur Kipps	A1227
Hilary Neville	Macbeth	Young Macduff	A653
	The Sound Of Music	Ensemble	A1033
Deborah Newbold	The Trial	Various	A1140
Madeleine Newbury	The Mousetrap	Mrs Boyle	A744
Andrew Newey	Miss Saigon	Marine	A727
Seamus Newham	Disobediently Yours	As Cast	A314
	Roman & Marys	As Cast	A934
Susanna Newham	Mansfield Park	Maria	A683
Anthony Newley	Once Upon A Song		A817
	Scrooge the Musical	Scrooge	A1039
Bill Newman	Sneeze	As Cast	A1018
Katharine Newman	King Lear In New York	TV Crew:Script Girl	A580
Philip Newman	The Invisible Man	Wicksted	A547
Steven Newman	World Upon The Moon	Cecco	A1241
Raul Newnie	Smile Orange	As Cast	A1017
Jonathan Newth	Hamlet	Player King	A466
	Romeo And Juliet	Capulet	A938
	'Tis Pity She's A Whore	Bonaventura	A1114
Jeremy Newton	Children Of Lesser God	Orin	A206
Peter Alex Newton	Five Guys Named Moe	No Moe	A407
Tim Newton	Ballad of Limehouse	As Cast	A88
Eileen Nicholas	House Among the Stars	Albertine	A512
	Revenger's Tragedy	Gratiana	A909
Paul Nicholas	Barnum	Barnum	A93
Peter Nicholas	Far From The Madding Crowd	Jan Coggan	A397
Hyacinth Nicholls	Biko	Ntsiki	A121
Michael Nicholson	And A Nightingale Sang	Eric	A43
	Death of A Salesman	Happy	A295
	On The Piste	Dave	A810
Lesley Nicol	Blue Remembered Hills	Audrey	A139
	Epsom Downs	Sharon	A375
	Feed	Edith/Jessie	A399
	Fuente Ovejuna	Barrildo	A423
	Romeo and Juliet	Lady Capulet	A935
Vincenzo Nicoli	Revenger's Tragedy	Lussurioso	A909
Jake Nightingale	Bouncers	Ralph	A151
Tim Nilsson-Page	Buddy	Ensemble	A169
	Goodnight Mr Tom	As cast	A450
	View From The Bridge	As Cast	A1170
Andy Nimmo	Spring Awakening	Robert/Gaston Prof. Flyswatter	A1037
Derek Nimmo	The Cabinet Minister	Cabinet Minister	A179
Isobil Nisbet	Cuttin' A Rug	Sadie	A266
Stuart Nisbet	Merlin, The Search	As Cast	A709
Nirupama Nityanandan	Les Atrides	As Cast	A609

Name	Play	Part	Ref
Paul Nivison	School For Wives	Horace	A958
Carol Noakes	Aladdin Bolton	Princess	A27
	Alfie	Siddie	A30
Garry Noakes	Starlight Express	Flat Top	A1043
Amanda Noar	Cinderella	Dandini	A225
Nigel Nobes	You Must Be The Husband	Alan	A1248
Cecilia Noble	Blues for Mr Charlie	Juanita	A143
	The Recruiting Officer	Rose	A896
Gabrielle Noble	Annie Get Your Gun	Ensemble	A51
Jee Hyun Noh	Carousel	As Cast	A190
Linda Nolan	Jack and the Beanstalk	Princess	A551
Pamela Nomvete	Fuente Ovejuna	Pascuala	A422
	Necklaces	As Cast	A774
Kathy Norcross	Radio Times	As Cast	A890
Hilde Norga	Miss Saigon	Go-Go Dancer	A727
Fenella Norman	Fiddler On The Roof	Shaindel	A401
Yolanda Norman	Far From The Madding Crowd	Liddy	A397
Andrew Normington	Kafka's Dick	Kafka	A571
	Rivals	Jack Absolute	A920
Hermione Norris	Pygmalion	Clara	A886
	Square Rounds	As Cast	A1038
David North	Macbeth	As Cast	A657
Roy North	Richard III	Edward	A912
Jeremy Northam	Gifts Of The Gorgon	Philip	A434
	La Bete	Elomire	A587
Robert Northwood	Starlight Express	As Cast	A1043
Adam Norton	The Double Bass	One Man Show	A334
	Henceforward...	Jerome	A491
Deborah Norton	Six Degrees...	Kitty	A1008
Graham Norton	EuroVision	As Cast	A381
Jim Norton	White Woman Street	Trooper O'Hara	A1202
Tim Norton	The Hatchet Man	As Cast	A478
David Nott	Robin Hood	Sherrif of Nottingham	A929
Cyril Ikechukwu Nri	The Road	Samson	A921
Andrew Nyman	Lust	Dorilant	A650
Daniel O'Brien	Fifteen Streets	Dominic O'Brien	A403
	Moll Flanders	As Cast	A730
	On The Piste	Chris	A811
	Three Musketeers	As Cast	A1107
	Tons Of Money	George Maitland	A1125
David O'Brien	World Upon The Moon	Buonafede	A1241
Maria O'Brien	Robin	Sisters Of Sodom	A927
Sean O'Brien	Phantom Of The Opera	Porter	A854
John O'Byrne	Doll's House	Nils Krogstad	A323
Richard O'Callaghan	Cerceau	Petushok (Rooster)	A195
	Cyrano De Bergerac	Raguenaud	A269
Sean O'Callaghan	Bright & Bold Design	Jim Rhys	A161
	Hobson's Choice	Dr MacFarlane	A499
	Julius Caesar	Casca	A564
Patrick O'Connell	Loot	Mcleavy	A638
Caroline O'Connor	West Side Story	Anita	A1193
Joseph O'Connor	Medea	Creon	A704
	Murmuring Judges	PC Raymond Beckett	A758
Michael O'Connor	In The Midnight Hour	Denny	A538
Terry O'Connor	Emanuelle Enchanted	As Cast	A363
Anthony O'Donnell	All's Well That Ends Well	Lavatch	A35
	As You Like It	Touchstone	A67
	The Beggar's Opera	Lockit	A106

Name	Play	Part	Ref
Rory O'Donnell	Twelfth Night	Orsino	A1151
Sally O'Donnell	Gormenghast	The Thing	A451
Kevin O'Donohue	Bad Blood	Firmin	A85
Peter O'Farrell	Richard III	Murderer	A912
Marie O'Flaherty	A Month In The Country	As Cast	A736
Michael O'Hagan	Wexford Trilogy	As Cast	A1194
David O'Hara	Colquhoun And MacBryde	Colquhoun	A235
Gerard O'Hare	Les Miserables	As Cast	A612
Brendan O'Hea	Becket	Saxon Boy	A103
	The Corn Is Green	Morgan Evans	A249
	Fiddler On The Roof	Perchick	A401
	A Midsummer Night's ..	Demetrius	A720
Patrick O'Kane	1953	Mussolini	A1
David O'Keefe	New World and Tears	Christian Religion Brother Boyle	A780
Robert O'Mahoney	All My Sons	Jim Bayliss	A33
Owen John O'Mahony	Cherry Orchard	Lopakhin	A202
	Loot	McLeavy	A637
Mark O'Malley	Les Miserables	Young Man/Feuilly	A611
Kate O'Mara	Cain	Eve	A181
	King Lear In New York	Jackie	A580
	Venus Observed	As Cast	A1168
Colette O'Neil	Time Of My Life	As Cast	A1112
Colm O'Neill	Jubilee	Tommy Pasmore	A562
Con O'Neill	Blues Brothers	Jake	A142
	The Fastest Clock...	Cougar Glass	A398
Fiona O'Neill	World Upon The Moon	Flaminia	A1241
Maggie O'Neill	Women Laughing	As Cast	A1235
Moya O'Shea	My Blood on Glass	As Cast	A761
Roy O'Shea	Buddy	Ensemble	A168
Stoli O'Shea	Buddy	Ensemble	A168
Sean O'Sullivan	Starlight Express	As Cast	A1043
Katherine O'Toole	Reflected Glory	Regina Melnick	A898
Peter O'Toole	Our Song	Roger	A833
David Oakley	The Card (A musical)	Calvert	A187
Robert Oates	Lust	Pinchwife	A650
Tracy Ann Oberman	The Beggar's Opera	Molly Brazen	A106
	A Jovial Crew	Beggar	A561
Vicky Ogden	The Tender Husband	Barsheba Tipkin	A1088
Toshie Ogura	Bodycount	Phan Thi Mao	A148
Pacer Oh	Miss Saigon	Barman	A727
Peter Oh	M. Butterfly	Kurogo 2	A651
Wale Ojo	Flamingo	As Cast	A408
Omar Okai	Five Guys Named Moe	Eat Moe	A407
Omar Okaybe	Elegies...	As Cast	A358
Sophie Okonedo	A Jovial Crew	Amie	A561
	The Odyssey	Nausicaa	A802
	Tamburlaine The Great	Anippe	A1067
Geoff Oldham	Romeo and Juliet	Montague	A936
	A View From The Bridge	Immigration Officer	A1172
Andrea Oliver	Elegies...	As Cast	A358
Horace Oliver	Five Guys Named Moe	Little Moe	A407
Jonathan Oliver	Devil's Only Sleeping	Barton	A303
	Stageland	MacShaugnassy Agent etc	A1041
Lyndi Oliver	Starlight Express	Volta	A1043
Prudence Oliver	Annie Get Your Gun	Minnie	A51
Guy Oliver-Watts	Blood Wedding	The Bridegroom	A134
Julie-Kate Olivier	Mansfield Park	Fanny Price	A683
	Rebecca	Mrs De Winter	A894
Tamsin Olivier	Pig In A Poke	Julie	A859

Name	Play	Part	Ref
Maggie **Ollerenshaw**	Your Sincerely	Vera Lynn	A1251
Gary **Olsen**	One The Ledge	As Cast	A821
Ayanbode **Oluwole**	The Road	Musician	A921
Ben **Onwukwe**	The Best Man	Patrick	A110
Clara **Onyemere**	Fuente Ovejuna	Woman	A422
Marvel **Opara**	Hound	Aysha	A510
Dhobi **Oparei**	The Winter's Tale	Polixenes	A1215
Lisa **Orgolini**	View From The Bridge	Catherine	A1170
Anders **Orhn**	The End Of The Tunnel	As Cast	A365
Linda **Ormiston**	The Mikado	Katisha	A722
Julia **Ormond**	Playing The Wife	As Cast	A865
Stephanie **Ormonde**	Don Quixote	As Cast	A328
Sunny **Ormonde**	The Maintenance Man	Christine	A674
Iain **Ormsby-Knox**	Metamorphosis	Mr Samsa	A714
Kenneth **Orr**	Les Miserables	Bishop of Digne	A611
Keith **Osborn**	Merchant of Venice	Gratiano	A708
	Noises Off	Gary Lejeune	A794
William **Osborne**	Frightened Lady	As Cast	A192
Steven **Osbourne**	Some Like It Hot	Spats Palazzo	A1025
Eddie **Osei**	Leave Taking	Broderick	A605
	Sidewalk Sidney	Sidney	A998
Nathan **Osgood**	Trouble in Mind	Eddie Fenton	A1142
Rachel **Osmon**	Diamonds in the Dust	As Cast	A306
Tony **Osoba**	Safe In Our Hands	Roland Dixon	A947
Cindy **Oswin**	Scenic Flights		A953
Tamzin **Outhwaite**	Radio Times	As Cast	A890
Indra **Ove**	A Midsummer Night's Dream	Hermia	A718
Clare **Owen**	Mansfield Park	Lady Bertram	A683
Steve **Owen**	Bouncers	Lucky Eric	A151
	Uncle Vanya	Telegin	A1158
Linda **Owen-Jones**	Frankenstein	Justine Moritz Agatha	A415
	The Tempest	Alonso/Juno	A1083
Ayse **Owens**	Self Catering	Bette Davis	A973
Kenneth **Owens**	On Golden Pond	Charlie	A809
Richard **Owens**	Goodnight Mr Tom	Tom Oakley	A450
William **Oxborrow**	The Hour Of The Lynx	The Boy	A511
Daphne **Oxenford**	Shades	Violet	A981
Christopher **Oxford**	Biboff	Dr Ziv	A117
Peter **Oxley**	Witness For The Prosecution	Policeman	A1218
Steven **Pacey**	Phantom of the Opera	Raoul	A853
Stephanie **Pack**	On The Piste	Melissa Southern	A812
Suzanne **Packer**	Blood Brothers	Mrs Johnston	A130
	Fuente Ovejuna	Alonso	A423
	Romeo and Juliet	Mercutio	A935
Anita **Packman**	Barnum	As Cast	A93
Graham **Padden**	Dangerous Corner	Robert Caplan	A277
	Grapes of Wrath	Casy	A454
	Wizard of Oz	Tin Man	A1224
John **Padden**	Bad Blood	Raphael	A85
	Marching Song	Boy	A685
	Six Degrees...	Trent	A1008
Simon **Padley**	Macbeth	Young Macduff	A658
Eileen **Page**	Elisabeth II	As Cast	A361
Helen **Pagett**	Happy As A Sandbag	As Cast	A473
Nicola **Pagett**	The Rules Of The Game	Silia	A943
Sylvie **Paladino**	Les Miserables	Eponine	A613
Lisa **Palfrey**	House Of America	Gwenny	A516
Irene **Palko**	Macbeth	As Cast	A660
Kevin **Pallister**	Robin Hood	Ivanhoe	A929

Name	Play	Part	Ref
Alan **Palmer**	Travelling Light	As Cast	A1135
Anna **Palmer**	Cut and Trust	Jnr Health Minister	A265
	Taming of the Shrew	Bianca	A1069
	Wizard of Oz	Dorothy	A1222
Audrey **Palmer**	The Sound Of Music	Ensemble	A1033
Michael **Palmer**	Hamlet	Laertes/Ghost	A463
	Heart	As Cast	A485
	King Lear	The Fool /Cornwall	A577
Toni **Palmer**	The Invisible Man	Mrs Hall	A547
	Phantom of the Opera	Madame Giry	A853
Nirmal **Chandra Pandey**	Heer Ranjha	As Cast	A489
Jack **Panter**	American Buffalo	Teach	A39
Chantal **Panto**	Doll's House	Ivy Helmer	A323
Dominique **Panto**	Doll's House	Emmy	A323
Evan **Pappas**	Merrily We Roll Along	As Cast	A711
Cuckoo **Parameswaran**	The Little Clay Cart	Vasantasena	A627
Judith **Paris**	Lust	Lady Fidget	A650
Diane **Parish**	Much Ado About Nothing	Hero	A752
	Romeo and Juliet	Balthasar	A935
Linda **Parish**	Blood Brothers	Linda	A130
Caroline **Parker**	Dead Heroic	Old Lady	A287
Iain **Parker**	Saint Oscar	Lord Alfred Douglas	A949
Oliver **Parker**	As You Like It	Orlando	A71
	The Barber Of Seville	Count	A89
	The Guardsman	An Actor	A461
	A Midsummer Night's ..	Demetrius	A721
	Trelawny Of The Wells	Tom Wrench	A1139
Tim **Parker**	Buddy	Ensemble	A169
Julian **Parkin**	The Tender Husband	Cpt Jack Clerimont	A1088
Wendy **Parkin**	Forbidden Planet	Petty Officer Lynn Gwyst	A904
Helen **Parkinson**	The Business Of Murder	Dee	A174
	The Maintenance Man	Chris	A673
	Stage Struck	Anne	A1040
Michael **Parkinson**	Porcelain	Voice IV	A871
Robin **Parkinson**	'Allo,'Allo	LeClere	A36
Jason **Parmenter**	Barnum	As Cast	A93
Brian **Parr**	Measure For Measure	Friar/Elbow Abhorson/Gent	A702
Suzanne **Parrott**	Man Outside	As Cast	A681
Danuta **Parsons**	Barnum	As Cast	A93
Grant **Parsons**	Pig In A Poke	Winstanley	A859
John **Partridge**	Starlight Express	Electra	A1043
Kimberley **Partridge**	Phantom Of The Opera	Meg Giry	A854
Richard **Pasco**	An Inspector Calls	Arthur Birling	A541
	Murmuring Judges	Sir Peter Edgecombe QC	A758
Anita **Pashley**	Aspects Of Love	Actress/Girlfriend Nun	A72
Ashley **Paske**	Aladdin	Aladdin	A18
Maria **Pastel**	Death of A Salesman	As Cast	A295
Anil **Patel**	Gulf Between Us	Militia	A462
Bill **Paterson**	Death and the Maiden	Gerardo Escobar	A293
	Misery	Paul Sheldon	A725
Antony **Patience**	School Of Night	Shakespeare	A960
James **Paton**	Elegies...	As Cast	A358
Anna **Patrick**	As You Like It	Phoebe	A71
	A Midsummer Night's ..	Helena	A721

Name	Play	Part	Ref
Helen **Patrick**	Stageland	Ethel/Actress/Aunt etc	A1041
Neil **Patterson**	Sophisticated Ladies	Ensemble	A1032
Robert **Patterson**	Murmuring Judges	Gerard McKinnon	A758
Scott **Pattison**	Starlight Express	As Cast	A1043
Debbie **Paul**	Barnstormers	Charlotte Deans	A92
Dorothy **Paul**	See That's Her!	One Woman Show	A972
Kate **Paul**	Merchant of Venice	Portia	A708
Sasha **Paul**	Steel Magnolias	Shelby	A1045
Gavin **Payne**	As You Like It	William	A71
	Curse Of The Mummy	Mr Smith	A263
	A Midsummer Night's ..	Snug	A721
Liz **Payne**	Don Juan In Hell	Donna Anna	A325
	Lady of the Lilacs	As Cast	A596
Harry **Peacock**	The Dark River	Mervyn Webb	A282
Philip **Peacock**	Hostages and Hamsters	Essa	A506
Tessa **Peake Jones**	Obsession	As Cast	A800
Eve **Pearce**	Time Windows	Sarah Gordon	A1113
Jacqueline **Pearce**	Shadowlands	Joy Davidman	A983
Joanne **Pearce**	The Alchemist	Doll Common	A28
	The Dybbuk	Leye	A349
	Hamlet	Ophelia	A466
	Henry IV Part 2	Doll Tearsheet	A493
	The Thebans	Antigone	A1095
Fred **Pearson**	Lulu	Doktor Schoen	A648
Helen **Pearson**	The Ballroom	As Cast	A1091
Mike **Pearson**	Patagonia	As Cast	A845
Patrick **Pearson**	Madness of George III	Henry Dundas	A669
Ian **Peart**	Gulf Between Us	Militia	A462
Anthony **Pedley**	Alfie	As Cast	A29
	The BFG	Father/The BFG	A116
Eddie **Peel**	Richard III	Clarence	A912
Marcus **Peerman**	Beardsley	Pierrot	A95
Kerry **Peers**	At Fifty She Discovered The Sea	The Daughter	A74
	Liaisons Dangereuses	Emile	A610
Rosaleen **Pelan**	Taming Of The Shrew	Bianca	A1070
Donald **Pelear**	As You Like It	Adam	A68
Valentine **Pelka**	Romeo And Juliet	Paris	A938
	A Woman Killed With Kindness	Sir Francis Acton	A1229
Andy **Pelos**	Happy As A Sandbag	As Cast	A473
Ron **Pember**	A Christmas Carol	Scrooge	A212
	Goin' Local	Waggy	A442
	Voysey Inheritance	Peacey	A1182
Antonia **Pemberton**	Uncle Vanya	Marina	A1157
Jonathan **Pembroke**	Blood Brothers	Sammy	A131
David **Pendlebury**	Leonardo	As Cast	A608
Marcel **Peneux**	The Cotton Club	Bill Bojangles Robinson	A250
Ann **Penfold**	The Revenger's Tragedy	Gratiana	A908
	Three Girls In Blue	Marya Filippovna	A1101
	Wicked Old Man	Jasmine	A1207
Vince **Penfold**	Sneeze	As Cast	A1018
Susan **Penhaligon**	Bedroom Farce	Susannah	A104
Simon **Penman**	Joseph...	Benjamin	A559
David **Penn**	Elephant	As Cast	A359
Garrett **Pennery**	Barnum	As Cast	A93
Christopher **Penney**	Measure For Measure	Claudio/Froth	A702
	Seagull	Constantine	A963
Ann **Pennington**	Single Spies	Coral Browne/The Queen	A1005
John **Pennington**	Three Musketeers	As Cast	A1107
Michael **Pennington**	Gifts Of The Gorgon	Lead Role	A434
George **Pensotti**	As You Like It	Corin	A71
	Curse Of The Mummy	Const/Prof Khan	A263
	A Midsummer Night's ..	Starveling	A721
Laura **Penta**	The Sound Of Music	Brigitta	A1033
Tom **Penta**	The Sound Of Music	Friedrich	A1033
Trevor **Penton**	Man, Beast and Virtue	Giglio	A682
Emma **Peploe-Williams**	Miss Saigon	Bar Girl	A727
Vicki **Pepperdine**	Beauty and the Beast	Sophia	A99
	The Winter's Tale	Emilia	A1215
Ian **Pepperell**	Grapes of Wrath	Connie	A454
	Playing by the Rules	Danny	A863
	Wizard of Oz	As Cast	A1224
Sharon **Percy**	Your Home In The West	Sharon	A1250
Jean **Perkins**	Chorus of Disapproval	Rebecca Huntley-Pike	A210
Tim **Perrin**	Don't Dress For Dinner	George	A331
David **Perry**	Hindsight	David	A495
Lynnette **Perry**	Grand Hotel	Flaemmchen	A453
Morris **Perry**	Hindsight	As Cast	A495
Patricia **Perry**	Savage Storm	As Cast	A952
Mandy **Perryment**	Some Like It Hot	Sugar	A1025
Stephen **Persaud**	Blues for Mr Charlie	Jimmy	A143
Dariel **Pertwee**	Becket	French Girl	A103
	A Midsummer Night's ..	Helena	A720
Jon **Pertwee**	Scrooge the Musical	Jacob Marley	A1039
Richard **Pescud**	Me And My Girl	Charles The Butler	A699
Fuschia **Peters**	Gamblers	Anna Candelabra	A424
Gordon **Peters**	Aladdin	Widow Twankey	A20
Jeremy **Peters**	Manslaughter	(Two-Hander)	A684
Michael **Peth**	Cats	Carbucketty	A194
	Miss Saigon	Marine/Dragon Acrobat	A727
Edward **Petherbridge**	Valentine's Day	William	A1165
Brian **Pettifer**	A Midsummer Night's Dream	Snout	A718
Yasmin **Pettigrew**	Stepping Out	Rose	A1046
Theresa **Petts**	Pygmalion	Lady	A886
	Square Rounds	As Cast	A1038
Peter **Peverley**	Time Windows	Peter	A1113
Phillipe **Peychaud**	Life Support		A621
David **Peyton-Bruhl**	Little Tramp	Bar Keep/Others	A634
	Roberto Calvi	As Cast	A926
Peggy **Phango**	Necklaces	As Cast	A774
David **Phelan**	Dangerous Corner	Gordon Whitehouse	A277
	Grapes of Wrath	Willy	A454
	Playing by the Rules	Steve	A863
	Wizard of Oz	As Cast	A1224
Edward **Phillips**	Some Like It Hot	Bienstock	A1025
Eryl **Phillips**	The Devils	De Laubardemont	A304
Gareth **Phillips**	Jack And The Beanstalk	As Cast	A552
Jacqueline **Phillips**	Beyond Reasonable Doubt	Court Usher	A114
	Don Juan	Charlotte	A327
	Goodnight Mr Tom	As Cast	A450
	Strippers	Michelle	A1057
Leslie **Phillips**	Painting Churches	Gardner Church	A842
Matthew **Phillips**	EuroVision	As Cast	A381
Sian **Phillips**	Painting Churches	Fanny Church	A842
Joanna **Phillips-Lane**	Henceforward...	Corinna	A491
	Snow Queen	The Snow Queen	A1021

Name	Play	Part	Ref
	Turkey Time	Mrs Pike	A1144
Mark **Phoenix**	Blood Wedding	Woodcutter	A134
	Under Milk Wood	As Cast	A1160
John **Phythian**	Death Of A Salesman	Biff	A297
Robert **Pickavance**	The Norman Conquests	Norman	A796
Donald **Pickering**	Our Song	Gumby T. Gumby	A833
Nicole **Picket**	Romeo and Juliet	Lady Capulet	A937
Carl **Picton**	The House Of Stairs	As cast	A513
Craig **Pinder**	All My Sons	Frank Lubey	A32
	Romeo and Juliet	Prince	A936
	A View From The Bridge	Lovis	A1172
Mark **Pinkosh**	Broken Folk		A164
	Death And Dancing	As Cast	A292
Steven **Pinner**	My Cousin Rachel	As Cast	A762
Harold **Pinter**	No Man's Land	Hirst	A789
Robin **Pirongs**	Grapes of Wrath	Deputy	A454
	Nervous Women	Sam	A776
	Playing by the Rules	Ape	A863
	Wizard of Oz	As Cast	A1224
Rachel **Pittman**	Ten In A Bed		A1086
Richie **Pitts**	Sophisticated Ladies	Ensemble	A1032
Nigel **Pivaro**	What The Butler Saw	Sgt Match	A1196
Carl **Pizie**	Elegies...	As Cast	A358
Raymond **Platt**	Wind In The Willows	Rupert	A1211
Angela **Pleasance**	Leo In Love	Blanche	A607
David **Plimmer**	Dead Man's Hat	As Cast	A288
Louise **Plowright**	Les Miserables	Madame Thenardier	A611
Tony **Plumridge**	Disobediently Yours	As Cast	A314
Glenn **Plunkett**	Eight to the Bar	As Cast	A356
Richard **Pocock**	Elegies...	As Cast	A358
Kathryn **Pogson**	Crackwalker	Sandy	A256
Alison **Pollard**	Annie Get Your Gun	Ensemble	A51
Su **Pollard**	Don't Dress For Dinner	Suzette	A331
Robin **Polley**	Cherry Orchard	Pischik	A202
	Doll's House	Torvald	A322
	Family Affair	Bolshov	A393
	Wizard of Oz	Lion	A1223
Eileen **Pollock**	Taste of Honey	Helen	A1074
Peter **Polycarpou**	Les Miserables	Thenardier	A613
	Phantom Of The Opera	The Phantom	A854
Simon **Pomara**	Mowgli - Enfant Loup	Mowgli	A745
Cassi **Pool**	Heart	As Cast	A485
Erika **Poole**	Macbeth	As Cast	A660
Michael **Poole**	Romeo And Juliet	Old Capulet	A938
	'Tis Pity She's A Whore	Cardinal	A1114
Tim **Poole**	The Golden Ass	Amyntas	A443
Kay **Pope**	Bright & Bold Design	Jessie Frost	A161
	Comedy of Errors	Adriana	A240
	Hobson's Choice	Alice Hobson	A499
	Jolly Potters	As Cast	A557
	Snow Queen	Robber Girl	A1021
	Turkey Time	Rose Adair	A1144
Natasha **Pope**	Blood Wedding	The Bride	A134
	Dead Soil	Daughter	A290
	Under Milk Wood	As Cast	A1160
B. **Poraj-Pstrokouski**	The Trial	Joseph Kafka	A1140
Charlotte **Porrass**	Miss Saigon	Tam	A727
Kate **Portal**	Hound	Desiree	A510
Robert **Portal**	Cain	Abel	A181
	Venus Observed	Dominic	A1168

Name	Play	Part	Ref
Peter **Porteous**	Fifteen Streets	James Llewellyn Father Bailey	A403
Ben **Porter**	Becket	Scribe	A103
Eric **Porter**	Uncle Vanya	Serebryakov	A1157
Nyree **Dawn Porter**	Beyond Reasonable Doubt	As Cast	A115
	The House Of Stairs	Elizabeth	A513
Russell **Porter**	Beyond Reasonable Doubt	Robert Pierson	A113
	What the Butler Saw	Nicholas Beckett	A1197
	Wicks's Folly	As Cast	A1208
Stewart **Porter**	Blue Remembered Hills	Raymond	A139
	Epsom Downs	Lord Rack	A375
	Fuente Ovejuna	Commander Fernando Gomez	A423
	Romeo and Juliet	Capulet	A935
Ruth **Posner**	Dybbuk	As Cast	A350
Pete **Postlethwaite**	Little Voice	Ray Say	A917
Melanie **Postma**	Cain	Zillah	A181
	King Lear In New York	As Cast	A580
Terri **Potoczna**	Shout Across The River	As Cast	A997
Tim **Potter**	The Sea	Thompson	A961
Andrew **Potts**	Man Outside	As Cast	A681
Graham **Pountney**	Travesties	Henry Carr	A1137
Gary **Powell**	Artists and Admirers	Migaev	A64
	Henry IV Part 1	Westmoreland	A492
	Henry IV Part 2	Westmoreland	A493
	Twelfth Night	Antonio	A1152
Shezwae **Powell**	70, Girls, 70	Melba	A4
	Cats	Grizabella	A194
Jack **Power**	Twelfth Night	Malvolio/Antonio Curio	A1149
Kevin **Power**	Elegies...	As Cast	A358
	Grand Hotel	Bellboy	A453
Pamela **Power**	Shirley Valentine	Shirley Valentine	A995
Corinna **Powlesland**	Blithe Spirit	Edith	A127
	Wizard of Oz	Wicked Witch	A1223
Mark **Powley**	Elegies...	As Cast	A358
Jerome **Pradon**	Miss Saigon	Chris	A727
Michael **Praed**	Aspects Of Love	Alex	A72
Robin **Pratt**	Frankenstein	The Monster	A415
	Monster He Made Me	Mussolini	A734
	The Tempest	Stephano/Antonio	A1083
Tim **Preece**	Safe In Our Hands	Trevor Robinson	A947
Robert **Preite**	Hapgood	Joe	A472
Catherine **Prendergast**	Blithe Spirit	Elvira	A128
	The Hostage	Teresa	A505
	Macbeth	Lady Macbeth	A661
Shaun **Prendergast**	Laurel and Hardy	As Cast	A603
Peter **Prentiss**	Leonardo	As Cast	A608
David **Prescott**	My Blood on Glass	As Cast	A761
	The Way of All Flesh	Theobald Pontifex	A1190
Paul **Prescott**	Blood Whispers	As Cast	A135
	A Distant Applause	As Cast	A315
Stan **Pretty**	Burbage and the Bard	Various	A172
Emlyn **Price**	Curse Of The Mummy	The Nurse	A263
Gareth **Tudor Price**	Office Party	Managing Director	A803
Ian **Price**	June Moon	As Cast	A567
Kenneth **Price**	Neville's Island	Roy	A777
	Out Of Order	Richard Willey MP	A835
	Rocket To The Moon	Ben Stark	A932

Name	Play	Part	Ref
Marianne Price	Buddy	Maria's Aunt	A168
Rebecca Price	Starlight Express	As Cast	A1043
Wyndham Price	House Of America	Labourer	A516
Sarah Prince	Fifteen Streets	Mary Llewellyn	A403
	On The Piste	Alison	A811
Stephanie Prince	Les Miserables	Ensemble	A611
Alfred Pringle	My Fair Lady	Alfred Doolittle	A763
Amanda Prior	Me And My Girl	Lady Jacqueline Carstone	A699
Philip Pritchard	Les Miserables	Farmer	A611
Robin Pritchard	Twelfth Night	Curio	A1151
Tessa Pritchard	Night Must Fall	Olivia Crayne	A784
	Tons Of Money	Jean Everard	A1125
Bernadine Pritchett	Carmen Jones	Card Player	A189
	Carousel	As Cast	A190
Colin Prockter	The Miser	Maitre Jaques	A724
Brian Protheroe	Schippel, The Plumber	Wolke	A954
Julian Protheroe	Macbeth	Malcolm	A658
	On The Piste	Dave	A811
Anthony Psaila	Telling Tales	As Cast	A1081
Ian Puleston-Davies	Seagull	James	A963
David Pullan	Beyond Reasonable Doubt	Robert Pierson	A114
	A Midsummer Night's Dream	Demetrius	A717
	Noises Off	Garry Lejeune	A795
	Women in Love	Gerald	A1233
John Purcell	Elvis - the Musical	Jordanaire	A362
Kay Purcell	It's A Girl	Eva	A549
Robert Purdy	Macbeth	As Cast	A660
James Purefoy	Back Up The Hearse	Brian	A84
Christian Pye	Elvis - the Musical	Jordanaire	A362
Jim Pyke	Man, Beast and Virtue	Belli	A682
Natasha Pyne	Alfie	As Cast	A29
Terry Quadling	The Imaginary Invalid	Beline	A529
Ernestina Quarcoo	Carmen Jones	Poncho's Girlfriend	A189
	Carousel	As Cast	A190
Kevin Quarmby	Les Miserables	Valjean	A612
	Water Music	Geoffrey	A1188
Hugh Quarshie	New World and Tears	Christopher Columbus	A780
	Someone Who'll Watch	Adam	A1028
Philip Quast	Les Miserables	Javert	A611
Jenny Quayle	Twelfth Night	Viola	A1148
John Quayle	Don't Dress For Dinner	Bernard	A331
	It Runs In The Family	Doctor Mortimer	A548
Caroline Quentin	Evening with Gary L.	Monica	A383
	Game of Love & Chance	Lisette	A425
John Quentin	The Family Reunion	Charles Piper	A394
Pooky Quesnel	Anna Karenina	Kitty	A50
Diana Quick	The Woman Destroyed	Murielle	A1225
Pearce Quigley	A Jovial Crew	Vincent	A561
	The Merry Wives Of Windsor	Slender	A713
	The Winter's Tale	Cleomenes	A1214
Denis Quilley	She Stoops To Conquer	Mr Hardcastle	A992
	Venus Observed	Reedbeck	A1168
Dennis Quilligan	Philadelphia Here I Come	Doogan	A856
Veronica Quilligan	Dancing At Lughnasa	Rose	A274
David Quilter	The Deep Blue Sea	William Collyer	A140

Name	Play	Part	Ref
Chris Quinn	The Sacred Penman	As Cast	A946
Elizabeth Quinn	Every Bit Of It	Georgia	A385
Gerard Quinn	Biko	Policeman	A121
James Quinn	Working	As Cast	A1239
John Quinn	Seagull	Cousin Gregory	A963
Debbie Radcliffe	Doll's House	Norma Helmer	A323
	Much Ado About Nothing	Beatrice	A750
Richard Radcliffe	Some Like It Hot	Reporter	A1025
Virginia Radcliffe	Measure For Measure	Mrs Overdone Francisca/Juliet	A702
Matthew Radford	Summer Lightning	Gally/Ronnie Fish	A1058
Thomas Radford	Hapgood	Joe	A472
Sian Radinger	Hamlet	As Cast	A466
	Henry IV Part 1	Traveller/Lady	A492
	Henry IV Part 2	Lady	A493
Nadine Raeburn	A Woman Plays ...		A1231
John Rafferty	Medea	Medea's Son	A704
Isobel Raine	Pond Life	Cassie	A869
Nickie Rainsford	The Sacred Penman	As Cast	A946
George Raistrick	Little Voice	Phone Man/Mr Boo	A917
Brian Ralph	Beyond Reasonable Doubt	Sir David Metcalfe QC	A114
	Noises Off	Frederick Fellowes	A795
Ian Ralph	Robin Hood	Friar Tuck	A929
Philip Ralph	Comedy of Errors	Merchant	A240
	Jolly Potters	As Cast	A557
John Rammage	The Mikado	The Mikado	A722
	Your Turn To Clean The Stairs	Brian	A1252
Lois Ramsay	On Top of the World		A814
Dennis Ramsden	It Runs In The Family	Sir Drake	A548
Mykal Rand	Starlight Express	Electra	A1043
Alan Randall	Turned Out Nice Again	George Formby	A1145
Celestine Randall	Madness of George III	Dr Ida MacAlpine	A669
Lynn Randolph	Carmen Jones	Jimmy the Photographer	A189
C Jay Ranger	Starlight Express	As Cast	A1043
Scott Ransome	Henry IV Part 1	Humphrey	A492
	Henry IV Part 2	Humphrey	A493
	Julius Caesar	Octavius	A566
	Romeo And Juliet	Peter	A938
Dale Rapley	Rocket To The Moon	Frenchy	A932
Stephen Rashbrook	As You Like It	Oliver	A68
Mindy Raskin	As Time Goes By	As Cast	A65
Ken Ratcliffe	Woman Of No Importance	Farquhar	A1230
Andrew Rattenbury	Loot	Dennis	A637
Paul Rattfield	Absurd Person Singular	As Cast	A11
Christophe Rauck	Les Atrides	As Cast	A609
Marsha Raven	Blues Angels	One Woman Show	A141
Raad Rawi	EuroVision	Sergio	A381
Adrian Rawlins	Hamlet	Laertes	A465
Brian Rawlinson	Hobson's Choice	Henry Hobson	A500
Janet Rawson	Ten Times Table	Philippa	A1087
Mary Ellen Ray	Blood Wedding	The Mother-In-Law	A134
Trevor Ray	Becket	Pope	A103
	Phoenix	Frankie	A857
Llewellyn Rayappen	Carmen Jones	Foreman	A189
Abi Rayment	My Heart's A Suitcase	Chris	A764
Emily Raymond	The Beggar's Opera	Mrs Vixen	A106
	The Changeling	Isabella	A197
	A Jovial Crew	Meriel	A561
Gary Raymond	A Little Night Music		A630

Name	Play	Part	Ref
Trevor **Raymond**	Grand Hotel	The Doorman	A453
Pam **Rayner**	The Kingfisher	Evelyn	A581
Tim **Raynham**	Cinderella	Lysteria	A225
Stephen **Rea**	Someone Who'll Watch	Edwards	A1028
David **Reakes**	Roadshow		A924
Alison **Reddihough**	Death Of A Salesman	Miss Forsythe	A297
Ian **Reddington**	Macbeth	Macbeth	A653
Ali **Redford**	Ghost Sonata	Young Lady	A431
Carol **Redford**	Hot Italian Nights	Ensemble	A507
	The Magic Storybook	Ensemble	A672
Ian **Redford**	Murder In Green Meadow	Jeff Symons	A757
Corin **Redgrave**	Love	Reader	A642
	Rosmersholm	Pastor Joahannes Rosmer	A939
Jemma **Redgrave**	As You Like It	Rosalind	A68
Vanessa **Redgrave**	Heartbreak House	Hesione Hushabye	A486
Darren Phillip **Redick**	Carousel	As Cast	A190
Nick **Reding**	Angels In America	Joseph Porter Pitt	A47
Amanda **Redman**	Private Lives	Amanda	A882
Joanne **Redman**	Moby Dick	Ishmael	A728
Ruth **Redman**	The Miser	Dame Claude	A724
Nicola **Redmond**	Body And Soul	Christine	A146
	Phoenix	Renata	A857
	Trelawny Of The Wells	Imogen Parrott	A1138
Manning **Redwood**	Ride Down Mt Morgan	Tom	A915
Carlene **Reed**	Hamlet	Gertrude	A463
	King Lear	Goneril	A577
Sarah **Reed**	Don't Rock The Boat	Shirley	A330
Angharad **Rees**	Cold Sweat	Elizabeth Mason	A234
Mark **Rees**	Patagonia	As Cast	A845
Richard **Rees**	New World and Tears	King Mohamed Tapirazu	A780
Yvette **Rees**	A Doll's House	Anne Marie	A324
Martin **Reeve**	Alfie	Harry/Mr Smith	A30
	A Marginal Affair	Nye Wilshaw	A687
Melvin **Reeves**	Buddy	Ensemble	A169
Neville **Reeves**	Bag Dancing	Neville Child	A87
Paul **Reeves**	Rocky Horror Show	Brad	A933
Saskia **Reeves**	'Tis Pity She's A Whore	Annabella	A1114
	Two Gents Of Verona	Silvia	A1154
	The Virtuoso	Miranda	A1176
	A Woman Killed With Kindness	Anne Frankford	A1229
Benji **Reid**	Heart	As Cast	A485
Sheila **Reid**	Romeo And Juliet	Nurse	A938
	'Tis Pity She's A Whore	Putana	A1114
	The Virtuoso	Mrs Figgup	A1176
Gabrielle **Reidy**	The Winter's Tale	Hermione	A1215
Jane **Reilly**	Exile	As Cast	A387
Robert **Reina**	Massa	Arthur Munby	A692
Ramon **Remedios**	Phantom Of The Opera	Ubaldo Piangi	A854
Michael **Remick**	The Card (A musical)	Jock	A187
Scott **Renderer**	Brace Up!	As Cast	A156
Elizabeth **Renihan**	The Beggar's Opera	Polly Peachum	A106
	A Jovial Crew	Beggar	A561
Grania **Renihan**	Aspects Of Love	Giulietta Trapansi	A72
Alan **Renwick**	Time Windows	Tom Beswick	A1113
Jan **Revere**	Hostages and Hamsters	Ellie	A506
	Some...Atomic Zombie		A1027

Name	Play	Part	Ref
Terese **Revill**	Leonardo	As Cast	A608
James **Reynard**	Molecatcher's Daughter	William Corder	A729
Philip **Rham**	Candide	Candide	A185
Zakaria **Riachi**	Mowgli - Enfant Loup	Baghera	A745
Mat **Ricardo**	The Three Musketeers	D'Artagnan	A1104
Emma **Rice**	House of Bernarda Alba	As Cast	A515
	Square Rounds	As Cast	A1038
	Tess Of The D'Urbervil	Marion	A1089
Reva **Rice**	Starlight Express	Pearl	A1043
Simon **Rice**	Carousel	As Cast	A190
Hallam **Rice-Edwards**	All My Sons	Bert	A33
Meredith **Rich**	Closer Than Ever	As Cast	A231
David **Richard-Fox**	The Best Man	Neil	A110
Angela **Richards**	A Swell Party	Mrs Cole Porter	A1060
Ben **Richards**	Radio Times	As Cast	A890
Corinna **Richards**	Daughters Of England	Castalia	A284
	Provoked Wife	Lady Brute	A884
Derek **Richards**	Grand Hotel	Scullery Worker Detective	A453
Gary **Richards**	Forever Yours	Leopold	A413
Graham **Richards**	Late Joys		A600
Lowri-Anne **Richards**	World Upon The Moon	Lisetta	A1241
Maurey **Richards**	Carmen Jones	Mr Higgins	A189
Ted **Richards**	The Hostage	Monsewer	A505
	Julius Caesar	Julius Caesar	A564
	Macbeth	Duncan	A661
	The Night Before The Morning After		A782
	The Threepenny Opera	Mr Peachum	A1109
Jo **Richardson**	Mansfield Park	Julia	A683
Lucy **Richardson**	Woman Who Cooked	Hilary	A1232
Miles **Richardson**	The Invisible Man	Wadger	A547
Sara **Richardson**	Alfie	As Cast	A29
Stephen **Richardson**	Biko	Donald Woods	A121
Doyle **Richmond**	Night in Tunisia	Older Morgan	A783
Kate **Richmond**	Lady Aoi	As Cast	A593
Robert **Richmond**	Merlin, The Search	As Cast	A709
Susannah **Rickards**	Hamlet	Ophelia	A467
Dominic **Rickhards**	Fuente Ovejuna	Second Alderman	A422
Alan **Rickman**	Hamlet	Hamlet	A465
Chris **Rickwood**	Roadshow		A924
Billy **Riddoch**	Tartuffe	As Cast	A1073
Paul **Rider**	Hamlet	Hamlet	A463
	King Lear	Edmund/Kent	A577
Joanna **Riding**	Carousel	Julie Jordan	A190
	Lady Be Good	Susie Trevor	A594
	Me And My Girl	Sally Smith	A699
Joanne **Ridley**	Les Miserables	As Cast	A612
Malcolm **Ridley**	Schmucks	As Cast	A955
Terence **Rigby**	Wind In The Willows	Albert	A1211
Diana **Rigg**	Berlin Bertie	Rosa Brine	A109
	Medea	Medea	A704
Julia **Righton**	Bright & Bold Design	Ada Lovatt	A161
	Julius Caesar	Calphurnia	A564
	The Night Before The Morning After		A782
	The Threepenny Opera	Low Dive Jenny	A1109
Eammon **Riley**	All My Sons	Frank Lubey	A33
Julie **Riley**	Raving Beauties	Jill	A893
Yvonne **Riley**	My Blood on Glass	As Cast	A761
Steve **Riley-Brough**	Macbeth	As Cast	A657
Helen **Rimmer**	Hecuba	Chorus	A488

Name	Play	Part	Ref
John Ringham	Death Of A Salesman	Willy Loman	A297
Roger Ringrose	Cabal and Love	Prince's Servant	A176
	Vincent	Vincent	A1175
Arthur Riordan	Digging for Fire	As Cast	A313
Aileen Ritchie	MacWizard Fae Oz	As Cast	A663
Paul Ritter	Seven Doors	As Cast	A978
Sonia Ritter	Enemy To The People	As Cast	A369
	The Snow Queen	As Cast	A1020
Chita Rivera	Kiss of Spiderwoman	Aurora	A584
Jamie Rivera	Miss Saigon	Kim	A727
Louisa Rix	The Pocket Dream	Titania	A868
Tanya Roach	Twelfth Night	Viola	A1151
Linus Roache	Love's Labour's Lost	Berowne	A645
Christopher Robbie	Hecuba	Talthybius	A488
	Indigo Mill	As Cast	A539
Heather Robbins	Carousel	As Cast	A190
Peter Robbins	Cinderella	Ugly Sister	A219
Beth Robert	Forever Yours	Carmen	A413
Eunice Roberts	Ten Times Table	Sophie	A1087
Adam Roberts	Haunted Hotel	Albert Denny	A479
Chrissy Roberts	The Virtuoso	Weaver	A1176
Christian Roberts	From A Jack To A King	Duke Box	A420
Ian Roberts	Carmen Jones	Dink	A189
Michael Roberts	Kafka's Dick	Brod	A571
	Little Shop Of Horrors	Mushnik	A632
Neil Roberts	As You Like It	As Cast	A68
Simon Roberts	The Devils	Adam/Prince Henri De Conde	A304
	The Rivals	Falkland	A919
Lynn Robertson Hay	Martin Chuzzlewit	Multiple Roles	A689
Ben Robertson	Bloody Poetry	Byron	A137
Gavin Robertson	The Three Musketeers	Various	A1105
Lesley Robertson	Eight to the Bar	As Cast	A356
Liz Robertson	The Sound Of Music	Maria Rainer	A1033
Margaret Robertson	Mrs Klein	As Cast	A749
Rachel Robertson	Lust	Margery Pinchwife	A650
	Spread A Little Happ	As Cast	A1035
Dee Robillard	Blood Brothers	Donna Marie/Miss Jones	A131
Jeremy Robins	Gravity Swing	As Cast	A457
Joanna Robinson	Pond Life	Pogo	A869
Leon Robinson	Carmen Jones	Dancer	A189
Lucius Robinson	Valdorama		A1164
Lucy Robinson	An Ideal Husband	Mrs Marchmont	A528
	Rivals	Lydia	A920
	Spring and Port Wine	Florence Crompton	A1036
Neville Robinson	Heart	As Cast	A485
Beth Robson	Cats	The Cats' Chorus	A194
	Radio Times	As Cast	A890
Vivienne Rochester	Great God Brown	Cubel	A459
	Hobson's Choice	Alice Hobson	A500
	Leave Taking	Mai	A605
Toby Rodin	Horse-Radish	As Cast	A504
Christian Rodska	Prisoner's Pumpkin	Jack	A879
Owen Roe	Cherry Orchard		A203
Maurice Roeves	Trouble in Mind	Al Manners	A1142
John Rogan	As You Like It	Duke Frederick	A68
	La Bete	Bejart	A587
Jean Rogers	Nightmare	As Cast	A787
Katharine Rogers	Measure For Measure	Isabella	A702
	Voysey Inheritance	Alice	A1182
Leigh Rogers	Confusions	Lucy/Paula/Milly etc	A246
Sally Rogers	Billy Liar	Liz	A122
	Murmuring Judges	PC Esther Bally	A758
Ian Rogerson	TO	As Cast	A1116
	Up 'N' Under	As Cast	A1163
Toby Rolt	School for Scandal	Charles Surface	A957
Patrick Romer	Outside Edge	Bob	A837
	Three Musketeers	Buckingham	A1106
	To Kill A Mockingbird	Judge Taylor	A1121
Matilde Romero	Blood Wedding	The Singer	A134
Shebah Ronay	Dog Days	As Cast	A319
Lynda Rooke	Raving Beauties	Diane	A893
	Stitched Up	Lizzie Drinkwater	A1050
Kevin Rooney	MacWizard Fae Oz	As Cast	A663
Lesley Rooney	Forever Yours	Marie Louse	A413
William Roose-Martin	Confusions	Terry/Martin/Vicar etc	A246
Amanda Root	Caesar And Cleopatra	Cleopatra	A180
David Roper	Anybody for Murder?	Max Harrington	A55
Lyon Roque	Miss Saigon	Vietnamese Customer	A727
Mary Roscoe	Trilby & Svengali	Mrs Bagot/Honorine	A1141
Alex Rose	Roadshow		A924
Clifford Rose	Hamlet	Ghost	A466
	Henry IV Part 1	Richard Scroop	A492
	Henry IV Part 2	Richard Scroop	A493
	The Thebans	Tiresias/Messenger	A1095
David Rose	The Sound Of Music	Franz	A1033
Jason Rose	Master Harold & The bo	Sam	A694
Lisa Rose	Ghosts	Regina	A432
Melanie Rose	Annie Get Your Gun	Ensemble	A51
Vanessa Rosenthal	Blodeuwedd	As Cast	A129
Emma Roskilly	The Sound Of Music	Louisa	A1033
Walter Ross Gower	Sneeze	As Cast	A1018
Ann-Louise Ross	Virginia Woolf	Martha	A1205
David Ross	Love's Labour's Lost	Holofernes	A645
	One The Ledge	As cast	A821
	The Recruiting Officer	Mr Balance	A896
	Wind In The Willows	Rat	A1211
Hugh Ross	Death and the Maiden	Dr Roberto Miranda	A293
Jane Rossington	Don't Rock The Boat	Carol Coombes	A330
Norman Rossington	Annie Get Your Gun	Charlie Davenport	A51
Pat Rossiter	Family Affair	Agrafena	A393
Beatrice Roth	Brace Up!	As Cast	A156
Liz Rothschild	The Choice	As Cast	A209
Alan Rothwell	Dangerous Obsession	John Barret	A281
	Spring and Port Wine	Rafe	A1036
Patricia Routledge	Carousel	Nettie Fowler	A190
	The Corn Is Green	Miss Moffat	A249
	Talking Heads	Irene	A1066
David Rowan	The Thin Soldier	As Cast	A1098
Dominic Rowan	Wit's End	Zagoretsky	A1216
Allison Rowe	Roaring Girl's Hamlet	Barnado	A925
Clive Rowe	Carousel	Enoch Snow	A190
	Fuente Ovejuna	Mengo	A422
Gordon Rowe	Love's Labour's Lost	Forester/Marcade	A645
Rosie Rowell	Self Catering	Marilyn Monroe	A973
	Weldon Rising	As Cast	A1192
Lucy Rowland	Doll's House	Emmy	A322
Paul Rowland	The Fancy Man	Mr Helliwell Jackie Diggle	A395

Name	Play	Part	Ref
Patsy **Rowlands**	Me And My Girl	The Duchess	A698
	Wind In The Willows	Hedghog Washerwoman	A1211
Amanda **Royle**	Penny for a Song	As Cast	A848
Carol **Royle**	Woman Of No Importance	Mrs Arbuthnot	A1230
David **Ruben**	In The Midnight Hour	Judd	A538
Thelma **Ruby**	Spread A Little Happ	As Cast	A1035
Pamela **Ruddock**	Rebecca	Mrs Danvers	A894
Laurence **Rudic**	1953	Eberhard	A1
Alison **Ruffelle**	Fiddler On The Roof	Chava	A401
Carole **Ruggier**	Julius Caesar	Portia	A564
	The Night Before The Morning After		A782
	The Threepenny Opera	Mrs Peachum	A1109
John **Rumney**	Fiddler On The Roof	Lazar Wolf	A401
	Fuente Ovejuna	King Ferdinand	A422
Candida **Rundle**	The Corn Is Green	Bessie Watty	A249
Jason **Rush**	Single Spies	Colin	A1005
Gillian **Rushton**	As You Like It	Country Girl	A71
	Lady Be Good	Shirley Vernon	A594
	A Midsummer Night's ..	Moth	A721
Fay **Rusling**	Don't Play With Love	Camille	A329
Catherine **Russell**	The Last Carnival	Aggie Willett	A598
Evan **Russell**	The Corn Is Green	Old Tom	A249
Jenna **Russell**	As You Like It	Court Lady Shepherdess	A67
	The Beggar's Opera	Lucy Lockit	A106
	The Winter's Tale	Dorcas	A1214
Peter **Russell**	Seagull	Dr Hickey	A963
Neil **Rutherford**	A Judgement In Stone	Giles	A563
Peter **Rutherford**	Radio Times	Bultitude	A890
Barrie **Rutter**	Richard III	Richard	A912
David **Ryall**	Sienna Red	As Cast	A999
	Water Music	Albert	A1188
Christopher **Ryan**	One The Ledge	As Cast	A821
Helen **Ryan**	Three Girls In Blue	Fyodorovna	A1101
Madge **Ryan**	Medea	The Nurse	A704
Rebecca **Ryan**	The Trial	Various	A1140
Sarah **Ryan**	Les Miserables	Ensemble	A613
Sue **Ryding**	Withering Looks	As Cast	A1217
Mark **Rylance**	Gamblers	Our Lady	A424
James **Ryland**	The Jungle Book	As Cast	A568
Peter **Rylands**	Beauty and the Beast	Silas Barker	A99
Mark **Saban**	Dragon	As Cast	A341
Kenn **Sabberton**	The Dybbuk	First Batlon	A349
	Henry IV Part 1	Bardolph	A492
	Henry IV Part 2	Bardolph	A493
	A Woman Killed With Kindness	Jenkin	A1229
Tim **Sabel**	Doll's House	Nils	A320
Hugh **Sachs**	Pig In A Poke	George	A859
Howard **Sadler**	Iago	Othello	A526
Martin **Sadler**	June Moon	As Cast	A567
Liza **Sadory**	Mrs Klein	As Cast	A749
Rebecca **Saire**	All's Well That Ends Well	Diana	A35
	A Jovial Crew	Rachel	A561
	School of Night	Audry Washington	A959
	The Taming Of The Shrew	Bianca	A1068
Clara **Salaman**	Courting Winnona	Winnona	A255
	Prin	Melanie	A876

Name	Play	Part	Ref
Pamela **Salem**	Macbeth	Lady Macbeth	A657
Gerard **Salih**	Bourgeois Gentilhomme	Student/Tailor Cook	A153
Ian **Salisbury**	Elvis - the Musical	Young Elvis	A362
Colin **Salmon**	Buddy	Ensemble	A169
Sylvester **Salmon**	Wicked Old Man	Rex	A1207
Ahmad **Saloum**	Gulf Between Us	Ancient	A462
John **Salthouse**	Absent Friends	John	A8
Neil **Salvage**	Bright & Bold Design	Hector Brabant	A161
	Hobson's Choice	Jim Heeler	A499
	Julius Caesar	Cicero	A564
	The Night Before The Morning After		A782
	The Threepenny Opera	Tiger Brown	A1109
Nick **Sampson**	Madness of George III	John Hoppner	A669
Robin **Samson**	Barnstormers	Thomas Naylor	A92
Chris **Samsworth**	Rivals	Faulkland	A920
Michael **Samuels**	Carmen Jones	Gloomy Soldier	A189
Sally **Sanders**	The Fancy Man	Mrs Mellowdew	A395
Jamie **Sandford**	The Imaginary Invalid	Dr Thomas Diaforus	A529
Myra **Sands**	Dead Flamingo Dancer	As Cast	A193
	Lust	Dainty Fidget	A650
Karin **Sang**	Miss Saigon	Yvonne	A727
Richard **Santhiri**	Much Ado About Nothing	Don John	A752
Cesar **Sarachu**	Street of Crocodiles	Joseph	A1056
Julio **Sarcane**	House Of The Spirits		A514
Valerie **Sarruf**	Henry IV Part 2	Lady Northumberland	A493
	The Thebans	Messenger/Eurydice	A1095
Lon **Satton**	Starlight Express	Poppa	A1043
Christopher **Saul**	The Thebans	Priest of Zeus	A1095
Julie **Saunders**	1953	Annette Le Skye	A1
	Macbeth	Third Witch	A655
	The Tempest	Miranda	A1082
Simone **Sauphanor**	Carmen Jones	Cindy Lou	A189
Joan **Savage**	70, Girls, 70	As Cast	A4
Martin **Savage**	Telling Tales	As Cast	A1081
Paul **Savage**	Elegies...	As Cast	A358
John **Savident**	The Card (A musical)	Duncalf	A187
Julian **Savill**	The Thin Soldier	As Cast	A1098
Anna **Savva**	Blood Wedding	The Servant	A134
	Dance Of Guns	As Cast	A273
	Kvetch	Donna	A586
George **Savvides**	House Of The Spirits		A514
Toby **Sawyer**	The English Kiss	Jocelyn	A370
James **Saxon**	Schippel, The Plumber	Schippel	A954
Rolf **Saxon**	Lost in Yonkers	As Cast	A641
Granville **Saxton**	Bulldog Drummond	Dr Lakington	A171
Ian **Saynor**	Fern Hill	John	A400
Malcolm **Scales**	Up 'N' Under	As Cast	A1163
Prunella **Scales**	The Mother Tongue	Dorothy	A743
	Some Singing Blood		A1026
Tony **Scannell**	Jack and the Beanstalk	Fleshcreep	A551
Adrian **Scarborough**	A Midsummer Night's Dream	Flute	A718
	The Recruiting Officer	Bullock	A896
	Wind In The Willows	Mole	A1211
John **Scarborough**	Death of A Salesman	As Cast	A295
Victoria **Scarborough**	Billy Liar	Barbara	A122
	La Ronde	(Two-hander)	A589
	The Rivals	Lydia Languish	A919
Steve **Scarron**	The Dorm	Vinny	A332

Name	Play	Part	Ref
Catherine Schaub	Les Atrides	As Cast	A609
Danny Scheinmann	Story of the Last	Various	A1053
Adrian Schiller	Bourgeois Gentilhomme	Tailor Apprentice	A153
	Wit's End	Chatsky	A1216
Sadie Schimmin	Schippel, The Plumber	Jenny	A954
Helen Schlesinger	Becket	Saxon Girl	A103
Katharine Schlesinger	Martin Chuzzlewit	Multiple Roles	A689
	Second From Last In The Sack Race	Cousin Hilda/Ada Pratt etc	A966
	A View From The Bridge	Catherine	A1171
Paul Schmidt	Brace Up!	As Cast	A156
Alister Schofield	Monster He Made Me	Paul	A734
Andrew Schofield	Self Catering	Clint Eastwood	A973
David Schofield	Blues for Mr Charlie	Lyle Britten	A143
	Murder In Green Meadow	Thomas Devereaux	A757
Mark Schofield	The Thin Soldier	As Cast	A1098
Peter Schofield	Wicks's Folly	As Cast	A1208
Phillip Schofield	Joseph...	Joseph	A559
Meriel Scholfield	Office Party	Accountant	A803
David Schonman	Daughters Of England	The Men	A284
Ida Schuster	Tartuffe	As Cast	A1073
Paul Scofield	Heartbreak House	Captain Shotover	A486
Sharon Scogings	The Maintenance Man	Diana	A673
	Teechers	Gail	A1076
Alex Scott	Coriolanus	As Cast	A248
Christopher Scott	Cinderella	Salmonella	A225
	Light in the Village	Mukhenjee	A622
Devon Scott	Television Programme	Beatrice	A1080
Dougray Scott	Unidentified Human	As Cast	A1162
Jackie Scott	Cats	Grizabella	A194
Lucy Scott	The Bells	Souzel	A108
	The Seagull	Masha	A962
	While The Sun Shines	Fiancee	A1201
Nicola Scott	A View From The Bridge	Beatrice	A1171
	The Winslow Boy	Miss Barnes	A1213
Shaun Scott	Heartbreak House	Randall Utterword	A486
Stuart Scott	Starlight Express	As Cast	A1043
Danny Scquiera	Courting Winnona	Stick	A255
Matthew Scurfield	Street of Crocodiles	The Father	A1056
Jenny Seagrove	The Guardsman	An Actress	A461
	King Lear In New York	Bett	A580
Nick Searle	Cats	Mungojerrie	A194
	Miss Saigon	Reporter	A727
Andrew Searr	The Baby	Simon	A82
Mitch Sebastian	Les Miserables	Montparnasse	A611
Carolyn Sebron	Carmen Jones	Frankie	A189
Andrew Secombe	The Invisible Man	Squire Burdock	A547
Katy Secombe	Blithe Spirit	Edith	A128
	The Hostage	Colette	A505
	Macbeth	Weird Sister/Lady Macduff	A661
Toby Sedgwick	The End Of The Tunnel	As Cast	A365
Graham Seed	Relatively Speaking	Greg	A900
Gary Sefton	Hobson's Choice	Albert Prosser	A500
	Importance of Being	Merriman	A532
	Metamorphosis	Gregor	A714
Jeffery Segal	Murmuring Judges	Judge	A758
	Wind In The Willows	Hedgehog Magistrate	A1211
Stella Segar	Joseph...	Gad's Wife	A559
Nicholas Selby	Breaking the Code	As Cast	A159

Name	Play	Part	Ref
Katherine Sellis	The Secret Rapture	Rhonda	A968
Robert Sena	Miss Saigon	Thuy	A727
Joanne Sergent	The Ecstacy	Dawn	A353
Andy Serkis	Hush	As Cast	A522
	The Revenger's Tragedy	Hippolito	A908
Steven Serlin	Elvis - the Musical	Hank Rich	A362
Bob Sessions	42nd Street	Julian Marsh	A2
George Sewell	Dick Whittington	Alderman Fitzwarren	A308
Rufus Sewell	Making It Better	Tomas Kratky	A677
Suchitra Sewrattan	Miss Saigon	Gigi	A727
Ian Sexon	End Of The Beginning	Various	A366
Sharon Shaffer	Elegies...	As Cast	A358
Patricia Shakesby	The Heiress	Mrs Elizabeth Almand	A490
Michael Shallard	Disobediently Yours	As Cast	A314
Jan Shand	Romeo And Juliet	Lady Capulet	A938
Jeff Shankley	Radio Times	Gary Strong	A890
Helen Shapiro	Jack And The Beanstalk	Jack	A552
Cyril Shaps	Madness of George III	Sir Lucas Pepys	A669
Gail Shapter	My Fair Lady	Flower Girl	A763
Gary Sharkey	Night Must Fall	Hurbert Laurie	A784
Lesley Sharp	Murmuring Judges	PC Sandra Bingham	A758
	Uncle Vanya	Sofya Alexandrovna	A1157
Nada Sharp	Woman Of No Importance	Alice	A1230
Richard Sharp	Carmen Jones	Sergeant Brown	A189
Allan Sharpe	Country Dance		A251
Ian Sharrock	The Fancy Man	Arthur Granville	A395
Michael Sharvell-Martin	Don't Rock The Boat	Arthur Bullhead	A330
	Goldilocks	Dame Gertie	A444
Louisa Shaw	Cats	Jennyanydots	A194
Martin Shaw	An Ideal Husband	Lord Goring	A527
	Sienna Red	Harry	A999
Michael Shaw	Ten Times Table	Eric	A1087
Olivia Shaw	The Sound Of Music	Ensemble	A1033
Ron Shaw	Merlin, The Search	As Cast	A709
David Shaw-Parker	Cyrano De Bergerac	A Marquis	A269
	A Dead Secret	Bert Vokes	A289
	Grand Hotel	Sandor	A453
Ellen Sheean	1953	Kate	A1
	Blood Wedding	The Mother	A134
	Under Milk Wood	As Cast	A1160
Lucy Sheen	M. Butterfly	Comrade Chin Suzuki/Shu Fang	A651
Michael Sheen	Romeo and Juliet	Romeo	A936
	A View From The Bridge	Submarine	A1172
Michael Sheldon	The Way of All Flesh	Overton	A1190
Ray Shell	Elegies...	As Cast	A358
Brian Shelley	Madness of George III	Fortnum	A669
Dave Shelley	Brace Up!	As Cast	A156
Paul Shelley	Liaisons Dangereuses	Le Vicomte de Valmont	A610
	Six Degrees...	Flan	A1008
Nadine Shenton	Story of the Last	Various	A1053
Jack Shepherd	Jane Eyre	Rochester	A555
Merlin Shepherd	Gravity Swing	As Cast	A457
Samantha Shepherd	The Imaginary Invalid	Louise	A529
Simon Shepherd	Spread A Little Happ	As Cast	A1035
Antony Sher	Tamburlaine The Great	Tamburlaine	A1067
	Uncle Vanya	Astrov	A1157
Dinah Sheridan	The Kingfisher	Evelyn	A582

Name	Play	Part	Ref
Susan **Sheridan**	Bedroom Farce	Jan	A104
Michael **Sherin**	The War In Heaven	As Cast	A1184
Di **Sherlock**	Gormenghast	Countess	A451
Maggie **Shevlin**	Seagull	Isobel	A963
Malcolm **Shields**	Beauty And The Beast	Billy The Dog/Lord Poultice	A97
	Merlin, The Search	As Cast	A709
Steve **Shill**	...Changed The Wires	Rob Bannerman	A1245
Richard **Shilling**	My Fair Lady	A Bystander	A763
	Phantom of the Opera	Ensemble	A853
Sadie **Shimmin**	The Guardsman	The Chamber Maid	A461
Aaron **Shirley**	Fuente Ovejuna	Soldier	A422
Charles **Shirvell**	Carousel	As Cast	A190
	Miss Saigon	Marine	A727
Estelle **Shohet**	Elisabeth II	As Cast	A361
Barrie **Shore**	Relative Values	Lady Hayling	A899
Peter **Shorey**	Hobson's Choice	Tubby Wadlow	A500
	Nervous Women	Jonathan	A776
	Wizard of Oz	The Wizard	A1224
Mandy **Short**	Kurt Weill Cabaret	As Cast	A585
John **Shrapnel**	The Dybbuk	Reb Azrielke	A349
	Hamlet	Claudius	A466
	The Thebans	Creon	A1095
William **Shrew**	Jack And The Beanstalk	The Giant	A553
Deborah **Shrimpton**	Joseph...	Mrs Potiphar	A559
Michael **Siberry**	All's Well That Ends Well	Parolles	A35
	As You Like It	Jaques	A67
	The Changeling	Alsemero	A197
David **Sibley**	A Month In The Country	As Cast	A736
Marlene **Sidaway**	Safe In Our Hands	Mrs Reed	A947
Carmen **Silvera**	'Allo,'Allo	Edith Artois	A36
	Cinderella	Fairy Godmother	A225
Peter **Silverleaf**	Gamblers	Sauerkraut	A424
	Savage Storm	As Cast	A952
Andrew **Simister**	Threepenny Story	Mr Peachum	A1108
	A View From The Bridge	Mike	A1169
James **Simmons**	Coriolanus	As Cast	A248
	Much Ado About Nothing	Benedick	A752
Paula **Simms**	King Lear	Fool	A578
	Threepenny Story	Mary Sawyer	A1108
	A View From The Bridge	Catherine	A1169
Stephen **Simms**	Macbeth	Banquo	A656
Charles **Simon**	Bourgeois Gentilhomme	Valet	A153
	School for Scandal	Rowley	A957
Nick **Simons**	Artists and Admirers	As Cast	A64
Charles **Simpson**	The Blue Angel	Hans	A138
	Iago	Iago	A526
	Macbeth	Malcolm	A655
	The Tempest	Ferdinand	A1082
Jane **Simpson**	Dead Heroic	Skin Diver	A287
Lee **Simpson**	The Comedy Store	Various	A242
	The Pocket Dream	Demetrius	A868
Angela **Sims**	The Card (A musical)	Widow Hullins	A187
Malcolm **Sinclair**	The Dark River	Alan Crocker	A282
Pamela **Sinclair**	The Three Musketeers	Queen Anne	A1104
Suzanne **Sinclair**	Stand Before You Naked	As Cast	A525
Donald **Sinden**	Venus Observed	The Duke Of Altair	A1168
Marc **Sinden**	Private Lives	Victor	A880
Guy **Siner**	'Allo,'Allo	Lieut Grober	A36
Aaron **Singer-Lee**	Romeo And Juliet	Child	A938
Terence **Singleton**	Stageland	Joe/Boatman/Actor etc	A1041
Fiona **Sinnott**	Les Miserables	Cosette	A611
Stuart **Skelding**	The Trial	Various	A1140
Matthew **Skilton**	Carousel	As Cast	A190
Claire **Skinner**	Measure For Measure	Isabella	A700
Karen **Skinns**	Merrily We Roll Along	As Cast	A711
Anna **Skye**	Blithe Spirit	As Cast	A125
	Far From The Madding Crowd	Bathsheba Everdine	A397
Michael **Skyers**	Starlight Express	As Cast	A1043
Paul **Slack**	Breaking the Code	As Cast	A159
	Gulf Between Us	Ryder	A462
	The Pope And The Witch	Det.Sgt. Zoff	A870
Nicola **Slade**	Doll's House	Anne-Marie	A320
	In The Midnight Hour	Mccaegy	A538
Lewis **Sladen**	Wind In The Willows	Portly	A1211
Claire **Slater**	The Sound Of Music	Gretl	A1033
Maxwell **Slater**	Aladdin	As Cast	A22
Paul **Slater**	42nd Street	As cast	A2
Simon **Slater**	The Baby	Derek	A82
Tony **Slattery**	Radio Times	Sammy	A890
Jane **Slavin**	Absent Friends	Evelyn	A8
William **Sleigh**	Our Song	The Maitre D'.	A833
Rob **Slinger**	The Ecstacy	Mike	A353
Michael **Small**	Joseph...	Apache Dancer	A559
Sharon **Small**	Little Shop Of Horrors	Audrey	A632
	School For Wives	Agnes	A958
	Travesties	Gwendolen	A1137
Tim **Smallwood**	Fool for Love	Eddie	A411
Anthony **Smee**	Thirteenth Night	As Cast	A1099
Derek **Smee**	The Recruiting Officer	Mr Scale	A896
	Wind In The Willows	Fox/Ticket Clerk	A1211
Jack **Smethurst**	Macbeth	Banquo	A657
Anna **Smith**	Good Rockin' Tonite	Iris	A449
Anne **Smith**	Robin	Morgana	A927
Annie **Smith**	Beauty And The Beast	Marrygolda	A98
Auriol **Smith**	A Dead Secret	Henrietta Spicer	A289
	Penny for a Song	As Cast	A848
	Who Was Hilary	Mrs Brute	A1204
Cathryn **Smith**	Some Like It Hot	Rossela	A1025
Clarence **Smith**	Blood Brothers	Eddie	A130
	Fuente Ovejuna	Captain Flores	A423
	Romeo and Juliet	Romeo	A935
Derek **Smith**	School for Scandal	Sir Oliver Surface	A957
	Twelfth Night	Sir Toby Belch	A1148
Doug **Smith**	The House Of Stairs	Mark	A513
	Indigo Mill	As Cast	A539
Duncan **Smith**	The Mikado	Pooh-Bah	A722
Graeme **Smith**	Barnum	As Cast	A93
Kay **Smith**	Carmen Jones	Card Player	A189
Kieran **Smith**	Ten In A Bed		A1086
Liz **Smith**	Just Between Ourselves	Marjorie	A569
Loveday **Smith**	Forbidden Planet	Ensign Lena Anne Fytter	A904
Martin **Smith**	A Swell Party		A106
Nicholas **Smith**	Me And My Girl	Sir John	A698
Penny **Smith**	Blood Whispers	As Cast	A135
Peyton **Smith**	Brace Up!	As Cast	A156
Rachel **Smith**	King Lear	Cordelia	A578
	Phantom Of The Opera	Ballet/Chorus	A854
Sally **Smith**	Phantom Of The Opera	Madame Giry	A854

Name	Play	Part	Ref
Tom Smith	Wind In The Willows	Portly	A1211
Jackie Smith-Wood	Over a Barrel	Jill	A840
Philippe Smolikowski	Dybbuk	As cast	A350
Ruby Snape	Sailor Beware!	Daphne Pink	A948
James Snell	Bulldog Drummond	Peterson	A171
	A Working Woman	Bazouge	A1238
Robin Sneller	The Recruiting Officer	Thomas	A896
Gareth Snook	Aspects Of Love	Hugo Le Meunier Alex's Friend	A72
	Assassins	As Cast	A73
	Merrily We Roll Along	Joe	A711
Philip Snowdon	Radio Times	As Cast	A890
Benjamin Soames	Serve Them All My Days	As Cast	A1123
Robin Soans	The Rivals	Sir Anthony Absolute	A919
	Three Birds Alighting	Various	A1100
Richard Sockett	Macbeth	Macduff	A653
David Solomon	Merchant of Venice	Launcelot	A708
Kate Somerby	Wind In The Willows	Rabbits	A1211
Geraldine Sommerville	Epsom Downs	Primrose	A375
	Fuente Ovejuna	Jacinta	A423
	Romeo and Juliet	Juliet	A935
	Three Birds Alighting	Various	A1100
Mia Soteriou	Don Quixote	As Cast	A328
Jon Sowden	A Dead Secret	Sir Arthur Lovecraft	A289
Peter Sowerbutts	Androcles And The Lion		A45
Helen Spackman	Mamahuhu?	As Cast	A678
Timothy Spall	Bourgeois Gentilhomme	Monsieur Jourdain	A153
	A Midsummer Night's Dream	Bottom	A718
Dave Spathaky	Gravity Swing	As Cast	A457
Steven Speirs	Frankie & Tommy	Tommy	A418
Dawn Spence	Death of A Salesman	As Cast	A295
	Grease	Marty	A458
	Moby Dick	As Cast	A728
Paul Spence	Playing The Wife	As Cast	A865
Dennis Spencer	Witness For The Prosecution	Myers	A1218
Rob Spendlove	No Remission	Derry	A790
Lisa Spenz	Blues Brothers	A Bluette	A142
Victor Spinetti	Goldilocks	Wicked Ringmaster	A444
Brian Spink	The Mousetrap	Major Metcalf	A744
Linda Spinner	La Bete	Marquise Theresa Du Par	A587
Kate Spiro	Building Blocks	Mary	A170
	Murder In Green Meadow	Joan Devereaux	A757
Samantha Spiro	As You Like It	Audrey	A71
	Lady Be Good	Daisy Parke	A594
	A Midsummer Night's ..	First Fairy	A721
	Tons Of Money	Simpson	A1125
Fiona Spreadborough	Safe In Our Hands	Sandy McDonough	A947
Joyce Springer	The Night Before The Morning After		A782
Peter Sproule	Dead Soil	Father/Older Actor	A290
	Medea	Aegeus	A704
Rachel Spry	Les Miserables	Old Woman	A611
Jill Spurrier	Birthday Party	As Cast	A124
Linda Spurrier	The Family Reunion	Mary	A394
	Pig In A Poke	Ernestine	A859
Guy-Paul St Germain	Cats	Mr Mistoffolees	A194

Name	Play	Part	Ref
Dinah Stabb	House of Bernarda Alba	As Cast	A515
Tim Stacey	Barnum	As Cast	A93
James Staddon	Cyrano De Bergerac	A Cadet/Etc	A269
	Miss Saigon	Marine	A727
Kathy Staff	Sailor Beware!	Edie Hornett	A948
Helen Stafford	Dance Of Guns	As Cast	A273
Ken Stafford	Cats	Victor	A194
Martyn Stanbridge	Intimate Exchanges	Toby	A544
John Standing	Hay Fever	David	A481
Richard Standing	Pond Life	Trevor	A869
Alan Stanford	Private Lives	Victor	A882
Gavin Stanley	Good Rockin' Tonite	Billy Fury	A449
Margot Stanley	And A Nightingale Sang	Peggy Stott	A43
	The Innocents	Mrs Grose	A540
Rachel Stanley	My Fair Lady	Lady Boxington	A763
Siobhan Stanley	Birthday Party	As Cast	A124
	Casanova	As Cast	A191
	Summer Lightning	Millicent Threepwood	A1058
Barry Stanton	Six Degrees...	Larkin	A1008
Sophie Stanton	Love's Labour's Lost	Jaquenetta	A645
Charles Stapley	The Kingfisher	Cecil	A582
Alvin Stardust	Slice Of Saturday...	Eric 'Rubberlegs'	A1015
Carol Starks	Fiddler On The Roof	Hodel	A401
Alison Steadman	Little Voice	Mari Hoff	A917
Barry Stearn	The Sea	Townspeople	A961
	Uncle Vanya	Yefim	A1157
Kate Steavenson-Payne	Molecatcher's Daughter	Maria Marten	A729
Maggie Steed	Game of Love & Chance	Silvia	A425
Deborah Steel	Buddy	Maria Elena	A169
Janet Steel	As You Desire Me		A66
	Ay Carmela!		A78
Christopher Steele	Les Miserables	Pimp/Claquesous	A611
Tommy Steele	Some Like It Hot	Joe	A1025
Matthew Steer	Shades	Alan	A981
Bernice Stegers	Marching Song	Catherine de Troyes	A685
	The Mother Tongue	Lettie	A743
Richard Stemp	No 3 Pied Piper Street	Luke	A788
Karlyn Stephen	Good Morning Bill	Marie	A447
	Merlin, The Search	As Cast	A709
Katy Stephens	Man Cub	As Cast	A679
Robert Stephens	Henry IV Part 1	Sir John Falstaff	A492
	Henry IV Part 2	Sir John Falstaff	A493
	Julius Caesar	Julius Caesar	A566
Sharon Stephens	Buddy	Ensemble	A168
Toby Stephens	All's Well That Ends Well	Bertram	A35
	Antony and Cleopatra	Pompey	A53
Tony Stephens	42nd Street	As cast	A2
Mike Sterling	Les Miserables	Marius	A611
David Sterne	To Kill A Mockingbird	Heck Tate	A1121
Benjamin Stertz	Games	As Cast	A426
Colin Stevens	Beauty And The Beast	Father/Spirit	A100
Dudley Stevens	Late Joys		A600
Gary Stevens	Name	As Cast	A772
Lucy Stevens	House Of The Spirits		A514
Ronnie Stevens	Becket	Cardinal	A103
	School for Scandal	Crabtree	A957
	Trelawny Of The Wells	Augustus Colpoys	A1139
Craig Stevenson	Forbidden Planet	Ensign Adam Amp	A904

Name	Play	Part	Ref
Jessica Stevenson	Fiddler On The Roof	Granma Tzeitel	A401
Juliet Stevenson	Death and the Maiden	Paulina Salas	A293
Marina Stevenson	Cats	Victoria	A194
Cameron Stewart	Beyond Reasonable Doubt	Dr Weeden	A113
	What the Butler Saw	Sergeant Match	A1197
Carola Stewart	You Must Be The Husband	Babs	A1248
Ewan Stewart	Phoenix	Paul	A857
	A Working Woman	Coupeau	A1238
Ian Stewart	Aspects Of Love	Actor	A72
Neil Stewart	Out Of Order	A Body	A835
Polly Stewart	Lettice & Lovage	The Woman	A614
Richard Stewart	The Bells	Walter	A108
Colin Stinton	Night of the Iguana	Jake Latta	A785
Frank Stirling	Stageland	Jephson/Fake Manager etc	A1041
Jackie Stirling	Man Cub	As Cast	A679
Paula Stockbridge	Liaisons Dangereuses	La Presidente de Tourvel	A610
	Necklaces	As Cast	A774
Jane Stoggles	Grand Hotel	Madam Peepee	A453
David Stoll	Noises Off	Selsdon Mowbray	A794
Jennie Stoller	At Fifty She Discovered The Sea	The Mother	A74
Graham Stone	Phantom Of The Opera	Innkeeper	A854
Richard Stone	Wizard of Oz	The Wizard	A1223
Jo Stone-Fewings	Fuente Ovejuna	Barrildo	A422
Joanne Stoner	Othello	Emelia	A827
	Richard III	Lady Anne	A912
	The School For Scandal	Lady Sneerwell	A956
Niall Stones	Miss Saigon	Marine	A727
Liz Stooke	Seagull	Pauline	A963
Charlotte Storey	In The Midnight Hour	Duffy	A538
	Too Much Too Young	As Cast	A1127
Ian Storey	World Upon The Moon	Ecclitico	A1241
Malcolm Storry	The Changeling	De Flores	A197
	Tamburlaine The Great	Bajazeth	A1067
Anthony Story	Macbeth	As Cast	A660
Ken Stott	Colquhoun And MacBryde	MacBryde	A235
	The Recruiting Officer	Kite	A896
	The Sea	Hatch	A961
Michaela Strachan	Goldilocks	Goldilocks	A444
Nadia Strahan	Joseph...	Mrs Potiphar	A559
John Straiton	Cuttin' A Rug	Phil	A266
	Hecuba	Ghost of Polydorus	A488
Peter Straker	Phantom of the Opera	The Phantom	A853
Michael Strassen	The Golden Ass	First Initiate	A443
Deirdre Strath	Ride Down Mt Morgan	Bessie	A915
Jon Strickland	Woman In Mind	As Cast	A1228
John Stride	King Lear In New York	Robert	A580
Virginia Stride	The House Of Stairs	Cosette	A513
Mark Strong	Fuente Ovejuna	Captain Flores	A422
Michael Stroud	Woman In Mind	As Cast	A1228
Imogen Stubbs	Heartbreak House	Ellie Dunn	A486
Una Stubbs	An Ideal Husband	Lady Markby	A528
Neil Stuke	Romeo and Juliet	Samson	A936
	A View From The Bridge	Immigration Officer	A1172
James Sturgess	Comedy of Errors	As Cast	A239
Sara Sugarman	Hamlet	As Cast	A465
	Handsome,Handicapped..	As Cast	A468
Graham Sullivan	Fooling About	As Cast	A412
Hugh Sullivan	Body And Soul	As Cast	A146
	Macbeth	Doctor	A655
	The Tempest	Gonzalo	A1082
Peter Sullivan	Measure For Measure	Lucio/Barnadine	A702
Marc Summers	Carmen Jones	Second Soldier	A189
Clare Summerskill	Buddy	Vi Petty	A169
Alexandra Sumner	Fiddler On The Roof	Tzeitel	A401
David Sumner	As You Like It	Duke	A71
	A Midsummer Night's ..	Theseus	A721
John Surman	Frankenstein	Alphonse Frankenstein	A415
	The Tempest	Prospero	A1083
Gil Sutherland	Cabal and Love	Baron von Walter (President)	A176
Peter Sutherland	Late Joys		A600
Julia Sutton	Late Joys		A600
Philip Sutton	My Fair Lady	Angry Man	A763
Sonia Swaby	Joseph...	Dan's Wife	A559
Roger Swaine	The Miser	Maitre Simon	A724
	Ten Times Table	Donald	A1087
Adrian Swann	Provoked Wife	Mademoiselle	A884
Susan Swayze	Twelfth Night	Feste	A1151
George Sweeney	Macbeth	Banquo	A653
Glynn Sweet	The Business Of Murder	As Cast	A175
Tracy Sweetinburgh	Saint Oscar	Lady Wilde	A949
	Shakers	Mel	A987
Caroline Swift	One For The Road	Pauline	A818
	Outside Edge	Miriam	A837
	To Kill A Mockingbird	Stephanie Crawford	A1121
Clive Swift	Marching Song	Harry Lancaster	A685
Jeremy Swift	Trilby & Svengali	Gecko/Sandy	A1141
Sarah Swingler	The Fancy Man	Edith Atkinson	A395
	Prin	Dibs	A876
Steve Swinscoe	Doll's House	Nils	A322
	Macbeth	Macduff	A658
Tim Swinton	The Recruiting Officer	Pluck	A897
Eric Sykes	19th Hole	The Secretary	A1090
Suzan Sylvester	All My Sons	Ann Deever	A33
	Life is a Dream	Rosaura	A619
	Love's Labour's Lost	Rosaline	A645
Vari Sylvester	End Of The Beginning	Various	A366
Cleo Sylvestre	Ten In A Bed		A1086
Paul Symington	Miss Saigon	Marine	A727
Amanda Symonds	In The Midnight Hour	Rita	A537
	In The Midnight Hour	Rita	A538
Sylvia Syms	The House Of Stairs	Cosette	A513
Jackie Sysum	Gravity Swing	As Cast	A457
Cindy Szegledy	Lady Aoi	As Cast	A593
Sheila Tait	And A Nightingale Sang	Helen Stott	A43
	On The Piste	Alison	A810
Simon Tait	The Mousetrap	Det Sgt Trotter	A744
John Tallents	Doll's House	Dr Rank	A323
	Much Ado About Nothing	Don Pedro	A750
Alfie Talman	Hapgood	Joe	A472
Christopher Talman	Hot Stuff	As Cast	A508
Tselane Tambo	Understanding The Dang	As Cast	A1161
Mark Tandy	Reflected Glory	James Wiley	A898
Leon Tanner	Cyrano De Bergerac	A Marquis/Etc	A269
Susan-Jane Tanner	As You Like It	Audrey	A67
	The Beggar's Opera	Mrs Peachum	A106
	The Odyssey	Athena	A802

Name	Play	Part	Ref
Terry **Taplin**	The House Of Stairs	As cast	A513
Paula **Tappenden**	As Time Goes By	As Cast	A65
Rory **Tapsell**	Elisabeth II	As Cast	A361
Jimmy **Tarbuck**	Dick Whittington	Idle Jim	A308
Liza **Tarbuck**	Bazaar and Rummage	Katrina	A94
Peter **Tate**	As You Desire Me		A66
	Master and Margarita	The Master	A693
Richard **Tate**	The Golden Ass	The Baker	A443
	Jack's Out	As Cast	A554
	Phantom of the Opera	Ensemble	A853
	The Professional	As Cast	A883
Stephen **Tate**	Forbidden Planet	Dr Prospero	A904
Andy **Taylor**	Evening with Gary L.	Bill	A383
Cheryl **Taylor**	Cinderella	Cinderella	A219
David **Taylor**	A Distant Applause	As Cast	A315
	Hostages and Hamsters	Kowalski	A506
	My Blood on Glass	As Cast	A761
Dominic **Taylor**	Fuente Ovejuna	First Alderman	A422
Gwen **Taylor**	The Mother Tongue	Harriet	A743
Ian **Taylor**	A Jovial Crew	Courtier/Beggar	A561
	The Winter's Tale	Lord	A1214
Kenneth **Alan Taylor**	Dick Whittington	Dame	A311
Mason **Taylor**	Some Like It Hot	Knuckles Spendoza	A1025
Patrice **Taylor**	The Sound Of Music	Sister Berthe	A1033
Polly **Taylor**	Body And Soul	As Cast	A146
Roberta **Taylor**	Casanova	As Cast	A191
Sally **Taylor**	Starlight Express	Dinah	A1043
Shirin **Taylor**	Three Birds Alighting	Various	A1100
Owen **Teale**	Henry IV Part 1	Hotspur	A492
	Henry IV Part 2	Hotspur	A493
	Julius Caesar	Mark Antony	A566
Adam **Tedder**	Buddy	Ensemble	A169
Akram **Telawe**	Gulf Between Us	Ismael	A462
James **Telfer**	Shadowlands	Alan Gregg	A984
	Strippers	Douggie	A1057
Peter **Temple**	The House Of Stairs	As cast	A513
	Road To Casablanca	Louis/Ferrari Ugarte	A923
David **Tennant**	Hay Fever	Simon Bliss	A482
	Merlin, The Search	As Cast	A709
	Tartuffe	As Cast	A1073
	Virginia Woolf	Nick	A1205
Nicholas **Tennant**	Billy Liar	Arthur	A122
David **Terence**	Henry IV Part 1	Gower	A492
	Henry IV Part 2	Ralph Moudly	A493
Kate **Terence**	Alfie	As Cast	A29
Malcolm **Terris**	After You With The Mlk	Fred	A16
	Rule Of The Game	Bernard O'Donnell	A942
	School for Scandal	Sir Peter Teazle	A957
Catherine **Terry**	Fiddler On The Roof	Fruma-Sarah	A401
Kathleen **Tessaro**	June Moon	As Cast	A567
Alex **Tetteh-Larteh**	Flamingo	As cast	A408
Josephine **Tewson**	See How They Run	Miss Skillen	A971
James **Thackwray**	Rivals	Thomas	A920
Eddie **Thengani**	Necklaces	As Cast	A774
David **Thewlis**	The Sea	Hollarcut	A961
Stephen **Thiebault**	Rocky Horror Show	Phantom	A933
Robert **Thirtle**	The Three Musketeers	Various	A1105
Adrienne **Thomas**	Cabal and Love	Lady Milford	A176
Anstey **Thomas**	A Doll's House	Helen	A324
	Understanding The Dang	As Cast	A1161
Ben **Thomas**	Fuente Ovejuna	Esteban	A422

Name	Play	Part	Ref
	Grace	Freddy	A452
	The Road	Professor	A921
Bill **Thomas**	Dragon	As Cast	A341
	What The Butler Saw	Dr Rance	A1196
Caroline **Thomas**	Witness For The Prosecution	The Other Woman	A1218
Chloe **Thomas**	Death Of A Salesman	The Woman	A297
Cloe **Thomas**	Hecuba	Chorus	A488
Debbie **Thomas**	Lloyd George	Various	A635
Eiry **Thomas**	Fern Hill	Nain/Linda	A400
Gareth **Thomas**	Dejavu	Cliff	A302
Giles **Thomas**	Colquhoun And MacBryde	As Cast	A235
Iwan **Thomas**	School for Scandal	Careless	A957
Nina **Thomas**	Play Strindberg	Alice	A861
	The Tender Husband	Mrs Clerimont	A1088
Sian **Thomas**	The Cutting	Judith	A267
	Square Rounds	As Cast	A1038
Frank **Thompson**	Cats	Admetus	A194
Jimmy **Thompson**	Run for Your Wife	As Cast	A944
John **Thompson**	Buddy	Jerry Allison	A169
Shelley **Thompson**	Murder In Green Meadow	Carolyn Thompson	A757
	Shadowlands	Joy Davidman	A985
Sophie **Thompson**	All's Well That Ends Well	Helena	A35
Vernon **Thompson**	My Cousin Rachel	James	A762
Debi **Thomson**	The Ballroom	As Cast	A1091
Barbara **Thorn**	Relative Values	Miranda	A899
Kraig **Thornber**	Forbidden Planet	Ariel	A904
Nigel **Thornbory**	Radio Times	Various	A889
Daniel **Thorndike**	Love	Reader	A642
Angela **Thorne**	Body And Soul	Glynis	A146
	Relatively Speaking	Sheila	A900
Simon **Thorne**	Call Blue Jane	As Cast	A182
Sophie **Thursfield**	A Doll's House	Nora	A324
Poppy **Tierney**	Miss Saigon	Bar Girl	A727
Tony **Timberlake**	Les Miserables	Thenardier	A611
Christopher **Timothy**	Building Blocks	David	A170
	Moment Of Weakness	Tony	A732
Rosie **Timpson**	Bright & Bold Design	Mab Cooper	A161
	Hobson's Choice	Maggie Hobson	A499
David **Timson**	Absent Friends	Colin	A10
	A Midsummer Night's Dream	Bottom	A717
	Penny for a Song	As Cast	A848
Stephen **Tindall**	Gaslight	Mr.Manningham	A429
Kate **Tindle**	Telling Tales	As Cast	A1081
Faith **Tingle**	Working	As Cast	A1239
Cassius **Tlhotlhalemajc**	Sikulu	Ensemble	A1001
Isaac **Tlhotlhalemaje**	Sikulu	Ensemble	A1001
Christopher **Toba**	Romeo and Juliet	Romeo	A937
Earl **Tobias**	Moby Dick	As Cast	A728
Heather **Tobias**	As You Like It	Audrey	A69
Anny **Tobin**	Dancing At Lughnasa	Kate	A274
Clifton **Todd**	Late Joys		A600
Richard **Todd**	Beyond Reasonable Doubt	As Cast	A115
	Sleuth	Andrew Wyke	A1013
	The Woman In Black	Arthur Kipps	A1226
Sandi **Toksvig**	The Comedy Store	Various	A242
	The Pocket Dream	Stage Manager	A868
Maria **Tolly**	Mrs Columbus	One-Woman Show	A747

Name	Play	Part	Ref
Audrey Tom	School for Scandal	Miss Verjuice	A957
Paul Tomany	Little Tramp	Joe, an agent Others	A634
Louise Tomkins	Bright & Bold Design	Joyce Murray	A161
	The Night Before The Morning After		A782
	Valentine's Day	Maisie	A1165
Gail Tomlinson	My Fair Lady	Queen Of Transylvania	A763
James Tomlinson	Rocket To The Moon	Mr Prince	A932
Paul Tompkinson	Joseph...	Butler	A559
Stephen Tompkinson	Absent Friends	John	A10
	Love's Labour's Lost	King of Navarre	A645
	Women Laughing	Tony	A1234
Fiona Tong	Hecuba	Chorus	A488
Rebbecca Toogood	Curse Of The Mummy	As cast	A263
Patrick Toomey	The Blue Angel	Paul	A138
	The Woman In Black	The Actor	A1227
Paul Tootnill	Dick Whittington	As Cast	A312
Gillian Topkins	On The Piste	Beverly Ryan	A812
Steve Toussaint	The Last Carnival	As Cast	A598
	Viva Detroit	Sonny	A1178
Harry Towb	Square Rounds	As Cast	A1038
	Trelawny Of The Wells	O'Dwyer	A1138
Stanley Townsend	Cherry Orchard		A203
	Double Dealer	As Cast	A335
	The Little Clay Cart	Sansthanaka	A627
Matthew Townshend	Chitty Bang Bang	The Child Catcher	A208
Jacquie Toye	Cinderella	As Cast	A222
	Fifteen Streets	Mary Ellen	A403
	Jubilee	Eileen	A562
	Little Tramp	Hannah	A634
Tim Tracey	The Hatchet Man	As Cast	A478
James Traherne	Animal Farm	Ensemble	A49
Chris Tranchell	The Golden Ass	Meretrix	A443
Mandy Travis	In The Midnight Hour	Beattie	A538
Aldan Treays	Cats	The Cats' Chorus	A194
Peter Treganna	Elephant	As Cast	A359
Lucy Tregear	Taming of the Shrew	Katherine	A1069
	Wizard of Oz	Aunt Em	A1222
David Trevena	Fiddler On The Roof	Rabbi	A401
Frederick Treves	Voysey Inheritance	Mr Voysey	A1182
Simon Treves	La Bete	De Brie	A587
Jack Tripp	Babes in the Wood	Nurse Ribena	A79
Jayne Trotman	Hecuba	Chorus	A488
Judi Trott	Mansfield Park	Mary Crawford	A683
David Troughton	Loot	Truscott	A638
Simon David Trout	Barnum	Tom Thumb	A93
Simeon Truby	Northern Trawl	Jim	A797
Paul Trussel	Liaisons Dangereuses	Azolan	A610
Menna Trussler	Sleeping With Mickey	One Woman Show	A1010
Len Trusty	Elegies...	As Cast	A358
Gregor Truter	Becket	1st Soldier	A103
	The Recruiting Officer	Mr Scale	A897
Rita Tsang	Miss Saigon	Mimi	A727
David Tse	Heer Ranjha	As Cast	A489
Reginald Tsiboe	Carmen Jones	Rum	A189
Rebecca Tuchner	Spring Awakening	Thea/Fastcrawler	A1037
James Tucker	Woman Of No Importance	Francis	A1230
Beth Tuckey	A Midsummer Night's Dream	Helena	A717
Iwan Tudor	The Corn Is Green	Ibwal Morris	A249
Nic Tudor	Mamahuhu?	As Cast	A678
Nicholas Tudor	Some...Atomic Zombie		A1027
Michael Tudor-Barnes	Beyond Reasonable Doubt	Metcalfe	A113
	Tons Of Money	Sprules	A1125
	What the Butler Saw	Dr Rance	A1197
Kevin Tuer	Cyrano De Bergerac	Cyrano De Bergerac	A268
Brian Tully	Death Of A Salesman	Uncle Ben	A297
	Fifteen Streets	Peter Bracken	A403
	Out Of Order	The Waiter	A835
	Shadowlands	Major W.H. Lewis	A984
Angela Tunstall	Square Rounds	As Cast	A1038
Darren Tunstall	The Recruiting Officer	Costar Pearmain	A897
Robert Tunstall	Hapgood	Blair	A472
Ester Turnage	Television Programme	Adel	A1080
John Turnbull	Marching Song	Father Anselm	A685
	School for Scandal	Snake	A957
Andrea Turner	Little Tramp	Lady Astor/Others	A634
Bridget Turner	The Best Man	Sylvie	A110
	Blithe Spirit	Madame Arcati	A127
	Trelawny Of The Wells	Miss Trafalgar Gower	A1138
Graham Turner	School of Night	Ingram Frizer	A959
	The Taming Of The Shrew	Hortensio	A1068
	The Winter's Tale	Young Shepherd	A1214
John Turner	Valentine's Day	Crampton	A1165
Lisa Turner	Beauty And The Beast	Sister/Spirit	A100
Maryann Turner	Strippers	Aunt Ada	A1057
Sally Turner	The Deep Blue Sea	Ann Welch	A140
Tony Turner	Othello	Iago	A827
	The School For Scandal	Sir Benjamin Backbite/Moses	A956
Zara Turner	The Revenger's Tragedy	Castiza	A908
	Six Degrees...	Elizabeth	A1008
Dorothy Tutin	The Seagull	Madame Arkadina	A962
Emma Tuvera	Miss Saigon	Tam	A727
Shadrack Twala	Sikulu	Ensemble	A1001
Todd Twala	Sikulu	Ensemble	A1001
Susan Twist	The Norman Conquests	Ruth	A796
	One For The Road	Jane	A818
	To Kill A Mockingbird	Mrs. Dubose	A1121
Thomas Tyler	Doll's House	Bobby	A322
Norman Tyrrell	A Midsummer Night's Dream	As Cast	A717
David Tysall	Gormenghast	Swelter	A451
	Porcelain	Voice I	A871
Toby Uffindell Phillips	The Sound Of Music	Kurt	A1033
Thomasina Unsworth	Women in Love	Gudrun	A1233
Jonathan Unwin	The Pope And The Witch	Alfredo	A870
Gareth Upton	Macbeth	Young Siward	A658
Joss Urch	Carousel	As Cast	A190
Tamara Ustinov	Love	Reader	A642
Summer V-Stralen	The Sound Of Music	Marta	A1033
Robert Vahey	Entertaining Mr Sloane	Kemp	A373
	Gaslight	Inspector Rough	A429
	Serve Them All My Days	As Cast	A1123
Ashley Valance	Comedy of Errors	As Cast	A239
Angela Vale	The Beggar's Opera	Mrs Slammekin	A106
	A Jovial Crew	Autem Mort	A561
	The Winter's Tale	Emilia	A1214

Name	Play	Part	Ref
Deborah **Vale**	Twelfth Night	Maria	A1149
Kate **Valk**	Brace Up!	As Cast	A156
Wendy **van der Plank**	The Rivals	Lucy	A918
Joanna **Van Gyseghem**	Lettice And Lovage	Lettice Douffet	A615
	Something's Burning	Nell	A1029
Walter **Vandyk**	Kurt Weill Cabaret	As Cast	A585
Zubin **Varla**	Lady Be Good	Jack Robinson	A594
Drew **Varley**	Cats	Bill Bailey	A194
Steven **Varnom**	Robin	Little John	A927
Paul **Vates**	Confusions	Waiter/Stewart Arthur	A246
Paul **Vaughan-Teague**	Play Strindberg	Edgar	A861
Vladimir **Vega**	New World and Tears	As Cast	A780
Camilla **Vella**	Happy As A Sandbag	As Cast	A473
Paul **Venables**	Evening With Gary L.	Ian	A382
	The Pope And The Witch	Monsignor Baggio Baresi	A870
Arturo **Venegas**	House Of The Spirits		A514
Wanda **Ventham**	It Runs In The Family	Rosemary Mortimore	A548
Laurie **Ventry**	Taming Of The Shrew	Grumio	A1070
Maria **Ventura**	Elegies...	As Cast	A358
Dorothy **Vernon**	Aspects Of Love	Elizabeth	A72
Richard **Vernon**	The Kingfisher	Cecil	A582
David **Verrey**	Comedy Of Errors	As Cast	A241
	The Recruiting Officer	Pluck	A896
Pamela **Vezey**	Anybody for Murder?	Mary Ticklewell	A55
Alan **Vicary**	The Mikado	Pish-Tush	A722
Pippa **Vickers**	As You Desire Me		A66
Nicola **Vickery**	Shakers	Adele	A987
Fiona **Victory**	Pygmies In The Ruins		A887
Susan **Vidler**	A Better Day	As Cast	A111
James **Villiers**	Madness of George III	Lord Thurlow	A669
Jay **Villiers**	Gaslight	Mr Manningham	A428
Dean **Viner**	Valentine's Day	Frank	A1165
Paul **Virah**	Three Girls In Blue	Valera	A1101
	Weldon Rising	As Cast	A1192
Henrietta **Voigts**	Happy Families	Rebecca/Lynn Sutton	A476
Tilly **Vosburgh**	Absent Friends	Marge	A10
Philip **Voss**	The Alchemist	Epicure Mammon	A28
	Artists and Admirers	Narokov	A64
	Columbus	Rodrigo Pulgar	A237
	Henry IV Part 1	Worcester/Lord Justice	A492
	Henry IV Part 2	Worcester/Lord Justice	A493
	The Thebans	Theseus	A1095
Voyd	Starlight Express	Buffy	A1043
Richard **Vranch**	The Comedy Store	Various	A242
Kevyn **Waby**	Starlight Express	Ruhrgold	A1043
Lisa **Waddingham**	Cats	Jemima	A194
Julian **Wadham**	Madness of George III	William Pitt	A669
Andrew C. **Wadsworth**	Closer Than Ever	As Cast	A231
	Les Miserables	Javert	A613
Mark **Waghorn**	Macbeth	Angus	A656
Kevin **Wainwright**	Carousel	As Cast	A190
	Miss Saigon	Marine	A727
Matthew **Wait**	Weldon Rising	As Cast	A1192
Martyn **Waites**	Shadowlands	Dr. Oakley	A984
	Strippers	Bernard	A1057
Colin **Wakefield**	Over a Barrel	Gordon	A840
	Shadowlands	As Cast	A983

Name	Play	Part	Ref
Ben **Walden**	Loot	Hal	A638
John **Walden**	Valentine's Day	Monty	A1165
Gary **Waldhorn**	Six Degrees...	Geoffrey/Detective	A1008
Patrick **Waldron**	Don't Play With Love	The Baron	A329
Carrie **Wale**	The Marvellous Boy	Sarah Chatterton	A690
Andrew **Walker**	Buddy	Ensemble	A168
Angelie **Walker**	Carmen Jones	Card Player	A189
Donald **Walker**	Beyond Reasonable Doubt	Court Attendant	A113
	Beyond Reasonable Doubt	Dr Weedon	A114
	Fifteen Streets	Joe Kelly/Doctor	A403
	Shadowlands	As Cast	A985
James **Walker**	As You Like It	Sir Oliver Martext	A67
	The Taming Of The Shrew	Landlord/Pedant	A1068
	The Winter's Tale	Dion	A1214
Joan **Walker**	Master and Margarita	Hella/Natasha	A693
Josie **Walker**	The Sound Of Music	A Postulant	A1033
Lucinda **Walker**	The Sound Of Music	Marta	A1033
Mark **Walker**	Starlight Express	Greaseball	A1043
Matthew **Walker**	Wit's End	Skalozub	A1216
Michael **Walker**	Beyond Reasonable Doubt	Anthony Blair-Booth, Q.C	A113
	What the Butler Saw	Dr Prentice	A1197
Pauline **Walker**	The Sound Of Music	Frau Schmidt	A1033
Rudolph **Walker**	The Odyssey	Blind Blue	A802
Timothy **Walker**	La Bete	Prince Conti	A587
	Why Things Happen	Greg	A1206
Zena **Walker**	Importance of Being	Lady Bracknell	A532
Kim **Wall**	Dick Whittington	As Cast	A312
Tamara **Wall**	The Sound Of Music	Louisa	A1033
Claire **Waller**	Beauty And The Beast	Beauty	A100
Tim **Wallers**	The Recruiting Officer	Mr Worthy	A897
Elizabeth **Walley**	Commodities	Catherine Brooks	A244
Bill **Wallis**	The Alchemist	Tribulation	A28
	Twelfth Night	Sir Toby Belch	A1152
Barry **Wallman**	Elisabeth II	As Cast	A361
Brian **Wallman**	Seven Doors	As Cast	A978
Angela **Walsh**	Roaring Girl's Hamlet	Gertrude	A925
Bradley **Walsh**	Aladdin	Wishey-Washey	A18
Dermot **Walsh**	The Revenger's Tragedy	Duke	A908
	The Rivals	Sir Anthony Absolute	A918
Genevieve **Walsh**	Bazaar and Rummage	Margaret	A94
Gerry **Walsh**	Cherry Orchard		A203
Valerie **Walsh**	Stepping Out	Maxine	A1046
Virginia **Walshaw**	While The Sun Shines	Hostess	A1201
Harriet **Walter**	Three Birds Alighting	Biddy	A1100
Simon **Walter**	Too Much Too Young	As Cast	A1127
Ewart **James Walters**	New World and Tears	Zelin/Heaven Duncanquellin	A780
John **Walters**	The House Of Stairs	Ivor/Maurice Esmond	A513
Sam **Walters**	Cerceau	Pasha	A195
Wally **Walters**	The Imaginary Invalid	Dr Diaforus	A529
Ali **Walton**	Peculiar People	Susan Baynard	A846
Clive **Walton**	June Moon	As Cast	A567
Kevin **Walton**	Assassins	As Cast	A73
Les **Want**	Some Like It Hot	Cop 2	A1025
Michael **Warburton**	Spring Awakening	Moritz, Herr Stiefel	A1037

Name	Play	Part	Ref
Howard **Ward**	Night of the Iguana	Hank	A785
Margaret **Ward**	Liaisons Dangereuses	Madame de Rosmonde	A610
Paddy **Ward**	The Kingfisher	Hawkins	A582
	Tons Of Money	Giles	A1125
Simon **Ward**	Don't Dress For Dinner	Robert	A331
Titania **Ward**	Stand Before You Naked	As cast	A525
Samantha **Warden**	A Midsummer Night's ..	Lady/Moth	A720
Gemma **Wardle**	Les Miserables	Ensemble	A611
Derek **Waring**	Witness For The Prosecution	Sir Wilfred	A1218
George **Waring**	Lettice & Lovage	Mr Bardolph	A614
Nick **Waring**	The Bells	Notary	A108
	Hay Fever	Simon	A481
	School for Scandal	Sir Benjamin Backbite	A957
	The Seagull	Konstantin	A962
Maria **Warner**	Frankenstein	Caroline Frankenstein/Mary	A415
	The Tempest	Gonzalo/Iris	A1083
Nicholas **Warnford**	A Midsummer Night's ..	Lord/Fairy Lord	A720
Anthony **Warren**	Killing Passion	Shridaman	A574
Marcia **Warren**	Happy Families	Liz Hickman	A476
	She Stoops To Conquer	As Cast	A991
Don **Warrington**	Hecuba	Polymestor	A488
Patrick **Warrington**	Twelfth Night	Sir Andrew Aguecheek	A1151
Richard **Warwick**	Cain	Adam	A181
	King Lear In New York	Alec	A580
Daniel **Washington**	Biko	Biko	A121
Jill **Washington**	The Mikado	Maid	A722
Jack **Waters**	As You Like It	Courtier	A67
	The Taming Of The Shrew	Rupert Llewellyn	A1068
Jan **Waters**	The Sound Of Music	Elsa Schraeder	A1033
Gwen **Watford**	Woman Of No Importance	Lady Hunstanton	A1230
Jason **Watkins**	The Rivals	Capt. Jack Absolute	A919
Roger **Watkins**	Beauty and the Beast	The Father	A99
	Prin	Director of Education	A876
Deborah **Watling**	Murder By Misadventure	Emma	A755
Dilys **Watling**	Bazaar and Rummage	Bell-Bell	A94
	Macbeth	Lady Macbeth	A658
Giles **Watling**	Witness For The Prosecution	Leonard Vole	A1218
Jack **Watling**	Our Song	Charles	A833
Andrew **Watson**	Blues for Mr Charlie	Ralph	A143
Colin **Watson**	La Ronde	(Two-hander)	A589
Derwent **Watson**	Happy Days	Willie	A475
Emily **Watson**	A Jovial Crew	Beggar	A561
	The Taming Of The Shrew	Mrs Ruth Banks Ellis	A1068
Fiona **Watson**	Metamorphosis	Mrs Samsa	A714
Julia **Watson**	Six Fools	As Cast	A1009
June **Watson**	Billy Liar	Alice Fisher	A122
Lydia **Watson**	Strange Domain	Yvonne	A1055
Michael **Watson**	Molecatcher's Daughter	Leading Roles	A729
Moray **Watson**	Body And Soul	As Cast	A146
Timothy **Watson**	Far From The Madding Crowd	Francis Troy	A397
	Penny for a Song	As Cast	A848
Tom **Watt**	Hobson's Choice	Will Mossop	A500

Name	Play	Part	Ref
	Scrooge the Musical	Bob Cratchit	A1039
Guy **Oliver Watts**	Hot Stuff	As Cast	A508
Sally **Watts**	All My Sons	Sue Bayliss	A32
Helen **Way**	Cats	Bombalurina	A194
Carl **Wayne**	Blood Brothers	Narrator	A131
Dig **Wayne**	Five Guys Named Moe	Nomax	A407
Dorothy **Wayne**	Turned Out Nice Again	Beryl Formby	A1145
Steven **Wayne**	Cats	George	A194
Andrew **Wear**	Richard III	Murderer	A912
	Spring and Port Wine	Wilfred Crompton	A1036
Philip **Weaver**	The Last Carnival	Antoine	A598
Anthony **Webb**	Body And Soul	As Cast	A146
Danny **Webb**	Back Up The Hearse	Steve	A84
	Death and the Maiden	Gerardo	A293
Christopher **Webber**	Wit's End	Famusov	A1216
David **Webber**	Merchant of Venice	Prince of Morocco	A708
	The Road	Say Tokyo Kid	A921
	Smile Orange	As Cast	A1017
Michael **Webber**	Ten In A Bed		A1086
Sian **Webber**	Haunted Hotel	Maria Cavenna	A479
	The Maintenance Man	Diana	A674
Kal **Weber**	Fool for Love	Martin	A411
Gary **Webster**	Alfie	Alfie	A30
	Cinderella	Prince	A221
Henry **Webster**	'Tis Pity She's A Whore	Citizen/Bandit	A1114
	Two Gents Of Verona	As Cast	A1154
Jeff **Webster**	Brace Up!	As Cast	A156
Leonard **Webster**	Peculiar People	Thomas Carter	A846
	Talk Of The Steamie	Andy	A1065
Paul **Webster**	The Changeling	Alibius	A197
	The Merry Wives Of Windsor	Sir Hugh Evans	A713
	The Taming Of The Shrew	Gremio	A1068
Stefan **Weclawek**	The Winter's Tale	Mamillius	A1214
Helen **Weir**	Beyond Reasonable Doubt	Lady Metcalfe	A113
Jonathan **Weir**	The Blue Angel	Lutz	A138
Ryan **Weir**	The Winslow Boy	Ronnie Winslow	A1213
Trudy **Weiss**	Toronto, Mississippi	As Cast	A1129
Fiona **Welburn**	Northern Trawl	Maureen	A797
Josephine **Welcome**	House Of The Spirits		A514
Hilary **Welles**	Evening With Gary L.	Birgitta	A382
Biddy **Wells**	The Night Before The Morning After		A782
	Romeo And Juliet	As Cast	A938
	The Threepenny Opera	Polly Peachum	A1109
	Two Gents Of Verona	As Cast	A1154
Colin **Wells**	Pelican	As Cast	A847
	Summer Lightning	Pilbiam	A1058
John **Wells**	Travel With My Aunt	As Cast	A1134
Anna **Welsh**	Eight to the Bar	As Cast	A356
Timothy **Welton**	Beyond Reasonable Doubt	Clerk of the Court	A113
	Dancing at Lughnasa	Gerry	A275
	Tons Of Money	James Chesterman	A1125
	The Winslow Boy	John Watherstone	A1213
Lawrence **Werber**	Grapes of Wrath	Pa	A454
	The Writing Game	Leo Rafkin	A1242
Roy **Weskin**	Hamlet	Claudius	A467
Peter **Wessen**	Lettice & Lovage	Surly Man	A614

Name	Play	Part	Ref
Alexander **West**	Taming Of The Shrew	Gremio	A1070
Karen **West**	Rocky Horror Show	Columbia	A933
Samuel **West**	Cain	Cain	A181
	The Sea	Willy Carson	A961
Sara **West**	Les Miserables	Ensemble	A611
Alan **Westaway**	Measure For Measure	Attendant	A702
	Merchant of Venice	Solanio	A708
David **Westbrook**	Hamlet	Polonius Gravedigger	A463
	King Lear	Edgar/France	A577
David **Westhead**	The Changeling	Antonio	A197
	A Jovial Crew	Randall	A561
	The Odyssey	Nestor	A802
	Tamburlaine The Great	Cosroe	A1067
George **Westhead**	All My Sons	George Deever	A33
Geoff **Westoby**	Ghosts	Pastor Manders	A432
David **Weston**	In Praise Of Love		A536
Debora **Weston**	Revenger's Tragedy	Duchess	A909
Steve **Weston**	Saint Oscar	Edward Carson	A949
Alec **Westwood**	Dragon	As Cast	A341
Valerie **Weyland**	My Blood on Glass	As Cast	A761
Jonathan **Whaley**	The Invisible Man	M.C.	A547
Denise **Wharmby**	Leonardo	As Cast	A608
John **Wheatley**	The Secret Rapture	Irwin	A968
Thomas **Wheatley**	Master and Margarita	Woland	A693
	Penny for a Song	As Cast	A848
Gary **Whelan**	Wexford Trilogy	Stapler	A1194
Jo-Leigh **Whelan**	Starlight Express	Volta/Sleeper	A1043
Stephen **Whinnery**	Chasing The Hypnotist	As Cast	A201
Andy **Whipp**	Roberto Calvi	As Cast	A926
Paul **Whitaker**	Starlight Express	As Cast	A1043
Harriet **Whitbread**	Stand Before You Naked	As Cast	A525
Peter **Whitbread**	The Family Reunion	Dr. Warburton	A394
Philip **Whitchurch**	A Month In The Country	As Cast	A736
	Stitched Up	Roger Drinkwater	A1050
Ali **White**	Double Dealer	As Cast	A335
	Pygmies In The Ruins		A887
Catherine **White**	Annie Get Your Gun	Jessie	A51
	Square Rounds	As Cast	A1038
Celia **White**	The Ballroom	As Cast	A1091
David **Andrew White**	Grand Hotel	Jimmy	A453
Gillian **White**	Twelfth Night	Maria	A1151
Jacinta **White**	Dick Whittington	Alice Fitzwarren	A308
Kerryann **White**	The Invisible Man	Millie	A547
Mark **White**	Moby Dick	English Captain	A728
Matthew **White**	The Card (A musical)	Parsloe	A187
	Merrily We Roll Along	As Cast	A711
Sharon **White**	No 3 Pied Piper Street	The Pied Piper	A788
	Some Like It Hot	Dolores	A1025
Lynn **Whitehead**	Barnstormers	Sarah Hodgson/Lady Mouthful	A92
	In The Midnight Hour	Beattie	A537
Toby **Whitehouse**	Devil's Only Sleeping	Bill Jinx	A303
Janet **Whiteside**	Blithe Spirit	Mrs Bradman	A127
	Martin Chuzzlewit	Multiple Roles	A689
June **Whitfield**	Babes in the Wood	Fairy Tinkle	A79
Melvin **Whitfield**	Carmen Jones	Worker	A189
	Carousel	As Cast	A190
Diane **Whitley**	Raving Beauties	Karen	A893
Peter **Whitman**	Merchant of Venice	Shylock	A708
Nigel **Whitmey**	Revenger's Tragedy	Hippolito	A909
Richard **Whitmore**	Chitty Bang Bang	The Baron	A208

Name	Play	Part	Ref
Tim **Whitnall**	Good Rockin' Tonite	Cliff Richard	A449
Benjamin **Whitrow**	The Merry Wives Of Windsor	Falstaff	A713
	The Winter's Tale	Camillo	A1214
Henrietta **Whitsun Jones**	Feed	Stephanie/Stella	A399
Sally **Whittaker**	Taste of Honey	Jo	A1075
Jane **Whittenshaw**	It's A Girl	Mina	A549
Christopher **Whittingham**	The Deep Blue Sea	Mr Miller	A140
	Confusions	Gosforth/Harry/Mr Pearce etc	A246
Matthew **Whittle**	The Jungle Book	As Cast	A568
	Pelican	As Cast	A847
	Summer Lightning	Hugo/Mason/Sir Gregory Parsloe	A1058
William **Whymper**	Beyond Reasonable Doubt	Anthony Blair-Booth QC	A114
	Shadowlands	As Cast	A985
Stephen **Whyte**	On Golden Pond	Billy Ray	A809
Graham **Wicinskj**	Endgame	As Cast	A368
Jeffry **Wickham**	An Ideal Husband	Lord Caversham	A528
Rupert **Wickham**	Three Musketeers	D'Artagnan	A1106
Steven **Wickham**	The Pope And The Witch	Understudy to Pope	A870
Victoria **Wicks**	As You Like It	Rosalind	A69
Richard **Wigfield**	Tess Of The D'Urbervil	Abraham	A1089
Peter **Wight**	Grace	Gavin Driver	A452
	Murmuring Judges	The Rt Hon Kevin Cumberland MP	A758
Andrew **Wightman**	Little Shop Of Horrors	Seymour	A632
Christopher **Wild**	Fiddler On The Roof	Fyedka	A401
John **Wild**	Comedy of Errors	Antipholus	A240
	Jolly Potters	As Cast	A557
Yasmin **Wilde**	Light in the Village	Sida	A622
David **Wilder**	Barnum	As Cast	A93
Carolyn **Wildi**	Breathless	Mina	A160
Rebecca **Wildish**	Wind In The Willows	Portly	A1211
Ian **Angus Wilkie**	A Better Day	Kier Hardie	A111
Ashley **Wilkinson**	Carmen Jones	Husky Miller	A189
Caroline **Wilkinson**	Name	As Cast	A772
Chris **Wilkinson**	Seagull	Peter	A963
Tara **Wilkinson**	Starlight Express	As Cast	A1043
Tom **Wilkinson**	King Lear	King Lear	A579
Paul **Willcocks**	Elephant	As Cast	A359
Toyah **Willcox**	The Choice		A209
	Memoirs of a Survivor	As Cast	A705
Dave **Willetts**	Les Miserables	Jean Valjean	A613
Shelly **Willetts**	Tess Of The D'Urbervil	Tess	A1089
Algernon **Williams**	Starlight Express	Rocky 2	A1043
Andrew **Williams**	Custer's Last Stand	Sheridan	A264
	Les Miserables	Ensemble	A611
Annabelle **Williams**	Carmen Jones	Card Player	A189
Bernadene **Williams**	Barnum	As Cast	A93
David **Williams**	Tess Of The D'Urbervil	Crick	A1089
Don **Williams**	Don Juan	Sganarelle	A327
	Goodnight Mr Tom	As Cast	A450
Gareth **Williams**	Macbeth	Seyton	A655
	The Tempest	Sebastian	A1082
Guy **Williams**	The Winter's Tale	Lord	A1214
Heather **Williams**	Epsom Downs	Maragret	A375
	Give You A Good Time	Lou	A437
	Lovers	The Woman	A647

Name	Play	Part	Ref
Jax Williams	Telling Tales	As Cast	A1081
Joan Carol Williams	Children Of Lesser God	Lydia	A206
John Williams	Ghosts	Jacob	A432
Jonathan Williams	Wit's End	The Prince	A1216
Kate Williams	Goin' Local	Nora	A442
	Talk Of The Steamie	Margaret	A1065
La Verne Williams	New World and Tears	Palca/The Devil Queen Isabella	A780
Maynard Williams	Starlight Express	As Cast	A1043
Nigel Williams	Beauty And The Beast	The Beast	A98
Olivia Williams	Bulldog Drummond	Phyllis	A171
Paul Williams	Endgame	As Cast	A368
Rory Williams	Starlight Express	Rocky 3	A1043
Sabra Williams	Enemy To The People	As Cast	A369
Sian Williams	Endangered Species	As Cast	A367
Simon Williams	Natural Causes	Walter	A773
Stuart Williams	Relative Values	The Admiral	A899
Sylvester Williams	Armed And Dangerous	As Cast	A59
Teohna Williams	Beauty and the Beast	Clarissa	A99
	The School For Scandal	Lady Teazle	A956
Dean Williamson	In The Midnight Hour	Creech	A537
Gary Williamson	Hecuba	Guard	A488
Jerome Willis	Killers	As Cast	A573
Johnson Willis	Julius Caesar	Artemidorus	A564
	The Threepenny Opera	Walter	A1109
Nuala Willis	Medea	The Chorus	A704
Richard Willis	Tess Of The D'Urbervil	Alec D'Urberville	A1089
David Willoughby	Animal Farm	Ensemble	A49
	Cyrano De Bergerac	Christian	A268
Bo Wills	Elvis - the Musical	Elvis	A362
Gary Wilmot	Carmen Jones	Joe	A189
	Me And My Girl	Bill Snibson	A698
Jonathan Wilmot	Bloody Poetry	Shelley	A137
	Spring Awakening	Hanschen, Herr Gabor	A1037
Victoria Wilmott	Androcles And The Lion		A45
Blair Wilson	Carmen Jones	Joe	A189
Britt Wilson	The Cotton Club	Andy Chambers	A250
Donna Wilson	Good Morning Bill	Sally Smith M.D.	A447
Esther Wilson	King Lear	Goneril	A578
Holly Wilson	Dangerous Obsession	As Cast	A278
	Reflected Glory	Susan Davis	A898
Judy Wilson	My Mother Said	Margaret	A767
K C Wilson	Grand Hotel	Preysing	A453
Monique Wilson	Miss Saigon	Kim	A727
Robert Wilson	42nd Street	As cast	A2
Sean Wilton	Lust	Sparkish	A650
Terence Wilton	'Tis Pity She's A Whore	Richardetto	A1114
	Two Gents Of Verona	Duke of Milan	A1154
Deborah Winckles	The Virtuoso	Mrs Flirt	A1176
Angela Windham-Lewis	Courting Winnona	Thelma Seager	A255
David Windle	Turned Out Nice Again	Ken from BBC	A1145
Ann Windsor	Goodnight Mr Tom	As Cast	A450
Barbara Windsor	Cinderella	Fairy Godmother	A220
	Music Hall		A759
Frank Windsor	Charley's Aunt	Colonel Sir Francis Chesney,	A200
Mark Wing-Davey	The Guardsman	A Critic	A461
Peter Wingfield	Game of Love & Chance	As Cast	A425
Michael Winsor	A Midsummer Night's Dream	As Cast	A717
Ben Winston	Macbeth	Young Macduff	A653
Sophia Winter	Dick Whittington	Alice Fitzwarren	A309
Sophia Winter	Leonardo	As Cast	A608
Bob Wisdom	Hapgood	Wates	A472
Anthony Wise	Grope	Bjorn Toulouse	A460
Ernie Wise	Sleeping Beauty	As Cast	A1012
Greg Wise	The Recruiting Officer	Captain Plume	A897
Michael Wisher	Savage Storm	As Cast	A952
	Six Fools	As Cast	A1009
Helene Witcombe	Les Miserables	Innkeeper's Wife	A611
Googie Withers	On Golden Pond	Ethel Thayer	A808
Rita Wolf	Beauty and the Beast	Beauty	A99
Emil Wolk	The Recruiting Officer	Captain Brazen	A897
Mark Womack	Romeo and Juliet	Tybalt	A936
	A View From The Bridge	Marco	A1172
Claire Wong	Madame Mao's Memories	Madame Mao	A667
Jade Wong	Miss Saigon	Tam	A727
Nigel Wong	Carmen Jones	Slappy	A189
Anne Wood	A Swell Party	As Cast	A1060
Jane Wood	Prisoner's Pumpkin	Sue	A879
Janine Wood	Penny for a Song	As Cast	A848
Ron Wood	When The Past Is Still	Robert Giles	A1199
Andrew Woodall	Murmuring Judges	First prisoner	A758
	Weldon Rising	As Cast	A1192
Ed Woodall	Life Support	As Cast	A621
Robert Woodall	Strange Domain	M. Seurel	A1055
Keith Woodason	Othello	Cassio	A827
	The School For Scandal	Joseph Surface	A956
Wendy Woodbridge	Carousel	As Cast	A190
Nicholas Woodeson	Berlin Bertie	Berlin Bertie	A109
Ann Woodfield	Barnum	As Cast	A93
Keith Woodhams	New World and Tears	King Ferdinand Idolatry/Aute	A780
Albie Woodington	The Alchemist	Drugger	A28
	Amphibians	Dribbler	A40
	Columbus	Juan Sanchez	A237
	Henry IV Part 2	Pistol	A493
Aubrey Woods	Joseph...	Jacob	A559
Darren Woods	42nd Street	As cast	A2
Eli Woods	Aladdin	Chinese Policeman	A18
John Woodvine	Dancing At Lughnasa	Jack	A274
	Macbeth	Duncan/Porter	A655
	The Tempest	Prospero	A1082
Mary Woodvine	Hecuba	Chorus	A488
Edward Woodward	A Dead Secret	Frederick	A289
Michael Woodward	Ghost Sonata	Bengtsson	A431
Peter Woodward	Bulldog Drummond	Bulldog	A171
	The Last Carnival	Victor Delafontaine	A598
Sarah Woodward	The Sea	Rose Jones	A961
Tim Woodward	Medea	Jason	A704
Karl Wooley	Julius Caesar	Carpenter	A564
Emily Woolf	Sex III	One-Woman Show	A980
Debbie Woolley	Angels & Amazons	As Cast	A48
James Woolley	Fallen Angels	Fred Sterroll	A391
Karl Woolley	Comedy of Errors	Dromio	A240
	Hobson's Choice	Albert Prosser	A499
	Jolly Potters	As Cast	A557
	Snow Queen	Kai	A1021
	Turkey Time	Luke Meate	A1144
Raymond Woolley	Bright & Bold Design	Raymond Parker	A161
Joanne Wooton	Shakers	Carol	A987

Name	Play	Part	Ref
David **Worley**	Barnum	As Cast	A93
Alexandra **Worrall**	Valentine's Day	Mabel	A1165
Julia **Worsley**	Les Miserables	Ensemble	A613
Victoria **Worsley**	Nervous Women	Celia	A776
	Wizard of Oz	As Cast	A1224
Kate **Worth**	Liar Liar	As Cast	A616
Jonathan **Wrather**	Lulu	Alva	A648
Christopher **Wren**	Cinderella	Prince Charming	A220
Steven **Wren**	Little Shop Of Horrors	Orin	A632
	On Golden Pond	Billy Ray Jnr	A809
Angus **Wright**	The Dybbuk	Second Batlon	A349
	Hamlet	As Cast	A466
	Henry IV Part 1	Archibald	A492
	Henry IV Part 2	Peter Bullcalf	A493
Bernard **Wright**	Comedy Of Errors	As Cast	A241
Chris **Wright**	Merchant of Venice	Bassanio	A708
	Taming of the Shrew	Petruchio	A1069
	Wizard of Oz	Hickory	A1222
	Working	As Cast	A1239
Derek **Wright**	Witness For The Prosecution	Mayhew	A1218
Michael **Wright**	Macbeth	Donalbain/Seyton	A653
Natalie **Wright**	Carousel	As Cast	A190
	Once Upon A Song	As Cast	A817
Nicola **Wright**	Iago	Emilia	A526
Philip **Wright**	The Best Man	Russell	A110
William **Wright**	It Runs In The Family	Leslie	A548
Bernard **Wrigley**	Aladdin Bolton	Abanazar	A27
Philip **Wrigley**	Merrily We Roll Along	As Cast	A711
Leo **Wringer**	Rosmersholm	Peder Mortensgaard	A939
	The Winter's Tale	Camillo	A1215
Peter **Wyatt**	Penny for a Song	As Cast	A848
Tessa **Wyatt**	The Chalk Garden	Olivia	A196
	Pig In A Poke	Martha	A859
Michael **Wyeth**	Valentine's Day	Morris	A1165
Paul **Wyett**	Billy Liar	Billy Fisher	A122
	Murmuring Judges	Keith Machin	A758
Ken **Wynne**	Twelfth Night	Feste	A1152
	The Virtuoso	Snarl	A1176
Michael **Wynne**	Androcles And The Lion		A45
Mark **Wynter**	Cats	Asparagus	A194
Jason **Yates**	Grapes of Wrath	Floyd	A454
	Playing by the Rules	Tony	A863
Louise **Yates**	My Mother Said...	Rosie Metcalfe	A766
	Nervous Women	Ali	A776
Marjorie **Yates**	All My Sons	Kate Keller	A33
	Glass Menagerie	Amanda	A440
	Stages	As Cast	A1042
Pauline **Yates**	Don't Rock The Boat	Mary	A330
Robert **Yeal**	Starlight Express	As Cast	A1043
Martin **Yeandle**	Happy As A Sandbag	As Cast	A473
Nelson **Yee**	Starlight Express	Krupp	A1043
David **Yelland**	An Ideal Husband	Sir Robert Chiltern	A527
	The Rules Of The Game	Guido	A943
Miltos **Yerolemou**	Metamorphosis	Chief Clerk/Lodger	A714
David **Yip**	White Woman Street	Nathaniel Yeshoev	A1202
Kati **Yla-Hokkala**	Gravity Swing	As Cast	A457
Daniel **York**	Hamlet	As Cast	A465
	Porcelain	John	A871
Eddie **York**	TO	As Cast	A1115
Edward **York**	Hobson's Choice	Timothy Wadlow	A499
Mark **York**	The English Kiss	Richard	A370
Amelia **Young**	Rimbaud And Verlaine	Cellist	A916
Benny **Young**	Six Fools	As Cast	A1009
Joe **Young**	Blood Brothers	Ensemble	A131
Jimmy **Yuill**	Coriolanus	As Cast	A248
Kirsty **Yuill**	End Of The Beginning	Various	A366
Richard **Zajdlic**	Turner's Crossing	Fraze	A1146
Kara **Zediker**	A Slip Of The Tongue	Teresa Kovac	A1016
Alexei **Zeitsev**	Stop in the Desert	As Cast	A1051
Matilda **Ziegler**	The Recruiting Officer	Melinda	A897
	Women Laughing	As Cast	A1235
Stephano **Zuki**	M. Butterfly	Kurogo 1	A651
Marjorie **Zuniga**	House Of The Spirits		A514

Produced exclusively for Plays & Players by SEARCHLINE

PLAYHOUSES

For a quick and easy reference guide, find your town and check which productions have been shown locally in 1992.

Listings show the month and year in which the play was in production, or if still in production ,the date to which it was booking at press time.

LONDON AREA

BARNET

Old Bull Arts

A738 *Moose* (3/92)
A510 *Hound* (4/92)
A258 *Crime of Love* (5/92)
A690 *The Marvellous Boy* (5/92)
A87 *Bag Dancing* (6/92)
A365 *The End Of The Tunnel* (10/92)
A953 *Scenic Flights* (10/92)
A1024 *The Solo Experience* (10/92)
A385 *Every Bit Of It* (12/92)

BATTERSEA

Bridge Lane Th

A133 *Blood Wedding* (3/92)
A324 *A Doll's House* (10/92)
A988 *Shame, Ignorance* (11/92)

BRENTFORD, MIDDX

Watermans

A589 *La Ronde* (3/92)
A1150 *Twelfth Night* (2-3/92)
A1104 *The Three Musketeers* (3-4/92)
A332 *The Dorm* (5/92)
A264 *Custer's Last Stand* (5/92)
A380 *Europeans* (7/92)
A639 *Lord of the Rings* (7-8/92)
A1051 *Stop in the Desert* (9/92)
A905 *Revelations* (9-10/92)
A747 *Mrs Columbus* (10/92)
A1088 *The Tender Husband* (11/92)
A865 *Playing The Wife* (11/92)
A307 *Dick Whittington* (12/92-1/93)

LONDON

Adelphi Th.

A699 *Me And My Girl* (2/85-93)

Albery Th.

A179 *The Cabinet Minister* (11/91-2/92)
A146 *Body And Soul* (5-6/92)
A868 *The Pocket Dream* (2-5/92)
A981 *Shades* (7/92-1/93)

Aldwych Th.

A250 *The Cotton Club* (1-6/92)
A1054 *Straight & Narrow* (6-9/92)
A917 *Little Voice* (10/92-2/93)

All Saints Arts

A273 *Dance Of Guns* (5/92)

Almeida Th.

A435 *The Gigli Concert* (1-2/92)
A477 *A Hard Heart* (2-4/92)
A943 *The Rules Of The Game* (5-6/92)
A704 *Medea* (9-10/92)
A789 *No Man's Land* (10-12/92)

Ambassadors Th.

A1111 *Thunderbirds FAB* (9/91-4/92)
A665 *Mad,Bad,And Dangerous* (5-7/92)
A420 *From A Jack To A King* (7/92-1/93)

Apollo Th.

A331 *Don't Dress For Dinner* (12/91-10/92)

Apollo Victoria

A1043 *Starlight Express* (3/84-2/93)

Arches Th.

A1166 *Valentine* (2/92)
A445 *Gone With The Wind II* (3-5/92)
A6 *Aba Daba Music Hall* (5-8/92)
A885 *Put That Light Out* (9-10/92)
A923 *Road To Casablanca* (10-11/92)
A215 *Christmas Rubbish* (11-12/92)
A101 *Beauty and the Bat* (1/93)

Arts Theatre

A147 *Body Talk* (2-4/92)
A470 *Hans C. Anderstories* (2-4/92)
A1086 *Ten In A Bed* (4/92)
A671 *The Magic Island* (2-3/93)
A550 *It's Not All Grimm* (2-4/93)
A1047 *Stig Of The Dump* (4-5/93)

Arts Theatre

A245 *The Complete Works* (3-10/92)

Attic Theatre

A1091 *The Ballroom* (4-5/92)
A585 *Kurt Weill Cabaret* (5-6/92)
A622 *Light in the Village* (6-7/92)

BAC

A451 *Gormenghast* (3-4/92)
A1190 *The Way of All Flesh* (4-5/92)
A684 *Manslaughter* (3-4/92)
A1081 *Telling Tales* (4-5/92)
A15 *Adult Child/Dead Child* (5/92)
A78 *Ay Carmela!* (5/92)
A409 *Flight To Finland* (6/92)
A87 *Bag Dancing* (6/92)
A1135 *Travelling Light* (7-8/92)
A955 *Schmucks* (7-8/92)
A824 *Orlando* (8/92)
A292 *Death And Dancing* (8-9/92)
A484 *Head-Rot Holiday* (10/92)
A800 *Obsession* (10/92)
A41 *An After Taste* (10/92)
A980 *Sex III* (10-11/92)
A413 *Forever Yours* (11/92)
A996 *Shoot The Women First* (12/92)
A560 *Josephine* (11/92-1/93)

BAC Studio 2

A843 *Paradise Garden* (6-7/92)
A165 *Broken Heads* (7-8/92)

Barbican Th.

A493 *Henry IV Part 2* (4-6/92)
A492 *Henry IV Part 1* (3-6/92)
A237 *Columbus* (7-9/92)
A28 *The Alchemist* (4-9/92)
A1095 *The Thebans* (8-11/92)
A938 *Romeo And Juliet* (6-11/92)
A1084 *The Tempest* (12/92)
A241 *Comedy Of Errors* (12/92)
A466 *Hamlet* (12/92-3/93)
A1154 *Two Gents Of Verona* (10/92-3/93)

Barbican/The Pit

A1114 *'Tis Pity She's A Whore* (4-6/92)
A1176 *The Virtuoso* (3-9/92)
A1229 *A Woman Killed With Kindness* (4-9/92)
A64 *Artists and Admirers* (10-11/92)
A40 *Amphibians* (8-11/92)
A349 *The Dybbuk* (7-11/92)
A434 *Gifts Of The Gorgon* (12/92-3/93)

A575 *King Baby* (1-3/93)

Barons Court Th.

A997 *Shout Across The River* (4-5/92)
A937 *Romeo and Juliet* (6-8/92)
A979 *Sex and Sadness* (8-9/92)
A731 *Moment of Madness* (8-9/92)
A596 *Lady of the Lilacs* (8-9/92)

Blackheath

A703 *Measure for Measure* (6/92)

Bloomsbury Th.

A141 *Blues Angels* (10/92)

Boulevard

A420 *From A Jack To A King* (2-5/92)
A370 *The English Kiss* (9-10/92)

Bush Th.

A267 *The Cutting* (2-3/92)
A313 *Digging for Fire* (3-4/92)
A1202 *White Woman Street* (4-5/92)
A869 *Pond Life* (6-7/92)
A857 *Phoenix* (7-8/92)
A554 *Jack's Out* (9/92)
A726 *Misogynist* (9-10/92)
A387 *Exile* (10/92)
A1194 *Wexford Trilogy* (11-12/92)

Cambridge Th.

A904 *Forbidden Planet* (9/89-1/93)

Canal Cafe Th.

A1055 *Strange Domain* (5-6/92)
A160 *Breathless* (7/92)
A1102 *Three Men in a Boat* (8/92)
A588 *La Muse* (8-9/92)
A913 *Richard's Cork Leg* (8-9/92)
A862 *The Player* (10/92)
A65 *As Time Goes By* (9-10/92)

Chelsea Centre

A511 *The Hour Of The Lynx* (4/92)
A155 *Boy's Own* (4-5/92)
A681 *Man Outside* (5-6/92)
A953 *Scenic Flights* (9/92)
A1024 *The Solo Experience* (11-12/92)

Chisenhale Gall.

A772 *Name* (10/92)

Clapham Common

A229 *Chinese State Circus* (10-11/92)

Cochrane Th

A921 *The Road* (2-3/92)
A1017 *Smile Orange* (4-5/92)
A774 *Necklaces* (10/92)
A644 *Love Space Demands* (10/92)
A1044 *State of Bewilderment* (1-2/93)

Cockpit Th.

A264 *Custer's Last Stand* (2-3/92)
A1225 *The Woman Destroyed* (2/92)
A1188 *Water Music* (9-10/92)
A931 *The Rock Station* (10-11/92)
A1141 *Trilby & Svengali* (11-12/92)

Collyer Hall Th.

A365 *The End Of The Tunnel* (10/92)

Comedy Th.

A1066 *Talking Heads* (1-3/92)
A870 *The Pope And The Witch* (4-5/92)
A302 *Dejavu* (6-8/92)
A1008 *Six Degrees...* (8-11/92)
A1139 *Trelawny Of The Wells* (12/92-1/93)

Court Th.

A828 *Othello* (7-8/92)
A517 *House of Bernarda Alba* (8/92)
A145 *Boardroom Shuffle* (9-10/92)

Criterion Th.

A371 *Ennio Marchetto* (10/92)
A677 *Making It Better* (10/92-1/93)
A725 *Misery* (12/92-3/93)

DOC Th. Club

A764 *My Heart's A Suitcase* (2/92)
A478 *The Hatchet Man* (3-4/92)
A946 *The Sacred Penman* (5-6/92)
A432 *Ghosts* (8-9/92)
A243 *Coming of Age* (9/92)
A654 *Macbeth* (9-10/92)
A715 *Metamorphosis* (10-11/92)
A823 *The Open Couple* (11-12/92)

Dominion

A36 *'Allo, 'Allo* (2-3/92)
A453 *Grand Hotel* (6-10/92)
A93 *Barnum* (12/92-1/93)

Donmar Warehouse

A73 *Assassins* (10/92-1/93)

Drill Hall

A48 *Angels & Amazons* (4-5/92)
A381 *EuroVision* (5-6/92)
A402 *Fierce Love* (6-7/92)
A218 *Christopher Street* (7-8/92)

Drury Lane Th.

A727 *Miss Saigon* (9/89-3/93)

Duchess Th.

A383 *Evening with Gary L.* (12/91-10/92)
A331 *Don't Dress For Dinner* (10/92-1/93)

Duke of York's

A293 *Death and the Maiden* (7/91-11/92)
A371 *Ennio Marchetto* (12/92)

Ecology Centre

A929 *Robin Hood* (2-3/92)
A1093 *The Refuge* (11/92)
A543 *Intimacy* (9/92-1/93)

Emerald Centre

A157 *Brand* (3/92)

Etcetera

A924 *Roadshow* (2-3/92)
A621 *Life Support* (2-3/92)
A524 *I Believe In Love* (3-4/92)
A662 *Macbett* (3-4/92)
A112 *Between the Lines* (4-5/92)
A871 *Porcelain* (5-6/92)
A504 *Horse-Radish* (5/92)
A123 *Billy the Kid* (5-6/92)
A844 *Passion of Marianne* (6-7/92)
A426 *Games* (7/92)
A692 *Massa* (7-8/92)
A969 *Section 2 Housing* (8/92)
A855 *Pharmaceutical* (8-9/92)
A333 *The Double D* (8-9/92)
A778 *New Man* (10-11/92)
A616 *Liar Liar* (10-11/92)
A1143 *Truth Games* (11/92)
A34 *All On Top* (11/92)
A1030 *Something Missing* (12/92)
A300 *Deceptions* (12/92)

Finborough Th.

A1129 *Toronto, Mississippi* (3-4/92)
A164 *Broken Folk* (4-5/92)
A455 *Grave Dancer* (5-6/92)
A1072 *Tango 'Til You're Sore* (6-7/92)
A734 *Monster He Made Me* (8/92)
A1199 *When The Past Is Still* (9-10/92)
A926 *Roberto Calvi* (10-11/92)

Fortune Th.

A1227 *The Woman In Black* (6/89-1/93)

French Institute

A329 *Don't Play With Love* (7/92)
A735 *Monstre, Va!* (10/92)

Garrick Th.

A274 *Dancing At Lughnasa* (12/91-1/93)

Gate Th. Club

A256 *Crackwalker* (3-4/92)
A408 *Flamingo* (4-5/92)
A85 *Bad Blood* (5/92)
A392 *False Servant* (6-7/92)
A1080 *Television Programme* (7-8/92)
A978 *Seven Doors* (8/92)
A488 *Hecuba* (9-10/92)
A515 *House of Bernarda Alba* (10-11/92)
A361 *Elisabeth II* (11-12/92)
A668 *Madness in Valencia* (12/92-1/93)

Globe Th.

A1032 *Sophisticated Ladies* (1-5/92)
A138 *The Blue Angel* (5-6/92)
A1165 *Valentine's Day* (9-10/92)

Globe Museum

A1151 *Twelfth Night* (11-12/92)

Grace Theatre

A1164 *Valdorama* (2/92)
A511 *The Hour Of The Lynx* (3/92)
A411 *Fool for Love* (7-8/92)
A659 *Macbeth* (10/92)

Greenwich Th.

A180 *Caesar And Cleopatra* (1-3/92)
A864 *Playing Sinatra* (3-4/92)
A249 *The Corn Is Green* (4/92)
A68 *As You Like It* (4-6/92)
A954 *Schippel, The Plumber* (6-7/92)
A743 *The Mother Tongue* (7-9/92)
A1203 *Who Shall I Be?* (9-10/92)
A569 *Just Between Ourselves* (10-12/92)
A878 *The Prisoner Of Zenda* (12/92-2/93)
A374 *Entertaining Mr Sloane* (2-3/93)
A378 *The Europeans* (3-4/93)

Hampstead Th.

A677 *Making It Better* (2-3/92)
A84 *Back Up The Hearse* (4-5/92)
A398 *The Fastest Clock...* (5-6/92)
A1028 *Someone Who'll Watch* (7-8/92)
A567 *June Moon* (9-10/92)
A631 *A Little Older* (10-11/92)
A452 *Grace* (12/92-1/93)

Haymarket
A103 Becket (10/91-3/92)
A486 Heartbreak House (3-6/92)
A1230 Woman Of No Importance (6-8/92)
A269 Cyrano De Bergerac (12/92-1/93)
Hen & Chickens
A39 American Buffalo (5-6/92)
A1174 Villain (6-7/92)
A1062 The Tailor-Made Man (10-11/92)
A314 Disobediently Yours (11-12/92)
Her Majesty's
A854 Phantom Of The Opera (10/86-9/93)
Holland Park Th.
A714 Metamorphosis (6/92)
A1195 What About Luv? (6/92)
A258 Crime of Love (6/92)
A577 King Lear (7/92)
A467 Hamlet (7/92)
A253 Country Wife (7/92)
Holloway Prison
A385 Every Bit Of It (12/92)
ICA
A1245 ...Changed The Wires (4/92)
A986 Shaker (4-5/92)
A326 Don Juan (5/92)
A31 Aliens 4 (10/92)
A363 Emanuelle Enchanted (10/92)
A1206 Why Things Happen (10/92)
A7 Abduction (11/92)
A182 Call Blue Jane (12/92)
A487 Heartless (12/92-1/93)
Jackson's Lane
A273 Dance Of Guns (4/92)
King's Head Th. Clu
A817 Once Upon A Song (2-3/92)
A196 The Chalk Garden (3-4/92)
A83 Baby Baby (5/92)
A856 Philadelphia Here I Come (5-7/92)
A591 La Voix Humaine (6/92)
A14 Adult Child/Dead Child (6/92)
A1128 Top of the Town (7/92)
A12 Acapulco (8-9/92)
A358 Elegies... (11-12/92)
La Bonne Crepe
A1027 Some...Atomic Zombie (2-3/92)
A75 The Author's Voice (4/92)
A506 Hostages and Hamsters (3-5/92)
A761 My Blood on Glass (5-6/92)
A315 A Distant Applause (9-10/92)
A135 Blood Whispers (10-11/92)
Lilian Baylis
A925 Roaring Girl's Hamlet (3-4/92)
A558 Jordan (4-5/92)
A1179 Voice of the Sea (8/92)
A365 The End Of The Tunnel (9/92)
A788 No 3 Pied Piper Street (10/92)
A648 Lulu (10-11/92)
A129 Blodeuwedd (11/92)
A463 Hamlet (12/92)
A577 King Lear (12/92)

Little Angel
A37 Amahal (1/92)
A228 Cindermouse (1/92)
A877 Prince And The Mouse (1-3/92)
A597 Lancelot The Lion (1-3/92)
A1210 Wild Night Of The Witches (3/92)
A792 Noah (4-5/92)
A1209 Wild Night Of The Witches (5/92)
A629 The Little Mermaid (9-10/92)
A676 Mak The Sheepstealer (10-11/92)
A227 Cindermouse (12/92-2/93)
A46 Angelo (12/92-2/93)
London Palladium
A559 Joseph... (6/91-1/93)
London Ark
A941 Ruby In The Dust (3/92)
A379 Europe my Country (5/92)
Lyric Ham'smith
A279 Dangerous Dolls-Mummys Little Girl (2/92)
A280 Dangerous Dolls-Soap Crazy (2-3/92)
A587 La Bete (1-3/92)
A176 Cabal and Love (3/92)
A1215 The Winter's Tale (4-5/92)
A87 Bag Dancing (5/92)
A87 Bag Dancing (5/92)
A638 Loot (5-6/92)
A563 A Judgement In Stone (6-7/92)
A8 Absent Friends (7-8/92)
A824 Orlando (9-10/92)
A670 Madras House (9-10/92)
A132 Blood Wedding (3-4/93)
Lyric Studio
A693 Master and Margarita (6-7/92)
A790 No Remission (7-8/92)
Lyric Studio
A1099 Thirteenth Night (10/92)
Lyric,Shaft.Ave.
A407 Five Guys Named Moe (10/90-1/93)
Man in the Moon
A1231 A Woman Plays ... (2/92)
A618 A Life In The Theatre (2/92)
A526 Iago (3/92)
A44 And Hunger For All (3/92)
A952 Savage Storm (3-4/92)
A154 Boy With Beer (4/92)
A1133 Traffic Hearts (6/92)
A1175 Vincent (8-9/92)
A1063 Taking of Liberty (8-9/92)
A1052 National Enquirer (7-9/92)
A993 She Ventures He Wins (8-9/92)
A1189 The Wax King (9-10/92)
A888 Queen Christina (10-11/92)
A184 The Candidate (11/92)
A1187 Watching And Weighting (12/92)
A1079 Telephonebelles (11-12/92)
Mermaid Th.
A861 Play Strindberg (2-3/92)
A204 Chester Mystery Plays (4-5/92)
A212 A Christmas Carol (12/92-1/93)

Mermaid Studio
A246 Confusions (4-5/92)
A1037 Spring Awakening (11/92)
Millfield Th.
A467 Hamlet (5/92)
A860 Pigspurt (12/92)
A552 Jack And The Beanstalk (12/92-1/93)
New End Th.
A653 Macbeth (2-3/92)
A66 As You Desire Me (3/92)
A1000 Signora Joyce (5/92)
A334 The Double Bass (4-5/92)
A431 Ghost Sonata (5-6/92)
A284 Daughters Of England (5-6/92)
A350 Dybbuk (6-7/92)
A244 Commodities (6-7/92)
A359 Elephant (7-8/92)
A884 Provoked Wife (8-9/92)
A1216 Wit's End (9-10/92)
A593 Lady Aoi (9-10/92)
A1053 Story of the Last (10-11/92)
A990 She Stoops To Conquer (11-12/92)
A347 The Duchess of Malfi (11-12/92)
New London Th.
A194 Cats (5/82-2/93)
North Peckham Ct
A694 Master Harold & The bo (11/92)
NT/Cottesloe
A627 The Little Clay Cart (3/92)
A1157 Uncle Vanya (3-4/92)
A775 Needles And Opium (4-6/92)
A422 Fuente Ovejuna (5-7/92)
A917 Little Voice (6-10/92)
A583 Kings (9-10/92)
A47 Angels In America (3-11/92)
A1056 Street of Crocodiles (8-12/92)
A122 Billy Liar (12/92-2/93)
A425 Game of Love & Chance (1-2/93)
A1042 Stages (11/92-2/93)
A285 The Day After Tomorrow (2/93)
A746 Mr A's Amazing Maze (2-3/93)
NT/Lyttelton
A961 The Sea (3-4/92)
A911 Richard III (5/92)
A153 Bourgeois Gentilhomme (4-8/92)
A785 Night of the Iguana (3-8/92)
A541 An Inspector Calls (9-10/92)
A669 Madness of George III (11/91-10/92)
A604 Le Baruffe Chiozzotte (10-11/92)
A1007 Six Characters (11/92)
A775 Needles And Opium (11/92)
A190 Carousel (12/92-3/93)
NT/Olivier
A1211 Wind In The Willows (3/92)
A758 Murmuring Judges (3-5/92)
A896 The Recruiting Officer (3-7/92)
A1038 Square Rounds (9-11/92)
A886 Pygmalion (4-11/92)
A718 A Midsummer Night's Dream (7-11/92)
A341 Dragon (10-11/92)
A541 An Inspector Calls (1-3/93)
A1138 Trelawny Of The Wells (2-3/93)

Offstage D/Stair
- A934 *Roman & Marys* (2-3/92)
- A525 *Stand Before You Naked* (3-4/92)
- A786 *Nightclub Puppets* (5/92)
- A95 *Beardsley* (6/92)
- A883 *The Professional* (11-12/92)

Old Red Lion Th.
- A396 *Fantasy Island* (1-2/92)
- A86 *Bad Girl* (2-3/92)
- A892 *Rat Play* (3-4/92)
- A255 *Courting Winnona* (6-7/92)
- A443 *The Golden Ass* (7-8/92)
- A283 *The Darling Family* (9-10/92)
- A546 *Invasion Werewolf* (10-11/92)
- A1009 *Six Fools* (11-12/92)

Old Vic
- A189 *Carmen Jones* (4/91-1/93)

Open Air Th.
- A594 *Lady Be Good* (7-9/92)
- A263 *Curse Of The Mummy* (8/92)
- A721 *A Midsummer Night's ..* (5-9/92)
- A71 *As You Like It* (6-9/92)

Palace Th.
- A613 *Les Miserables* (12/85-3/93)

Pentameters
- A421 *Frozen Chicken* (4-5/92)
- A353 *The Ecstacy* (11/92)
- A1034 *Speed-The-Plow* (11-12/92)

Phoenix Th.
- A131 *Blood Brothers* (7/88-3/93)

Piccadilly Th.
- A728 *Moby Dick* (2-7/92)
- A1200 *Which Witch* (10/92-4/93)

Players Th.
- A98 *Beauty And The Beast* (12/91-2/92)
- A600 *Late Joys* (2/92)

Playhouse
- A842 *Painting Churches* (1-2/92)
- A449 *Good Rockin' Tonite* (3-7/92)
- A548 *It Runs In The Family* (8/92-1/93)

Polka Th.
- A45 *Androcles And The Lion* (2-3/92)
- A891 *The Ransom & The Golden Chicken* (3-4/92)
- A664 *Mad Mash One* (4/92)
- A1249 *The Young Man Of Cury* (4/92)
- A539 *Indigo Mill* (4-6/92)
- A436 *Giraffe, Pelly, & Me* (6-8/92)
- A344 *Dreams of Anne Frank* (10-11/92)
- A1221 *Wizard of Oz* (11/92-2/93)
- A158 *Brave Magicians* (2-3/93)

Poly of E London
- A273 *Dance Of Guns* (5/92)

Prince Edward
- A1025 *Some Like It Hot* (3-6/92)
- A257 *Crazy For You* (2-9/93)

Prince of Wales Th.
- A72 *Aspects Of Love* (4/89-6/92)
- A449 *Good Rockin' Tonite* (7-11/92)
- A51 *Annie Get Your Gun* (11/92-2/93)

Purcell Room
- A1105 *The Three Musketeers* (8/92)

Queen's Th.
- A1001 *Sikulu* (4-7/92)
- A890 *Radio Times* (10/92-4/93)

Redbridge Centre
- A788 *No 3 Pied Piper Street* (11/92)

Riverside Std.
- A108 *The Bells* (1/92)
- A414 *Four Marys* (2/92)
- A860 *Pigspurt* (3/92)
- A339 *Down And Out...* (3-4/92)
- A457 *Gravity Swing* (4/92)
- A121 *Biko* (6/92)
- A465 *Hamlet* (9-10/92)
- A1236 *Women Of The Dust* (11/92)

Royal Court Th.
- A389 *Faith Healer* (1-2/92)
- A887 *Pygmies In The Ruins* (2-3/92)
- A109 *Berlin Bertie* (4-5/92)
- A1008 *Six Degrees...* (8-10/92)
- A871 *Porcelain* (8/92)
- A522 *Hush* (8-9/92)
- A945 *Sab* (9-10/92)
- A198 *The Changing Reason* (9-10/92)
- A390 *Faith Over Reason* (9-10/92)
- A235 *Colquhoun And MacBryde* (9-10/92)
- A779 *New Voices* (10/92)
- A1100 *Three Birds Alighting* (11-12/92)
- A579 *King Lear* (1-3/93)

Royalty Theatre
- A1082 *The Tempest* (11-12/92)
- A655 *Macbeth* (11-12/92)
- A624 *Lion Witch & Wardrobe* (12/92-1/93)

Rudolf Steiner
- A329 *Don't Play With Love* (7-8/92)
- A459 *Great God Brown* (9/92)

Saatchi Coll.
- A1184 *The War In Heaven* (9/92)

Sadler's Wells
- A1033 *The Sound Of Music* (6-9/92)

Seven Dials Ctre
- A70 *As You Like It* (11-12/92)

Shaftesbury Th.
- A853 *Phantom of the Opera* (12/91-3/92)
- A1016 *A Slip Of The Tongue* (4-8/92)
- A584 *Kiss of Spiderwoman* (10/92-1/93)

Spitalfields Mkt
- A1184 *The War In Heaven* (10/92)

LONDON N11

Springfield Th.
- A496 *His Brother's Keeper* (3-4/92)

LONDON

St Martin's Th.
- A744 *The Mousetrap* (11/52-92)

Strand Th.
- A449 *Good Rockin' Tonite* (1-3/92)
- A641 *Lost in Yonkers* (11/92-5/93)

Tabard Th.
- A316 *Doctor Faustus* (3/92)
- A521 *Howard Johnson* (3-4/92)
- A576 *King Lear* (4-5/92)
- A1244 *Wuthering Heights* (6/92)
- A38 *American Heart* (7-8/92)
- A660 *Macbeth* (9-10/92)

Th. Museum
- A372 *Enter The Tragic Muse* (3/92)
- A233 *Clown For A Day* (3/92)
- A519 *House That Henry Built* (3-4/92)
- A642 *Love* (4/92)
- A96 *Beardsley* (4-5/92)
- A13 *The Actor's Nightmare* (5-6/92)
- A1159 *Uncle Vanya* (6-8/92)
- A964 *The Seagull* (6-8/92)
- A950 *Salonika* (6-8/92)
- A841 *Pains of Youth* (6-8/92)
- A52 *Antigone* (6-8/92)
- A1006 *Sisters* (9/92)

Th. Upstairs
- A839 *Outside of Heaven* (1-3/92)
- A1026 *Some Singing Blood* (3-4/92)
- A845 *Patagonia* (5/92)
- A572 *Karate Billy...Home* (4-5/92)
- A1235 *Women Laughing* (9-10/92)
- A1192 *Weldon Rising* (11-12/92)
- A573 *Killers* (11/92)
- A686 *Marching For Fausa* (1-2/93)
- A836 *Out Of The Ordinary* (3-4/93)

The Courtyard
- A1092 *The Great Exhibition* (9/92)
- A410 *Flowers For Algernon* (10-11/92)

The Diorama
- A259 *Punishment Of Animals* (3-4/92)

The Grove
- A468 *Handsome,Handicapped..* (3/92)

The Link
- A484 *Head-Rot Holiday* (11/92)

The Vox Theatre
- A201 *Chasing The Hypnotist* (4-5/92)

Theatre Centre
- A1240 *World...Upside Down* (2-4/92)
- A617 *The Lie Of The Land* (2-4/92)

Theatro Technis
- A117 *Biboff* (9/92)

Tower Theatre
- A951 *Same Time Next Year* (10/92)
- A712 *Merry Wives Of Windsor* (11/92)
- A535 *In Celebration* (11/92)

Tricycle Th.
- A1178 *Viva Detroit* (2-3/92)
- A50 *Anna Karenina* (3-4/92)
- A87 *Bag Dancing* (5/92)
- A825 *Oscar* (5/92)
- A643 *Love and a Bottle* (6/92)
- A1156 *Una Pooka* (7-8/92)
- A424 *Gamblers* (9-10/92)
- A1142 *Trouble in Mind* (10-11/92)

Turtle Key Arts
- A695 *Mayor of Casterbridge* (6/92)

Turtle Key Arts
- A678 *Mamahuhu?* (7-8/92)
- A137 *Bloody Poetry* (9/92)

Vaudeville Th.
A1060 *A Swell Party* (10/91-3/92)
A898 *Reflected Glory* (4-6/92)
A755 *Murder By Misadventure* (7-9/92)
A1028 *Someone Who'll Watch* (9-12/92)
A567 *June Moon* (11/92-1/93)
Victoria Palace Th.
A169 *Buddy* (10/89-1/93)
Village Theatre
A323 *Doll's House* (5-6/92)
A384 *Everlasting Rose* (6/92)
A750 *Much Ado About Nothing* (9-10/92)
A729 *Molecatcher's Daughter* (11-12/92)
Waltham Forest
A273 *Dance Of Guns* (5/92)
Westminster Th.
A953 *Scenic Flights* (10/92)
White Bear
A1161 *Understanding The Dang* (6/92)
Whitehall Th.
A142 *Blues Brothers* (8/91-6/92)
A1035 *Spread A Little Happ* (6-7/92)
A755 *Murder By Misadventure* (9/92-1/93)
Wimbledon Th.
A933 *Rocky Horror Show* (2/92)
A1218 *Witness For The Prosecution* (3/92)
A1046 *Stepping Out* (3/92)
A94 *Bazaar and Rummage* (4/92)
A200 *Charley's Aunt* (5/92)
A1163 *Up 'N' Under* (6/92)
A1248 *You Must Be The Husband* (6/92)
A508 *Hot Stuff* (7/92)
A367 *Endangered Species* (9/92)
A803 *Office Party* (9-10/92)
A803 *Office Party* (9-10/92)
A473 *Happy As A Sandbag* (11/92)
A444 *Goldilocks* (12/92-1/93)
Wyndhams Th.
A915 *Ride Down Mt Morgan* (10/91-2/92)
A1054 *Straight & Narrow* (3-6/92)
A1134 *Travel With My Aunt* (11/92-3/93)
A856 *Philadelphia Here I Come* (7/92-11/93)
Young Vic Th.
A33 *All My Sons* (1-2/92)
A700 *Measure For Measure* (3-4/92)
A538 *In The Midnight Hour* (5-7/92)
A939 *Rosmersholm* (9-10/92)
A1020 *The Snow Queen* (11/92-1/93)
Young Vic Studio
A485 *Heart* (1/92)
RICHMOND
Georgian Theatre Royal
A463 *Hamlet* (7/92)
A679 *Man Cub* (7/92)
A459 *Great God Brown* (9/92)
A1088 *The Tender Husband* (10/92)
Orange Tree Th.
A974 *Self Portrait* (2-3/92)
A282 *The Dark River* (3-4/92)
A1204 *Who Was Hilary* (5/92)
A195 *Cerceau* (4-6/92)
A1103 *Three More Sleepless* (6/92)
A497 *His Majesty* (9-10/92)
A348 *Dutch Courtesan* (10-11/92)
A848 *Penny for a Song* (12/92-1/93)
A63 *The Artifice* (2-3/93)
A901 *Return of the Prodigal* (4-5/93)
Richmond Th.
A1230 *Woman Of No Importance* (2/92)
A807 *On Approval* (2/92)
A665 *Mad,Bad,And Dangerous* (3/92)
A724 *The Miser* (3/92)
A672 *The Magic Storybook* (3/92)
A507 *Hot Italian Nights* (3/92)
A607 *Leo In Love* (3-4/92)
A289 *A Dead Secret* (4/92)
A104 *Bedroom Farce* (4/92)
A513 *The House Of Stairs* (4-5/92)
A249 *The Corn Is Green* (5/92)
A999 *Sienna Red* (5/92)
A981 *Shades* (6/92)
A651 *M. Butterfly* (6/92)
A995 *Shirley Valentine* (6/92)
A655 *Macbeth* (6-7/92)
A1148 *Twelfth Night* (6-7/92)
A490 *The Heiress* (7-8/92)
A808 *On Golden Pond* (8/92)
A4 *70, Girls, 70* (8/92)
A159 *Breaking the Code* (8-9/92)
A994 *Sherlock Holmes* (9/92)
A830 *Otherwise Engaged* (9/92)
A1134 *Travel With My Aunt* (9/92)
A391 *Fallen Angels* (9-10/92)
A907 *Revenge* (10/92)
A907 *Revenge* (10/92)
A677 *Making It Better* (10/92)
A641 *Lost in Yonkers* (10/92)
A527 *An Ideal Husband* (10/92)
A481 *Hay Fever* (11/92)
A773 *Natural Causes* (11/92)
A275 *Dancing at Lughnasa* (11/92)
A1023 *Snow White* (12/92-1/93)
STRATFORD EAST
Th. Royal
A783 *Night in Tunisia* (1-2/92)
A442 *Goin' Local* (3-4/92)
A265 *Cut and Trust* (4-5/92)
A111 *A Better Day* (6-7/92)
A547 *The Invisible Man* (9-10/92)
A489 *Heer Ranjha* (10-11/92)
UXBRIDGE
The Nave
A574 *Killing Passion* (3/92)
A467 *Hamlet* (5/92)

SOUTH EAST ENGLAND

ALDERSHOT
West End Centre
A48 *Angels & Amazons* (4/92)
A1190 *The Way of All Flesh* (5/92)
A889 *Radio Times* (11/92)
A836 *Out Of The Ordinary* (2/93)
AYLESBURY
Limelight Th
A1232 *Woman Who Cooked* (4/92)
A1241 *World Upon The Moon* (9/92)
A1217 *Withering Looks* (10/92)
A418 *Frankie & Tommy* (10/92)
A385 *Every Bit Of It* (12/92)
BANBURY
Mill Theatre
A1130 *Tottering Towers* (10/92)
BASILDON
Towngate Th.
A672 *The Magic Storybook* (2/92)
A507 *Hot Italian Nights* (2/92)
A200 *Charley's Aunt* (3-4/92)
A1190 *The Way of All Flesh* (4/92)
A762 *My Cousin Rachel* (4-5/92)
A748 *Mrs Klein* (6/92)
BASINGSTOKE
Central Studio
A365 *The End Of The Tunnel* (10/92)
A388 *Experiment In Contra.* (10/92)
A88 *Ballad of Limehouse* (10/92)
A824 *Orlando* (11/92)
Haymarket Th.
A126 *Blithe Spirit* (1-2/92)
A733 *Monday After Miracle* (3/92)
A634 *Little Tramp* (4/92)
BATTLE
Battle Festival
A172 *Burbage and the Bard* (5/92)
BEDS.
Arts Centre
A953 *Scenic Flights* (10/92)
BRACKNELL
South Hill Park
A510 *Hound* (4/92)
A714 *Metamorphosis* (5/92)
A920 *Rivals* (10/92)
Wilde Th.
A1178 *Viva Detroit* (3-4/92)
A364 *Emperor's New Clothes* (7-8/92)
A463 *Hamlet* (9/92)
A577 *King Lear* (9/92)
A1217 *Withering Looks* (9/92)
A1117 *TO* (11/92)
BRECON
Guildhall Th.
A400 *Fern Hill* (6/92)
A463 *Hamlet* (9/92)
A577 *King Lear* (9/92)
A100 *Beauty And The Beast* (11/92)
A418 *Frankie & Tommy* (11/92)
A268 *Cyrano De Bergerac* (12/92)
BRIGHTON
Bhasvic Studio
A1180 *Voices at Her Elbow* (5/92)
Gardner Arts Ctr
A369 *Enemy To The People* (3/92)
A714 *Metamorphosis* (5/92)
A1105 *The Three Musketeers* (5/92)
A1237 *Women on Top* (6/92)

A122 *Billy Liar* (10/92)
A129 *Blodeuwedd* (11/92)
A418 *Frankie & Tommy* (12/92)

Pavillion

A14 *Adult Child/Dead Child* (6/92)

Th. Royal

A464 *Hamlet* (2/92)
A464 *Hamlet* (2/92)
A820 *One Over The Eight* (2/92)
A820 *One Over The Eight* (2/92)
A1054 *Straight & Narrow* (2/92)
A755 *Murder By Misadventure* (3/92)
A898 *Reflected Glory* (3/92)
A607 *Leo In Love* (3/92)
A146 *Body And Soul* (3-4/92)
A1230 *Woman Of No Importance* (4/92)
A94 *Bazaar and Rummage* (4/92)
A275 *Dancing at Lughnasa* (4/92)
A490 *The Heiress* (5/92)
A104 *Bedroom Farce* (5/92)
A4 *70, Girls, 70* (6/92)
A513 *The House Of Stairs* (6/92)
A330 *Don't Rock The Boat* (6/92)
A981 *Shades* (6/92)
A1134 *Travel With My Aunt* (7/92)
A1046 *Stepping Out* (7/92)
A1015 *Slice Of Saturday...* (7/92)
A651 *M. Butterfly* (7/92)
A1218 *Witness For The Prosecution* (7-8/92)
A1111 *Thunderbirds FAB* (8/92)
A808 *On Golden Pond* (8/92)
A294 *Death and the Maiden* (8/92)
A592 *Ladies' Night* (8/92)
A382 *Evening With Gary L.* (9/92)
A159 *Breaking the Code* (9/92)
A301 *The Decorator* (9/92)
A391 *Fallen Angels* (10/92)
A594 *Lady Be Good* (10/92)
A900 *Relatively Speaking* (11/92)
A1139 *Trelawny Of The Wells* (11/92)
A220 *Cinderella* (12/92-1/93)

Theatre Events

A292 *Death And Dancing* (10/92)
A960 *School Of Night* (10/92)

BROADSTAIRS

Island Arts

A48 *Angels & Amazons* (4/92)
A1178 *Viva Detroit* (5/92)
A129 *Blodeuwedd* (10/92)

BROMLEY

Churchill Th.

A762 *My Cousin Rachel* (1-2/92)
A490 *The Heiress* (2-3/92)
A1218 *Witness For The Prosecution* (3/92)
A193 *Dead Flamingo Dancer* (3-4/92)
A651 *M. Butterfly* (4/92)
A104 *Bedroom Farce* (5/92)
A942 *Rule Of The Game* (5-6/92)
A362 *Elvis - the Musical* (6-7/92)
A907 *Revenge* (8/92)
A1134 *Travel With My Aunt* (8/92)
A513 *The House Of Stairs* (9/92)
A1046 *Stepping Out* (9/92)
A759 *Music Hall* (10/92)
A834 *Out Of Order* (11/92)
A308 *Dick Whittington* (12/92-1/93)

BUNTINGFORD

Ward Freeman Sch

A268 *Cyrano De Bergerac* (11/92)

CANTERBURY

C'bury Cathedral

A771 *Mystery Plays* (7-8/92)

Gulbenkian Th.

A578 *King Lear* (3/92)
A748 *Mrs Klein* (4/92)
A1217 *Withering Looks* (10/92)
A122 *Billy Liar* (10/92)
A968 *The Secret Rapture* (10/92)
A268 *Cyrano De Bergerac* (11/92)

Marlowe Th.

A571 *Kafka's Dick* (3/92)
A745 *Mowgli - Enfant Loup* (3/92)
A755 *Murder By Misadventure* (3/92)
A116 *The BFG* (3-4/92)
A94 *Bazaar and Rummage* (4-5/92)
A651 *M. Butterfly* (5/92)
A200 *Charley's Aunt* (5/92)
A513 *The House Of Stairs* (5/92)
A1015 *Slice Of Saturday...* (6/92)
A275 *Dancing at Lughnasa* (6/92)
A4 *70, Girls, 70* (7/92)
A1218 *Witness For The Prosecution* (7/92)
A1041 *Stageland* (7-8/92)
A907 *Revenge* (9/92)
A391 *Fallen Angels* (11/92)

CHELMSFORD

Civic Th.

A473 *Happy As A Sandbag* (9/92)
A94 *Bazaar and Rummage* (10/92)
A803 *Office Party* (10/92)

CHELMSFORD

Riverside Leis.

A1172 *A View From The Bridge* (6/92)
A936 *Romeo and Juliet* (6/92)

CHICHESTER

Festival Th.

A1082 *The Tempest* (1/92)
A655 *Macbeth* (1/92)
A104 *Bedroom Farce* (3/92)
A248 *Coriolanus* (5-6/92)
A1168 *Venus Observed* (5-7/92)
A580 *King Lear In New York* (7-9/92)
A1046 *Stepping Out* (9-10/92)
A992 *She Stoops To Conquer* (8-10/92)
A159 *Breaking the Code* (10/92)

Minerva Studio

A697 *Me and My Friend* (6-8/92)
A338 *Double Take* (7-8/92)
A1177 *Vita and Virginia* (9/92)
A181 *Cain* (9/92)
A122 *Billy Liar* (9/92)

CLACTON

West Cliff Th.

A1031 *Song of Provence* (10/92)
A268 *Cyrano De Bergerac* (12/92)

COLCHESTER

Colchester Arts

A738 *Moose* (4/92)
A48 *Angels & Amazons* (6/92)
A953 *Scenic Flights* (10/92)
A87 *Bag Dancing* (11/92)

Mercury Th.

A1197 *What the Butler Saw* (1-2/92)
A113 *Beyond Reasonable Doubt* (2-3/92)
A1213 *The Winslow Boy* (3/92)
A1125 *Tons Of Money* (4/92)
A1208 *Wicks's Folly* (5/92)
A784 *Night Must Fall* (5-6/92)
A1107 *Three Musketeers* (8-9/92)
A811 *On The Piste* (9-10/92)
A403 *Fifteen Streets* (10/92)
A562 *Jubilee* (11/92)
A222 *Cinderella* (12/92-1/93)

Mercury Studio

A730 *Moll Flanders* (11/92)

Univ. of Essex

A578 *King Lear* (3/92)
A748 *Mrs Klein* (5/92)
A467 *Hamlet* (5/92)
A1206 *Why Things Happen* (11/92)

CRANLEIGH

Arts Centre

A268 *Cyrano De Bergerac* (11/92)

CRAWLEY

The Hawth

A578 *King Lear* (3/92)
A94 *Bazaar and Rummage* (3-4/92)
A755 *Murder By Misadventure* (4/92)
A748 *Mrs Klein* (5/92)
A933 *Rocky Horror Show* (5/92)
A738 *Moose* (5/92)
A714 *Metamorphosis* (6/92)
A1190 *The Way of All Flesh* (6/92)
A1046 *Stepping Out* (6/92)
A1218 *Witness For The Prosecution* (7/92)
A1218 *Witness For The Prosecution* (7/92)
A301 *The Decorator* (9/92)
A968 *The Secret Rapture* (9/92)
A752 *Much Ado About Nothing* (9-10/92)
A382 *Evening With Gary L.* (10/92)
A275 *Dancing at Lughnasa* (11/92)
A1044 *State of Bewilderment* (11/92)
A803 *Office Party* (2/93)
A836 *Out Of The Ordinary* (3/93)

CROYDON

Ashcroft Th.

A60 *Arms and the Man* (1-2/92)
A55 *Anybody for Murder?* (2-3/92)
A724 *The Miser* (3/92)
A275 *Dancing at Lughnasa* (3/92)
A1248 *You Must Be The Husband* (3/92)
A657 *Macbeth* (5/92)
A1145 *Turned Out Nice Again* (5/92)

A1218 *Witness For The Prosecution* (6/92)
A4 *70, Girls, 70* (6/92)
A1041 *Stageland* (7/92)
A159 *Breaking the Code* (9/92)
A787 *Nightmare* (9/92)
A592 *Ladies' Night* (9-10/92)
A513 *The House Of Stairs* (10/92)
A1090 *19th Hole* (11/92)
A479 *Haunted Hotel* (11/92)
A1022 *Snow White...* (12/92-1/93)

Warehouse Th.

A1104 *The Three Musketeers* (2-3/92)
A404 *Fighting For The Dunghill* (3-5/92)
A1146 *Turner's Crossing* (5-6/92)
A814 *On Top of the World* (6-7/92)
A960 *School Of Night* (9-10/92)
A110 *The Best Man* (10-11/92)
A328 *Don Quixote* (12/92-1/93)

DARTFORD

Orchard Th.

A933 *Rocky Horror Show* (3/92)
A513 *The House Of Stairs* (3/92)
A610 *Liaisons Dangereuses* (3-4/92)
A1046 *Stepping Out* (4-5/92)
A1218 *Witness For The Prosecution* (5/92)
A457 *Gravity Swing* (5/92)
A330 *Don't Rock The Boat* (6/92)
A116 *The BFG* (6-7/92)
A592 *Ladies' Night* (7/92)
A479 *Haunted Hotel* (10/92)
A362 *Elvis - the Musical* (11/92)
A803 *Office Party* (1/93)
A746 *Mr A's Amazing Maze* (5/93)

E. OXFORD

Pegasus Theatre

A1130 *Tottering Towers* (10/92)
A385 *Every Bit Of It* (11/92)

EASTBOURNE

Arts Centre

A1190 *The Way of All Flesh* (4/92)

Congress Th. The

A803 *Office Party* (11/92)

Devonshire Park Th.

A1248 *You Must Be The Husband* (3/92)
A880 *Private Lives* (3/92)
A200 *Charley's Aunt* (3/92)
A762 *My Cousin Rachel* (3-4/92)
A1218 *Witness For The Prosecution* (4/92)
A395 *The Fancy Man* (4/92)
A1041 *Stageland* (6/92)
A1132 *Towards Zero* (6/92)
A850 *Peril At End House* (6/92)
A1131 *Touch of Danger* (6/92)
A756 *A Murder Arranged* (6-7/92)
A501 *The Hollow* (7-9/92)
A970 *See How They Run* (7-9/92)
A927 *Robin* (12/92)

Winter Gardens

A94 *Bazaar and Rummage* (11/92)

EPSOM

Epsom Playhouse

A479 *Haunted Hotel* (9/92)

Playhouse

A767 *My Mother Said* (6/92)
A55 *Anybody for Murder?* (6/92)
A690 *The Marvellous Boy* (6/92)
A1149 *Twelfth Night* (10/92)

FAREHAM

Ashcroft Centre

A369 *Enemy To The People* (3/92)
A1178 *Viva Detroit* (4/92)
A1217 *Withering Looks* (10/92)
A578 *King Lear* (10/92)
A365 *The End Of The Tunnel* (10/92)
A824 *Orlando* (11/92)
A916 *Rimbaud And Verlaine* (11/92)
A385 *Every Bit Of It* (12/92)
A836 *Out Of The Ordinary* (2/93)
A213 *A Christmas Carol*

Fareham Community College

A418 *Frankie & Tommy* (11/92)

FARNHAM

Redgrave Th.

A1005 *Single Spies* (2-3/92)
A330 *Don't Rock The Boat* (4-5/92)
A683 *Mansfield Park* (5-6/92)
A995 *Shirley Valentine* (6/92)
A1163 *Up 'N' Under* (6-7/92)
A1251 *Your Sincerely* (7/92)
A1248 *You Must Be The Husband* (7/92)
A752 *Much Ado About Nothing* (7/92)
A881 *Private Lives* (8-9/92)
A239 *Comedy of Errors* (10/92)
A210 *Chorus of Disapproval* (11-12/92)
A498 *Hobbit* (12/92-1/93)

The Maltings

A369 *Enemy To The People* (3/92)

GAINSBOROUGH

Trinity Arts

A48 *Angels & Amazons* (4/92)
A767 *My Mother Said* (6/92)
A1088 *The Tender Husband* (10/92)
A467 *Hamlet* (11/92)

GRAYS

Thameside Th.

A1206 *Why Things Happen* (11/92)
A100 *Beauty And The Beast* (12/92)

GUILDFORD

Civic Hall

A657 *Macbeth* (6/92)

Yvonne Arnaud

A1066 *Talking Heads* (1/92)
A1230 *Woman Of No Importance* (1-2/92)
A807 *On Approval* (2/92)
A486 *Heartbreak House* (2-3/92)
A146 *Body And Soul* (3/92)
A724 *The Miser* (3/92)
A755 *Murder By Misadventure* (3-4/92)
A909 *Revenger's Tragedy* (4/92)
A249 *The Corn Is Green* (4-5/92)
A1029 *Something's Burning* (5/92)
A4 *70, Girls, 70* (5/92)
A808 *On Golden Pond* (6/92)
A942 *Rule Of The Game* (6/92)
A42 *John Mills* (6/92)
A1041 *Stageland* (6-7/92)
A907 *Revenge* (7/92)
A159 *Breaking the Code* (7-8/92)
A301 *The Decorator* (8/92)
A830 *Otherwise Engaged* (8-9/92)
A743 *The Mother Tongue* (9/92)
A641 *Lost in Yonkers* (9-10/92)
A1134 *Travel With My Aunt* (10/92)
A900 *Relatively Speaking* (10/92)
A1139 *Trelawny Of The Wells* (10-11/92)
A481 *Hay Fever* (11/92)
A773 *Natural Causes* (11-12/92)

HARLOW

Studio Theatre

A1077 *Teechers* (9/92)
A252 *Country Wife* (11/92)

The Playhouse

A672 *The Magic Storybook* (3/92)
A507 *Hot Italian Nights* (3/92)
A1145 *Turned Out Nice Again* (3/92)
A92 *Barnstormers* (3/92)
A657 *Macbeth* (4-5/92)
A971 *See How They Run* (5/92)
A762 *My Cousin Rachel* (5/92)
A354 *Eductaing Rita* (6/92)
A105 *Bedside Manners* (6/92)
A502 *Home At Seven* (6/92)
A648 *Lulu* (9/92)
A1044 *State of Bewilderment* (9/92)
A238 *Come On Sinderby* (9/92)
A1088 *The Tender Husband* (9-10/92)
A920 *Rivals* (10/92)
A752 *Much Ado About Nothing* (10/92)
A463 *Hamlet* (11/92)
A577 *King Lear* (11/92)
A100 *Beauty And The Beast* (11/92)
A1218 *Witness For The Prosecution* (11/92)
A268 *Cyrano De Bergerac* (11-12/92)

HARROW

Harrow Arts

A88 *Ballad of Limehouse* (11/92)
A418 *Frankie & Tommy* (12/92)

HASTINGS

White Rock Th.

A971 *See How They Run* (6/92)

HAYES, MIDDX

Beck Th.

A1046 *Stepping Out* (2/92)
A49 *Animal Farm* (3/92)
A762 *My Cousin Rachel* (4/92)
A1218 *Witness For The Prosecution* (4/92)
A513 *The House Of Stairs* (5/92)
A330 *Don't Rock The Boat* (7/92)
A275 *Dancing at Lughnasa* (10/92)
A100 *Beauty And The Beast* (11/92)

HAYWARDS HEATH

Platform Theatre

A1044 *State of Bewilderment* (9/92)
A467 *Hamlet* (11/92)
A980 *Sex III* (11/92)
A100 *Beauty And The Beast* (1/93)
A836 *Out Of The Ordinary* (2/93)

HEMEL/HEMP

Old Town Hall

A1105 *The Three Musketeers* (5/92)
A87 *Bag Dancing* (5/92)
A748 *Mrs Klein* (5/92)
A767 *My Mother Said* (6/92)
A1031 *Song of Provence* (9/92)
A953 *Scenic Flights* (10/92)
A968 *The Secret Rapture* (11/92)
A824 *Orlando* (11/92)
A1206 *Why Things Happen* (11/92)
A385 *Every Bit Of It* (11/92)
A1088 *The Tender Husband* (12/92)
A836 *Out Of The Ordinary* (2/93)

HODDESDON

Broxbourne Arts Centre

A1105 *The Three Musketeers* (5/92)

HORNCHURCH

Queen's Th.

A894 *Rebecca* (3/92)
A234 *Cold Sweat* (4-5/92)
A144 *Blues In The Night* (5/92)
A1015 *Slice Of Saturday...* (7-8/92)
A592 *Ladies' Night* (8/92)
A1065 *Talk Of The Steamie* (9/92)
A428 *Gaslight* (10/92)
A788 *No 3 Pied Piper Street* (11/92)
A650 *Lust* (10-11/92)
A805 *Old Mother Hubbard* (12/92-1/93)

HORSHAM

Arts Centre

A578 *King Lear* (1/92)
A762 *My Cousin Rachel* (3/92)
A55 *Anybody for Murder?* (4/92)
A467 *Hamlet* (5/92)
A1195 *What About Luv?* (6/92)
A767 *My Mother Said* (7/92)
A1018 *Sneeze* (9/92)
A1218 *Witness For The Prosecution* (10/92)
A1149 *Twelfth Night* (10/92)
A473 *Happy As A Sandbag* (10/92)
A268 *Cyrano De Bergerac* (11/92)
A26 *Aladdin* (12/92-1/93)

Christ's Hosp.

A968 *The Secret Rapture* (10/92)
A1088 *The Tender Husband* (10/92)

Harlequin Th.

A968 *The Secret Rapture* (10/92)

HOUNSLOW

Centrespace

A824 *Orlando* (11/92)

ISLE OF WIGHT

Ryde Theatre

A987 *Shakers* (5/92)

LEATHERHEAD

Casson Room

A822 *One-Man Shows* (11/92)

Thorndike Th.

A1226 *The Woman In Black* (2/92)
A513 *The House Of Stairs* (3/92)
A651 *M. Butterfly* (3-4/92)
A1045 *Steel Magnolias* (4-5/92)
A302 *Dejavu* (5/92)
A657 *Macbeth* (5/92)
A529 *The Imaginary Invalid* (6/92)
A1134 *Travel With My Aunt* (6-7/92)
A1132 *Towards Zero* (7/92)
A850 *Peril At End House* (7/92)
A291 *Deadly Nightcap* (7/92)
A756 *A Murder Arranged* (7-8/92)
A391 *Fallen Angels* (8/92)
A527 *An Ideal Husband* (8-9/92)
A1090 *19th Hole* (10/92)
A1147 *Twelfth Night* (10-11/92)
A1098 *The Thin Soldier* (10-11/92)
A115 *Beyond Reasonable Doubt* (11-12/92)
A19 *Aladdin* (12/92-1/93)

LEIGHTON BUZZ.

Library Theatre

A987 *Shakers* (4/92)
A748 *Mrs Klein* (5/92)
A1031 *Song of Provence* (11/92)

LONDON

Questors

A590 *La Ronde* (9/92)
A1126 *Too Clever By Half* (10/92)

The Lost Theatre

A1149 *Twelfth Night* (10/92)

LUTON

St George's Th.

A1220 *The Wizard of Oz* (2/92)
A1178 *Viva Detroit* (4/92)
A365 *The End Of The Tunnel* (10/92)
A87 *Bag Dancing* (10/92)
A418 *Frankie & Tommy* (10/92)
A577 *King Lear* (11/92)

MAIDSTONE

Hazlitt Theatre

A325 *Don Juan In Hell* (5/92)
A1149 *Twelfth Night* (10/92)

NEWBURY

Arts Workshop

A48 *Angels & Amazons* (4/92)
A824 *Orlando* (11/92)

Watermill Th.

A971 *See How They Run* (3-5/92)
A495 *Hindsight* (5-6/92)
A140 *The Deep Blue Sea* (6-7/92)
A187 *The Card (A musical)* (7-9/92)
A656 *Macbeth* (9-10/92)
A260 *Crucifer* (10-11/92)
A760 *Music Hall* (11/92)

OXFORD

Apollo

A1082 *The Tempest* (2/92)
A655 *Macbeth* (2/92)
A2 *42nd Street* (2-3/92)
A698 *Me And My Girl* (4/92)
A763 *My Fair Lady* (4-5/92)
A116 *The BFG* (5/92)
A94 *Bazaar and Rummage* (5/92)
A657 *Macbeth* (6/92)
A1218 *Witness For The Prosecution* (8/92)
A93 *Barnum* (10-11/92)
A18 *Aladdin* (12/92-1/93)

College of F.E.

A824 *Orlando* (10/92)

Old Fire Station

A199 *Charlemagne* (4/92)
A608 *Leonardo* (10/92)
A975 *Selling Out* (11/92)

Oxford Playhouse

A60 *Arms and the Man* (2/92)
A200 *Charley's Aunt* (3/92)
A1215 *The Winter's Tale* (3/92)
A607 *Leo In Love* (3/92)
A507 *Hot Italian Nights* (4/92)
A275 *Dancing at Lughnasa* (5/92)
A909 *Revenger's Tragedy* (5/92)
A513 *The House Of Stairs* (6-7/92)
A490 *The Heiress* (7/92)
A1163 *Up 'N' Under* (7/92)
A457 *Gravity Swing* (7/92)
A752 *Much Ado About Nothing* (8/92)
A648 *Lulu* (9/92)
A122 *Billy Liar* (9/92)
A594 *Lady Be Good* (9-10/92)
A1088 *The Tender Husband* (10/92)
A1141 *Trilby & Svengali* (10/92)
A859 *Pig In A Poke* (10/92)
A1044 *State of Bewilderment* (10/92)
A294 *Death and the Maiden* (11/92)
A425 *Game of Love & Chance* (11/92)
A412 *Fooling About* (12/92-1/93)
A746 *Mr A's Amazing Maze* (5/93)

St Catherine's

A975 *Selling Out* (10/92)

PORTSMOUTH

Hornpipe Arts

A1190 *The Way of All Flesh* (5/92)
A767 *My Mother Said* (6/92)
A388 *Experiment In Contra.* (10/92)

New Th. Royal

A369 *Enemy To The People* (3/92)

POTTERS BAR, HERTS

Willyotts Arts C

A467 *Hamlet* (10/92)

RAMSGATE

Granville Th.

A55 *Anybody for Murder?* (2/92)

READING

21 South Street

A48 *Angels & Amazons* (4/92)
A1178 *Viva Detroit* (5/92)
A385 *Every Bit Of It* (12/92)

The Hexagon
A880 *Private Lives* (3/92)
A610 *Liaisons Dangereuses* (3/92)
A933 *Rocky Horror Show* (4/92)
A1148 *Twelfth Night* (5/92)
A655 *Macbeth* (5/92)
A275 *Dancing at Lughnasa* (6/92)
A1046 *Stepping Out* (7/92)
A467 *Hamlet* (9/92)
A242 *The Comedy Store* (10/92)
A382 *Evening With Gary L.* (11/92)
A551 *Jack and the Beanstalk* (12/92-1/93)

REDHILL
The Harlequin Theatre
A578 *King Lear* (1/92)
A417 *Frankie & Johnny* (3/92)
A369 *Enemy To The People* (3/92)
A766 *My Mother Said...* (5/92)
A971 *See How They Run* (5/92)
A1088 *The Tender Husband* (10/92)

RICHMOND
Duke's Head
A849 *Pepys - The Diarist* (3-4/92)
A534 *In Camera* (5-6/92)
A483 *He's So at Peace...* (6-7/92)
A1018 *Sneeze* (7-8/92)
A1006 *Sisters* (9-10/92)

SEVENOAKS
Sevenoaks Fest.
A258 *Crime of Love* (6/92)

SOUTHAMPTON
Mayflower
A1148 *Twelfth Night* (3/92)
A655 *Macbeth* (3/92)
A168 *Buddy* (5/92)
A93 *Barnum* (7-9/92)
A763 *My Fair Lady* (9/92)
A382 *Evening With Gary L.* (10/92)
A241 *Comedy Of Errors* (12/92)
Nuffield Th.
A607 *Leo In Love* (2/92)
A171 *Bulldog Drummond* (3-4/92)
A780 *New World and Tears* (4-5/92)
A757 *Murder In Green Meadow* (5-6/92)
A170 *Building Blocks* (9-10/92)
A1141 *Trilby & Svengali* (10-11/92)
A480 *Hawks & Doves* (11-12/92)
A1003 *Sindbad's Arabian..* (12/92-1/93)
A628 *Little Foxes* (2/93)
Nuffield Studio
A1024 *The Solo Experience* (10/92)
A88 *Ballad of Limehouse* (11/92)
The Gantry
A1178 *Viva Detroit* (5/92)
A48 *Angels & Amazons* (5/92)
A578 *King Lear* (10/92)
A1088 *The Tender Husband* (10/92)
A824 *Orlando* (11/92)
A836 *Out Of The Ordinary* (3/93)

SOUTHSEA
King's Theatre
A762 *My Cousin Rachel* (3/92)
A94 *Bazaar and Rummage* (3/92)
A55 *Anybody for Murder?* (3-4/92)
A1041 *Stageland* (6/92)

ST ALBANS
Arena Theatre
A624 *Lion Witch & Wardrobe* (11/92)
Maltings Arts
A157 *Brand* (3/92)
A748 *Mrs Klein* (5/92)
A459 *Great God Brown* (11/92)
A1206 *Why Things Happen* (11/92)
A824 *Orlando* (11/92)
A1217 *Withering Looks* (11/92)
A100 *Beauty And The Beast* (11/92)

STEVENAGE
Gordon Craig Th.
A762 *My Cousin Rachel* (5/92)
A971 *See How They Run* (5/92)
A582 *The Kingfisher* (6/92)
A208 *Chitty Bang Bang* (8/92)
A657 *Macbeth* (9/92)
A1218 *Witness For The Prosecution* (9-10/92)
A479 *Haunted Hotel* (10/92)

STOWE, BUCKS
State Music Room
A1241 *World Upon The Moon* (9/92)

SUTTON
Charles Cryer Studio Theatre
A1178 *Viva Detroit* (5/92)
A1018 *Sneeze* (9/92)

SUTTON, SURREY
Seacombe Centre
A418 *Frankie & Tommy* (12/92)

SWINDON
Arts Centre
A748 *Mrs Klein* (5/92)

THAME, OXON
Sports & Arts C.
A467 *Hamlet* (10/92)

TUNBRIDGE WELLS
Assembly Hall
A1111 *Thunderbirds FAB* (9-10/92)
Trinity Arts
A369 *Enemy To The People* (4/92)
A748 *Mrs Klein* (4/92)
A968 *The Secret Rapture* (9/92)
A122 *Billy Liar* (10/92)
A87 *Bag Dancing* (10/92)
A1088 *The Tender Husband* (10/92)
A1044 *State of Bewilderment* (11/92)

WALTON-ON-TH
Riverhouse Barn
A369 *Enemy To The People* (4/92)
A748 *Mrs Klein* (5/92)
A1190 *The Way of All Flesh* (6/92)
A459 *Great God Brown* (11/92)

WATFORD
Palace Th.
A696 *Me And Mamie O'Rourke* (1-2/92)
A89 *The Barber Of Seville* (3/92)
A1050 *Stitched Up* (4/92)
A82 *The Baby* (5/92)
A192 *Frightened Lady* (9/92)
A32 *All My Sons* (10/92)
A736 *A Month In The Country* (11/92)
A17 *Aladdin* (12/92-1/93)
A804 *Old Country* (1-2/93)

WELWYN GDN CITY
Campus West
A268 *Cyrano De Bergerac* (12/92)

WINCHESTER
John Stripe Th.
A1178 *Viva Detroit* (5/92)
Th. Royal
A417 *Frankie & Johnny* (2/92)
A1248 *You Must Be The Husband* (3/92)
A762 *My Cousin Rachel* (3/92)
A1215 *The Winter's Tale* (3/92)
A909 *Revenger's Tragedy* (4/92)
A1190 *The Way of All Flesh* (5/92)
A859 *Pig In A Poke* (5/92)
A479 *Haunted Hotel* (9/92)
A968 *The Secret Rapture* (10/92)
A824 *Orlando* (10/92)
A920 *Rivals* (11/92)
A1044 *State of Bewilderment* (11/92)
A657 *Macbeth* (11-12/92)
A803 *Office Party* (2/93)

WINDSOR
Arts Centre
A767 *My Mother Said* (6/92)
A258 *Crime of Love* (6/92)

WINDSOR, BERKS
Th. Royal
A1218 *Witness For The Prosecution* (2-3/92)
A1228 *Woman In Mind* (2-3/92)
A1029 *Something's Burning* (4-5/92)
A490 *The Heiress* (4/92)
A808 *On Golden Pond* (5/92)
A548 *It Runs In The Family* (6/92)
A294 *Death and the Maiden* (7-8/92)
A812 *On The Piste* (8/92)
A1046 *Stepping Out* (8-9/92)
A319 *Dog Days* (9-10/92)
A773 *Natural Causes* (10-11/92)
A900 *Relatively Speaking* (11/92)
A1012 *Sleeping Beauty* (12/92-1/93)

WINSLOW
Evans Theatre
A824 *Orlando* (10/92)

WOKING
New Victoria Th.
A981 *Shades* (6/92)
A490 *The Heiress* (6/92)
A1015 *Slice Of Saturday...* (7/92)
A651 *M. Butterfly* (7/92)
A808 *On Golden Pond* (7-8/92)
A1046 *Stepping Out* (8/92)

A1013 *Sleuth* (9/92)
A1218 *Witness For The Prosecution* (9/92)
A391 *Fallen Angels* (10/92)
A1082 *The Tempest* (10/92)
A655 *Macbeth* (10/92)
A94 *Bazaar and Rummage* (11/92)
A927 *Robin* (11/92)
A362 *Elvis - the Musical* (12/92)
A803 *Office Party* (3/93)

WOODHAM

William Ferrers

A748 *Mrs Klein* (5/92)

WORTHING

Connaught Th.

A1046 *Stepping Out* (2/92)
A762 *My Cousin Rachel* (2/92)
A1215 *The Winter's Tale* (3/92)
A672 *The Magic Storybook* (3/92)
A507 *Hot Italian Nights* (3/92)
A599 *The Late Edwina Black* (3-4/92)
A395 *The Fancy Man* (5/92)
A909 *Revenger's Tragedy* (5/92)
A1105 *The Three Musketeers* (5/92)
A971 *See How They Run* (6/92)
A767 *My Mother Said* (6/92)
A582 *The Kingfisher* (6/92)
A1041 *Stageland* (7/92)
A1218 *Witness For The Prosecution* (9/92)
A648 *Lulu* (9/92)
A1044 *State of Bewilderment* (10/92)
A859 *Pig In A Poke* (10/92)
A425 *Game of Love & Chance* (11/92)
A968 *The Secret Rapture* (11/92)
A866 *Please Sir!* (11/92)
A745 *Mowgli - Enfant Loup* (11/92)
A479 *Haunted Hotel* (11/92)
A309 *Dick Whittington* (12/92-1/93)

Pavilion Th.

A960 *School Of Night* (9/92)
A1111 *Thunderbirds FAB* (11/92)

SOUTH WEST ENGLAND

ANDOVER

Cricklade Th.

A369 *Enemy To The People* (3/92)
A510 *Hound* (4/92)
A889 *Radio Times* (5/93)

ARUNDEL

Open Air Theatre

A752 *Much Ado About Nothing* (9/92)

AXMINSTER

The Guildhall

A288 *Dead Man's Hat* (10/92)

BARNSTAPLE

North Devon Col.

A288 *Dead Man's Hat* (10/92)
A365 *The End Of The Tunnel* (10/92)

Park School

A415 *Frankenstein* (4/92)

Queens Hall Th

A1083 *The Tempest* (3/92)

BATH

Th. Royal

A1230 *Woman Of No Importance* (2/92)
A607 *Leo In Love* (3/92)
A762 *My Cousin Rachel* (3/92)
A755 *Murder By Misadventure* (3/92)
A909 *Revenger's Tragedy* (4/92)
A200 *Charley's Aunt* (4-5/92)
A4 *70, Girls, 70* (5/92)
A1148 *Twelfth Night* (5/92)
A655 *Macbeth* (5/92)
A669 *Madness of George III* (5/92)
A999 *Sienna Red* (6/92)
A249 *The Corn Is Green* (6/92)
A513 *The House Of Stairs* (6/92)
A981 *Shades* (6-7/92)
A1134 *Travel With My Aunt* (7/92)
A582 *The Kingfisher* (7/92)
A159 *Breaking the Code* (8/92)
A808 *On Golden Pond* (8/92)
A1182 *Voysey Inheritance* (8/92)
A391 *Fallen Angels* (9/92)
A527 *An Ideal Husband* (10/92)
A833 *Our Song* (10/92)
A641 *Lost in Yonkers* (11/92)
A481 *Hay Fever* (11/92)
A541 *An Inspector Calls* (11/92)
A773 *Natural Causes* (12/92)
A224 *Cinderella* (12/92-1/93)

Ustinov Studio

A865 *Playing The Wife* (11-12/92)

BEAFORD, DEVON

Beaford Art Ctr.

A48 *Angels & Amazons* (4/92)

BIDEFORD

College Theatre

A574 *Killing Passion* (3/92)
A415 *Frankenstein* (5/92)
A1083 *The Tempest* (5/92)
A288 *Dead Man's Hat* (10/92)

BLANDFORD

Bryanston Arts

A415 *Frankenstein* (5/92)
A467 *Hamlet* (9/92)
A441 *Glassparts* (11/92)

BOGNOR REGIS

Alexandra Th.

A599 *The Late Edwina Black* (4-5/92)
A690 *The Marvellous Boy* (5/92)

BOURNEMOUTH

Jellicoe Theatre

A824 *Orlando* (10/92)

Pavilion Theatre

A1218 *Witness For The Prosecution* (3/92)
A960 *School Of Night* (5/92)
A1145 *Turned Out Nice Again* (6/92)
A1111 *Thunderbirds FAB* (7/92)
A362 *Elvis - the Musical* (7-9/92)
A219 *Cinderella* (12/92-1/93)

Russell-Cotes

A415 *Frankenstein* (5/92)

BOVEY TRACEY

The Town Hall

A288 *Dead Man's Hat* (10/92)

BRIDGWATER

Bridgwater Arts Centre

A574 *Killing Passion* (2/92)
A1149 *Twelfth Night* (10/92)

BRISTOL

Albany Centre

A510 *Hound* (5/92)

Bristol Old Vic

A935 *Romeo and Juliet* (1-2/92)
A1230 *Woman Of No Importance* (3/92)
A423 *Fuente Ovejuna* (3/92)
A375 *Epsom Downs* (4/92)
A139 *Blue Remembered Hills* (4-6/92)
A275 *Dancing at Lughnasa* (8/92)
A440 *Glass Menagerie* (9/92)
A1085 *Tempest* (9-10/92)
A532 *Importance of Being* (11/92)
A25 *Aladdin* (12/92-1/93)

Glynne Wickham

A986 *Shaker* (4/92)
A987 *Shakers* (6/92)
A824 *Orlando* (10/92)

Hippodrome

A898 *Reflected Glory* (3/92)
A168 *Buddy* (3/92)
A116 *The BFG* (4-5/92)
A763 *My Fair Lady* (5/92)
A657 *Macbeth* (7-8/92)
A94 *Bazaar and Rummage* (9/92)
A382 *Evening With Gary L.* (9-10/92)
A1082 *The Tempest* (10/92)
A655 *Macbeth* (10/92)
A698 *Me And My Girl* (2/93)

Hope Theatre

A574 *Killing Passion* (3/92)
A1083 *The Tempest* (6/92)
A415 *Frankenstein* (6/92)

New Vic

A437 *Give You A Good Time* (2-3/92)
A1071 *Tamoyos* (3/92)
A148 *Bodycount* (4/92)
A1246 *Yerma* (4-5/92)
A647 *Lovers* (5-6/92)
A130 *Blood Brothers* (5-6/92)
A690 *The Marvellous Boy* (6/92)
A1190 *The Way of All Flesh* (6-7/92)
A879 *Prisoner's Pumpkin* (9-10/92)
A1236 *Women Of The Dust* (10/92)
A1127 *Too Much Too Young* (11/92)
A207 *Chimes* (12/92-1/93)

Redgrave Theatre

A288 *Dead Man's Hat* (10/92)
A1149 *Twelfth Night* (10/92)

BUDE

The Parkhouse Centre

A415 *Frankenstein* (6/92)

Produced exclusively for Plays & Players by SEARCHLINE

CASTLE CARY
Ansford College
A288 Dead Man's Hat (10/92)
CHELTENHAM
Everyman Th.
A544 Intimate Exchanges (3/92)
A393 Family Affair (4/92)
A202 Cherry Orchard (4-5/92)
A614 Lettice & Lovage (6/92)
A1015 Slice Of Saturday... (7/92)
A840 Over a Barrel (8/92)
A595 Lady Macbeth (8-9/92)
A603 Laurel and Hardy (9/92)
A1078 Teechers (9/92)
A1120 TO (9-10/92)
A322 Doll's House (10/92)
A1111 Thunderbirds FAB (10/92)
A658 Macbeth (10-11/92)
A1223 Wizard of Oz (12/92-1/93)
Shaftesbury Hall
A772 Name (6/92)
CIRENCESTER
Cirencester Sch
A369 Enemy To The People (5/92)
CORNWALL,
Arts Centre
A388 Experiment In Contra. (12/92)
DARTINGTON
Barn Theatre
A369 Enemy To The People (5/92)
A1083 The Tempest (5/92)
DORCHESTER
Corn Exchange
A1083 The Tempest (3/92)
A415 Frankenstein (5/92)
Town Hall
A288 Dead Man's Hat (10/92)
DORSET
Powell Theatre
A824 Orlando (10/92)
Sherbourne School
A574 Killing Passion (2/92)
DRIFFIELD
Old Town Hall
A268 Cyrano De Bergerac (11/92)
EXETER
Barnfield Th.
A258 Crime of Love (6/92)
Drama Studio
A365 The End Of The Tunnel (10/92)
Northcott
A818 One For The Road (2/92)
A1083 The Tempest (3-4/92)
A759 Music Hall (4/92)
A415 Frankenstein (4/92)
A1106 Three Musketeers (7-8/92)
A837 Outside Edge (8-9/92)
A1121 To Kill A Mockingbird (9-10/92)
A288 Dead Man's Hat (10/92)
A706 Merchant of Venice (11/92)
A930 Robin of the Wood (12/92-1/93)
Plough Theatre
A369 Enemy To The People (5/92)
A682 Man, Beast and Virtue (5/92)
A288 Dead Man's Hat (10/92)
St Luke's Th.
A388 Experiment In Contra. (12/92)
EXFORD
Memorial Hall
A288 Dead Man's Hat (10/92)
FALMOUTH
Arts Centre
A1083 The Tempest (3/92)
A415 Frankenstein (5/92)
A968 The Secret Rapture (10/92)
A288 Dead Man's Hat (11/92)
A388 Experiment In Contra. (12/92)
FROME
Merlin
A578 King Lear (3/92)
A1083 The Tempest (3/92)
A415 Frankenstein (6/92)
A1149 Twelfth Night (10/92)
A129 Blodeuwedd (10/92)
A418 Frankie & Tommy (12/92)
GLOUCESTER
Brewery Arts
A1149 Twelfth Night (10/92)
Guildhall Arts
A824 Orlando (10/92)
HAVANT
Havant Arts Centre
A767 My Mother Said (6/92)
ILFRACOMBE
Victoria Pavilio
A1083 The Tempest (3/92)
A415 Frankenstein (6/92)
A288 Dead Man's Hat (10/92)
KETTERING
Corn Market Hall
A1149 Twelfth Night (10/92)
LAUNCESTON
Launceston Coll.
A288 Dead Man's Hat (10/92)
LEIGH
Leigh Drama Ctre
A48 Angels & Amazons (6/92)
LITTLEHAMPTON
Barn Arts Centre
A1149 Twelfth Night (10/92)
LIVERPOOL
Hugh Baird Coll.
A1169 A View From The Bridge (3/92)
LYNTON
Town Hall
A415 Frankenstein (6/92)
MARLBOROUGH
M'brough College
A467 Hamlet (9/92)
MINEHEAD
The Regal Th.
A415 Frankenstein (6/92)
A288 Dead Man's Hat (10/92)
NEW MILTON
Forest Arts Ctre
A748 Mrs Klein (5/92)
A578 King Lear (9/92)
NEWQUAY
Treviglas School
A1083 The Tempest (3/92)
A415 Frankenstein (6/92)
A288 Dead Man's Hat (11/92)
NR TOTNES
Kingsbridge Leis
A1172 A View From The Bridge (5-6/92)
A936 Romeo and Juliet (5-6/92)
OKEHAMPTON
The Octagon
A1083 The Tempest (3/92)
A415 Frankenstein (5/92)
A288 Dead Man's Hat (11/92)
PENZANCE
Acorn Arts Ctre
A1083 The Tempest (3/92)
A415 Frankenstein (5/92)
A288 Dead Man's Hat (11/92)
PLYMOUTH
Drum Theatre
A417 Frankie & Johnny (2/92)
A1083 The Tempest (3/92)
A1118 TO (3-4/92)
A415 Frankenstein (4/92)
A577 King Lear (6/92)
A463 Hamlet (6/92)
A288 Dead Man's Hat (11/92)
Lipson Comm Coll
A369 Enemy To The People (5/92)
Th. Royal
A880 Private Lives (2/92)
A732 Moment Of Weakness (3/92)
A289 A Dead Secret (3-4/92)
A116 The BFG (4/92)
A755 Murder By Misadventure (4/92)
A630 A Little Night Music (4-5/92)
A490 The Heiress (5/92)
A513 The House Of Stairs (5/92)
A1218 Witness For The Prosecution (6/92)
A51 Annie Get Your Gun (8-9/92)
A301 The Decorator (9/92)
A94 Bazaar and Rummage (9/92)
A275 Dancing at Lughnasa (9-10/92)
A1082 The Tempest (10/92)
A655 Macbeth (10/92)
A362 Elvis - the Musical (10/92)
A168 Buddy (11-12/92)
POOLE
Towngate Th.
A60 Arms and the Man (2/92)
A472 Hapgood (2-3/92)
A610 Liaisons Dangereuses (3/92)
A672 The Magic Storybook (3-4/92)
A507 Hot Italian Nights (3-4/92)
A607 Leo In Love (4/92)
A417 Frankie & Johnny (4/92)
A417 Frankie & Johnny (4/92)

A395 *The Fancy Man* (4/92)
A92 *Barnstormers* (4/92)
A909 *Revenger's Tragedy* (4-5/92)
A859 *Pig In A Poke* (5/92)
A116 *The BFG* (5/92)
A762 *My Cousin Rachel* (5/92)
A1046 *Stepping Out* (5/92)
A582 *The Kingfisher* (6/92)
A1218 *Witness For The Prosecution* (6/92)
A1015 *Slice Of Saturday...* (6/92)
A55 *Anybody for Murder?* (6-7/92)
A55 *Anybody for Murder?* (6-7/92)
A1134 *Travel With My Aunt* (9/92)
A1013 *Sleuth* (9/92)
A920 *Rivals* (9-10/92)
A648 *Lulu* (10/92)
A592 *Ladies' Night* (10/92)
A425 *Game of Love & Chance* (10/92)
A657 *Macbeth* (11/92)
A223 *Cinderella* (12/92-1/93)
A746 *Mr A's Amazing Maze* (4/93)

SALISBURY, WILTS.
Arts Centre
A467 *Hamlet* (5/92)
A1190 *The Way of All Flesh* (6/92)

SALISBURY
Playhouse Th.
A339 *Down And Out...* (1-2/92)
A16 *After You With The Mlk* (2-3/92)
A209 *The Choice* (3/92)
A346 *Driving Miss Daisy* (3-4/92)
A50 *Anna Karenina* (4/92)
A690 *The Marvellous Boy* (5/92)
A336 *Double Double* (4-5/92)
A899 *Relative Values* (5-6/92)
A762 *My Cousin Rachel* (7-8/92)
A62 *Arsenic and Old Lace* (8/92)
A1004 *Single Spies* (9/92)
A716 *A Midsummer Night's Dream* (9-10/92)
A320 *Doll's House* (10-11/92)
A1087 *Ten Times Table* (11-12/92)
A740 *Mother Goose* (12/92-1/93)
A803 *Office Party* (4/93)
Salberg Studio
A705 *Memoirs of a Survivor* (9/92)
A299 *Decadence* (10/92)
A474 *Happy Days* (11-12/92)

SHAFTESBURY
Arts Centre
A1083 *The Tempest* (4/92)
A288 *Dead Man's Hat* (10/92)

SHERBORNE, DORSET
Digby Hall
A1083 *The Tempest* (4/92)
A415 *Frankenstein* (5/92)

SHROPS
Ludlow Festival
A69 *As You Like It* (6-7/92)

SIDMOUTH
Manor Pavilion
A415 *Frankenstein* (6/92)
A1083 *The Tempest* (6/92)

SOUTH MOLTON
Sth Molton Cllge
A1083 *The Tempest* (3/92)

STREET, SOMERSET
Strode Theatre
A574 *Killing Passion* (2/92)
A48 *Angels & Amazons* (4/92)
A824 *Orlando* (10/92)

SWANAGE
Mowlem Theatre
A415 *Frankenstein* (5/92)
A1083 *The Tempest* (5/92)
A288 *Dead Man's Hat* (10/92)

SWINDON
Link Arts Studio
A441 *Glassparts* (11/92)
Wyvern Th.
A1046 *Stepping Out* (2/92)
A607 *Leo In Love* (3/92)
A987 *Shakers* (4/92)
A457 *Gravity Swing* (5/92)
A971 *See How They Run* (6/92)
A762 *My Cousin Rachel* (6-7/92)
A1218 *Witness For The Prosecution* (7/92)
A1111 *Thunderbirds FAB* (7-8/92)
A752 *Much Ado About Nothing* (10/92)
A418 *Frankie & Tommy* (11/92)

TAUNTON
Brewhouse Th.
A417 *Frankie & Johnny* (2/92)
A672 *The Magic Storybook* (2/92)
A507 *Hot Italian Nights* (2/92)
A50 *Anna Karenina* (4/92)
A415 *Frankenstein* (6/92)
A909 *Revenger's Tragedy* (6/92)
A582 *The Kingfisher* (6-7/92)
A648 *Lulu* (9/92)
A467 *Hamlet* (9/92)
A479 *Haunted Hotel* (9/92)
A1044 *State of Bewilderment* (10/92)
A968 *The Secret Rapture* (10/92)
A288 *Dead Man's Hat* (10/92)
A752 *Much Ado About Nothing* (10/92)
A441 *Glassparts* (11/92)
A122 *Billy Liar* (11/92)

TAVISTOCK
Town Hall
A1083 *The Tempest* (3/92)

TORQUAY
Princess Theatre
A657 *Macbeth* (4/92)
A762 *My Cousin Rachel* (6/92)

TOTNES
Dartington Arts
A48 *Angels & Amazons* (4/92)
The Civic Hall
A415 *Frankenstein* (5/92)

TRURO, CORNWALL
Truro City Hall
A589 *La Ronde* (3-4/92)

WARMINSTER
West Wilts Arts Centre
A589 *La Ronde* (3/92)
A1190 *The Way of All Flesh* (6/92)

WELLINGBOROUGH
The Tithe Barn
A1149 *Twelfth Night* (10/92)

WESTON-S-MARE
Playhouse Th.
A457 *Gravity Swing* (4/92)
A657 *Macbeth* (9/92)
A473 *Happy As A Sandbag* (9-10/92)

WEYMOUTH
Drama Hall
A574 *Killing Passion* (2/92)
Ocean Room
A48 *Angels & Amazons* (6/92)

YEOVIL
Octagon
A1248 *You Must Be The Husband* (2/92)
A417 *Frankie & Johnny* (3-4/92)
A971 *See How They Run* (5/92)
A1105 *The Three Musketeers* (5/92)
A457 *Gravity Swing* (6/92)
A714 *Metamorphosis* (6/92)
A657 *Macbeth* (6/92)
A767 *My Mother Said* (7/92)
A467 *Hamlet* (7/92)
A968 *The Secret Rapture* (9/92)

MIDLANDS

ASHBOURNE
Q E Grammar Sch
A1233 *Women in Love* (11/92)

ASHBY-DE-LA-ZOUCH
Venture Th
A1233 *Women in Love* (11/92)

ASHBY/ZOUCH
Theatregoers
A303 *Devil's Only Sleeping* (11/92)

AVERHAM
Robin Hood Th.
A172 *Burbage and the Bard* (4/92)

B/HAM
King Edward VI School
A303 *Devil's Only Sleeping* (11/92)

BARTON-UNDER-NEEDWOOD
Barton Village Hall
A1233 *Women in Love* (10/92)

BEDFORD
Alexander Sports
A1172 *A View From The Bridge* (6/92)
A936 *Romeo and Juliet* (6/92)
Bowen West Th.
A738 *Moose* (5/92)
A1044 *State of Bewilderment* (9/92)
A365 *The End Of The Tunnel* (10/92)
A1206 *Why Things Happen* (10/92)
A968 *The Secret Rapture* (10/92)
A292 *Death And Dancing* (10/92)
A860 *Pigspurt* (11/92)
A485 *Heart* (11/92)

A467 *Hamlet* (11/92)
A388 *Experiment In Contra.* (11/92)
A88 *Ballad of Limehouse* (12/92)
A836 *Out Of The Ordinary* (3/93)

BEESTON

Roundhill School

A100 *Beauty And The Beast* (12/92)

BIRMINGHAM

Alexandra Th.

A898 *Reflected Glory* (2/92)
A807 *On Approval* (3/92)
A1230 *Woman Of No Importance* (3/92)
A724 *The Miser* (3/92)
A146 *Body And Soul* (3/92)
A275 *Dancing at Lughnasa* (4-5/92)
A999 *Sienna Red* (5/92)
A249 *The Corn Is Green* (6/92)
A1218 *Witness For The Prosecution* (6/92)
A762 *My Cousin Rachel* (6/92)
A1046 *Stepping Out* (6/92)
A490 *The Heiress* (6-7/92)
A651 *M. Butterfly* (7/92)
A513 *The House Of Stairs* (7/92)
A159 *Breaking the Code* (7/92)
A808 *On Golden Pond* (7/92)
A582 *The Kingfisher* (7-8/92)
A1134 *Travel With My Aunt* (8-9/92)
A382 *Evening With Gary L.* (9/92)
A830 *Otherwise Engaged* (9-10/92)
A391 *Fallen Angels* (10/92)
A907 *Revenge* (10/92)
A641 *Lost in Yonkers* (10/92)
A1039 *Scrooge the Musical* (11/92-1/93)

Arts Centre

A574 *Killing Passion* (3/92)
A987 *Shakers* (3-4/92)
A1232 *Woman Who Cooked* (4/92)
A510 *Hound* (4-5/92)
A666 *Madame Mao's Memories* (5/92)
A1178 *Viva Detroit* (6/92)
A1190 *The Way of All Flesh* (6/92)
A48 *Angels & Amazons* (6/92)
A365 *The End Of The Tunnel* (10/92)
A1024 *The Solo Experience* (10/92)
A1088 *The Tender Husband* (10/92)
A100 *Beauty And The Beast* (11/92)
A388 *Experiment In Contra.* (11/92)
A788 *No 3 Pied Piper Street* (11/92-1/93)
A88 *Ballad of Limehouse* (12/92)
A836 *Out Of The Ordinary* (3/93)

Birm.Rep. Studio

A339 *Down And Out...* (2/92)
A925 *Roaring Girl's Hamlet* (3/92)
A1140 *The Trial* (3-4/92)
A863 *Playing by the Rules* (9/92)
A1136 *Travelling Light* (9-10/92)
A1122 *To My Country A Child* (10/92)
A303 *Devil's Only Sleeping* (10/92)
A776 *Nervous Women* (11/92)
A352 *East Lynne* (12/92-1/93)

Birmingham Rep.

A571 *Kafka's Dick* (1-2/92)
A500 *Hobson's Choice* (2-3/92)
A766 *My Mother Said...* (4/92)
A918 *The Rivals* (5/92)
A121 *Biko* (5-6/92)
A99 *Beauty and the Beast* (6-7/92)
A598 *The Last Carnival* (7-8/92)
A890 *Radio Times* (9-10/92)
A454 *Grapes of Wrath* (10/92)
A277 *Dangerous Corner* (11/92)
A1224 *Wizard of Oz* (12/92-1/93)
A118 *Big Maggie* (2/93)

Hippodrome

A763 *My Fair Lady* (3/92)
A933 *Rocky Horror Show* (5/92)
A508 *Hot Stuff* (6-7/92)
A116 *The BFG* (7/92)
A1218 *Witness For The Prosecution* (8/92)
A51 *Annie Get Your Gun* (9-10/92)
A362 *Elvis - the Musical* (11/92)
A698 *Me And My Girl* (3-4/93)

Holyhead School

A303 *Devil's Only Sleeping* (11/92)

Old Rep Th.

A1201 *While The Sun Shines* (9-10/92)

Perry Common School

A303 *Devil's Only Sleeping* (10/92)

BLYTH

Blyth Tynedale High School

A418 *Frankie & Tommy* (11/92)

BRADFORD

Theatre in the Mill

A332 *The Dorm* (5/92)

BROMYARD

Conquest Theatre

A1149 *Twelfth Night* (10/92)

BUCKS

The Elgiva

A690 *The Marvellous Boy* (6/92)

BURTON-ON-TRENT

Brewhouse Th.

A1169 *A View From The Bridge* (2/92)
A1108 *Threepenny Story* (2/92)
A172 *Burbage and the Bard* (5/92)
A679 *Man Cub* (6/92)
A463 *Hamlet* (7/92)
A1217 *Withering Looks* (8/92)
A87 *Bag Dancing* (10/92)
A122 *Billy Liar* (10/92)
A509 *Houdini* (11/92)
A1233 *Women in Love* (11/92)
A1149 *Twelfth Night* (12/92)
A268 *Cyrano De Bergerac* (12/92)
A100 *Beauty And The Beast* (12/92)

BURTON/TRENT

Meadowside Leis.

A1172 *A View From The Bridge* (5/92)
A936 *Romeo and Juliet* (5/92)
A910 *Richard III* (9-10/92)

CASTLE DONINGTON

Village Hall

A1233 *Women in Love* (11/92)

CHESHIRE

Civic Theatre

A1145 *Turned Out Nice Again* (5/92)

CHIPPING NORTON

The Theatre

A742 *Mother Goose*
A369 *Enemy To The People* (3/92)
A1178 *Viva Detroit* (4/92)
A48 *Angels & Amazons* (4/92)
A748 *Mrs Klein* (4/92)
A1145 *Turned Out Nice Again* (4/92)
A325 *Don Juan In Hell* (5/92)
A1241 *World Upon The Moon* (7/92)
A365 *The End Of The Tunnel* (9/92)
A1088 *The Tender Husband* (10/92)
A788 *No 3 Pied Piper Street* (10/92)
A459 *Great God Brown* (11/92)
A968 *The Secret Rapture* (11/92)

CHRISTCHURCH

Regent Centre

A369 *Enemy To The People* (3/92)

CHURCH EATON

Village Inst.

A303 *Devil's Only Sleeping* (11/92)

CIRENCESTER

Niccol Centre

A1190 *The Way of All Flesh* (6/92)
A824 *Orlando* (10/92)

COVENTRY

Belgrade Th.

A406 *Firestone* (2/92)
A104 *Bedroom Farce* (3/92)
A947 *Safe In Our Hands* (4/92)
A1015 *Slice Of Saturday...* (4-5/92)
A605 *Leave Taking* (5/92)
A275 *Dancing at Lughnasa* (5-6/92)
A755 *Murder By Misadventure* (6/92)
A1017 *Smile Orange* (6/92)
A1248 *You Must Be The Husband* (6-7/92)
A11 *Absurd Person Singular* (9/92)
A944 *Run for Your Wife* (9-10/92)
A983 *Shadowlands* (10/92)
A306 *Diamonds in the Dust* (11/92)
A513 *The House Of Stairs* (11/92)
A741 *Mother Goose* (12/92-1/93)
A688 *Martin Chuzzlewit* (2/93)
A150 *Bouncers* (3/93)

Belgrade Studio

A832 *Our Ellen* (4/92)
A1153 *A Twitch On The Thread* (5/92)

Warwick Arts

A578 *King Lear* (1/92)
A574 *Killing Passion* (1/92)
A672 *The Magic Storybook* (2/92)
A507 *Hot Italian Nights* (2/92)
A1148 *Twelfth Night* (2/92)
A655 *Macbeth* (3/92)
A457 *Gravity Swing* (4/92)
A1105 *The Three Musketeers* (4-5/92)

A845 *Patagonia* (5/92)
A909 *Revenger's Tragedy* (5/92)
A1178 *Viva Detroit* (5/92)
A690 *The Marvellous Boy* (5/92)
A1024 *The Solo Experience* (10/92)
A752 *Much Ado About Nothing* (10/92)
A365 *The End Of The Tunnel* (10/92)
A1044 *State of Bewilderment* (10/92)
A968 *The Secret Rapture* (10/92)
A122 *Billy Liar* (10/92)
A803 *Office Party* (11/92)
A385 *Every Bit Of It* (11/92)
A363 *Emanuelle Enchanted* (11/92)
A1217 *Withering Looks* (11/92)
A425 *Game of Love & Chance* (11/92)
A216 *Christmas Cat* (12/92-1/93)
A836 *Out Of The Ordinary* (2/93)
A746 *Mr A's Amazing Maze* (5/93)

CREWE

Lyceum Th.

A92 *Barnstormers* (3/92)
A724 *The Miser* (4/92)
A490 *The Heiress* (5/92)
A55 *Anybody for Murder?* (5/92)
A920 *Rivals* (9/92)
A907 *Revenge* (9-10/92)
A1088 *The Tender Husband* (11/92)
A803 *Office Party* (3/93)

DERBY

Chellaston Coll

A1233 *Women in Love* (11/92)

College of H.E.

A1233 *Women in Love* (11/92)

Derby Studio

A1233 *Women in Love* (11/92)
A601 *Laurel and Hardy* (1-2/93)
A419 *Frankie and Johnny...* (4-5/93)

Guildhall Th.

A577 *King Lear* (11/92)

Playhouse

A43 *And A Nightingale Sang* (2-3/92)
A769 *My Sister Next Door* (2-3/92)
A540 *The Innocents* (4/92)
A397 *Far From The Madding Crowd* (5-6/92)
A125 *Blithe Spirit* (6/92)
A458 *Grease* (8-9/92)
A295 *Death of A Salesman* (10/92)
A810 *On The Piste* (10-11/92)
A211 *Chorus of Disapproval* (2-3/93)
A633 *Little Shop of Horrors* (3-4/93)
A205 *Children of a Lesser..* (5-6/93)
A838 *Outside Edge* (6-7/93)

Tertiary College

A1233 *Women in Love* (11/92)

DERRY

Templemore Sports Complex

A430 *Gaudeamus* (5/92)
A422 *Fuente Ovejuna* (6/92)

DUDLEY

Crestwood School

A303 *Devil's Only Sleeping* (11/92)

DURSLEY, GLOS.

Prema Arts Ctr.

A48 *Angels & Amazons* (4/92)
A363 *Emanuelle Enchanted* (10/92)

ETWALL

John Port Sch

A1233 *Women in Love* (11/92)

GRANTHAM

Guildhall Centre

A748 *Mrs Klein* (5/92)
A369 *Enemy To The People* (5/92)
A1190 *The Way of All Flesh* (5/92)
A1088 *The Tender Husband* (10/92)
A100 *Beauty And The Beast* (11/92)

Live Arts

A1105 *The Three Musketeers* (4/92)
A467 *Hamlet* (10/92)

HALIFAX

Square Chapel

A509 *Houdini* (10/92)

HANLEY

Th. Royal

A933 *Rocky Horror Show* (4-5/92)
A94 *Bazaar and Rummage* (11/92)

HAY-ON-WYE

Hay-on-Wye Fest.

A172 *Burbage and the Bard* (5/92)
A369 *Enemy To The People* (5/92)

ILKESTON

Derby College

A1233 *Women in Love* (11/92)

KIDDERMINSTER

Rose Theatre

A824 *Orlando* (10/92)

LEAMINGTON SPA

Royal Theatre

A1145 *Turned Out Nice Again* (4/92)

LEEK

Westwood High School

A303 *Devil's Only Sleeping* (11/92)

LEICESTER

Haymarket Th.

A711 *Merrily We Roll Along* (4-5/92)
A394 *The Family Reunion* (5-6/92)
A508 *Hot Stuff* (8-9/92)
A745 *Mowgli - Enfant Loup* (9-10/92)
A991 *She Stoops To Conquer* (9-10/92)
A134 *Blood Wedding* (10/92)
A1011 *Sleeping Beauty/Beast* (12/92-1/93)
A1193 *West Side Story* (11/92-1/93)
A836 *Out Of The Ordinary* (3/93)

Haymarket Studio

A50 *Anna Karenina* (2/92)
A290 *Dead Soil* (3-4/92)
A1232 *Woman Who Cooked* (4/92)
A1178 *Viva Detroit* (5/92)
A369 *Enemy To The People* (5/92)
A88 *Ballad of Limehouse* (9/92)
A772 *Name* (10/92)
A772 *Name* (10/92)
A949 *Saint Oscar* (10-11/92)
A1160 *Under Milk Wood* (11-12/92)

A416 *Frankenstein* (12/92-1/93)

Phoenix Arts

A441 *Glassparts* (11/92)
A363 *Emanuelle Enchanted* (11/92)
A1044 *State of Bewilderment* (12/92)

LICHFIELD

Lichfield Civic Hall

A55 *Anybody for Murder?* (3/92)

LIVERPOOL

St George's Hall

A465 *Hamlet* (11/92)

MALVERN

Malvern Festival Th.

A732 *Moment Of Weakness* (2/92)
A755 *Murder By Misadventure* (3/92)
A146 *Body And Soul* (4/92)
A94 *Bazaar and Rummage* (5/92)
A490 *The Heiress* (5/92)
A325 *Don Juan In Hell* (5/92)
A582 *The Kingfisher* (7/92)
A4 *70, Girls, 70* (7/92)
A391 *Fallen Angels* (9/92)
A1218 *Witness For The Prosecution* (10/92)
A479 *Haunted Hotel* (11/92)
A275 *Dancing at Lughnasa* (11/92)
A425 *Game of Love & Chance* (12/92)

MANSFIELD

All Saints Schoo

A577 *King Lear* (9/92)

MATLOCK

Highfields Sch

A1233 *Women in Love* (11/92)

MATLOCK, DERBYS

The Crown

A172 *Burbage and the Bard* (4/92)

MELTON MOWBRAY

Melton Th.

A1233 *Women in Love* (11/92)

MILTON KEYNES

Woughton Centre

A1232 *Woman Who Cooked* (4/92)
A418 *Frankie & Tommy* (10/92)
A385 *Every Bit Of It* (11/92)

NEW/U/LYME

New Victoria Th.

A867 *The Plough & The Stars* (3/93)
A768 *My Mother Said* (2/93)
A376 *Eric The Epic* (2/93)
A782 *The Night Before The Morning After* (12/91-3/92)
A925 *Roaring Girl's Hamlet* (3/92)
A1109 *The Threepenny Opera* (2-3/92)
A564 *Julius Caesar* (3-4/92)
A499 *Hobson's Choice* (5-6/92)
A161 *Bright & Bold Design* (4-6/92)
A1115 *TO* (4-8/92)
A557 *Jolly Potters* (8/92)
A485 *Heart* (10/92)
A240 *Comedy of Errors* (11/92)
A1144 *Turkey Time* (11/92)
A491 *Henceforward...* (11/92)
A1021 *Snow Queen* (12/92-1/93)

NEWARK

Magdalene Sch

A100 *Beauty And The Beast* (11/92)

Palace Theatre

A906 *The Revenger's Tragedy* (3/92)
A451 *Gormenghast* (4/92)
A682 *Man, Beast and Virtue* (4/92)
A457 *Gravity Swing* (6/92)
A577 *King Lear* (10/92)
A1044 *State of Bewilderment* (10/92)
A1044 *State of Bewilderment* (10/92)
A24 *Aladdin* (1/93)

NEWCASTLE UNDER LYME

Stephen Joseph Studio

A836 *Out Of The Ordinary* (3/92)
A372 *Enter The Tragic Muse* (12/92)
A469 *Hanging Around* (12/92)

NORTHAMPTON

Derngate

A1082 *The Tempest* (1/92)
A275 *Dancing at Lughnasa* (3/92)
A513 *The House Of Stairs* (4/92)
A116 *The BFG* (6/92)
A508 *Hot Stuff* (7/92)
A301 *The Decorator* (8-9/92)
A1111 *Thunderbirds FAB* (9/92)

Royal Th.

A175 *The Business Of Murder* (1-2/92)
A966 *Second From Last In The Sack Race* (3/92)
A689 *Martin Chuzzlewit* (4/92)
A1171 *A View From The Bridge* (5/92)
A127 *Blithe Spirit* (5-6/92)
A749 *Mrs Klein* (8-9/92)
A1123 *Serve Them All My Days* (8-9/92)
A373 *Entertaining Mr Sloane* (9-10/92)
A1014 *Slice of Saturday* (10/92)
A278 *Dangerous Obsession* (11-12/92)
A312 *Dick Whittington* (12/92-1/93)
A286 *Day After The Fair* (1-2/93)
A531 *The Importance Of Being Earnest* (2-3/93)
A765 *My Mother Said* (3-4/93)
A982 *Shadowlands* (4-5/93)
A520 *How The Other Half Loves* (5-6/93)

The Menagerie

A1241 *World Upon The Moon* (9/92)

NORTHANTS

Victoria Centre

A1178 *Viva Detroit* (5/92)

NOTTINGHAM

Clarendon College

A1024 *The Solo Experience* (10/92)

Th. Royal

A1082 *The Tempest* (2/92)
A655 *Macbeth* (2/92)
A807 *On Approval* (3/92)
A732 *Moment Of Weakness* (3/92)
A275 *Dancing at Lughnasa* (4/92)
A168 *Buddy* (4-5/92)
A933 *Rocky Horror Show* (5/92)
A2 *42nd Street* (5-6/92)
A116 *The BFG* (6/92)
A1218 *Witness For The Prosecution* (6-7/92)
A513 *The House Of Stairs* (7/92)
A1111 *Thunderbirds FAB* (7/92)
A508 *Hot Stuff* (7-8/92)
A657 *Macbeth* (8/92)
A1013 *Sleuth* (9/92)
A159 *Breaking the Code* (9/92)
A294 *Death and the Maiden* (9/92)
A301 *The Decorator* (10/92)
A241 *Comedy Of Errors* (10/92)
A93 *Barnum* (11/92)

The Playhouse

A868 *The Pocket Dream* (2/92)
A1196 *What The Butler Saw* (2-3/92)
A612 *Les Miserables* (4/92)
A430 *Gaudeamus* (4-5/92)
A442 *Goin' Local* (5/92)
A563 *A Judgement In Stone* (5/92)
A919 *The Rivals* (6/92)
A803 *Office Party* (9/92)
A456 *Grave Plots* (10/92)
A465 *Hamlet* (10/92)
A317 *Doctor Faustus* (11/92)
A311 *Dick Whittington* (12/92-1/93)
A188 *The Caretaker* (1-2/93)
A821 *One The Ledge* (2-3/93)
A119 *Big Night Out* (3-4/93)

Toot Hill Th.

A577 *King Lear* (10/92)

NOTTS

Kimberley Comp. School

A463 *Hamlet* (9/92)

Netherfield Comm

A1108 *Threepenny Story* (3/92)

NUNEATON

Barleston Ctre

A1233 *Women in Love* (11/92)

OAKHAM

Oakham Festival

A987 *Shakers* (6/92)

PETERBOROUGH

Stahl Theatre

A1169 *A View From The Bridge* (3/92)
A1105 *The Three Musketeers* (5/92)
A968 *The Secret Rapture* (9/92)
A1141 *Trilby & Svengali* (10/92)
A1088 *The Tender Husband* (10/92)
A578 *King Lear* (10/92)

REDBRIDGE

Redbridge Drama

A385 *Every Bit Of It* (12/92)

ROTHERHAM

Civic Theatre

A1145 *Turned Out Nice Again* (5/92)

S.NORMANTON

Picture Palace

A1233 *Women in Love* (11/92)

SANDWELL

Holly Lodge Sch

A303 *Devil's Only Sleeping* (11/92)

SHREWSBURY

Ashton Theatre

A418 *Frankie & Tommy* (10/92)

English Bridge Workshops

A303 *Devil's Only Sleeping* (11/92)

Music Hall

A1169 *A View From The Bridge* (3/92)
A268 *Cyrano De Bergerac* (12/92)

SOLIHULL

Library Theatre

A49 *Animal Farm* (3/92)

SOUTHPORT

Little Theatre

A753 *Much Ado About Nothing* (8/92)

SPALDING

Sth Holland Ctr.

A748 *Mrs Klein* (5/92)
A987 *Shakers* (6/92)
A1190 *The Way of All Flesh* (6/92)
A467 *Hamlet* (9/92)

STAFFORDSHIRE

Belgrave School

A1149 *Twelfth Night* (10/92)

STAFFORD

Gatehouse Th.

A467 *Hamlet* (11/92)

STAFFORDSHIRE

Prince Of Wales

A1145 *Turned Out Nice Again* (4/92)
A1105 *The Three Musketeers* (6/92)
A1149 *Twelfth Night* (10/92)

STAMFORD

Rutland Open Air

A719 *A Midsummer Night's Dream* (6-8/92)
A646 *Love's Labour's Lost* (6-8/92)
A565 *Julius Caesar* (6-8/92)

Stamford Arts C.

A157 *Brand* (4/92)
A1190 *The Way of All Flesh* (5/92)
A459 *Great God Brown* (10/92)
A1024 *The Solo Experience* (10/92)
A268 *Cyrano De Bergerac* (11/92)
A1031 *Song of Provence* (11/92)
A1088 *The Tender Husband* (11/92)

STOKE

Sixth Form College

A303 *Devil's Only Sleeping* (10/92)

STOURBRIDGE

Haybridge School

A172 *Burbage and the Bard* (6/92)

STRATFORD-UPON-AVON

Civic Hall

A1145 *Turned Out Nice Again* (5/92)

RST

A1046 *Stepping Out* (2/92)
A1068 *The Taming Of The Shrew* (3-9/92)
A713 *The Merry Wives Of Windsor* (8-9/92)
A67 *As You Like It* (4/92-1/93)
A1214 *The Winter's Tale* (6/92-1/93)
A53 *Antony and Cleopatra* (10/92-1/93)

Swan Th.
A1215 *The Winter's Tale* (2/92)
A561 *A Jovial Crew* (4-9/92)
A1067 *Tamburlaine The Great* (8/92-1/93)
A197 *The Changeling* (10/92-1/93)
A106 *The Beggar's Opera* (3/92-1/93)
A35 *All's Well That Ends Well* (6/92-1/93)

STRATFORD/AVON
The Other Place
A910 *Richard III* (8-9/92)
A802 *The Odyssey* (6/92-1/93)
A959 *School of Night* (10/92-1/93)

STROUD
Forest...College
A369 *Enemy To The People* (5/92)
A418 *Frankie & Tommy* (11/92)

SUTTON COLDFIELD
Highbury Th
A303 *Devil's Only Sleeping* (10/92)

SUTTON IN ASHFIELD
Sutton Centre
A418 *Frankie & Tommy* (11/92)
A100 *Beauty And The Beast* (12/92)

UPPINGHAM
Uppingham Th.
A987 *Shakers* (6/92)

W. BRIDGEFORD
Rushcliffe Leisure Centre
A100 *Beauty And The Beast* (12/92)

WALSALL
Garage Arts & Media Centre
A418 *Frankie & Tommy* (12/92)

WARWICK
Arts Centre
A60 *Arms and the Man* (2/92)
A925 *Roaring Girl's Hamlet* (3/92)
A748 *Mrs Klein* (5/92)

WHITCHURCH
Civic Centre
A365 *The End Of The Tunnel* (10/92)

WOLVERHAMPTON
Arena Th.
A1169 *A View From The Bridge* (2/92)
A1108 *Threepenny Story* (2/92)
A925 *Roaring Girl's Hamlet* (3/92)
A589 *La Ronde* (3/92)
A738 *Moose* (4/92)
A1190 *The Way of All Flesh* (5/92)
A578 *King Lear* (10/92)
A1024 *The Solo Experience* (10/92)
A365 *The End Of The Tunnel* (10/92)
A303 *Devil's Only Sleeping* (11/92)
A824 *Orlando* (11/92)
A385 *Every Bit Of It* (11/92)
A459 *Great God Brown* (11/92)
A418 *Frankie & Tommy* (12/92)
A836 *Out Of The Ordinary* (3/93)

Grand Theatre
A1082 *The Tempest* (2/92)
A610 *Liaisons Dangereuses* (3/92)
A1046 *Stepping Out* (3/92)
A1218 *Witness For The Prosecution* (3-4/92)
A94 *Bazaar and Rummage* (4/92)
A513 *The House Of Stairs* (4/92)
A395 *The Fancy Man* (5/92)
A1111 *Thunderbirds FAB* (6/92)
A467 *Hamlet* (6/92)
A242 *The Comedy Store* (10/92)
A275 *Dancing at Lughnasa* (11/92)
A657 *Macbeth* (11/92)
A927 *Robin* (11-12/92)
A803 *Office Party* (12/92)

WOMBOURNE
Ounsdale Sch
A303 *Devil's Only Sleeping* (11/92)

WORCESTER
Arts Workshop
A953 *Scenic Flights* (10/92)

Swan Theatre
A343 *The Dramatic Attitudes* (2/92)
A262 *Curse of Mummy's Tomb* (3/92)
A1048 *Stig Of The Dump* (4/92)
A457 *Gravity Swing* (5/92)
A56 *Anzacs Over England* (9-10/92)
A637 *Loot* (10/92)
A439 *Glass Menagerie* (11/92)
A803 *Office Party* (11/92)
A23 *Aladdin* (12/92-1/93)
A902 *Return of the Native* (2-3/93)
A819 *One For The Road* (3-4/93)

WORCS.
Bewdley Festival
A418 *Frankie & Tommy* (10/92)

WORKSOP
Regal Arts Ctre
A49 *Animal Farm* (3/92)
A1190 *The Way of All Flesh* (6/92)
A463 *Hamlet* (10/92)
A418 *Frankie & Tommy* (10/92)
A268 *Cyrano De Bergerac* (11/92)
A100 *Beauty And The Beast* (12/92)

EAST ANGLIA

B. ST EDMUNDS
The Metropolitan
A467 *Hamlet* (11/92)
A268 *Cyrano De Bergerac* (11/92)
A100 *Beauty And The Beast* (12/92)

BENWICK
Village Hall
A100 *Beauty And The Beast* (11/92)

BURY ST EDMUNDS
Th. Royal
A200 *Charley's Aunt* (2/92)
A1215 *The Winter's Tale* (3/92)
A672 *The Magic Storybook* (3/92)
A507 *Hot Italian Nights* (3/92)
A457 *Gravity Swing* (5/92)
A748 *Mrs Klein* (5/92)
A714 *Metamorphosis* (6/92)
A987 *Shakers* (6/92)
A1163 *Up 'N' Under* (7/92)
A968 *The Secret Rapture* (9/92)
A752 *Much Ado About Nothing* (9/92)
A1044 *State of Bewilderment* (10/92)
A803 *Office Party* (10/92)
A648 *Lulu* (10/92)
A467 *Hamlet* (11/92)
A859 *Pig In A Poke* (11/92)
A1031 *Song of Provence* (11/92)
A1088 *The Tender Husband* (12/92)

CAMBRIDGE
ADC Theatre
A1217 *Withering Looks* (7/92)

Arts Th.
A60 *Arms and the Man* (1-2/92)
A457 *Gravity Swing* (3/92)
A1215 *The Winter's Tale* (3/92)
A724 *The Miser* (3-4/92)
A200 *Charley's Aunt* (4/92)
A451 *Gormenghast* (4/92)
A275 *Dancing at Lughnasa* (4/92)
A1046 *Stepping Out* (5/92)
A1111 *Thunderbirds FAB* (5/92)
A909 *Revenger's Tragedy* (5-6/92)
A1163 *Up 'N' Under* (6/92)
A651 *M. Butterfly* (7/92)
A752 *Much Ado About Nothing* (7-8/92)
A294 *Death and the Maiden* (9/92)
A513 *The House Of Stairs* (9/92)
A270 *Cyrano De Bergerac* (9/92)
A648 *Lulu* (9-10/92)
A920 *Rivals* (10/92)
A594 *Lady Be Good* (10/92)
A859 *Pig In A Poke* (10/92)
A1044 *State of Bewilderment* (11/92)
A803 *Office Party* (11/92)
A425 *Game of Love & Chance* (11-12/92)
A225 *Cinderella* (12/92-1/93)

Cambridge Fest.
A467 *Hamlet* (7/92)

Drama Centre
A1088 *The Tender Husband* (10/92)
A268 *Cyrano De Bergerac* (11/92)

The Junction
A510 *Hound* (4/92)
A48 *Angels & Amazons* (4/92)
A1206 *Why Things Happen* (11/92)
A385 *Every Bit Of It* (12/92)
A836 *Out Of The Ordinary* (3/93)

DAVENTRY
Tertiary College
A1149 *Twelfth Night* (10/92)

ELY
The Tithe Barn
A467 *Hamlet* (9/92)

FRIDAY BRIDGE
Village Hall
A100 *Beauty And The Beast* (11/92)

HUNSTANTON
Hunstanton Fest.
A172 *Burbage and the Bard* (6/92)

Princess Th.
A1031 *Song of Provence* (11/92)

IPSWICH

Regent Th.

A116 *The BFG* (6/92)
A242 *The Comedy Store* (10/92)

Sir J. Mills Th.

A846 *Peculiar People* (3/92)

Wolsey Theatre

A1225 *The Woman Destroyed* (3/92)
A10 *Absent Friends* (2-3/92)
A717 *A Midsummer Night's Dream* (3-4/92)
A1178 *Viva Detroit* (4/92)
A985 *Shadowlands* (4-5/92)
A321 *A Dolls House* (5/92)
A795 *Noises Off* (6/92)
A114 *Beyond Reasonable Doubt* (7/92)
A298 *Deathtrap* (9/92)
A183 *Candida* (9-10/92)
A1031 *Song of Provence* (10/92)
A1170 *View From The Bridge* (10-11/92)
A450 *Goodnight Mr Tom* (11-12/92)
A276 *Dangerous Corner* (1-2/93)
A494 *High Society* (12/92-2/93)

Wolsey Studio

A1094 *The Slicing Edge* (3/92)
A327 *Don Juan* (10-11/92)
A816 *Once In A While* (11-12/92)
A640 *The Lost Child* (12/92-1/93)
A798 *The Nose* (1/93)
A922 *Road* (2/93)

KING'S LYNN

King's Lynn Arts

A48 *Angels & Amazons* (4/92)
A369 *Enemy To The People* (4/92)
A467 *Hamlet* (7/92)
A968 *The Secret Rapture* (9/92)
A1031 *Song of Provence* (10/92)
A268 *Cyrano De Bergerac* (11/92)
A1088 *The Tender Husband* (11/92)

LOWESTOFT

The Marina Th.

A971 *See How They Run* (6/92)
A1111 *Thunderbirds FAB* (10/92)
A657 *Macbeth* (10/92)
A467 *Hamlet* (11/92)

NORWICH

Hewitt School

A369 *Enemy To The People* (4/92)

Norwich Art Ctr.

A369 *Enemy To The People* (4/92)
A467 *Hamlet* (9-10/92)
A418 *Frankie & Tommy* (11/92)

Norwich Puppet

A1110 *Thumbelina* (12/91-2/92)
A471 *Hansel And Gretel* (12/91-2/92)
A570 *Just So* (9/92)
A1019 *Snow Queen* (11/92-1/93)
A858 *The Pied Piper* (11/92-1/93)

Th. Royal

A382 *Evening With Gary L.* (12/92)
A221 *Cinderella* (12/92-1/93)
A803 *Office Party* (2/93)

PARSONS DROVE

Village Hall

A100 *Beauty And The Beast* (11/92)

PETERBOROUGH

Arts Centre

A1178 *Viva Detroit* (5/92)
A748 *Mrs Klein* (5/92)

Key Theatre

A762 *My Cousin Rachel* (4/92)
A345 *Driving Miss Daisy* (5/92)
A657 *Macbeth* (6/92)
A592 *Ladies' Night* (7/92)
A1015 *Slice Of Saturday...* (7/92)
A1248 *You Must Be The Husband* (7/92)
A831 *Our Day Out* (8/92)
A1218 *Witness For The Prosecution* (8-9/92)
A944 *Run for Your Wife* (9/92)
A803 *Office Party* (10/92)
A382 *Evening With Gary L.* (11/92)
A739 *Mother Goose* (12/92-1/93)

SUDBURY

Quay Theatre

A748 *Mrs Klein* (4/92)
A1190 *The Way of All Flesh* (5/92)
A325 *Don Juan In Hell* (5/92)
A767 *My Mother Said* (6/92)
A1217 *Withering Looks* (10/92)
A418 *Frankie & Tommy* (10/92)
A1031 *Song of Provence* (10/92)

WESTCLIFF-ON-SEA

Dixon Studio

A268 *Cyrano De Bergerac* (12/92)

Palace Th.

A835 *Out Of Order* (2/92)
A337 *Double Double* (3/92)
A49 *Animal Farm* (3/92)
A984 *Shadowlands* (5/92)
A1057 *Strippers* (5-6/92)
A1041 *Stageland* (7/92)
A582 *The Kingfisher* (8/92)
A1248 *You Must Be The Husband* (8/92)
A9 *Absent Friends* (9-10/92)
A1113 *Time Windows* (10/92)
A297 *Death Of A Salesman* (11/92)
A102 *Beauty And The Beast* (12/92-1/93)
A754 *Muder At The Vicerage* (1-2/93)

WISBECH,CAMBS

Angles Centre

A418 *Frankie & Tommy* (11/92)
A88 *Ballad of Limehouse* (12/92)

WISBECH

Empire Theatre

A1145 *Turned Out Nice Again* (4/92)

NORTH WEST

ALTRINCHAM

Club Theatre

A577 *King Lear* (10/92)

ASHTON-UNDER-LYNE

Tameside Th

A55 *Anybody for Murder?* (5/92)
A388 *Experiment In Contra.* (11/92)

BAILRIGG

Nuffield Studio

A824 *Orlando* (11/92)

BARROW-IN-FURNESS

Forum 28

A657 *Macbeth* (5/92)
A987 *Shakers* (6/92)
A920 *Rivals* (11/92)
A385 *Every Bit Of It* (11/92)

BLACKPOOL

Grand Th.

A60 *Arms and the Man* (2/92)
A200 *Charley's Aunt* (3/92)
A738 *Moose* (4/92)
A762 *My Cousin Rachel* (4/92)
A1105 *The Three Musketeers* (4/92)
A563 *A Judgement In Stone* (6/92)
A1111 *Thunderbirds FAB* (6/92)
A107 *Belle Reprieve* (8-9/92)
A594 *Lady Be Good* (11/92)
A1088 *The Tender Husband* (11/92)
A1044 *State of Bewilderment* (12/92)
A541 *An Inspector Calls* (12/92)
A803 *Office Party* (3/93)

Opera House

A168 *Buddy* (7-11/92)

BOLTON

Octopus Studio

A469 *Hanging Around* (12/92)

Octagon Th.

A1036 *Spring and Port Wine* (2-3/92)
A745 *Mowgli - Enfant Loup* (3/92)
A206 *Children Of Lesser God* (4/92)
A796 *The Norman Conquests* (5-6/92)
A399 *Feed* (9-10/92)
A1075 *Taste of Honey* (10/92)
A30 *Alfie* (11/92)
A27 *Aladdin Bolton* (12/92-1/93)
A542 *Inspector Calls* (1-2/93)
A296 *Death of A Salesman* (2-3/93)

BOWNESS

Old Laundry Th

A100 *Beauty And The Beast* (12/92)

BRADFORD

Alhambra Th.

A339 *Down And Out...* (3/92)
A933 *Rocky Horror Show* (3/92)
A807 *On Approval* (3/92)
A168 *Buddy* (3-4/92)
A430 *Gaudeamus* (4/92)
A1033 *The Sound Of Music* (5/92)
A669 *Madness of George III* (5/92)
A249 *The Corn Is Green* (6/92)
A763 *My Fair Lady* (6-7/92)
A116 *The BFG* (7/92)
A159 *Breaking the Code* (8/92)
A275 *Dancing at Lughnasa* (9/92)
A1111 *Thunderbirds FAB* (9/92)
A641 *Lost in Yonkers* (10/92)
A465 *Hamlet* (10/92)
A362 *Elvis - the Musical* (11/92)
A541 *An Inspector Calls* (11/92)

A241 *Comedy Of Errors* (12/92)
A928 *Robin Hood* (12/92-2/93)
A821 *One The Ledge* (4/93)

Alhambra St

A1105 *The Three Musketeers* (6/92)
A294 *Death and the Maiden* (8/92)
A418 *Frankie & Tommy* (10/92)
A1088 *The Tender Husband* (10/92)
A270 *Cyrano De Bergerac* (10/92)
A122 *Billy Liar* (3/93)

Robin Mills

A609 *Les Atrides* (7/92)

St George's Hall

A1015 *Slice Of Saturday...* (6/92)

BROUGHTON

Victory Hall

A509 *Houdini* (11/92)

BURNLEY

Mechanics Theatr

A1145 *Turned Out Nice Again* (5/92)

BUXTON

Opera House

A417 *Frankie & Johnny* (2/92)
A906 *The Revenger's Tragedy* (3/92)
A231 *Closer Than Ever* (5/92)
A657 *Macbeth* (5/92)
A502 *Home At Seven* (5/92)
A354 *Eductaing Rita* (5/92)
A105 *Bedside Manners* (5/92)
A1111 *Thunderbirds FAB* (6/92)
A55 *Anybody for Murder?* (6/92)
A1015 *Slice Of Saturday...* (6-7/92)
A577 *King Lear* (9/92)
A463 *Hamlet* (9/92)
A787 *Nightmare* (9/92)
A294 *Death and the Maiden* (9-10/92)
A473 *Happy As A Sandbag* (10/92)
A1044 *State of Bewilderment* (12/92)

CHESTER

Gateway Th.

A472 *Hapgood* (1-2/92)
A429 *Gaslight* (2-3/92)
A674 *The Maintenance Man* (4-5/92)
A549 *It's A Girl* (5-6/92)
A152 *Bouncers* (7-8/92)
A615 *Lettice And Lovage* (9-10/92)
A701 *Measure For Measure* (11/92)
A1155 *The Ugly Duckling* (12/92-1/93)

CHESTERFIELD

Pomegranate Th.

A1145 *Turned Out Nice Again* (4/92)
A473 *Happy As A Sandbag* (11/92)

CHESTER

The Cathedral

A770 *Mystery Plays* (6-7/92)

CREWE

Alsager Arts C.

A363 *Emanuelle Enchanted* (11/92)
A388 *Experiment In Contra.* (11/92)

Shavington Sport

A1172 *A View From The Bridge* (6/92)
A936 *Romeo and Juliet* (6/92)

CUMBRIA

Brewery Arts Cen

A578 *King Lear* (1/92)

ELLESMERE

Ellesmere Arts C

A418 *Frankie & Tommy* (10/92)
A268 *Cyrano De Bergerac* (11/92)

ELLESMERE PORT

Grange Arts Ctre

A510 *Hound* (5/92)

KNUTSFORD

Little Theatre

A463 *Hamlet* (10/92)

LANCASTER

Dukes Theatre

A271 *Daisy Pulls it Off* (9-10/92)
A318 *Doctor Faustus* (10-11/92)
A226 *Cinderella* (12/92-1/93)

Grand Th.

A94 *Bazaar and Rummage* (10/92)

Nuffield Theatre

A738 *Moose* (5/92)
A363 *Emanuelle Enchanted* (10/92)
A577 *King Lear* (10/92)
A388 *Experiment In Contra.* (11/92)

LANCASTER

Williamson Park

A1069 *Taming of the Shrew* (6-7/92)
A1222 *Wizard of Oz* (7-8/92)

LIVERPOOL

Bluecoat Arts

A1232 *Woman Who Cooked* (4/92)
A48 *Angels & Amazons* (5/92)

Empire Th.

A763 *My Fair Lady* (4/92)
A698 *Me And My Girl* (4-5/92)
A116 *The BFG* (5/92)
A657 *Macbeth* (6-7/92)
A168 *Buddy* (11/92)

Everyman Th.

A827 *Othello* (1-2/92)
A956 *The School For Scandal* (3-4/92)
A448 *Good Person Of Sezuan* (4-5/92)
A510 *Hound* (5/92)
A185 *Candide* (5-6/92)
A751 *Much Ado About Nothing* (10-11/92)
A680 *Man in the Moon* (11-12/92)
A1219 *Wizard of Oz* (12/92-1/93)

Melling Tithebarn

A388 *Experiment In Contra.* (11/92)

Playhouse

A815 *Once A Catholic* (2-3/92)
A5 *99, Heyworth Street* (3/92)
A77 *Awfully Big Adventure* (3-4/92)
A513 *The House Of Stairs* (5/92)
A651 *M. Butterfly* (5/92)
A1046 *Stepping Out* (5/92)
A893 *Raving Beauties* (6/92)
A690 *The Marvellous Boy* (6/92)
A530 *Imagine* (7-8/92)
A812 *On The Piste* (8-9/92)
A1090 *19th Hole* (9-10/92)
A927 *Robin* (10/92)
A791 *No Trams To Lime St.* (9-10/92)
A995 *Shirley Valentine* (10-11/92)
A1147 *Twelfth Night* (11-12/92)
A74 *At Fifty She Discovered The Sea* (11-12/92)

Playhouse Studio

A973 *Self Catering* (9-10/92)
A1192 *Weldon Rising* (10-11/92)

Unity Theatre

A365 *The End Of The Tunnel* (10/92)
A578 *King Lear* (10-11/92)
A88 *Ballad of Limehouse* (11/92)

MACCLESFIELD

Mad's Little The

A418 *Frankie & Tommy* (10/92)

MANCHESTER

Contact Th.

A272 *The Dance & Railroad* (3/92)
A702 *Measure For Measure* (4-5/92)
A232 *Cloud 9* (5-6/92)
A1178 *Viva Detroit* (6/92)
A258 *Crime of Love* (6/92)
A386 *Excess XS* (9-10/92)
A122 *Billy Liar* (10/92)
A963 *Seagull* (10-11/92)
A360 *Elidor* (12/92-1/93)

Forum Th.

A687 *A Marginal Affair* (3/92)
A55 *Anybody for Murder?* (4/92)
A794 *Noises Off* (9-10/92)
A281 *Dangerous Obsession* (10-11/92)
A852 *Peter Pan* (12/92-1/93)
A545 *Into The Woods* (2/93)
A813 *On The Piste* (3/93)

Granada Car Park

A229 *Chinese State Circus* (9-10/92)

Grange Arts Ctr.

A467 *Hamlet* (11/92)

Library Th.

A1242 *The Writing Game* (3-4/92)
A231 *Closer Than Ever* (4-5/92)
A1239 *Working* (5/92)
A1217 *Withering Looks* (9/92)
A163 *Broadway Bound* (9-10/92)
A708 *Merchant of Venice* (10-11/92)
A217 *Christmas Carol* (11/92-1/93)
A433 *Ghosts* (1-2/93)

Opera House

A36 *'Allo, 'Allo* (3/92)
A168 *Buddy* (11/91-2/92)
A763 *My Fair Lady* (2-3/92)
A610 *Liaisons Dangereuses* (3/92)
A200 *Charley's Aunt* (4/92)
A1145 *Turned Out Nice Again* (4/92)
A1015 *Slice Of Saturday...* (5/92)
A592 *Ladies' Night* (6/92)
A116 *The BFG* (6/92)
A490 *The Heiress* (6/92)
A4 *70, Girls, 70* (6-7/92)

A657 *Macbeth* (7/92)
A808 *On Golden Pond* (8/92)
A1218 *Witness For The Prosecution* (8/92)
A275 *Dancing at Lughnasa* (8/92)
A391 *Fallen Angels* (9/92)
A93 *Barnum* (9-10/92)
A933 *Rocky Horror Show* (11/92)
A242 *The Comedy Store* (11/92)
A29 *Alfie* (11-12/92)
A20 *Aladdin* (12/92-2/93)
A903 *Forbidden Planet(Tour)* (5/93)

Palace Th.
A898 *Reflected Glory* (3/92)
A1054 *Straight & Narrow* (3-4/92)
A611 *Les Miserables* (4-10/92)

Royal Exchange
A998 *Sidewalk Sidney* (1-2/92)
A936 *Romeo and Juliet* (2-3/92)
A1172 *A View From The Bridge* (4/92)
A1234 *Women Laughing* (4-5/92)
A897 *The Recruiting Officer* (5-6/92)
A528 *An Ideal Husband* (7-8/92)
A645 *Love's Labour's Lost* (9-10/92)
A143 *Blues for Mr Charlie* (10-11/92)
A801 *Odd Women* (11-12/92)
A737 *Moonstone* (12/92-1/93)
A166 *Brothers Kramazov* (2/93)

Royal Northern
A1111 *Thunderbirds FAB* (9/92)

The Green Room
A48 *Angels & Amazons* (4/92)
A1232 *Woman Who Cooked* (4/92)
A510 *Hound* (5/92)
A772 *Name* (6/92)
A14 *Adult Child/Dead Child* (6/92)
A578 *King Lear* (10/92)
A388 *Experiment In Contra.* (11/92)
A363 *Emanuelle Enchanted* (11/92)

MANSFIELD

Civic Theatre
A340 *Dracula Spectacular* (6/92)

NORTHWICH

Harlequin Th
A574 *Killing Passion* (3/92)
A1232 *Woman Who Cooked* (4/92)
A48 *Angels & Amazons* (6/92)
A1046 *Stepping Out* (9/92)
A577 *King Lear* (10/92)

Village Hall
A268 *Cyrano De Bergerac* (11/92)

OLDHAM

Coliseum Th.
A1217 *Withering Looks* (10/92)

OSWALDTWISTLE

Civic Theatre
A48 *Angels & Amazons* (6/92)

PRESTON

Charter Th.
A571 *Kafka's Dick* (2/92)
A417 *Frankie & Johnny* (3/92)
A1046 *Stepping Out* (4/92)
A1145 *Turned Out Nice Again* (5/92)
A762 *My Cousin Rachel* (5/92)
A657 *Macbeth* (6/92)
A473 *Happy As A Sandbag* (11/92)
A920 *Rivals* (11/92)
A746 *Mr A's Amazing Maze* (5/93)

Poly Arts Centre
A268 *Cyrano De Bergerac* (11/92)

SKELMERSDALE

Library Arts Th.
A157 *Brand* (4/92)

ST ANNE'S

Blackpool Coll
A268 *Cyrano De Bergerac* (11/92)

STOCKPORT

Centre Stage
A268 *Cyrano De Bergerac* (11/92)

Davenport Th.
A553 *Jack And The Beanstalk* (12/92-1/93)

STOCKTON ON TEES

Dovecot
A1088 *The Tender Husband* (10/92)
A418 *Frankie & Tommy* (11/92)

TELFORD

Madeley Court Theatre
A418 *Frankie & Tommy* (10/92)

New College
A303 *Devil's Only Sleeping* (10/92)

Oakengates Th
A100 *Beauty And The Beast* (11/92)

TIVERTON

Blundells School
A288 *Dead Man's Hat* (11/92)

ULVERSTON

Coronation Hall
A509 *Houdini* (11/92)

WARRINGTON

Nth.Cheshire Col
A388 *Experiment In Contra.* (11/92)

WARRINGTON, CHESHIRE

Parr Hall
A48 *Angels & Amazons* (4/92)
A418 *Frankie & Tommy* (10/92)

WIDNES

Halton Guildhall
A510 *Hound* (5/92)

NORTH EAST

UK Tour
A797 *Northern Trawl* (11/92-3/93)

BILLINGHAM

Forum Theatre
A933 *Rocky Horror Show* (3/92)
A1046 *Stepping Out* (3-4/92)
A513 *The House Of Stairs* (4/92)
A104 *Bedroom Farce* (4/92)
A651 *M. Butterfly* (4-5/92)
A275 *Dancing at Lughnasa* (5/92)
A1015 *Slice Of Saturday...* (5/92)
A1218 *Witness For The Prosecution* (7/92)
A907 *Revenge* (9/92)
A94 *Bazaar and Rummage* (10/92)
A391 *Fallen Angels* (10/92)
A927 *Robin* (11/92)

BRADFORD

Treadwell's
A460 *Grope* (10-11/92)

CHESTERFIELD

Arts Centre
A268 *Cyrano De Bergerac* (11/92)

DARLINGTON

Civic Theatre
A898 *Reflected Glory* (2/92)
A1148 *Twelfth Night* (3/92)
A655 *Macbeth* (3/92)
A200 *Charley's Aunt* (3/92)
A2 *42nd Street* (4/92)
A490 *The Heiress* (6/92)
A987 *Shakers* (6/92)
A762 *My Cousin Rachel* (6/92)
A1218 *Witness For The Prosecution* (9/92)
A594 *Lady Be Good* (9/92)
A301 *The Decorator* (10/92)
A787 *Nightmare* (10/92)
A745 *Mowgli - Enfant Loup* (11/92)
A382 *Evening With Gary L.* (11/92)
A81 *Babes In The Wood* (12/92-1/93)

DONCASTER

Civic Theatre
A1145 *Turned Out Nice Again* (5/92)
A340 *Dracula Spectacular* (6/92)

GRIMSBY

Caxton Theatre
A268 *Cyrano De Bergerac* (12/92)

Grimsby Leis.
A1172 *A View From The Bridge* (5/92)
A936 *Romeo and Juliet* (5/92)
A467 *Hamlet* (10/92)

HARROGATE

Harrogate Th.
A1217 *Withering Looks* (7/92)
A128 *Blithe Spirit* (9-10/92)
A661 *Macbeth* (10/92)
A505 *The Hostage* (10-11/92)
A90 *The Barber of Seville* (11-12/92)
A310 *Dick Whittington* (12/92-1/93)

HARTLEPOOL

Town Hall
A510 *Hound* (5/92)

HORNCASTLE

Lion Theatre
A418 *Frankie & Tommy* (11/92)

HORNSEA

Hornsea School
A268 *Cyrano De Bergerac* (12/92)

HUDDERSFIELD

Venn Street
A925 *Roaring Girl's Hamlet* (3/92)
A385 *Every Bit Of It* (11/92)

HULL

Hull New Th.
A168 *Buddy* (2-3/92)
A2 *42nd Street* (3-4/92)
A933 *Rocky Horror Show* (4/92)

A1046 *Stepping Out* (4/92)
A655 *Macbeth* (4-5/92)
A275 *Dancing at Lughnasa* (5/92)
A762 *My Cousin Rachel* (6/92)
A971 *See How They Run* (6-7/92)
A592 *Ladies' Night* (9/92)
A94 *Bazaar and Rummage* (9-10/92)
A368 *Endgame* (10/92)
A301 *The Decorator* (10/92)
A29 *Alfie* (10/92)
A1082 *The Tempest* (11/92)
A927 *Robin* (11/92)
A362 *Elvis - the Musical* (11-12/92)

M.Rawlings Ctre
A268 *Cyrano De Bergerac* (12/92)

Marina Boat Head
A912 *Richard III* (6/92)

Spring St. Th.
A589 *La Ronde* (3/92)
A49 *Animal Farm* (3-4/92)
A58 *April In Paris* (4-5/92)
A1116 *TO* (5-6/92)
A690 *The Marvellous Boy* (6/92)
A151 *Bouncers* (7-8/92)
A418 *Frankie & Tommy* (9-10/92)
A577 *King Lear* (10/92)
A463 *Hamlet* (10/92)
A48 *Angels & Amazons* (10/92)
A797 *Northern Trawl* (11/92)
A803 *Office Party* (12/92-1/93)
A427 *Gargling With Jelly* (12/92-1/93)

LANCS

College of F.E.
A467 *Hamlet* (9/92)

LEEDS

Grand Th.
A1230 *Woman Of No Importance* (3/92)
A880 *Private Lives* (3/92)
A898 *Reflected Glory* (3/92)
A104 *Bedroom Farce* (3-4/92)
A592 *Ladies' Night* (6/92)
A808 *On Golden Pond* (7/92)
A4 *70, Girls, 70* (7/92)
A1046 *Stepping Out* (7-8/92)
A508 *Hot Stuff* (8/92)
A242 *The Comedy Store* (10/92)
A29 *Alfie* (11/92)
A1082 *The Tempest* (11/92)
A655 *Macbeth* (11/92)

The Polytechnic
A385 *Every Bit Of It* (11/92)

W/Yorks Playh.
A462 *Gulf Between Us* (1-2/92)
A50 *Anna Karenina* (2/92)
A908 *The Revenger's Tragedy* (2-3/92)
A918 *The Rivals* (3-4/92)
A476 *Happy Families* (2-4/92)
A1101 *Three Girls In Blue* (4-5/92)
A1089 *Tess Of The D'Urbervil* (4-5/92)
A619 *Life is a Dream* (5-6/92)
A8 *Absent Friends* (6-7/92)
A1207 *Wicked Old Man* (6-7/92)
A586 *Kvetch* (7-8/92)
A876 *Prin* (9-10/92)
A1238 *A Working Woman* (11-12/92)
A401 *Fiddler On The Roof* (11/92-1/93)
A803 *Office Party* (3/93)

LINCOLN

Th. Royal
A1248 *You Must Be The Husband* (3/92)
A507 *Hot Italian Nights* (4/92)
A672 *The Magic Storybook* (4/92)
A1218 *Witness For The Prosecution* (4/92)
A599 *The Late Edwina Black* (4/92)
A714 *Metamorphosis* (5/92)
A340 *Dracula Spectacular* (6/92)
A55 *Anybody for Murder?* (6/92)
A473 *Happy As A Sandbag* (10/92)
A1111 *Thunderbirds FAB* (10/92)
A594 *Lady Be Good* (10/92)
A803 *Office Party* (5/93)

The Lawn
A467 *Hamlet* (9/92)

MANSFIELD

Comm. Arts Centr
A172 *Burbage and the Bard* (5/92)

Mansfield Leis.
A1172 *A View From The Bridge* (5/92)
A936 *Romeo and Juliet* (5/92)
A679 *Man Cub* (6/92)
A459 *Great God Brown* (10/92)
A100 *Beauty And The Beast* (12/92)

MIDDLESBOROUGH

Little Theatre
A577 *King Lear* (5/92)
A463 *Hamlet* (5/92)
A457 *Gravity Swing* (6/92)
A679 *Man Cub* (8/92)
A994 *Sherlock Holmes* (9/92)
A467 *Hamlet* (10/92)
A129 *Blodeuwedd* (10/92)
A968 *The Secret Rapture* (11/92)

NEWCASTLE/TYNE

Gulbenkian Th.
A690 *The Marvellous Boy* (5/92)
A666 *Madame Mao's Memories* (5/92)
A1190 *The Way of All Flesh* (6/92)
A1217 *Withering Looks* (10/92)
A788 *No 3 Pied Piper Street* (10/92)

NEWCASTLE/U/TYNE

Live Theatre
A510 *Hound* (5/92)
A1250 *Your Home In The West* (10/92)
A509 *Houdini* (11/92)
A385 *Every Bit Of It* (11/92)

NEWCASTLE/TYNE

New Tyne Th.
A200 *Charley's Aunt* (5/92)
A1041 *Stageland* (5/92)
A463 *Hamlet* (6/92)
A577 *King Lear* (6/92)
A657 *Macbeth* (10/92)
A362 *Elvis - the Musical* (10/92)

NEWCASTLE/U/TYNE

Playhouse
A1176 *The Virtuoso* (2/92)
A28 *The Alchemist* (3/92)
A1095 *The Thebans* (3/92)
A1154 *Two Gents Of Verona* (3/92)
A92 *Barnstormers* (3-4/92)
A1105 *The Three Musketeers* (4/92)
A987 *Shakers* (5/92)
A803 *Office Party* (12/92-1/93)

Th. Royal
A732 *Moment Of Weakness* (3/92)

Th. Royal
A938 *Romeo And Juliet* (3/92)
A566 *Julius Caesar* (3/92)
A1152 *Twelfth Night* (3/92)
A933 *Rocky Horror Show* (3-4/92)
A669 *Madness of George III* (4/92)
A655 *Macbeth* (5/92)
A1033 *The Sound Of Music* (5-6/92)
A275 *Dancing at Lughnasa* (6-7/92)
A116 *The BFG* (7/92)
A159 *Breaking the Code* (7/92)
A763 *My Fair Lady* (8-9/92)
A641 *Lost in Yonkers* (10/92)
A541 *An Inspector Calls* (10/92)
A29 *Alfie* (11/92)
A821 *One The Ledge* (4/93)

NOTTINGHAM

Minster School
A577 *King Lear* (9/92)
A100 *Beauty And The Beast* (12/92)

Powerhouse
A363 *Emanuelle Enchanted* (11/92)

RICHMOND

Georgian Theatre
A748 *Mrs Klein* (6/92)
A172 *Burbage and the Bard* (6/92)

ROTHERHAM

Rawmarsh School
A987 *Shakers* (6/92)

Rotherham Arts
A738 *Moose* (3/92)
A385 *Every Bit Of It* (11/92)
A88 *Ballad of Limehouse* (11/92)

SCARBOROUGH

Futurist Theatre
A1145 *Turned Out Nice Again* (5/92)

Nth.Riding Coll.
A363 *Emanuelle Enchanted* (11/92)
A463 *Hamlet* (11/92)
A577 *King Lear* (11/92)

S. Joseph Studio
A120 *Bigger Slice of Pie* (7-9/92)
A1173 *Village Wooing* (7-9/92)
A57 *Apple Blossom Aftern'n* (7-9/92)
A989 *The Shawl* (8-9/92)

Stephen Joseph
A932 *Rocket To The Moon* (4-7/92)
A1112 *Time Of My Life* (4-8/92)
A777 *Neville's Island* (6-9/92)

SCUNTHORPE

Civic Theatre

A803 *Office Party* (2/92)
A55 *Anybody for Murder?* (4-5/92)
A467 *Hamlet* (5/92)
A582 *The Kingfisher* (6/92)
A479 *Haunted Hotel* (9-10/92)

SELBY

Selby High Sch.

A369 *Enemy To The People* (4-5/92)

SHEFFIELD

Crucible Th.

A1049 *Stirrings in Sheffield on Sat Night* (1-2/92)
A1046 *Stepping Out* (3/92)
A995 *Shirley Valentine* (3/92)
A759 *Music Hall* (3/92)
A104 *Bedroom Farce* (3/92)
A275 *Dancing at Lughnasa* (3-4/92)
A457 *Gravity Swing* (5/92)
A463 *Hamlet* (6/92)
A577 *King Lear* (6/92)
A177 *Cabaret* (6/92)
A967 *Diary Of Adrian Mole* (7/92)
A720 *A Midsummer Night's ..* (10/92)
A59 *Armed And Dangerous* (10/92)
A1111 *Thunderbirds FAB* (10/92)
A555 *Jane Eyre* (11/92)
A851 *Peter Pan* (12/92-1/93)

Library Theatre

A1178 *Viva Detroit* (4/92)

Lyceum Th.

A1230 *Woman Of No Importance* (2/92)
A168 *Buddy* (2/92)
A513 *The House Of Stairs* (3-4/92)
A807 *On Approval* (3-4/92)
A490 *The Heiress* (4/92)
A200 *Charley's Aunt* (4/92)
A669 *Madness of George III* (4-5/92)
A249 *The Corn Is Green* (5/92)
A1015 *Slice Of Saturday...* (6/92)
A4 *70, Girls, 70* (6/92)
A752 *Much Ado About Nothing* (7/92)
A592 *Ladies' Night* (7/92)
A1218 *Witness For The Prosecution* (8/92)
A1013 *Sleuth* (8/92)
A391 *Fallen Angels* (8/92)
A944 *Run for Your Wife* (8-9/92)
A382 *Evening With Gary L.* (9/92)
A159 *Breaking the Code* (9/92)
A527 *An Ideal Husband* (9-10/92)
A362 *Elvis - the Musical* (10/92)
A541 *An Inspector Calls* (11/92)
A29 *Alfie* (11/92)
A900 *Relatively Speaking* (12/92)
A21 *Aladdin* (12/92-1/93)

Merlin Theatre

A157 *Brand* (4/92)
A459 *Great God Brown* (10/92)

Montgomery Th.

A400 *Fern Hill* (7/92)

The Leadmill

A772 *Name* (6/92)
A365 *The End Of The Tunnel* (10/92)
A363 *Emanuelle Enchanted* (11/92)

WAKEFIELD

Theatre Royal

A1116 *TO* (4-5/92)
A58 *April In Paris* (5/92)
A1044 *State of Bewilderment* (9/92)
A479 *Haunted Hotel* (10/92)
A473 *Happy As A Sandbag* (11/92)

WHITLEY

Whitley Bay P/h.

A679 *Man Cub* (8/92)
A788 *No 3 Pied Piper Street* (11/92)
A122 *Billy Liar* (12/92)

YORK

Theatre Royal

A995 *Shirley Valentine* (5/92)
A104 *Bedroom Farce* (5/92)
A1247 *York Mystery Plays* (6-7/92)
A1198 *What The Butler Saw* (7-8/92)
A606 *Lend Me A Tenor* (8-9/92)
A533 *Imp. Of Being Earnest* (9-10/92)
A94 *Bazaar and Rummage* (10/92)
A275 *Dancing at Lughnasa* (10/92)
A803 *Office Party* (10/92)
A537 *In The Midnight Hour* (10-11/92)
A80 *Babes in the Wood* (12/92-1/93)
A873 *Price* (2/93)

York Arts Centre

A418 *Frankie & Tommy* (12/92)

NORTHERN COUNTIES

ASHINGTON

Ashington Leis.

A1172 *A View From The Bridge* (3-5/92)
A936 *Romeo and Juliet* (5/92)

BARROW IN FURNESS

Bradie's

A465 *Hamlet* (10/92)

BARROW-IN-FURNESS

VI Form Coll

A1190 *The Way of All Flesh* (6/92)
A418 *Frankie & Tommy* (10/92)
A465 *Hamlet* (10/92)

CARLISLE

Stanwix Arts Th

A578 *King Lear* (1/92)
A1169 *A View From The Bridge* (3/92)
A1108 *Threepenny Story* (3/92)
A738 *Moose* (4/92)
A1190 *The Way of All Flesh* (6/92)
A509 *Houdini* (10/92)
A365 *The End Of The Tunnel* (10/92)
A467 *Hamlet* (10/92)
A418 *Frankie & Tommy* (11/92)

The Sands Centre

A1172 *A View From The Bridge* (5/92)
A936 *Romeo and Juliet* (5/92)

CLEVELAND

Town Hall Theatr

A1145 *Turned Out Nice Again* (4/92)

CUMBRIA

Eden Arts Trust

A1083 *The Tempest* (6/92)
A415 *Frankenstein* (6/92)

HEXHAM

Queens Hall Arts

A451 *Gormenghast* (2/92)
A738 *Moose* (5/92)
A457 *Gravity Swing* (8/92)
A994 *Sherlock Holmes* (8/92)
A994 *Sherlock Holmes* (8/92)
A577 *King Lear* (10/92)
A463 *Hamlet* (10/92)
A1088 *The Tender Husband* (11/92)

ISLE OF MAN

Gaiety Th.

A395 *The Fancy Man* (5/92)
A1041 *Stageland* (6/92)
A657 *Macbeth* (2/93)

KENDAL

Kendal Town Hall

A1169 *A View From The Bridge* (3/92)
A509 *Houdini* (11/92)

KESWICK

Blue Box Th. By The Lake

A679 *Man Cub* (6/92)

Century Th.

A186 *Caprice* (3/92)
A679 *Man Cub* (6/92)
A1064 *Taking Steps* (7-9/92)
A173 *Business of Murder* (7-9/92)
A91 *Barefoot in the Park* (8-9/92)

SOUTH SHIELDS

Library Theatre

A509 *Houdini* (11/92)

SUNDERLAND

Empire Theatre

A94 *Bazaar and Rummage* (5/92)

TYNESIDE

Buddle Arts Ctre

A510 *Hound* (5/92)

SCOTLAND

ABERDEEN

Arts Centre

A258 *Crime of Love* (6/92)
A679 *Man Cub* (7/92)
A366 *End Of The Beginning* (11/92)

Haddo House

A366 *End Of The Beginning* (11/92)

His Majesty's Th.

A762 *My Cousin Rachel* (2/92)
A1033 *The Sound Of Music* (2-3/92)
A1082 *The Tempest* (3/92)
A655 *Macbeth* (3/92)
A2 *42nd Street* (5/92)
A763 *My Fair Lady* (6/92)
A592 *Ladies' Night* (7-8/92)
A275 *Dancing at Lughnasa* (9/92)

Produced exclusively for Plays & Players by SEARCHLINE

A391 *Fallen Angels* (9/92)
A362 *Elvis - the Musical* (10/92)
Lemon Tree
A88 *Ballad of Limehouse* (10/92)
ACHARACLE,H'LANDS
Village Hall
A467 *Hamlet* (7/92)
ARDRISHAIG
Ardishaig Hall
A366 *End Of The Beginning* (11/92)
AYR
Borderline Th
A366 *End Of The Beginning* (11/92)
Civic Th.
A157 *Brand* (4/92)
A48 *Angels & Amazons* (4/92)
A258 *Crime of Love* (5/92)
A459 *Great God Brown* (9/92)
Gaiety Theatre
A55 *Anybody for Murder?* (3/92)
A592 *Ladies' Night* (9/92)
BALLACHULISH, H'LAND
Village Hall
A1097 *Therese Raquin* (4/92)
BERWICK-U-TWEED
The Maltings
A463 *Hamlet* (10/92)
A577 *King Lear* (10/92)
A388 *Experiment In Contra.* (11/92)
A1088 *The Tender Husband* (11/92)
BOWNESS
The Old Laundry
A509 *Houdini* (10/92)
CASTLE DOUGLAS
High School
A366 *End Of The Beginning* (10/92)
CLYDEBANK
St Andrews Sch
A366 *End Of The Beginning* (11/92)
CUMBERNAULD
Cumbernauld Th.
A157 *Brand* (4/92)
A1119 *TO* (6-7/92)
A509 *Houdini* (10/92)
DINGWALL
Town Hall
A1097 *Therese Raquin* (4/92)
DUNDEE
Arts Centre
A366 *End Of The Beginning* (11/92)
Dundee Repertory
A536 *In Praise Of Love* (2-3/92)
A251 *Country Dance* (3/92)
A1097 *Therese Raquin* (4/92)
A1252 *Your Turn To Clean The Stairs* (4/92)
A972 *See That's Her!* (4-5/92)
A1041 *Stageland* (5/92)
A254 *Couples* (8/92)
A1183 *Walter* (8-9/92)
A270 *Cyrano De Bergerac* (9/92)
A1205 *Virginia Woolf* (9-10/92)
A1073 *Tartuffe* (10-11/92)

A710 *Merlin the Magnificent* (11/92-1/93)
DURNESS
Village Hall
A467 *Hamlet* (7/92)
EDINBURGH
The Pleasance (2)
A960 *School Of Night* (9/92)
Assembly Rooms
A1217 *Withering Looks* (8-9/92)
Assembly Hall
A422 *Fuente Ovejuna* (8-9/92)
George Square Theatre
A1111 *Thunderbirds FAB* (8-9/92)
A151 *Bouncers* (9/92)
King's Th.
A490 *The Heiress* (4-5/92)
A168 *Buddy* (6/92)
A4 *70, Girls, 70* (7-8/92)
A357 *Ein Traum, Was Sonst?* (8/92)
A669 *Madness of George III* (9/92)
A275 *Dancing at Lughnasa* (9/92)
A159 *Breaking the Code* (9-10/92)
A51 *Annie Get Your Gun* (10/92)
A29 *Alfie* (11/92)
Playhouse Th.
A933 *Rocky Horror Show* (3/92)
A763 *My Fair Lady* (6/92)
A698 *Me And My Girl* (12/92-2/93)
Royal Lyceum Th. Co
A1158 *Uncle Vanya* (3/92)
A709 *Merlin, The Search* (4/92)
A266 *Cuttin' A Rug* (4-5/92)
A447 *Good Morning Bill* (5-6/92)
A1137 *Travesties* (6-7/92)
A482 *Hay Fever* (7-8/92)
A1182 *Voysey Inheritance* (8/92)
A670 *Madras House* (8/92)
A958 *School For Wives* (9/92)
A806 *Old Times* (10/92)
A1070 *Taming Of The Shrew* (10-11/92)
A602 *Laurel and Hardy* (11-12/92)
A97 *Beauty And The Beast* (12/92-1/93)
A875 *Prime of Miss Jean* (1/93)
A874 *Price* (2/93)
A723 *Mirandolina* (3/93)
St Bride's Centre
A497 *His Majesty* (8/92)
A509 *Houdini* (10/92)
Th. Workshop
A366 *End Of The Beginning* (11/92)
Traverse Th.
A925 *Roaring Girl's Hamlet* (2-3/92)
A1191 *We* (3/92)
A872 *Powershifts* (3/92)
A332 *The Dorm* (3/92)
A1252 *Your Turn To Clean The Stairs* (4/92)
A905 *Revelations* (8-9/92)
A270 *Cyrano De Bergerac* (8-9/92)
A977 *Serpent Kills* (8-9/92)
A667 *Madame Mao's Memories* (8-9/92)
A620 *Life of Stuff* (8-9/92)
A236 *Columbus* (7-9/92)

A518 *House That Jack Bought* (9/92)
A230 *Clockwork Orange* (9-10/92)
A512 *House Among the Stars* (10-11/92)
A292 *Death And Dancing* (11/92)
A167 *Buchanan* (11-12/92)
A1162 *Unidentified Human* (11-12/92)
A385 *Every Bit Of It* (1/93)
FAROE ISLES
The Faroe Isles
A467 *Hamlet* (8/92)
FIFE
Fife College
A1097 *Therese Raquin* (4/92)
FINDHORN, H'LANDS
Village Hall
A467 *Hamlet* (7/92)
GALASHIELS
Volunteer Hall
A1097 *Therese Raquin* (4/92)
GLASGOW
Arches Th.
A1232 *Woman Who Cooked* (5/92)
A914 *Richard's Cork Leg* (10-11/92)
Bishoploch Hall
A366 *End Of The Beginning* (11/92)
Citz. Second Th.
A1 *1953* (2-3/92)
A191 *Casanova* (3-4/92)
A523 *Hypochondriacs* (4-5/92)
A1124 *Tomorrow We Do The Sky* (6-7/92)
A3 *47* (7/92)
A1185 *Wasp Factory* (9/92)
A799 *Not About Heroes* (10-11/92)
A124 *Birthday Party* (11-12/92)
A261 *Crying For The Moon* (12/92)
Citz. Third Th.
A781 *Niagara* (2-3/92)
A847 *Pelican* (3-4/92)
A829 *Other Places* (4-5/92)
A503 *Home Show Pieces* (9/92)
A1167 *Venus and Adonis* (10-11/92)
A247 *Conundrum* (11-12/92)
Citz. First Th.
A1058 *Summer Lightning* (2-3/92)
A649 *Lulu* (3-4/92)
A355 *Edward II* (5/92)
A652 *Macbeth* (5-6/92)
A356 *Eight to the Bar* (6-7/92)
A663 *MacWizard Fae Oz* (7/92)
A675 *Major Barbara* (9/92)
A1059 *Sweet Bird of Youth* (10-11/92)
A475 *Happy Days* (11/92)
A568 *The Jungle Book* (12/92-1/93)
Community Venue
A366 *End Of The Beginning* (11/92)
Dolphin Arts
A366 *End Of The Beginning* (11/92)
Drama Centre
A258 *Crime of Love* (5/92)

King's Th.
A1230 *Woman Of No Importance* (4/92)
A1033 *The Sound Of Music* (4-5/92)
A168 *Buddy* (6-7/92)
A763 *My Fair Lady* (8/92)
A51 *Annie Get Your Gun* (11/92)
Mercat Theatre
A366 *End Of The Beginning* (10/92)
New Athenaeum
A714 *Metamorphosis* (4/92)
Old Athenaeum Th
A369 *Enemy To The People* (3/92)
A366 *End Of The Beginning* (11/92)
Th. Royal
A104 *Bedroom Farce* (4-5/92)
A513 *The House Of Stairs* (6/92)
A1148 *Twelfth Night* (6/92)
A655 *Macbeth* (6/92)
A490 *The Heiress* (7/92)
A1111 *Thunderbirds FAB* (11/92)
A541 *An Inspector Calls* (11-12/92)
A821 *One The Ledge* (3-4/93)
The CCA
A388 *Experiment In Contra.* (12/92)
Tramway
A339 *Down And Out...* (4/92)
A1097 *Therese Raquin* (4/92)
A514 *House Of The Spirits* (4/92)
A430 *Gaudeamus* (5/92)
A845 *Patagonia* (5/92)
A563 *A Judgement In Stone* (5/92)
A516 *House Of America* (10/92)
A156 *Brace Up!* (10-11/92)
Tron Th.
A136 *Bloody Chamber* (5/92)
A446 *Good* (5/92)
A556 *Jesuit* (5/92)
A287 *Dead Heroic* (6/92)
A972 *See That's Her!* (6/92)
A626 *Lions of Lisbon* (6/92)
A1119 *TO* (6/92)
A48 *Angels & Amazons* (6-7/92)
A270 *Cyrano De Bergerac* (9-10/92)
A122 *Billy Liar* (11/92)
A385 *Every Bit Of It* (1/93)
HAMILTON
Whitehill Ctr
A366 *End Of The Beginning* (11/92)
INVERNESS
Eden Court Th.
A1082 *The Tempest* (3/92)
A655 *Macbeth* (3/92)
A610 *Liaisons Dangereuses* (4/92)
A116 *The BFG* (4/92)
A200 *Charley's Aunt* (5/92)
A467 *Hamlet* (8-9/92)
A275 *Dancing at Lughnasa* (9/92)
A958 *School For Wives* (10/92)
A1218 *Witness For The Prosecution* (11/92)

KILMARNOCK
Palace Th.
A1097 *Therese Raquin* (4/92)
KIRKCALDY
Adam Smith Th.
A610 *Liaisons Dangereuses* (4/92)
KIRKWALL
St Magnus Festival
A467 *Hamlet* (6/92)
LOCHCARRON
Village Hall
A467 *Hamlet* (7/92)
MALLAIG, H'LAND
High School
A1097 *Therese Raquin* (4/92)
NEWTON STEWART
D. Stewart Sch
A366 *End Of The Beginning* (10/92)
PAISLEY
Arts Centre
A1097 *Therese Raquin* (4/92)
A366 *End Of The Beginning* (10/92)
PENICUIK, LOTHIAN
Town Hall
A1097 *Therese Raquin* (5/92)
PERTH
Perth Th.
A438 *The Glass Menagerie* (2/92)
A793 *Noises Off* (2-3/92)
A1243 *Wuthering Heights* (3-4/92)
A632 *Little Shop Of Horrors* (4-5/92)
A1096 *Then There Were None* (7-8/92)
A722 *The Mikado* (8-9/92)
A691 *Mary Queen of Scots* (10/92)
A1186 *Wasting Reality* (10-11/92)
PITLOCHRY, TAYSIDE
Town Hall
A1097 *Therese Raquin* (4/92)
ROSEHALL, H'LANDS
Village Hall
A467 *Hamlet* (7/92)
ROTHSHIRE, H'LAND
Village Hall
A1097 *Therese Raquin* (4/92)
SHETLAND ISLES
Shetland Island
A467 *Hamlet* (6/92)
SKYE, H'LAND
Broadford Hall
A1097 *Therese Raquin* (4/92)
A467 *Hamlet* (7/92)
SOUTHPORT
Arts Centre
A268 *Cyrano De Bergerac* (11/92)
A100 *Beauty And The Beast* (1/93)
ST ANDREWS
Byre Theatre
A1097 *Therese Raquin* (4/92)
A1181 *Voyage Round Para* (5-6/92)
A809 *On Golden Pond* (6-7/92)
A1212 *Wind in the Willows* (7-8/92)
A162 *Brighton Beach Memoirs* (8-9/92)

A826 *Othello* (9-10/92)
STIRLING
Cowane Centre
A388 *Experiment In Contra.* (12/92)
MacRobert Arts
A48 *Angels & Amazons* (4/92)
A1097 *Therese Raquin* (5/92)
A752 *Much Ado About Nothing* (9/92)
STRANRAER
Ryan Centre
A48 *Angels & Amazons* (3/92)
THORNHILL
Wallace Hall
A366 *End Of The Beginning* (10/92)
THURSO
Mill
A1097 *Therese Raquin* (4/92)
A467 *Hamlet* (6/92)
ULLAPOOL
Leisure Centre
A48 *Angels & Amazons* (6/92)
A467 *Hamlet* (7/92)
ULLAPOOL, H'LAND
Village Hall
A1097 *Therese Raquin* (4/92)
A467 *Hamlet* (7/92)
WICK
Lyth Arts Centre
A467 *Hamlet* (6/92)

WALES

ABERFAN
Community Centre
A418 *Frankie & Tommy* (10/92)
ABERGAVENNY
Borough Theatre
A369 *Enemy To The People* (3/92)
A400 *Fern Hill* (7/92)
ABERYSTWYTH
Aberystwyth Arts Centre
A714 *Metamorphosis* (5/92)
A55 *Anybody for Murder?* (5/92)
A400 *Fern Hill* (6/92)
A824 *Orlando* (10/92)
A479 *Haunted Hotel* (10/92)
A463 *Hamlet* (11/92)
A577 *King Lear* (11/92)
A803 *Office Party* (12/92)
AMMANFORD, DYFED
Aman Centre
A1002 *The Sin Eaters* (5/92)
BANGOR
Theatr Gwynedd
A707 *Merchant Of Venice* (4/92)
A400 *Fern Hill* (6/92)
A577 *King Lear* (11/92)
A268 *Cyrano De Bergerac* (11/92)
A100 *Beauty And The Beast* (11/92)
A463 *Hamlet* (12/92)

BUILTH WELLS
Wyeside Arts C.
A1105 *The Three Musketeers* (5/92)
A400 *Fern Hill* (7/92)
A824 *Orlando* (10/92)
A463 *Hamlet* (11/92)
A577 *King Lear* (11/92)
CARDIFF
Chapter Arts
A516 *House Of America* (10/92)
Llanover Hall
A1002 *The Sin Eaters* (5/92)
New Th.
A1230 *Woman Of No Importance* (3/92)
A763 *My Fair Lady* (3-4/92)
A1148 *Twelfth Night* (4/92)
A116 *The BFG* (4/92)
A513 *The House Of Stairs* (6/92)
A651 *M. Butterfly* (6/92)
A249 *The Corn Is Green* (6-5/92)
A2 *42nd Street* (6-7/92)
A527 *An Ideal Husband* (10/92)
A655 *Macbeth* (10/92)
A907 *Revenge* (10/92)
A541 *An Inspector Calls* (11/92)
A362 *Elvis - the Musical* (11/92)
A275 *Dancing at Lughnasa* (11-12/92)
A79 *Babes in the Wood* (12/92-1/93)
A1082 *The Tempest* (2/93)
Sherman Th.
A707 *Merchant Of Venice* (2-3/92)
A589 *La Ronde* (3/92)
A925 *Roaring Girl's Hamlet* (3/92)
A400 *Fern Hill* (5/92)
A510 *Hound* (5/92)
A987 *Shakers* (5/92)
A1178 *Viva Detroit* (5/92)
A1010 *Sleeping With Mickey* (7/92)
A129 *Blodeuwedd* (9-10/92)
A377 *Erogenous Zones* (9-10/92)
A122 *Billy Liar* (11/92)
A418 *Frankie & Tommy* (11/92)
A385 *Every Bit Of It* (1/93)
CARDIGAN
Theatr Mwldan
A400 *Fern Hill* (6/92)
A463 *Hamlet* (9/92)
A824 *Orlando* (10/92)
A129 *Blodeuwedd* (10/92)
A418 *Frankie & Tommy* (11/92)
CHEPSTOW, GWENT
Drill Hall
A1002 *The Sin Eaters* (5/92)
COLWYN BAY
Theatr Colwyn
A400 *Fern Hill* (6-7/92)
A174 *The Business Of Murder* (7-8/92)
A1076 *Teechers* (8/92)
A1040 *Stage Struck* (8/92)
A581 *The Kingfisher* (8/92)
A673 *The Maintenance Man* (8/92)
A976 *September In The Rain* (9/92)
A635 *Lloyd George* (10/92)
A268 *Cyrano De Bergerac* (11/92)
A22 *Aladdin* (12/92-1/93)
GWENT
Blackwood Miners'Inst
A418 *Frankie & Tommy* (10/92)
Congress Th.
A418 *Frankie & Tommy* (10/92)
Drama Centre
A1002 *The Sin Eaters* (5/92)
GWYNEDD
Theatr Ardudwy
A400 *Fern Hill* (6/92)
A577 *King Lear* (11/92)
A418 *Frankie & Tommy* (11/92)
LAMPETER
Theatr Felinfach
A400 *Fern Hill* (6/92)
A577 *King Lear* (11/92)
A418 *Frankie & Tommy* (11/92)
MERTHYR TYDFIL
Technical Coll.
A577 *King Lear* (10/92)
MILFORD HAVEN
Torch Theatre
A707 *Merchant Of Venice* (2/92)
A54 *Antony And Cleopatra* (2-3/92)
A400 *Fern Hill* (6/92)
A305 *Dial M for Murder* (8/92)
A405 *Mamie Stewart* (10/92)
A965 *Season's Greetings* (11/92)
A623 *Lion, Witch & Wardrobe* (12/92-1/93)
MOLD
Th.Clywd Studio
A351 *Return Journey* (4-5/92)
A1074 *Taste of Honey* (9-10/92)
A304 *The Devils* (11-12/92)
Theatr Clwyd
A755 *Murder By Misadventure* (1-2/92)
A461 *The Guardsman* (1-2/92)
A685 *Marching Song* (2-3/92)
A948 *Sailor Beware!* (3-4/92)
A962 *The Seagull* (5/92)
A1163 *Up 'N' Under* (6/92)
A957 *School for Scandal* (9/92)
A481 *Hay Fever* (10/92)
A388 *Experiment In Contra.* (11/92)
A382 *Evening With Gary L.* (11/92)
A214 *Christmas Carol* (12/92-1/93)
NANTYMOEL
Berwyn Centre
A418 *Frankie & Tommy* (10/92)
A577 *King Lear* (10/92)
NEWPORT, I O W
Medina Theatre
A657 *Macbeth* (10/92)
NEWPORT, GWENT
Newport Centre
A1002 *The Sin Eaters* (5/92)
NEWTOWN
Theatr Hafren
A578 *King Lear* (2/92)
A1215 *The Winter's Tale* (3/92)
A738 *Moose* (3/92)
A714 *Metamorphosis* (4/92)
A987 *Shakers* (6/92)
A400 *Fern Hill* (6/92)
A968 *The Secret Rapture* (10/92)
A788 *No 3 Pied Piper Street* (11/92)
A467 *Hamlet* (11/92)
A388 *Experiment In Contra.* (11/92)
A1141 *Trilby & Svengali* (11/92)
A122 *Billy Liar* (2/93)
PONTYPRIDD
Municipal Hall
A577 *King Lear* (10/92)
A418 *Frankie & Tommy* (10/92)
RHYL
New Pavilion
A657 *Macbeth* (5/92)
A1111 *Thunderbirds FAB* (6-7/92)
SWANSEA
Counterpoint
A889 *Radio Times* (10/92)
Grand Th.
A610 *Liaisons Dangereuses* (2/92)
A1046 *Stepping Out* (3/92)
A395 *The Fancy Man* (4-5/92)
A933 *Rocky Horror Show* (5/92)
A116 *The BFG* (5/92)
A457 *Gravity Swing* (6/92)
A508 *Hot Stuff* (7/92)
A655 *Macbeth* (9-10/92)
A1082 *The Tempest* (9-10/92)
A382 *Evening With Gary L.* (10/92)
A657 *Macbeth* (11/92)
A29 *Alfie* (12/92)
Miners Hall
A463 *Hamlet* (11/92)
Penyrheol Theatr
A1149 *Twelfth Night* (10/92)
A418 *Frankie & Tommy* (12/92)
Taliesin Arts C.
A578 *King Lear* (2/92)
A400 *Fern Hill* (5/92)
A467 *Hamlet* (11/92)
Theatre Cwmtawe
A369 *Enemy To The People* (3/92)
Ystradgynglais W
A400 *Fern Hill* (6/92)
TREORCHY
Parc & Dare Th.
A577 *King Lear* (10/92)
YSTRAD MYNACH
Lewis Girls Sch.
A577 *King Lear* (10/92)

N.IRELAND & EIRE

BELFAST
Arts Theatre
A578 *King Lear* (2/92)

A987 *Shakers* (4/92)
A714 *Metamorphosis* (6/92)
A714 *Metamorphosis* (6/92)
A178 *Cabaret* (9/92)
A1141 *Trilby & Svengali* (11/92)
A122 *Billy Liar* (11/92)
A388 *Experiment In Contra.* (11/92)

Lyric Players
A61 *Arms And The Man* (10/92)
A940 *Round The Big Clock* (11/92)
A625 *Lion Witsh & Wardrobe* (12/92-1/93)

Old Museum Arts Centre
A1232 *Woman Who Cooked* (4-5/92)

Opera House
A610 *Liaisons Dangereuses* (4/92)
A168 *Buddy* (5-6/92)
A362 *Elvis - the Musical* (9-10/92)
A159 *Breaking the Code* (10/92)
A1218 *Witness For The Prosecution* (10/92)
A1111 *Thunderbirds FAB* (11-12/92)

Stranmillis Th
A865 *Playing The Wife* (11/92)

CO FERMANAGH

Ardhowen Th.
A578 *King Lear* (2/92)

COLERAINE

Riverside Th.
A578 *King Lear* (2/92)
A987 *Shakers* (4/92)
A509 *Houdini* (10/92)
A122 *Billy Liar* (11/92)

CORK

Cork Opera House
A275 *Dancing at Lughnasa* (2-3/92)

Everyman Palace
A987 *Shakers* (4/92)

CORK, EIRE

Triskel Arts Ctr
A1002 *The Sin Eaters* (4-5/92)

DUBLIN

Abbey Th.
A342 *Drama At Inish* (6-7/92)

DUBLIN 2

Andrews Lane Studio Th.
A895 *Rebels And Friends* (2/92)
A1061 *Sylvia* (9/92)

DUBLIN

Andrews Lane
A636 *London Vertigo* (1-2/92)
A88 *Ballad of Limehouse* (10/92)

City Centre
A1002 *The Sin Eaters* (4/92)

Gate Theatre
A882 *Private Lives* (3-5/92)
A203 *Cherry Orchard* (5-6/92)
A335 *Double Dealer* (12/92-1/93)

Peacock Th.
A149 *Bold Girls* (6-7/92)
A76 *Away Alone* (7-8/92)

Riverbank Theatre
A122 *Billy Liar* (10/92-1/93)

NEWRY

Newry Arts Centre
A509 *Houdini* (10/92)

SLIGO

Hawk's Well Th.
A987 *Shakers* (4-5/92)

CHANNEL ISLANDS

ST HELIER

Arts Centre
A589 *La Ronde* (3/92)
A748 *Mrs Klein* (5/92)
A1083 *The Tempest* (5/92)
A415 *Frankenstein* (5/92)
A767 *My Mother Said* (6/92)
A1044 *State of Bewilderment* (12/92)

INTERNATIONAL

BELGIUM

Antwerp, Belgium
A1105 *The Three Musketeers* (5/92)

BREST

Brest, Brittany
A1002 *The Sin Eaters* (5/92)

LESNEVEN, BRITTANY

Lesneven
A1002 *The Sin Eaters* (5/92)

NEUSS (GERMANY)

Globe Theatre
A467 *Hamlet* (6/92)

PARIS

Glennevilliers
A339 *Down And Out...* (4/92)

SEVILLE, SPAIN

T. Lope de Vega
A422 *Fuente Ovejuna* (6/92)

SWEDEN

Linkoping
A457 *Gravity Swing* (5-6/92)

TOKYO, JAPAN

Globe
A463 *Hamlet* (7-8/92)
A577 *King Lear* (7-8/92)
A752 *Much Ado About Nothing* (11/92)

TUNISIA

Tunisia
A1105 *The Three Musketeers* (5/92)

PLAYWRIGHTS

All the playwrights we are aware of who have had plays in production in 1992.
Use the cross-referencing to identify where plays were produced.

William Shakespeare (82)				
All's Well That Ends Well	*A35*			
Antony And Cleopatra (2)	*A53*	*A54*		
As You Like It (5)	*A67*	*A68*	*A69*	*A70*
	A71			
Comedy Of Errors (3)	*A239*	*A240*	*A241*	
The Complete Works	*A245*			
Coriolanus	*A248*			
Hamlet (5)	*A463*	*A464*	*A465*	*A466*
	A467			
Henry IV Part 2	*A493*			
Iago	*A526*			
Julius Caesar (3)	*A564*	*A565*	*A566*	
King Lear (3)	*A576*	*A578*	*A579*	
Love's Labour's Lost (2)	*A645*	*A646*		
Macbeth (9)	*A652*	*A653*	*A654*	*A655*
	A656	*A657*	*A658*	*A660*
	A661			
Measure for Measure (4)	*A700*	*A701*	*A702*	*A703*
Merchant of Venice (3)	*A706*	*A707*	*A708*	
The Merry Wives Of Windsor (2)	*A712*	*A713*		
A Midsummer Night's .. (6)	*A716*	*A717*	*A718*	*A719*
	A720	*A721*		
Much Ado About Nothing (3)	*A750*	*A751*	*A753*	
Othello (3)	*A826*	*A827*	*A828*	
Richard III (3)	*A910*	*A911*	*A912*	
Roaring Girl's Hamlet	*A925*			
Romeo And Juliet (4)	*A935*	*A936*	*A937*	*A938*
Taming Of The Shrew (2)	*A1068*	*A1070*		
Tempest (4)	*A1082*	*A1083*	*A1084*	*A1085*
Twelfth Night (5)	*A1147*	*A1149*	*A1150*	*A1151*
	A1152			
Two Gents Of Verona	*A1154*			
Venus and Adonis	*A1167*			
The Wax King	*A1189*			
The Winter's Tale (2)	*A1214*	*A1215*		
Alan Ayckbourn (21)				
Absent Friends (3)	*A8*	*A9*	*A10*	
Absurd Person Singular	*A11*			
Bedroom Farce	*A104*			
Between the Lines	*A112*			
Chorus of Disapproval (2)	*A210*	*A211*		
Confusions	*A246*			
Henceforward...	*A491*			
How The Other Half Loves	*A520*			
Intimate Exchanges	*A544*			
Just Between Ourselves	*A569*			
Mr A's Amazing Maze	*A746*			
The Norman Conquests	*A796*			
Relatively Speaking	*A900*			
Season's Greetings	*A965*			
Taking Steps	*A1064*			
Ten Times Table	*A1087*			
Time Of My Life	*A1112*			
Woman In Mind	*A1228*			
John Godber (16)				
April In Paris	*A58*			
Bouncers (3)	*A150*	*A151*	*A152*	
Happy Families	*A476*			
Office Party	*A803*			
On The Piste (4)	*A810*	*A811*	*A812*	*A813*
September In The Rain	*A976*			
Shakers	*A987*			
Teechers (3)	*A1076*	*A1077*	*A1078*	
Up 'N' Under	*A1163*			
RSC (16)				
Amphibians	*A40*			
Antony and Cleopatra	*A53*			
Artists and Admirers	*A64*			
The Changeling	*A197*			
Columbus	*A237*			
Comedy Of Errors	*A241*			
Gifts Of The Gorgon	*A434*			
Julius Caesar	*A566*			
King Baby	*A575*			
Richard III	*A910*			
Romeo And Juliet	*A938*			
School of Night	*A959*			
The Tempest	*A1084*			
The Thebans	*A1095*			
Twelfth Night	*A1152*			
The Winter's Tale	*A1214*			
Arthur Miller (12)				
All My Sons (2)	*A32*	*A33*		
Death Of A Salesman (3)	*A295*	*A296*	*A297*	
Price (2)	*A873*	*A874*		
Ride Down Mt Morgan	*A915*			
A View From The Bridge (4)	*A1169*	*A1170*	*A1171*	*A1172*

Noel Coward (11)				
Blithe Spirit (4)	*A125*	*A126*	*A127*	*A128*
Fallen Angels	*A391*			
Hay Fever (2)	*A481*	*A482*		
Private Lives (3)	*A880*	*A881*	*A882*	
Relative Values	*A899*			
RNT (10)				
Billy Liar	*A122*			
Bourgeois Gentilhomme	*A153*			
Carousel	*A190*			
Dragon	*A341*			
An Inspector Calls	*A541*			
Kings	*A583*			
One The Ledge	*A821*			
Richard III	*A911*			
Square Rounds	*A1038*			
Stages	*A1042*			
George Bernard Shaw (10)				
Arms And The Man (2)	*A60*	*A61*		
Caesar And Cleopatra	*A180*			
Candida	*A183*			
Don Juan In Hell	*A325*			
Heartbreak House	*A486*			
Major Barbara	*A675*			
Pygmalion	*A886*			
Valentine's Day	*A1165*			
Village Wooing	*A1173*			
Henrik Ibsen (9)				
Brand	*A157*			
A Doll's House (5)	*A320*	*A321*	*A322*	*A323*
	A324			
Ghosts (2)	*A432*	*A433*		
Rosmersholm	*A939*			
Jim Cartwright (8)				
Little Voice	*A917*			
Road	*A922*			
TO (6)	*A1115*	*A1116*	*A1117*	*A1118*
	A1119	*A1120*		
Anton Chekhov (8)				
Cherry Orchard (2)	*A202*	*A203*		
The Seagull (3)	*A962*	*A963*	*A964*	
Sneeze	*A1018*			
Uncle Vanya (2)	*A1158*	*A1159*		
Richard Harris (8)				
The Business Of Murder (3)	*A173*	*A174*	*A175*	
The Maintenance Man (2)	*A673*	*A674*		
Outside Edge (2)	*A837*	*A838*		
Stepping Out	*A1046*			
Joe Orton (7)				
Entertaining Mr Sloane (2)	*A373*	*A374*		
Loot (2)	*A637*	*A638*		
What The Butler Saw (3)	*A1196*	*A1197*	*A1198*	
Willy Russell (7)				
Blood Brothers (2)	*A130*	*A131*		
Eductaing Rita	*A354*			
One For The Road (2)	*A818*	*A819*		
Our Day Out	*A831*			
Shirley Valentine	*A995*			
Devised By The Company (7)				
Beauty And The Beast	*A100*			
Call Blue Jane	*A182*			
Diamonds in the Dust	*A306*			
Emanuelle Enchanted	*A363*			
Hot Italian Nights	*A507*			
The Marvellous Boy	*A690*			
World...Upside Down	*A1240*			
Alan Bennett (6)				
Kafka's Dick	*A571*			
Madness of George III	*A669*			
Old Country	*A804*			
Single Spies (2)	*A1004*	*A1005*		
Talking Heads	*A1066*			
Agatha Christie (6)				
The Hollow	*A501*			
The Mousetrap	*A744*			
Peril At End House	*A850*			
Then There Were None	*A1096*			
Towards Zero	*A1132*			
Witness For The Prosecution	*A1218*			
Brian Friel (6)				
Dancing at Lughnasa (2)	*A274*	*A275*		
Faith Healer	*A389*			
London Vertigo	*A636*			
Lovers	*A647*			
Philadelphia Here I Come	*A856*			
Moliere (6)				
Bourgeois Gentilhomme	*A153*			
Don Juan	*A327*			
The Imaginary Invalid	*A529*			
The Miser	*A724*			
School For Wives	*A958*			
Tartuffe	*A1073*			
Oscar Wilde (6)				
An Ideal Husband (2)	*A527*	*A528*		
Imp. Of Being Earnest (3)	*A531*	*A532*	*A533*	
Woman Of No Importance	*A1230*			
Mr Andrew Lloyd Webber (5)				
Aspects Of Love	*A72*			
Cats	*A194*			
Joseph...	*A559*			
Phantom Of The Opera	*A854*			
Starlight Express	*A1043*			
Federico Garcia Lorca (5)				
Blood Wedding (3)	*A132*	*A133*	*A134*	
House of Bernarda Alba (2)	*A515*	*A517*		
Harold Pinter (5)				
Birthday Party	*A124*			
The Caretaker	*A188*			
No Man's Land	*A789*			
Old Times	*A806*			
Other Places	*A829*			
Richard Brinsley Sheridan (5)				
Rivals (3)	*A918*	*A919*	*A920*	
School for Scandal (2)	*A956*	*A957*		
Aline Waites (5)				
Aba Daba Music Hall	*A6*			
Beauty and the Bat	*A101*			
Christmas Rubbish	*A215*			
Put That Light Out	*A885*			
Road To Casablanca	*A923*			
Tennessee Williams (5)				
Glass Menagerie (3)	*A438*	*A439*	*A440*	
Night of the Iguana	*A785*			
Sweet Bird of Youth	*A1059*			

Hans Christian Andersen (4)

- The Little Mermaid — *A629*
- The Snow Queen (2) — *A1019* *A1020*
- The Thin Soldier — *A1098*

Steven Berkoff (4)

- Acapulco — *A12*
- Decadence — *A299*
- Kvetch — *A586*
- Metamorphosis — *A715*

Howard Brenton (4)

- Berlin Bertie — *A109*
- Bloody Poetry — *A137*
- Epsom Downs — *A375*
- Thirteenth Night — *A1099*

The Heather Brothers (4)

- Cold Sweat — *A234*
- Lust — *A650*
- Slice Of Saturday... (2) — *A1014* *A1015*

Bob Carlton (4)

- Aladdin Bolton — *A27*
- From A Jack To A King — *A420*
- Forbidden Planet (2) — *A903* *A904*

Ray Cooney (4)

- It Runs In The Family — *A548*
- Out Of Order (2) — *A834* *A835*
- Run for Your Wife — *A944*

Lope de Vega (4)

- Fuente Ovejuna (2) — *A422* *A423*
- Madness in Valencia — *A668*
- New World and Tears — *A780*

Charlotte Keatley (4)

- My Mother Said (4) — *A765* *A766* *A767* *A768*

Bernard Kops (4)

- Androcles And The Lion — *A45*
- Dreams of Anne Frank — *A344*
- Playing Sinatra — *A864*
- Who Shall I Be? — *A1203*

David Mamet (4)

- American Buffalo — *A39*
- A Life In The Theatre — *A618*
- The Shawl — *A989*
- Speed-The-Plow — *A1034*

Christopher Marlowe (4)

- Doctor Faustus (3) — *A316* *A317* *A318*
- Tamburlaine The Great — *A1067*

Tom McGrath (4)

- Buchanan — *A167*
- Laurel and Hardy (3) — *A601* *A602* *A603*

William Nicholson (4)

- Shadowlands (4) — *A982* *A983* *A984* *A985*

Luigi Pirandello (4)

- As You Desire Me — *A66*
- Man, Beast and Virtue — *A682*
- The Rules Of The Game — *A943*
- Six Characters — *A1007*

Paul Prescott (4)

- Blood Whispers — *A135*
- A Distant Applause — *A315*
- My Blood on Glass — *A761*
- Some...Atomic Zombie — *A1027*

J.B. Priestley (4)

- Dangerous Corner (2) — *A276* *A277*
- Inspector Calls (2) — *A541* *A542*

Terence Rattigan (4)

- The Deep Blue Sea — *A140*
- In Praise Of Love — *A536*
- While The Sun Shines — *A1201*
- The Winslow Boy — *A1213*

Neil Simon (4)

- Barefoot in the Park — *A91*
- Brighton Beach Memoirs — *A162*
- Broadway Bound — *A163*
- Lost in Yonkers — *A641*

David Anderson (3)

- 47 — *A3*
- Eight to the Bar — *A356*
- House That Jack Bought — *A518*

Jeffrey Archer (3)

- Beyond Reasonable Doubt (3) — *A113* *A114* *A115*

Mr Harley Granville Barker (3)

- His Majesty — *A497*
- Madras House — *A670*
- Voysey Inheritance — *A1182*

Brendan Behan (3)

- The Hostage — *A505*
- Richard's Cork Leg (2) — *A913* *A914*

Mr Bertolt Brecht (3)

- Edward II — *A355*
- Good Person Of Sezuan — *A448*
- The Threepenny Opera — *A1109*

Ms Claire Dowie (3)

- Adult Child/Dead Child (2) — *A14* *A15*
- Death And Dancing — *A292*

Bob Eaton (3)

- Curse of Mummy's Tomb — *A262*
- Imagine — *A530*
- The Night Before The Morning After — *A782*

George Farquhar (3)

- Love and a Bottle — *A643*
- The Recruiting Officer (2) — *A896* *A897*

Dario Fo (3)

- The Open Couple — *A823*
- The Pope And The Witch — *A870*
- A Woman Plays ... — *A1231*

Michael Frayn (3)

- Noises Off (2) — *A793* *A794*
- Noises Off — *A795*

Oliver Goldsmith (3)

- Prince And The Mouse — *A877*
- She Stoops To Conquer (2) — *A991* *A992*

Simon Gray (3)

- Dog Days — *A319*
- Otherwise Engaged — *A830*
- Stage Struck — *A1040*

David Hare (3)

- Murmuring Judges — *A758*
- The Secret Rapture — *A968*
- The Great Exhibition — *A1092*

Robin Hunter (3)

- Beauty and the Bat — *A101*
- Put That Light Out — *A885*
- Road To Casablanca — *A923*

Mike Kenny (3)

- Bag Dancing — *A87*
- Fern Hill — *A400*
- The Lost Child — *A640*

Noel Greig (2)
- Dead Heroic — *A287*
- The Lie Of The Land — *A617*

Willis Hall (2)
- Billy Liar — *A122*
- The Card (A musical) — *A187*

Patrick Hamilton (2)
- Gaslight (2) — *A428* *A429*

Michael Harding (2)
- Misogynist — *A726*
- Una Pooka — *A1156*

Thomas Hardy (2)
- Far From The Madding Crowd — *A397*
- Tess Of The D'Urbervil — *A1089*

Robin Hawdon (2)
- Don't Rock The Boat — *A330*
- Revenge — *A907*

Ken Hill (2)
- The Invisible Man — *A547*
- Phantom of the Opera — *A853*

David Holman (2)
- Beauty and the Beast — *A99*
- Christmas Carol — *A217*

Roy Hudd (2)
- Aladdin — *A17*
- Babes in the Wood — *A79*

David Henry Hwang (2)
- The Dance & Railroad — *A272*
- M. Butterfly — *A651*

Debbie Isitt (2)
- Out Of The Ordinary — *A836*
- Woman Who Cooked — *A1232*

Alan Janes (2)
- Buddy (2) — *A168* *A169*

David Kelsey (2)
- Gone With The Wind II — *A445*
- Road To Casablanca — *A923*

Bill Kenwright (2)
- Dejavu — *A302*
- Twelfth Night — *A1147*

Philip King (2)
- See How They Run (2) — *A970* *A971*

Rudyard Kipling (2)
- The Jungle Book — *A568*
- Just So — *A570*

Carlo Lange (2)
- A Distant Applause — *A315*
- Hostages and Hamsters — *A506*

Pete Lawson (2)
- Telephonebelles — *A1079*
- Traffic Hearts — *A1133*

Claire Luckham (2)
- The Choice — *A209*
- The Dramatic Attitudes — *A343*

David Maclennan (2)
- Eight to the Bar — *A356*
- House That Jack Bought — *A518*

Pierre Marivaux (2)
- False Servant — *A392*
- Game of Love & Chance — *A425*

Joe Masteroff (2)
- Cabaret (2) — *A177* *A178*

Terrence McNally (2)
- Frankie and Johnny... (2) — *A417* *A419*

Mark Medoff (2)
- Children Of Lesser God (2) — *A205* *A206*

Alan Menken (2)
- Little Shop of Horrors (2) — *A632* *A633*

Thomas Middleton (2)
- The Changeling — *A197*
- Revenger's Tragedy — *A909*

Ted Moore (2)
- Travelling Light (2) — *A1135* *A1136*

Jacqueline Mulhallen (2)
- Rebels And Friends — *A895*
- Sylvia — *A1061*

Rona Munro (2)
- Bold Girls — *A149*
- Your Turn To Clean The Stairs — *A1252*

Sean O'Casey (2)
- End Of The Beginning — *A366*
- The Plough & The Stars — *A867*

Henry Ong (2)
- Madame Mao's Memories (2) — *A666* *A667*

Louise Page (2)
- Hawks & Doves — *A480*
- Salonika — *A950*

Stuart Paterson (2)
- Beauty And The Beast — *A97*
- Merlin the Magnificent — *A710*

Ronald Selwyn Phillips (2)
- Moment of Madness — *A731*
- Sex and Sadness — *A979*

Sir Arthur Wing Pinero (2)
- Trelawny Of The Wells (2) — *A1138* *A1139*

Stephen Poliakoff (2)
- Shout Across The River — *A997*
- Sienna Red — *A999*

Cole Porter (2)
- High Society — *A494*
- A Swell Party — *A1060*

Billy Roche (2)
- Amphibians — *A40*
- Wexford Trilogy — *A1194*

Philip Ryan (2)
- In The Midnight Hour (2) — *A537* *A538*

Jean-Paul Sartre (2)
- In Camera — *A534*
- Intimacy — *A543*

Arthur Schnitzler (2)
- La Ronde (2) — *A589* *A590*

Sam Shepard (2)
- Fool for Love — *A411*
- The War In Heaven — *A1184*

Steve Shill (2)
- The Caretaker — *A188*
- ...Changed The Wires — *A1245*

Dave Simpson (2)
- A Marginal Affair — *A687*
- Raving Beauties — *A893*

Roy Smiles (2)
- Roberto Calvi — *A926*
- Schmucks — *A955*

Arthur Smith (2)
- Evening with Gary L. (2) *A382* *A383*

Nick Stafford (2)
- Devil's Only Sleeping *A303*
- The Snow Queen *A1020*

Tom Stoppard (2)
- Hapgood *A472*
- Travesties *A1137*

Botho Strauss (2)
- Hypochondriacs *A523*
- Seven Doors *A978*

August Strindberg (2)
- Ghost Sonata *A431*
- Pelican *A847*

Kenneth Alan Taylor (2)
- Cinderella *A226*
- Dick Whittington *A311*

Ernest Thompson (2)
- On Golden Pond (2) *A808* *A809*

Sandi Toksvig (2)
- Big Night Out *A119*
- The Pocket Dream *A868*

Cyril Tourneur (2)
- Revenger's Tragedy (2) *A908* *A909*

Sue Townsend (2)
- Bazaar and Rummage *A94*
- Diary Of Adrian Mole *A967*

Ben Travers (2)
- After You With The Mlk *A16*
- Turkey Time *A1144*

Michel Tremblay (2)
- Forever Yours *A413*
- House Among the Stars *A512*

Alfred Uhry (2)
- Driving Miss Daisy (2) *A345* *A346*

John van Druten (2)
- Cabaret (2) *A177* *A178*

Frank Vickery (2)
- Erogenous Zones *A377*
- Sleeping With Mickey *A1010*

Michael Wall (2)
- Women Laughing (2) *A1234* *A1235*

Peter Whelan (2)
- Bright & Bold Design *A161*
- School of Night *A959*

William Wycherley (2)
- Country Wife (2) *A252* *A253*

Sheila Yeger (2)
- A Better Day *A111*
- Self Portrait *A974*

Kerryson & Norris Hot Stuff *A508*
Bernstein, Sondheim & Robbins West Side Story *A1193*
Clemens & Spooner Anybody for Murder? *A55*
Roel Adam The Day After Tomorrow *A285*
Alan Ahlberg Ten In A Bed *A1086*
Mr Sholom Alaichem Fiddler On The Roof *A401*
Edward Albee Virginia Woolf *A1205*
Alonso Alegria Niagara *A781*
Tariq Ali Necklaces *A774*
Marion Andre Savage Storm *A952*
William Archibald The Innocents *A540*
Ariadne She Ventures He Wins *A993*
Ronald Armstrong Voyage Round Para *A1181*
Howard Ashma Little Shop of Horrors *A633*
Howard Ashman Little Shop Of Horrors *A632*
Ian Auld Lions of Lisbon *A626*
Jane Austen Mansfield Park *A683*
Enid Bagnold The Chalk Garden *A196*
Beryl Bainbridge Awfully Big Adventure *A77*
James Baldwin Blues for Mr Charlie *A143*
Robert Ballard The Three Musketeers *A1104*
Julie Balloo Dangerous Dolls-Soap Crazy *A280*
Biyi Bandele- Thomas Marching For Fausa *A686*
Iain Banks Wasp Factory *A1185*
Miss Deborah Barnard Shoot The Women First *A996*
Douglas Barron The Cotton Club *A250*
Sebastian Barry White Woman Street *A1202*
Neil Bartlett A Judgement In Stone *A563*
Frank Baum The Wizard of Oz *A1220*
Lee Beagley Threepenny Story *A1108*
Belgrade Theatre Our Ellen *A832*
Derek Benfield Bedside Manners *A105*
Thomas Bernhard Elisabeth II *A361*
Marsha Raven & Beverly Andrews Blues Angels *A141*
Jean Binnie Lady Macbeth *A595*
Mitch Binns Barnstormers *A92*
Paul Bishop Billy the Kid *A123*
Simon Black The Ecstacy *A353*
Mt Bryan Blackburn Dick Whittington *A308*
Simon Blake Broken Heads *A165*
Sydnee Blake Stand Before You Naked *A525*
Mr Alan Bleasdale One The Ledge *A821*
Paul Boakye Boy With Beer *A154*
Mr Jerry Bock Fiddler On The Roof *A401*
Edward Bond The Sea *A961*
Mary Bonner And Hunger For All *A44*
Jan Booth He's So at Peace... *A483*
Wolfgang Borchert Man Outside *A681*
Saskia Bosch La Muse *A500*
Mr Colin Bostock-Smith You Must Be The Husband *A1248*
Alain Boublil Les Miserables *A613*
John Boyd Round The Big Clock *A940*
Mr Mike Bradwell Grace *A452*
Melvyn Bragg King Lear In New York *A580*
Mark Brailsford As Time Goes By *A65*
Marcus Brent All On Top *A34*
Will Brenton Mother Goose *A741*
Elly Brewer The Pocket Dream *A868*
Broadway Gravity Swing *A457*
Emily Bronte Wuthering Heights *A1243*
Blake Brooker Serpent Kills *A977*
Pip Broughton Big Night Out *A119*
Ian Brown Wasting Reality *A1186*
Robin Brown Manslaughter *A684*
Ferdinand Bruckner Pains of Youth *A841*
Mr John Bryan 99, Heyworth Street *A5*
Mr Tony Bryan 99, Heyworth Street *A5*
David Bryer Women on Top *A1237*
Moira Buffini Jordan *A558*
Clayton Buffoni Telling Tales *A1081*
Wendy Buonaventura Revelations *A905*
Michael Burrell My Sister Next Door *A769*
John Burrows It's A Girl *A549*
Jill Burrows Wicks's Folly *A1208*
Samuel Butler The Way of All Flesh *A1190*
Dan Butler Dead Flamingo Dancer *A193*

Michael Butt Monster He Made Me *A734*
Jez Butterworth I Believe In Love *A524*
Devised by cast Tottering Towers *A1130*
Mr Steve Byrne Bag Dancing *A87*
George Byron Cain *A181*
John Caird Trelawny Of The Wells *A1138*
Calderon Life is a Dream *A619*
Richard Cameron Pond Life *A869*
Jimmy Camicia Christopher Street *A218*
Marc Camoletti Don't Dress For Dinner *A331*
Ken Campbell Pigspurt *A860*
Jon Canter The Baby *A82*
Mr Gary Carpenter Goodnight Mr Tom *A450*
Ruth Carter Women Of The Dust *A1236*
Warren Casey Grease *A458*
Ben Caudell Truth Games *A1143*
Michele Celeste Columbus *A236*
Susannah Centlivre The Artifice *A63*
Maureen Chadwick Josephine *A560*
Joseph Chaikin The War In Heaven *A1184*
Mlle Denise Chalem At Fifty She Discovered The Sea *A74*
Daniel Chambers Selling Out *A975*
Patrice Chaplin Ruby In The Dust *A941*
Alice Childress Trouble in Mind *A1142*
Jimmie Chinn Straight & Narrow *A1054*
Michael Church The English Kiss *A370*
Caryl Churchill Three More Sleepless *A1103*
Anthony Clark The Day After Tomorrow *A285*
Mr Noel Clark The Day After Tomorrow *A285*
Jeff Clarke Mother Goose *A742*
Stephen Clarke A Twitch On The Thread *A1153*
Mr Tony Clayton Mother Goose *A739*
John Clifford Light in the Village *A622*
Marvin Close Working *A1239*
James Clutton Oscar *A825*
Wilkie Collins Haunted Hotel *A479*
Theatre of Comedy Out Of Order *A834*
William Congreve Double Dealer *A335*
John Constable Gormenghast *A451*
David Conville Curse Of The Mummy *A263*
Michael Cook Sab *A945*
Judith Cook The Slicing Edge *A1094*
Thomas Coyle The Hatchet Man *A478*
Ted Craig Don Quixote *A328*
Rupert Creed Northern Trawl *A797*
David Croft 'Allo,'Allo *A36*
Carol Crowther Enter The Tragic Muse *A372*
Marty Cruikshank Why Things Happen *A1206*
Hugh Cruttwell Something Missing *A1030*
Alan Cullen Stirrings in Sheffield on Sat Night *A1049*
Andrew Cullen Self Catering *A973*
Geoffrey Cush Punishment Of Animals *A259*
Wally Daly Roman & Marys *A934*
Sarah Daniels Head-Rot Holiday *A484*
Adam Darius Rimbaud And Verlaine *A916*
Jennie Darnell Traffic Hearts *A1133*
Andrew Davies Prin *A876*
Luther Davis Grand Hotel *A453*
Andrew Dawson Thunderbirds FAB *A1111*
Simone De Beauvoir The Woman Destroyed *A1225*
Andy de la Tour Safe In Our Hands *A947*
Bartholome De Las Casas New World and Tears *A780*
Denise Deegan Daisy Pulls it Off *A271*
Julie Denny Emperor's New Clothes *A364*
John Denny Emperor's New Clothes *A364*
Peter Denyer Dick Whittington *A307*
Chris Denys Aladdin *A25*
Steven Deproost Voices at Her Elbow *A1180*
Shelia Dewey Turner's Crossing *A1146*
Miss Gillian Diamond Twelfth Night *A1147*
Marjorie Dickinson Lloyd George *A635*
William Diner The Late Edwina Black *A599*
Simon Donald Life of Stuff *A620*
Mary Agnes Donoghue Me And Mamie O'Rourke *A696*
Tankred Dorst Merlin, The Search *A709*
Dostoyevsky Brothers Kramazov *A166*
George Du Maurier Trilby & Svengali *A1141*
Martin Duncan Four Marys *A414*
Rod Dungate Playing by the Rules *A863*
Russell Dunlop Leonardo *A608*
Christopher Durang The Actor's Nightmare *A13*
Friedrich Durrenmatt Play Strindberg *A861*
Terry Eagleton Saint Oscar *A949*
Mr Brian Eastman Misery *A725*
Fred Ebb Kiss of Spiderwoman *A584*
Jenny Eclair Dangerous Dolls-Mummys Little Girl *A279*
Dic Edwards Casanova *A191*
Miss Sian Edwards Six Fools *A1009*
Eric Elice Double Double *A337*
T.S. Eliot The Family Reunion *A394*
Jane Eller Grope *A460*
Duke Ellington Sophisticated Ladies *A1032*
Tom Elliott Feed *A399*
Paul Elliott Elvis - the Musical *A362*
Per Enquist The Hour Of The Lynx *A511*
Sheldon Epps Blues In The Night *A144*
Euripides Hecuba *A488*
Miss Sian Evans At Fifty She Discovered The Sea *A74*
Sean Eve American Heart *A38*
Richard Everett Hindsight *A495*
Richard Fawkes Biko *A121*
Kevin Fegan Excess XS *A386*
Mr Andrew Fell Forbidden Planet(Tour) *A903*
Georges Feydeau Pig In A Poke *A859*
Jonathan Field Courting Winnona *A255*
Amy Finegan Voice of the Sea *A1179*
Nick Fisher Indigo Mill *A539*
Ger FitzGibbon The Rock Station *A931*
Raymund FitzSimon Houdini *A509*
Sean Foley Moose *A738*
John Ford 'Tis Pity She's A Whore *A1114*
Maggie Fox Withering Looks *A1217*
Mr Vince Foxall Don Quixote *A328*
Alan Franks The Mother Tongue *A743*
Gilly Fraser Give You A Good Time *A437*
Brad Fraser Unidentified Human *A1162*
Christopher Fry Venus Observed *A1168*
Athol Fugard Master Harold & The bo *A694*
Michael Futcher Disobediently Yours *A314*
Mr David Gale Abduction *A7*
Grizelda Gambaro Bad Blood *A85*
John Gay The Beggar's Opera *A106*
Pam Gems Queen Christina *A888*
Ira Gershwin Lady Be Good *A594*
William Gibson Monday After Miracle *A733*
Jean Giono Song of Provence *A1031*

Paul Giovanni Crucifer A260
Paul Godfrey Once In A While A816
Sheila Goff Understanding The Dang A1161
Mr Nicolai Gogol Gamblers A424
Carlo Goldoni Le Baruffe Chiozzotte A604
Steve Gooch Massa A692
Jack Good Good Rockin' Tonite A449
David Gooderson Curse Of The Mummy A263
David Goodland Anzacs Over England A56
Susan Gott Watching And Weighting A1187
Michael Gow On Top of the World A814
Kenneth Grahame Wind In The Willows A1211
Richard Greenburgh The Author's Voice A75
David Greenspan Home Show Pieces A503
Griboedev Wit's End A1216
Linda Griffiths The Darling Family A283
Trevor Griffiths Gulf Between Us A462
The Brothers Grimm It's Not All Grimm A550
John Guare Six Degrees... A1008
Yossi Hadar Biboff A117
Miss Kate Hale Shoot The Women First A996
John Halstead Old Mother Hubbard A805
Godfrey Hamilton Broken Folk A164
Oscar Hammerstein Carmen Jones A189
Rodgers & Hammerstein II The Sound Of Music A1033
Christopher Hampton Liaisons Dangereuses A610
John Hankin Return of the Prodigal A901
James Harding I Believe In Love A524
Robert Harling Steel Magnolias A1045
Mr Sheldon Harnick Fiddler On The Roof A401
Chris Harris Aladdin A25
Tony Harrison Square Rounds A1038
Mr Charles Hart Phantom Of The Opera A854
Ronald Harwood Reflected Glory A898
Leah Hausman Glassparts A441
Giles Havergal The Jungle Book A568
Jim Hawkins Northern Trawl A797
Josef Haydn World Upon The Moon A1241
Ronald Hayman Playing The Wife A865
Lillian Hellman Little Foxes A628
Kimberley Ann Herd His Brother's Keeper A496
Mr Brian Hewitt-Jones Cinderella A219
Thomas Heywood A Woman Killed With Kindness A1229
Susan Hill The Woman In Black A1226
Hugh Hodgart Beauty And The Beast A97
Mr Guy Holland No 3 Pied Piper Street A788
Vilma Hollingbery Dick Whittington A312
Anthony Hope The Prisoner Of Zenda A878
Michele Howarth Grope A460
Tina Howe Painting Churches A842
Stewart Howson Sherlock Holmes A994
Declan Hughes Digging for Fire A313
Dusty Hughes A Slip Of The Tongue A1016
Victor Hugo Les Miserables A612
Sarah Hunter Faith Over Reason A390
Ron Hutchinson Pygmies In The Ruins A887
Tunde Ikoli Goin' Local A442
Eugene Ionesco Macbett A662
Jim Jacobs Grease A458
Henry James The Heiress A490
Ludovic Janvier Monstre, Va! A735
Guy Jenkin Fighting For The Dunghill A404
Catherine Johnson Too Much Too Young A1127
J. Madison Johnston His Brother's Keeper A496
Ben Jonson The Alchemist A28
Kafka The Trial A1140
Sergei Kaladin Gaudeamus A430
Berwick Kaler Babes in the Wood A80
John Kander Kiss of Spiderwoman A584
John Kane A Swell Party A1060
David Kane Grave Plots A456
George Kaufman June Moon A567
Jackie Kay Every Bit Of It A385
John B. Keane Big Maggie A118
Mark Keegan Coming of Age A243
Tom Kempinski When The Past Is Still A1199
Roy Kendall Body And Soul A146
James Kennaway Country Dance A251
Sharon Kennet The Sacred Penman A946
Mary Kerridge Sleeping Beauty A1012
Paul Kerryson Saint Oscar A949
Joseph Kesselring Arsenic and Old Lace A62
Daniel Keyes Flowers For Algernon A410
Derek Killeen Mother Goose A739
Gerald Killingworth The Golden Ass A443
Peter King The Ballroom A1091
Mr Clive King Stig Of The Dump A1047
Mr Stephen King Misery A725
King & Carey Sailor Beware! A948
Mr Bob Kingdom Return Journey A351
Stash Kirkbride The Candidate A184
Frederick Knott Dial M for Murder A305
Dusan Kovacevic The Professional A883
Franz Xavier Kroetz Dead Soil A290
Tony Kushner Angels In America A47
Damian Landi Oscar A825
Mr Harry Landis In Celebration A535
Bob Larbey Building Blocks A170
Ring Lardner June Moon A567
Iain Lauchlan Mother Goose A741
Karoline Leach Robin of the Wood A930
Mr Tom Leatherbarrow Molecatcher's Daughter A729
Miss Elizabeth LeCompte Brace Up! A156
Ken Lee Happy As A Sandbag A473
Robin Lefevre One The Ledge A821
Robert Lepage Needles And Opium A775
Ira Levin Deathtrap A298
Saunders Lewis Blodeuwedd A129
Miss Peta Lily Glassparts A441
David Lodge The Writing Game A1242
Christopher Logue Kings A583
Mark Long The Solo Experience A1024
Tony Longhurst Villain A1174
Frederick Lonsdale On Approval A807
Frederico Garcia Lorca Yerma A1246
Mr Doug Lucie Grace A452
Ken Ludwig Lend Me A Tenor A606
Tim Luscombe EuroVision A381
Miss Lorelei Lynn Wizard of Oz A1224
Garry Lyons Frankie & Tommy A418
Noel MacAoidh The Changing Reason A198
Claire MacDonald Heartless A487
Stephen MacDonald Not About Heroes A799
Miss Marianne MacDonald Liar Liar A616
Sharman MacDonald Shades A981
Robert David MacDonald Conundrum A247

Roy MacGregor Phoenix *A857*
Joan MacLeod Toronto, Mississippi *A1129*
Mr Kenneth MacMillan Carousel *A190*
Claudio Macor The Tailor-Made Man *A1062*
Michelle Magorian Goodnight Mr Tom *A450*
Willy Maley Lions of Lisbon *A626*
Steven Mallatratt The Woman In Black *A1227*
Andrew Manley Dick Whittington *A310*
Jennifer Manley Dick Whittington *A310*
John Marston Dutch Courtesan *A348*
Sue Sutton Mayo Christmas Carol *A217*
Antony McCarten Ladies' Night *A592*
Jane McCulloch Mad,Bad,And Dangerous *A665*
Stuart McEnzie Hostages and Hamsters *A506*
Douglas McFarren Obsession *A800*
John McGrath Wicked Old Man *A1207*
Frank McGuinness Someone Who'll Watch *A1028*
Richard McInerny Shaker *A986*
Clare McIntyre My Heart's A Suitcase *A764*
Mr Gerard McLarnon Brothers Kramazov *A166*
Mr Jim McManus Top of the Town *A1128*
Alan McMurtrie Prisoner's Pumpkin *A879*
Terence McNally Kiss of Spiderwoman *A584*
Randhi McWilliams Sidewalk Sidney *A998*
Michael Mears Tomorrow We Do The Sky *A1124*
Menotti Amahal *A37*
Philip Michell Mamie Stewart *A405*
Lizzie Mickery Grave Dancer *A455*
Sarah Miles Charlemagne *A199*
Danny Miller Jack's Out *A554*
Mr Jonathan Miller Double Dealer *A335*
Graeme Miller ...Changed The Wires *A1245*
Jonathan Milton Burbage and the Bard *A172*
Betsuyaka Minoru Elephant *A359*
Yukio Mishima Lady Aoi *A593*
Tean Mitchell Radio Times *A889*
Greg & Tommy Moeller Leonardo *A608*
Deborah Moggach Double Take *A338*
Ferenc Molnar The Guardsman *A461*
Mr Simon Moore Misery *A725*
Mr Chris Moreno Cinderella *A219*
Lyndon Morgans Water Music *A1188*
Sheridan Morley Spread A Little Happ *A1035*
Deirdra Morris Revelations *A905*
William Morum The Late Edwina Black *A599*
Miss Cheryl Moskowitz No 3 Pied Piper Street *A788*
Roger S. Moss Nightmare *A787*
Tom Murphy The Gigli Concert *A435*
Robert Murray Robin Hood *A929*
Phyllis Nagy Weldon Rising *A1192*
Mr Terry Neason Crying For The Moon *A261*
Richard Nelson Columbus *A237*
David Ian Neville Exile *A387*
Anthony Newley Once Upon A Song *A817*
Tim Newton Ballad of Limehouse *A88*
Leonard Nimoy Vincent *A1175*
Janet Noble Away Alone *A76*
Adam Norton The Double Bass *A334*
Richard O'Brien Rocky Horror Show *A933*
Maureen O'Brien The Cutting *A267*
G. O'Connor Signora Joyce *A1000*
Mary O'Malley Once A Catholic *A815*
Eugene O'Neill Great God Brown *A459*
Joyce Carol Oates Stand Before You Naked *A525*
Clifford Odets Rocket To The Moon *A932*
Kenn Oldfield Dick Whittington *A308*
Donald Oliver Dead Flamingo Dancer *A193*
Donald S Olson Beardsley *A95*
Geoffrey Osborn La Muse *A588*
Brian Osborne Voyage Round Para *A1181*
John Osborne Dejavu *A302*
Mr Richard Osbourne Our Ellen *A832*
Maria Oshodi Hound *A510*
Peter Oswald Valdorama *A1164*
Cindy Oswin Scenic Flights *A953*
Brian Parr Cinderella *A222*
Brian Patten Gargling With Jelly *A427*
Dorothy Paul See That's Her! *A972*
Barbara Perkins The Refuge *A1093*
Adam Pernak Killers *A573*
Peter Howarth Robin *A927*
Tony Peters Beardsley *A96*
Clarke Peters Five Guys Named Moe *A407*
Ludmilla Petrushevskaya Three Girls In Blue *A1101*
Peter Pilbeam Section 2 Housing *A969*
Winsome Pinnock Leave Taking *A605*
Mr Stephen Plaice School Of Night *A960*
J. Planche Beauty And The Beast *A98*
Gillian Plowman Me and My Friend *A697*
Klaus Pohl Karate Billy...Home *A572*
David Pomeranz Little Tramp *A634*
Douglas Post Murder In Green Meadow *A757*
Dennis Potter Blue Remembered Hills *A139*
Vince Powell Turned Out Nice Again *A1145*
Stan Pretty Burbage and the Bard *A172*
Patrick Prior Cut and Trust *A265*
Craig Raine 1953 *A1*
Franca Rame The Open Couple *A823*
France Rame A Woman Plays ... *A1231*
Alan Randall Turned Out Nice Again *A1145*
Nina Rapi Dance Of Guns *A273*
Andy Rashleigh Body Talk *A147*
Kenneth Rea Brave Magicians *A158*
Tracy Redraws Section 2 Housing *A969*
Elice & Rees Double Double *A336*
Roger Rees Double Double *A337*
Anna Reynolds Jordan *A558*
Trevor Rhone Smile Orange *A1017*
David Richard-Fox The Best Man *A110*
Philip Ridley The Fastest Clock... *A398*
Robert Rigby Peculiar People *A846*
Peter Robert One Over The Eight *A820*
Meade Roberts Lady of the Lilacs *A596*
Gavin Robertson Thunderbirds FAB *A1111*
Rony Robinson Eric The Epic *A376*
James Robson King Baby *A575*
Cheryl Robson Taking of Liberty *A1063*
Toby Rodin Horse-Radish *A504*
Tony Roper Talk Of The Steamie *A1065*
Ian Rowlands The Sin Eaters *A1002*
William Rowley The Changeling *A197*
Mr Myles Rudge The Jungle Book *A568*
Daryl Runswick The Bells *A108*
Bill Russell Elegies... *A358*
Sue Ryding Withering Looks *A1217*
Martin Sadofski Outside of Heaven *A839*

DIRECTORS

All the directors we are aware of who have had plays in production in 1992.
Use the cross-referencing to link plays and playhouses.

Christopher Dunham (8)

Absent Friends	*A9*	
Beauty And The Beast	*A102*	
Death Of A Salesman	*A297*	
Muder At The Vicerage	*A754*	
Out Of Order	*A835*	
Shadowlands	*A984*	
Strippers	*A1057*	
Time Windows	*A1113*	

Paul Kerryson (8)

70, Girls, 70	*A4*	
Hot Stuff	*A508*	
Ladies' Night	*A592*	
Merrily We Roll Along	*A711*	
Saint Oscar	*A949*	
She Stoops To Conquer	*A991*	
Sleeping Beauty/Beast	*A1011*	
West Side Story	*A1193*	

Trevor Nunn (8)

Aspects Of Love	*A72*	
The Blue Angel	*A138*	
Cats	*A194*	
Heartbreak House	*A486*	
Les Miserables (2)	*A611*	*A613*
Measure For Measure	*A700*	
Starlight Express	*A1043*	

Patrick Sandford (8)

Building Blocks	*A170*	
Hawks & Doves	*A480*	
Leo In Love	*A607*	
Little Foxes	*A628*	
Murder In Green Meadow	*A757*	
New World and Tears	*A780*	
Painting Churches	*A842*	
Sindbad's Arabian..	*A1003*	

Pat Trueman (8)

Aladdin	*A23*	
Anzacs Over England	*A56*	
Curse of Mummy's Tomb	*A262*	
The Dramatic Attitudes	*A343*	
Glass Menagerie	*A439*	
One For The Road	*A819*	
Return of the Native	*A902*	
Stig Of The Dump	*A1048*	

Antony Tuckey (8)

Beyond Reasonable Doubt	*A114*
Candida	*A183*
Dangerous Corner	*A276*
Don Juan	*A327*
Goodnight Mr Tom	*A450*
High Society	*A494*
Noises Off	*A795*
Shadowlands	*A985*

Hettie MacDonald (7)

Absent Friends	*A10*
Deathtrap	*A298*
A Dolls House	*A321*
The Nose	*A798*
Once In A While	*A816*
Road	*A922*
View From The Bridge	*A1170*

Lawrence Till (7)

Alfie	*A30*
Children Of Lesser God	*A206*
Death of A Salesman	*A296*
Feed	*A399*
Inspector Calls	*A542*
Spring and Port Wine	*A1036*
Taste of Honey	*A1075*

Gareth ap Gwylim (6)

The Business Of Murder	*A174*
The Kingfisher	*A581*
The Maintenance Man	*A673*
September In The Rain	*A976*
Stage Struck	*A1040*
Teechers	*A1076*

Ian Hastings (6)

Chimes	*A207*
Epsom Downs	*A375*
Give You A Good Time	*A437*
Glass Menagerie	*A440*
Importance of Being	*A532*
Lovers	*A647*

Gwenda Hughes (6)

Beauty and the Beast	*A99*
Big Maggie	*A118*
Dangerous Corner	*A277*
East Lynne	*A352*
Hobson's Choice	*A500*

Travelling Light	*A1136*
Aline Waites (6)	
Aba Daba Music Hall	*A6*
Beauty and the Bat	*A101*
Christmas Rubbish	*A215*
Gone With The Wind II	*A445*
Put That Light Out	*A885*
Valentine	*A1166*
Michael Winter (6)	
Beyond Reasonable Doubt	*A113*
Cinderella	*A222*
Fifteen Streets	*A403*
Three Musketeers	*A1107*
What the Butler Saw	*A1197*
Wicks's Folly	*A1208*
Ken Alexander (5)	
Brighton Beach Memoirs	*A162*
Little Shop Of Horrors	*A632*
Mary Queen of Scots	*A691*
Then There Were None	*A1096*
Wuthering Heights	*A1243*
Julia Bardsley (5)	
Blood Wedding	*A134*
Dead Soil	*A290*
The Family Reunion	*A394*
Frankenstein	*A416*
Under Milk Wood	*A1160*
Michael Brown (5)	
Dangerous Obsession	*A278*
Day After The Fair	*A286*
Dick Whittington	*A312*
Second From Last In The Sack Race	*A966*
Serve Them All My Days	*A1123*
Annie Castledine (5)	
A Better Day	*A111*
The Choice	*A209*
Jane Eyre	*A555*
Rosmersholm	*A939*
Self Portrait	*A974*
Peter Cheeseman (5)	
Bright & Bold Design	*A161*
The Double Bass	*A334*
Jolly Potters	*A557*
The Plough & The Stars	*A867*
Turkey Time	*A1144*
Mark Clements (5)	
And A Nightingale Sang	*A43*
Blithe Spirit	*A125*
Far From The Madding Crowd	*A397*
Grease	*A458*
On The Piste	*A810*
John Durnin (5)	
Merchant of Venice	*A706*
One For The Road	*A818*
Robin of the Wood	*A930*
Three Musketeers	*A1106*
To Kill A Mockingbird	*A1121*
John Godber (5)	
April In Paris	*A58*
Happy Families	*A476*
Office Party	*A803*
Shakers	*A987*
Up 'N' Under	*A1163*
Roger Haines (5)	
Broadway Bound	*A163*
Closer Than Ever	*A231*
Into The Woods	*A545*
Peter Pan	*A852*
Sophisticated Ladies	*A1032*
Hugh Hodgart (5)	
Good Morning Bill	*A447*
Hay Fever	*A482*
Mirandolina	*A723*
Old Times	*A806*
Uncle Vanya	*A1158*
Martin Houghton (5)	
Cherry Orchard	*A202*
Doll's House	*A322*
Family Affair	*A393*
Lady Macbeth	*A595*
Macbeth	*A658*
Nicholas Hytner (5)	
Carousel	*A190*
Madness of George III	*A669*
Miss Saigon	*A727*
The Recruiting Officer	*A896*
Wind In The Willows	*A1211*
Ian Kellgren (5)	
Awfully Big Adventure	*A77*
Good Rockin' Tonite	*A449*
Imagine	*A530*
Sleuth	*A1013*
The Woman In Black	*A1226*
Andrew Manley (5)	
The Barber of Seville	*A90*
Blithe Spirit	*A128*
Dick Whittington	*A310*
The Hostage	*A505*
Macbeth	*A661*
Sam Mendes (5)	
The Alchemist	*A28*
Assassins	*A73*
Richard III	*A910*
Little Voice	*A917*
The Sea	*A961*
Braham Murray (5)	
Brothers Kramazov	*A166*
The Cabinet Minister	*A179*
The Miser	*A724*
Odd Women	*A801*
The Recruiting Officer	*A897*
Derek Nicholls (5)	
Babes in the Wood	*A80*
Imp. Of Being Earnest	*A533*
In The Midnight Hour	*A537*
Lend Me A Tenor	*A606*
What The Butler Saw	*A1198*
Adrian Noble (5)	
Hamlet	*A466*
Henry IV Part 1	*A492*
Henry IV Part 2	*A493*
The Thebans	*A1095*
The Winter's Tale	*A1214*
Jon Pope (5)	
Cinderella	*A226*
Doctor Faustus	*A318*

Lulu A649
Taming of the Shrew A1069
Wizard of Oz A1222

Paul Prescott (5)
Blood Whispers A135
A Distant Applause A315
Hostages and Hamsters A506
My Blood on Glass A761
Some...Atomic Zombie A1027

Rob Swain (5)
Eric The Epic A376
Henceforward... A491
Hobson's Choice A499
The Threepenny Opera A1109
TO A1115

Charles Vance (5)
Bedside Manners A105
Eductaing Rita A354
Home At Seven A502
My Cousin Rachel A762
Witness For The Prosecution A1218

Sam Walters (5)
The Artifice A63
The Dark River A282
Dutch Courtesan A348
His Majesty A497
Penny for a Song A848

Graham Watkins (5)
Comedy of Errors A239
Don't Rock The Boat A330
Hobbit A498
Mansfield Park A683
Revenge A907

John Caird (4)
Antony and Cleopatra A53
The Beggar's Opera A106
Columbus A237
Les Miserables A611

Anthony Clark (4)
Grapes of Wrath A454
My Mother Said... A766
Nervous Women A776
Playing by the Rules A863

Martin Connor (4)
Aladdin A17
Dead Flamingo Dancer A193
Noises Off A794
Stepping Out A1046

Damian Cruden (4)
Bouncers A151
Frankie & Tommy A418
Gargling With Jelly A427
TO A1116

John Doyle (4)
Candide A185
Much Ado About Nothing A751
Othello A827
The School For Scandal A956

Matthew Francis (4)
Caesar And Cleopatra A180
The Corn Is Green A249
The Prisoner Of Zenda A878
Who Shall I Be? A1203

Sonia Fraser (4)
Arsenic and Old Lace A62
Driving Miss Daisy A346
Horse-Radish A504
Tomorrow We Do The Sky A1124

Sir Peter Hall (4)
All's Well That Ends Well A35
Gifts Of The Gorgon A434
An Ideal Husband A527
Sienna Red A999

Giles Havergal (4)
Major Barbara A675
Other Places A829
Summer Lightning A1058
Travel With My Aunt A1134

Malcolm Hebden (4)
Apple Blossom Aftern'n A57
Rocket To The Moon A932
The Shawl A989
Village Wooing A1173

Peter James (4)
Absent Friends A8
Loot A638
Madras House A670
Sailor Beware! A948

Ellis Jones (4)
Barefoot in the Park A91
Business of Murder A173
Intimate Exchanges A544
Taking Steps A1064

Sheila Mander (4)
Laurel and Hardy A603
Lettice & Lovage A614
Over a Barrel A840
Wizard of Oz A1223

Val May (4)
Body And Soul A146
The Decorator A301
Moment Of Weakness A732
Murder By Misadventure A755

Robin Midgley (4)
The Innocents A540
Just Between Ourselves A569
Rivals A920
Robin Hood A928

Deborah Paige (4)
After You With The Mlk A16
A Midsummer Night's Dream A716
Mother Goose A740
Relative Values A899

Philip Prowse (4)
1953 A1
Edward II A355
Sweet Bird of Youth A1059
Woman Of No Importance A1230

Max Stafford-Clark (4)
Hush A522
A Jovial Crew A561
King Lear A579
Three Birds Alighting A1100

Kit Thacker (4)
Antony And Cleopatra A54
Dial M for Murder A305

Lion, Witch & Wardrobe	A623	
Season's Greetings	A965	
David Thacker (4)		
All My Sons	A33	
As You Like It	A67	
The Merry Wives Of Windsor	A713	
Two Gents Of Verona	A1154	
Bob Tomson (4)		
Blood Brothers	A131	
On The Piste	A812	
Raving Beauties	A893	
Scrooge the Musical	A1039	
Colin Watkeys (4)		
Adult Child/Dead Child	A15	
Broken Folk	A164	
Death And Dancing	A292	
Pigspurt	A860	
Alan Ayckbourn (3)		
One Over The Eight	A820	
Selling Out	A975	
Time Of My Life	A1112	
Richard Baron (3)		
Laurel and Hardy	A602	
Price	A874	
Travesties	A1137	
Michael Bogdanov (3)		
Cherry Orchard	A203	
Macbeth	A655	
The Tempest	A1082	
Ian Brown (3)		
Columbus	A236	
House Among the Stars	A512	
Unidentified Human	A1162	
Marina Caldarone (3)		
Cold Sweat	A234	
Old Mother Hubbard	A805	
Talk Of The Steamie	A1065	
Graham Callan (3)		
Crucifer	A260	
Hapgood	A472	
Ten Times Table	A1087	
Simon Callow (3)		
Carmen Jones	A189	
My Fair Lady	A763	
Shades	A981	
Penny Ciniewicz (3)		
Outside of Heaven	A839	
Prin	A876	
Weldon Rising	A1192	
Phil Clark (3)		
Erogenous Zones	A377	
Fern Hill	A400	
Sleeping With Mickey	A1010	
John David (3)		
The Heiress	A490	
Private Lives (2)	A880	A881
Richard Eyre (3)		
Murmuring Judges	A758	
Night of the Iguana	A785	
Richard III	A911	
David Gilmore (3)		
Radio Times	A890	
A Swell Party	A1060	
The Ballroom	A1091	
Hamish Glen (3)		
Tartuffe	A1073	
Walter	A1183	
Virginia Woolf	A1205	
Andrew Hay (3)		
Blue Remembered Hills	A139	
Fuente Ovejuna	A423	
Romeo and Juliet	A935	
Gregory Hersov (3)		
Blues for Mr Charlie	A143	
Romeo and Juliet	A936	
A View From The Bridge	A1172	
Chris Honer (3)		
Merchant of Venice	A708	
Working	A1239	
The Writing Game	A1242	
Jude Kelly (3)		
The Pope And The Witch	A870	
The Revenger's Tragedy	A908	
Wicked Old Man	A1207	
Derek Killeen (3)		
Driving Miss Daisy	A345	
Our Day Out	A831	
Steel Magnolias	A1045	
Maggie Kinloch (3)		
On Golden Pond	A809	
Othello	A826	
Voyage Round Para	A1181	
Brigid Larmour (3)		
Excess XS	A386	
Measure For Measure	A702	
Seagull	A963	
Robin Lefevre (3)		
Private Lives	A882	
Someone Who'll Watch	A1028	
Wexford Trilogy	A1194	
David Leveaux (3)		
No Man's Land	A789	
Romeo And Juliet	A938	
'Tis Pity She's A Whore	A1114	
Phyllida Lloyd (3)		
Artists and Admirers	A64	
Six Degrees...	A1008	
The Virtuoso	A1176	
Robert David MacDonald (3)		
Casanova	A191	
Conundrum	A247	
Niagara	A781	
James Maxwell (3)		
An Ideal Husband	A528	
Moonstone	A737	
Sidewalk Sidney	A998	
Katie Mitchell (3)		
The Dybbuk	A349	
House of Bernarda Alba	A515	
A Woman Killed With Kindness	A1229	
Elijah Moshinsky (3)		
Becket	A103	
Cyrano De Bergerac	A269	
Reflected Glory	A898	

Michael Napier Brown (3)

The Fancy Man	*A395*	
Martin Chuzzlewit	*A689*	
A View From The Bridge	*A1171*	

Mike Ockrent (3)

Crazy For You	*A257*	
Me And My Girl (2)	*A698*	*A699*

Mark Piper (3)

Natural Causes	*A773*	
Sleeping Beauty	*A1012*	
Something's Burning	*A1029*	

Lindsay Posner (3)

Colquhoun And MacBryde	*A235*	
Death and the Maiden (2)	*A293*	*A294*

Roger Redfarn (3)

Annie Get Your Gun	*A51*	
A Dead Secret	*A289*	
A Little Night Music	*A630*	

John Retallack (3)

Fooling About	*A412*	
Hot Italian Nights	*A507*	
The Magic Storybook	*A672*	

Ian Rickson (3)

Killers	*A573*	
Me and My Friend	*A697*	
Sab	*A945*	

Neil Sissons (3)

Hamlet	*A463*	
King Lear	*A577*	
The Revenger's Tragedy	*A906*	

Euan Smith (3)

The Deep Blue Sea	*A140*	
Hindsight	*A495*	
Macbeth	*A656*	

Lou Stein (3)

All My Sons	*A32*	
The Baby	*A82*	
The Barber Of Seville	*A89*	

Ian Talbot (3)

Lady Be Good	*A594*	
A Midsummer Night's ..	*A721*	
You Must Be The Husband	*A1248*	

Derek Wax (3)

As You Desire Me	*A66*	
Man, Beast and Virtue	*A682*	
No Remission	*A790*	

Richard Williams (3)

Body Talk	*A147*	
Hans C. Anderstories	*A470*	
Ten In A Bed	*A1086*	

Ian Wooldridge (3)

Merlin, The Search	*A709*	
School For Wives	*A958*	
Taming Of The Shrew	*A1070*	

John Adams (2)

Kafka's Dick	*A571*	
The Last Carnival	*A598*	

Maria Aitken (2)

As You Like It	*A71*	
School for Scandal	*A957*	

Bill Alexander (2)

School of Night	*A959*	
The Taming Of The Shrew	*A1068*	

Mike Alfreds (2)

Game of Love & Chance	*A425*	
Revenger's Tragedy	*A909*	

Michael Attenborough (2)

Amphibians	*A40*	
The Changeling	*A197*	

Neil Bartlett (2)

Game of Love & Chance	*A425*	
A Judgement In Stone	*A563*	

Lee Beagley (2)

King Lear	*A578*	
Threepenny Story	*A1108*	

Ruth Ben-Tovim (2)

Ballad of Limehouse	*A88*	
Dance Of Guns	*A273*	

Peter Benedict (2)

Country Wife	*A253*	
Punishment Of Animals	*A259*	

Rob Bettinson (2)

Buddy (2)	*A168*	*A169*

John Binnie (2)

A Little Older	*A631*	
MacWizard Fae Oz	*A663*	

Kate Bone (2)

King Lear	*A576*	
Macbeth	*A660*	

Laurence Boswell (2)

Hecuba	*A488*	
Madness in Valencia	*A668*	

Yvonne Brewster (2)

Love Space Demands	*A644*	
The Road	*A921*	

June Brown (2)

The Double D	*A333*	
Pharmaceutical	*A855*	

Bill Buffery (2)

Dead Man's Hat	*A288*	
Frankenstein	*A415*	

Geoff Bullen (2)

Jubilee	*A562*	
The Winslow Boy	*A1213*	

Topher Campbell (2)

Flamingo	*A408*	
Necklaces	*A774*	

Bob Carlton (2)

Forbidden Planet	*A904*	
Stitched Up	*A1050*	

Alan Cohen (2)

As You Like It	*A69*	
Peter Pan	*A851*	

Roger Cook (2)

Moment of Madness	*A731*	
Sex and Sadness	*A979*	

Audrey Cooke (2)

Evening with Gary L. (2)	*A382*	*A383*

Anthony Cornish (2)

The Duchess of Malfi	*A347*	
She Stoops To Conquer	*A990*	

Ted Craig (2)

Playing Sinatra	*A864*	
Turner's Crossing	*A1146*	

Patrick Mason (2)		
Dancing at Lughnasa (2)	*A274*	*A275*
Mr David Massarella (2)		
Doll's House	*A320*	
Single Spies	*A1004*	
Christopher Masters (2)		
Mrs Klein	*A748*	
The Secret Rapture	*A968*	
Sue Sutton Mayo (2)		
Ghosts	*A433*	
A Marginal Affair	*A687*	
Ken McClymont (2)		
Jack's Out	*A554*	
Rat Play	*A892*	
Jane McCulloch (2)		
Chorus of Disapproval	*A210*	
Mad,Bad,And Dangerous	*A665*	
Antony McDonald (2)		
Birthday Party	*A124*	
Why Things Happen	*A1206*	
Nancy Meckler (2)		
Anna Karenina	*A50*	
Trilby & Svengali	*A1141*	
John Mitchell (2)		
Buchanan	*A167*	
Life of Stuff	*A620*	
Maggie Norris (2)		
Daisy Pulls it Off	*A271*	
Josephine	*A560*	
Charles Nowosielski (2)		
Arms And The Man	*A61*	
Lion Witsh & Wardrobe	*A625*	
Sean O'Connor (2)		
Blues In The Night	*A144*	
Gaslight	*A428*	
Richard Olivier (2)		
M. Butterfly	*A651*	
Shirley Valentine	*A995*	
Connal Orton (2)		
Bigger Slice of Pie	*A120*	
Neville's Island	*A777*	
Richard Osborne (2)		
Fighting For The Dunghill	*A404*	
Memoirs of a Survivor	*A705*	
Lynne Parker (2)		
Digging for Fire	*A313*	
Love and a Bottle	*A643*	
Sue Parrish (2)		
Every Bit Of It	*A385*	
Roaring Girl's Hamlet	*A925*	
Jonathon Petherbridge (2)		
Good Person Of Sezuan	*A448*	
Measure for Measure	*A703*	
Nick Philippou (2)		
Arms and the Man	*A60*	
Lulu	*A648*	
Steven Pimlott (2)		
Joseph...	*A559*	
Julius Caesar	*A566*	
Harold Prince (2)		
Kiss of Spiderwoman	*A584*	
Phantom Of The Opera	*A854*	
Christopher Renshaw (2)		
Fallen Angels	*A391*	
On Golden Pond	*A808*	
Adrian Reynolds (2)		
Little Tramp	*A634*	
Monday After Miracle	*A733*	
Toby Robertson (2)		
The Seagull	*A962*	
Trelawny Of The Wells	*A1139*	
Kate Rowland (2)		
Bad Blood	*A85*	
Self Catering	*A973*	
Michael Rudman (2)		
Making It Better	*A677*	
A Midsummer Night's ..	*A720*	
Jeremy Sams (2)		
Entertaining Mr Sloane	*A374*	
Schippel, The Plumber	*A954*	
Rumu Sen-Gupta (2)		
Leave Taking	*A605*	
Shadowlands	*A983*	
Ceri Sherlock (2)		
Blodeuwedd	*A129*	
La Ronde	*A589*	
Caroline Smith (2)		
Bedroom Farce	*A104*	
Indigo Mill	*A539*	
Julia Smith (2)		
Metamorphosis	*A714*	
The Trial	*A1140*	
Richard Stone (2)		
Teechers	*A1078*	
TO	*A1120*	
Alan Strachan (2)		
Hay Fever	*A481*	
June Moon	*A567*	
Tim Supple (2)		
Billy Liar	*A122*	
Coriolanus	*A248*	
Malcolm Sutherland (2)		
Venus and Adonis	*A1167*	
Wasp Factory	*A1185*	
Kenneth Alan Taylor (2)		
Dick Whittington	*A311*	
The House Of Stairs	*A513*	
Jeff Teare (2)		
Cut and Trust	*A265*	
Night in Tunisia	*A783*	
Wendy Toye (2)		
See How They Run	*A971*	
The Sound Of Music	*A1033*	
Ultz (2)		
Dragon	*A341*	
What The Butler Saw	*A1196*	
Simon Usher (2)		
King Baby	*A575*	
Pond Life	*A869*	
Jatinder Verma (2)		
Heer Ranjha	*A489*	
The Little Clay Cart	*A627*	
Michael Walling (2)		
Beardsley	*A95*	
Great God Brown	*A459*	

Graham Watts (2)
- Moll Flanders *A730*
- On The Piste *A811*

Patrick Wilde (2)
- Cabal and Love *A176*
- Deceptions *A300*

Richard Wilson (2)
- Women Laughing (2) *A1234* *A1235*

Peter Wilson (2)
- Charley's Aunt *A200*
- Cinderella *A221*

Stuart Wood (2)
- New Man *A778*
- Paradise Garden *A843*

Yuval Zamir (2)
- Blood Wedding *A133*
- Spring Awakening *A1037*

Martin Duncan & Ian Spink Four Marys *A414*
James Alby Killing Passion *A574*
William Alderson Rebels And Friends *A895*
David Alexander Pepys - The Diarist *A849*
Foz Allan Blood Brothers *A130*
Stuart Allen Shame, Ignorance *A988*
Michael Almaz Intimacy *A543*
Lindsay Anderson Stages *A1042*
David Anderson House That Jack Bought *A518*
Beverly Andrews Blues Angels *A141*
Annabel Arden The Winter's Tale *A1215*
Alex Armitage Radio Times *A890*
Gareth Armstrong The Business Of Murder *A175*
Graham Ashe Enter The Tragic Muse *A372*
Mike Ashman The Golden Ass *A443*
Charles Augins Five Guys Named Moe *A407*
Liane Aukin Kings *A583*
Robert Ballard The Three Musketeers *A1104*
Frith Banbury Frightened Lady *A192*
Lynda Baron Aladdin *A26*
Romy Baskerville The Norman Conquests *A796*
Ben Benison Hamlet *A467*
Alan Bennett Talking Heads *A1066*
Mary Benning La Voix Humaine *A591*
Leon Berger Mamahuhu? *A678*
Steven Berkoff Acapulco *A12*
Damian Bermingham Wuthering Heights *A1244*
Adrian Berry Endgame *A368*
Jonathan Best Speed-The-Plow *A1034*
Jon Best Provoked Wife *A884*
Paul Besterman Grope *A460*
John Bett Country Dance *A251*
Natasha Betteridge Forever Yours *A413*
David Bidmead I Believe In Love *A524*
Michael Birch Three Girls In Blue *A1101*
Anna Birch Bad Girl *A86*
Jennifer Black Therese Raquin *A1097*
Paul Blackman Schmucks *A955*
Lionel Blair Cinderella *A221*
Simon Blake Broken Heads *A165*
Sydnee Blake Stand Before You Naked *A525*
Michael Blakemore Ride Down Mt Morgan *A915*
Ian Blower Cinderella *A226*
Keith Boak Water Music *A1188*
Krzystof Borowiec Stop in the Desert *A1051*
Peter Bowles Otherwise Engaged *A830*
Michael Boyd Good *A446*
Danny Boyle Berlin Bertie *A109*
Mark Bramble Barnum *A93*
Andrew Breakwell The Lost Child *A640*
John Brett See That's Her! *A972*
Alexander Bridge The Late Edwina Black *A599*
Richard Bridges Lord of the Rings *A639*
Richard Bridgland All On Top *A34*
Adrian Brine Cerceau *A195*
Blake Brooker Serpent Kills *A977*
Pip Broughton The Pocket Dream *A868*
David Bryer Women on Top *A1237*
Fiona Buffini Jordan *A558*
Clayton Buffoni Telling Tales *A1081*
Cliff Burnett Wind in the Willows *A1212*
Lynton Burns Sikulu *A1001*
Michael Burrell My Sister Next Door *A769*
Josette Bushell-Mingo King Lear *A578*
Burt Caesar Cloud 9 *A232*
John Cameron No Trams To Lime St. *A791*
Jimmy Camicia Christopher Street *A218*
Ken Campbell Pigspurt *A860*
Robert Cantarella Monstre, Va! *A735*
Tim Carroll Enemy To The People *A369*
Les Carruthers TO *A1119*
James Robert Carson As You Like It *A68*
Jo Carter Mayor of Casterbridge *A695*
Karen Cass Daughters Of England *A284*
Burt Ceaser Faith Over Reason *A390*
Duggie Chapman Turned Out Nice Again *A1145*
Bob Cheeseman Mystery Plays *A770*
Robert Chetwyn Me And Mamie O'Rourke *A696*
Graham Chinn Travelling Light *A1135*
Robert Clare Much Ado About Nothing *A753*
Jeff Clarke World Upon The Moon *A1241*
Paul Clarkson Women in Love *A1233*
Brian Clemens Anybody for Murder? *A55*
Janine Clements The Refuge *A1093*
Roger Clissold Beyond Reasonable Doubt *A115*
Tom Conti Dog Days *A319*
David Conville Tons Of Money *A1125*
Ray Cooney It Runs In The Family *A548*
Richard Cotterell The Mother Tongue *A743*
Vivienne Cottrell She Ventures He Wins *A993*
Vivienne Cozens Between the Lines *A112*
David Craik Play Strindberg *A861*
Tony Craven 19th Hole *A1090*
Peter Craze The Professional *A883*
Rupert Creed Northern Trawl *A797*
Michael Cross Our Day Out *A831*
Hugh Cruttwell Something Missing *A1030*
Adam Darius Rimbaud And Verlaine *A916*
Howard Davies Pygmalion *A886*
Tudor Davies Goldilocks *A444*
Allan Davis Straight & Narrow *A1054*
Sue Davis Angels & Amazons *A48*
Gabrielle Daws Disobediently Yours *A314*
Andrew Dawson Thunderbirds FAB *A1111*
Eric de Dadelsen Mowgli - Enfant Loup *A745*
Roger Delves-Broughton The Barber of Seville *A90*
Julie Denny Emperor's New Clothes *A364*
Matthew Devitt From A Jack To A King *A420*
Ian Dickens Macbeth *A657*

Richard Digby-Day What the Butler Saw *A1197*
Luke Dixon Salonika *A950*
Stephen Dobbin Liaisons Dangereuses *A610*
Lev Dodin Gaudeamus *A430*
Gregory Doran The Odyssey *A802*
Dennis Douglas Tottering Towers *A1130*
Joe Dowling Faith Healer *A389*
Kay Dudeny The Imaginary Invalid *A529*
Han Duijvendak Barnstormers *A92*
Frank Dunlop Alfie *A29*
Janice Dunn Diamonds in the Dust *A306*
Brian Elsley Elidor *A360*
Tim Etchells Emanuelle Enchanted *A363*
Caroline Eves Taste of Honey *A1074*
David Farr Seven Doors *A978*
Vicky Featherstone Kvetch *A586*
Don Fellows Fool for Love *A411*
Alan Ferris The English Kiss *A370*
Vanessa Fielding The Woman Destroyed *A1225*
Peter Fieldson Wizard of Oz *A1219*
Jonas Finley Ghost Sonata *A431*
Chris Fisher Thirteenth Night *A1099*
Lucie Fitchett The Tender Husband *A1088*
Caroline Fitzgerald White Woman Street *A1202*
Fionnula Flannagan Away Alone *A76*
David Fleeshman Dangerous Obsession *A281*
Vanessa Ford Lion Witch & Wardrobe *A624*
Lisa Forrell Charlemagne *A199*
Helen Fotheringham Liar Liar *A616*
Malcolm Frederick Viva Detroit *A1178*
Judy Friel London Vertigo *A636*
Michael Friend Stageland *A1041*
Peter Gale House of Bernarda Alba *A517*
Caroline Gardiner Macbeth *A654*
Ruth Garnault The Sin Eaters *A1002*
Jamie Garven Merchant Of Venice *A707*
William Gaskill Voysey Inheritance *A1182*
Phillipe Gaulier The End Of The Tunnel *A365*
Chris Geelan Macbeth *A653*
Goh Siew Geok The Dance & Railroad *A272*
Richard Georgeson Tango 'Til You're Sore *A1072*
John Ghent Happy As A Sandbag *A473*
Jane Gibson A Working Woman *A1238*
Kate Gielgud The Ecstacy *A353*
David Giles On Approval *A807*
David Gillies Twelfth Night *A1150*
David Glass Gormenghast *A451*
Oliver Goldsmith She Stoops To Conquer *A990*
Jack Good Good Rockin' Tonite *A449*
Elizabeth Goria My Mother Said *A767*
Andy Graham Animal Farm *A49*
David Graham-Young Master and Margarita *A693*
Rumin Gray At Fifty She Discovered The Sea *A74*
Lennox Greaves Loot *A637*
Richard Gregory Excess XS *A386*
Annie Griffin Shaker *A986*
Trevor Griffiths Gulf Between Us *A462*
Robbie Gringrass Story of the Last *A1053*
Philip Grout Blithe Spirit *A126*
Claire Grove It's A Girl *A549*
Bob Grove Coming of Age *A243*
Kirstie Gulick National Enquirer *A1052*
Tamsin Habety Twelfth Night *A1151*
Richard Haddon Bazaar and Rummage *A94*
Piers Haggard Which Witch *A1200*
Edward Hall Cain *A181*
Julia Hallawell Richard's Cork Leg *A913*
Hugh Halliday Leonardo *A608*
Liam Halligan Kurt Weill Cabaret *A585*
Gillian Hambleton Sherlock Holmes *A994*
Gloria Hamilton Master Harold & The bo *A694*
Bryan Hands You Must Be The Husband *A1248*
Terry Hands Tamburlaine The Great *A1067*
Michael Harding Misogynist *A726*
Michelle Hardy Cinderella *A225*
Jean Harley A Midsummer Night's Dream *A719*
Simon Harris Forever Yours *A413*
Jon Harris Daughters Of England *A284*
John Harris Commodities *A244*
Tony Harrison Square Rounds *A1038*
Deidre Harrison Courting Winnona *A255*
Wayne Harrison On Top of the World *A814*
Leah Hausman A Judgement In Stone *A563*
Andy Hay Too Much Too Young *A1127*
Jamie Hayes Oscar *A825*
Lea Heather Slice Of Saturday... *A1015*
Philip Hedley Goin' Local *A442*
Ian Herbert Sisters *A1006*
Mark Heron My Heart's A Suitcase *A764*
Theresa Heskins Devil's Only Sleeping *A303*
Caroline Hetherington Bloody Poetry *A137*
Karl Hibbert The Maintenance Man *A674*
Dominic Hill Three More Sleepless *A1103*
Astrid Hilne Brand *A157*
Friedrich Hollander The Blue Angel *A138*
Jasper Holmes Flowers For Algernon *A410*
Anthony Hopkins Return Journey *A351*
Cathryn Horn Monster He Made Me *A734*
Jos Houben Moose *A738*
Roy Hudd Babes in the Wood *A79*
Tom Hunsinger Dangerous Dolls-Mummys Little Girl *A279*
Johnny Hutch Endangered Species *A367*
Dalia Ibelhauptaite Gamblers *A424*
Kenny Ireland The Europeans *A378*
Polly Irvin A Doll's House *A324*
Debbie Isitt Woman Who Cooked *A1232*
Mike James Marnie Stewart *A405*
Jeremy James Beauty And The Beast *A100*
Eve Jamieson End Of The Beginning *A366*
Roland Jaquarello Gaslight *A429*
Adrian Johnston Wizard of Oz *A1222*
Larry Jones Metamorphosis *A715*
Deb Jones Signora Joyce *A1000*
Brenda Jones Country Wife *A252*
Richard Jones Bourgeois Gentilhomme *A153*
Wyn Jones Mrs Klein *A749*
Wilfred Judd Biko *A121*
Ian Judge Comedy Of Errors *A241*
Rachel Kavanaugh Who Was Hilary *A1204*
Tim Keenan Elephant *A359*
Penelope Keith Relatively Speaking *A900*
David Kelsey Road To Casablanca *A923*
Sharon Kennet The Sacred Penman *A946*
Bill Kenwright Robin *A927*
Delena Kidd Curse Of The Mummy *A263*
Jonathan Kiley Babes In The Wood *A81*

Mark Lambert Una Pooka *A1156*
Kristine Langdon-Smith Women Of The Dust *A1236*
Stephen Langridge The Bells *A108*
Jean-Marc Lanteri Don't Play With Love *A329*
Iain Lauchlan Mother Goose *A741*
Andy Lavender Man Outside *A681*
Pete Lawson Telephonebelles *A1079*
Jenny Lee Light in the Village *A622*
Sue Lefton A Working Woman *A1238*
Josephine LeGrice The Hatchet Man *A478*
David Leland Blues Brothers *A142*
Leslie Lawton Out Of Order *A834*
Christopher Lillicrap Christmas Cat *A216*
Julia Limer The Marvellous Boy *A690*
John Link Confusions *A246*
Bonnie Lithgoe Jack And The Beanstalk *A552*
Kristine London-Smith Bodycount *A148*
Robert Longden Moby Dick *A728*
Pat Lower Ghosts *A432*
Tim Luscombe EuroVision *A381*
Jake Lushington Wit's End *A1216*
Jerzy Luzynski Stop in the Desert *A1051*
Alan Lyddiard The Dance & Railroad *A272*
Gillian Lynne Valentine's Day *A1165*
Stephen MacDonald Not About Heroes *A799*
David MacLellen House That Jack Bought *A518*
David Maclennan Eight to the Bar *A356*
Claudio Macor The Tailor-Made Man *A1062*
Christopher Malcolm Rocky Horror Show *A933*
Patrick Marmion American Heart *A38*
Ewan Marshall Hound *A510*
Brian Marshall Jack and the Beanstalk *A551*
Jonathan Martin False Servant *A392*
Chris Martin Comedy of Errors *A240*
Libby Mason The Lie Of The Land *A617*
Mr David Massarella Happy Days *A474*
Sean Mathias Uncle Vanya *A1157*
Simon Mawdsley Teechers *A1077*
Joan-Ann Maynard An After Taste *A41*
Libby McArthur Lions of Lisbon *A626*
Simon McBurney Street of Crocodiles *A1056*
Michael McCaffey Hamlet *A464*
Phelim McDermott Doctor Faustus *A317*
Ian McDiarmid A Hard Heart *A477*
James McDonald Crackwalker *A256*
Dave McVicar Merlin the Magnificent *A710*
Simon Meadon Too Clever By Half *A1126*
Peter Meineck Villain *A1174*
Gabriele Meini Understanding The Dang *A1161*
Michael Merwitzer Endangered Species *A367*
Jonathan Meth The Sacred Penman *A946*
Kenn Michaels Dick Whittington *A307*
Les Miller The Hour Of The Lynx *A511*
Jonathan Milton Burbage and the Bard *A172*
Ariane Mnouchkine Les Atrides *A609*
Cordelia Monsey Roman & Marys *A934*
Abigail Morris The Rock Station *A931*
Stanley Morris Billy the Kid *A123*
Gerry Mulgrew Cyrano De Bergerac *A270*
Robert Murray Robin Hood *A929*
Silvio Narizzano Lady of the Lilacs *A596*
David Ian Neville Exile *A387*
Anthony Newley Once Upon A Song *A817*
Yukio Ninagawa The Tempest *A1084*
Peter D Norman Games *A426*
Kate Normington Manslaughter *A684*
Eoin O'Callaghan Pygmies In The Ruins *A887*
Anatol Orient A Life In The Theatre *A618*
Alastair Palmer Twelfth Night *A1149*
Tony Palmer Dejavu *A302*
Lucy Parker The Guardsman *A461*
Julia Pascal Dybbuk *A350*
Mark Pearson Patagonia *A845*
Mary Peate Grave Dancer *A455*
Birte Pedersen Gravity Swing *A457*
Ron Pember A Christmas Carol *A212*
Michael Pennington Twelfth Night *A1148*
Clive Perry The Mikado *A722*
Kenneth Pickering Mystery Plays *A771*
Tim Pigott-Smith Playing The Wife *A865*
Paul Pinson The Dorm *A332*
Stephen Powell The Tempest *A1083*
Michael Poyner Round The Big Clock *A940*
Andrew Pratt Queen Christina *A888*
Hana-Maria Pravda Savage Storm *A952*
Stan Pretty Burbage and the Bard *A172*
Colin Prockter Lloyd George *A635*
Bill Pryde Obsession *A800*
Peter Quigley Cabaret *A178*
Matthew Radford Venus and Adonis *A1167*
Sita Ramamurthy World...Upside Down *A1240*
Paulette Randall Head-Rot Holiday *A484*
Sarah Ream Double Double *A336*
David Evans Rees Romeo and Juliet *A937*
Roland Rees Ruby In The Dust *A941*
Karel Reisz The Gigli Concert *A435*
Tim Reynolds Massa *A692*
Trevor Rhone Smile Orange *A1017*
Griff Rhys Jones Twelfth Night *A1152*
Steffyni Rigold Voice of the Sea *A1179*
Roger Ringrose Vincent *A1175*
David Roberts Love's Labour's Lost *A646*
Gavin Robertson Thunderbirds FAB *A1111*
Tony Robertson Marching Song *A685*
Kevin Robertson Your Sincerely *A1251*
Jonathan Robinson American Buffalo *A39*
James Roose-Evans Venus Observed *A1168*
Michael Rose Cinderella *A223*
Peter Rowe Les Miserables *A612*
Tal Rubins Rebecca *A894*
Bill Russell Elegies... *A358*
Barrie Rutter Richard III *A912*
Christopher G Sandford Christmas Carol *A214*
Granville Saxton While The Sun Shines *A1201*
Tessa Schneideman Ay Carmela! *A78*
Buddy Schwab Barnum *A93*
Ned Seago The Author's Voice *A75*
Toby Sedgwick The Three Musketeers *A1105*
Ong Keng Sen Madame Mao's Memories *A667*
Phil Setren Dangerous Dolls-Soap Crazy *A280*
Deborah Shaw Breathless *A160*
Rehan Sheikh The Player *A862*
Peter Shepherd Diary Of Adrian Mole *A967*
Ned Sherrin Our Song *A833*
Robert Sian Bouncers *A152*
Charles Siegel Toronto, Mississippi *A1129*

Lee Simpson Doctor Faustus *A317*
Jeremy Sinden Bulldog Drummond *A171*
Alexander Sisters Fantasy Island *A396*
Roger Smith Old Country *A804*
Julie Somers As You Like It *A70*
Noreen Spall Merry Wives Of Windsor *A712*
Ian Spink Pelican *A847*
Eric Standidge Double Double *A337*
Tommy Steele Some Like It Hot *A1025*
Roman Stefanski Giraffe, Pelly, & Me *A436*
Karen Stephens In The Midnight Hour *A538*
Dudley Stevens Beauty And The Beast *A98*
Mr Gary Stevens Name *A772*
Simon Stokes A Slip Of The Tongue *A1016*
Claire Storey As Time Goes By *A65*
Georgio Strehler Le Baruffe Chiozzotte *A604*
John Strehlow Much Ado About Nothing *A750*
Jo Stuart Truth Games *A1143*
Robert Sturua Hamlet *A465*
Sara Sugarman Handsome,Handicapped.. *A468*
Liz Swift We *A1191*
Toby Swift Custer's Last Stand *A264*
Colin Swift Sneeze *A1018*
David Taylor Lost in Yonkers *A641*
Gerry Tebutt High Society *A494*
The Company Fierce Love *A402*
Bardy Thomas The Best Man *A110*
Jens Thordal Adult Child/Dead Child *A14*
Carole Todd Elvis - the Musical *A362*
David Toguri Lust *A650*
Matthew Townshend Chitty Bang Bang *A208*
Gregor Truter Roberto Calvi *A926*
Tommy Tune Grand Hotel *A453*
David Turner The Mousetrap *A744*
Benjamin Twist Cuttin' A Rug *A266*
Stephen Unwin Karate Billy...Home *A572*
Helena Uren School Of Night *A960*
Marc Urquhart Strange Domain *A1055*
Micheline van de Poel Moose *A738*
Simone Vause Sylvia *A1061*
Simon Vincenzi Heartless *A487*
Phil Viner Chasing The Hypnotist *A201*
Terry Wale In Praise Of Love *A536*
Matthew Warchus Life is a Dream *A619*
Debbie Wastling Dracula Spectacular *A340*
Diane Watson Julius Caesar *A565*
Helen Watson Music Hall *A760*
Peter Westbury Same Time Next Year *A951*
Matthew Westwood The Double D *A333*
Joe White To My Country A Child *A1122*
Chris White In The Midnight Hour *A538*
David Whybrow Section 2 Housing *A969*
Clifford Williams Breaking the Code *A159*
Phil Willmott The Wax King *A1189*
Phil Wilmott Iago *A526*
Billy Wilson The Cotton Club *A250*
Kay Winterbourne Love's Labour's Lost *A646*
Denise Wong Heart *A485*
Beth Wood The Thin Soldier *A1098*
Peter Wood She Stoops To Conquer *A992*
David Wood The BFG *A116*
David Woods Three Men in a Boat *A1102*
Hugh Wooldridge Double Take *A338*
Johnny Worthy Slice of Saturday *A1014*
Christopher Wren Cinderella *A220*
Jules Wright Some Singing Blood *A1026*
Janine Wunsche The Darling Family *A283*
Stephen Wyllie The Candidate *A184*
Madeleine Wynn When The Past Is Still *A1199*
Shai Bar Yaacov Biboff *A117*
Robin Yarnton Voices at Her Elbow *A1180*
Tony Yates Boy's Own *A155*
Susannah York Revelations *A905*
Jeff Young Man in the Moon *A680*
Esty Zakhem And Hunger For All *A44*
Franco Zeffirelli Six Characters *A1007*

PRODUCERS

All the producers we are aware of who have had plays in production in 1992. Use the cross-referencing to link plays and playhouses.

Bill Kenwright Ltd (15)		
Bedroom Farce	*A104*	
Blood Brothers	*A131*	
Dancing at Lughnasa (2)	*A274*	*A275*
Death and the Maiden	*A294*	
Fallen Angels	*A391*	
Good Rockin' Tonite	*A449*	
The House Of Stairs	*A513*	
An Ideal Husband	*A527*	
M. Butterfly	*A651*	
On Golden Pond	*A808*	
On The Piste	*A812*	
Shirley Valentine	*A995*	
Sienna Red	*A999*	
Travel With My Aunt	*A1134*	
RSC (14)		
The Alchemist	*A28*	
All's Well That Ends Well	*A35*	
As You Like It	*A67*	
Henry IV Part 1	*A492*	
Henry IV Part 2	*A493*	
Liaisons Dangereuses	*A610*	
Measure For Measure	*A700*	
The Merry Wives Of Windsor	*A713*	
The Odyssey	*A802*	
Tamburlaine The Great	*A1067*	
The Taming Of The Shrew	*A1068*	
'Tis Pity She's A Whore	*A1114*	
Two Gents Of Verona	*A1154*	
A Woman Killed With Kindness	*A1229*	
Duncan C Weldon (12)		
John Mills	*A42*	
Becket	*A103*	
Breaking the Code	*A159*	
The Cabinet Minister	*A179*	
The Corn Is Green	*A249*	
Cyrano De Bergerac	*A269*	
Heartbreak House	*A486*	
Lost in Yonkers	*A641*	
The Miser	*A724*	
Talking Heads	*A1066*	
Trelawny Of The Wells	*A1139*	
Woman Of No Importance	*A1230*	
RNT (11)		
Angels In America	*A47*	
Game of Love & Chance	*A425*	
The Little Clay Cart	*A627*	
Madness of George III	*A669*	
Murmuring Judges	*A758*	
Night of the Iguana	*A785*	
Pygmalion	*A886*	
The Recruiting Officer	*A896*	
The Sea	*A961*	
Uncle Vanya	*A1157*	
Wind In The Willows	*A1211*	
Cameron Mackintosh (8)		
The Card (A musical)	*A187*	
Cats	*A194*	
Five Guys Named Moe	*A407*	
Les Miserables (2)	*A611*	*A613*
Miss Saigon	*A727*	
Moby Dick	*A728*	
Phantom Of The Opera	*A854*	
Mark Furness Ltd (7)		
'Allo,'Allo	*A36*	
The Blue Angel	*A138*	
Body And Soul	*A146*	
Don't Dress For Dinner	*A331*	
Little Tramp	*A634*	
Reflected Glory	*A898*	
Some Like It Hot	*A1025*	
Paul Elliott (6)		
Buddy (2)	*A168*	*A169*
Cinderella	*A224*	
Goldilocks	*A444*	
Snow White (2)	*A1022*	*A1023*
Charles Vance (5)		
Bedside Manners	*A105*	
Eductaing Rita	*A354*	
Home At Seven	*A502*	
My Cousin Rachel	*A762*	
Witness For The Prosecution	*A1218*	
Michael Rose (4)		
Cinderella	*A223*	
Closer Than Ever	*A231*	
Nightmare	*A787*	
Sophisticated Ladies	*A1032*	

Royal Court Theatre (4)
- Death and the Maiden *A293*
- Six Degrees... *A1008*
- Weldon Rising *A1192*
- Women Laughing *A1235*

Sacha Brooks (3)
- Madame Mao's Memories *A666*
- Passion of Marianne *A844*
- Porcelain *A871*

Theatre of Comedy (3)
- Hay Fever *A481*
- June Moon *A567*
- The Pocket Dream *A868*

Bush Theatre Company (3)
- The Cutting *A267*
- Phoenix *A857*
- Wexford Trilogy *A1194*

Pola Jones (3)
- Me And My Girl *A698*
- My Fair Lady *A763*
- Forbidden Planet *A904*

Aline Waites (3)
- Gone With The Wind II *A445*
- Road To Casablanca *A923*
- Valentine *A1166*

Watermill Theatre (3)
- The Deep Blue Sea *A140*
- The Card (A musical) *A187*
- See How They Run *A971*

Lee Dean Associates (2)
- The Heiress *A490*
- Private Lives *A880*

Nigel Barden (2)
- Blood Wedding *A133*
- Spring Awakening *A1037*

Michael Codron (2)
- 70, Girls, 70 *A4*
- Little Voice *A917*

Dan Crawford (2)
- Lust *A650*
- Once Upon A Song *A817*

Buddy Dalton (2)
- The Professional *A883*
- Roman & Marys *A934*

Gloria (2)
- Game of Love & Chance *A425*
- A Judgement In Stone *A563*

Icy Productions (2)
- Dangerous Dolls-Soap Crazy (2) *A279* *A280*

Bill Kenwright (2)
- Aladdin *A19*
- Stepping Out *A1046*

Carlo Lange (2)
- Blood Whispers *A135*
- My Blood on Glass *A761*

Ronald Lee (2)
- Annie Get Your Gun *A51*
- The Sound Of Music *A1033*

John Newman (2)
- 70, Girls, 70 *A4*
- The Blue Angel *A138*

Peter D Norman (2)
- Games *A426*
- Section 2 Housing *A969*

Stage One (2)
- Beardsley *A95*
- Great God Brown *A459*

Palace Theatre (2)
- Aladdin *A17*
- Me And Mamie O'Rourke *A696*

Howard Panter (2)
- Shades *A981*
- A Slip Of The Tongue *A1016*

David Pugh Ltd (2)
- Blues Brothers *A142*
- Someone Who'll Watch *A1028*

PW Productions (2)
- Evening with Gary L. (2) *A382* *A383*

Really Useful Group (2)
- Aspects Of Love *A72*
- Joseph... *A559*

Turnstyle (2)
- Carmen Jones *A189*
- A Slip Of The Tongue *A1016*

Osney Mead Valdorama *A1164*
Not The Abbey Theatre Richard's Cork Leg *A913*
Arts Admin Heartless *A487*
William Alderson Rebels And Friends *A895*
Foz Allan Prisoner's Pumpkin *A879*
Alex Armitage Me And My Girl *A699*
International Artistes Ltd Jack And The Beanstalk *A553*
Arts Theatre Prod. Cabaret *A178*
Michael Attenborough The Beggar's Opera *A106*
Daryl Back Anybody for Murder? *A55*
Barmont Productions Rat Play *A892*
Barbara Barringer Strange Domain *A1055*
David Bidmead Between the Lines *A112*
Bonne Crepe Some...Atomic Zombie *A1027*
Arthur Bostrom Bazaar and Rummage *A94*
Brian Brolly Valentine's Day *A1165*
Bryan Hands Productions Ltd You Must Be The Husband *A1248*
Nica Burns The Comedy Store *A242*
Cafe Theatre Company Intimacy *A543*
Tindrum Company Flowers For Algernon *A410*
Barry Clayman Concerts 42nd Street *A2*
Ben Crocker The Tender Husband *A1088*
Allan Davis Ltd Straight & Narrow *A1054*
Lee Dean Revenge *A907*
Simon Drysdale Adult Child/Dead Child *A14*
Paul du Fer Revenge *A907*
Dual Control International Theatre Mowgli - Enfant Loup *A745*
Emmy Enterprises Inc The Professional *A883*
Etcetera Theatre Company Between the Lines *A112*
Excalibur Productions Don't Rock The Boat *A330*
Robert Fox Ltd Ride Down Mt Morgan *A915*
Freeshooter The Pope And The Witch *A870*
Michael Friend Productions Stageland *A1041*
Roger Gartland My Mother Said *A767*
Frank & Woji Gero Sophisticated Ladies *A1032*
Syd Golder Strange Domain *A1055*
Fenton Gray What About Luv? *A1195*
M.I. Group Painting Churches *A842*
Ivan Hale Slice Of Saturday... *A1015*
Abigail Harrison Fool for Love *A411*

Thelma Holt Hamlet *A465*
Hot Show Ltd Phantom of the Opera *A853*
Edwardian Hotels Oscar *A825*
Inner City Th. Co. The Hour Of The Lynx *A511*
Richard Jackson Beardsley *A95*
Harvey Kass Talk Of The Steamie *A1065*
Gerald Killingworth The Golden Ass *A443*
David Kirk The Fancy Man *A395*
Linnit Productions Straight & Narrow *A1054*
Stuart Littlewood Robin Hood *A928*
LIVENT Kiss of Spiderwoman *A584*
Rocky Horror London Ltd Rocky Horror Show *A933*
Rough Magic Digging for Fire *A313*
Manchester Theatres Ltd Aladdin *A20*
Tina Marshall Speed-The-Plow *A1034*
Peter Matthews Robin Hood *A929*
Raphael McAuliffe Bloody Poetry *A137*
Carl Miller The Changing Reason *A198*
Katie Mitchell House of Bernarda Alba *A515*
Annette Moscowitz Watching And Weighting *A1187*
Annette Moskowitz Brand *A157*
Graham Mulvin Ltd. Scrooge the Musical *A1039*
James Nederlander Grand Hotel *A453*
Nick Thomas Productions Jack and the Beanstalk *A551*
City of Nottingham Hamlet *A465*
Old Vic Theatre Company Fuente Ovejuna *A423*
Orchard Theatre Company Frankenstein *A415*
Nicky Pallot A Jovial Crew *A561*
Sarah Parkin As You Like It *A69*
Pencon On Approval *A807*
Perth Theatre Mary Queen of Scots *A691*
Notingham Playhouse Grave Plots *A456*
Pocket Theatre Cumbria Man Cub *A679*
Powerhouse Pictures As You Desire Me *A66*
Titan Productions Thunderbirds FAB *A1111*
E & B Productions Rule Of The Game *A942*
Newpalm Productions Ladies' Night *A592*
Muffin Productions Cinderella *A225*
Carnival Productions Grave Plots *A456*
Waldgrave Productions Radio Times *A890*
West Stage Productions From A Jack To A King *A420*
BK Productions Disobediently Yours *A314*
New Pantomime Productions Aladdin *A26*
Theatre Productions Ltd Which Witch *A1200*
Warwick Productions Ltd The Complete Works *A245*
Excalibur Productions Ltd Murder By Misadventure *A755*
PW Productions Ltd The Woman In Black *A1227*
Queen's Theatre Gaslight *A428*
Alexander Racolin Brand *A157*
Alexander E Racolin Watching And Weighting *A1187*
Redgrave Theatre Company Single Spies *A1005*
Michael Redington Our Song *A833*
Alex Rose Roadshow *A924*
Barrie Rutter Richard III *A912*
Peter Saunders Ltd The Mousetrap *A744*
ATC & Sherman Theatre Blodeuwedd *A129*
Showpeople 90 A Swell Party *A1060*
Charles H. Simpson Bazaar and Rummage *A94*
Edward Snape The Complete Works *A245*
Rebecca Snell The Candidate *A184*
Lance Spiro The Chalk Garden *A196*
Barry Stacey The Late Edwina Black *A599*
Stardust Productions The Cotton Club *A250*
Barrie C Stead Aladdin *A18*
Charles Stephens The Complete Works *A245*
Mr Gary Stevens Name *A772*
James Tapp Bazaar and Rummage *A94*
The Warehouse Theatre Company The Three Musketeers *A1104*
Theatr Clywd Sailor Beware! *A948*
Hampstead Theatre June Moon *A567*
Praxis Theatre Co. The Sacred Penman *A946*
Really Useful Theatre Co.Ltd. Starlight Express *A1043*
Theatre Royal Plymouth A Dead Secret *A289*
Theatre Royal Presentations The Woman Destroyed *A1225*
Nick Thomas Babes In The Wood *A81*
Sponsored by Unilever Hamlet *A466*
West Yorkshire Playhouse Happy Families *A476*
Westhead Chester Mystery Plays *A204*
Michael White Mad,Bad,And Dangerous *A665*
Rebecca Wolman Story of the Last *A1053*
Wolsey Theatre Company Ltd Absent Friends *A10*
Kevin Wood Prod. Cinderella *A220*
Ridiculous Woods Three Men in a Boat *A1102*
Emily Woolf Sex III *A980*

Photo Credits

SECTION	PHOTO	PHOTOGRAPHER
	NEW PLAYERS OF THE YEAR:-	
	Ned Sherrin	Robert Workman
	Rachel Robertson	Alastair Muir
	WHO DOES WHAT:-	
	Cameron Mackintosh	Michael LePoer Trench
	Philip Prowse	John Vere Brown
	HOW THEATRE HAPPENS	
	Henry IV Part One	Richard Mildenhall
	Joseph	Michael LePoer Trench
	Hedda Gabler	John Haynes
	Pygmalion	Richard Mildenhall
	Fuente Ovejuna	Robert Workman
	DIRECTORS & DESIGNERS:-	
	Six Degrees of Separation	Martha Swope
	Heartbreak House	Ivan Kyncl
WEST END		
	MUSICALS:-	
	Assassins	Michael LePoer Trench
	Lady Be Good	Alastair Muir
	Grand Hotel	Michael LePoer Trench
	The Phantom of the Opera (Hill)	Clive Barda
	Starlight Express	Nobby Clark
	Me and My Girl	Mike Martin
	Les Miserables	Michael LePoer Trench
	The Phantom of the Opera (Webber)	Clive Barda
	Blood Brothers	Alastair Muir
	Miss Saigon	Michael LePoer Trench
	Aspects of Love	Clive Barda
	Carmen Jones	John Haynes
	Joseph & His Technicolour etc	Michael LePoer Trench
	Moby Dick	Michael LePoer Trench
	Valentine's Day	John Haynes
	Blood Wedding	Richard H Smith
WEST END -		
	ENTERTAINMENTS:-	
	Complete Works of W Shakespeare	Stuart Morris
	Five Guys Named Moe	Anthony Crickmay
	Sophisticated Ladies	Nobby Clark
	Mad, Bad and Dangerous to Know	Chris Daniels
	Rachel Robertson	Tristram Kenton

SECTION	PHOTO	PHOTOGRAPHER
WEST END - PLAY:-	It Runs in the Family	Reg Wilson
	La Bete	Tristram Kenton
	Dancing at Lughnasa	Simon Annand
	A Ride Down Mount Morgan	Inge Morath
	Painting Churches	Paul Carter
	Straight and Narrow	Catherine Ashmore
	The Pope and the Witch	Stuart Colwill
	A Slip of the Tongue	Chris Ridley
	The Blue Angel	Clive Barda
WEST END -	REVIVALS AND CLASSICS:-	
	As You Like It	Alastair Muir
	The Cabinet Minister	John Haynes
	The Pocket Dream	Hugo Glendinning
	Don't Dress for Dinner	Gordon Rainsford
	A Midsummer Night's Dream	Alastair Muir
	Heartbreak House	Ivan Kyncl
	A Woman of No Importance	Ivan Kyncl
	Cyrano de Bergerac	Nobby Clark
FRINGE -	ALMEIDA:-	
	The Gigli Concert	Ivan Kyncl
	A Hard Heart	Ivan Kyncl
	The Rules of the Game	Ivan Kyncl
	Medea	Ivan Kyncl
	BUSH:-	
	The Cutting	Sarah Leigh Lewis
	Digging for Fire	Amelia Stein
	White Woman Street	Mark Douet
	Phoenix	Mark Douet
	THE GATE:-	
	Walpurgis Night	Carole Latimer
	Crackwalker	Simon Annand
	Flamingo	Simon Annand
	The False Servant	Simon Annand
	The Television Programme	Simon Annand
	GREENWICH:-	
	Caesar and Cleopatra	Nobby Clark
	As You Like It	Paul Thompson
	Schippel The Plumber	Paul Thompson
	The Mother Tongue	Paul Thompson
	Who Shall I Be Tomorrow	Paul Thompson
	HAMPSTEAD:-	
	Making it Better	John Haynes
	Back Up The Hearse	John Haynes
	The Fastest Clock in the Universe	John Haynes
	Someone who'll Watch Over Me	John Haynes

SECTION	PHOTO	PHOTOGRAPHER
	KING'S HEAD:-	
	Once Upon A Song	Adam Lawrence
	The Chalk Garden	Tristram Kenton
	Baby Baby	Ute Klaphake
	Philadelphia, Here I Come!	Alastair Muir
	RIVERSIDE STUDIOS:-	
	Four Marys	Chris Nash
	Down and Out in Paris & London	Hugo Glendinning
	The Gravity Swing	Martin Cole
	THEATRE ROYAL, STRATFORD EAST:-	
	A Night in Tunisia	Alastair Muir
	Goin' Local	Alastair Muir
	Cut and Thrust	Alastair Muir
	Armed and Dangerous	Alastair Muir
	A Better Day	Alastair Muir
	YOUNG VIC:-	
	All My Sons	Alastair Muir
	Measure for Measure	Clive Barda
	In the Midnight Hour	Gordon Rainsford
	Caucasion Chalk Circle	Gordon Rainsford
	Guys and Dolls	Gordon Rainsford
	B A C:-	
	Mary Stuart	Stuart Colwill
	Manslaughter	John Kellett
	CROYDON WAREHOUSE:-	
	Fighting for the Dunghill	Paul Thompson
	On Top of the World	Paul Thompson
	TRICYCLE:-	
	Love and a Bottle	Amelia Stein
	Gamblers	Richard H. Smith
BEYOND THE FRINGE:-		
	Jordan	Hugo Glendinning
	A Stop in the Desert	Geraint Lewis
	Gormenghast	Graham Fudger
	Sweet Temptations	Joseph Gallus Rittenberg
THE ROYAL COURT:-		
	Outside of Heaven	Sheila Burnett
	Some Singing Blood	Sheila Burnett
	Berlin Bertie	John Haynes
	Karate Billy Comes Home	John Haynes
	Six Degrees of Separation	Robert Workman
	Hush	John Haynes
	Colquhoun and MacBride	John Haynes
THE NATIONAL THEATRE:-		
	ALL PHOTOGRAPHS SUPPLIED BY THE PRESS OFFICE OF THE NATIONAL	

SECTION PHOTO	PHOTOGRAPHER
THE R S C-ALL PHOTOGRAPHS SUPPLIED BY THE PRESS OFFICE OF THE R S C	
REGIONS -	
SCOTLAND -	
CITIZENS, GLASGOW	
Niagara	James Graham
1953	James Graham
Summer Lightning	James Graham
The Pelican	James Graham
Casanova Undone	James Graham
Lulu	James Graham
Other Places	James Graham
Edward II	James Graham
ROYAL LYCEUM, EDINBURGH:-	
All Photographs Taken By Sean Hudson	
TRAVERSE, EDINBURGH:-	
Your Turn to Clean the Stair	Colin Usher
Columbus:Blooding the Ocean	Sean Hudson
The Life of Stuff	Sean Hudson
DUNDEE REP:-	
Walter	Alex "Tug" Wilson
Tartuffe	Andrew Olney
PERTH THEATRE:-	
Wuthering Heights	Louis Flood
Little Shop of Horrors	Louis Flood
PITLOCHRY:-	
The Norman Conquests	Sean Hudson
The Dominion of Fancy	Sean Hudson
TRON GLASGOW:-	
Good	Sean Hudson
The Bloody Chamber	Alan Crumlish
NORTHERN IRELAND -	
LYRIC BELFAST:-	
Dockers	Christopher Hill
Rebecca	Christopher Hill
Pygmies in the Ruins	Christopher Hill
CIVIC ARTS:-	
A Slice of Saturday Night	Christopher Hill
THE NORTH WEST:-	
THE ROYAL EXCHANGE:-	
All Photographs by Stephen Vaughan	
THE LIBRARY THEATRE:-	
Two Way Mirror	Gerry Murray
The Writing Games	Gerry Murray
All others by Phil Cutts	
LIVERPOOL EVERYMAN:-	
Othello	Sol Pepper
Candide	Phil Cutts

SECTION	PHOTO	PHOTOGRAPHER
	LIVERPOOL PLAYHOUSE:-	
	Imagine	Phil Cutts
THE NORTH EAST-		
	WEST YORKSHIRE PLAYHOUSE:-	
	Cinderella	Simon Warner
	The Revenger's Tragedy	Simon Warner
	Happy Families	Simon Warner
	The Wicked Old Man	Simon Warner
	When We Are Married	Simon Warner
	Absent Friends	Tristram Kenton
	Life is a Dream	Ivan Kyncl
	Three Girls in Blue	Gerry Murray
	STEPHEN JOSEPH THEATRE:-	
	All Photographs by Adrian Gatie	
	Except James Tonlinson Supplied by	Pemberton Associates
	THE CRUCIBLE:-	
	All Photographs by Gerry Murray	
	HARROGATE THEATRE:-	
	Blithe Spirit	John McPherson
THE MIDLANDS -		
	BIRMINGHAM REP	
	My Mother Said I Never Should	Robert Day
	Playing By the Rules	Alan Wood
	BELGRADE THEATRE:-	
	Firestone	Robert Lapworth
	Safe in Our Hands	Richard Sadler
	A Twitch on the Thread	Robert Lapworth
	Leave Taking	Robert Lapworth
	DERBY PLAYHOUSE:-	
	On the Piste	Robert Day
	And a Nightingale Sang	Robert Day
	Far From the Madding Crowd	Robert Day
	LEICESTER HAYMARKET:-	
	Hot Stuff	Gerry Murray
	Merrily We Roll Along	Gerry Murray
	NOTTINGHAM PLAYHOUSE:-	
	All Photographs by Gerry Murray	
	EVERYMAN CHELTENHAM:-	
	A Family Affair	Robert Workman
	Over a Barrel	Alan Wood
	NEW VICTORIA THEATRE:-	
	All photographs by Robert Day	
	THE ROYAL THEATRE, NORTHAMPTON:-	
	All photographs by John Roan	

SECTION	PHOTO	PHOTOGRAPHER
WALES -		
	SHERMAN THEATRE:-	
	Fern Hill	Brian Tarr
	The Merchant of Venice	Brian Tarr
	Sleeping with Mickey Mouse	Mark Johnson
	Blodeuwedd	Mark Johnson
	THEATRE CLWYD:-	
	The Guardsman	Mark Douet
	Marching Song	Mark Douet
	The Seagull	Mark Douet
	The Devils	Phil Cutts
	THEATRE GEYNEDD:-	
	The Druid's Rest	Dylan Rowlands
	The Glass Menagerie	Dyland Rowlands
	TORCH THEATRE:-	
	Antony And Cleopatra	Martin Cavaney
THE EAST -		
	QUEENS THEATRE, HORNCHURCH:-	
	Rebecca	Roy Squire
THE SOUTH WEST -		
	BRISTOL OLD VIC	
	Andy Hay	James Barke
	NORTHCOTT THEATRE:-	
	Inventing a New Colour	Alan Winn
	SALISBURY PLAYHOUSE:-	
	Relative Values	Peter Brown
	PLYMOUTH, THEATRE ROYAL	
	All Photographs by Eric Thompson	
THE SOUTH AND SOUTH EAST -		
	CHICHESTER FESTIVAL THEATRE:-	
	Venus Observed	John Haynes
	She Stoops to Conquer	John Haynes
	King Lear in New York	John Timbers
	Double Take	Paul Carter
	Me and My Girl	Paul Carter
	NUFFIELD THEATRE:-	
	All Photographs by Paul Carter	
	PALACE THEATRE, WATFORD:-	
	All Photographs by Donald Cooper	
COMMERCIAL TOURS -		
	Annie Get Your Gun	Michael LePoer Trench
	The Haunted Hotel	Sheila Burnett
TOURING COMPANIES -		
	ACTORS TOURING COMPANY:-	
	All Photographs by Alastair Muir	

SECTION	PHOTO	PHOTOGRAPHER
	BRITH GOF:-	
	All Photographs by Brian Tarr	
	CAMBRIDGE THEATRE COMPANY:-	
	The Game of Love and Chance	Simon Annand
	CLEAN BREAK THEATRE COMPANY:-	
	Head-Rot Holiday	Sarah Ainslie
	GLORIA:-	
	A Judgement in Stone (Survey Photo)	Sean Hudson
	A Judgement in Stone (Show Photo)	Mike Laye
	GRAEAE:-	
	Maria Oshodi	Eddie Carr
	Hound	Simon Gould
	HULL TRUCK:-	
	All Photographs by Adrian Gatie	
	KABOODLE:-	
	Company Photograph by Charlie Baker	
	LONDON BUBBLE:-	
	The Good Person of Sezuan	Sol Papadopoulos
	MEETING GROUND:-	
	Directors	Keith Pattison
	MILLSTREAM:-	
	All Photographs by Marylin Kingwill	
	PAINES PLOUGH:-	
	Augustine	Hugo Glendinning
	RED SHIFT:-	
	Orlando (Survey Photo)	Henrietta Butler
	Orlando (Show Photo)	Stuart Colwill
	RENAISSANCE:-	
	All Photographs by Richard H Smith	
	7:84:-	
	All Photographs by Eileen Heraghty	
	SHARED EXPERIENCE:-	
	Anna Karenina	Paul Carter
	SPHINX;-	
	Sue Parrish & Harriet Walter	Sheila Burnett
	TARA ARTS:-	
	Artistic Director	Coneyl Jay
	Heer Ranjha	Nick Liseiko
FESTIVALS -		
	EDINBURGH:-	
	Frankie and Tommy	Adrian Gatie
	Play, Boy!	John Stark
	Studs	Derek Speirs
	MAYFEST:-	
	The World's Edge	Roberto Cavieres
	BARCLAY'S NEW STAGES:-	
	Stomp	Steve McNicholas
	Birthday	Chris Nash

SECTION	PHOTO	PHOTOGRAPHER
CHILDREN'S THEATRE -		
	PANTOMIME-	
The Snow Queen		Carol Baugh
	Mother Goose	Alastair Muir
	POLKA THEATRE:-	
	Anne Frank	Jeanette Pritchard
	PUPPET THEATRE:-	
	Angelo	John Roberts
	The Snow Queen	Stephen Lorenc
	COMMERCIAL TOUR:-	
	The Wild West Show	Douglas Robertson
	The Lion, the Witch & the Wardrobe	Gerry Murray
	TOURING COMPANIES:-	
	Greenfingers	Trish Morrissey
	Bagdancing	Trich Morrissey
INTERNATIONAL -		
	JAPAN:-	
	Macbeth	Yung Wen-Chin
	REPUBLIC OF IRELAND:-	
	A Month in the Country	Tom Lawlor
	U.S.A.:-	
	Jelly's Last Jam	Martha Swope
	FORMER EASTERN BLOC:-	
	Vaclav Havel	Ivan Kyncl
MEDIA -		
	T.V:-	
	An Ungentlemanly Act	John Green
	Natural Lies	Sven Arnstein
AN ACTOR'S LIFE-		
	John Arthur	Robert Workman
	DRAMA SCHOOLS:-	
	Guildhall	Laurence Burns
WHERE ACTING HELPS -		
	T.I.E :-	
	Geese	Peter Corbett
	An Audience Reaction	Mike Blenkinsop
OBITUARIES -		
	Geoffrey Axworthy	Brian Tarr
	Gwen Ffrancon-Davies	Angus McBean